W9-CPE-743

THEORIES OF ETHICS

PAUL A. NEWBERRY

California State University, Bakersfield

Mayfield Publishing Company
Mountain View, California
London • Toronto

To Joanne and Madeline with love

Copyright © 1999 by Mayfield Publishing Company

All rights reserved. No portion of this book may be reproduced in any form or by any means without written permission of the publisher.

Library of Congress Cataloging-in-Publication Data
Newberry, Paul A.
   Theories of ethics / Paul A. Newberry.
      p. cm.
   Includes bibliographical references.
   ISBN 1-55934-965-4
   1. Ethics.   I. Title.
BJ1012.N49   1998   98-17926
170—dc21   CIP

Manufactured in the United States of America
10 9 8 7 6 5 4 3 2 1

Mayfield Publishing Company
1280 Villa Street
Mountain View, California 94041

Sponsoring editor, Kenneth King; production, Publication Services; manuscript editor, Katherine Coyle; art director, Jeanne M. Schreiber; text designer, Donna Davis; cover designer, Leslie Thomas Fitch; manufacturing manager, Randy Hurst. The text was set in 10/12 Berkeley Book by Publication Services and printed on 45# Baycoat Velvet by The Banta Book Group.

Cover image: Poussin, Nicolas (1593–1665). Three shepherds and a shepherdess try to decipher the inscription "Et in Arcadia Ego" on an ancient sarcophagus. Oil on canvas (around 1650), 85 × 121 cm. The Louvre, Paris, France. Photo (c) by Erich Lessing.

Credits and acknowledgments continue on page 650, which constitutes an extension of the copyright page.

PREFACE

This book puts under one cover as many as possible of the core works in Western ethical theory in as complete a form as space will allow. These works, which may be considered the canonical texts in philosophical ethics, trace the development of ethical theories from Socrates to the present era. Thus, I have chosen works from the history of ethics that remain influential, seriously studied, and widely anthologized. Although it is difficult to predict which products of the twentieth century will have similar lasting value, I have selected readings that appear likely to represent influential trends in contemporary ethical theory.

A word is necessary about the reason this book contains only the core works from the history of Western philosophy. The canonical approach to philosophy has come under justified attack in recent years for ignoring the voices of women, people of color, and non-Western writers and thinkers. Thus, my initial hope in setting out to compile a text for an ethical theory course was to include underrepresented thinkers along with the more standard writers in the Western tradition of ethics. However, I soon was disabused of this notion, as the number of unquestionable core works in ethics is so great that inclusion of the lesser-known works, either those within or without Western ethics, would result in a book that does too little by trying to do too much. To do justice to those writers whose visibility and study should be encouraged but who are not considered part of the canonical core of ethics, one must devote an entire reader to them. Compiling a reader of this kind is of great interest to me, but it will have to wait until the present work is completed. The works I have selected for this reader will always remain important, even though they may not be all that is important.

Although historical approaches to philosophy have been deemphasized in recent years, such an approach is valuable in an ethics class, especially one examining theories of ethics. How can one better appreciate the complexity and wonder of ethics than to study the historical development of the theories? The student can read about ideas in context, as they arose, often in response to arguments and theories that came before. If one were to use an issues approach to ethics, the student would read Mill and Nozick, for example, as if they were contemporaries. Although this approach may be appropriate for some situations and for many subjects, it runs the risk of confirming the student in his or her prejudice that many illustrious philosophers were simply silly. Students can better appreciate and understand ethical theories if they read the most influential works chronologically.

Four signature features of this book make it appropriate as a text in an undergraduate or advanced undergraduate course in ethics or ethical theory. First, it is arranged chronologically to emphasize the historical development of Western ethical theory from the time of Socrates through the latter part of this century. Major ethical traditions from the past are included along with the major developments within our own century. Second, the majority of the selections are core works from the Western ethical tradition. Some other selections, less central to the tradition, are included to allow the instructor as much flexibility in approach as possible.

Third, the selections are relatively lengthy so that the reader will gain a sense of both the context of the particular reading and the style of the philosopher. This approach avoids the reduction of important philosophical works to the equivalent of "sound bites" that may leave out important information and be misleading. Finally, concise yet informative introductions to the readings connect each selection to its tradition as well as to general ethical theories in Western philosophy.

A brief explanation is in order concerning the choice of works in the final section. Although the first half of this century was concerned primarily with metaethics—the logic and language of ethics—interest in normative ethical theories was renewed by mid-century. So much important work has been done and continues to be done in moral philosophy that it is almost impossible to focus on only a dozen readings to represent this work. The articles included here are meant not necessarily as the best or most important work in the last few decades, but rather as representing the kinds of issues important in contemporary ethical theory. For example, included here are articles on the most prominent ethical theories: utilitarianism, Kantian deontology, social contract theory, and virtue ethics. Also included are articles representing interesting work that is not based on such prominent theories, for example, an article concerning the ethics of the Stoics and two articles on feminist ethics. Together these works give a picture of the kinds of normative ethical work currently being engaged in. The purpose of the section is to demonstrate to the reader that normative ethical theory is alive and has vibrant historical roots.

This book is intended primarily for an advanced undergraduate ethical theory course in which ethics is studied historically, but it is also appropriate for an introductory course, perhaps with shorter readings assigned. Despite its chronological ordering, the material is adaptable to ethics courses that do not treat the subject historically. Following is a suggestion for reading order in a course studying the prominent ethical theories:

1. Utilitarianism: Bentham, Mill, Sidgwick, Moore, Smart, and Williams
2. Kantian deontology: Kant, Hill, and O'Neill (and possibly Ross for an alternative version of a deontological theory)
3. Virtue ethics: Aristotle, Anscombe, and Wolf
4. Social contract theory: Hobbes, Rawls, and Gauthier

Thanks are due to the following individuals for their insightful reviews of the manuscript: Marcia Baron, University of Illinois at Urbana–Champaign; Richard Eggerman, Oklahoma State University; Richard Fumerton, University of Iowa; Joyce Henricks, Central Michigan University; Bruce Landesman, University of Utah; Walter H. O'Briant, formerly of University of Georgia; Hal Walberg, Mankato State University; and Edward Walter, University of Missouri–Kansas City.

I would like to acknowledge the people who helped make this book possible. My colleagues at California State University, Bakersfield, Norman Prigge and Gary Kessler, read the prospective table of contents and offered helpful suggestions. Janice Daurio and Jerrold Caplan of Moorpark College gave useful advice on the introductions. Of course, any remaining mistakes are mine alone. Another colleague, Lorna Clymer of California State University, Bakersfield, offered wise counsel and editing throughout the process. My thanks go to Ken King and the rest of the Mayfield staff, who gave me great advice and support from start to finish. Finally, and most important, thanks to my wife, Joanne (who wielded the red pencil), and daughter, Madeline, for their unceasing support and love.

CONTENTS

PART V. EARLY TWENTIETH-CENTURY ETHICS

PART VI. CURRENT DEVELOPMENTS IN ETHICAL THEORY

SOCRATES

FROM *Plato*, Euthyphro

Socrates was born around 470 B.C. in Athens and died there famously in 399 B.C. by drinking hemlock, condemned to death by an Athenian court. This legendary philosopher marks the beginning of moral philosophy. In some ways it is odd that he should be so considered. The first philosophers lived some one hundred and fifty years prior to his birth. Why not associate the beginning of moral philosophy with Democritus, Heraclitus, Pythagoras, or another pre-Socratic? After all, some of them wrote about ethics. Further, since Socrates did not write anything, his thought is available to us only through the writing of others. How do we know the moral philosophy of Socrates, and how should we represent it in an anthology of ethical theory?

At least three reasons support the selection of Socrates as the first practitioner of moral philosophy. First of all, even though Democritus, Heraclitus, and Pythagoras wrote on issues we clearly should classify as moral philosophy, Socrates is the first to concentrate almost exclusively on moral issues. For the pre-Socratics, the question of how we ought to live was not a central one as it was for Socrates. Even though Socrates did not leave us a "theory of ethics" or a comprehensive account of moral philosophy, he was the first to enumerate critical questions in ethics that have continued to be asked by philosophers for nearly 2500 years: What kind of life should one live? How do we know what is the good life? What are the meanings of various terms in morality, such as "good," "bad," "courage," "piety," "virtue," and "justice"? We might say that Socrates was the first to ask the questions vital to the development of moral philososphy and that Plato decisively developed and continued the inquiry.

Another reason to view Socrates as the beginning of moral philosophy is the importance of the Socratic method for subsequent moral philosophy. It was through the "dialectic," in which Socrates would question a friend about the meaning of some concept, such as justice, and then refute each definition he was given, that Socrates demonstrated that most who claim to have knowledge do not. The truly wise person knows first his own ignorance (see the Apology). By questioning those who act as if they know what is good, Socrates reveals to us the need to question moral knowledge in the same way that we question other claims to knowledge. Part of what makes the philosophical study of ethics unique is just this sense that we must take seriously the need to question.

In Socrates we see a man for whom moral philosophy was not merely an intellectual concern but a facet of life. This makes Socrates a good choice for the title of "first moral philosopher." Knowing what constitutes a good life is not among the ways one can live a good life but a necessary part of it. Recall his famous dictum "the unexamined life is not worth living." Socrates made a career of questioning others about the lives they led and urging them to learn what was good so that they could live a good life. The ultimate statement of moral philosophy's importance to a good life is represented by the manner of

Socrates' death. Rather than escape the Athenian jail, which would have required him to break the law and thus leave him disgraced in his own eyes and without integrity, Socrates chose death and thus became a symbol for two and a half millennia (See the Crito). What better example of a moral philosopher could we find?

Even if we grant that moral philosophy begins rightly with Socrates, finding a way to represent his thoughts poses a somewhat more difficult question. Socrates is the main character in many of Plato's dialogues, but do these writings represent the thoughts and teachings of Socrates or those of Plato? Or are they a combination of the two? It is generally agreed that the earlier dialogues, due to difference in style and substance, most likely portray the philosophy of Socrates and the later dialogues represent Plato's refinements, additions, and concerns built upon the thoughts of his teacher. Thus, to represent Socrates' contribution to moral philosophy, the reading presented here is the Euthyphro, one of Plato's earlier dialogues. The Euthyphro is a fine representation of the Socratic method as Socrates challenges Euthyphro to define piety. A later dialogue, the Republic, will be used to showcase the deeper philosophical reflections of Plato.

Socrates is no exception to the rule that philosophers and their inquiries are shaped by the times in which they live. The two main forces that shaped Socrates' thought on moral philosophy are the forces of tradition on the one hand and the new power and importance of the Sophists on the other. The Sophists were paid teachers whose job it was to provide training for the up-and-coming members of this democratic city-state. The training they provided was in "human excellence" or virtue. The Sophists undercut the traditional code of honor embraced by the aristocrats by inculcating in their students the notion that values are subjective and that might makes right.

Socrates shared with the Sophists an insistence that rules of conduct be subjected to rational scrutiny. But, unlike the Sophists, Socrates believed that objective rules of conduct could be found and articulated. Even though Socrates was unable to find these rules of conduct applicable to all people, he made clear that such rules are necessary for the justification of moral conduct.

Those whose moral philosophy was directly affected by the teachings of Socrates include the members of the four schools founded by former students. The Megarian school of Euclides, Aristippus and the Cyrenaics, Antisthenese and the Cynics, and the Academy of Plato were all influenced by the teachings of Socrates, though they emphasized different aspects. Indirectly, Socrates' teachings influenced Aristotle (through his teacher Plato). The Stoics (who are represented in this volume by Epictetus) considered their own philosophy to be influenced by both Plato and the Cynics. Even in our own day the great civil rights leader Martin Luther King, Jr., invokes the memory of Socrates in his famous "Letter from the Birmingham Jail" and reminds us that the life and death of Socrates give testimony to his deep moral convictions and his belief in the incorruptibility of philosophy.

PERSONS OF THE DIALOGUE

Socrates.   Euthyphro.

SCENE:—The Porch of The King Archon

Euthyphro. WHY have you left the Lyceum, Socrates? and what are you doing in the porch of the King Archon? Surely you can not be engaged in an action before the king, as I am.

Socrates. Not in an action, Euthyphro; impeachment is the word which the Athenians use.

Euth. What! I suppose that some one has been prosecuting you, for I can not believe that you are the prosecutor of another.

Soc. Certainly not.

Euth. Then some one else has been prosecuting you?

Soc. Yes.

Euth. And who is he?

Soc. A young man who is little known, Euthyphro; and I hardly know him: his name is Meletus, and he is of the deme of Pitthis. Perhaps you may remember his appearance; he has a beak, and long straight hair, and a beard which is ill grown.

Euth. No, I do not remember him, Socrates. And what is the charge which he brings against you?

Soc. What is the charge? Well, a very serious charge, which shows a good deal of character in the young man, and for which he is certainly not to be despised. He says he knows how the youth are corrupted and who are their corruptors. I fancy that he must be a wise man, and seeing that I am anything but a wise man, he has found me out, and is going to accuse me of corrupting his young friends. And of this our mother the state is to be the judge. Of all our political men he is the only one who seems to me to begin in the right way, with the cultivation of virtue in youth; he is a good husbandman, and takes care of the shoots first, and clears away us who are the destroyers of them. That is the first step; he will afterwards attend to the elder branches; and if he goes on as he has begun, he will be a very great public benefactor.

Euth. I hope that he may; but I rather fear, Socrates, that the reverse will turn out to be the truth. My opinion is that in attacking you he is simply aiming a blow at the state in a sacred place. But in what way does he say that you corrupt the young?

Soc. He brings a wonderful accusation against me, which at first hearing excites surprise: he says that I am a poet or maker of gods, and that I make new gods and deny the existence of old ones; this is the ground of his indictment.

Euth. I understand, Socrates; he means to attack you about the familiar sign which occasionally, as you say, comes to you. He thinks that you are a neologian, and he is going to have you up before the court for this. He knows that such a charge is readily received, for the world is always jealous of novelties in religion. And I know that when I myself speak in the assembly about divine things, and foretell the future to them, they laugh at me as a madman; and yet every word that I say is true. But they are jealous of all of us. I suppose that we must be brave and not mind them.

Soc. Their laughter, friend Euthyphro, is not a matter of much consequence. For a man may be thought wise; but the Athenians, I suspect, do not I care much about this, until he begins to make other men wise; and then for some reason or other, perhaps, as you say, from jealousy, they are angry.

Euth. I have no desire to try conclusions with them about this.

Soc. I dare say that you don't make yourself common, and are not apt to impart your wisdom. But I have a benevolent habit of pouring out myself to everybody, and would even pay for a listener, and I am afraid that the Athenians know this; and therefore, as I was saying, if the Athenians would only laugh at me as you say that they laugh at you, the time might pass gaily enough in the court; but perhaps they may be in earnest, and then what the end will be you soothsayers only can predict.

Euth. I dare say that the affair will end in nothing, Socrates, and that you will win your cause; and I think that I shall win mine.

Soc. And what is your suit? and are you the pursuer or defendant, Euthyphro?

Euth. I am pursuer.

Soc. Of whom?

Euth. You will think me mad when I tell you whom I am pursuing.

Soc. Why, has the fugitive wings?

Euth. Nay, he is not very volatile at his time of life.

Soc. Who is he?

Euth. My father.

Soc. Your father! good heavens, you don't mean that?

Euth. Yes.

Soc. And of what is he accused?

Euth. Murder, Socrates.

Soc. By the powers, Euthyphro! how little does the common herd know of the nature of right and truth. A man must be an extraordinary man and have made great strides in wisdom, before he could have seen his way to this.

Euth. Indeed, Socrates, he must have made great strides.

Soc. I suppose that the man whom your father murdered was one of your relatives; if he had been a stranger you would never have thought of prosecuting him.

Euth. I am amused, Socrates, at your making a distinction between one who is a relation and one who is not a relation; for surely the pollution is the same in either ease, if you knowingly associate with the murderer when you ought to clear yourself by proceeding against him. The real question is whether the murdered man has been justly slain. If justly, then your duty is to let the matter alone; but if unjustly, then even if the murderer is under the same roof with you and eats at the same table, proceed against him. Now the man who is dead was a poor dependant of mine who worked for us as a field laborer at Naxos, and one day in a fit of drunken passion he got into a quarrel with one of our domestic servants and slew him. My father bound him hand and foot and threw him into a ditch, and then sent to Athens to ask of a diviner what he should do with him. Meantime he had no care or thought of him, being under the impression that he was a murderer; and that even if he did die there would be no great harm. And this was just what happened. For such was the effect of cold and hunger and chains upon him, that before the messenger returned from the diviner, he was dead. And my father and family are angry with me for taking the part of the murderer and prosecuting my father. They say that he did not kill him, and if he did, the dead man was but a murderer, and I ought not to take any notice, for that a son is impious who prosecutes a father. That shows, Socrates, how little they know of the opinions of the gods about piety and impiety.

Soc. Good heavens, Euthyphro! and have you such a precise knowledge of piety and impiety, and of divine things in general, that, supposing the circumstances to be as you state, you are not afraid that you too may be doing an impious thing in bringing an action against your father?

Euth. The best of Euthyphro, and that which distinguishes him, Socrates, from other men, is his exact knowledge of all these matters. What should I be good for without that?

Soc. Rare friend! I think that I can not do better than be your disciple, before the trial with Meletus comes on. Then I shall challenge him, and say that I have always had a great interest in religious questions, and now, as he charges me with rash imaginations and innovations in religion, I have become your disciple. Now you, Meletus, as I shall say to him, acknowledge Euthyphro to be a great theologian, and sound in his opinions; and if you think that of him you ought to think the same of me, and not have me into court; you should begin by indicting him who is my teacher, and who is the real corruptor, not of the young, but of the old; that is to say, of myself whom he instructs, and of his old father whom he admonishes and chastises. And if Meletus refuses to listen to me, but will go on, and will not shift the indictment from me to you, I can not do better than say in the court that I challenged him in this way.

Euth. Yes, Socrates; and if he attempts to indict me I am mistaken if I don't find a flaw in him; the court shall have a great deal more to say to him than to me.

Soc. I know that, dear friend; and that is the reason why I desire to be your disciple. For I observe that no one, not even Meletus, appears to notice you; but his sharp eyes have found me out at once, and he has indicted me for impiety. And therefore, I adjure you to tell me the nature of piety and impiety, which you said that you knew so well, and of murder, and the rest of them. What are they? Is not piety in every action always the same? and impiety, again, is not that always the opposite of piety, and also the same with itself, having, as impiety, one notion which includes whatever is impious?

Euth. To be sure, Socrates.

Soc. And what is piety, and what is impiety?

Euth. Piety is doing as I am doing; that is to say, prosecuting any one who is guilty of murder, sacrilege, or of any other similar crime—whether he be your father or mother, or some other person, that makes no difference—and not prosecuting them is impiety. And please to consider, Socrates, what a notable proof I will give you of the truth of what I am saying, which I have already given to others:—of the truth, I mean, of the principle that the impious, whoever he may be, ought not to go unpunished. For do not men regard Zeus as the best and most righteous of the gods?—and even they admit that he bound his father (Cronos) because he wickedly devoured his sons, and that he too had punished his own father (Uranus) for a similar reason, in a nameless manner. And yet when I proceed against my father, they are angry with me. This is their inconsistent way of talking when the gods are concerned, and when I am concerned.

Soc. May not this be the reason, Euthyphro, why I am charged with impiety—that I can not away with these stories about the gods? and therefore I suppose that people think me wrong. But, as you who are well informed about them approve of them, I can not do better than assent to your superior wisdom. For what else can I say, confessing as I do, that I know nothing of them. I wish you would tell me whether you really believe that they are true?

Euth. Yes, Socrates; and things more wonderful still, of which the world is in ignorance.

Soc. And do you really believe that the gods fought with one another, and had dire quarrels, battles, and the like, as the poets say, and as you may see represented in the works of great artists? The temples are full of them; and notably the robe of Athene, which is carried up to the Acropolis at the great Panathenaea, is embroidered with them. Are all these tales of the gods true, Euthyphro?

Euth. Yes, Socrates; and, as I was saying, I can tell you, if you would like to hear them, many other things about the gods which would quite amaze you.

Soc. I dare say; and you shall tell me them at some other time when I have leisure. But just at present I would rather hear from you a more precise answer, which you have not as yet given, my friend, to the question, What is "piety"? In reply, you only say that piety is, Doing as you do, charging your father with murder?

Euth. And that is true, Socrates.

Soc. I dare say, Euthyphro, but there are many other pious acts.

Euth. There are.

Soc. Remember that I did not ask you to give me two or three examples of piety, but to explain the general idea which makes all pious things to be pious. Do you not recollect that there was one idea which made the impious impious, and the pious pious?

Euth. I remember.

Soc. Tell me what this is, and then I shall have a standard to which I may look, and by which I may measure the nature of actions, whether yours or any one's else, and say that this action is pious, and that impious?

Euth. I will tell you, if you like.

Soc. I should very much like.

Euth. Piety, then, is that which is dear to the gods, and impiety is that which is not dear to them.

Soc. Very good, Euthyphro; you have now given me just the sort of answer which I wanted. But whether it is true or not I can not as yet tell, although I make no doubt that you will prove the truth of your words.

Euth. Of course.

Soc. Come, then, and let us examine what we are saying. That thing or person which is dear to the gods is pious, and that thing or person which is hateful to the gods is impious. Was not that said?

Euth. Yes, that was said.

Soc. And that seems to have been very well said too?

Euth. Yes, Socrates, I think that; it was certainly said.

Soc. And further, Euthyphro, the gods were admitted to have enmities and hatreds and differences—that was also said?

Euth. Yes, that was said.

Soc. And what sort of difference creates enmity and anger? Suppose for example that you and I, my good friend, differ about a number; do differences of this sort make us enemies and set us at variance with one another? Do we not go at once to calculation, and end them by a sum?

Euth. True.

Soc. Or suppose that we differ about magnitudes, do we not quickly put an end to that difference by measuring?

Euth. That is true.

Soc. And we end a controversy about heavy and light by resorting to a weighing-machine?

Euth. To be sure.

Soc. But what differences are those which, because they can not be thus decided, make us angry and set us at enmity with one another? I dare say the answer does not occur to you at the moment, and therefore I will suggest that this happens when the matters of difference are the just and unjust, good and evil, honorable and dishonorable. Are not these the points about which, when differing, and unable satisfactorily to decide our differences, we quarrel, when we do quarrel, as you and I and all men experience?

Euth. Yes, Socrates, that is the nature of the differences about which we quarrel.

Soc. And the quarrels of the gods, noble Euthyphro, when they occur, are of a like nature?

Euth. They are.

Soc. They have differences of opinion, as you say, about good and evil, just and unjust, honorable and dishonorable: there would have been no quarrels among them, if there had been no such differences—would there now?

Euth. You are quite right.

Soc. Does not every man love that which he deems noble and just and good, and hate the opposite of them?

Euth. Very true.

Soc. But then, as you say, people regard the same things, some as just and others as unjust; and they dispute about this, and there arise wars and fightings among them.

Euth. Yes, that is true.

Soc. Then the same things, as appears, are hated by the gods and loved by the gods, and are both hateful and dear to them?

Euth. True.

Soc. Then upon this view the same things, Euthyphro, will be pious and also impious?

Euth. That, I suppose, is true.

Soc. Then, my friend, I remark with surprise that you have not answered what I asked. For I certainly did not ask what was that which is at once pious and impious: and that which is loved by the gods appears also to be hated by them. And therefore, Euthyphro, in thus chastising your father you may very likely be doing what is agreeable to Zeus but disagreeable to Cronos or Uranus, and what is acceptable to Hephaestus but unacceptable to Here, and there may be other gods who have similar differences of opinion.

Euth. But I believe, Socrates, that all the gods would be agreed as to the propriety of punishing a murderer: there would be no difference of opinion about that.

Soc. Well, but speaking of men, Euthyphro, did you ever hear any one arguing that a murderer or any sort of evil-doer ought to be let off?

Euth. I should rather say that they are always arguing this, especially in courts of law: they commit all sorts of crimes, and there is nothing that they will not do or say in order to escape punishment.

Soc. But do they admit their guilt, Euthyphro, and yet say that they ought not to be punished?

Euth. No; they do not.

Soc. Then there are some things which they do not venture to say and do: for they do not venture to argue that the guilty are to be unpunished, but they deny their guilt, do they not?

Euth. Yes.

Soc. Then they do not argue that the evil-doer should not be punished, but they argue about the fact of who the evil-doer is, and what he did and when?

Euth. True.

Soc. And the gods are in the same case, if as you imply they quarrel about just and unjust, and some of them say that they wrong one another, and others of them deny this. For surely neither God nor man will ever venture to say that the doer of evil is not to be punished:—you don't mean to tell me that?

Euth. That is true, Socrates, in the main.

Soc. But they join issue about particulars; and this applies not only to men but to the gods; if they dispute at all they dispute about some act which is called in question, and which some affirm to be just, others to be unjust. Is not that true?

Euth. Quite true.

Soc. Well then, my dear friend Euthyphro, do tell me, for my better instruction and information, what proof have you that in the opinion of all the gods a servant who is guilty of murder, and is put in chains by the master of the dead man, and dies because he is put in chains before his corrector can learn from the interpreters what he ought to do with him, dies unjustly; and that on behalf of such an one a son ought to proceed against his father and accuse him of murder. How would you show that all the gods absolutely agree in approving of his act? Prove to me that, and I will applaud your wisdom as long as you live.

Euth. That would not be an easy task, although I could make the matter very clear indeed to you.

Soc. I understand; you mean to say that I am not so quick of apprehension as the judges: for to them you will be sure to prove that the act is unjust, and hateful to the gods.

Euth. Yes indeed, Socrates; at least if they will listen to me.

Soc. But they will be sure to listen if they find that you are a good speaker. There was a notion that came into my mind while you were speaking; I said to myself: "Well, and what if Euthyphro does prove to me that all the gods regarded the death of the serf as unjust, how do I know anything more of the nature of piety and impiety? for granting that this action may be hateful to the gods, still these distinctions have no bearing on the definition of piety and impiety, for that which is hateful to the gods has been shown to be also pleasing and dear to them." And therefore, Euthyphro, I don't ask you to prove this; I will suppose, if you like, that all the gods condemn and abominate such an action. But I will amend the definition so far as to say that what

all the gods hate is impious, and what they love pious or holy; and what some of them love and others hate is both or neither. Shall this be our definition of piety and impiety?

Euth. Why not, Socrates?

Soc. Why not! certainly, as far as I am concerned, Euthyphro. But whether this admission will greatly assist you in the task of instructing me as you promised, is a matter for you to consider.

Euth. Yes, I should say that what all the gods love is pious and holy, and the opposite which they all hate, impious.

Soc. Ought we to inquire into the truth of this, Euthyphro, or simply to accept the mere statement on our own authority and that of others?

Euth. We should inquire; and I believe that the statement will stand the test of inquiry.

Soc. That, my good friend, we shall know better in a little while. The point which I should first wish to understand is whether the pious or holy is beloved by the gods because it is holy, or holy because it is beloved of the gods.

Euth. I don't understand your meaning, Socrates.

Soc. I will endeavor to explain: we speak of carrying and we speak of being carried, of leading and being led, seeing and being seen. And here is a difference, the nature of which you understand.

Euth. I think that I understand.

Soc. And is not that which is beloved distinct from that which loves?

Euth. Certainly.

Soc. Well; and now tell me, is that which is carried in this state of carrying because it is carried, or for some other reason?

Euth. No; that is the reason.

Soc. And the same is true of that which is led and of that which is seen?

Euth. True.

Soc. And a thing is not seen because it is visible, but conversely, visible because it is seen; nor is a thing in the state of being led because it is led, or in the state of being carried because it is carried, but the converse of this. And now I think, Euthyphro, that my meaning will be intelligible; and my meaning is, that any state of action or passion implies previous action or passion. It does not become because it is becoming, but it is becoming because it comes; neither does it suffer because it is in a state of suffering, but it is in a state of suffering because it suffers. Do you admit that?

Euth. Yes.

Soc. Is not that which is loved in some state either of becoming or suffering?

Euth. Yes.

Soc. And the same holds as in the previous instances; the state of being loved follows the act of being loved, and not the act the state.

Euth. That is certain.

Soc. And what do you say of piety, Euthyphro: is not piety, according to your definition, loved by all the gods?

Euth. Yes.

Soc. Because it is pious or holy, or for some other reason?

Euth. No, that is the reason.

Soc. It is loved because it is holy, not holy because it is loved?

Euth. Yes.

Soc. And that which is in a state to be loved of the gods, and is dear to them, is in a state to be loved of them because it is loved of them?

Euth. Certainly.

Soc. Then that which is loved of God, Euthyphro, is not holy, nor is that which is holy loved of God, as you affirm; but they are two different things.

Euth. How you mean, Socrates?

Soc. I mean to say that the holy has been acknowledged by us to be loved of God because it is holy, not to be holy because it is loved.

Euth. Yes.

Soc. But that which is dear to the gods is dear to them because it is loved by them, not loved by them because it is dear to them.

Euth. True.

Soc. But, friend Euthyphro, if that which is holy is the same as that which is dear to God, and that

which is holy is loved as being holy, then that which is dear to God would have been loved as being dear to God; but if that which is dear to God is dear to him because loved by him, then that which is holy would have been holy because loved by him. But now you see that the reverse is the case, and that they are quite different from one another. For one (θεοφιλὲς) is of a kind to be loved because it is loved, and the other (ὅσιον) is loved because it is of a kind to be loved. Thus you appear to me, Euthyphro, when I ask you what is the essence of holiness, to offer an attribute only, and not the essence—the attribute of being loved by all the gods. But you still refuse to explain to me the nature of piety. And therefore, if you please, I will ask you not to hide your treasure, but to tell me once more what piety or holiness really is, whether dear to the gods or not (for that is a matter about which we will not quarrel). And what is impiety?

Euth. I really do not know, Socrates, how to say what I mean. For somehow or other our arguments, on whatever ground we rest them, seem to turn round and walk away.

Soc. Your words, Euthyphro, are like the handiwork of my ancestor Daedalus; and if I were the sayer or propounder of them, you might say that this comes of my being his relation; and that this is the reason why my arguments walk away and won't remain fixed where they are placed. But now, as the notions are your own, you must find some other gibe, for they certainly, as you yourself allow, show an inclination to be on the move.

Euth. Nay, Socrates, I shall still say that you are the Daedalus who sets arguments in motion; not I, certainly, make them move or go round, for they would never have stirred, as far as I am concerned.

Soc. Then I must be a greater than Daedalus; for whereas he only made his own inventions to move, I move those of other people as well. And the beauty of it is, that I would rather not. For I would give the wisdom of Daedalus, and the wealth of Tantalus, to be able to detain them and keep them fixed. But enough of this. As I perceive that you are indolent, I will myself endeavor to show you how you might instruct me in the nature of piety; and I hope that you will not grudge your labor. Tell me, then,—Is not that which is pious necessarily just?

Euth. Yes.

Soc. And is, then, all which is just pious? or, is that which is pious all just, but that which is just only in part and not all pious?

Euth. I don't understand you, Socrates.

Soc. And yet I know that you are as much wiser than I am, as you are younger. But, as I was saying, revered friend, the abundance of your wisdom makes you indolent. Please to exert yourself, for there is no real difficulty in understanding me. What I mean I may explain by an illustration of what I do not mean. The poet (Stasinus) sings—
"Of Zeus, the author and creator of all these things, You will not tell: for where there is fear there is also reverence."
And I disagree with this poet. Shall I tell you in what I disagree?

Euth. By all means.

Soc. I should not say that where there is fear there is also reverence; for I am sure that many persons fear poverty and disease, and the like evils, but I do not perceive that they reverence the objects of their fear.

Euth. Very true.

Soc. But where reverence is, there is fear; for he who has a feeling of reverence and shame about the commission of any action, fears and is afraid of an ill reputation.

Euth. No doubt.

Soc. Then we are wrong in saying that where there is fear there is also reverence; and we should say, where there is reverence there is also fear. But there is not always reverence where there is fear; for fear is a more extended notion, and reverence is a part of fear, just as the odd is a part of number, and number is a more extended notion than the odd. I suppose that you follow me now?

Euth. Quite well.

Soc. That was the sort of question which I meant to raise when asking whether the just is the pious, or the pious the just; and whether there may not be justice where there is not always piety; for justice is the more extended notion of which piety is only a part. Do you agree in that?

Euth. Yes; that, I think, is correct.

Soc. Then, now, if piety is a part of justice, I suppose that we inquire what part? If you had pursued the injury in the previous cases; for instance, if you had asked me what is an even number, and what part of number the even is, I should have had no difficulty in replying, a number which represents a figure having two equal sides. Do you agree?

Euth. Yes.

Soc. In like manner, I want you to tell me what part of justice is piety or holiness; that I may be able to tell Meletus not to do me injustice, or indict me for impiety; as I am now adequately instructed by you in the nature of piety or holiness, and their opposites.

Euth. Piety or holiness, Socrates, appears to me to be that part of justice which attends to the gods, as there is the other part of justice which attends to men.

Soc. That is good, Euthyphro; yet still there is a little point about which I should like to have further information, What is the meaning of "attention"? For attention can hardly be used in the same sense when applied to the gods as when applied to other things. For instance, horses are said to require attention, and not every person is able to attend to them, but only a person skilled in horsemanship. Is not that true?

Euth. Quite true.

Soc. I should suppose that the art of horsemanship is the art of attending to horses?

Euth. Yes.

Soc. Nor is every one qualified to attend to dogs, but only the huntsman.

Euth. True.

Soc. And I should also conceive that the art of the huntsman is the art of attending to dogs?

Euth. Yes.

Soc. As the art of the oxherd is the art of attending to oxen?

Euth. Very true.

Soc. And as holiness or piety is the art of attending to the gods?—that would be your meaning, Euthyphro?

Euth. Yes.

Soc. And is not attention always designed for the good or benefit of that to which the attention is given? As in the case of horses, you may observe that when attended to by the horseman's art they are benefited and improved, are they not?

Euth. True.

Soc. As the dogs are benefited by the huntsman's art, and the oxen by the art of the oxherd, and all other things are tended or attended for their good and not for their hurt?

Euth. Certainly, not for their hurt.

Soc. But for their good?

Euth. Of course.

Soc. And does piety or holiness, which has been defined as the art of attending to the gods, benefit or improve them? Would you say that when you do a holy act you make any of the gods better?

Euth. No, no; that is certainly not my meaning.

Soc. Indeed, Euthyphro, I did not suppose that this was your meaning; far otherwise. And that was the reason why I asked you the nature of this attention, because I thought that this was not your meaning.

Euth. You do me justice, Socrates; for that is not my meaning.

Soc. Good: but I must still ask what is this attention to the gods which is called piety?

Euth. It is such, Socrates, as servants show to their masters.

Soc. I understand—a sort of ministration to the gods.

Euth. Exactly.

Soc. Medicine is also a sort of ministration or service, tending to the attainment of some object—would you not say health?

Euth. Yes.

Soc. Again, there is an art which ministers to the ship-builder with a view to the attainment of some result?

Euth. Yes, Socrates, with a view to the building of a ship.

Soc. As there is an art which ministers to the house-builder with a view to the building of a house?

Euth. Yes.

Soc. And now tell me, my good friend, about this art which ministers to the gods: what work does that help to accomplish? For you must surely know if, as you say, you are of all men living the one who is best instructed in religion.

Euth. And that is true, Socrates.

Soc. Tell me then, oh tell me—what is that fair work which the gods do by the help of us as their ministers?

Euth. Many and fair, Socrates, are the works which they do.

Soc. Why, my friend, and so are those of a general. But the chief of them is easily told. Would you not say that victory in war is the chief of them?

Euth. Certainly.

Soc. Many and fair, too, are the works of the husbandman, if I am not mistaken; but his chief work is the production of food from the earth?

Euth. Exactly.

Soc. And of the many and fair things which the gods do, which is the chief and principal one?

Euth. I have told you already, Socrates, that to learn all these things accurately will be very tiresome. Let me simply say that piety is learning how to please the gods in word and deed, by prayers and sacrifices. That is piety, which is the salvation of families and states, just as the impious, which is unpleasing to the gods, is their ruin and destruction.

Soc. I think that you could have answered in much fewer words the chief question which I asked, Euthyphro, if you had chosen. But I see plainly that you are not disposed to instruct me: else why, when we had reached the point, did you turn aside? Had you only answered me I should have learned of you by this time the nature of piety. Now, as the asker of a question is necessarily dependent on the answerer, whither he leads I must follow; and can only ask again, what is the pious, and what is piety? Do you mean that they are a sort of science of praying and sacrificing?

Euth. Yes, I do.

Soc. And sacrificing is giving to the gods, and prayer is asking of the gods?

Euth. Yes, Socrates.

Soc. Upon this view, then, piety is a science of asking and giving?

Euth. You understand me capitally, Socrates.

Soc. Yes, my friend; the reason is that I am a votary of your science, and give my mind to it, and therefore nothing which you say will be thrown away upon me. Please then to tell me, what is the nature of this service to the gods? Do you mean that we prefer requests and give gifts to them?

Euth. Yes, I do.

Soc. Is not the right way of asking to ask of them what we want?

Euth. Certainly.

Soc. And the right way of giving is to give to them in return what they want of us. There would be no meaning in an art which gives to any one that which he does not want.

Euth. Very true, Socrates.

Soc. Then piety, Euthyphro, is an art which gods and men have of doing business with one another?

Euth. That is an expression which you may use, if you like.

Soc. But I have no particular liking for anything but the truth. I wish, however, that you would tell me what benefit accrues to the gods from our gifts. That they are the givers of every good to us is clear; but how we can give any good thing to them in return is far from being equally clear. If they give everything and we give nothing, that must be an affair of business in which we have very greatly the advantage of them.

Euth. And do you imagine, Socrates, that any benefit accrues to the gods from what they receive of us?

Soc. But if not, Euthyphro, what sort of gifts do we confer upon the gods?

Euth. What should we confer upon them, but tributes of honor; and, as I was just now saying, what is pleasing to them?

Soc. Piety, then, is pleasing to the gods, but not beneficial or dear to them?

Euth. I should say that nothing could be dearer.

Soc. Then once more the assertion is repeated that piety is dear to the gods?

Euth. No doubt.

Soc. And when you say this, can you wonder at your words not standing firm, but walking away? Will you accuse me of being the Daedalus who makes them walk away, not perceiving that there is another and far greater artist than Daedalus who makes them go round in a circle; and that is yourself: for the argument, as you will perceive, comes round to the same point. I think that you must remember our saying that the holy or pious was not the same as that which is loved of the gods. Do you remember that?

Euth. I do.

Soc. And do you not see that what is loved of the gods is holy, and that this is the same as what is dear to them?

Euth. True.

Soc. Then either we were wrong in that admission; or, if we were right then, we are wrong now.

Euth. I suppose that is the case.

Soc. Then we must begin again and ask, What is piety? That is an inquiry which I shall never be weary of pursuing as far as in me lies; and I entreat you not to scorn me, but to apply your mind to the utmost and tell me the truth. For, if any man knows, you are he; and therefore I shall detain you, like Proteus, until you tell. For if you had not certainly known the nature of piety and impiety, I am confident that you would never, on behalf of a serf, have charged your aged father with murder. You would not have run such a risk of doing wrong in the sight of the gods, and you would have had too much respect for the opinions of men. I am sure, therefore, that you know the nature of piety and impiety. Speak out then, my dear Euthyphro, and do not hide your knowledge.

Euth. Another time, Socrates; for I am in a hurry, and must go now.

Soc. Alas! my companion, and will you leave me in despair? I was hoping that you would instruct me in the nature of piety and impiety, so that I might have cleared myself of Meletus and his in-dictment. Then I might have proved to him that I had been converted by Euthyphro, and had done

with rash innovations and speculations, in which I had indulged through ignorance, and was about to lead a better life.

PLATO

Republic, *Books I, II, IV, VI, VII, and IX*

Plato (427–327 B.C.), student of Socrates and teacher of Aristotle, was one of the greatest intellects of all time. Western philosophy, said Alfred North Whitehead, is but a footnote to Plato. In the some two dozen dialogues he wrote in the fifty years following the death of Socrates, Plato considers many important ethical issues. In the Crito, *for example, Socrates' refusal to escape what his followers saw as an unjust death sentence ordered by an Athenian court plants the seeds of a modern social contract theory of ethics. Socrates does not escape because he has, in essence, a contract with the state that has raised and protected him in much the same way that a child has obligations to his or her parents. In other dialogues various virtue-related terms such as "piety," "courage," and "justice" are subjected to the dialectic (or Socratic method), in which various attempts to define these terms are met with relentless cross-examination. Yet it is in the* Republic, *a much longer dialogue than most, where we see the most profound expression of Plato's mature moral philosophy.*

The Republic *can be read on two levels. First, it is a characterization of Plato's ideal state—a paradigm that describes not how states are constructed, but how they should be if they are to be perfectly just. The ideal rulers in this republic are those who are trained in reasoning—the philosophers will rule over the workers and auxiliaries. On another level, the* Republic *describes the ideal person: the one in whom reason rules over passions and desires. Whether this work is principally a political treatise or a work in moral psychology is the subject of continuing debate (see the introduction to Waterfield's translation of* Republic*).*

Key to Plato's moral philosophy are his metaphysics and epistemology, particularly the theory of Forms (or Ideas). For Plato, the objects of knowledge are divided into two hierarchical realms: those changing, sensible objects and the unchanging ideas called "Forms." The objects, which we perceive through our senses, are less real than the Forms, which we know through reason. These two realms are further divided into two levels. The lower realm (of objects) is divided into a lower section of images and an upper section of natural objects. The realm of Forms is also divided, into a lower realm of mathematical Forms and an upper realm of ethical Forms. Plato's hierarchical order places ethics at the top, crowned only by the Form of the Good, in relation to which all other Forms must be understood. Thus, ethical knowledge is both the highest kind of knowledge and the most difficult to attain. In the Republic, *Plato sets out his theory of Forms in the allegorical discussions of the Divided Line, the Sun, and the Cave in Books VI and VII, which provide the foundation for his claim that knowledge of the good is both a necessary and sufficient condition for doing good.*

Even though Platonic metaphysics is no longer a particularly viable theory in philosophical circles, its influence is still widely felt in many of our common notions, such as the superiority of reason over sense experience and the immortality of an immaterial soul contained within a material body. Plato's influence on moral philosophy cannot be discounted. It was he who first framed many of the important issues in moral philosophy that still interest us today; the fact/value distinction, the objectivity or subjectivity of values, the attainment of moral knowledge, and understanding moral responsibility are just a few of the still vibrant issues that concerned Plato. Many consider Plato to be the founder of political philosophy and the Republic its founding document.

In addition to Plato's indirect influence on the history of ethical theory, he directly influenced the moral philosophy of his most famous student, Aristotle, as well as the ancient Stoics. Through the Neoplatonists, Plato's thought also influenced Augustine and thereby the entire history of Christianity. In the late seventeenth century, a group of British moralists, notably Ralph Cudworth and Henry More, were known collectively as the Cambridge Platonists for their adherence to Platonic philosophy. And in the intuitionism of G. E. Moore at the end of the nineteenth century we can find the influence of Plato.

Book I

PERSONS OF THE DIALOGUE

Socrates, *who is the narrator.*
Glaucon.
Adeimantus.
Polemarchus.
Cephalus.
Thrasymachus.
Cleitophon.

And others who are mute auditors.

The scene is laid in the house of Cephalus at the Piraeus; and the whole dialogue is narrated by Socrates the day after it actually took place to Timaeus, Hermocrates, Critias, and a nameless person, who are introduced in the Timaeus.

I went down yesterday to the Piraeus with Glaucon the son of Ariston, that I might offer up my prayers to the goddess; and also because I wanted to see in what manner they would celebrate the festival, which was a new thing. I was delighted with the procession of the inhabitants; but that of the Thracians was equally, if not more, beautiful. When we had finished our prayers and viewed the spectacle, we turned in the direction of the city; and at that instant Polemarchus the son of Cephalus chanced to catch sight of us from a distance as we were starting on our way home, and told his servant to run and bid us wait for him. The servant took hold of me by the cloak behind, and said: Polemarchus desires you to wait.

I turned round, and asked him where his master was.

There he is, said the youth, coming after you, if you will only wait.

Certainly we will, said Glaucon; and in a few minutes Polemarchus appeared, and with him Adeimantus, Glaucon's brother, Niceratus the son of Nicias, and several others who had been at the procession.

Polemarchus said to me: I perceive, Socrates, that you and your companion are already on your way to the city.

You are not far wrong, I said.

But do you see, he rejoined, how many we are?

Of course.

And are you stronger than all these? for if not, you will have to remain where you are.

May there not be the alternative, I said, that we may persuade you to let us go?

But can you persuade us, if we refuse to listen to you? he said.

Certainly not, replied Glaucon.

Then we are not going to listen; of that you may be assured.

Adeimantus added: Has no one told you of the torch-race on horseback in honor of the goddess which will take place in the evening?

With horses! I replied: That is a novelty. Will horsemen carry torches and pass them one to another during the race?

Yes, said Polemarchus, and not only so, but a festival will be celebrated at night, which you certainly ought to see. Let us rise soon after supper and see this festival; there will be a gathering of young men, and we will have a good talk. Stay then, and do not be perverse.

Glaucon said: I suppose, since you insist, that we must.

Very good, I replied.

Accordingly we went with Polemarchus to his house; and there we found his brothers Lysias and Euthydemus, and with them Thrasymachus the Chalcedonian, Charmantides the Paeanian, and Cleitophon the son of Aristonymus. There too was Cephalus the father of Polemarchus, whom I had not seen for a long time, and I thought him very much aged. He was seated on a cushioned chair, and had a garland on his head, for he had been sacrificing in the court; and there were some other chairs in the room arranged in a semicircle, upon which we sat down by him. He saluted me eagerly, and then he said:—

You don't come to see me, Socrates, as often as you ought: If I were still able to go and see you I would not ask you to come to me. But at my age I can hardly get to the city, and therefore you should come oftener to the Piraeus. For let me tell you, that the more the pleasures of the body fade away, the greater to me is the pleasure and charm of conversation. Do not then deny my request, but make our house your resort and keep company with these young men; we are old friends, and you will be quite at home with us.

I replied: There is nothing which for my part I like better, Cephalus, than conversing with aged men; for I regard them as travellers who have gone a journey which I too may have to go, and of whom I ought to inquire, whether the way is smooth and easy, or rugged and difficult. And this is a question which I should like to ask of you who have arrived at that time which the poets call the "threshold of old age"—Is life harder towards the end, or what report do you give of it?

I will tell you, Socrates, he said, what my own feeling is. Men of my age flock together; we are birds of a feather, as the old proverb says; and at our meetings the tale of my acquaintance commonly is—I can not eat, I can not drink; the pleasures of youth and love are fled away: there was a good time once, but now that is gone, and life is no longer life. Some complain of the slights which are put upon them by relations, and they will tell you sadly of how many evils their old age is the cause. But to me, Socrates, these complainers seem to blame that which is not really in fault. For if old age were the cause, I too being old, and every other old man, would have felt as they do. But this is not my own experience, nor that of others whom I have known. How well I remember the aged poet Sophocles, when in answer to the question, How does love suit with age, Sophocles,—are you still the man you were? Peace, he replied; most gladly have I escaped the thing of which you speak; I feel as if I had escaped from a mad and furious master. His words have often occurred to my mind since, and they seem as good to me now as at the time when he uttered them. For certainly old age has a great sense of calm and freedom; when the passions relax their hold, then, as Sophocles says, we are freed from the grasp not of one mad master only, but of many. The truth is, Socrates, that these regrets, and also the complaints about relations, are to be attributed to the same cause, which is not old age, but men's characters and tempers; for he who is of a calm and happy nature will hardly feel the pressure of age, but to him who is of an opposite disposition youth and age are equally a burden.

I listened in admiration, and wanting to draw him out, that he might go on—Yes, Cephalus, I said; but I rather suspect that people in general are not convinced by you when you speak thus; they think that old age sits lightly upon you, not because of your happy disposition, but because you are rich, and wealth is well known to be a great comforter.

You are right, he replied; they are not convinced: and there is something in what they say; not, however, so much as they imagine. I might answer them as Themistocles answered the Seriphian who was abusing him and saying that he was famous, not for his own merits but because he was an Athenian: "If you had been a native of my country or I of yours, neither of us would have been famous." And to those who are not rich and are impatient of old age, the same reply may be made; for to the good poor man old age can not be a light burden, nor can a bad rich man ever have peace with himself.

May I ask, Cephalus, whether your fortune was for the most part inherited or acquired by you?

Acquired! Socrates; do you want to know how much I acquired? In the art of making money I have been midway between my father and grandfather: for my grandfather, whose name I bear, doubled and trebled the value of his patrimony, that which he inherited being much what I possess now; but my father Lysanias reduced the property below what it is at present: and I shall be satisfied if I leave to these my sons not less but a little more than I received.

That was why I asked you the question, I replied, because I see that you are indifferent about money, which is a characteristic rather of those who have inherited their fortunes than of those who have acquired them; the makers of fortunes have a second love of money as a creation of their own, resembling the affection of authors for their own poems, or of parents for their children, besides that natural love of it for the sake of use and profit which is common to them and all men. And hence they are very bad company, for they can talk about nothing but the praises of wealth.

That is true, he said.

Yes, that is very true, but may I ask another question?—What do you consider to be the greatest blessing which you have reaped from your wealth?

One, he said, of which I could not expect easily to convince others. For let me tell you, Socrates, that when a man thinks himself to be near death, fears and cares enter into his mind which he never had before; the tales of a world below and the punishment which is exacted there of deeds done here were once a laughing matter to him, but now he is tormented with the thought that they may be true: either from the weakness of age, or because he is now drawing nearer to that other place, he has a clearer view of these things; suspicions and alarms crowd thickly upon him, and he begins to reflect and consider what wrongs he has done to others. And when he finds that the sum of his transgressions is great he will many a time like a child start up in his sleep for fear, and he is filled with dark forebodings. But to him who is conscious of no sin, sweet hope, as Pindar charmingly says, is the kind nurse of his age:

> "Hope," he says, "cherishes the soul of him who lives in justice and holiness, and is the nurse of his age and the companion of his journey;—hope which is mightiest to sway the restless soul of man."

How admirable are his words! And the great blessings of riches, I do not say to every man, but to a good man, is, that he has had no occasion to deceive or to defraud others, either intentionally or unintentionally; and when he departs to the world below he is not in any apprehension about offerings due to the gods or debts which he owes to men. Now to this peace of mind the possession of wealth greatly contributes; and therefore I say, that, setting one thing against another, of the many advantages which wealth has to give, to a man of sense this is in my opinion the greatest.

Well said, Cephalus, I replied; but as concerning justice, what is it?—to speak the truth and to pay your debts—no more than this? And even to this are there not exceptions? Suppose that a friend when in his right mind has deposited arms with me and he asks for them when he is not in his right mind, ought I to give them back to him? No one would say that I ought or that I should be right in doing so, any more than they would say that I ought always to speak the truth to one who is in his condition.

You are quite right, he replied.

But then, I said, speaking the truth and paying your debts is not a correct definition of justice.

Quite correct, Socrates, if Simonides is to be believed, said Polemarchus interposing.

I fear, said Cephalus, that I must go now, for I have to look after the sacrifices, and I hand over the argument to Polemarchus and the company.

Is not Polemarchus your heir? I said.

To be sure, he answered, and went away laughing to the sacrifices.

Tell me then, O thou heir of the argument, what did Simonides say, and according to you truly say, about justice?

He said that the repayment of a debt is just, and in saying so he appears to me to be right.

I should be sorry to doubt the word of such a wise and inspired man, but his meaning, though probably clear to you, is the reverse of clear to me. For he certainly does not mean, as we were just now saying, that I ought to return a deposit of arms or of anything else to one who asks for it when he is not in his right senses; and yet a deposit can not be denied to be a debt.

True.

Then when the person who asks me is not in his right mind I am by no means to make the return?

Certainly not.

When Simonides said that the repayment of a debt was justice, he did not mean to include that case?

Certainly not; for he thinks that a friend ought always to do good to a friend and never evil.

You mean that the return of a deposit of gold which is to the injury of the receiver, if the two parties are friends, is not the repayment of a debt,—that is what you would imagine him to say?

Yes.

And are enemies also to receive what we owe to them?

To be sure, he said, they are to receive what we owe them, and an enemy, as I take it, owes to an enemy that which is due or proper to him—that is to say, evil.

Simonides, then, after the manner of poets, would seem to have spoken darkly of the nature of justice; for he really meant to say that justice is the giving to each man what is proper to him, and this he termed a debt.

That must have been his meaning, he said.

By heaven! I replied; and if we asked him what due or proper thing is given by medicine, and to whom, what answer do you think that he would make to us?

He would surely reply that medicine gives drugs and meat and drink to human bodies.

And what due or proper thing is given by cookery and to what?

Seasoning to food.

And what is that which justice gives, and to whom?

If, Socrates, we are to be guided at all by the analogy of the preceding instances, then justice is the art which gives good to friends and evil to enemies.

That is his meaning then?

I think so.

And who is best able to do good to his friends and evil to his enemies in time of sickness?

The physician.

Or when they are on a voyage, amid the perils of the sea?

The pilot.

And in what sort of actions or with a view to what result is the just man most able to do harm to his enemy and good to his friend?

In going to war against the one and in making alliances with the other.

But when a man is well, my dear Polemarchus, there is no need of a physician?

No.

And he who is not on a voyage has no need of a pilot?

No.

Then in time of peace justice will be of no use?

I am very far from thinking so.

You think that justice may be of use in peace as well as in war?

Yes.

Like husbandry for the acquisition of corn?

Yes.

Or like shoemaking for the acquisition of shoes,—that is what you mean?

Yes.

And what similar use or power of acquisition has justice in time of peace?

In contracts, Socrates, justice is of use.

And by contracts you mean partnerships?

Exactly.

But is the just man or the skilful player a more useful and better partner at a game of draughts?

The skilful player.

And in the laying of bricks and stones is the just man a more useful or better partner than the builder?

Quite the reverse.

Then in what sort of partnership is the just man a better partner than the harp-player, as in playing the harp the harp-player is certainly a better partner than the just man?

In a money partnership.

Yes, Polemarchus, but surely not in the use of money; for you do not want a just man to be your counsellor in the purchase or sale of a horse; a man who is knowing about horses would be better for that, would he not?

Certainly.

And when you want to buy a ship, the shipwright or the pilot would be better?

True.

Then what is that joint use of silver or gold in which the just man is to be preferred?

When you want a deposit to be kept safely.

You mean when money is not wanted, but allowed to lie?

Precisely.

That is to say, justice is useful when money is useless?

That is the inference.

And when you want to keep a pruning-hook safe, then justice is useful to the individual and to the state; but when you want to use it, then the art of the vine-dresser?

Clearly.

And when you want to keep a shield or a lyre, and not to use them, you would say that justice is useful; but when you want to use them, then the art of the soldier or of the musician?

Certainly.

And so of all other things;—justice is useful when they are useless, and useless when they are useful?

That is the inference.

Then justice is not good for much. But let us consider this further point: Is not he who can best strike a blow in a boxing match or in any kind of fighting best able to ward off a blow?

Certainly.

And he who is most skilful in preventing or escaping from a disease is best able to create one?

True.

And he is the best guard of a camp who is best able to steal a march upon the enemy?

Certainly.

Then he who is a good keeper of anything is also a good thief?

That, I suppose, is to be inferred.

Then if the just man is good at keeping money, he is good at stealing it?

That is implied in the argument.

Then after all the just man has turned out to be a thief. And this is a lesson which I suspect you must have learned out of Homer; for he, speaking of Autolycus, the maternal grandfather of Odysseus, who is a favorite of his, affirms that

He was excellent above all men in theft and perjury.

And so, you and Homer and Simonides are agreed that justice is an art of theft; to be practised however "for the good of friends and for the harm of enemies,"—that was what you were saying?

No, certainly not that, although I do not now know what I did say; but I still stand by the latter words.

Well, there is another question: By friends and enemies do we mean those who are so really, or only in seeming?

Surely, he said, a man may be expected to love those whom he thinks good, and to hate those whom he thinks evil.

Yes, but do not persons often err about good and evil: many who are not good seem to be so, and conversely?

That is true.

Then to them the good will be enemies and the evil will be their friends?

True.

And in that case they will be right in doing good to the evil and evil to the good?

Clearly.

But the good are just and would not do an injustice?

True.

Then according to your argument it is just to injure those who do no wrong?

Nay, Socrates; the doctrine is immoral.

Then I suppose that we ought to do good to the just and harm to the unjust?

I like that better.

But see the consequence:—Many a man who is ignorant of human nature has friends who are bad friends, and in that case he ought to do harm to them; and he has good enemies whom he ought to benefit; but, if so, we shall be saying the very opposite of that which we affirmed to be the meaning of Simonides.

Very true, he said; and I think that we had better correct an error into which we seem to have fallen in the use of the words "friend" and "enemy."

What was the error, Polemarchus? I asked.

We assumed that he is a friend who seems to be or who is thought good.

And how is the error to be corrected?

We should rather say that he is a friend who is, as well as seems, good; and that he who seems only, and is not good, only seems to be and is not a friend; and of an enemy the same may be said.

You would argue that the good are our friends and the bad our enemies?

Yes.

And instead of saying simply as we did at first, that it is just to do good to our friends and harm to our enemies, we should further say: It is just to do good to our friends when they are good and harm to our enemies when they are evil?

Yes, that appears to me to be the truth.

But ought the just to injure any one at all?

Undoubtedly he ought to injure those who are both wicked and his enemies.

When horses are injured, are they improved or deteriorated?

The latter.

Deteriorated, that is to say, in the good qualities of horses, not of dogs?

Yes, of horses.

And dogs are deteriorated in the good qualities of dogs, and not of horses?

Of course.

And will not men who are injured be deteriorated in that which is the proper virtue of man?

Certainly.

And that human virtue is justice?

To be sure.

Then men who are injured are of necessity made unjust?

That is the result.

But can the musician by his art make men unmusical?

Certainly not.

Or the horseman by his art make them bad horsemen?

Impossible.

And can the just by justice make men unjust, or speaking generally, can the good by virtue make them bad?

Assuredly not.

Any more than heat can produce cold?

It cannot.

Or drought moisture?

Clearly not.

Nor can the good harm any one?

Impossible.

And the just is the good?

Certainly.

Then to injure a friend or any one else is not the act of a just man, but of the opposite, who is the unjust?

I think that what you say is quite true, Socrates.

Then if a man says that justice consists in the repayment of debts, and that good is the debt which a just man owes to his friends, and evil the debt which he owes to his enemies,—to say this is not wise; for it is not true, if, as has been clearly shown, the injuring of another can be in no case just.

I agree with you, said Polemarchus.

Then you and I are prepared to take up arms against any one who attributes such a saying to Simonides or Bias or Pittacus, or any other wise man or seer?

I am quite ready to do battle at your side, he said.

Shall I tell you whose I believe the saying to be?

Whose?

I believe that Periander or Perdiccas or Xerxes or Ismenias the Theban, or some other rich and mighty man, who had a great opinion of his own power, was the first to say that justice is "doing good to your friends and harm to your enemies."

Most true, he said.

Yes, I said; but if this definition of justice also breaks down, what other can be offered?

Several times in the course of the discussion Thrasymachus had made an attempt to get the argument into his own hands, and had been put down by the rest of the company, who wanted to hear the end. But when Polemarchus and I had done speaking and there was a pause, he could no longer hold his peace; and, gathering himself up, he came at us like a wild beast, seeking to devour us. We were quite panic-stricken at the sight of him.

He roared out to the whole company: What folly, Socrates, has taken possession of you all? And why, sillybillies, do you knock under to one another? I say that if you want really to know what justice is, you should not only ask but answer, and you should not seek honor to yourself from the refutation of an opponent, but have your own answer; for there is many a one who can ask and can not answer. And now I will not have you say that justice is duty or advantage or profit or gain or interest, for this sort of nonsense will not do for me; I must have clearness and accuracy.

I was panic-stricken at his words, and could not look at him without trembling. Indeed I believe that if I had not fixed my eye upon him, I should have been struck dumb: but when I saw his fury rising, I looked at him first, and was therefore able to reply to him.

Thrasymachus, I said, with a quiver, don't be hard upon us. Polemarchus and I may have been guilty of a little mistake in the argument, but I can assure you that the error was not intentional. If we were seeking for a piece of gold, you would not imagine that we were "knocking under to one another," and so losing our chance of finding it. And why, when we are seeking for justice, a thing more precious than many pieces of gold, do you say that we are weakly yielding to one another and not doing our utmost to get at the truth? Nay, my good friend, we are most willing and anxious to do so, but the fact is that we can not. And if so, you people who know all things should pity us and not be angry with us.

How characteristic of Socrates! he replied, with a bitter laugh;—that's your ironical style! Did I not foresee—have I not already told you, that whatever he was asked he would refuse to answer, and try irony or any other shuffle, in order that he might avoid answering?

You are a philosopher, Thrasymachus, I replied, and well know that if you ask a person what numbers make up twelve, taking care to prohibit him whom you ask from answering twice six, or three times four, or six times two, or four times three, "for this sort of nonsense will not do for me,"—then obviously, if that is your way of putting the question, no one can answer you. But suppose that he were to retort, "Thrasymachus, what do you mean? If one of these numbers which you interdict be the true answer to the question, am I falsely to say some other number which is not the right one?—is that your meaning?"—How would you answer him?

Just as if the two cases were at all alike! he said.

Why should they not be? I replied; and even if they are not, but only appear to be so to the person who is asked, ought he not to say what he thinks, whether you and I forbid him or not?

I presume then that you are going to make one of the interdicted answers?

I dare say that I may, notwithstanding the danger, if upon reflection I approve of any of them.

But what if I give you an answer about justice other and better, he said, than any of these? What do you deserve to have done to you?

Done to me!—as becomes the ignorant, I must learn from the wise—that is what I deserve to have done to me.

What, and no payment! a pleasant notion!

I will pay when I have the money, I replied.

But you have, Socrates, said Glaucon: and you, Thrasymachus, need be under no anxiety about money, for we will all make a contribution for Socrates.

Yes, he replied, and then Socrates will do as he always does—refuse to answer himself, but take and pull to pieces the answer of some one else.

Why, my good friend, I said, how can any one answer who knows and says that he knows, just nothing; and who, even if he has some faint notions of his own, is told by a man of authority not to utter them? The natural thing is, that the speaker should be some one like yourself who professes to know and can tell what he knows. Will you then kindly answer, for the edification of the company and of myself?

Glaucon and the rest of the company joined in my request, and Thrasymachus, as any one might see, was in reality eager to speak; for he thought that he had an excellent answer, and would distinguish himself. But at first he affected to insist on my answering; at length he consented to begin. Behold, he said, the wisdom of Socrates; he refuses to teach himself, and goes about learning of others, to whom he never even says Thank you.

That I learn of others, I replied, is quite true; but that I am ungrateful I wholly deny. Money I have none, and therefore I pay in praise, which is all I have; and how ready I am to praise any one who appears to me to speak well you will very soon find out when you answer; for I expect that you will answer well.

Listen, then, he said; I proclaim that justice is nothing else than the interest of the stronger. And now why do you not praise me? But of course you won't.

Let me first understand you, I replied. Justice, as you say, is the interest of the stronger. What, Thrasymachus, is the meaning of this? You can not mean to say that because Polydamas, the pancratiast, is stronger than we are, and finds the eating of beef conducive to his bodily strength, that to eat beef is therefore equally for our good who are weaker than he is, and right and just for us?

That's abominable of you, Socrates; you take the words in the sense which is most damaging to the argument.

Not at all, my good sir, I said; I am trying to understand them; and I wish that you would be a little clearer.

Well, he said, have you never heard that forms of government differ; there are tyrannies, and there are democracies, and there are aristocracies?

Yes, I know.

And the government is the ruling power in each state?

Certainly.

And the different forms of government make laws democratical, aristocratical, tyrannical, with a view to their several interests; and these laws, which are made by them for their own interests, are the justice which they deliver to their subjects, and him who transgresses them they punish as a breaker of the law, and unjust. And that is what I mean when I say that in all states there is the same principle of justice, which is the interest of the government; and as the government must be supposed to have power, the only reasonable conclusion is, that everywhere there is one principle of justice, which is the interest of the stronger.

Now I understand you, I said; and whether you are right or not I will try to discover. But let me remark, that in defining justice you have yourself used the word "interest" which you forbade me to use. It is true, however, that in your definition the words "of the stronger" are added.

A small addition, you must allow, he said.

Great or small, never mind about that: we must first inquire whether what you are saying is the truth. Now we are both agreed that justice is interest of some sort, but you go on to say "of the stronger"; about this addition I am not so sure, and must therefore consider further.

Proceed.

I will; and first tell me, Do you admit that it is just for subjects to obey their rulers?

I do.

But are the rulers of states absolutely infallible, or are they sometimes liable to err?

To be sure, he replied, they are liable to err.

Then in making their laws they may sometimes make them rightly, and sometimes not?

True.

When they make them rightly, they make them agreeably to their interest; when they are mistaken, contrary to their interest; you admit that?

Yes.

And the laws which they make must be obeyed by their subjects,—and that is what you call justice?

Doubtless.

Then justice, according to your argument, is not only obedience to the interest of the stronger but the reverse?

What is that you are saying? he asked.

I am only repeating what you are saying, I believe. But let us consider: Have we not admitted that the rulers may be mistaken about their own interest in what they command, and also that to obey them is justice? Has not that been admitted?

Yes.

Then you must also have acknowledged justice not to be for the interest of the stronger, when the rulers unintentionally command things to be done which are to their own injury. For if, as you say, justice is the obedience which the subject renders to their com-

mands, in that case, O wisest of men, is there any escape from the conclusion that the weaker are commanded to do, not what is for the interest, but what is for the injury of the stronger?

Nothing can be clearer, Socrates, said Polemarchus.

Yes, said Cleitophon, interposing, if you are allowed to be his witness.

But there is no need of any witness, said Polemarchus, for Thrasymachus himself acknowledges that rulers may sometimes command what is not for their own interest, and that for subjects to obey them is justice.

Yes, Polemarchus,—Thrasymachus said that for subjects to do what was commanded by their rulers is just.

Yes, Cleitophon, but he also said that justice is the interest of the stronger, and, while admitting both these propositions, he further acknowledged that the stronger may command the weaker who are his subjects to do what is not for his own interest; whence follows that justice is the injury quite as much as the interest of the stronger.

But, said Cleitophon, he meant by the interest of the stronger what the stronger thought to be his interest,—this was what the weaker had to do; and this was affirmed by him to be justice.

Those were not his words, rejoined Polemarchus.

Never mind, I replied, if he now says that they are, let us accept his statement. Tell me, Thrasymachus, I said, did you mean by justice what the stronger thought to be his interest, whether really so or not?

Certainly not, he said. Do you suppose that I call him who is mistaken the stronger at the time when he is mistaken?

Yes, I said, my impression was that you did so, when you admitted that the ruler was not infallible but might be sometimes mistaken.

You argue like an informer, Socrates. Do you mean, for example, that he who is mistaken about the sick is a physician in that he is mistaken? or that he who errs in arithmetic or grammar is an arithmetician or grammarian at the time when he is making the mistake, in respect of the mistake? True, we say that the physician or arithmetician or grammarian has made a mistake, but this is only a way of speaking; for the fact is that neither the grammarian nor any other person of skill ever makes a mistake in so far as he is what his name implies; they none of them err unless their skill fails them, and then they cease to be skilled artists. No artist or sage or ruler errs at the time when he is what his name implies; though he is commonly said to err, and I adopted the common mode of speaking. But to be perfectly accurate, since you are such a lover of accuracy, we should say that the ruler, in so far as he is ruler, is unerring, and, being unerring, always commands that which is for his own interest; and the subject is required to execute his commands; and therefore, as I said at first and now repeat, justice is the interest of the stronger.

Indeed, Thrasymachus, and do I really appear to you to argue like an informer?

Certainly, he replied.

And do you suppose that I ask these questions with any design of injuring you in the argument?

Nay, he replied, "suppose" is not the word—I know it; but you will be found out, and by sheer force of argument you will never prevail.

I shall not make the attempt, my dear man; but to avoid any misunderstanding occurring between us in future, let me ask, in what sense do you speak of a ruler or stronger whose interest, as you were saying, he being the superior, it is just that the inferior should execute—is he a ruler in the popular or in the strict sense of the term?

In the strictest of all senses, he said. And now cheat and play the informer if you can; I ask no quarter at your hands. But you never will be able, never.

And do you imagine, I said, that I am such a madman as to try and cheat Thrasymachus? I might as well shave a lion.

Why, he said, you made the attempt a minute ago, and you failed.

Enough, I said, of these civilities. It will be better that I should ask you a question: Is the physician, taken in that strict sense of which you are speaking, a healer of the sick or a maker of money? And remember that I am now speaking of the true physician.

A healer of the sick, he replied.

And the pilot—that is to say, the true pilot—is he a captain of sailors or a mere sailor?

A captain of sailors.

The circumstance that he sails in the ship is not to be taken into account; neither is he to be called a sailor; the name pilot by which he is distinguished has nothing to do with sailing, but is significant of his skill and of his authority over the sailors.

Very true, he said.

Now, I said, every art has an interest?

Certainly.

For which the art has to consider and provide?

Yes, that is the aim of art.

And the interest of any art is the perfection of it—this and nothing else?

What do you mean?

I mean what I may illustrate negatively by the example of the body. Suppose you were to ask me whether the body is self-sufficing or has wants, I should reply: Certainly the body has wants; for the body may be ill and require to be cured, and has therefore interests to which the art of medicine ministers; and this is the origin and intention of medicine, as you will acknowledge. Am I not right?

Quite right, he replied.

But is the art of medicine or any other art faulty or deficient in any quality in the same way that the eye may be deficient in sight or the ear fail of hearing, and therefore requires another art to provide for the interests of seeing and hearing—has art in itself, I say, any similar liability to fault or defect, and does every art require another supplementary art to provide for its interests, and that another and another without end? Or have the arts to look only after their own interests? Or have they no need either of themselves or of another?—having no faults or defects, they have no need to correct them, either by the exercise of their own art or of any other; they have only to consider the interest of their subject-matter. For every art remains pure and faultless while remaining true—that is to say, while perfect and unimpaired. Take the words in your precise sense, and tell me whether I am not right.

Yes, clearly.

Then medicine does not consider the interest of medicine, but the interest of the body?

True, he said.

Nor does the art of horsemanship consider the interests of the art of horsemanship, but the interests of the horse; neither do any other arts care for themselves, for they have no needs; they care only for that which is the subject of their art?

True, he said.

But surely, Thrasymachus, the arts are the superiors and rulers of their own subjects?

To this he assented with a good deal of reluctance.

Then, I said, no science or art considers or enjoins the interest of the stronger or superior, but only the interest of the subject and weaker?

He made an attempt to contest this proposition also, but finally acquiesced.

Then, I continued, no physician, in so far as he is a physician, considers his own good in what he prescribes, but the good of his patient; for the true physician is also a ruler having the human body as a subject, and is not a mere money-maker; that has been admitted?

Yes.

And the pilot likewise, in the strict sense of the term, is a ruler of sailors and not a mere sailor.

That has been admitted.

And such a pilot and ruler will provide and prescribe for the interest of the sailor who is under him, and not for his own or the ruler's interest?

He gave a reluctant "Yes."

Then, I said, Thrasymachus, there is no one in any rule who, in so far as he is a ruler, considers or enjoins what is for his own interest, but always what is for the interest of his subject or suitable to his art; to that he looks, and that alone he considers in everything which he says and does.

When we had got to this point in the argument, and every one saw that the definition of justice had been completely upset, Thrasymachus, instead of replying to me, said: Tell me, Socrates, have you got a nurse?

Why do you ask such a question, I said, when you ought rather to be answering?

Because she leaves you to snivel, and never wipes your nose: she has not even taught you to know the shepherd from the sheep.

What makes you say that? I replied.

Because you fancy that the shepherd or neatherd fattens or tends the sheep or oxen with a view to their own good and not to the good of himself or his master; and you further imagine that the rulers of states, if they are true rulers, never think of their subjects as sheep, and that they are not studying their own advantage day and night. Oh, no; and so entirely astray are you in your ideas about the just and unjust as not even to know that justice and the just are in reality another's good; that is to say, the interest of the ruler and stronger, and the loss of the subject and servant; and injustice the opposite; for the unjust is lord over the truly simple and just: he is the stronger, and his subjects do what is for his interest, and minister to his happiness, which is very far from being their own. Consider further, most foolish Socrates, that the just is always a loser in comparison with the unjust. First of all, in private contracts: wherever the unjust is the partner of the just you will find that, when the partnership is dissolved, the unjust man has always more and the just less. Secondly, in their dealings with the State: when there is an income-tax, the just man will pay more and the unjust less on the same amount of income; and when there is anything to be received the one gains nothing and the other much. Observe also what happens when they take an office; there is the just man neglecting his affairs and perhaps suffering other losses and getting nothing out of the public, because he is just; moreover he is hated by his friends and acquaintance for refusing to serve them in unlawful ways. But all this is reversed in the case of the unjust man. I am speaking, as before, of injustice on a large scale in which the advantage of the unjust is most apparent; and my meaning will be most clearly seen if we turn to that highest form of injustice in which the criminal is the happiest of men, and the sufferers or those who refuse to do injustice are the most miserable—that is to say tyranny, which by fraud and force takes away the property of others, not little by little but wholesale; comprehending in one, things sacred as well as profane, private and public; for which acts of wrong, if he were detected perpetrating any of them singly, he would be punished and incur great disgrace—they who do such wrong in particular cases are called robbers of temples, and man-stealers and burglars and swindlers and thieves. But when a man besides taking away the money of the citizens has made slaves of them, then, instead of these names of reproach, he is termed happy and blessed, not only by the citizens but by all who hear of his having achieved the consummation of injustice. For mankind censure injustice, fearing that they may be victims of it and not because they shrink from committing it. And thus, as I have shown, Socrates, injustice, when on a sufficient scale, has more strength and freedom and mastery than justice; and, as I said at first, justice is the interest of the stronger, whereas injustice is a man's own profit and interest.

Thrasymachus, when he had thus spoken, having, like a bath-man, deluged our ears with his words, had a mind to go away. But the company would not let him; they insisted that he should remain and defend his position; and I myself added my own humble request that he would not leave us.

Thrasymachus, I said to him, excellent man, how suggestive are your remarks! And are you going to run away before you have fairly taught or learned whether they are true or not? Is the attempt to determine the way of man's life so small a matter in your eyes—to determine how life may be passed by each one of us to the greatest advantage?

And do I differ from you, he said, as to the importance of the inquiry?

You appear rather, I replied, to have no care or thought about us, Thrasymachus—whether we live better or worse from not knowing what you say you know, is to you a matter of indifference. Prithee, friend, do not keep your knowledge to yourself; we are a large party; and any benefit which you confer upon us will be amply rewarded. For my own part I openly declare that I am not convinced, and that I do not believe injustice to be more gainful than justice, even if uncontrolled and allowed to have free play. For, granting that there may be an unjust man who is able to commit injustice either by fraud or force, still this does not convince me of the superior advantage of injustice, and there may be others who are in the same predicament with myself. Perhaps we may be wrong; if so, you in your wisdom should convince us that we are mistaken in preferring justice to injustice.

And how am I to convince you, he said, if you are not already convinced by what I have just said; what more can I do for you? Would you have me put the proof bodily into your souls?

Heaven forbid! I said; I would only ask you to be consistent; or, if you change, change openly and let there be no deception. For I must remark, Thrasymachus, if you will recall what was previously said, that although you began by defining the true physician in an exact sense, you did not observe a like exactness when speaking of the shepherd; you thought that the shepherd as a shepherd tends the sheep not with a view to their own good, but like a mere diner or banqueter with a view to the pleasures of the table; or, again, as a trader for sale in the market, and not as a shepherd. Yet surely the art of the shepherd is concerned only with the good of his subjects; he has only to provide the best for them, since the perfection of the art is already ensured whenever all the requirements of it are satisfied. And that was what I was saying just now about the ruler. I conceived that the art of the ruler, considered as ruler, whether in a state or in private life, could only regard the good of his flock or subjects; whereas you seem to think that the rulers in states, that is to say, the true rulers, like being in authority.

Think! Nay, I am sure of it.

Then why in the case of lesser offices do men never take them willingly without payment, unless under the idea that they govern for the advantage not of themselves but of others? Let me ask you a question: Are not the several arts different, by reason of their each having a separate function? And, my dear illustrious friend, do say what you think, that we may make a little progress.

Yes, that is the difference, he replied.

And each art gives us a particular good and not merely a general one—medicine, for example, gives us health; navigation, safety at sea, and so on?

Yes, he said.

And the art of payment has the special function of giving pay: but we do not confuse this with other arts, any more than the art of the pilot is to be confused with the art of medicine, because the health of the pilot may be improved by a sea voyage. You would not be inclined to say, would you, that navigation is the art of medicine, at least if we are to adopt your exact use of language?

Certainly not.

Or because a man is in good health when he receives pay you would not say that the art of payment is medicine?

I should not.

Nor would you say that medicine is the art of receiving pay because a man takes fees when he is engaged in healing?

Certainly not.

And we have admitted, I said, that the good of each art is specially confined to the art?

Yes.

Then, if there be any good which all artists have in common, that is to be attributed to something of which they all have the common use?

True, he replied.

And when the artist is benefited by receiving pay the advantage is gained by an additional use of the art of pay, which is not the art professed by him?

He gave a reluctant assent to this.

Then the pay is not derived by the several artists from their respective arts. But the truth is, that while the art of medicine gives health, and the art of the builder builds a house, another art attends them which is the art of pay. The various arts may be doing their own business and benefiting that over which they preside, but would the artist receive any benefit from his art unless he were paid as well?

I suppose not.

But does he therefore confer no benefit when he works for nothing?

Certainly, he confers a benefit.

Then now, Thrasymachus, there is no longer any doubt that neither arts nor governments provide for their own interests; but, as we were before saying, they rule and provide for the interests of their subjects who are the weaker and not the stronger—to their good they attend and not to the good of the superior. And this is the reason, my dear Thrasymachus, why, as I was just now saying, no one is willing to govern; because no one likes to take in hand the reformation of evils which are not his concern without remuneration. For, in the execution of his work, and in giving his orders to another, the true artist does not regard his own interest, but always that of his subjects; and therefore in order that rulers may be willing to rule, they must be paid in one of three modes of payment, money or honor, or a penalty for refusing.

What do you mean, Socrates? said Glaucon. The first two modes of payment are intelligible enough, but what the penalty is I do not understand, or how a penalty can be a payment.

You mean that you do not understand the nature of this payment which to the best men is the great inducement to rule? Of course you know that ambition and avarice are held to be, as indeed they are, a disgrace?

Very true.

And for this reason, I said, money and honor have no attraction for them; good men do not wish to be openly demanding payment for governing and so to get the name of hirelings, nor by secretly helping themselves out of the public revenues to get the name of thieves. And not being ambitious they do not care about honor. Wherefore necessity must be laid upon them, and they must be induced to serve from the fear of punishment. And this, as I imagine, is the reason why the forwardness to take office, instead of waiting to be compelled, has been deemed dishonorable. Now the worst part of the punishment is that he who refuses to rule is liable to be ruled by one who is worse than himself. And the fear of this, as I conceive,

induces the good to take office, not because they would, but because they can not help—not under the idea that they are going to have any benefit or enjoyment themselves, but as a necessity, and because they are not able to commit the task of ruling to any one who is better than themselves, or indeed as good. For there is reason to think that if a city were composed entirely of good men, then to avoid office would be as much an object of contention as to obtain office is at present; then we should have plain proof that the true ruler is not meant by nature to regard his own interest, but that of his subjects; and every one who knew this would choose rather to receive a benefit from another than to have the trouble of conferring one. So far am I from agreeing with Thrasymachus that justice is the interest of the stronger. This latter question need not be further discussed at present; but when Thrasymachus says that the life of the unjust is more advantageous than that of the just, his new statement appears to me to be of a far more serious character. Which of us has spoken truly? And which sort of life, Glaucon, do you prefer?

I for my part deem the life of the just to be the more advantageous, he answered.

Did you hear all the advantages of the unjust which Thrasymachus was rehearsing?

Yes, I heard him, he replied, but he has not convinced me.

Then shall we try to find some way of convincing him, if we can, that he is saying what is not true?

Most certainly, he replied.

If, I said, he makes a set speech and we make another recounting all the advantages of being just, and he answers and we rejoin, there must be a numbering and measuring of the goods which are claimed on either side, and in the end we shall want judges to decide; but if we proceed in our inquiry as we lately did, by making admissions to one another, we shall unite the offices of judge and advocate in our own persons.

Very good, he said.

And which method do I understand you to prefer? I said.

That which you propose.

Well, then, Thrasymachus, I said, suppose you begin at the beginning and answer me. You say that perfect injustice is more gainful than perfect justice?

Yes, that is what I say, and I have given you my reasons.

And what is your view about them? Would you call one of them virtue and the other vice?

Certainly.

I suppose that you would call justice virtue and injustice vice?

What a charming notion! So likely too, seeing that I affirm injustice to be profitable and justice not.

What else then would you say?

The opposite, he replied.

And would you call justice vice?

No, I would rather say sublime simplicity.

Then would you call injustice malignity?

No; I would rather say discretion.

And do the unjust appear to you to be wise and good?

Yes, he said; at any rate those of them who are able to be perfectly unjust, and who have the power of subduing states and nations; but perhaps you imagine me to be talking of cutpurses. Even this profession if undetected has advantages, though they are not to be compared with those of which I was just now speaking.

I do not think that I misapprehend your meaning, Thrasymachus, I replied; but still I can not hear without amazement that you class injustice with wisdom and virtue, and justice with the opposite.

Certainly, I do so class them.

Now, I said, you are on more substantial and almost unanswerable ground; for if the injustice which you were maintaining to be profitable had been admitted by you as by others to be vice and deformity, an answer might have been given to you on received principles; but now I perceive that you will call injustice honorable and strong, and to the unjust you will attribute all the qualities which were attributed by us before to the just, seeing that you do not hesitate to rank injustice with wisdom and virtue.

You have guessed most infallibly, he replied.

Then I certainly ought not to shrink from going through with the argument so long as I have reason to think that you, Thrasymachus, are speaking your real mind; for I do believe that you are now in earnest and are not amusing yourself at our expense.

I may be in earnest or not, but what is that to you?—to refute the argument is your business.

Very true, I said; that is what I have to do: But will you be so good as answer yet one more question? Does the just man try to gain any advantage over the just?

Far otherwise; if he did he would not be the simple amusing creature which he is.

And would he try to go beyond just action?

He would not.

And how would he regard the attempt to gain an advantage over the unjust; would that be considered by him as just or unjust?

He would think it just, and would try to gain the advantage; but he would not be able.

Whether he would or would not be able, I said, is not to the point. My question is only whether the just man, while refusing to have more than another just man, would wish and claim to have more than the unjust?

Yes, he would.

And what of the unjust—does he claim to have more than the just man and to do more than is just?

Of course, he said, for he claims to have more than all men.

And the unjust man will strive and struggle to obtain more than the unjust man or action, in order that he may have more than all?

True.

We may put the matter thus, I said—the just does not desire more than his like but more than his unlike, whereas the unjust desires more than both his like and his unlike?

Nothing, he said, can be better than that statement.

And the unjust is good and wise, and the just is neither?

Good again, he said.

And is not the unjust like the wise and good and the just unlike them?

Of course, he said, he who is of a certain nature, is like those who are of a certain nature; he who is not, not.

Each of them, I said, is such as his like is?

Certainly, he replied.

Very good, Thrasymachus, I said; and now to take the case of the arts: you would admit that one man is a musician and another not a musician?

Yes.

And which is wise and which is foolish?

Clearly the musician is wise, and he who is not a musician is foolish.

And he is good in as far as he is wise, and bad in as far as he is foolish?

Yes.

And you would say the same sort of thing of the physician?

Yes.

And do you think, my excellent friend, that a musician when he adjusts the lyre would desire or claim to exceed or go beyond a musician in the tightening and loosening the strings?

I do not think that he would.

But he would claim to exceed the non-musician?

Of course.

And what would you say of the physician? In prescribing meats and drinks would he wish to go beyond another physician or beyond the practice of medicine?

He would not.

But he would wish to go beyond the non-physician?

Yes.

And about knowledge and ignorance in general; see whether you think that any man who has knowledge ever would wish to have the choice of saying or doing more than another man who has knowledge. Would he not rather say or do the same as his like in the same case?

That, I suppose, can hardly be denied.

And what of the ignorant? would he not desire to have more than either the knowing or the ignorant?

I dare say.

And the knowing is wise?

Yes.

And the wise is good?

True.

Then the wise and good will not desire to gain more than his like, but more than his unlike and opposite?

I suppose so.

Whereas the bad and ignorant will desire to gain more than both?

Yes.

But did we not say, Thrasymachus, that the unjust goes beyond both his like and unlike? Were not these your words?

They were.

And you also said that the just will not go beyond his like but his unlike?

Yes.

Then the just is like the wise and good, and the unjust like the evil and ignorant?

That is the inference.

And each of them is such as his like is?

That was admitted.

Then the just has turned out to be wise and good and the unjust evil and ignorant.

Thrasymachus made all these admissions, not fluently, as I repeat them, but with extreme reluctance; it was a hot summer's day, and the perspiration poured from him in torrents; and then I saw what I had never seen before, Thrasymachus blushing. As we were now agreed that justice was virtue and wisdom, and injustice vice and ignorance, I proceeded to another point:

Well, I said, Thrasymachus, that matter is now settled; but were we not also saying that injustice had strength; do you remember?

Yes, I remember, he said, but do not suppose that I approve of what you are saying or have no answer; if however I were to answer, you would be quite certain to accuse me of haranguing; therefore either permit me to have my say out, or if you would rather ask, do so, and I will answer "Very good," as they say to story-telling old women, and will nod "Yes" and "No."

Certainly not, I said, if contrary to your real opinion.

Yes, he said, I will, to please you, since you will not let me speak. What else would you have?

Nothing in the world, I said; and if you are so disposed I will ask and you shall answer.

Proceed.

Then I will repeat the question which I asked before, in order that our examination of the relative nature of justice and injustice may be carried on regularly. A statement was made that injustice is stronger and more powerful than justice, but now justice, having been identified with wisdom and virtue, is easily shown to be stronger than injustice, if injustice is ignorance; this can no longer be questioned by any one. But I want to view the matter, Thrasymachus, in a different way: You would not deny that a state may be unjust and may be unjustly attempting to enslave other states; or may have already enslaved them, and may be holding many of them in subjection?

True, he replied; and I will add that the best and most perfectly unjust state will be most likely to do so.

I know, I said, that such was your position; but what I would further consider is, whether this power which is possessed by the superior state can exist or be exercised without justice or only with justice.

If you are right in your view, and justice is wisdom, then only with justice; but if I am right, then without justice.

I am delighted, Thrasymachus, to see you not only nodding assent and dissent, but making answers which are quite excellent.

That is out of civility to you, he replied.

You are very kind, I said; and would you have the goodness also to inform me, whether you think that a state, or an army, or a band of robbers and thieves, or any other gang of evil-doers could act at all if they injured one another?

No indeed, he said, they could not.

But if they abstained from injuring one another, then they might act together better?

Yes.

And this is because injustice creates divisions and hatreds and fighting, and justice imparts harmony and friendship; is not that true, Thrasymachus?

I agree, he said, because I do not wish to quarrel with you.

How good of you, I said; but I should like to know also whether injustice, having this tendency to arouse hatred, wherever existing, among slaves or among freemen, will not make them hate one another and set them at variance and render them incapable of common action?

Certainly.

And even if injustice be found in two only, will they not quarrel and fight, and become enemies to one another and to the just?

They will.

And suppose injustice abiding in a single person, would your wisdom say that she loses or that she retains her natural power?

Let us assume that she retains her power.

Yet is not the power which injustice exercises of such a nature that wherever she takes up her abode, whether in a city, in an army, in a family, or in any other body, that body is, to begin with, rendered incapable of united action by reason of sedition and distraction; and does it not become its own enemy and at variance with all that opposes it, and with the just? Is not this the case?

Yes, certainly

And is not injustice equally fatal when existing in a single person; in the first place rendering him incapable of action because he is not at unity with himself, and in the second place making him an enemy to himself and the just? Is not that true, Thrasymachus?

Yes.

And O my friend, I said, surely the gods are just? Granted that they are.

But if so, the unjust will be the enemy of the gods, and the just will be their friends?

Feast away in triumph, and take your fill of the argument; I will not oppose you, lest I should displease the company.

Well then, proceed with your answers, and let me have the remainder of my repast. For we have already shown that the just are clearly wiser and better and abler than the unjust, and that the unjust are incapable of common action; nay more, that to speak as we did of men who are evil acting at any time vigorously together, is not strictly true, for if they had been perfectly evil, they would have laid hands upon one another; but it is evident that there must have been some remnant of justice in them, which enabled them to combine; if there had not been they would have injured one another as well as their victims; they were but half-villains in their enterprises; for had they been whole villains, and utterly unjust, they would have been utterly incapable of action. That, as I believe, is the truth of the matter, and not what you said at first. But whether the just have a better and happier life than the unjust is a further question which we also proposed to consider. I think that they have, and for the reasons which I have given; but still I should like to examine further, for no light matter is at stake, nothing less than the rule of human life.

Proceed.

I will proceed by asking a question: Would you not say that a horse has some end?

I should.

And the end or use of a horse or of anything would be that which could not be accomplished or not so well accomplished, by any other thing?

I do not understand, he said.

Let me explain: Can you see, except with the eye? Certainly not.

Or hear, except with the ear?

No.

These then may be truly said to be the ends of these organs?

They may.

But you can cut off a vine-branch with a dagger or with a chisel, and in many other ways?

Of course.

And yet not so well as with a pruning-hook made for the purpose?

True.

May we not say that this is the end of a pruning-hook?

We may.

Then now I think you will have no difficulty in understanding my meaning when I asked the question whether the end of anything would be that which could not be accomplished, or not so well accomplished, by any other thing?

I understand your meaning, he said, and assent.

And that to which an end is appointed has also an excellence? Need I ask again whether the eye has an end?

It has.

And has not the eye an excellence?

Yes.

And the ear has an end and an excellence also?

True.

And the same is true of all other things; they have each of them an end and a special excellence?

That is so.

Well, and can the eyes fulfill their end if they are wanting in their own proper excellence and have a defect instead?

How can they, he said, if they are blind and can not see?

You mean to say, if they have lost their proper excellence, which is sight, but I have not arrived at that point yet. I would rather ask the question more generally, and only inquire whether the things which fulfill their ends fulfill them by their own proper excellence, and fail of fulfilling them by their own defect?

Certainly, he replied.

I might say the same of the ears; when deprived of their own proper excellence they can not fulfill their end?

True.

And the same observation will apply to all other things?

I agree.

Well; and has not the soul an end which nothing else can fulfill? for example, to superintend and command and deliberate and the like. Are not these functions proper to the soul, and can they rightly be assigned to any other?

To no other.

And is not life to be reckoned among the ends of the soul?

Assuredly, he said.

And has not the soul an excellence also?

Yes.

And can she or can she not fulfill her own ends when deprived of that excellence?

She can not.

Then an evil soul must necessarily be an evil ruler and superintendent, and the good soul a good ruler?

Yes, necessarily.

And we have admitted that justice is the excellence of the soul, and injustice the defect of the soul?

That has been admitted.

Then the just soul and the just man will live well, and the unjust man will live ill?

That is what your argument proves.

And he who lives well is blessed and happy, and he who lives ill the reverse of happy?

Certainly.

Then the just is happy, and the unjust miserable?

So be it.

But happiness and not misery is profitable.

Of course.

Then, my blessed Thrasymachus, injustice can never be more profitable than justice.

Let this, Socrates, he said, be your entertainment at the Bendidea.

For which I am indebted to you, I said, now that you have grown gentle towards me and have left off scolding. Nevertheless, I have not been well entertained; but that was my own fault and not yours. As an epicure snatches a taste of every dish which is successively brought to table, he not having allowed himself time to enjoy the one before, so have I gone from one subject to another without having discovered what I sought at first, the nature of justice. I left that inquiry and turned away to consider whether justice is virtue and wisdom or evil and folly; and when there arose a further question about the comparative advantages of justice and injustice, I could not refrain from passing on to that. And the result of the whole discussion has been that I know nothing at all. For I know not what justice is, and therefore I am not likely to know whether it is or is not a virtue, nor can I say whether the just man is happy or unhappy.

Book II

With these words I was thinking that I had made an end of the discussion; but the end, in truth, proved to be only a beginning. For Glaucon, who is always the most pugnacious of men, was dissatisfied at Thrasymachus' retirement; he wanted to have the battle out. So he said to me: Socrates, do you wish really to persuade us, or only to seem to have persuaded us, that to be just is always better than to be unjust?

I should wish really to persuade you, I replied, if I could.

Then you certainly have not succeeded. Let me ask you now:—How would you arrange goods—are there not some which we welcome for their own sakes, and independently of their consequences, as, for example, harmless pleasures and enjoyments, which delight us at the time, although nothing follows from them?

I agree in thinking that there is such a class, I replied.

Is there not also a second class of goods, such as knowledge, sight, health, which are desirable not only in themselves, but also for their results?

Certainly, I said.

And would you not recognize a third class, such as gymnastic, and the care of the sick, and the physician's art; also the various ways of money-making—these do us good but we regard them as disagreeable; and no one would choose them for their own sakes, but only for the sake of some reward or result which flows from them?

There is, I said, this third class also. But why do you ask?

Because I want to know in which of the three classes you would place justice?

In the highest class, I replied,—among those goods which he who would be happy desires both for their own sake and for the sake of their results.

Then the many are of another mind; they think that justice is to be reckoned in the troublesome class, among goods which are to be pursued for the sake of rewards and of reputation, but in themselves are disagreeable and rather to be avoided.

I know, I said, that this is their manner of thinking, and that this was the thesis which Thrasymachus was maintaining just now, when he censured justice and praised injustice. But I am too stupid to be convinced by him.

I wish, he said, that you would hear me as well as him, and then I shall see whether you and I agree. For Thrasymachus seems to me, like a snake, to have been charmed by your voice sooner than he ought to have been; but to my mind the nature of justice and injus-

tice have not yet been made clear. Setting aside their rewards and results, I want to know what they are in themselves, and how they inwardly work in the soul. If you please, then, I will revive the argument of Thrasymachus. And first I will speak of the nature and origin of justice according to the common view of them. Secondly, I will show that all men who practices justice do so against their will, of necessity, but not as a good. And thirdly, I will argue that there is reason in this view, for the life of the unjust is after all better far than the life of the just—if what they say is true, Socrates, since I myself am not of their opinion. But still I acknowledge that I am perplexed when I hear the voices of Thrasymachus and myriads of others dinning in my ears; and, on the other hand, I have never yet heard the superiority of justice to injustice maintained by any one in a satisfactory way. I want to hear justice praised in respect of itself; then I shall be satisfied, and you are the person from whom I think that I am most likely to hear this; and therefore I will praise the unjust life to the utmost of my power, and my manner of speaking will indicate the manner in which I desire to hear you too praising justice and censuring injustice. Will you say whether you approve of my proposal?

Indeed I do; nor can I imagine any theme about which a man of sense would oftener wish to converse.

I am delighted, he replied, to hear you say so, and shall begin by speaking, as I proposed, of the nature and origin of justice.

They say that to do injustice is, by nature, good; to suffer injustice, evil; but that the evil is greater than the good. And so when men have both done and suffered injustice and have had experience of both, not being able to avoid the one and obtain the other, they think that they had better agree among themselves to have neither; hence there arise laws and mutual covenants; and that which is ordained by law is termed by them lawful and just. This they affirm to be the origin and nature of justice;—it is a mean or compromise, between the best of all, which is to do injustice and not be punished, and the worst of all, which is to suffer injustice without the power of retaliation; and justice, being at a middle point between the two, is tolerated not as a good, but as the lesser evil, and honored by reason of the inability of men to do injustice. For no man who is worthy to be called a man would ever submit to such an agreement if he were able to resist; he would be mad if he did. Such is the received account, Socrates, of the nature and origin of justice.

͵ Now that those who practise justice do so involuntarily and because they have not the power to be unjust will best appear if we imagine something of this kind: having given both to the just and the unjust power to do what they will, let us watch and see whither desire will lead them; then we shall discover in the very act the just and unjust man to be preceeding along the same road, following their interest, which all natures deem to be their good, and are only diverted into the path of justice by the force of law. The liberty which we are supposing may be most completely given to them in the form of such a power as is said to have been possessed by Gyges, the ancestor of Croesus the Lydian. According to the tradition, Gyges was a shepherd in the service of the king of Lydia; there was a great storm, and an earthquake made an opening in the earth at the place where he was feeding his flock. Amazed at the sight, he descended into the opening, where, among other marvels, he beheld a hollow brazen horse, having doors, at which he stooping and looking in saw a dead body of stature, as appeared to him, more than human, and having nothing on but a gold ring; this he took from the finger of the dead and reascended. Now the shepherds met together, according to custom, that they might send their monthly report about the flocks to the king; into their assembly he came having the ring on his finger, and as he was sitting among them he chanced to turn the collet of the ring inside his hand, when instantly he became invisible to the rest of the company and they began to speak of him as if he were no longer present. He was astonished at this, and again touching the ring he turned the collet outwards and reappeared; he made several trials of the ring, and always with the same result when he turned the collet inwards he became invisible, when outwards he reappeared. Whereupon he contrived to be chosen one of the messengers who were sent to the court; where as soon as he arrived he seduced the queen, and with her help conspired against the king and slew him, and took the kingdom. Suppose now that there were two such magic rings, and the just put on one of them and the unjust the other; no man can be imagined to be of such an iron nature that he would stand fast in justice. No man would keep his hands off what was not his own when he could safely take what he liked out of the market, or go into houses and lie with any one at

his pleasure, or kill or release from prison whom he would, and in all respects be like a God among men. Then the actions of the just would be as the actions of the unjust; they would both come at last to the same point. And this we may truly affirm to be a great proof that a man is just, not willingly or because he thinks that justice is any good to him individually, but of necessity, for wherever any one thinks that he can safely be unjust, there he is unjust. For all men believe in their hearts that injustice is far more profitable to the individual than justice, and he who argues as I have been supposing, will say that they are right. If you could imagine any one obtaining this power of becoming invisible, and never doing any wrong or touching what was another's, he would be thought by the lookers-on to be a most wretched idiot, although they would praise him to one another's faces, and keep up appearances with one another from a fear that they too might suffer injustice. Enough of this.

Now, if we are to form a real judgment of the life of the just and unjust, we must isolate them; there is no other way; and how is the isolation to be effected? I answer: Let the unjust man be entirely unjust, and the just man entirely just; nothing is to be taken away from either of them, and both are to be perfectly furnished for the work of their respective lives. First, let the unjust be like other distinguished masters of craft; like the skilful pilot or physician, who knows intuitively his own powers and keeps within their limits, and who, if he fails at any point, is able to recover himself. So let the unjust make his unjust attempts in the right way, and lie hidden if he means to be great in his injustice: (he who is found out is nobody:) for the highest reach of injustice is, to be deemed just when you are not. Therefore I say that in the perfectly unjust man we must assume the most perfect injustice; there is to be no deduction, but we must allow him, while doing the most unjust acts, to have acquired the greatest reputation for justice. If he have taken a false step he must be able to recover himself; he must be one who can speak with effect, if any of his deeds come to light, and who can force his way where force is required by his courage and strength, and command of money and friends. And at his side let us place the just man in his nobleness and simplicity, wishing, as Æschylus says, to be and not to seem good. There must be no seeming, for if he seem to be just he will he honored and rewarded, and then we shall not know whether he is just for the sake of justice or for the sake of honors and rewards; therefore, let him be clothed in justice only, and have no other covering; and he must be imagined in a state of life the opposite of the former. Let him be the best of men, and let him be thought the worst; then he will have been put to the proof; and we shall see whether he will be affected by the fear of infamy and its consequences. And let him continue thus to the hour of death; being just and seeming to be unjust. When both have reached the uttermost extreme, the one of justice and the other of injustice, let judgment be given which of them is the happier of the two.

Heavens! my dear Glaucon, I said, how energetically you polish them up for the decision, first one and then the other, as if they were two statues.

I do my best, he said. And now that we know what they are like there is no difficulty in tracing out the sort of life which awaits either of them. This I will proceed to describe; but as you may think the description a little too coarse, I ask you to suppose, Socrates, that the words which follow are not mine.—Let me put them into the mouths of the eulogists of injustice: They will tell you that the just man who is thought unjust will be scourged, racked, bound—will have his eyes burned out; and, at last, after suffering every kind of evil, he will be impaled: Then he will understand that he ought to seem only, and not to be, just; the words of Æschylus may be more truly spoken of the unjust than of the just. For the unjust is pursuing a reality; he does not live with a view to appearances—he wants to be really unjust and not to seem only:—

"His mind has a soil deep and fertile,
Out of which spring his prudent counsels."

In the first place, he is thought just, and therefore bears rule in the city; he can marry whom he will, and give in marriage to whom he will; also he can trade and deal where he likes, and always to his own advantage, because he has no misgivings about injustice; and at every contest, whether in public or private, he gets the better of his antagonists, and gains at their expense, and is rich, and out of his gains he can benefit his friends, and harm his enemies; moreover, he can offer sacrifices, and dedicate gifts to the gods abundantly and magnificently, and can honor the gods or any man whom he wants to honor in a far better style than the just, and therefore he is likely to be dearer than they are to the gods. And thus, Socrates, gods and men are said to unite in making the life of the unjust better than the life of the just.

I was going to say something in answer to Glaucon, when Adeimantus, his brother, interposed: Socrates, he said, you do not suppose that there is nothing more to be urged?

Why, what else is there? I answered.

The strongest point of all has not been even mentioned, he replied.

Well, then, according to the proverb, "Let brother help brother"—if he fails in any part do you assist him; although I must confess that Glaucon has already said quite enough to lay me in the dust, and take from me the power of helping justice.

Nonsense, he replied. But let me add something more: There is another side to Glaucon's argument about the praise and censure of justice and injustice, which is equally required in order to bring out what I believe to be his meaning. Parents and tutors are always telling their sons and their wards that they are to be just; but why? Not for the sake of justice, but for the sake of character and reputation; in the hope of obtaining for him who is reputed just some of those offices, marriages, and the like which Glaucon has enumerated among the advantages accruing to the unjust from the reputation of justice. More, however, is made of appearances by this class of persons than by the others; for they throw in the good opinion of the gods, and will tell you of a shower of benefits which the heavens, as they say, rain upon the pious; and this accords with the testimony of the noble Hesiod and Homer, the first of whom says, that the gods make the oaks of the just—

"To bear acorns at their summit, and bees in the middle;
And the sheep are bowed down with the weight of their fleeces,"

and many other blessings of a like kind are provided for them. And Homer has a very similar strain; for he speaks of one whose fame is—

"As the fame of some blameless king who, like a god,
Maintains justice; to whom the black earth brings forth
Wheat and barley, whose trees are bowed with fruit,
And his sheep never fail to bear, and the sea gives him fish."

Still grander are the gifts of heaven which Musaeus and his son vouchsafe to the just; they take them down into the world below, where they have the saints lying on couches at a feast, everlastingly drunk, crowned with garlands; their ideas seem to be that an immortality of drunkenness is the highest meed of virtue. Some extend their rewards yet further; the posterity, as they say, of the faithful and just shall survive to the third and fourth generation. This is the style in which they praise justice. But about the wicked there is another strain; they bury them in a slough in Hades, and make them carry water in a sieve; also while they are yet living they bring them to infamy, and inflict upon them the punishments which Glaucon described as the portion of the just who are reputed to be unjust; nothing else does their invention supply. Such is their manner of praising the one and censuring the other.

Once more, Socrates, I will ask you to consider another way of speaking about justice and injustice, which is not confined to the poets, but is found in prose writers. The universal voice of mankind is always declaring that justice and virtue are honorable, but grievous and toilsome; and that the pleasures of vice and injustice are easy of attainment, and are only censured by law and opinion. They say also that honesty is for the most part less profitable than dishonesty; and they are quite ready to call wicked men happy, and to honor them both in public and private when they are rich or in any other way influential, while they despise and overlook those who may be weak and poor, even though acknowledging them to be better than the others. But most extraordinary of all is their mode of speaking about virtue and the gods: they say that the gods apportion calamity and misery to many good men, and good and happiness to the wicked. And mendicant prophets go to rich men's doors and persuade them that they have a power committed to them by the gods of making an atonement for a man's own or his ancestors' sins by sacrifices or charms, with rejoicings and feasts; and they promise to harm an enemy, whether just or unjust, at a small cost; with magic arts and incantations binding heaven, as they say, to execute their will. And the poets are the authorities to whom they appeal, now smoothing the path of vice with the words of Hesiod:—

"Vice may be had in abundance without trouble; the way is smooth and her dwelling-place is near. But before virtue the gods have set toil,"

and a tedious and uphill road: then citing Homer as a witness that the gods may be influenced by men; for he also says:—

"The gods, too, may be turned from their purpose; and men pray to them and avert their wrath by sacrifices and soothing entreaties, and by libations and the odor of fat, when they have sinned and transgressed."

And they produce a host of books written by Musaeus and Orpheus, who were children of the Moon and the Muses—that is what they say—according to which they perform their ritual, and persuade not only individuals, but whole cities, that expiations and atonements for sin may be made by sacrifices and amusements which fill a vacant hour, and are equally at the service of the living and the dead; the latter sort they call mysteries, and they redeem us from the pains of hell, but if we neglect them no one knows what awaits us.

He proceeded: And now when the young hear all this said about virtue and vice, and the way in which gods and men regard them, how are their minds likely to be affected, my dear Socrates,—those of them, I mean, who are quickwitted, and, like bees on the wing, light on every flower, and from all that they hear are prone to draw conclusions as to what manner of persons they should be and in what way they should walk if they would make the best of life? Probably the youth will say to himself in the words of Pindar—

"Can I by justice or by crooked ways of deceit ascend a loftier tower which may be a fortress to me all my days?"

For what men say is that, if I am really just and am not also thought just, profit there is none, but the pain and loss on the other hand are unmistakable. But if, though unjust, I acquire the reputation of justice, a heavenly life is promised to me. Since then, as philosophers prove, appearance tyrannizes over truth and is lord of happiness, to appearance I must devote myself. I will describe around me a picture and shadow of virtue to be the vestibule and exterior of my house; behind I will trail the subtle and crafty fox, as Archilochus, greatest of sages, recommends. But I hear some one exclaiming that the concealment of wickedness is often difficult; to which I answer, Nothing great is easy. Nevertheless, the argument indicates this, if we would be happy, to be the path along which we should proceed. With a view to concealment we will establish secret brotherhoods and political clubs. And there are professors of rhetoric who teach the art of persuading courts and assemblies; and so, partly by persuasion and partly by force, I shall make unlawful gains and not be punished. Still I hear a voice saying that thy gods can not be deceived, neither can they be compelled. But what if there are no gods? or, suppose them to have no care of human things—why in either case should we mind about concealment? And even if there are gods, and they do care about us, yet we know of them only from tradition and the genealogies of the poets; and these are the very persons who say that they may be influenced and turned by "sacrifices and soothing entreaties and by offerings." Let us be consistent then, and believe both or neither. If the poets speak truly, why then we had better be unjust and offer of the fruits of injustice; for if we are just, although we may escape the vengeance of heaven, we shall lose the gains of injustice; but, if we are unjust, we shall keep the gains, and by our sinning and praying, and praying and sinning, the gods will be propitiated, and we shall not be punished. "But there is a world below in which either we or our posterity will suffer for our unjust deeds." Yes, my friend, will be the reflection, but there are mysteries and atoning deities, and these have great power. That is what mighty cities declare; and the children of the gods, who were their poets and prophets, bear a like testimony.

On what principle, then, shall we any longer choose justice rather than the worst injustice? when, if we only unite the latter with a deceitful regard to appearances, we shall fare to our mind both with gods and men, in life and after death, as the most numerous and the highest authorities tell us. Knowing all this, Socrates, how can a man who has any superiority of mind or person or rank or wealth, be willing to honor justice; or indeed to refrain from laughing when he hears justice praised? And even if there should be some one who is able to disprove the truth of my words, and who is satisfied that justice is best, still he is not angry with the unjust, but is very ready to forgive them, because he also knows that men are not just of their own free will; unless, peradventure, there be some one whom the divinity within him may have inspired with a hatred of injustice, or who has attained knowledge of the truth—but no other man. He only blames injustice who, owing to cowardice or age or some weakness, has not the power of being unjust. And this is proved by the fact that when he obtains the power, he immediately becomes unjust as far as he can be.

The cause of all this, Socrates, was indicated by us at the beginning of the argument, when my brother and I told you how astonished we were to find that of all the professing panegyrists of justice—beginning with the ancient heroes of whom any memorial has been preserved to us, and ending with the men of our own time—no one has ever blamed injustice or praised justice except with a view to the glories, honors, and benefits which flow from them. No one has ever adequately described either in verse or prose the true essential nature of either of them abiding in the soul, and invisible to any human or divine eye; or shown that of all the things of a man's soul which he has within him, justice is the greatest good, and injustice the greatest evil. Had this been the universal strain, had you sought to persuade us of this from our youth upwards, we should not have been on the watch to keep one another from doing wrong, but every one would have been his own watchman, because afraid, if he did wrong, of harboring in himself the greatest of evils. I dare say that Thrasymachus and others would seriously hold the language which I have been merely repeating, and words even stronger than these about justice and injustice, grossly, as I conceive, perverting their true nature. But I speak in this vehement manner, as I must frankly confess to you, because I want to hear from you the opposite side; and I would ask you to show not only the superiority which justice has over injustice, but what effect they have on the possessor of them which makes the one to be a good and the other an evil to him. And please, as Glaucon requested of you, to exclude reputations; for unless you take away from each of them his true reputation and add on the false, we shall say that you do not praise justice, but the appearance of it; we shall think that you are only exhorting us to keep injustice dark, and that you really agree with Thrasymachus in thinking that justice is another's good and the interest of the stronger, and that injustice is a man's own profit and interest, though injurious to the weaker. Now as you have admitted that justice is one of that highest class of goods which are desired indeed for their results, but in a far greater degree for their own sakes—like sight or hearing or knowledge or health, or any other real and natural and not merely conventional good—I would ask you in your praise of justice to regard one point only: I mean the essential good and evil which justice and injustice work in the possessors of them. Let others praise justice and censure injustice, magnifying the rewards and honors of the one and abusing the other; that is a manner of arguing which, coming from them, I am ready to tolerate, but from you who have spent your whole life in the consideration of this question, unless I hear the contrary from your own lips, I expect something better. And therefore, I say, not only prove to us that justice is better than injustice, but show what they either of them do to the possessor of them, which makes the one to be a good and the other an evil, whether seen or unseen by gods and men.

I had always admired the genius of Glaucon and Adeimantus, but on hearing these words I was quite delighted, and said: Sons of an illustrious father, that was not a bad beginning of the Elegiac verses which the admirer of Glaucon made in honor of you after you had distinguished yourselves at the battle of Megara:

> "Sons of Ariston," he sang, "divine offspring of an illustrious hero."

The epithet is very appropriate, for there is something truly divine in being able to argue as you have done for the superiority of injustice, and remaining unconvinced by your own arguments. And I do believe that you are not convinced—this I infer from your general character, for had I judged only from your speeches I should have mistrusted you. But now, the greater my confidence in you, the greater is my difficulty in knowing what to say. For I am in a strait between two; on the one hand I feel that I am unequal to the task; and my inability is brought home to me by the fact that you were not satisfied with the answer which I made to Thrasymachus, proving, as I thought, the superiority which justice has over injustice. And yet I can not refuse to help, while breath and speech remain to me; I am afraid that there would be an impiety in being present when justice is evil spoken of and not lifting up a hand in her defense. And therefore I had best give such help as I can.

Glaucon and the rest entreated me by all means not to let the question drop, but to proceed in the investigation. They wanted to arrive at the truth, first, about the nature of justice and injustice, and secondly, about their relative advantages. I told them, what I really thought, that the inquiry would be of a serious nature, and would require very good eyes. Seeing then, I said, that we are no great wits, I think that we had better adopt a method which I may illustrate thus; suppose that a short-sighted person had been asked by some one to read small letters from a distance; and it occurred to some one else that they might be found in another place which was larger and in which the letters were larger—if they were the same and he could read the larger letters first, and then proceeds to the lesser—this would have been thought a rare piece of good fortune.

Very true, said Adeimantus; but how does the illustration apply to our inquiry?

I will tell you, I replied; justice, which is the subject of our inquiry, is, as you know, sometimes spoken of as the virtue of an individual, and sometimes as the virtue of a State.

True, he replied.

And is not a State larger than an individual?

It is.

Then in the larger the quantity of justice is likely to be larger and more easily discernible. I propose therefore that we inquire into the nature of justice and injustice, first as they appear in the State, and secondly in the individual, proceeding from the greater to the lesser and comparing them.

That, he said, is an excellent proposal.

And if we imagine the State in process of creation, we shall see the justice and injustice of the State in process of creation also.

I dare say.

When the State is completed there may be a hope that the object of our search will be more easily discovered.

Yes, far more easily.

But ought we to attempt to construct one? I said; for to do so, as I am inclined to think, will be a very serious task. Reflect therefore.

I have reflected, said Adeimantus, and am anxious that you should proceed.

A State, I said, arises, as I conceive, out of the needs of mankind; no one is self-sufficing, but all of us have many wants. Can any other origin of a State be imagined?

There can be no other.

Then, as we have many wants, and many persons are needed to supply them, one takes a helper for one purpose and another for another; and when these partners and helpers are gathered together in one habitation the body of inhabitants is termed a State.

True, he said.

And they exchange with one another, and one gives, and another receives, under the idea that the exchange will be for their good.

Very true.

Then, I said, let us begin and create in idea a State; and yet the true creator is necessity, who is the mother of our invention.

Of course, he replied.

Now the first and greatest of necessities is food, which is the condition of life and existence.

Certainly.

The second is a dwelling, and the third clothing and the like.

True.

And now let us see how our city will be able to supply this great demand: We may suppose that one man is a husbandman, another a builder, some one else a weaver—shall we add to them a shoemaker, or perhaps some other purveyor to our bodily wants?

Quite right.

The barest notion of a State must include four or five men.

Clearly.

And how will they proceed? Will each bring the result of his labors into a common stock?—the individual husbandman, for example, producing for four and laboring four times as long and as much as he need in the provision of food with which he supplies others as well as himself; or will he have nothing to do with others and not be at the trouble of producing for them, but provide for himself alone a fourth of the food in a fourth of the time, and in the remaining three fourths of his time be employed in making a house or a coat or a pair of shoes, having no partnership with others, but supplying himself all his own wants?

Adeimantus thought that he should aim at producing food only and not at producing everything.

Probably, I replied, that would be the better way; and when I hear you say this, I am myself reminded that we are not all alike; there are diversities of natures among us which are adapted to different occupations.

Very true.

And will you have a work better done when the workman has many occupations, or when he has only one?

When he has only one.

Further, there can be no doubt that a work is spoiled when not done at the right time?

No doubt.

For business is not disposed to wait until the doer of the business is at leisure; but the doer must follow up what he is doing, and make the business his first object.

He must.

And if so, we must infer that all things are produced more plentifully and easily and of a better quality when one man does one thing which is natural to him, and does it at the right time, and leaves other things.

Undoubtedly.

Then more than our citizens will be required; for the husbandman will not make his own plough or mattock, or other implements of agriculture, if they are to be good for anything. Neither will the builder make his tools—and he too needs many; and in like manner the weaver and shoemaker.

True.

Then carpenters, and smiths, and many other artisans, will be sharers in our little State, which is already beginning to grow?

True.

Yet even if we add neatherds, shepherds, and other herdsmen, in order that our husbandmen may have oxen to plough with, and builders as well as husbandmen may have draught cattle, and curriers and weavers fleeces and hides,—still our State will not be very large.

That is true; yet neither will it be a very small State which contains all these.

Then, again, there is the situation of the city—to find a place where nothing need be imported is well-nigh impossible.

Impossible.

Then there must be another class of citizens who will bring the required supply from another city?

There must.

But if the trader goes empty-handed, having nothing which they require who would supply his need, he will come back empty-handed.

That is certain.

And therefore what they produce at home must be not only enough for themselves, but such both in quantity and quality as to accommodate those from whom their wants are supplied.

Very true.

Then more husbandmen and more artisans will be required?

They will.

Not to mention the importers and exporters, who are called merchants?

Yes.

Then we shall want merchants?

We shall.

And if merchandise is to be carried over the sea, skilful sailors will also be needed, and in considerable numbers?

Yes, in considerable numbers.

Then, again, within the city, how will they exchange their productions? To secure such an exchange was, as you will remember, one of our principal objects when we formed them into a society and constituted a State.

Clearly they will buy and sell.

Then they will need a market-place, and a money-token for purposes of exchange.

Certainly.

Suppose now that a husbandman, or an artisan, brings some production to market, and he comes at a time when there is no one to exchange with him,— is he to leave his calling and sit idle in the marketplace?

Not at all; he will find people there who, seeing the want, undertake the office of salesmen. In well-ordered states they are commonly those who are the weakest in bodily strength, and therefore of little use for any other purpose; their duty is to be in the market, and to give money in exchange for goods to those who desire to sell and to take money from those who desire to buy.

This want, then, creates a class of retail-traders in our State. Is not "retailer" the term which is applied to those who sit in the market-place engaged in buying and selling, while those who wander from one city to another are called merchants?

Yes, he said.

And there is another class of servants, who are intellectually hardly on the level of companionship; still they have plenty of bodily strength for labor, which accordingly they sell, and are called, if I do not mistake, hirelings, hire being the name which is given to the price of their labor.

True.

Then hirelings will help to make up our population?

Yes.

And now, Adeimantus, is our State matured and perfected?

I think so.

Where, then, is justice, and where is injustice, and in what part of the State did they spring up?

Probably in the dealings of these citizens with one another. I can not imagine that they are more likely to be found anywhere else.

I dare say that you are right in your suggestion, I said; we had better think the matter out, and not shrink from the inquiry

Let us then consider, first of all, what will be their way of life, now that we have thus established them. Will they not produce corn, and wine, and clothes, and shoes, and build houses for themselves? And when they are housed, they will work, in summer, commonly, stripped and barefoot, but in winter substantially clothed and shod. They will feed on barley-meal and flour of wheat, baking and kneading them, making noble cakes and loaves; these they will serve up on a mat of reeds or on clean leaves, themselves reclining the while upon beds strewn with yew or myrtle. And they and their children will feast, drinking of the wine which they have made, wearing garlands on their heads, and hymning the praises of the gods, in happy converse with one another. And they will take care that their families do not exceed their means; having an eye to poverty or war.

But, said Glaucon, interposing, you have not given them a relish to their meal.

True, I replied, I had forgotten; of course they must have a relish — salt, and olives, and cheese, and they will boil roots and herbs such as country people prepare; for a dessert we shall give them figs, and peas, and beans; and they will roast myrtle-berries and acorns at the fire, drinking in moderation. And with such a diet they may be expected to live in peace and health to a good old age, and bequeath a similar life to their children after them.

Yes, Socrates, he said, and if you were providing for a city of pigs, how else would you feed the beasts?

But what would you have, Glaucon? I replied.

Why, he said, you should give them the ordinary conveniences of life. People who are to be comfortable are accustomed to lie on sofas, and dine off tables, and they should have sauces and sweets in the modern style.

Yes, I said, now I understand: the question which you would have me consider is, not only how a State, but how a luxurious State is created; and possibly there is no harm in this, for in such a State we shall be more likely to see how justice and injustice originate. In my opinion the true and healthy constitution of the State is the one which I have described.

But if you wish also to see a State at fever-heat, I have no objection. For I suspect that many will not be satisfied with the simpler way of life. They will be for adding sofas, and tables, and other furniture; also dainties, and perfumes, and incense, and courtesans, and cakes, all these not of one sort only, but in every variety; we must go beyond the necessaries of which I was at first speaking, such as houses, and clothes, and shoes: the arts of the painter and the embroiderer will have to be set in motion, and gold and ivory and all sorts of materials must be procured.

True, he said.

Then we must enlarge our borders; for the original healthy State is no longer sufficient. Now will the city have to fill and swell with a multitude of callings which are not required by any natural want; such as the whole tribe of hunters and actors, of whom one large class have to do with forms and colors; another will be the votaries of music—poets and their attendant train of rhapsodists, players, dancers, contractors; also makers of divers kinds of articles, including women's dresses. And we shall want more servants. Will not tutors be also in request, and nurses wet and dry, tirewomen and barbers, as well as confectioners and cooks; and swineherds, too, who were not needed and therefore had no place in the former edition of our State, but are needed now? They must not be forgotten: and there will be animals of many other kinds, if people eat them.

Certainly.

And living in this way we shall have much greater need of physicians than before?

Much greater.

And the country which was enough to support the original inhabitants will be too small now, and not enough?

Quite true.

Then a slice of our neighbors' land will be wanted by us for pasture and tillage, and they will want a slice of ours, if, like ourselves, they exceed the limit of necessity, and give themselves up to the unlimited accumulation of wealth?

That, Socrates, will be inevitable.

And so we shall go to war, Glaucon. Shall we not?

Most certainly, he replied.

Then, without determining as yet whether war does good or harm, thus much we may affirm, that now we have discovered war to be derived from causes which are also the causes of almost all the evils in States, private as well as public.

Undoubtedly.

And our State must once more enlarge; and this time the enlargement will be nothing short of a whole army, which will have to go out and fight with the invaders for all that we have, as well as for the things and persons whom we were describing above.

Why? he said; are they not capable of defending themselves?

No, I said; not if we were right in the principle which was acknowledged by all of us when we were framing the State: the principle, as you will remember, was that one man can not practise many arts with success.

Very true, he said.

But is not war an art?

Certainly.

And an art requiring as much attention as shoemaking?

Quite true.

And the shoemaker was not allowed by us to be a husbandman, or a weaver, or a builder—in order that we might have our shoes well made; but to him and to every other worker was assigned one work for which he was by nature fitted, and at that he was to continue working all his life long and at no other; he was not to let opportunities slip, and then he would become a good workman. Now nothing can be more important than that the work of a soldier should be well done. But is war an art so easily acquired that a man may be a warrior who is also a husbandman, or shoemaker, or other artisan; although no one in the world would be a good dice or draught player who merely took up the game as a recreation, and had not from his earliest years devoted himself to this and nothing else? No tools will make a man a skilled workman, or master of defence, nor be of any use to him who has not learned how to handle them, and has never bestowed any attention upon them. How then will he who takes up a shield or other implement of war become a good fighter all in a day, whether with heavy-armed or any other kind of troops?

Yes, he said, the tools which would teach men their own use would be beyond price.

And the higher the duties of the guardian, I said, the more time, and skill, and art, and application will be needed by him?

No doubt, he replied.

Will he not also require natural aptitude for his calling?

Certainly.

Then it will be our duty to select, if we can, natures which are fitted for the task of guarding the city?

It will.

And the selection will be no easy matter, I said; but we must be brave and do our best.

We must.

Is not the noble youth very like a well-bred dog in respect of guarding and watching?

What do you mean?

I mean that both of them ought to be quick to see, and swift to overtake the enemy when they see him; and strong too if, when they have caught him, they have to fight with him.

All these qualities, he replied, will certainly be required by them.

Well, and your guardian must be brave if he is to fight well?

Certainly.

And is he likely to be brave who has no spirit, whether horse or dog or any other animal? Have you never observed how invincible and unconquerable is spirit and how the presence of it makes the soul of any creature to be absolutely fearless and indomitable?

I have.

Then now we have a clear notion of the bodily qualities which are required in the guardian.

True.

And also of the mental ones; his soul is to be full of spirit?

Yes.

But are not these spirited natures apt to be savage with one another, and with everybody else?

A difficulty by no means easy to overcome, he replied.

Whereas, I said, they ought to be dangerous to their enemies, and gentle to their friends; if not, they will destroy themselves without waiting for their enemies to destroy them.

True, he said.

What is to be done then? I said; how shall we find a gentle nature which has also a great spirit, for the one is the contradiction of the other?

True.

He will not be a good guardian who is wanting in either of these two qualities; and yet the combination of them appears to be impossible; and hence we must infer that to be a good guardian is impossible.

I am afraid that what you say is true, he replied.

Here feeling perplexed I began to think over what had preceded.—My friend, I said, no wonder that we are in a perplexity; for we have lost sight of the image which we had before us.

What do you mean? he said.

I mean to say that there do exist natures gifted with those opposite qualities.

And where do you find them?

Many animals, I replied, furnish examples of them; our friend the dog is a very good one: you know that well-bred dogs are perfectly gentle to their familiars and acquaintances, and the reverse to strangers.

Yes, I know.

Then there is nothing impossible or out of the order of nature in our finding a guardian who has a similar combination of qualities?

Certainly not.

Would not he who is fitted to be a guardian, besides the spirited nature, need to have the qualities of a philosopher?

I do not apprehend your meaning.

The trait of which I am speaking, I replied, may be also seen in the dog, and is remarkable in the animal.

What trait?

Why, a dog, whenever he sees a stranger, is angry; when an acquaintance, he welcomes him, although the one has never done any harm, nor the other any good. Did this never strike you as curious?

The matter never struck me before; but I quite recognize the truth of your remark.

And surely this instinct of the dog is very charming;—your dog is a true philosopher.

Why?

Why, because he distinguishes the face of a friend and of an enemy only by the criterion of knowing and not knowing. And must not an animal be a lover of learning who determines what he likes and dislikes by the test of knowledge and ignorance?

Most assuredly.

And is not the love of learning the love of wisdom, which is philosophy?

They are the same, he replied.

And may we not say confidently of man also, that he who is likely to be gentle to his friends and acquaintances, must by nature be a lover of wisdom and knowledge?

That we may safely affirm.

Then he who is to be a really good and noble guardian of the State will require to unite in himself philosophy and spirit and swiftness and strength?

Undoubtedly.

Then we have found the desired natures; and now that we have found them, how are they to be reared and educated? Is not this an inquiry which may be expected to throw light on the greater inquiry which is our final end—How do justice and injustice grow up in States? for we do not want either to omit what is to the point or to draw out the argument to an inconvenient length.

Adeimantus thought that the inquiry would be of great service to us.

Then, I said, my dear friend, the task must not be given up, even if somewhat long.

Certainly not.

Come then, and let us pass a leisure hour in story-telling, and our story shall be the education of our heroes.

By all means.

And what shall be their education? Can we find a better than the traditional sort?—and this has two divisions, gymnastic for the body, and music for the soul.

True.

Shall we begin education with music, and go on to gymnastic afterwards?

By all means.

And when you speak of music, do you include literature or not?

I do.

And literature may be either true or false?

Yes.

And the young should be trained in both kinds, and we begin with the false?

I do not understand your meaning, he said.

You know, I said, that we begin by telling children stories which, though not wholly destitute of truth, are in the main fictitious; and these stories are told them when they are not of an age to learn gymnastics.

Very true.

That was my meaning when I said that we must teach music before gymnastics.

Quite right, he said.

You know also that the beginning is the most important part of any work, especially in the case of a young and tender thing; for that is the time at which the character is being formed and the desired impression is more readily taken.

Quite true.

And shall we just carelessly allow children to hear any casual tales which may be devised by casual persons, and to receive into their minds ideas for the most part the very opposite of those which we should wish them to have when they are grown up?

We can not.

Then the first thing will be to establish a censorship of the writers of fiction, and let the censors receive any tale of fiction which is good, and reject the bad; and we will desire mothers and nurses to tell their children the authorized ones only. Let them fashion the mind with such tales, even more fondly than they mould the body with their hands; but most of those which are now in use must be discarded.

Of what tales are you speaking? he said.

You may find a model of the lesser in the greater, I said; for they are necessarily of the same type, and there is the same spirit in both of them.

Very likely, he replied; but I do not as yet know what you would term the greater.

Those, I said, which are narrated by Homer and Hesiod, and the rest of the poets, who have ever been the great story-tellers of mankind.

But which stories do you mean, he said; and what fault do you find with them?

A fault which is most serious, I said; the fault of telling a lie, and, what is more, a bad lie.

But when is this fault committed?

Whenever an erroneous representation is made of the nature of gods and heroes,—as when a painter paints a portrait not having the shadow of a likeness to the original.

Yes, he said, that sort of thing is certainly very blamable; but what are the stories which you mean?

First of all, I said, there was that greatest of all lies in high places, which the poet told about Uranus, and which was a bad lie too,—I mean what Hesiod says that Uranus did, and how Cronus retaliated on him. The doings of Cronus, and the sufferings which in turn his son inflicted upon him, even if they were true, ought certainly not to be lightly told to young and thoughtless persons; if possible, they had better be buried in silence. But if there is an absolute necessity for their mention, a chosen few might hear them in a mystery, and they should sacrifice not a common pig, but some huge and unprocurable victim; and then the number of the hearers will be very few indeed.

Why, yes, said he, those stories are extremely objectionable.

Yes, Adeimantus, they are stories not to be repeated in our State; the young man should not be told that in committing the worst of crimes he is far from doing anything outrageous; and that even if he chastises his father when he does wrong, in whatever manner, he will only be following the example of the first and greatest among the gods.

I entirely agree with you, he said; in my opinion those stories are quite unfit to be repeated.

Neither, if we mean our future guardians to regard the habit of quarrelling among themselves as of all things the basest, should any word be said to them of the wars in heaven, and of the plots and fightings of the gods against one another, for they are not true. No, we shall never mention the battles of the giants, or let them be embroidered on garments; and we shall be silent about the innumerable other quarrels of gods and heroes with their friends and relatives. If they would only believe us we would tell them that quarrelling is unholy, and that never up to this time has there been any quarrel between citizens; this is what old men and old women should begin by telling children; and when they grow up, the poets also should be told to compose for them in a similar spirit. But the narrative of Hephaestus binding Here his mother, or how on another occasion Zeus sent him flying for taking her part when she was being beaten, and all the battles of the gods in Homer—these tales must not be admitted into our State, whether they are supposed to have an allegorical meaning or not. For a young person can not judge what is allegorical and what is literal; anything that he receives into his mind at that age is likely to become indelible and unalterable; and therefore it is most important that the tales which the young first hear should be models of virtuous thoughts.

There you are right, he replied; but if any one asks where are such models to be found and of what tales are you speaking—how shall we answer him?

I said to him, You and I, Adeimantus, at this moment are not poets, but founders of a State: now the founders of a State ought to know the general forms in which poets should cast their tales, and the limits which must be observed by them, but to make the tales is not their business.

Very true, he said; but what are these forms of theology which you mean?

Something of this kind, I replied:—God is always to be represented as he truly is, whatever be the sort of poetry, epic, lyric or tragic, in which the representation is given.

Right.

And is he not truly good? and must he not be represented as such?

Certainly.

And no good thing is hurtful?

No, indeed.

And that which is not hurtful hurts not?

Certainly not.

And that which hurts not does no evil?

No.

And can that which does no evil be a cause of evil?

Impossible.

And the good is advantageous?

Yes.

And therefore the cause of well-being?

Yes.

It follows therefore that the good is not the cause of all things, but of the good only?

Assuredly.

Then God, if he be good, is not the author of all things, as the many assert, but he is the cause of a few things only, and not of most things that occur to men. For few are the goods of human life, and many are the evils, and the good is to be attributed to God alone; of the evils the causes are to be sought elsewhere, and not in him.

That appears to me to be most true, he said.

Then we must not listen to Homer or to any other poet who is guilty of the folly of saying that two casks

"Lie at the threshold of Zeus, full of lots, one of good, the other of evil lots,"

and that he to whom Zeus gives a mixture of the two

"Sometimes meets with evil fortune, at other times with good;"

but that he to whom is given the cup of unmingled ill,

"Him wild hunger drives o'er the beauteous earth."

And again—

"Zeus, who is the dispenser of good and evil to us."

And if any one asserts that the violation of oaths and treaties, which was really the work of Pandarus, was brought about by Athene and Zeus, or that the strife and contention of the gods was instigated by Themis and Zeus, he shall not have our approval; neither will we allow our young men to hear the words of Æschylus, that

> "God plants guilt among men when he desires utterly to destroy a house."

And if a poet writes of the sufferings of Niobe—the subject of the tragedy in which these iambic verses occur—or of the house of Pelops, or of the Trojan war or on any similar theme, either we must not permit him to say that these are the works of God, or if they are of God, he must devise some explanation of them such as we are seeking; he must say that God did what was just and right, and they were the better for being punished; but that those who are punished are miserable, and that God is the author of their misery—the poet is not to be permitted to say; though he may say that the wicked are miserable because they require to be punished, and are benefited by receiving punishment from God; but that God being good is the author of evil to any one is to be strenuously denied, and not to be said or sung or heard in verse or prose by any one whether old or young in any well-ordered commonwealth. Such a fiction is suicidal, ruinous, impious.

I agree with you, he replied, and am ready to give my assent to the law.

Let this then be one of our rules and principles concerning the gods, to which our poets and reciters will be expected to conform,—that God is not the author of all things, but of good only.

That will do, he said.

And what do you think of a second principle? Shall I ask you whether God is a magician, and of a nature to appear insidiously now in one shape, and now in another—sometimes himself changing and passing into many forms, sometimes deceiving us with the semblance of such transformations; or is he one and the same immutably fixed in his own proper image?

I can not answer you, he said, without more thought.

Well, I said; but if we suppose a change in anything, that change must be effected either by the thing itself, or by some other thing?

Most certainly.

And things which are at their best are also least liable to be altered or discomposed; for example, when healthiest and strongest, the human frame is least liable to be affected by meats and drinks, and the plant which is in the fullest vigor also suffers least from winds or the heat of the sun or any similar causes.

Of course.

And will not the bravest and wisest soul be least confused or deranged by any external influence?

True.

And the same principle, as I should suppose, applies to all composite things—furniture, houses, garments: when good and well made, they are least altered by time and circumstances.

Very true.

Then everything which is good, whether made by art or nature, or both, is least liable to suffer change from without?

True.

But surely God and the things of God are in every way perfect?

Of course they are.

Then he can hardly be compelled by external influence to take many shapes?

He can not.

But may he not change and transform himself?

Clearly, he said, that must be the case if he is changed at all.

And will he then change himself for the better and fairer, or for the worse and more unsightly?

If he change at all he can only change for the worse, for we can not suppose him to be deficient either in virtue or beauty.

Very true, Adeimantus; but then, would any one, whether God or man, desire to make himself worse?

Impossible.

Then it is impossible that God should ever be willing to change; being, as is supposed, the fairest and best that is conceivable, every God remains absolutely and forever in his own form.

That necessarily follows, he said, in my judgment.

Then, I said, my dear friend, let none of the poets tell us that

> "The gods, taking the disguise of strangers from other lands, walk up and down cities in all sorts of forms;"

and let no one slander Proteus and Thetis, neither let any one, either in tragedy or in any other kind of poetry, introduce Here disguised in the likeness of a priestess asking an alms

"For the life-giving daughters of Inachus the river of Argos;"

—let us have no more lies of that sort. Neither must we have in mothers under the influence of the poets scaring their children with a bad version of these myths—telling how certain gods, as they say, "Go about by night in the likeness of so many strangers and in divers forms"; but let them take heed lest they make cowards of their children, and at the same time speak blasphemy against the gods.

Heaven forbid, he said.

But although the gods are themselves unchangeable, still by witchcraft and deception they may make us think that they appear in various forms?

Perhaps, he replied.

Well, but can you imagine that God will be willing to lie, whether in word or deed, or to put forth a phantom of himself?

I can not say, he replied.

Do you not know, I said, that the true lie, if such an expression may be allowed, is hated of gods and men?

What do you mean? he said.

I mean that no one is willingly deceived in that which is the truest and highest part of himself, or about the truest and highest matters; there, above all, he is most afraid of a lie having possession of him.

Still, he said, I do not comprehend you.

The reason is, I replied, that you attribute some profound meaning to my words; but I am only saying that deception, or being deceived or uninformed about the highest realities in the highest part of themselves, which is the soul, and in that part of them to have and to hold the lie, is what mankind least like;—that, I say, is what they utterly detest.

There is nothing more hateful to them.

And, as I was just now remarking, this ignorance in the soul of him who is deceived may be called the true lie; for the lie in words is only a kind of imitation and shadowy image of a previous affection of the soul, not pure unadulterated falsehood. Am I not right?

Perfectly right.

The true lie is hated not only by the gods, but also by men?

Yes.

Whereas the lie in words is in certain cases useful and not hateful; in dealing with enemies—that would

be an instance; or again, when those whom we call our friends in a fit of madness or illusion are going to do some harm, then it is useful and is a sort of medicine or preventive; also in the tales of mythology, of which we were just now speaking—because we do not know the truth about ancient times, we make falsehood as much like truth as we can, and so turn it to account.

Very true, he said.

But can any of these reasons apply to God? Can we suppose that he is ignorant of antiquity, and therefore has recourse to invention?

That would be ridiculous, he said.

Then the lying poet has no place in our idea of God?

I should say not.

Or perhaps he may tell a lie because he is afraid of enemies?

That is inconceivable.

But he may have friends who are senseless or mad?

But no mad or senseless person can be a friend of God.

Then no motive can be imagined why God should lie?

None whatever.

Then the superhuman and divine is absolutely incapable of falsehood?

Yes.

Then is God perfectly simple and true both in word and deed; he changes not; he deceives not, either by sign or word, by dream or waking vision.

Your thoughts, he said, are the reflection of my own.

You agree with me then, I said, that this is the second type or form in which we should write and speak about divine things. The gods are not magicians who transform themselves, neither do they deceive mankind in any way.

I grant that.

Then, although we are admirers of Homer, we do not admire the lying dream which Zeus sends to Agamemnon; neither will we praise the verses of Æschylus in which Thetis says that Apollo at her nuptials

"Was celebrating in song her fair progeny whose days were to be long, and to know no sickness. And when he had spoken of my lot as in all things blessed of heaven he raised a note of triumph and cheered my soul. And I thought that the word of Phoebus, being divine and full of prophecy, would not fail. And now he himself who uttered the strain, he who was present at the banquet; and who said this—he it is who has slain my son."

These are the kind of sentiments about the gods which will arouse our anger; and he who utters them shall be refused a chorus; neither shall we allow teachers to make use of them in the instruction of the young, meaning, as we do, that our guardians, as far as men can be, should be true worshippers of the gods and like them.

I entirely agree, he said, in these principles, and promise to make them my laws.

...

Book IV

Here Adeimantus interposed a question: How would you answer, Socrates, said he, if a person were to say that you are making these people miserable, and that they are the cause of their own unhappiness; the city in fact belongs to them, but they are none the better for it; whereas other men acquire lands, and build large and handsome houses, and have everything handsome about them, offering sacrifices to the gods on their own account, and practising hospitality; moreover, as you were saying just now, they have gold and silver, and all that is usual among the favorites of fortune; but our poor citizens are no better than mercenaries who are quartered in the city and are always mounting guard?

Yes, I said; and you may add that they are only fed, and not paid in addition to their food, like other men; and therefore they can not, if they would, take a journey of pleasure; they have no money to spend on a mistress or any other luxurious fancy, which, as the world goes, is thought to be happiness; and many other accusations of the same nature might be added.

But, said he, let us suppose all this to be included in the charge.

You mean to ask, I said, what will be our answer?

Yes.

If we proceed along the old path, my belief, I said, is that we shall find the answer. And our answer will be that, even as they are, our guardians may very likely be the happiest of men; but that our aim in founding the State was not the disproportionate happiness of any one class, but the greatest happiness of the whole; we thought that in a State which is ordered with a view to the good of the whole we should be most likely to find justice, and in the ill-ordered State injustice: and, having found them, we might then decide which of the two is the happier. At present, I take it, we are fashioning the happy State, not piecemeal, or with a view of making a few happy citizens, but as a whole; and by-and-by we will proceed to view the opposite kind of State. Suppose that we were painting a statue, and some one came up to us and said, Why do you not put the most beautiful colors on the most beautiful parts of the body—the eyes ought to be purple, but you have made them black—to him we might fairly answer, Sir, you would not surely have us beautify the eyes to such a degree that they are no longer eyes; consider rather whether, by giving this and the other features their due proportion, we make the whole beautiful. And so I say to you, do not compel us to assign to the guardians a sort of happiness which will make them anything but guardians; for we too can clothe our husbandmen in royal apparel, and set crowns of gold on their heads, and bid them till the ground as much as they like, and no more. Our potters also might be allowed to repose on couches, and feast by the fireside, passing round the winecup, while their wheel is conveniently at hand, and working at pottery only as much as they like; in this way we might make every class happy—and then, as you imagine, the whole State would be happy. But do not put this idea into our heads; for, if we listen to you, the husbandman will be no longer a husbandman, the potter will cease to be a potter, and no one will have the character of any distinct class in the State. Now this is not of much consequence where the corruption of society, and pretension to be what you are not, is confined to cobblers; but when the guardians of the laws and of the government are only seeming and not real guardians, then see how they turn the State upside down; and on the other hand they alone have the power of giving order and happiness to the State. We mean our guardians to be true saviors and not the destroyers of the State, whereas our opponent is thinking of peasants at a festival, who are enjoying a life of revelry, not of citizens who are doing their duty to the State. But, if so, we mean different things, and he is speaking of something which is not a State. And therefore we must consider whether in appointing our guardians we would look to their greatest happiness individually, or whether this principle of happiness does not rather reside in the State as a whole. But if the latter be the truth, then the guardians and auxiliaries, and all others equally with them, must be compelled or induced to do their own work in the best way. And thus the whole State will grow up in a noble order, and the several classes will receive the proportion of happiness which nature assigns to them.

I think that you are quite right.

I wonder whether you will agree with another remark which occurs to me.

What may that be?

There seem to be two causes of the deterioration of the arts.

What are they?

Wealth, I said, and poverty.

How do they act?

The process is as follows: When a potter becomes rich, will he, think you, any longer take the same pains with his art?

Certainly not.

He will grow more and more indolent and careless?

Very true.

And the result will be that he becomes a worse potter?

Yes; he greatly deteriorates.

But, on the other hand, if he has no money, and can not provide himself with tools or instruments, he will not work equally well himself, nor will he teach his sons or apprentices to work equally well.

Certainly not.

Then, under the influence either of poverty or of wealth, workmen and their work are equally liable to degenerate?

That is evident.

Here, then, is a discovery of new evils, I said, against which the guardians will have to watch, or they will creep into the city unobserved.

What evils?

Wealth, I said, and poverty; the one is the parent of luxury and indolence, and the other of meanness and viciousness, and both of discontent.

That is very true, he replied; but still I should like to know, Socrates, how our city will be able to go to war, especially against an enemy who is rich and powerful, if deprived of the sinews of war.

There would certainly be a difficulty, I replied, in going to war with one such enemy; but there is no difficulty where there are two of them.

How so? he asked.

In the first place, I said, if we have to fight, our side will be trained warriors fighting against an army of rich men.

That is true, he said.

And do you not suppose, Adeimantus, that a single boxer who was perfect in his art would easily be a match for two stout and well-to-do gentlemen who were not boxers?

Hardly, if they came upon him at once.

What, not, I said, if he were able to run away and then turn and strike at the one who first came up? And supposing he were to do this several times under the heat of a scorching sun, might he not, being an expert, overturn more than one stout personage?

Certainly, he said, there would be nothing wonderful in that.

And yet rich men probably have a greater superiority in the science and practise of boxing than they have in military qualities.

Likely enough.

Then we may assume that our athletes will be able to fight with two or three times their own number?

I agree with you, for I think you right.

And suppose that, before engaging, our citizens send an embassy to one of the two cities, telling them what is the truth: Silver and gold we neither have nor are permitted to have, but you may; do you therefore come and help us in war, and take the spoils of the other city: Who, on hearing these words, would choose to fight against lean wiry dogs, rather than, with the dogs on their side, against fat and tender sheep?

That is not likely; and yet there might be a danger to the poor State if the wealth of many States were to be gathered into one.

But how simple of you to use the term State at all of any but our own!

Why so?

You ought to speak of other States in the plural number; not of them is a city, but many cities, as they say in the game. For indeed any city, however small, is in fact divided into two, one the city of the poor, the other of the rich; these are at war with one another; and in either there are many smaller divisions, and you would be altogether beside the mark if you treated them all as a single State. But if you deal with them as many, and give the wealth or power or persons of the one to the others, you will always have a great many friends and not many enemies. And your State, while the wise order which has now been prescribed continues to prevail in her, will be the greatest of States, I do not mean to say in reputation or appearance, but in deed and truth, though she number not more than a thousand defenders. A single State which is her equal you will hardly find, either among Hellenes or barbarians, though many that appear to be as great and many times greater.

That is most true, he said.

And what, I said, will be the best limit for our rulers to fix when they are considering the size of the State and the amount of territory which they are to include, and beyond which they will not go?

What limit would you propose?

I would allow the State to increase so far as is consistent with unity; that, I think, is the proper limit.

Very good, he said.

Here then, I said, is another order which will have to be conveyed to our guardians: Let our city be accounted neither large nor small, but one and self-sufficing.

And surely, said he, this is not a very severe order which we impose upon them.

And the other, said I, of which we were speaking before is lighter still,—I mean the duty of degrading the offspring of the guardians when inferior, and of elevating into the rank of guardians the offspring of the lower classes, when naturally superior. The intention was, that, in the case of the citizens generally, each individual should be put to the use for which nature intended him, one to one work, and then every man would do his own business, and be one and not many; and so the whole city would be one and not many.

Yes, he said; that is not so difficult.

The regulations which we are prescribing, my good Adeimantus, are not, as might be supposed, a number of great principles, but trifles all, if care be taken, as the saying is, of the one great thing,—a thing, however, which I would rather call, not great, but sufficient for our purpose.

What may that be? he asked.

Education, I said, and nurture: If our citizens are well educated, and grow into sensible men, they will easily see their way through all these, as well as other matters which I omit; such, for example, as marriage, the possession of women and the procreation of children, which will all follow the general principle that friends have all things in common, as the proverb says.

That will be the best way of settling them.

Also, I said, the State, if once started well, moves with accumulating force like a wheel. For good nurture and education implant good constitutions, and these good constitutions taking root in a good education improve more and more, and this improvement affects the breed in man as in other animals.

Very possibly, he said.

Then to sum up: This is the point to which, above all, the attention of our rulers should be directed,—that music and gymnastic be preserved in their original form, and no innovation made. They must do their utmost to maintain them intact. And when any one says that mankind most regard

"The newest song which the singers have,"

they will be afraid that he may be praising, not new songs, but a new kind of song; and this ought not to be praised, or conceived to be the meaning of the poet; for any musical innovation is full of danger to the whole State, and ought to be prohibited. So Damon tells me, and I can quite believe him;—he says that when modes of music change, the fundamental laws of the State always change with them.

Yes, said Adeimantus; and you may add my suffrage to Damon's and your own.

Then, I said, our guardians must lay the foundations of their fortress in music?

Yes, he said; the lawlessness of which you speak too easily steals in.

Yes, I replied, in the form of amusement; and at first sight it appears harmless.

Why, yes, he said, and there is no harm; were it not that little by little this spirit of license, finding a home, imperceptibly penetrates into manners and customs; whence, issuing with greater force, it invades contracts between man and man, and from contracts goes on to laws and constitutions, in utter recklessness, ending at last, Socrates, by an overthrow of all rights, private as well as public.

Is that true? I said.

That is my belief, he replied.

Then, as I was saying, our youth should be trained from the first in a stricter system, for if amusements become lawless, and the youths themselves become lawless, they can never grow up into well-conducted and virtuous citizens.

Very true, he said.

And when they have made a good beginning in play, and by the help of music have gained the habit of good order, then this habit of order, in a manner how unlike the lawless play of the others! will accompany them in all their actions and be a principle of growth to them, and if there be any fallen places in the State will raise them up again.

Very true, he said.

Thus educated, they will invent for themselves any lesser rules which their predecessors have altogether neglected.

What do you mean?

I mean such things as these:—when the young are to be silent before their elders; how they are to show respect to them by standing and making them sit; what honor is due to parents; what garments or shoes are to be worn; the mode of dressing the hair; deportment and manners in general. You would agree with me?

Yes.

But there is, I think, small wisdom in legislating about such matters,—I doubt if it is ever done; nor are any precise written enactments about them likely to be lasting.

Impossible.

It would seem, Adeimantus, that the direction in which education starts a man, will determine his future life. Does not like always attract like?

To be sure.

Until some one rare and grand result is reached which may be good, and may be the reverse of good?

That is not to be denied.

And for this reason, I said, I shall not attempt to legislate further about them.

Naturally enough, he replied.

Well, and about the business of the agora, and the ordinary dealings between man and man, or again about agreements with artisans; about insult and injury, or the commencement of actions, and the appointment of juries, what would you say? there may also arise questions about any impositions and exactions of market and harbor dues which may be required, and in general about the regulations of markets, police, harbors, and the like. But, oh heavens! shall we condescend to legislate on any of these particulars?

I think, he said, that there is no need to impose laws about them on good men; what regulations are necessary they will find out soon enough for themselves.

Yes, I said, my friend, if God will only preserve to them the laws which we have given them.

And without divine help, said Adeimantus, they will go on forever making and mending their laws and their lives in the hope of attaining perfection.

You would compare them, I said, to those invalids who, having no self-restraint, will not leave off their habits of intemperance?

Exactly.

Yes, I said; and what a delightful life they lead! they are always doctoring and increasing and complicating their disorders, and always fancying that they will be cured by any nostrum which anybody advises them to try.

Such cases are very common, he said, with invalids of this sort.

Yes, I replied; and the charming thing is that they deem him their worst enemy who tells them the truth, which is simply that, unless they give up eating and drinking and wenching and idling, neither drug nor cautery nor spell nor amulet nor any other remedy will avail.

Charming! he replied. I see nothing charming in going into a passion with a man who tells you what is right.

These gentlemen, I said, do not seem to be in your good graces.

Assuredly not.

Nor would you praise the behavior of States which act like the men whom I was just now describing. For are there not ill-ordered States in which the citizens are forbidden under pain of death to alter the constitution; and yet he who most sweetly courts those who live under this regime and indulges them and fawns upon them and is skilful in anticipating and gratifying their humors is held to be a great and good statesman—do not these States resemble the persons whom I was describing?

Yes, he said; the States are as bad as the men; and I am very far from praising them.

But do you not admire, I said, the coolness and dexterity of these ready ministers of political corruption?

Yes, he said, I do; but not of all of them, for there are some whom the applause of the multitude has deluded into the belief that they are really statesmen, and these are not much to be admired.

What do you mean? I said; you should have more feeling for them. When a man can not measure, and a great many others who can not measure declare that he is four cubits high, can he help believing what they say?

Nay, he said, certainly not in that case.

Well, then, do not be angry with them; for are they not as good as a play, trying their hand at paltry reforms such as I was describing; they are always fancying that by legislation they will make an end of frauds in contracts, and the other rascalities which I was mentioning, not knowing that they are in reality cutting off the heads of a hydra?

Yes, he said; that is just what they are doing.

I conceive, I said, that the true legislator will not trouble himself with this class of enactments whether concerning laws or the constitution either in an ill-ordered or in a well-ordered State; for in the former they are quite useless, and in the latter there will be no difficulty in devising them; and many of them will naturally flow out of our previous regulations.

What, then, he said, is still remaining to us of the work of legislation?

Nothing to us, I replied; but to Apollo, the god of Delphi, there remains the ordering of the greatest and noblest and chiefest things of all.

Which are they? he said.

The institution of temples and sacrifices, and the entire service of gods, demigods, and heroes; also the ordering of the repositories of the dead, and the rites which have to be observed by him who would propitiate the inhabitants of the world below. These are matters of which we are ignorant ourselves, and as founders of a city we should be unwise in trusting them to any interpreter but our ancestral deity. He is the god who sits in the centre, on the navel of the earth, and he is the interpreter of religion to all mankind.

You are right, and we will do as you propose.

But where, amid all this, is justice? son of Ariston, tell me where. Now that our city has been made habitable, light a candle and search, and get your brother and Polemarchus and the rest of our friends to help, and let us see where in it we can discover justice and where injustice, and in what they differ from one another, and which of them the man who would be happy should have for his portion, whether seen or unseen by gods and men.

Nonsense, said Glaucon: did you not promise to search yourself, saying that for you not to help justice in her need would be an impiety?

I do not deny that I said so; and as you remind me, I will be as good as my word; but you must join.

We will, he replied.

Well, then, I hope to make the discovery in this way: I mean to begin with the assumption that our State, if rightly ordered, is perfect.

That is most certain.

And, being perfect, is therefore wise and valiant and temperate and just.

That is likewise clear.

And whichever of these qualities we find in the State, the one which is not found will be the residue?

Very good.

If there were four things, and we were searching for one of them, wherever it might be, the one sought for might be known to us from the first, and there would be no further trouble; or we might know the other three first, and then the fourth would clearly be the one left.

Very true, he said.

And is not a similar method to be pursued about the virtues, which are also four in number?

Clearly.

First among the virtues found in the State, wisdom comes into view, and in this I detect a certain peculiarity.

What is that?

The State which we have been describing is said to be wise as being good in counsel?

Very true.

And good counsel is clearly a kind of knowledge, for not by ignorance, but by knowledge, do men counsel well?

Clearly.

And the kinds of knowledge in a State are many and diverse?

Of course.

There is the knowledge of the carpenter; but is that the sort of knowledge which gives a city the title of wise and good in counsel?

Certainly not; that would only give a city the reputation of skill in carpentering.

Then a city is not to be called wise because possessing a knowledge which counsels for the best about wooden implements?

Certainly not.

Nor by reason of a knowledge which advises about brazen pots, he said, nor as possessing any other similar knowledge?

Not by reason of any of them, he said.

Nor yet by reason of a knowledge which cultivates the earth; that would give the city the name of agricultural?

Yes.

Well, I said, and is there any knowledge in our recently-founded State among any of the citizens which advises, not about any particular thing in the State, but about the whole, and considers how a State can best deal with itself and with other States?

There certainly is.

And what is this knowledge, and among whom is it found? I asked.

It is the knowledge of the guardians, he replied, and is found among those whom we were just now describing as perfect guardians.

And what is the name which the city derives from the possession of this sort of knowledge?

The name of good in counsel and truly wise.

And will there be in our city more of these true guardians or more smiths?

The smiths, he replied, will be far more numerous.

Will not the guardians be the smallest of all the classes who receive a name from the profession of some kind of knowledge?

Much the smallest.

And so by reason of the smallest part or class, and of the knowledge which resides in this presiding and ruling part of itself, the whole State, being thus constituted according to nature, will be wise; and this, which has the only knowledge worthy to be called wisdom, has been ordained by nature to be of all classes the least.

Most true.

Thus, then, I said, the nature and place in the State of one of the four virtues has somehow or other been discovered.

And, in my humble opinion, very satisfactorily discovered, he replied.

Again, I said, there is no difficulty in seeing the nature of courage, and in what part that quality resides which gives the name of courageous to the State.

How do you mean?

Why, I said, every one who calls any State courageous or cowardly, will be thinking of the part which fights and goes out to war on the State's behalf.

No one, he replied, would ever think of any other.

The rest of the citizens may be courageous or may be cowardly, but their courage or cowardice will not, as I conceive, have the effect of making the city either the one or the other.

Certainly not.

The city will be courageous in virtue of a portion of herself which preserves under all circumstances that opinion about the nature of things to be feared and not to be feared in which our legislator educated them; and this is what you term courage.

I should like to hear what you are saying once more, for I do not think that I perfectly understand you.

I mean that courage is a kind of salvation.

Salvation of what?

Of the opinion respecting things to be feared, what they are and of what nature, which the law implants through education; and I mean by the words "under all circumstances" to intimate that in pleasure or in pain, or under the influence of desire or fear, a man preserves and does not lose this opinion. Shall I give you an illustration?

If you please.

You know, I said, that dyers, when they want to dye wool for making the true sea-purple, begin by selecting their white color first; this they prepare and dress with much care and pains, in order that the white ground may take the purple hue in full perfection. The dyeing then proceeds; and whatever is dyed in this manner becomes a fast color, and no washing either with lyes or without them can take away the bloom. But, when the ground has not been duly prepared, you will have noticed how poor is the look either of purple or of any other color.

Yes, he said; I know that they have a washed-out and ridiculous appearance.

Then now, I said, you will understand what our object was in selecting our soldiers, and educating them in music and gymnastic; we were contriving influences which would prepare them to take the dye of the laws in perfection, and the color of their opinion about dangers and of every other opinion was to be indelibly fixed by their nurture and training, not to be washed away by such potent lyes as pleasure—mightier agent far in washing the soul than any soda or lye; or by sorrow, fear, and desire, the mightiest of all other solvents. And this sort of universal saving power of true opinion in conformity with law about real and false dangers I call and maintain to be courage, unless you disagree.

But I agree, he replied; for I suppose that you mean to exclude mere uninstructed courage, such as that of a wild beast or of a slave—this, in your opinion, is not the courage which the law ordains, and ought to have another name.

Most certainly:

Then I may infer courage to be such as you describe?

Why, yes, said I, you may, and if you add the words "of a citizen," you will not be far wrong;—hereafter, if you like, we will carry the examination further, but at present we are seeking not for courage but justice; and for the purpose of our inquiry we have said enough.

You are right, he replied.

Two virtues remain to be discovered in the State—first, temperance, and then justice, which is the end of our search.

Very true.

Now, can we find justice without troubling ourselves about temperance?

I do not know how that can be accomplished, he said, nor do I desire that justice should be brought to light and temperance lost sight of; and therefore I wish that you would do me the favor of considering temperance first.

Certainly, I replied, I should not be justified in refusing your request.

Then consider, he said.

Yes, I replied; I will; and as far as I can at present see, the virtue of temperance has more of the nature of harmony and symphony than the preceding.

How so? he asked.

Temperance, I replied, is the ordering or controlling of certain pleasures and desires; this is curiously enough implied in the saying of "a man being his own master"; and other traces of the same notion may be found in language.

No doubt, he said.

There is something ridiculous in the expression "master of himself"; for the master is also the servant and the servant the master; and in all these modes of speaking the same person is denoted.

Certainly.

The meaning is, I believe, that in the human soul there is a better and also a worse principle; and when the better has the worse under control, then a man is said to be master of himself; and this is a term of praise: but when, owing to evil education or association, the better principle, which is also the smaller, is overwhelmed by the greater mass of the worse—in this case he is blamed and is called the slave of self and unprincipled.

Yes, there is reason in that.

And now, I said, look at our newly-created State, and there you will find one of these two conditions realized; for the State, as you will acknowledge, may be justly called master of itself, if the words "temperance" and "self-mastery" truly express the rule of the better part over the worse.

Yes, he said, I see that what you say is true.

Let me further note that the manifold and complex pleasures and desires and pains are generally found in children and women and servants, and in the freemen so called who are of the lowest and more numerous class.

Certainly, he said.

Whereas the simple and moderate desires which follow reason, and are under the guidance of mind and true opinion, are to be found only in a few, and those the best born and best educated.

Very true.

These two, as you may perceive, have a place in our State; and the meaner desires of the many are held down by the virtuous desires and wisdom of the few.

That I perceive, he said.

Then if there be any city which may be described as master of its own pleasures and desires, and master of itself, ours may claim such a designation?

Certainly, he replied.

It may also be called temperate, and for the same reasons?

Yes.

And if there be any State in which rulers and subjects will be agreed as to the question who are to rule, that again will be our State?

Undoubtedly.

And the citizens being thus agreed among themselves, in which class will temperance be found—in the rulers or in the subjects?

In both, as I should imagine, he replied.

Do you observe that we were not far wrong in our guess that temperance was a sort of harmony?

Why so?

Why, because temperance is unlike courage and wisdom, each of which resides in a part only, the one making the State wise and the other valiant; not so temperance, which extends to the whole, and runs through all the notes of the scale, and produces a harmony of the weaker and the stronger and the middle class, whether you suppose them to be stronger or weaker in wisdom or power or numbers or wealth, or anything else. Most truly then may we deem temperance to be the agreement of the naturally superior and inferior, as to the right to rule of either, both in states and individuals.

I entirely agree with you.

And so, I said, we may consider three out of the four virtues to have been discovered in our State. The last of those qualities which make a state virtuous must be justice, if we only knew what that was.

The inference is obvious.

The time then has arrived, Glaucon, when, like huntsmen, we should surround the cover, and look sharp that justice does not steal away, and pass out of sight and escape us; for beyond a doubt she is somewhere in this country: watch therefore and strive to catch a sight of her, and if you see her first, let me know.

Would that I could! but you should regard me rather as a follower who has just eyes enough to see what you show him—that is about as much as I am good for.

Offer up a prayer with me and follow.

I will, but you must show me the way.

Here is no path, I said, and the wood is dark and perplexing; still we must push on.

Let us push on.

Here I saw something: Halloo! I said, I begin to perceive a track, and I believe that the quarry will not escape.

Good news, he said.

Truly, I said, we are stupid fellows.

Why so?

Why, my good sir, at the beginning of our inquiry, ages ago, there was justice tumbling out at our feet, and we never saw her; nothing could be more ridiculous. Like people who go about looking for what they have in their hands—that was the way with us—we looked not at what we were seeking, but at what was far off in the distance; and therefore, I suppose, we missed her.

What do you mean?

I mean to say that in reality for a long time past we have been talking of justice, and have failed to recognize her.

I grow impatient at the length of your exordium.

Well then, tell me, I said, whether I am right or not: You remember the original principle which we were always laying down at the foundation of the State, that one man should practise one thing only, the thing to which his nature was best adapted;—now justice is this principle or a part of it.

Yes, we often said that one man should do one thing only.

Further, we affirmed that justice was doing one's own business, and not being a busybody; we said so again and again, and many others have said the same to us.

Yes, we said so.

Then to do one's own business in a certain way may be assumed to be justice. Can you tell me whence I derive this inference?

I can not, but I should like to be told.

Because I think that this is the only virtue which remains in the State when the other virtues of temperance and courage and wisdom are abstracted; and, that this is the ultimate cause and condition of the existence of all of them, and while remaining in them is also their preservative; and we were saying that if the three were discovered by us, justice would be the fourth or remaining one.

That follows of necessity.

If we are asked to determine which of these four qualities by its presence contributes most to the excellence of the State, whether the agreement of rulers and subjects, or the preservation in the soldiers of the opinion which the law ordains about the true nature of dangers, or wisdom and watchfulness in the rulers, or whether this other which I am mentioning, and which is found in children and women, slave and freeman, artisan, ruler, subject,—the quality, I mean, of every one doing his own work, and not being a busybody, would claim the palm—the question is not so easily answered.

Certainly, he replied, there would be a difficulty in saying which.

Then the power of each individual in the State to do his own work appears to compete with the other political virtues, wisdom, temperance, courage.

Yes, he said.

And the virtue which enters into this competition is justice?

Exactly.

Let us look at the question from another point of view: Are not the rulers in a State those to whom you would entrust the office of determining suits at law?

Certainly.

And are suits decided on any other ground but that a man may neither take what is another's, nor be deprived of what is his own?

Yes; that is their principle.

Which is a just principle?

Yes.

Then on this view also justice will be admitted to be the having and doing what is a man's own, and belongs to him?

Very true.

Think, now, and say whether you agree with me or not. Suppose a carpenter to be doing the business of a cobbler, or a cobbler of a carpenter; and suppose them to exchange their implements or their duties, or the same person to be doing the work of both, or whatever be the change; do you think that any great harm would result to the State?

Not much.

But when the cobbler or any other man whom nature designed to be a trader, having his heart lifted up by wealth or strength or the number of his followers, or any like advantage, attempts to force his way into the class of warriors, or a warrior into that of legislators and guardians, for which he is unfitted, and either to take the implements or the duties of the other; or when one man is trader, legislator, and warrior all in one, then I think you will agree with me in saying that this interchange and this meddling of one with another is the ruin of the State.

Most true.

Seeing then, I said, that there are three distinct classes, any meddling of one with another, or the change of one into another, is the greatest harm to the State, and may be most justly termed evil-doing?

Precisely.

And the greatest degree of evil-doing to one's own city would be termed by you injustice?

Certainly.

This then is injustice; and on the other hand when the trader, the auxiliary, and the guardian each do their own business, that is justice, and will make the city just.

I agree with you.

We will not, I said, be over-positive as yet; but if, on trial, this conception of justice be verified in the individual as well as in the State, there will be no longer any room for doubt; if it be not verified, we must have a fresh inquiry. First let us complete the old investigation, which we began, as you remember, under the impression that, if we could previously examine justice on the larger scale, there would be less difficulty in discerning her in the individual. That larger example appeared to be the State, and accordingly we constructed as good a one as we could, knowing well that in the good State justice would be found. Let the discovery which we made be now applied to the individual—if they agree, we shall be satisfied; or, if there be a difference in the individual, we will come back to the State and have another trial of the theory. The friction of the two when rubbed together may possibly strike a light in which justice will shine forth, and the vision which is then revealed we will fix in our souls.

That will be in regular course; let us do as you say.

I proceeded to ask: When two things, a greater and less, are called by the same name, are they like or unlike in so far as they are called the same?

Like, he replied.

The just man then, if we regard the idea of justice only, will be like the just State?

He will.

And a State was thought by us to be just when the three classes in the State severally did their own business; and also thought to be temperate and valiant and wise by reason of certain other affections and qualities of these same classes?

True, he said.

And so of the individual; we may assume that he has the same three principles in his own soul which are found in the State; and he may be rightly described in the same terms, because he is affected in the same manner?

Certainly, he said.

Once more then, O my friend, we may have alighted upon an easy question—whether the soul has these three principles or not?

An easy question! Nay, rather, Socrates, the proverb holds that hard is the good.

Very true, I said; and I do not think that the method which we are employing is at all adequate to the accurate solution of this question; the true method is another and a longer one. Still we may arrive at a solution not below the level of the previous inquiry.

May we not be satisfied with that? he said;—under the circumstances, I am quite content.

I too, I replied, shall be extremely well satisfied.

Then faint not in pursuing the speculation, he said.

Must we not acknowledge, I said, that in each of us there are the same principles and habits which there are in the State; and that from the individual they pass into the State?—how else can they come there? Take the quality of passion or spirit;—it would be ridiculous to imagine that this quality, when found in States, is not derived from the individuals who are supposed to possess it, e.g., the Thracians, Scythians, and in general the northern nations; and the same may be said of the love of knowledge, which is the special characteristic of our part of the world, or of the love of money, which may, with equal truth, be attributed to the Phoenicians and Egyptians.

Exactly so, he said.

There is no difficulty in understanding this.

None whatever.

But the question is not quite so easy when we proceed to ask whether these principles are three or one; whether, that is to say, we learn with one part of our nature, are angry with another, and with a third part desire the satisfaction of our natural appetites: or whether the whole soul comes into play in each sort of action—to determine that is the difficulty.

Yes, he said; there lies the difficulty.

Then let us now try and determine whether they are the same or different.

How can we? he asked.

I replied as follows: The same thing clearly can not act or be acted upon in the same part or in relation to the same thing at the same time, in contrary ways; and therefore whenever this contradiction occurs in things apparently the same, we know that they are really not the same, but different.

Good.

For example, I said, can the same thing be at rest and in motion at the same time in the same part?

Impossible.

Still, I said, let us have a more precise statement of terms, lest we should hereafter fall out by the way. Imagine the case of a man who is standing and also moving his hands and his head, and suppose a person to say that one and the same person is in motion and at rest at the same moment—to such a mode of speech we should object, and should rather say that one part of him is in motion while another is at rest.

Very true.

And suppose the objector to refine still further, and to draw the nice distinction that not only parts of tops, but whole tops, when they spin round with their pegs fixed on the spot, are at rest and in motion at the same time (and he may say the same of anything which revolves in the same spot), his objection would not be admitted by us, because in such cases things are not at rest and in motion in the same parts of themselves; we should rather say that they have both an axis and a circumference; and that the axis stands still, for there is no deviation from the perpendicular; and that the circumference goes round. But if, while revolving, the axis inclines either to the right or left, forwards or backwards, then in no point of view can they be at rest.

That is the correct mode of describing them, he replied.

Then none of these objections will confuse us, or incline us to believe that the same thing at the same time, in the same part or in relation to the same thing, can act or be acted upon in contrary ways.

Certainly not, according to my way of thinking.

Yet, I said, that we may not be compelled to examine all such objections, and prove at length that they are untrue, let us assume their absurdity, and go forward on the understanding that hereafter, if this assumption turn out to be untrue, all the consequences which follow shall be withdrawn.

Yes, he said, that will be the best way.

Well, I said, would you not allow that assent and dissent, desire and aversion, attraction and repulsion, are all of them opposites, whether they are regarded as active or passive (for that makes no difference in the fact of their opposition)?

Yes, he said, they are opposites.

Well, I said, and hunger and thirst, and the desires in general, and again willing and wishing, all these you would refer to the classes already mentioned. You would say—would you not?—that the soul of him who desires is seeking after the object of his desire; or that he is drawing to himself the thing which he wishes to possess: or again, when a person wants anything to be given him, his mind, longing for the realization of his desire, intimates his wish to have it by a nod of assent, as if he had been asked a question?

Very true.

And what would you say of unwillingness and dislike and the absence of desire; should not these be referred to the opposite class of repulsion and rejection?

Certainly.

Admitting this to be true of desire generally, let us suppose a particular class of desires, and out of these we will select hunger and thirst, as they are termed, which are the most obvious of them?

Let us take that class, he said.

The object of one is food, and of the other drink?

Yes.

And here comes the point: is not thirst the desire which the soul has of drink, and of drink only; not of drink qualified by anything else; for example, warm or cold, or much or little, or, in a word, drink of any particular sort: but if the thirst be accompanied by heat, then the desire is of cold drink; or, if accompanied by cold, then of warm drink; or, if the thirst be excessive, then the drink which is desired will be excessive; or, if not great, the quantity of drink will also be small: but thirst pure and simple will desire drink pure and simple, which is the natural satisfaction of thirst, as food is of hunger?

Yes, he said; the simple desire is, as you say, in every case of the simple object, and the qualified desire of the qualified object.

But here a confusion may arise; and I should wish to guard against an opponent starting up and saying that no man desires drink only, but good drink, or food only, but good food; for good is the universal object of desire, and thirst being a desire, will necessarily be thirst after good drink; and the same is true of every other desire.

Yes, he replied, the opponent might have something to say.

Nevertheless I should still maintain, that of relatives some have a quality attached to either term of the relation; others are simple and have their correlatives simple.

I do not know what you mean.

Well, you know of course that the greater is relative to the less?

Certainly.

And the much greater to the much less?

Yes.

And the sometime greater to the sometime less, and the greater that is to be to the less that is to be?

Certainly, he said.

And so of more and less, and of other correlative terms, such as the double and the half, or again, the heavier and the lighter, the swifter and the slower; and of hot and cold, and of any other relatives;—is not this true of all of them?

Yes.

And does not the same principle hold in the sciences? The object of science is knowledge (assuming that to be the true definition), but the object of a particular science is a particular kind of knowledge; I mean, for example, that the science of housebuilding is a kind of knowledge which is defined and distinguished from other kinds and is therefore termed architecture.

Certainly

Because it has a particular quality which no other has?

Yes.

And it has this particular quality because it has an object of a particular kind; and this is true of the other arts and sciences?

Yes.

Now, then, if I have made myself clear, you will understand my original meaning in what I said about relatives. My meaning was, that if one term of a relation is taken alone, the other is taken alone; if one term is qualified, the other is also qualified. I do not mean to say that relatives may not be disparate, or that the science of health is healthy, or of disease necessarily diseased, or that the sciences of good and evil are therefore good and evil; but only that, when the term science is no longer used absolutely, but has a qualified object which in this case is the nature of health and disease, it becomes defined, and is hence called not merely science, but the science of medicine.

I quite understand, and I think as you do.

Would you not say that thirst is one of these essentially relative terms, having clearly a relation—

Yes, thirst is relative to drink.

And a certain kind of thirst is relative to a certain kind of drink; but thirst taken alone is neither of much nor little, nor of good nor bad, nor of any particular kind of drink, but of drink only?

Certainly.

Then the soul of the thirsty one, in so far as he is thirsty, desires only drink; for this he yearns and tries to obtain it?

That is plain.

And if you suppose something which pulls a thirsty soul away from drink, that must be different from the thirsty principle which draws him like a beast to drink: for, as we were saying, the same thing can not at the same time with the same part of itself act in contrary ways about the same.

Impossible.

No more than you can say that the hands of the archer push and pull the bow at the same time, but what you say is that one hand pushes and the other pulls.

Exactly so, he replied.

And might a man be thirsty, and yet unwilling to drink?

Yes, he said, it constantly happens.

And in such a case what is one to say? Would you not say that there was something in the soul bidding a man to drink, and something else forbidding him, which is other and stronger than the principle which bids him?

I should say so.

And the forbidding principle is derived from reason, and that which bids and attracts proceeds from passion and disease?

Clearly.

Then we may fairly assume that they are two, and that they differ from one another; the one with which a man reasons, we may call the rational principle of the soul, the other, with which he loves and hungers and thirsts and feels the flutterings of any other desire, may be termed the irrational or appetitive, the ally of sundry pleasures and satisfactions?

Yes, he said, we may fairly assume them to be different.

Then let us finally determine that there are two principles existing in the soul. And what of passion, or spirit? Is it a third, or akin to one of the preceding?

I should be inclined to say—akin to desire.

Well, I said, there is a story which I remember to have heard, and in which I put faith. The story is, that Leontius, the son of Aglaion, coming up one day from the Piraeus, under the north wall on the outside, observed some dead bodies lying on the ground at the place of execution. He felt a desire to see them, and also a dread and abhorrence of them; for a time he struggled and covered his eyes, but at length the desire got the better of him; and forcing them open, he ran up to the dead bodies, saying, Look, ye wretches, take your fill of the fair sight.

I have heard the story myself, he said.

The moral of the tale is, that anger at times goes to war with desire, as though they were two distinct things.

Yes; that is the meaning, he said.

And are there not many other cases in which we observe that when a man's desires violently prevail over his reason, he reviles himself, and is angry at the violence within him, and that in this struggle, which is like the struggle of factions in a State, his spirit is on the side of his reason;—but for the passionate or spirited element to take part with the desires when reason decides that she should not be opposed, is a sort of thing which I believe that you never observed occurring in yourself, nor, as I should imagine in any one else?

Certainly not.

Suppose that a man thinks he has done a wrong to another, the nobler he is the less able is he to feel indignant at any suffering, such as hunger, or cold, or any other pain which the injured person may inflict upon him—these he deems to be just, and, as I say, his anger refuses to be excited by them.

True, he said.

But when he thinks that he is the sufferer of the wrong, then he boils and chafes, and is on the side of what he believes to be justice; and because he suffers hunger or cold or other pain he is only the more determined to persevere and conquer. His noble spirit will not be quelled until he either slays or is slain; or until he hears the voice of the shepherd, that is, reason, bidding his dog bark no more.

The illustration is perfect, he replied; and in our State, as we were saying, the auxiliaries were to be dogs, and to hear the voice of the rulers, who are their shepherds.

I perceive, I said, that you quite understand me; there is, however, a further point which I wish you to consider.

What point?

You remember that passion or spirit appeared at first sight to be a kind of desire, but now we should say quite the contrary; for in the conflict of the soul spirit is arrayed on the side of the rational principle.

Most assuredly.

But a further question arises: Is passion different from reason also, or only a kind of reason; in which latter case, instead of three principles in the soul, there will be only two, the rational and the concupiscent; or rather, as the State was composed of three classes, traders, auxiliaries, counsellors, so may there not be in the individual soul a third element which is passion or spirit, and when not corrupted by bad education is the natural auxiliary of reason?

Yes, he said, there must be a third.

Yes, I replied, if passion, which has already been shown to be different from desire, turn out also to be different from reason.

But that is easily proved:—We may observe even in young children that they are full of spirit almost as soon as they are born, whereas some of them never seem to attain to the use of reason, and most of them late enough.

Excellent, I said, and you may see passion equally in brute animals, which is a further proof of the truth of what you are saying. And we may once more appeal to the words of Homer, which have been already quoted by us,

"He smote his breast, and thus rebuked his soul;"

for in this verse Homer has clearly supposed the power which reasons about the better and worse to be different from the unreasoning anger which is rebuked by it.

Very true, he said.

And so, after much tossing, we have reached land, and are fairly agreed that the same principles which exist in the State exist also in the individual, and that they are three in number.

Exactly.

Must we not then infer that the individual is wise in the same way, and in virtue of the same quality which makes the State wise?

Certainly.

Also that the same quality which constitutes courage in the State constitutes courage in the individual, and that both the State and the individual bear the same relation to all the other virtues?

Assuredly.

And the individual will be acknowledged by us to be just in the same way in which the State is just?

That follows of course.

We can not but remember that the justice of the State consisted in each of the three classes doing the work of its own class?

We are not very likely to have forgotten, he said.

We must recollect that the individual in whom the several qualities of his nature do their own work will be just, and will do his own work?

Yes, he said, we must remember that too.

And ought not the rational principle, which is wise, and has the care of the whole soul, to rule, and the passionate or spirited principle to be the subject and ally?

Certainly.

And, as we were saying, the united influence of music and gymnastic will bring them into accord, nerving and sustaining the reason with noble words and lessons, and moderating and soothing and civilizing the wildness of passion by harmony and rhythm?

Quite true, he said.

And these two, thus nurtured and educated, and having learned truly to know their own functions, will rule over the concupiscent, which in each of us is the largest part of the soul and by nature most insatiable of gain; over this they will keep guard, lest, waxing great and strong with the fulness of bodily pleasures, as they are termed, the concupiscent soul, no longer confined to her own sphere, should attempt to enslave and rule those who are not her natural-born subjects, and overturn the whole life of man?

Very true, he said.

Both together will they not be the best defenders of the whole soul and the whole body against attacks from without; the one counselling, and the other fighting under his leader, and courageously executing his commands and counsels?

True.

And he is to be deemed courageous whose spirit retains in pleasure and in pain the commands of reason about what he ought or ought not to fear?

Right, he replied.

And him we call wise who has in him that little part which rules, and which proclaims these commands; that part too being supposed to have a knowledge of what is for the interest of each of the three parts and of the whole?

Assuredly.

And would you not say that he is temperate who has these same elements in friendly harmony, in whom the one ruling principle of reason, and the two subject ones of spirit and desire are equally agreed that reason ought to rule, and do not rebel?

Certainly, he said, that is the true account of temperance whether in the State or individual.

And surely, I said, we have explained again and again how and by virtue of what quality a man will be just.

That is very certain.

And is justice dimmer in the individual, and is her form different, or is she the same which we found her to be in the State?

There is no difference in my opinion, he said.

Because, if any doubt is still lingering in our minds, a few commonplace instances will satisfy us of the truth of what I am saying.

What sort of instances do you mean?

If the case is put to us, must we not admit that the just State, or the man who is trained in the principles of such a State, will be less likely than the unjust to make away with a deposit of gold or silver? Would any one deny this?

No one, he replied.

Will the just man or citizen ever be guilty of sacrilege or theft, or treachery either to his friends or to his country?

Never.

Neither will he ever break faith where there have been oaths or agreements?

Impossible.

No one will be less likely to commit adultery, or to dishonor his father and mother, or to fail in his religious duties?

No one.

And the reason is that each part of him is doing its own business, whether in ruling or being ruled?

Exactly so.

Are you satisfied then that the quality which makes such men and such states is justice, or do you hope to discover some other?

Not I, indeed.

Then our dream has been realized; and the suspicion which we entertained at the beginning of our work of construction, that some divine power must have conducted us to a primary form of justice, has now been verified?

Yes, certainly.

And the division of labor which required the carpenter and the shoemaker and the rest of the citizens to be doing each his own business, and not another's, was a shadow of justice, and for that reason it was of use?

Clearly.

But in reality justice was such as we were describing, being concerned however, not with the outward man, but with the inward, which is the true self and concernment of man: for the just man does not permit the several elements within him to interfere with one another, or any of them to do the work of others,—he

sets in order his own inner life, and is his own master and his own law, and at peace with himself; and when he has bound together the three principles within him, which may be compared to the higher, lower, and middle notes of the scale, and the intermediate intervals—when he has bound all these together, and is no longer many, but has become one entirely temperate and perfectly adjusted nature, then he proceeds to act, if he has to act, whether in a matter of property, or in the treatment of the body, or in some affair of politics or private business; always thinking and calling that which preserves and cooperates with this harmonious condition, just and good action, and the knowledge which presides over it, wisdom, and that which at any time impairs this condition, he will call unjust action, and the opinion which presides over it ignorance.

You have said the exact truth, Socrates.

Very good; and if we were to affirm that we had discovered the just man and the just State, and the nature of justice in each of them, we should not be telling a falsehood?

Most certainly not.

May we say so, then?

Let us say so.

And now, I said, injustice has to be considered.

Clearly.

Must not injustice be a strife which arises among the three principles—a meddlesomeness, and interference, and rising up of a part of the soul against the whole, an assertion of unlawful authority, which is made by a rebellious subject against a true prince, of whom he is the natural vassal,—what is all this confusion and delusion but injustice, and intemperance and cowardice and ignorance, and every form of vice?

Exactly so.

And if the nature of justice and injustice be known, then the meaning of acting unjustly and being unjust, or, again, of acting justly, will also be perfectly clear?

What do you mean? he said.

Why, I said, they are like disease and health; being in the soul just what disease and health are in the body.

How so? he said.

Why, I said, that which is healthy causes health, and that which is unhealthy causes disease.

Yes.

And just actions cause justice, and unjust actions cause injustice?

That is certain.

And the creation of health is the institution of a natural order and government of one by another in the parts of the body; and the creation of disease is the production of a state of things at variance with this natural order?

True.

And is not the creation of justice the institution of a natural order and government of one by another in the parts of the soul, and the creation of injustice the production of a state of things at variance with the natural order?

Exactly so, he said.

Then virtue is the health and beauty and well-being of the soul, and vice the disease and weakness and deformity of the same?

True.

And do not good practices lead to virtue, and evil practices to vice?

Assuredly.

Still our old question of the comparative advantage of justice and injustice has not been answered: Which is the more profitable, to be just and act justly and practise virtue, whether seen or unseen of gods and men, or to be unjust and act unjustly, if only unpunished and unreformed?

In my judgment, Socrates, the question has now become ridiculous. We know that, when the bodily constitution is gone, life is no longer endurable, though pampered with all kinds of meats and drinks, and having all wealth and all power; and shall we be told that when the very essence of the vital principle is undermined and corrupted, life is still worth having to a man, if only he be allowed to do whatever he likes with the single exception that he is not to acquire justice and virtue, or to escape from injustice and vice; assuming them both to be such as we have described?

Yes, I said, the question is, as you say, ridiculous. Still, as we are near the spot at which we may see the truth in the clearest manner with our own eyes, let us not faint by the way.

Certainly not, he replied.

Come up hither, I said, and behold the various forms of vice, those of them, I mean, which are worth looking at.

I am following you, he replied: proceed.

I said, The argument seems to have reached a height from which, as from some tower of specula-tion, a man may look down and see that virtue is one, but that the forms of vice are innumerable; there being four special ones which are deserving of note.

What do you mean? he said.

I mean, I replied, that there appear to be as many forms of the soul as there are distinct forms of the State.

How many?

There are five of the State, and five of the soul, I said.

What are they?

The first, I said, is that which we have been describing, and which may be said to have two names, monarchy and aristocracy, accordingly as rule is exercised by one distinguished man or by many.

True, he replied.

But I regard the two names as describing one form only; for whether the government is in the hands of one or many, if the governors have been trained in the manner which we have supposed, the fundamental laws of the State will be maintained.

That is true, he replied.

. . .

Book VI

And thus, Glaucon, after the argument has gone a weary way, the true and the false philosophers have at length appeared in view.

I do not think, he said, that the way could have been shortened.

I suppose not, I said; and yet I believe that we might have had a better view of both of them if the discussion could have been confined to this one subject and if there were not many other questions awaiting us, which he who desires to see in what respect the life of the just differs from that of the unjust must consider.

And what is the next question? he asked.

Surely, I said, the one which follows next in order. Inasmuch as philosophers only are able to grasp the eternal and unchangeable, and those who wander in the region of the many and variable are not philosophers, I must ask you which of the two classes should be the rulers of our State?

And how can we rightly answer that question?

Whichever of the two are best able to guard the laws and institutions of our State—let them be our guardians.

Very good.

Neither, I said, can there be any question that the guardian who is to keep anything should have eyes rather than no eyes?

There can be no question of that.

And are not those who are verily and indeed wanting in the knowledge of the true being of each thing, and who have in their souls no clear pattern, and are unable as with a painter's eye to look at the absolute truth and to that original to repair, and having perfect vision of the other world to order the laws about beauty, goodness, justice in this, if not already ordered, and to guard and preserve the order of them—are not such persons, I ask, simply blind?

Truly, he replied, they are much in that condition.

And shall they be our guardians when there are others who, besides being their equals in experience and falling short of them in no particular of virtue, also know the very truth of each thing?

There can be no reason, he said, for rejecting those who have this greatest of all great qualities; they must always have the first place unless they fail in some other respect.

Suppose then, I said, that we determine how far they can unite this and the other excellences.

By all means.

In the first place, as we began by observing, the nature of the philosopher has to be ascertained. We must come to an understanding about him, and, when we have done so, then, if I am not mistaken, we shall also acknowledge that such an union of qualities is possible, and that those in whom they are united, and those only, should be rulers in the State.

What do you mean?

Let us suppose that philosophical minds always love knowledge of a sort which shows them the eternal nature not varying from generation and corruption.

Agreed.

And further, I said, let us agree that they are lovers of all true being; there is no part whether greater or less, or more or less honorable, which they are willing to renounce; as we said before of the lover and the man of ambition.

True.

And if they are to be what we were describing, is there not another quality which they should also possess?

What quality?

Truthfulness: they will never intentionally receive into their mind falsehood, which is their detestation, and they will love the truth.

Yes, that may be safely affirmed of them.

"May be," my friend, I replied, is not the word; say rather, "must be affirmed": for he whose nature is amorous of anything can not help loving all that belongs or is akin to the object of his affections.

Right, he said.

And is there anything more akin to wisdom than truth?

How can there be?

Can the same nature be a lover of wisdom and a lover of falsehood?

Never.

The true lover of learning then must from his earliest youth, as far as in him lies, desire all truth?

Assuredly.

But then again, as we know by experience, he whose desires are strong in one direction will have them weaker in others; they will be like a stream which has been drawn off into another channel.

True.

He whose desires are drawn towards knowledge in every form will be absorbed in the pleasures of the soul, and will hardly feel bodily pleasure—I mean, if he be a true philosopher and not a sham one.

That is most certain.

Such an one is sure to be temperate and the reverse of covetous; for the motives which make another man desirous of having and spending, have no place in his character.

Very true.

Another criterion of the philosophical nature has also to be considered.

What is that?

There should be no secret corner of illiberality; nothing can be more antagonistic than meanness to a soul which is ever longing after the whole of things both divine and human.

Most true, he replied.

Then how can he who has magnificence of mind and is the spectator of all time and all existence, think much of human life?

He can not.

Or can such an one account death fearful?

No indeed.

Then the cowardly and mean nature has no part in true philosophy?

Certainly not.

Or again: can he who is harmoniously constituted, who is not covetous or mean, or a boaster, or a coward—can he, I say, ever be unjust or hard in his dealings?

Impossible.

Then you will soon observe whether a man is just and gentle, or rude and unsociable; these are the signs which distinguish even in youth the philosophical nature from the unphilosophical.

True.

There is another point which should be remarked.

What point?

Whether he has or has not a pleasure in learning; for no one will love that which gives him pain, and in which after much toil he makes little progress.

Certainly not.

And again, if he is forgetful and retains nothing of what he learns, will he not be an empty vessel?

That is certain.

Laboring in vain, he must end in hating himself and his fruitless occupation?

Yes.

Then a soul which forgets can not be ranked among genuine philosophic natures; we must insist that the philosopher should have a good memory?

Certainly.

And once more, the inharmonious and unseemly nature can only tend to disproportion?

Undoubtedly.

And do you consider truth to be akin to proportion or to disproportion?

To proportion.

Then, besides other qualities, we must try to find a naturally well-proportioned and gracious mind, which will move spontaneously towards the true being of everything.

Certainly.

Well, and do not all these qualities, which we have been enumerating, go together, and are they not, in a manner, necessary to a soul, which is to have a full and perfect participation of being?

They are absolutely necessary, he replied.

And must not that be a blameless study which he only can pursue who has the gift of a good memory, and is quick to learn,—noble, gracious, the friend of truth, justice, courage, temperance, who are his kindred?

The god of jealousy himself, he said, could find no fault with such a study.

And to men like him. I said, when perfected by years and education, and to these only you will entrust the State.

Here Adeimantus interposed and said: To these statements, Socrates, no one can offer a reply; but when you talk in this way, a strange feeling passes over the minds of your hearers: They fancy that they are led astray a little at each step in the argument, owing to their own want of skill in asking and answering questions; these littles accumulate, and at the end of the discussion they are found to have sustained a mighty overthrow and all their former notions appear to be turned upside down. And as unskilful players of draughts are at last shut up by their more skilful adversaries and have no piece to move, so they too find themselves shut up at last; for they have nothing to say in this new game of which words are the counters; and yet all the time they are in the right. The observation is suggested to me by what is now occurring. For any one of us might say, that although in words he is not able to meet you at each step of the argument, he sees as a fact that the votaries of philosophy, when they carry on the study, not only in youth as a part of education, but as the pursuit of their maturer years, most of them become strange monsters, not to say utter rogues, and that those who may be considered the best of them are made useless to the world by the very study which you extol.

Well, and do you think that those who say so are wrong?

I can not tell, he replied; but I should like to know what is your opinion.

Hear my answer; I am of opinion that they are quite right.

Then how can you be justified in saying that cities will not cease from evil until philosophers rule in them, when philosophers are acknowledged by us to be of no use to them?

You ask a question, I said, to which a reply can only be given in a parable.

Yes, Socrates; and that is a way of speaking to which you are not at all accustomed, I suppose.

I perceive, I said, that you are vastly amused at having plunged me into such a hopeless discussion; but now hear the parable, and then you will be still more amused at the meagreness of my imagination: for the manner in which the best men are treated in their own States is so grievous that no single thing on earth is comparable to it; and therefore, if I am to plead their cause, I must have recourse to fiction, and put together a figure made up of many things, like the fabulous unions of goats and stags which are found in pictures. Imagine then a fleet or a ship in which there is a captain who is taller and stronger than any of the crew, but he is a little deaf and has a similar infirmity in sight, and his knowledge of navigation is not much better. The sailors are quarrelling with one another about the steering—every one is of opinion that he has a right to steer, though he has never learned the art of navigation and can not tell who taught him or when he learned, and will further assert that it can not be taught, and they are ready to cut in pieces any one who says the contrary. They throng about the captain, begging and praying him to commit the helm to them; and if at any time they do not prevail, but others are preferred to them, they kill the others or throw them overboard, and having first chained up the noble captain's senses with drink or some narcotic drug, they mutiny and take possession of the ship and make free with the stores; thus, eating and drinking, they proceed on their voyage in such manner as might be expected of them. Him who is their partisan and cleverly aids them in their plot for getting the ship out of the captain's hands into their own whether by force or persuasion, they compliment with the name of sailor, pilot, able seaman, and abuse the other sort of man, whom they call a good-for-nothing; but that the true pilot must pay attention to the year and seasons and sky and stars and winds, and whatever else belongs to his art, if he intends to be really qualified for the command of a ship, and that he must and will be the steerer, whether other people like or not—the possibility of this union of authority with the steerer's art has never seriously entered into their thoughts or been made part of their calling. Now in vessels which are in a state of mutiny and by sailors who are mutineers, how will the true pilot be regarded? Will he not be called by them a prater, a star-gazer, a good-for-nothing?

Of course, said Adeimantus.

Then you will hardly need, I said, to hear the interpretation of the figure, which describes the true philosopher in his relation to the State; for you understand already.

Certainly.

Then suppose you now take this parable to the gentleman who is surprised at finding that philosophers have no honor in their cities; explain it to him and try to convince him that their having honor would be far more extraordinary.

I will.

Say to him, that, in deeming the best votaries of philosophy to be useless to the rest of the world, he is right; but also tell him to attribute their uselessness to the fault of those who will not use them, and not to themselves. The pilot should not humbly beg the sailors to be commanded by him—that is not the order of nature; neither are "the wise to go to the doors of the rich"—the ingenious author of this saying told a lie—but the truth is, that, when a man is ill, whether he be rich or poor, to the physician he must go, and he who wants to be governed, to him who is able to govern. The ruler who is good for anything ought not to beg his subjects to be ruled by him; although the present governors of mankind are of a different stamp; they may be justly compared to the mutinous sailors, and the true helmsmen to those who are called by them good-for-nothings and star-gazers.

Precisely so, he said.

For these reasons, and among men like these, philosophy, the noblest pursuit of all, is not likely to be much esteemed by those of the opposite faction; not that the greatest and most lasting injury is done to her by her opponents, but by her own professing followers, the same of whom you suppose the accuser to say, that the greater number of them are arrant rogues, and the best are useless; in which opinion I agreed.

Yes.

And the reason why the good are useless has now been explained?

True.

Then shall we proceed to show that the corruption of the majority is also unavoidable, and that this is not to be laid to the charge of philosophy any more than the other?

By all means.

And let us ask and answer in turn, first going back to the description of the gentle and noble nature. Truth, as you will remember, was his leader, whom he followed always and in all things; failing in this, he was an impostor, and had no part or lot in true philosophy.

Yes, that was said.

Well, and is not this one quality, to mention no others, greatly at variance with present notions of him?

Certainly, he said.

And have we not a right to say in his defence, that the true lover of knowledge is always striving after being—that is his nature; he will not rest in the multiplicity of individuals, which is an appearance only, but will go on—the keen edge will not be blunted, nor the force of his desire abate until he have attained the knowledge of the true nature of every essence by a sympathetic and kindred power in the soul, and by that power drawing near and mingling and becoming incorporate with very being, having begotten mind and truth, he will have knowledge and will live and grow truly, and then, and not till then, will he cease from his travail.

Nothing, he said, can be more just than such a description of him.

And will the love of a lie be any part of a philosopher's nature? Will he not utterly hate a lie?

He will.

And when truth is the captain, we can not suspect any evil of the band which he leads?

Impossible.

Justice and health of mind will be of the company, and temperance will follow after?

True, he replied.

Neither is there any reason why I should again set in array the philosopher's virtues, as you will doubtless remember that courage, magnificence, apprehension, memory, were his natural gifts. And you objected that, although no one could deny what I then said, still, if you leave words and look at facts, the persons who are thus described are some of them manifestly useless, and the greater number utterly depraved; we were then led to inquire into the grounds of these accusations, and have now arrived at the point of asking why are the majority bad, which question of necessity brought us back to the examination and definition of the true philosopher.

Exactly.

And we have next to consider the corruptions of the philosophic nature, why so many are spoiled and so few escape spoiling—I am speaking of those who were

said to be useless but not wicked—and, when we have done with them, we will speak of the imitators of philosophy, what manner of men are they who aspire after a profession which is above them and of which they are unworthy, and then, by their manifold inconsistencies, bring upon philosophy, and upon all philosophers, that universal reprobation of which we speak.

What are these corruptions? he said.

I will see if I can explain them to you. Every one will admit that a nature having in perfection all the qualities which we required in a philosopher, is a rare plant which is seldom seen among men.

Rare indeed.

And what numberless and powerful causes tend to destroy these rare natures!

What causes?

In the first place there are their own virtues, their courage, temperance, and the rest of them, every one of which praiseworthy qualities (and this is a most singular circumstance) destroys and distracts from philosophy the soul which is the possessor of them.

That is very singular, he replied.

Then there are all the ordinary goods of life—beauty, wealth, strength, rank, and great connections in the State—you understand the sort of things—these also have a corrupting and distracting effect.

I understand; but I should like to know more precisely what you mean about them.

Grasp the truth as a whole, I said, and in the right way; you will then have no difficulty in apprehending the preceding remarks, and they will no longer appear strange to you.

And how am I to do so? he asked.

Why, I said, we know that all germs or seeds, whether vegetable or animal, when they fail to meet with proper nutriment or climate or soil, in proportion to their vigor, are all the more sensitive to the want of a suitable environment, for evil is a greater enemy to what is good than to what is not.

Very true.

There is reason in supposing that the finest natures, when under alien conditions, receive more injury than the inferior, because the contrast is greater.

Certainly.

And may we not say, Adeimantus, that the most gifted minds, when they are ill-educated, become pre-eminently bad? Do not great crimes and the spirit of pure evil spring out of a fulness of nature ruined by education rather than from any inferiority, whereas weak natures are scarcely capable of any very great good or very great evil?

There I think that you are right.

And our philosopher follows the same analogy—he is like a plant which, having proper nurture, must necessarily grow and mature into all virtue, but, if sown and planted in an alien soil, becomes the most noxious of all weeds, unless he be preserved by some divine power. Do you really think, as people so often say, that our youth are corrupted by Sophists, or that private teachers of the art corrupt them in any degree worth speaking of? Are not the public who say these things the greatest of all Sophists? And do they not educate to perfection young and old, men and women alike, and fashion them after their own hearts?

When is this accomplished? he said.

When they meet together, and the world sits down at an assembly, or in a court of law, or a theatre, or a camp, or in any other popular resort, and there is a great uproar, and they praise some things which are being said or done, and blame other things, equally exaggerating both, shouting and clapping their hands, and the echo of the rocks and the place in which they are assembled redoubles the sound of the praise or blame—at such a time will not a young man's heart, as they say, leap within him? Will any private training enable him to stand firm against the overwhelming flood of popular opinion? or will he be carried away by the stream? Will he not have the notions of good and evil which the public in general have—he will do as they do, and as they are, such will he be?

Yes, Socrates; necessity will compel him.

And yet, I said, there is a still greater necessity, which has not been mentioned.

What is that?

The gentle force of attainder or confiscation or death, which, as you are aware, these new Sophists and educators, who are the public, apply when their words are powerless.

Indeed they do; and in right good earnest.

Now what opinion of any other Sophist, or of any private person, can be expected to overcome in such an unequal contest?

None, he replied.

No, indeed, I said, even to make the attempt is a great piece of folly; there neither is, nor has been, nor is ever likely to be, any different type of character which has had no other training in virtue but that which is supplied by public opinion—I speak, my friend, of human virtue only; what is more than human, as the proverb says, is not included: for I would not have you ignorant that, in the present evil state of governments, whatever is saved and comes to good is saved by the power of God, as we may truly say.

I quite assent, he replied.

Then let me crave your assent also to a further observation.

What are you going to say?

Why, that all those mercenary individuals, whom the many call Sophists and whom they deem to be their adversaries, do, in fact, teach nothing but the opinion of the many, that is to say, the opinions of their assemblies; and this is their wisdom. I might compare them to a man who should study the tempers and desires of a mighty strong beast who is fed by him—he would learn how to approach and handle him, also at what times and from what causes he is dangerous or the reverse, and what is the meaning of his several cries, and by what sounds, when another utters them, he is soothed or infuriated; and you may suppose further, that when, by continually attending upon him, he has become perfect in all this, he calls his knowledge wisdom, and makes of it a system or art, which he proceeds to teach, although he has no real notion of what he means by the principles or passions of which he is speaking, but calls this honorable and that dishonorable, or good or evil, or just or unjust, all in accordance with the tastes and tempers of the great brute. Good he pronounces to be that in which the beast delights and evil to be that which he dislikes; and he can give no other account of them except that the just and noble are the necessary, having never himself seen, and having no power of explaining to others the nature of either, or the difference between them, which is immense. By heaven, would not such an one be a rare educator?

Indeed he would.

And in what way does he who thinks that wisdom is the discernment of the tempers and tastes of the motley multitude, whether in painting or music, or, finally, in politics, differ from him whom I have been describing? For when a man consorts with the many, and exhibits to them his poem or other work of art or the service which he has done the State, making them his judges when he is not obliged, the so-called necessity of Diomede will oblige him to produce whatever they praise. And yet the reasons are utterly ludicrous which they give in confirmation of their own notions about the honorable and good. Did you ever hear any of them which were not?

No, nor am I likely to hear.

You recognize the truth of what I have been saying? Then let me ask you to consider further whether the world will ever be induced to believe in the existence of absolute beauty rather than of the many beautiful, or of the absolute in each kind rather than of the many in each kind?

Certainly not.

Then the world can not possibly be a philosopher?

Impossible.

And therefore philosophers must inevitably fall under the censure of the world?

They must.

And of individuals who consort with the mob and seek to please them?

That is evident.

Then, do you see any way in which the philosopher can be preserved in his calling to the end? and remember what we were saying of him, that he was to have quickness and memory and courage and magnificence—these were admitted by us to be the true philosopher's gifts.

Yes.

Will not such an one from his early childhood be in all things first among all, especially if his bodily endowments are like his mental ones?

Certainly, he said.

And his friends and fellow-citizens will want to use him as he gets older for their own purposes?

No question.

Falling at his feet, they will make requests to him and do him honor and flatter him, because they want to get into their hands now, the power which he will one day possess.

That often happens, he said.

And what will a man such as he is be likely to do under such circumstances, especially if he be a citizen of a great city, rich and noble, and a tall proper youth? Will he not be full of boundless aspirations, and fancy himself able to manage the affairs of Hellenes and of barbarians, and having got such notions into his head will he not dilate and elevate himself in the fulness of vain pomp and senseless pride?

To be sure he will.

Now, when he is in this state of mind, if some one gently comes to him and tells him that he is a fool and must get understanding, which can only be got by slaving for it, do you think that, under such adverse circumstances, he will be easily induced to listen?

Far otherwise.

And even if there be some one who through inherent goodness or natural reasonableness has had his eyes opened a little and is humbled and taken captive by philosophy, how will his friends behave when they think that they are likely to lose the advantage which they were hoping to reap from his companionship? Will they not do and say anything to prevent him from yielding to his better nature and to render his teacher powerless, using to this end private intrigues as well as public prosecutions?

There can be no doubt of it.

And how can one who is thus circumstanced ever become a philosopher?

Impossible.

Then were we not right in saying that even the very qualities which make a man a philosopher may, if he be ill-educated, divert him from philosophy no less than riches and their accompaniments and the other so-called goods of life?

We were quite right.

Thus, my excellent friend, is brought about all that ruin and failure which I have been describing of the natures best adapted to the best of all pursuits; they are natures which we maintain to be rare at any time; this being the class out of which come the men who are the authors of the greatest evil to States and individuals; and also of the greatest good when the tide carries them in that direction; but a small man never was the doer of any great thing either to individuals or to States.

That is most true, he said.

And so philosophy is left desolate, with her marriage rite incomplete: for her own have fallen away and forsaken her, and while they are leading a false and unbecoming life, other unworthy persons, seeing that she has no kinsmen to be her protectors, enter in and dishonor her; and fasten upon her the reproaches which, as you say, her reprovers utter, who affirm of her votaries that some are good for nothing, and that the greater number deserve the severest punishment.

That is certainly what people say.

Yes; and what else would you expect, I said, when you think of the puny creatures who, seeing this land open to them—a land well stocked with fair names and showy titles—like prisoners running out of prison into a sanctuary, take a leap out of their trades into philosophy; those who do so being probably the cleverest hands at their own miserable crafts? For, although philosophy be in this evil case, still there remains a dignity about her which is not to be found in the arts. And many are thus attracted by her whose natures are imperfect and whose souls are maimed and disfigured by their meannesses, as their bodies are by their trades and crafts. Is not this unavoidable?

Yes.

Are they not exactly like a bald little tinker who has just got out of durance and come into a fortune; he takes a bath and puts on a new coat, and is decked out as a bridegroom going to marry his master's daughter, who is left poor and desolate?

A most exact parallel.

What will be the issue of such marriages? Will they not be vile and bastard?

There can be no question of it.

And when persons who are unworthy of education approach philosophy and make an alliance with her who is in a rank above them, what sort of ideas and opinions are likely to be generated? Will they not be sophisms captivating to the ear, having nothing in them genuine, or worthy of or akin to true wisdom?

No doubt, he said.

Then, Adeimantus, I said, the worthy disciples of philosophy will be but a small remnant: perchance some noble and well-educated person, detained by exile in her service, who in the absence of corrupting influences remains devoted to her; or some lofty soul born in a mean city, the politics of which he contemns and neglects; and there may be a gifted few who leave the arts, which they justly despise, and come to her;—or peradventure there are some who are restrained by our friend Theages' bridle; for everything in the life of Theages conspired to divert him from philosophy; but ill-health kept him away from politics. My own case of the internal sign is hardly worth mentioning, for rarely, if ever, has such a monitor been given to any other man. Those who belong to this small class have tasted how sweet and blessed a possession philosophy is, and have also seen enough of the madness of the multitude; and they know that no politician is honest, nor is there any champion of justice at whose side they may fight and be saved. Such an one may be compared to a man who has fallen among wild beasts—he will not join in the wickedness of his fellows, but neither is he able singly to resist all their fierce natures, and therefore seeing that he would be of no use to the State or to his friends, and reflecting that he would have to throw away his life without doing any good either to himself or others, he holds his peace, and goes his own way. He is like one who, in the storm of dust and sleet which the driving wind hurries along, retires under the shelter of a wall; and seeing the rest of mankind full of wickedness, he is content, if only he can live his own life and be pure from evil or unrighteousness, and depart in peace and good-will, with bright hopes.

Yes, he said, and he will have done a great work before he departs.

A great work—yes; but not the greatest, unless he find a State suitable to him; for in a State which is suitable to him, he will have a larger growth and be the savior of his country, as well as of himself.

The causes why philosophy is in such an evil name have now been sufficiently explained: the injustice of the charges against her has been shown—is there anything more which you wish to say?

Nothing more on that subject, he replied; but I should like to know which of the governments now existing is in your opinion the one adapted to her.

Not any of them I said; and that is precisely the accusation which I bring against them—not one of them is worthy of the philosophic nature, and hence that nature is warped and estranged;—as the exotic seed which is sown in a foreign land becomes denaturalized, and is wont to be overpowered and to lose itself in the new soil, even so this growth of philosophy, instead of persisting, degenerates and receives another character. But if philosophy ever finds in the State that perfection which she herself is, then will be seen that she is in truth divine, and that all other things, whether natures of men or institutions, are but human;—and now, I know, that you are going to ask, What that State is:

No, he said; there you are wrong, for I was going to ask another question—whether it is the State of which we are the founders and inventors, or some other?

Yes, I replied, ours in most respects; but you may remember my saying before, that some living authority would always be required in the State having the same idea of the constitution which guided you when as legislator you were laying down the laws.

That was said, he replied.

Yes, but not in a satisfactory manner; you frightened us by interposing objections, which certainly showed that the discussion would be long and difficult; and what still remains is the reverse of easy.

What is there remaining?

The question how the study of philosophy may be so ordered as not to be the ruin of the State: All great attempts are attended with risk; "hard is the good," as men say.

Still, he said, let the point be cleared up, and the inquiry will then be complete.

I shall not be hindered, I said, by any want of will, but, if at all, by a want of power: my zeal you may see for yourselves; and please to remark in what I am about to say how boldly and unhesitatingly I declare that States should pursue philosophy, not as they do now, but in a different spirit.

In what manner?

At present, I said, the students of philosophy are quite young; beginning when they are hardly past childhood, they devote only the time saved from moneymaking and housekeeping to such pursuits; and even those of them who are reputed to have most of the philosophic spirit, when they come within sight of the great difficulty of the subject, I mean dialectic, take themselves off. In after life when invited by some one else, they may, perhaps, go and hear a lecture, and about this they make much ado, for philosophy is not considered by them to be their proper business: at last, when they grow old, in most cases they are extinguished more truly than Heracleitus' sun, inasmuch as they never light up again.

But what ought to be their course?

Just the opposite. In childhood and youth their study, and what philosophy they learn, should be suited to their tender years: during this period while they are growing up towards manhood, the chief and special care should be given to their bodies that they may have them to use in the service of philosophy; as life advances and the intellect begins to mature, let them increase the gymnastics of the soul; but when the strength of our citizens fails and is past civil and military duties, then let them range at will and engage in no serious labor, as we intend them to live happily here, and to crown this life with a similar happiness in another.

How truly in earnest you are, Socrates! he said; I am sure of that; and yet most of your hearers, if I am not mistaken, are likely to be still more earnest in their opposition to you, and will never be convinced; Thrasymachus least of all.

Do not make a quarrel, I said, between Thrasymachus and me, who have recently become friends, although, indeed, we were never enemies; for I shall go on striving to the utmost until I either convert him and other men, or do something which may profit them against the day when they live again, and hold the like discourse in another state of existence.

You are speaking of a time which is not very near.

Rather, I replied, of a time which is as nothing in comparison with eternity. Nevertheless, I do not wonder that the many refuse to believe; for they have never seen that of which we are now speaking realized; they have seen only a conventional imitation of philosophy, consisting of words artificially brought together, not like these of ours having a natural unity. But a human being who in word and work is perfectly moulded, as far as can be, into the proportion and likeness of virtue—such a man ruling in a city which bears the same image, they have never yet seen, neither one nor many of them—do you think that they ever did?

No indeed.

No, my friend, and they have seldom, if ever, heard free and noble sentiments; such as men utter when they are earnestly and by every means in their power seeking after truth for the sake of knowledge, while they look coldly on the subtleties of controversy, of which the end is opinion and strife, whether they meet with them in the courts of law or in society.

They are strangers, he said, to the words of which you speak.

And this was what we foresaw, and this was the reason why truth forced us to admit, not without fear and hesitation, that neither cities nor States nor individuals will ever attain perfection until the small class of philosophers whom we termed useless but not corrupt are providentially compelled, whether they will or not, to take care of the State, and until a like necessity be laid on the State to obey them; or until kings, or if not kings, the sons of kings or princes, are divinely inspired with a true love of true philosophy. That either or both of these alternatives are impossible, I see no reason to affirm: if they were so, we might indeed be justly ridiculed as dreamers and visionaries. Am I not right?

Quite right.

If then, in the countless ages of the past, or at the present hour in some foreign clime which is far away and beyond our ken, the perfected philosopher is or has been or hereafter shall be compelled by a superior power to have the charge of the State, we are ready to assert to the death, that this our constitution has been, and is—yea, and will be whenever the Muse of Philosophy is queen. There is no impossibility in all this; that there is a difficulty, we acknowledge ourselves.

My opinion agrees with yours, he said.

But do you mean to say that this is not the opinion of the multitude?

I should imagine not, he replied.

O my friend, I said, do not attack the multitude: they will change their minds, if, not in an aggressive spirit, but gently and with the view of soothing them and removing their dislike of over-education, you show them your philosophers as they really are and describe as you were just now doing their character and profession, and then mankind will see that he of whom you are speaking is not such as they supposed—if they view him in this new light, they will surely change their notion of him, and answer in another strain. Who can be at enmity with one who loves them, who that is himself gentle and free from envy will be jealous of one in whom there is no jealousy? Nay, let me answer for you, that in a few this harsh temper may be found but not in the majority of mankind.

I quite agree with you, he said.

And do you not also think, as I do, that the harsh feeling which the many entertain towards philosophy originates in the pretenders, who rush in uninvited, and are always abusing them, and finding fault with them, who make persons instead of things the theme of their conversation? and nothing can be more unbecoming in philosophers than this.

It is most unbecoming.

For he, Adeimantus, whose mind is fixed upon true being, has surely no time to look down upon the affairs of earth, or to be filled with malice and envy, contending against men; his eye is ever directed towards things fixed and immutable, which he sees neither injuring nor injured by one another, but all in order moving according to reason; these he imitates, and to these he will, as far as he can, conform himself. Can a man help imitating that with which he holds reverential converse?

Impossible.

And the philosopher holding converse with the divine order, becomes orderly and divine, as far as the nature of man allows; but like every one else, he will suffer from detraction.

Of course.

And if a necessity be laid upon him of fashioning, not only himself, but human nature generally, whether in States or individuals, into that which he beholds elsewhere, will he, think you, be an unskilful artificer of justice, temperance, and every civil virtue?

Anything but unskilful.

And if the world perceives that what we are saying about him is the truth, will they be angry with philosophy? Will they disbelieve us, when we tell them that no State call be happy which is not designed by artists who imitate the heavenly pattern?

They will not be angry if they understand, he said. But how will they draw out the plan of which you are speaking?

They will begin by taking the State and the manners of men, from which, as from a tablet, they will rub out the picture, and leave a clean surface. This is no easy task. But whether easy or not, herein will lie the difference between them and every other legislator,—they will have nothing to do either with individual or State, and will inscribe no laws, until they have either found, or themselves made, a clean surface.

They will be very right, he said.

Having effected this, they will proceed to trace an outline of the constitution?

No doubt.

And when they are filling in the work, as I conceive, they will often turn their eyes upwards and downwards: I mean that they will first look at absolute justice and beauty and temperance, and again at the human copy; and will mingle and temper the various elements of life into the image of a man; and this they will conceive according to that other image, which, when existing among men, Homer calls the form and likeness of God.

Very true, he said.

And one feature they will erase, and another they will put in, until they have made the ways of men, as far as possible, agreeable to the ways of God?

Indeed, he said, in no way could they make a fairer picture.

And now, I said, are we beginning to persuade those whom you described as rushing at us with might and main, that the painter of constitutions is such an one as we were praising; at whom they were so very indignant because to his hands we committed the State; and are they growing a little calmer at what they have just heard?

Much calmer, if there is any sense in them.

Why, where can they still find any ground for objection? Will they doubt that the philosopher is a lover of truth and being?

They would not be so unreasonable.

Or that his nature, being such as we have delineated, is akin to the highest good?

Neither can they doubt this.

But again, will they tell us that such a nature, placed under favorable circumstances, will not be perfectly good and wise if any ever was? Or will they prefer those whom we have rejected?

Surely not.

Then will they still be angry at our saying, that, until philosophers bear rule, States and individuals will have no rest from evil, nor will this our imaginary State ever be realized?

I think that they will be less angry.

Shall we assume that they are not only less angry but quite gentle, and that they have been converted and for very shame, if for no other reason, can not refuse to come to terms?

By all means, he said.

Then let us suppose that the reconciliation has been effected. Will any one deny the other point, that there may be sons of kings or princes who are by nature philosophers?

Surely no man, he said.

And when they have come into being will any one say that they must of necessity be destroyed; that they can hardly be saved is not denied even by us; but that in the whole course of ages no single one of them can escape—who will venture to affirm this?

Who indeed!

But, said I, one is enough; let there be one man who has a city obedient to his will, and he might bring into existence the ideal polity about which the world is so incredulous.

Yes, one is enough.

The ruler may impose the laws and institutions which we have been describing, and the citizens may possibly be willing to obey them?

Certainly.

And that others should approve, of what we approve, is no miracle or impossibility?

I think not.

But we have sufficiently shown, in what has preceded, that all this, if only possible, is assuredly for the best.

We have.

And now we say not only that our laws, if they could be enacted, would be for the best, but also that the enactment of them, though difficult, is not impossible.

Very good.

And so with pain and toil we have reached the end of one subject, but more remains to be discussed;—how and by what studies and pursuits will the saviors of the constitution be created, and at what ages are they to apply themselves to their several studies?

Certainly.

I omitted the troublesome business of the possession of women, and the procreation of children, and the appointment of the rulers, because I knew that the perfect State would be eyed with jealousy and was difficult of attainment; but that piece of cleverness was not of much service to me, for I had to discuss them all the same. The women and children are now disposed of, but the other question of the rulers must be investigated from the very beginning. We were saying, as you will remember, that they were to be lovers of their country, tried by the test of pleasures and pains, and neither in hardships, nor in dangers, nor at any other critical moment were to lose their patriotism—he was to be rejected who failed, but he who always came forth pure, like gold tried in the refiner's fire, was to be made a ruler, and to receive honors and rewards in life and after death. This was the sort of thing which was being said, and then the argument turned aside and veiled her face; not liking to stir the question which has now arisen.

I perfectly remember, he said.

Yes, my friend, I said, and I then shrank from hazarding the bold word; but now let me dare to say—that the perfect guardian must be a philosopher.

Yes, he said, let that be affirmed.

And do not suppose that there will be many of them; for the gifts which were deemed by us to be essential rarely grow together; they are mostly found in shreds and patches.

What do you mean? he said.

You are aware, I replied, that quick intelligence, memory, sagacity, cleverness, and similar qualities, do not often grow together, and that persons who possess them and are at the same time high-spirited and magnanimous are not so constituted by nature as to live orderly and in a peaceful and settled manner; they are driven any way by their impulses, and all solid principle goes out of them.

Very true, he said.

On the other hand, those steadfast natures which can better be depended upon, which in a battle are impregnable to fear and immovable, are equally immovable when there is anything to be learned; they are always in a torpid state, and are apt to yawn and go to sleep over any intellectual toil.

Quite true.

And yet we were saying that both qualities were necessary in those to whom the higher education is to be imparted, and who are to share in any office or command.

Certainly, he said.

And will they be a class which is rarely found?

Yes, indeed.

Then the aspirant must not only be tested in those labors and dangers and pleasures which we mentioned before, but there is another kind of probation which we did not mention—he must be exercised also in many kinds of knowledge, to see whether the soul will be able to endure the highest of all, or will faint under them, as in any other studies and exercises.

Yes, he said, you are quite right in testing him. But what do you mean by the highest of all knowledge?

You may remember, I said, that we divided the soul into three parts; and distinguished the several natures of justice, temperance, courage, and wisdom?

Indeed, he said, if I had forgotten, I should not deserve to hear more.

And do you remember the word of caution which preceded the discussion of them?

To what do you refer?

We were saying, if I am not mistaken, that he who wanted to see them in their perfect beauty must take a longer and more circuitous way, at the end of which they would appear; but that we could add on a popular exposition of them on a level with the discussion which had preceded. And you replied that such an exposition would be enough for you, and so the inquiry was continued in what to me seemed to be a very inaccurate manner; whether you were satisfied or not, it is for you to say.

Yes, he said, I thought and the others thought that you gave us a fair measure of truth.

But, my friend, I said, a measure of such things which in any degree falls short of the whole truth is not fair measure; for nothing imperfect is the measure of anything, although persons are too apt to be contented and think that they need search no further.

Not an uncommon case when people are indolent.

Yes, I said; and there can not be any worse fault in a guardian of the State and of the laws.

True.

The guardian then, I said, must be required to take the longer circuit, and toil at learning as well as at gymnastics, or he will never reach the highest knowledge of all, which, as we were just now saying, is his proper calling.

What, he said, is there a knowledge still higher than this—higher than justice and the other virtues?

Yes, I said, there is. And of the virtues too we must behold not the outline merely, as at present—nothing short of the most finished picture should satisfy us. When little things are elaborated with an infinity of pains, in order that they may appear in their full beauty and utmost clearness, how ridiculous that we should not think the highest truths worthy of attaining the highest accuracy!

A right noble thought; but do you suppose that we shall refrain from asking you what is this highest knowledge?

Nay, I said, ask if you will; but I am certain that you have heard the answer many times, and now you either do not understand me or, as I rather think, you are disposed to be troublesome; for you have often been told that the idea of good is the highest knowledge, and that all other things become useful and advantageous only by their use of this. You can hardly be ignorant that of this I was about to speak, concerning which, as you have often heard me say, we know so little; and, without which, any other knowledge or possession of any kind will profit us nothing. Do you think that the possession of all other things is of any value if we do not possess the good? or the knowledge of all other things if we have no knowledge of beauty and goodness?

Assuredly not.

You are further aware that most people affirm pleasure to be the good, but the finer sort of wits say it is knowledge?

Yes.

And you are aware too that the latter can not explain what they mean by knowledge, but are obliged after all to say knowledge of the good?

How ridiculous!

Yes, I said, that they should begin by reproaching us with our ignorance of the good, and then presume our knowledge of it—for the good they define to be knowledge of the good, just as if we understood them when they use the term "good"—this is of course ridiculous.

Most true, he said.

And those who make pleasure their good are in equal perplexity; for they are compelled to admit that there are bad pleasures as well as good.

Certainly.

And therefore to acknowledge that bad and good are the same?

True.

There can be no doubt about the numerous difficulties in which this question is involved.

There can be none.

Further, do we not see that many are willing to do or to have or to seem to be what is just and honorable without the reality; but no one is satisfied with the appearance of good—the reality is what they seek; in the case of the good, appearance is despised by every one.

Very true, he said.

Of this then, which every soul of man pursues and makes the end of all his actions, having a presentiment that there is such an end, and yet hesitating because neither knowing the nature nor having the same assurance of this as of other things, and therefore losing whatever good there is in other things,—of a principle such and so great as this ought the best men in our State, to whom everything is entrusted, to be in the darkness of ignorance?

Certainly not, he said.

I am sure, I said, that he who dies not know how the beautiful and the just are likewise good will be but a sorry guardian of them; and I suspect that no one who is ignorant of the good will have a true knowledge of them.

That, he said, is a shrewd suspicion of yours.

And if we only have a guardian who has this knowledge our State will be perfectly ordered?

Of course, he replied; but I wish that you would tell me whether you conceive this supreme principle of the good to be knowledge or pleasure, or different from either?

Aye, I said, I knew all along that a fastidious gentleman like you would not be contented with the thoughts of other people about these matters.

True, Socrates; but I must say that one who like you has passed a lifetime in the study of philosophy should not be always repeating the opinions of others, and never telling his own.

Well, but has any one a right to say positively what he does not know?

Not, he said, with the assurance of positive certainty; he has no right to do that: but he may say what he thinks, as a matter of opinion.

And do you not know, I said, that all mere opinions are bad, and the best of them blind? You would not deny that those who have any true notion without intelligence are only like blind men who feel their way along the road?

Very true.

And do you wish to behold what is blind and crooked and base, when others will tell you of brightness and beauty?

Still, I must implore you, Socrates, said Glaucon, not to turn away just as you are reaching the goal; if you will only give such an explanation of the good as you have already given of justice and temperance and the other virtues, we shall be satisfied.

Yes, my friend, and I shall be at least equally satisfied, but I can not help fearing that I shall fail, and that my indiscreet zeal will bring ridicule upon me. No, sweet sirs, let us not at present ask what is the actual nature of the good, for to reach what is now in my thoughts would be an effort too great for me. But of the child of the good who is likest him, I would fain speak, if I could be sure that you wished to hear—otherwise, not.

By all means, he said, tell us about the child, and you shall remain in our debt for the account of the parent.

I do indeed wish, I replied, that I could pay, and you receive, the account of the parent, and not, as now, of the offspring only; take, however, this latter by way of interest, and at the same time have a care that I do not render a false account, although I have no intention of deceiving you.

Yes, we will take all the care that we can: proceed.

Yes, I said, but I must first come to an understanding with you, and remind you of what I have mentioned in the course of this discussion, and at many other times.

What?

The old story, that there is a many beautiful and a many good, and so of other things which we describe and define; to all of them the term "many" is applied.

True, he said.

And there is an absolute beauty and an absolute good, and of other things to which the term "many" is applied there is an absolute; for they may be brought under a single idea, which is called the essence of each.

Very true.

The many, as we say, are seen but not known, and the ideas are known but not seen.

Exactly.

And what is the organ with which we see the visible things?

The sight, he said.

And with the hearing, I said, we hear, and with the other senses perceive the other objects of sense?

True.

But have you remarked that sight is by far the most costly and complex piece of workmanship which the artificer of the senses ever contrived?

No, I never have, he said.

Then reflect: has the ear or voice need of any third or additional nature in order that the one may be able to hear and the other to be heard?

Nothing of the sort.

No, indeed, I replied; and the same is true of most, if not all, the other senses—you would not say that any of them requires such an addition?

Certainly not.

But you see that without the addition of some other nature there is no seeing or being seen?

How do you mean?

Sight being, as I conceive, in the eyes, and he who has eyes wanting to see; color being also present in them, still unless there be a third nature specially adapted to the purpose, the owner of the eyes will see nothing and the colors will be invisible.

Of what nature are you speaking?

Of that which you term light, I replied.

True, he said.

Noble, then, is the bond which links together sight and visibility, and great beyond other bonds by no small difference of nature; for light is their bond, and light is no ignoble thing?

Nay, he said, the reverse of ignoble.

And which, I said, of the gods in heaven would you say was the lord of this element? Whose is that light which makes the eye to see perfectly and the visible to appear?

You mean the sun, as you and all mankind say.

May not the relation of sight to this deity be described as follows?

How?

Neither sight nor the eye in which sight resides is the sun?

No.

Yet of all the organs of sense the eye is the most like the sun?

By far the most like.

And the power which the eye possesses is a sort of effluence which is dispensed from the sun?

Exactly.

Then the sun is not sight, but the author of sight who is recognized by sight?

True, he said.

And this is he whom I call the child of the good, whom the good begat in his own likeness, to be in the visible world, in relation to sight and the things of sight, what the good is in the intellectual world in relation to mind and the things of mind:

Will you be a little more explicit? he said.

Why, you know, I said, that the eyes, when a person directs them towards objects on which the light of day is no longer shining but the moon and stars only, see dimly, and are nearly blind; they seem to have no clearness of vision in them?

Very true.

But when they are directed towards objects on which the sun shines, they see clearly and there is sight in them?

Certainly.

● And the soul is like the eye: when resting upon that on which truth and being shine, the soul perceives and understands, and is radiant with intelligence; but when turned towards the twilight of becoming and perishing, then she has opinion only, and goes blinking about, and is first of one opinion and then of another, and seems to have no intelligence?

Just so.

Now, that which imparts truth to the known and the power of knowing to the knower is what I would have you term the idea of good, and this you will deem to be the cause of science, and of truth in so far as the latter becomes the subject of knowledge; beautiful too, as are both truth and knowledge, you will be right in esteeming this other nature as more beautiful than either; and, as in the previous instance, light and sight may be truly said to be like the sun, and yet not to be the sun, so in this other sphere, science and truth may be deemed to be like the good, but not the good; the good has a place of honor yet higher.

What a wonder of beauty that must be, he said, which is the author of science and truth, and yet surpasses them in beauty; for you surely can not mean to say that pleasure is the good?

God forbid, I replied; but may I ask you to consider the image in another point of view?

In what point of view?

You would say, would you not, that the sun is not only the author of visibility in all visible things, but of generation and nourishment and growth, though he himself is not generation?

Certainly.

In like manner the good may be said to be not only the author of knowledge to all things known, but of their being and essence, and yet the good is not essence, but far exceeds essence in dignity and power.

Glaucon said, with a ludicrous earnestness: By the light of heaven, how amazing!

Yes, I said, and the exaggeration may be set down to you; for you made me utter my fancies.

And pray continue to utter them; at any rate let us hear if there is anything more to be said about the similitude of the sun.

Yes, I said, there is a great deal more.

Then omit nothing, however slight.

I will do my best, I said; but I should think that a great deal will have to be omitted.

I hope not, he said.

You have to imagine, then, that there are two ruling powers, and that one of them is set over the intellectual world, the other over the visible. I do not

say heaven, lest you should fancy upon the name (οὐρανός, ὁρατός). you have this distinction of the v ble fixed in your mind?

I have.

Now take a line which has been cut into two unequal parts, and divide each of them again in the same proportion, and suppose the two main divisions to answer, one to the visible and the other to the intelligible, and then compare the subdivisions in respect of their clearness and want of clearness, and you will find that the first section in the sphere of the visible consists of images. And by images I mean, in the first place, shadows, and in the second place, reflections in water and in solid, smooth and polished bodies and the like: Do you understand?

Yes, I understand.

Imagine, now, the other section, of which this is only the resemblance, to include the animals which we see, and everything that grows or is made.

Very good.

Would you not admit that both the sections of this division have different degrees of truth, and that the copy is to the original as the sphere of opinion is to the sphere of knowledge?

Most undoubtedly.

Next proceed to consider the manner in which the sphere of the intellectual is to be divided.

In what manner?

Thus:—There are two subdivisions, in the lower of which the soul uses the figures given by the former division as images; the inquiry can only be hypothetical, and instead of going upwards to a principle descends to the other end; in the higher of the two, the soul passes out of hypotheses, and goes up to a principle which is above hypotheses, making no use of images as in the former case, but proceeding only in and through the ideas themselves.

I do not quite understand your meaning, he said.

Then I will try again; you will understand me better when I have made some preliminary remarks. You are aware that students of geometry, arithmetic, and the kindred sciences assume the odd and the even and the figures and three kinds of angles and the like in their several branches of science; these are their hypotheses, which they and everybody are supposed to know, and therefore they do not deign to give any account of them either to themselves or others; but they begin with them, and go on until they

ve at last, and in a consistent manner, at their
conclusion?

Yes, he said, I know.

And do you not know also that although they
make use of the visible forms and reason about them,
they are thinking not of these, but of the ideals which
they resemble; not of the figures which they draw, but
of the absolute square and the absolute diameter, and
so on—the forms which they draw or make, and
which have shadows and reflections in water of their
own, are converted by them into images, but they are
really seeking to behold the things themselves, which
can only be seen with the eye of the mind?

That is true.

And of this I spoke as the intelligible, although in
the search after it the soul is compelled to use hypotheses; not ascending to a first principle, because
she is unable to rise above the region of hypothesis, but
employing the objects of which the shadows below are
resemblances in their turn as images, they having in
relation to the shadows and reflections of them a
greater distinctness, and therefore a higher value.

I understand, he said, that you are speaking of the
province of geometry and the sister arts.

And when I speak of the other division of the intelligible, you will understand me to speak of that
other sort of knowledge which reason herself attains
by the power of dialectic, using the hypotheses not
as first principles, but only as hypotheses—that is to
say, as steps and points of departure into a world
which is above hypotheses, in order that she may
soar beyond them to the first principle of the whole;
and clinging to this and then to that which depends
on this, by successive steps she descends again
without the aid of any sensible object, from ideas,
through ideas, and in ideas she ends.

I understand you, he replied; not perfectly, for
you seem to me to be describing a task which is really tremendous; but, at any rate, I understand you
to say that knowledge and being, which the science
of dialectic contemplates, are clearer than the notions of the arts, as they are termed, which proceed
from hypotheses only: these are also contemplated
by the understanding, and not by the senses: yet, because they start from hypotheses and do not ascend
to a principle, those who contemplate them appear
to you not to exercise the higher reason upon them,
although when a first principle is added to them they
are cognizable by the higher reason. And the habit

which is concerned with geometry and the cognate
sciences I suppose that you would term understanding and not reason, as being intermediate between
opinion and reason.

You have quite conceived my meaning, I said; and
now, corresponding to these four divisions, let there
be four faculties in the soul—reason answering to
the highest, understanding to the second, faith (or
conviction) to the third, and perception of shadows
to the last—and let there be a scale of them, and let
us suppose that the several faculties have clearness
in the same degree that their objects have truth.

I understand, he replied, and give my assent, and
accept your arrangement.

. . .

Book VII

And now, I said, let me show in a figure how far our
nature is enlightened or unenlightened:—Behold!
human beings living in an underground den, which
has a mouth open towards the light and reaching all
along the den; here they have been from their childhood, and have their legs and necks chained so that
they can not move, and can only see before them,
being prevented by the chains from turning round
their heads. Above and behind them a fire is blazing
at a distance, and between the fire and the prisoners
there is a raised way; and you will see, if you look, a
low wall built along the way, like the screen which
marionette players have in front of them, over which
they show the puppets.

I see.

And do you see, I said, men passing along the
wall carrying all sorts of vessels, and statues and figures of animals made of wood and stone and various
materials, which appear over the wall? Some of them
are talking, others silent.

You have shown me a strange image, and they are
strange prisoners.

Like ourselves, I replied; and they see only their
own shadows, or the shadows of one another; which
the fire throws on the opposite wall of the cave?

True, he said; how could they see anything but
the shadows if they were never allowed to move their
heads?

And of the objects which are being carried in like
manner they would only see the shadows?

Yes, he said.

And if they were able to converse with one another, would they not suppose that they were naming what was actually before them?

Very true.

And suppose further that the prison had an echo which came from the other side, would they not be sure to fancy when one of the passers-by spoke that the voice which they heard came from the passing shadow?

No question, he replied.

To them, I said, the truth would be literally nothing but the shadows of the images.

That is certain.

And now look again, and see what will naturally follow if the prisoners are released and disabused of their error. At first, when any of them is liberated and compelled suddenly to stand up and turn his neck round and walk and look towards the light, he will suffer sharp pains; the glare will distress him, and he will be unable to see the realities of which in his former state he had seen the shadows; and then conceive some one saying to him, that what he saw before was an illusion, but that now, when he is approaching nearer to being and his eye is turned towards more real existence, he has a clearer vision,—what will be his reply? And you may further imagine that his instructor is pointing to the objects as they pass and requiring him to name them,—will he not be perplexed? Will he not fancy that the shadows which he formerly saw are truer than the objects which are now shown to him?

Far truer.

And if he is compelled to look straight at the light, will he not have a pain in his eyes which will make him turn away to take refuge in the objects of vision which he can see, and which he will conceive to be in reality clearer than the things which are now being shown to him?

True, he said.

And suppose once more, that he is reluctantly dragged up a steep and rugged ascent, and held fast until he is forced into the presence of the sun himself, is he not likely to be pained and irritated? When he approaches the light his eyes will be dazzled, and he will not be able to see anything at all of what are now called realities.

Not all in a moment, he said.

He will require to grow accustomed to the sight of the upper world. And first he will see the shadows best, next the reflections of men and other objects in the water, and then the objects themselves; then he will gaze upon the light of the moon and the stars and the spangled heaven; and he will see the sky and the stars by night better than the sun or the light of the sun by day?

Certainly.

Last of all he will be able to see the sun, and not mere reflections of him in the water, but he will see him in his own proper place, and not in another; and he will contemplate him as he is.

Certainly.

He will then proceed to argue that this is he who gives the season and the years, and is the guardian of all that is in the visible world, and in a certain way the cause of all things which he and his fellows have been accustomed to behold?

Clearly, he said, he would first see the sun and then reason about him.

And when he remembered his old habitation, and the wisdom of the den and his fellow-prisoners, do you not suppose that he would felicitate himself on the change, and pity them?

Certainly, he would.

And if they were in the habit of conferring honors among themselves on those who were quickest to observe the passing shadows and to remark which of them went before, and which followed after, and which were together; and who were therefore best able to draw conclusions as to the future, do you think that he would care for such honors and glories, or envy the possessors of them? Would he not say with Homer,

"Better to be the poor servant of a poor master,"

and to endure anything, rather than think as they do and live after their manner?

Yes, he said, I think that he would rather suffer anything than entertain these false notions and live in this miserable manner.

Imagine once more, I said, such an one coming suddenly out of the sun to be replaced in his old situation; would he not be certain to have his eyes full of darkness?

To be sure, he said.

And if there were a contest, and he had to compete in measuring the shadows with the prisoners who had never moved out of the den, while his sight was still weak, and before his eyes had become steady (and the time which would be needed to acquire this new habit of sight might be very considerable), would he not be ridiculous? Men would say of him that up he went and down he came without his eyes; and that it was better not even to think of ascending; and if any one tried to loose another and lead him up to the light, let them only catch the offender, and they would put him to death.

No question, he said.

This entire allegory, I said, you may now append, dear Glaucon, to the previous argument; the prison-house is the world of sight, the light of the fire is the sun, and you will not misapprehend me if you interpret the journey upwards to be the ascent of the soul into the intellectual world according to my poor belief, which, at your desire, I have expressed— whether rightly or wrongly God knows. But, whether true or false, my opinion is that in the world of knowledge the idea of good appears last of all, and is seen only with an effort; and, when seen, is also inferred to be the universal author of all things beautiful and right, parent of light and of the lord of light in this visible world, and the immediate source of reason and truth in the intellectual; and that this is the power upon which he who would act rationally either in public or private life must have his eye fixed.

I agree, he said, as far as I am able to understand you.

Moreover, I said, you must not wonder that those who attain to this beatific vision are unwilling to descend to human affairs; for their souls are ever hastening into the upper world where they desire to dwell; which desire of theirs is very natural, if our allegory may be trusted.

Yes, very natural.

And is there anything surprising in one who passes from divine contemplations to the evil state of man, misbehaving himself in a ridiculous manner; if, while his eyes are blinking and before he has become accustomed to the surrounding darkness, he is compelled to fight in courts of law, or in other places, about the images or the shadows of images of justice, and is endeavoring to meet the conceptions of those who have never yet seen absolute justice?

Anything but surprising, he replied.

Any one who has common sense will remember that the bewilderments of the eyes are of two kinds, and arise from two causes, either from coming out of the light or from going into the light, which is true of the mind's eye, quite as much as of the bodily eye; and he who remembers this when he sees any one whose vision is perplexed and weak, will not be too ready to laugh; he will first ask whether that soul of man has come out of the brighter life, and is unable to see because unaccustomed to the dark, or having turned from darkness to the day is dazzled by excess of light. And he will count the one happy in his condition and state of being, and he will pity the other; or, if he have a mind to laugh at the soul which comes from below into the light, there will be more reason in this than in the laugh which greets him who returns from above out of the light into the den.

That, he said, is a very just distinction.

But then, if I am right, certain professors of education must be wrong when they say that they can put a knowledge into the soul which was not there before, like sight into blind eyes.

They undoubtedly say this, he replied.

Whereas, our argument shows that the power and capacity of learning exists in the soul already; and that just as the eye was unable to turn from darkness to light without the whole body, so too the instrument of knowledge can only by the movement of the whole soul be turned from the world of becoming into that of being, and learn by degrees to endure the sight of being, and of the brightest and best of being, or in other words, of the good.

Very true.

And must there not be some art which will effect conversion in the easiest and quickest manner; not implanting the faculty of sight, for that exists already, but has been turned in the wrong direction, and is looking away from the truth?

Yes, he said, such an art may be presumed.

And whereas the other so-called virtues of the soul seem to be akin to bodily qualities, for even when they are not originally innate they can be implanted later by habit and exercise, the virtue of wisdom more than anything else contains a divine element which always remains, and by this conversion is rendered useful and profitable; or, on the other hand, hurtful and useless. Did you never observe the narrow intelligence flashing from the keen eye of a clever rogue—how eager he is, how clearly his paltry soul sees the way to his end; he is the reverse of blind, but his keen eye-sight is forced into the service of evil, and he is mischievous in proportion to his cleverness?

Very true, he said.

But what if there had been a circumcision of such natures in the days of their youth; and they had been severed from those sensual pleasures, such as eating and drinking, which, like leaden weights, were attached to them at their birth, and which drag them down and turn the vision of their souls upon the things that are below—if, I say, they had been released from these impediments and turned in the opposite direction, the very same faculty in them would have seen the truth as keenly as they see what their eyes are turned to now.

Very likely.

Yes, I said; and there is another thing which is likely, or rather a necessary inference from what has preceded, that neither the uneducated and uninformed of the truth, nor yet those who never make an end of their education, will be able ministers of State; not the former, because they have no single aim of duty which is the rule of all their actions, private as well as public; nor the latter, because they will not act at all except upon compulsion, fancying that they are already dwelling apart in the islands of the blest.

Very true, he replied.

Then, I said, the business of us who are the founders of the State will be to compel the best minds to attain that knowledge which we have already shown to be the greatest of all—they must continue to ascended until they arrive at the good; but when they have ascended and seen enough we must not allow them to do as they do now.

What do you mean?

I mean that they remain in the upper world: but this must not be allowed; they must be made to descend again among the prisoners in the den, and partake of their labors and honors, whether they are worth having or not.

But is not this unjust? he said; ought we to give them a worse life, when they might have a better?

You have again forgotten, my friend, I said, the intention of the legislator, who did not aim at making any one class in the State happy above the rest; the happiness was to be in the whole State, and he held the citizens together by persuasion and necessity, making them benefactors of the State, and therefore benefactors of one another; to this end he created them, not to please themselves, but to be his instruments in binding up the State.

True, he said, I had forgotten.

Observe, Glaucon, that there will be no injustice in compelling our philosophers to have a care and providence of others; we shall explain to them that in other States, men of their class are not obliged to share in the toils of politics: and this is reasonable, for they grow up at their own sweet will, and the government would rather not have them. Being self-taught, they can not be expected to show any gratitude for a culture which they have never received. But we have brought you into the world to be rulers of the hive, kings of yourselves and of the other citizens, and have educated you far better and more perfectly than they have been educated, and you are better able to share in the double duty. Wherefore each of you, when his turn comes, must go down to the general underground abode, and get the habit of seeing in the dark. When you have acquired the habit, you will see ten thousand times better than the inhabitants of the den, and you will know what the several images are, and what they represent, because you have seen the beautiful and just and good in their truth. And thus our State, which is also yours, will be a reality, and not a dream only, and will be administered in a spirit unlike that of other States, in which men fight with one another about shadows only and are distracted in the struggle for power, which in their eyes is a great good. Whereas the truth is that the State in which the rulers are most reluctant to govern is always the best and most quietly governed, and the State in which they are most eager, the worst.

Quite true, he replied.

And will our pupils, when they hear this, refuse to take their turn at the toils of State, when they are allowed to spend the greater part of their time with one another in the heavenly light?

Impossible, he answered; for they are just men, and the commands which we impose upon them are just; there can be no doubt that every one of them will take office as a stern necessity, and not after the fashion of our present rulers of State.

Yes, my friend, I said; and there lies the point. You must contrive for your future rulers another and a better life than that of a ruler, and then you may have a well-ordered State; for only in the State which offers this, will they rule who are truly rich, not in silver and gold, but in virtue and wisdom, which are the true blessings of life. Whereas if they go to the administration of public affairs, poor and hungering after their own private advantage, thinking that hence they are to snatch the chief good, order there can never be; for they will be fighting about office, and the civil and domestic broils which thus arise will be the ruin of the rulers themselves and of the whole State.

Most true, he replied.

And the only life which looks down upon the life of political ambition is that of true philosophy. Do you know of any other?

Indeed, I do not, he said.

And those who govern ought not to be lovers of the task? For, if they are, there will be rival lovers, and they will fight.

No question.

Who then are those whom we shall compel to be guardians? Surely they will be the men who are wisest about affairs of State, and by whom the State is best administered, and who at the same time have other honors and another and a better life than that of politics?

They are the men, and I will choose them, he replied.

And now shall we consider in what way such guardians will be produced, and how they are to be brought from darkness to light,—as some are said to have ascended from the world below to the gods?

By all means, he replied.

The process, I said, is not the turning over of an oyster-shell, but the turning round of a soul passing from a day which is little better than night to the true day of being, that is, the ascent from below, which we affirm to be true philosophy?

Quite so.

And should we not inquire what sort of knowledge has the power of effecting such a change?

Certainly.

What sort of knowledge is there which would draw the soul from becoming to being? And another consideration has just occurred to me: You will remember that our young men are to be warrior athletes?

Yes, that was said.

Then this new kind of knowledge must have an additional quality?

What quality?

Usefulness in war.

Yes, if possible.

There were two parts in our former scheme of education, were there not?

Just so.

There was gymnastic, which presided over the growth and decay of the body, and may therefore be regarded as having to do with generation and corruption?

True.

Then that is not the knowledge which we are seeking to discover?

No.

But what do you say of music, what also entered to a certain extent into our former scheme?

Music, he said, as you will remember, was the counterpart of gymnastic, and trained the guardians by the influences of habit, by harmony making them harmonious, by rhythm rhythmical, but not giving them science; and the words, whether fabulous or possibly true, had kindred elements of rhythm and harmony in them. But in music there was nothing which tended to that good which you are now seeking.

You are most accurate, I said, in your recollection; in music there certainly was nothing of the kind. But what branch of knowledge is there, my dear Glaucon, which is of the desired nature; since all the useful arts were reckoned mean by us?

Undoubtedly; and yet if music and gymnastic are excluded, and the arts are also excluded, what remains?

Well, I said, there may be nothing left of our special subjects; and then we shall have to take something which is not special, but of universal application.

What may that be?

A something which all arts and sciences and intelligences use in common, and which every one first has to learn among the elements of education.

What is that?

The little matter of distinguishing one, two, and three—in a word, number and calculation:—do not all arts and sciences necessarily partake of them?

Yes.

Then the art of war partakes of them?

To be sure.

Then Palamedes, whenever he appears in tragedy, proves Agamemnon ridiculously unfit to be a general. Did you never remark how he declares that he had invented number, and had numbered the ships and set in array the ranks of the army at Troy; which implies that they had never been numbered before, and Agamemnon must be supposed literally to have been incapable of counting his own feet—how could he if he was ignorant of number? And if that is true, what sort of general must he have been?

I should say a very strange one, if this was as you say.

Can we deny that a warrior should have a knowledge of arithmetic?

Certainly he should, if he is to have the smallest understanding of military tactics, or indeed, I should rather say, if he is to be a man at all.

I should like to know whether you have the same notion which I have of this study?

What is your notion?

It appears to me to be a study of the kind which we are seeking, and which leads naturally to reflection, but never to have been rightly used; for the true use of it is simply to draw the soul towards being.

Will you explain your meaning? he said.

I will try, I said; and I wish you would share the inquiry with me, and say "yes" or "no" when I attempt to distinguish in my own mind what branches of knowledge have this attracting power, in order that we may have clearer proof that arithmetic is, as I suspect, one of them.

Explain, he said.

I mean to say that objects of sense are of two kinds; some of them do not invite thought because the sense is an adequate judge of them; while in the case of other objects sense is so untrustworthy that further inquiry is imperatively demanded.

You are clearly referring, he said, to the manner in which the senses are imposed upon by distance, and by painting in light and shade.

No, I said, that is not at all my meaning.

Then what is your meaning?

When speaking of uninviting objects, I mean those which do not pass from one sensation to the opposite; inviting objects are those which do; in this latter case the sense coming upon the object, whether at a distance or near, gives no more vivid idea of anything in particular than of its opposite. An illustration will make my meaning clearer:—here are three fingers—a little finger, a second finger, and a middle finger.

Very good.

You may suppose that they are seen quite close: And here comes the point.

What is it?

Each of them equally appears a finger, whether seen in the middle or at the extremity, whether white or black, or thick or thin—it makes no difference; a finger is a finger all the same. In these cases a man is not compelled to ask of thought the question what is a finger? for the sight never intimates to the mind that a finger is other than a finger.

True.

And therefore, I said, as we might expect, there is nothing here which invites or excites intelligence.

There is not, he said.

But is this equally true of the greatness and smallness of the fingers? Can sight adequately perceive them? and is no difference made by the circumstance that one of the fingers is in the middle and another at the extremity? And in like manner does the touch adequately perceive the qualities of thickness or thinness, of softness or hardness? And so of the other senses; do they give perfect intimations of such matters? Is not their mode of operation on this wise—the sense which is concerned with the quality of hardness is necessarily concerned also with the quality of softness, and only intimates to the soul that the same thing is felt to be both hard and soft?

You are quite right, he said.

And must not the soul be perplexed at this intimation which the sense gives of a hard which is also soft? What, again, is the meaning of light and heavy, if that which is light is also heavy, and that which is heavy, light?

Yes, he said, these intimations which the soul receives are very curious and require to be explained.

Yes, I said, and in these perplexities the soul naturally summons to her aid calculation and intelligence, that she may see whether the several objects announced to her are one or two.

True.

And if they turn out to be two, is not each of them one and different?

Certainly.

And if each is one, and both are two, she will conceive the two as in a state of division, for if they were undivided they could only be conceived of as one?

True.

The eye certainly did see both small and great, but only in a confused manner; they were not distinguished.

Yes.

Whereas the thinking mind, intending to light up the chaos, was compelled to reverse the process, and look at small and great as separate and not confused.

Very true.

Was not this the beginning of the inquiry "What is great?" and "What is small?"

Exactly so.

And thus arose the distinction of the visible and the intelligible.

Most true.

This was what I meant when I spoke of impressions which invited the intellect, or the reverse—those which are simultaneous with opposite impressions, invite thought; those which are simultaneous do not.

I understand, he said, and agree with you.

And to which class do unity and number belong?

I do not know, he replied.

Think a little and you will see that what has preceded will supply the answer; for if simple unity could be adequately perceived by the sight or by any other sense, then, as we were saying in the case of the finger, there would be nothing to attract towards being; but when there is some contradiction always present, and one is the reverse of one and involves the conception of plurality, then thought begins to be aroused within us, and the soul perplexed and wanting to arrive at a decision asks "What is absolute unity?" This is the way in which the study of the one has a power of drawing and converting the mind to the contemplation of true being.

And surely, he said, this occurs notably in the case of one; for we see the same thing to be both one and infinite in multitude?

Yes, I said; and this being true of one must be equally true of all number?

Certainly.

And all arithmetic and calculation have to do with number?

Yes.

And they appear to lead the mind towards truth?

Yes, in a very remarkable manner.

Then this is knowledge of the kind for which we are seeking, having a double use, military and philosophical; for the man of war must learn the art of number or he will not know how to array his troops, and the philosopher also, because he has to rise out of the sea of change and lay hold of true being, and therefore he must be an arithmetician.

That is true.

And our guardian is both warrior and philosopher?

Certainly.

Then this is a kind of knowledge which legislation may fitly prescribe; and we must endeavor to persuade those who are to be the principal men of our State to go and learn arithmetic, not as amateurs, but they must carry on the study until they see the nature of numbers with the mind only; nor again, like merchants or retail-traders, with a view to buying or selling, but for the sake of their military use, and of the soul herself; and because this will be the easiest way for her to pass from becoming to truth and being.

That is excellent, he said.

Yes, I said, and now having spoken of it, I must add how charming the science is! and in how many ways it conduces to our desired end, if pursued in the spirit of a philosopher, and not of a shopkeeper!

How do you mean?

I mean, as I was saying, that arithmetic has a very great and elevating effect, compelling the soul to reason about abstract number, and rebelling against the introduction of visible or tangible objects into the argument. You know how steadily the masters of the art repel and ridicule any one who attempts to divide absolute unity when he is calculating, and if you divide, they multiply, taking care that one shall continue one and not become lost in fractions.

That is very true.

Now, suppose a person were to say to them: O my friends, what are these wonderful numbers about which you are reasoning, in which, as you say, there is a unity such as you demand, and each unit is equal, invariable, indivisible,—what would they answer?

They would answer, as I should conceive, that they were speaking of those numbers which can only be realized in thought.

Then you see that this knowledge may be truly called necessary, necessitating as it clearly does the use of the pure intelligence in the attainment of pure truth?

Yes; that is a marked characteristic of it.

And have you further observed, that those who have a natural talent for calculation are generally quick at every other kind of knowledge; and even the dull, if they have had an arithmetical training, although they may derive no other advantage from it, always become much quicker than they would otherwise have been.

Very true, he said.

And indeed, you will not easily find a more difficult study, and not many as difficult.

You will not.

And, for all these reasons, arithmetic is a kind of knowledge in which the best natures should be trained, and which must not be given up.

I agree.

Let this then be made one of our subjects of education. And next, shall we inquire whether the kindred science also concerns us?

You mean geometry?

Exactly so.

Clearly, he said, we are concerned with that part of geometry which relates to war; for in pitching a camp, or taking up a position, or closing or extending the lines of an army, or any other military manœuvre, whether in actual battle or on a march, it will make all the difference whether a general is or is not a geometrician.

Yes, I said, but for that purpose a very little of either geometry or calculation will be enough; the question relates rather to the greater and more advanced part of geometry—whether that tends in any degree to make more easy the vision of the idea of good; and thither, as I was saying, all things tend which compel the soul to turn her gaze towards that place, where is the full perfection of being, which she ought, by all means, to behold.

True, he said.

Then if geometry compels us to view being, it concerns us; if becoming only, it does not concern us?

Yes, that is what we assert.

Yet anybody who has the least acquaintance with geometry will not deny that such a conception of the science is in flat contradiction to the ordinary language of geometricians.

How so?

They have in view practice only, and are always speaking, in a narrow and ridiculous manner, of squaring and extending and applying and the like—they confuse the necessities of geometry with those of daily life; whereas knowledge is the real object of the whole science.

Certainly, he said.

Then must not a further admission be made?

What admission?

That the knowledge at which geometry aims is knowledge of the eternal, and not of aught perishing and transient.

That, he replied, may be readily allowed, and is true.

Then, my noble friend, geometry will draw the soul towards truth, and create the spirit of philoso-phy, and raise up that which is now unhappily allowed to fall down.

Nothing will be more likely to have such an effect.

Then nothing should be more sternly laid down than that the inhabitants of your fair city should by all means learn geometry. Moreover the science has indirect effects, which are not small.

Of what kind? he said.

There are the military advantages of which you spoke, I said; and in all departments of knowledge, as experience proves, any one who has studied geometry is infinitely quicker of apprehension than one who has not.

Yes indeed, he said, there is an infinite difference between them.

Then shall we propose this as a second branch of knowledge which our youth will study?

Let us do so, he replied.

And suppose we make astronomy the third—what do you say?

I am strongly inclined to it, he said; the observation of the seasons and of months and years is as essential to the general as it is to the farmer or sailor.

I am amused, I said, at your fear of the world, which makes you guard against the appearance of insisting upon useless studies; and I quite admit the difficulty of believing that in every man there is an eye of the soul which, when by other pursuits lost and dimmed, is by these purified and re-illumined; and is more precious far than ten thousand bodily eyes, for by it alone is truth seen. Now there are two classes of persons: one class of those who will agree with you and will take your words as a revelation; another class to whom they will be utterly unmeaning, and who will naturally deem them to be idle tales, for they see no sort of profit which is to be obtained from them. And therefore you had better decide at once with which of the two you are proposing to argue. You will very likely say with neither, and that your chief aim in carrying on the argument is your own improvement; at the same time you do not grudge to others any benefit which they may receive.

I think that I should prefer to carry on the argument mainly on my own behalf.

Then take a step backward, for we have gone wrong in the order of the sciences.

What was the mistake? he said.

After plane geometry, I said, we proceeded at once to solids in revolution, instead of taking solids in themselves; whereas after the second dimension the third, which is concerned with cubes and dimensions of depth, ought to have followed.

That is true, Socrates; but so little seems to be known as yet about these subjects.

Why, yes, I said, and for two reasons:—in the first place, no government patronizes them; this leads to a want of energy in the pursuit of them, and they are difficult; in the second place, students can not learn them unless they have a director. But then a director can hardly be found, and even if he could, as matters now stand, the students, who are very conceited, would not attend to him. That, however, would be otherwise if the whole State became the director of these studies and gave honor to them; then disciples would want to come, and there would be continuous and earnest search, and discoveries would be made; since even now, disregarded as they are by the world, and maimed of their fair proportions, and although none of their votaries can tell the use of them, still these studies force their way by their natural charm, and very likely, if they had the help of the State, they would some day emerge into light.

Yes, he said, there is a remarkable charm in them. But I do not clearly understand the change in the order. First you began with a geometry of plane surfaces?

Yes, I said.

And you placed astronomy next, and then you made a step backward?

Yes, and I have delayed you by my hurry; the ludicrous state of solid geometry, which in natural order, should have followed, made me pass over this branch and go on to astronomy, or motion of solids.

True, he said.

Then assuming that the science now omitted would come into existence if encouraged by the State, let us go on to astronomy, which will be fourth.

The right order, he replied. And now, Socrates, as you rebuked the vulgar manner in which I praised astronomy before, my praise shall be given in your own spirit. For every one, as I think, must see that astronomy compels the soul to look upwards and leads us from this world to another.

Every one but myself, I said; to every one else this may be clear, but not to me.

And what then would you say?

I should rather say that those who elevate astronomy into philosophy appear to me to make us look downwards and not upwards.

What do you mean? he asked.

You, I replied, have in your mind a truly sublime conception of our knowledge of the things above. And I dare say that if a person were to throw his head back and study the fretted ceiling, you would still think that his mind was the percipient, and not his eyes. And you are very likely right, and I may be a simpleton: but, in my opinion, that knowledge only which is of being and of the unseen can make the soul look upwards, and whether a man gapes at the heavens or blinks on the ground, seeking to learn some particular of sense, I would deny that he can learn, for nothing of that sort is matter of science; his soul is looking downwards, not upwards, whether his way to knowledge is by water or by land, whether he floats, or only lies on his back.

I acknowledge, he said, the justice of your rebuke. Still, I should like to ascertain how astronomy can be learned in any manner more conducive to that knowledge of which we are speaking?

I will tell you, I said: The starry heaven which we behold is wrought upon a visible ground, and therefore, although the fairest and most perfect of visible things, must necessarily be deemed inferior far to the true motions of absolute swiftness and absolute slowness, which are relative to each other, and carry with them that which is contained in them, in the true number and in every true figure. Now, these are to be apprehended by reason and intelligence, but not by sight.

True, he replied.

The spangled heavens should be used as a pattern and with a view to that higher knowledge; their beauty is like the beauty of figures or pictures excellently wrought by the hand of Daedalus, or some other great artist, which we may chance to behold; any geometrician who saw them would appreciate the exquisiteness of their workmanship, but he would never dream of thinking that in them he could find the true equal or true double, or the truth of any other proportion.

No, he replied, such an idea would be ridiculous.

And will not a true astronomer have the same feeling when he looks at the movements of the stars? Will he not think that heaven and the things in heaven are framed by the Creator of them in the most perfect manner? But he will never imagine that the proportions of night and day, or of both to the month, or of the month to the year, or of the stars to these and to one another, and any other things that are material and visible can also be eternal and subject to no deviation—that would be absurd; and it is equally absurd to take so much pains in investigating their exact truth.

I quite agree, though I never thought of this before.

Then, I said, in astronomy, as in geometry, we should employ problems, and let the heavens alone if we would approach the subject in the right way and so make the natural gift of reason to be any of real use.

That, he said, is a work infinitely beyond our present astronomers.

Yes, I said; and there are many other things which must also have a similar extension given to them, if our legislation is to be of any value. But can you tell me of any other suitable study?

No, he said, not without thinking.

Motion, I said, has many forms, and not one only; two of them are obvious enough even to wits no better than ours; and there are others, as I imagine, which may be left to wiser persons.

But where are the two?

There is a second, I said, which is the counterpart of the one already named.

And what may that be?

The second, I said, would seem relatively to the ears to be what the first is to the eyes; for I conceive that as the eyes are designed to look up at the stars, so are the ears to hear harmonious motions; and these are sister sciences—as the Pythagoreans say, and we, Glaucon, agree with them?

Yes, he replied.

But this, I said, is a laborious study, and therefore we had better go and learn of them; and they will tell us whether there are any other applications of these sciences. At the same time, we must not lose sight of our own higher object.

What is that?

There is a perfection which all knowledge ought to reach, and which our pupils ought also to attain, and not to fall short of, as I was saying that they did in astronomy. For in the science of harmony, as you probably know, the same thing happens. The teachers of harmony compare the sounds and consonances which are heard only, and their labor, like that of the astronomers, is in vain.

Yes, by heaven! he said; and 'tis as good as a play to hear them talking about their condensed notes, as they call them; they put their ears close alongside of the strings like persons catching a sound from their neighbor's wall—one set of them declaring that they distinguish an intermediate note and have found the least interval which should be the unit of measurement; the others insisting that the two sounds have passed into the same—either party setting their ears before their understanding.

You mean, I said, those gentlemen who tease and torture the strings and rack them on the pegs of the instrument: I might carry on the metaphor and speak after their manner of the blows which the plectrum gives, and make accusations against the strings, both of backwardness and forwardness to sound; but this would be tedious, and therefore I will only say that these are not the men, and that I am referring to the Pythagoreans, of whom I was just now proposing to inquire about harmony. For they too are in error, like the astronomers; they investigate the numbers of the harmonies which are heard, but they never attain to problems—that is to say, they never reach the natural harmonies of number, or reflect why some numbers are harmonious and others not.

That, he said, is a thing of more than mortal knowledge.

A thing, I replied, which I would rather call useful; that is, if sought after with a view to the beautiful and good; but if pursued in any other spirit, useless.

Very true, he said.

Now, when all these studies reach the point of intercommunion and connection with one another, and come to be considered in their mutual affinities, then, I think, but not till then, will the pursuit of them have a value for our objects; otherwise there is no profit in them.

I suspect so; but you are speaking, Socrates, of a vast work.

What do you mean? I said; the prelude or what? Do you not know that all this is but the prelude to the actual strain which we have to learn? For you surely would not regard the skilled mathematician as a dialectician?

Assuredly not, he said; I have hardly ever known a mathematician who was capable of reasoning.

But do you imagine that men who are unable to give and take a reason will have the knowledge which we require of them?

Neither can this be supposed.

And so, Glaucon, I said, we have at last arrived at the hymn of dialectic. This is that strain which is of the intellect only, but which the faculty of sight will nevertheless be found to imitate; for sight, as you may remember, was imagined by us after a while to behold the real animals and stars, and last of all the sun himself. And so with dialectic; when a person starts on the discovery of the absolute by the light of reason only, and without any assistance of sense, and perseveres until by pure intelligence he arrives at the perception of the absolute good, he at last finds himself at the end of the intellectual world, as in the case of sight at the end of the visible.

Exactly, he said.

Then this is the progress which you call dialectic?

True.

But the release of the prisoners from chains, and their translation from the shadows to the images and to the light, and the ascent from the underground den to the sun, while in his presence they are vainly trying to look on animals and plants and the light of the sun, but are able to perceive even with their weak eyes the images in the water [which are divine], and are the shadows of true existence (not shadows of images cast by a light of fire, which compared with the sun is only an image)—this power of elevating the highest principle in the soul to the contemplation of that which is best in existence, with which we may compare the raising of that faculty which is the very light of the body to the sight of that which is brightest in the material and visible world—this power is given, as I was saying, by all that study and pursuit of the arts which has been described.

I agree in what you are saying, he replied, which may be hard to believe, yet, from another point of view, is harder still to deny. This however is not a theme to be treated of in passing only, but will have to be discussed again and again. And so, whether our conclusion be true or false, let us assume all this, and proceed at once from the prelude or preamble to the chief strain, and describe that in like manner. Say, then, what is the nature and what are the divisions of dialectic, and what are the paths which lead thither; for these paths will also lead to our final rest.

Dear Glaucon, I said, you will not be able to follow me here, though I would do my best, and you should behold not an image only but the absolute truth, according to my notion. Whether what I told you would or would not have been a reality I can not venture to say; but you would have seen something like reality; of that I am confident.

Doubtless, he replied.

But I must also remind you, that the power of dialectic alone can reveal this, and only to one who is a disciple of the previous sciences.

Of that assertion you may be as confident as of the last.

And assuredly no one will argue that there is any other method of comprehending by any regular process all true existence or of ascertaining what each thing is in its own nature; for the arts in general are concerned with the desires or opinions of men, or are cultivated with a view to production and construction, or for the preservation of such productions and constructions; and as to the mathematical sciences which, as we were saying, have some apprehension of true being—geometry and the like—they only dream about being, but never can they behold the waking reality so long as they leave the hypotheses which they use unexamined, and are unable to give an account of them. For when a man knows not his own first principle, and when the conclusion and intermediate steps are also constructed out of he knows not what, how can he imagine that such a fabric of convention can ever become science?

Impossible, he said.

Then dialectic, and dialectic alone, goes directly to the first principle and is the only science which does away with hypotheses in order to make her ground secure; the eye of the soul, which is literally buried in an outlandish slough, is by her gentle aid lifted upwards; and she uses as handmaids and helpers in the work of conversion, the sciences which we have been discussing. Custom terms them sciences, but they ought to have some other name, implying greater clearness than opinion and less clearness than science: and this, in our previous sketch, was called understanding. But why should we dispute about names when we have realities of such importance to consider?

Why indeed, he said, when any name will do which expresses the thought of the mind with clearness?

At any rate, we are satisfied, as before, to have four divisions; two for intellect and two for opinion, and to call the first division science, the second understanding, the third belief, and the fourth perception of shadows, opinion being concerned with becoming, and intellect with being; and so to make a proportion:

> As being is to becoming, so is pure intellect to opinion. And as intellect is to opinion, so is science to belief, and understanding to the perception of shadows.

But let us defer the further correlation and subdivision of the subjects of opinion and of intellect, for it will be a long inquiry, many times longer than this has been.

As far as I understand, he said, I agree.

And do you also agree, I said, in describing the dialectician as one who attains a conception of the essence of each thing? And he who does not possess and is therefore unable to impart this conception, in whatever degree he fails, may in that degree also be said to fail in intelligence? Will you admit so much?

Yes, he said; how can I deny it?

And you would say the same of the conception of the good? Until the person is able to abstract and define rationally the idea of good, and unless he can run the gauntlet of all objections, and is ready to disprove them, not by appeals to opinion, but to absolute truth, never faltering at any step of the argument—unless he can do all this, you would say that he knows neither the idea of good nor any other good; he apprehends only a shadow, if anything at all, which is given by opinion and not by science;—dreaming and slumbering in this life, before he is well awake here, he arrives at the world below, and has his final quietus.

In all that I should most certainly agree with you.

And surely you would not have the children of your ideal State, whom you are nurturing and educating—if the ideal ever becomes a reality—you would not allow the future rulers to be like posts, having no reason in them, and yet to be set in authority over the highest matters?

Certainly not.

Then you will make a law that they shall have such an education as will enable them to attain the greatest skill in asking and answering questions?

Yes, he said, you and I together will make it.

Dialectic, then, as you will agree, is the coping-stone of the sciences, and is set over them; no other science can be placed higher—the nature of knowledge can no further go?

I agree, he said.

But to whom we are to assign these studies, and in what way they are to be assigned, are questions which remain to be considered.

Yes, clearly.

You remember, I said, how the rulers were chosen before?

Certainly, he said.

The same natures must still be chosen, and the preference again given to the surest and the bravest, and, if possible, to the fairest; and, having noble and generous tempers, they should also have the natural gifts which will facilitate their education.

And what are these?

Such gifts as keenness and ready powers of acquisition; for the mind more often faints from the severity of study than from the severity of gymnastics: the toil is more entirely the mind's own, and is not shared with the body.

Very true, he replied.

Further, he of whom we are in search should have a good memory, and be an unwearied solid man who is a lover of labor in any line; or he will never be able to endure the great amount of bodily exercise and to go through all the intellectual discipline and study which we require of him.

Certainly, he said; he must have natural gifts.

The mistake at present is, that those who study philosophy have no vocation, and this, as I was before saying, is the reason why she has fallen into disrepute: her true sons should take her by the hand and not bastards.

What do you mean?

In the first place, her votary should not have a lame or halting industry—I mean, that he should not be half industrious and half idle: as, for example, when a man is a lover of gymnastic and hunting, and all other bodily exercises, but a hater rather than a lover of the labor of learning or listening or inquiring. Or the occupation to which he devotes himself may be of an opposite kind, and he may have the other sort of lameness.

Certainly, he said.

And as to truth, I said, is not a soul equally to be deemed halt and lame which hates voluntary falsehood and is extremely indignant at herself and others when they tell lies, but is patient of involuntary falsehood, and does not mind wallowing like a swinish beast in the mire of ignorance, and has no shame at being detected?

To be sure.

And, again, in respect of temperance, courage, magnificence, and every other virtue, should we not carefully distinguish between the true son and the bastard? for where there is no discernment of such qualities states and individuals unconsciously err; and the state makes a ruler, and the individual a friend, of one who, being defective in some part of virtue, is in a figure lame or a bastard.

That is very true, he said.

All these things, then, will have to be carefully considered by us; and if only those whom we introduce to this vast system of education and training are sound in body and mind, justice herself will have nothing to say against us, and we shall be the saviors of the constitution and of the State; but, if our pupils are men of another stamp, the reverse will happen, and we shall pour a still greater flood of ridicule on philosophy than she has to endure at present.

That would not be creditable.

Certainly not, I said; and yet perhaps, in thus turning jest into earnest I am equally ridiculous.

In what respect?

I had forgotten, I said, that we were not serious and spoke with too much excitement. For when I saw philosophy so undeservedly trampled under foot of men I could not help feeling a sort of indignation at the authors of her disgrace: and my anger made me too vehement.

Indeed! I was listening, and did not think so.

But I, who am the speaker, felt that I was. And now let me remind you that, although in our former selection we chose old men, we must not do so in this. Solon was under a delusion when he said that a man when he grows old may learn many things—for he can no more learn much than he can run much; youth is the time for any extraordinary toil.

Of course.

And, therefore, calculation and geometry and all the other elements of instruction, which are a preparation for dialectic, should be presented to the mind in childhood; not, however, under any notion of forcing our system of education.

Why not?

Because a freeman ought not to be a slave in the acquisition of knowledge of any kind. Bodily exercise, when compulsory, does no harm to the body; but knowledge which is acquired under compulsion obtains no hold on the mind.

Very true.

Then, my good friend, I said, do not use compulsion, but let early education be a sort of amusement; you will the be better able to find out the natural bent.

That is a very rational notion, he said.

Do you remember that the children, too, were to be taken to see the battle on horseback; and that if there were no danger they were to be brought close up and, like young hounds, have a taste of blood given them?

Yes, I remember.

The same practice may be followed, I said, in all these things—labors, lessons, dangers—and he who is most at home in all of them ought to be enrolled in a select number.

At what age?

At the age when the necessary gymnastics are over: the period whether of two or three years which passes in this sort of training is useless for any other purpose; for sleep and exercise are unpropitious to learning; and the trial of who is first in gymnastic exercises is one of the most important tests to which our youth are subjected.

Certainly, he replied.

After that time those who are selected from the class of twenty years old will be promoted to higher honor, and the sciences which they learned without any order in their early education will now be brought together, and they will be able to see the natural relationship of them to one another and to true being.

Yes, he said, that is the only kind of knowledge which takes lasting root.

Yes, I said; and the capacity for such knowledge is the great criterion of dialectical talent; the comprehensive mind is always the dialectical.

I agree with you, he said.

These, I said, are the points which you must consider; and those who have most of this comprehension, and who are most steadfast in their learning, and in their military and other appointed duties, when they have arrived at the age of thirty will have to be chosen by you out of the select class, and elevated to higher honor; and you will have to prove them by the help of dialectic, in order to learn which of them is able to give up the use of sight and the other senses, and in company with truth to attain absolute being: And here, my friend, great caution is required.

Why great caution?

Do you not remark, I said, how great is the evil which dialectic has introduced?

What evil? he said.

The students of the art are filled with lawlessness.

Quite true, he said.

Do you think that there is anything so very unnatural or inexcusable in their case? or will you make allowance for them?

In what way make allowance?

I want you, I said, by way of parallel, to imagine a supposititious son who is brought up in great wealth; he is one of a great and numerous family, and has many flatterers. When he grows up to manhood, he learns that his alleged are not his real parents; but who the real are he is unable to discover. Can you guess how he will be likely to behave towards his flatterers and his supposed parents, first of all during the period when he is ignorant of the false relation, and then again when he knows? Or shall I guess for you?

If you please.

Then I should say, that while he is ignorant of the truth he will be likely to honor his father and his mother and his supposed relations more than the flatterers; he will be less inclined to neglect them when in need, or to do or say anything against them; and he will be less willing to disobey them in any important matter.

He will.

But when he has made the discovery, I should imagine that he would diminish his honor and regard for them, and would become more devoted to the flatterers; their influence over him would greatly increase; he would now live after their ways, and openly associate with them, and, unless he were of an unusually good disposition, he would trouble himself no more about his supposed parents or other relations.

Well, all that is very probable. But how is the image applicable to the disciples of philosophy?

In this way: you know that there are certain principles about justice and honor, which were taught us in childhood, and under their parental authority we have been brought up, obeying and honoring them.

That is true.

There are also opposite maxims and habits of pleasure which flatter and attract the soul, but do not influence those of us who have any sense of right, and they continue to obey and honor the maxims of their fathers.

True.

Now, when a man is in this state, and the questioning spirit asks what is fair or honorable, and he answers as the legislator has taught him, and then arguments many and diverse refute his words, until he is driven into believing that nothing is honorable any more than dishonorable, or just and good any more than the reverse, and so of all the notions which he most valued, do you think that he will still honor and obey them as before?

Impossible.

And when he ceases to think them honorable and natural as heretofore, and he fails to discover the true, can he be expected to pursue any life other than that which flatters his desires?

He can not.

And from being a keeper of the law he is converted into a breaker of it?

Unquestionably.

Now all this is very natural in students of philosophy such as I have described, and also, as I was just now saying, most excusable.

Yes, he said; and, I may add, pitiable.

Therefore, that your feelings may not be moved to pity about our citizens who are now thirty years of age, every care must be taken in introducing them to dialectic.

Certainly.

There is a danger lest they should taste the dear delight too early; for youngsters, as you may have observed, when they first get the taste in their mouths, argue for amusement, and are always contradicting and refuting others in imitation of those who refute them; like puppy-dogs, they rejoice in pulling and tearing at all who come near them.

Yes, he said, there is nothing which they like better.

And when they have made many conquests and received defeats at the hands of many, they violently and speedily get into a way of not believing anything which they believed before, and hence, not only they, but philosophy and all that relates to it is apt to have a bad name with the rest of the world.

Too true, he said.

But when a man begins to get older, he will no longer be guilty of such insanity; he will imitate the dialectician who is seeking for truth, and not the eristic, who is contradicting for the sake of amusement; and the greater moderation of his character will increase instead of diminishing the honor of the pursuit.

Very true, he said.

And did we not make special provision for this, when we said that the disciples of philosophy were to be orderly and steadfast, not, as now, any chance aspirant or intruder?

Very true.

Suppose, I said, the study of philosophy to take the place of gymnastics and to be continued diligently and earnestly and exclusively for twice the number of years which were passed in bodily exercise—will that be enough?

Would you say six or four years? he asked.

Say five years, I replied; at the end of the time they must be sent down again into the den and compelled to hold any military or other office which young men are qualified to hold: in this way they will get their experience of life, and there will be an opportunity of trying whether, when they are drawn all manner of ways by temptation, they will stand firm or flinch.

And how long is this stage of their lives to last?

Fifteen years, I answered; and when they have reached fifty years of age, then let those who still survive and have distinguished themselves in every action of their lives and in every branch of knowledge come at last to their consummation: the time has now arrived at which they must raise the eye of the soul to the universal light which lightens all things, and behold the absolute good; for that is the pattern according to which they are to order the State and the lives of individuals, and the remainder of their own lives also; making philosophy their chief pursuit, but, when their turn comes, toiling also at politics and ruling for the public good, not as though they were performing some heroic action, but simply as a matter of duty; and when they have brought up in each generation others like themselves and left them in their place to be governors of the State, then they will depart to the Islands of the Blest and dwell there; and the city will give them public memorials and sacrifices and honor them, if the Pythian oracle consent, as demigods, but if not, as in any case blessed and divine.

You are a sculptor, Socrates, and have made statues of our governors faultless in beauty.

Yes, I said, Glaucon, and of our governesses too; for you must not suppose that what I have been saying applies to men only and not to women as far as their natures can go.

There you are right, he said, since we have made them to share in all things like the men.

Well, I said, and you would agree (would you not?) that what has been said about the State and the government is not a mere dream, and although difficult not impossible, but only possible in the way which has been supposed; that is to say, when the true philosopher kings are born in a State, one or more of them, despising the honors of this present world which they deem mean and worthless, esteeming above all things right and the honor that springs from right, and regarding justice as the greatest and most necessary of all things, whose ministers they are, and whose principles will be exalted by them when they set in order their own city?

How will they proceed?

They will begin by sending out into the country all the inhabitants of the city who are more than ten years old, and will take possession of their children, who will be unaffected by the habits of their parents; these they will train in their own habits and laws, I mean in the laws which we have given them: and in this way the State and constitution of which we were speaking will soonest and most easily attain happiness, and the nation which has such a constitution will gain most.

Yes, that will be the best way. And I think, Socrates, that you have very well described how, if ever, such a constitution might come into being.

Enough then of the perfect State, and of the man who bears its image—there is no difficulty in seeing how we shall describe him.

There is no difficulty, he replied; and I agree with you in thinking that nothing more need be said.

. . .

Book IX

Last of all comes the tyrannical man; about whom we have once more to ask, how is he formed out of the democratical? and how does he live, in happiness or in misery?

Yes, he said, he is the only one remaining.

There is, however, I said, a previous question which remains unanswered.

What question?

I do not think that we have adequately determined the nature and number of the appetites, and until this is accomplished the inquiry will always be confused.

Well, he said, it is not too late to supply the omission.

Very true, I said; and observe the point which I want to understand: Certain of the unnecessary pleasures and appetites I conceive to be unlawful; every one appears to have them, but in some persons they are controlled by the laws and by reason, and the better desires prevail over them—either they are wholly banished or they become few and weak; while in the case of others they are stronger, and there are more of them.

Which appetites do you mean?

I mean those which are awake when the reasoning and human and ruling power is asleep; then the wild beast within us, gorged with meat or drink, starts up and having shaken off sleep, goes forth to satisfy his desires; and there is no conceivable folly or crime—not excepting incest or any other unnatural union, or parricide, or the eating of forbidden food—which at such a time, when he has parted company with all shame and sense, a man may not be ready to commit.

Most true, he said.

But when a man's pulse is healthy and temperate, and when before going to sleep he has awakened his rational powers, and fed them on noble thoughts and inquiries, collecting himself in meditation; after having first indulged his appetites neither too much nor too little, but just enough to lay them to sleep, and prevent them and their judgments and pains from interfering with the higher principle—which he leaves in the solitude of pure abstraction, free to contemplate and aspire to the knowledge of the unknown, whether in past, present, or future: when again he has allayed the passionate element, if he has a quarrel against any one—I say, when, after pacifying the two irrational principles, he rouses up the third, which is reason, before he takes his rest, then, as you know, he attains truth most nearly, and is least likely to be the sport of fantastic and lawless visions.

I quite agree.

In saying this I have been running into a digression; but the point which I desire to note is that in all of us, even in good men, there is a lawless wild-beast nature, which peers out in sleep. Pray, consider whether I am right, and you agree with me.

Yes, I agree.

And now remember the character which we attributed to the democratic man. He was supposed from his youth upwards to have been trained under a miserly parent, who encouraged the saving appetites in him, but discountenanced the unnecessary, which aim only at amusement and ornament?

True.

And then he got into the company of a more refined, licentious sort of people, and taking to all their wanton ways rushed into the opposite extreme from an abhorrence of his father's meanness. At last, being a better man than his corruptors, he was drawn in both directions until he halted midway and led a life, not of vulgar and slavish passion, but of what he deemed moderate indulgence in various pleasures. After this manner the democrat was generated out of the oligarch?

Yes, he said; that was our view of him, and is so still.

And now, I said, years will have passed away, and you must conceive this man, such as he is, to have a son, who is brought up in his father's principles.

I can imagine him.

Then you must further imagine the same thing to happen to the son which has already happened to the father:—he is drawn into a perfectly lawless life, which by his seducers is termed perfect liberty; and his father and friends take part with his moderate desires, and the opposite party assist the opposite ones. As soon as these dire magicians and tyrant-makers find that they are losing their hold on him, they contrive to implant in him a master passion, to be lord over his idle and spendthrift lusts—a sort of monstrous winged drone—that is the only image which will adequately describe him.

Yes, he said, that is the only adequate image of him.

And when his other lusts, amid clouds of incense and perfumes and garlands and wines, and all the pleasures of a dissolute life, now let loose, come buzzing around him, nourishing to the utmost the sting of desire which they implant in his drone-like nature, then at last this lord of the soul, having Madness for the captain of his guard, breaks out into a frenzy; and if he finds in himself any good opinions or appetites in process of formation, and there is in him any sense of shame remaining, to these better principles he puts an end, and casts them forth until he has purged away temperance and brought in madness to the full.

Yes, he said, that is the way in which the tyrannical man is generated.

And is not this the reason why of old love has been called a tyrant?

I should not wonder.

Further, I said, has not a drunken man also the spirit of a tyrant?

He has.

And you know that a man who is deranged and not right in his mind, will fancy that he is able to rule, not only over men, but also over the gods?

That he will.

And the tyrannical man in the true sense of the word comes into being when, either under the influence of nature, or habit, or both, he becomes drunken, lustful, passionate? O my friend, is not that so?

Assuredly.

Such is the man and such is his origin. And next, how does he live?

Suppose, as people facetiously say, you were to tell me.

I imagine, I said, at the next step in his progress, that there will be feasts and carousals and revellings and courtezans, and all that sort of thing; Love is the lord of the house within him, and orders all the concerns of his soul.

That is certain.

Yes; and every day and every night desires grow up many and formidable, and their demands are many.

They are indeed, he said.

His revenues, if he has any, are soon spent.

True.

Then comes debt and the cutting down of his property.

Of course.

When he has nothing left, must not his desires, crowding in the nest like young ravens, be crying aloud for food; and he, goaded on by them, and especially by love himself, who is in a manner the captain of them, is in a frenzy, and would fain discover whom he can defraud or despoil of his property, in order that he may gratify them?

Yes, that is sure to be the case.

He must have money, no matter how, if he is to escape horrid pains and pangs.

He must.

And as in himself there was a succession of pleasures, and the new got the better of the old and took away their rights, so he being younger will claim to have more than his father and his mother, and if he has spent his own share of the property, he will take a slice of theirs.

No doubt he will.

And if his parents will not give way, then he will try first of all to cheat and deceive them.

Very true.

And if he fails, then he will use force and plunder them.

Yes, probably.

And if the old man and woman fight for their own, what then, my friend? Will the creature feel any compunction at tyrannizing over them?

Nay, he said, I should not feel at all comfortable about his parents.

But, O heavens! Adeimantus, on account of some new-fangled love of a harlot, who is anything but a necessary connection, can you believe that he would strike the mother who is his ancient friend and necessary to his very existence, and would place her under the authority of the other, when she is brought under the same roof with her; or that, under like circumstances, he would do the same to his withered old father, first and most indispensable of friends, for the sake of some newly-found blooming youth who is the reverse of indispensable?

Yes, indeed, he said; I believe that he would.

Truly, then, I said, a tyrannical son is a blessing to his father and mother.

He is indeed, he replied.

He first takes their property, and when that fails, and pleasures are beginning to swarm in the hive of his soul, then he breaks into a house, or steals the garments of some nightly wayfarer; next he proceeds to clear a temple. Meanwhile the old opinions which he had when a child, and which gave judgment about good and evil, are overthrown by those others which have just been emancipated, and are now the bodyguard of love and share his empire. These in his democratic days, when he was still subject to the laws and to his father, were only let loose in the dreams of sleep. But now that he is under the dominion of Love, he becomes always and in waking reality what he was then very rarely and in a dream only; he will commit the foulest murder, or eat forbidden food, or be guilty of any other horrid act. Love is his tyrant, and lives lordly in him and lawlessly, and being himself a king, leads him on, as a tyrant leads a State, to the performance of any reckless deed by which he can maintain himself and the rabble of his associates, whether those whom evil communications have brought in from without, or those whom he himself has allowed to break loose within him by reason of a similar evil nature in himself. Have we not here a picture of his way of life?

Yes, indeed, he said.

And if there are only a few of them in the State, and the rest of the people are well disposed, they go away and become the body-guard or mercenary soldiers of some other tyrant who may probably want them for a war; and if there is no war, they stay at home and do many little pieces of mischief in the city.

What sort of mischief?

For example, they are the thieves, burglars, cutpurses, foot-pads, robbers of temples, man-stealers of the community; or if they are able to speak they turn informers, and bear false witness, and take bribes.

A small catalogue of evils, even if the perpetrators of them are few in number.

Yes, I said; but small and great are comparative terms, and all these things, in the misery and evil which they inflict upon a State, do not come within a thousand miles of the tyrant; when this noxious class and their followers grow numerous and become conscious of their strength, assisted by the infatuation of the people, they choose from among themselves the one who has most of the tyrant in his own soul, and him they create their tyrant.

Yes, he said, and he will be the most fit to be a tyrant.

If the people yield, well and good; but if they resist him, as he began by beating his own father and mother, so now, if he has the power, he beats them, and will keep his dear old fatherland or motherland, as the Cretans say, in subjection to his young retainers whom he has introduced to be their rulers and masters. This is the end of his passions and desires.

Exactly.

When such men are only private individuals and before they get power, this is their character; they associate entirely with their own flatterers or ready tools; or if they want anything from anybody, they in their turn are equally ready to bow down before them: they profess every sort of affection for them; but when they have gained their point they know them no more.

Yes, truly.

They are always either the masters or servants and never the friends of anybody; the tyrant never tastes of true freedom or friendship.

Certainly not.

And may we not rightly call such men treacherous?

No question.

Also they are utterly unjust, if we were right in our notion of justice?

Yes, he said, and we were perfectly right.

Let us then sum up in a word, I said, the character of the worst man: he is the waking reality of what we dreamed.

Most true.

And this is he who being by nature most of a tyrant bears rule, and the longer he lives the more of a tyrant he becomes.

That is certain, said Glaucon, taking his turn to answer.

And will not he who has been shown to be the wickedest, be also the most miserable? and he who has tyrannized longest and most, most continually and truly miserable; although this may not be the opinion of men in general?

Yes, he said, inevitably.

And must not the tyrannical man be like the tyrannical State, and the democratical man like the democratical State and the same of the others?

Certainly.

And as State is to State in virtue and happiness, so is man in relation to man?

To be sure.

Then comparing our original city, which was under a king, and the city which is under a tyrant, how do they stand as to virtue?

They are the opposite extremes, he said, for one is the very best and the other is the very worst.

There can be no mistake, I said, as to which is which, and therefore I will at once inquire whether you would arrive at a similar decision about their relative happiness and misery. And here we must not allow ourselves to be panic-stricken at the apparition of the tyrant, who is only a unit and may perhaps have a few retainers about him; but let us go as we ought into every corner of the city and look all about, and then we will give our opinion.

A fair invitation, he replied; and I see, as every one must, that a tyranny is the wretchedest form of government, and the rule of a king the happiest.

And in estimating the men too, may I not fairly make a like request, that I should have a judge whose mind can enter into and see through human nature? he must not be like a child who looks at the outside and is dazzled at the pompous aspect which the tyrannical nature assumes to the beholder, but let him be one who has a clear insight. May I suppose that the judgment is given in the hearing of us all by one who is able to judge, and has dwelt in the same place with him, and been present at his daily life and known him in his family relations, where he may be seen stripped of his tragedy attire, and again in the hour of public danger—he shall tell us about the happiness and misery of the tyrant when compared with other men?

That again, he said, is a very fair proposal.

Shall I assume that we ourselves are able and experienced judges and have before now met with such a person? We shall then have some one who will answer our inquiries.

By all means.

Let me ask you not to forget the parallel of the individual and the State; bearing this in mind, and glancing in turn from one to the other of them, will you tell me their respective conditions?

What do you mean? he asked.

Beginning with the State, I replied, would you say that a city which is governed by a tyrant is free or enslaved?

No city, he said, can be more completely enslaved.

And yet, as you see, there are freemen as well as masters in such a State?

Yes, he said, I see that there are—a few; but the people, speaking generally, and the best of them are miserably degraded and enslaved.

Then if the man is like the State, I said, must not the same rule prevail? his soul is full of meanness and vulgarity—the best elements in him are enslaved; and there is a small ruling part, which is also the worst and maddest.

Inevitably.

And would you say that the soul of such an one is the soul of a freeman, or of a slave?

He has the soul of a slave, in my opinion.

And the State which is enslaved under a tyrant is utterly incapable of acting voluntarily?

Utterly incapable.

And also the soul which is under a tyrant (I am speaking of the soul taken as a whole) is least capable of doing what she desires; there is a gadfly which goads her, and she is full of trouble and remorse?

Certainly.

And is the city which is under a tyrant rich or poor?

Poor.

And the tyrannical soul must be always poor and insatiable?

True.

And must not such a State and such a man be always full of fear?

Yes, indeed.

Is there any State in which you will find more of lamentation and sorrow and groaning and pain?

Certainly not.

And is there any man in whom you will find more of this sort of misery than in the tyrannical man, who is in a fury of passions and desires?

Impossible.

Reflecting upon these and similar evils, you held the tyrannical State to be the most miserable of States?

And I was right, he said.

Certainly, I said. And when you see the same evils in the tyrannical man, what do you say of him?

I say that he is by far the most miserable of all men.

There, I said, I think that you are beginning to go wrong.

What do you mean?

I do not think that he has as yet reached the utmost extreme of misery

Then who is more miserable?

One of whom I am about to speak.

Who is that?

He who is of a tyrannical nature, and instead of leading a private life has been cursed with the further misfortune of being a public tyrant.

From what has been said, I gather that you are right.

Yes, I replied, but in this high argument you should be a little more certain, and should not conjecture only; for of all questions, this respecting good and evil is the greatest.

Very true, he said.

Let me then offer you an illustration, which may, I think, throw a light upon this subject.

What is your illustration?

The case of rich individuals in cities who possess many slaves: from them you may form an idea of the tyrant's condition, for they both have slaves; the only difference is that he has more slaves.

Yes, that is the difference.

You know that they live securely and have nothing to apprehend from their servants?

What should they fear?

Nothing. But do you observe the reason of this?

Yes; the reason is, that the whole city is leagued together for the protection of each individual.

Very true, I said. But imagine one of these owners, the master say of some fifty slaves, together with his family and property and slaves, carried off by a god into the wilderness, where there are no freemen to help him—will he not be in an agony of fear lest he and his wife and children should be put to death by his slaves?

Yes, he said, he will be in the utmost fear.

The time has arrived when he will be compelled to flatter divers of his slaves, and make many promises to them of freedom and other things, much against his will—he will have to cajole his own servants.

Yes, he said, that will be the only way of saving himself.

And suppose the same god, who carried him away, to surround him with neighbors who will not suffer one man to be the master of another, and who, if they could catch the offender, would take his life?

His case will be still worse, if you suppose him to be everywhere surrounded and watched by enemies.

And is not this the sort of prison in which the tyrant will be bound—he who being by nature such as we have described, is full of all sorts of fears and lusts? His soul is dainty and greedy, and yet alone, of all men in the city, he is never allowed to go on a journey, or to see the things which other freemen desire to see, but he lives in his hole like a woman hidden in the house, and is jealous of any other citizen who goes into foreign parts and sees anything of interest.

Very true, he said.

And amid evils such as these will not he who is ill-governed in his own person—the tyrannical man, I mean—whom you just now decided to be the most miserable of all—will not he be yet more miserable when, instead of leading a private life, he is constrained by fortune to be a public tyrant? He has to be master of others when he is not master of himself: he is like a diseased or paralytic man who is compelled to pass his life, not in retirement, but fighting and combating with other men.

Yes, he said, the similitude is most exact.

Is not his case utterly miserable? and does not the actual tyrant lead a worse life than he whose life you determined to be the worst?

Certainly.

He who is the real tyrant, whatever men may think, is the real slave, and is obliged to practice the greatest adulation and servility, and to be the flatterer of the vilest of mankind. He has desires which he is utterly unable to satisfy, and has more wants than any one, and is truly poor, if you know how to inspect the whole soul of him: all his life long he is beset with fear and is full of convulsions and distractions, even as the State which he resembles: and surely the resemblance holds?

Very true, he said.

Moreover, as we were saying before, he grows worse from having power: he becomes and is of necessity more jealous, more faithless, more unjust, more friendless, more impious, than he was at first; he is the purveyor and cherisher of every sort of vice, and the consequence is that he is supremely miserable, and that he makes everybody else as miserable as himself.

No man of any sense will dispute your words.

Come then, I said, and as the general umpire in theatrical contests proclaims the result, do you also decide who in your opinion is first in the scale of happiness, and who second, and in what order the others follow: there are five of them in all—they are the royal, timocratical, oligarchical, democratical, tyrannical.

The decision will be easily given, he replied; they shall be choruses coming on the stage, and I must judge them in the order in which they enter, by the criterion of virtue and vice, happiness and misery.

Need we hire a herald, or shall I announce, that the son of Ariston [the best] has decided that the best and justest is also the happiest, and that this is he who is the most royal man and king over himself; and that the worst and most unjust man is also the most miserable, and that this is he who being the greatest tyrant of himself is also the greatest tyrant of his State?

Make the proclamation yourself, he said.

And shall I add, "whether seen or unseen by gods and men"?

Let the words be added.

Then this, I said, will be our first proof; and there is another, which may also have some weight.

What is that?

The second proof is derived from the nature of the soul: seeing that the individual soul, like the State, has been divided by us into three principles, the division may, I think, furnish a new demonstration.

Of what nature?

It seems to me that to these three principles three pleasures correspond; also three desires and governing powers.

How do you mean? he said.

There is one principle with which, as we were saying, a man learns, another with which he is angry; the third, having many forms, has no special name, but is denoted by the general term appetitive, from the extraordinary strength and vehemence of the desires of eating and drinking and the other sensual appetites which are the main elements of it; also money-loving, because such desires are generally satisfied by the help of money.

That is true, he said.

If we were to say that the loves and pleasures of this third part were concerned with gain, we should then be able to fall back on a single notion; and might truly and intelligibly describe this part of the soul as loving gain or money.

I agree with you.

Again, is not the passionate element wholly set on ruling and conquering and getting fame?

True.

Suppose we call it the contentious or ambitious— would the term be suitable?

Extremely suitable.

On the other hand, every one sees that the principle of knowledge is wholly directed to the truth, and cares less than either of the others for gain or fame.

Far less.

"Lover of wisdom," "lover of knowledge," are titles which we may fitly apply to that part of the soul?

Certainly.

One principle prevails in the souls of one class of men, another in others, as may happen?

Yes.

Then we may begin by assuming that there are three classes of men—lovers of wisdom, lovers of honor, lovers of gain?

Exactly.

And there are three kinds of pleasure, which are their several objects?

Very true.

Now, if you examine the three classes of men, and ask of them in turn which of their lives is pleasantest, each will be found praising his own and depreciating that of others: the money-maker will contrast the vanity of honor or of learning if they bring no money with the solid advantages of gold and silver?

True, he said.

And the lover of honor—what will be his opinion? Will he not think that the pleasure of riches is vulgar, while the pleasure of learning, if it brings no distinction, is all smoke and nonsense to him?

Very true

And are we to suppose, I said, that the philosopher sets any value on other pleasures in comparison with the pleasure of knowing the truth, and in that pursuit abiding, ever learning, not so far indeed from the heaven of pleasure? Does he not call the other pleasures necessary, under the idea that if there were no necessity for them, he would rather not have them?

There can be no doubt of that, he replied.

Since, then, the pleasures of each class and the life of each are in dispute, and the question is not which life is more or less honorable, or better or worse, but which is the more pleasant or painless—how shall we know who speaks truly?

I can not myself tell, he said.

Well, but what ought to be the criterion? Is any better than experience and wisdom and reason?

There can not be a better, he said.

Then, I said, reflect. Of the three individuals, which has the greatest experience of all the pleasures which we enumerated? Has the lover of gain, in learning the nature of essential truth, greater experience of the pleasure of knowledge than the philosopher has of the pleasure of gain?

The philosopher, he replied, has greatly the advantage; for he has of necessity always known the taste of the other pleasures from his childhood upwards: but the lover of gain in all his experience has not of necessity tasted—or, I should rather say, even had he desired, could hardly have tasted—the sweetness of learning and knowing truth.

Then the lover of wisdom has a great advantage over the lover of gain, for he has a double experience?

Yes, very great.

Again, has he greater experience of the pleasures of honor, or the lover of honor of the pleasures of wisdom?

Nay, he said, all three are honored in proportion as they attain their object; for the rich man and the brave man and the wise man alike have their crowd of admirers, and as they all receive honor they all have experience of the pleasures of honor; but the delight which is to be found in the knowledge of true being is known to the philosopher only.

His experience, then, will enable him to judge better than any one?

Far better.

And he is the only one who has wisdom as well as experience?

Certainly.

Further, the very faculty which is the instrument of judgment is not possessed by the covetous or ambitious man, but only by the philosopher?

What faculty?

Reason, with whom, as we were saying, the decision ought to rest.

Yes.

And reasoning is peculiarly his instrument?

Certainly.

If wealth and gain were the criterion, then the praise or blame of the lover of gain would surely be the most trustworthy?

Assuredly.

Or if honor or victory or courage, in that case the judgment of the ambitious or pugnacious would be the truest?

Clearly.

But since experience and wisdom and reason are the judges—

The only inference possible, he replied, is that pleasures which are approved by the lover of wisdom and reason are the truest.

And so we arrive at the result, that the pleasure of the intelligent part of the soul is the pleasantest of the three, and that he of us in whom this is the ruling principle has the pleasantest life.

Unquestionably, he said, the wise man speaks with authority when he approves of his own life.

And what does the judge affirm to be the life which is next, and the pleasure which is next?

Clearly that of the soldier and lover of honor; who is nearer to himself than the money-maker.

Last comes the lover of gain?

Very true, he said.

Twice in succession, then, has the just man overthrown the unjust in this conflict; and now comes the third trial, which is dedicated to Olympian Zeus the savior: a sage whispers in my ear that no pleasure except that of the wise is quite true and pure—all others are a shadow only; and surely this will prove the greatest and most decisive of falls?

Yes, the greatest; but will you explain yourself?

I will work out the subject and you shall answer my questions.

Proceed.

Say, then, is not pleasure opposed to pain?

True.

And there is a neutral state which is neither pleasure nor pain?

There is.

A state which is intermediate, and a sort of repose of the soul about either—that is what you mean?

Yes.

You remember what people say when they are sick?

What do they say?

That after all nothing is pleasanter than health. But then they never knew this to be the greatest of pleasures until they were ill.

Yes, I know, he said.

And when persons are suffering from acute pain, you must have heard them say that there is nothing pleasanter than to get rid of their pain?

I have.

And there are many other cases of suffering in which the mere rest and cessation of pain, and not any positive enjoyment, is extolled by them as the greatest pleasure?

Yes, he said; at the time they are pleased and well content to be at rest.

Again, when pleasure ceases, that sort of rest or cessation will be painful?

Doubtless, he said.

Then the intermediate state of rest will be pleasure and will also be pain?

So it would seem.

But can that which is neither become both?

I should say not.

And both pleasure and pain are motions of the soul, are they not?

Yes.

But that which is neither was just now shown to be rest and not motion, and in a mean between them?

Yes.

How, then, can we be right in supposing that the absence of pain is pleasure, or that the absence of pleasure is pain?

Impossible.

This then is an appearance only and not a reality; that is to say, the rest is pleasure at the moment and in comparison of what is painful, and painful in comparison of what is pleasant; but all these representations, when tried by the test of true pleasure, are not real but a sort of imposition?

That is the inference.

Look at the other class of pleasures which have no antecedent pains and you will no longer suppose, as you perhaps may at present, that pleasure is only the cessation of pain, or pain of pleasure.

What are they, he said, and where shall I find them?

There are many of them: take as an example the pleasures of smell, which are very great and have no antecedent pains; they come in a moment, and when they depart leave no pain behind them.

Most true, he said.

Let us not, then, be induced to believe that pure pleasure is the cessation of pain, or pain of pleasure.

No.

Still, the more numerous and violent pleasures which reach the soul through the body are generally of this sort—they are reliefs of pain.

That is true.

And the anticipations of future pleasures and pains are of a like nature?

Yes.

Shall I give you an illustration of them?

Let me hear.

You would allow, I said, that there is in nature an upper and lower and middle region?

I should.

And if a person were to go from the lower to the middle region, would he not imagine that he is going up; and he who is standing in the middle and sees whence he has come, would imagine that he is already in the upper region, if he has never seen the true upper world?

To be sure, he said; how can he think otherwise?

But if he were taken back again he would imagine, and truly imagine, that he was descending?

No doubt.

All that would arise out of his ignorance of the true upper and middle and lower regions?

Yes.

Then can you wonder that persons who are inexperienced in the truth, as they have wrong ideas about many other things, should also have wrong ideas about pleasure and pain and the intermediate state; so that when they are only being drawn towards the painful they feel pain and think the pain which they experience to be real, and in like manner, when drawn away from pain to the neutral or intermediate state, they firmly believe that they have reached the goal of satiety and pleasure; they, not knowing pleasure, err in contrasting pain with the absence of pain, which is like contrasting black with gray instead of white—can you wonder, I say, at this?

No, indeed; I should be much more disposed to wonder at the opposite.

Look at the matter thus:—Hunger, thirst, and the like, are inanitions of the bodily state?

Yes.

And ignorance and folly are inanitions of the soul?

True.

And food and wisdom are the corresponding satisfactions of either?

Certainly.

And is the satisfaction derived from that which has less or from that which has more existence the truer?

Clearly, from that which has more.

What classes of things have a greater share of pure existence in your judgment—those of which food and drink and condiments and all kinds of sustenance are examples, or the class which contains true opinion and knowledge and mind and all the different kinds of virtue? Put the question in this way:—Which has a more pure being—that which is concerned with the invariable, the immortal, and the true, and is of such a nature, and is found in such natures; or that which is concerned with and found in the variable and mortal, and is itself variable and mortal?

Far purer, he replied, is the being of that which is concerned with the invariable.

And does the essence of the invariable partake of knowledge in the same degree as of essence?

Yes, of knowledge in the same degree.

And of truth in the same degree?

Yes.

And, conversely, that which has less of truth will also have less of essence?

Necessarily.

Then, in general, those kinds of things which are in the service of the body have less of truth and essence than those which are in the service of the soul?

Far less.

And has not the body itself less of truth and essence than the soul?

Yes.

What is filled with more real existence, and actually has a more real existence, is more really filled than that which is filled with less real existence and is less real?

Of course.

And if there be a pleasure in being filled with that which is according to nature, that which is more really filled with more real being will more really and truly enjoy true pleasure; whereas that which participates in less real being will be less truly and surely satisfied, and will participate in an illusory and less real pleasure?

Unquestionably.

Those then who know not wisdom and virtue, and are always busy with gluttony and sensuality, go down and again as far as the mean; and in this region they move at random throughout life, but they never pass into the true upper world; thither they neither look, nor do they ever find their way, neither are they truly filled with true being, nor do they taste of pure and abiding pleasure. Like cattle, with their eyes always looking down and their heads stooping to the earth, that is, to the dining table, they fatten and feed and breed, and, in their excessive love of these delights, they kick and butt at one another with horns and hoofs which are made of iron; and they kill one another by reason of their insatiable lust. For they fill themselves with that which is not substantial, and the part of themselves which they fill is also unsubstantial and incontinent.

Verily, Socrates, said Glaucon, you describe the life of the many like an oracle.

Their pleasures are mixed with pains—how can they be otherwise? For they are mere shadows and pictures of the true, and are colored by contrast, which exaggerates both light and shade, and so they implant in the minds of fools insane desires of themselves; and they are fought about as Stesichorus says that the Greeks fought about the shadow of Helen at Troy in ignorance of the truth.

Something of that sort must inevitably happen.

And must not the like happen with the spirited or passionate element of the soul? Will not the passionate man who carries his passion into action, be in the like case, whether he is envious and ambitious, or violent and contentious, or angry and discontented, if he be seeking to attain honor and victory and the satisfaction of his anger without reason or sense?

Yes, he said, the same will happen with the spirited element also.

Then may we not confidently assert that the lovers of money and honor, when they seek their pleasures under the guidance and in the company of reason and knowledge, and pursue after and win the pleasures which wisdom shows them, will also have the truest pleasures in the highest degree which is attainable to them, inasmuch as they follow truth; and they will have the pleasures which are natural to them, if that which is best for each one is also most natural to him?

Yes, certainly; the best is the most natural.

And when the whole soul follows the philosophical principle, and there is no division, the several parts are just, and do each of them their own business, and enjoy severally the best and truest pleasures of which they are capable?

Exactly.

But when either of the two other principles prevails, it fails in attaining its own pleasure, and compels the rest to pursue after a pleasure which is a shadow only and which is not their own?

True.

And the greater the interval which separates them from philosophy and reason, the more strange and illusive will be the pleasure?

Yes.

And is not that farthest from reason which is at the greatest distance from law and order?

Clearly.

And the lustful and tyrannical desires are, as we saw, at the greatest distance?

Yes.

And the royal and orderly desires are nearest?

Yes.

Then the tyrant will live at the greatest distance from true or natural pleasure, and the king at the least?

Certainly.

But if so, the tyrant will live most unpleasantly, and the king most pleasantly?

Inevitably.

Would you know the measure of the interval which separates them?

Will you tell me?

There appear to be three pleasures, one genuine and two spurious: now the transgression of the tyrant reaches a point beyond the spurious; he has run away from the region of law and reason, and taken up his abode with certain slave pleasures which are his satellites, and the measure of his inferiority can only be expressed in a figure.

How do you mean?

I assume, I said, that the tyrant is in the third place from the oligarch; the democrat was in the middle?

Yes.

And if there is truth in what has preceded, he will be wedded to an image of pleasure which is thrice removed as to truth from the pleasure of the oligarch?

He will.

And the oligarch is third from the royal; since we count as one royal and aristocratical?

Yes, he is third.

Then the tyrant is removed from true pleasure by the space of a number which is three times three?

Manifestly.

The shadow then of tyrannical pleasure determined by the number of length will be a plane figure.

Certainly.

And if you raise the power and make the plane a solid, there is no difficulty in seeing how vast is the interval by which the tyrant is parted from the king.

Yes; the arithmetician will easily do the sum.

Or if some person begins at the other end and measures the interval by which the king is parted from the tyrant in truth of pleasure, he will find him, when the multiplication is completed, living 729 times more pleasantly, and the tyrant more painfully by this same interval.

What a wonderful calculation! And how enormous is the distance which separates the just from the unjust in regard to pleasure and pain!

Yet a true calculation, I said, and a number which nearly concerns human life, if human beings are concerned with days and nights and months and years.

Yes, he said, human life is certainly concerned with them.

Then if the good and just man be thus superior in pleasure to the evil and unjust, his superiority will be infinitely greater in propriety of life and in beauty and virtue?

Immeasurably greater.

Well, I said, and now having arrived at this stage of the argument, we may revert to the words which brought us hither: Was not some one saying that injustice was a gain to the perfectly unjust who was reputed to be just?

Yes, that was said.

Now then, having determined the power and quality of justice and injustice, let us have a little conversation with him.

What shall we say to him?

Let us make an image of the soul, that he may have his own words presented before his eyes.

Of what sort?

An ideal image of the soul, like the composite creations of ancient mythology, such as the Chimera or Scylla or Cerberus, and there are many others in which two or more different natures are said to grow into one.

There are said to have been such unions.

Then do you now model the form of a multitudinous, many-headed monster, having a ring of heads of all manner of beasts, tame and wild, which he is able to generate and metamorphose at will.

You suppose marvelous powers in the artist; but, as language is more pliable than wax or any similar substance, let there be such a model as you propose.

Suppose now that you make a second form as of a lion, and a third of a man, the second smaller than the first, and the third smaller than the second.

That, he said, is an easier task; and I have made them as you say.

And now join them, and let the three go into one.

That has been accomplished.

Next fashion the outside of them into a single image, as of a man, so that he who is not able to look within, and sees only the outer hull, may believe the beast to be a single human creature.

I have done so, he said.

And now, to him who maintains that it is profitable for the human creature to be unjust, and unprofitable to be just, let us reply that, if he be right, it is profitable for this creature to feast the multitudinous monster and strengthen the lion and the lion-like qualities, but to starve and weaken the man, who is consequently liable to be dragged about at the mercy of either of the other two; and he is not to attempt to familiarize or harmonize them with one another—he ought rather to suffer them to fight and bite and devour one another.

Certainly, he said; that is what the approver of injustice says.

To him the supporter of justice makes answer that he should ever so speak and act as to give the man within him in some way or other the most complete mastery over the entire human creature. He should watch over the many-headed monster like a good husbandman, fostering and cultivating the gentle qualities, and preventing the wild ones from growing; he should be making the lion-heart his ally, and in common care of them all should be uniting the several parts with one another and with himself.

Yes, he said, that is quite what the maintainer of justice will say.

And so from every point of view, whether of pleasure, honor, or advantage, the approver of justice is right and speaks the truth, and the disapprover is wrong and false and ignorant?

Yes, from every point of view.

Come, now, and let us gently reason with the unjust, who is not intentionally in error. "Sweet Sir," we will say to him, "what think you of things esteemed noble and ignoble? Is not the noble that which subjects the beast to the man, or rather to the god in man; and the ignoble that which subjects the man to the beast?" He can hardly avoid saying Yes—can he now?

Not if he has any regard for my opinion.

But, if he agrees so far, we may ask him to answer another question: "Then how would a man profit if he received gold and silver on the condition that he was to enslave the noblest part of him to the worst? Who can imagine that a man who sold his son or daughter into slavery for money, especially if he sold them into the hands of fierce and evil men, would be the gainer, however large might be the sum which he received? And will any one say that he is not a miserable caitiff who remorselessly sells his own divine being to that which is most godless and detestable? Eriphyle took the necklace as the price of her husband's life, but he is taking a bribe in order to compass a worse ruin.

Yes, said Glaucon, far worse—I will answer for him.

Has not the intemperate been censured of old, because in him the huge multiform monster is allowed to be too much at large?

Clearly.

And men are blamed for pride and bad temper when the lion and serpent element in them disproportionately grows and gains strength?

Yes.

And luxury and softness are blamed, because they relax and weaken this same creature, and make a coward of him?

Very true.

And is not a man reproached for flattery and meanness who subordinates the spirited animal to the unruly monster, and, for the sake of money, of which he can never have enough, habituates him in the days of his youth to be trampled in the mire, and from being a lion to become a monkey?

True, he said.

And why are mean employments and manual arts a reproach? Only because they imply a natural weakness of the higher principle; the individual is unable to control the creatures within him, but has to court them, and his great study is how to flatter them.

Such appears to be the reason.

And therefore, being desirous of placing him under a rule like that of the best, we say that he ought to be the servant of the best, in whom the Divine rules; not as Thrasymachus supposed, to the injury of the servant, but because every one had better be ruled by divine wisdom dwelling within him; or, if this be impossible, then by an external authority, in order that we may be all, as far as possible, under the same government, friends and equals.

True, he said.

And this is clearly seen to be the intention of the law, which is the ally of the whole city; and is seen also in the authority which we exercise over children, and the refusal to let them be free until we have established in them a principle analogous to the constitution of a state, and by cultivation of this higher element have set up in their hearts a guardian and ruler like our own, and when this is done they may go their ways.

Yes, he said, the purpose of the law is manifest.

From what point of view, then, and on what ground can we say that a man is profited by injustice or intemperance or other baseness, which will make him a worse man, even though he acquire money or power by his wickedness?

From no point of view at all.

What shall he profit, if his injustice be undetected and unpunished? He who is undetected only gets worse, whereas he who is detected and punished has the brutal part of his nature silenced and humanized; the gentler element in him is liberated, and his whole soul is perfected and ennobled by the acquirement of justice and temperance and wisdom, more than the body ever is by receiving gifts of beauty, strength and health, in proportion as the soul is more honorable than the body.

Certainly, he said.

To this nobler purpose the man of understanding will devote the energies of his life. And in the first place, he will honor studies which impress these qualities on his soul, and will disregard others?

Clearly, he said.

In the next place, he will regulate his bodily habit and training, and so far will he be from yielding to brutal and irrational pleasures, that he will regard even health as quite a secondary matter; his first object will be not that he may be fair or strong or well, unless he is likely thereby to gain temperance, but he will always desire so to attemper the body as to preserve the harmony of the soul?

Certainly he will, if he has true music in him.

And in the acquisition of wealth there is a principle of order and harmony which he will also observe; he will not allow himself to be dazzled by the foolish applause of the world, and heap up riches to his own infinite harm?

Certainly not, he said.

He will look at the city which is within him, and take heed that no disorder occur in it, such as might arise either from superfluity or from want; and upon this principle he will regulate his property and gain or spend according to his means.

Very true.

And, for the same reason, he will gladly accept and enjoy such honors as he deems likely to make him a better man; but those, whether private or public, which are likely to disorder his life, he will avoid?

Then, if that is his motive, he will not be a statesman.

By the dog of Egypt, he will! in the city which is his own he certainly will, though in the land of his birth perhaps not, unless he have a divine call.

I understand; you mean that he will be a ruler in the city of which we are the founders, and which exists in idea only; for I do not believe that there is such an one anywhere on earth?

In heaven, I replied, there is laid up a pattern of it, methinks, which he who desires may behold, and beholding, may set his own house in order. But whether such an one exists, or ever will exist in fact is no matter; for he will live after the manner of that city, having nothing to do with any other.

I think so, he said.

ARISTOTLE

Nicomachean Ethics

Aristotle was born in 384 B.C. in Stagira, Macedonia, where his father was court physician to the king. He was sent at the age of seventeen to Plato's Academy where he remained as student and teacher for twenty years. After Plato's death, Aristotle left Athens. Among his activities at that time were extensive biological and zoological investigations and a year spent as tutor for the son of Philip II of Macedonia, a young man who later became known to the world as Alexander the Great. Aristotle returned to Athens in 336 B.C. after Alexander ascended to the throne, and he founded his own school, the Lyceum. His students became known as Peripatetics since instruction was often given under the covered walks—peripatoi, in Greek—of the school where he would walk and lecture. Of Aristotle's writings, only fragments of dialogues and some letters remain. The main body of his work, some twelve volumes in English, consists of lecture notes thought to have been recorded by his students. This fact may account for the rather dry nature of the prose even as it expresses the brilliance of his thought. Aristotle died in self-imposed exile in 322 B.C. at the age of 62, only a year after fleeing anti-Macedonian feeling in Athens.

Having been a student of Plato, Aristotle reflects Platonic issues in his writing. But he often disagrees with his teacher; for example, he denies the doctrine of the Forms. While Aristotle holds that universals exist as well as sensible particulars, he argues that this does not entail that universals are Ideas or Forms. Since, as we've seen, Plato's ethics is built upon the foundation of his metaphysics, and Aristotle rejects the core of Plato's metaphysics, Aristotle's moral philosophy naturally diverges from that of Plato.

Aristotle's ethical writings are found in three works: the Eudemian Ethics, Nicomachean Ethics, *and* Politics. *Since the* Nicomachean Ethics *(named for Aristotle's son) supercede the* Eudemian Ethics, *and the* Politics *concerns the practical application of ethics in a political system, the Nicomachean Ethics is usually seen as the best expression of Aristotle's moral philosophy. It is from this work that the readings in our text are taken.*

Aristotle begins the Ethics *with an observation he thinks is beyond dispute: Everyone, says Aristotle, agrees that what is good is whatever is aimed at. Thus, the good for humankind is whatever people in fact naturally seek. The term* eudaimonia, *which rather unfortunately is translated into English as "happiness" but means something more like "well-being," is the word he uses to formally identify that at which humankind naturally aims. For Aristotle, the real problem in ethics is discovering just what constitutes* eudaimonia. *This means we must identify the function of a human being, because things are good if they perform the function for which they exist and bad if they fail to fulfill that function. For example, just as a hammer is a good hammer as long as it functions properly as a hammer, a person is a good person as long as he or she functions as a human being ought to function. The proper functioning of the human he defines as the exercise of natural human faculties in accordance with virtue. And again, just as in the case of his teacher, Plato, the governance of reason is crucial in the acquisition and exercise of virtue.*

Like his teacher Plato, and Socrates before him, Aristotle has profoundly affected the history of Western moral philosophy. As we consider Plato to be the original source of religious and idealistic ethics, Aristotle is the source of naturalistic ethics. His moral philosophy most directly influenced the Stoics and, later, St. Thomas Aquinas. In the latter half of the twentieth century, a renewed interest in Aristotle's ethics has arisen due to the emergence of Virtue Ethics. In this text, readings by Anscombe and by Wolf represent current voices taking up an ancient theme.

Book I

Every art and every inquiry, and similarly every action and pursuit, is thought to aim at some good; and for this reason the good has rightly been declared to be that at which all things aim. But a certain difference is found among ends; some are activities, others are products apart from the activities that produce them. Where there are ends apart from the actions, it is the nature of the products to be better than the activities. Now, as there are many actions, arts, and sciences, their ends also are many; the end of the medical art is health, that of shipbuilding a vessel, that of strategy victory, that of economics wealth. But where such arts fall under a single capacity—as bridle-making and the other arts concerned with the equipment of horses fall under the art of riding, and this and every military action under strategy, in the same way other arts fall under yet others—in all of these the ends of the master arts are to be preferred to all the subordinate ends; for it is for the sake of the former that the latter are pursued.

It makes no difference whether the activities themselves are the ends of the actions, or something else apart from the activities, as in the case of the sciences just mentioned.

If, then, there is some end of the things we do, which we desire for its own sake (everything else being desired for the sake of this), and if we do not choose everything for the sake of something else (for at that rate the process would go on to infinity, so that our desire would be empty and vain), clearly this must be the good and the chief good. Will not the knowledge of it, then, have a great influence on life? Shall we not, like archers who have a mark to aim at, be more likely to hit upon what is right? If so, we must try, in outline at least, to determine what it is, and of which of the sciences or capacities it is the object. It would seem to belong to the most authoritative art and that which is most truly the master art. And politics appears to be of this nature; for it is this that ordains which of the sciences should be studied in a state, and which each class of citizens should learn and up to what point they should learn them; and we see even the most highly esteemed of capacities to fall under this, e.g. strategy, economics, rhetoric; now, since politics uses the rest of the sciences, and since, again, it legislates as to what we are to do and what we are to abstain from, the end of this science must include those of the others, so that this end must be the good for man. For even if the end is the same for a single man and for a state, that of the state seems at all events something greater and more complete whether to attain or to preserve; though it is worth while to attain the end merely for one man, it is finer and more godlike to attain it for a nation or for city-states. These, then, are the ends at which our inquiry aims, since it is political science, in one sense of that term.

Our discussion will be adequate if it has as much clearness as the subject-matter admits of, for precision is not to be sought for alike in all discussions, any more than in all the products of the crafts. Now fine and just actions, which political science investigates, admit of much variety and fluctuation of opinion, so that they may be thought to exist only by convention, and not by nature. And goods also give rise to a similar fluctuation because they bring harm to many people; for before now men have been undone by reason of their wealth, and others by reason of their courage. We must be content, then, in speaking of such subjects and with such premises to indicate the truth roughly and in outline, and in speaking about things which are only for the most part true and with premises of the same kind to reach conclusions that are no better. In the same spirit, therefore, should each type of statement be *received;* for it is the mark of an educated man to look for precision in each class of things just so far as the nature of the subject admits; it is evidently equally foolish to accept probable reasoning from a mathematician and to demand from a rhetorician scientific proofs.

Now each man judges well the things he knows, and of these he is a good judge. And so the man who has been educated in a subject is a good judge of that subject, and the man who has received an all-round education is a good judge in general. Hence a young man is not a proper hearer of lectures on political science; for he is inexperienced in the actions that occur in life, but its discussions start from these and are about these; and, further, since he tends to follow his passions, his study will be vain and unprofitable, because the end aimed at is not knowledge but action. And it makes no difference whether he is young in years or youthful in character; the defect does not depend on time, but on his living, and pursuing each successive object, as passion directs. For to such persons, as to the incontinent, knowledge brings no profit; but to those who desire and act in accordance with a rational principle knowledge about such matters will be of great benefit.

These remarks about the student, the sort of treatment to be expected, and the purpose of the inquiry, may be taken as our preface.

Let us resume our inquiry and state, in view of the fact that all knowledge and every pursuit aims at some good, what it is that we say political science aims at and what is the highest of all goods achievable by action. Verbally there is very general agreement; for both the general run of men and people of superior refinement say that it is happiness, and identify living well and doing well with being happy; but with regard to what happiness is they differ, and the many do not give the same account as the wise. For the former think it is some plain and obvious thing, like pleasure, wealth, or honour; they differ, however, from one another—and often even the same man identifies it with different things, with health when he is ill, with wealth when he is poor; but, conscious of their ignorance, they admire those who proclaim some great ideal that is above their comprehension. Now some thought that apart from these many goods there is another which is self-subsistent and causes the goodness of all these as well. To examine all the opinions that have been held were perhaps somewhat fruitless; enough to examine those that are most prevalent or that seem to be arguable.

Let us not fail to notice, however, that there is a difference between arguments from and those to the first principles. For Plato, too, was right in raising this question and asking, as he used to do, 'are we on the way from or to the first principles?' There is a difference, as there is in a racecourse between the course from the judges to the turning point and the way back. For, while we must begin with what is known, things are objects of knowledge in two senses—some to us, some without qualification. Presumably, then, *we* must begin with things known to *us*. Hence any one who is to listen intelligently to lectures about what is noble and just and, generally, about the subjects of political science must have been brought up in good habits. For the fact is the starting-point, and if this is sufficiently plain to him, he will not at the start need the reason as well; and the man who has been well brought up has or can easily get starting-points. And as for him who neither has nor can get them, let him hear the words of Hesiod:

> Far best is he who knows all things himself;
> Good, he that hearkens when men counsel right;
> But he who neither knows, nor lays to heart
> Another's wisdom, is a useless wight.

Let us, however, resume our discussion from the point at which we digressed. To judge from the lives that men lead, most men, and men of the most vulgar type, seem (not without some ground) to identify the good, or happiness, with pleasure; which is the reason why they love the life of enjoyment. For there are, we may say, three prominent types of life—that just mentioned, the political, and thirdly the contemplative life. Now the mass of mankind are evidently quite slavish in their tastes, preferring a life suitable to beasts, but they get some ground for their view from the fact that many of those in high places share the tastes of Sardanapallus. A consideration of the prominent types of life shows that people of superior refinement and of active disposition identify happiness with honour; for this is, roughly speaking, the end of the political life. But it seems too superficial to be what we are looking for, since it is thought to depend on those who bestow honour rather than on him who receives it, but the good we divine to be something proper to a man and not easily taken from him. Further, men seem to pursue honour in order that they may be assured of their goodness; at least it is by men of practical wisdom that they seek to be honoured, and among those who know them, and on the ground of their virtue; clearly, then, according to them, at any rate, virtue is better. And perhaps one might even suppose this to be, rather than honour, the end of the political life. But even this appears somewhat incomplete; for possession of virtue seems actually compatible with being asleep, or with lifelong inactivity, and, further, with the greatest sufferings and misfortunes; but a man who was living so no one would call happy, unless he were maintaining a thesis at all costs. But enough of this; for the subject has been sufficiently treated even in the current discussions. Third comes the contemplative life, which we shall consider later.

The life of money-making is one undertaken under compulsion, and wealth is evidently not the good we are seeking; for it is merely useful and for the sake of something else. And so one might rather take the aforenamed objects to be ends; for they are loved for themselves. But it is evident that not even these are ends; yet many arguments have been thrown away in support of them. Let us leave this subject, then.

We had perhaps better consider the universal good and discuss thoroughly what is meant by it, although such an inquiry is made an uphill one by the fact that the Forms have been introduced by friends of our own. Yet it would perhaps be thought to be better, indeed to be our duty, for the sake of maintaining the truth even to destroy what touches us closely, especially as we are philosophers or lovers of wisdom; for, while both are dear, piety requires us to honour truth above our friends.

The men who introduced this doctrine did not posit Ideas of classes within which they recognized priority and posteriority (which is the reason why they did not maintain the existence of an Idea embracing all numbers); but the term 'good' is used both in the category of substance and in that of quality and in that of relation, and that which is *per se*, i.e. substance, is prior in nature to the relative (for the latter is like an offshoot and accident of being); so that there could not be a common Idea set over all these goods. Further, since 'good' has as many senses as 'being' (for it is predicated both in the category of substance, as of God and of reason, and in quality, i.e. of the virtues, and in quantity, i.e. of that which is moderate, and in relation, i.e. of the useful, and in time, i.e. of the right opportunity, and in place, i.e. of the right locality and the like), clearly it cannot be something universally present in all cases and single; for then it could not have been predicated in all the categories but in one only. Further, since of the things answering to one Idea there is one science, there would have been one science of all the goods; but as it is there are many sciences even of the things that fall under one category, e.g. of opportunity, for opportunity in war is studied by strategics and in disease by medicine, and the moderate in food is studied by medicine and in exercise by the science of gymnastics. And one might ask the question, what in the world they *mean* by 'a thing itself,' if (as is the case) in 'man himself' and in a particular man the account of man is one and the same. For in so far as they are man, they will in no respect differ; and if this is so, neither will 'good itself' and particular goods, in so far as they are good. But again it will not be good any the more for being eternal, since that which lasts long is no whiter than that which perishes in a day. The Pythagoreans seem to give a more plausible account of the good, when they place the one in the column of goods; and it is they that Speusippus seems to have followed.

But let us discuss these matters elsewhere; an objection to what we have said, however, may be discerned in the fact that the Platonists have not been speaking about *all* goods, and that the goods that are pursued and loved for themselves are called good by reference to a single Form, while those which tend to produce or to preserve these somehow or to prevent their contraries are called so by reference to these, and in a secondary sense. Clearly, then, goods must be spoken of in two ways, and some must be good in themselves, the others by reason of these. Let us separate, then, things good in themselves from things useful, and consider whether the former are called good by reference to a single Idea. What sort of goods would one call good in themselves? Is it those that are pursued

even when isolated from others, such as intelligence, sight, and certain pleasures and honours? Certainly, if we pursue these also for the sake of something else, yet one would place them among things good in themselves. Or is nothing other than the Idea of good good in itself? In that case the Form will be empty. But if the things we have named are also things good in themselves, the account of the good will have to appear as something identical in them all, as that of whiteness is identical in snow and in white lead. But of honour, wisdom, and pleasure, just in respect of their goodness, the accounts are distinct and diverse. The good, therefore, is not some common element answering to one Idea.

But what then do we mean by the good? It is surely not like the things that only chance to have the same name. Are goods one, then, by being derived from one good or by all contributing to one good, or are they rather one by analogy? Certainly as sight is in the body, so is reason in the soul, and so on in other cases. But perhaps these subjects had better be dismissed for the present; for perfect precision about them would be more appropriate to another branch of philosophy. And similarly with regard to the Idea; even if there is some one good which is universally predicable of goods or is capable of separate and independent existence, clearly it could not be achieved or attained by man; but we are now seeking something attainable. Perhaps, however, some one might think it worth while to recognize this with a view to the goods that *are* attainable and achievable; for having this as a sort of pattern we shall know better the goods that are good for us, and if we know them shall attain them. This argument has some plausibility, but seems to clash with the procedure of the sciences; for all of these, though they aim at some good and seek to supply the deficiency of it, leave on one side the knowledge of *the* good. Yet that all the exponents of the arts should be ignorant of, and should not even seek, so great an aid is not probable. It is hard, too, to see how a weaver or a carpenter will be benefited in regard to his own craft by knowing this 'good itself,' or how the man who has viewed the Idea itself will be a better doctor or general thereby. For a doctor seems not even to study health in this way, but the health of man, or perhaps rather the health of a particular man; it is individuals that he is healing. But enough of these topics.

Let us again return to the good we are seeking, and ask what it can be. It seems different in different actions and arts; it is different in medicine, in strategy, and in the other arts likewise. What then is the good of each? Surely that for whose sake everything else is done. In medicine this is health, in strategy victory, in architecture a house, in any other sphere something else, and in every action and pursuit the end; for it is for the sake of this that all men do whatever else they do. Therefore, if there is an end for all that we do, this will be the good achievable by action, and if there are more than one, these will be the goods achievable by action.

So the argument has by a different course reached the same point; but we must try to state this even more clearly. Since there are evidently more than one end, and we choose some of these (e.g. wealth, flutes, and in general instruments) for the sake of something else, clearly not all ends are final ends; but the chief good is evidently something final. Therefore, if there is only one final end, this will be what we are seeking, and if there are more than one, the most final of these will be what we are seeking. Now we call that which is in itself worthy of pursuit more final than that which is worthy of pursuit for the sake of something else, and that which is never desirable for the sake of something else more final than the things that are desirable both in themselves and for the sake of that other thing, and therefore we call final without qualification that which is always desirable in itself and never for the sake of something else.

Now such a thing happiness, above all else, is held to be; for this we choose always for itself and never for the sake of something else, but honour, pleasure, reason, and every virtue we choose indeed for themselves (for if nothing resulted from them we should still choose each of them), but we choose them also for the sake of happiness, judging that by means of them we shall be happy. Happiness, on the other hand, no one chooses for the sake of these, nor, in general, for anything other than itself.

From the point of view of self-sufficiency the same result seems to follow; for the final good is thought to be self-sufficient. Now by self-sufficient we do not mean that which is sufficient for a man by himself, for one who lives a solitary life, but also for parents, children, wife, and in general for his friends and fellow citizens, since man is born for citizenship.

But some limit must be set to this; for if we extend our requirement to ancestors and descendants and friends' friends we are in for an infinite series. Let us examine this question, however, on another occasion; the self-sufficient we now define as that which when isolated makes life desirable and lacking in nothing; and such we think happiness to be; and further we think it most desirable of all things, without being counted as one good thing among others—if it were so counted it would clearly be made more desirable by the addition of even the least of goods; for that which is added becomes an excess of goods, and of goods the greater is always more desirable. Happiness, then, is something final and self-sufficient, and is the end of action.

Presumably, however, to say that happiness is the chief good seems a platitude, and a clearer account of what it is is still desired. This might perhaps be given, if we could first ascertain the function of man. For just as for a flute-player, a sculptor, or any artist, and, in general, for all things that have a function or activity, the good and the 'well' is thought to reside in the function, so would it seem to be for man, if he has a function. Have the carpenter, then, and the tanner certain functions or activities, and has man none? Is he born without a function? Or as eye, hand, foot, and in general each of the parts evidently has a function, may one lay it down that man similarly has a function apart from all these? What then can this be? Life seems to be common even to plants, but we are seeking what is peculiar to man. Let us exclude, therefore, the life of nutrition and growth. Next there would be a life of perception, but it also seems to be common even to the horse, the ox, and every animal. There remains, then, an active life of the element that has a rational principle; of this, one part has such a principle in the sense of being obedient to one, the other in the sense of possessing one and exercising thought. And as 'life of the rational element' also has two meanings, we must state that life in the sense of activity is what we mean; for this seems to be the more proper sense of the term. Now if the function of man is an activity of soul which follows or implies a rational principle, and if we say 'a so-and-so' and 'a good so-and-so' have a function which is the same in kind, e.g. a lyre-player and a good lyre-player, and so without qualification in all cases, eminence in respect of goodness being added to the name of the function (for the function of a lyre-player is to play the lyre, and that of a good lyre-player is to do so well): if this is the case, [and we state the function of man to be a certain kind of life, and this to be an activity or actions of the soul implying a rational principle, and the function of a good man to be the good and noble performance of these, and if any action is well performed when it is performed in accordance with the appropriate excellence: if this is the case,] human good turns out to be activity of soul in accordance with virtue, and if there are more than one virtue, in accordance with the best and most complete.

But we must add 'in a complete life.' For one swallow does not make a summer, nor does one day; and so too one day, or a short time, does not make a man blessed and happy.

Let this serve as an outline of the good; for we must presumably first sketch it roughly, and then later fill in the details. But it would seem that any one is capable of carrying on and articulating what has once been well outlined, and that time is a good discoverer or partner in such a work; to which facts the advances of the arts are due; for any one can add what is lacking. And we must also remember what has been said before, and not look for precision in all things alike, but in each class of things such precision as accords with the subject-matter, and so much as is appropriate to the inquiry. For a carpenter and a geometer investigate the right angle in different ways; the former does so in so far as the right angle is useful for his work, while the latter inquires what it is or what sort of thing it is; for he is a spectator of the truth. We must act in the same way, then, in all other matters as well, that our main task may not be subordinated to minor questions. Nor must we demand the cause in all matters alike; it is enough in some cases that the *fact* be well established, as in the case of the first principles; the fact is the primary thing or first principle. Now of first principles we see some by induction, some by perception, some by a certain habituation, and others too in other ways. But each set of principles we must try to investigate in the natural way, and we must take pains to state them definitely, since they have a great influence on what follows. For the beginning is thought to be more than half of the whole, and many of the questions we ask are cleared up by it.

We must consider it, however, in the light not only of our conclusion and our premises, but also of what is commonly said about it; for with a true view all the data harmonize, but with a false one the facts soon clash. Now goods have been divided into three classes, and some are described as external, others as relating to soul or to body; we call those that relate to soul most properly and truly goods, and psychical actions and activities we class as relating to soul. Therefore our account must be sound, at least according to this view, which is an old one and agreed on by philosophers. It is correct also in that we identify the end with certain actions and activities; for thus it falls among goods of the soul and not among external goods. Another belief which harmonizes with our account is that the happy man lives well and does well; for we have practically defined happiness as a sort of good life and good action. The characteristics that are looked for in happiness seem also, all of them, to belong to what we have defined happiness as being. For some identify happiness with virtue, some with practical wisdom, others with a kind of philosophic wisdom, others with these, or one of these, accompanied by pleasure or not without pleasure; while others include also external prosperity. Now some of these views have been held by many men and men of old, others by a few eminent persons; and it is not probable that either of these should be entirely mistaken, but rather that they should be right in at least some one respect or even in most respects.

With those who identify happiness with virtue or some one virtue our account is in harmony; for to virtue belongs virtuous activity. But it makes, perhaps, no small difference whether we place the chief good in possession or in use, in state of mind or in activity. For the state of mind may exist without producing any good result, as in a man who is asleep or in some other way quite inactive, but the activity cannot; for one who has the activity will of necessity be acting, and acting well. And as in the Olympic Games it is not the most beautiful and the strongest that are crowned but those who compete (for it is some of these that are victorious), so those who act win, and rightly win, the noble and good things in life.

Their life is also in itself pleasant. For pleasure is a state of *soul*, and to each man that which he is said to be a lover of is pleasant; e.g. not only is a horse pleasant to the lover of horses, and a spectacle to the lover of sights, but also in the same way just acts are pleasant to the lover of justice and in general virtuous acts to the lover of virtue. Now for most men their pleasures are in conflict with one another because these are not by nature pleasant, but the lovers of what is noble find pleasant the things that are by nature pleasant; and virtuous actions are such, so that these are pleasant for such men as well as in their own nature. Their life, therefore, has no further need of pleasure as a sort of adventitious charm, but has its pleasure in itself. For, besides what we have said, the man who does not rejoice in noble actions is not even good; since no one would call a man just who did not enjoy acting justly, nor any man liberal who did not enjoy liberal actions; and similarly in all other cases. If this is so, virtuous actions must be in themselves pleasant. But they are also *good* and *noble,* and have each of these attributes in the highest degree, since the good man judges well about these attributes; his judgement is such as we have described. Happiness then is the best, noblest, and most pleasant thing in the world, and these attributes are not severed as in the inscription at Delos—

> Most noble is that which is justest, and best is health;
> But pleasantest is it to win what we love.

For all these properties belong to the best activities; and these, or one—the best—of these, we identify with happiness.

Yet evidently, as we said, it needs the external goods as well; for it is impossible, or not easy, to do noble acts without the proper equipment. In many actions we use friends and riches and political power as instruments; and there are some things the lack of which takes the lustre from happiness, as good birth, goodly children, beauty; for the man who is very ugly in appearance or ill-born or solitary and childless is not very likely to be happy, and perhaps a man would be still less likely if he had thoroughly bad children or friends or had lost good children or friends by death. As we said, then, happiness seems to need this sort of prosperity in addition; for which reason some identify happiness with good fortune, though others identify it with virtue.

For this reason also the question is asked, whether happiness is to be acquired by learning or by habituation or some other sort of training, or comes in virtue of some divine providence or again by chance. Now if there is *any* gift of the gods to

men, it is reasonable that happiness should be god-given, and most surely god-given of all human things inasmuch as it is the best. But this question would perhaps be more appropriate to another inquiry; happiness seems, however, even if it is not god-sent but comes as a result of virtue and some process of learning or training, to be among the most godlike things; for that which is the prize and end of virtue seems to be the best thing in the world, and something godlike and blessed.

It will also on this view be very generally shared; for all who are not maimed as regards their potentiality for virtue may win it by a certain kind of study and care. But if it is better to be happy thus than by chance, it is reasonable that the facts should be so, since everything that depends on the action of nature is by nature as good as it can be, and similarly everything that depends on art or any rational cause, and especially if it depends on the best of all causes. To entrust to chance what is greatest and most noble would be a very defective arrangement.

The answer to the question we are asking is plain also from the definition of happiness; for it has been said to be a virtuous activity of soul, of a certain kind. Of the remaining goods, some must necessarily pre-exist as conditions of happiness, and others are naturally co-operative and useful as instruments. And this will be found to agree with what we said at the outset; for we stated the end of political science to be the best end, and political science spends most of its pains on making the citizens to be of a certain character, viz. good and capable of noble acts.

It is natural, then, that we call neither ox nor horse nor any other of the animals happy; for none of them is capable of sharing in such activity. For this reason also a boy is not happy; for he is not yet capable of such acts, owing to his age; and boys who are called happy are being congratulated by reason of the hopes we have for them. For there is required, as we said, not only complete virtue but also a complete life, since many changes occur in life, and all manner of chances, and the most prosperous may fall into great misfortunes in old age, as is told of Priam in the Trojan Cycle; and one who has experienced such chances and has ended wretchedly no one calls happy.

Must no one at all, then, be called happy while he lives; must we, as Solon says, see the end? Even if we are to lay down this doctrine, is it also the case that a man *is* happy when he is *dead?* Or is not this quite absurd, especially for us who say that happiness is an activity? But if we do not call the dead man happy, and if Solon does not mean this, but that one can then safely *call* a man blessed as being at last beyond evils and misfortunes, this also affords matter for discussion; for both evil and good are thought to exist for a dead man, as much as for one who is alive but not aware of them; e. g. honours and dishonours and the good or bad fortunes of children and in general of descendants. And this also presents a problem; for though a man has lived happily up to old age and has had a death worthy of his life, many reverses may befall his descendants—some of them may be good and attain the life they deserve, while with others the opposite may be the case; and clearly too the degrees of relationship between them and their ancestors may vary indefinitely. It would be odd, then, if the dead man were to share in these changes and become at one time happy, at another wretched; while it would also be odd if the fortunes of the descendants did not for *some* time have *some* effect on the happiness of their ancestors.

But we must return to our first difficulty; for perhaps by a consideration of it our present problem might be solved. Now if we must see the end and only then call a man happy, not as being happy but as having been so before, surely this is a paradox, that when he is happy the attribute that belongs to him is not to be truly predicated of him because we do not wish to call living men happy, on account of the changes that may befall them, and because we have assumed happiness to be something permanent and by no means easily changed, while a single man may suffer many turns of fortune's wheel. For clearly if we were to keep pace with his fortunes, we should often call the same man happy and again wretched, making the happy man out to be a 'chameleon and insecurely based.' Or is this keeping pace with his fortunes quite wrong? Success or failure in life does not depend on these, but human life, as we said, needs these as mere additions, while virtuous activities or their opposites are what constitute happiness or the reverse.

The question we have now discussed confirms our definition. For no function of man has so much permanence as virtuous activities (these are thought to be more durable even than knowledge of the sciences), and of these themselves the most valuable are more durable because those who are happy spend their life most readily and most continuously in these; for this seems to be the reason why we do not forget them. The attribute in question, then, will belong to the happy man, and he will be happy throughout his life; for always, or by preference to everything else, he will be engaged in virtuous action and contemplation, and he will bear the chances of life most nobly and altogether decorously, if he is 'truly good' and 'foursquare beyond reproach.'

Now many events happen by chance, and events differing in importance; small pieces of good fortune or of its opposite clearly do not weigh down the scales of life one way or the other, but a multitude of great events if they turn out well will make life happier (for not only are they themselves such as to add beauty to life, but the way a man deals with them may be noble and good), while if they turn out ill they crush and maim happiness; for they both bring pain with them and hinder many activities. Yet even in these nobility shines through, when a man bears with resignation many great misfortunes, not through insensibility to pain but through nobility and greatness of soul.

If activities are, as we said, what gives life its character, no happy man can become miserable; for he will never do the acts that are hateful and mean. For the man who is truly good and wise, we think, bears all the chances of life becomingly and always makes the best of circumstances, as a good general makes the best military use of the army at his command and a good shoemaker makes the best shoes out of the hides that are given him; and so with all other craftsmen. And if this is the case, the happy man can never become miserable—though he will not reach *blessedness,* if he meet with fortunes like those of Priam.

Nor, again, is he many-coloured and changeable; for neither will he be moved from his happy state easily or by any ordinary misadventures, but only by many great ones, nor, if he has had many great misadventures, will he recover his happiness in a short time, but if at all, only in a long and complete one in which he has attained many splendid successes.

Why then should we not say that he is happy who is active in accordance with complete virtue and is sufficiently equipped with external goods, not for some chance period but throughout a complete life? Or must we add 'and who is destined to live thus and die as befits his life'? Certainly the future is obscure to us while happiness, we claim, is an end and something in every way final. If so, we shall call happy those among living men in whom these conditions are, and are to be, fulfilled—but happy *men*. So much for these questions.

That the fortunes of descendants and of all a man's friends should not affect his happiness at all seems a very unfriendly doctrine, and one opposed to the opinions men hold; but since the events that happen are numerous and admit of all sorts of difference, and some come more near to us and others less so, it seems a long—nay, an infinite—task to discuss each in detail; a general outline will perhaps suffice. If, then, as some of a man's own misadventures have a certain weight and influence on life while others are, as it were, lighter, so too there are differences among the misadventures of our friends taken as a whole, and it makes a difference whether the various sufferings befall the living or the dead (much more even than whether lawless and terrible deeds are presupposed in a tragedy or done on the stage), this difference also must be taken into account; or rather, perhaps, the fact that doubt is felt whether the dead share in any good or evil. For it seems, from these considerations, that even if anything whether good or evil penetrates to them, it must be something weak and negligible, either in itself or for them, or if not, at least it must be such in degree and kind as not to make happy those who are not happy nor to take away their blessedness from those who are. The good or bad fortunes of friends, then, seem to have some effects on the dead, but effects of such a kind and degree as neither to make the happy unhappy nor to produce any other change of the kind.

These questions having been definitely answered, let us consider whether happiness is among the things that are praised or rather among the things that are prized; for clearly it is not to be placed among *potentialities*. Everything that is praised seems to be praised because it is of a certain kind and is related somehow to something else; for we praise the just or brave man and in general both the good man and virtue itself because of the actions and functions involved, and we praise the strong man, the good runner, and so on, because he is of a certain kind and is related in a certain way to something good and important. This is clear also from the praises of

the gods; for it seems absurd that the gods should be referred to our standard, but this *is* done because praise involves a reference, as we said, to something else. But if praise is for things such as we have described, clearly what applies to the best things is not praise, but something greater and better, as is indeed obvious; for what we do to the gods and the most godlike of men is to call them blessed and happy. And so too with good *things*; no one praises happiness as he does justice, but rather calls it blessed, as being something more divine and better.

Eudoxus also seems to have been right in his method of advocating the supremacy of pleasure; he thought that the fact that, though a good, it is not praised indicated it to be better than the things that are praised, and that this is what God and the good are; for by reference to these all other things are judged. *Praise* is appropriate to virtue, for as a result of virtue men tend to do noble deeds; but *encomia* are bestowed on acts, whether of the body or of the soul. But perhaps nicety in these matters is more proper to those who have made a study of encomia; to us it is clear from what has been said that happiness is among the things that are prized and perfect. It seems to be so also from the fact that it is a first principle; for it is for the sake of this that we all do all that we do, and the first principle and cause of goods is, we claim, something prized and divine.

Since happiness is an activity of soul in accordance with perfect virtue, we must consider the nature of virtue; for perhaps we shall thus see better the nature of happiness. The true student of politics, too, is thought to have studied virtue above all things; for he wishes to make his fellow citizens good and obedient to the laws. As an example of this we have the lawgivers of the Cretans and the Spartans, and any others of the kind that there may have been. And if this inquiry belongs to political science, clearly the pursuit of it will be in accordance with our original plan. But clearly the virtue we must study is human virtue; for the good we were seeking was human good and the happiness human happiness. By human virtue we mean not that of the body but that of the soul; and happiness also we call an activity of soul. But if this is so, clearly the student of politics must know somehow the facts about soul, as the man who is to heal the eyes or the body as a whole must know about the eyes or the body; and all the more since politics is more prized and better than medicine; but even among doctors the best educated spend much labour on acquiring knowledge of the body. The student of politics, then, must study the soul, and must study it with these objects in view, and do so just to the extent which is sufficient for the questions we are discussing; for further precision is perhaps something more laborious than our purposes require.

Some things are said about it, adequately enough, even in the discussions outside our school, and we must use these; e.g. that one element in the soul is irrational and one has a rational principle. Whether these are separated as the parts of the body or of anything divisible are, or are distinct by definition but by nature inseparable, like convex and concave in the circumference of a circle, does not affect the present question.

Of the irrational element one division seems to be widely distributed, and vegetative in its nature, I mean that which causes nutrition and growth; for it is this kind of power of the soul that one must assign to all nurslings and to embryos, and this same power to full-grown creatures; this is more reasonable than to assign some different power to them. Now the excellence of this seems to be common to all species and not specifically human; for this part or faculty seems to function most in sleep, while goodness and badness are least manifest in sleep (whence comes the saying that the happy are no better off than the wretched for half their lives; and this happens naturally enough, since sleep is an inactivity of the soul in that respect in which it is called good or bad), unless perhaps to a small extent some of the movements actually penetrate to the soul, and in this respect the dreams of good men are better than those of ordinary people. Enough of this subject, however; let us leave the nutritive faculty alone, since it has by its nature no share in human excellence.

There seems to be also another irrational element in the soul—one which in a sense, however, shares in a rational principle. For we praise the rational principle of the continent man and of the incontinent, and the part of their soul that has such a principle, since it urges them aright and towards the best objects; but there is found in them also another element naturally opposed to the rational principle, which fights against and resists that principle. For exactly as paralyzed limbs when we intend to move them to the right turn on the contrary to the left, so is it with the soul; the impulses of incontinent people move in contrary directions. But while in the body we see that which moves astray, in the soul we do not. No doubt, however, we must none the less suppose that in the soul too there is something contrary to the rational principle, resisting and opposing it. In what sense it is distinct from the other elements does not concern us. Now even this seems to have a share in a rational principle, as we said; at any rate in the continent man it obeys the rational principle—and presumably in the temperate and brave man it is still more obedient; for in him it speaks, on all matters, with the same voice as the rational principle.

Therefore the irrational element also appears to be twofold. For the vegetative element in no way shares in a rational principle, but the appetitive and in general the desiring element in a sense shares in it, in so far as it listens to and obeys it; this is the sense in which we speak of 'taking account' of one's father or one's friends, not that in which we speak of 'accounting' for a mathematical property. That the irrational element is in some sense persuaded by a rational principle is indicated also by the giving of advice and by all reproof and exhortation. And if this element also must be said to have a rational principle, that which has a rational principle (as well as that which has not) will be twofold, one subdivision having it in the strict sense and in itself, and the other having a tendency to obey as one does one's father.

Virtue too is distinguished into kinds in accordance with this difference; for we say that some of the virtues are intellectual and others moral, philosophic wisdom and understanding and practical wisdom being intellectual, liberality and temperance moral. For in speaking about a man's character we do not say that he is wise or has understanding but that he is good-tempered or temperate; yet we praise the wise man also with respect to his state of mind; and of states of mind we call those which merit praise virtues.

Book II

Virtue, then, being of two kinds, intellectual and moral, intellectual virtue in the main owes both its birth and its growth to teaching (for which reason it requires experience and time), while moral virtue comes about as a result of habit, whence also its name (ἠθική) is one that is formed by a slight variation from the word ἔθος (habit). From this it is also plain that none of the moral virtues arises in us by nature; for nothing that exists by nature can form a habit contrary to its nature. For instance the stone which by nature moves downwards cannot be habituated to move upwards, not even if one tries to train it by throwing it up ten thousand times; nor can fire be habituated to move downwards, nor can anything else that by nature behaves in one way be trained to behave in another. Neither by nature, then, nor contrary to nature do the virtues arise in us; rather we are adapted by nature to receive them, and are made perfect by habit.

Again, of all the things that come to us by nature we first acquire the potentiality and later exhibit the activity (this is plain in the case of the senses; for it was not by often seeing or often hearing that we got these senses, but on the contrary we had them before we used them, and did not come to have them by using them); but the virtues we get by first exercising them, as also happens in the case of the arts as well. For the things we have to learn before we can do them, we learn by doing them, e.g. men become builders by building and lyre-players by playing the lyre; so too we become just by doing just acts, temperate by doing temperate acts, brave by doing brave acts.

This is confirmed by what happens in states; for legislators make the citizens good by forming habits in them, and this is the wish of every legislator, and those who do not effect it miss their mark, and it is in this that a good constitution differs from a bad one.

Again, it is from the same causes and by the same means that every virtue is both produced and destroyed, and similarly every art; for it is from playing the lyre that both good and bad lyre-players are produced. And the corresponding statement is true of builders and of all the rest; men will be good or bad builders as a result of building well or badly. For if this were not so, there would have been no need of a teacher, but all men would have been born good or bad at their craft. This, then, is the case with the virtues also; by doing the acts that we do in our transactions with other men we become just or unjust, and by doing the acts that we do in the presence of danger, and being habituated to feel fear or confidence, we become brave or cowardly. The same is true of appetites and feelings of anger; some men become temperate and good-tempered, others self-indulgent and irascible, by behaving in one way or the other in the appropriate circumstances. Thus, in one word, states of character arise out of like activities. This is why the activities we exhibit must be of a certain kind; it is because the states of character correspond to the differences between these. It makes no small difference, then, whether we form habits of one kind or of another from our very youth; it makes a very great difference, or rather *all* the difference.

Since, then, the present inquiry does not aim at theoretical knowledge like the others (for we are inquiring not in order to know what virtue is, but in order to become good, since otherwise our inquiry would have been of no use), we must examine the nature of actions, namely how we ought to do them; for these determine also the nature of the states of character that are produced, as we have said. Now, that we must act according to the right rule is a common principle and must be assumed—it will be discussed later, i.e. both what the right rule is, and how it is related to the other virtues. But this must be agreed upon beforehand, that the whole account of matters of conduct must be given in outline and not precisely, as we said at the very beginning that the accounts we demand must be in accordance with the subject-matter; matters concerned with conduct and questions of what is good for us have no fixity, any more than matters of health. The general account being of this nature, the account of particular cases is yet more lacking in exactness; for they do not fall under any art or precept but the agents themselves must in each case consider what is appropriate to the occasion, as happens also in the art of medicine or of navigation.

But though our present account is of this nature we must give what help we can. First, then, let us consider this, that it is the nature of such things to be destroyed by defect and excess, as we see in the case of strength and of health (for to gain light on things imperceptible we must use the evidence of sensible things); both excessive and defective exercise destroys the strength, and similarly drink or food which is above or below a certain amount destroys the health, while that which is proportionate both produces and increases and preserves it. So too is it, then, in the case of temperance and courage and the other virtues. For the man who flies from and fears everything and does not stand his ground against anything becomes a coward, and the man who fears nothing at all but goes to meet every danger becomes rash; and similarly the man who indulges in every pleasure and abstains from none becomes self-indulgent, while the man who shuns every pleasure, as boors do, becomes in a way insensible; temperance and courage, then, are destroyed by excess and defect, and preserved by the mean.

But not only are the sources and causes of their origination and growth the same as those of their destruction, but also the sphere of their actualization will be the same; for this is also true of the things which are more evident to sense, e.g. of strength; it is produced by taking much food and undergoing much exertion, and it is the strong man that will be most able to do these things. So too is it with the virtues; by abstaining from pleasures we become temperate, and it is when we have become so that we are most able to abstain from them; and similarly too in the case of courage; for by being habituated to despise things that are terrible and to stand our ground against them we become brave, and it is when we have become so that we shall be most able to stand our ground against them.

We must take as a sign of states of character the pleasure or pain that ensues on acts; for the man who abstains from bodily pleasures and delights in this very fact is temperate, while the man who is annoyed at it is self-indulgent, and he who stands his ground against things that are terrible and delights in this or at least is not pained is brave, while the man who is pained is a coward. For moral excellence is concerned with pleasures and pains; it is on account of the pleasure that we do bad things, and on account of the pain that we abstain from noble ones. Hence we ought to have been brought up in a particular way from our very youth, as Plato says, so as both to delight in and to be pained by the things that we ought; for this is the right education.

Again, if the virtues are concerned with actions and passions, and every passion and every action is accompanied by pleasure and pain, for this reason also virtue will be concerned with pleasures and pains. This is indicated also by the fact that punishment is inflicted by these means; for it is a kind of cure, and it is the nature of cures to be effected by contraries.

Again, as we said but lately, every state of soul has a nature relative to and concerned with the kind of things by which it tends to be made worse or better; but it is by reason of pleasures and pains that men become bad, by pursuing and avoiding these—either the pleasures and pains they ought not or when they ought not or as they ought not, or by going wrong in one of the other similar ways that may be distinguished. Hence men even define the virtues as certain states of impassivity and rest; not well, however, because they speak absolutely, and do not say 'as one ought' and 'as one ought not' and 'when one ought or ought not,' and the other things that may be added. We assume, then, that this kind of excellence tends to do what is best with regard to pleasures and pains, and vice does the contrary.

The following facts also may show us that virtue and vice are concerned with these same things. There being three objects of choice and three of avoidance, the noble, the advantageous, the pleasant, and their contraries, the base, the injurious, the painful, about all of these the good man tends to go right and the bad man to go wrong, and especially about pleasure; for this is common to the animals, and also it accompanies all objects of choice; for even the noble and the advantageous appear pleasant.

Again, it has grown up with us all from our infancy; this is why it is difficult to rub off this passion, engrained as it is in our life. And we measure even our actions, some of us more and others less, by the rule of pleasure and pain. For this reason, then, our whole inquiry must be about these; for to feel delight and pain rightly or wrongly has no small effect on our actions.

Again, it is harder to fight with pleasure than with anger, to use Heraclitus' phrase, but both art and virtue are always concerned with what is harder; for even the good is better when it is harder. Therefore for this reason also the whole concern both of virtue and of political science is with pleasures and pains; for the man who uses these well will be good, he who uses them badly bad.

That virtue, then, is concerned with pleasures and pains, and that by the acts from which it arises it is both increased and, if they are done differently, destroyed, and that the acts from which it arose are those in which it actualizes itself—let this be taken as said.

The question might be asked, what we mean by saying that we must become just by doing just acts, and temperate by doing temperate acts; for if men do just and temperate acts, they are already just and temperate, exactly as, if they do what is in accordance with the laws of grammar and of music, they are grammarians and musicians.

Or is this not true even of the arts? It is possible to do something that is in accordance with the laws of grammar, either by chance or at the suggestion of another. A man will be a grammarian, then, only when he has both done something grammatical and done it grammatically; and this means doing it in accordance with the grammatical knowledge in himself.

Again, the case of the arts and that of the virtues are not similar; for the products of the arts have their goodness in themselves, so that it is enough that they should have a certain character, but if the acts that are in accordance with the virtues have themselves a certain character it does not follow that they are done justly or temperately. The agent also must be in a certain condition when he does them; in the first place he must have knowledge, secondly he must choose the acts, and choose them for their own sakes, and thirdly his action must proceed from a firm and unchangeable character. These are not reckoned in as conditions of the possession of the arts, except the bare knowledge; but as a condition of the possession of the virtues knowledge has little or no weight, while the other conditions count not for a little but for everything, i.e. the very conditions which result from often doing just and temperate acts.

Actions, then, are called just and temperate when they are such as the just or the temperate man would do; but it is not the man who does these that is just and temperate, but the man who also does them *as* just and temperate men do them.•It is well said, then, that it is by doing just acts that the just man is produced, and by doing temperate acts the temperate man; without doing these no one would have even a prospect of becoming good.

•But most people do not do these, but take refuge in theory and think they are being philosophers and will become good in this way, behaving somewhat like patients who listen attentively to their doctors, but do none of the things they are ordered to do. As the latter will not be made well in body by such a course of treatment, the former will not be made well in soul by such a course of philosophy.

Next we must consider what virtue is. Since things that are found in the soul are of three kinds— passions, faculties, states of character, virtue must be one of these. By passions I mean appetite, anger, fear, confidence, envy, joy, friendly feeling, hatred, longing, emulation, pity, and in general the feelings that are accompanied by pleasure or pain; by faculties the things in virtue of which we are said to be capable of feeling these, e.g. of becoming angry or being pained or feeling pity; by states of character the things in virtue of which we stand well or badly with reference to the passions, e.g. with reference to anger we stand badly if we feel it violently or too weakly, and well if we feel it moderately; and similarly with reference to the other passions.

Now neither the virtues nor the vices are *passions,* because we are not called good or bad on the ground of our passions, but are so called on the ground of our virtues and our vices, and because we are neither praised nor blamed for our passions (for the man who feels fear or anger is not praised, nor is the man who simply feels anger blamed, but the man who feels it in a certain way), but for our virtues and our vices we *are* praised or blamed.

Again, we feel anger and fear without choice, but the virtues are modes of choice or involve choice. Further, in respect of the passions we are said to be moved, but in respect of the virtues and the vices we are said not to be moved but to be disposed in a particular way.

For these reasons also they are not *faculties;* for we are neither called good nor bad, nor praised nor blamed, for the simple capacity of feeling the passions; again, we have the faculties by nature, but we are not made good or bad by nature; we have spoken of this before.

If, then, the virtues are neither passions nor faculties, all that remains is that they should be *states of character.*

Thus we have stated what virtue is in respect of its genus.

We must, however, not only describe virtue as a state of character, but also say what sort of state it is. We may remark, then, that every virtue or excellence both brings into good condition the thing of which it is the excellence and makes the work of that thing be done well; e.g. the excellence of the eye makes both the eye and its work good; for it is by the excellence of the eye that we see well. Similarly the excellence of the horse makes a horse both good in itself and good at running and at carrying its rider and at awaiting the attack of the enemy. Therefore, if this is true in every case, the virtue of man also will be the state of character which makes a man good and which makes him do his own work well.

How this is to happen we have stated already, but it will be made plain also by the following consideration of the specific nature of virtue. In everything that is continuous and divisible it is possible to take more, less, or an equal amount, and that either in terms of the thing itself or relatively to us; and the equal is an intermediate between excess and defect. By the intermediate in the object I mean that which is equidistant from each of the extremes, which is one and the same for all men; by the intermediate relatively to us that which is neither too much nor too little—and this is not one, nor the same for all. For instance, if ten is many and two is few, six is the intermediate, taken in terms of the object; for it exceeds and is exceeded by an equal amount; this is intermediate according to arithmetical proportion. But the intermediate relatively to us is not to be taken so; if ten pounds are too much for a particular person to eat and two too little, it does not follow that the trainer will order six pounds; for this also is perhaps too much for the person who is to take it, or too little—too little for Milo, too much for the beginner in athletic exercises. The same is true of running and wrestling. Thus a master of any art avoids excess and defect, but seeks the intermediate and chooses this—the intermediate not in the object but relatively to us.

If it is thus, then, that every art does its work well—by looking to the intermediate and judging its works by this standard (so that we often say of good works of art that it is not possible either to take away or to add anything, implying that excess and defect destroy the goodness of works of art, while the mean preserves it; and good artists, as we say, look to this in their work), and if, further, virtue is more exact and better than any art, as nature also is, then virtue must have the quality of aiming at the intermediate. I mean moral virtue; for it is this that is concerned with passions and actions, and in these there is excess, defect, and the intermediate. For instance, both fear and confidence and appetite and anger and pity and in general pleasure and pain may be felt both too much and too little, and in both cases not well; but to feel them at the right times, with reference to the right objects, towards the right people, with the right motive, and in the right way, is what is both intermediate and best, and this is characteristic of virtue. Similarly with regard to actions also there is excess, defect, and the intermediate. Now virtue is concerned with passions and actions, in which excess is a form of failure, and so is defect, while the intermediate is praised and is a form of success; and being praised and being successful are both characteristics of virtue. Therefore virtue is a kind of mean, since, as we have seen, it aims at what is intermediate.

Again, it is possible to fail in many ways (for evil belongs to the class of the unlimited, as the Pythagoreans conjectured, and good to that of the limited), while to succeed is possible only in one way (for which reason also one is easy and the other difficult—to miss the mark easy, to hit it difficult); for these reasons also, then, excess and defect are characteristic of vice, and the mean of virtue;

For men are good in but one way, but bad in many.

Virtue, then, is a state of character concerned with choice, lying in a mean, i.e. the mean relative to us, this being determined by a rational principle, and by that principle by which the man of practical wisdom would determine it. Now it is a mean between two vices, that which depends on excess and that which depends on defect; and again it is a mean because the vices respectively fall short of or exceed what is right in both passions and actions, while virtue both finds and chooses that which is intermediate. Hence in respect of its substance and the definition which states its essence virtue is a mean, with regard to what is best and right an extreme.

But not every action nor every passion admits of a mean; for some have names that already imply badness, e.g. spite, shamelessness, envy, and in the case of actions adultery, theft, murder; for all of these and suchlike things imply by their names that they are themselves bad, and not the excesses or deficiencies of them. It is not possible, then, ever to be right with regard to them; one must always be wrong. Nor does goodness or badness with regard to such things depend on committing adultery with the right woman, at the right time, and in the right way, but simply to do any of them is to go wrong. It would be equally absurd, then, to expect that in unjust, cowardly, and voluptuous action there should be a mean, an excess, and a deficiency; for at that rate there would be a mean of excess and of deficiency, an excess of excess, and a deficiency of deficiency. But as there is no excess and deficiency of temperance and courage because what is intermediate is in a sense an extreme, so too of the actions we have mentioned there is no mean nor any excess and deficiency, but however they are done they are wrong; for in general there is neither a mean of excess and deficiency, nor excess and deficiency of a mean.

We must, however, not only make this general statement, but also apply it to the individual facts. For among statements about conduct those which are general apply more widely, but those which are particular are more genuine, since conduct has to do with individual cases, and our statements must harmonize with the facts in these cases. We may take these cases from our table. With regard to feelings of fear and confidence courage is the mean; of the people who exceed, he who exceeds in fearlessness has no name (many of the states have no name), while the man who exceeds in confidence is rash, and he who exceeds in fear and falls short in confidence is a coward. With regard to pleasures and pains—not all of them, and not so much with regard to the pains— the mean is temperance, the excess self-indulgence. Persons deficient with regard to the pleasures are not often found; hence such persons also have received no name. But let us call them 'insensible.'

With regard to giving and taking of money the mean is liberality, the excess and the defect prodigality and meanness. In these actions people exceed and fall short in contrary ways; the prodigal exceeds in spending and falls short in taking, while the mean man exceeds in taking and falls short in spending. (At present we are giving a mere outline or summary, and are satisfied with this; later these states will be more exactly determined.) With regard to money there are also other dispositions—a mean, magnificence (for the magnificent man differs from the liberal man; the former deals with large sums, the latter with small ones), an excess, tastelessness and vulgarity, and a deficiency, niggardliness; these differ from the states opposed to liberality, and the mode of their difference will be stated later.

With regard to honour and dishonour the mean is proper pride, the excess is known as a sort of 'empty vanity,' and the deficiency is undue humility; and as we said liberality was related to magnificence, differ-

ing from it by dealing with small sums, so there is a state similarly related to proper pride, being concerned with small honours while that is concerned with great. For it is possible to desire honour as one ought, and more than one ought, and less, and the man who exceeds in his desires is called ambitious, the man who falls short unambitious, while the intermediate person has no name. The dispositions also are nameless, except that that of the ambitious man is called ambition. Hence the people who are at the extremes lay claim to the middle place; and we ourselves sometimes call the intermediate person ambitious and sometimes unambitious, and sometimes praise the ambitious man and sometimes the unambitious. The reason of our doing this will be stated in what follows; but now let us speak of the remaining states according to the method which has been indicated.

With regard to anger also there is an excess, a deficiency, and a mean. Although they can scarcely be said to have names, yet since we call the intermediate person good-tempered let us call the mean good temper; of the persons at the extremes let the one who exceeds be called irascible, and his vice irascibility, and the man who falls short an inirascible sort of person, and the deficiency inirascibility.

There are also three other means, which have a certain likeness to one another, but differ from one another: for they are all concerned with intercourse in words and actions, but differ in that one is concerned with truth in this sphere, the other two with pleasantness; and of this one kind is exhibited in giving amusement, the other in all the circumstances of life. We must therefore speak of these too, that we may the better see that in all things the mean is praise-worthy, and the extremes neither praiseworthy nor right, but worthy of blame. Now most of these states also have no names, but we must try, as in the other cases, to invent names ourselves so that we may be clear and easy to follow. With regard to truth, then, the intermediate is a truthful sort of person and the mean may be called truthfulness, while the pretence which exaggerates is boastfulness and the person characterized by it a boaster, and that which understates is mock modesty and the person characterized by it mock-modest. With regard to pleasantness in the giving of amusement the intermediate person is ready-witted and the disposition ready wit, the excess is buffoonery and the person characterized by it a buffoon, while the man who falls short is a sort of boor and his state is boorishness. With regard to the remaining kind of pleasantness, that which is exhibited in life in general, the man who is pleasant in the right way is friendly and the mean is friendliness, while the man who exceeds is an obsequious person if he has no end in view, a flatterer if he is aiming at his own advantage, and the man who falls short and is unpleasant in all circumstances is a quarrelsome and surly sort of person.

There are also means in the passions and concerned with the passions; since shame is not a virtue, and yet praise is extended to the modest man. For even in these matters one man is said to be intermediate, and another to exceed, as for instance the bashful man who is ashamed of everything; while he who falls short or is not ashamed of anything at all is shameless, and the intermediate person is modest. Righteous indignation is a mean between envy and spite, and these states are concerned with the pain and pleasure that are felt at the fortunes of our neighbours; the man who is characterized by righteous indignation is pained at undeserved good fortune, the envious man, going beyond him, is pained at all good fortune, and the spiteful man falls so far short of being pained that he even rejoices. But these states there will be an opportunity of describing elsewhere; with regard to justice, since it has not one simple meaning, we shall, after describing the other states, distinguish its two kinds and say how each of them is a mean; and similarly we shall treat also of the rational virtues.

There are three kinds of disposition, then, two of them vices, involving excess and deficiency respectively, and one a virtue, viz. the mean, and all are in a sense opposed to all; for the extreme states are contrary both to the intermediate state and to each other, and the intermediate to the extremes; as the equal is greater relatively to the less, less relatively to the greater, so the middle states are excessive relatively to the deficiencies, deficient relatively to the excesses, both in passions and in actions. For the brave man appears rash relatively to the coward, and cowardly relatively to the rash man; and similarly the temperate man appears self-indulgent relatively to the insensible man, insensible relatively to the self-indulgent, and the liberal man prodigal relatively to the mean man, mean relatively to the prodigal. Hence also the people at the extremes push the in-termediate man each over to the other, and the brave man is called rash by the coward, cowardly by the rash man, and correspondingly in the other cases.

These states being thus opposed to one another, the greatest contrariety is that of the extremes to each other, rather than to the intermediate; for these are further from each other than from the intermediate, as the great is further from the small and the small from the great than both are from the equal. Again, to the intermediate some extremes show a certain likeness, as that of rashness to courage and that of prodigality to liberality; but the extremes show the greatest unlikeness to each other; now contraries are defined as the things that are furthest from each other, so that things that are further apart are more contrary.

To the mean in some cases the deficiency, in some the excess is more opposed; e.g. it is not rashness, which is an excess, but cowardice, which is a deficiency, that is more opposed to courage, and not insensibility, which is a deficiency, but self-indulgence, which is an excess, that is more opposed to temperance. This happens from two reasons, one being drawn from the thing itself; for because one extreme is nearer and liker to the intermediate, we oppose not this but rather its contrary to the intermediate. E.g., since rashness is thought liker and nearer to courage, and cowardice more unlike, we oppose rather the latter to courage; for things that are further from the intermediate are thought more contrary to it. This, then, is one cause, drawn from the thing itself; another is drawn from ourselves; for the things to which we ourselves more naturally tend seem more contrary to the intermediate. For instance, we ourselves tend more naturally to pleasures, and hence are more easily carried away towards self-indulgence than towards propriety. We describe as contrary to the mean, then, rather the directions in which we more often go to great lengths; and therefore self-indulgence, which is an excess, is the more contrary to temperance.

That moral virtue is a mean, then, and in what sense it is so, and that it is a mean between two vices, the one involving excess, the other deficiency, and that it is such because its character is to aim at what is intermediate in passions and in actions, has been sufficiently stated. Hence also it is no easy task to be good. For in everything it is no easy task to find the middle, e.g. to find the middle of a circle is not for every one but for him who knows; so, too, any one can get angry—that is easy—or give or spend money; but to do this to the right person, to the right extent, at the right time, with the right motive, and in the right way, *that* is not for every one, nor is it easy; wherefore goodness is both rare and laudable and noble.

Hence he who aims at the intermediate must first depart from what is the more contrary to it, as Calypso advises—

Hold the ship out beyond that surf and spray.

For of the extremes one is more erroneous, one less so; therefore, since to hit the mean is hard in the extreme, we must as a second best, as people say, take the least of the evils; and this will be done best in the way we describe.

But we must consider the things towards which we ourselves also are easily carried away; for some of us tend to one thing, some to another; and this will be recognizable from the pleasure and the pain we feel. We must drag ourselves away to the contrary extreme; for we shall get into the intermediate state by drawing well away from error, as people do in straightening sticks that are bent.

Now in everything the pleasant or pleasure is most to be guarded against; for we do not judge it impartially. We ought, then, to feel towards pleasure as the elders of the people felt towards Helen, and in all circumstances repeat their saying; for if we dismiss pleasure thus we are less likely to go astray. It is by doing this, then, (to sum the matter up) that we shall best be able to hit the mean.

But this is no doubt difficult, and especially in individual cases; for it is not easy to determine both how and with whom and on what provocation and how long one should be angry; for we too sometimes praise those who fall short and call them good-tempered, but sometimes we praise those who get angry and call them manly. The man, however, who deviates little from goodness is not blamed, whether he do so in the direction of the more or of the less, but only the man who deviates more widely; for *he* does not fail to be noticed. But up to what point and to what extent a man must deviate before he becomes blameworthy it is not easy to determine by reasoning, any more than anything else that is perceived by the senses; such things depend on particular facts, and the decision rests with perception. So much,

then, is plain, that the intermediate state is in all things to be praised, but that we must incline sometimes towards the excess, sometimes towards the deficiency; for so shall we most easily hit the mean and what is right.

Book III

Since virtue is concerned with passions and actions, and on voluntary passions and actions praise and blame are bestowed, on those that are involuntary pardon, and sometimes also pity, to distinguish the voluntary and the involuntary is presumably necessary for those who are studying the nature of virtue, and useful also for legislators with a view to the assigning both of honours and of punishments.

Those things, then, are thought involuntary, which take place under compulsion or owing to ignorance; and that is compulsory of which the moving principle is outside, being a principle in which nothing is contributed by the person who is acting or is feeling the passion, e.g. if he were to be carried somewhere by a wind, or by men who had him in their power.

But with regard to the things that are done from fear of greater evils or for some noble object (e.g. if a tyrant were to order one to do something base, having one's parents and children in his power, and if one did the action they were to be saved, but otherwise would be put to death), it may be debated whether such actions are involuntary or voluntary. Something of the sort happens also with regard to the throwing of goods overboard in a storm; for in the abstract no one throws goods away voluntarily, but on condition of its securing the safety of himself and his crew any sensible man does so. Such actions, then, are mixed, but are more like voluntary actions; for they are worthy of choice at the time when they are done, and the end of an action is relative to the occasion. Both the terms, then, 'voluntary' and 'involuntary,' must be used with reference to the moment of action. Now the man acts voluntarily; for the principle that moves the instrumental parts of the body in such actions is in him, and the things of which the moving principle is in a man himself are in his power to do or not to do. Such actions, therefore, are voluntary, but in the abstract perhaps involuntary; for no one would choose any such act in itself.

For such actions men are sometimes even praised, when they endure something base or painful in return for great and noble objects gained; in the opposite case they are blamed, since to endure the greatest indignities for no noble end or for a trifling end is the mark of an inferior person. On some actions praise indeed is not bestowed, but pardon is, when one does what he ought not under pressure which overstrains human nature and which no one could withstand. But some acts, perhaps, we cannot be forced to do, but ought rather to face death after the most fearful sufferings; for the things that 'forced' Euripides' Alcmaeon to slay his mother seem absurd. It is difficult sometimes to determine what should be chosen at what cost, and what should be endured in return for what gain, and yet more difficult to abide by our decisions; for as a rule what is expected is painful, and what we are forced to do is base, whence praise and blame are bestowed on those who have been compelled or have not.

What sort of acts, then, should be called compulsory? We answer that without qualification actions are so when the cause is in the external circumstances and the agent contributes nothing. But the things that in themselves are involuntary, but now and in return for these gains are worthy of choice, and whose moving principle is in the agent, are in themselves involuntary, but now and in return for these gains voluntary. They are more like voluntary acts; for actions are in the class of particulars, and the particular acts here are voluntary. What sort of things are to be chosen, and in return for what, it is not easy to state; for there are many differences in the particular cases.

But if some one were to say that pleasant and noble objects have a compelling power, forcing us from without, all acts would be for him compulsory; for it is for these objects that all men do everything they do. And those who act under compulsion and unwillingly act with pain, but those who do acts for their pleasantness and nobility do them with pleasure; it is absurd to make external circumstances responsible, and not oneself, as being easily caught by such attractions, and to make oneself responsible for noble acts but the pleasant objects responsible for base acts. The compulsory, then, seems to be that whose moving principle is outside, the person compelled contributing nothing.

Everything that is done by reason of ignorance is *not* voluntary; it is only what produces pain and repentance that is *in*voluntary. For the man who has done something owing to ignorance, and feels not the least vexation at his action, has not acted voluntarily, since he did not know what he was doing, nor yet involuntarily, since he is not pained. Of people, then, who act by reason of ignorance he who repents is thought an involuntary agent, and the man who does not repent may, since he is different, be called a not voluntary agent; for, since he differs from the other, it is better that he should have a name of his own.

Acting by reason of ignorance seems also to be different from acting *in* ignorance; for the man who is drunk or in a rage is thought to act as a result not of ignorance but of one of the causes mentioned, yet not knowingly but in ignorance.

Now every wicked man is ignorant of what he ought to do and what he ought to abstain from, and it is by reason of error of this kind that men become unjust and in general bad; but the term 'involuntary' tends to be used not if a man is ignorant of what is to his advantage—for it is not mistaken purpose that causes involuntary action (it leads rather to wickedness), nor ignorance of the universal (for *that* men are *blamed*), but ignorance of particulars, i.e. of the circumstances of the action and the objects with which it is concerned. For it is on these that both pity and pardon depend, since the person who is ignorant of any of these acts involuntarily.

Perhaps it is just as well, therefore, to determine their nature and number. A man may be ignorant, then, of who he is, what he is doing, what or whom he is acting on, and sometimes also what (e.g. what instrument) he is doing it with, and to what end (e.g. he may think his act will conduce to some one's safety), and how he is doing it (e.g. whether gently or violently). Now of all of these no one could be ignorant unless he were mad, and evidently also he could not be ignorant of the agent; for how could he not know himself? But of what he is doing a man might be ignorant, as for instance people say 'it slipped out of their mouths as they were speaking,' or 'they did not know it was a secret,' as Aeschylus said of the mysteries, or a man might say he 'let it go off when he merely wanted to show its working,' as the man did with the catapult. Again, one might think one's son was an enemy, as Merope did, or that a pointed spear had a button on it, or that a stone was pumice-stone; or one might give a man a draught to save him, and really kill him; or one might want to touch a man, as people do in sparring, and really wound him. The ignorance may relate, then, to any of these things, i.e. of the circumstances of the action, and the man who was ignorant of any of these is thought to have acted involuntarily, and especially if he was ignorant on the most important points; and these are thought to be the circumstances of the action and its end. Further, the doing of an act that is called involuntary in virtue of ignorance of this sort must be painful and involve repentance.

Since that which is done under compulsion or by reason of ignorance is involuntary, the voluntary would seem to be that of which the moving principle is in the agent himself, he being aware of the particular circumstances of the action. Presumably acts done by reason of anger or appetite are not rightly called involuntary. For in the first place, on that showing none of the other animals will act voluntarily, nor will children; and secondly, is it meant that we do not do voluntarily *any* of the acts that are due to appetite or anger, or that we do the noble acts voluntarily and the base acts involuntarily? Is not this absurd, when one and the same thing is the cause? But it would surely be odd to describe as involuntary the things one ought to desire; and we ought both to be angry at certain things and to have an appetite for certain things, e.g. for health and for learning. Also what is involuntary is thought to be painful, but what is in accordance with appetite is thought to be pleasant. Again, what is the difference in respect of involuntariness between errors committed upon calculation and those committed in anger? Both are to be avoided, but the irrational passions are thought not less human than reason is, and therefore also the actions which proceed from anger or appetite are the man's actions. It would be odd, then, to treat them as involuntary.

Both the voluntary and the involuntary having been delimited, we must next discuss choice; for it is thought to be most closely bound up with virtue and to discriminate characters better than actions do.

Choice, then, seems to be voluntary, but not the same thing as the voluntary; the latter extends more widely. For both children and the lower animals share in voluntary action, but not in choice, and acts done on the spur of the moment we describe as voluntary, but not as chosen.

Those who say it is appetite or anger or wish or a kind of opinion do not seem to be right. For choice is not common to irrational creatures as well, but appetite and anger are. Again, the incontinent man acts with appetite, but not with choice; while the continent man on the contrary acts with choice, but not with appetite. Again, appetite is contrary to choice, but not appetite to appetite. Again, appetite relates to the pleasant and the painful, choice neither to the painful nor to the pleasant.

Still less is it anger; for acts due to anger are thought to be less than any others objects of choice.

But neither is it wish, though it seems near to it; for choice cannot relate to impossibles, and if any one said he chose them he would be thought silly; but there may be a wish even for impossibles, e.g. for immortality. And wish may relate to things that could in no way be brought about by one's own efforts, e.g. that a particular actor or athlete should win in a competition; but no one chooses such things, but only the things that he thinks could be brought about by his own efforts. Again, wish relates rather to the end, choice to the means; for instance, we wish to be healthy, but we choose the acts which will make us healthy, and we wish to be happy and say we do, but we cannot well say we choose to be so; for, in general, choice seems to relate to the things that are in our own power.

For this reason, too, it cannot be opinion; for opinion is thought to relate to all kinds of things, no less to eternal things and impossible things than to things in our own power; and it is distinguished by its falsity or truth, not by its badness or goodness, while choice is distinguished rather by these.

Now with opinion in general perhaps no one even says it is identical. But it is not identical even with any kind of opinion; for by choosing what is good or bad we are men of a certain character, which we are not by holding certain opinions. And we choose to get or avoid something good or bad, but we have opinions about what a thing is or whom it is good for or how it is good for him; we can hardly be said to opine to get or avoid anything. And choice is praised for being related to the right object rather than for being rightly related to it, opinion for being truly related to its object. And we choose what we best know to be good, but we opine what we do not quite know; and it is not the same people that are thought to make the best choices and to have the best opinions, but some are thought to have fairly good opinions, but by reason of vice to choose what they should not. If opinion precedes choice or accompanies it, that makes no difference; for it is not this that we are considering, but whether it is *identical* with some kind of opinion.

What, then, or what kind of thing is it, since it is none of the things we have mentioned? It seems to be voluntary, but not all that is voluntary to be an object of choice. Is it, then, what has been decided on by previous deliberation? At any rate choice involves a rational principle and thought. Even the name seems to suggest that it is what is chosen before other things.

Do we deliberate about everything, and is everything a possible subject of deliberation, or is deliberation impossible about some things? We ought presumably to call not what a fool or a madman would deliberate about, but what a sensible man would deliberate about, a subject of deliberation. Now about eternal things no one deliberates, e.g. about the material universe or the incommensurability of the diagonal and the side of a square. But no more do we deliberate about the things that involve movement but always happen in the same way, whether of necessity or by nature or from any other cause, e.g. the solstices and the risings of the stars; nor about things that happen now in one way, now in another, e.g. droughts and rains; nor about chance events, like the finding of treasure. But we do not deliberate even about all human affairs; for instance, no Spartan deliberates about the best constitution for the Scythians. For none of these things can be brought about by our own efforts.

We deliberate about things that are in our power and can be done; and these are in fact what is left. For nature, necessity, and chance are thought to be causes, and also reason and everything that depends on man. Now every class of men deliberates about the things that can be done by their own efforts. And in the case of exact and self-contained sciences there is no deliberation, e.g. about the letters of the alphabet (for we have no doubt how they should be written); but the things that are brought about by our own efforts, but not always in the same way, are the things about which we deliberate, e.g. questions of medical treatment or of money-making. And we do

so more in the case of the art of navigation than in that of gymnastics, inasmuch as it has been less exactly worked out, and again about other things in the same ratio, and more also in the case of the arts than in that of the sciences; for we have more doubt about the former. Deliberation is concerned with things that happen in a certain way for the most part, but in which the event is obscure, and with things in which it is indeterminate. We call in others to aid us in deliberation on important questions, distrusting ourselves as not being equal to deciding.

We deliberate not about ends but about means. For a doctor does not deliberate whether he shall heal, nor an orator whether he shall persuade, nor a statesman whether he shall produce law and order, nor does any one else deliberate about his end. They assume the end and consider how and by what means it is to be attained; and if it seems to be produced by several means they consider by which it is most easily and best produced, while if it is achieved by one only they consider how it will be achieved by this and by what means *this* will be achieved, till they come to the first cause, which in the order of discovery is last. For the person who deliberates seems to investigate and analyse in the way described as though he were analysing a geometrical construction (not all investigation appears to be deliberation—for instance mathematical investigations—but all deliberation is investigation), and what is last in the order of analysis seems to be first in the order of becoming. And if we come on an impossibility, we give up the search, e.g. if we need money and this cannot be got; but if a thing appears possible we try to do it. By 'possible' things I mean things that might be brought about by our own efforts; and these in a sense include things that can be brought about by the efforts of our friends, since the moving principle is in ourselves. The subject of investigation is sometimes the instruments, sometimes the use of them; and similarly in the other cases—sometimes the means, sometimes the mode of using it or the means of bringing it about. It seems, then, as has been said, that man is a moving principle of actions; now deliberation is about the things to be done by the agent himself, and actions are for the sake of things other than themselves. For the end cannot be a subject of deliberation, but only the means; nor indeed can the particular facts be a subject of it, as whether this is bread or has been baked as it should; for these are matters of perception. If we are to be always deliberating, we shall have to go on to infinity.

The same thing is deliberated upon and is chosen, except that the object of choice is already determinate, since it is that which has been decided upon as a result of deliberation that is the object of choice. For every one ceases to inquire how he is to act when he has brought the moving principle back to himself and to the ruling part of himself; for this is what chooses. This is plain also from the ancient constitutions, which Homer represented; for the kings announced their choices to the people. The object of choice being one of the things in our own power which is desired after deliberation, choice will be deliberate desire of things in our own power; for when we have decided as a result of deliberation, we desire in accordance with our deliberation.

We may take it, then, that we have described choice in outline, and stated the nature of its objects and the fact that it is concerned with means.

That *wish* is for the end has already been stated; some think it is for the good, others for the apparent good. Now those who say that the good is the object of wish must admit in consequence that that which the man who does not choose aright wishes for is not an object of wish (for if it is to be so, it must also be good; but it was, if it so happened, bad); while those who say the apparent good is the object of wish must admit that there is no natural object of wish, but only what seems good to each man. Now different things appear good to different people, and, if it so happens, even contrary things.

If these consequences are unpleasing, are we to say that absolutely and in truth the good is the object of wish, but for each person the apparent good; that that which is in truth an object of wish is an object of wish to the good man, while any chance thing may be so to the bad man, as in the case of bodies also the things that are in truth wholesome are wholesome for bodies which are in good condition, while for those that are diseased other things are wholesome—or bitter or sweet or hot or heavy, and so on; since the good man judges each class of things rightly, and in each the truth appears to him? For each state of character has its own ideas of the noble and the pleasant, and perhaps the good man differs from others most by seeing the truth in each class of things, being as it were the norm and measure of them. In most things the error seems to be due to

pleasure; for it appears a good when it is not. We therefore choose the pleasant as a good, and avoid pain as an evil.

The end, then, being what we wish for, the means what we deliberate about and choose, actions concerning means must be according to choice and voluntary. Now the exercise of the virtues is concerned with means. Therefore virtue also is in our own power, and so too vice. For where it is in our power to act it is also in our power not to act, and *vice versa*; so that, if to act, where this is noble, is in our power, not to act, which will be base, will also be in our power, and if not to act, where this is noble, is in our power, to act, which will be base, will also be in our power. Now if it is in our power to do noble or base acts, and likewise in our power not to do them, and this was what being good or bad meant, then it is in our power to be virtuous or vicious.

The saying that 'no one is voluntarily wicked nor involuntarily happy' seems to be partly false and partly true; for no one is involuntarily happy, but wickedness *is* voluntary. Or else we shall have to dispute what has just been said, at any rate, and deny that man is a moving principle or begetter of his actions as of children. But if these facts are evident and we cannot refer actions to moving principles other than those in ourselves, the acts whose moving principles are in us must themselves also be in our power and voluntary.

Witness seems to be borne to this both by individuals in their private capacity and by legislators themselves; for these punish and take vengeance on those who do wicked acts (unless they have acted under compulsion or as a result of ignorance for which they are not themselves responsible), while they honour those who do noble acts, as though they meant to encourage the latter and deter the former. But no one is encouraged to do the things that are neither in our power nor voluntary; it is assumed that there is no gain in being persuaded not to be hot or in pain or hungry or the like, since we shall experience these feelings none the less. Indeed, we punish a man for his very ignorance, if he is thought responsible for the ignorance, as when penalties are doubled in the case of drunkenness; for the moving principle is in the man himself, since he had the power of not getting drunk and his getting drunk was the cause of his ignorance. And we punish those who are ignorant of anything in the laws that they ought to know and that is not difficult, and so too in the case of anything else that they are thought to be ignorant of through carelessness; we assume that it is in their power not to be ignorant, since they have the power of taking care.

But perhaps a man is the kind of man not to take care. Still they are themselves by their slack lives responsible for becoming men of that kind, and men make themselves responsible for being unjust or self-indulgent, in the one case by cheating and in the other by spending their time in drinking bouts and the like; for it is activities exercised on particular objects that make the corresponding character. This is plain from the case of people training for any contest or action; they practise the activity the whole time. Now not to know that it is from the exercise of activities on particular objects that states of character are produced is the mark of a thoroughly senseless person. Again, it is irrational to suppose that a man who acts unjustly does not wish to be unjust or a man who acts self-indulgently to be self-indulgent. But if *without* being ignorant a man does the things which will make him unjust, he will be unjust voluntarily. Yet it does not follow that if he wishes he will cease to be unjust and will be just. For neither does the man who is ill become well on those terms. We may suppose a case in which he is ill voluntarily, through living incontinently and disobeying his doctors. In that case it was *then* open to him not to be ill, but not now, when he has thrown away his chance, just as when you have let a stone go it is too late to recover it; but yet it was in your power to throw it, since the moving principle was in you. So, too, to the unjust and to the self-indulgent man it was open at the beginning not to become men of this kind, and so they are unjust and self-indulgent voluntarily; but now that they have become so it is not possible for them not to be so.

But not only are the vices of the soul voluntary, but those of the body also for some men, whom we accordingly blame; while no one blames those who are ugly by nature, we blame those who are so owing to want of exercise and care. So it is, too, with respect to weakness and infirmity; no one would reproach a man blind from birth or by disease or from a blow, but rather pity him, while every one would blame a man who was blind from drunkenness or some other form of self-indulgence. Of vices of the body, then, those in our own power are blamed,

those not in our power are not. And if this be so, in the other cases also the vices that are blamed must be in our own power.

Now some one may say that all men desire the apparent good, but have no control over the appearance, but the end appears to each man in a form answering to his character. We reply that if each man is somehow responsible for his state of mind, he will also be himself somehow responsible for the appearance; but if not, no one is responsible for his own evildoing, but every one does evil acts through ignorance of the end, thinking that by these he will get what is best, and the aiming at the end is not self-chosen but one must be born with an eye, as it were, by which to judge rightly and choose what is truly good, and he is well endowed by nature who is well endowed with this. For it is what is greatest and most noble, and what we cannot get or learn from another, but must have just such as it was when given us at birth, and to be well and nobly endowed with this will be perfect and true excellence of natural endowment. If this is true, then, how will virtue be more voluntary than vice? To both men alike, the good and the bad, the end appears and is fixed by nature or however it may be, and it is by referring everything else to this that men do whatever they do.

Whether, then, it is not by nature that the end appears to each man such as it does appear, but something also depends on him, or the end is natural but because the good man adopts the means voluntarily virtue is voluntary, vice also will be none the less voluntary; for in the case of the bad man there is equally present that which depends on himself in his actions even if not in his end. If, then, as is asserted, the virtues are voluntary (for we are ourselves somehow partly responsible for our states of character, and it is by being persons of a certain kind that we assume the end to be so and so), the vices also will be voluntary; for the same is true of them.

With regard to the virtues in *general* we have stated their genus in outline, viz. that they are means and that they are states of character, and that they tend, and by their own nature, to the doing of the acts by which they are produced, and that they are in our power and voluntary, and act as the right rule prescribes. But actions and states of character are not voluntary in the same way; for we are masters of our actions from the beginning right to the end, if we know the particular facts, but though we control the beginning of our states of character the gradual progress is not obvious, any more than it is in illnesses; because it was in our power, however, to act in this way or not in this way, therefore the states are voluntary.

Let us take up the several virtues, however, and say which they are and what sort of things they are concerned with and how they are concerned with them; at the same time it will become plain how many they are. And first let us speak of courage.

That it is a mean with regard to feelings of fear and of confidence has already been made evident; and plainly the things we fear are terrible things, and these are, to speak without qualification, evils; for which reason people even define fear as expectation of evil. Now we fear all evils, e.g. disgrace, poverty, disease, friendlessness, death, but the brave man is not thought to be concerned with all; for to fear some things is even right and noble, and it is base not to fear them—e.g. disgrace; he who fears this is good and modest, and he who does not is shameless. He is, however, by some people called brave, by a transference of the word to a new meaning; for he has in him something which is like the brave man, since the brave man also is a fearless person. Poverty and disease we perhaps ought not to fear, nor in general the things that do not proceed from vice and are not due to a man himself. But not even the man who is fearless of these is brave. Yet we apply the word to him also in virtue of a similarity; for some who in the dangers of war are cowards are liberal and are confident in face of the loss of money. Nor is a man a coward if he fears insult to his wife and children or envy or anything of the kind; nor brave if he is confident when he is about to be flogged. With what sort of terrible things, then, is the brave man concerned? Surely with the greatest; for no one is more likely than he to stand his ground against what is awe-inspiring. Now death is the most terrible of all things; for it is the end, and nothing is thought to be any longer either good or bad for the dead. But the brave man would not seem to be concerned even with death in *all* circumstances, e.g. at sea or in disease. In what circumstances, then? Surely in the noblest. Now such deaths are those in battle; for these take place in the greatest and noblest danger. And these are correspondingly honoured in city-states and at the courts of monarchs. Properly, then, he will be called brave who is fearless in face of a noble death, and of all emergen-

cies that involve death; and the emergencies of war are in the highest degree of this kind. Yet at sea also, and in disease, the brave man is fearless, but not in the same way as the seamen; for he has given up hope of safety, and is disliking the thought of death in this shape, while they are hopeful because of their experience. At the same time, we show courage in situations where there is the opportunity of showing prowess or where death is noble; but in these forms of death neither of these conditions is fulfilled.

What is terrible is not the same for all men; but we say there are things terrible even beyond human strength. These, then, are terrible to every one—at least to every sensible man; but the terrible things that are *not* beyond human strength differ in magnitude and degree, and so too do the things that inspire confidence. Now the brave man is as dauntless as man may be. Therefore, while he will fear even the things that are not beyond human strength, he will face them as he ought and as the rule directs, for honour's sake; for this is the end of virtue. But it is possible to fear these more, or less, and again to fear things that are not terrible as if they were. Of the faults that are committed one consists in fearing what one should not, another in fearing as we should not, another in fearing when we should not, and so on; and so too with respect to the things that inspire confidence. The man, then, who faces and who fears the right things and from the right motive, in the right way and at the right time, and who feels confidence under the corresponding conditions, is brave; for the brave man feels and acts according to the merits of the case and in whatever way the rule directs. Now the end of every activity is conformity to the corresponding state of character. This is true, therefore, of the brave man as well as of others. But courage is noble. Therefore the end also is noble; for each thing is defined by its end. Therefore it is for a noble end that the brave man endures and acts as courage directs.

Of those who go to excess he who exceeds in fearlessness has no name (we have said previously that many states of character have no names), but he would be a sort of madman or insensible person if he feared nothing, neither earthquakes nor the waves, as they say the Celts do not; while the man who exceeds in confidence about what really is terrible is rash. The rash man, however, is also thought to be boastful and only a pretender to courage; at all events, as the brave man *is* with regard to what is terrible, so the rash man wishes to *appear;* and so he imitates him in situations where he can. Hence also most of them are a mixture of rashness and cowardice; for, while in these situations they display confidence, they do not hold their ground against what is really terrible. The man who exceeds in fear is a coward; for he fears both what he ought not and as he ought not, and all the similar characterizations attach to him. He is lacking also in confidence; but he is more conspicuous for his excess of fear in painful situations. The coward, then, is a despairing sort of person; for he fears everything. The brave man, on the other hand, has the opposite disposition; for confidence is the mark of a hopeful disposition. The coward, the rash man, and the brave man, then, are concerned with the same objects but are differently disposed towards them; for the first two exceed and fall short, while the third holds the middle, which is the right, position; and rash men are precipitate, and wish for dangers beforehand but draw back when they are in them, while brave men are keen in the moment of action, but quiet beforehand.

As we have said, then, courage is a mean with respect to things that inspire confidence or fear, in the circumstances that have been stated; and it chooses or endures things because it is noble to do so, or because it is base not to do so. But to die to escape from poverty or love or anything painful is not the mark of a brave man, but rather of a coward; for it is softness to fly from what is troublesome, and such a man endures death not because it is noble but to fly from evil.

Courage, then, is something of this sort, but the name is also applied to five other kinds. (1) First comes the courage of the citizen-soldier; for this is most like true courage. Citizen-soldiers seem to face dangers because of the penalties imposed by the laws and the reproaches they would otherwise incur, and because of the honours they win by such action; and therefore those peoples seem to be bravest among whom cowards are held in dishonour and brave men in honour. This is the kind of courage that Homer depicts, e.g. in Diomede and in Hector:

First will Polydamas be to heap reproach on me then; and

For Hector one day 'mid the Trojans shall utter
 his vaulting harangue:

"Afraid was Tydeides, and fled from my face."

This kind of courage is most like to that which we described earlier, because it is due to virtue; for it is due to shame and to desire of a noble object (i.e. honour) and avoidance of disgrace, which is ignoble. One might rank in the same class even those who are compelled by their rulers; but they are inferior, inasmuch as they do what they do not from shame but from fear, and to avoid not what is disgraceful but what is painful; for their masters compel them, as Hector does:

But if I shall spy any dastard that cowers far from the
 fight,
Vainly will such an one hope to escape from the dogs.

And those who give them their posts, and beat them if they retreat, do the same, and so do those who draw them up with trenches or something of the sort behind them; all of these apply compulsion. But one ought to be brave not under compulsion but because it is noble to be so.

(2) Experience with regard to particular facts is also thought to be courage; this is indeed the reason why Socrates thought courage was knowledge. Other people exhibit this quality in other dangers, and professional soldiers exhibit it in the dangers of war, for there seem to be many empty alarms in war, of which these have had the most comprehensive experience; therefore they seem brave, because the others do not know the nature of the facts. Again, their experience makes them most capable in attack and in defense, since they can use their arms and have the kind that are likely to be best both for attack and for defense; therefore they fight like armed men against unarmed or like trained athletes against amateurs; for in such contests too it is not the bravest men that fight best, but those who are strongest and have their bodies in the best condition. Professional soldiers turn cowards, however, when the danger puts too great a strain on them and they are inferior in numbers and equipment; for they are the first to fly, while citizen-forces die at their posts, as in fact happened at the temple of Hermes. For to the latter flight is disgraceful and death is preferable to safety on those terms; while the former from the very beginning faced the danger on the assumption that they were stronger, and when they know the facts they fly, fearing death more than disgrace; but the brave man is not that sort of person.

(3) Passion also is sometimes reckoned as courage; those who act from passion, like wild beasts rushing at those who have wounded them, are thought to be brave, because brave men also are passionate; for passion above all things is eager to rush on danger, and hence Homer's 'put strength into his passion' and 'aroused their spirit and passion' and 'hard he breathed panting' and 'his blood boiled.' For all such expressions seem to indicate the stirring and onset of passion. Now brave men act for honour's sake, but passion aids them; while wild beasts act under the influence of pain; for they attack because they have been wounded or because they are afraid, since if they are in a forest they do not come near one. Thus they are not brave because, driven by pain and passion, they rush on danger without foreseeing any of the perils, since at that rate even asses would be brave when they are hungry; for blows will not drive them from their food; and lust also makes adulterers do many daring things. [Those creatures are not brave, then, which are driven on to danger by pain or passion.] The 'courage' that is due to passion seems to be the most natural, and to be courage if choice and motive be added.

Men, then, as well as beasts, suffer pain when they are angry, and are pleased when they exact their revenge; those who fight for these reasons, however, are pugnacious but not brave; for they do not act for honour's sake nor as the rule directs, but from strength of feeling; they have, however, something akin to courage.

(4) Nor are sanguine people brave; for they are confident in danger only because they have conquered often and against many foes. Yet they closely resemble brave men, because both are confident; but brave men are confident for the reasons stated earlier, while these are so because they think they are the strongest and can suffer nothing. (Drunken men also behave in this way; they become sanguine.) When their adventures do not succeed, however, they run away; but it was the mark of a brave man to face things that are, and seem, terrible for a man, because it is noble to do so and disgraceful not to do so. Hence also it is thought the mark of a braver man to be fearless and undisturbed in sudden alarms than to be so in those that are foreseen; for it must have proceeded more from a state of character, because less from preparation; acts that are foreseen may be chosen by calculation and rule, but sudden actions must be in accordance with one's state of character.

(5) People who are ignorant of the danger also appear brave, and they are not far removed from those of a sanguine temper, but are inferior inasmuch as they have no self-reliance while these have. Hence also the sanguine hold their ground for a time; but those who have been deceived about the facts fly if they know or suspect that these are different from what they supposed, as happened to the Argives when they fell in with the Spartans and took them for Sicyonians.

We have, then, described the character both of brave men and of those who are thought to be brave.

Though courage is concerned with feelings of confidence and of fear, it is not concerned with both alike, but more with the things that inspire fear; for he who is undisturbed in face of these and bears himself as he should towards these is more truly brave than the man who does so towards the things that inspire confidence. It is for facing what is painful, then, as has been said, that men are called brave. Hence also courage involves pain, and is justly praised; for it is harder to face what is painful than to abstain from what is pleasant. Yet the end which courage sets before it would seem to be pleasant, but to be concealed by the attending circumstances, as happens also in athletic contests; for the end at which boxers aim is pleasant—the crown and the honours—but the blows they take are distressing to flesh and blood, and painful, and so is their whole exertion; and because the blows and the exertions are many the end, which is but small, appears to have nothing pleasant in it. And so, if the case of courage is similar, death and wounds will be painful to the brave man and against his will, but he will face them because it is noble to do so or because it is base not to do so. And the more he is possessed of virtue in its entirety and the happier he is, the more he will be pained at the thought of death; for life is best worth living for such a man, and he is knowingly losing the greatest goods, and this is painful. But he is none the less brave, and perhaps all the more so, because he chooses noble deeds of war at that cost. It is not the case, then, with all the virtues that the exercise of them is pleasant, except in so far as it reaches its end. But it is quite possible that the best soldiers may be not men of this sort but those who are less brave but have no other good; for these are ready to face danger, and they sell their life for trifling gains.

So much, then, for courage; it is not difficult to grasp its nature in outline, at any rate, from what has been said.

After courage let us speak of temperance; for these seem to be the virtues of the irrational parts. We have said that temperance is a mean with regard to pleasures (for it is less, and not in the same way, concerned with pains); self-indulgence also is manifested in the same sphere. Now, therefore, let us determine with what sort of pleasures they are concerned. We may assume the distinction between bodily pleasures and those of the soul, such as love of honour and love of learning; for the lover of each of these delights in that of which he is a lover, the body being in no way affected, but rather the mind; but men who are concerned with such pleasures are called neither temperate nor self-indulgent. Nor, again, are those who are concerned with the other pleasures that are not bodily; for those who are fond of hearing and telling stories and who spend their days on anything that turns up are called gossips, but not self-indulgent, nor are those who are pained at the loss of money or of friends.

Temperance must be concerned with bodily pleasures, but not all even of these; for those who delight in objects of vision, such as colours and shapes and painting, are called neither temperate nor self-indulgent; yet it would seem possible to delight even in these either as one should or to excess or to a deficient degree.

And so too is it with objects of hearing; no one calls those who delight extravagantly in music or acting self-indulgent, nor those who do so as they ought temperate.

Nor do we apply these names to those who delight in odour, unless it be incidentally; we do not call those self-indulgent who delight in the odour of apples or roses or incense, but rather those who delight in the odour of unguents or of dainty dishes; for self-indulgent people delight in these because these remind them of the objects of their appetite. And one may see even other people, when they are hungry, delighting in the smell of food; but to delight in this kind of thing is the mark of the self-indulgent man; for these are objects of appetite to him.

Nor is there in animals other than man any pleasure connected with these senses, except incidentally. For dogs do not delight in the scent of hares, but in the eating of them, but the scent told them the hares were there; nor does the lion delight in the lowing of the ox, but in eating it; but he perceived by the lowing that it was near, and therefore appears to delight in the lowing; and similarly he does not delight because he sees 'a stag or a wild goat,' but because he is going to make a meal of it. Temperance and self-indulgence, however, are concerned with the kind of pleasures that the other animals share in, which therefore appear slavish and brutish; these are touch and taste. But even of taste they appear to make little or no use; for the business of taste is the discriminating of flavours, which is done by wine-tasters and people who season dishes; but they hardly take pleasure in making these discriminations, or at least self-indulgent people do not, but in the actual enjoyment, which in all cases comes through touch, both in the case of food and in that of drink and in that of sexual intercourse. This is why a certain gourmand prayed that his throat might become longer than a crane's, implying that it was the contact that he took pleasure in. Thus the sense with which self-indulgence is connected is the most widely shared of the senses; and self-indulgence would seem to be justly a matter of reproach, because it attaches to us not as men but as animals. To delight in such things, then, and to love them above all others, is brutish. For even of the pleasures of touch the most liberal have been eliminated, e.g. those produced in the gymnasium by rubbing and by the consequent heat; for the contact characteristic of the self-indulgent man does not affect the whole body but only certain parts.

Of the appetites some seem to be common, others to be peculiar to individuals and acquired; e.g. the appetite for food is natural, since every one who is without it craves for food or drink, and sometimes for both, and for love also (as Homer says) if he is young and lusty; but not every one craves for this or that kind of nourishment or love, nor for the same things. Hence such craving appears to be our very own. Yet it has of course something natural about it; for different things are pleasant to different kinds of people, and some things are more pleasant to every one than chance objects. Now in the natural appetites few go wrong, and only in one direction, that of excess; for to eat or drink whatever offers itself till one is surfeited is to exceed the natural amount, since natural appetite is the replenishment of one's deficiency. Hence these people are called belly-gods, this implying that they fill their belly beyond what is right. It is people of entirely slavish character that become like this. But with regard to the pleasures peculiar to individuals many people go wrong and in many ways. For while the people who are 'fond of so and so' are so called because they delight either in the wrong things, or more than most people do, or in the wrong way, the self-indulgent exceed in all three ways; they both delight in some things that they ought not to delight in (since they are hateful), and if one ought to delight in some of the things they delight in, they do so more than one ought and than most men do.

Plainly, then, excess with regard to pleasures is self-indulgence and is culpable; with regard to pains one is not, as in the case of courage, called temperate for facing them or self-indulgent for not doing so, but the self-indulgent man is so called because he is pained more than he ought at not getting pleasant things (even his pain being caused by pleasure), and the temperate man is so called because he is not pained at the absence of what is pleasant and at his abstinence from it.

The self-indulgent man, then, craves for all pleasant things or those that are most pleasant, and is led by his appetite to choose these at the cost of everything else; hence he is pained both when he fails to get them and when he is merely craving for them (for appetite involves pain); but it seems absurd to be pained for the sake of pleasure. People who fall short with regard to pleasures and delight in them less than they should are hardly found; for such insensibility is not human. Even the other animals distinguish different kinds of food and enjoy some and not others; and if there is any one who finds nothing pleasant and nothing more attractive than anything else, he must be something quite different from a man; this sort of person has not received a name because he hardly occurs. The temperate man occupies a middle position with regard to these objects. For he neither enjoys the things that the self-indulgent man enjoys most—but rather dislikes them—nor in general the things that he should not, nor anything of this sort to excess, nor does he feel pain or craving when they are absent, or does so only to a moderate degree, and not more than he should, nor when he should not, and so on; but the things that,

being pleasant, make for health or for good condition, he will desire moderately and as he should, and also other pleasant things if they are not hindrances to these ends, or contrary to what is noble, or beyond his means. For he who neglects these conditions loves such pleasures more than they are worth, but the temperate man is not that sort of person, but the sort of person that the right rule prescribes.

Self-indulgence is more like a voluntary state than cowardice. For the former is actuated by pleasure, the latter by pain of which the one is to be chosen and the other to be avoided; and pain upsets and destroys the nature of the person who feels it, while pleasure does nothing of the sort. Therefore self-indulgence is more voluntary. Hence also it is more a matter of reproach; for it is easier to become accustomed to its objects, since there are many things of this sort in life, and the process of habituation to them is free from danger, while with terrible objects the reverse is the case. But cowardice would seem to be voluntary in a different degree from its particular manifestations; for it is itself painless, but in these we are upset by pain, so that we even throw down our arms and disgrace ourselves in other ways; hence our acts are even thought to be done under compulsion. For the self-indulgent man, on the other hand, the particular acts are voluntary (for he does them with craving and desire), but the whole state is less so; for no one craves to be self-indulgent.

The name self-indulgence is applied also to childish faults; for they bear a certain resemblance to what we have been considering. Which is called after which, makes no difference to our present purpose; plainly, however, the later is called after the earlier. The transference of the name seems not a bad one; for that which desires what is base and which develops quickly ought to be kept in a chastened condition, and these characteristics belong above all to appetite and to the child, since children in fact live at the beck and call of appetite, and it is in them that the desire for what is pleasant is strongest. If, then, it is not going to be obedient and subject to the ruling principle, it will go to great lengths; for in an irrational being the desire for pleasure is insatiable even if it tries every source of gratification, and the exercise of appetite increases its innate force, and if appetites are strong and violent they even expel the power of calculation. Hence they should be moderate and few, and should in no way oppose the rational principle—and this is what we call an obedient and chastened state—and as the child should live according to the direction of his tutor, so the appetitive element should live according to rational principle. Hence the appetitive element in a temperate man should harmonize with the rational principle; for the noble is the mark at which both aim, and the temperate man craves for the things he ought, as he ought, and when he ought; and this is what rational principle directs.

Here we conclude our account of temperance.

. . .

Book VI

Since we have previously said that one ought to choose that which is intermediate, not the excess nor the defect, and that the intermediate is determined by the dictates of the right rule, let us discuss the nature of these dictates. In all the states of character we have mentioned, as in all other matters, there is a mark to which the man who has the rule looks, and heightens or relaxes his activity accordingly, and there is a standard which determines the mean states which we say are intermediate between excess and defect, being in accordance with the right rule. But such a statement, though true, is by no means clear; for not only here but in all other pursuits which are objects of knowledge it is indeed true to say that we must not exert ourselves nor relax our efforts too much nor too little, but to an intermediate extent and as the right rule dictates; but if a man had only this knowledge he would be none the wiser—e.g. we should not know what sort of medicines to apply to our body if some one were to say 'all those which the medical art prescribes, and which agree with the practice of one who possesses the art.' Hence it is necessary with regard to the states of the soul also not only that this true statement should be made, but also that it should be determined what is the right rule and what is the standard that fixes it.

We divided the virtues of the soul and said that some are virtues of character and others of intellect. Now we have discussed in detail the moral virtues; with regard to the others let us express our view as follows, beginning with some remarks about the soul. We said before that there are two parts of the soul—that which grasps a rule or rational principle, and the irrational; let us now draw a similar distinc-

tion within the part which grasps a rational principle. And let it be assumed that there are two parts which grasp a rational principle—one by which we contemplate the kind of things whose originative causes are invariable, and one by which we contemplate variable things; for where objects differ in kind the part of the soul answering to each of the two is different in kind, since it is in virtue of a certain likeness and kinship with their objects that they have the knowledge they have. Let one of these parts be called the scientific and the other the calculative; for to deliberate and to calculate are the same thing, but no one deliberates about the invariable. Therefore the calculative is one part of the faculty which grasps rational principles. We must, then, learn what is the best state of each of these two parts; for this is the virtue of each.

The virtue of a thing is relative to its proper work. Now there are three things in the soul which control action and truth—sensation, reason, desire.

Of these sensation originates no action; this is plain from the fact that the lower animals have sensation but no share in action.

What affirmation and negation are in thinking, pursuit and avoidance are in desire; so that since moral virtue is a state of character concerned with choice, and choice is deliberate desire, therefore both the reasoning must be true and the desire right, if the choice is to be good, and the latter must pursue just what the former asserts. Now this kind of intellect and of truth is practical; of the intellect which is contemplative, not practical nor productive, the good and the bad state are truth and falsity respectively (for this is the work of everything intellectual); while of the part which is practical and intellectual the good state is truth in agreement with right desire.

The origin of action—its efficient, not its final cause—is choice, and that of choice is desire and reasoning with a view to an end. This is why choice cannot exist either without reason and intellect or without a moral state; for good action and its opposite cannot exist without a combination of intellect and character. Intellect itself, however, moves nothing, but only the intellect which aims at an end and is practical; for this rules the productive intellect as well, since every one who makes makes for an end, and that which is made is not an end in the unqualified sense (but only an end in a particular relation, and the end of a particular operation)—only that which is *done* is that; for good action is an end, and desire aims at this. Hence choice is either desiderative reason or ratiocinative desire, and such an origin of action is a man. (It is to be noted that nothing that is past is an object of choice, e.g. no one chooses to have sacked Troy;. for no one *deliberates* about the past, but about what is future and capable of being otherwise, while what is past is not capable of not having taken place; hence Agathon is right in saying

> For this alone is lacking even to God,
> To make undone things that have once been done.)

The work of both the intellectual parts, then, is truth. Therefore the states that are most strictly those in respect of which each of these parts will reach truth are the virtues of the two parts.

Let us begin, then, from the beginning, and discuss these states once more. Let it be assumed that the states by virtue of which the soul possesses truth by way of affirmation or denial are five in number, i.e. art, scientific knowledge, practical wisdom, philosophic wisdom, intuitive reason; we do not include judgement and opinion because in these we may be mistaken.

Now what *scientific knowledge* is, if we are to speak exactly and not follow mere similarities, is plain from what follows. We all suppose that what we know is not even capable of being otherwise; of things capable of being otherwise we do not know, when they have passed outside our observation, whether they exist or not. Therefore the object of scientific knowledge is of necessity. Therefore it is eternal; for things that are of necessity in the unqualified sense are all eternal; and things that are eternal are ungenerated and imperishable. Again, every science is thought to be capable of being taught, and its object of being learned. And all teaching starts from what is already known, as we maintain in the *Analytics* also; for it proceeds sometimes through induction and sometimes by syllogism. Now induction is the starting-point which knowledge even of the universal presupposes, while syllogism proceeds *from* universals. There are therefore starting-points from which syllogism proceeds, which are not reached by syllogism; it is therefore by induction that they are acquired. Scientific knowledge is, then, a state of capacity to demonstrate, and has the other limiting characteristics which we specify in the *Analytics;* for

it is when a man believes in a certain way and the starting-points are known to him that he has scientific knowledge, since if they are not better known to him than the conclusion, he will have his knowledge only incidentally.

Let this, then, be taken as our account of scientific knowledge.

In the variable are included both things made and things done; making and acting are different (for their nature we treat even the discussions outside our school as reliable); so that the reasoned state of capacity to act is different from the reasoned state of capacity to make. Hence too they are not included one in the other; for neither is acting making nor is making acting. Now since architecture is an art and is essentially a reasoned state of capacity to make, and there is neither any art that is not such a state nor any such state that is not an art, *art* is identical with a state of capacity to make, involving a true course of reasoning. All art is concerned with coming into being, i.e. with contriving and considering how something may come into being which is capable of either being or not being, and whose origin is in the maker and not in the thing made; for art is concerned neither with things that are, or come into being, by necessity, nor with things that do so in accordance with nature (since these have their origin in themselves). Making and acting being different, art must be a matter of making, not of acting. And in a sense chance and art are concerned with the same objects; as Agathon says, 'art loves chance and chance loves art.' Art, then, as has been said, is a state concerned with making, involving a true course of reasoning, and lack of art on the contrary is a state concerned with making, involving a false course of reasoning; both are concerned with the variable.

Regarding *practical wisdom* we shall get at the truth by considering who are the persons we credit with it. Now it is thought to be the mark of a man of practical wisdom to be able to deliberate well about what is good and expedient for himself, not in some particular respect, e.g. about what sorts of thing conduce to health or to strength, but about what sorts of thing conduce to the good life in general. This is shown by the fact that we credit men with practical wisdom in some particular respect when they have calculated well with a view to some good end which is one of those that are not the object of any art. It follows that in the general sense also the man who is capable of deliberating has practical wisdom. Now no one deliberates about things that are invariable, nor about things that it is impossible for him to do. Therefore, since scientific knowledge involves demonstration, but there is no demonstration of things whose first principles are variable (for all such things might actually be otherwise), and since it is impossible to deliberate about things that are of necessity, practical wisdom cannot be scientific knowledge nor art; not science because that which can be done is capable of being otherwise, not art because action and making are different kinds of thing. The remaining alternative, then, is that it is a true and reasoned state of capacity to act with regard to the things that are good or bad for man. For while making has an end other than itself, action cannot; for good action itself is its end. It is for this reason that we think Pericles and men like him have practical wisdom, viz. because they can see what is good for themselves and what is good for men in general; we consider that those can do this who are good at managing households or states. (This is why we call temperance (σωφροσύνη) by this name; we imply that it preserves one's practical wisdom (σῴζουσα τὴν φρόνησιν). Now what it preserves is a judgement of the kind we have described. For it is not any and every judgement that pleasant and painful objects destroy and pervert, e.g. the judgement that the triangle has or has not its angles equal to two right angles, but only judgements about what is to be done. For the originating causes of the things that are done consist in the end at which they are aimed; but the man who has been ruined by pleasure or pain forthwith fails to see any such originating cause—to see that for the sake of this or because of this he ought to choose and do whatever he chooses and does; for vice is destructive of the originating cause of action.)

Practical wisdom, then, must be a reasoned and true state of capacity to act with regard to human goods. But further, while there is such a thing as excellence in art, there is no such thing as excellence in practical wisdom; and in art he who errs willingly is preferable, but in practical wisdom, as in the virtues, he is the reverse. Plainly, then, practical wisdom is a virtue and not an art. There being two parts of the soul that can follow a course of reasoning, it must be the virtue of one of the two, i.e. of that part which forms opinions; for opinion is about the variable and so is

practical wisdom. But yet it is not only a reasoned state; this is shown by the fact that a state of that sort may be forgotten but practical wisdom cannot.

Scientific knowledge is judgement about things that are universal and necessary, and the conclusions of demonstration, and all scientific knowledge, follow from first principles (for scientific knowledge involves apprehension of a rational ground). This being so, the first principle from which what is scientifically known follows cannot be an object of scientific knowledge, of art, or of practical wisdom; for that which can be scientifically known can be demonstrated, and art and practical wisdom deal with things that are variable. Nor are these first principles the objects of philosophic wisdom, for it is a mark of the philosopher to have *demonstration* about some things. If, then, the states of mind by which we have truth and are never deceived about things invariable or even variable are scientific knowledge, practical wisdom, philosophic wisdom, and intuitive reason, and it cannot be any of the three (i.e. practical wisdom, scientific knowledge, or philosophic wisdom), the remaining alternative is that it is *intuitive reason* that grasps the first principles.

Wisdom (1) in the arts we ascribe to their most finished exponents, e.g. to Phidias as a sculptor and to Polyclitus as a maker of portrait-statues, and here we mean nothing by wisdom except excellence in art; but (2) we think that some people are wise in general, not in some particular field or in any other limited respect, as Homer says in the *Margites,*

Him did the gods make neither a digger nor yet a
    ploughman
Nor wise in anything else.

Therefore wisdom must plainly be the most finished of the forms of knowledge. It follows that the wise man must not only know what follows from the first principles, but must also possess truth about the first principles. Therefore wisdom must be intuitive reason combined with scientific knowledge—scientific knowledge of the highest objects which has received as it were its proper completion.

Of the highest objects, we say; for it would be strange to think that the art of politics, or practical wisdom, is the best knowledge, since man is not the best thing in the world. Now if what is healthy or good is different for men and for fishes, but what is white or straight is always the same, any one would say that what is wise is the same but what is practically wise is different; for it is to that which observes well the various matters concerning itself that one ascribes practical wisdom, and it is to this that one will entrust such matters. This is why we say that some even of the lower animals have practical wisdom, viz. those which are found to have a power of foresight with regard to their own life. It is evident also that philosophic wisdom and the art of politics cannot be the same; for if the state of mind concerned with a man's own interests is to be called philosophic wisdom, there will be many philosophic wisdoms; there will not be one concerned with the good of all animals (any more than there is one art of medicine for all existing things), but a different philosophic wisdom about the good of each species.

But if the argument be that man is the best of the animals, this makes no difference; for there are other things much more divine in their nature even than man, e.g., most conspicuously, the bodies of which the heavens are framed. From what has been said it is plain, then, that philosophic wisdom is scientific knowledge, combined with intuitive reason, of the things that are highest by nature. This is why we say Anaxagoras, Thales, and men like them have philosophic but not practical wisdom, when we see them ignorant of what is to their own advantage, and why we say that they know things that are remarkable, admirable, difficult, and divine, but useless; viz. because it is not human goods that they seek.

Practical wisdom on the other hand is concerned with things human and things about which it is possible to deliberate; for we say this is above all the work of the man of practical wisdom, to deliberate well, but no one deliberates about things invariable, nor about things which have not an end, and that a good that can be brought about by action. The man who is without qualification good at deliberating is the man who is capable of aiming in accordance with calculation at the best for man of things attainable by action. Nor is practical wisdom concerned with universals only—it must also recognize the particulars; for it is practical, and practice is concerned with particulars. This is why some who do not know, and especially those who have experience, are more practical than others who know; for if a man knew that light meats are digestible and wholesome, but did not know which sorts of meat are light, he would not produce health, but the man who knows that

chicken is wholesome is more likely to produce health.

Now practical wisdom is concerned with action; therefore one should have both forms of it, or the latter in preference to the former. But of practical as of philosophic wisdom there must be a controlling kind.

Political wisdom and practical wisdom are the same state of mind, but their essence is not the same. Of the wisdom concerned with the city, the practical wisdom which plays a controlling part is legislative wisdom, while that which is related to this as particulars to their universal is known by the general name 'political wisdom;' this has to do with action and deliberation, for a decree is a thing to be carried out in the form of an individual act. This is why the exponents of this art are alone said to 'take part in politics;' for these alone 'do things' as manual labourers 'do things.'

Practical wisdom also is identified especially with that form of it which is concerned with a man himself—with the individual; and this is known by the general name 'practical wisdom;' of the other kinds one is called household management, another legislation, the third politics, and of the latter one part is called deliberative and the other judicial. Now knowing what is good for oneself will be one kind of knowledge, but it is very different from the other kinds; and the man who knows and concerns himself with his own interests is thought to have practical wisdom, while politicians are thought to be busybodies; hence the words of Euripides,

> But how could I be wise, who might at ease,
> Numbered among the army's multitude,
> Have had an equal share? . . .
> For those who aim too high and do too much. . . .

Those who think thus seek their own good, and consider that one ought to do so. From this opinion, then, has come the view that such men have practical wisdom; yet perhaps one's own good cannot exist without household management, nor without a form of government. Further, how one should order one's own affairs is not clear and needs inquiry.

What has been said is confirmed by the fact that while young men become geometricians and mathematicians and wise in matters like these, it is thought that a young man of practical wisdom cannot be found. The cause is that such wisdom is concerned not only with universals but with particulars, which become familiar from experience, but a young man has no experience, for it is length of time that gives experience; indeed one might ask this question too, why a boy may become a mathematician, but not a philosopher or a physicist. Is it because the objects of mathematics exist by abstraction, while the first principles of these other subjects come from experience, and because young men have no conviction about the latter but merely use the proper language, while the essence of mathematical objects is plain enough to them?

Further, error in deliberation may be either about the universal or about the particular; we may fail to know either that all water that weighs heavy is bad, or that this particular water weighs heavy.

That practical wisdom is not scientific knowledge is evident; for it is, as has been said, concerned with the ultimate particular fact, since the thing to be done is of this nature. It is opposed, then, to intuitive reason; for intuitive reason is of the limiting premisses, for which no reason can be given, while practical wisdom is concerned with the ultimate particular, which is the object not of scientific knowledge but of perception—not the perception of qualities peculiar to one sense but a perception akin to that by which we perceive that the particular figure before us is a triangle; for in that direction as well as in that of the major premiss there will be a limit. But this is rather perception than practical wisdom, though it is another kind of perception than that of the qualities peculiar to each sense.

There is a difference between inquiry and deliberation; for deliberation is inquiry into a particular kind of thing. We must grasp the nature of excellence in deliberation as well—whether it is a form of scientific knowledge, or opinion, or skill in conjecture, or some other kind of thing. *Scientific knowledge* it is not; for men do not inquire about the things they know about, but good deliberation is a kind of deliberation, and he who deliberates inquires and calculates. Nor is it *skill in conjecture;* for this both involves no reasoning and is something that is quick in its operation, while men deliberate a long time, and they say that one should carry out quickly the conclusions of one's deliberation, but should deliberate slowly. Again, *readiness of mind* is different from excellence in deliberation; it is a sort of skill in conjecture. Nor again is excellence in deliberation *opinion*

of any sort. But since the man who deliberates badly makes a mistake, while he who deliberates well does so correctly, excellence in deliberation is clearly a kind of correctness, but neither of knowledge nor of opinion; for there is no such thing as correctness of knowledge (since there is no such thing as error of knowledge), and correctness of opinion is truth; and at the same time everything that is an object of opinion is already determined. But again excellence in deliberation involves reasoning. The remaining alternative, then, is that it is *correctness of thinking;* for this is not yet assertion, since, while even opinion is not inquiry but has reached the stage of assertion, the man who is deliberating, whether he does so well or ill, is searching for something and calculating.

But excellence in deliberation is a certain correctness of deliberation; hence we must first inquire what deliberation is and what it is about. And, there being more than one kind of correctness, plainly excellence in deliberation is not any and every kind; for (1) the incontinent man and the bad man, if he is clever, will reach as a result of his calculation what he sets before himself, so that he will have deliberated correctly, but he will have got for himself a great evil. Now to have deliberated well is thought to be a good thing; for it is this kind of correctness of deliberation that is excellence in deliberation, viz. that which tends to attain what is good. But (2) it is possible to attain even good by a false syllogism, and to attain what one ought to do but not by the right means, the middle term being false; so that this too is not yet excellence in deliberation—this state in virtue of which one attains what one ought but not by the right means. Again (3) it is possible to attain it by long deliberation while another man attains it quickly. Therefore in the former case we have not yet got excellence in deliberation, which is rightness with regard to the expedient—rightness in respect both of the end, the manner, and the time. (4) Further it is possible to have deliberated well either in the unqualified sense or with reference to a particular end. Excellence in deliberation in the unqualified sense, then, is that which succeeds with reference to what is the end in the unqualified sense, and excellence in deliberation in a particular sense is that which succeeds relatively to a particular end. If, then, it is characteristic of men of practical wisdom to have deliberated well, excellence in deliberation will be correctness with regard to what conduces to the end of which practical wisdom is the true apprehension.

Understanding, also, and goodness of understanding, in virtue of which men are said to be men of understanding or of good understanding, are neither entirely the same as opinion or scientific knowledge (for at that rate all men would have been men of understanding), nor are they one of the particular sciences, such as medicine, the science of things connected with health, or geometry, the science of spatial magnitudes. For understanding is neither about things that are always and are unchangeable, nor about any and every one of the things that come into being, but about things which may become subjects of questioning and deliberation. Hence it is about the same objects as practical wisdom; but understanding and practical wisdom are not the same. For practical wisdom issues commands, since its end is what ought to be done or not to be done; but understanding only judges. (Understanding is identical with goodness of understanding, men of understanding with men of good understanding.) Now understanding is neither the having nor the acquiring of practical wisdom; but as learning is called understanding when it means the exercise of the faculty of knowledge, so 'understanding' is applicable to the exercise of the faculty of opinion for the purpose of judging of what some one else says about matters with which practical wisdom is concerned—and of judging soundly; for 'well' and 'soundly' are the same thing. And from this has come the use of the name 'understanding' in virtue of which men are said to be 'of good understanding,' viz. from the application of the word to the grasping of scientific truth; for we often call such grasping understanding.

What is called judgement, in virtue of which men are said to 'be sympathetic judges' and to 'have judgement,' is the right discrimination of the equitable. This is shown by the fact that we say the equitable man is above all others a man of sympathetic judgement, and identify equity with sympathetic judgement about certain facts. And sympathetic judgement is judgement which discriminates what is equitable and does so correctly; and correct judgement is that which judges what is true.

Now all the states we have considered converge, as might be expected, to the same point; for when we speak of judgement and understanding and practical wisdom and intuitive reason we credit the same people with possessing judgement and having reached years of reason and with having practical wisdom and understanding. For all these faculties deal with ultimates, i.e. with particulars; and being a man of understanding and of good or sympathetic judgement consists in being able to judge about the things with which practical wisdom is concerned; for the equities are common to all good men in relation to other men. Now all things which have to be done are included among particulars or ultimates; for not only must the man of practical wisdom know particular facts, but understanding and judgement are also concerned with things to be done, and these are ultimates. And intuitive reason is concerned with the ultimates in both directions; for both the first terms and the last are objects of intuitive reason and not of argument, and the intuitive reason which is presupposed by demonstrations grasps the unchangeable and first terms, while the intuitive reason involved in practical reasonings grasps the last and variable fact, i.e. the minor premiss. For these variable facts are the starting-points for the apprehension of the end, since the universals are reached from the particulars; of these therefore we must have perception, and this perception is intuitive reason.

This is why these states are thought to be natural endowments—why, while no one is thought to be a philosopher by nature, people are thought to have by nature judgement, understanding, and intuitive reason. This is shown by the fact that we think our powers correspond to our time of life, and that a particular age brings with it intuitive reason and judgement; this implies that nature is the cause. [Hence intuitive reason is both beginning and end; for demonstrations are from these and about these.] Therefore we ought to attend to the undemonstrated sayings and opinions of experienced and older people or of people of practical wisdom not less than to demonstrations; for because experience has given them an eye they see aright.

We have stated, then, what practical and philosophic wisdom are, and with what each of them is concerned, and we have said that each is the virtue of a different part of the soul.

Difficulties might be raised as to the utility of these qualities of mind. For (1) philosophic wisdom will contemplate none of the things that will make a man happy (for it is not concerned with any coming into being), and though practical wisdom has *this* merit, for what purpose do we need it? Practical wisdom is the quality of mind concerned with things just and noble and good for man, but these are the things which it is the mark of a *good* man to do, and we are none the more able to act for *knowing* them if the virtues are states of *character,* just as we are none the better able to act for knowing the things that are healthy and sound, in the sense not of producing but of issuing from the state of health; for we are none the more able to act for having the art of medicine or of gymnastics. But (2) if we are to say that a man should have practical wisdom not for the sake of knowing moral truths but for the sake of becoming good, practical wisdom will be of no use to those who *are* good; but again it is of no use to those who have *not* virtue; for it will make no difference whether they have practical wisdom themselves or obey others who have it, and it would be enough for us to do what we do in the case of health; though we wish to become healthy, yet we do not learn the art of medicine. (3) Besides this, it would be thought strange if practical wisdom, being inferior to philosophic wisdom, is to be put in authority over it, as seems to be implied by the fact that the art which produces anything rules and issues commands about that thing.

These, then, are the questions we must discuss; so far we have only stated the difficulties.

(1) Now first let us say that in themselves these states must be worthy of choice because they are the virtues of the two parts of the soul respectively, even if neither of them produce anything.

(2) Secondly, they do produce something, not as the art of medicine produces health, however, but as health produces health, so does philosophic wisdom produce happiness; for, being a part of virtue entire, by being possessed and by actualizing itself it makes a man happy.

(3) Again, the work of man is achieved only in accordance with practical wisdom as well as with moral virtue; for virtue makes us aim at the right mark, and practical wisdom makes us take the right means. (Of the fourth part of the soul—the nutritive—there is no such virtue; for there is nothing which it is in its power to do or not to do.)

(4) With regard to our being none the more able to do because of our practical wisdom what is noble and just, let us begin a little further back, starting with the following principle. As we say that some

people who do just acts are not necessarily just, i.e. those who do the acts ordained by the laws either unwillingly or owing to ignorance or for some other reason and not for the sake of the acts themselves (though, to be sure, they do what they should and all the things that the good man ought), so is it, it seems, that in order to be good one must be in a certain state when one does the several acts, i.e. one must do them as a result of choice and for the sake of the acts themselves. Now virtue makes the choice right, but the question of the things which should naturally be done to carry out our choice belongs not to virtue but to another faculty. We must devote our attention to these matters and give a clearer statement about them. There is a faculty which is called cleverness; and this is such as to be able to do the things that tend towards the mark we have set before ourselves, and to hit it. Now if the mark be noble, the cleverness is laudable, but if the mark be bad, the cleverness is mere smartness; hence we call even men of practical wisdom clever or smart. Practical wisdom is not the faculty, but it does not exist without this faculty. And this eye of the soul acquires its formed state not without the aid of virtue, as has been said and is plain; for the syllogisms which deal with acts to be done are things which involve a starting-point, viz. 'since the end, i.e. what is best, is of such and such a nature,' whatever it may be (let it for the sake of argument be what we please); and this is not evident except to the good man; for wickedness perverts us and causes us to be deceived about the starting-points of action. Therefore it is evident that it is impossible to be practically wise without being good.

We must therefore consider virtue also once more; for virtue too is similarly related; as practical wisdom is to cleverness—not the same, but like it— so is natural virtue to virtue in the strict sense. For all men think that each type of character belongs to its possessors in some sense by nature; for from the very moment of birth we are just or fitted for self-control or brave or have the other moral qualities; but yet we seek something else as that which is good in the strict sense—we seek for the presence of such qualities in another way. For both children and brutes have the natural dispositions to these qualities, but without reason these are evidently hurtful. Only we seem to see this much, that, while one may be led astray by them, as a strong body which moves without sight may stumble badly because of its lack of sight, still, if a man once acquires reason, that makes a difference in action; and his state, while still like what it was, will then be virtue in the strict sense. Therefore, as in the part of us which forms opinions there are two types, cleverness and practical wisdom, so too in the moral part there are two types, natural virtue and virtue in the strict sense, and of these the latter involves practical wisdom. This is why some say that all the virtues are forms of practical wisdom, and why Socrates in one respect was on the right track while in another he went astray; in thinking that all the virtues were forms of practical wisdom he was wrong, but in saying they implied practical wisdom he was right. This is confirmed by the fact that even now all men, when they define virtue, after naming the state of character and its objects add 'that (state) which is in accordance with the right rule'; now the right rule is that which is in accordance with practical wisdom. All men, then, seem somehow to divine that this kind of state is virtue, viz. that which is in accordance with practical wisdom. But we must go a little further. For it is not merely the state in accordance with the right rule, but the state that implies the *presence* of the right rule, that is virtue; and practical wisdom is a right rule about such matters. Socrates, then, thought the virtues were rules or rational principles (for he thought they were, all of them, forms of scientific knowledge), while we think they *involve* a rational principle.

It is clear, then, from what has been said, that it is not possible to be good in the strict sense without practical wisdom, nor practically wise without moral virtue. But in this way we may also refute the dialectical argument whereby it might be contended that the virtues exist in separation from each other; the same man, it might be said, is not best equipped by nature for all the virtues, so that he will have already acquired one when he has not yet acquired another. This is possible in respect of.the natural virtues, but not in respect of those in respect of which a man is called without qualification good; for with the presence of the one quality, practical wisdom, will be given all the virtues. And it is plain that, even if it were of no practical value, we should have needed it because it is the virtue of the part of us in question; plain too that the choice will not be right without practical wisdom any more than without virtue; for

the one determines the end and the other makes us do the things that lead to the end.

But again it is not *supreme* over philosophic wisdom, i.e. over the superior part of us, any more than the art of medicine is over health; for it does not use it but provides for its coming into being; it issues orders, then, for its sake, but not to it. Further, to maintain its supremacy would be like saying that the art of politics rules the gods because it issues orders about all the affairs of the state.

. . .

Book X

After these matters we ought perhaps next to discuss pleasure. For it is thought to be most intimately connected with our human nature, which is the reason why in educating the young we steer them by the rudders of pleasure and pain; it is thought, too, that to enjoy the things we ought and to hate the things we ought has the greatest bearing on virtue of character. For these things extend right through life, with a weight and power of their own in respect both to virtue and to the happy life, since men choose what is pleasant and avoid what is painful; and such things, it will be thought, we should least of all omit to discuss, especially since they admit of much dispute. For some say pleasure is the good, while others, on the contrary, say it is thoroughly bad—some no doubt being persuaded that the facts are so, and others thinking it has a better effect on our life to exhibit pleasure as a bad thing even if it is not; for most people (they think) incline towards it and are the slaves of their pleasures, for which reason they ought to lead them in the opposite direction, since thus they will reach the middle state. But surely this is not correct. For arguments about matters concerned with feelings and actions are less reliable than facts: and so when they clash with the facts of perception they are despised, and discredit the truth as well; if a man who runs down pleasure is once seen to be aiming at it, his inclining towards it is thought to imply that it is all worthy of being aimed at; for most people are not good at drawing distinctions. True arguments seem, then, most useful, not only with a view to knowledge, but with a view to life also; for since they harmonize with the facts they are believed, and so they stimulate those who understand them to live according to them.—Enough of such questions; let us proceed to review the opinions that have been expressed about pleasure.

Eudoxus thought pleasure was the good because he saw all things, both rational and irrational, aiming at it, and because in all things that which is the object of choice is what is excellent, and that which is most the object of choice the greatest good; thus the fact that all things moved towards the same object indicated that this was for all things the chief good (for each thing, he argued, finds its own good, as it finds its own nourishment); and that which is good for all things and at which all aim was *the* good. His arguments were credited more because of the excellence of his character than for their own sake; he was thought to be remarkably self-controlled, and therefore it was thought that he was not saying what he did say as a friend of pleasure, but that the facts really were so. He believed that the same conclusion followed no less plainly from a study of the contrary of pleasure; pain was in itself an object of aversion to all things, and therefore its contrary must be similarly an object of choice. And again that is most an object of choice which we choose not because or for the sake of something else, and pleasure is admittedly of this nature; for no one asks to what end he is pleased, thus implying that pleasure is in itself an object of choice. Further, he argued that pleasure when added to any good, e.g. to just or temperate action, makes it more worthy of choice, and that it is only by itself that the good can be increased.

This argument seems to show it to be one of the goods, and no more a good than any other; for every good is more worthy of choice along with another good than taken alone. And so it is by an argument of this kind that Plato proves the good *not* to be pleasure; he argues that the pleasant life is more desirable with wisdom than without, and that if the mixture is better, pleasure is not the good; for the good cannot become more desirable by the addition of anything to it. Now it is clear that nothing else, any more than pleasure, can be the good if it is made more desirable by the addition of any of the things that are good in themselves. What, then, is there that satisfies this criterion, which at the same time we can participate in? It is something of this sort that we are looking for.

Those who object that that at which all things aim is not necessarily good are, we may surmise, talking nonsense. For we say that that which every one thinks really is so; and the man who attacks this belief will hardly have anything more credible to maintain instead. If it is senseless creatures that desire the things in question, there might be something in what they say; but if intelligent creatures do so as well, what sense can there be in this view? But perhaps even in inferior creatures there is some natural good stronger than themselves which aims at their proper good.

Nor does the argument about the contrary of pleasure seem to be correct. They say that if pain is an evil it does not follow that pleasure is a good; for evil is opposed to evil and at the same time both are opposed to the neutral state—which is correct enough but does not apply to the things in question. For if both pleasure and pain belonged to the class of evils they ought both to be objects of aversion, while if they belonged to the class of neutrals neither should be an object of aversion or they should both be equally so; but in fact people evidently avoid the one as evil and choose the other as good; that then must be the nature of the opposition between them.

Nor again, if pleasure is not a quality, does it follow that it is not a good; for the activities of virtue are not qualities either, nor is happiness.

They say, however, that the good is determinate, while pleasure is indeterminate, because it admits of degrees. Now if it is from the feeling of pleasure that they judge thus, the same will be true of justice and the other virtues, in respect of which we plainly say that people of a certain character are so more or less, and act more or less in accordance with these virtues; for people may be more just or brave, and it is possible also to act justly or temperately more or less. But if their judgement is based on the various pleasures, surely they are not stating the real cause, if in fact some pleasures are unmixed and others mixed. Again, just as health admits of degrees without being indeterminate, why should not pleasure? The same proportion is not found in all things, nor a single proportion always in the same thing, but it may be relaxed and yet persist up to a point, and it may differ in degree. The case of pleasure also may therefore be of this kind.

Again, they assume that the good is perfect while movements and comings into being are imperfect, and try to exhibit pleasure as being a movement and a coming into being. But they do not seem to be right even in saying that it is a movement. For speed and slowness are thought to be proper to every movement, and if a movement, e.g. that of the heavens, has not speed or slowness in itself, it has it in relation to something else; but of pleasure neither of these things is true. For while we may *become* pleased quickly as we may become angry quickly, we cannot *be* pleased quickly, not even in relation to some one else, while we *can* walk, or grow, or the like, quickly. While, then, we can change quickly or slowly into a state of pleasure, we cannot quickly exhibit the activity of pleasure, i.e. be pleased. Again, how can it be a coming into being? It is not thought that any chance thing can come out of any chance thing, but that a thing is dissolved into that out of which it comes into being; and pain would be the destruction of that of which pleasure is the coming into being.

They say, too, that pain is the lack of that which is according to nature, and pleasure is replenishment. But these experiences are bodily. If then pleasure is replenishment with that which is according to nature, that which feels pleasure will be that in which the replenishment takes place, i.e. the body; but that is not thought to be the case; therefore the replenishment is not pleasure, though one would be pleased when replenishment was taking place, just as one would be pained if one was being operated on. This opinion seems to be based on the pains and pleasures connected with nutrition; on the fact that when people have been short of food and have felt pain beforehand they are pleased by the replenishment. But this does not happen with all pleasures; for the pleasures of learning and, among the sensuous pleasures, those of smell, and also many sounds and sights, and memories and hopes, do not presuppose pain. Of what then will these be the coming into being? There has not been lack of anything of which they could be the supplying anew.

In reply to those who bring forward the disgraceful pleasures one may say that these are not pleasant; if things are pleasant to people of vicious constitution, we must not suppose that they are also pleasant to others than these, just as we do not reason so about the things that are wholesome or sweet or bitter to sick people, or ascribe whiteness to the things that seem white to those suffering from a disease of the eye. Or one might answer thus—that the pleasures are desirable, but not from *these* sources, as wealth is desirable, but not as the reward of betrayal,

and health, but not at the cost of eating anything and everything. Or perhaps pleasures differ in kind; for those derived from noble sources are different from those derived from base sources, and one cannot get the pleasure of the just man without being just, nor that of the musical man without being musical, and so on.

The fact, too, that a friend is different from a flatterer seems to make it plain that pleasure is not a good or that pleasures are different in kind; for the one is thought to consort with us with a view to the good, the other with a view to our pleasure, and the one is reproached for his conduct while the other is praised on the ground that he consorts with us for different ends. And no one would choose to live with the intellect of a child throughout his life, however much he were to be pleased at the things that children are pleased at, nor to get enjoyment by doing some most disgraceful deed, though he were never to feel any pain in consequence. And there are many things we should be keen about even if they brought no pleasure; e.g. seeing, remembering, knowing, possessing the virtues. If pleasures necessarily do accompany these, that makes no odds; we should choose these even if no pleasure resulted. It seems to be clear, then, that neither is pleasure the good nor is all pleasure desirable, and that some pleasures *are* desirable in themselves, differing in kind or in their sources from the others. So much for the things that are said about pleasure and pain.

What pleasure is, or what kind of thing it is, will become plainer if we take up the question again from the beginning. Seeing seems to be at any moment complete, for it does not lack anything which coming into being later will complete its form; and pleasure also seems to be of this nature. For it is a whole, and at no time can one find a pleasure whose form will be completed if the pleasure lasts longer. For this reason, too, it is not a movement. For every movement (e.g. that of building) takes time and is for the sake of an end, and is complete when it has made what it aims at. It is complete, therefore, only in the whole time or at that final moment. In their parts and during the time they occupy, all movements are incomplete, and are different in kind from the whole movement and from each other. For the fitting together of the stones is different from the fluting of the column, and these are both different from the making of the temple; and the making of the temple is complete (for it lacks nothing with a view to the end proposed), but the making of the base or of the triglyph is incomplete; for each is the making of only a part. They differ in kind, then, and it is not possible to find at any and every time a movement complete in form, but if at all, only in the whole time. So, too, in the case of walking and all other movements. For if locomotion is a movement from here to there, it, too, has differences in kind— flying, walking, leaping, and so on. And not only so, but in walking itself there are such differences; for the whence and whither are not the same in the whole racecourse and in a part of it, nor in one part and in another, nor is it the same thing to traverse this line and that; for one traverses not only a line but one which is in a place, and this one is in a different place from that. We have discussed movement with precision in another work, but it seems that it is not complete at any and every time, but that the many movements are incomplete and different in kind, since the whence and whither give them their form. But of pleasure the form is complete at any and every time. Plainly, then, pleasure and movement must be different from each other, and pleasure must be one of the things that are whole and complete. This would seem to be the case, too, from the fact that it is not possible to move otherwise than in time, but it *is* possible to be pleased; for that which takes place in a moment is a whole.

From these considerations it is clear, too, that these thinkers are not right in saying there is a movement or a coming into being *of* pleasure. For these cannot be ascribed to all things, but only to those that are divisible and not wholes; there is no coming into being of seeing nor of a point nor of a unit, nor is any of these a movement or coming into being; therefore there is no movement or coming into being of pleasure either; for it is a whole.

Since every sense is active in relation to its object, and a sense which is in good condition acts perfectly in relation to the most beautiful of its objects (for perfect activity seems to be ideally of this nature; whether we say that *it* is active, or the organ in which it resides, may be assumed to be immaterial), it follows that in the case of each sense the best activity is that of the best-conditioned organ in relation to the finest of its objects. And this activity will be the most complete and pleasant. For, while there is pleasure in respect of any sense, and in respect of thought and

contemplation no less, the most complete is pleasantest, and that of a well-conditioned organ in relation to the worthiest of its objects is the most complete; and the pleasure completes the activity. But the pleasure does not complete it in the same way as the combination of object and sense, both good, just as health and the doctor are not in the same way the cause of a man's being healthy. (That pleasure is produced in respect to each sense is plain; for we speak of sights and sounds as pleasant. It is also plain that it arises most of all when both the sense is at its best and it is active in reference to an object which corresponds; when both object and perceiver are of the best there will always be pleasure, since the requisite agent and patient are both present.) Pleasure completes the activity not as the corresponding permanent state does, by its immanence, but as an end which supervenes as the bloom of youth does on those in the flower of their age. So long, then, as both the intelligible or sensible object and the discriminating or contemplative faculty are as they should be, the pleasure will be involved in the activity; for when both the passive and the active factor are unchanged and are related to each other in the same way, the same result naturally follows.

How, then, is it that no one is continuously pleased? Is it that we grow weary? Certainly all human things are incapable of continuous activity. Therefore pleasure also is not continuous; for it accompanies activity. Some things delight us when they are new, but later do so less, for the same reason; for at first the mind is in a state of stimulation and intensely active about them, as people are with respect to their vision when they look hard at a thing, but afterwards our activity is not of this kind, but has grown relaxed; for which reason the pleasure also is dulled.

One might think that all men desire pleasure because they all aim at life; life is an activity, and each man is active about those things and with those faculties that he loves most; e.g. the musician is active with his hearing in reference to tunes, the student with his mind in reference to theoretical questions, and so on in each case; now pleasure completes the activities, and therefore life, which they desire. It is with good reason, then, that they aim at pleasure too, since for every one it completes life, which is desirable. But whether we choose life for the sake of pleasure or pleasure for the sake of life is a question we may dismiss for the present. For they seem to be bound up together and not to admit of separation, since without activity pleasure does not arise, and every activity is completed by the attendant pleasure.

For this reason pleasures seem, too, to differ in kind. For things different in kind are, we think, completed by different things (we see this to be true both of natural objects and of things produced by art, e.g. animals, trees, a painting, a sculpture, a house, an implement); and, similarly, we think that activities differing in kind are completed by things differing in kind. Now the activities of thought differ from those of the senses, and both differ among themselves, in kind; so, therefore, do the pleasures that complete them.

This may be seen, too, from the fact that each of the pleasures is bound up with the activity it completes. For an activity is intensifed by its proper pleasure, since each class of things is better judged of and brought to precision by those who engage in the activity with pleasure; e.g. it is those who enjoy geometrical thinking that become geometers and grasp the various propositions better, and, similarly, those who are fond of music or of building, and so on, make progress in their proper function by enjoying it; so the pleasures intensify the activities, and what intensifies a thing is proper to it, but things different in kind have properties different in kind.

This will be even more apparent from the fact that activities are hindered by pleasures arising from other sources. For people who are fond of playing the flute are incapable of attending to arguments if they overhear some one playing the flute, since they enjoy flute-playing more than the activity in hand; so the pleasure connected with flute-playing destroys the activity concerned with argument. This happens, similarly, in all other cases, when one is active about two things at once; the more pleasant activity drives out the other, and if it is much more pleasant does so all the more, so that one even ceases from the other. This is why when we enjoy anything very much we do not throw ourselves into anything else, and do one thing only when we are not much pleased by another; e.g. in the theatre the people who eat sweets do so most when the actors are poor. Now since activities are made precise and more enduring and better by their proper pleasure, and injured by alien pleasures, evidently the two kinds of pleasure are far apart. For alien pleasures do pretty much what proper pains do, since activities are destroyed by

their proper pains; e.g. if a man finds writing or doing sums unpleasant and painful, he does not write, or does not do sums, because the activity is painful. So an activity suffers contrary effects from its proper pleasures and pains, i.e. from those that supervene on it in virtue of its own nature. And alien pleasures have been stated to do much the same as pain; they destroy the activity, only not to the same degree.

Now since activities differ in respect of goodness and badness, and some are worthy to be chosen, others to be avoided, and others neutral, so, too, are the pleasures; for to each activity there is a proper pleasure. The pleasure proper to a worthy activity is good and that proper to an unworthy activity bad; just as the appetites for noble objects are laudable, those for base objects culpable. But the pleasures involved in activities are more proper to them than the desires; for the latter are separated both in time and in nature, while the former are close to the activities, and so hard to distinguish from them that it admits of dispute whether the activity is not the same as the pleasure. (Still, pleasure does not seem to *be* thought or perception—that would be strange; but because they are not found apart they appear to some people the same.) As activities are different, then, so are the corresponding pleasures. Now sight is superior to touch in purity, and hearing and smell to taste; the pleasures, therefore, are similarly superior, and those of thought superior to these, and within each of the two kinds some are superior to others.

Each animal is thought to have a proper pleasure, as it has a proper function; viz. that which corresponds to its activity. If we survey them species by species, too, this will be evident; horse, dog, and man have different pleasures, as Heraclitus says 'asses would prefer sweepings to gold;' for food is pleasanter than gold to asses. So the pleasures of creatures different in kind differ in kind, and it is plausible to suppose that those of a single species do not differ. But they vary to no small extent, in the case of men at least; the same things delight some people and pain others, and are painful and odious to some, and pleasant to and liked by others. This happens, too, in the case of sweet things; the same things do not seem sweet to a man in a fever and a healthy man—nor hot to a weak man and one in good condition. The same happens in other cases. But in all such matters that which appears to the good man is thought to be really so. If this is correct, as it seems to be, and virtue and the good man as such are the measure of each thing, those also will be pleasures which appear so to him, and those things pleasant which he enjoys. If the things he finds tiresome seem pleasant to some one, that is nothing surprising; for men may be ruined and spoilt in many ways; but the things are not pleasant, but only pleasant to these people and to people in this condition. Those which are admittedly disgraceful plainly should not be said to be pleasures, except to a perverted taste; but of those that are thought to be good what kind of pleasure or what pleasure should be said to be that proper to man? Is it not plain from the corresponding activities? The pleasures follow these. Whether, then, the perfect and supremely happy man has one or more activities, the pleasures that perfect these will be said in the strict sense to be pleasures proper to man, and the rest will be so in a secondary and fractional way, as are the activities.

Now that we have spoken of the virtues, the forms of friendship, and the varieties of pleasure, what remains is to discuss in outline the nature of happiness, since this is what we state the end of human nature to be. Our discussion will be the more concise if we first sum up what we have said already. We said, then, that it is not a disposition; for if it were it might belong to some one who was asleep throughout his life, living the life of a plant, or, again, to some one who was suffering the greatest misfortunes. If these implications are unacceptable, and we must rather class happiness as an activity, as we have said before, and if some activities are necessary, and desirable for the sake of something else, while others are so in themselves, evidently happiness must be placed among those desirable in themselves, not among those desirable for the sake of something else; for happiness does not lack anything, but is self-sufficient. Now those activities are desirable in themselves from which nothing is sought beyond the activity. And of this nature virtuous actions are thought to be; for to do noble and good deeds is a thing desirable for its own sake.

Pleasant amusements also are thought to be of this nature; we choose them not for the sake of other things; for we are injured rather than benefited by them, since we are led to neglect our bodies and our property. But most of the people who are deemed happy take refuge in such pastimes, which is the reason why those who are ready-witted at them are highly esteemed at the courts of tyrants; they make themselves pleasant companions in the tyrants' favourite pursuits, and that is the sort of man they want. Now these things are thought to be of the nature of happiness because people in despotic positions spend their leisure in them, but perhaps such people prove nothing; for virtue and reason, from which good activities flow, do not depend on despotic position; nor, if these people, who have never tasted pure and generous pleasure, take refuge in the bodily pleasures, should these for that reason be thought more desirable; for boys, too, think the things that are valued among themselves are the best. It is to be expected, then, that, as different things seem valuable to boys and to men, so they should to bad men and to good. Now, as we have often maintained, those things are both valuable and pleasant which are such to the good man; and to each man the activity in accordance with his own disposition is most desirable, and, therefore, to the good man that which is in accordance with virtue. Happiness, therefore, does not lie in amusement; it would, indeed, be strange if the end were amusement, and one were to take trouble and suffer hardship all one's life in order to amuse oneself. For, in a word, everything that we choose we choose for the sake of something else—except happiness, which is an end. Now to exert oneself and work for the sake of amusement seems silly and utterly childish. But to amuse oneself in order that one may exert oneself, as Anacharsis puts it, seems right; for amusement is a sort of relaxation, and we need relaxation because we cannot work continuously. Relaxation, then, is not an end; for it is taken for the sake of activity.

The happy life is thought to be virtuous; now a virtuous life requires exertion, and does not consist in amusement. And we say that serious things are better than laughable things and those connected with amusement, and that the activity of the better of any two things—whether it be two elements of our being or two men—is the more serious; but the activity of the better is *ipso facto* superior and more of the nature of happiness. And any chance person—even a slave—can enjoy the bodily pleasures no less than the best man; but no one assigns to a slave a share in happiness—unless he assigns to him also a share in human life. For happiness does not lie in such occupations, but, as we have said before, in virtuous activities.

If happiness is activity in accordance with virtue, it is reasonable that it should be in accordance with the highest virtue; and this will be that of the best thing in us. Whether it be reason or something else that is this element which is thought to be our natural ruler and guide and to take thought of things noble and divine, whether it be itself also divine or only the most divine element in us, the activity of this in accordance with its proper virtue will be perfect happiness. That this activity is contemplative we have already said.

Now this would seem to be in agreement both with what we said before and with the truth. For, firstly, this activity is the best (since not only is reason the best thing in us, but the objects of reason are the best of knowable objects); and, secondly, it is the most continuous, since we can contemplate truth more continuously than we can *do* anything. And we think happiness has pleasure mingled with it, but the activity of philosophic wisdom is admittedly the pleasantest of virtuous activities; at all events the pursuit of it is thought to offer pleasures marvellous for their purity and their enduringness, and it is to be expected that those who know will pass their time more pleasantly than those who inquire. And the self-sufficiency that is spoken of must belong most to the contemplative activity. For while a philosopher, as well as a just man or one possessing any other virtue, needs the necessaries of life, when they are sufficiently equipped with things of that sort the just man needs people towards whom and with whom he shall act justly, and the temperate man, the brave man, and each of the others is in the same case, but the philosopher, even when by himself, can contemplate truth, and the better the wiser he is; he can perhaps do so better if he has fellow-workers, but still he is the most self-sufficient. And this activity alone would seem to be loved for its own sake; for nothing arises from it apart from the contemplating, while from practical activities we gain more or less apart from the action. And happiness is thought to depend on leisure; for we are busy that we may have leisure, and make war that we may live in peace. Now the activity of the practical virtues is exhibited in political or military affairs, but the actions concerned with these seem to be unleisurely. Warlike actions are completely so (for no one chooses to be at war, or provokes war, for the sake of being at war; any one would seem absolutely murderous if he were to make enemies of his friends in order to bring about battle and slaughter); but the action of the statesman is also unleisurely, and—apart from the political action itself—aims at despotic power and honours, or at all events happiness, for him and his fellow citizens—a happiness different from political action, and evidently sought as being different. So if among virtuous actions political and military actions are distinguished by nobility and greatness, and these are unleisurely and aim at an end and are not desirable for their own sake, but the activity of reason, which is contemplative, seems both to be superior in serious worth and to aim at no end beyond itself, and to have its pleasure proper to itself (and this augments the activity), and the self-sufficiency, leisureliness, unweariedness (so far as this is possible for man), and all the other attributes ascribed to the supremely happy man are evidently those connected with this activity, it follows that this will be the complete happiness of man, if it be allowed a complete term of life (for none of the attributes of happiness is *in*complete).

But such a life would be too high for man; for it is not in so far as he is man that he will live so, but in so far as something divine is present in him; and by so much as this is superior to our composite nature is its activity superior to that which is the exercise of the other kind of virtue. If reason is divine, then, in comparison with man, the life according to it is divine in comparison with human life. But we must not follow those who advise us, being men, to think of human things, and, being mortal, of mortal things, but must, so far as we can, make ourselves immortal, and strain every nerve to live in accordance with the best thing in us; for even if it be small in bulk, much more does it in power and worth surpass everything. This would seem, too, to be each man himself, since it is the authoritative and better part of him. It would be strange, then, if he were to choose not the life of his self but that of something else. And what we said before will apply now; that which is proper to each thing is by nature best and most pleasant for each thing; for man, therefore, the life according to reason is best and pleasantest, since reason more than anything else *is* man. This life therefore is also the happiest.

But in a secondary degree the life in accordance with the other kind of virtue is happy; for the activities in accordance with this befit our human estate. Just and brave acts, and other virtuous acts, we do in relation to each other, observing our respective duties with regard to contracts and services and all manner of actions and with regard to passions; and all of these seem to be typically human. Some of them seem even to arise from the body, and virtue of character to be in many ways bound up with the passions. Practical wisdom, too, is linked to virtue of character, and this to practical wisdom, since the principles of practical wisdom are in accordance with the moral virtues and rightness in morals is in accordance with practical wisdom. Being connected with the passions also, the moral virtues must belong to our composite nature; and the virtues of our composite nature are human; so, therefore, are the life and the happiness which correspond to these. The excellence of the reason is a thing apart; we must be content to say this much about it, for to describe it precisely is a task greater than our purpose requires. It would seem, however, also to need external equipment but little, or less than moral virtue does. Grant that both need the necessaries, and do so equally, even if the statesman's work is the more concerned with the body and things of that sort; for there will be little difference there; but in what they need for the exercise of their activities there will be much difference. The liberal man will need money for the doing of his liberal deeds, and the just man too will need it for the returning of services (for wishes are hard to discern, and even people who are not just pretend to wish to act justly); and the brave man will need power if he is to accomplish any of the acts that correspond to his virtue, and the temperate man will need opportunity; for how else is either he or any of the others to be recognized? It is debated, too, whether the will or the deed is more essential to virtue, which is assumed to involve both; it is surely clear that its perfection involves both; but for deeds many things are needed, and more, the greater and nobler the deeds are. But the man who is contemplating the truth needs no such thing, at least with a view to the exercise of his activity; indeed they are, one may say, even hindrances, at all events to his contemplation; but in so far as he is a man and lives with a number of people, he chooses to do virtuous acts; he will therefore need such aids to living a human life.

But that perfect happiness is a contemplative activity will appear from the following consideration as well. We assume the gods to be above all other be-

ings blessed and happy; but what sort of actions must we assign to them? Acts of justice? Will not the gods seem absurd if they make contracts and return deposits, and so on? Acts of a brave man, then, confronting dangers and running risks because it is noble to do so? Or liberal acts? To whom will they give? It will be strange if they are really to have money or anything of the kind. And what would their temperate acts be? Is not such praise tasteless, since they have no bad appetites? If we were to run through them all, the circumstances of action would be found trivial and unworthy of gods. Still, every one supposes that they *live* and therefore that they are active; we cannot suppose them to sleep like Endymion. Now if you take away from a living being action, and still more production, what is left but contemplation? Therefore the activity of God, which surpasses all others in blessedness, must be contemplative; and of human activities, therefore, that which is most akin to this must be most of the nature of happiness.

This is indicated, too, by the fact that the other animals have no share in happiness, being completely deprived of such activity. For while the whole life of the gods is blessed, and that of men too in so far as some likeness of such activity belongs to them, none of the other animals is happy, since they in no way share in contemplation. Happiness extends, then, just so far as contemplation does, and those to whom contemplation more fully belongs are more truly happy, not as a mere concomitant but in virtue of the contemplation; for this is in itself precious. Happiness, therefore, must be some form of contemplation.

But, being a man, one will also need external prosperity; for our nature is not self-sufficient for the purpose of contemplation, but our body also must be healthy and must have food and other attention. Still, we must not think that the man who is to be happy will need many things or great things, merely because he cannot be supremely happy without external goods; for self-sufficiency and action do not involve excess, and we can do noble acts without ruling earth and sea; for even with moderate advantages one can act virtuously (this is manifest enough; for private persons are thought to do worthy acts no less than despots—indeed even more); and it is enough that we should have so much as that; for the life of the man who is active in accordance with virtue will be happy. Solon, too, was perhaps sketching well the happy man when he described him as moderately furnished with externals but as having done (as Solon thought) the noblest acts, and lived temperately; for one can with but moderate possessions do what one ought. Anaxagoras also seems to have supposed the happy man not to be rich nor a despot, when he said that he would not be surprised if the happy man were to seem to most people a strange person; for they judge by externals, since these are all they perceive. The opinions of the wise seem, then, to harmonize with our arguments. But while even such things carry some conviction, the truth in practical matters is discerned from the facts of life; for these are the decisive factor. We must therefore survey what we have already said, bringing it to the test of the facts of life, and if it harmonizes with the facts we must accept it, but if it clashes with them we must suppose it to be mere theory. Now he who exercises his reason and cultivates it seems to be both in the best state of mind and most dear to the gods. For if the gods have any care for human affairs, as they are thought to have, it would be reasonable both that they should delight in that which was best and most akin to them (i.e. reason) and that they should reward those who love and honour this most, as caring for the things that are dear to them and acting both rightly and nobly. And that all these attributes belong most of all to the philosopher is manifest. He, therefore, is the dearest to the gods. And he who is that will presumably be also the happiest; so that in this way too the philosopher will more than any other be happy.

If these matters and the virtues, and also friendship and pleasure, have been dealt with sufficiently in outline, are we to suppose that our programme has reached its end? Surely, as the saying goes, where there are things to be done the end is not to survey and recognize the various things, but rather to do them; with regard to virtue, then, it is not enough to know, but we must try to have and use it, or try any other way there may be of becoming good. Now if arguments were in themselves enough to make men good, they would justly, as Theognis says, have won very great rewards, and such rewards should have been provided; but as things are, while they seem to have power to encourage and stimulate the generous-minded among our youth, and to make a character which is gently born, and a true lover of what is

noble, ready to be possessed by virtue, they are not able to encourage the many to nobility and goodness. For these do not by nature obey the sense of shame, but only fear, and do not abstain from bad acts because of their baseness but through fear of punishment; living by passion they pursue their own pleasures and the means to them, and avoid the opposite pains, and have not even a conception of what is noble and truly pleasant, since they have never tasted it. What argument would remould such people? It is hard, if not impossible, to remove by argument the traits that have long since been incorporated in the character; and perhaps we must be content if, when all the influences by which we are thought to become good are present, we get some tincture of virtue.

Now some think that we are made good by nature, others by habituation, others by teaching. Nature's part evidently does not depend on us, but as a result of some divine causes is present in those who are truly fortunate; while argument and teaching, we may suspect, are not powerful with all men, but the soul of the student must first have been cultivated by means of habits for noble joy and noble hatred, like earth which is to nourish the seed. For he who lives as passion directs will not hear argument that dissuades him, nor understand it if he does; and how can we persuade one in such a state to change his ways? And in general passion seems to yield not to argument but to force. The character, then, must somehow be there already with a kinship to virtue, loving what is noble and hating what is base.

But it is difficult to get from youth up a right training for virtue if one has not been brought up under right laws; for to live temperately and hardily is not pleasant to most people, especially when they are young. For this reason their nurture and occupations should be fixed by law; for they will not be painful when they have become customary. But it is surely not enough that when they are young they should get the right nurture and attention; since they must, even when they are grown up, practise and be habituated to them, we shall need laws for this as well, and generally speaking to cover the whole of life; for most people obey necessity rather than argument, and punishments rather than the sense of what is noble.

This is why some think that legislators ought to stimulate men to virtue and urge them forward by the motive of the noble, on the assumption that those who have been well advanced by the formation of habits will attend to such influences; and that punishments and penalties should be imposed on those who disobey and are of inferior nature, while the incurably bad should be completely banished. A good man (they think), since he lives with his mind fixed on what is noble, will submit to argument, while a bad man, whose desire is for pleasure, is corrected by pain like a beast of burden. This is, too, why they say the pains inflicted should be those that are most opposed to the pleasures such men love.

However that may be, if (as we have said) the man who is to be good must be well trained and habituated, and go on to spend his time in worthy occupations and neither willingly nor unwillingly do bad actions, and if this can be brought about if men live in accordance with a sort of reason and right order, provided this has force,—if this be so, the paternal command indeed has not the required force or compulsive power (nor in general has the command of one man, unless he be a king or something similar), but the *law* has compulsive power, while it is at the same time a rule proceeding from a sort of practical wisdom and reason. And while people hate *men* who oppose their impulses, even if they oppose them rightly, the law in its ordaining of what is good is not burdensome.

In the Spartan state alone, or almost alone, the legislator seems to have paid attention to questions of nurture and occupations; in most states such matters have been neglected, and each man lives as he pleases, Cyclops-fashion, 'to his own wife and children dealing law.' Now it is best that there should be a public and proper care for such matters; but if they are neglected by the community it would seem right for each man to help his children and friends towards virtue, and that they should have the power, or at least the will, to do this.

It would seem from what has been said that he can do this better if he makes himself capable of legislating. For public control is plainly effected by laws, and good control by good laws; whether written or unwritten would seem to make no difference, nor whether they are laws providing for the education of individuals or of groups—any more than it does in the case of music or gymnastics and other such pursuits. For as in cities laws and prevailing types of character have force, so in households do

the injunctions and the habits of the father, and these have even more because of the tie of blood and the benefits he confers; for the children start with a natural affection and disposition to obey. Further, private education has an advantage over public, as private medical treatment has; for while in general rest and abstinence from food are good for a man in a fever, for a particular man they may not be; and a boxer presumably does not prescribe the same style of fighting to all his pupils. It would seem, then, that the detail is worked out with more precision if the control is private; for each person is more likely to get what suits his case.

But the details can be best looked after, one by one, by a doctor or gymnastic instructor or any one else who has the general knowledge of what is good for every one or for people of a certain kind (for the sciences both are said to be, and are, concerned with what is universal); not but what some particular detail may perhaps be well looked after by an unscientific person, if he has studied accurately in the light of experience what happens in each case, just as some people seem to be their own best doctors, though they could give no help to any one else. None the less, it will perhaps be agreed that if a man does wish to become master of an art or science he must go to the universal, and come to know it as well as possible; for, as we have said, it is with this that the sciences are concerned.

And surely he who wants to make men, whether many or few, better by his care must try to become capable of legislating, if it is through laws that we can become good. For to get any one whatever—any one who is put before us—into the right condition is not for the first chance comer; if any one can do it, it is the man who knows, just as in medicine and all other matters which give scope for care and prudence.

Must we not, then, next examine whence or how one can learn how to legislate? Is it, as in all other cases, from statesmen? Certainly it was thought to be a part of statesmanship. Or is a difference apparent between statesmanship and the other sciences and arts? In the others the same people are found offering to teach the arts and practising them, e.g. doctors or painters; but while the sophists profess to teach politics, it is practised not by any of them but by the politicians, who would seem to do so by dint of a certain skill and experience rather than of thought;

for they are not found either writing or speaking about such matters (though it were a nobler occupation perhaps than composing speeches for the lawcourts and the assembly), nor again are they found to have made statesmen of their own sons or any other of their friends. But it was to be expected that they should if they could; for there is nothing better than such a skill that they could have left to their cities, or could prefer to have for themselves, or, therefore, for those dearest to them. Still, experience seems to contribute not a little; else they could not have become politicians by familiarity with politics; and so it seems that those who aim at knowing about the art of politics need experience as well.

But those of the sophists who profess the art seem to be very far from teaching it. For, to put the matter generally, they do not even know what kind of thing it is nor what kinds of things it is about; otherwise they would not have classed it as identical with rhetoric or even inferior to it, nor have thought it easy to legislate by collecting the laws that are thought well of; they say it is possible to select the best laws, as though even the selection did not demand intelligence and as though right judgement were not the greatest thing, as in matters of music. For while people experienced in any department judge rightly the works produced in it, and understand by what means or how they are achieved, and what harmonizes with what, the inexperienced must be content if they do not fail to see whether the work has been well or ill made—as in the case of painting. Now laws are as it were the 'works' of the political art; how then can one learn from them to be a legislator, or judge which are best? Even medical men do not seem to be made by a study of text-books. Yet people try, at any rate, to state not only the treatments, but also how particular classes of people can be cured and should be treated—distinguishing the various habits of body; but while this seems useful to experienced people, to the inexperienced it is valueless. Surely, then, while collections of laws, and of constitutions also, may be serviceable to those who can study them and judge what is good or bad and what enactments suit what circumstances, those who go through such collections without a practised faculty will not have right judgement (unless it be as a spontaneous gift of nature), though they may perhaps become more intelligent in such matters.

Now our predecessors have left the subject of legislation to us unexamined; it is perhaps best, therefore, that we should ourselves study it, and in general study the question of the constitution, in order to complete to the best of our ability our philosophy of human nature. First, then, if anything has been said well in detail by earlier thinkers, let us try to review it; then in the light of the constitutions we have collected let us study what sorts of influence preserve and destroy states, and what sorts preserve or destroy the particular kinds of constitution, and to what causes it is due that some are well and others ill administered. When these have been studied we shall perhaps be more likely to see with a comprehensive view, which constitution is best, and how each must be ordered, and what laws and customs it must use, if it is to be at its best. Let us make a beginning of our discussion.

EPICURUS

To Menoeceus and Principal Doctrines

In the 500 years between the death of Aristotle and the rise of Christianity, two main philosophical systems predominated: Epicureanism, the subject of this chapter, and Stoicism, the subject of the next. Epicureanism identifies a philosophy first taught by Epicurus (c. 341–270 B.C.), who established a community in Athens in 306 B.C. called "the Garden." The social and political turmoil that followed the death of Alexander the Great in 326 B.C. had profound effects on the intellectual and artistic life of Athens. In an age of growing uncertainty, Epicurus sought certainty. It was his aim to find a firm foundation for a philosophical system that could counter both the emerging skepticism and the reigning idealism This he created with a hedonistic ethics adapted from the Cyrenaics and supported by a foundation of the physics of Democritus.

Like the Cyrenaics, who attributed their ethical system to the teachings of Socrates, Epicurus taught that pleasure is the sole good. Thus, like the Cyrenaics, he held that one should always choose the more pleasurable alternative except when the consequences of doing so will be more painful. Further, both Cyrenaics and Epicureans agreed that pain should never be chosen except when doing so will lead to greater pleasure. However, unlike the Cyrenaics, Epicurus did not promote a merely sensualist hedonism.

Pleasure may be the sole good, but the active pleasure sought by the Cyrenaics was inferior to what Epicurus termed ataraxia, *or tranquility. It is tranquility, the absence of unsatisfied desires, that should be sought. What prevents our attainment of tranquility, or peace of mind? Most often, says Epicurus, it is worries about the future. And the worries of the future that are most destructive of tranquility are the related fears of death and of punishment by the gods. For Epicurus and his followers, it is by helping individuals overcome the obstacles to tranquility that philosophy finds its function. By arguing for the Atomistic theory of physics learned from Democritus, he tries to demonstrate that these fears of the gods and fears of our own deaths are empty fears.*

The Atomists held that everything, even the human, was built of infinitesimal particles, or atoms. Such a mechanistic account of the cosmos left no place for a creator. Gods existed, for Epicurus, but they had no regard for humankind. Thus, worries about the actions of the gods in the form of rewards or punishments after death were unfounded. Also, according to Epicurus, since humans are but atoms, they come into and go out of being when the necessary conditions are met. Death, then, is really nothing to us, and therefore not to be feared. The best life is one devoted to achieving tranquility in the here and now, not one spent worrying about the future.

Only fragments remain of the reported 300 volumes written by Epicurus. Summaries of Epicurus' philosophy have been preserved in Diogenes Laertius' Life of Epicurus. A letter entitled To Menoeceus, *on the topic of ethics, and a collection of aphorisms called* Principal Doctrines *are included in this chapter.*

Epicurus' moral philosophy stood the test of time. His teaching quickly spread throughout the Greek-speaking world, and even his critics admired the cultivation of friendship so important to the Epicureans. His system continued to be influential for over half a millennium, established in Rome in the first century B.C. by Lucretius, whose book On the Nature of Things *proved influential among the Roman aristocracy. Longer-range effects of Epicureanism appear in the moral philosophy of the Utilitarians and other hedonistic theories of ethics.*

Epicurus to Menoeceus

Let no one when young delay to study philosophy, nor when he is old grow weary of his study. For no one can come too early or too late to secure the health of his soul. And the man who says that the age for philosophy has either not yet come or has gone by is like the man who says that the age for happiness is not yet come to him, or has passed away. Wherefore both when young and old a man must study philosophy, that as he grows old he may be young in blessings through the grateful recollection of what has been, and that in youth he may be old as well, since he will know no fear of what is to come.

We must then meditate on the things that make our happiness, seeing that when that is with us we have all, but when it is absent we do all to win it.

The things which I used unceasingly to commend to you, these do and practise, considering them to be the first principles of the good life. First of all believe that god is a being immortal and blessed, even as the common idea of a god is engraved on men's minds, and do not assign to him anything alien to his immortality or ill-suited to his blessedness: but believe about him everything that can uphold his blessedness and immortality. For gods there are, since the knowledge of them is by clear vision. But they are not such as the many believe them to be: for indeed they do not consistently represent them as they believe them to be. And the impious man is not he who denies the gods of the many, but he who attaches to the gods the beliefs of the many. For the statements of the many about the gods are not conceptions derived from sensation, but false suppositions, according to which the greatest misfortunes befall the wicked and the greatest blessings the good by the gift of the gods. For men being accustomed always to their own virtues welcome those like themselves, but regard all that is not of their nature as alien.

Become accustomed to the belief that death is nothing to us. For all good and evil consists in sensation, but death is deprivation of sensation. And therefore a right understanding that death is nothing to us makes the mortality of life enjoyable, not because it adds to it an infinite span of time, but because it takes away the craving for immortality. For there is nothing terrible in life for the man who has truly comprehended that there is nothing terrible in not living. So that the man speaks but idly who says that he fears death not because it will be painful when it comes, but because it is painful in anticipation. For that which gives no trouble when it comes, is but an empty pain in anticipation. So death, the most terrifying of ills, is nothing to us, since so long as we exist death is not with us; but when death comes, then we do not exist. It does not then concern either the living or the dead, since for the former it is not, and the latter are no more.

But the many at one moment shun death as the greatest of evils, at another yearn for it as a respite from the evils in life. But the wise man neither seeks to escape life nor fears the cessation of life, for neither does life offend him nor does the absence of life seem to be any evil. And just as with food he does not seek simply the larger share and nothing else, but rather the most pleasant, so he seeks to enjoy not the longest period of time, but the most pleasant.

And he who counsels the young man to live well, but the old man to make a good end, is foolish, not merely because of the desirability of life, but also because it is the same training which teaches to live well and to die well. Yet much worse still is the man who says it is good not to be born, but

'once born make haste to pass the gates of Death.'
(Theognis, 427)

For if he says this from conviction why does he not pass away out of life? For it is open to him to do so, if he had firmly made up his mind to this. But if he speaks in jest, his words are idle among men who cannot receive them.

We must then bear in mind that the future is neither ours, nor yet wholly not ours, so that we may not altogether expect it as sure to come, nor abandon hope of it, as if it will certainly not come.

We must consider that of desires some are natural, others vain, and of the natural some are necessary and others merely natural; and of the necessary some are necessary for happiness, others for the repose of the body, and others for very life. The right understanding of these facts enables us to refer all choice and avoidance to the health of the body and the soul's freedom from disturbance, since this is the aim of the life of blessedness. For it is to obtain this end that we always act, namely, to avoid pain and fear. And when this is once secured for us, all the tempest of the soul is dispersed, since the living creature has not to wander as though in search of something that is missing, and to look for some other thing by which he can fulfil the good of the soul and the good of the body. For it is then that we have need of pleasure, when we feel pain owing to the absence of pleasure; but when we do not feel pain, we no longer need pleasure. And for this cause we call pleasure the beginning and end of the blessed life. For we recognize pleasure as the first good innate in us, and from pleasure we begin every act of choice and avoidance, and to pleasure we return again, using the feeling as the standard by which we judge every good.

And since pleasure is the first good and natural to us, for this very reason we do not choose every pleasure, but sometimes we pass over many pleasures, when greater discomfort accrues to us as the result of them: and similarly we think many pains better than pleasures, since a greater pleasure comes to us when we have endured pains for a long time. Every pleasure then because of its natural kinship to us is good, yet not every pleasure is to be chosen: even as every pain also is an evil, yet not all are always of a nature to be avoided. Yet by a scale of comparison and by the consideration of advantages and disadvantages we must form our judgement on all these matters. For the good on certain occasions we treat as bad, and conversely the bad as good.

And again independence of desire we think a great good—not that we may at all times enjoy but a few things, but that, if we do not possess many, we may enjoy the few in the genuine persuasion that those have the sweetest pleasure in luxury who least need it, and that all that is natural is easy to be obtained, but that which is superfluous is hard. And so plain savours bring us a pleasure equal to a luxurious diet, when all the pain due to want is removed; and bread and water produce the highest pleasure, when one who needs them puts them to his lips. To grow accustomed therefore to simple and not luxurious diet gives us health to the full, and makes a man alert for the needful employments of life, and when after long intervals we approach luxuries, disposes us better towards them, and fits us to be fearless of fortune.

When, therefore, we maintain that pleasure is the end, we do not mean the pleasures of profligates and those that consist in sensuality, as is supposed by some who are either ignorant or disagree with us or do not understand, but freedom from pain in the body and from trouble in the mind. For it is not continuous drinkings and revellings, nor the satisfaction of lusts, nor the enjoyment of fish and other luxuries of the wealthy table, which produce a pleasant life, but sober reasoning, searching out the motives for all choice and avoidance, and banishing mere opinions, to which are due the greatest disturbance of the spirit.

Of all this the beginning and the greatest good is prudence. Wherefore prudence is a more precious thing even than philosophy: for from prudence are sprung all the other virtues, and it teaches us that it is not possible to live pleasantly without living prudently and honourably and justly, nor, again, to live a life of prudence, honour, and justice without living pleasantly. For the virtues are by nature bound up with the pleasant life, and the pleasant life is inseparable from them. For indeed who, think you, is a better man than he who holds reverent opinions concerning the gods and is at all times free from fear of death, and has reasoned out the end ordained by nature? He understands that the limit of good things is easy to fulfil and easy to attain, whereas the course of ills is either short in time or slight in pain: he laughs at destiny, whom some have introduced as the mistress of all things. He thinks that with us lies the chief power in determining events, some of which happen by necessity and some by chance, and some are within our control; for while necessity cannot be called to account, he sees that chance is inconstant, but that which is in our control is subject to no master, and to it are naturally attached praise and blame. For, indeed, it were better to follow the myths about the gods than to become a slave to the destiny of the natural philosophers; for the former suggests a hope of placating the gods by worship, whereas the latter involves a necessity which knows no placation. As to chance, he does not regard it as a god as most men do (for in god's acts there is no disorder), nor as an uncertain cause of all things: for he does not believe that good and evil are given by chance to man for the framing of a blessed life, but that opportunities for great good and great evil are afforded by it. He therefore thinks it better to be unfortunate in reasonable action than to prosper in unreason. For it is better in a man's actions that what is well chosen should fail, rather than that what is ill chosen should be successful owing to chance.

Meditate therefore on these things and things akin to them night and day by yourself, and with a companion like to yourself, and never shall you be disturbed waking or asleep, but you shall live like a god among men. For a man who lives among immortal blessings is not like to a mortal being.

Principal Doctrines

I. The blessed and immortal nature knows no trouble itself nor causes trouble to any other, so that it is never constrained by anger or favour. For all such things exist only in the weak.

II. Death is nothing to us: for that which is dissolved is without sensation; and that which lacks sensation is nothing to us.

III. The limit of quantity in pleasures is the removal of all that is painful. Wherever pleasure is present, as long as it is there, there is neither pain of body nor of mind, nor of both at once.

IV. Pain does not last continuously in the flesh, but the acutest pain is there for a very short time, and even that which just exceeds the pleasure in the flesh does not continue for many days at once. But chronic illnesses permit a predominance of pleasure over pain in the flesh.

V. It is not possible to live pleasantly without living prudently and honourably and justly, nor again to live a life of prudence, honour, and justice without living pleasantly. And the man who does not possess the pleasant life, is not living prudently and honourably and justly, and the man who does not possess the virtuous life, cannot possibly live pleasantly.

VI. To secure protection from men anything is a natural good, by which you may be able to attain this end.

VII. Some men wished to become famous and conspicuous, thinking that they would thus win for themselves safety from other men. Wherefore if the life of such men is safe, they have obtained the good which nature craves; but if it is not safe, they do not possess that for which they strove at first by the instinct of nature.

VIII. No pleasure is a bad thing in itself; but the means which produce some pleasures bring with them disturbances many times greater than the pleasures.

IX. If every pleasure could be intensified so that it lasted and influenced the whole organism or the most essential parts of our nature, pleasures would never differ from one another.

X. If the things that produce the pleasures of profligates could dispel the fears of the mind about the phenomena of the sky and death and its pains, and also teach the limits of desires and of pains, we should never have cause to blame them: for they would be filling themselves full with pleasures from every source and never have pain of body or mind, which is the evil of life.

XI. If we were not troubled by our suspicions of the phenomena of the sky and about death, fearing that it concerns us, and also by our failure to grasp the limits of pains and desires, we should have no need of natural science.

XII. A man cannot dispel his fear about the most important matters if he does not know what is the nature of the universe but suspects the truth of some mythical story. So that without natural science it is not possible to attain our pleasures unalloyed.

XIII. There is no profit in securing protection in relation to men, if things above and things beneath the earth and indeed all in the boundless universe remain matters of suspicion.

XIV. The most unalloyed source of protection from men, which is secured to some extent by a certain force of expulsion, is in fact the immunity which results from a quiet life and the retirement from the world.

XV. The wealth demanded by nature is both limited and easily procured; that demanded by idle imaginings stretches on to infinity.

XVI. In but few things chance hinders a wise man, but the greatest and most important matters reason has ordained and throughout the whole period of life does and will ordain.

XVII. The just man is most free from trouble, the unjust most full of trouble.

XVIII. The pleasure in the flesh is not increased, when once the pain due to want is removed, but is only varied: and the limit as regards pleasure in the mind is begotten by the reasoned understanding of these very pleasures and of the emotions akin to them, which used to cause the greatest fear to the mind.

XIX. Infinite time contains no greater pleasure than limited time, if one measures by reason the limits of pleasure.

XX. The flesh perceives the limits of pleasure as unlimited and unlimited time is required to supply it. But the mind, having attained a reasoned understanding of the ultimate good of the flesh and its limits and having dissipated the fears concerning the time to come, supplies us with the complete life, and we have no further need of infinite time: but neither does the mind shun pleasure, nor, when circumstances begin to bring about the departure from life, does it approach its end as though it fell short in any way of the best life.

XXI. He who has learned the limits of life knows that that which removes the pain due to want and makes the whole of life complete is easy to obtain; so that there is no need of actions which involve competition.

XXII. We must consider both the real purpose and all the evidence of direct perception, to which we always refer the conclusions of opinion; otherwise, all will be full of doubt and confusion.

XXIII. If you fight against all sensations, you will have no standard by which to judge even those of them which you say are false.

XXIV. If you reject any single sensation and fail to distinguish between the conclusion of opinion as to the appearance awaiting confirmation and that which is actually given by the sensation or feeling, or each intuitive apprehension of the mind, you will confound all other sensations as well with the same groundless opinion, so that you will reject every standard of judgement. And if among the mental images created by your opinion you affirm both that which awaits confirmation and that which does not, you will not escape error, since you will have preserved the whole cause of doubt in every judgement between what is right and what is wrong.

XXV. If on each occasion instead of referring your actions to the end of nature, you turn to some other nearer standard when you are making a choice or an avoidance, your actions will not be consistent with your principles.

XXVI. Of desires, all that do not lead to a sense of pain, if they are not satisfied, are not necessary, but involve a craving which is easily dispelled, when the object is hard to procure or they seem likely to produce harm.

XXVII. Of all the things which wisdom acquires to produce the blessedness of the complete life, far the greatest is the possession of friendship.

XXVIII. The same conviction which has given us confidence that there is nothing terrible that lasts for ever or even for long, has also seen the protection of friendship most fully completed in the limited evils of this life.

XXIX. Among desires some are natural and necessary, some natural but not necessary, and others neither natural nor necessary, but due to idle imagination.

XXX. Wherever in the case of desires which are physical, but do not lead to a sense of pain, if they are not fulfilled, the effort is intense, such pleasures are due to idle imagination, and it is not owing to their own nature that they fail to be dispelled, but owing to the empty imaginings of the man.

XXXI. The justice which arises from nature is a pledge of mutual advantage to restrain men from harming one another and save them from being harmed.

XXXII. For all living things which have not been able to make compacts not to harm one another or be harmed, nothing ever is either just or unjust; and likewise too for all tribes of men which have been unable or unwilling to make compacts not to harm or be harmed.

XXXIII. Justice never is anything in itself, but in the dealings of men with one another in any place whatever and at any time it is a kind of compact not to harm or be harmed.

XXXIV. Injustice is not an evil in itself, but only in consequence of the fear which attaches to the apprehension of being unable to escape those appointed to punish such actions.

XXXV. It is not possible for one who acts in secret contravention of the terms of the compact not to harm or be harmed, to be confident that he will escape detection, even if at present he escapes a thousand times. For up to the time of death it cannot be certain that he will indeed escape.

XXXVI. In its general aspect justice is the same for all, for it is a kind of mutual advantage in the dealings of men with one another: but with reference to the individual peculiarities of a country or any other circumstances the same thing does not turn out to be just for all.

XXXVII. Among actions which are sanctioned as just by law, that which is proved on examination to be of advantage in the requirements of men's dealings with one another, has the guarantee of justice, whether it is the same for all or not. But if a man makes a law and it does not turn out to lead to advantage in men's dealings with each other, then it no longer has the essential nature of justice. And even if the advantage in the matter of justice shifts from one side to the other, but for a while accords with the general concept, it is none the less just for that period in the eyes of those who do not confound themselves with empty sounds but look to the actual facts.

XXXVIII. Where, provided the circumstances have not been altered, actions which were considered just, have been shown not to accord with the general concept in actual practice, then they are not just. But where, when circumstances have changed, the same actions which were sanctioned as just no longer lead to advantage, there they were just at the time when they were of advantage for the dealings of fellow-citizens with one another; but subsequently they are no longer just, when no longer of advantage.

XXXIX. The man who has best ordered the element of disquiet arising from external circumstances has made those things that he could akin to himself and the rest at least no alien: but with all to which he could not do even this, he has refrained from mixing, and has expelled from his life all which it was of advantage to treat thus.

XL. As many as possess the power to procure complete immunity from their neighbours, these also live most pleasantly with one another, since they have the most certain pledge of security, and after they have enjoyed the fullest intimacy, they do not lament the previous departure of a dead friend, as though he were to be pitied.

EPICTETUS

The Encheiridion

Founded in Athens in 300 B.C. and named after the Painted Porch (Stoa Poikile in Greek) from which Zeno lectured, Stoicism, along with rival Epicureanism, became one of the two chief schools of philosophy during the Hellenistic and Roman eras. Zeno, and later Chryssipus and Cleanthes, established the groundwork of the Stoic system during that period now known as the Early Stoa. The foundations they constructed exhibit a variety of influences. Stoic physics originated with Heraclitus of Ephesus; Stoic logic comes by way of the logic of the Megarians; the ethics of the Stoics was derived from the philosophy of the Cynics. And at the root of all of these influences lay the teachings of the master himself—Socrates. Of the philosophers of the Early Stoa, no writings remain.

Ethics, the central feature of Stoic philosophy, is compared to the fruit of the tree that logic and physics support. The perfectly virtuous being, known as the Sage, had attained the one true virtue—wisdom of the good. Since the capacity for rational understanding is a spark of the divine that makes up the universe, acting morally is simply a matter of acting in accord with reason, and, hence, living in accord with nature itself. By choosing a life harmonious with the orderliness and benevolence of the universe, we adapt ourselves to its order and fulfill our purpose. The contemporary meaning of the word "stoic" reveals one aspect of the life of the Stoic Sage. Today's stoic remains undeterred in the face of danger or suffering. This meaning reflects the belief of the Stoic philosophers that emotions or passions are inferior to reason and thus not in harmony with the cosmos. When one yields to emotions, whether those of sorrow and pity or even joy and happiness, one turns away from rationality, order, and virtue.

The universal law, which establishes the rules of virtuous living, entails that all events are determined: a paradoxical conclusion for the Stoic. If all outcomes are determined, how can anyone be morally responsible for what happens? The Stoics answered with characteristic aplomb: I may not be able to change what happens, but I can choose my reaction to it. Even though we cannot govern what occurs, we can control the way we feel about it. Thus the Stoic strove for complete indifference (apatheia) to everything but the wisdom of the law of nature. We must accept the universe as it is and resolutely find it now perfect.

Epictetus (c. 50–130), belongs to the Roman period of Stoicism, the Late Stoa. Along with Seneca and Marcus Aurelius, Epictetus helped spread the Stoic teaching throughout the Roman world, where it eventually grew into the semi-official philosophy of the establishment. Born into slavery, Epictetus was granted his freedom sometime after the death of Nero in 68 A.D. True to the philosophy he advocated, he lived a disciplined, materialistically simple life and became widely admired for his loving and humble nature. Although he was not active politically, he was a moral activist, urging his followers to examine the morality of their actions since responsibility for one's choices rests on the individual alone. The ability to choose our response to what happens, granted to humans in an otherwise completely determined universe, was so powerful that even Zeus could not interfere with it. The virtuous Sage understands this fact and lives accordingly.

Like Socrates, Epictetus published nothing himself. For his teachings we must rely on the class notes of Flavius Arrianeus, one of his pupils. Perhaps most influential was the model of the good life that Epictetus both lived and preached. The Stoic philosophy thrived for over 500 years, having a profound influence on the Christian ethics that eventually replaced both it and Epicureanism throughout most of the Western world. Some renewed interest in Stoic philosophy has arisen, represented in this volume by a recent article from Martha Nussbaum, "The Stoics on the Extirpation of the Passions."

I.

Of things some are in our power, and others are not. In our power are opinion, movement toward a thing, desire, aversion (turning from a thing); and in a word, whatever are our own acts: not in our power are the body, property, reputation, offices (magisterial power), and in a word, whatever are not our own acts. And the things in our power are by nature free, not subject to restraint nor hindrance: but the things not in our power are weak, slavish, subject to restraint, in the power of others. Remember then that if you think the things which are by nature slavish to be free, and the things which are in the power of others to be your own, you will be hindered, you will lament, you will be disturbed, you will blame both gods and men: but if you think that only which is your own to be your own, and

if you think that what is another's, as it really is, belongs to another, no man will ever compel you, no man will hinder you, you will never blame any man, you will accuse no man, you will do nothing involuntarily (against your will), no man will harm you, you will have no enemy, for you will not suffer any harm.

If then you desire (aim at) such great things, remember that you must not (attempt to) lay hold of them with a small effort; but you must leave alone some things entirely, and postpone others for the present. But if you wish for these things also (such great things), and power (office) and wealth, perhaps you will not gain even these very things (power and wealth) because you aim also at those former things (such great things): certainly you will fail in those things through which alone happiness and freedom are secured. Straightway then practice saying to every harsh appearance, You are an appearance, and in no manner what you appear to be. Then examine it by the rules which you possess, and by this first and chiefly, whether it relates to the things which are in our power or to the things which are not in our power: and if it relates to anything which is not in our power, be ready to say, that it does not concern you.

II.

Remember that desire contains in it the profession (hope) of obtaining that which you desire; and the profession (hope) in aversion (turning from a thing) is that you will not fall into that which you attempt to avoid: and he who fails in his desire is unfortunate; and he who falls into that which he would avoid, is unhappy. If then you attempt to avoid only the things contrary to nature which are within your power, you will not be involved in any of the things which you would avoid. But if you attempt to avoid disease or death or poverty, you will be unhappy. Take away then aversion from all things which are not in our power, and transfer it to the things contrary to nature which are in our power. But destroy desire completely for the present. For if you desire anything which is not in our power, you must be unfortunate: but of the things in our power, and which it would be good to desire, nothing yet is before you. But employ only the power of moving toward an object and retiring from it; and these powers indeed only slightly and with exceptions and with remission.

III.

In everything which pleases the soul, or supplies a want, or is loved, remember to add this to the (description, notion); what is the nature of each thing, beginning from the smallest? If you love an earthen vessel, say it is an earthen vessel which you love; for when it has been broken, you will not be disturbed. If you are kissing your child or wife, say that it is a human being whom you are kissing, for when the wife or child dies, you will not be disturbed.

IV.

When you are going to take in hand any act, remind yourself what kind of an act it is. If you are going to bathe, place before yourself what happens in the bath: some splashing the water, others pushing against one another, others abusing one another, and some stealing: and thus with more safety you will undertake the matter, if you say to yourself, I now intend to bathe, and to maintain my will in a manner comfortable to nature. And so you do in every act: for thus if any hindrance to bathing shall happen, let this thought be ready; it was not this only that I intended, but I intended also to maintain my will in a way comfortable to nature; but I shall not maintain it so, if I am vexed at what happens.

V.

Men are disturbed not by the things which happen, but by the opinions about the things: for example, death is nothing terrible, for if it were, it would have seemed so to Socrates; for the opinion about death, that it is terrible, is the terrible thing. When then we are impeded or disturbed or grieved, let us never blame others, but ourselves, that is, our opinions. It is the act of an ill-instructed man to blame others for his own bad condition; it is the act of one who has begun to be instructed, to lay the blame on himself; and of one whose instruction is completed, neither to blame another, nor himself.

VI.

Be not elated at any advantage (excellence), which belongs to another. If a horse when he is elated should say, I am beautiful, one might endure it. But when you are elated, and say, I have a beautiful horse, you must know that you are elated at having a good horse. What then is your own? The use of appearances. Consequently when in the use of appearances you are conformable to nature, then be elated, for then you will be elated at something good which is your own.

VII.

As on a voyage when the vessel has reached a port, if you go out to get water, it is an amusement by the way to pick up a shell-fish or some bulb, but your thoughts ought to be directed to the ship, and you ought to be constantly watching if the captain should call, and then you must throw away all those things, that you may not be bound and pitched into the ship like sheep: so in life also, if there be given to you instead of a little bulb and a shell a wife and child, there will be nothing to prevent (you from taking them). But if the captain should call, run to the ship, and leave all those things without regard to them. But if you are old, do not even go far from the ship, lest when you are called you make default.

VIII.

Seek not that the things which happen should happen as you wish; but wish the things which happen to be as they are, and you will have a tranquil flow of life.

IX.

Disease is an impediment to the body, but not to the will, unless the will itself chooses. Lameness is an impediment to the leg, but not to the will. And add this reflection on the occasion of everything that happens; for you will find it an impediment to something else, but not to yourself.

X.

On the occasion of every accident (event) that befalls you, remember to turn to yourself and inquire what power you have for turning it to use. If you see a fair man or a fair woman, you will find that the power to resist is temperance (continence). If labor (pain) be presented to you, you will find that it is endurance. If it be abusive words, you will find it to be patience. And if you have been thus formed to the (proper) habit, the appearances will not carry you along with them.

XI.

Never say about anything, I have lost it, but say I have restored it. Is your child dead? It has been restored. Is your wife dead? She has been restored. Has your estate been taken from you? Has not then this also been restored? But he who has taken it from me is a bad man. But what is it to you, by whose hands the giver demanded it back? So long as he may allow you, take care of it as a thing which belongs to another, as travelers do with their inn.

XII.

If you intend to improve, throw away such thoughts as these: if I neglect my affairs, I shall not have the means of living: unless I chastise my slave, he will be bad. For it is better to die of hunger and so be released from grief and fear than to live in abundance with perturbation; and it is better for your slave to be bad than for you to be unhappy. Begin then from little things. Is the oil spilled? Is a little wine stolen? Say on the occasion, at such price is sold freedom from perturbation; at such price is sold tranquillity, but nothing is got for nothing. And when you call your slave, consider that it is possible that he does not hear; and if he does hear, that he will do nothing which you wish. But matters are not so well with him, but altogether well with you, that it should be in his power for you to be not disturbed.

XIII.

If you would improve, submit to be considered without sense and foolish with respect to externals. Wish to be considered to know nothing: and if you shall seem to some to be a person of importance, distrust yourself. For you should know that it is not easy both to keep your will in a condition conformable to nature and (to secure) external things; but if a man is careful about the one, it is an absolute necessity that he will neglect the other.

XIV.

If you would have your children and your wife and your friends to live forever, you are silly; for you would have the things which are not in your power to be in your power, and the things which belong to others to be yours. So if you would have your slave to be free from faults, you are a fool; for you would have badness not to be badness, but something else. But if you wish not to fail in your desires, you are able to do that. Practice then this which you are able to do. He is the master of every man who has the power over the things, which another person wishes or does not wish, the power to confer them on him or to take them away. Whoever then wishes to be free, let him neither wish for anything nor avoid anything which depends on others: if he does not observe this rule, he must be a slave.

XV.

Remember that in life you ought to behave as at a banquet. Suppose that something is carried round and is opposite to you. Stretch out your hand and take a portion with decency. Suppose that it passes by you. Do not detain it. Suppose that it is not yet come to you. Do not send your desire forward to it, but wait till it is opposite to you. Do so with respect to children, so with respect to a wife, so with respect to magisterial offices, so with respect to wealth, and you will be some time a worthy partner of the banquets of the gods. But if you take none of the things which are set before you, and even despise them, then you will be not only a fellow-banqueter with the gods, but also a partner with them in power. For by acting thus Diogenes and Heracleitus and those like them were deservedly divine, and were so called.

XVI.

When you see a person weeping in sorrow either when a child goes abroad or when he is dead, or when the man has lost his property, take care that the appearance do not hurry you away with it, as if he were suffering in external things. But straightway make a distinction in your own mind, and be in readiness to say, it is not that which has happened that afflicts this man, for it does not afflict another, but it is the opinion about this thing which afflicts the man. So far as words then do not be unwilling to show him sympathy, and even if it happens so, to lament with him. But take care that you do not lament internally also.

XVII.

Remember that thou art an actor in a play of such a kind as the teacher (author) may choose; if short, of a short one; if long, of a long one: if he wishes you to act the part of a poor man, see that you act the part naturally; if the part of a lame man, of a magistrate, of a private person, (do the same). For this is your duty, to act well the part that is given to you; but to select the part, belongs to another.

XVIII.

When a raven has croaked inauspiciously, let not the appearance hurry you away with it: but straightway make a distinction in your mind and say, None of these things is signified to me, but either to my poor body, or to my small property, or to my reputation, or to my children or to my wife: but to me all significations are auspicious if I choose. For whatever of these things results, it is in my power to derive benefit from it.

XIX.

You can be invincible, if you enter into no contest in which it is not in your power to conquer. Take care then when you observe a man honored before others or possessed of great power or highly esteemed for any reason, not to suppose him happy, and be not carried away by the appearance. For if the nature of the good is in our power, neither envy nor jealousy will have a place in us. But you yourself will not wish to be a general or senator or consul, but a free man: and there is only one way to this, to despise (care not for) the things which are not in our power.

XX.

Remember that it is not he who reviles you or strikes you, who insults you, but it is your opinion about these things as being insulting. When then a man irritates you, you must know that it is your own opinion which has irritated you. Therefore especially try not to be carried away by the appearance. For if you once gain time and delay, you will more easily master yourself.

XXI.

Let death and exile and every other thing which appears dreadful be daily before your eyes; but most of all death: and you will never think of anything mean nor will you desire anything extravagantly.

XXII.

If you desire philosophy, prepare yourself from the beginning to be ridiculed, to expect that many will sneer at you, and say, He has all at once returned to us as a philosopher; and whence does he get this supercilious look for us? Do you not show a supercilious look; but hold on to the things which seem to you best as one appointed by God to this station. And remember that if you abide in the same principles, these men who first ridiculed will afterward admire you: but if you shall have been overpowered by them, you will bring on yourself double ridicule.

XXIII.

If it should ever happen to you to be turned to externals in order to please some person, you must know that you have lost your purpose in life. Be satisfied then in everything with being a philosopher; and if you wish to seem also to any person to be a philosopher, appear so to yourself, and you will be able to do this.

XXIV.

Let not these thoughts afflict you, I shall live unhonored and be nobody nowhere. For if want of honor (ἀτιμία) is an evil, you cannot be in evil through the means (fault) of another any more than you can be involved in anything base. Is it then your business to obtain the rank of magistrate, or to be received at a banquet? By no means. How then can this be want of honor (dishonor)? And how will you be nobody nowhere, when you ought to be somebody in those things only which are in your power, in which indeed it is permitted to you to be a man of the greatest worth? But your friends will be without assistance! What do you mean by being without assistance? They will not receive money from you, nor will you make them Roman citizens. Who then told you that these are among the things which are in our power, and not in the power of others? And who can give to another what he has not himself? Acquire money then, your friends say, that we also may have something. If I can acquire money and also keep myself modest, and faithful and magnanimous, point out the way, and I will acquire it. But if you ask me to lose the things which are good and my own, in order that you may gain the things which are not good, see how unfair and silly you are. Besides, which would you rather have, money or a faithful and modest friend? For this end then rather help me to be such a man, and do not ask me to do this by which I shall lose that character. But my country, you say, as far as it depends on me, will be without my help. I ask again, what help do you mean? It will not have porticoes or baths through you. And what does this mean? For it is not furnished with shoes by means of a smith, nor with arms by means of a shoemaker. But it is enough if every man fully discharges the work that is his own: and if you provided

it with another citizen faithful and modest, would you not be useful to it? Yes. Then you also cannot be useless to it. What place then, you say, shall I hold in the city? Whatever you can, if you maintain at the same time your fidelity and modesty. But if when you wish to be useful to the state, you shall lose these qualities, what profit could you be to it, if you were made shameless and faithless?

XXV.

Has any man been preferred before you at a banquet, or in being saluted, or in being invited to a consultation? If these things are good, you ought to rejoice that he has obtained them: but if bad, be not grieved because you have not obtained them; and remember that you cannot, if you do not the same things in order to obtain what is not in our power, be considered worthy of the same (equal) things. For how can a man obtain an equal share with another when he does not visit a man's doors as that other man does, when he does not attend him when he goes abroad, as the other man does; when he does not praise (flatter) him as another does? You will be unjust then and insatiable, if you do not part with the price, in return for which those things are sold, and if you wish to obtain them for nothing. Well, what is the price of lettuces? An obolus perhaps. If then a man gives up the obolus, and recieves the lettuces, and if you do not give up the obolus and do not obtain the lettuces, do not suppose that you recieve less than he who has got the lettuces; for as he has the lettuces, so you have the obolus which you did not give. In the same way then in the other matter also you have not been invited to a man's feast, for you did not give to the host the price at which the supper is sold; but he sells it for praise (flattery), he sells it for personal attention. Give then the price, if it is for your interest, for which it is sold. But if you wish both not to give the price and to obtain the things, you are insatiable and silly. Have you nothing then in place of the supper? You have indeed, you have the not flattering of him, whom you did not choose to flatter; you have the not enduring of the man when he enters the room.

XXVI.

We may learn the wish (will) of nature from the things in which we do not differ from one another; for instance, when your neighbor's slave has broken his cup, or anything else, we are ready to say forthwith, that it is one of the things which happen. You must know then that when your cup also is broken, you ought to think as you did when your neighbor's cup was broken. Transfer this reflection to greater things also. Is another man's child or wife dead? There is no one who would not say, this is an event incident to man. But when a man's own child or wife is dead, forthwith he calls out, Woe to me, how wretched I am. But we ought to remember how we feel when we hear that it has happened to others.

XXVII.

As a mark is not set up for the purpose of missing the aim, so neither does the nature of evil exist in the world.

XXVIII.

If any person was intending to put your body in the power of any man whom you fell in with on the way, you would be vexed: but that you put your understanding in the power of any man whom you meet, so that if he should revile you, it is disturbed and troubled, are you not ashamed at this?

XXIX.

In every act observe the things which come first, and those which follow it; and so proceed to the act. If you do not, at first you will approach it with alacrity, without having thought of the things which will follow; but afterward, when certain base (ugly) things have shown themselves, you will be ashamed. A man wishes to conquer at the Olympic games. I also wish indeed, for it is a fine thing. But observe both the things which come first, and the things which follow; and then begin the act. You must do everything according to rule, eat according to strict orders, abstain from delicacies, exercise yourself as you are bid at appointed times, in heat, in cold, you must not drink cold water, nor wine as you choose; in a word, you must deliver yourself up to the exercise master as you do to the physician, and then proceed to the contest. And sometimes you will strain the hand, put the ankle out of joint, swallow much dust, sometimes be flogged, and after all this be defeated. When

you have considered all this, if you still choose, go to the contest: if you do not, you will behave like children, who at one time play at wrestlers, another time as flute players, again as gladiators, then as trumpeters, then as tragic actors: so you also will be at one time an athlete, at another a gladiator, then a rhetorician, then a philosopher, but with your whole soul you will be nothing at all; but like an ape you imitate everything that you see, and one thing after another pleases you. For you have not undertaken anything with consideration, nor have you surveyed it well; but carelessly and with cold desire. Thus some who have seen a philosopher and having heard one speak, as Euphrates speaks,—and who can speak as he does?—they wish to be philosophers themselves also. My man, first of all consider what kind of thing it is: and then examine your own nature, if you are able to sustain the character. Do you wish to be a pentathlete or a wrestler? Look at your arms, your thighs, examine your loins. For different men are formed by nature for different things. Do you think that if you do these things, you can eat in the same manner, drink in the same manner, and in the same manner loathe certain things? You must pass sleepless nights, endure toil, go away from your kinsmen, be despised by a slave, in everything have the inferior part, in honour, in office, in the courts of justice, in every little matter. Consider these things, if you would exchange for them, freedom from passions, liberty, tranquillity. If not, take care that, like little children, you be not now a philosopher, then a servant of the publicani, then a rhetorician, then a procurator (manager) for Caesar. These things are not consistent. You must be one man, either good or bad. You must either cultivate your own ruling faculty, or external things; you must either exercise your skill on internal things or on external things; that is you must either maintain the position of a philosopher or that of a common person.

XXX.

Duties are universally measured by relations. Is a man a father? The precept is to take care of him, to yield to him in all things, to submit when he is reproachful, when he inflicts blows. But suppose that he is a bad father. Were you then by nature made akin to a good father? No; but to a father. Does a brother wrong you? Maintain then your own position toward him, and do not examine what he is doing, but what you must do that your will shall be conformable to nature. For another will not damage you unless you choose: but you will be damaged then when you shall think that you are damaged. In this way then you will discover your duty from the relation of a neighbor, from that of a citizen, from that of a general, if you are accustomed to contemplate the relations.

XXXI.

As to piety toward the Gods you must know that this is the chief thing: to have right opinions about them, to think that they exist, and that they administer the All well and justly; and you must fix yourself in this principle (duty), to obey them, and yield to them in everything which happens, and voluntarily to follow it as being accomplished by the wisest intelligence. For if you do so, you will never either blame the Gods, nor will you accuse them of neglecting you. And it is not possible for this to be done in any other way than by withdrawing from the things which are not in our power, and by placing the good and the evil only in those things which are in our power. For if you think that any of the things which are not in our power is good or bad, it is absolutely necessary that, when you do not obtain what you wish, and when you fall into those things which you do not wish, you will find fault and hate those who are the cause of them; for every animal is formed by nature to this, to fly from and to turn from the things which appear harmful and the things which are the cause of the harm, but to follow and admire the things which are useful and the causes of the useful. It is impossible then for a person who thinks that he is harmed to be delighted with that which he thinks to be the cause of the harm, as it is also impossible to be pleased with the harm itself. For this reason also a father is reviled by his son, when he gives no part to his son of the things which are considered to be good: and it was this which made Polynices and Eteocles enemies, the opinion that royal power was a good. It is for this reason that the cultivator of the earth reviles the Gods, for this reason the sailor does, and the merchant, and for this reason those who lose their wives and their children. For where the useful (your interest) is, there also piety is. Consequently he who takes care to desire as he ought and to avoid as he ought, at the same time also cares after piety. But to

make libations and to sacrifice and to offer first fruits according to the custom of our fathers, purely and not meanly nor carelessly nor scantily nor above our ability, is a thing which belongs to all to do.

XXXII.

When you have recourse to divination, remember that you do not know how it will turn out, but that you are come to inquire from the diviner. But of what kind it is, you know when you come, if indeed you are a philosopher. For if it is any of the things which are not in our power, it is absolutely necessary that it must be neither good nor bad. Do not then bring to the diviner desire or aversion (ἔκκλισιν): if you do, you will approach him with fear. But having determined in your mind that everything which shall turn out (result) is indifferent, and does not concern you, and whatever it may be, for it will be in your power to use it well, and no man will hinder this, come then with confidence to the Gods as your advisers. And then when any advice shall have been given, remember whom you have taken as advisers, and whom you will have neglected, if you do not obey them. And go to divination, as Socrates said that you ought, about those matters in which all the inquiry has reference to the result, and in which means are not given either by reason nor by any other art for knowing the thing which is the subject of the inquiry. Wherefore when we ought to share a friend's danger or that of our country, you must not consult the diviner whether you ought to share it. For even if the diviner shall tell you that the signs of the victims are unlucky, it is plain that this is a token of death or mutilation of part of the body or of exile. But reason prevails that even with these risks we should share the dangers of our friend and of our country. Therefore attend to the greater diviner, the Pythian God, who ejected from the temple him who did not assist his friend when he was being murdered.

XXXIII.

Immediately prescribe some character and some form to yourself, which you shall observe both when you are alone and when you meet with men.

And let silence be the general rule, or let only what is necessary be said, and in few words. And rarely and when the occasion calls we shall say something; but about none of the common subjects, nor about gladiators, nor horse-races, nor about athletes, nor about eating or drinking, which are the usual subjects; and especially not about men, as blaming them or praising them, or comparing them. If then you are able, bring over by your conversation the conversation of your associates to that which is proper; but if you should happen to be confined to the company of strangers, be silent.

Let not your laughter be much, nor on many occasions, nor excessive.

Refuse altogether to take an oath, if it is possible: if it is not, refuse as far as you are able.

Avoid banquets which are given by strangers and by ignorant persons. But if ever there is occasion to join in them, let your attention be carefully fixed, that you slip not into the manners of the vulgar (the uninstructed). For you must know, that if your companion be impure, he also who keeps company with him must become impure, though he should happen to be pure.

Take (apply) the things which relate to the body as far as the bare use, as food, drink, clothing, house, and slaves: but exclude everything which is for show, or luxury.

As to pleasure with women, abstain as far as you can before marriage: but if you do indulge in it, do it in the way which is conformable to custom. Do not however be disagreeable to those who indulge in these pleasures, or reprove them; and do not often boast that you do not indulge in them yourself.

If a man has reported to you, that a certain person speaks ill of you, do not make any defense (answer) to what has been told you: but reply, The man did not know the rest of my faults, for he would not have mentioned these only.

It is not necessary to go to the theaters often: but if there is ever a proper occasion for going, do not show yourself as being a partisan of any man except yourself, that is, desire only that to be done which is done, and for him only to gain the prize who gains the prize; for in this way you will meet with no hindrance. But abstain entirely from shouts and laughter at any (thing or person), or violent emotions. And when you are come away, do not talk much about what has passed on the stage, except about that which may lead to your own improvement. For it is plain, if you do talk much that you admired the spectacle (more than you ought).

Do not go to the hearing of certain persons' recitations nor visit them readily. But if you do attend, observe gravity and sedateness, and also avoid making yourself disagreeable.

When you are going to meet with any person and particularly one of those who are considered to be in a superior condition, place before yourself what Socrates or Zeno would have done in such circumstances, and you will have no difficulty in making a proper use of the occasion.

When you are going to any of those who are in great power, place before yourself that you will not find the man at home, that you will be excluded, that the door will not be opened to you, that the man will not care about you. And if with all this it is your duty to visit him, bear what happens, and never say to yourself that it was not worth the trouble. For this is silly, and marks the character of a man who is offended by externals.

In company take care not to speak much and excessively about your own acts or dangers: for as it is pleasant to you to make mention of your dangers, it is not so pleasant to others to hear what has happened to you. Take care also not to provoke laughter; for this is a slippery way toward vulgar habits, and is also adapted to diminish the respect of your neighbors. It is a dangerous habit also to approach obscene talk. When then anything of this kind happens, if there is a good opportunity, rebuke the man who has proceeded to this talk: but if there is not an opportunity, by your silence at least, and blushing and expression of dissatisfaction by your countenance, show plainly that you are displeased at such talk.

XXXIV.

If you have received the impression of any pleasure, guard yourself against being carried away by it; but let the thing wait for you, and allow yourself a certain delay on your own part. Then think of both times, of the time when you will enjoy the pleasure, and of the time after the enjoyment of the pleasure when you will repent and will reproach yourself. And set against these things how you will rejoice if you have abstained from the pleasure, and how you will commend yourself. But if it seem to you seasonable to undertake (do) the thing, take care that the charm of it, and the pleasure, and the attraction of it shall not conquer you: but set on the other side the consideration how much better it is to be conscious that you have gained this victory.

XXXV.

When you have decided that a thing ought to be done and are doing it, never avoid being seen doing it, though the many shall form an unfavorable opinion about it. For if it is not right to do it, avoid doing the thing; but if it is right, why are you afraid of those who shall find fault wrongly?

XXXVI.

As the proposition it is either day or it is night is of great importance for the disjunctive argument, but for the conjunctive is of no value, so in a symposium (entertainment) to select the larger share is of great value for the body, but for the maintenance of the social feeling is worth nothing. When then you are eating with another, remember to look not only to the value for the body of the things set before you, but also to the value of the behavior toward the host which ought to be observed.

XXXVII.

If you have assumed a character above your strength, you have both acted in this matter in an unbecoming way, and you have neglected that which you might have fulfilled.

XXXVIII.

In walking about as you take care not to step on a nail or to sprain your foot, so take care not to damage your own ruling faculty: and if we observe this rule in every act, we shall undertake the act with more security.

XXXIX.

The measure of possession (property) is to every man the body, as the foot is of the shoe. If then you stand on this rule (the demands of the body), you will maintain the measure: but if you pass beyond it, you must then of necessity be hurried as it were down a precipice. As also in the matter of the shoe, if you go beyond the (necessities of the) foot, the shoe is gilded, then of a purple color, then embroidered: for there is no limit to that which has once passed the true measure.

XL.

Women forthwith from the age of fourteen are called by the men mistresses (dominae). Therefore since they see that there is nothing else that they can obtain, but only the power of lying with men, they begin to decorate themselves, and to place all their hopes in this. It is worth our while then to take care that they may know that they are valued (by men) for nothing else than appearing (being) decent and modest and discreet.

XLI.

It is a mark of a mean capacity to spend much time on the things which concern the body, such as much exercise, much eating, much drinking, much easing of the body, much copulation. But these things should be done as subordinate things: and let all your care be directed to the mind.

XLII.

When any person treats you ill or speaks ill of you, remember that he does this or says this because he thinks that it is his duty. It is not possible then for him to follow that which seems right to you, but that which seems right to himself. Accordingly if he is wrong in his opinion, he is the person who is hurt, for he is the person who has been deceived; for if a man shall suppose the true conjunction to be false, it is not the conjunction which is hindered, but the man who has been deceived about it. If you proceed then from these opinions, you will be mild in temper to him who reviles you: for say on each occasion, It seemed so to him.

XLIII.

Everything has two handles, the one by which it may be borne, the other by which it may not. If your brother acts unjustly, do not lay hold of the act by that handle wherein he acts unjustly, for this is the handle which cannot be borne; but lay hold of the other, that he is your brother, that he was nurtured with you, and you will lay hold of the thing by that handle by which it can be borne.

XLIV.

These reasonings do not cohere: I am richer than you, therefore I am better than you; I am more eloquent than you, therefore I am better than you. On the contrary these rather cohere, I am richer than you, therefore my possessions are greater than yours: I am more eloquent than you, therefore my speech is superior to yours. But you are neither possession nor speech.

XLV.

Does a man bathe quickly (early)? do not say that he bathes badly, but that he bathes quickly. Does a man drink much wine? do not say that he does this badly, but say that he drinks much. For before you shall have determined the opinion, how do you know whether he is acting wrong? Thus it will not happen to you to comprehend some appearances which are capable of being comprehended, but to assent to others.

XLVI.

On no occasion call yourself a philosopher, and do not speak much among the uninstructed about theorems (philosophical rules, precepts): but do that which follows from them. For example at a banquet do not say how a man ought to eat, but eat as you ought to eat. For remember that in this way Socrates also altogether avoided ostentation: persons used to come to him and ask to be recommended by him to philosophers, and he used to take them to philosophers: so easily did he submit to being overlooked. Accordingly if any conversation should arise among uninstructed persons about any theorem, generally be silent; for there is great danger that you will immediately vomit up what you have not digested. And when a man shall say to you, that you know nothing, and you are not vexed, then be sure that you have begun the work (of philosophy). For even sheep do not vomit up their grass and show to the shepherds how much they have eaten; but when they have internally digested the pasture, they produce externally wool and milk. Do you also show not your theorems to the uninstructed, but show the acts which come from their digestion.

XLVII.

When at a small cost you are supplied with everything for the body, do not be proud of this; nor, if you drink water, say on every occasion, I drink water. But consider first how much more frugal the poor are than we, and how much more enduring of labor. And if you ever wish to exercise yourself in labor and endurance, do it for yourself, and not for others: do not embrace statues. But if you are ever very thirsty, take a draught of cold water, and spit it out, and tell no man.

XLVIII.

The condition and characteristic of an uninstructed person is this: he never expects from himself profit (advantage) nor harm, but from externals. The condition and characteristic of a philosopher is this: he expects all advantage and all harm from himself. The signs (marks) of one who is making progress are these: he censures no man, he praises no man, he blames no man, he accuses no man, he says nothing about himself as if he were somebody or knew something; when he is impeded at all or hindered, he blames himself: if a man praises him, he ridicules the praiser to himself: if a man censures him, he makes no defense: he goes about like weak persons, being careful not to move any of the things which are placed, before they are firmly fixed: he removes all desire from himself, and he transfers aversion ἔπλιον to those things only of the things within our power which are contrary to nature: he employs a moderate movement toward everything: whether he is considered foolish or ignorant, he cares not: and in a word he watches himself as if he were an enemy and lying in ambush.

XLIX.

When a man is proud because he can understand and explain the writings of Chrysippus, say to yourself If Chrysippus had not written obscurely, this man would have had nothing to be proud of. But what is it that I wish? To understand Nature and to follow it. I inquire therefore who is the interpreter: and when I have heard that it is Chrysippus, I come to him (the interpreter). But I do not understand what is written, and therefore I seek the interpreter. And so far there is yet nothing to be proud of. But when I shall have found the interpreter, the thing that remains is to use the precepts (the lessons). This itself is the only thing to be proud of. But if I shall admire the exposition, what else have I been made unless a grammarian instead of a philosopher? except in one thing, that I am explaining Chrysippus instead of Homer. When then any man says to me, Read Chrysippus to me, I rather blush, when I cannot show my acts like to and consistent with his words.

L.

Whatever things (rules) are proposed to you (for the conduct of life) abide by them, as if they were laws, as if you would be guilty of impiety if you transgressed any of them. And whatever any man shall say about you, do not attend to it: for this is no affair of yours. How long will you then still defer thinking yourself worthy of the best things, and in no matter transgressing the distinctive reason? Have you accepted the theorems (rules), which it was your duty to agree to, and have you agreed to them? what teacher then do you still expect that you defer to him the correction of yourself? You are no longer a youth, but already a full-grown man. If then you are negligent and slothful, and are continually making procrastination after procrastination, and proposal (intention) after proposal, and fixing day after day, after which you will attend to yourself, you will not know that you are not making improvement, but you will continue ignorant (uninstructed) both while you live and till you die. Immediately then think it right to live as a full-grown man, and one who is making proficiency, and let everything which appears to you to be the best be to you a law which must not be transgressed. And if anything laborious, or pleasant or glorious or inglorious be presented to you, remember that now is the contest, now are the Olympic games, and they cannot be deferred; and that it depends on one defeat and one giving way

that progress is either lost or maintained. Socrates in this way became perfect, in all things improving himself, attending to nothing except to reason. But you, though you are not yet a Socrates, ought to live as one who wishes to be a Socrates.

LI.

The first and most necessary place (part) in philosophy is the use of theorems (precepts), for instance, that we must not lie: the second part is that of demonstrations, for instance, How is it proved that we ought not to lie: the third is that which is confirmatory of these two and explanatory, for example, How is this a demonstration? For what is demonstration, what is consequence, what is contradiction, what is truth, what is falsehood? The third part (topic) is necessary on account of the second, and the second on account of the first; but the most necessary and that on which we ought to rest is the first. But we do the contrary. For we spend our time on the third topic, and all our earnestness is about it: but we entirely neglect the first. Therefore we lie; but the demonstration that we ought not to lie we have ready to hand.

LII.

In every thing (circumstance) we should hold these maxims ready to hand:

> Lead me, O Zeus, and thou O Destiny,
> The way that I am bid by you to go:
> To follow I am ready. If I choose not,
> I make myself a wretch, and still must follow.

> But whoso nobly yields unto necessity,
> We hold him wise, and skill'd in things divine.

And the third also: O Crito, if so it pleases the Gods, so let it be; Anytus and Melitus are able indeed to kill me, but they cannot harm me.

ST. AUGUSTINE

FROM *The City of God*

Early Christian ethics not only had an enormous impact on modern moral philosophy, but was in turn greatly influenced by the ethical systems of the classical philosophers. This dual influence is seen clearly in the work of St. Augustine (354–430), who most effectively wedded the moral philosophy of the classical world to Christian ethics in the early church—a marriage of reason and faith.

From the second to fourth centuries, Christianity spread throughout the Roman empire, offering hope of otherworldly happiness for great numbers of oppressed people. By the fourth century, the masses were largely won over, and it fell to such early church fathers as Augustine, Clement of Alexandria, Origen, and Tertullian to interpret the Christian message for the intellectuals. Since Christianity arose in the Roman empire, the resulting ethics in the early Christian religion was thus a combination of Judaism and Greco-Roman philosophies. Christianity brought together two divergent sources of moral command—divine will and human reason.

Aurelius Augustinus, later St. Augustine, was born in the Roman province of Numidia, near Carthage, in North Africa. His mother was a Christian (later canonized as St. Monica) and his father was a pagan. In his Confessions, he famously relates his intellectual search for truth amidst a life of sin that he finally abandoned with a conversion to Christianity in 386. It is said that he had many times tried and failed to alter his sinful ways, but that it was the words of a child that awakened him to God. Weeping one day with helplessness, he heard in the distance a child chanting, "Take and read; Take and read." Believing this to be a sign from God, he opened the New Testament and his eyes fell on a passage from Romans. Herein he had at last found the strength to turn himself away from his evil life and to embrace the path of God. Embrace the path of God he did, eventually rising in the church to the office of bishop of Hippo.

Morality is a central concern in the thought of St. Augustine. This is because he saw happiness as the goal of human life yet contended that happiness attained only in an earthly sphere was not true happiness. What actually brings happiness is following the will of God, which depends upon both true thinking and right actions. Augustine's ethics was, in large part, under the influence of the tradition of the Christian (i.e., Catholic) church. What makes his thinking so important in philosophical ethical theory is the way he interpreted the classical philosophers, particularly Plato, in light of the Christian tradition. For example, he saw Plato as identifying the supreme good as God. Classical philosophy thus influenced, and was influenced by, Christian theology.

Since St. Augustine blends the worlds of Christianity and philosophy, it is not surprising to find parallels in each. He accepted the four cardinal virtues put forward by Plato: temperance, justice, wisdom, and courage. Like the Greco-Roman philosophers, he believed that people are responsible for their actions and have the freedom to choose between alternative courses. Yet he differs from the philosophers in crucial respects. The cardinal virtues are to be admired, but unless they are inspired by a faith in Christ, they are of no worth. Yes, people are responsible for their actions, but for Augustine people are rewarded or punished by their motives, depending on whether they move in their actions toward God or away from God. And free will operates in a being who is a complex mix of different desires, drives, and impulses. Due to the sin of Adam and the fall of man, these impulses are disordered and out of harmony with the universe. If we act morally, we use our will to harmonize those impulses and make possible an eternal life of blessedness guided by the divine order of creation.

Augustine's major works are the Confessions, The City of God, Enchiridion, *and* On Freedom of the Will. *His influence on Christian thought was enormous. His writings provided not only the cornerstones of the Catholic faith, but were influential in the formation of Protestantism as well. In European moral philosophy he remains, along with St. Thomas Aquinas, one of the two most influential minds of the Middle Ages.*

Book XII

5. That in All Natures, of Every Kind and Rank, God Is Glorified

All natures, then, inasmuch as they are, and have therefore a rank and species of their own, and a kind of internal harmony, are certainly good. And when they are in the places assigned to them by the order of their nature, they preserve such being as they have received. And those things which have not received everlasting being, are altered for better or for worse, so as to suit the wants and motions of those things to which the Creator's law has made them subservient; and thus they tend in the divine providence to that end which is embraced in the general scheme of the government of the universe. So that, though the corruption of transitory and perishable things brings them to utter destruction, it does not prevent their producing that which was designed to be their result. And this being so, God, who supremely is, and who therefore created every being which has not supreme existence (for that which was made of nothing could not be equal to Him, and indeed could not be at all had He not made it), is not to be found fault with on account of the creature's faults, but is to be praised in view of the natures He has made.

6. What the Cause of the Blessedness of the Good Angels Is, and What the Cause of the Misery of the Wicked

Thus the true cause of the blessedness of the good angels is found to be this, that they cleave to Him who supremely is. And if we ask the cause of the misery of the bad, it occurs to us, and not unreasonably, that they are miserable because they have forsaken Him who supremely is, and have turned to themselves who have no such essence. And this vice, what else is it called than pride? For "pride is the beginning of sin." They were unwilling, then, to preserve their strength for God; and as adherence to God was the condition of their enjoying an ampler being, they diminished it by preferring themselves to Him. This was the first defect, and the first impoverishment, and the first flaw of their nature, which was created, not indeed supremely existent, but finding its blessedness in the enjoyment of the Supreme Being; whilst by abandoning Him it should become, not indeed no nature at all, but a nature with a less ample existence, and therefore wretched.

If the further question be asked, What was the efficient cause of their evil will? there is none. For what is it which makes the will bad, when it is the will itself which makes the action bad? And consequently the bad will is the cause of the bad action, but nothing is the efficient cause of the bad will. For if anything is the cause, this thing either has or has not a will. If it has, the will is either good or bad. If good, who is so left to himself as to say that a good will makes a will bad? For in this case a good will would be the cause of sin; a most absurd supposition. On the other hand, if this hypothetical thing has a bad will, I wish to know what made it so; and that we may not go on for ever, I ask at once, what made the *first* evil will bad? For that is not the first which was itself corrupted by an evil will, but that is the first which was made evil by no other will. For if it were preceded by that which made it evil, that will was first which made the other evil. But if it is replied, "Nothing made it evil; it always was evil," I ask if it has been existing in some nature. For if not, then it did not exist at all; and if it did exist in some nature, then it vitiated and corrupted it, and injured it, and consequently deprived it of good. And therefore the evil will could not exist in an evil nature, but in a nature at once good and mutable, which this vice could injure. For if it did no injury, it was no vice; and consequently the will in which it was, could not be called evil. But if it did injury, it did it by taking away or diminishing good. And therefore there could not be from eternity, as was suggested, an evil will in that thing in which there had been previously a natural good, which the evil will was able to diminish by corrupting it. If, then, it was not from eternity, who, I ask, made it? The only thing that can be suggested in reply is, that something which itself had no will, made the will evil. I ask, then, whether this thing was superior, inferior, or equal to it? If superior, then it is better. How, then, has it no will, and not rather a good will? The same reasoning applies if it was equal; for so long as two things have equally a good will, the one cannot produce in the other an evil will. Then remains the supposition that that which corrupted the will of the angelic nature which first sinned, was itself an inferior thing without a will. But that thing, be it of the lowest and most earthly kind, is certainly itself good, since it is a nature and being, with a form and rank of its own in its own kind and order. How, then, can a good thing be the efficient cause of an evil will? How, I say, can good be the cause of evil? For when the will abandons what is above itself, and turns to what is lower, it becomes evil—not because that is evil to which it turns, but because the turning itself is wicked. Therefore it is not an inferior thing which has made the will evil, but it is itself which has become so by wickedly and inordinately desiring an inferior thing. For if two men, alike in physical and moral constitution, see the same corporal beauty, and one of them is excited by the sight to desire an illicit enjoyment, while the other stedfastly maintains a modest restraint of his will, what do we suppose brings it about, that there is an evil will in the one and not in the other? What produces it in the man in whom it exists? Not the bodily beauty, for

that was presented equally to the gaze of both, and yet did not produce in both an evil will. Did the flesh of the one cause the desire as he looked? But why did not the flesh of the other? Or was it the disposition? But why not the disposition of both? For we are supposing that both were of a like temperament of body and soul. Must we, then, say that the one was tempted by a secret suggestion of the evil spirit? As if it was not by his own will that he consented to this suggestion and to any inducement whatever! This consent, then, this evil will which he presented to the evil suasive influence—what was the cause of it, we ask? For, not to delay on such a difficulty as this, if both are tempted equally, and one yields and consents to the temptation, while the other remains unmoved by it, what other account can we give of the matter than this, that the one is willing, the other unwilling, to fall away from chastity? And what causes this but their own wills, in cases at least such as we are supposing, where the temperament is identical? The same beauty was equally obvious to the eyes of both; the same secret temptation pressed on both with equal violence. However minutely we examine the case, therefore, we can discern nothing which caused the will of the one to be evil. For if we say that the man himself made his will evil, what was the man himself before his will was evil but a good nature created by God, the unchangeable good? Here are two men who, before the temptation, were alike in body and soul, and of whom one yielded to the tempter who persuaded him, while the other could not be persuaded to desire that lovely body which was equally before the eyes of both. Shall we say of the successfully tempted man that he corrupted his own will, since he was certainly good before his will became bad? Then, why did he do so? Was it because his will was a nature, or because it was made of nothing? We shall find that the latter is the case. For if a nature is the cause of an evil will, what else can we say than that evil arises from good, or that good is the cause of evil? And how can it come to pass that a nature, good though mutable, should produce any evil—that is to say, should make the will itself wicked?

7. That We Ought Not to Expect to Find Any Efficient Cause of the Evil Will

Let no one, therefore, look for an efficient cause of the evil will; for it is not efficient, but deficient, as the will itself is not an effecting of something, but a defect. For defection from that which supremely is, to that which has less of being—this is to begin to have an evil will. Now, to seek to discover the causes of these defections—causes, as I have said, not efficient, but deficient—is as if some one sought to see darkness, or hear silence. Yet both of these are known by us, and the former by means only of the eye, the latter only by the ear; but not by their positive actuality, but by their want of it. Let no one, then, seek to know from me what I know that I do not know; unless he perhaps wishes to learn to be ignorant of that of which all we know is, that it cannot be known. For those things which are known not by their actuality, but by their want of it, are known, if our expression may be allowed and understood, by not knowing them, that by knowing them they may be not known. For when the eyesight surveys objects that strike the sense, it nowhere sees darkness but where it begins not to see. And so no other sense but the ear can perceive silence, and yet it is only perceived by not hearing. Thus, too, our mind perceives intelligible forms by understanding them; but when they are deficient, it knows them by not knowing them; for "who can understand defects?"

8. Of the Misdirected Love Whereby the Will Fell Away from the Immutable to the Mutable Good

This I do know, that the nature of God can never, nowhere, nowise be defective, and that natures made of nothing can. These latter, however, the more being they have, and the more good they do (for then they do something positive), the more they have efficient causes; but in so far as they are defective in being, and consequently do evil (for then what is their work but vanity?), they have deficient causes. And I know likewise, that the will could not become evil, were it unwilling to become so; and therefore its failings are justly punished, being not necessary, but voluntary. For its defections are not to evil things, but are themselves evil; that is to say, are not towards things that are naturally and in themselves evil, but the defection of the will is evil, because it is contrary to the order of nature, and an abandonment of that which has supreme being for that which has less. For avarice is not a fault inherent in gold, but in the man who inordinately loves gold, to the detriment of justice, which ought to be

held in incomparably higher regard than gold. Neither is luxury the fault of lovely and charming objects, but of the heart that inordinately loves sensual pleasures, to the neglect of temperance, which attaches us to objects more lovely in their spirituality, and more delectable by their incorruptibility. Nor yet is boasting the fault of human praise, but of the soul that is inordinately fond of the applause of men, and that makes light of the voice of conscience. Pride, too, is not the fault of him who delegates power, nor of power itself, but of the soul that is inordinately enamoured of its own power, and despises the more just dominion of a higher authority. Consequently he who inordinately loves the good which any nature possesses, even though he obtain it, himself becomes evil in the good, and wretched because deprived of a greater good.

· · ·

Book XIV

25. Of True Blessedness, Which this Present Life Cannot Enjoy

However, if we look at this a little more closely, we see that no one lives as he wishes but the blessed, and that no one is blessed but the righteous. But even the righteous himself does not live as he wishes, until he has arrived where he cannot die, be deceived, or injured, and until he is assured that this shall be his eternal condition. For this nature demands; and nature is not fully and perfectly blessed till it attains what it seeks. But what man is at present able to live as he wishes, when it is not in his power so much as to live? He wishes to live, he is compelled to die. How, then, does he live as he wishes who does not live as long as he wishes? or if he wishes to die, how can he live as he wishes, since he does not wish even to live? Or if he wishes to die, not because he dislikes life, but that after death he may live better, still he is not yet living as he wishes, but only has the prospect of so living when, through death, he reaches that which he wishes. But admit that he lives as he wishes, because he has done violence to himself, and forced himself not to wish what he cannot obtain, and to wish only what he can (as Terence has it, "Since you cannot do what you will, will what you can"), is he therefore blessed because he is patiently wretched? For a blessed life is possessed only by the man who loves it. If it is loved and possessed, it must necessarily be more ardently loved than all besides; for whatever else is loved must be loved for the sake of the blessed life. And if it is loved as it deserves to be—and the man is not blessed who does not love the blessed life as it deserves—then he who so loves it cannot but wish it to be eternal. Therefore it shall then only be blessed when it is eternal.

. . .

28. Of the Nature of the Two Cities, the Earthly and the Heavenly

Accordingly, two cities have been formed by two loves: the earthly by the love of self, even to the contempt of God; the heavenly by the love of God, even to the contempt of self. The former, in a word, glories in itself, the latter in the Lord. For the one seeks glory from men; but the greatest glory of the other is God, the witness of conscience. The one lifts up its head in its own glory; the other says to its God, "Thou art my glory, and the lifter up of mine head." In the one, the princes and the nations it subdues are ruled by the love of ruling; in the other, the princes and the subjects serve one another in love, the latter obeying, while the former take thought for all. The one delights in its own strength, represented in the persons of its rulers; the other says to its God, "I will love Thee, O Lord, my strength." And therefore the wise men of the one city, living according to man, have sought for profit to their own bodies or souls, or both, and those who have known God "glorified Him not as God, neither were thankful, but became vain in their imaginations, and their foolish heart was darkened; professing themselves to be wise"— that is, glorying in their own wisdom, and being possessed by pride—"they became fools, and changed the glory of the incorruptible God into an image made like to corruptible man, and to birds, and four-footed beasts, and creeping things." For they were either leaders or followers of the people in adoring images, "and worshipped and served the creature more than the Creator, who is blessed for ever." But

in the other city there is no human wisdom, but only godliness, which offers due worship to the true God, and looks for its reward in the society of the saints, of holy angels as well as holy men, "that God may be all in all."

. . .

Book XIX

4. What the Christians Believe Regarding the Supreme Good and Evil, in Opposition to the Philosophers, Who Have Maintained that the Supreme Good Is in Themselves

If, then, we be asked what the city of God has to say upon these points, and, in the first place, what its opinion regarding the supreme good and evil is, it will reply that life eternal is the supreme good, death eternal the supreme evil, and that to obtain the one and escape the other we must live rightly. And thus it is written, "The just lives by faith," for we do not as yet see our good, and must therefore live by faith; neither have we in ourselves power to live rightly, but can do so only if He who has given us faith to believe in His help do help us when we believe and pray. As for those who have supposed that the sovereign good and evil are to be found in this life, and have placed it either in the soul or the body, or in both, or, to speak more explicitly, either in pleasure or in virtue, or in both; in repose or in virtue, or in both; in pleasure and repose, or in virtue, or in all combined; in the primary objects of nature, or in virtue, or in both—all these have, with a marvellous shallowness, sought to find their blessedness in this life and in themselves. Contempt has been poured upon such ideas by the Truth, saying by the prophet, "The Lord knoweth the thoughts of men" (or, as the Apostle Paul cites the passage, "The Lord knoweth the thoughts of the *wise*") "that they are vain."

For what flood of eloquence can suffice to detail the miseries of this life? Cicero, in the *Consolation* on the death of his daughter, has spent all his ability in lamentation; but how inadequate was even his ability here? For when, where, how, in this life can these primary objects of nature be possessed so that they may not be assailed by unforeseen accident? Is the body of the wise man exempt from any pain which may dispel pleasure, from any disquietude which may banish repose? The amputation or decay of the members of the body puts an end to its integrity, deformity blights its beauty, weakness its health, lassitude its vigour, sleepiness or sluggishness its activity—and which of these is it that may not assail the flesh of the wise man? Comely and fitting attitudes and movements of the body are numbered among the prime natural blessings; but what if some sickness makes the members tremble? what if a man suffers from curvature of the spine to such an extent that his hands reach the ground, and he goes upon all-fours like a quadruped? Does not this destroy all beauty and grace in the body, whether at rest or in motion? What shall I say of the fundamental blessings of the soul, sense and intellect, of which the one is given for the perception, and the other for the comprehension of truth? But what kind of sense is it that remains when a man becomes deaf and blind? where are reason and intellect when disease makes a man delirious? We can scarcely, or not at all, refrain from tears, when we think of or see the actions and words of such frantic persons, and consider how different from and even opposed to their own sober judgment and ordinary conduct their present demeanour is. And what shall I say of those who suffer from demoniacal possession? Where is their own intelligence hidden and buried while the malignant spirit is using their body and soul according to his own will? And who is quite sure that no such thing can happen to the wise man in this life? Then, as to the perception of truth, what can we hope for even in this way while in the body, as we read in the true book of Wisdom, "The corruptible body weigheth down the soul, and the earthly tabernacle presseth down the mind that museth upon many things"? And eagerness, or desire of action, if this is the right meaning to put upon the Greek ὁρμή, is also reckoned among the primary advantages of nature; and yet is it not this which produces those pitiable movements of the insane, and those actions which we shudder to see, when sense is deceived and reason deranged?

In fine, virtue itself, which is not among the primary objects of nature, but succeeds to them as the result of learning, though it holds the highest place among human good things, what is its occupation save to wage perpetual war with vices—not those that are outside of us, but within; not other men's, but our own—a war which is waged especially by that virtue which the Greeks call σωφροσύνη, and we temperance, and which bridles carnal lusts, and prevents them from winning the consent of the spirit to wicked deeds? For we must not fancy that there is no vice in us, when, as the apostle says, "The flesh lusteth against the spirit"; for to this vice there is a contrary virtue, when, as the same writer says, "The spirit lusteth against the flesh." "For these two," he says, "are contrary one to the other, so that you cannot do the things which you would." But what is it we wish to do when we seek to attain the supreme good, unless that the flesh should cease to lust against the spirit, and that there be no vice in us against which the spirit may lust? And as we cannot attain to this in the present life, however ardently we desire it, let us by God's help accomplish at least this, to preserve the soul from succumbing and yielding to the flesh that lusts against it, and to refuse our consent to the perpetration of sin. Far be it from us, then, to fancy that while we are still engaged in this intestine war, we have already found the happiness which we seek to reach by victory. And who is there so wise that he has no conflict at all to maintain against his vices?

What shall I say of that virtue which is called prudence? Is not all its vigilance spent in the discernment of good from evil things, so that no mistake may be admitted about what we should desire and what avoid? And thus it is itself a proof that we are in the midst of evils, or that evils are in us; for it teaches us that it is an evil to consent to sin, and a good to refuse this consent. And yet this evil, to which prudence teaches and temperance enables us not to consent, is removed from this life neither by prudence nor by temperance. And justice, whose office it is to render to every man his due, whereby there is in man himself a certain just order of nature, so that the soul is subjected to God, and the flesh to the soul, and consequently both soul and flesh to God—does not this virtue demonstrate that it is as yet rather labouring towards its end than resting in its finished work? For the soul is so much the less subjected to God as it is less occupied with the thought of God; and the flesh is so much the less subjected to the spirit as it lusts more vehemently against the spirit. So long, therefore, as we are beset by this weakness, this plague, this disease, how shall we dare to say that we are safe? and if not safe, then how can we be already enjoying our final beatitude? Then that virtue which goes by the name of fortitude is the plainest proof of the ills of life, for it is these ills which it is compelled to bear patiently. And this holds good, no matter though the ripest wisdom co-exists with it. And I am at a loss to understand how the Stoic philosophers can presume to say that these are no ills, though at the same time they allow the wise man to commit suicide and pass out of this life if they become so grievous that he cannot or ought not to endure them. But such is the stupid pride of these men who fancy that the supreme good can be found in this life, and that they can become happy by their own resources, that their wise man, or at least the man whom they fancifully depict as such, is always happy, even though he become blind, deaf, dumb, mutilated, racked with pains, or suffer any conceivable calamity such as may compel him to make away with himself; and they are not ashamed to call the life that is beset with these evils happy. O happy life, which seeks the aid of death to end it! If it is happy, let the wise man remain in it; but if these ills drive him out of it, in what sense is it happy? Or how can they say that these are not evils which conquer the virtue of fortitude, and force it not only to yield, but so to rave that it in one breath calls life happy and recommends it to be given up? For who is so blind as not to see that if it were happy it would not be fled from? And if they say we should flee from it on account of the infirmities that beset it, why then do they not lower their pride and acknowledge that it is miserable? Was it, I would ask, fortitude or weakness which prompted Cato to kill himself? for he would not have done so had he not been too weak to endure Cæsar's victory. Where, then, is his fortitude? It has yielded, it has succumbed, it has been so thoroughly overcome as to abandon, forsake, flee this happy life. Or was it no longer happy? Then it was miserable. How, then, were these not evils which made life miserable, and a thing to be escaped from?

And therefore those who admit that these are evils, as the Peripatetics do, and the Old Academy, the sect with Varro advocates, express a more intelligible doctrine; but theirs also is a surprising mistake, for they contend that this is a happy life which is beset by these evils, even though they be so great that he who endures them should commit suicide to escape them. "Pains and anguish of body," says Varro, "are evils, and so much the worse in proportion to their severity; and to escape them you must quit this life." What life, I pray? This life, he says, which is oppressed by such evils. Then it is happy in the midst of these very evils on account of which you say we must quit it? Or do you call it happy because you are at liberty to escape these evils by death? What, then, if by some secret judgment of God you were held fast and not permitted to die, nor suffered to live without these evils? In that case, at least, you would say that such a life was miserable. It is soon relinquished, no doubt, but this does not make it not miserable; for were it eternal, you yourself would pronounce it miserable. Its brevity, therefore, does not clear it of misery; neither ought it to be called happiness because it is a brief misery. Certainly there is a mighty force in these evils which compel a man—according to them, even a wise man—to cease to be a man that he may escape them, though they say, and say truly, that it is as it were the first and strongest demand of nature that a man cherish himself, and naturally therefore avoid death, and should so stand his own friend as to wish and vehemently aim at continuing to exist as a living creature, and subsisting in this union of soul and body. There is a mighty force in these evils to overcome this natural instinct by which death is by every means and with all a man's efforts avoided, and to overcome it so completely that what was avoided is desired, sought after, and if it cannot in any other way be obtained, is inflicted by the man on himself. There is a mighty force in these evils which make fortitude a homicide—if, indeed, that is to be called fortitude which is so thoroughly overcome by these evils, that it not only cannot preserve by patience the man whom it undertook to govern and defend, but is itself obliged to kill him. The wise man, I admit, ought to bear death with patience, but when it is inflicted by another. If, then, as these men maintain, he is obliged to inflict it on himself, certainly it must be owned that the ills which compel him to this are not only evils, but intorerable evils. The life, then, which is either subject to accidents, or environed with evils so considerable and grievous, could never have been called happy, if the men who give it this name had condescended to yield to the truth, and to be conquered by valid arguments, when they inquired after the happy life, as they yield to unhappiness, and are overcome by overwhelming evils, when they put themselves to death, and if they had not fancied that the supreme good was to be found in this mortal life; for the very virtues of this life, which are certainly its best and most useful possessions, are all the more telling proofs of its miseries in proportion as they are helpful against the violence of its dangers, toils, and woes. For if these are true virtues—and such cannot exist save in those who have true piety—they do not profess to be able to deliver the men who possess them from all miseries; for true virtues tell no such lies, but they profess that by the hope of the future world this life, which is miserably involved in the many and great evils of this world, is happy as it is also safe. For if not yet safe, how could it be happy? And therefore the Apostle Paul, speaking not of men without prudence, temperance, fortitude, and justice, but of those whose lives were regulated by true piety, and whose virtues were therefore true, says, "For we are saved by hope: now hope which is seen is not hope; for what a man seeth, why doth he yet hope for? But if we hope for that we see not, then do we with patience wait for it." As, therefore, we are saved, so we are made happy by hope. And as we do not as yet possess a present, but look for a future salvation, so is it with our happiness, and this "with patience"; for we are encompassed with evils, which we ought patiently to endure, until we come to the ineffable enjoyment of unmixed good; for there shall be no longer anything to endure. Salvation, such as it shall be in the world to come, shall itself be our final happiness. And this happiness these philosophers refuse to believe in, because they do not see it, and attempt to fabricate for themselves a happiness in this life, based upon a virtue which is as deceitful as it is proud.

. . .

rather because the Psalmist says of the city of God, the subject of this laborious work, "Praise the Lord, O Jerusalem; praise thy God, O Zion: for He hath strengthened the bars of thy gates; He hath blessed thy children within thee; who hath made thy borders peace." For when the bars of her gates shall be strengthened, none shall go in or come out from her; consequently we ought to understand the peace of her borders as that final peace we are wishing to declare. For even the mystical name of the city itself, that is, *Jerusalem,* means, as I have already said, "Vision of Peace." But as the word peace is employed in connection with things in this world in which certainly life eternal has no place, we have preferred to call the end or supreme good of this city life eternal rather than peace. Of this end the apostle says, "But now, being freed from sin, and become servants to God, ye have your fruit unto holiness, and the end life eternal." But, on the other hand, as those who are not familiar with Scripture may suppose that the life of the wicked is eternal life, either because of the immortality of the soul, which some of the philosophers even have recognised, or because of the endless punishment of the wicked, which forms a part of our faith, and which seems impossible unless the wicked live for ever, it may therefore be advisable, in order that every one may readily understand what we mean, to say that the end or supreme good of this city is either peace in eternal life, or eternal life in peace. For peace is a good so great, that even in this earthly and mortal life there is no word we hear with such pleasure, nothing we desire with such zest, or find to be more thoroughly gratifying. So that if we dwell for a little longer on this subject, we shall not, in my opinion, be wearisome to our readers, who will attend both for the sake of understanding what is the end of this city of which we speak, and for the sake of the sweetness of peace which is dear to all.

. . .

11. Of the Happiness of the Eternal Peace, Which Constitutes the End or True Perfection of the Saints

And thus we may say of peace, as we have said of eternal life, that it is the end of our good; and the

13. Of the Universal Peace Which the Law of Nature Preserves through All Disturbances, and by Which Every One Reaches His Desert in a Way Regulated by the Just Judge

The peace of the body then consists in the duly proportioned arrangement of its parts. The peace of the irrational soul is the harmonious repose of the appetites, and that of the rational soul the harmony of knowledge and action. The peace of body and soul is the well-ordered and harmonious life and health of the living creature. Peace between man and God is the well-ordered obedience of faith to eternal law. Peace between man and man is well-ordered concord. Domestic peace is the well-ordered concord between those of the family who rule and those who obey. Civil peace is a similar concord among the citizens. The peace of the celestial city is the perfectly ordered and harmonious enjoyment of God, and of one another in God. The peace of all things is the tranquillity of order. Order is the distribution which allots things equal and unequal, each to its own place. And hence, though the miserable, in so far as they are such, do certainly not enjoy peace, but are severed from that tranquillity of order in which there is no disturbance, nevertheless, inasmuch as they are deservedly and justly miserable, they are by their very misery connected with order. They are not, indeed, conjoined with the blessed, but they are disjoined from them by the law of order. And though they are disquieted, their circumstances are notwithstanding adjusted to them, and consequently they have some tranquillity of order, and therefore some peace. But they are wretched because, although not wholly miserable, they are not in that place where any mixture of misery is impossible. They would, however, be more wretched if they had not that peace which arises from being in harmony with the natural order of things. When they suffer, their peace is in so far disturbed; but their peace continues in so far as they do not suffer, and in so far as their nature continues to exist. As, then, there may be life without pain, while there cannot be pain without some kind of life, so there may be peace without war, but there cannot be war without some kind of peace, because war supposes the existence of some natures to wage it, and these natures cannot exist without peace of one kind or other.

And therefore there is a nature in which evil does not or even cannot exist; but there cannot be a nature in which there is no good. Hence not even the nature of the devil himself is evil, in so far as it is nature, but it was made evil by being perverted. Thus he did not abide in the truth, but could not escape the judgment of the Truth; he did not abide in the tranquillity of order, but did not therefore escape the power of the Ordainer. The good imparted by God to his nature did not screen him from the justice of God by which order was preserved in his punishment; neither did God punish the good which He had created but the evil which the devil had committed. God did not take back all He had imparted to his nature, but something He took and something He left, that there might remain enough to be sensible of the loss of what was taken. And this very sensibility to pain is evidence of the good which has been taken away and the good which has been left. For, were nothing good left, there could be no pain on account of the good which had been lost. For he who sins is still worse if he rejoices in his loss of righteousness. But he who is in pain, if he derives no benefit from it, mourns at least the loss of health. And as righteousness and health are both good things, and as the loss of any good thing is matter of grief, not of joy—if, at least, there is no compensation, as spiritual righteousness may compensate for the loss of bodily health—certainly it is more suitable for a wicked man to grieve in punishment than to rejoice in his fault. As, then, the joy of a sinner who has abandoned what is good is evidence of a bad will, so his grief for the good he has lost when he is punished is evidence of a good nature. For he who laments the peace his nature has lost is stirred to do so by some relics of peace which make his nature friendly to itself. And it is very just that in the final punishment the wicked and godless should in anguish bewail the loss of the natural advantages they enjoyed, and should perceive that they were most justly taken from them by that God whose benign liberality they had despised. God, then, the most wise Creator and most just Ordainer of all natures, who placed the human race upon earth as its greatest ornament, imparted to men some good things adapted to this life, to wit, temporal peace, such as we enjoy in this life from health and safety and human fellowship, and all things needful for the preservation and recovery of this peace, such the objects which are accommodated to our outward senses, light, night, the air, and waters suitable for us, and everything the body requires to sustain, shelter, heal, or beautify it: and all under this most equitable condition, that every man who made a good use of these advantages suited to the peace of his mortal condition, should receive ampler and better blessings, namely, the peace of immortality, accompanied by glory and honour in an endless life made fit for the enjoyment of God and of one another in God; but that he who used the present blessings badly should both lose them and should not receive the others.

14. Of the Order and Law Which Obtain in Heaven and Earth, whereby It Comes to Pass That Human Society Is Served by Those Who Rule It

The whole use, then, of things temporal has a reference to this result of earthly peace in the earthly community, while in the city of God it is connected with eternal peace. And therefore, if we were irrational animals, we should desire nothing beyond the proper arrangement of the parts of the body and the satisfaction of the appetites—nothing, therefore, but bodily comfort and abundance of pleasures, that the peace of the body might contribute to the peace of the soul. For if bodily peace be awanting, a bar is put to the peace even of the irrational soul, since it cannot obtain the gratification of its appetites. And these two together help out the mutual peace of soul and body, the peace of harmonious life and health. For as animals, by shunning pain, show that they love bodily peace, and, by pursuing pleasure to gratify their appetites, show that they love peace of soul, so their shrinking from death is a sufficient indication of their intense love of that peace which binds soul and body in close alliance. But, as man has a rational soul, he subordinates all this which he has in common with the beasts to the peace of his rational soul, that his intellect may have free play and may regulate his actions, and that he may thus enjoy the well-ordered harmony of knowledge and action which constitutes, as we have said, the peace of the rational soul. And for this purpose he must desire to be neither molested by pain, nor disturbed by desire, nor extinguished by death, that he may arrive at some useful knowledge by which he may regulate his life and manners. But, owing to the liability of the human mind to fall into mistakes, this very pursuit of knowledge may be a snare to him unless he has a divine Master, whom he may obey without misgiving, and who may at the same time give him such help as to preserve his own freedom. And because, so long as he is in this mortal body, he is a stranger to God, he walks by faith, not by sight; and he therefore refers all peace, bodily or spiritual or both, to that peace which mortal man has with the immortal God, so that he exhibits the well-ordered obedience of faith to eternal law. But as this divine Master inculcates two precepts—the love of God and the love of our neighbour—and as in these precepts a man finds three things he has to love—God, himself, and his neighbour—and that he who loves God loves himself thereby, it follows that he must endeavour to get his neighbour to love God, since he is ordered to love his neighbour as himself. He ought to make this endeavour in behalf of his wife, his children, his household, all within his reach, even as he would wish his neighbour to do the same for him if he needed it; and consequently he will be at peace, or in well-ordered concord, with all men, as far as in him lies. And this is the order of this concord, that a man, in the first place, injure no one, and, in the second, do good to every one he can reach. Primarily, therefore, his own household are his care, for the law of nature and of society gives him readier access to them and greater opportunity of serving them. And hence the apostle says, "Now, if any provide not for his own, and specially for those of his own house, he hath denied the faith, and is worse than an infidel." This is the origin of domestic peace, or the well-ordered concord of those in the family who rule and those who obey. For they who care for the rest rule—the husband the wife, the parents the children, the masters the servants; and they who are cared for obey—the women their husbands, the children their parents, the servants their masters. But in the family of the just man who lives by faith and is as yet a pilgrim journeying on to the celestial city, even those who rule serve those whom they seem to command; for they rule not from a love of power, but from a sense of the duty they owe to others—not because they are proud of authority, but because they love mercy.

15. Of the Liberty Proper to Man's Nature, and the Servitude Introduced by Sin,—a Servitude in Which the Man Whose Will Is Wicked Is the Slave of His Own Lust, Though He Is Free so Far as Regards Other Men

This is prescribed by the order of nature: it is thus that God has created man. For "let them," He says, "have dominion over the fish of the sea, and over the fowl of the air, and over every creeping thing which creepeth on the earth." He did not intend that His rational creature, who was made in His image, should have dominion over anything but the irrational creation—not man over man, but man over the beasts. And hence the righteous men in primitive times were made shepherds of cattle rather than kings of men, God intending thus to teach us what the relative position of the creatures is, and what the desert of sin; for it is with justice, we believe, that the condition of slavery is the result of sin. And this is why we do not find the word "slave" in any part of Scripture until righteous Noah branded the sin of his son with this name. It is a name, therefore, introduced by sin and not by nature. The origin of the Latin word for slave is supposed to be found in the circumstance that those who by the law of war were liable to be killed were sometimes preserved by their victors, and were hence called servants. And these circumstances could never have arisen save through sin. For even when we wage a just war, our adversaries must be sinning; and every victory, even though gained by wicked men, is a result of the first judgment of God, who humbles the vanquished either for the sake of removing or of punishing their sins. Witness that man of God, Daniel, who, when he was in captivity, confessed to God his own sins and the sins of his people, and declares with pious grief that these were the cause of the captivity. The prime cause, then, of slavery is sin, which brings man under the dominion of his fellow—that which does not happen save by the judgment of God, with whom is no unrighteousness, and who knows how to award fit punishments to every variety of offence. But our Master in heaven says, "Every one who doeth sin is the servant of sin." And thus there are many wicked masters who have religious men as their slaves, and who are yet themselves in bondage; "for of whom a man is overcome, of the same is he brought in bondage." And beyond question it is a happier thing to be the slave of a man than of a lust; for even this very lust of ruling, to mention no others, lays waste men's hearts with the most ruthless dominion. Moreover, when men are subjected to one another in a peaceful order, the lowly position does as much good to the servant as the proud position does harm to the master. But by nature, as God first created us, no one is the slave either of man or of sin. This servitude is, however, penal, and is appointed by that law which enjoins the preservation of the natural order and forbids its disturbance; for if nothing had been done in violation of that law, there would have been nothing to restrain by penal servitude. And therefore the apostle admonishes slaves to be subject to their masters, and to serve them heartily and with good-will, so that, if they cannot be freed by their masters, they may themselves make their slavery in some sort free, by serving not in crafty fear, but in faithful love, until all unrighteousness pass away, and all principality and every human power be brought to nothing, and God be all in all.

. . .

17. What Produces Peace, and What Discord, between the Heavenly and Earthly Cities

But the families which do not live by faith seek their peace in the earthly advantages of this life; while the families which live by faith look for those eternal blessings which are promised, and use as pilgrims such advantages of time and of earth as do not fascinate and divert them from God, but rather aid them to endure with greater ease, and to keep down the number of those burdens of the corruptible body which weigh upon the soul. Thus the things necessary for this mortal life are used by both kinds of men and families alike, but each has its own peculiar and widely different aim in using them. The earthly city, which does not live by faith, seeks an earthly peace, and the end it proposes, in the well-ordered concord of civic obedience and rule, is the combination of men's wills to attain the things which are helpful to this life. The heavenly city, or rather the part of it which sojourns on earth and lives by faith, makes use of this peace only because it must, until this mortal condition which necessitates it shall pass away. Consequently, so long as it lives like a captive and a stranger in the earthly city, though it has already received the promise of redemption, and the gift of the Spirit as the earnest of it, it makes no scruple to obey the laws of the earthly city, whereby the things necessary for the maintenance of this mortal life are administered; and thus, as this life is common to both cities, so there is a harmony between them in regard to what belongs to it. But, as the earthly city has had some philosophers whose doctrine is condemned by the divine teaching, and who, being deceived either by their own conjectures or by demons, supposed that many gods must be invited to take an interest in human affairs, and assigned to each a separate function and a separate department—to one the body, to another the soul; and in the body itself, to one the head, to another the neck, and each of the other members to one of the gods; and in like manner, in the soul, to one god the natural capacity was assigned, to another education, to another anger, to another lust; and so the various affairs of life were assigned—cattle to one, corn to another, wine to another, oil to another, the woods to another, money to another, navigation to another, wars and victories to another, marriages to another, births and fecundity to another, and other things to other gods: and as the celestial city, on the other hand, knew that one God only was to be worshipped, and that to Him alone was due that service which the Greeks call λατρεία, and which can be given only to a god, it has come to pass that the two cities could not have common laws of religion, and that the heavenly city has been compelled in this matter to dissent, and to become obnoxious to those who think differently, and to stand the brunt of their anger and hatred and persecutions, except in so far as the minds of their enemies have been alarmed by the multitude of the Christians and quelled by the manifest protection of God accorded to them. This heavenly city, then, while it sojourns on earth, calls citizens out of all nations, and gathers together a society of pilgrims of all languages, not scrupling about diversities in the manners, laws, and institutions whereby earthly peace is secured and maintained, but recognising that, however various these are, they all tend to one and the same end of earthly peace. It therefore is so far from rescinding and abolishing these diversities, that it even preserves and adapts them, so long only as no hindrance to the worship of the one supreme and true God is thus introduced. Even the heavenly city, therefore, while in its state of pilgrimage, avails itself of the peace of earth, and, so far as it can without injuring faith and godliness, desires and maintains a common agreement among men regarding the acquisition of the necessaries of life, and makes this earthly peace bear upon the peace of heaven; for this alone can be truly called and esteemed the peace of the reasonable creatures, consisting as it does in the perfectly ordered and harmonious enjoyment of God and of one another in God. When we shall have reached that peace, this mortal life shall give place to one that is eternal, and our body shall be no more this animal body which by its corruption weighs down the soul, but a spiritual body feeling no want, and in all its members subjected to the will. In its pilgrim state the heavenly city possesses this peace by faith; and by this faith it lives righteously when it refers to the attainment of that peace every good action towards God and man; for the life of the city is a social life.

ST. THOMAS AQUINAS

FROM THE *Summa Theologica*

In the twelfth and thirteenth centuries, European civilization experienced advances on many fronts. Artistic and educational innovations coincided with improvements in agriculture and commerce. Philosophy, too, experienced a resurgence. The classic works of the Greek philosophers, long maintained by Jewish and Muslim scholars, were available for the first time to the Christian world in Latin translation. By 1250, the chief works of Aristotle had been translated, along with commentaries by his Jewish and Muslim followers; this provided Catholic scholars with a dilemma. How should they respond to these works that were, in many ways, in opposition to the teachings of Augustine and Catholic theology? Virtually all Christian scholars of this day belonged to either the Dominican or Franciscan orders, each of which had a different reaction to these new works.

The Franciscans, most notably in the works of St. Bonaventure, declared Aristotle's teachings to be a combination of half-truths and outright falsehoods. Since, in their view, Aristotle opposed Augustine, the Franciscan stance toward his work was critical. The Dominicans, especially in the person of St. Thomas Aquinas, took a different view. They thought the philosophy of Aristotle reconcilable with Catholic dogma. In fact, Aquinas revered the thought of Aristotle so much that he referred to him as the Philosopher.

Thomas Aquinas (c. 1224–1274) was born at Roccasecca, Italy, near Aquino. Born into an aristocratic family, he was educated first in Italy and later at the University of Paris, where he eventually attained a professorship. In 1244, he entered the Dominican order. It was natural that he should turn his brilliant mind to the work of Aristotle. Aquinas studied under a Dominican scholar named Albert, who later became St. Albert the Great, whose commentaries on Aristotle helped bring the Greek thinker to the attention of Christendom.

The foremost philosopher of the medieval period, St. Thomas Aquinas achieved his goal of proving the compatibility of Aristotle's philosophy with Church theology by constructing a unified view of humans, nature, and God. Aquinas' philosophy is a rethinking of Aristotelianism, but with significant influences from Augustinism, Stoicism, and Neoplatonism. He was innovative in his reworking of the philosophies of his predecessors into a coherent whole that shows both the stamp of his own intelligence and the influence of his religious commitment.

In the field of ethics, reconciling Augustine and Aristotle would appear a difficult enterprise indeed. Aristotle's moral philosophy is relativistic, rational, and prudential while the ethics of Augustine is absolutist, grounded in faith, and independent of consequences. Yet Aquinas did not conclude that at least one of these two views was necessarily in error. Instead, he reconciled the two systems by making room for two kinds of ethical principles and concepts. Thus, for Aquinas two kinds of virtues exist. Natural virtues are attained by reason and training; theological virtues require faith and God's grace. The natural virtues lead to worldly happiness, the theological virtues to eternal happiness.

At the center of Aquinas' ethics is the concept of natural law. Natural law is the divine law discovered by human intelligence. We learn of the natural moral law and its requirements through the use of our practical reason. However, since intelligence may not always be reliable, God has spelled out his law in two forms: the Old Law given to Moses, and the New Law taught by Christ. Thus, synthesized by Aquinas under the concept of natural law, the ethics of Augustine and Aristotle now provide complementary, rather than competing, standards of moral conduct. Aquinas unified the precepts of the Catholic church and the natural philosophy of Aristotle. His optimistic view of the power of knowledge and intelligent action to improve human life contributed to the rebirth of natural science in the thirteenth century.

Aquinas' works fill twenty-five volumes in their original Latin. Along with commentaries, letters, sermons, devotionals, and other writings, Aquinas produced two great comprehensive treatises: Summa Contra Gentiles and the Summa Theologica. The term "summa" indicates an ordered synthesis of knowledge covering a wide field. The Summa Contra Gentiles is a synthesis of theology and philosophy designed to guide Dominican missionaries in arguing against the Muslims. The Summa Theologica, begun around 1264, runs to five volumes but was never completed; it aims to systematize theology for beginners in the subject. It is from the latter work that our excerpts are taken.

Question XC
On the Essence of Law
(In Four Articles)

We have now to consider the extrinsic principles of acts. Now the extrinsic principle inclining to evil is the devil, of whose temptations we have spoken in the First Part. But the extrinsic principle moving to good is God, Who both instructs us by means of His Law, and assists us by His Grace. Therefore, in the first place, we must speak of law; in the second place, of grace.

Concerning law, we must consider (1) law itself in general; (2) its parts. Concerning law in general three points offer themselves for our consideration: (1) its essence; (2) the different kinds of law; (3) the effects of law.

Under the first head there are four points of inquiry: (1) Whether law is something pertaining to reason? (2) Concerning the end of law. (3) Its cause. (4) The promulgation of law.

First Article
Whether Law Is Something
Pertaining to Reason?

We proceed thus to the First Article:—

Objection 1. It would seem that law is not something pertaining to reason. For the Apostle says (*Rom.* vii. 23): *I see another law in my members,* etc. But nothing pertaining to reason is in the members, since the reason does not make use of a bodily organ. Therefore law is not something pertaining to reason.

Obj. 2. Further, in the reason there is nothing else but power, habit and act. But law is not the power itself of reason. In like manner, neither is it a habit of reason, because the habits of reason are the intellectual virtues, of which we have spoken above. Nor again is it an act of reason, because then law would cease when the act of reason ceases, for instance, while we are asleep. Therefore law is nothing pertaining to reason.

Obj. 3. Further, the law moves those who are subject to it to act rightly. But it belongs properly to the will to move to act, as is evident from what has been said above. Therefore law pertains, not to the reason, but to the will, according to the words of the Jurist: *Whatsoever pleaseth the sovereign has the force of law.*

On the contrary, It belongs to the law to command and to forbid. But it belongs to reason to command, as was stated above. Therefore law is something pertaining to reason.

I answer that, Law is a rule and measure of acts, whereby man is induced to act or is restrained from acting; for *lex* [law] is derived from *ligare* [to bind], because it binds one to act. Now the rule and measure of human acts is the reason, which is the first principle of human acts, as is evident from what has been stated above. For it belongs to the reason to direct to the end, which is the first principle in all matters of action, according to the Philosopher. Now that which is the principle in any genus is the rule and measure of that genus: for instance unity in the genus of numbers, and the first movement in the genus of movements. Consequently, it follows that law is something pertaining to reason.

Reply Obj. 1. Since law is a kind of rule and measure, it may be in something in two ways. First, as in that which measures and rules; and since this is proper to reason, it follows that, in this way, law is in the reason alone. Secondly, as in that which is measured and ruled. In this way, law is in all those things that are inclined to something because of some law; so that any inclination arising from a law may be called a law, not essentially, but by participation as it were. And thus the inclination of the members to concupiscence is called *the law the members.*

Reply Obj. 2. Just as, in external acts, we may consider the work and the work done, for instance, the work of building and the house built, so in the acts of reason, we may consider the act itself of reason, i.e., to understand and to reason, and something produced by this act. With regard to the speculative reason, this is first of all the definition; secondly, the proposition; thirdly, the syllogism or argument. And since the practical reason also makes use of the syllogism in operable matters, as we have stated above and as the Philosopher teaches, hence we find in the practical reason something that holds the same position in regard to operations as, in the speculative reason, the proposition holds in regard to conclusions. Such universal propositions of the practical reason that are directed to operations have the nature of law. And these propositions are sometimes under our actual consideration, while sometimes they are retained in the reason by means of a habit.

Reply Obj. 3. Reason has its power of moving from the will, as was stated above; for it is due to the fact that one wills the end, that the reason issues its commands as regards things ordained to the end. But in order that the volition of what is commanded may have the nature of law, it needs to be in accord with some rule of reason. And in this sense is to be understood the saying that the will of the sovereign has the force of law; or otherwise the sovereign's will would savor of lawlessness rather than of law.

Second Article
Whether Law Is Always Directed to the Common Good?

We proceed thus to the Second Article:—

Objection 1. It would seem that law is not always directed to the common good as to its end. For it belongs to law to command and to forbid. But commands are directed to certain individual goods. Therefore the end of law is not always the common good.

Obj. 2. Further, law directs man in his actions. But human actions are concerned with particular matters. Therefore law is directed to some particular good.

Obj. 3. Further, Isidore says: *If law is based on reason, whatever is based on reason will be a law.* But reason is the foundation not only of what is ordained to the common good, but also of that which is directed to private good. Therefore law is not directed only to the good of all, but also to the private good of an individual.

On the contrary, Isidore says that *laws are enacted for no private profit, but for the common benefit of the citizens.*

I answer that, As we have stated above, law belongs to that which is a principle of human acts, because it is their rule and measure. Now as reason is a principle of human acts, so in reason itself there is something which is the principle in respect of all the rest. Hence to this principle chiefly and mainly law must needs be referred. Now the first principle in practical matters, which are the object of the practical reason, is the last end: and the last end of human life is happiness or beatitude, as we have stated above. Consequently, law must needs concern itself mainly with the order that is in beatitude. Moreover, since every part is ordained to the whole as the imperfect to the perfect, and since one man is a part of the perfect community, law must needs concern itself properly with the order directed to universal happiness. Therefore the Philosopher, in the above definition of legal matters, mentions both happiness and the body politic, since he says that we call those legal matters *just which are adapted to produce and preserve happiness and its parts for the body politic.* For the state is a perfect community, as he says in *Politics* i.

Now, in every genus, that which belongs to it chiefly is the principle of the others, and the others belong to that genus according to some order towards that thing. Thus fire, which is chief among hot things, is the cause of heat in mixed bodies, and these are said to be hot in so far as they have a share of fire. Consequently, since law is chiefly ordained to the common good, any other precept in regard to some individual work must needs be devoid of the nature of a law, save in so far as it regards the common good. Therefore every law is ordained to the common good.

Reply Obj. 1. A command denotes the application of a law to matters regulated by law. Now the order to the common good, at which law aims, is applicable to particular ends. And in this way commands are given even concerning particular matters.

Reply Obj. 2. Actions are indeed concerned with particular matters, but those particular matters are referable to the common good, not as to a common genus or species, but as to a common final cause, according as the common good is said to be the common end.

Reply Obj. 3. Just as nothing stands firm with regard to the speculative reason except that which is traced back to the first indemonstrable principles, so nothing stands firm with regard to the practical reason, unless it be directed to the last end which is the common good. Now whatever stands to reason in this sense has the nature of a law.

Third Article
Whether the Reason of Any Man Is Competent to Make Laws?

We proceed thus to the Third Article:—

Objection 1. It would seem that the reason of any man is competent to make laws. For the Apostle says (*Rom.* ii. 14) that *when the Gentiles, who have not the law, do by nature those things that are of the law, . . . they are a law to themselves.* Now he says this of all in general. Therefore anyone can make a law for himself.

Obj. 2. Further, as the Philosopher says, *the intention of the lawgiver is to lead men to virtue.* But every man can lead another to virtue. Therefore the reason of any man is competent to make laws.

Obj. 3. Further, just as the sovereign of a state governs the state, so every father of a family governs his household. But the sovereign of a state can make laws for the state. Therefore every father of a family can make laws for his household.

On the contrary, Isidore says, and the *Decretals* repeat: *A law is an ordinance of the people, whereby something is sanctioned by the Elders together with the Commonalty.* Therefore not everyone can make laws.

I answer that, A law, properly speaking, regards first and foremost the order to the common good. Now to order anything to the common good belongs either to the whole people, or to someone who is the vicegerent of the whole people. Hence the making of a law belongs either to the whole people or to a public personage who has care of the whole people; for in all other matters the directing of anything to the end concerns him to whom the end belongs.

Reply Obj. 1. As was stated above, a law is in a person not only as in one that rules, but also, by participation, as in one that is ruled. In the latter way, each one is a law to himself, in so far as he shares the direction that he receives from one who rules him. Hence the same text goes on: *Who show the work of the law written in their hearts* (*Rom.* ii. 15).

Reply Obj. 2. A private person cannot lead another to virtue efficaciously; for he can only advise, and if his advice be not taken, it has no coercive power, such as the law should have, in order to prove an efficacious inducement to virtue, as the Philosopher says. But this coercive power is vested in the whole people or in some public personage, to whom it belongs to inflict penalties, as we shall state further on. Therefore the framing of laws belongs to him alone.

Reply Obj. 3. As one man is a part of the household, so a household is a part of the state; and the state is a perfect community, according to *Politics* 1. Therefore, just as the good of one man is not the last end, but is ordained to the common good, so too the good of one household is ordained to the good of a single state, which is a perfect community. Consequently, he that governs a family can indeed make certain commands or ordinances, but not such as to have properly the nature of law.

Fourth Article
Whether Promulgation Is Essential to Law?

We proceed thus to the Fourth Article:—

Objection 1. It would seem that promulgation is not essential to law. For the natural law, above all, has the character of law. But the natural law needs no promulgation. Therefore it is not essential to law that it be promulgated.

Obj. 2. Further, it belongs properly to law to bind one to do or not to do something. But the obligation of fulfilling a law touches not only those in whose presence it is promulgated, but also others. Therefore promulgation is not essential to law.

Obj. 3. Further, the binding force of law extends even to the future, since *laws are binding in matters of the future,* as the jurists say. But promulgation concerns those who are present. Therefore it is not essential to law.

On the contrary, It is laid down in the *Decretals* that *laws are established when they are promulgated.*

I answer that, As was stated above, a law is imposed on others as a rule and measure. Now a rule or measure is imposed by being applied to those who are to be ruled and measured by it. Therefore, in order that a law obtain the binding force which is proper to a law, it must needs be applied to the men who have to be ruled by it. But such application is made by its being made known to them by promulgation. Therefore promulgation is necessary for law to obtain its force.

Thus, from the four preceding articles, the definition of law may be gathered. Law is nothing else than an ordinance of reason for the common good, promulgated by him who has the care of the community.

Reply Obj. 1. The natural law is promulgated by the very fact that God instilled it into man's mind so as to be known by him naturally.

Reply Obj. 2. Those who are not present when a law is promulgated are bound to observe the law, in so far as it is made known or can be made known to them by others, after it has been promulgated.

Reply Obj. 3. The promulgation that takes place in the present extends to future time by reason of the durability of written characters, by which means it is continually promulgated. Hence Isidore says that *lex* [law] *is derived from legere* [to read] *because it is written.*

Question XCI
On the Various Kinds of Law
(In Six Articles)

We must now consider the various kinds of law, under which head there are six points of inquiry: (1) Whether there is an eternal law? (2) Whether there is a natural law? (3) Whether there is a human law? (4) Whether there is a divine law? (5) Whether there is one divine law, or several? (6) Whether there is a law of sin?

First Article
Whether There Is an Eternal Law?

We proceed thus to the First Article:—

Objection 1. It would seem that there is no eternal law. For every law is imposed on someone. But there was not someone from eternity on whom a law could be imposed, since God alone was from eternity. Therefore no law is eternal.

Obj. 2. Further, promulgation is essential to law. But promulgation could not be from eternity, because there was no one to whom it could be promulgated from eternity. Therefore no law can be eternal.

Obj. 3. Further, law implies order to an end. But nothing ordained to an end is eternal, for the last end alone is eternal. Therefore no law is eternal.

On the contrary, Augustine says: *That Law which is the Supreme Reason cannot be understood to be otherwise than unchangeable and eternal.*

I answer that, As we have stated above, law is nothing else but a dictate of practical reason emanating from the ruler who governs a perfect community. Now it is evident, granted that the world is ruled by divine providence, as was stated in the First Part, that the whole community of the universe is governed by the divine reason. Therefore the very notion of the government of things in God, the rule of the universe, has the nature of a law. And since the divine reason's conception of things is not subject to time, but is eternal, according to *Prov.* viii. 23, therefore it is that this kind of law must be called eternal.

Reply Obj. 1. Those things that do not exist in themselves exist in God, inasmuch as they are known and preordained by Him, according to *Rom.* iv. 17: *Who calls those things that are not, as those that are.* Accordingly, the eternal concept of the divine law bears the character of an eternal law in so far as it is ordained by God to the government of things foreknown by Him.

Reply Obj. 2. Promulgation is made by word of mouth or in writing, and in both ways the eternal law is promulgated, because both the divine Word and the writing of the Book of Life are eternal. But the promulgation cannot be from eternity on the part of the creature that hears or reads.

Reply Obj. 3. Law implies order to the end actively, namely, in so far as it directs certain things to the end; but not passively,—that is to say, the law itself is not ordained to the end, except accidentally, in a governor whose end is extrinsic to him, and to which end his law must needs be ordained. But the end of the divine government is God Himself, and His law is not something other than Himself. Therefore the eternal law is not ordained to another end.

Second Article
Whether There Is in Us a Natural Law?

We proceed thus to the Second Article:

Objection 1. It would seem that there is no natural law in us. For man is governed sufficiently by the eternal law, since Augustine says that *the eternal law is that by which it is right that all things should be most orderly.* But nature does not abound in superfluities as neither does she fail in necessaries. Therefore man has no natural law.

Obj. 2. Further, by the law man is directed, in his acts, to the end, as was stated above. But the directing of human acts to their end is not a function of nature, as is the case in irrational creatures, which act for an end solely by their natural appetite; whereas man acts for an end by his reason and will. Therefore man has no natural law.

Obj. 3. Further, the more a man is free, the less is he under the law. But man is freer than all the animals because of his free choice, with which he is endowed in distinction from all other animals. Since, therefore, other animals are not subject to a natural law, neither is man subject to a natural law.

On the contrary, the *Gloss* on *Rom.* ii. 14 (*When the Gentiles, who have not the law, do by nature those things that are of the law*) comments as follows: *Although they have no written law, yet they have the natural law, whereby each one knows, and is conscious of, what is good and what is evil.*

I answer that, As we have stated above, law, being a rule and measure, can be in a person in two ways: in one way, as in him that rules and measures; in another way, as in that which is ruled and measured, since a thing is ruled and measured in so far as it partakes of the rule or measure. Therefore, since all things subject to divine providence are ruled and measured by the eternal law, as was stated above, it is evident that all things partake in some way in the eternal law, in so far as, namely, from its being imprinted on them, they de-

rive their respective inclinations to their proper acts and ends. Now among all others, the rational creature is subject to divine providence in a more excellent way, in so far as it itself partakes of a share of providence, by being provident both for itself and for others. Therefore it has a share of the eternal reason, whereby it has a natural inclination to its proper act and end; and this participation of the eternal law in the rational creature is called the natural law. Hence the Psalmist, after saying (*Ps.* iv. 6): *Offer up the sacrifice of justice,* as though someone asked what the works of justice are, adds: *Many say, Who showeth us good things?* in answer to which question he says: *The light of Thy countenance, O Lord, is signed upon us.* He thus implies that the light of natural reason, whereby we discern what is good and what is evil, which is the function of the natural law, is nothing else than an imprint on us of the divine light. It is therefore evident that the natural law is nothing else than the rational creature's participation of the eternal law.

Reply Obj. 1. This argument would hold if the natural law were something different from the eternal law; whereas it is nothing but a participation thereof, as we have stated above.

• *Reply Obj.* 2. Every act of reason and will in us is based on that which is according to nature, as was stated above. For every act of reasoning is based on principles that are known naturally, and every act of appetite in respect of the means is derived from the natural appetite in respect of the last end. Accordingly, the first direction of our acts to their end must needs be through the natural law.

Reply Obj. 3. Even irrational animals partake in their own way of the eternal reason, just as the rational creature does. But because the rational creature partakes thereof in an intellectual and rational manner, therefore the participation of the eternal law in the rational creature is properly called a law, since a law is something pertaining to reason, as was stated above. Irrational creatures, however, do not partake thereof in a rational manner, and therefore there is no participation of the eternal law in them, except by way of likeness.

Third Article
Whether There Is a Human Law?

We proceed thus to the Third Article:—

Objection 1. It would seem that there is not a human law. For the natural law is a participation of the eternal law, as was stated above. Now through the eternal law *all things are most orderly,* as

Augustine states. Therefore the natural law suffices for the ordering of all human affairs. Consequently there is no need for a human law.

Obj. 2. Further, law has the character of a measure, as was stated above. But human reason is not a measure of things, but *vice versa,* as is stated in *Metaph.* x. Therefore no law can emanate from the human reason.

Obj. 3. Further, a measure should be most certain, as is stated in *Metaph.* x. But the dictates of the human reason in matters of conduct are uncertain, according to *Wis.* ix. 14: *The thoughts of mortal men are fearful, and our counsels uncertain.* Therefore no law can emanate from the human reason.

On the contrary, Augustine distinguishes two kinds of law, the one eternal, the other temporal, which he calls human.

I answer that, As we have stated above, a law is a dictate of the practical reason. Now it is to be observed that the same procedure takes place in the practical and in the speculative reason, for each proceeds from principles to conclusions, as was stated above. Accordingly, we conclude that, just as in the speculative reason, from naturally known indemonstrable principles we draw the conclusions of the various sciences, the knowledge of which is not imparted to us by nature, but acquired by the efforts of reason, so too it is that from the precepts of the natural law, as from common and indemonstrable principles, the human reason needs to proceed to the more particular determination of certain matters. These particular determinations, devised by human reason, are called human laws, provided that the other essential conditions of law be observed, as was stated above. Therefore Tully says in his *Rhetoric* that *justice has its source in nature; thence certain things came into custom by reason of their utility; afterwards these things which emanated from nature, and were approved by custom, were sanctioned by fear and reverence for the law.*

Reply Obj. 1. The human reason cannot have a full participation of the dictate of the divine reason, but according to its own mode, and imperfectly. Consequently, just as on the part of the speculative reason, by a natural participation of divine wisdom, there is in us the knowledge of certain common principles, but not a proper knowledge of each single truth, such as that contained in the divine wisdom, so, too, on the part of the practical reason, man has a natural participation of the eternal law, according to certain common principles, but not as regards the particular determinations of individual cases, which are, however, contained in the eternal law. Hence the need for human reason to proceed further to sanction them by law.

Reply Obj. 2. Human reason is not, of itself, the rule of things. But the principles impressed on it by nature are the general rules and measures of all things relating to human conduct, of which the natural reason is the rule and measure, although it is not the measure of things that are from nature.

Reply Obj. 3. The practical reason is concerned with operable matters, which are singular and contingent, but not with necessary things, with which the speculative reason is concerned. Therefore human laws cannot have that inerrancy that belongs to the demonstrated conclusions of the sciences. Nor is it necessary for every measure to be altogether unerring and certain, but according as it is possible in its own particular genus.

Fourth Article
Whether There Was Any Need for a Divine Law?

We proceed thus to the Fourth Article:—

Objection 1. It would seem that there was no need for a divine law. For, as was stated above, the natural law is a participation in us of the eternal law. But the eternal law is the divine law, as was stated above. Therefore there is no need for a divine law in addition to the natural law and to human laws derived therefrom.

Obj. 2. Further, it is written (*Ecclus.* xv. 14) that *God left man in the hand of his own counsel.* Now counsel is an act of reason, as was stated above. Therefore man was left to the direction of his reason. But a dictate of human reason is a human law, as was stated above. Therefore there is no need for man to be governed also by a divine law.

Obj. 3. Further, human nature is more self-sufficing than irrational creatures. But irrational creatures have no divine law besides the natural inclination impressed on them. Much less, therefore, should the rational creature have a divine law in addition to the natural law.

On the contrary, David prayed God to set His law before him, saying (*Ps.* cxviii 33): *Set before me for a law the way of Thy justifications, O Lord.*

I answer that, Besides the natural and the human law it was necessary for the directing of human conduct to have a divine law. And this for four reasons.

First, because it is by law that man is directed how to perform his proper acts in view of his last end. Now if man were ordained to no other end than that which is proportionate to his natural ability, there would be no need for man to have any further direction, on the part of his reason, in addition to the natural law and humanly devised law which is derived from it. But since man is ordained to an end of eternal happiness which exceeds man's natural ability, as we have stated above, therefore it was necessary that, in addition to the natural and the human law, man should be directed to his end by a law given by God.

Secondly, because, by reason of the uncertainty of human judgment, especially on contingent and particular matters, different people form different judgments on human acts; whence also different and contrary laws result. In order, therefore, that man may know without any doubt what he ought to do and what he ought to avoid, it was necessary for man to be directed in his proper acts by a law given by God, for it is certain that such a law cannot err.

Thirdly, because man can make laws in those matters of which he is competent to judge. But man is not competent to judge of interior movements, that are hidden, but only of exterior acts which are observable; and yet for the perfection of virtue it is necessary for man to conduct himself rightly in both kinds of acts. Consequently, human law could not sufficiently curb and direct interior acts, and it was necessary for this purpose that a divine law should supervene.

Fourthly, because, as Augustine says, human law cannot punish or forbid all evil deeds, since, while aiming at doing away with all evils, it would do away with many good things, and would hinder the advance of the common good, which is necessary for human living. In order, therefore, that no evil might remain unforbidden and unpunished, it was necessary for the divine law to supervene, whereby all sins are forbidden.

And these four causes are touched upon in *Ps.* cxviii. 8, where it is said: *The law of the Lord is unspotted,* i.e., allowing no foulness of sin; *converting souls,* because it directs not only exterior, but also interior, acts; *the testimony of the Lord is faithful,* because of the certainty of what is true and right; *giving wisdom to little ones,* by directing man to an end supernatural and divine.

Reply Obj. 1. By the natural law the eternal law is participated proportionately to the capacity of human nature. But to his supernatural end man needs to be directed in a yet higher way. Hence the additional law given by God, whereby man shares more perfectly in the eternal law.

Reply Obj. 2. Counsel is a kind of inquiry, and hence must proceed from some principles. Nor is it enough for it to proceed from principles imparted by nature, which are the precepts of the natural law, for the reasons given above; but there is need for certain additional principles, namely, the precepts of the divine law.

Reply Obj. 3. Irrational creatures are not ordained to an end higher than that which is proportionate to their natural powers. Consequently the comparison fails.

Fifth Article
Whether There Is but One Divine Law?

We proceed thus to the Fifth Article:—

Objection 1. It would seem that there is but one divine law. For, where there is one king in one kingdom, there is but one law. Now the whole of mankind is compared to God as to one king, according to *Ps.* xlvi. 8: *God is the King of all the earth.* Therefore there is but one divine law.

Obj. 2. Further, every law is directed to the end which the lawgiver intends for those for whom he makes the law. But God intends one and the same thing for all men, since according to *1 Tim.* ii. 4: *He will have all men to be saved, and to come to the knowledge of the truth.* Therefore there is but one divine law.

Obj. 3. Further, the divine law seems to be more akin to the eternal law, which is one, than the natural law, according as the revelation of grace is of a higher order than natural knowledge. But natural law is one for all men. Therefore much more is the divine law but one.

On the contrary, The Apostle says (*Heb.* vii. 12): *The priesthood being translated, it is necessary that a translation also be made of the law.* But the priesthood is twofold, as stated in the same passage, viz., the levitical priesthood, and the priesthood of Christ. Therefore the divine law is twofold, namely, the Old Law and the New Law.

I answer that, As we have stated in the First Part, distinction is the cause of number. Now things may be distinguished in two ways. First, as those things that are altogether specifically different, *e.g.,* a horse and an ox. Secondly, as perfect and imperfect in the same species, *e.g.,* a boy and a man; and in this way the divine law is distinguished into Old and New. Hence the Apostle (*Gal.* iii. 24, 25) compares the state of man under the Old Law to that of a child *under a pedagogue;* but the state under the New Law, to that of a full grown man, who is *no longer under a pedagogue.*

Now the perfection and imperfection of these two laws is to be taken in connection with the three conditions pertaining to law, as was stated above. For, in the first place, it belongs to law to be directed to the common good as to its end, as was stated above. This good may be twofold. It may be a sensible and earthly good, and to this man was directly ordained by the Old Law. Hence it is that, at the very outset of the Law, the people were invited to the earthly kingdom of the Chananæans (*Exod.* iii. 8, 17). Again it may be an intelligible and heavenly good, and to this, man is ordained by the New Law. Therefore, at the very beginning of His preaching, Christ invited men to the kingdom of heaven, saying (*Matt.* iv. 17): *Do penance, for the kingdom of heaven is at hand.* Hence Augustine says that *promises of temporal goods are contained in the Old Testament, for which reason it is called old; but the promise of eternal life belongs to the New Testament.*

Secondly, it belongs to law to direct human acts according to the order of justice; wherein also the New Law surpasses the Old Law, since it directs our internal acts, according to *Matt.* v. 20: *Unless your justice abound more than that of the Scribes and Pharisees, you shall not enter into the kingdom of heaven.* Hence the saying that *the Old Law restrains the hand, but the New Law controls the soul.*

Thirdly, it belongs to law to induce men to observe its commandments. This the Old Law did by the fear of punishment, but the New Law, by love, which is poured into our hearts by the grace of Christ, bestowed in the New Law, but foreshadowed in the Old. Hence Augustine says that *there is little difference between the Law and the Gospel—fear* [timor] *and love* [amor]

Reply Obj. 1. As the father of a family issues different commands to the children and to the adults, so also the one King, God, in His one kingdom, gave one law to men while they were yet imperfect, and another more perfect law when, by the preceding law, they had been led to a greater capacity for divine things.

Reply Obj. 2. The salvation of man could not be achieved otherwise than through Christ, according to *Acts* iv. 12: *There is no other name . . . given to men, whereby we must be saved.* Consequently, the law that brings all to salvation could not be given until after the coming of Christ. But before His coming it was necessary to give to the people, of whom Christ was to be born, a law containing certain rudiments of justice unto salvation, in order to prepare them to receive Him.

Reply Obj. 3. The natural law directs man by way of certain general precepts, common to both the perfect and the imperfect. Hence it is one and the same for all. But the divine law directs man also in certain particular matters, to which the perfect and imperfect do not stand in the same relation. Hence the necessity for the divine law to be twofold, as we have already explained.

Sixth Article
Whether There Is a Law in the *Fomes* of Sin?

We proceed thus to the Sixth Article:—

Objection 1. It would seem that there is no law of the 'fomes' of sin. For Isidore says that the *law is based on reason.* But the 'fomes' of sin is not based on reason, but deviates from it. Therefore the 'fomes' has not the nature of a law.

Obj. 2. Further, every law is binding, so that those who do not obey it are called transgressors. But man is not called a transgressor from not following the instigations of the 'fomes,' but rather from his following them. Therefore the 'fomes' has not the nature of a law.

Obj. 3. Further, law is ordained to the common good, as was stated above. But the 'fomes' inclines us, not to the common good, but to our own private good. Therefore the 'fomes' has not the nature of law.

On the contrary, The Apostle says (*Rom.* vii. 23): *I see another law in my members, fighting against the law of my mind.*

I answer that, As we have stated above, law, as to its essence, resides in him that rules and measures, but, by way of participation, in that which is ruled and measured; so that every inclination or ordination which may be found in things subject to law is called a law by participation, as was stated above. Now those who are subject to law may receive a twofold inclination from the lawgiver. First, in so far as he directly inclines his subjects to something. According to this, he directs different subjects to different acts; and in this way we may say that there is a military law and a mercantile law. Secondly, indirectly, and thus by the very fact that a lawgiver deprives a subject of some dignity, the latter passes into another order, so as to be under another law, as it were. For example, if a soldier be turned out of the army, he will become a subject of rural or of mercantile legislation.

Accordingly, under the divine Lawgiver, various creatures have various natural inclinations, so that what is, as it were, a law for one, is against the law for another. Thus, I might say that fierceness is, in a way, the law of a dog, but against the law of a sheep or another meek animal. And so the law of man, which, by the divine ordinance, is allotted to him according to his proper natural condition, is that he should act in accordance with reason; and this law was so effective in man's first state, that nothing either outside or against reason could take man unawares. But when man turned his back on God, he fell under the influence of his sensual impulses. In fact, this happens to each one individually, according as he has the more departed from the path of reason; so that, after a fashion, he is likened to the beasts that are led by the impulse of sensuality, according to Ps. xlviii. 21: *Man, when he was in honor, did not understand: he hath been compared to senseless beasts, and made like to them.*

Accordingly, then, this very inclination of sensuality, which is called the 'fomes,' in other animals has absolutely the nature of law, yet only in so far as we may consider as law what is an inclination subject to law. But in man, it has not the nature of law in this way; rather is it a deviation from the law of reason. But since, by the just sentence of God, man is deprived of original justice, and his reason bereft of its vigor, this impulse of sensuality, whereby he is led, has the nature of a law in so far as it is a penalty following from the divine law depriving man of his proper dignity.

Reply Obj. I. This argument considers the 'fomes' in itself as an incentive to evil. It is not thus that it has the nature of a law, as we have stated above, but according as it results from the justice of the divine law; much as though we were to say that it is a law that a nobleman should be made subject to menial labor because of some misdeed.

Reply Obj. 2. This argument considers law in the light of a rule or measure; for it is in this sense that those who deviate from the law become transgressors. But the 'fomes' is not a law in this respect, but by a kind of participation, as was stated above.

Reply Obj. 3. This argument considers the 'fomes' as to its proper inclination, and not as to its origin. And yet if the inclination of sensuality be considered as it is in other animals, thus it is ordained to the common good, namely, to the preservation of nature in the species or in the individual. This is true in man also, in so far as sensuality is subject to reason. But it is called the 'fomes' in so far as it departs from the order of reason.

Question XCII
On the Effects of Law
(In Two Articles)

We must now consider the effects of law, under which head there are two points of inquiry: (1) Whether it is an effect of law to make men good? (2) Whether the *effects of law are to command, to forbid, to permit and to punish,* as the Jurist states?

First Article
Whether It Is an Effect of
Law to Make Men Good?

We proceed thus to the First Article:—

Objection 1. It seems that it is not an effect of law to make men good. For men are good through virtue, since virtue, as is stated in *Ethics* ii., is *that which makes its subject good.* But virtue is in man from God alone, because He it is Who *works it in us without us,* as was stated above in the definition of virtue. Therefore it does not belong to law to make men good.

Obj. 2. Further, Law does not profit a man unless he obeys it. But the very fact that a man obeys a law is due to his being good. Therefore in man goodness is presupposed to the law. Therefore the law does not make men good.

Obj. 3. Further, Law is ordained to the common good, as was stated above. But some behave well in things regarding the community, who behave ill in things regarding themselves. Therefore it does not belong to law to make men good.

Obj. 4. Further, some laws are tyrannical, as the Philosopher says. But a tyrant does not intend the good of his subjects, but considers only his own profit. Therefore law does not make men good.

On the contrary, The Philosopher says that the *intention of every lawgiver is to make men good.*

I answer that, As we have stated above, a law is nothing else than a dictate of reason in the ruler by whom his subjects are governed. Now the virtue of any being that is a subject consists in its being well subordinated to that by which it is regulated; and thus we see that the virtue of the irascible and concupiscible powers consists in their being obedient to reason. In the same way, *the virtue of every subject consists in his being well subjected to his ruler,* as the Philosopher says. But every law aims at being obeyed by those who are subject to it. Consequently it is evident that the proper effect of law is to lead its subjects to their proper virtue; and since virtue is *that which makes its subject good,* it follows that the proper effect of law is to make those, to whom it is given, good, either absolutely or in some particular respect. For if the intention of the lawgiver is fixed on a true good, which is the common good regulated according to divine justice, it follows that the effect of law is to make men good absolutely. If, however, the intention of the lawgiver is fixed on that which is not good absolutely, but useful or pleasurable to himself, or in opposition to divine justice, then law does not make men good absolutely, but in a relative way, namely, in relation to that particular government. In this way good is found even in things that are bad of themselves. Thus a man is called a good robber, because he works in a way that is adapted to his end.

Reply Obj. 1. Virtue is twofold, as was explained above, viz., acquired and infused. Now the fact of being accustomed to an action contributes to both, but in different ways; for it causes the acquired virtue, while it disposes to infused virtue, and preserves and fosters it when it already exists. And since law is given for the purpose of directing human acts, insofar as human acts conduce to virtue, so far does law make men good. Therefore the Philosopher says in the second book of the *Politics* that *lawgivers make men good by habituating them to good works.*

Reply Obj. 2. It is not always through the perfect goodness of virtue that one obeys the law, but sometimes it is through fear of punishment, and sometimes from the mere dictate of reason, which is a beginning of virtue, as we have stated above.

Reply Obj. 3. The goodness of any part is considered in its relation with the whole; and hence Augustine says that *unseemly is the part that harmonizes not with the whole to which it belongs.* Since, then, every man is a part of the state, it is impossible that a man be good, unless he be well ordered to the common good, nor can the whole be well ordered unless its parts be proportioned to it. Consequently, the common good of the state cannot flourish, unless the citizens be virtuous, at least those whose business it is to govern. But it is enough for the good of the community that the other citizens be so far virtuous that they obey the commands of their rulers. Hence the Philosopher says that *the virtue of a sovereign is the same as that of a good man, but the virtue of any common citizen is not the same as that of a good man.*

Reply Obj. 4. A tyrannical law, through not being according to reason, is not a law, absolutely speaking, but rather a perversion of law; and yet in so far as it is something in the nature of a law, its aim is that the citizens be good. For it has the nature of law only in so far as it is an ordinance made by a superior to his subjects, and aims at being obeyed by them; and this is to make them good, not absolutely, but with respect to that particular government.

Second Article
Whether the Acts of Law Are Suitably Assigned?

We proceed thus to the Second Article:—

Objection 1. It would seem that the acts of law are not suitably assigned as consisting in *command, prohibition, permission and punishment.* For *every law is a general precept,* as the Jurist states. But command and precept are the same. Therefore the other three are superfluous.

Obj. 2. Further, the effect of law is to induce its subjects to be good, as was stated above. But counsel aims at a higher good than a command does. Therefore it belongs to law to counsel rather than to command.

Obj. 3. Further, just as punishment stirs a man to good deeds, so does reward. Therefore, if to punish is reckoned an effect of law, so also is to reward.

Obj. 4. Further, the intention of a lawgiver is to make men good, as was stated above. But he that obeys the law merely through fear of being punished is not good; because, *although a good deed may be done through servile fear, i.e., fear of punishment, it is not done well,* as Augustine says. Therefore punishment is not a proper effect of law.

On the contrary, Isidore says: *Every law either permits something, as: 'A brave man may demand his reward'; or forbids something, as: 'No man may ask a consecrated virgin in marriage'; or punishes, as: 'Let him that commits a murder be put to death.'*

I answer that, Just as an enunciation is a dictate of reason as asserting something, so a law is a dictate of reason as commanding something. Now it is proper to reason to lead from one thing to another. Therefore, just as, in the demonstrative sciences, the reason leads us from certain principles to assent to the conclusion, so it induces us by some means to assent to the precept of the law.

Now the precepts of law are concerned with human acts, in which the law directs, as stated above. But there are three kinds of human acts. For, as was stated above, some acts are good of their nature, viz., acts of virtue, and in respect of these the act of the law is a precept or command, for *the law commands all acts of virtue.* Other acts are evil of their nature, viz., acts of vice, and in respect of these the law forbids. And other acts are, of their nature, indifferent, and in respect of these the law permits. (We may add that all acts that are either not distinctly good or not distinctly bad may be called indifferent.) Furthermore, it is the fear of punishment that law makes use of in order to ensure obedience; and in this respect punishment is an effect of law.

Reply Obj. 1. Just as to cease from evil is a kind of good, so a prohibition is a kind of precept; and, accordingly, taking precept in a wide sense, every law is regularly called a precept.

Reply Obj. 2. To advise is not a proper act of law, but may be within the competence even of a private person, who cannot make a law. Hence, the Apostle, after giving a certain counsel (*1 Cor.* vii. 12) says: *I speak, not the Lord.* Consequently, it is not reckoned as an effect of law.

Reply Obj. 3. To reward may also pertain to anyone, but to punish pertains to none but the administrator of the law, by whose authority the pain is inflicted. Therefore to reward is not reckoned an effect of law, but only to punish.

Reply Obj. 4. From becoming accustomed to avoid evil and fulfill what is good, through fear of punishment, one is sometimes led on to do so likewise with pleasure and of one's own accord. Accordingly, law, even by punishing, leads men on to being good.

. . .

Question XCIV
The Natural Law
(In Six Articles)

We must now consider the natural law, concerning which there are six points of inquiry: (1) What is the natural law? (2) What are the precepts of the natural law? (3) Whether all the acts of the virtues are prescribed by the natural law? (4) Whether the natural law is the same in all? (5) Whether it is changeable? (6) Whether it can be abolished from the mind of man?

First Article
Whether the Natural Law Is a Habit?

We proceed thus to the First Article:—

Objection 1. It would seem that the natural law is a habit. For, as the Philosopher says, *there are three things in the soul, power, habit and passion.* But the natural law is not one of the soul's powers, nor is it one of the passions, as we may see by going through them one by one. Therefore the natural law is a habit.

Obj. 2. Further, Basil says that the *conscience or synderesis is the law of our mind;* which can apply only to the natural law. But *synderesis* is a habit, as was shown in the First Part. Therefore the natural law is a habit.

Obj. 3. Further, the natural law abides in man always, as will be shown further on. But man's reason, which the law regards, does not always think about the natural law. Therefore the natural law is not an act, but a habit.

On the contrary, Augustine says that *a habit is that whereby something is done when necessary.* But such is not the natural law, since it is in infants and in the damned who cannot act by it. Therefore the natural law is not a habit.

I answer that, A thing may be called a habit in two ways. First, properly and essentially, and thus the natural law is not a habit. For it has been stated above that the natural law is something appointed by reason, just as a proposition is a work of reason. Now that which a man does is not the same as that whereby he does it, for he makes a becoming speech by the habit of grammar. Since, then, a habit is that by which we act, a law cannot be a habit properly and essentially.

Secondly, the term habit may be applied to that which we hold by a habit. Thus *faith* may mean *that which we hold by faith*. Accordingly, since the precepts of the natural law are sometimes considered by reason actually, while sometimes they are in the reason only habitually, in this way the natural law may be called a habit. So, too, in speculative matters, the indemonstrable principles are not the habit itself whereby we hold these principles; they are rather the principles of which we possess the habit.

Reply Obj. 1. The Philosopher proposes there to discover the genus of virtue; and since it is evident that virtue is a principle of action, he mentions only those things which are principles of human acts, viz., powers, habits and passions. But there are other things in the soul besides these three: *e.g.,* acts, as *to will* is in the one that wills; again, there are things known in the knower; moreover its own natural properties are in the soul, such as immortality and the like.

Reply Obj. 2. *Synderesis* is said to be the law of our intellect because it is a habit containing the precepts of the natural law, which are the first principles of human actions.

Reply Obj. 3. This argument proves that the natural law is held habitually; and this is granted.

To the argument advanced in the contrary sense we reply that sometimes a man is unable to make use of that which is in him habitually, because of some impediment. Thus, because of sleep, a man is unable to use the habit of science. In like manner, through the deficiency of his age, a child cannot use the habit of the understanding of principles, or the natural law, which is in him habitually.

Second Article
Whether the Natural Law Contains Several Precepts, or Only One?

We proceed thus to the Second Article:—

Objection 1. It would seem that the natural law contains, not several precepts, but only one. For law is a kind of precept, as was stated above. If therefore there were many precepts of the natural law, it would follow that there are also many natural laws.

Obj. 2. Further, the natural law is consequent upon human nature. But human nature, as a whole, is one, though, as to its parts, it is manifold. Therefore, either there is but one precept of the law of nature because of the unity of nature as a whole, or there are many by reason of the number of parts of human nature. The result would be that even things relating to the inclination of the concupiscible power would belong to the natural law.

Obj. 3. Further, law is something pertaining to reason, as was stated above. Now reason is but one in man. Therefore there is only one precept of the natural law.

On the contrary, The precepts of the natural law in man stand in relation to operable matters as first principles do to matters of demonstration. But there are several first indemonstrable principles. Therefore there are also several precepts of the natural law.

I answer that, As was stated above, the precepts of the natural law are to the practical reason what the first principles of demonstrations are to the speculative reason, because both are self-evident principles. Now a thing is said to be self-evident in two ways: first, in itself; secondly, in relation to us. Any proposition is said to be self-evident in itself, if its predicate is contained in the notion of the subject; even though it may happen that to one who does not know the definition of the subject, such a proposition is not self-evident. For instance, this proposition, *Man is a rational being,* is, in its very nature, self-evident, since he who says *man,* says *a rational being;* and yet to one who does not know what a man is, this proposition is not self-evident. Hence it is that, as Boethius says, certain axioms or propositions are universally self-evident to all; and such are the propositions whose terms are known to all, as, *Every whole is greater than its part,* and, *Things equal to one and the same are equal to one another.* But some propositions are self-evident only to the wise, who understand the meaning of the terms of such propositions. Thus to one who understands that an angel is not a body, it is self-evident that an angel is not circumscriptively in a place. But this is not evident to the unlearned, for they cannot grasp it.

Now a certain order is to be found in those things that are apprehended by men. For that which first falls under apprehension is *being,* the understanding of which is included in all things whatsoever a man apprehends. Therefore the first indemonstrable principle is that *the same thing cannot be affirmed and denied at the same time,* which is based on the notion of *being* and *not-being:* and on this principle all others are based, as is stated in *Metaph.* iv. Now as *being* is the first thing that falls under the apprehension absolutely, so *good* is the first thing that falls under the apprehension of the practical reason, which is directed to action (since every agent acts for an end, which has the nature of good). Consequently, the first principle in the practical reason is one founded on the nature of good, viz., that *good is that which all things seek after.* Hence this is the first precept of law, that *good is to be done and promoted, and evil is to be avoided.* All other precepts of the natural law are based upon this; so that all the things which the practical reason naturally apprehends as man's good belong to the precepts of the natural law under the form of things to be done or avoided.

Since, however, good has the nature of an end, and evil, the nature of the contrary, hence it is that all those things to which man has a natural inclination are naturally apprehended by reason as being good, and consequently as objects of pursuit, and their contraries as evil, and objects of avoidance. Therefore, the order of the precepts of the natural law is according to the order of natural inclinations. For there is in man, first of all, an inclination to good in accordance with the nature which he has in common with all substances, inasmuch, namely, as every substance seeks the preservation of its own being, according to its nature; and by reason of this inclination, whatever is a means of preserving human life, and of warding off its obstacles, belongs to the natural law. Secondly, there is in man an inclination to things that pertain to him more specially, according to that nature which he has in common with other animals; and in virtue of this inclination, those things are said to belong to the natural law *which nature has taught to all animals,* such as sexual intercourse, the education of offspring and so forth. Thirdly, there is in man an inclination to good according to the nature of his reason, which nature is proper to him. Thus man has a natural inclination to know the truth about God, and to live in society; and in this respect, whatever pertains to this inclination belongs to the natural law: *e.g.,* to shun ignorance, to avoid offending those among whom one has to live, and other such things regarding the above inclination.

Reply Obj. 1. All these precepts of the law of nature have the character of one natural law, inasmuch as they flow from one first precept.

Reply Obj. 2. All the inclinations of any parts whatsoever of human nature, *e.g.,* of the concupiscible and irascible parts, in so far as they are ruled by reason, belong to the natural law, and are reduced to one first precept, as was stated above. And thus the precepts of the natural law are many in themselves, but they are based on one common foundation.

Reply Obj. 3. Although reason is one in itself, yet it directs all things regarding man; so that whatever can be ruled by reason is contained under the law of reason.

Third Article
Whether All the Acts of the Virtues Are Prescribed by the Natural Law?

We proceed thus to the Third Article:—

Objection 1. It would seem that not all the acts of the virtues are prescribed by the natural law. For, as was stated above, it is of the nature of law that it be ordained to the common good. But some acts of the virtues are ordained to the private good of the individual, as is evident especially in regard to acts of temperance. Therefore, not all the acts of the virtues are the subject of natural law.

Obj. 2. Further, every sin is opposed to some virtuous act. If therefore all the acts of the virtues are prescribed by the natural law, it seems to follow that all sins are against nature; whereas this applies to certain special sins.

Obj. 3. Further, those things which are according to nature are common to all. But the acts of the virtues are not common to all, since a thing is virtuous in one, and vicious in another. Therefore, not all the acts of the virtues are prescribed by the natural law.

On the contrary, Damascene says that *virtues are natural.* Therefore virtuous acts also are subject to the natural law.

I answer that, We may speak of virtuous acts in two ways: first, in so far as they are virtuous; secondly, as such and such acts considered in their proper species. If, then, we are speaking of the acts of the virtues in so far as they are virtuous, thus all virtuous acts belong to the natural law. For it has been stated that to the natural law belongs everything to which a man is inclined according to his nature. Now each thing is inclined naturally to an operation that is suitable to it according to its form: *e.g.,* fire is inclined to give heat. Therefore, since the rational soul is the proper form of man, there is in every man a natural inclination to act according to reason; and this is to act according to virtue. Consequently, considered thus, all the acts of the virtues are prescribed by the natural law, since each one's reason naturally dictates to him to act virtuously. But if we speak of virtuous acts, considered in themselves, *i.e.,* in their proper species, thus not all virtuous acts are prescribed by the natural law. For many things are done virtuously, to which nature does not primarily incline, but which, through the inquiry of reason, have been found by men to be conducive to well-living.

Reply Obj. 1. Temperance is about the natural concupiscences of food, drink and sexual matters, which are indeed ordained to the common good of nature, just as other matters of law are ordained to the moral common good.

Reply Obj. 2. By human nature we may mean either that which is proper to man, and in this sense all sins, as being against reason, are also against nature, as Damascene states; or we may mean that nature which is common to man and other animals, and in this sense, certain special sins are said to be against nature: *e.g.* contrary to sexual intercourse, which is natural to all animals, is unisexual lust, which has received the special name of the unnatural crime.

Reply Obj. 3. This argument considers acts in themselves. For it is owing to the various conditions of men that certain acts are virtuous for some, as being proportioned and becoming to them, while they are vicious for others, as not being proportioned to them.

Fourth Article
Whether the Natural Law Is the Same in All Men?

We proceed thus to the Fourth Article:—

Objection 1. It would seem that the natural law is not the same in all. For it is stated in the *Decretals* that *the natural law is that which is contained in the Law and the Gospel.* But this is not common to all men, because, as it is written (*Rom.* x. 16), *all do not obey the gospel.* Therefore the natural law is not the same in all men.

Obj. 2. Further, *Things which are according to the law are said to be just,* as is stated in *Ethics* v. But it is stated in the same book that nothing is so just for all as not to be subject to change in regard to some

men. Therefore even the natural law is not the same in all men.

Obj. 3. Further, as was stated above, to the natural law belongs everything to which a man is inclined according to his nature. Now different men are naturally inclined to different things,—some to the desire of pleasures, others to the desire of honors, and other men to other things. Therefore, there is not one natural law for all.

On the contrary, Isidore says: *The natural law is common to all nations.*

I answer that, As we have stated above, to the natural law belong those things to which a man is inclined naturally; and among these it is proper to man to be inclined to act according to reason. Now it belongs to the reason to proceed from what is common to what is proper, as is stated in *Physics* i. The speculative reason, however, is differently situated, in this matter, from the practical reason. For, since the speculative reason is concerned chiefly with necessary things, which cannot be otherwise than they are, its proper conclusions, like the universal principles, contain the truth without fail. The practical reason, on the other hand, is concerned with contingent matters, which is the domain of human actions; and, consequently, although there is necessity in the common principles, the more we descend towards the particular, the more frequently we encounter defects. Accordingly, then, in speculative matters truth is the same in all men, both as to principles and as to conclusions; although the truth is not known to all as regards the conclusions, but only as regards the principles which are called *common notions.* But in matters of action, truth or practical rectitude is not the same for all as to what is particular, but only as to the common principles; and where there is the same rectitude in relation to particulars, it is not equally known to all.

It is therefore evident that, as regards the common principles whether of speculative or of practical reason, truth or rectitude is the same for all, and is equally known by all. But as to the proper conclusions of the speculative reason, the truth is the same for all, but it is not equally known to all. Thus, it is true for all that the three angles of a triangle are together equal to two right angles, although it is not known to all. But as to the proper conclusions of the practical reason, neither is the truth or rectitude the same for all, nor, where it is the same, is it equally known by all. Thus, it is right and true for all to act according to reason, and from this principle it follows, as a proper conclusion, that goods entrusted to another should be restored to their owner. Now this is true for the majority of cases. But it may happen in a particular case that it would be injurious, and therefore unreasonable, to restore goods held in trust; for instance, if they are claimed for the purpose of fighting against one's country. And this principle will be found to fail the more, according as we descend further towards the particular, *e.g.*, if one were to say that goods held in trust should be restored with such and such a guarantee, or in such and such a way; because the greater the number of conditions added, the greater the number of ways in which the principle may fail, so that it be not right to restore or not to restore.

Consequently, we must say that the natural law, as to the first common principles, is the same for all, both as to rectitude and as to knowledge. But as to certain more particular aspects, which are conclusions, as it were, of those common principles, it is the same for all in the majority of cases, both as to rectitude and as to knowledge; and yet in some few cases it may fail, both as to rectitude, by reason of certain obstacles (just as natures subject to generation and corruption fail in some few cases because of some obstacle), and as to knowledge, since in some the reason is perverted by passion, or evil habit, or an evil disposition of nature. Thus at one time theft, although it is expressly contrary to the natural law, was not considered wrong among the Germans, as Julius Cæsar relates.

Reply Obj. 1. The meaning of the sentence quoted is not that whatever is contained in the Law and the Gospel belongs to the natural law, since they contain many things that are above nature; but that whatever belongs to the natural law is fully contained in them. Therefore Gratian, after saying that *the natural law is what is contained in the Law and the Gospel,* adds at once, by way of example, *by which everyone is commanded to do to others as he would be done by.*

Reply Obj. 2. The saying of the Philosopher is to be understood of things that are naturally just, not as common principles, but as conclusions drawn from them, having rectitude in the majority of cases, but failing in a few.

Reply Obj. 3: Just as in man reason rules and commands the other powers, so all the natural inclina-

tions belonging to the other powers must needs be directed according to reason. Therefore it is universally right for all men that all their inclinations should be directed according to reason.

Fifth Article
Whether the Natural Law Can Be Changed?

We proceed thus to the Fifth Article:—

Objection 1. It would seem that the natural law can be changed. For on *Ecclus.* xvii. 9 (*He gave them instructions, and the law of life*) the *Gloss* says: *He wished the law of the letter to be written, in order to correct the law of nature.* But that which is corrected is changed. Therefore the natural law can be changed.

Obj. 2. Further, the slaying of the innocent, adultery and theft are against the natural law. But we find these things changed by God: as when God commanded Abraham to slay his innocent son (*Gen.* xxii. 2); and when He ordered the Jews to borrow and purloin the vessels of the Egyptians (*Exod.* xii. 35); and when He commanded Osee to take to himself a *wife of fornications* (*Osee* i. 2). Therefore the natural law can be changed.

Obj. 3. Further, Isidore says that *the possession of all things in common, and universal freedom, are matters of natural law.* But these things are seen to be changed by human laws. Therefore it seems that the natural law is subject to change.

On the contrary, It is said in the *Decretals: The natural law dates from the creation of the rational creature. It does not vary according to time, but remains unchangeable.*

I answer that, A Change in the natural law may be understood in two ways. First, by way of addition. In this sense, nothing hinders the natural law from being changed, since many things for the benefit of human life have been added over and above the natural law, both by the divine law and by human laws.

Secondly, a change in the natural law may be understood by way of subtraction, so that what previously was according to the natural law, ceases to be so. In this sense, the natural law is altogether unchangeable in its first principles. But in its secondary principles, which, as we have said, are certain detailed proximate conclusions drawn from the first principles, the natural law is not changed so that what it prescribes be not right in most cases. But it may be changed in some particular cases of rare occurrence, through some special causes hindering the observance of such precepts, as was stated above.

Reply Obj. 1. The written law is said to be given for the correction of the natural law, either because it supplies what was wanting to the natural law, or because the natural law was so perverted in the hearts of some men, as to certain matters, that they esteemed those things good which are naturally evil; which perversion stood in need of correction.

Reply Obj. 2. All men alike, both guilty and innocent, die the death of nature; which death of nature is inflicted by the power of God because of original sin, according to *I Kings* ii. 6: *The Lord killeth and maketh alive.* Consequently, by the command of God, death can be inflicted on any man, guilty or innocent, without any injustice whatever.—In like manner, adultery is intercourse with another's wife; who is allotted to him by the law emanating from God. Consequently intercourse with any woman, by the command of God, is neither adultery nor fornication.—The same applies to theft, which is the taking of another's property. For whatever is taken by the command of God, to Whom all things belong, is not taken against the will of its owner, whereas it is in this that theft consists.—Nor is it only in human things that whatever is commanded by God is right; but also in natural things, whatever is done by God is, in some way, natural, as was stated in the First Part.

Reply Obj. 3. A thing is said to belong to the natural law in two ways. First, because nature inclines thereto: *e.g.,* that one should not do harm to another. Secondly, because nature did not bring with it the contrary. Thus, we might say that for man to be naked is of the natural law, because nature did not give him clothes, but art invented them. In this sense, *the possession of all things in common and universal freedom* are said to be of the natural law, because, namely, the distinction of possessions and slavery were not brought in by nature, but devised by human reason for the benefit of human life. Accordingly, the law of nature was not changed in this respect, except by addition.

Sixth Article
Whether the Natural Law Can Be Abolished from the Heart of Man?

We proceed thus to the Sixth Article:—

Objection 1. It would seem that the natural law can be abolished from the heart of man. For on *Rom.* ii. 14 (*When the Gentiles who have not the law,* etc.) the *Gloss* says that *the law of justice, which sin had blotted out, is graven on the heart of man when he is restored by grace.* But the law of justice is the law of nature. Therefore the law of nature can be blotted out.

Obj. 2. Further, the law of grace is more efficacious than the law of nature. But the law of grace is blotted out by sin. Much more, therefore, can the law of nature be blotted out.

Obj. 3. Further, that which is established by law is proposed as something just. But many things are enacted by men which are contrary to the law of nature. Therefore the law of nature can be abolished from the heart of man.

On the contrary, Augustine says: *Thy law is written in the hearts of men, which iniquity itself effaces not.* But the law which is written in men's hearts is the natural law. Therefore the natural law cannot be blotted out.

I answer that, As we have stated above, there belong to the natural law, first, certain most common precepts that are known to all; and secondly, certain secondary and more particular precepts, which are, as it were, conclusions following closely from first principles. As to the common principles, the natural law, in its universal meaning, cannot in any way be blotted out from men's hearts. But it is blotted out in the case of a particular action, in so far as reason is hindered from applying the common principle to the particular action because of concupiscence or some other passion, as was stated above.—But as to the other, *i.e.,* the secondary precepts, the natural law can be blotted out from the human heart, either by evil persuasions, just as in speculative matters errors occur in respect of necessary conclusions; or by vicious customs and corrupt habits, as, among some men, theft, and even unnatural vices, as the Apostle states (*Rom.* i. 24), were not esteemed sinful.

Reply Obj. 1. Sin blots out the law of nature in particular cases, not universally, except perchance in regard to the secondary precepts of the natural law, in the way stated above.

Reply Obj. 2. Although grace is more efficacious than nature, yet nature is more essential to man, and therefore more enduring.

Reply Obj. 3. This argument is true of the secondary precepts of the natural law, against which some legislators have framed certain enactments which are unjust.

Question XCV
Human Law
(In Four Articles)

WE must now consider human law, and (1) concerning this law considered in itself; (2) its power; (3) its mutability. Under the first head there are four points of inquiry: (1) Its utility. (2) Its origin. (3) Its quality. (4) Its division.

First Article
Whether It Was Useful for
Laws to Be Framed by Men?

We proceed thus to the First Article:—

Objection 1. It would seem that it was not useful for laws to be framed by men; For the purpose of every law is that man be made good thereby, as was stated above. But men are more to be induced to be good willingly by means of admonitions, than against their will, by means of laws. Therefore there was no need to frame laws.

Obj. 2. Further, As the Philosopher says, *men have recourse to a judge as to animate justice*. But animate justice is better than inanimate justice, which is contained in laws. Therefore it would have been better for the execution of justice to be entrusted to the decision of judges than to frame laws in addition.

Obj. 3. Further, every law is framed for the direction of human actions, as is evident from what has been stated above. But since human actions are about singulars, which are infinite in number, matters pertaining to the direction of human actions cannot be taken into sufficient consideration except by a wise man, who looks into each one of them. Therefore it would have been better for human acts to be directed by the judgment of wise men, than by the framing of laws. Therefore there was no need of human laws.

On the contrary, Isidore says: *Laws were made that in fear thereof human audacity might be held in check, that innocence might be safeguarded in the midst of wickedness, and that the dread of punishment might prevent the wicked from doing harm.* But these things are most necessary to mankind. Therefore it was necessary that human laws should be made.

I answer that, As we have stated above, man has a natural aptitude for virtue; but the perfection of virtue must be acquired by man by means of some kind of training. Thus we observe that a man is helped by diligence in his necessities, for instance, in food and clothing. Certain beginnings of these he has from nature, viz., his reason and his hands; but he has not the full complement, as other animals have, to whom nature has given sufficiently of clothing and food. Now it is difficult to see how man could suffice for himself in the matter of this training, since the perfection of virtue consists chiefly in withdrawing man from undue pleasures, to which above all man is inclined, and especially the young, who are more capable of being trained. Consequently a man needs to receive this training from another, whereby to arrive at the perfection of virtue. And as to those young people who are inclined to acts of virtue by their good natural disposition, or by custom, or rather by the gift of God, paternal training suffices, which is by admonitions. But since some are found to be dissolute and prone to vice, and not easily amenable to words, it was necessary for such to be restrained from evil by force and fear, in order that, at least, they might desist from evil-doing, and leave others in peace, and that they themselves, by being habituated in this way, might be brought to do willingly what hitherto they did from fear, and thus become virtuous. Now this kind of training, which compels through fear of punishment, is the discipline of laws. Therefore, in order that man might have peace and virtue, it was necessary for laws to be framed; for, as the Philosopher says, *as man is the most noble of animals if he be perfect in virtue, so he is the lowest of all, if he be severed from law and justice.* For man can use his reason to devise means of satisfying his lusts and evil passions, which other animals are unable to do.

Reply Obj. 1. Men who are well disposed are led willingly to virtue by being admonished better than by coercion; but men whose disposition is evil are not led to virtue unless they are compelled.

Reply Obj. 2. As the Philosopher says, *it is better that all things be regulated by law, than left to be decided by judges.* And this for three reasons. First, because it is easier to find a few wise men competent to frame right laws, than to find the many who would be necessary to judge rightly of each single case.—Secondly, because those who make laws consider long beforehand what laws to make, whereas judgment on each single case has to be pronounced as soon as it arises; and it is easier for man to see what is right, by taking many instances into consideration, than by considering one solitary instance.—Thirdly, because lawgivers judge universally and about future events, whereas those who sit in judgment judge of things present, towards which they are affected by love, hatred, or some kind of cupidity; and thus their judgment becomes perverted.

Since, then, the animated justice of the judge is not found in every man, and since it can be bent, therefore it was necessary, whenever possible, for the law to determine how to judge, and for very few matters to be left to the decision of men.

Reply Obj. 3. Certain individual facts which cannot be covered by the law *have necessarily to be committed to judges,* as the Philosopher says in the same passage: *e.g., concerning something that has happened or not happened,* and the like.

Second Article
Whether Every Human Law Is Derived from the Natural Law?

We proceed thus to the Second Article:—

Objection 1. It would seem that not every human law is derived from the natural law. For the Philosopher says that *the legal just is that which originally was a matter of indifference.* But those things which arise from the natural law are not matters of indifference. Therefore the enactments of human laws are not all derived from the natural law.

Obj. 2. Further, positive law is divided against natural law, as is stated by Isidore and the Philosopher. But those things which flow as conclusions from the common principles of the natural law belong to the natural law, as was stated above. Therefore that which is established by human law is not derived from the natural law.

Obj. 3. Further, the law of nature is the same for all, since the Philosopher says that *the natural just is that which is equally valid everywhere.* If therefore human laws were derived from the natural law, it would follow that they too are the same for all; which is clearly false.

Obj. 4. Further, it is possible to give a reason for things which are derived from the natural law. But *it is not possible to give the reason for all the legal enactments of the lawgivers,* as the Jurist says. Therefore not all human laws are derived from the natural law.

On the contrary, Tully says: *Things which emanated from nature, and were approved by custom, were sanctioned by fear and reverence for the laws.*

I answer that, As Augustine says, *that which is not just seems to be no law at all.* Hence the force of a law depends on the extent of its justice. Now in human affairs a thing is said to be just from being right, according to the rule of reason. But the first rule of reason is the law of nature, as is clear from what has been stated above. Consequently, every human law has just so much of the nature of law as it is derived from the law of nature. But if in any point it departs from the law of nature, it is no longer a law but a perversion of law.

But it must be noted that something may be derived from the natural law in two ways: first, as a conclusion from principles; secondly, by way of a determination of certain common notions. The first way is like to that by which, in the sciences, demonstrated conclusions are drawn from the principles; while the second is likened to that whereby, in the arts, common forms are determined to some particular. Thus, the craftsman needs to determine the common form of a house to the shape of this or that particular house. Some things are therefore derived from the common principles of the natural law by way of conclusions: *e.g.,* that *one must not kill* may be derived as a conclusion from the principle that *one should do harm to no man;* while some are derived therefrom by way of determination: *e.g.,* the law of nature has it that the evil-doer should be punished, but that he be punished in this or that way is a determination of the law of nature.

Accordingly, both modes of derivation are found in the human law. But those things which are derived in the first way are contained in human law, not as emanating therefrom exclusively, but as having some force from the natural law also. But those things which are derived in the second way have no other force than that of human law.

Reply Obj. 1. The Philosopher is speaking of those enactments which are by way of determination or specification of the precepts of the natural law.

Reply Obj. 2. This argument holds for those things that are derived from the natural law by way of conclusion.

Reply Obj. 3. The common principles of the natural law cannot be applied to all men in the same way because of the great variety of human affairs;

and hence arises the diversity of positive laws among various people.

Reply Obj. 4. These words of the Jurist are to be understood as referring to the decisions of rulers in determining particular points of the natural law; and to these determinations the judgment of expert and prudent men is related as to its principles, in so far, namely, as they see at once what is the best thing to decide. Hence the Philosopher says that, in such matters, *we ought to pay as much attention to the undemonstrated sayings and opinions of persons who surpass us in experience, age and prudence, as to their demonstrations.*

Third Article
Whether Isidore's Description of the Quality of Positive Law Is Appropriate?

We proceed thus to the Third Article:—

Objection 1. It would seem that Isidore's description of the quality of positive law is not appropriate, when he says: *Law shall be virtuous, just, possible to nature, according to the custom of the country, suitable to place and time, necessary, useful; clearly expressed, lest by its obscurity it lead to misunderstanding; framed for no private benefit, but for the common good.* For he had previously expressed the quality of law in three conditions, saying that *law is anything founded on reason, provided that it foster religion, be helpful to discipline, and further the common welfare.* Therefore it was needless to add any further conditions to these.

Obj. 2. Further, Justice is included in virtue [*honestas*], as Tully says. Therefore, after saying *virtuous,* it was superfluous to add *just.*

Obj. 3. Further, written law is co-divided against custom, according to Isidore. Therefore it should not be stated in the definition of law that it is *according to the custom of the country.*

Obj. 4. Further, a thing may be necessary in two ways. It may be necessary absolutely, because it cannot be otherwise; and that which is necessary in this way is not subject to human judgment. Hence human law is not concerned with necessity of this kind. Again, a thing may be necessary for an end, and this necessity is the same as usefulness. Therefore it is superfluous to say both *necessary* and *useful.*

On the contrary stands the authority of Isidore.

I answer that, Whenever a thing is for an end, its form must be determined proportionately to that end; as the form of a saw is such as to be suitable for cut-

ting. Again, everything that is ruled and measured must have a form proportioned to its rule and measure. Now both these conditions are verified in human law, since it is both something ordained to an end, and it is also a rule or measure ruled or measured by a higher measure. Now this higher measure is twofold, viz., the divine law and the natural law, as was explained above. But the end of human law is to be useful to man, as the Jurist states. Therefore Isidore, in determining the nature of law, first lays down three conditions; viz., that it *foster religion,* inasmuch as it is proportioned to the divine law; that it be *helpful to discipline,* inasmuch as it is proportioned to the natural law; and that it *further the common welfare,* inasmuch as it is proportioned to the utility of mankind.

All the other conditions mentioned by him are reduced to these three. For it is called virtuous because it fosters religion. And when he goes on to say that it should be *just, possible to nature, according to the customs of the country, adapted to place and time,* he implies that it should be suitable to discipline. For human discipline depends, first, on the order of reason, to which he refers by saying *just.* Secondly, it depends on the ability of the agent, because discipline should be adapted to each one according to his ability, taking also into account the ability of nature (for the same burdens should not be laid on children as on adults); and it should be according to human customs, since man cannot live alone in society, paying no heed to others. Thirdly, it depends on certain circumstances, in respect of which he says, *adapted to place and time.* The remaining words, *necessary, useful,* etc., mean that law should further the common welfare: so that *necessity* refers to the removal of evils, *usefulness,* to the attainment of good, *clearness of expression,* to the need of preventing any harm ensuing from the law itself. And since, as was stated above, law is ordained to the common good, this is expressed in the last part of the description.

This suffices for the Replies to the Objections.

Fourth Article
Whether Isidore's Division of Human Laws Is Appropriate?

We proceed thus to the Fourth Article:—

Objection 1. It would seem that Isidore divided human statutes or human law wrongly. For under this law he includes the *law of nations,* so called, because, as he says, *nearly all nations use it*. But, as he says, *natural law is that which is common to all nations*. Therefore the law of nations is not contained under positive human law, but rather under natural law.

Obj. 2. Further, those laws which have the same force seem to differ, not formally, but only materially. But *statutes, decrees of the commonalty, senatorial decrees,* and the like which he mentions, all have the same force. Therefore they do not differ, except materially. But art takes no notice of such a distinction, since it may go on to infinity. Therefore this division of human laws is not appropriate.

Obj. 3. Further, just as, in the state, there are princes, priests and soldiers, so there are other human offices. Therefore it seems that, as this division includes *military law,* and *public law,* referring to priests and magistrates, so also it should include other laws pertaining to other offices of the state.

Obj. 4. Further, those things that are accidental should be passed over. But it is accidental to law that it be framed by this or that man. Therefore it is unreasonable to divide laws according to the names of lawgivers, so that one be called the *Cornelian* law, another the *Falcidian* law, etc.

On the contrary, The authority of Isidore suffices.

I answer that, A thing can be divided essentially in respect of something contained in the notion of that thing. Thus a soul, either rational or irrational, is contained in the notion of animal; and therefore animal is divided properly and essentially in respect of its being rational or irrational, but not in the point of its being white or black, which are entirely outside the notion of animal. Now, in the notion of human law, many things are contained, in respect of any of which human law can be divided properly and essentially. For, in the first place, it belongs to the notion of human law to be derived from the law of nature, as was explained above. In this respect positive law is divided into the *law of nations* and *civil law,* according to the two ways in which something may be derived from the law of nature, as was stated above. For to the law of nations belong those things which are derived from the law of nature as conclusions from principles, *e.g.,* just buyings and sellings, and the like, without which men cannot live together; and this belongs to the law of nature, since man is by nature a social animal, as is proved in *Politics* i. But those things which are derived from the law of nature by way of particular determination belong to the civil law, according as each state decides on what is best for itself.

Secondly, it belongs to the notion of human law to be ordained to the common good of the state. In this respect, human law may be divided according to the different kinds of men who work in a special way for the common good: *e.g.,* priests, by praying to God for the people; princes, by governing the people; soldiers, by fighting for the safety of the people. Therefore certain special kinds of law are adapted to these men.

Thirdly, it belongs to the notion of human law to be framed by the one who governs the community of the state, as was shown above. In this respect, there are various human laws according to the various forms of government. Of these, according to the Philosopher, one is *monarchy, i.e.,* when the state is governed by one; and then we have *Royal Ordinances.* Another form is *aristocracy, i.e.,* government by the best men or men of highest rank; and then we have the *Authoritative legal opinions* [*Responsa Prudentum*] and *Decrees of the Senate* [*Senatus consulta*]. Another form is *oligarchy, i.e.,* government by a few rich and powerful men; and then we have *Prætorian,* also called *Honorary,* law. Another form of government is that of the people, which is called democracy, and there we have *Decrees of the commonalty* [*Plebiscita*]. There is also tyrannical government, which is altogether corrupt, which, therefore, has no corresponding law. Finally, there is a form of government made up of all these, and which is the best; and in this respect we have *law sanctioned by the Lords and Commons,* as is stated by Isidore.

Fourthly, it belongs to the notion of human law to direct human actions. In this respect, according to the various matters of which the law treats, there are various kinds of laws, which are sometimes named after their authors. Thus we have the *Lex Julia* about adultery, the *Lex Cornelia* concerning assassins, and so on, differentiated in this way, not because of the authors, but because of the matters to which they refer.

Reply Obj. 1. The law of nations is indeed, in some way, natural to man, in so far as he is a reasonable being, because it is derived from the natural law by way of a conclusion that is not very remote from its principles. Therefore men easily agreed thereto. Nevertheless, it is distinct from the natural law, especially from that natural law which is c6mmon to all animals.

The Replies to the other Objections are evident from what has been said.

Question XCVI
On the Power of Human Law
(In Six Articles)

We must now consider the power of human law. Under this head there are six points of inquiry: (1) Whether human law should be framed in a common way? (2) Whether human law should repress all vices? (3) Whether human law is competent to direct the acts of all the virtues? (4) Whether it binds man in conscience? (5) Whether all men are subject to human law? (6) Whether those who are under the law may act outside the letter of the law?

First Article
Whether Human Law Should Be Framed in a Common Way Rather Than in the Particular?

We proceed thus to the First Article:—

Objection 1. It would seem that human law should be framed, not in a common way, but rather in the particular. For the Philosopher says that *the legal just . . . includes all particular acts of legislation . . . and all those matters which are the subject of decrees,* which are also individual matters, since decrees are framed about individual actions. Therefore law is framed not only in a common way, but also in the particular.

Obj. 2. Further, law is the director of human acts, as was stated above. But human acts are about individual matters. Therefore human laws should be framed, not in a common way, but rather in the particular.

Obj. 3. Further, law is a rule and measure of human acts, as was stated above. But a measure should be most certain, as is stated in *Metaph.* x. Since, therefore, in human acts no universal proposition can be so certain as not to fail in some individual cases, it seems that laws should be framed, not in a common way, but in the particular.

On the contrary, The Jurist says that *laws should be made to suit the majority of instances; and they are not framed according to what may possibly happen in an individual case.*

I answer that, Whatever is for an end should be proportioned to that end. Now the end of law is the common good, because, as Isidore says, *law should be framed, not for any private benefit, but for the common*

good of all the citizens. Hence human laws should be proportioned to the common good. Now the common good comprises many things. Therefore law should take account of many things, as to persons, as to matters, and as to times. For the community of the state is composed of many persons, and its good is procured by many actions; nor is it established to endure for only a short time, but to last for all time by the citizens succeeding one another, as Augustine says.

Reply Obj. 1. The Philosopher divides the legal just, *i.e.,* positive law, into three parts. For some things are laid down absolutely in a common way, and these are the common laws. Of these he says that *the legal is that which originally was a matter of indifference, but which, when enacted, is so no longer:* e.g., the fixing of the ransom of a captive.—Some things affect the community in one respect, and individuals in another. These are called *privileges, i.e., private laws,* as it were, because they regard private persons, although their power extends to many matters; and in regard to these, he adds, *and further, all particular acts of legislation.*—Other matters are legal, not through being laws, but through being applications of common laws to particular cases. Such are decrees which have the force of law; and in regard to these he adds, *all matters subject to decrees.*

Reply Obj. 2. A principle of direction should be applicable to many. Hence the Philosopher says that all things belonging to one genus are measured by one, which is the principle in that genus. For if there were as many rules or measures as there are things measured or ruled, they would cease to be of use, since their use consists in being applicable to many things. Hence law would be of no use, if it did not extend further than to one single act. For the decrees of prudent men are made for the purpose of directing individual actions, whereas law is a *common precept,* as was stated above.

Reply Obj. 3. We must not seek the same degree of certainty in all things. Consequently, in contingent matters, such as natural and human things, it is enough for a thing to be certain, as being true in the greater number of instances, though at times, and less frequently, it fail.

Second Article
Whether It Belongs to Human Law to Repress All Vices?

We proceed thus to the Second Article.—

Objection 1. It would seem that it belongs to human law to repress all vices. For Isidore says that *laws were made in order that, in fear thereof, man's audacity might be held in check.* But it would not be held in check sufficiently unless all evils were repressed by law. Therefore human law should repress all evils.

Obj. 2. Further, the intention of the lawgiver is to make the citizens virtuous. But a man cannot be virtuous unless he forbear from all kinds of vice. Therefore it belongs to human law to repress all vices.

Obj. 3. Further, human law is derived from the natural law, as was stated above. But all vices are contrary to the law of nature. Therefore human law should repress all vices.

On the contrary, We read in *De Libero Arbitrio,* i: *It seems to me that the law which is written for the governing of the people rightly permits these things, and that divine providence punishes them.* But divine providence punishes nothing but vices. Therefore human law rightly allows some vices, by not repressing them.

I answer that, As was stated above, law is framed as a rule or measure of human acts. Now a measure should be homogeneous with that which it measures, as is stated in *Metaph.* x., since different things are measured by different measures. Therefore laws imposed on men should also be in keeping with their condition, for, as Isidore says, law should be *possible both according to nature, and according to the customs of the country.* Now the ability or facility of action is due to an interior habit or disposition, since the same thing is not possible to one who has not a virtuous habit, as is possible to one who has. Thus the same thing is not possible to a child as to a full-grown man, and for which reason the law for children is not the same as for adults, since many things are permitted to children, which in an adult are punished by law or at any rate are open to blame. In like manner, many things are permissible to men not perfect in virtue, which would be intolerable in a virtuous man.

Now human law is framed for the multitude of human beings, the majority of whom are not perfect in virtue. Therefore human laws do not forbid all vices, from which the virtuous abstain, but only the more grievous vices, from which it is possible for the majority to abstain; and chiefly those that are injurious to others, without the prohibition of which human society could not be maintained. Thus human law prohibits murder, theft and the like.

Reply Obj. 1. Audacity seems to refer to the assailing of others. Consequently, it belongs to those sins chiefly whereby one's neighbor is injured. These sins are forbidden by human law, as was stated.

Reply Obj. 2. The purpose of human law is to lead men to virtue, not suddenly, but gradually. Therefore it does not lay upon the multitude of imperfect men the burdens of those who are already virtuous, viz., that they should abstain from all evil. Otherwise these imperfect ones, being unable to bear such precepts, would break out into yet greater evils. As it is written (*Prov.* xxx. 33): *He that violently bloweth his nose, bringeth out blood;* again (*Matt.* ix. 17): *if new wine, i.e.,* precepts of a perfect life, is *put into old bottles, i.e.,* into imperfect men, *the bottles break, and the wine runneth out, i.e.,* the precepts are despised, and those men, from contempt, break out into evils worse still.

Reply Obj. 3. The natural law is a participation in us of the eternal law, while human law falls short of the eternal law. For Augustine says: *The law which is framed for the government of states allows and leaves unpunished many things that are punished by divine providence. Nor, if this law does not attempt to do everything, is this a reason why it should be blamed for what it does.* Therefore, human law likewise does not prohibit everything that is forbidden by the natural law.

Third Article
Whether Human Law Prescribes the Acts of All the Virtues?

We proceed thus to the Third Article:—

Objection 1. It would seem that human law does not prescribe the acts of all the virtues. For vicious acts are contrary to acts of virtue. But human law does not prohibit all vices, as was stated above. Therefore neither does it prescribe all acts of virtue.

Obj. 2. Further, a virtuous act proceeds from a virtue. But virtue is the end of law, so that whatever is from a virtue cannot come under a precept of law. Therefore human law does not prescribe all acts of virtue.

Obj. 3. Further, law is ordained to the common good, as was stated above. But some acts of virtue are ordained, not to the common good, but to private good. Therefore law does not prescribe all acts of virtue.

On the contrary, The Philosopher says that law *prescribes the performance of the acts of a brave man, . . . and the acts of the temperate man, . . . and the acts of the meek man; and in like manner as regards the other virtues and vices, prescribing the former, forbidding the latter.*

I answer that, The species of virtues are distinguished by their objects, as was explained above. Now all the objects of the virtues can be referred either to the private good of an individual, or to the common good of the multitude. Thus, matters of fortitude may be achieved either for the safety of the state, or for upholding the rights of a friend; and in like manner with the other virtues. But law, as was stated above, is ordained to the common good. Therefore, there is no virtue whose acts cannot be prescribed by the law. Nevertheless, human law does not prescribe concerning all the acts of every virtue, but only in regard to those that are ordainable to the common good,—either immediately, as when certain things are done directly for the common good,—or mediately, as when a lawgiver prescribes certain things pertaining to good order, whereby the citizens are directed in the upholding of the common good of justice and peace.

Reply Obj. 1. Human law does not forbid all vicious acts, by the obligation of a precept, as neither does it prescribe all acts of virtue. But it forbids certain acts of each vice, just as it prescribes some acts of each virtue.

Reply Obj. 2. An act is said to be an act of virtue in two ways. First, from the fact that a man does something virtuous; and thus the act of justice is to do what is right, and an act of fortitude is to do brave things. In this way law prescribes certain acts of virtue.—Secondly, an act of virtue is so called when a man does a virtuous thing in a way in which a virtuous man does it. Such an act always proceeds from virtue. Nor does it come under a precept of law, but is the end at which every lawgiver aims.

Reply Obj. 3. There is no virtue whose act is not ordainable to the common good, as was stated above, either mediately or immediately.

Fourth Article
Whether Human Law Binds a Man in Conscience?

We proceed thus to the Fourth Article:—

Objection 1. It would seem that human law does not bind a man in conscience. For an inferior power cannot impose its law on the judgment of a higher power. But the power of man, which frames human law, is beneath the divine power. Therefore human law cannot impose its precept on a divine judgment, such as is the judgment of conscience.

Obj. 2. Further, the judgment of conscience depends chiefly on the commandments of God. But sometimes God's commandments are made void by human laws, according to *Matt.* xv. 6: *You have made void the commandment of God for your tradition.* Therefore human law does not bind a man in conscience.

Obj. 3. Further, human laws often bring loss of character and injury on man, according to *Isa.* x. 1, 2: *Woe to them that make wicked laws, and when they write, write injustice; to oppress the poor in judgment, and do violence to the cause of the humble of My people.* But it is lawful for anyone to avoid oppression and violence. Therefore human laws do not bind man in conscience.

On the contrary, It is written (*I Pet.* ii. 19): *This is thanksworthy, if for conscience . . . a man endure sorrows, suffering wrongfully.*

I answer that, Laws framed by man are either just or unjust. If they be just, they have the power of binding in conscience from the eternal law whence they are derived, according to *Prov.* viii. 15: *By Me kings reign, and lawgivers decree just things.* Now laws are said to be just, both from the end (when, namely, they are ordained to the common good), from their author (that is to say, when the law that is made does not exceed the power of the lawgiver), and from their form (when, namely, burdens are laid on the subjects according to an equality of proportion and with a view to the common good). For, since one man is a part of the community, each man, in all that he is and has, belongs to the community; just as a part, in all that it is, belongs to the whole. So, too, nature inflicts a loss on the part in order to save the whole; so that for this reason such laws as these, which impose proportionate burdens, are just and binding in conscience, and are legal laws.

On the other hand, laws may be unjust in two ways: first, by being contrary to human good, through being opposed to the things mentioned above:—either in respect of the end, as when an authority imposes on his subjects burdensome laws, conducive, not to the common good, but rather to his own cupidity or vainglory; or in respect of the author, as when a man makes a law that goes beyond the power committed to him; or in respect of the form, as when burdens are imposed unequally on the community, although with a view to the common good. Such are acts of violence rather than laws, because, as Augustine says, *a law that is not just seems to be no law at all.* Therefore, such laws do not bind in conscience, except perhaps in order to avoid scandal or disturbance, for which cause a man should even yield his right, according to *Matt.* v. 40, 41: *If a man . . . take away thy coat, let go thy cloak also unto him; and whosoever will force thee one mile, go with him other two.*

Secondly, laws may be unjust through being opposed to the divine good. Such are the laws of tyrants inducing to idolatry, or to anything else contrary to the divine law. Laws of this kind must in no way be observed, because, as is stated in *Acts* v. 29, *we ought to obey God rather than men.*

Reply Obj. 1. As the Apostle says (*Rom.* xiii. 1, 2), all human power is from God . . . *therefore he that resisteth the power,* in matters that are within its scope, *resisteth the ordinance of God;* so that he becomes guilty in conscience.

Reply Obj. 2. This argument is true of laws that are contrary to the commandments of God, which is beyond the scope of [human] power. Therefore in such matters human law should not be obeyed.

Reply Obj. 3. This argument is true of a law that inflicts an unjust burden on its subjects. Furthermore, the power that man holds from God does not extend to this. Hence neither in such matters is man bound to obey the law, provided he avoid giving scandal or inflicting a more grievous injury.

Fifth Article
Whether All Are Subject to Law?

We proceed thus to the Fifth Article:—

Objection 1. It would seem that not all are subject to the law. For those alone are subject to a law for whom a law is made. But the Apostle says (1 *Tim.* i. 9): *The law is not made for the just man.* Therefore the just are not subject to human law.

Obj. 2. Further, Pope Urban says (this is also found in the *Decretals*): *He that is guided by a private law need not for any reason be bound by the public law.* Now all spiritual men are led by the private law of the Holy Ghost, for they are the sons of God, of whom it is said (*Rom.* viii. 14): *Whosoever are led by the Spirit of God, they are the sons of God.* Therefore not all men are subject to human law.

Obj. 3. Further, the Jurist says that *the sovereign is exempt from the laws.* But he that is exempt from the law is not bound thereby. Therefore not all are subject to law.

On the contrary, The Apostle says (*Rom.* xiii. I): *Let every soul be subject to the higher powers.* But subjection to a power seems to imply subjection to the laws framed by that power. Therefore all men should be subject to law.

I answer that, As was stated above, the notion of law contains two things: first, that it is a rule of human acts; secondly, that it has coercive power. Therefore a man may be subject to law in two ways. First, as the regulated is subject to the regulator; and whoever is subject to a power in this way is subject to the law framed by that power. But it may happen in two ways that one is not subject to a power. In one way, by being altogether free from its authority. And so it happens that the subjects of one city or kingdom are not bound by the laws of the sovereign of another city or kingdom, since they are not subject to his authority. In another way, by being under a yet higher law. Thus the subject of a proconsul should be ruled by his command, but not in those matters in which the subject receives his orders from the emperor; for in these matters he is not bound by the mandate of the lower authority, since he is directed by that of a higher. In this way, one who is subject absolutely to a law may not be subject thereto in certain matters, in respect of which he is ruled by a higher law.

Secondly, a man is said to be subject to a law as the coerced is subject to the coercer. In this way the virtuous and righteous are not subject to law, but only the wicked. For coercion and violence are contrary to the will; but the will of the good is in harmony with law, whereas the will of the wicked is discordant from it. Therefore in this sense the good are not subject to law, but only the wicked.

Reply Obj. 1. This argument is true of subjection by way of coercion, for, in this way, *the law is not made for the just men,* because *they are a law to themselves,* since they *show the work of the law written in their hearts,* as the Apostle says (*Rom.* ii. 14, 15). Consequently law does not coerce them in the way that it does the wicked.

Reply Obj. 2. The law of the Holy Ghost is above all law framed by man, and therefore spiritual men, in so far as they are led by the law of the Holy Ghost, are not subject to the law in those matters that are inconsistent with the guidance of the Holy Ghost. Nevertheless, it is an effect of the guidance of the Holy Ghost that spiritual men are subject to human laws, according to *1 Pet.* ii. 13: *Be ye subject . . . to every human creature for God's sake.*

Reply Obj. 3. The sovereign is said to be *exempt from the law,* as to its coercive power, since, properly speaking, no man is coerced by himself, and law has no coercive power save from the authority of the sovereign. Thus is the sovereign said to be exempt from the law because none is competent to pass sentence on him, if he acts against the law. Therefore on *Ps.* 1.6 (*To Thee only have I sinned*) the *Gloss* says that *there is no man who can judge the deeds of a king*. But as to the directive force of law, the sovereign is subject to the law by his own will, according to the statement that *whatever law a man makes for another, he should keep himself*. And the authority of a wise man says: *Obey the law that thou makest thyself.* Moreover the Lord reproaches those *who say and do not*; and who *bind heavy burdens and lay them on men's shoulders, but with a finger of their own they will not move them* (*Matt.* xxiii. 3, 4). Hence, in the judgment of God, the sovereign is not exempt from the law, as to its directive force; but he should fulfill it voluntarily, and not of constraint. Again, the sovereign is above the law, in so far as, when it is expedient, he can change the law, and rule within it according to time and place.

Sixth Article
Whether He Who Is Under a Law May Act Outside the Letter of the Law?

We proceed thus to the Sixth Article:—

Objection 1. It seems that he who is subject to a law may not act outside the letter of the law. For Augustine says: *Although men judge about temporal laws when they make them, yet when once they are made they must pass judgment, not on them, but according to them.* But if anyone disregard the letter of the law, saying that he observes the intention of the lawgiver, he seems to pass judgment on the law. Therefore it is not right for one who is under a law to disregard the letter of the law, in order to observe the intention of the lawgiver.

Obj. 2. Further, he alone is competent to interpret the law who can make the law. But those who are subject to the law cannot make the law. Therefore they have no right to interpret the intention of the lawgiver, but should always act according to the letter of the law.

Obj. 3. Further, every wise man knows how to explain his intention by words. But those who framed the laws should be reckoned wise, for Wisdom says (*Prov.* viii. 15): *By Me kings reign, and lawgivers decree just things.* Therefore we should not judge of the intention of the lawgiver otherwise than by the words of the law.

On the contrary, Hilary says: *The meaning of what is said is according to the motive for saying it; because things are not subject to speech, but speech to things.* Therefore we should take account of the motive of the lawgiver, rather than of his very words.

I answer that, As was stated above, every law is directed to the common welfare of men, and derives the force and nature of law accordingly; but in so far as it fails of this common welfare, it is without binding power. Hence the Jurist says: *By no reason of law, or favor of equity, is it allowable for us to interpret harshly, and render burdensome, those useful measures which have been enacted for the welfare of man.* Now it often happens that the observance of some point of law conduces to the common welfare in the majority of instances, and yet, in some cases, is very injurious. Since, then, the lawgiver cannot have in view every single case, he shapes the law according to what happens most frequently, by directing his attention to the common good. Hence, if a case arise wherein the observance of that law would be injurious to the general welfare, it should not be observed. For instance, suppose that in a besieged city it be an established law that the gates of the city are to be kept closed, this is good for public welfare as a general rule; but if it were to happen that the enemy are in pursuit of certain citizens, who are defenders of the city, it would be a great calamity for the city if the gates were not opened to them; and so in that case the gates ought to be opened, contrary to the letter of the law, in order to maintain the common welfare, which the lawgiver had in view.

Nevertheless, it must be noted that if the observance of the law according to the letter does not involve any sudden risk, needing instant remedy, it is not permissible for everyone to expound what is useful and what is not useful to the state; rather those alone can do this who are in authority, and who, in the event of such cases, have the power to dispense from the laws. If, however, the peril be so sudden as not to allow the delay involved in referring the matter to authority, the necessity itself carries with it a dispensation, since necessity knows no law.

Reply Obj. 1. He who in a case of necessity acts outside the letter of the law does not judge of the law; but he judges of a particular case in which he sees that the letter of the law is not to be observed.

Reply Obj. 2. He who follows the intention of the lawgiver does not interpret the law absolutely; but he interprets the law in a case in which it is evident, by reason of the manifest harm, that the lawgiyer intended otherwise. For if it be a matter of doubt, he must either act according to the letter of the law, or consult those in power.

Reply Obj. 3. No man is so wise as to be able to consider every single case; and therefore he is not able sufficiently to express in words all those things that are suitable for the end he has in view. And even if a lawgiver were able to take all the cases into consideration, he ought not to mention them all, in order to avoid confusion; but he should frame the law according to that which is of most common occurrence.

THOMAS HOBBES

FROM *Leviathan*

Often called the father of modern analytic philosophy, Thomas Hobbes was born in England in 1588, the year England fought off invasion by Spain's Invincible Armada. This period of social and political ferment into which Hobbes was born was likewise a period of increased philosophical activity. Philosophical interest, especially in ethics, tends to expand during periods of social crisis because traditional beliefs and values are brought into question. In the sixteenth and seventeenth centuries, both the Catholic church and Aristotle were under fire from all sides: The Galilean and Copernican revolutions in science, the Reformation, and the decline in medieval feudalism and the advent of industrial democracy all threatened the entrenched orthodoxy.

Hobbes joined in the search for an ethical method that was founded on reason and could be universally accepted. Hobbes was sent when he was only 14 to Magdellan College, Oxford. Even though he was educated under the Aristotelian system, he was largely unimpressed by it. When, in 1610, he made his first visit to the Continent, he discovered for himself the disfavor into which Aristotle's teachings had fallen: The scientific method being employed by Kepler, Descartes, Galileo, and Francis Bacon appeared to be a more reliable way to attain truth. At the same time, he was impressed by the ability of the geometric method to arrive at indubitable conclusions in mathematics. Determined to adapt to philosophy what he had learned, Hobbes combined scientific and geometric methods to uncover truths of humankind and society.

The concept of natural law, divinely sanctioned objective truths of the universe discoverable by reason, was the primary target of Hobbes' criticism. Hobbes argued for a new understanding of natural law that was not divine—a law inherent in the nature of humankind. That law has as its cornerstone the inherent desire we all possess for self-preservation.

Since he defined "good" as the object of any human desire, that which humans naturally desire (self-preservation) is the primary good. Moral rules, then, for Hobbes, are merely societal inventions to discourage those actions that lead to personal destruction or that imperil the means to self-preservation. But Hobbes' innovation lies not in this hedonistic view of ethics, which is merely a modern version of Epicureanism. Rather, what is novel in Hobbes is the view that moral rules require general observance, impossible without the intervention of government. Societies adopt moral rules because rational people recognize that without such rules society gives way to a war of all against all in which everyone suffers. What ensures that each person's tendencies to greed, envy, and aggression are brought under control is the power of the state. Each person obeys the law because he or she knows that punishment by the state will be the cost of disobedience. The people are willing to accept the power of the state because the alternative is so grim.

The Leviathan, *from which the textual selections are excerpted, is Hobbes' major work. He was at the center of a number of philosophical and theological disputes in his day, and by the time of his death at the age of 91, he was a veritable English institution. His influence on ethical theory was enormous. By rejecting ethics' reliance on revealed theology, Hobbes returned philosophy to the concerns that had engaged Socrates and the Sophists. But now these concerns were raised to a higher level by Hobbes, profiting from both the Christian insights into the obligatory force of moral principles and the refinements of scientific method.*

The mainstream of English ethics begins with Hobbes and the replies and criticisms he provoked. A whole group of English philosophers collectively known as the British Moralists criticized the pessimistic view of man given by Hobbes, contending instead that benevolence was just as primary an emotion for humankind as self-interest. We can trace the threads of Hobbesian thought up to our own day, most clearly in hedonistic theories like utilitarianism and ethical egoism, and in the ethical theory of contractarianism (or social contract theory), discussed by Plato in the Crito *and influential today in the ethics of John Rawls, David Gauthier, and others.*

Chapter VI. Of the Interior Beginnings of Voluntary Motions; Commonly Called the Passions; and the Speeches by Which They Are Expressed

There be in animals, two sorts of *motions* peculiar to them: one called *vital*; begun in generation, and continued without interruption through their whole life; such as are the *course* of the *blood*, the *pulse*, the *breathing*, the *concoction, nutrition, excretion,* &c., to which motions there needs no help of imagination: the other is *animal motion*, otherwise called *voluntary motion*; as to *go*, to *speak*, to *move* any of our limbs, in such manner as is first fancied in our minds. That sense is motion in the organs and interior parts of man's body, caused by the action of the things we see, hear, &c.; and that fancy is but the relics of the same motion, remaining after sense, has been al-ready said in the first and second chapters. And because *going, speaking,* and the like voluntary motions, depend always upon a precedent thought of *whither, which way,* and *what;* it is evident, that the imagination is the first internal beginning of all voluntary motion. And although unstudied men do not conceive any motion at all to be there, where the thing moved is invisible; or the space it is moved in is, for the shortness of it, insensible; yet that doth not hinder, but that such motions are. For let a space be never so little, that which is moved over a greater space, whereof that little one is part, must first be moved over that. These small beginnings of motion, within the body of man, before they appear in walking, speaking, striking, and other visible actions, are commonly called ENDEAVOUR.

This endeavour, when it is toward something which causes it, is called APPETITE, or DESIRE; the latter, being the general name; and the other oftentimes restrained to signify the desire of food, namely *hunger* and *thirst.* And when the endeavour is fromward something, it is generally called AVERSION. These words, *appetite* and *aversion,* we have from the Latins; and they both of them signify the motions, one of approaching, the other of retiring. So also do the Greek words for the same, which are ὁρμή and ἀφορμή. For nature itself does often press upon men those truths, which afterwards, when they look for somewhat beyond nature, they stumble at. For the Schools find in mere appetite to go, or move, no actual motion at all: but because some motion they must acknowledge, they call it metaphorical motion; which is but an absurd speech: for though words may be called metaphorical; bodies and motions can not.

That which men desire, they are also said to LOVE: and to HATE those things for which they have aversion. So that desire and love are the same thing; save that by desire, we always signify the absence of the object; by love, most commonly the presence of the same. So also by aversion, we signify the absence; and by hate, the presence of the object.

Of appetites and aversions, some are born with men; as appetite of food, appetite of excretion, and exoneration, which may also and more properly be called aversions, from somewhat they feel in their bodies; and some other appetites, not many. The rest, which are appetites of particular things, proceed from experience, and trial of their effects upon themselves or other men. For of things we know not at all, or believe not to be, we can have no further desire, than to taste and try. But aversion we have for things, not only which we know have hurt us, but also that we do not know whether they will hurt us, or not.

Those things which we neither desire, nor hate, we are said to *contemn;* CONTEMPT being nothing else but an immobility, or contumacy of the heart, in resisting the action of certain things; and proceeding from that the heart is already moved otherwise, by other more potent objects; or from want of experience of them.

And because the constitution of a man's body is in continual mutation, it is impossible that all the same things should always cause in him the same appetites, and aversions: much less can all men consent, in the desire of almost any one and the same object.

But whatsoever is the object of any man's appetite or desire, that is it which he for his part calleth *good:* and the object of his hate and aversion, evil; and of his contempt, *vile* and *inconsiderable.* For these words of good, evil, and contemptible, are ever used with relation to the person that useth them: there being nothing simply and absolutely so; nor any common rule of good and evil, to be taken from the nature of the objects themselves; but from the person of the man, where there is no commonwealth; or, in a commonwealth, from the person that representeth; it or from an arbitrator or judge, whom men disagreeing shall by consent set up, and make his sentence the rule thereof.

The Latin tongue has two words, whose significations approach to those of good and evil; but are not precisely the same; and those are *pulchrum* and *turpe.* Whereof the former signifies that, which by some apparent signs promiseth good; and the latter, that which promiseth evil. But in our tongue we have not so general names to express them by. But for *pulchrum* we say in some things, *fair;* in others, *beautiful,* or *handsome,* or *gallant,* or *honourable,* or *comely,* or *amiable;* and for *turpe, foul, deformed, ugly, base, nauseous,* and the like, as the subject shall require; all which words, in their proper places, signify nothing else but the *mien,* or countenance, that promiseth good and evil. So that of good there be three kinds; good in the promise, that is *pulchrum;* good in effect, as the end desired, which is called *jucundum, delightful;* and good as the means, which is called *utile, profitable;* and as many of evil: for *evil* in promise, is that they call *turpe;* evil in effect, and end, is *molestum, unpleasant, troublesome;* and evil in the means, *inutile, unprofitable, hurtful.*

As, in sense, that which is really within us, is, as I have said before, only motion, caused by the action of external objects, but in apparence; to the sight, light and colour; to the ear, sound; to the nostril, odour, &c.: so, when the action of the same object is continued from the eyes, ears, and other organs to the heart, the real effect there is nothing but motion, or endeavour; which consisteth in appetite, or aversion, to or from the object moving. But the apparence, or sense of that motion, is that we either call *delight,* or *trouble of mind.*

This motion, which is called appetite, and for the apparence of it *delight,* and *pleasure,* seemeth to be a corroboration of vital motion, and a help thereunto;

and therefore such things as caused delight, were not improperly called *jucunda, a juvando,* from helping or fortifying; and the contrary, *molesta, offensive,* from hindering, and troubling the motion vital.

Pleasure therefore, or *delight,* is the apparence, or sense of good; and *molestation,* or *displeasure,* the apparence, or sense of evil. And consequently all appetite, desire, and love, is accompanied with some delight more or less; and all hatred and aversion, with more or less displeasure and offence.

Of pleasures or delights, some arise from the sense of an object present; and those may be called *pleasure of sense;* the word *sensual,* as it is used by those only that condemn them, having no place till there be laws. Of this kind are all onerations and exonerations of the body; as also all that is pleasant, in the *sight, hearing, smell, taste,* or *touch.* Others arise from the expectation, that proceeds from foresight of the end, or consequence of things; whether those things in the sense please or displease. And these are *pleasures of the mind* of him that draweth those consequences, and are generally called JOY. In the like manner, displeasures are some in the sense, and called PAIN; others in the expectation of consequences, and are called GRIEF.

These simple passions called *appetite, desire, love, aversion, hate, joy,* and *grief,* have their names for divers considerations diversified. As first, when they one succeed another, they are diversely called from the opinion men have of the likelihood of attaining what they desire. Secondly, from the object loved or hated. Thirdly, from the consideration of many of them together. Fourthly, from the alteration or succession itself.

For *appetite,* with an opinion of attaining, is called HOPE.

The same, without such opinion, DESPAIR.

Aversion, with opinion of HURT from the object, FEAR.

The same, with hope of avoiding that hurt by resistance, COURAGE.

Sudden *courage,* ANGER.

Constant *hope,* CONFIDENCE of ourselves.

Constant *despair,* DIFFIDENCE of ourselves.

Anger for great hurt done to another, when we conceive the same to be done by injury, INDIGNATION.

Desire of good to another, BENEVOLENCE, GOOD WILL, CHARITY. If to man generally, GOOD NATURE.

Desire of riches, COVETOUSNESS; a name used always in signification of blame; because men contending for them, are displeased with one another attaining them; though the desire in itself be to be blamed, or allowed, according to the means by which these riches are sought.

Desire of office, or precedence, AMBITION: a name used also in the worse sense, for the reason before mentioned.

Desire of things that conduce but a little to our ends, and fear of things that are of but little hindrance, PUSILLANIMITY.

Contempt of little helps and hindrances, MAGNANIMITY.

Magnanimity, in danger of death or wounds, VALOUR, FORTITUDE.

Magnanimity in the use of riches, LIBERALITY.

Pusillanimity in the same, WRETCHEDNESS, MISERABLENESS, or PARSIMONY; as it is liked or disliked.

Love of persons for society, KINDNESS.

Love of persons for pleasing the sense only, NATURAL LUST.

Love of the same, acquired from rumination, that is, imagination of pleasure past, LUXURY.

Love of one singularly, with desire to be singularly beloved, THE PASSION OF LOVE. The same, with fear that the love is not mutual, JEALOUSY.

Desire, by doing hurt to another, to make him condemn some fact of his own, REVENGEFULNESS.

Desire to know why, and how, CURIOSITY; such as is in no living creature but *man:* so that man is distinguished, not only by his reason, but also by this singular passion from other *animals;* in whom the appetite of food, and other pleasures of sense, by predominance, take away the care of knowing causes; which is a lust of the mind, that by a perseverance of delight in the continual and indefatigable generation of knowledge, exceedeth the short vehemence of any carnal pleasure.

Fear of power invisible, feigned by the mind, or imagined from tales publicly allowed, RELIGION; not allowed, SUPERSTITION. And when the power imagined, is truly such as we imagine, TRUE RELIGION.

Fear, without the apprehension of why, or what, PANIC TERROR, called so from the fables, that make Pan the author of them; whereas, in truth, there is always in him that so feareth first, some apprehension of the cause, though the rest run away by example, every one supposing his fellow to know why. And therefore this passion happens to none but in a throng, or multitude of people.

Joy, from apprehension of novelty, ADMIRATION; proper to man, because it excites the appetite of knowing the cause.

Joy, arising from imagination of a man's own power and ability, is that exultation of the mind which is called GLORYING: which if grounded upon the experience of his own former actions, is the same with *confidence:* but if grounded on the flattery of others; or only supposed by himself, for delight in the consequences of it, is called VAIN-GLORY: which name is properly given; because a well grounded *confidence* begetteth attempt; whereas the supposing of power does not, and is therefore rightly called *vain.*

Grief, from opinion of want of power, is called DEJECTION of mind.

The *vain-glory* which consisteth in the feigning or supposing of abilities in ourselves, which we know are not, is most incident to young men, and nourished by the histories, or fictions of gallant persons; and is corrected oftentimes by age, and employment.

Sudden glory, is the passion which maketh those *grimaces* called LAUGHTER; and is caused either by some sudden act of their own, that pleaseth them; or by the apprehension of some deformed thing in another, by comparison whereof they suddenly applaud themselves. And it is incident most to them, that are conscious of the fewest abilities in themselves; who are forced to keep themselves in their own favour, by observing the imperfections of other men. And therefore much laughter at the defects of others, is a sign of pusillanimity. For of great minds, one of the proper works is, to help and free others from scorn; and compare themselves only with the most able.

On the contrary, *sudden dejection,* is the passion that causeth WEEPING; and is caused by such accidents, as suddenly take away some vehement hope, or some prop of their power: and they are most subject to it, that rely principally on helps external, such as are women, and children. Therefore some weep for the loss of friends; others for their unkindness; others for the sudden stop made to their thoughts of revenge, by reconciliation. But in all cases, both laughter, and weeping, are sudden motions; custom taking them both away. For no man laughs at old jests; or weeps for an old calamity.

Grief, for the discovery of some defect of ability, is SHAME, or the passion that discovereth itself in BLUSHING; and consisteth in the apprehension of some thing dishonourable; and in young men, is a sign of the love of good reputation, and commendable; in old men it is a sign of the same; but because it comes too late, not commendable.

The *contempt* of good reputation is called IMPUDENCE.

Grief, for the calamity of another, is PITY; and ariseth from the imagination that the like calamity may befall himself; and therefore is called also COMPASSION, and in the phrase of this present time a FELLOW-FEELING: and therefore for calamity arriving from great wickedness, the best men have the least pity; and for the same calamity those hate pity, that think themselves least obnoxious to the same.

Contempt, or little sense of the calamity of others, is that which men call CRUELTY; proceeding from security of their own fortune. For, that any man should take pleasure in other men's great harms; without other end of his own, I do not conceive it possible.

Grief, for the success of a competitor in wealth, honour, or other good, if it be joined with endeavour to enforce our own abilities to equal or exceed him, is called EMULATION: but joined with endeavour to supplant, or hinder a competitor, ENVY.

When in the mind of man, appetites, and aversions, hopes, and fears, concerning one and the same thing, arise alternately; and divers good and evil consequences of the doing, or omitting the thing propounded, come successively into our thoughts; so that sometimes we have an appetite to it; sometimes an aversion from it; sometimes hope to be able to do it; sometimes despair, or fear to attempt it; the whole sum of desires, aversions, hopes and fears continued till the thing be either done, or thought impossible, is that we call DELIBERATION.

Therefore of things past, there is no *deliberation;* because manifestly impossible to be changed: nor of things known to be impossible, or thought so; because men know, or think such deliberation vain. But of things impossible, which we think possible, we may deliberate; not knowing it is in vain. And it is called *deliberation;* because it is a putting an end to the *liberty* we had of doing, or omitting, according to our own appetite, or aversion.

This alternate succession of appetites, aversions, hopes and fears, is no less in other living creatures than in man: and therefore beasts also deliberate.

Every *deliberation* is then said to *end,* when that whereof they deliberate, is either done, or thought impossible; because till then we retain the liberty of doing, or omitting; according to our appetite, or aversion.

In *deliberation,* the last appetite, or aversion, immediately adhering to the action, or to the omission thereof, is that we call the WILL; the act, not the faculty, of *willing.* And beasts that have *deliberation,* must necessarily also have *will.* The definition of the *will,* given commonly by the Schools, that it is a *rational appetite,* is not good. For if it were, then could there be no voluntary act against reason. For a *voluntary act* is that, which proceedeth from the *will,* and no other. But if instead of a rational appetite, we shall say an appetite resulting from a precedent deliberation, then the definition is the same that I have given here. *Will,* therefore, *is the last appetite in deliberating.* And though we say in common discourse, a man had a will once to do a thing, that nevertheless he forbore to do; yet that is properly but an inclination, which makes no action voluntary; because the action depends not of it, but of the last inclination, or appetite. For if the intervenient appetites, make any action voluntary; then by the same reason all intervenient aversions, should make the same action involuntary; and so one and the same action, should be both voluntary and involuntary.

By this it is manifest, that not only actions that have their beginning from covetousness, ambition, lust, or other appetites to the thing propounded; but also those that have their beginning from aversion, or fear of those consequences that follow the omission, are *voluntary actions.*

The forms of speech by which the passions are expressed, are partly the same, and partly different from those, by which we express our thoughts. And first, generally all passions may be expressed *indicatively;* as *I love, I fear, I joy, I deliberate, I will, I command:* but some of them have particular expressions by themselves, which nevertheless are not affirmations, unless it be when they serve to make other inferences, besides that of the passion they proceed from. Deliberation is expressed *subjunctively;* which is a speech proper to signify suppositions, with their consequences; as, *if this be done, then this will follow;* and differs not from the language of reasoning, save that reasoning is in general words; but deliberation for the most part is of particulars. The language of desire, and aversion, is *imperative;* as *do this, forbear that;* which when the party is obliged to do, or for-

bear, is *command;* otherwise *prayer;* or else *counsel.* The language of vain-glory, of indignation, pity and revengefulness, *optative:* but of the desire to know, there is a peculiar expression called *interrogative;* as, *what is it, when shall it, how is it done,* and *why so?* other language of the passions I find none: for cursing, swearing, reviling, and the like, do not signify as speech; but as the actions of a tongue accustomed.

These forms of speech, I say, are expressions, or voluntary significations of our passions: but certain signs they be not; because they may be used arbitrarily, whether they that use them, have such passions or not. The best signs of passions present, are either in the countenance, motions of the body, actions, and ends, or aims, which we otherwise know the man to have.

And because in deliberation, the appetites, and aversions, are raised by foresight of the good and evil consequences, and sequels of the action whereof we deliberate; the good or evil effect thereof dependeth on the foresight of a long chain of consequences, of which very seldom any man is able to see the end. But for so far as a man seeth, if the good in those consequences be greater than the evil, the whole chain is that which writers call *apparent,* or *seeming good.* And contrarily, when the evil exceedeth the good, the whole is *apparent,* or *seeming evil:* so that he who hath by experience, or reason, the greatest and surest prospect of consequences, deliberates best himself; and is able when he will, to give the best counsel unto others.

Continual success in obtaining those things which a man from time to time desireth, that is to say, continual prospering, is that men call FELICITY; I mean the felicity of this life. For there is no such thing as perpetual tranquillity of mind, while we live here; because life itself is but motion, and can never be without desire, nor without fear, no more than without sense. What kind of felicity God hath ordained to them that devoutly honour Him, a man shall no sooner know, than enjoy; being joys, that now are as incomprehensible, as the word of school-men *beatifical vision* is unintelligible.

The form of speech whereby men signify their opinion of the goodness of anything, is PRAISE. That whereby they signify the power and greatness of anything, is MAGNIFYING. And that whereby they signify the opinion they have of a man's felicity, is by the

Greeks called μαχαρισμός, for which we have no name in our tongue. And thus much is sufficient for the present purpose, to have been said of the PASSIONS.

. . .

Chapter XIII. Of the Natural Condition of Mankind as Concerning Their Felicity, and Misery

Nature hath made men so equal, in the faculties of the body, and mind; as that though there be found one man sometimes manifestly stronger in body, or of quicker mind than another; yet when all is reckoned together, the difference between man, and man, is not so considerable, as that one man can thereupon claim to himself any benefit, to which another may not pretend, as well as he. For as to the strength of body, the weakest has strength enough to kill the strongest, either by secret machination, or by confederacy with others, that are in the same danger with himself.

And as to the faculties of the mind, setting aside the arts grounded upon words, and especially that skill of proceeding upon general, and infallible rules, called science; which very few have, and but in few things; as being not a native faculty, born with us; nor attained, as prudence, while we look after somewhat else, I find yet a greater equality amongst men, than that of strength. For prudence, is but experience; which equal time, equally bestows on all men, in those things they equally apply themselves unto. That which may perhaps make such equality incredible, is but a vain conceit of one's own wisdom, which almost all men think they have in a greater degree, than the vulgar; that is, than all men but themselves, and a few others, whom by fame, or for concurring with themselves, they approve. For such is the nature of men, that howsoever they may acknowledge many others to be more witty, or more eloquent, or more learned; yet they will hardly believe there be many so wise as themselves; for they see their own wit at hand, and other men's at a distance. But this proveth rather that men are in that point equal, than unequal. For there is not ordinarily a greater sign of the equal distribution of any thing, than that every man is contented with his share.

From this equality of ability, ariseth equality of hope in the attaining of our ends. And therefore if any two men desire the same thing, which nevertheless they cannot both enjoy, they become enemies; and in the way to their end, which is principally their own conservation, and sometimes their delectation only, endeavour to destroy, or subdue one another. And from hence it comes to pass, that where an invader hath no more to fear, than another man's single power; if one plant, sow, build, or possess a convenient seat, others may probably be expected to come prepared with forces united, to dispossess, and deprive him, not only of the fruit of his labour, but also of his life, or liberty. And the invader again is in the like danger of another.

And from this diffidence of one another, there is no way for any man to secure himself, so reasonable, as anticipation; that is, by force, or wiles, to master the persons of all men he can, so long, till he see no other power great enough to endanger him: and this is no more than his own conservation requireth, and is generally allowed. Also because there be some, that taking pleasure in contemplating their own power in the acts of conquest, which they pursue farther than their security requires; if others, that otherwise would be glad to be at ease within modest bounds, should not by invasion increase their power, they would not be able, long time, by standing only on their defence, to subsist. And by consequence, such augmentation of dominion over men being necessary to a man's conservation, it ought to be allowed him.

Again, men have no pleasure, but on the contrary a great deal of grief, in keeping company, where there is no power able to over-awe them all. For every man looketh that his companion should value him, at the same rate he sets upon himself: and upon all signs of contempt, or undervaluing, naturally endeavours, as far as he dares, (which amongst them that have no common power to keep them in quiet, is far enough to make them destroy each other), to extort a greater value from his contemners, by damage; and from others, by the example.

So that in the nature of man, we find three principal causes of quarrel. First, competition; second, diffidence; thirdly, glory.

The first, maketh men invade for gain; the second, for safety; and the third, for reputation. The first use violence, to make themselves masters of other men's persons, wives, children, and cattle; the second, to defend them; the third, for trifles, as a word, a smile, a different opinion, and any other sign of undervalue, either direct in their persons, or by reflection in their kindred, their friends, their nation, their profession, or their name.

Hereby it is manifest, that during the time men live without a common power to keep them all in awe, they are in that condition which is called war; and such a war, as is of every man, against every man. For WAR, consisteth not in battle only, or the act of fighting; but in a tract of time, wherein the will to contend by battle is sufficiently known: and therefore the notion of *time,* is to be considered in the nature of war; as it is in the nature of weather. For as the nature of foul weather, lieth not in a shower or two of rain; but in an inclination thereto of many days together: so the nature of war, consisteth not in actual fighting; but in the known disposition thereto, during all the time there is no assurance to the contrary. All other time is PEACE.

Whatsoever therefore is consequent to a time of war, where every man is enemy to every man; the same is consequent to the time, wherein men live without other security, than what their own strength, and their own invention shall furnish them withal. In such condition, there is no place for industry; because the fruit thereof is uncertain: and consequently no culture of the earth; no navigation, nor use of the commodities that may be imported by sea; no commodious building; no instruments of moving, and removing, such things as require much force; no knowledge of the face of the earth; no account of time; no arts; no letters; no society; and which is worst of all, continual fear, and danger of violent death; and the life of man, solitary, poor, nasty, brutish, and short.

It may seem strange to some man, that has not well weighed these things; that nature should thus dissociate, and render men apt to invade, and destroy one another: and he may therefore, not trusting to this inference, made from the passions, desire perhaps to have the same confirmed by experience. Let him therefore consider with himself, when taking a journey, he arms himself, and seeks to go well accompanied; when going to sleep, he locks his doors; when even in his house he locks his chests; and this when he knows there be laws, and public officers, armed, to revenge all injuries shall be done him; what opinion he has of his fellow-subjects, when he rides armed; of his fellow citizens, when he locks his doors; and of his children, and servants, when he locks his chests. Does he not there as much accuse mankind by his actions, as I do by my words? But neither of us accuse man's nature in it. The desires, and other passions of man, are in themselves no sin. No more are the actions, that proceed from those passions, till they know a law that forbids them: which till laws be made they cannot know: nor can any law be made, till they have agreed upon the person that shall make it.

It may peradventure be thought, there was never such a time, nor condition of war as this; and I believe it was never generally so, over all the world: but there are many places, where they live so now. For the savage people in many places of America, except the government of small families, the concord whereof dependeth on natural lust, have no government at all; and live at this day in that brutish manner, as I said before. Howsoever, it may be perceived what manner of life there would be, where there were no common power to fear, by the manner of life, which men that have formerly lived under a peaceful government, use to degenerate into, in a civil war.

But though there had never been any time, wherein particular men were in a condition of war one against another; yet in all times, kings, and persons of sovereign authority, because of their independency, are in continual jealousies, and in the state and posture of gladiators; having their weapons pointing, and their eyes fixed on one another; that is, their forts, garrisons, and guns upon the frontiers of their kingdoms; and continual spies upon their neighbours; which is a posture of war. But because they uphold thereby, the industry of their subjects; there does not follow from it, that misery, which accompanies the liberty of particular men.

To this war of every man, against every man, this also is consequent; that nothing can be unjust. The notions of right and wrong, justice and injustice have there no place. Where there is no common power, there is no law: where no law, no injustice. Force, and fraud, are in war the two cardinal virtues. Justice, and injustice are none of the faculties neither of the body, nor mind. If they were, they might be in a man that were alone in the world, as well as his senses, and passions. They are qualities, that relate to men in society, not in solitude. It is consequent also to the same condition, that there be no propriety, no dominion, no *mine* and *thine* distinct; but only that to be every man's, that he can get; and for so long, as he can keep it. And thus much for the ill condition, which man by mere nature is actually placed in; though with a possibility to come out of it, consisting partly in the passions, partly in his reason.

The passions that incline men to peace, are fear of death; desire of such things as are necessary to commodious living; and a hope by their industry to obtain them. And reason suggesteth convenient articles of peace, upon which men may be drawn to agreement. These articles, are they, which otherwise are called the Laws of Nature: whereof I shall speak more particularly, in the two following chapters.

. . .

Chapter XIV. Of the First and Second Natural Laws, and of Contracts

The RIGHT OF NATURE, which writers commonly call *jus naturale,* is the liberty each man hath, to use his own power, as he will himself, for the preservation of his own nature; that is to say, of his own life; and consequently, of doing anything, which in his own judgment, and reason, he shall conceive to be the aptest means thereunto.

By LIBERTY, is understood, according to the proper signification of the word, the absence of external impediments: which impediments, may oft take away part of a man's power to do what he would; but cannot hinder him from using the power left him, according as his judgment, and reason shall dictate to him.

A LAW OF NATURE, *lex naturalis,* is a precept or general rule, found out by reason, by which a man is forbidden to do that, which is destructive of his life, or taketh away the means of preserving the same; and to

omit that, by which he thinketh it may be best preserved. For though they that speak of this subject, use to confound *jus,* and *lex, right* and *law:* yet they ought to be distinguished; because RIGHT, consisteth in liberty to do, or to forbear; whereas LAW, determineth, and bindeth to one of them: so that law, and right, differ as much, as obligation, and liberty; which in one and the same matter are inconsistent.

And because the condition of man, as hath been declared in the precedent chapter, is a condition of war of every one against every one; in which case every one is governed by his own reason; and there is nothing he can make use of, that may not be a help unto him, in preserving his life against his enemies; it followeth, that in such a condition, every man has a right to every thing; even to one another's body. And therefore, as long as this natural right of every man to every thing endureth, there can be no security to any man, how strong or wise so ever he be, of living out the time, which nature ordinarily alloweth men to live. And consequently it is a precept, or general rule of reason, *that every man, ought to endeavour peace, as far as he has hope of obtaining it; and when he cannot obtain it, that he may seek, and use, all helps, and advantages of war.* The first branch of which rule, containeth the first, and fundamental law of nature; which is, *to seek peace, and follow it.* The second, the sum of the right of nature; which is, *by all means we can, to defend ourselves.*

From this fundamental law of nature, by which men are commanded to endeavour peace, is derived this second law; *that a man be willing, when others are so too, as far forth, as for peace, and defence of himself he shall think it necessary, to lay down this right to all things; and be contented with so much liberty against other men, as he would allow other men against himself.* For as long as every man holdeth this right, of doing any thing he liketh; so long are all men in the condition of war. But if other men will not lay down their right, as well as he; then there is no reason for anyone, to divest himself of his: for that were to expose himself to prey, which no man is bound to, rather than to dispose himself to peace. This is that law of the Gospel; *whatsoever you require that others should do to you, that do ye to them.* And that law of all men, *quod tibi fieri non vis, alteri ne feceris.*

To *lay down* a man's *right* to any thing, is to *divest* himself of the *liberty,* of hindering another of the benefit of his own right to the same. For he that renounceth, or passeth away his own right, giveth not to any other man a right which he had not before; because there is nothing to which every man had not right by nature: but only standeth out of his way, that he may enjoy his own original right, without hindrance from him; not without hindrance from another. So that the effect which redoundeth to one man, by another man's defect of right, is but so much diminution of impediments to the use of his own right original.

Right is laid aside, either by simply renouncing it; or by transferring it to another. By *simply* RE-NOUNCING; when he cares not to whom the benefit thereof redoundeth. By TRANSFERRING; when he intendeth the benefit thereof to some certain person, or persons. And when a man hath in either manner abandoned, or granted away his right; then is he said to be OBLIGED, or BOUND, not to hinder those, to whom such right is granted, or abandoned, from the benefit of it: and that he *ought,* and it is his DUTY, not to make void that voluntary act of his own: and that such hindrance is INJUSTICE, and INJURY, as being *sine jure;* the right being before renounced, or transferred. So that *injury,* or *injustice,* in the controversies of the world, is somewhat like to that, which in the disputations of scholars is called *absurdity.* For as it is there called an absurdity, to contradict what one maintained in the beginning: so in the world, it is called injustice, and injury, voluntarily to undo that, which from the beginning he had voluntarily done. The way by which a man either simply renounceth, or transferreth his right, is a declaration, or signification, by some voluntary and sufficient sign, or signs, that he doth so renounce, or transfer; or hath so renounced, or transferred the same, to him that accepteth it. And these signs are either words only, or actions only; or, as it happeneth most often, both words, and actions. And the same are the BONDS, by which men are bound, and obliged: bonds, that have their strength, not from their own nature, for nothing is more easily broken than a man's word, but from fear of some evil consequence upon the rupture.

Whensoever a man transferreth his right, or renounceth it; it is either in consideration of some right reciprocally transferred to himself; or for some other good he hopeth for thereby. For it is a voluntary act: and of the voluntary acts of every man, the object is some *good to himself.* And therefore there be

some rights, which no man can be understood by any words, or other signs, to have abandoned, or transferred. As first a man cannot lay down the right of resisting them, that assault him by force, to take away his life; because he cannot be understood to aim thereby, at any good to himself. The same may be said of wounds, and chains, and imprisonment; both because there is no benefit consequent to such patience; as there is to the patience of suffering another to be wounded, or imprisoned: as also because a man cannot tell, when he seeth men proceed against him by violence, whether they intend his death or not. And lastly the motive, and end for which this renouncing, and transferring of right is introduced, is nothing else but the security of a man's person, in his life, and in the means of so preserving life, as not to be weary of it. And therefore if a man by words, or other signs, seem to despoil himself of the end, for which those signs were intended; he is not to be understood as if he meant it, or that it was his will; but that he was ignorant of how such words and actions were to be interpreted.

The mutual transferring of right, is that which men call CONTRACT.

There is difference between transferring of right to the thing; and transferring, or tradition, that is delivery of the thing itself. For the thing may be delivered together with the translation of the right; as in buying and selling with ready-money; or exchange of goods, or lands: and it may be delivered some time after.

Again, one of the contractors, may deliver the thing contracted for on his part, and leave the other to perform his part at some determinate time after, and in the mean time be trusted; and then the contract on his part, is called PACT, or COVENANT: or both parts may contract now, to perform hereafter: in which cases, he that is to perform in time to come, being trusted, his performance is called *keeping of promise,* or faith; and the failing of performance, if it be voluntary, *violation of faith.*

When the transferring of right, is not mutual: but one of the parties transferreth, in hope to gain thereby friendship, or service from another, or from his friends; or in hope to gain the reputation of charity, or magnanimity; or to deliver his mind from the pain of compassion; or in hope of reward in heaven; this is not contract, but GIFT, FREE-GIFT, GRACE: which words signify one and the same thing.

Signs of contract, are either *express,* or *by inference.* Express, are words spoken with understanding of what they signify: and such words are either of the time *present,* or *past; as, I give, I grant, I have given, I have granted, I will that this be yours:* or of the future; as, *I will give, I will grant:* which words of the future are called PROMISE.

Signs by inference, are sometimes the consequence of words; sometimes the consequence of silence; sometimes the consequence of actions; sometimes the consequence of forbearing an action: and generally a sign by inference, of any contract, is whatsoever sufficiently argues the will of the contractor.

Words alone, if they be of the time to come, and contain a bare promise, are an insufficient sign of a free-gift, and therefore not obligatory. For if they be of the time to come, as *to-morrow I will give,* they are a sign I have not given yet, and consequently that my right is not transferred, but remaineth till I transfer it by some other act. But if the words be of the time present, or past, as, *I have given,* or, *do give to be delivered to-morrow,* then is my to-morrow's right given away to-day; and that by the virtue of the words, though there were no other argument of my will. And there is a great difference in the signification of these words, *volo hoc tuum esse cras,* and *cras dabo;* that is, between *I will that this be thine to-morrow,* and, *I will give it thee to-morrow;* for the word *I will,* in the former manner of speech, signifies an act of the will present; but in the latter, it signifies a promise of an act of the will to come: and therefore the former words, being of the present, transfer a future right; the latter, that be of the future, transfer nothing. But if there be other signs of the will to transfer a right, besides words; then, though the gift be free, yet may the right be understood to pass by words of the future: as if a man propound a prize to him that comes first to the end of a race, the gift is free; and though the words be of the future, yet the right passeth: for if he would not have his words so be understood, he should not have let them run.

In contracts, the right passeth, not only where the words are of the time present, or past, but also where they are of the future: because all contract is mutual translation, or change of right; and therefore he that promiseth only, because he hath already received the benefit for which he promiseth, is to be understood as if he intended the right should pass: for unless he

had been content to have his words so understood, the other would not have performed his part. And for that cause, in buying, and selling, and other acts of contract, a promise is equivalent to a covenant; and therefore obligatory.

He that performeth first in the case of a contract, is said to MERIT that which he is to receive by the performance of the other; and he hath it as *due.* Also when a prize is propounded to many, which is to be given to him only that winneth; or money is thrown amongst many, to be enjoyed by them that catch it; though it is to be a free gift; yet so to win, or so to catch, is to *merit,* and to have it as DUE. For the right is transferred in the propounding of the prize, and in throwing down the money; though it not be determined to whom, but by the event of the contention. But there is between these two sorts of merit, this difference, that in contract, I merit by virtue of my own power, and the contractor's need; but in the case of free gift, I am enabled to merit only by the benignity of the giver: in contract, I merit at the contractor's hand that he should part with his right; in this case of gift, I merit not that the giver should part with his right; but that when he has parted with it, it should be mine, rather than another's. And this I think to be the meaning of that distinction of the Schools, between *meritum congrui,* and *meritum condigni.* For God Almighty, having promised Paradise to those men, hoodwinked with carnal desires, that can walk through this world according to the precepts, and limits prescribed by him; they say, he that shall so walk, shall merit Paradise *ex congruo.* But because no man can demand a right to it, by his own righteousness, or any power in himself, but by the free grace of God only; they say, no man can merit Paradise *ex condigno.* This I say, I think is the meaning of that distinction; but because disputers do not agree upon the signification of their own terms of art, longer than it serves their turn; I will not affirm any thing of their meaning: only this I say; when a gift is given indefinitely, as a prize to be contended for, he that winneth meriteth, and may claim the prize as due.

If a covenant be made, wherein neither of the parties perform presently, but trust one another; in the condition of mere nature, which is a condition of war of every man against every man, upon any reasonable suspicion, it is void: but if there be a common power set over them both, with right and force sufficient to compel performance, it is not void. For he that performeth first, has no assurance the other will perform after; because the bonds of words are too weak to bridle men's ambition, avarice, anger, and other passions, without the fear of some coercive power; which in the condition of mere nature, where all men are equal, and judges of the justness of their own fears, cannot possibly be supposed. And therefore he which performeth first, does but betray himself to his enemy; contrary to the right, he can never abandon, of defending his life, and means of living.

But in a civil estate, where there is a power set up to constrain those that would otherwise violate their faith, that fear is no more reasonable; and for that cause, he which by the covenant is to perform first, is obliged so to do.

The cause of fear, which maketh such a covenant invalid, must be always something arising after the covenant made; as some new fact, or other sign of the will not to perform: else it cannot make the covenant void. For that which could not hinder a man from promising, ought not to be admitted as a hindrance of performing.

He that transferreth any right, transferreth the means of enjoying it, as far as lieth in his power. As he that selleth land, is understood to transfer the herbage, and whatsoever grows upon it: nor can he that sells a mill turn away the stream that drives it. And they that give to a man the right of government in sovereignty, are understood to give him the right of levying money to maintain soldiers; and of appointing magistrates for the administration of justice.

To make covenants with brute beasts, is impossible; because not understanding our speech, they understand not, nor accept of any translation of right; nor can translate any right to another: and without mutual acceptation, there is no covenant.

To make covenant with God, is impossible, but by mediation of such as God speaketh to, either by revelation supernatural, or by his lieutenants that govern under him, and in his name: for otherwise we know not whether our covenants be accepted, or not. And therefore they that vow anything contrary to any law of nature, vow in vain; as being a thing unjust to pay such vow. And if it be a thing commanded by the law of nature, it is not the vow, but the law that binds them.

The matter, or subject of a covenant, is always something that falleth under deliberation; for to covenant, is an act of the will; that is to say, an act, and the last act of deliberation; and is therefore always understood to be something to come; and which is judged possible for him that covenanteth, to perform.

And therefore, to promise that which is known to be impossible, is no covenant. But if that prove impossible afterwards, which before was thought possible, the covenant is valid, and bindeth, though not to the thing itself, yet to the value; or, if that also be impossible, to the unfeigned endeavour of performing as much as is possible: for to more no man can be obliged.

Men are freed of their covenants two ways; by performing; or by being forgiven. For performance, is the natural end of obligation; and forgiveness, the restitution of liberty; as being a retransferring of that right, in which the obligation consisted.

Covenants entered into by fear, in the condition of mere nature, are obligatory. For example, if I covenant to pay a ransom, or service, for my life, to an enemy; I am bound by it: for it is a contract, wherein one receiveth the benefit of life; the other is to receive money, or service for it; and consequently, where no other law, as in the condition of mere nature, forbiddeth the performance, the covenant is valid. Therefore prisoners of war, if trusted with the payment of their ransom, are obliged to pay it: and if a weaker prince, make a disadvantageous peace with a stronger, for fear; he is bound to keep it; unless, as hath been said before, there ariseth some new, and just cause of fear, to renew the war. And even in commonwealths, if I be forced to redeem myself from a thief by promising him money, I am bound to pay it, till the civil law discharge me. For whatsoever I may lawfully do without obligation, the same I may lawfully covenant to do through fear: and what I lawfully covenant, I cannot lawfully break.

A former covenant, makes void a later. For a man that hath passed away his right to one man to-day, hath it not to pass to-morrow to another: and therefore the later promise passeth no right, but is null.

A covenant not to defend myself from force, by force, is always void. For, as I have showed before, no man can transfer, or lay down his right to save himself from death, wounds, imprisonment, the avoiding whereof is the only end of laying down any right; and therefore the promise of not resisting force, in no covenant transferreth any right; nor is obliging. For though a man may covenant thus, *unless I do so, or so, kill me;* he cannot covenant thus, *un-*

less I do so, or so, I will not resist you, when you come to kill me. For man by nature chooseth the lesser evil, which is danger of death in resisting; rather than the greater, which is certain and present death in not resisting. And this is granted to be true by all men, in that they lead criminals to execution, and prison, with armed men, notwithstanding that such criminals have consented to the law, by which they are condemned.

A covenant to accuse oneself, without assurance of pardon, is likewise invalid. For in the condition of nature, where every man is judge, there is no place for accusation: and in the civil state, the accusation is followed with punishment; which being force, a man is not obliged not to resist. The same is also true, of the accusation of those, by whose condemnation a man falls into misery; as of a father, wife, or benefactor. For the testimony of such an accuser, if it be not willingly given, is presumed to be corrupted by nature; and therefore not to be received: and where a man's testimony is not to be credited, he is not bound to give it. Also accusations upon torture, are not to be reputed as testimonies. For torture is to be used but as means of conjecture, and light, in the further examination, and search of truth: and what is in that ease confessed, tendeth to the case of him that is tortured; not to the informing of the torturers: and therefore ought not to have the credit of a sufficient testimony: for whether he deliver himself by true, or false accusation, he does it by the right of preserving his own life.

The force of words, being, as I have formerly noted, too weak to hold men to the performance of their covenants; there are in man's nature, but two imaginable helps to strengthen it. And those are either a fear of the consequence of breaking their word; or a glory, or pride in appearing not to need to break it. This latter is a generosity too rarely found to be presumed on, especially in the pursuers of wealth, command, or sensual pleasure; which are the greatest part of mankind. The passion to be reckoned upon, is fear; whereof there be two very general objects: one, the power of spirits invisible; the other, the power of those men they shall therein offend. Of these two, though the former be the greater power, yet the fear of the latter is commonly the greater fear. The fear of the former is in every man, his own religion: which hath place in the nature of man before civil society. The latter hath not so; at least not place enough, to keep men to their promises; because in the condition of mere nature,

the inequality of power is not discerned, but by the event of battle. So that before the time of civil society, or in the interruption thereof by war, there is nothing can strengthen a covenant of peace agreed on, against the temptations of avarice, ambition, lust, or other strong desire, but the fear of that invisible power, which they every one worship as God; and fear as a revenger of their perfidy. All therefore that can be done between two men not subject to civil power, is to put one another to swear by the God he feareth: which *swearing,* or OATH, is a *form of speech, added to a promise; by which he that promiseth, signifieth, that unless he perform, he renounceth the mercy of his God, or calleth to him for vengeance on himself.* Such was the heathen form, *Let* Jupiter *kill me else, as I kill this beast.* So is our form, *I shall do thus, and thus, so help me God.* And this, with the rites and ceremonies, which every one useth in his own religion, that the fear of breaking faith might be the greater.

By this it appears, that an oath taken according to any other form, or rite, than his, that sweareth, is in vain; and no oath: and that there is no swearing by any thing which the swearer thinks not God. For though men have sometimes used to swear by their kings, for fear, or flattery; yet they would have it thereby understood, they attributed to them divine honour. And that swearing unnecessarily by God, is but prophaning of his name: and swearing by other things, as men do in common discourse, is not swearing, but an impious custom, gotten by too much vehemence of talking.

It appears also, that the oath adds nothing to the obligation. For a covenant, if lawful, binds in the sight of God, without the oath, as much as with it: if unlawful, bindeth not at all; though it be confirmed with an oath.

. . .

Chapter XV. Of Other Laws of Nature

From that law of nature, by which we are obliged to transfer to another, such rights, as being retained, hinder the peace of mankind, there followeth a third; which is this, *that men perform their covenants made:* without which, covenants are in vain, and but empty words; and the right of all men to all things remaining, we are still in the condition of war.

And in this law of nature, consisteth the fountain and original of JUSTICE. For where no covenant hath preceded, there hath no right being transferred, and every man has right to every thing; and consequently, no action can be unjust. But when a covenant is made, then to break it is *unjust:* and the definition of INJUSTICE, is no other than *the not performance of covenant.* And whatsoever is not unjust, is *just.*

But because covenants of mutual trust, where there is a fear of not performance on either part, as hath been said in the former chapter, are invalid; though the original of justice be the making of covenants; yet injustice actually there can be none, till the cause of such fear be taken away; which while men are in the natural condition of war, cannot be done. Therefore before the names of just, and unjust can have place, there must be some coercive power, to compel men equally to the performance of their covenants, by the terror of some punishment, greater than the benefit they expect by the breach of their covenant; and to make good that propriety, which by mutual contract men acquire, in recompense of the universal right they abandon: and such power there is none before the erection of a commonwealth. And this is also to be gathered out of the ordinary definition of justice in the Schools: for they say, that *justice is the constant will of giving to every man his own.* And therefore where there is no *own,* that is no propriety, there is no injustice; and where is no coercive power erected, that is, where there is no commonwealth, there is no propriety; all men having right to all things: therefore where there is no commonwealth, there nothing is unjust. So that the nature of justice, consisteth in keeping of valid covenants: but the validity of covenants begins not but with the constitution of a civil power, sufficient to compel men to keep them: and then it is also that propriety begins.

The fool hath said in his heart, there is no such thing as justice; and sometimes also with his tongue; seriously alleging, that every man's conservation, and contentment, being committed to his own care, there could be no reason, why every man might not do what he thought conduced thereunto: and therefore also to make, or not make; keep, or not keep covenants, was not against reason, when it conduced to one's benefit. He does not therein deny, that there be covenants; and that they are sometimes broken, sometimes kept; and that such breach of them may

be called injustice, and the observance of them justice: but he questioneth, whether injustice, taking away the fear of God, for the same fool hath said in his heart there is no God, may not sometimes stand with that reason, which dictateth to every man his own good; and particularly then, when it conduceth to such a benefit, as shall put a man in a condition, to neglect not only the dispraise, and revilings, but also the power of other men. The kingdom of God is gotten by violence: but what if it could be gotten by unjust violence? were it against reason so to get it, when it is impossible to receive hurt by it? and if it be not against reason, it is not against justice; or else justice is not to be approved for good. From such reasoning as this, successful wickedness hath obtained the name of virtue: and some that in all other things have disallowed the violation of faith; yet have allowed it, when it is for the getting of a kingdom. And the heathen that believed, that Saturn was deposed by his son Jupiter, believed nevertheless the same Jupiter to be the avenger of injustice: somewhat like to a piece of law in Coke's *Commentaries on Littleton;* where he says, if the right heir of the crown be attainted of treason; yet the crown shall descend to him, and *eo instante* the attainder be void: from which instances a man will be very prone to infer; that when the heir apparent of a kingdom, shall kill him that is in possession, though his father; you may call it injustice, or by what other name you will; yet it can never be against reason, seeing all the voluntary actions of men tend to the benefit of themselves; and those actions are most reasonable, that conduce most to their ends. This specious reasoning is nevertheless false.

For the question is not of promises mutual, where there is no security of performance on either side; as when there is no civil power erected over the parties promising; for such promises are no covenants: but either where one of the parties has performed already; or where there is a power to make him perform; there is the question whether it be against reason, that is, against the benefit of the other to perform, or not. And I say it is not against reason. For the manifestation whereof, we are to consider; first, that when a man doth a thing, which notwithstanding anything can be foreseen, and reckoned on, tendeth to his own destruction, howsoever some accident which he could not expect, arriving may turn it to his benefit; yet such events do not make it reasonably or wisely done. Secondly, that in a condition of war, wherein every man to every man, for want of a common power to keep them all in awe, is an enemy, there is no man who can hope by his own strength, or wit, to defend himself from destruction, without the help of confederates; where everyone expects the same defence by the confederation, that any one else does: and therefore he which declares he thinks it reason to deceive those that help him, can in reason expect no other means of safety, than what can be had from his own single power. He therefore that breaketh his covenant, and consequently declareth that he thinks he may with reason do so, cannot be received into any society, that unite themselves for peace and defense, but by the error of them that receive him; nor when he is received, be retained in it, without seeing the danger of their error; which errors a man cannot reasonably reckon upon as the means of his security: and therefore if he be left, or cast out of society, he perisheth; and if he live in society, it is by the errors of other men, which he could not foresee, nor reckon upon; and consequently against the reason of his preservation; and so, as all men that contribute not to his destruction, forbear him only out of ignorance of what is good for themselves.

As for the instance of gaining the secure and perpetual felicity of heaven, by any way; it is frivolous: there being but one way imaginable; and that is not breaking, but keeping of covenant.

And for the other instance of attaining sovereignty by rebellion; it is manifest, that though the event follow, yet because it cannot reasonably be expected, but rather the contrary; and because by gaining it so, others are taught to gain the same in like manner, the attempt thereof is against reason. Justice therefore, that is to say, keeping of covenant, is a rule of reason, by which we are forbidden to do any thing destructive to our life; and consequently a law of nature.

There be some that proceed further; and will not have the law of nature, to be those rules which conduce to the preservation of man's life on earth; but to the attaining of an eternal felicity after death; to which they think the breach of covenant may conduce; and consequently be just and reasonable; such are they that think it a work of merit to kill, or depose, or rebel against, the sovereign power constituted over them by their own consent. But because

there is no natural knowledge of man's estate after death; much less of the reward that is then to be given to breach of faith; but only a belief grounded upon other men's saying, that they know it supernaturally, or that they know those, that knew them, that knew others, that knew it supernaturally; breach of faith cannot be called a precept of reason, or nature.

Others, that allow for a law of nature, the keeping of faith, do nevertheless make exception of certain persons; as heretics, and such as use not to perform their covenant to others: and this also is against reason. For if any fault of a man, be sufficient to discharge our covenant made; the same ought in reason to have been sufficient to have hindered the making of it.

The names of just, and unjust, when they are attributed to men, signify one thing; and when they are attributed to actions, another. When they are attributed to men, they signify conformity, or inconformity of manners, to reason. But when they are attributed to actions, they signify the conformity, or inconformity to reason, not of manners, or manner of life, but of particular actions. A just man therefore, is he that taketh all the care he can, that his actions may be all just: and an unjust man, is he that neglecteth it. And such men are more often in our language styled by the names of righteous, and unrighteous; than just, and unjust; though the meaning be the same. Therefore a righteous man, does not lose that title, by one, or a few unjust actions, that proceed from sudden passion, or mistake of things, or persons: nor does an unrighteous man, lose his character, for such actions, as he does, or forbears to do, for fear: because his will is not framed by the justice, but by the apparent benefit of what he is to do. That which gives to human actions the relish of justice, is a certain nobleness or gallantness of courage, rarely found, by which a man scorns to be beholden for the contentment of his life, to fraud, or breach of promise. This justice of the manners, is that which is meant, where justice is called a virtue; and injustice a vice.

But the justice of actions denominates men, not just, but *guiltless*; and the injustice of the same, which is also called injury, gives them but the name of *guilty*.

Again, the injustice of manners, is the disposition, or aptitude to do injury; and is injustice before it proceed to act; and without supposing any individual person injured. But the injustice of an action, that is to say injury, supposeth an individual person injured; namely him, to whom the covenant was made: and therefore many times the injury is received by one man, when the damage redoundeth to another. As when the master commandeth his servant to give money to a stranger; if it be not done, the injury is done to the master, whom he had before covenanted to obey; but the damage redoundeth to the stranger, to whom he had no obligation; and therefore could not injure him. And so also in commonwealths, private men may remit to one another their debts; but not robberies or other violences, whereby they are endamaged; because the detaining of debt, is an injury to themselves; but robbery and violence, are injuries to the person of the commonwealth.

Whatsoever is done to a man, conformable to his own will signified to the doer, is no injury to him. For if he that doeth it, hath not passed away his original right to do what he please, by some antecedent covenant, there is no breach of covenant; and therefore no injury done him. And if he have: then his will to have it done being signified, is a release of that covenant: and so again there is no injury done him.

Justice of actions, is by writers divided into *commutative,* and *distributive:* and the former they say consisteth in proportion arithmetical; the latter in proportion geometrical. Commutative therefore, they place in the equality of value of the things contracted for; and distributive, in the distribution of equal benefit, to men of equal merit. As if it were injustice to sell dearer than we buy; or to give more to a man than he merits. The value of all things contracted for, is measured by the appetite of the contractors: and therefore the just value, is that which they be contented to give. And merit, besides that which is by covenant, where the performance on one part, meriteth the performance of the other part, and falls under justice commutative, not distributive, is not due by justice; but is rewarded of grace only. And therefore this distinction, in the sense wherein it useth to be expounded, is not right. To speak properly, commutative justice, is the justice, of a contractor; that is, a performance of covenant, in buying, and selling; hiring, and letting to hire; lending, and borrowing; exchanging, bartering, and other acts of contract.

And distributive justice, the justice of an arbitrator; that is to say, the act of defining what is just. Wherein, being trusted by them that make him arbitrator, if he perform his trust, he is said to distribute to every man his own: and this is indeed just distribution, and may be called, though improperly, distributive justice; but more properly equity; which also is a law of nature, as shall be shown in due place.

As justice dependeth on antecedent covenant; so does GRATITUDE depend on antecedent grace; that is to say, antecedent free gift: and is the fourth law of nature; which may be conceived in this form, *that a man which receiveth benefit from another of mere grace, endeavour that he which giveth it, have no reasonable cause to repent him of his good will.* For no man giveth, but with intention of good to himself; because gift is voluntary; and of all voluntary acts, the object is to every man his own good; of which if men see they shall be frustrated, there will be no beginning of benevolence, or trust; nor consequently of mutual help; nor of reconciliation of one man to another; and therefore they are to remain still in the condition of *war;* which is contrary to the first and fundamental law of nature, which commandeth men to *seek peace.* The breach of this law, is called *ingratitude;* and hath the same relation to grace, that injustice hath to obligation by covenant.

A fifth law of nature, is COMPLAISANCE; that is to say, *that every man strive to accommodate himself to the rest.* For the understanding whereof, we may consider, that there is in men's aptness to society, a diversity of nature, rising from their diversity of affections; not unlike to that we see in stones brought together for building of an edifice. For as that stone which by the asperity, and irregularity of figure, takes more room from others, than itself fills; and for the hardness, cannot be easily made plain, and thereby hindereth the building, is by the builders cast away as unprofitable, and troublesome: so also, a man that by asperity of nature, will strive to retain those things which to himself are superfluous, and to others necessary; and for the stubbornness of his passions, cannot be corrected, is to be left, or cast out of society, as cumbersome thereunto. For seeing every man, not only by right, but also by necessity of nature, is supposed to endeavour all he can, to obtain that which is necessary for his conservation; he that shall oppose himself against it, for things superfluous, is guilty of the war that thereupon is to follow; and therefore doth that, which is contrary to the fundamental law of nature, which commandeth *to seek peace.* The observers of this law, may be called SOCIABLE, the Latins call them *commodi;* the contrary, *stubborn, insociable, froward, intractable.*

A sixth law of nature, is this, *that upon caution of the future time, a man ought to pardon the offences past of them that repenting, desire it.* For PARDON, is nothing but granting of peace; which though granted to them that persevere in their hostility, be not peace, but fear; yet not granted to them that give caution of the future time, is sign of an aversion to peace; and therefore contrary to the law of nature.

A seventh is, *that in revenges,* that is, retribution of evil for evil, *men look not at the greatness of the evil past, but the greatness of the good to follow.* Whereby we are forbidden to inflict punishment with any other design, than for correction of the offender, or direction of others. For this law is consequent to the next before it, that commandeth pardon, upon security of the future time. Besides, revenge without respect to the example, and profit to come, is a triumph, or glorying in the hurt of another, tending to no end; for the end is always somewhat to come; and glorying to no end, is vain-glory, and contrary to reason, and to hurt without reason, tendeth to the introduction of war; which is against the law of nature; and is commonly styled by the name of *cruelty.*

And because all signs of hatred, or contempt, provoke to fight; insomuch as most men choose rather to hazard their life, than not to be revenged; we may in the eighth place, for a law of nature, set down this precept, *that no man by deed, word, countenance, or gesture, declare hatred, or contempt of another.* The breach of which law, is commonly called *contumely.*

The question who is the better man, has no place in the condition of mere nature; where, as has been shewn before, all men are equal. The inequality that now is, has been introduced by the laws civil. I know that Aristotle in the first book of his *Politics,* for a foundation of his doctrine, maketh men by nature, some more worthy to command, meaning the wiser sort, such as he thought himself to be for his philosophy; others to serve, meaning those that had strong bodies, but were not philosophers as he; as if master and servant were not introduced by consent of men, but by difference of wit: which is not only against reason; but also against experience. For there are

very few so foolish, that had not rather govern themselves, than be governed by others: nor when the wise in their own conceit, contend by force, with them who distrust their own wisdom, do they always, or often, or almost at any time, get the victory. If nature therefore have made men equal, that equality is to be acknowledged: or if nature have made men unequal; yet because men that think themselves equal, will not enter into conditions of peace, but upon equal terms, such equality must be admitted. And therefore for the ninth law of nature, I put this, *that every man acknowledge another for his equal by nature.* The breach of this precept is *pride.*

On this law, dependeth another, *that at the entrance into conditions of peace, no man require to reserve to himself any right, which he is not content should be reserved to every one of the rest.* As it is necessary for all men that seek peace, to lay down certain rights of nature; that is to say, not to have liberty to do all they list: so is it necessary for man's life, to retain some; as right to govern their own bodies; enjoy air, water, motion, ways to go from place to place; and all things else, without which a man cannot live, or not live well. If in this case, at the making of peace, men require for themselves, that which they would not have to be granted to others, they do contrary to the precedent law, that commandeth the acknowledgment of natural equality, and therefore also against the law of nature. The observers of this law, are those we call *modest,* and the breakers *arrogant* men. The Greeks call the violation of this law πλεονεξία; that is, a desire of more than their share.

Also if *a man be trusted to judge between man and man,* it is a precept of the law of nature, *that he deal equally between them.* For without that, the controversies of men cannot be determined but by war. He therefore that is partial in judgment, doth what in him lies, to deter men from the use of judges, and arbitrators; and consequently, against the fundamental law of nature, is the cause of war.

The observance of this law, from the equal distribution to each man, of that which in reason belongeth to him, is called EQUITY, and, as I have said before, distributive justice: the violation, *acception of persons,* προσωποληψία.

And from this followeth another law, *that such things as cannot be divided, be enjoyed in common, if it can be; and if the quantity of the thing permit, without stint; otherwise proportionably to the number of them that have right.* For otherwise the distribution is unequal, and contrary to equity.

But some things there be, that can neither be divided, nor enjoyed in common. Then, the law of nature, which prescribeth equity, requireth, *that the entire right; or else, making the use alternate, the first possession, be determined by lot.* For equal distribution, is of the law of nature; and other means of equal distribution cannot be imagined.

Of *lots* there be two sorts, *arbitrary,* and *natural.* Arbitrary, is that which is agreed on by the competitors: natural, is either *primogeniture,* which the Greek calls κληρονομία, which signifies, *given by lot;* or *first seizure.*

And therefore those things which cannot be enjoyed in common, nor divided ought to be adjudged to the first possessor; and in some cases to the first born, as acquired by lot.

It is also a law of nature, *that all men that mediate peace, be allowed safe conduct.* For the law that commandeth peace, as the *end,* commandeth intercession, as the *means;* and to intercession the means is safe conduct.

And because, though men be never so willing to observe these laws, there may nevertheless arise questions concerning a man's action; first, whether it were done, or not done; secondly, if done, whether against the law, or not against the law: the former whereof, is called a question *of fact:* the latter a question *of right,* therefore unless the parties to the question, covenant mutually to stand to the sentence of another, they are as far from peace as ever. This other to whose sentence they submit is called an ARBITRATOR. And therefore it is of the law of nature, *that they that are at controversy, submit their right to the judgment of an arbitrator.*

And seeing every man is presumed to do all things in order to his own benefit, no man is a fit arbitrator in his own cause; and if he were never so fit; yet equity allowing to each party equal benefit, if one be admitted to be judge, the other is to be admitted also; and so the controversy, that is, the cause of war, remains, against the law of nature.

For the same reason no man in any cause ought to be received for arbitrator, to whom greater profit, or honour, or pleasure apparently ariseth out of the victory of one party, than of the other: for he hath taken, though an unavoidable bribe, yet a bribe; and no man can be obliged to trust him. And thus also

the controversy, and the condition of war remaineth, contrary to the law of nature.

And in a controversy of *fact,* the judge being to give more credit to one, than to the other, if there be no other arguments, must give credit to a third; or to a third and fourth; or more: for else the question is undecided, and left to force, contrary to the law of nature.

These are the laws of nature, dictating peace, for a means of the conservation of men in multitudes; and which only concern the doctrine of civil society. There be other things tending to the destruction of particular men; as drunkenness, and all other parts of intemperance; which may therefore also be reckoned amongst those things which the law of nature hath forbidden; but are not necessary to be mentioned, nor are pertinent enough to this place.

And though this may seem too subtle a deduction of the laws of nature, to be taken notice of by all men; whereof the most part are too busy in getting food, and the rest too negligent to understand; yet to leave all men inexcusable, they have been contracted into one easy sum, intelligible even to the meanest capacity; and that is, *Do not that to another, which thou wouldst not have done to thyself;* which sheweth him, that he has no more to do in learning the laws of nature, but, when weighing the actions of other men with his own, they seem too heavy, to put them into the other part of the balance, and his own into their place, that his own passions, and self-love, may add nothing to the weight; and then there is none of these laws of nature that will not appear unto him very reasonable.

The laws of nature oblige *in foro interno;* that is to say, they bind to a desire they should take place: but *in foro externo;* that is, to the putting them in act, not always. For he that should be modest, and tractable, and perform all he promises, in such time, and place, where no man else should do so, should but make himself a prey to others, and procure his own certain ruin, contrary to the ground of all laws of nature, which tend to nature's preservation. And again, he that having sufficient security, that others shall observe the same laws towards him, observes them not himself, seeketh not peace, but war; and consequently the destruction of his nature by violence.And whatsoever laws bind *in foro interno,* may be broken, not only by a fact contrary to the law, but also by a fact according to it, in case a man think it contrary. For though his action in this case, be according to the law; yet his purpose was against the law; which, where the obligition is *in foro interno,* is a breach.

The laws of nature are immutable and eternal; for injustice, ingratitude, arrogance, pride, iniquity, acception of persons, and the rest, can never be made lawful. For it can never be that war shall preserve life, and peace destroy it.

The same laws, because they oblige only to a desire, and endeavour, I mean an unfeigned and constant endeavour, are easy to be observed. For in that they require nothing but endeavour, he that endeavoureth their performance, fulfilleth them, and he that fulfilleth the law, is just.

And the science of them, is the true and only moral philosophy. For moral philosophy is nothing else but the science of what is *good,* and *evil,* in the conversation, and society of mankind. *Good,* and *evil,* are names that signify our appetites, and aversions; which in different tempers, customs, and doctrines of men, are different: and divers men, differ not only in their judgment, on the senses of what is pleasant, and unpleasant to the taste, smell, hearing, touch, and sight; but also of what is conformable, or disagreeable to reason, in the actions of common life. Nay, the same man, in divers times, differs from himself; and one time praiseth, that is, calleth good, what another time he dispraiseth, and calleth evil:

from whence arise disputes, controversies, and at last war. And therefore so long as a man is in the condition of mere nature, which is a condition of war, his private appetite is the measure of good, and evil: and consequently all men agree on this, that peace is good, and therefore also the way, or means of peace, which, as I have shewed before, are *justice, gratitude, modesty, equity, mercy,* and the rest of the laws of nature, are good; that is to say; *moral virtues;* and their contrary *vices,* evil. Now the science of virtue and vice, is moral philosophy; and therefore the true doctrine of the laws of nature, is the true moral philosophy. But the writers of moral philosophy, though they acknowledge the same virtues and vices; yet not seeing wherein consisted their goodness; nor that they come to be praised, as the means of peaceable, sociable, and comfortable living, place them in a mediocrity of passions: as if not the cause, but the degree of daring, made fortitude; or not the cause, but the quantity of a gift, made liberality.

These dictates of reason, men used to call by the name of laws, but improperly: for they are but conclusions, or theorems concerning what conduceth to the conservation and defence of themselves; whereas law, properly, is the word of him, that by right hath command over others. But yet if we consider the same theorems, as delivered in the word of God, that by right commandeth all things; then are they properly called laws.

DAVID HUME

FROM *An Enquiry Concerning the Principles of Morals*

One of the greatest of all English moralists was David Hume. He was born in Edinburgh, Scotland, in 1711, the youngest of three children whose father owned a small estate and whose mother came from a family of lawyers. It was to the study of law that young Hume was directed, but his interests lay elsewhere. Instead, he sought a literary career, and by 1729 was convinced that he had a momentous idea for a major work in philosophy.

After five years of intensive study at home followed by three more years spent writing, his philosophical composition was published in 1739 as A Treatise of Human Nature. *He intended the work to be widely read: in his age one could expect that all educated people were able to understand and read philosophy, economics, science, and other topics now relegated to the specialist. To Hume's great disappointment, however, the book failed to ignite the philosophical controversy he had imagined. In fact, the book went almost completely unnoticed. Convinced that the work's failure was due to literary style, Hume undertook revisions, publishing the reworked first part of the* Treatise *in 1748 as* An Enquiry Concerning Human Understanding *and the revised third part (on morality and politics) three years later as* An Enquiry Concerning the Principles of Morals. *The publication of these two works, along with some polite essays, secured fame and a degree of fortune for Hume. In later life he published a long and controversial history of England and, posthumously,* Dialogues Concerning Natural Religion. *Even though the* Treatise *contains valuable insights into the formulation of Hume's thought, he declared at the end of his life that the second* Enquiry *was by far his best work. For that reason, it is from the later work that the selections in the present text are chosen.*

Formulated during the Age of Enlightenment, Hume's philosophy was an accurate reflection of his time (although he was more radical in his atheism than most Enlightenment writers). He wrote in opposition to the great rationalistic metaphysics of Descartes, Spinoza, and Leibniz, as well as in opposition to religion. He was positively influenced by his English empiricist predecessors such as Locke, Hutcheson, and Joseph Butler as well as by the emerging scientific method. It was especially the experimental method employed by Sir Isaac Newton, whose Principia *had been published in 1689, that captured his interest. Hume's philosophical aim was to combine the Newtonian experimental method with an empiricist philosophical investigation into the principles of the human mind.*

Hume's goal in moral philosophy was to understand both human nature and the world without reference to religious doctrine. In opposition to the influential and prevalent Calvinist view, he argued that morality, being agreeable and useful, could lead to an enjoyable life in the present. Calvin and his followers preached that one should disdain the present life in favor of the next. With scientific understanding of human nature, people could be freed, Hume thought, from the superstitious and pernicious influence of Calvin and others of his kind.

What Hume discovered when he directed the scientific method of Newton to the study of human moral life, he argued, is that moral judgments are not the result of reason, but rather of feeling. When we evaluate an action as virtuous or vicious, we are merely indicating how we feel about it. This is because moral judgments are meant to motivate us to action, and reason lacks such ability to motivate. It is moral sentiment, not reason, that contains the requisite motivational properties required by moral judgments. And the moral sentiment is brought about by what is pleasant or useful.

Hume's influence on subsequent ethical theory, like his influence in all philosophy, was and is enormous. However, the continuation of Hume's moral philosophy proceeds primarily in two directions. His view that the powers of reason are limited and that the human world should be explained in terms of feelings, not reason, sets the course for subjectivism in ethics, prevalent in the twentieth century. Alternatively, Hume's utilitarian theory of good situates him near the beginning of the utilitarian school of moral philosophy, later formulated in detail by Jeremy Bentham and John Stuart Mill.

Section I.—Of the General Principles of Morals.

Disputes with men, pertinaciously obstinate in their principles, are, of all others, the most irksome; except, perhaps, those with persons, entirely disingenuous, who really do not believe the opinions they defend, but engage in the controversy, from affectation, from a spirit of opposition, or from a desire of showing wit and ingenuity, superior to the rest of mankind. The same blind adherence to their own arguments is to be expected in both; the same contempt of their antagonists; and the same passionate vehemence, in inforcing sophistry and falsehood. And as reasoning is not the source, whence either disputant derives his tenets; it is in vain to expect, that any logic, which speaks not to the affections, will ever engage him to embrace sounder principles.

Those who have denied the reality of moral distinctions, may be ranked among the disingenuous disputants; nor is it conceivable, that any human creature could ever seriously believe, that all characters and actions were alike entitled to the affection and regard of every one. The difference, which nature has placed between one man and another, is so wide, and this difference is still so much farther widened, by education, example, and habit, that, where the opposite extremes come at once under our apprehension, there is no scepticism so scrupulous, and scarce any assurance so determined, as absolutely to deny all distinction between them. Let a man's insensibility be ever so great, he must often be touched with the images of RIGHT and WRONG; and let his prejudices be ever so obstinate, he must observe, that others are susceptible of like impressions. The only way, therefore, of converting an antagonist of this kind, is to leave him to himself. For, finding that no body keeps up the controversy with him, it is probable he will, at last, of himself, from mere weariness, come over to the side of common sense and reason.

There has been a controversy started of late, much better worth examination, concerning the general foundation of MORALS; whether they be derived from REASON, or from SENTIMENT; whether we attain the knowledge of them by a chain of argument and induction, or by an immediate feeling and finer internal sense; whether, like all sound judgment of truth and falsehood, they should be the same to every rational intelligent being; or whether, like the perception of beauty and deformity, they be founded entirely on the particular fabric and constitution of the human species.

The ancient philosophers, though they often affirm, that virtue is nothing but conformity to reason, yet, in general, seem to consider morals as deriving their existence from taste and sentiment. On the other hand, our modern enquirers, though they also talk much of the beauty of virtue, and deformity of vice, yet have commonly endeavoured to account for these distinctions by metaphysical reasonings, and by deductions from the most abstract principles of the understanding. Such confusion reigned in these subjects, that an opposition of the greatest consequence could prevail between one system and another, and even in the parts of almost each individual system; and yet no body, till very lately, was ever sensible of it. The elegant Lord SHAFTESBURY, who first gave occasion to remark this distinction, and who, in general, adhered to the principles of the ancients, is not, himself, entirely free from the same confusion.

It must be acknowledged, that both sides of the question are susceptible of specious arguments. Moral distinctions, it may be said, are discernible by pure *reason:* Else, whence the many disputes that reign in common life, as well as in philosophy, with regard to this subject: The long chain of proofs often produced on both sides; the examples cited, the authorities appealed to, the analogies employed, the fallacies detected, the inferences drawn, and the several conclusions adjusted to their proper principles. Truth is disputable; not taste: What exists in the nature of things is the standard of our judgment; what each man feels within himself is the standard of sentiment. Propositions in geometry may be proved, systems in physics may be controverted; but the harmony of verse, the tenderness of passion, the brilliancy of wit, must give immediate pleasure. No man reasons concerning another's beauty; but frequently concerning the justice or injustice of his actions. In every criminal trial the first object of the prisoner is to disprove the facts alleged, and deny the actions imputed to him: The second to prove, that, even if these actions were real, they might be justified, as innocent and lawful. It is confessedly by deductions of the understanding, that the first point is ascertained: How can we suppose that a different faculty of the mind is employed in fixing the other?

On the other hand, those who would resolve all moral determinations into *sentiment,* may endeavour to show, that it is impossible for reason ever to draw conclusions of this nature. To virtue, say they, it belongs to be *amiable,* and vice *odious.* This forms their very nature or essence. But can reason or argumentation distribute these different epithets to any subjects, and pronounce before-hand, that this must produce love, and that hatred? Or what other reason can we ever assign for these affections, but the original fabric and formation of the human mind, which is naturally adapted to receive them?

The end of all moral speculations is to teach us our duty; and, by proper representations of the deformity of vice and beauty of virtue, beget correspondent habits, and engage us to avoid the one, and embrace the other. But is this ever to be expected from inferences and conclusions of the understanding, which of themselves have no hold of the affections or set in motion the active powers of men? They discover truths: But where the truths which they discover are indifferent, and beget no desire or aversion, they can have no influence on conduct and behaviour. What is honourable, what is fair, what is becoming, what is noble, what is generous, takes possession of the heart, and animates us to embrace and maintain it. What is intelligible, what is evident, what is probable, what is true, procures only the cool assent of the understanding; and gratifying a speculative curiosity, puts an end to our researches.

Extinguish all the warm feelings and prepossessions in favour of virtue, and all disgust or aversion to vice: Render men totally indifferent towards these distinctions; and morality is no longer a practical study, nor has any tendency to regulate our lives and actions.

These arguments on each side (and many more might be produced) are so plausible, that I am apt to suspect, they may, the one as well as the other, be solid and satisfactory, and that *reason* and *sentiment* concur in almost all moral determinations and conclusions. The final sentence, it is probable, which pronounces characters and actions amiable or odious, praise-worthy or blameable; that which stamps on them the mark of honour or infamy, approbation or censure; that which renders morality an active principle, and constitutes virtue our happiness, and vice our misery: It is probable, I say, that this final sentence depends on some internal sense or feeling, which nature has made universal in the whole species. For what else can have an influence of this nature? But in order to pave the way for such a sentiment, and give a proper discernment of its object, it is often necessary, we find, that much reasoning should precede, that nice distinctions be made, just conclusions drawn, distant comparisons formed, complicated relations examined, and general facts fixed and ascertained. Some species of beauty, especially the natural kinds, on their first appearance, command our affection and approbation; and where they fail of this effect, it is impossible for any reasoning to redress their influence, or adapt them better to our taste and sentiment. But in many orders of beauty, particularly those of the finer arts, it is requisite to employ much reasoning, in order to feel the proper sentiment; and a false relish may frequently be corrected by argument and reflection. There are just grounds to conclude, that moral beauty partakes much of this latter species, and demands the assistance of our intellectual faculties, in order to give it a suitable influence on the human mind.

But though this question, concerning the general principles of morals, be curious and important, it is needless for us, at present, to employ farther care in our researches concerning it. For if we can be so happy, in the course of this enquiry, as to discover the true origin of morals, it will then easily appear how far either sentiment or reason enters into all determinations of this nature.[1] In order to attain this purpose, we shall endeavour to follow a very simple method: We shall analyse that complication of mental qualities, which form what, in common life, we call PERSONAL MERIT: We shall consider every attribute of the mind, which renders a man an object either of esteem and affection, or of hatred and contempt; every habit or sentiment or faculty, which, if ascribed to any person, implies either praise or blame, and may enter into any panegyric or satire of his character and manners. The quick sensibility, which, on this head, is so universal among mankind, gives a philosopher sufficient assurance, that he can never be considerably mistaken in framing the catalogue, or incur any danger of misplacing the objects of his contemplation: He needs only enter into his own breast for a moment, and consider whether or not he should desire to have this or that quality as-

---

1. See Appendix I. Concerning Moral Sentiment.

cribed to him, and whether such or such an imputation would proceed from a friend or an enemy. The very nature of language guides us almost infallibly in forming a judgment of this nature; and as every tongue possesses one set of words which are taken in a good sense, and another in the opposite, the least acquaintance with the idiom suffices, without any reasoning, to direct us in collecting and arranging the estimable or blameable qualities of men. The only object of reasoning is to discover the circumstances on both sides, which are common to these qualities; to observe that particular in which the estimable qualities agree on the one hand, and the blameable on the other; and thence to reach the foundation of ethics, and find those universal principles, from which all censure or approbation is ultimately derived. As this is a question of fact, not of abstract science, we can only expect success, by following the experimental method, and deducing general maxims from a comparison of particular instances. The other scientifical method, where a general abstract principle is first established, and is afterwards branched out into a variety of inferences and conclusions, may be more perfect in itself, but suits less the imperfection of human nature, and is a common source of illusion and mistake in this as well as in other subjects. Men are now cured of their passion for hypotheses and systems in natural philosophy, and will hearken to no arguments but those which are derived from experience. It is full time they should attempt a like reformation in all moral disquisitions; and reject every system of ethics, however subtile or ingenious, which is not founded on fact and observation.

We shall begin our enquiry on this head by the consideration of social virtues, benevolence and justice. The explication of them will probably give us an opening by which others may be accounted for.

Section II.—Of Benevolence.

Part I.

It may be esteemed, perhaps, a superfluous task to prove, that the benevolent or softer affections are ESTIMABLE; and wherever they appear, engage the approbation, and good-will of mankind. The epithets *sociable, good-natured, humane, merciful, grateful, friendly, generous, beneficent,* or their equivalents, are known in all languages, and universally express the highest merit, which *human nature* is capable of attaining. Where these amiable qualities are attended with birth and power and eminent abilities, and display themselves in the good government or useful instruction of mankind, they seem even to raise the possessors of them above the rank of *human nature,* and make them approach in some measure to the divine. Exalted capacity, undaunted courage, prosperous success; these may only expose a hero or politician to the envy or ill-will of the public: But as soon as the praises are added of humane and beneficent; when instances are displayed of lenity, tenderness, or friendship: envy itself is silent, or joins the general voice of approbation and applause.

When Pericles, the great Athenian statesman and general, was on his death-bed, his surrounding friends, deeming him now insensible, began to indulge their sorrow for their expiring patron, by enumerating his great qualities and successes, his conquests and victories, the unusual length of his administration, and his nine trophies erected over the enemies of the republic. *You forget,* cries the dying hero, who had heard all, *you forget the most eminent of my praises, while you dwell so much on those vulgar advantages, in which fortune had a principal share. You have not observed, that no citizen has ever yet worne mourning on my account.*

In men of more ordinary talents and capacity, the social virtues become, if possible, still more essentially requisite; there being nothing eminent, in that case, to compensate for the want of them, or preserve the person from our severest hatred, as well as contempt. A high ambition, an elevated courage, is apt, says Cicero, in less perfect characters, to degenerate into a turbulent ferocity. The more social and softer virtues are there chiefly to be regarded. These are always good and amiable.

The principal advantage, which Juvenal discovers in the extensive capacity of the human species is, that it renders our benevolence also more extensive, and gives us larger opportunities of spreading our kindly influence than what are indulged to the inferior creation. It must, indeed, be confessed, that by doing good only, can a man truly enjoy the advantages of being eminent. His exalted station, of itself, but the more exposes him to danger and tempest. His sole prerogative is to afford shelter to inferiors, who repose themselves under his cover and protection.

But I forget, that it is not my present business to recommend generosity and benevolence, or to paint, in their true colours, all the genuine charms of the social virtues. These, indeed, sufficiently engage every heart, on the first apprehension of them; and it is difficult to abstain from some sally of panegyric, as often as they occur in discourse or reasoning. But our object here being more the speculative, than the practical part of morals, it will suffice to remark, (what will readily, I believe, be allowed) that no qualities are more intitled to the general good-will and approbation of mankind than benevolence and humanity, friendship and gratitude, natural affection and public spirit, or whatever proceeds from a tender sympathy with others, and a generous concern for our kind and species. These, wherever they appear, seem to transfuse themselves, in a manner, into each beholder, and to call forth, in their own behalf, the same favourable and affectionate sentiments, which they exert on all around.

Part II.

We may observe, that, in displaying the praises of any humane, beneficent man, there is one circumstance which never fails to be amply insisted on, namely, the happiness and satisfaction, derived to society from his intercourse and good offices. To his parents, we are apt to say, he endears himself by his pious attachment and duteous care, still more than by the connexions of nature. His children never feel his authority, but when employed for their advantage. With him, the ties of love are consolidated by beneficence and friendship. The ties of friendship approach, in a fond observance of each obliging office, to those of love and inclination. His domestics and dependants have in him a sure resource; and no longer dread the power of fortune, but so far as she exercises it over him. From him the hungry receive food, the naked cloathing, the ignorant and slothful skill and industry. Like the sun, an inferior minister of providence, he cheers, invigorates, and sustains the surrounding world.

If confined to private life, the sphere of his activity is narrower; but his influence is all benign and gentle. If exalted into a higher station, mankind and posterity reap the fruit of his labours.

As these topics of praise never fail to be employed, and with success, where we would inspire esteem for any one; may it not thence be concluded, that the UTILITY, resulting from the social virtues, forms, at least, a *part* of their merit, and is one source of that approbation and regard so universally paid to them?

When we recommend even an animal or a plant as *useful* and *beneficial,* we give it an applause and recommendation suited to its nature. As, on the other hand, reflection on the baneful influence of any of these inferior beings always inspires us with the sentiment of aversion. The eye is pleased with the prospect of corn-fields and loaded vineyards; horses grazing, and flocks pasturing: But flies the view of briars and brambles, affording shelter to wolves and serpents.

A machine, a piece of furniture, a vestment, a house well contrived for use and conveniency, is so far beautiful, and is contemplated with pleasure and approbation. An experienced eye is here sensible to many excellencies, which escape persons ignorant and uninstructed.

Can anything stronger be said in praise of a profession, such as merchandize or manufacture, than to observe the advantages which it procures to society? And is not a monk and inquisitor enraged when we treat his order as useless or pernicious to mankind?

The historian exults in displaying the benefit arising from his labours. The writer of romance alleviates or denies the bad consequences ascribed to his manner of composition.

In general, what praise is implied in the simple epithet *useful!* What reproach in the contrary!

Your Gods, says CICERO, in opposition to the EPICUREANS, cannot justly claim any worship or adoration, with whatever imaginary perfections you may suppose them endowed. They are totally useless and unactive. Even the EGYPTIANS, whom you so much ridicule, never consecrated any animal but on account of its utility.

The sceptics assert, though absurdly, that the origin of all religious worship was derived from the utility of inanimate objects, as the sun and moon, to the support and well-being of mankind. This is also the common reason assigned by historians, for the deification of eminent heroes and legislators.

To plant a tree, to cultivate a field, to beget children; meritorious acts, according to the religion of ZOROASTER.

In all determinations of morality, this circumstance of public utility is ever principally in view; and wherever disputes arise, either in philosophy or common life, concerning the bounds of duty, the question cannot, by any means, be decided with greater certainty, than by ascertaining, on any side, the true interests of mankind. If any false opinion, embraced from appearances, has been found to prevail; as soon as farther experience and sounder reasoning have given us juster notions of human affairs; we retract our first sentiment, and adjust anew the boundaries of moral good and evil.

Giving alms to common beggars is naturally praised; because it seems to carry relief to the distressed and indigent: But when we observe the encouragement thence arising to idleness and debauchery, we regard that species of charity rather as a weakness than a virtue.

Tyrannicide, or the assassination of usurpers and oppressive princes, was highly extolled in ancient times; because it both freed mankind from many of these monsters, and seemed to keep the others in awe, whom the sword or poinard could not reach. But history and experience having since convinced us, that this practice encreases the jealousy and cruelty of princes, a TIMOLEON and a BRUTUS, though treated with indulgence on account of the prejudices of their times, are now considered as very improper models for imitation.

Liberality in princes is regarded as a mark of beneficence: But when it occurs, that the homely bread of the honest and industrious is often thereby converted into delicious cates for the idle and the prodigal, we soon retract our heedless praises. The regrets of a prince, for having lost a day, were noble and generous: But had he intended to have spent it in acts of generosity to his greedy courtiers, it was better lost than misemployed after that manner.

Luxury, or a refinement on the pleasures and conveniencies of life, had long been supposed the source of every corruption in government, and the immediate cause of faction, sedition, civil wars, and the total loss of liberty. It was, therefore, universally regarded as a vice, and was an object of declamation to all satyrists, and severe moralists. Those, who prove, or attempt to prove, that such refinements rather tend to the encrease of industry, civility, and arts, regulate anew our *moral* as well as *political* sentiments, and represent, as laudable or innocent, what had formerly been regarded as pernicious and blameable.

Upon the whole, then, it seems undeniable, *that* nothing can bestow more merit on any human creature than the sentiment of benevolence in an eminent degree; and *that a part,* at least, of its merit arises from its tendency to promote the interests of our species, and bestow happiness on human society. We carry our view into the salutary consequences of such a character and disposition; and whatever has so benign an influence, and forwards so desirable an end, is beheld with complacency and pleasure. The social virtues are never regarded without their beneficial tendencies, nor viewed as barren and unfruitful. The happiness of mankind, the order of society, the harmony of families, the mutual support of friends, are always considered as the result of their gentle dominion over the breasts of men.

How considerable a *part* of their merit we ought to ascribe to their utility, will better appear from future disquisitions;[1] as well as the reason, why this circumstance has such a command over our esteem and approbation.[2]

Section III.—Of Justice.

Part I.

That Justice is useful to society, and consequently that *part* of its merit, at least, must arise from that consideration, it would be a superfluous undertaking to prove. That public utility is the *sole* origin of justice, and that reflections on the beneficial consequences of this virtue are the *sole* foundation of its merit; this proposition, being more curious and important, will better deserve our examination and enquiry.

Let us suppose, that nature has bestowed on the human race such profuse *abundance* of all *external* conveniencies, that, without any uncertainty in the event, without any care or industry on our part, every individual finds himself fully provided with whatever his most voracious appetites can want, or luxurious imagination wish or desire. His natural beauty, we shall suppose, surpasses all acquired ornaments: The

---

1. Sect. 3d . . . Of Justice. . . .

2. Sect. 5th. Why Utility Pleases.

perpetual clemency of the seasons renders useless all cloaths or covering: The raw herbage affords him the most delicious fare; the clear fountain, the richest beverage. No laborious occupation required: No tillage: No navigation. Music, poetry, and contemplation, form his sole business: Conversation, mirth, and friendship his sole amusement.

It seems evident, that, in such a happy state, every other social virtue would flourish, and receive tenfold encrease; but the cautious, jealous virtue of justice would never once have been dreamed of. For what purpose make a partition of goods, where every one has already more than enough? Why give rise to property, where there cannot possibly be any injury? Why call this object *mine,* when, upon the seizing of it by another, I need but stretch out my hand to possess myself of what is equally valuable? Justice, in that case, being totally USELESS, would be an idle ceremonial, and could never possibly have place in the catalogue of virtues.

We see, even in the present necessitous condition of mankind, that, wherever any benefit is bestowed by nature in an unlimited abundance, we leave it always in common among the whole human race, and make no subdivisions of right and property. Water and air, though the most necessary of all objects, are not challenged as the property of individuals; nor can any man commit injustice by the most lavish use and enjoyment of these blessings. In fertile extensive countries, with few inhabitants, land is regarded on the same footing. And no topic is so much insisted on by those, who defend the liberty of the seas, as the unexhausted use of them in navigation. Were the advantages, procured by navigation, as inexhaustible, these reasoners had never had any adversaries to refute; nor had any claims ever been advanced of a separate, exclusive dominion over the ocean.

It may happen, in some countries, at some periods, that there be established a property in water, none in land;[1] if the latter be in greater abundance than can be used by the inhabitants, and the former be found, with difficulty, and in very small quantities.

Again; suppose, that, though the necessities of human race continue the same as at present, yet the mind is so enlarged, and so replete with friendship and generosity, that every man has the utmost tenderness for every man, and feels no more concern for his own interest than for that of his fellows: It seems evident, that the USE of justice would, in this case, be suspended by such an extensive benevolence, nor would the divisions and barriers of property and obligation have ever been thought of. Why should I bind another, by a deed or promise, to do me any good office, when I know that he is already prompted, by the strongest inclination, to seek my happiness, and would, of himself, perform the desired service; except the hurt, he thereby receives, be greater than the benefit accruing to me? in which case, he knows, that, from my innate humanity and friendship, I should be the first to oppose myself to his imprudent generosity. Why raise land-marks between my neighbour's field and mine, when my heart has made no division between our interests; but shares all his joys and sorrows with the same force and vivacity as if originally my own? Every man, upon this supposition, being a second self to another, would trust all his interests to the discretion of every man; without jealousy, without partition, without distinction. And the whole human race would form only one family; where all would lie in common, and be used freely, without regard to property; but cautiously too, with as entire regard to the necessities of each individual, as if our own interests were most intimately concerned.

In the present disposition of the human heart, it would, perhaps, be difficult to find compleat instances of such enlarged affections; but still we may observe, that the case of families approaches towards it; and the stronger the mutual benevolence is among the individuals, the nearer it approaches; till all distinction of property be, in a great measure, lost and confounded among them. Between married persons, the cement of friendship is by the laws supposed so strong as to abolish all division of possessions: and has often, in reality, the force ascribed to it. And it is observable, that, during the ardour of new enthusiasms, when every principle is inflamed into extravagance, the community of goods has frequently been attempted: and nothing but experience of its inconveniencies, from the returning or disguised selfishness of men, could make the imprudent fanatics adopt anew the ideas of justice and of separate property. So true is it, that this virtue derives its existence entirely from its necessary *use* to the intercourse and social state of mankind.

---

1. GENESIS, chap. xiii. and xxi.

To make this truth more evident, let us reverse the foregoing suppositions; and carrying every thing to the opposite extreme, consider what would be the effect of these new situations. Suppose a society to fall into such want of all common necessaries, that the utmost frugality and industry cannot preserve the greater number from perishing, and the whole from extreme misery: It will readily, I believe, be admitted, that the strict laws of justice are suspended, in such a pressing emergence, and give place to the stronger motives of necessity and self-preservation. Is it any crime, after a shipwreck, to seize whatever means or instrument of safety one can lay hold of, without regard to former limitations of property? Or if a city besieged were perishing with hunger; can we imagine, that men will see any means of preservation before them, and lose their lives, from a scrupulous regard to what, in other situations, would be the rules of equity and justice? The USE and TENDENCY of that virtue is to procure happiness and security, by preserving order in society: But where the society is ready to perish from extreme necessity, no greater evil can be dreaded from violence and injustice; and every man may now provide for himself by all the means, which prudence can dictate, or humanity permit. The public, even in less urgent necessities, opens granaries, without the consent of proprietors; as justly supposing, that the authority of magistracy may, consistent with equity, extend so far: But were any number of men to assemble, without the tye of laws or civil jurisdiction; would an equal partition of bread in a famine, though effected by power and even violence, be regarded as criminal or injurious?

Suppose likewise, that it should be a virtuous man's fate to fall into the society of ruffians, remote from the protection of laws and government; what conduct must he embrace in that melancholy situation? He sees such a desperate rapaciousness prevail; such a disregard to equity, such contempt of order, such stupid blindness to future consequences, as must immediately have the most tragical conclusion, and must terminate in destruction to the greater number, and in a total dissolution of society to the rest. He, mean while, can have no other expedient than to arm himself, to whomever the sword he seizes, or the buckler, may belong: To make provision of all means of defence and security: And his particular regard to justice being no longer of USE to

his own safety or that of others, he must consult the dictates of self-preservation alone, without concern for those who no longer merit his care and attention.

When any man, even in political society, renders himself, by his crimes, obnoxious to the public, he is punished by the laws in his goods and person; that is, the ordinary rules of justice are, with regard to him, suspended for a moment, and it becomes equitable to inflict on him, for the *benefit* of society, what, otherwise, he could not suffer without wrong or injury.

The rage and violence of public war; what is it but a suspension of justice among the warring parties, who perceive, that this virtue is now no longer of any *use* or advantage to them? The laws of war, which then succeed to those of equity and justice, are rules calculated for the *advantage* and *utility* of that particular state, in which men are now placed. And were a civilized nation engaged with barbarians, who observed no rules even of war; the former must also suspend their observance of them, where they no longer serve to any purpose; and must render every action or encounter as bloody and pernicious as possible to the first aggressors.

Thus, the rules of equity or justice depend entirely on the particular state and condition, in which men are placed, and owe their origin and existence to that UTILITY, which results to the public from their strict and regular observance. Reverse, in any considerable circumstance, the condition of men: Produce extreme abundance or extreme necessity: Implant in the human breast perfect moderation and humanity, or perfect rapaciousness and malice: By rendering justice totally *useless,* you thereby totally destroy its essence, and suspend its obligation upon mankind.

The common situation of society is a medium amidst all these extremes. We are naturally partial to ourselves, and to our friends; but are capable of learning the advantage resulting from a more equitable conduct. Few enjoyments are given us from the open and liberal hand of nature; but by art, labour, and industry, we can extract them in great abundance. Hence the ideas of property become necessary in all civil society: Hence justice derives its usefulness to the public: And hence alone arises its merit and moral obligation.

These conclusions are so natural and obvious, that they have not escaped even the poets, in their descriptions of the felicity, attending the golden age or the reign of SATURN. The seasons, in that first period of nature, were so temperate, if we credit these agreeable fictions, that there was no necessity for men to provide themselves with cloaths and houses, as a security against the violence of heat and cold: The rivers flowed with wine and milk: The oaks yielded honey; and nature spontaneously produced her greatest delicacies. Nor were these the chief advantages of that happy age. Tempests were not alone removed from nature; but those more furious tempests were unknown to human breasts, which now cause such uproar, and engender such confusion. Avarice, ambition, cruelty, selfishness, were never heard of: Cordial affection, compassion, sympathy, were the only movements with which the mind was yet acquainted. Even the punctilious distinction of *mine* and *thine* was banished from among that happy race of mortals, and carried with it the very notion of property and obligation, justice and injustice.

This *poetical* fiction of the *golden age is,* in some respects, of a piece with the *philosophical* fiction of the *state of nature;* only that the former is represented as the most charming and most peaceable condition, which can possibly be imagined; whereas the latter is painted out as a state of mutual war and violence, attended with the most extreme necessity. On the first origin of mankind, we are told, their ignorance and savage nature were so prevalent, that they could give no mutual trust, but must each depend upon himself, and his own force or cunning for protection and security. No law was heard of: No rule of justice known: No distinction of property regarded: Power was the only measure of right; and a perpetual war of all against all was the result of men's untamed selfishness and barbarity.[1]

Whether such a condition of human nature could ever exist, or if it did, could continue so long as to merit the appellation of a *state,* may justly be doubted. Men are necessarily born in a family-society, at least; and are trained up by their parents to some rule of conduct and behaviour. But this must be admitted, that, if such a state of mutual war and violence was ever real, the suspension of all laws of justice, from their absolute inutility, is a necessary and infallible consequence.

The more we vary our views of human life, and the newer and more unusual the lights are, in which we survey it, the more shall we be convinced, that the origin here assigned for the virtue of justice is real and satisfactory.

Were there a species of creatures, intermingled with men, which, though rational, were possessed of such inferior strength, both of body and mind, that they were incapable of all resistance, and could never, upon the highest provocation, make us feel the effects of their resentment; the necessary consequence, I think, is, that we should be bound, by the laws of humanity, to give gentle usage to these creatures, but should not, properly speaking, lie under

---

1. This fiction of a state of nature, as a state of war, was not first started by Mr. HOBBES, as is commonly imagined. PLATO endeavours to refute an hypothesis very like it in the 2nd, 3rd, and 4th books de republica. CICERO, on the contrary, supposes it certain and universally acknowledged in the following passage. 'Quis enim vestrûm, judices, ignorat, ita naturam rerum tulisse, ut quodam tempore homines, nondum neque naturali, neque civili jure descripto, fusi per agros, ac dispersi vagarentur tantumque haberent quantum manu ac viribus, per cædem ac vulnera, aut eripere, aut retinere potuissent? Qui igitur primi virtute et consilio præstanti extiterunt, ii perspecto genere humanæ docilitatis atque ingenii, dissipatos, unum in locum congregarunt, eosque ex feritate illa ad justitiam ac mansuetudinem transduxerunt. Tum res ad communem utilitatem, quas publicas appellamus, tum conventicula hominum, quae postea civitates nominatæ sunt, tum domicilia conjuncta, quas urbes dicamus, invento et divino et humano jure, mœnibus sepserunt. Atque inter hanc vitam, perpolitam humanitate, et illam immanem, nihil tam interest quam JUS atque VIS. Horum utro uti nolimus, altero est utendum. Vim volumus extingui? Jus valeat necesse est, id est, judicia, quibus omne jus contine-

tur. Judicia displicent, aut nulla sunt? Visdominetur necesse est. Hæc vident omnes.' . . . [Can there be anyone among you, jurors, who does not know that nature had brought things about so that, at one time, before natural or civil law was discerned, scattered and landless men roamed the country-side, men who had just as much as they had been able to snatch by force and defend by bloodshed and violence? Then those men who first stood out for their exceptional virtue and judgment, having recognized men's natural talent for training and ingenuity, brought the nomads together and led them from savagery into justice and mildness. And after human and divine law were discovered, then matters were arranged for the general good, which we call public affairs, then common meeting places, which were later called communities, and eventually homes were brought within walls, which we call cities. And so there is no more difference between this orderly civilized life, and that former savagery, than there is between LAW and VIOLENCE. If we prefer not to use one of these, we must use the other. Do we want violence eradicated? Then law must prevail, i.e., the verdicts in which all law is contained. Are the verdicts disliked or ignored? Then violence must prevail. Everyone understands this.]

any restraint of justice with regard to them, nor could they possess any right or property, exclusive of such arbitrary lords. Our intercourse with them could not be called society, which supposes a degree of equality; but absolute command on the one side, and servile obedience on the other. Whatever we covet, they must instantly resign: Our permission is the only tenure, by which they hold their possessions: Our compassion and kindness the only check, by which they curb our lawless will: And as no inconvenience ever results from the exercise of a power, so firmly established in nature, the restraints of justice and property, being totally *useless*, would never have place in so unequal a confederacy.

This is plainly the situation of men, with regard to animals; and how far these may be said to possess reason, I leave it to others to determine. The great superiority of civilized EUROPEANS above barbarous INDIANS, tempted us to imagine ourselves on the same footing with regard to them, and made us throw off all restraints of justice, and even of humanity, in our treatment of them. In many nations, the female sex are reduced to like slavery, and are rendered incapable of all property, in opposition to their lordly masters. But though the males, when united, have, in all countries, bodily force sufficient to maintain this severe tyranny; yet such are the insinuation, address, and charms of their fair companions, that women are commonly able to break the confederacy, and share with the other sex in all the rights and privileges of society.

Were the human species so framed by nature as that each individual possessed within himself every faculty, requisite both for his own preservation and for the propagation of his kind: Were all society and intercourse cut off between man and man, by the primary intention of the supreme Creator: It seems evident, that so solitary a being would be as much incapable of justice, as of social discourse and conversation. Where mutual regards and forbearance serve to no manner of purpose, they would never direct the conduct of any reasonable. man. The headlong course of the passions would be checked by no reflection on future consequences. And as each man is here supposed to love himself alone, and to depend only on himself and his own activity for safety and happiness, he would, on every occasion to the utmost of his power, challenge the preference above every other being, to none of which he is bound by any ties, either of nature or of interest.

But suppose the conjunction of the sexes to be established in nature, a family immediately arises; and particular rules being found requisite for its subsistence, these are immediately embraced; though without comprehending the rest of mankind within their prescriptions. Suppose, that several families unite together into one society, which is totally disjoined from all others, the rules, which preserve peace and order, enlarge themselves to the utmost extent of that society; but becoming then entirely useless, lose their force when carried one step farther. But again suppose, that several distinct societies maintain a kind of intercourse for mutual convenience and advantage, the boundaries of justice still grow larger, in proportion to the largeness of men's views, and the force of their mutual connexions. History, experience, reason sufficiently instruct us in this natural progress of human sentiments, and in the gradual enlargement of our regards to justice, in proportion as we become acquainted with the extensive utility of that virtue.

Part II.

If we examine the *particular* laws, by which justice is directed, and property determined; we shall still be presented with the same conclusion. The good of mankind is the only object of all these laws and regulations. Not only it is requisite, for the peace and interest of society, that men's possessions should be separated; but the rules, which we follow, in making the separation, are such as can best be contrived to serve farther the interests of society.

We shall suppose, that a creature, possessed of reason, but unacquainted with human nature, deliberates with himself what RULES of justice or property would best promote public interest, and establish peace and security among mankind: His most obvious thought would be, to assign the largest possessions to the most extensive virtue, and give every one the power of doing good, proportioned to his inclination. In a perfect theocracy, where a being, infinitely intelligent, governs by particular volitions, this rule would certainly have place, and might serve to the wisest purposes: But were mankind to execute such a law; so great is the uncertainty of merit, both from its natural obscurity, and from the self-conceit of each individual, that no determinate rule of conduct would ever result from it; and the total dissolution of society must be the immediate consequence. Fanatics may suppose, *that dominion is founded on grace,* and *that saints alone inherit the earth;* but the civil magistrate very justly puts these sublime theorists on the same footing with common robbers, and teaches them by the severest discipline, that a rule, which, in speculation, may seem the most advantageous to society, may yet be found, in practice, totally pernicious and destructive.

That there were *religious* fanatics of this kind in ENGLAND, during the civil wars, we learn from history; though it is probable, that the obvious *tendency* of these principles excited such horror in mankind, as soon obliged the dangerous enthusiasts to renounce, or at least conceal their tenets. Perhaps, the *levellers,* who claimed an equal distribution of property, were a kind of *political* fanatics, which arose from the religious species, and more openly avowed their pretensions; as carrying a more plausible appearance, of being practicable in themselves, as well as useful to human society.

It must, indeed, be confessed, that nature is so liberal to mankind, that, were all her presents equally divided among the species, and improved by art and industry, every individual would enjoy all the necessaries, and even most of the comforts of life; nor would ever be liable to any ills, but such as might accidentally arise from the sickly frame and constitution of his body. It must also be confessed, that, wherever we depart from this equality, we rob the poor of more satisfaction than we add to the rich, and that the slight gratification of a frivolous vanity, in one individual, frequently costs more than bread to many families, and even provinces. It may appear withal, that the rule of equality, as it would be highly *useful,* is not altogether *impracticable;* but has taken place, at least in an imperfect degree, in some republics; particularly that of SPARTA; where it was attended, it is said, with the most beneficial consequences. Not to mention, that the AGRARIAN laws, so frequently claimed in ROME, and carried into execution in many GREEK cities, proceeded, all of them, from a general idea of the utility of this principle.

But historians, and even common sense, may inform us, that, however specious these ideas of *perfect* equality may seem, they are really, at bottom, *impracticable;* and were they not so, would be extremely *pernicious* to human society. Render

possessions ever so equal, men's different degrees of art, care, and industry will immediately break that equality. Or if you check these virtues, you reduce society to the most extreme indigence; and instead of preventing want and beggary in a few, render it unavoidable to the whole community. The most rigorous inquisition too is requisite to watch every inequality on its first appearance; and the most severe jurisdiction, to punish and redress it. But besides, that so much authority must soon degenerate into tyranny, and be exerted with great partialities; who can possibly be possessed of it, in such a situation as is here supposed? Perfect equality of possessions, destroying all subordination, weakens extremely the authority of magistracy, and must reduce all power nearly to a level, as well as property.

We may conclude, therefore, that, in order to establish laws for the regulation of property, we must be acquainted with the nature and situation of man; must reject appearances, which may be false, though specious; and must search for those rules, which are, on the whole, most *useful* and *beneficial.* Vulgar sense and slight experience are sufficient for this purpose; where men give not way to too selfish avidity, or too extensive enthusiasm.

Who sees not, for instance, that whatever is produced or improved by a man's art or industry ought, for ever, to be secured to him, in order to give encouragement to such *useful* habits and accomplishments? That the property ought also to descend to children and relations, for the same *useful* purpose? That it may be alienated by consent, in order to beget that commerce and intercourse, which is so *beneficial* to human society? And that all contracts and promises ought carefully to be fulfilled, in order to secure mutual trust and confidence, by which the general *interest* of mankind is so much promoted?

Examine the writers on the laws of nature; and you will always find, that, whatever principles they set out with, they are sure to terminate here at last, and to assign, as the ultimate reason for every rule which they establish, the convenience and necessities of mankind. A concession thus extorted, in opposition to systems, has more authority, than if it had been made in prosecution of them.

What other reason, indeed, could writers ever give, why this must be *mine* and that *yours;* since uninstructed nature, surely, never made any such distinction? The objects, which receive those appellations, are, of themselves, foreign to us; they are totally disjoined and separated from us; and nothing but the general interests of society can form the connexion.

Sometimes, the interests of society may require a rule of justice in a particular case; but may not determine any particular rule, among several, which are all equally beneficial. In that case, the slightest *analogies* are laid hold of, in order to prevent that indifference and ambiguity, which would be the source of perpetual dissention. Thus possession alone, and first possession, is supposed to convey property, where no body else has any preceding claim and pretension. Many of the reasonings of lawyers are of this analogical nature, and depend on very slight connexions of the imagination.

Does any one scruple, in extraordinary cases, to violate all regard to the private property of individuals, and sacrifice to public interest a distinction, which had been established for the sake of that interest? The safety of the people is the supreme law: All other particular laws are subordinate to it, and dependant on it: And if, in the *common* course of things, they be followed and regarded; it is only because the public safety and interest *commonly* demand so equal and impartial an administration.

Sometimes both *utility* and *analogy* fail, and leave the laws of justice in total uncertainty. Thus, it is highly requisite, that prescription or long possession should convey property; but what number of days or months or years should be sufficient for that purpose, it is impossible for reason alone to determine. *Civil laws* here supply the place of the natural *code*, and assign different terms for prescription, according to the different *utilities*, proposed by the legislator. Bills of exchange and promissory notes, by the laws of most countries, prescribe sooner than bonds, and mortgages, and contracts of a more formal nature.

In general, we may observe, that all questions of property are subordinate to authority of civil laws, which extend, restrain, modify, and alter the rules of natural justice, according to the particular *convenience* of each community. The laws have, or ought to have, a constant reference to the constitution of government, the manners, the climate, the religion, the commerce, the situation of each society. A late author of genius, as well as of learning, has prosecuted this subject at large, and has established, from these principles, a system of political knowledge, which abounds in ingenious and brilliant thoughts, and is not wanting in solidity.[1]

What is a man's property? Any thing, which it is lawful for him, and for him alone, to use. *But what rule have we, by which we can distinguish these objects?* Here we must have recourse to statutes, customs, precedents, analogies, and a hundred other circumstances; some of which are constant and inflexible, some variable and arbitrary. But the ultimate point, in which they all professedly terminate, is, the interest and happiness of human society. Where this enters not into consideration, nothing can appear more whimsical, unnatural, and even superstitious, than all or most of the laws of justice and of property.

Those, who ridicule vulgar superstitions, and expose the folly of particular regards to meats, days, places, postures, apparel, have an easy task; while

---

1. The author of *L'Esprit des Loix.* This illustrious writer. however, sets out with a different theory, and supposes all right to be founded on certain *rapports* or relations; which is a system, that, in my opinion, never will be reconciled with true philosophy. Father MALEBRANCHE, as far as I can learn, was the first that started this abstract theory of morals, which was afterwards adopted by CUDWORTH, CLARKE, and others; and as it excludes all sentiment, and pretends to found every thing on reason, it has not wanted followers in this philosophic age. See Section 1. and Appendix I. With regard to justice, the virtue here treated of, the inference against this theory seems short and conclusive. Property is allowed to be dependent on civil laws; civil laws are allowed to have no other object, but the interest of society: This therefore must be allowed to be the sole foundation of property and justice. Not to mention, that our obligation itself to obey the magistrate and his laws is founded on nothing but the interests of society.

If the ideas of justice, sometimes, do not follow the dispositions of civil law: we shall find, that these cases, instead of objections, are confirmations of the theory delivered above. Where a civil law is so perverse as to cross all the interests of society, it loses all its authority, and men judge by the ideas of natural justice, which are conformable to those interests. Sometimes also civil laws, for useful purposes, require a ceremony or form to any deed; and where that is wanting, their decrees run contrary to the usual tenour of justice; but one who takes advantage of such chicanes, is not commonly regarded as an honest man. Thus, the interests of society require, that contracts be fulfilled; and there is not a more material article either of natural or civil justice: But the omission of a trifling circumstance will often, by law, invalidate a contract, *in foro humano,* but not *in foro conscientiæ,* as divines express themselves. In these cases, the magistrate is supposed only to withdraw his power of enforcing the right, not to have altered the right. Where his intention extends to the right, and is conformable to the interests of society; it never fails to alter the right; a clear proof of the origin of justice and of property, as assigned above.

they consider all the qualities and relations of the objects, and discover no adequate cause for that affection or antipathy, veneration or horror, which have so mighty an influence over a considerable part of mankind. A SYRIAN would have starved rather than taste pigeon; an EGYPTIAN would not have approached bacon: But if these species of food be examined by the senses of sight, smell, or taste, or scrutinized by the sciences of chymistry, medicine, or physics; no difference is ever found between them and any other species, nor can that precise circumstance be pitched on, which may afford a just foundation for the religious passion. A fowl on Thursday is lawful food; on Friday abominable: Eggs, in this house, and in this diocese, are permitted during Lent; a hundred paces farther, to eat them is a damnable sin. This earth or building, yesterday was profane; to-day, by the muttering of certain words, it has become holy and sacred. Such reflections as these, in the mouth of a philosopher, one may safely say, are too obvious to have any influence; because they must always, to every man, occur at first sight; and where they prevail not, of themselves, they are surely obstructed by education, prejudice, and passion, not by ignorance or mistake.

It may appear to a careless view, or rather a too abstracted reflection, that there enters a like superstition into all the sentiments of justice; and that, if a man expose its object, or what we call property, to the same scrutiny of sense and science, he will not, by the most accurate enquiry, find any foundation for the difference made by moral sentiment. I may lawfully nourish myself from this tree; but the fruit of another of the same species, ten paces off, it is criminal for me to touch. Had I worne this apparel an hour ago, I had merited the severest punishment; but a man, by pronouncing a few magical syllables, has now rendered it fit for my use and service. Were this house placed in the neighbouring territory, it had been immoral for me to dwell in it; but being built on this side of the river, it is subject to a different municipal law, and, by its becoming mine, I incur no blame or censure. The same species of reasoning, it may be thought, which so successfully exposes superstition, is also applicable to justice; nor is it possible, in the one case more than in the other, to point out, in the object, that precise quality or circumstance, which is the foundation of the sentiment.

But there is this material difference between *superstition* and *justice,* that the former is frivolous, useless, and burdensome; the latter is absolutely requisite to the well-being of mankind and existence of society. When we abstract from this circumstance (for it is too apparent ever to be overlooked) it must be confessed, that all regards to right and property, seem entirely without foundation, as much as the grossest and most vulgar superstition. Were the interests of society nowise concerned, it is as unintelligible, why another's articulating certain sounds implying consent, should change the nature of my actions with regard to a particular object, as why the reciting of a liturgy by a priest, in a certain habit and posture, should dedicate a heap of brick and timber, and render it, thenceforth and for ever, sacred.[1]

---

1. It is evident, that the will or consent alone never transfers property, nor causes the obligation of a promise (for the same reasoning extends to both) but the will must be expressed by words or signs, in order to impose a tye upon any man. The expression being once brought in as subservient to the will, soon becomes the principal part of the promise; nor will a man be less bound by his word, though he secretly give a different direction to his intention, and with-hold the assent of his mind. But though the expression makes, on most occasions, the whole of the promise, yet it does not always so; and one who should make use of any expression, of which he knows not the meaning, and which he uses without any sense of the consequences, would not certainly be bound by it. Nay, though he know its meaning, yet if he use it in jest only, and with such signs as evidently. show, that he has no serious intention of binding himself, he would not lie under any obligation of performance; but it is necessary, that the words be a perfect expression of the will, without any contrary signs. Nay, even this we must not carry so far as to imagine, that one, whom, by our quickness of understanding, we conjecture, from certain signs, to have an intention of deceiving us, is not bound by his expression or verbal promise, if we accept of it; but must limit this conclusion to those cases where the signs are of a different nature from those of deceit. All these contradictions are easily accounted for, if justice arise entirely from its usefulness to society; but will never be explained on any other hypothesis.

It is remarkable, that the moral decisions of the *Jesuits* and other relaxed casuists, were commonly formed in prosecution of some such subtilties of reasoning as are here pointed out, and proceed as much from the habit of scholastic refinement as from any corruption of the heart, if we may follow the authority of Mons. BAYLE. See his Dictionary, article LOYOLA. And why has the indignation of mankind risen so high against these casuists; but because every one perceived, that human society could not subsist were such practices authorized, and that morals must always be handled with a view to public interest, more than philosophical regularity? If the secret direction of the intention, said every man

These reflections are far from weakening the obligations of justice, or diminishing any thing from the most sacred attention to property. On the contrary, such sentiments must acquire new force from the present reasoning. For what stronger foundation can be desired or conceived for any duty, than to observe, that human society, or even human nature could not subsist, without the establishment of it; and will still arrive at greater degrees of happiness and perfection, the more inviolable the regard is, which is paid to that duty?

The dilemma seems obvious: As justice evidently tends to promote public utility and to support civil society, the sentiment of justice is either derived from our reflecting on that tendency, or like hunger, thirst, and other appetites, resentment, love of life, attachment to offspring, and other passions, arises from a simple original instinct in the human breast, which nature has implanted for like salutary purposes. If the latter be the case, it follows, that property, which is the object of justice, is also distinguished by a simple, original instinct, and is not ascertained by any argument or reflection. But who is there that ever heard of such an instinct? Or is this a subject, in which new discoveries can be made? We may as well attempt to discover, in the body, new senses, which had before escaped the observation of all mankind.

of sense, could invalidate a contract; where is our security? And yet a metaphysical schoolman might think, that where an intention was supposed to be requisite, if that intention really had not place, no consequence ought to follow, and no obligation be imposed. The casuistical subtilties may not be greater than the subtilties of lawyers, hinted at above; but as the former are *pernicious* and the latter *innocent* and even *necessary,* this is the reason of the very different reception they meet with from the world.

It is a doctrine of the church of ROME, that the priest, by a secret direction of his intention, can invalidate any sacrament. This position is derived from a strict and regular prosecution of the obvious truth, that empty words alone, without any meaning or intention in the speaker, can never be attended with any effect. If the same conclusion be not admitted in reasonings concerning civil contracts, where the affair is allowed to be of so much less consequence than the eternal salvation of thousands, it proceeds entirely from men's sense of the danger and inconvenience of the doctrine in the former case: And we may thence observe, that however positive, arrogant, and dogmatical any superstition may appear, it never can convey any thorough persuasion of the reality of its objects, or put them, in any degree, on a balance with the common incidents of life. which we learn from daily observation and experimental reasoning.

But farther, though it seems a very simple proposition to say, that nature, by an instinctive sentiment, distinguishes property, yet in reality we shall find, that there are required for that purpose ten thousand different instincts, and these employed about objects of the greatest intricacy and nicest discernment. For when a definition of *property* is required, that relation is found to resolve itself into any possession acquired by occupation, by industry, by prescription, by inheritance, by contract, &c. Can we think, that nature, by an original instinct, instructs us in all these methods of acquisition?

These words too, inheritance and contract, stand for ideas infinitely complicated; and to define them exactly, a hundred volumes of laws, and a thousand volumes of commentators, have not been found sufficient. Does nature, whose instincts in men are simple, embrace such complicated and artificial objects, and create a rational creature, without trusting any thing to the operation of his reason?

But even though all this were admitted, it would not be satisfactory. Positive laws can certainly transfer property. Is it by another original instinct, that we recognize the authority of kings and senates, and mark all the boundaries of their jurisdiction? Judges too, even though their sentence be erroneous and illegal, must be allowed, for the sake of peace and order, to have decisive authority, and ultimately to determine property. Have we original, innate ideas of prætors and chancellors and juries? Who sees not, that all these institutions arise merely from the necessities of human society?

All birds of the same species, in every age and country, build their nests alike: In this we see the force of instinct. Men, in different times and places, frame their houses differently: Here we perceive the influence of reason and custom. A like inference may be drawn from comparing the instinct of generation and the institution of property.

How great soever the variety of municipal laws, it must be confessed, that their chief out-lines pretty regularly concur; because the purposes, to which they tend, are every where exactly similar. In like manner, all houses have a roof and walls, windows and chimneys; though diversified in their shape, figure, and materials. The purposes of the latter, directed to the conveniences of human life, discover not more plainly their origin from reason and reflection, than do those of the former, which point all to a like end.

I need not mention the variations, which all the rules of property receive from the finer turns and connexions of the imagination, and from the subtilties and abstractions of law-topics and reasonings. There is no possibility of reconciling this observation to the notion of original instincts.

What alone will beget a doubt concerning the theory, on which I insist, is the influence of education and acquired habits, by which we are so accustomed to blame injustice, that we are not, in every instance, conscious of any immediate reflection on the pernicious consequences of it. The views the most familiar to us are apt, for that very reason, to escape us; and what we have very frequently performed from certain motives, we are apt likewise to continue mechanically, without recalling, on every occasion, the reflections, which first determined us. The convenience, or rather necessity, which leads to justice, is so universal, and every where points so much to the same rules, that the habit takes place in all societies; and it is not without some scrutiny, that we are able to ascertain its true origin. The matter, however, is not so obscure, but that, even in common life, we have, every moment, recourse to the principle of public utility, and ask, *What must become of the world, if such practices prevail? How could society subsist under such disorders?* Were the distinction or separation of possessions entirely useless, can any one conceive, that it ever should have obtained in society?

Thus we seem, upon the whole, to have attained a knowledge of the force of that principle here insisted on, and can determine what degree of esteem or moral approbation may result from reflections on public interest and utility. The necessity of justice to the support of society is the SOLE foundation of that virtue; and since no moral excellence is more highly esteemed, we may conclude, that this circumstance of usefulness has, in general, the strongest energy, and most entire command over our sentiments. It must, therefore, be the source of a considerable part of the merit ascribed to humanity, benevolence, friendship, public spirit, and other social virtues of that stamp; as it is the SOLE source of the moral approbation paid to fidelity, justice, veracity, integrity, and those other estimable and useful qualities and principles. It is entirely agreeable to the rules of philosophy, and even of common reason; where any principle has been found to have a great force and energy in one instance, to ascribe to it a like energy

in all similar instances. This indeed is NEWTON'S chief rule of philosophizing.[1]

. . .

Section V.—Why Utility Pleases.

Part I.

It seems so natural a thought to ascribe to their utility the praise, which we bestow on the social virtues, that one would expect to meet with this principle every where in moral writers, as the chief foundation of their reasoning and enquiry. In common life, we may observe, that the circumstance of utility is always appealed to; nor is it supposed, that a greater eulogy can be given to any man, than to display his usefulness to the public, and enumerate the services, which he has performed to mankind and society. What praise, even of an inanimate form, if the regularity and elegance of its parts destroy not its fitness for any useful purpose! And how satisfactory an apology for any disproportion or seeming deformity, if we can show the necessity of that particular construction for the use intended! A ship appears more beautiful to an artist, or one moderately skilled in navigation, where its prow is wide and swelling beyond its poop, than if it were framed with a precise geometrical regularity, in contradiction to all the laws of mechanics. A building, whose doors and windows were exact squares, would hurt the eye by that very proportion; as ill adapted to the figure of a human creature, for whose service the fabric was intended. What wonder then, that a man, whose habits and conduct are hurtful to society, and dangerous or pernicious to every one who has an intercourse with him, should, on that account, be an object of disapprobation, and communicate to every spectator the strongest sentiment of disgust and hatred.[2]

---

1. Principia. . . .

2. We ought not to imagine, because an inanimate object may be useful as well as a man, that therefore it ought also, according to this system, to merit the appellation of *virtuous*. The sentiments, excited by utility, are, in the two cases, very different; and the one is mixed with affection, esteem, approbation, &c. and not the other. In like manner, an inanimate object may have good colour and proportions as well as a human figure. But can we ever be in

But perhaps the difficulty of accounting for these effects of usefulness, or its contrary, has kept philosophers from admitting them into their systems of ethics, and has induced them rather to employ any other principle, in explaining the origin of moral good and evil. But it is no just reason for rejecting any principle, confirmed by experience, that we cannot give a satisfactory account of its origin, nor are able to resolve it into other more general principles. And if we would employ a little thought on the present subject, we need be at no loss to account for the influence of utility, and to deduce it from principles, the most known and avowed in human nature.

From the apparent usefulness of the social virtues, it has readily been inferred by sceptics, both ancient and modern, that all moral distinctions arise from education, and were, at first, invented, and afterwards encouraged, by the art of politicians, in order to render men tractable, and subdue their natural ferocity and selfishness, which incapacitated them for society. This principle, indeed, of precept and education, must so far be owned to have a powerful influence, that it may frequently encrease or diminish, beyond their natural standard, the sentiments of approbation or dislike; and may even, in particular instances, create, without any natural principle, a new sentiment of this kind; as is evident in all superstitious practices and observances: But that *all* moral affection or dislike arises from this origin, will never surely be allowed by any judicious enquirer. Had nature made no such distinction, founded on the original constitution of the mind, the words, *honourable* and *shameful, lovely* and *odious, noble* and *despicable,* had never

had place in any language; nor could politicians, had they invented these terms, ever have been able to render them intelligible, or make them convey any idea to the audience. So that nothing can be more superficial than this paradox of the sceptics; and it were well, if, in the abstruser studies of logic and metaphysics, we could as easily obviate the cavils of that sect, as in the practical and more intelligible sciences of politics and morals.

The social virtues must, therefore, be allowed to have a natural beauty and amiableness, which, at first, antecedent to all precept or education, recommends them to the esteem of uninstructed mankind, and engages their affections. And as the public utility of these virtues is the chief circumstance, whence they derive their merit, it follows, that the end, which they have a tendency to promote, must be some way agreeable to us, and take hold of some natural affection. It must please, either from considerations of self-interest, or from more generous motives and regards.

It has often been asserted, that, as every man has a strong connexion with society, and perceives the impossibility of his solitary subsistence, he becomes, on that account, favourable to all those habits or principles, which promote order in society, and insure to him the quiet possession of so inestimable a blessing. As much as we value our own happiness and welfare, as much must we applaud the practice of justice and humanity, by which alone the social confederacy can be maintained, and every man reap the fruits of mutual protection and assistance.

This deduction of morals from self-love, or a regard to private interest, is an obvious thought, and has not arisen wholly from the wanton sallies and sportive assaults of the sceptics. To mention no others, POLYBIUS, one of the gravest and most judicious, as well as most moral writers of antiquity, has assigned this selfish origin to all our sentiments of virtue.[1] But though the solid, practical sense of that author, and his aversion to all vain subtilties, render

---

love with the former? There are a numerous set of passions and sentiments, of which thinking rational beings are, by the original constitution of nature, the only proper objects: And though the very same qualities be transferred to an insensible, inanimate being, they will not excite the same sentiments. The beneficial qualities of herbs and minerals are, indeed, sometimes called their *virtues;* but this is an effect of the caprice of language, which ought not to be regarded in reasoning. For though there be a species of approbation attending even inanimate objects when beneficial, yet this sentiment is so weak, and so different from that which is directed to beneficent magistrates or statesmen, that they ought not to be ranked under the same class or appellation.

A very small variation of the object, even where the same qualities are preserved, will destroy a sentiment. Thus, the same beauty transferred to a different sex, excites no amorous passion, where nature is not extremely perverted.

---

1. Undutifulness to parents is disapproved of by mankind, προορωμένους τὸ μέλλον, καῖ συλλογιζομένους, ὅτι τὸ παραπλήσιον ἑκάστοις αὐτῶν συγκυρήσει. [. . . looking to the future and inferring that something similar will happen to each of them . . .] Ingratitude for a like reason (though he seems there to mix a more generous regard) συναγανακτοῦντας μὲν τῷ πέλας, ἀναφέροντος δ᾽ ἐπ᾽ αὐτοὺς τὸ παραπλήσιον. ἐξ ὧν ὑπογίγνεταί τις ἔννοια παρ᾽ ἑκάστῳ τοῦ καθήκοντος δυνάμεως καὶ θεωρίας. [. . . rallying around

his authority on the present subject very considerable; yet is not this an affair to be decided by authority, and the voice of nature and experience seems plainly to oppose the selfish theory.

We frequently bestow praise on virtuous actions, performed in very distant ages and remote countries; where the utmost subtilty of imagination would not discover any appearance of self-interest, or find any connexion of our present happiness and security with events so widely separated from us.

A generous, a brave, a noble deed, performed by an adversary, commands our approbation; while in its consequences it may be acknowledged prejudicial to our particular interest.

Where private advantage concurs with general affection for virtue, we readily perceive and avow the mixture of these distinct sentiments, which have a very different feeling and influence on the mind. We praise, perhaps, with more alacrity, where the generous, humane action contributes to our particular interest: But the topics of praise, which we insist on, are very wide of this circumstance. And we may attempt to bring over others to our sentiments, without endeavouring to convince them, that they reap any advantage from the actions which we recommend to their approbation and applause.

Frame the model of a praise-worthy character, consisting of all the most amiable moral virtues: Give instances, in which these display themselves after an eminent and extraordinary manner: You readily engage the esteem and approbation of all your audience, who never so much as enquire in what age and country the person lived, who possessed these noble qualities: A circumstance, however, of all others, the most material to self-love, or a concern for our own individual happiness.

Once on a time, a statesman, in the shock and contest of parties, prevailed so far as to procure, by his eloquence, the banishment of an able adversary; whom he secretly followed, offering him money for his support during his exile, and soothing him with topics of consolation in his misfortunes. *Alas!* cries

the banished statesman, *with what regret must I leave my friends in this city, where even enemies are so generous!* Virtue, though in an enemy, here pleased him: And we also give it the just tribute of praise and approbation; nor do we retract these sentiments, when we hear, that the action passed at ATHENS, about two thousand years ago, and that the persons' names were ESCHINES and DEMOSTHENES.

What is that to me? There are few occasions, when this question is not pertinent: And had it that universal, infallible influence supposed, it would turn into ridicule every composition, and almost every conversation, which contain any praise or censure of men and manners.

It is but a weak subterfuge, when pressed by these facts and arguments, to say, that we transport ourselves, by the force of imagination, into distant ages and countries, and consider the advantage, which we should have reaped from these characters, had we been contemporaries, and had any commerce with the persons. It is not conceivable, how a *real* sentiment or passion can ever arise from a known *imaginary* interest; especially when our *real* interest is still kept in view, and is often acknowledged to be entirely distinct from the imaginary, and even sometimes opposite to it.

A man, brought to the brink of a precipice, cannot look down without trembling; and the sentiment of *imaginary* danger actuates him, in opposition to the opinion and belief of *real* safety. But the imagination is here assisted by the presence of a striking object; and yet prevails not, except it be also aided by novelty, and the unusual appearance of the object. Custom soon reconciles us to heights and precipices, and wears off these false and delusive terrors. The reverse is observable in the estimates, which we form of characters and manners; and the more we habituate ourselves to an accurate scrutiny of morals, the more delicate feeling do we acquire of the most minute distinctions between vice and virtue. Such frequent occasion, indeed, have we, in common life, to pronounce all kinds of moral determinations, that no object of this kind can be new or unusual to us; nor could any *false* views or prepossessions maintain their ground against an experience, so common and familiar. Experience being chiefly what forms the association of ideas, it is impossible, that any association could establish and support itself, in direct opposition to that principle.

their neighbour and imagining the same injury happening to themselves. From this there arises gradually in each man an idea of the meaning and concept of duty.] . . . Perhaps the historian only meant, that our sympathy and humanity was more enlivened, by our considering the similarity of our case with that of the person suffering; which is a just sentiment.

Usefulness is agreeable, and engages our approbation. This is a matter of fact, confirmed by daily observation. But, *useful?* For what? For some body's interest, surely. Whose interest then? Not our own only: For our approbation frequently extends farther. It must, therefore, be the interest of those, who are served by the character or action approved of; and these we may conclude, however remote, are not totally indifferent to us. By opening up this principle, we shall discover one great source of moral distinctions.

Part II.

Self-love is a principle in human nature of such extensive energy, and the interest of each individual is, in general, so closely connected with that of the community, that those philosophers were excusable, who fancied, that all our concern for the public might be resolved into a concern for our own happiness and preservation. They saw every moment, instances of approbation or blame, satisfaction or displeasure towards characters and actions; they denominated the objects of these sentiments, *virtues,* or *vices;* they observed, that the former had a tendency to encrease the happiness, and the latter the misery of mankind; they asked, whether it were possible that we could have any general concern for society, or any disinterested resentment of the welfare or injury of others; they found it simpler to consider all these sentiments as modifications of self-love; and they discovered a pretence, at least, for this unity of principle, in that close union of interest, which is so observable between the public and each individual.

But notwithstanding this frequent confusion of interests, it is easy to attain what natural philosophers, after lord BACON, have affected to call the *experimentum crucis,* or that experiment, which points out the right way in any doubt or ambiguity. We have found instances, in which private interest was separate from public; in which it was even contrary: And yet we observed the moral sentiment to continue, notwithstanding this disjunction of interests. And wherever these distinct interests sensibly concurred, we always found a sensible encrease of the sentiment, and a more warm affection to virtue, and detestation of vice, or what we properly call, *gratitude* and *revenge.* Compelled by these instances, we must renounce the theory, which accounts for every

moral sentiment by the principle of self-love. We must adopt a more public affection, and allow, that the interests of society are not, even on their own account, entirely indifferent to us. Usefulness is only a tendency to a certain end; and it is a contradiction in terms, that any thing pleases as means to an end, where the end itself no wise affects us. If usefulness, therefore, be a source of moral sentiment, and if this usefulness be not always considered with a reference to self; it follows, that every thing, which contributes to the happiness of society, recommends itself directly to our approbation and good-will. Here is a principle, which accounts, in great part, for the origin of morality: And what need we seek for abstruse and remote systems, when there occurs one so obvious and natural?[1]

Have we any difficulty to comprehend the force of humanity and benevolence? Or to conceive, that the very aspect of happiness, joy, prosperity, gives pleasure; that of pain, suffering, sorrow, communicates uneasiness? The human countenance, says HORACE,[2] borrows smiles or tears from the human countenance. Reduce a person to solitude, and he loses all enjoyment, except either of the sensual or speculative kind; and that because the movements of his heart are not forwarded by correspondent movements in his fellow-creatures. The signs of sorrow and mourning, though arbitrary, affect us with melancholy; but the natural symptoms, tears and cries and groans, never fail to infuse compassion and uneasiness. And if the effects of misery touch us in so lively a manner; can we be supposed altogether

---

1. It is needless to push our researches so far as to ask, why we have humanity or a fellow-feeling with others. It is sufficient, that this is experienced to be a principle in human nature. We must stop somewhere in our examination of causes; and there are, in every science, some general principles, beyond which we cannot hope to find any principle more general. No man is absolutely indifferent to the happiness and misery of others. The first has a natural tendency to give pleasure; the second, pain. This every one may find in himself. It is not probable, that these principles can be resolved into principles more simple and universal, whatever attempts may have been made to that purpose. But if it were possible, it belongs not to the present subject; and we may here safely consider these principles as original: Happy, if we can render all the consequences sufficiently plain and perspicuous!

2. Uti ridentibus arrident, ita flentibus adflent. [As men's faces smile with those who smile, so they weep with those who weep.) Humani vultus. . . .

insensible or indifferent towards its causes; when a malicious or treacherous character and behaviour are presented to us?

We enter, I shall suppose, into a convenient, warm, well-contrived apartment: We necessarily receive a pleasure from its very survey; because it presents us with the pleasing ideas of ease, satisfaction, and enjoyment. The hospitable, good-humoured, humane landlord appears. This circumstance surely must embellish the whole: nor can we easily forbear reflecting, with pleasure, on the satisfaction which results to every one from his intercourse and good-offices.

His whole family, by the freedom, ease, confidence, and calm enjoyment, diffused over their countenances, sufficiently express their happiness. I have a pleasing sympathy in the prospect of so much joy, and can never consider the source of it, without the most agreeable emotions.

He tells me, that an oppressive and powerful neighbour had attempted to dispossess him of his inheritance, and had long disturbed all his innocent and social pleasures. I feel an immediate indignation arise in me against such violence and injury

But it is no wonder, he adds, that a private wrong should proceed from a man, who had enslaved provinces, depopulated cities, and made the field and scaffold stream with human blood. I am struck with horror at the prospect of so much misery, and am actuated by the strongest antipathy against its author.

In general, it is certain, that, wherever we go, whatever we reflect on or converse about, every thing still presents us with the view of human happiness or misery, and excites in our breast a sympathetic movement of pleasure or uneasiness. In our serious occupations, in our careless amusements, this principle still exerts its active energy.

A man, who enters the theatre, is immediately struck with the view of so great a multitude participating of one common amusement; and experiences, from their very aspect, a superior sensibility or disposition of being affected with every sentiment, which he shares with his fellow-creatures.

He observes the actors to be animated by the appearance of a full audience, and raised to a degree of enthusiasm, which they cannot command in any solitary or calm moment.

Every movement of the theatre, by a skilful poet, is communicated, as it were by magic, to the specta-tors; who weep, tremble, resent, rejoice, and are enflamed with all the variety of passions, which actuate the several personages of the drama.

Where any event crosses our wishes, and interrupts the happiness of the favorite characters, we feel a sensible anxiety and concern. But where their sufferings proceed from the treachery, cruelty, or tyranny of an enemy, our breasts are affected with the liveliest resentment against the author of these calamities.

It is here esteemed contrary to the rules of art to represent any thing cool and indifferent. A distant friend, or a confident, who has no immediate interest in the catastrophe, ought, if possible, to be avoided by the poet; as communicating a like indifference to the audience, and checking the progress of the passions.

Few species of poetry are more entertaining than *pastoral;* and every one is sensible, that the chief source of its pleasure arises from those images of a gentle and tender tranquillity, which it represents in its personages, and of which it communicates a like sentiment to the reader. SANNAZARIUS, who transferred the scene to the sea-shore, though he presented the most magnificent object in nature, is confessed to have erred in his choice. The idea of toil, labour, and danger, suffered by the fishermen, is painful; by an unavoidable sympathy, which attends every conception of human happiness or misery.

When I was twenty, says a FRENCH poet, OVID was my favourite: Now I am forty, I declare for HORACE. We enter, to be sure, more readily into sentiments, which resemble those we feel every day: But no passion, when well represented, can be entirely indifferent to us; because there is none, of which every man has not, within him, at least the seeds and first principles. It is the business of poetry to bring every affection near to us by lively imagery and representation, and make it look like truth and reality: A certain proof, that, wherever that reality is found, our minds are disposed to be strongly affected by it.

Any recent event or piece of news, by which the fate of states, provinces, or many individuals is affected, is extremely interesting even to those whose welfare is not immediately engaged. Such intelligence is propagated with celerity, heard with avidity, and enquired into with attention and concern. The interest of society appears, on this occasion, to be, in some degree, the interest of each individual. The imagination is sure to be affected; though the passions excited may not always be so strong and steady as to have great influence on the conduct and behaviour.

The perusal of a history seems a calm entertainment; but would be no entertainment at all, did not our hearts beat with correspondent movements to those which are described by the historian.

THUCYDIDES and GUICCIARDIN support with difficulty our attention; while the former describes the trivial rencounters of the small cities of GREECE, and the latter the harmless wars of PISA. The few persons interested, and the small interest fill not the imagination, and engage not the affections. The deep distress of the numerous ATHENIAN army before SYRACUSE; the danger which so nearly threatens VENICE; these excite compassion; these move terror and anxiety.

The indifferent, uninteresting stile of SUETONIUS, equally with the masterly pencil of TACITUS, may convince us of the cruel depravity of NERO or TIBERIUS: But what a difference of sentiment! While the former coldly relates the facts; and the latter sets before our eyes the venerable figures of a SORANUS and a THRASEA, intrepid in their fate, and only moved by the melting sorrows of their friends and kindred. What sympathy then touches every human heart! What indignation against the tyrant, whose causeless fear or unprovoked malice gave rise to such detestable barbarity!

If we bring these subjects nearer: If we remove all suspicion of fiction and deceit: What powerful concern is excited, and how much superior, in many instances, to the narrow attachments of self-love and private interest! Popular sedition, party zeal, a devoted obedience to factious leaders; these are some of the most visible, though less laudable effects of this social sympathy in human nature.

The frivolousness of the subject too, we may observe, is not able to detach us entirely from what carries an image of human sentiment and affection.

When a person stutters, and pronounces with difficulty, we even sympathize with this trivial uneasiness, and suffer for him. And it is a rule in criticism, that every combination of syllables or letters, which gives pain to the organs of speech in the recital, appears also, from a species of sympathy, harsh and disagreeable to the ear. Nay, when we run over a book with our eye, we are sensible of such unhar-

monious composition; because we still imagine, that a person recites it to us, and suffers from the pronunciation of these jarring sounds. So delicate is our sympathy!

Easy and unconstrained postures and motions are always beautiful: An air of health and vigour is agreeable: Cloaths which warm, without burdening the body; which cover, without imprisoning the limbs, are well-fashioned. In every judgment of beauty, the feelings of the person affected enter into consideration, and communicate to the spectator similar touches of pain or pleasure.[1] What wonder, then, if we can pronounce no judgment concerning the character and conduct of men, without considering the tendencies of their actions, and the happiness or misery which thence arises to society? What association of ideas would ever operate, were that principle here totally unactive.[2]

If any man from a cold insensibility, or narrow selfishness of temper, is unaffected with the images of human happiness or misery, he must be equally indifferent to the images of vice and virtue: As, on the other hand, it is always found, that a warm concern for the interests of our species is attended with a del-

---

1. 'Decentior equus cujus astricta sunt ilia; sed idem velocior. Pulcher aspectu sit athleta, cujus lacertos exercitatio expressit; idem certamini paratior. Nunquam enim *species* ab *utilitate* dividitur. Sed hoc quidem discernere modici judicii est.' [A horse whose flanks are well-knit is more graceful, but is also faster. The wrestler who has built up his muscles in training is a handsome sight, but he is also better prepared for the match. Indeed beauty is never distinct from usefulness. But no great degree of insight is needed to see this.] QUINTILIAN. . . .

2. In proportion to the station which a man possesses, according to the relations in which he is placed; we always expect from him a greater or less degree of good, and when disappointed, blame his inutility; and much more do we blame him, if any ill or prejudice arise from his conduct and behaviour. When the interests of one country interfere with those of another, we estimate the merits of a statesman by the good or ill, which results to his own country from his measures and councils, without regard to the prejudice which he brings on his enemies and rivals. His fellow-citizens are the objects, which lie nearest the eye, while we determine his character. And as nature has implanted in every one a superior affection to his own country, we never expect any regard to distant nations, where a competition arises. Not to mention, that, while every man consults the good of his own community, we are sensible, that the general interest of mankind is better promoted, than by loose indeterminate views to the good of a species, whence no beneficial action could ever result, for want of a duly limited object, on which they could exert themselves.

icate feeling of all moral distinctions; a strong resentment of injury done to men; a lively approbation of their welfare. In this particular, though great superiority is observable of one man above another; yet none are so entirely indifferent to the interest of their fellow-creatures, as to perceive no distinctions of moral good and evil, in consequence of the different tendencies of actions and principles. How, indeed, can we suppose it possible in any one, who wears a human heart, that if there be subjected to his censure, one character or system of conduct, which is beneficial, and another, which is pernicious, to his species or community, he will not so much as give a cool preference to the former, or ascribe to it the smallest merit or regard? Let us suppose such a person ever so selfish; let private interest have ingrossed ever so much his attention; yet in instances, where that is not concerned, he must unavoidably feel *some* propensity to the good of mankind, and make it an object of choice, if everything else be equal. Would any man, who is walking along, tread as willingly on another's gouty toes, whom he has no quarrel with, as on the hard flint and pavement? There is here surely a difference in the case. We surely take into consideration the happiness and misery of others, in weighing the several motives of action, and incline to the former, where no private regards draw us to seek our own promotion or advantage by the injury of our fellow-creatures. And if the principles of humanity are capable, in many instances, of influencing our actions, they must, at all times, have *some* authority over our sentiments, and give us a general approbation of what is useful to society, and blame of what is dangerous or pernicious. The degrees of these sentiments may be the subject of controversy; but the reality of their existence, one should think, must be admitted, in every theory or system.

A creature, absolutely malicious and spiteful, were there any such in nature, must be worse than indifferent to the images of vice and virtue. All his sentiments must be inverted, and directly opposite to those, which prevail in the human species. Whatever contributes to the good of mankind as it crosses the constant bent of his wishes and desires, must produce uneasiness and disapprobation; and on the contrary, whatever is the source of disorder and misery in society, must, for the same reason, be regarded with pleasure and complacency. TIMON, who, probably from his affected spleen, more than any inveterate malice, was denominated the man-hater, embraced ALCIBIADES, with great fondness. *Go on my boy!* cried he, *acquire the confidence of the people: You will one day, I foresee, be the cause of great calamities to them*[1]: Could we admit the two principles of the MANICHEANS, it is an infallible consequence, that their sentiments of human actions, as well as of every thing else, must be totally opposite, and that every instance of justice and humanity, from its necessary tendency, must please the one deity and displease the other. All mankind so far resemble the good principle, that, where interest or revenge or envy perverts not our disposition, we are always inclined, from our natural philanthropy, to give the preference to the happiness of society, and consequently to virtue, above its opposite. Absolute, unprovoked, disinterested malice has never, perhaps, place in any human breast; or if it had, must there pervert all the sentiments of morals, as well as the feelings of humanity. If the cruelty of NERO be allowed entirely voluntary, and not rather the effect of constant fear and resentment; it is evident, that TIGELLINUS, preferably to SENECA or BURRHUS, must have possessed his steady and uniform approbation.

A statesman or patriot, who serves our own country, in our own time, has always a more passionate regard paid to him, than one whose beneficial influence operated on distant ages or remote nations; where the good, resulting from his generous humanity, being less connected with us, seems more obscure, and affects us with a less lively sympathy. We may own the merit to be equally great, though our sentiments are not raised to an equal height, in both cases. The judgment here corrects the inequalities of our internal emotions and perceptions; in like manner, as it preserves us from error, in the several variations of images, presented to our external senses. The same object, at a double distance, really throws on the eye a picture of but half the bulk; yet we imagine that it appears of the same size in both situations; because we know, that, on our approach to it, its image would expand on the eye, and that the difference consists not in the object itself, but in our position with regard to it. And, indeed, without such a correction of appearances, both in internal and external sentiment, men could never think or talk

---

1. PLUTARCH. . . .

steadily on any subject; while their fluctuating situations produce a continual variation on objects, and throw them into such different and contrary lights and positions.[1]

The more we converse with mankind, and the greater social intercourse we maintain, the more shall we be familiarized to these general preferences and distinctions, without which our conversation and discourse could scarcely be rendered intelligible to each other. Every man's interest is peculiar to himself, and the aversions and desires, which result from it, cannot be supposed to affect others in a like degree. General language, therefore, being formed for general use, must be moulded on some more general views, and must affix the epithets of praise or blame, in conformity to sentiments, which arise from the general interests of the community. And if these sentiments, in most men, be not so strong as those, which have a reference to private good; yet still they must make some distinction, even in persons the most depraved and selfish; and must attach the notion of good to a beneficent conduct, and of evil to the contrary. Sympathy, we shall allow, is much fainter than our concern for ourselves, and sympathy with persons remote from us, much fainter than that with persons near and contiguous; but for this very reason, it is necessary for us, in our calm judgments and discourse concerning the characters of men, to neglect all these differences, and render our sentiments more public and social. Besides, that we ourselves often change our situation in this particular, we every day meet with persons, who are in a situation different from us, and who could never converse with us, were we to remain constantly in that position and point of view, which is peculiar to ourselves. The intercourse of sentiments, therefore, in society and conversation, makes us form some general unalterable standard, by which we may approve or disapprove of characters and manners. And though the heart takes not part with those general notions, nor regulates all its love and hatred, by the universal, abstract differences of vice and virtue, without regard to self, or the persons with whom we are more intimately connected; yet have these moral differences a considerable influence, and being sufficient, at least, for discourse, serve all our purposes in company, in the pulpit, on the theatre, and in the schools.[2]

Thus, in whatever light we take this subject, the merit, ascribed to the social virtues, appears still uniform, and arises chiefly from that regard, which the natural sentiment of benevolence engages us to pay to the interests of mankind and society. If we consider the principles of the human make, such as they appear to daily experience and observation, we must, *à priori,* conclude it impossible for such a creature as man to be totally indifferent to the well or ill-being of his fellow creatures, and not readily, of himself, to pronounce, where nothing gives him any particular byass, that what promotes their happiness is good, what tends to their misery is evil, without any farther regard or consideration. Here then are the faint rudiments, at least, or out-lines, of a *general* distinction between actions; and in proportion as the humanity of the person is supposed to encrease, his connexion with those who are injured or benefited, and his lively conception of their misery or happiness; his consequent censure or approbation acquires proportionable vigour. There is no necessity, that a generous action, barely mentioned in an old history or remote gazette, should communicate any

---

1. For a like reason, the tendencies of actions and characters, not their real accidental consequences, are alone regarded in our determinations or general judgments; though in our real feeling or sentiment, we cannot help paying greater regard to one whose station, joined to virtue, renders him really useful to society, than to one, who exerts the social virtues only in good intentions and benevolent affections. Separating the character from the fortune, by an easy and necessary effort of thought, we pronounce these persons alike, and give them the same general praise. The judgment corrects or endeavours to correct the appearance: But is not able entirely to prevail over sentiment.

Why is this peach-tree said to be better than that other; but because it produces more or better fruit? And would not the same praise be given it, though snails or vermin had destroyed the peaches, before they came to full maturity? In morals too, is not *the tree known by the fruit?* And cannot we easily distinguish between nature and accident, in the one case as well as in the other?

2. It is wisely ordained by nature, that private connexions should commonly prevail over universal views and considerations; otherwise our affections and actions would be dissipated and lost, for want of a proper limited object. Thus a small benefit done to ourselves, or our near friends, excites more lively sentiments of love and approbation than a great benefit done to a distant commonwealth: But still we know here, as in all the senses, to correct these inequalities by reflection, and retain a general standard of vice and virtue, founded chiefly on general usefulness.

strong feelings of applause and admiration. Virtue, placed at such a distance, is liked a fixed star, which, though to the eye of reason, it may appear as luminous as the sun in his meridian, is so infinitely removed, as to affect the senses, neither with light nor heat. Bring this virtue nearer, by our acquaintance or connexion with the persons, or even by an eloquent recital of the case; our hearts are immediately caught, our sympathy enlivened, and our cool approbation converted into the warmest sentiments of friendship and regard. These seem necessary and infallible consequences of the general principles of human nature, as discovered in common life and practice.

Again; reverse these views and reasonings: Consider the matter *à posteriori;* and weighing the consequences, enquire if the merit of social virtue be not, in a great measure, derived from the feelings of humanity, with which it affects the spectators. It appears to be matter of fact, that the circumstance of *utility,* in all subjects, is a source of praise and approbation: That it is constantly appealed to in all moral decisions concerning the merit and demerit of actions: That it is the *sole* source of that high regard paid to justice, fidelity, honour, allegiance, and chastity: That it is inseparable from all the other social virtues, humanity, generosity, charity, affability, lenity, mercy, and moderation: And, in a word, that it is a foundation of the chief part of morals, which has a reference to mankind and our fellow-creatures.

It appears also, that in our general approbation of characters and manners, the useful tendency of the social virtues moves us not by any regards to self-interest, but has an influence much more universal and extensive. It appears, that a tendency to public good, and to the promoting of peace, harmony, and order in society, does always, by affecting the benevolent principles of our frame, engage us on the side of the social virtues. And it appears, as an additional confirmation, that these principles of humanity and sympathy enter so deeply into all our sentiments, and have so powerful an influence, as may enable them to excite the strongest censure and applause. The present theory is the simple result of all these inferences, each of which seems founded on uniform experience and observation.

Were it doubtful, whether there were any such principle in our nature as humanity or a concern for others, yet when we see, in numberless instances, that whatever has a tendency to promote the interests of society, is so highly approved of, we ought thence to learn the force of the benevolent principle; since it is impossible for any thing to please as means to an end, where the end is totally indifferent. On the other hand, were it doubtful, whether there were, implanted in our nature, any general principle of moral blame and approbation, yet when we see, in numberless instances, the influence of humanity, we ought thence to conclude, that it is impossible, but that every thing, which promotes the interest of society, must communicate pleasure, and what is pernicious give uneasiness. But when these different reflections and observations concur in establishing the same conclusion, must they not bestow an undisputed evidence upon it?

It is however hoped, that the progress of this argument will bring a farther confirmation of the present theory, by showing the rise of other sentiments of esteem and regard from the same or like principles.

Section VI.—Of Qualities Useful to Ourselves.

Part I.

It seems evident, that where a quality or habit is subjected to our examination, if it appear, in any respect, prejudicial to the person possessed of it, or such as incapacitates him for business and action, it is instantly blamed, and ranked among his faults and imperfections. Indolence, negligence, want of order and method, obstinacy, fickleness, rashness, credulity; these qualities were never esteemed by any one indifferent to a character; much less, extolled as accomplishments or virtues. The prejudice, resulting from them, immediately strikes our eye, and gives us the sentiment of pain and disapprobation.

No quality, it is allowed, is absolutely either blameable or praiseworthy. It is all according to its degree. A due medium, say the PERIPATETICS, is the characteristic of virtue. But this medium is chiefly determined by utility. A proper celerity, for instance, and dispatch in business, is commendable. When defective, no progress is ever made in the execution of any purpose: When excessive, it engages us in precipitate and ill-concerted measures and enterprises: By such reasons, we fix the proper and commendable mediocrity in all moral and prudential disquisitions; and never lose view of the advantages, which result from any character or habit.

Now as these advantages are enjoyed by the person possessed of the character, it can never be *self-love* which renders the prospect of them agreeable to us, the spectators, and prompts our esteem and approbation. No force of imagination can convert us into another person, and make us fancy, that we, being that person, reap benefit from those valuable qualities, which belong to him. Or if it did, no celerity of imagination could immediately transport us back, into ourselves, and make us love and esteem the person, as different from us. Views and sentiments, so opposite to known truth, and to each other, could never have place, at the same time, in the same person. All suspicion, therefore, of selfish regards, is here totally excluded. It is a quite different principle, which actuates our bosom, and interests us in the felicity of the person whom we contemplate. Where his natural talents and acquired abilities give us the prospect of elevation, advancement, a figure in life, prosperous success, a steady command over fortune, and the execution of great or advantageous undertakings; we are struck with such agreeable images and feel a complacency and regard immediately arise towards him. The ideas of happiness, joy, triumph, prosperity, are connected with every circumstance of his character and diffuse over our minds a pleasing sentiment of sympathy and humanity.[1]

Let us suppose a person originally framed so as to have no manner of concern for his fellow-creatures, but to regard the happiness and misery of all sensible beings with greater indifference than even two contiguous shades of the same colour. Let us suppose, if the prosperity of nations were laid on the one hand, and their ruin on the other, and he were desired to choose; that he would stand, like the schoolman's ass, irresolute and undetermined, between equal motives; or rather, like the same ass between two pieces of wood or marble, without any inclination or propensity to either side. The consequence, I believe, must be allowed just, that such a person, being absolutely unconcerned, either for the public good of a community or the private utility of others, would look on every quality, however pernicious, or however beneficial, to society, or to its possessor, with the same indifference as on the most common and uninteresting object.

But if, instead of this fancied monster, we suppose a *man* to form a judgment or determination in the case, there is to him a plain foundation of preference, where every thing else is equal; and however cool his choice may be, if his heart be selfish, or if the persons interested be remote from him; there must still be a choice or distinction between what is useful, and what is pernicious. Now this distinction is the same in all its parts, with the *moral distinction,* whose foundation has been so often, and so much in vain, enquired after. The same endowments of the mind, in every circumstance, are agreeable to the sentiment of morals and to that of humanity; the same temper is susceptible of high degrees of the one sentiment and of the other; and the same alteration in the objects, by their nearer approach or by connexions, enlivens the one and the other. By all the rules of philosophy, therefore, we must conclude, that these sentiments are originally the same; since, in each particular, even the most minute, they are governed by the same laws, and are moved by the same objects.

Why do philosophers infer, with the greatest certainty, that the moon is kept in its orbit by the same force of gravity, that makes bodies fall near the surface of the earth, but because these effects are, upon computation, found similar and equal? And must not this argument bring as strong conviction, in moral as in natural disquisitions?

To prove, by any long detail, that all the qualities, useful to the possessor, are approved of, and the contrary censured, would be superfluous. The least reflection on what is every day experienced in life, will be sufficient. We shall only mention a few in-

---

1. One may venture to affirm, that there is no human creature, to whom the appearance of happiness (where envy or revenge has no place) does not give pleasure, that of misery, uneasiness. This seems inseparable from our make and constitution. But they are only the more generous minds, that are thence prompted to seek zealously the good of others, and to have a real passion for their welfare. With men of narrow and ungenerous spirits, this sympathy goes not beyond a slight feeling of the imagination, which serves only to excite sentiments of complacency or censure, and makes them apply to the object either honourable or dishonourable appellations. A griping miser, for instance, praises extremely *industry* and *frugality* even in others, and sets them, in his estimation, above all the other virtues. He knows the good that results from them, and feels that species of happiness with a more lively sympathy, than any other you could represent to him; though perhaps he would not part with a shilling to make the fortune of the industrious man, whom he praises so highly.

stances, in order to remove, if possible, all doubt and hesitation.

The quality, the most necessary for the execution of any useful enterprise, is DISCRETION; by which we carry on a safe intercourse with others, give due attention to our own and to their character, weigh each circumstance of the business which we undertake, and employ the surest and safest means for the attainment of any end or purpose. To a CROMWELL, perhaps or a DE RETZ, discretion may appear an alderman-like virtue, as Dr. SWIFT calls it; and being incompatible with those vast designs, to which their courage and ambition prompted them, it might really, in them, be a fault or imperfection. But in the conduct of ordinary life, no virtue is more requisite, not only to obtain success, but to avoid the most fatal miscarriages and disappointments. The greatest parts without it, as observed by an elegant writer, may be fatal to their owner; as POLYPHEMUS, deprived of his eye, was only the more exposed, on account of his enormous strength and stature.

The best character, indeed, were it not rather too perfect for human nature, is that which is not swayed by temper of any kind; but alternately employs enterprise and caution, as each is *useful* to the particular purpose intended. Such is the excellence which ST. EVREMOND ascribes to mareschal TURENNE, who displayed every campaign, as he grew older, more temerity in his military enterprises; and being now, from long experience, perfectly acquainted with every incident in war, he advanced with greater firmness and security, in a road so well known to him. Fabius, says MACHIAVEL, was cautious; Scipio enterprising: And both succeeded, because the situation of the ROMAN affairs, during the command of each, was peculiarly adapted to his genius; but both would have failed, had these situations been reversed. He is happy, whose circumstances suit his temper; but he is more excellent, who can suit his temper to any circumstances.

What need is there to display the praises of IN-DUSTRY, and to extol its advantages, in the acquisition of power and riches, or in raising what we call a *fortune* in the world? The tortoise, according to the fable, by his perseverance, gained the race of the hare, though possessed of much superior swiftness. A man's time, when well husbanded, is like a cultivated field, of which a few acres produce more of what is useful to life, than extensive provinces, even

of the richest soil, when over-run with weeds and brambles.

But all prospect of success in life, or even of tolerable subsistence, must fail, where a reasonable FRUGALITY is wanting. The heap, in stead of encreasing, diminishes daily, and leaves its possessor so much more unhappy, as, not having been able to confine his expences to a large revenue, he will still less be able to live contentedly on a small one. The souls of men, according to PLATO,[1] inflamed with impure appetites, and losing the body, which alone afforded means of satisfaction, hover about the earth, and haunt the places where their bodies are deposited; possessed with a longing desire to recover the lost organs of sensation. So may we see worthless prodigals, having consumed their fortune in wild debauches, thrusting themselves into every plentiful table, and every party of pleasure, hated even by the vicious, and despised even by fools.

The one extreme of frugality is *avarice,* which, as it both deprives a man of all use of his riches, and checks hospitality and every social enjoyment, is justly censured on a double account. *Prodigality,* the other extreme, is commonly more hurtful to a man himself; and each of these extremes is blamed above the other, according to the temper of the person who censures, and according to his greater or less sensibility to pleasure, either social or sensual.

QUALITIES often derive their merit from complicated sources. *Honesty, fidelity, truth,* are praised for their immediate tendency to promote the interests of society; but after those virtues are once established upon this foundation, they are also considered as advantageous to the person himself, and as the source of that trust and confidence, which can alone give a man any consideration in life. One becomes contemptible, no less than odious, when he forgets the duty, which, in this particular, he owes to himself as well as to society.

Perhaps, this consideration is one *chief* source of the high blame, which is thrown on any instance of failure among women in point of *chastity*. The greatest regard, which can be acquired by that sex, is derived from their fidelity; and a woman becomes cheap and vulgar, loses her rank, and is exposed to every insult, who is deficient in this particular. The

---

1. Phaedo. . . .

smallest failure is here sufficient to blast her character. A female has so many opportunities of secretly indulging these appetites, that nothing can give us security but her absolute modesty and reserve; and where a breach is once made, it can scarcely ever be fully repaired. If a man behave with cowardice on one occasion, a contrary conduct reinstates him in his character. But by what action can a woman, whose behaviour has once been dissolute, be able to assure us, that she has formed better resolutions, and has self-command enough to carry them into execution?

All men, it is allowed, are equally desirous of happiness; but few are successful in the pursuit: One considerable cause is the want of STRENGTH of MIND, which might enable them to resist the temptation of present ease or pleasure, and carry them forward in the search of more distant profit and enjoyment. Our affections, on a general prospect of their objects, form certain rules of conduct, and certain measures of preference of one above another: And these decisions, though really the result of our calm passions and propensities, (for what else can pronounce any object eligible or the contrary?) are yet said, by a natural abuse of terms, to be the determinations of pure *reason* and reflection. But when some of these objects approach nearer to us, or acquire the advantages of favourable lights and positions, which catch the heart or imagination; our general resolutions are frequently confounded, a small enjoyment preferred, and lasting shame and sorrow entailed upon us. And however poets may employ their wit and eloquence, in celebrating present pleasure, and rejecting all distant views to fame, health, or fortune; it is obvious, that this practice is the source of all dissoluteness and disorder, repentance and misery. A man of a strong and determined temper adheres tenaciously to his general resolutions, and is neither seduced by the allurements of pleasure, nor terrified by the menaces of pain; but keeps still in view those distant pursuits, by which he, at once, ensures his happiness and his honour.

Self-satisfaction, at least in some degree, is an advantage, which equally attends the FOOL and the WISE MAN: But it is the only one; nor is there any other circumstance in the conduct of life, where they are upon an equal footing. Business, books, conversation; for all of these, a fool is totally incapacitated, and except condemned by his station to the coarsest drudgery, remains a *useless* burthen upon the earth. Accordingly, it is found, that men are extremely jealous of their character in this particular; and many instances are seen of profligacy and treachery, the most avowed and unreserved; none of bearing patiently the imputation of ignorance and stupidity. DICAEARCHUS, the MACEDONIAN general, who, as POLYBIUS tells us, openly erected one altar to impiety, another to injustice, in order to bid defiance to mankind; even he, I am well assured, would have started at the epithet of *fool,* and have meditated revenge for so injurious an appellation. Except the affection of parents, the strongest and most indissoluble bond in nature, no connexion has strength sufficient to support the disgust arising from this character. Love itself, which can subsist under treachery, ingratitude, malice, and infidelity, is immediately extinguished by it, when perceived and acknowledged; nor are deformity and old age more fatal to the dominion of that passion. So dreadful are the ideas of an utter incapacity for any purpose or undertaking, and of continued error and misconduct in life!

When it is asked, whether a quick or a slow apprehension be most valuable? Whether one, that, at first view, penetrates far into a subject, but can perform nothing upon study; or a contrary character, which must work out every thing by dint of application? Whether a clear head or a copious invention? Whether a profound genius or a sure judgment? In short, what character, or peculiar turn of understanding is more excellent than another? It is evident, that we can answer none of these questions, without considering which of those qualities capacitates a man best for the world, and carries him farthest in any undertaking.

If refined sense and exalted sense be not so *useful* as common sense, their rarity, their novelty, and the nobleness of their objects make some compensation, and render them the admiration of mankind: As gold, though less serviceable than iron, acquires, from its scarcity, a value, which is much superior.

The defects of judgment can be supplied by no art or invention; but those of MEMORY frequently may, both in business and in study, by method and industry, and by diligence in committing every thing to writing; and we scarcely ever hear a short memory given as a reason for a man's failure in any undertaking. But in ancient times, when no man could make a figure without the talent of speaking, and when the audience were too delicate to bear such crude, undigested harangues as our extemporary orators offer to public assemblies; the faculty of memory was then of the utmost consequence, and was accordingly much more valued than at present. Scarce any great genius is mentioned in antiquity, who is not celebrated for this talent; and CICERO enumerates it among the other sublime qualities of CÆSAR himself.[1]

Particular customs and manners alter the usefulness of qualities: They also alter their merit. Particular situations and accidents have, in some degree, the same influence. He will always be more esteemed, who possesses those talents and accomplishments, which suit his station and profession, than he whom fortune has misplaced in the part which she has assigned him. The private or selfish virtues are, in this respect, more arbitrary than the public and social. In other respects, they are, perhaps, less liable to doubt and controversy.

In this kingdom, such continued ostentation, of late years, has prevailed among men in *active* life with regard to *public spirit,* and among those in *speculative* with regard to *benevolence;* and so many false pretensions to each have been, no doubt, detected, that men of the world are apt, without any bad intention, to discover a sullen incredulity on the head of those moral endowments, and even sometimes absolutely to deny their existence and reality. In like manner, I find, that, of old, the perpetual cant of the *Stoics* and *Cynics* concerning *virtue,* their magnificent professions and slender performances, bred a disgust in mankind; and LUCIAN, who, though licentious with regard to pleasure, is yet, in other respects, a very moral writer, cannot, sometimes, talk of virtue, so much boasted, without betraying symptoms of spleen and irony.[2] But surely this peevish delicacy, whence-ever it arises, can never be carried so far as to make us deny the existence of every species of merit, and all distinction of manners and behaviour. Besides *discretion, caution, enterprise, industry, as-*

siduity, frugality, economy, good-sense, prudence, discernment; besides these endowments, I say, whose very names force an avowal of their merit, there are many others, to which the most determined scepticism cannot, for a moment, refuse the tribute of praise and approbation. *Temperance, sobriety, patience, constancy, perseverance, forethought, considerateness, secrecy, order, insinuation, address, presence of mind, quickness of conception, facility of expression;* these, and a thousand more of the same kind, no man will ever deny to be excellencies and perfections. As their merit consists in their tendency to serve the person, possessed of them, without any magnificent claim to public and social desert, we are the less jealous of their pretensions, and readily admit them into the catalogue of laudable qualities. We are not sensible, that, by this concession, we have paved the way for all the other moral excellencies, and cannot confidently hesitate any longer, with regard to disinterested benevolence, patriotism, and humanity.

It seems, indeed, certain, that first appearances are here, as usual, extremely deceitful, and that it is more difficult, in a speculative way, to resolve into self-love the merit, which we ascribe to the selfish virtues above-mentioned, than that even of the social virtues, justice and beneficence. For this latter purpose, we need but say, that whatever conduct promotes the good of the community is loved, praised, and esteemed by the community, on account of that utility and interest, of which every one partakes: And though this affection and regard be, in reality, gratitude, not self-love, yet a distinction, even of this obvious nature, may not readily be made by superficial reasoners; and there is room, at least, to support the cavil and dispute for a moment. But as qualities, which tend only to the utility of their possessor, without any reference to us, or to the community, are yet esteemed and valued; by what theory or system can we account for this sentiment from self love, or deduce it from that

---

1. Fuit in illo ingenium, ratio, memoria, literæ, cura, cogitatio, diligentia, &c. PHILIP. . . . [That man had genius, judgment, memory, learning, compassion, understanding and industry, etc.]

2. Ἀρετήν τινα καὶ ἀσώματα καὶ λήρους μεγάλη τῇ ξυνειρόντων. [. . . droning on and on in a grand voice about some virtue and immaterial substances, and other nonsense.] Luc. TIMON. . . . Again, Καὶ συναγάγοντες (οἱ φιλόσοφοι) εὐεξαπάτητα μειράκια τήν

τε πολυθμλλήτον ἀρετὴν τραγωδοῦσι. [. . . and gathering the young, so easily deceived, around them, they (the philosophers) soliloquize on the hackneyed theme of virtue.] ICARO-MEN. . . . In another place, "Ἡ πού γάρ ἐστιν ἡ πολυθρύλλητος ἀρετὴ, καὶ φύσις, καὶ εἱμαρμένη, καὶ τύχη, ἀνυπόστατα καὶ κενὰ πραγμάτων ὀνόματα. [Where then is that hackneyed virtue and nature and destiny and fortune, words empty of substance?] Deor. Concil. . .

favourite origin? There seems here a necessity for confessing that the happiness and misery of others are not spectacles entirely indifferent to us; but that the view of the former, whether in its causes or effects, like sun-shine or the prospect of well-cultivated plains, (to carry our pretensions no higher) communicates a secret joy and satisfaction; the appearance of the latter, like a lowering cloud or barren landskip, throws a melancholy damp over the imagination. And this concession being once made, the difficulty is over; and a natural unforced interpretation of the phænomena of human life will afterwards, we may hope, prevail among all speculative enquirers.

Part II.

It may not be improper, in this place, to examine the influence of bodily endowments, and of the goods of fortune, over our sentiments of regard and esteem, and to consider whether these phænomena fortify or weaken the present theory. It will naturally be expected, that the beauty of the body, as is supposed by all ancient moralists, will be similar, in some respects, to that of the mind; and that every kind of esteem, which is paid to a man, will have something similar in its origin, whether it arise from his mental endowments, or from the situation of his exterior circumstances.

It is evident, that one considerable source of *beauty* in all animals is the advantage, which they reap from the particular structure of their limbs and members, suitably to the particular manner of life, to which they are by nature destined. The just proportions of a horse, described by XENOPHON and VIRGIL, are the same, that are received at this day by our modern jockeys; because the foundation of them is the same, namely, experience of what is detrimental or useful in the animal.

Broad shoulders, a lank belly, firm joints, taper legs; all these are beautiful in our species, because signs of force and vigour. Ideas of utility and its contrary, though they do not entirely determine what is handsome or deformed, are evidently the source of a considerable part of approbation or dislike.

In ancient times, bodily strength and dexterity, being of greater *use* and importance in war, was also much more esteemed and valued, than at present. Not to insist on HOMER and the poets, we may observe, that

historians scruple not to mention *force of body* among the other accomplishments even of EPAMINONDAS, whom they acknowledge to be the greatest hero, statesman, and general of all the GREEKS.[1] A like praise is given to POMPEY, one of the greatest of the ROMANS.[2] This instance is similar to what we observed above, with regard to memory.

What derision and contempt, with both sexes, attend *impotence;* while the unhappy object is regarded as one deprived of so capital a pleasure in life, and at the same time, as disabled from communicating it to others. *Barrenness* in women, being also a species of *inutility,* is a reproach, but not in the same degree: Of which the reason is very obvious, according to the present theory.

There is no rule in painting or statuary more indispensable than that of balancing the figures, and placing them with the greatest exactness of their proper center of gravity. A figure, which is not justly balanced, is ugly; because it conveys the disagreeable ideas of fall, harm, and pain.[3]

A disposition or turn of mind, which qualifies a man to rise in the world, and advance his fortune, is

---

1. DIODORUS SICULUS. . . . It may not be improper to give the character of EPAMINONDAS, as drawn by the historian, in order to show the ideas of perfect merit, which prevailed in those ages. In other illustrious men, says he, you will observe, that each possessed some one shining quality, which was the foundation of his fame: In EPAMINONDAS all the *virtues* are found united; force of body, eloquence of expression, vigour of mind, contempt of riches, gentleness of disposition, and *what is chiefly to be regarded,* courage and conduct in war.

2. *Cum alacribus. saltu; cum velocibus, cursu; cum validis recte certabat.* [He competed with the agile at jumping, the swift at running and the strong with honor.] SALLUST apud VEGET. . . .

3. All men are equally liable to pain and disease and sickness; and may again recover health and ease. These circumstances, as they make no distinction between one man and another, are no source of pride or humility, regard or contempt. But comparing our own species to superior ones, it is a very mortifying consideration, that we should all be so liable to diseases and infirmities; and divines accordingly employ this topic, in order to depress self-conceit and vanity. They would have more success, if the common bent of our thoughts were not perpetually turned to compare ourselves with others. The infirmities of old age are mortifying; because a comparison with the young may take place. The king's evil is industriously concealed, because it affects others, and is often transmitted to posterity. The case is nearly the same with such diseases as convey any nauseous or frightful images; the epilepsy, for instance, ulcers, sores, scabs, etc.

entitled to esteem and regard, as has already been explained. It may, therefore, naturally be supposed, that the actual possession of riches and authority will have a considerable influence over these sentiments.

Let us examine any hypothesis, by which we can account for the regard paid to the rich and powerful: We shall find none satisfactory, but that which derives it from the enjoyment communicated to the spectator by the images of prosperity, happiness, ease, plenty, authority, and the gratification of every appetite. Self-love, for instance, which some affect so much to consider as the source of every sentiment, is plainly insufficient for this purpose. Where no good-will or friendship appears, it is difficult to conceive on what we can found our hope of advantage from the riches of others; though we naturally respect the rich, even before they discover any such favourable disposition towards us.

We are affected with the same sentiments, when we lie so much out of the sphere of their activity, that they cannot even be supposed to possess the power of serving us. A prisoner of war, in all civilised nations, is treated with a regard suited to his condition; and riches, it is evident, go far towards fixing the condition of any person. If birth and quality enter for a share, this still affords us an argument to our present purpose. For what is it we call a man of birth, but one who is descended from a long succession of rich and powerful ancestors, and who acquires our esteem by his connexion with persons whom we esteem? His ancestors, therefore, though dead, are respected, in some measure, on account of their riches; and consequently, without any kind of expectation.

But not to go so far as prisoners of war or the dead, to find instances of this disinterested regard of riches; we may only observe, with a little attention, those phænomena, which occur in common life and conversation. A man, who is himself, we shall suppose, of a competent fortune, and of no profession, being introduced to a company of strangers, naturally treats them with different degrees of respect, as he is informed of their different fortunes and conditions; though it is impossible that he can so suddenly propose, and perhaps he would not accept of, any pecuniary advantage from them. A traveller is always admitted into company, and meets with civility, in proportion as his train and equipage speak him a man of great or moderate fortune. In short, the dif-

ferent ranks of men are, in a great measure, regulated by riches; and that with regard to superiors as well as inferiors, strangers as well acquaintance.

What remains, therefore, but to conclude, that, as riches are desired for ourselves only as the means of gratifying our appetites, either at present or in some imaginary future period; they beget esteem in others merely from their having that influence. This indeed is their very nature or essence: They have a direct reference to the commodities, conveniencies, and pleasures of life: The bill of a banker, who is broke, or gold in a desert island, would otherwise be full as valuable. When we approach a man, who is, as we say, at his ease, we are presented with the pleasing ideas of plenty, satisfaction, cleanliness, warmth; a chearful house, elegant furniture, ready service, and whatever is desirable in meat, drink, or apparel. On the contrary, when a poor man appears, the disagreeable images of want, penury, hard labour, dirty furniture, coarse or ragged cloaths, nauseous meat and distasteful liquor, immediately strike our fancy. What else do we mean by saying that one is rich, the other poor? And as regard or contempt is the natural consequence of those different situations in life; it is easily seen what additional light and evidence this throws on our preceding theory, with regard to all moral distinctions.[1]

A man, who has cured himself of all ridiculous prepossessions, and is fully, sincerely, and steadily convinced, from experience as well as philosophy, that the difference of fortune makes less difference in happiness than is vulgarly imagined; such a one does

---

1. There is something extraordinary, and seemingly unaccountable in the operation of our passions, when we consider the fortune and situation of others. Very often another's advancement and prosperity produces envy, which has a strong mixture of hatred, and arises chiefly from the comparison of ourselves with the person. At the very same time, or at least in very short intervals, we may feel the passion of respect, which is a species of affection or good-will, with a mixture of humility. On the other hand, the misfortunes of our fellows often cause pity, which has in it a strong mixture of good-will. This sentiment of pity is nearly allied to contempt, which is a species of dislike, with a mixture of pride. I only point out these phenomena, as a subject of speculation to such as are curious with regard to moral enquiries. It is sufficient for the present purpose to observe in general, that power and riches commonly cause respect, poverty and meanness contempt, though particular views and incidents may sometimes raise the passions of envy and of pity.

not measure out degrees of esteem according to the rent-rolls of his acquaintance. He may, indeed, externally pay a superior deference to the great lord above the vassal; because riches are the most convenient, being the most fixed and determinate, source of distinction: But his internal sentiments are more regulated by the personal characters of men, than by the accidental and capricious favours of fortune.

In most countries of EUROPE, family, that is, hereditary riches, marked with titles and symbols from the sovereign, is the chief source of distinction. In ENGLAND, more regard is paid to present opulence and plenty. Each practice has its advantages and disadvantages. Where birth is respected, unactive, spiritless minds remain in haughty indolence, and dream of nothing but pedigrees and genealogies: The generous and ambitious seek honour and authority and reputation and favour. Where riches are the chief idol, corruption, venality, rapine prevail: Arts, manufactures, commerce, agriculture flourish. The former prejudice, being favourable to military virtue, is more suited to monarchies. The latter, being the chief spur to industry, agrees better with a republican government. And we accordingly find, that each of these forms of government, by varying the *utility* of those customs, has commonly a proportionable effect on the sentiments of mankind.

. . .

Sect. IX.—Conclusion.

Part I.

It may justly appear surprising, that any man, in so late an age, should find it requisite to prove, by elaborate reasoning, that PERSONAL MERIT consists altogether in the possession of mental qualities, *useful* or *agreeable* to the *person himself* or to *others*. It might be expected, that this principle would have occurred even to the first rude, unpractised enquirers concerning morals, and been received from its own evidence, without any argument or disputation. Whatever is valuable in any kind, so naturally classes itself under the division of *useful* or *agreeable,* the *utile* or the *dulce,* that it is not easy to imagine, why we should ever seek farther, or consider the question as a matter of nice research or enquiry. And as every

thing useful or agreeable must possess these qualities with regard either to the *person himself* or to *others,* the compleat delineation or description of merit seems to be performed as naturally as a shadow is cast by the sun, or an image is reflected upon water. If the ground, on which the shadow is cast, be not broken and uneven; nor the surface, from which the image is reflected, disturbed and confused; a just figure is immediately presented, without any art or attention. And it seems a reasonable presumption, that systems and hypotheses have perverted our natural understanding; when a theory, so simple and obvious, could so long have escaped the most elaborate examination.

But however the case may have fared with philosophy; in common life, these principles are still implicitly maintained, nor is any other topic of praise or blame ever recurred to, when we employ any panegyric or satire, any applause or censure of human action and behaviour. If we observe men, in every intercourse of business or pleasure, in every discourse and conversation; we shall find them no where, except in the schools, at any loss upon this subject. What so natural, for instance, as the following dialogue? You are very happy, we shall suppose one to say, addressing himself to another, that you have given your daughter to CLEANTHES. He is a man of honour and humanity. Every one, who has any intercourse with him, is sure of *fair* and *kind* treatment.[1] I congratulate you too, says another on the promising expectations of this son-in-law; whose assiduous application to the study of the laws, whose quick penetration and early knowledge both of men and business, prognosticate the greatest honours and advancement.[2] You surprise me, replies a third, when you talk of CLEANTHES as a man of business and application. I met him lately in a circle of the gayest company, and he was the very life and soul of our conversation: So much wit with good manners; so much gallantry without affectation; so much ingenious knowledge so genteelly delivered, I have never before observed in any one.[3] You would admire him still more, says a fourth, if you knew him more familiarly. That chearfulness, which you might remark in

_____

1. Qualities useful to others.

2. Qualities useful to the person himself. Section VI.

3. Qualities immediately agreeable to others. . . .

him, is not a sudden flash struck out by company: It runs through the whole tenor of his life, and preserves a perpetual serenity on his countenance, and tranquillity in his soul. He has met with severe trials, misfortunes as well as dangers; and by his greatness of mind, was still superior to all of them.[1] The image, gentlemen, which you have here delineated of CLEANTHES, cry'd I, is that of accomplished merit. Each of you has given a stroke of the pencil to his figure; and you have unawares exceeded all the pictures drawn by GRATIAN or CASTIGLIONE. A philosopher might select this character as a model of perfect virtue.

And as every quality, which is useful or agreeable to ourselves or others, is, in common life, allowed to be a part of personal merit; so no other will ever be received, where men judge of things by their natural, unprejudiced reason, without the delusive glosses of superstition and false religion. Celibacy, fasting, penance, mortification, self-denial, humility, silence, solitude, and the whole train of monkish virtues; for what reason are they every where rejected by men of sense, but because they serve to no manner of purpose; neither advance a man's fortune in the world, nor render him a more valuable member of society; neither qualify him for the entertainment of company, nor increase his power of self-enjoyment? We observe, on the contrary, that they cross all these desirable ends; stupify the understanding and harden the heart, obscure the fancy and sour the temper. We justly, therefore, transfer them to the opposite column, and place them in the catalogue of vices; nor has any superstition force sufficient among men of the world, to pervert entirely these natural sentiments. A gloomy, harebrained enthusiast, after his death, may have a place in the calendar; but will scarcely ever be admitted, when alive, into intimacy and society, except by those who are as delirious and dismal as himself.

It seems a happiness in the present theory, that it enters not into that vulgar dispute concerning the *degrees* of benevolence or self-love, which prevail in human nature; a dispute which is never likely to have any issue, both because men, who have taken part, are not easily convinced, and because the phænomena, which can be produced on either side, are so dispersed, so uncertain, and subject to so many interpretations, that it is scarcely possible accurately to compare them, or draw from them any determinate inference or conclusion. It is sufficient for our present purpose, if it be allowed, what surely, without the greatest absurdity, cannot be disputed, that there is some benevolence, however small, infused into our bosom; some spark of friendship for human kind; some particle of the dove, kneaded into our frame, along with the elements of the wolf and serpent. Let these generous sentiments be supposed ever so weak; let them be insufficient to move even a hand or finger of our body; they must still direct the determinations of our mind, and where every thing else is equal, produce a cool preference of what is useful and serviceable to mankind, above what is pernicious and dangerous. A *moral distinction*, therefore, immediately arises; a general sentiment of blame and approbation; a tendency, however faint, to the objects of the one, and a proportionable aversion to those of the other. Nor will those reasoners, who so earnestly maintain the predominant selfishness of human kind, be any wise scandalized at hearing of the weak sentiments of virtue, implanted in our nature. On the contrary, they are found as ready to maintain the one tenet as the other; and their spirit of satire (for such it appears, rather than of corruption) naturally gives rise to both opinions; which have, indeed, a great and almost an indissoluble connexion together.

Avarice, ambition, vanity, and all passions vulgarly, though improperly, comprized under the denomination of *self-love,* are here excluded from our theory concerning the origin of morals, not because they are too weak, but because they have not a proper direction, for that purpose. The notion of morals, implies some sentiment common to all mankind, which recommends the same object to general approbation, and makes every man, or most men, agree in the same opinion or decision concerning it. It also implies some sentiment, so universal and comprehensive as to extend to all mankind, and render the actions and conduct, even of the persons the most remote, an object of applause or censure, according as they agree or disagree with that rule of right which is established. These two requisite circumstances belong alone to the sentiment of humanity here insisted on. The other passions produce, in every breast, many strong sentiments of desire and aversion, affection and hatred; but these neither are felt so much in common, nor are so comprehensive,

---

1. Qualities immediately agreeable to the person himself. . . .

as to be the foundation of any general system and established theory of blame or approbation.

When a man denominates another his *enemy*, his *rival*, his *antagonist*, his *adversary*, he is understood to speak the language of self-love, and to express sentiments, peculiar to himself, and arising from his particular circumstances and situation. But when he bestows on any man the epithets of *vicious* or *odious* or *depraved*, he then speaks another language, and expresses sentiments, in which, he expects, all his audience are to concur with him. He must here, therefore, depart from his private and particular situation, and must chuse a point of view, common to him with others: He must move some universal principle of the human frame, and touch a string, to which all mankind have an accord and symphony. If he mean, therefore, to express, that this man possesses qualities, whose tendency is pernicious to society, he has chosen this common point of view, and has touched the principle of humanity, in which every man, in some degree, concurs. While the human heart is compounded of the same elements as at present, it will never be wholly indifferent to public good, nor entirely unaffected with the tendency of characters and manners. And though this affection of humanity may not generally be esteemed so strong as vanity or ambition, yet, being common to all men, it can alone be the foundation of morals, or of any general system of blame or praise. One man's ambition is not another's ambition; nor will the same event or object satisfy both: But the humanity of one man is the humanity of every one; and the same object touches this passion in all human creatures.

But the sentiments, which arise from humanity, are not only the same in all human creatures, and produce the same approbation or censure; but they also comprehend all human creatures; nor is there any one whose conduct or character is not, by their means, an object, to every one, of censure or approbation. On the contrary, those other passions, commonly denominated selfish, both produce different sentiments in each individual, according to his particular situation; and also contemplate the greater part of mankind with the utmost indifference and unconcern. Whoever has a high regard and esteem for me flatters my vanity; whoever expresses contempt mortifies and displeases me: But as my name is known but to a small part of mankind, there are few, who come within the sphere of this passion, or

excite, on its account, either my affection or disgust. But if you represent a tyrannical, insolent, or barbarous behaviour, in any country or in any age of the world; I soon carry my eye to the pernicious tendency of such a conduct, and feel the sentiment of repugnance and displeasure towards it. No character can be so remote as to be, in this light, wholly indifferent to me. What is beneficial to society or to the person himself must still be preferred. And every quality or action, of every human being, must, by this means, be ranked under some class or denomination, expressive of general censure or applause.

What more, therefore, can we ask to distinguish the sentiments, dependent on humanity, from those connected with any other passion, or to satisfy us, why the former are the origin of morals, not the latter? Whatever conduct gains my approbation, by touching my humanity, procures also the applause of all mankind, by affecting the same principle in them: But what serves my avarice or ambition pleases these passions in me alone, and affects not the avarice and ambition of the rest of mankind. There is no circumstance of conduct in any man, provided it have a beneficial tendency, that is not agreeable to my humanity, however remote the person: But every man, so far removed as neither to cross nor serve my avarice and ambition, is regarded as wholly indifferent by those passions. The distinction, therefore, between these species of sentiment being so great and evident, language must soon be moulded upon it, and must invent a peculiar set of terms, in order to express those universal sentiments of censure or approbation, which arise from humanity, or from views of general usefulness and its contrary. VIRTUE and VICE become then known: Morals are recognized: Certain general ideas are framed of human conduct and behaviour: Such measures are expected from men, in such situations: This action is determined to be conformable to our abstract rule; that other, contrary. And by such universal principles are the particular sentiments of self-love frequently controuled and limited.[1]

From instances of popular tumults, seditions, factions, panics, and of all passions, which are shared

---

1. It seems certain, both from reason and experience, that a rude, untaught savage regulates chiefly his love and hatred by the ideas of private utility and injury, and has but faint conceptions of a general rule or system of behaviour. The man who stands opposite to him in battle, he hates heartily, not only for the present moment,

with a multitude; we may learn the influence of society, in exciting and supporting any emotion; while
the most ungovernable disorders are raised, we find,
by that means, from the slightest and most frivolous
occasions. SOLON was not very cruel, though perhaps, an unjust legislator, who punished neuters in
civil wars; and few, I believe, would, in such cases,
incur the penalty, were their affection and discourse
allowed sufficient to absolve them. No selfishness,
and scarce any philosophy, have their force sufficient
to support a total coolness and indifference; and he
must be more or less than man, who kindles not in
the common blaze. What wonder, then, that moral
sentiments are found of such influence in life;
though springing from principles, which may appear, at first sight, somewhat small and delicate? But
these principles, we must remark, are social and universal: They form, in a manner, the *party* of humankind against vice or disorder, its common enemy:
And as the benevolent concern for others is diffused,
in a greater or less degree, over all men, and is the
same in all, it occurs more frequently in discourse, is
cherished by society and conversation, and the
blame and approbation, consequent on it, are
thereby rouzed from that lethargy, into which they
are probably lulled, in solitary and uncultivated nature. Other passions, though perhaps originally
stronger, yet being selfish and private, are often overpowered by its force, and yield the dominion of our
breast to those social and public principles.

   Another spring of our constitution, that brings a
great addition of force to moral sentiment, is, the
love of fame; which rules, with such uncontrolled

authority, in all generous minds, and is often the
grand object of all their designs and undertakings.
By our continual and earnest pursuit of a character,
a name, a reputation in the world, we bring our own
deportment and conduct frequently in review, and
consider how they appear in the eyes of those who
approach and regard us. This constant habit of surveying ourselves, as it were, in reflection, keeps alive
all the sentiments of right and wrong, and begets, in
noble natures, a certain reverence for themselves as
well as others; which is the surest guardian of every
virtue. The animal conveniencies and pleasures sink
gradually in their value; while every inward beauty
and moral grace is studiously acquired, and the
mind is accomplished in every perfection, which can
adorn or embellish a rational creature.

   Here is the most perfect morality with which we
are acquainted: Here is displayed the force of many
sympathies. Our moral sentiment is itself a feeling
chiefly of that nature: And our regard to a character
with others seems to arise only from a care of preserving a character with ourselves; and in order to attain this end, we find it necessary to prop our
tottering judgment on the correspondent approbation of mankind.

   But, that we may accommodate matters, and remove, if possible, every difficulty, let us allow all
these reasonings to be false. Let us allow, that, when
we resolve the pleasure, which arises from views of
utility, into the sentiments of humanity and sympathy, we have embraced a wrong hypothesis. Let us
confess it necessary to find some other explication of
that applause, which is paid to objects, whether
inanimate, animate, or rational, if they have a tendency to promote the welfare and advantage of
mankind. However difficult it be to conceive, that an
object is approved of on account of its tendency to a
certain end, while the end itself is totally indifferent;
let us swallow this absurdity, and consider what are
the consequences. The preceding delineation or definition of PERSONAL MERIT must still retain its evidence and authority: It must still be allowed, that
every quality of the mind, which is *useful* or *agreeable*
to the *person himself* or to *others,* communicates a
pleasure to the spectator, engages his esteem, and is
admitted under the honourable denomination of
virtue or merit. Are not justice, fidelity, honour, veracity, allegiance, chastity, esteemed solely on account of their tendency to promote the good of

---

which is almost unavoidable, but for ever after; nor is he satisfied
without the most extreme punishment and vengeance. But we, accustomed to society, and to more enlarged reflections, consider,
that this man is serving his own country and community; that any
man, in the same situation, would do the same; that we ourselves,
in like circumstances, observe a like conduct; that, in general,
human society is best supported on such maxims: And by these
suppositions and views, we correct, in some measure, our ruder
and narrower passions. And though much of our friendship and
enmity be still regulated by private considerations of benefit and
harm, we pay, at least, this homage to general rules, which we are
accustomed to respect, that we commonly pervert our adversary's
conduct, by imputing malice or injustice to him, in order to give
vent to those passions, which arise from self-love and private interest. When the heart is full of rage, it never wants pretences of
this nature; though sometimes as frivolous, as those from which
HORACE, being almost crushed by the fall of a tree, affects to accuse of parricide the first planter of it.

society? Is not that tendency inseparable from humanity, benevolence, lenity, generosity, gratitude, moderation, tenderness, friendship, and all the other social virtues? Can it possibly be doubted, that industry, discretion, frugality, secrecy, order, perseverance, forethought, judgment, and this whole class of virtues and accomplishments, of which many pages would not contain the catalogue; can it be doubted, I say, that the tendency of these qualities to promote the interest and happiness of their possessor, is the sole foundation of their merit? Who can dispute that a mind, which supports a perpetual serenity and chearfulness, a noble dignity and undaunted spirit, a tender affection and goodwill to all around; as it has more enjoyment within itself, is also a more animating and rejoicing spectacle, than if dejected with melancholy, tormented with anxiety, irritated with rage, or sunk into the most abject baseness and degeneracy? And as to the qualities, immediately *agreeable to others,* they speak sufficiently for themselves; and he must be unhappy, indeed, either in his own temper, or in his situation and company, who has never perceived the charms of a facetious wit or flowing affability, of a delicate modesty or decent genteelness of address and manner.

I am sensible, that nothing can be more unphilosophical than to be positive or dogmatical on any subject; and that, even if *excessive* scepticism could be maintained, it would not be more destructive to all just reasoning and enquiry. I am convinced, that, where men are the most sure and arrogant, they are commonly the most mistaken, and have there given reins to passion, without that proper deliberation and suspence, which can alone secure them from the grossest absurdities. Yet, I must confess, that this enumeration puts the matter in so strong a light, that I cannot, *at present,* be more assured of any truth, which I learn from reasoning and argument, than that personal merit consists entirely in the usefulness or agreeableness of qualities to the person himself possessed of them, or to others, who have any intercourse with him. But when. I reflect, that, though the bulk and figure of the earth have been measured and delineated, though the motions of the tides have been accounted for, the order and œconomy of the heavenly bodies subjected to their proper laws, and INFINITE itself reduced to calculation; yet men still dispute concerning the foundation of their moral duties: When I reflect on this, I say, I fall back into diffidence and scepticism, and suspect, that an hypothesis, so obvious, had it been a true one, would, long ere now, have been received by the unanimous suffrage and consent of mankind.

Part II.

Having expressed the moral *approbation* attending merit or virtue, there remains nothing, but briefly to consider our interested *obligation* to it, and to enquire, whether every man, who has any regard to his own happiness and welfare, will not best find his account in the practice of every moral duty. If this can be clearly ascertained from the foregoing theory, we shall have the satisfaction to reflect, that we have advanced principles, which not only, it is hoped, will stand the test of reasoning and enquiry, but may contribute to the amendment of men's lives, and their improvement in morality and social virtue. And though the philosophical truth of any proposition by no means depends on its tendency to promote the interests of society; yet a man has but a bad grace, who delivers a theory, however true, which, he must confess, leads to a practice dangerous and pernicious. Why rake into those corners of nature, which spread a nuisance all around? Why dig up the pestilence from the pit, in which it is buried? The ingenuity of your researches may be admired; but your systems will be detested: And mankind will agree, if they cannot refute them, to sink them, at least, in eternal silence and oblivion. Truths, which are *pernicious* to society, if any such there be, will yield to errors, which are salutary and *advantageous.*

But what philosophical truths can be more advantageous to society, than those here delivered, which represent virtue in all her genuine and most engaging charms, and make us approach her with ease, familiarity, and affection? The dismal dress falls off, with which many divines, and some philosophers have covered her; and nothing appears but gentleness, humanity, beneficence, affability; nay even, at proper intervals, play, frolic, and gaiety. She talks not of useless austerities and rigours, suffering and self-denial. She declares, that her sole purpose is, to make her votaries and all mankind, during every instant of their existence, if possible, cheerful and happy; nor does she ever willingly part with any pleasure but in hopes of ample compensation in some other period of their lives. The sole trouble, which she demands, is that of just calculation, and a steady preference of the greater happiness. And if any austere pretenders approach her, enemies to joy and pleasure, she either rejects them as hypocrites and deceivers; or if she admit them in her train, they are ranked however, among the least favoured of her votaries.

And, indeed, to drop all figurative expression, what hopes can we ever have of engaging mankind to a practice, which we confess full of austerity and rigour? Or what theory of morals can ever serve any useful purpose, unless it can show, by a particular detail, that all the duties, which it recommends, are also the true interest of each individual? The peculiar advantage of the foregoing system seems to be, that it furnishes proper mediums for that purpose.

That the virtues which are immediately *useful* or *agreeable* to the person possessed of them, are desirable in a view to self-interest, it would surely be superfluous to prove. Moralists, indeed, may spare themselves all the pains, which they often take in recommending these duties. To what purpose collect arguments to evince, that temperance is advantageous, and the excesses of pleasure hurtful? When it appears, that these excesses are only denominated such, because they are hurtful; and that, if unlimited use of strong liquors, for instance, no more impaired health or the faculties of mind and body than the use of air or water, it would not be a whit more vicious or blameable.

It seems equally superfluous to prove, that the *companionable* virtues of good manners and wit, decency and genteelness, are more desirable than the contrary qualities. Vanity alone, without any other consideration, is a sufficient motive to make us wish for the possession of these accomplishments. No man was ever willingly deficient in this particular. All our failures here proceed from bad education, want of capacity, or a perverse and unpliable disposition. Would you have your company coveted, admired, followed; rather than hated, despised, avoided? Can any one seriously deliberate in the case? As no enjoyment is sincere, without some reference to company and society; so no society can be agreeable, or even tolerable, where a man feels his presence unwelcome, and discovers all around him symptoms of disgust and aversion.

But why, in the greater society or confederacy of mankind, should not the case be the same as in particular clubs and companies? Why is it more doubtful, that the enlarged virtues of humanity, generosity, beneficence, are desirable with a view to happiness and self-interest, than the limited endowments of ingenuity and politeness? Are we apprehensive, lest those social affections interfere, in a greater and more immediate degree than any other pursuits, with private utility, and cannot be gratified, without some important sacrifice of honour and advantage? If so, we are but ill instructed in the nature of the human passions, and are more influenced by verbal distinctions than by real differences.

Whatever contradiction may vulgarly be supposed between the *selfish* and *social* sentiments or dispositions, they are really no more opposite than selfish and ambitious, selfish and revengeful, selfish and vain. It is requisite, that there be an original propensity of some kind, in order to be a basis to self-love, by giving a relish to the objects of its pursuit; and none more fit for this purpose than benevolence or humanity. The goods of fortune are spent in one gratification or another: The miser, who accumulates his annual income, and lends it out at interest, has really spent it in the gratification of his avarice. And it would be difficult to show, why a man is more a loser by a generous action, than by any other method of expence; since the utmost which he can attain, by the most elaborate selfishness, is the indulgence of some affection.

Now if life, without passion, must be altogether insipid and tiresome; let a man suppose that he has full power of modelling his own disposition, and let him deliberate what appetite or desire he would choose for the foundation of his happiness and enjoyment. Every affection, he would observe, when gratified by success, gives a satisfaction proportioned to its force and violence: but besides this advantage, common to all, the immediate feeling of benevolence and friendship, humanity and kindness, is sweet, smooth, tender, and agreeable, independent of all fortune and accidents. These virtues are besides attended with a pleasing consciousness or remembrance, and keep us in humour with ourselves as well as others; while we retain the agreeable reflection of having done our part towards mankind and society. And though all men show a jealousy of our success in the pursuits of avarice and ambition; yet are we almost sure of their good-will and good-wishes, so long as we persevere in the paths of virtue, and employ ourselves in the execution of generous plans and purposes. What other passion is there where we shall find so many advantages united; an agreeable sentiment, a pleasing consciousness, a good reputation? But of these truths, we may observe, men are, of themselves, pretty much convinced; nor are they deficient in their duty to society, because they would not wish to be generous, friendly, and humane; but because they do not feel themselves such.

Treating vice with the greatest candour, and making it all possible concessions, we must acknowledge, that there is not, in any instance, the smallest pretext for giving it the preference above virtue, with a view to self-interest; except, perhaps, in the case of justice, where a man, taking things in a certain light, may often seem to be a loser by his integrity. And though it is allowed, that, without a regard to property, no society could subsist; yet, according to the imperfect way in which human affairs are conducted, a sensible knave, in particular incidents, may think, that an act of iniquity or infidelity will make a considerable addition to his fortune, without causing any considerable breach in the social union and confederacy. That *honesty is the best policy,* may be a good general rule; but is liable to many exceptions: And he, it may, perhaps, be thought, conducts himself with most wisdom, who observes the general rule, and takes advantage of all the exceptions.

I must confess, that, if a man think, that this reasoning much requires an answer, it will be a little difficult to find any, which will to him appear satisfactory and convincing. If his heart rebel not against such pernicious maxims, if he feel no reluctance to the thoughts of villany or baseness, he has indeed lost a considerable motive to virtue; and we may expect, that his practice will be answerable to his speculation. But in all ingenuous natures, the antipathy to treachery and roguery is too strong to be counterbalanced by any views of profit or pecuniary advantage. Inward peace of mind, consciousness of integrity, a satisfactory review of our own conduct; these are circumstances very requisite to happiness, and will be cherished and cultivated by every honest man, who feels the importance of them.

Such a one has, besides, the frequent satisfaction of seeing knaves, with all their pretended cunning and abilities, betrayed by their own maxims; and while they purpose to cheat with moderation and secrecy, a tempting incident occurs, nature is frail, and they give into the snare; whence they can never extricate themselves, without a total loss of reputation, and the forfeiture of all future trust and confidence with mankind.

But were they ever so secret and successful, the honest man, if he has any tincture of philosophy, or even common observation and reflection, will discover that they themselves are, in the end, the greatest dupes, and have sacrificed the invaluable enjoyment of a character, with themselves at least, for the acquisition of worthless toys and gewgaws. How little is requisite to supply the *necessities* of nature? And in a view to *pleasure,* what comparison between the unbought satisfaction of conversation, society, study, even health and the common beauties of nature, but above all the peaceful reflection on one's own conduct: What comparison, I say, between these, and the feverish, empty amusements of luxury and expence? These natural pleasures, indeed, are really without price; both because they are below all price in their attainment, and above it in their enjoyment.

Appendix I.—Concerning Moral Sentiment.

If the foregoing hypothesis be received, it will now be easy for us to determine the question first started,[1] concerning the general principles of morals; and though we postponed the decision of that question, lest it should then involve us in intricate speculations, which are unfit for moral discourses, we may resume it at present, and examine how far either *reason* or *sentiment* enters into all decisions of praise or censure.

One principal foundation of moral praise being supposed to lie in the usefulness of any quality or action; it is evident, that *reason* must enter for a considerable share in all decisions of this kind; since nothing but that faculty can instruct us in the tendency of qualities and actions, and point out their beneficial consequences to society and to their possessor. In many cases, this is an affair liable to great controversy: Doubts may arise; opposite interests may occur; and a preference must be given to one side, from very nice views, and a small overbalance

---

1. Sect. I. Of the General Principles of Morals.

of utility. This is particularly remarkable in questions with regard to justice; as is, indeed, natural to suppose, from that species of utility, which attends this virtue.[1] Were every single instance of justice, like that of benevolence, useful to society; this would be a more simple state of the case, and seldom liable to great controversy. But as single instances of justice are often pernicious in their first and immediate tendency, and as the advantage to society results only from the observance of the general rule, and from the concurrence and combination of several persons in the same equitable conduct; the case here becomes more intricate and involved. The various circumstances of society; the various consequences of any practice; the various interests, which may be proposed: These, on many occasions, are doubtful, and subject to great discussion and enquiry. The object of municipal laws is to fix all the questions with regard to justice: The debates of civilians; the reflections of politicians; the precedents of history and public records, are all directed to the same purpose. And a very accurate *reason* or *judgment* is often requisite, to give the true determination, amidst such intricate doubts arising from obscure or opposite utilities.

But though reason, when fully assisted and improved, be sufficient to instruct us in the pernicious or useful tendency of qualities and actions; it is not alone sufficient to produce any moral blame or approbation. Utility is only a tendency to a certain end; and were the end totally indifferent to us, we should feel the same indifference towards the means. It is requisite a *sentiment* should here display itself, in order to give a preference to the useful above the pernicious tendencies. This sentiment can be no other than a feeling for the happiness of mankind, and a resentment of their misery; since these are the different ends which virtue and vice have a tendency to promote. Here, therefore, *reason* instructs us in the several tendencies of actions, and *humanity* makes a distinction in favour to those which are useful and beneficial.

This partition between the faculties of understanding and sentiment, in all moral decisions, seems clear from the preceding hypothesis. But I shall suppose that hypothesis false: It will then be requisite to look out for some other theory, that may be satisfactory; and I dare venture to affirm, that none such will ever be found, so long as we suppose reason to be the sole source of morals. To prove this, it will be proper to weigh the five following considerations.

I. It is easy for a false hypothesis to maintain some appearance of truth, while it keeps wholly in generals, makes use of undefined terms, and employs comparisons, instead of instances. This is particularly remarkable in that philosophy, which ascribes the discernment of all moral distinctions to reason alone, without the concurrence of sentiment. It is impossible that, in any particular instance, this hypothesis can so much as be rendered intelligible; whatever specious figure it may make in general declamations and discourses. Examine the crime of *ingratitude,* for instance; which has place, wherever we observe good-will, expressed and known, together with good-offices performed, on the one side, and a return of ill-will or indifference, with ill-offices or neglect on the other: Anatomize all these circumstances, and examine, by your reason alone, in what consists the demerit or blame: You never will come to any issue or conclusion.

Reason judges either of *matter of fact* or of *relations.* Enquire then, *first,* where is that matter of fact, which we here call *crime;* point it out; determine the time of its existence; describe its essence or nature; explain the sense or faculty, to which it discovers itself. It resides in the mind of the person, who is ungrateful. He must, therefore, feel it, and be conscious of it. But nothing is there, except the passion of ill-will or absolute indifference. You cannot say, that these, of themselves, always, and in all circumstances, are crimes. No: They are only crimes, when directed towards persons, who have before expressed and displayed good-will towards us. Consequently, we may infer, that the crime of ingratitude is not any particular individual *fact;* but arises from a complication of circumstances, which, being presented to the spectator, excites the *sentiment* of blame, by the particular structure and fabric of his mind.

This representation, you say, is false. Crime, indeed, consists not in a particular *fact,* of whose reality we are assured by *reason:* But it consists in certain *moral relations,* discovered by reason, in the same manner as we discover, by reason, the truths of

---

1. See Appendix III. Some farther Considerations with regard to Justice.

geometry or algebra. But what are the relations, I ask, of which you here talk? In the case stated above, I see first good-will and good-offices in one person; then ill-will and ill-offices in the other. Between these, there is the relation of *contrariety*. Does the crime consist in that relation? But suppose a person bore me ill-will or did me ill-offices; and I, in return, were indifferent towards him, or did him good-offices: Here is the same relation of *contrariety;* and yet my conduct is often highly laudable. Twist and turn this matter as much as you will, you can never rest the morality on relation; but must have recourse to the decisions of sentiment.

When it is affirmed, that two and three are equal to the half of ten; this relation of equality, I understand perfectly. I conceive, that if ten be divided into two parts, of which one has as many units as the other; and if any of these parts be compared to two added to three, it will contain as many units as that compound number. But when you draw thence a comparison to moral relations, I own that I am altogether at a loss to understand you. A moral action, a crime, such as ingratitude, is a complicated object. Does morality consist in the relation of its parts to each other? How? After what manner? Specify the relation: Be more particular and explicit in your propositions; and you will easily see their falsehood.

No, say you, the morality consists in the relation of actions to the rule of right; and they are denominated good or ill, according as they agree or disagree with it. What then is this rule of right? In what does it consist? How is it determined? By reason, you say, which examines the moral relations of actions. So that moral relations are determined by the comparison of actions to a rule. And that rule is determined by considering the moral relations of objects. Is not this fine reasoning?

All this is metaphysics, you cry: That is enough: There needs nothing more to give a strong presumption of falsehood. Yes, reply I: Here are metaphysics surely: But they are all on your side, who advance an abstruse hypothesis, which can never be made intelligible, nor quadrate with any particular instance or illustration. The hypothesis which we embrace is plain. It maintains, that morality is determined by sentiment. It defines virtue to be *whatever mental action or quality gives to a spectator the pleasing sentiment of approbation;* and vice the contrary. We then pro-

ceed to examine a plain matter of fact, to wit, what actions have this influence: We consider all the circumstances, in which these actions agree: And thence endeavour to extract some general observations with regard to these sentiments. If you call this metaphysics, and find any thing abstruse here, you need only conclude, that your turn of mind is not suited to the moral sciences.

II. When a man, at any time, deliberates concerning his own conduct (as, whether he had better, in a particular emergence, assist a brother or a benefactor), he must consider these separate relations, with all the circumstances and situations of the persons, in order to determine the superior duty and obligation: And in order to determine the proportion of lines in any triangle, it is necessary to examine the nature of that figure, and the relations which its several parts bear to each other. But notwithstanding this appearing similarity in the two cases, there is, at bottom, an extreme difference between them. A speculative reasoner concerning triangles or circles considers the several known and given relations of the parts of these figures; and thence infers some unknown relation, which is dependent on the former. But in moral deliberations, we must be acquainted, before-hand, with all the objects, and all their relations to each other; and from a comparison of the whole, fix our choice or approbation. No new fact to be ascertained: No new relation to be discovered. All the circumstances of the case are supposed to be laid before us, ere we can fix any sentence of blame or approbation. If any material circumstance be yet unknown or doubtful, we must first employ our enquiry or intellectual faculties to assure us of it; and must suspend for a time all moral decision or sentiment. While we are ignorant, whether a man were aggressor or not, how can we determine whether the person who killed him, be criminal or innocent? But after every circumstance, every relation is known, the understanding has no farther room to operate, nor any object on which it could employ itself. The approbation or blame, which then ensues, cannot be the work of the judgment, but of the heart; and is not a speculative proposition or affirmation, but an active feeling or sentiment. In the disquisitions of the understanding, from known circumstances and relations, we infer some new and unknown. In moral decisions, all the circumstances and relations must be previously known; and the mind, from the contemplation of the whole, feels some new impression of affection or disgust, esteem or contempt, approbation or blame.

Hence the great difference between a mistake of *fact* and one of *right;* and hence the reason why the one is commonly criminal and not the other. When OEDIPUS killed LAIUS, he was ignorant of the relation, and from circumstances, innocent and involuntary, formed erroneous opinions concerning the action which he committed. But when Nero killed AGRIPPINA, all the relations between himself and the person, and all the circumstances of the fact, were previously known to him: But the motive of revenge, or fear, or interest, prevailed in his savage heart over the sentiments of duty and humanity. And when we express that detestation against him, to which he, himself, in a little time, became insensible; it is not, that we see any relations, of which he was ignorant; but that, from the rectitude of our disposition, we feel sentiments, against which he was hardened, from flattery and a long perseverance in the most enormous crimes. In these sentiments, then, not in a discovery of relations of any kind, do all moral determinations consist. Before we can pretend to form any decision of this kind, every thing must be known and ascertained on the side of the object or action. Nothing remains but to feel, on our part, some sentiment of blame or approbation; whence we pronounce the action criminal or virtuous.

III. This doctrine will become still more evident, if we compare moral beauty with natural, to which, in many particulars, it bears so near a resemblance. It is on the proportion, relation, and position of parts, that all natural beauty depends; but it would be absurd thence to infer, that the perception of beauty, like that of truth in geometrical problems, consists wholly in the perception of relations, and was performed entirely by the understanding or intellectual faculties. In all the sciences, our mind, from the known relations, investigates the unknown: But in all decisions of taste or external beauty, all the relations are before-hand obvious to the eye; and we thence proceed to feel a sentiment of complacency or disgust, according to the nature of the object, and disposition of our organs.

EUCLID has fully explained all the qualities of the circle; but has not, in any proposition, said a word of its beauty. The reason is evident. The beauty is not a quality of the circle. It lies not in any part of the line, whose parts are equally distant from a common center. It is only the effect, which that figure produces upon the mind, whose peculiar fabric or structure renders it susceptible of such sentiments. In vain would you look for it in the circle, or seek it, either by your senses or by mathematical reasonings, in all the properties of that figure.

Attend to PALLADIO and PERRAULT, while they explain all the parts and proportions of a pillar: They talk of the cornice and frieze and base and entablature and shaft and architrave; and give the description and position of each of these members. But should you ask the description and position of its beauty, they would readily reply, that the beauty is not in any of the parts or members of a pillar, but results from the whole, when that complicated figure is presented to an intelligent mind, susceptible to those finer sensations. 'Till such a spectator appear, there is nothing but a figure of such particular dimensions and proportions: From his sentiments alone arise its elegance and beauty.

Again; attend to CICERO, while he paints the crimes of a VERRES or a CATILINE; you must acknowledge that the moral turpitude results, in the same manner, from the contemplation of the whole, when presented to a being, whose organs have such a particular structure and formation. The orator may paint rage, insolence, barbarity on the one side: Meekness, suffering, sorrow, innocence on the other: But if you feel no indignation or compassion arise in you from this complication of circumstances, you would in vain ask him, in what consists the crime or villany, which he so vehemently exclaims against: At what time, or on what subject it first began to exist: And what has a few months afterwards become of it, when every disposition and thought of all the actors is totally altered, or annihilated. No satisfactory answer can be given to any of these questions, upon the abstract hypothesis of morals; and we must at last acknowledge, that the crime of immorality is no particular fact or relation, which can be the object of the understanding: But arises entirely from the sentiment of disapprobation, which, by the structure of human nature, we unavoidably feel on the apprehension of barbarity or treachery.

IV. Inanimate objects may bear to each other all the same relations, which we observe in moral agents; though the former can never be the object of love or hatred, nor are consequently susceptible of merit or iniquity. A young tree, which over-tops and destroys its parent, stands in all the same relations with NERO, when he murdered AGRIPPINA; and if morality consisted merely in relations, would, no doubt, be equally criminal.

V. It appears evident, that the ultimate ends of human actions can never, in any case, be accounted for by *reason*, but recommend themselves entirely to the sentiments and affections of mankind, without any dependance on the intellectual faculties. Ask a man, *why he uses exercise;* he will answer, *because he desires to keep his health.* If you then enquire, *why he desires health,* he will readily reply, *because sickness is painful.* If you push your enquiries farther, and desire a reason, *why he hates pain,* it is impossible he can ever give any. This is an ultimate end, and is never referred to any other object.

Perhaps, to your second question, *why he desires health,* he may also reply, that *it is necessary for the exercise of his calling.* If you ask, *why he is anxious on that head,* he will answer, *because he desires to get money.* If you demand *Why? It is the instrument of pleasure,* says he. And beyond this it is an absurdity to ask for a reason. It is impossible there can be a progress *in infinitum;* and that one thing can always be a reason, why another is desired. Something must be desirable on its own account, and because of its immediate accord or agreement with human sentiment and affection.

Now as virtue is an end, and is desirable on its own account, without fee or reward, merely, for the immediate satisfaction which it conveys; it is requisite that there should be some sentiment, which it touches; some internal taste or feeling, or whatever you please to call it, which distinguishes moral good and evil, and which embraces the one and rejects the other.

Thus the distinct boundaries and offices of *reason* and of *taste* are easily ascertained. The former conveys the knowledge of truth and falsehood: The latter gives the sentiment of beauty and deformity, vice and virtue. The one discovers objects, as they really stand in nature, without addition or diminution: The other has a productive faculty, and gilding or staining all natural objects with the colours, borrowed from internal sentiment, raises, in a manner, a new creation. Reason, being cool and disengaged, is no motive to action, and directs only the impulse re-

ceived from appetite or inclination, by showing us the means of attaining happiness or avoiding misery: Taste, as it gives pleasure or pain, and thereby constitutes happiness or misery, becomes a motive to action, and is the first spring or impulse to desire and volition. From circumstances and relations, known or supposed, the former leads us to the discovery of the concealed and unknown: After all circumstances and relations are laid before us, the latter makes us feel from the whole a new sentiment of blame or approbation. The standard of the one, being founded on the nature of things, is eternal and inflexible, even by the will of the Supreme Being: The standard of the other, arising from the internal frame and constitution of animals, is ultimately derived from that Supreme Will, which bestowed on each being its peculiar nature, and arranged the several classes and orders of existence.

Appendix II.—Of Self-love.

There is a principle, supposed to prevail among many, which is utterly incompatible with all virtue or moral sentiment; and as it can proceed from nothing but the most depraved disposition, so in its turn it tends still further to encourage that depravity. This principle is, that all *benevolence* is mere hypocrisy, friendship a cheat, public spirit a farce, fidelity a snare to procure trust and confidence; and that, while all of us, at bottom, pursue only our private interest, we wear these fair disguises, in order to put others off their guard, and expose them the more to our wiles and machinations. What heart one must be possessed of who professes such principles, and who feels no internal sentiment that belies so pernicious a theory, it is easy to imagine: And also, what degree of affection and benevolence he can bear to a species, whom he represents under such odious colours, and supposes so little susceptible of gratitude or any return of affection. Or if we should not ascribe these principles wholly to a corrupted heart, we must, at least, account for them from the most careless and precipitate examination. Superficial reasoners, indeed, observing many false pretences, among mankind, and feeling, perhaps, no very strong restraint in their own disposition, might draw a general and a hasty conclusion, that all is equally corrupted, and that men, different from all other animals, and indeed from all other species of existences, admit of no degrees of good or bad, but are, in every instance, the same creatures under different disguises and appearances.

There is another principle, somewhat resembling the former; which has been much insisted on by philosophers, and has been the foundation of many a system; that, whatever affection one may feel, or imagine he feels for others, no passion is, or can be disinterested; that the most generous friendship, however sincere, is a modification of self-love; and that, even unknown to ourselves, we seek only our own gratification, while we appear the most deeply engaged in schemes for the liberty and happiness of mankind. By a turn of imagination, by a refinement of reflection, by an enthusiasm of passion, we seem to take part in the interests of others, and imagine ourselves divested of all selfish considerations: But, at bottom, the most generous patriot and most niggardly miser, the bravest hero and most abject coward, have, in every action, an equal regard to their own happiness and welfare.

Whoever concludes from the seeming tendency of this opinion, that those, who make profession of it, cannot possibly feel the true sentiments of benevolence, or have any regard for genuine virtue, will often find himself, in practice, very much mistaken. Probity and honour were no strangers to EPICURUS and his sect. ATTICUS and HORACE seem to have enjoyed from nature, and cultivated by reflection, as generous and friendly dispositions as any disciple of the austerer schools. And among the modern, HOBBES and LOCKE, who maintained the selfish system of morals, lived irreproachable lives; though the former lay not under any restraint of religion, which might supply the defects of his philosophy

An EPICUREAN or a HOBBIST readily allows, that there is such a thing as friendship in the world, without hypocrisy or disguise; though he may attempt, by a philosophical chymistry, to resolve the elements of this passion, if I may so speak, into those of another, and explain every affection to be self-love, twisted and moulded, by a particular turn of imagination, into a variety of appearances. But as the same turn of imagination prevails not in every man, nor gives the same direction to the original passion; this is sufficient, even according to the selfish system, to make the widest difference in human characters, and denominate one man virtuous and humane, another vicious and meanly interested. I esteem the man, whose self-love, by whatever means, is so directed as to give him a concern for others, and render him serviceable to society: As I hate or despise him, who has no regard to any thing beyond his own gratifications and enjoyments. In vain would you suggest, that these characters, though seemingly opposite, are, at bottom, the same, and that a very inconsiderable turn of thought forms the whole difference between them. Each character, notwithstanding these inconsiderable differences, appears to me, in practice, pretty durable and untransmutable. And I find not in this more than in other subjects, that the natural sentiments, arising from the general appearances of things, are easily destroyed by subtile reflections concerning the minute origin of these appearances. Does not the lively, chearful colour of a countenance inspire me with complacency and pleasure; even though I learn from philosophy, that all difference of complexion arises from the most minute differences of thickness, in the most minute parts of the skin; by means of which a superficies is qualified to reflect one of the original colours of light, and absorb the others?

But though the question, concerning the universal or partial selfishness of man be not so material, as is usually imagined, to morality and practice, it is certainly of consequence in the speculative science of human nature, and is a proper object of curiosity and enquiry. It may not, therefore, be unsuitable, in this place, to bestow a few reflections upon it.[1]

The most obvious objection to the selfish hypothesis, is, that, as it is contrary to common feeling and our most unprejudiced notions, there is required the highest stretch of philosophy to establish so extraordinary a paradox. To the most careless observer, there appear to be such dispositions as benevolence and generosity; such affections as love, friendship,

---

1. Benevolence naturally divides into two kinds, the *general* and the *particular*. The first is, where we have no friendship or connexion or esteem for the person, but feel only a general sympathy with him or a compassion for his pains, and a congratulation with his pleasures. The other species of benevolence is founded on an opinion of virtue, on services done us, or on some particular connexions. Both these sentiments must be allowed real in human nature; but whether they will resolve into some nice considerations of self-love, is a question more curious than important. The former sentiment, to wit, that of general benevolence, or humanity, or sympathy, we shall have occasion frequently to treat of in the course of this enquiry; and I assume it as real, from general experience, without any other proof.

compassion, gratitude. These sentiments have their causes, effects, objects, and operations, marked by common language and observation, and plainly distinguished from those of the selfish passions. And as this is the obvious appearance of things, it must be admitted; till some hypothesis be discovered, which, by penetrating deeper into human nature, may prove the former affections to be nothing but modifications of the latter. All attempts of this kind have hitherto proved fruitless, and seem to have proceeded entirely, from that love of *simplicity*, which has been the source of much false reasoning in philosophy. I shall not here enter into any detail on the present subject. Many able philosophers have shown the insufficiency of these systems. And I shall take for granted what, I believe, the smallest reflection will make evident to every impartial enquirer.

But the nature of the subject furnishes the strongest presumption, that no better system will ever, for the future, be invented, in order to account for the origin of the benevolent from the selfish affections, and reduce all the various emotions of the human mind to a perfect simplicity. The case is not the same in this species of philosophy as in physics. Many an hypothesis in nature, contrary to first appearances, has been found, on more accurate scrutiny, solid and satisfactory. Instances of this kind are so frequent, that a judicious, as well as witty philosopher,[1] has ventured to affirm, if there be more than one way, in which any phænomenon may be produced, that there is a general presumption for its arising from the causes, which are the least obvious and familiar. But the presumption always lies on the other side, in all enquiries concerning the origin of our passions, and of the internal operations of the human mind. The simplest and most obvious cause, which can there be assigned for any phænomenon, is probably the true one. When a philosopher, in the explication of his system, is obliged to have recourse to some very intricate and refined reflections, and to suppose them essential to the production of any passion or emotion, we have reason to be extremely on our guard against so fallacious an hypothesis. The affections are not susceptible of any impression from the refinements of reason or imagination; and it is always found, that a vigorous exertion of the latter faculties, necessarily, from the narrow capacity of the human mind, destroys all activity in the former. Our predominant motive or intention is, indeed, frequently concealed from ourselves, when it is mingled and confounded with other motives, which the mind, from vanity or self-conceit, is desirous of supposing more prevalent: But there is no instance, that a concealment of this nature has ever arisen from the abstruseness and intricacy of the motive. A man, that has lost a friend and patron, may flatter himself, that all his grief arises from generous sentiments, without any mixture of narrow or interested considerations: But a man, that grieves for a valuable friend, who needed his patronage and protection; how can we suppose, that his passionate tenderness arises from some metaphysical regards to a self-interest, which has no foundation or reality? We may as well imagine, that minute wheels and springs, like those of a watch, give motion to a loaded waggon, as account for the origin of passion from such abstruse reflections.

Animals are found susceptible of kindness, both to their own species and to ours; nor is there, in this case, the least suspicion of disguise or artifice. Shall we account for all *their* sentiments too, from refined deductions of self-interest? Or if we admit a disinterested benevolence in the inferior species, by what rule of analogy can we refuse it in the superior?

Love between the sexes begets a complacency and good-will, very distinct from the gratification of an appetite. Tenderness to their offspring, in all sensible beings, is commonly able alone to counterbalance the strongest motives of self-love, and has no manner of dependance on that affection. What interest can a fond mother have in view, who loses her health by assiduous attendance on her sick child, and afterwards languishes and dies of grief, when freed, by its death, from the slavery of that attendance?

Is gratitude no affection of the human breast, or is that a word merely, without any meaning or reality? Have we no satisfaction in one man's company above another's, and no desire of the welfare of our friend, even though absence or death should prevent us from all participation it it? Or what is it commonly, that gives us any participation in it, even while alive and present, but our affection and regard to him?

These and a thousand other instances are marks of a general benevolence in human nature, where no *real* interest binds us to the object. And how an *imag-*

---

1. Mons. FONTENELLE.

inary interest, known and avowed for such, can be the origin of any passion or emotion, seems difficult to explain. No satisfactory hypothesis of this kind has yet been discovered; nor is there the smallest probability, that the future industry of men will ever be attended with more favourable success.

But farther, if we consider rightly of the matter, we shall find, that the hypothesis, which allows of a disinterested benevolence, distinct from self-love, has really more *simplicity* in it, and is more conformable to the analogy of nature, than that which pretends to resolve all friendship and humanity into this latter principle. There are bodily wants or appetites, acknowledged by every one, which necessarily precede all sensual enjoyment, and carry us directly to seek possession of the object. Thus, hunger and thirst have eating and drinking for their end; and from the gratification of these primary appetites arises a pleasure, which may become the object of another species of desire or inclination, that is secondary and interested. In the same manner, there are mental passions, by which we are impelled immediately to seek particular objects, such as fame, or power, or vengeance, without any regard to interest; and when these objects are attained, a pleasing enjoyment ensues, as the consequence of our indulged affections. Nature must, by the internal frame and constitution of the mind, give an original propensity to fame, ere we can reap any pleasure from that acquisition, or pursue it from motives of self-love, and a desire of happiness. If I have no vanity, I take no delight in praise: If I be void of ambition, power gives me no enjoyment: If I be not angry, the punishment of an adversary is totally indifferent to me. In all these cases, there is a passion, which points immediately to the object, and constitutes it our good or happiness; as there are other secondary passions, which afterwards arise, and pursue it as a part of our happiness, when once it is constituted such by our original affections. Were there no appetite of any kind antecedent to self-love, that propensity could scarcely ever exert itself; because we should, in that case, have felt few and slender pains or pleasures, and have little misery or happiness to avoid or to pursue.

Now where is the difficulty in conceiving, that this may likewise be the case with benevolence and friendship and that, from the original frame of our temper, we may feel a desire of another's happiness or good, which, by means of that affection, becomes our own good, and is afterwards pursued, from the combined motives of benevolence and self-enjoyment? Who sees not that vengeance, from the force alone of passion, may be so eagerly pursued, as to make us knowingly neglect every consideration of ease, interest, or safety; and, like some vindictive animals, infuse our very souls into the wounds we give an enemy?[1] And what a malignant philosophy must it be, that will not allow, to humanity and friendship, the same privileges, which are undisputably granted to the darker passions of enmity and resentment? Such a philosophy is more like a satyr than a true delineation or description of human nature; and may be a good foundation for paradoxical wit and raillery, but is a very bad one for any serious argument or reasoning.

Appendix III.—Some Farther Considerations with Regard to Justice.

The intention of this Appendix is to give some more particular explication of the origin and nature of Justice, and to mark some differences between it and the other virtues.

The social virtues of humanity and benevolence exert their influence immediately, by a direct tendency or instinct, which chiefly keeps in view the simple object, moving the affections, and comprehends not any scheme or system, nor the consequences resulting from the concurrence, imitation, or example of others. A parent flies to the relief of his child; transported by that natural sympathy, which actuates him, and which affords no leisure to reflect on the sentiments or conduct of the rest of mankind in like circumstances. A generous man chearfully embraces an opportunity of serving his friend; because he then feels himself under the dominion of the beneficent affections, nor is he concerned whether any other person in the universe were ever before actuated by such noble motives, or will ever afterwards prove their influence. In all these cases, the social passions have in view a single individual object, and pursue the safety or happiness alone of the person loved and esteemed. With this they are satisfied: In this, they acquiesce. And as the good, resulting from their benign influence, is in itself com-

---

1. Animasque in vulnere ponunt [. . . and put their souls in the wounds.] VIRG. . . . Dum alteri noceat, sui negligens [. . . careless of itself, as long as it can hurt another.], says SENECA of Anger. . . .

pleat and entire, it also excites the moral sentiment of approbation, without any reflection on farther consequences, and without any more enlarged views of the concurrence or imitation of the other members of society. On the contrary, were the generous friend or disinterested patriot to stand alone in the practice of beneficence; this would rather enhance his value in our eyes, and join the praise of rarity and novelty to his other more exalted merits.

The case is not the same with the social virtues of justice and fidelity. They are highly useful, or indeed absolutely necessary to the well-being of mankind: But the benefit, resulting from them, is not the consequence of every individual single act; but arises from the whole scheme or system, concurred in by the whole, or the greater part of the society. General peace and order are the attendants of justice or a general abstinence from the possessions of others: But a particular regard to the particular right of one individual citizen may frequently, considered in itself, be productive of pernicious consequences. The result of the individual acts is here, in many instances, directly opposite to that of the whole system of actions; and the former may be extremely hurtful, while the latter is, to the highest degree, advantageous. Riches, inherited from a parent, are, in a bad man's hand, the instrument of mischief. The right of succession may, in one instance, be hurtful. Its benefit arises only from the observance of the general rule; and it is sufficient, if compensation be thereby made for all the ills and inconveniencies, which flow from particular characters and situations.

CYRUS, young and unexperienced, considered only the individual case before him, and reflected on a limited fitness and convenience, when he assigned the long coat to the tall boy, and the short coat to the other of smaller size. His governor instructed him better; while he pointed out more enlarged views and consequences, and informed his pupil of the general, inflexible rules, necessary to support general peace and order in society.

The happiness and prosperity of mankind, arising from the social virtue of benevolence and its subdivisions, may be compared to a wall, built by many hands; which still rises by each stone, that is heaped upon it, and receives increase proportional to the diligence and care of each workman. The same happiness, raised by the social virtue of justice and its subdivisions, may be compared to the building of a vault, where each individual stone would, of itself, fall to the ground; nor is the whole fabric supported but by the mutual assistance and combination of its corresponding parts.

All the laws of nature, which regulate property, as well as all civil laws, are general, and regard alone some essential circumstances of the case, without taking into consideration the characters, situations, and connexions of the person concerned, or any particular consequences which may result from the determination of these laws, in any particular case which offers. They deprive, without scruple, a beneficent man of all his possessions, if acquired by mistake, without a good title; in order to bestow them on a selfish miser, who has already heaped up immense stores of superfluous riches. Public utility requires, that property should be regulated by general inflexible rules; and though such rules are adopted as best serve the same end of public utility, it is impossible for them to prevent all particular hardships, or make beneficial consequences result from every individual case. It is sufficient, if the whole plan or scheme be necessary to the support of civil society, and if the balance of good, in the main, do thereby preponderate much above that of evil. Even the general laws of the universe, though planned by infinite wisdom, cannot exclude all evil or inconvenience, in every particular operation.

It has been asserted by some, that justice arises from HUMAN CONVENTIONS, and proceeds from the voluntary choice, consent, or combination of mankind. If by *convention* be here meant a *promise* (which is the most usual sense of the word) nothing can be more absurd than this position. The observance of promises is itself one of the most considerable parts of justice; and we are not surely bound to keep our word, because we have given our word to keep it. But if by convention be meant a sense of common interest; which sense each man feels in his own breast, which he remarks in his fellows, and which carries him, in concurrence with others, into a general plan or system of actions, which tends to public utility; it must be owned, that, in this sense, justice arises from human conventions. For if it be allowed (what is, indeed, evident) that the particular consequences of a particular act of justice may be hurtful to the public as well as to individuals; it follows, that every man, in embracing that virtue, must have an eye to the whole plan or system, and must expect the concurrence of his fellows in the same conduct and behaviour. Did all his views terminate in the consequences of each act of his own, his benevolence and humanity as well as his self-love, might often prescribe to him measures of conduct very different from those, which are agreeable to the strict rules of right and justice.

Thus two men pull the oars of a boat by common convention, for common interest, without any promise or contract: Thus gold and silver are made the measures of exchange; thus speech and words and language are fixed by human convention and agreement. Whatever is advantageous to two or more persons, if all perform their part; but what loses all advantage, if only one perform, can arise from no other principle. There would otherwise be no motive for any one of them to enter into that scheme of conduct.[1]

The word, *natural,* is commonly taken in so many senses, and is of so loose a signification, that it seems vain to dispute, whether justice be natural or not. If self-love, if benevolence be natural to man; if reason and forethought be also natural; then may the same epithet he applied to justice, order, fidelity, property, society. Men's inclination, their necessities lead them to combine; their understanding and experience tell them, that this combination is impossible, where each governs himself by no rule, and pays no regard to the possessions of others: And from these passions and re-flections conjoined, as soon as we observe like passions and reflections in others, the sentiment of justice, throughout all ages, has infallibly and certainly had place, to some degree or other, in every individual of the human species. In so sagacious an animal, what necessarily arises from the exertion of his intellectual faculties, may justly be esteemed natural.[2]

Among all civilized nations, it has been the constant endeavour to remove every thing arbitrary and partial from the decision of property, and to fix the sentence of judges by such general views and considerations, as may be equal to every member of the society. For besides, that nothing could be more dangerous than to accustom the bench, even in the smallest instance, to regard private friendship or enmity; it is certain, that men, where they imagine, that there was no other reason for the preference of their adversary but personal favour, are apt to entertain the strongest ill-will against the magistrates and judges. When natural reason, therefore, points out no fixed view of public utility, by which a controversy of property can be decided, positive laws are often framed to supply its place, and direct the procedure of all courts of judicature. Where these too fail, as often happens, precedents are called for; and a former decision, though given itself without any sufficient reason, justly becomes a sufficient reason for a new decision. If direct laws and precedents be wanting, imperfect and indirect ones are brought in

---

1. This theory concerning the origin of property, and consequently of justice, is, in the main, the same with that hinted at and adopted by GROTIUS. 'Hinc discimus, quæ fuerit causa, ob quam a primæva communione rerum primo mobilium, deinde & immobilium discessum est: nimirum quod cum non content homines vesci sponte natis, antra habitare, corpore aut nudo agere, aut corticibus arborum ferarumve pellibus vestito, vita genus exquisitus delegissent, industria opus fuit, quam singuli rebus singulis adhiberent: Quo minus autem fructus in commune conferrentur, primum obstitit locorum, in quæ homines discesserunt, distantia, deinde justitiæ & amoris defectus, per quem fiebat, ut nec in labore, nec in consumtione fructuum, quæ debebat, æqualitas servaretur. Simul discimus, quomodo res in proprietatem iverint; non animi actu solo, neque enim scire alii poterant, quid alii suum esse vellent, ut eo abstinerent, & idem velle plures poterant; sed pacto quodam aut expresso, ut per divisionem, aut tacito, ut per occupationem. [From this we learn how it happened that primitive communal ownership was abandoned, first of moveable and then of immoveable goods. No doubt after becoming dissatisfied with eating whatever grew wild, living in caves, going naked or dressing in tree bark or animal skins, men chose a civilized way of life, so then organization became necessary, that each individual might apply himself to a single task. At first few goods could be brought together for general use because the remote distances at which men were scattered stood in the way; and further, because of the decline of justice and love, the necessary equity of work and of consumption of produce could not be maintained. Likewise we see how property arose, not by a single act of mind, for men could not know what others wanted for themselves, and so abstain from it, and it often happened that many wanted the same thing, but rather by agreement either explicit as in distribution, or tacit, as in possession.] Do Jure Belli & Pacis. . . .

2. Natural may be opposed, either to what is *unusual, miraculous,* or *artificial.* In the two former senses, justice and property are undoubtedly natural. But as they suppose reason, forethought, design, and a social union and confederacy among men, perhaps, that epithet cannot strictly, in the last sense, be applied to them. Had men lived without society, property had never been known, and neither justice nor injustice had ever existed. But society among human creatures, had been impossible, without reason, and forethought. Inferior animals, that unite, are guided by instinct, which supplies the place of reason. But all these disputes are merely verbal.

aid; and the controverted case is ranged under them, by analogical reasonings and comparisons, and similitudes, and correspondencies, which are often more fanciful than real. In general, it may safely be affirmed, that jurisprudence is, in this respect, different from all the sciences; and that in many of its nicer questions, there cannot properly be said to be truth or falsehood on either side. If one pleader bring the case under any former law or precedent, by a refined analogy or comparison; the opposite pleader is not at a loss to find an opposite analogy or comparison: And the preference given by the judge is often founded more on taste and imagination than on any solid argument. Public utility is the general object of all courts of judicature; and this utility too requires a stable rule in all controversies. But where several rules, nearly equal and indifferent, present themselves, it is a very slight turn of thought, which fixes the decision in favour of either party.[1]

We may just observe, before we conclude this subject, that, after the laws of justice are fixed by views of general utility, the injury, the hardship, the harm, which result to any individual from a violation of them, enter very much into consideration, and are a great source of that universal blame, which attends every wrong or iniquity. By the laws of society this coat, this horse, is mine, and *ought* to remain perpetually in my possession: I reckon on the secure enjoyment of it: By depriving me of it, you disappoint my expectations, and doubly displease me, and offend every bystander. It is a public wrong, so far as the rules of equity are violated: It is

---

1. That there be a separation or distinction of possessions. and that this separation be steady and constant; this is absolutely required by the interests of society, and hence the origin of justice and property. What possessions are assigned to particular persons; this is, generally speaking, pretty indifferent; and is often determined by very frivolous views and considerations. We shall mention a few particulars.

Were a society formed among several independent members, the most obvious rule, which could be agreed on, would be to annex property to *present* possession, and leave every one a right to what he at present enjoys. The relation of possession, which takes place between the person and the object, naturally draws on the relation of property.

For a like reason, occupation or first possession becomes the foundation of property.

Where a man bestows labour and industry upon any object, which before belonged to no body; as in cutting down and shaping a tree, in cultivating a field, &c., the alteration which he produces, causes a relation between him and the object, and naturally engages us to annex it to him by the new relation of property. This cause here concurs with the public utility, which consists in the encouragement given to industry and labour.

Perhaps too, private humanity towards the possessor, concurs, in this instance, with the other motives, and engages us to leave with him what he has acquired by his sweat and labour; and what he has flattered himself in the constant enjoyment of. For though private humanity can, by no means, be the origin of justice; since the latter virtue so often contradicts the former; yet when the rule of separate and constant possession is once formed by the indispensable necessities of society, private humanity, and an aversion to the doing a hardship to another may, in a particular instance, give rise to a particular rule of property.

I am much inclined to think, that the right of succession or inheritance much depends on those connexions of the imagination and that the relation to a former proprietor begetting a relation to the object, is the cause why the property is transferred to a man after the death of his kinsman. It is true; industry is more encouraged by the transference of possession to children or near relations: But this consideration will only have place in a cultivated society; whereas the right of succession is regarded even among thegreatestBarbarians.

Acquisition of property by *accession* can be explained no way but by having recourse to the relations and connexions of the imagination.

The property of rivers, by the laws of most nations, and by the natural turn of our thought, is attributed to the proprietors of their banks, excepting such vast rivers as the RHINE or the DANUBE, which seem too large to follow as an accession to the property of the neighbouring fields. Yet even these rivers are considered as the property of that nation, through whose dominions they run; the idea of a nation being of a suitable bulk to correspond with them, and bear them such a relation in the fancy.

The accessions, which are made to land, bordering upon rivers, follow the land, say the civilians, provided it be made by what they call *alluvion,* that is, insensibly and imperceptibly; which are circumstances, that assist the imagination in the conjunction.

Where there is any considerable portion torn at once from one bank and added to another, it becomes not his property, whose land it falls on, till it unite with the land, and till the trees and plants have spread their roots into both. Before that, the thought does not sufficiently join them.

In short, we must ever distinguish between the necessity of a separation and constancy in men's possession, and the rules, which assign particular objects to particular persons. The first necessity is obvious, strong, and invincible: The latter may depend on a public utility more light and frivolous, on the sentiment of private humanity and aversion to private hardship. on positive laws, on precedents, analogies, and very fine connexions and turns of the imagination.

a private harm, so far as an individual is injured. And though the second consideration could have no place, were not the former previously established: For otherwise the distinction of *mine* and *thine* would be unknown in society: Yet there is no question, but the regard to general good is much en- forced by the respect to particular. What injures the community, without hurting any individual, is often more lightly thought of. But where the greatest public wrong is also conjoined with a considerable private one, no wonder the highest disapprobation attends so iniquitous a behaviour.

IMMANUEL KANT

Fundamental Principles of the Metaphysics of Morals

The tradition inspired by Locke and Hume, utilitarianism, was to become the predominant moral theory in England. Meanwhile, on the continent, in Germany, originated what was to become utilitarianism's main rival: the moral philosophy of Immanuel Kant (1724–1804). By the nineteenth century, the debate between these two traditions dominated moral philosophy, and the argument still churns.

    Born in Konigsberg in East Prussia, Kant was educated at the university there and stayed on to become lecturer and, eventually, professor. He was the first major modern philosopher to earn his living as a teacher of philosophy. Although he lived in a time of great social turmoil, Kant was a man of conservative habit who never married and lived always in the town of his birth. Yet his conservative nature did not prevent his admiration, if only from afar, of Rousseau and the French revolution.

    Kant's initial academic duties lay in teaching such subjects as physics and mathematics as well as philosophy. His early published work mostly concerned what we now would call natural science; it wasn't until after 1760 that his mind turned its full attention to philosophical issues in the modern sense. His varied early interests, though, were later to enliven his philosophical lectures, delivered to audiences filled with students and others who frequently had traveled from distant parts of Germany just to hear the great thinker. That his lectures were entertaining may come as a surprise to those who know Kant only through his often turgid writing. This writing style resulted from his adopting the scholastic manner common in his day, not from an inherent dullness in the master.

    The philosophical work of Kant is typically divided into two periods: the "precritical period" before 1770 and the "critical period" in 1770 and after. The critical period is so named because Kant himself described his mature philosophy as a form of "critical idealism," an idealism founded on a critique of the powers of reason. His primary written work begins with the publication in 1780 of his magnum opus, the eagerly awaited Critique of

Pure Reason. *Even though Kant had an established reputation by the time of the publication of this work, its arrival was met mostly with bewilderment and confusion. Few could understand his ideas, due partly to his formal argumentation style and partly to the highly abstract nature of his subject matter. To remedy this confusion, he reiterated the main argument in a more simplified manner in a short work, the* Prolegomena to Every Future Metaphysics, *published in 1783. His major contributions to ethical theory appeared soon after. By 1790 he had published his three main works: the* Fundamental Principles of the Metaphysics of Morals *(1785), followed by the* Critique of Practical Reason *in 1788 and the* Critique of Judgment *in 1790.*

Like many of his contemporaries, Kant embraced the Enlightenment belief in the power of reason over authority and tradition, especially in its respect for the advances of science. But unlike them, he was mostly alone in recognizing the challenge that the determinism implicit in Newtonian physics creates for ethics. Kant was determined to combine the insights of science with the autonomy of morality. This he began with a short work, the Fundamental Principles, *reprinted here in its entirety.*

If he had published nothing other than his Fundamental Principles, *Kant would have assured himself a place in the history of ethics. His sole aim in this work, as he states in the Preface, is "to seek out and establish the supreme principle of morality." This he does by investigating the special features of the situation wherein moral decisions are made in order to discover the unique features of those decisions. As Kant sees it, man is a creature who is half sensual and half rational. Although sensual impulses determine many of our actions, and in these actions reason takes, as Hume said, the role of "handmaiden," not all acts are of this kind. In moral actions, the roles of reason and impulse are reversed. We act morally when we act, not out of an interest in the consequences of that act, but out of respect for moral principle. We may not be able to choose our inclinations and desires, yet we can choose between acting from inclination or from duty. It is in this choice that morality lies.*

Kant's deontological ethical theory is one of the primary theories in the moral philosophy of our day, and even his opponents must acknowledge the powerful influence of his thought. Utilitarians, for example, still must address the challenge from Kant's theory. A host of Kantians continue to promote, understand, and repair his ethical theory, while others see his thought as, at least in part, the root of their own. Of the twentieth-century representatives of Kantianism, Onora O'Neill and Thomas E. Hill, Jr., are included in this volume. The contractarian theory of John Rawls, an influential theory inspired by Kantian principles, is also present in this volume.

Preface

Ancient Greek Philosophy was divided into three sciences: Physics, Ethics, and Logic. This division is perfectly suitable to the nature of the thing, and the only improvement that can be made in it is to add the principle on which it is based, so that we may both satisfy ourselves of its completeness, and also be able to determine correctly the necessary subdivisions.

All rational knowledge is either *material* or *formal*: the former considers some object, the latter is concerned only with the form of the understanding and of the reason itself, and with the universal laws of thought in general without distinction of its objects. Formal philosophy is called Logic. Material philosophy, however, which has to do with determinate objects and the laws to which they are subject, is again two-fold; for these laws are either laws of *nature* or of *freedom*. The science of the former is Physics, that of the latter, Ethics; they are also called *natural philosophy* and *moral philosophy* respectively.

Logic cannot have any empirical part; that is, a part in which the universal and necessary laws of thought should rest on grounds taken from experience: otherwise it would not be logic, *i.e.* a canon for the understanding or the reason, valid for all thought, and capable of demonstration. Natural and moral philosophy, on the contrary, can each have their empirical part, since the former has to determine the laws of nature as an object of experience; the latter the laws of the human will, so far as it is affected by nature: the former, however, being laws according to which everything does happen; the latter, laws according to which everything ought to happen. Ethics, however, must also consider the conditions under which what ought to happen frequently does not.

We may call all philosophy *empirical,* so far as it is based on grounds of experience: on the other hand, that which delivers its doctrines from *à priori* principles alone we may call *pure* philosophy. When the latter is merely formal it is *logic;* if it is restricted to definite objects of the understanding it is *metaphysic.*

In this way there arises the idea of a two-fold metaphysic—a *metaphysic of nature* and a *metaphysic of morals.* Physics will thus have an empirical and also a rational part. It is the same with Ethics; but here the empirical part might have the special name of *practical anthropology,* the name *morality* being appropriated to the rational part.

All trades, arts, and handiworks have gained by division of labour, namely, when, instead of one man doing everything, each confines himself to a certain kind of work distinct from others in the treatment it requires, so as to be able to perform it with greater facility and in the greatest perfection. Where the different kinds of work are not so distinguished and divided, where everyone is a jack-of-all-trades, there manufactures remain still in the greatest barbarism. It might deserve to be considered whether pure philosophy in all its parts does not require a man specially devoted to it, and whether it would not be better for the whole business of science if those who, to please the tastes of the public, are wont to blend the rational and empirical elements together, mixed in all sorts of proportions unknown to themselves, and who call themselves independent thinkers, giving the name of minute philosophers to those who apply themselves to the rational part only—if these, I say,

were warned not to carry on two employments together which differ widely in the treatment they demand, for each of which perhaps a special talent is required, and the combination of which in one person only produces bunglers. But I only ask here whether the nature of science does not require that we should always carefully separate the empirical from the rational part, and prefix to Physics proper (or empirical physics) a metaphysic of nature, and to practical anthropology a metaphysic of morals, which must be carefully cleared of everything empirical, so that we may know how much can be accomplished by pure reason in both cases, and from what sources it draws this its *à priori* teaching, and that whether the latter inquiry is conducted by all moralists (whose name is legion), or only by some who feel a calling thereto.

As my concern here is with moral philosophy, I limit the question suggested to this: Whether it is not of the utmost necessity to construct a pure moral philosophy, perfectly cleared of everything which is only empirical, and which belongs to anthropology? for that such a philosophy must be possible is evident from the common idea of duty and of the moral laws. Everyone must admit that if a law is to have moral force, *i.e.* to be the basis of an obligation, it must carry with it absolute necessity; that, for example, the precept, 'Thou shalt not lie,' is not valid for men alone, as if other rational beings had no need to observe it; and so with all the other moral laws properly so called; that, therefore, the basis of obligation must not be sought in the nature of man, or in the circumstances in the world in which he is placed, but *à priori* simply in the conceptions of pure reason; and although any other precept which is founded on principles of mere experience may be in certain respects universal, yet, in as far as it rests even in the least degree on an empirical basis, perhaps only as to a motive, such a precept, while it may be a practical rule, can never be called a moral law.

Thus not only are moral laws with their principles essentially distinguished from every other kind of practical knowledge in which there is anything empirical, but all moral philosophy rests wholly on its pure part. When applied to man, it does not borrow the least thing from the knowledge of man himself (anthropology), but gives laws *à priori* to him as a rational being. No doubt these laws require a judgment sharpened by experience, in order on the one hand to distinguish in what cases they are applicable, and on the other to procure for them access to the will of the man, and effectual influence on conduct; since man is acted on by so many inclinations that, though capable of the idea of a practical pure reason, he is not so easily able to make it effective *in concreto* in his life.

A metaphysic of morals is therefore indispensably necessary, not merely for speculative reasons, in order to investigate the sources of the practical principles which are to be found *à priori* in our reason, but also because morals themselves are liable to all sorts of corruption, as long as we are without that clue and supreme canon by which to estimate them correctly. For, in order that an action should be morally good, it is not enough that it *conform* to the moral law, but it must also be done *for the sake of the law,* otherwise that conformity is only very contingent and uncertain; since a principle which is not moral, although it may now and then produce actions conformable to the law, will also often produce actions which contradict it. Now it is only in a pure philosophy that we can look for the moral law in its purity and genuineness (and, in a practical matter, this is of the utmost consequence): we must, therefore, begin with pure philosophy (metaphysic), and without it there cannot be any moral philosophy at all. That which mingles these pure principles with the empirical does not deserve the name of philosophy (for what distinguishes philosophy from common rational knowledge is, that it treats in separate sciences what the latter only comprehends confusedly); much less does it deserve that of moral philosophy, since by this confusion it even spoils the purity of morals themselves, and counteracts its own end.

Let it not be thought, however, that what is here demanded is already extant in the propædeutic prefixed by the celebrated Wolf to his moral philosophy, namely, his so-called *general practical philosophy,* and that, therefore, we have not to strike into an entirely new field. Just because it was to be a general practical philosophy, it has not taken into consideration a will of any particular kind—say one which should be determined solely from *à priori* principles without any empirical motives, and which we might call a pure will, but volition in general, with all the actions and conditions which belong to it in this general signification. By this it is distinguished from a metaphysic of morals, just as general logic, which treats of the acts and canons of thought *in general,* is distinguished from transcendental philosophy, which treats of the particular acts and canons of *pure* thought, *i.e.* that whose cognitions are altogether *à priori*. For the metaphysic of morals has to examine the idea and the principles of a possible *pure* will, and not the acts and conditions of human volition generally, which for the most part are drawn from psychology. It is true that moral laws and duty are spoken of in the general practical philosophy (contrary indeed to all fitness). But this is no objection, for in this respect also the authors of that science remain true to their idea of it; they do not distinguish the motives which are prescribed as such by reason alone altogether *à priori,* and which are properly moral, from the empirical motives which the under-standing raises to general conceptions merely by comparison of experiences; but without noticing the difference of their sources, and looking on them all as homogeneous, they consider only their greater or less amount. It is in this way they frame their notion of *obligation,* which, though anything but moral, is all that can be asked for in a philosophy which passes no judgment at all on the *origin* of all possible practical concepts, whether they are *à priori,* or only *à posteriori*.

Intending to publish hereafter a metaphysic of morals, I issue in the first instance these fundamental principles. Indeed there is properly no other foundation for it than the *critical examination of a pure practical reason;* just as that of metaphysics is the critical examination of the pure speculative reason, already published. But in the first place the former is not so absolutely necessary as the latter, because in moral concerns human reason can easily be brought to a high degree of correctness and completeness, even in the commonest understanding, while on the contrary in its theoretic but pure use it is wholly dialectical; and in the second place if the critique of a pure practical reason is to be complete, it must be possible at the same time to show its identity with the speculative reason in a common principle, for it can ultimately be only one and the same reason which has to be distinguished merely in its application. I could not, however, bring it to such completeness here, without introducing considerations of a wholly different kind, which would be perplexing to the reader. On this account I have adopted the title of *Fundamental Principles of the Metaphysic of Morals,* instead of that of *Critical Examination of the pure practical Reason.*

But in the third place, since a metaphysic of morals, in spite of the discouraging title, is yet capable of being presented in a popular form, and one adapted to the common understanding, I find it useful to separate from it this preliminary treatise on its fundamental principles, in order that I may not hereafter have need to introduce these necessarily subtle discussions into a book of a more simple character.

The present treatise is, however, nothing more than the investigation and establishment of *the supreme principle of morality,* and this alone constitutes a study complete in itself, and one which ought to be kept apart from every other moral investigation. No doubt my conclusions on this weighty question, which has hitherto been very unsatisfactorily examined, would receive much light from the application of the same principle to the whole system, and would be greatly confirmed by the adequacy which it exhibits throughout; but I must forego this advantage, which indeed would be after all more gratifying than useful, since the easy applicability of a principle and its apparent adequacy give no very certain proof of its soundness, but rather inspire a certain partiality, which prevents us from examining and estimating it strictly in itself, and without regard to consequences.

I have adopted in this work the method which I think most suitable, proceeding analytically from common knowledge to the determination of its ultimate principle, and again descending synthetically from the examination of this principle and its sources to the common knowledge in which we find it employed. The division will, therefore, be as follows:—

1. *First section.*—Transition from the common rational knowledge of morality to the philosophical.

2. *Second section.*—Transition from popular moral philosophy to the metaphysic of morals.

3. *Third section.*—Final step from the metaphysic of morals to the critique of the pure practical reason.

First Section. Transition from the Common Rational Knowledge of Morality to the Philosophical.

Nothing can possibly be conceived in the world, or even out of it, which can be called good without qualification, except a Good Will. Intelligence, wit,

judgment, and the other *talents* of the mind, however they may be named, or courage, resolution, perseverance, as qualities of temperament, are undoubtedly good and desirable in many respects; but these gifts of nature may also become extremely bad and mischievous if the will which is to make use of them, and which, therefore, constitutes what is called *character,* is not good. It is the same with the *gifts of fortune.* Power, riches, honour, even health, and the general well-being and contentment with one's condition which is called *happiness,* inspire pride, and often presumption, if there is not a good will to correct the influence of these on the mind, and with this also to rectify the whole principle of acting, and adapt it to its end. The sight of a being who is not adorned with a single feature of a pure and good will, enjoying unbroken prosperity, can never give pleasure to an impartial rational spectator. Thus a good will appears to constitute the indispensable condition even of being worthy of happiness.

There are even some qualities which are of service to this good will itself, and may facilitate its action, yet which have no intrinsic unconditional value, but always presuppose a good will, and this qualifies the esteem that we justly have for them, and does not permit us to regard them as absolutely good. Moderation in the affections and passions, self-control and calm deliberation are not only good in many respects, but even seem to constitute part of the intrinsic worth of the person; but they are far from deserving to be called good without qualification, although they have been so unconditionally praised by the ancients. For without the principles of a good will, they may become extremely bad, and the coolness of a villain not only makes him far more dangerous, but also directly makes him more abominable in our eyes than he would have been without it.

A good will is good not because of what it performs or effects, not by its aptness for the attainment of some proposed end, but simply by virtue of the volition, that is, it is good in itself, and considered by itself is to be esteemed much higher than all that can be brought about by it in favour of any inclination, nay, even of the sum total of all inclinations. Even if it should happen that, owing to special disfavour of fortune, or the niggardly provision of a step-motherly nature, this will should wholly lack power to accomplish its purpose, if with its greatest efforts it should yet achieve nothing, and there should remain only the good will (not to be sure, a mere wish, but the summoning of all means in our power), then, like a jewel, it would still shine by its own light, as a thing which has its whole value in itself. Its usefulness or fruitlessness can neither add to nor take away anything from this value. It would be, as it were, only the setting to enable us to handle it the more conveniently in common commerce or to attract to it the attention of those who are not yet connoisseurs, but not to recommend it to true connoisseurs, or to determine its value.

There is, however, something so strange in this idea of the absolute value of the mere will, in which no account is taken of its utility, that notwithstanding the thorough assent of even common reason to the idea, yet a suspicion must arise that it may perhaps really be the product of mere high-flown fancy, and that we may have misunderstood the purpose of nature in assigning reason as the governor of our will. Therefore we will examine this idea from this point of view.

In the physical constitution of an organized being, that is, a being adapted suitably to the purposes of life, we assume it as a fundamental principle that no organ for any purpose will be found but what is also the fittest and best adapted for that purpose. Now in a being which has reason and a will, if the proper object of nature were its *conservation,* its *welfare,* in a word, its *happiness,* then nature would have hit upon a very bad arrangement in selecting the reason of the creature to carry out this purpose. For all the actions which the creature has to perform with a view to this purpose, and the whole rule of its conduct, would be far more surely prescribed to it by instinct, and that end would have been attained thereby much more certainly than it ever can be by reason. Should reason have been communicated to this favoured creature over and above, it must only have served it to contemplate the happy constitution of its nature, to admire it, to congratulate itself thereon, and to feel thankful for it to the beneficent cause, but not that it should subject its desires to that weak and delusive guidance, and meddle bunglingly with the purpose of nature. In a word, nature would have taken care that reason should not break forth into *practical exercise,* nor have the presumption, with its weak insight, to think out for itself the plan of happiness, and of the means of attaining it. Nature would not only have taken on herself the choice of the ends, but also of the means, and with wise fore-sight would have entrusted both to instinct.

And, in fact, we find that the more a cultivated reason applies itself with deliberate purpose to the enjoyment of life and happiness, so much the more does the man fail of true satisfaction. And from this circumstance there arises in many, if they are candid enough to confess it, a certain degree of *misology,* that is, hatred of reason, especially in the case of those who are most experienced in the use of it, because after calculating all the advantages they derive, I do not say from the invention of all the arts of common luxury, but even from the sciences (which seem to them to be after all only a luxury of the understanding), they find that they have, in fact, only brought more trouble on their shoulders, rather than gained in happiness; and they end by envying, rather than despising, the more common stamp of men who keep closer to the guidance of mere instinct, and do not allow their reason much influence on their conduct. And this we must admit, that the judgment of those who would very much lower the lofty eulogies of the advantages which reason gives us in regard to the happiness and satisfaction of life, or who would even reduce them below zero, is by no means morose or ungrateful to the goodness with which the world is governed, but that there lies at the root of these judgments the idea that our existence has a different and far nobler end, for which, and not for happiness, reason is properly intended, and which must, therefore, be regarded as the supreme condition to which the private ends of man must, for the most part, be postponed.

For as reason is not competent to guide the will with certainty in regard to its objects and the satisfaction of all our wants (which it to some extent even multiplies), this being an end to which an implanted instinct would have led with much greater certainty; and since, nevertheless, reason is imparted to us as a practical faculty, *i.e.* as one which is to have influence on the *will,* therefore, admitting that nature generally in the distribution of her capacities has adapted the means to the end, its true destination must be to produce a *will,* not merely good as a *means* to something else, but *good in itself,* for which reason was absolutely necessary. This will then, though not indeed the sole and complete good, must be the supreme good and the condition of every other, even of the desire of happiness. Under these circumstances, there is nothing inconsistent with the wisdom of nature in the fact that the cultivation of the reason, which is requisite for the first and unconditional purpose, does in many ways interfere, at least in this life, with the attainment of the second, which is always conditional, namely, happiness. Nay, it may even reduce it to nothing, without nature thereby failing of her purpose. For reason recognises the establishment of a good will as its highest practical destination, and in attaining this purpose is capable only of a satisfaction of its own proper kind, namely, that from the attainment of an end, which end again is determined by reason only, notwithstanding that this may involve many a disappointment to the ends of inclination.

We have then to develop the notion of a will which deserves to be highly esteemed for itself, and is good without a view to anything further, a notion which exists already in the sound natural understanding, requiring rather to be cleared up than to be taught, and which in estimating the value of our actions always takes the first place, and constitutes the condition of all the rest. In order to do this we will take the notion of duty, which includes that of a good will, although implying certain subjective restrictions and hindrances. These, however, far from concealing it, or rendering it unrecognisable, rather bring it out by contrast, and make it shine forth so much the brighter.

I omit here all actions which are already recognised as inconsistent with duty, although they may be useful for this or that purpose, for with these the question whether they are done *from duty* cannot arise at all, since they even conflict with it. I also set aside those actions which really conform to duty, but to which men have *no* direct *inclination,* performing them because they are impelled thereto by some other inclination. For in this case we can readily distinguish whether the action which agrees with duty is done *from duty,* or from a selfish view. It is much harder to make this distinction when the action accords with duty, and the subject has besides a *direct* inclination to it. For example, it is always a matter of duty that a dealer should not overcharge an inexperienced purchase; and wherever there is much commerce the prudent tradesman does not overcharge, but keeps a fixed price for everyone, so that a child

buys of him as well as any other. Men are thus *honestly* served; but this is not enough to make us believe that the tradesman has so acted from duty and from principles of honesty his own advantage required it: it is out of the question in this case to suppose that he might besides have a direct inclination in favour of the buyers, so that, as it were, from love he should give no advantage to one over another. Accordingly the action was done neither from duty nor from direct inclination, but merely with a selfish view.

On the other hand, it is a duty to maintain one's life; and, in addition, every one has also a direct inclination to do so. But on this account the often anxious care which most men take for it has no intrinsic worth, and their maxim has no moral import. They preserve their life *as duty requires,* no doubt, but not *because duty requires.* On the other hand, if adversity and hopeless sorrow have completely taken away the relish for life, if the unfortunate one, strong in mind, indignant at his fate rather than desponding or dejected, wishes for death, and yet preserves his life without loving it—not from inclination or fear, but from duty—then his maxim has a moral worth.

To be beneficent when we can is a duty; and besides this, there are many minds so sympathetically constituted that, without any other motive of vanity or self-interest, they find a pleasure in spreading joy around them, and can take delight in the satisfaction of others so far as it is their own work. But I maintain that in such a case an action of this kind, however proper, however amiable it may be, has nevertheless no true moral worth, but is on a level with other inclinations, *e.g.* the inclination to honour, which, if it is happily directed to that which is in fact of public utility and accordant with duty, and consequently honourable, deserves praise and encouragement, but not esteem. For the maxim lacks the moral import, namely, that such actions be done *from duty,* not from inclination. Put the case that the mind of that philanthropist were clouded by sorrow of his own extinguishing all sympathy with the lot of others, and that while he still has the power to benefit others in distress, he is not touched by their trouble because he is absorbed with his own; and now suppose that he tears himself out of this dead insensibility, and performs the action without any inclination to it, but simply from duty, then first has his action its genuine moral worth. Further still; if nature has put little sympathy in the heart of this or that man; if he, supposed to be an upright man, is by temperament cold and indifferent to the sufferings of others, perhaps because in respect of his own he is provided with the special gift of patience and fortitude, and supposes, or even requires, that others should have the same—and such a man would certainly not be the meanest product of nature—but if nature had not specially framed him for a philanthropist, would he not still find in himself a source from whence to give himself a far higher worth than that of a good-natured temperament could be? Unquestionably. it is just in this that the moral worth of the character is brought out which is incomparably the highest of all, namely, that he is beneficent, not from inclination, but from duty.

To secure one's own happiness is a duty, at least indirectly; for discontent with one's condition, under a pressure of many anxieties and amidst unsatisfied wants, might easily become a *great temptation to transgression of duty*. But here again, without looking to duty, all men have already the strongest and most intimate inclination to happiness, because it is just in this idea that all inclinations are combined in one total. But the precept of happiness is often of such a sort that it greatly interferes with some inclinations, and yet a man cannot form any definite and certain conception of the sum of satisfaction of all of them which is called happiness. It is not then to be wondered at that a single inclination, definite both as to what it promises and as to the time within which it can be gratified, is often able to overcome such a fluctuating idea, and that a gouty patient, for instance, can choose to enjoy what he likes, and to suffer what he may, since, according to his calculation, on this occasion at least, he has [only] not sacrificed the enjoyment of the present moment to a possibly mistaken expectation of a happiness which is supposed to be found in health. But even in this case, if the general desire for happiness did not influence his will, and supposing that in his particular case health was not a necessary element in this calculation, there yet remains in this, as in all other cases, this law, namely, that he should promote his happiness not from inclination but from duty, and by this would his conduct first acquire true moral worth.

It is in this manner, undoubtedly, that we are to understand those passages of Scripture also in which we are commanded to love our neighbour, even our enemy. For love, as an affection, cannot be com-

manded, but beneficence for duty's sake may; even though we are not impelled to it by any inclination—nay, are even repelled by a natural and unconquerable aversion. This is *practical* love, and not *pathological*—a love which is seated in the will, and not in the propensions of sense—in principles of action and not of tender sympathy; and it is this love alone which can be commanded.

The second proposition is: That an action done from duty derives its moral worth, *not from the purpose* which is to be attained by it, but from the maxim by which it is determined, and therefore does not depend on the realization of the object of the action, but merely on the *principle of volition* by which the action has taken place, without regard to any object of desire. It is clear from what precedes that the purposes which we may have in view in our actions, or their effects regarded as ends and springs of the will, cannot give to actions any unconditional or moral worth. In what, then, can their worth lie, if it is not to consist in the will and in reference to its expected effect? It cannot lie anywhere but in the *principle of the will* without regard to the ends which can be attained by the action. For the will stands between its *à priori* principle, which is formal, and its *à posteriori* spring, which is material, as between two roads, and as it must be determined by something, it follows that it must be determined by the formal principle of volition when an action is done from duty, in which case every material principle has been withdrawn from it.

The third proposition, which is a consequence of the two preceding, I would express thus: *Duty is the necessity of acting from respect for the law.* I may have *inclination* for an object as the effect of my proposed action, but I cannot have *respect* for it, just for this reason, that it is an effect and not an energy of will. Similarly, I cannot have respect for inclination, whether my own or another's; I can at most, if my own, approve it; if another's, sometimes even love it; *i.e.* look on it as favourable to my own interest. It is only what is connected with my will as a principle, by no means as an effect—what does not subserve my inclination, but overpowers it, or at least in case of choice excludes it from its calculation—in other words, simply the law of itself which can be an object of respect, and hence a command. Now an action done from duty must wholly exclude the influence of inclination, and with it every object of the will, so that nothing remains which can determine the will except objectively the *law,* and subjectively *pure respect* for this practical law, and consequently the maxim[1] that I should follow this law even to the thwarting of all my inclinations.

Thus the moral worth of an action does not lie in the effect expected from it, nor in any principle of action which requires to borrow its motive from this expected effect. For all these effects—agreeableness of one's condition, and even the promotion of the happiness of others—could have been also brought about by other causes, so that for this there would have been no need of the will of a rational being; whereas it is in this alone that the supreme and unconditional good can be found. The pre-eminent good which we call moral can therefore consist in nothing else than the *conception of law* in itself, *which certainly is only possible in a rational being,* in so far as this conception, and not the expected effect, determines the will. This is a good which is already present in the person who acts accordingly, and we have not to wait for it to appear first in the result.[2]

But what sort of law can that be, the conception of which must determine the will, even without paying any regard to the effect expected from it, in order that this will may be called good absolutely and without qualification? As I have deprived the will of every impulse which could arise to it from obedience to any law, there remains nothing but the universal conformity of its actions to law in general, which alone is to serve the will as a principle, *i.e.* I am never to act otherwise than so *that I could also will that my maxim should become a universal law.* Here now, it is the simple conformity to law in general, without as-

suming any particular law applicable to certain actions, that serves the will as its principle, and must so serve it, if duty is not to be a vain delusion and a chimerical notion. The common reason of men in its practical judgments perfectly coincides with this, and always has in view the principle here suggested. Let the question be, for example: May I when in distress make a promise with the intention not to keep it? I readily distinguish here between the two significations which the question may have: Whether it is prudent, or whether it is right, to make a false promise. The former may undoubtedly often be the case. I see clearly indeed that it is not enough to extricate myself from a present difficulty by means of this subterfuge, but it must be well considered whether there may not hereafter spring from this lie much greater inconvenience than that from which I now free myself, and as, with all my supposed *cunning,* the consequences cannot be so easily foreseen but that credit once lost may be much more injurious to me than any mischief which I seek to avoid at present, it should be considered whether it would not be more *prudent* to act herein according to a universal maxim, and to make it a habit to promise nothing except with the intention of keeping it. But it is soon clear to me that such a maxim will still only be based on the fear of consequences. Now it is a wholly different thing to be truthful from duty, and to be so from apprehension of injurious consequences. In the first case, the very notion of the action already implies a law for me; in the second case, I must first look about elsewhere to see what results may be combined with it which would affect myself. For to deviate from the principle of duty is beyond

---

1. A *maxim* is the subjective principle of volition. The objective principle (*i.e.* that which would also serve subjectively as a practical principle to all rational beings if reason had full power over the faculty of desire) is the practical *law.*

2. It might be here objected to me that I take refuge behind the word *respect* in an obscure feeling, instead of giving a distinct solution of the question by a concept of the reason. But although respect is a feeling, it is not a feeling *received* through influence, but is *self-wrought* by a rational concept, and, therefore, is specifically distinct from all feelings of the former kind, which may be referred either to inclination or. Fear what I recognise immediately as a law for me, I recognise with respect. This merely signifies the consciousness that my will is *subordinate* to a law, without the intervention of other influences on my sense. The immediate determination of the will by the law, and the consciousness of this is called *respect,* so that this is

regarded as an *effect* of the law on the subject, and not as the *cause* of it. Respect is properly the conception of a worth which thwarts my self-love. Accordingly it is something which is considered neither as an object of inclination nor of fear, although it has something analogous to both. The *object* of respect is the *law* only, and that, the law which we impose on *ourselves,* and yet recognise as necessary in itself. As a law, we are subjected to it without consulting self-love; as imposed by us on ourselves, it is a result of our will. In the former aspect it has an analogy to fear, in the latter to inclination. Respect for a person is properly only respect for the law (of honesty, &c.), of which he gives us an example. Since we also look on the improvement of our talents as a duty, we consider that we see in a person of talents, as it were, the *example of a law* (viz. to become like him in this by exercise), and this constitutes our respect. All so-called moral interest consists simply in respect for the law.

all doubt wicked; but to be unfaithful to my maxim of prudence may often be very advantageous to me, although to abide by it is certainly safer. The shortest way, however, and an unerring one, to discover the answer to this question whether a lying promise is consistent with duty, is to ask myself, Should I be content that my maxim (to extricate myself from difficulty by a false promise) should hold good as a universal law, for myself as well as for others? and should I be able to say to myself, "Every one may make a deceitful promise when he finds himself in a difficulty from which he cannot otherwise extricate himself"? Then I presently become aware that while I can will the lie, I can by no means will that lying should be a universal law. For with such a law there would be no promises at all, since it would be in vain to allege my intention in regard to my future actions to those who would not believe this allegation, or if they over-hastily did so would pay me back in my own coin. Hence my maxim, as soon as it should be made a universal law, would necessarily destroy itself.

I do not, therefore, need any far-reaching penetration to discern what I have to do in order that my will may be morally good. Inexperienced in the course of the world, incapable of being prepared for all its contingencies, I only ask myself: Canst thou also will that thy maxim should be a universal law? If not, then it must be rejected, and that not because of a disadvantage accruing from it to myself or even to others, but because it cannot enter as a principle into a possible universal legislation, and reason extorts from me immediate respect for such legislation. I do not indeed as yet *discern* on what this respect is based (this the philosopher may inquire), but at least I understand this, that it is an estimation of the worth which far outweighs all worth of what is recommended by inclination, and that the necessity of acting from *pure* respect for the practical law is what constitutes duty, to which every other motive must give place, because it is the condition of a will being good *in itself,* and the worth of such a will is above everything.

Thus, then, without quitting the moral knowledge of common human reason, we have arrived at its principle. And although, no doubt, common men do not conceive it in such an abstract and universal form, yet they always have it really before their eyes, and use it as the standard of their decision. Here it would be easy to show how, with this compass in hand, men are well able to distinguish, in every case that occurs, what is good, what bad, conformably to duty or inconsistent with it, if, without in the least teaching them anything new, we only, like Socrates, direct their attention to the principle they themselves employ; and that therefore we do not need science and philosophy to know what we should do to be honest and good, yea, even wise and virtuous. Indeed we might well have conjectured beforehand that the knowledge of what every man is bound to do, and therefore also to know, would be within the reach of every man, even the commonest. Here we cannot forbear admiration when we see how great an advantage the practical judgment has over the theoretical in the common understanding of men. In the latter, if common reason ventures to depart from the laws of experience and from the perceptions of the senses it falls into mere inconceivabilities and self-contradictions, at least into a chaos of uncertainty, obscurity, and instability. But in the practical sphere it is just when the common understanding excludes all sensible springs from practical laws that its power of judgment begins to show itself to advantage. It then becomes even subtle, whether it be that it chicanes with its own conscience or with other claims respecting what is to be called right, or whether it desires for its own instruction to determine honestly the worth of actions; and, in the latter case, it may even have as good a hope of hitting the mark as any philosopher whatever can promise himself. Nay, it is almost more sure of doing so, because the philosopher cannot have any other principle, while he may easily perplex his judgment by a multitude of considerations foreign to the matter, and so turn aside from the right way. Would it not therefore be wiser in moral concerns to acquiesce in the judgment of common reason, or at most only to call in philosophy for the purpose of rendering the system of morals more complete and intelligible, and its rules more convenient for use (especially for disputation), but not so as to draw off the common understanding from its happy simplicity, or to bring it by means of philosophy into a new path of inquiry and instruction?

Innocence is indeed a glorious thing, only, on the other hand, it is very sad that it cannot well maintain itself, and is easily seduced. On this account even wisdom—which otherwise consists more in conduct than in knowledge—yet has need of science, not in order to learn from it, but to secure for its precepts admission and permanence. Against all the commands of duty which reason represents to man as so deserving of respect, he feels in himself a powerful counterpoise in his wants and inclinations, the entire satisfaction of which he sums up under the name of happiness. Now reason issues its commands unyieldingly, without promising anything to the inclinations, and, as it were, with disregard and contempt for these claims, which are so impetuous, and at the same time so plausible, and which will not allow themselves to be suppressed by any command. Hence there arises a natural *dialectic,* i.e. a disposition to argue against these strict laws of duty and to question their validity, or at least their purity and strictness; and, if possible, to make them more accordant with our wishes and inclinations, that is to say, to corrupt them at their very source, and entirely to destroy their worth—a thing which even common practical reason cannot ultimately call good.

Thus is the *common reason of man* compelled to go out of its sphere, and to take a step into the field of a *practical philosophy,* not to satisfy any speculative want (which never occurs to it as long as it is content to be mere sound reason), but even on practical grounds, in order to attain in it information and clear instruction respecting the source of its principle, and the correct determination of it in opposition to the maxims which are based on wants and inclinations, so that it may escape from the perplexity of opposite claims, and not run the risk of losing all genuine moral principles through the equivocation into which it easily falls. Thus, when practical reason cultivates itself, there insensibly arises in it a dialectic which forces it to seek aid in philosophy, just as happens to it in its theoretic use; and in this case, therefore, as well as in the other, it will find rest nowhere but in a thorough critical examination of our reason.

Second Section. Transition from Popular Moral Philosophy to the Metaphysic of Morals.

If we have hitherto drawn our notion of duty from the common use of our practical reason, it is by no means to be inferred that we have treated it as an empirical notion. On the contrary, if we attend to the experience of men's conduct, we meet frequent and, as we ourselves allow, just complaints that one cannot find a single certain example of the disposition to act from pure duty. Although many things are done in *conformity* with what *duty* prescribes, it is never-

theless always doubtful whether they are done strictly *from duty,* so as to have a moral worth. Hence there have, at all times, been philosophers who have altogether denied that this disposition actually exists at all in human actions, and have ascribed everything to a more or less refined self-love. Not that they have on that account questioned the soundness of the conception of morality; on the contrary, they spoke with sincere regret of the frailty and corruption of human nature, which though noble enough to take as its rule an idea so worthy of respect, is yet too weak to follow it, and employs reason, which ought to give it the law only for the purpose of providing for the interest of the inclinations, whether singly or at the best in the greatest possible harmony with one another.

In fact, it is absolutely impossible to make out by experience with complete certainty a single case in which the maxim of an action, however right in itself, rested simply on moral grounds and on the conception of duty. Sometimes it happens that with the sharpest self-examination we can find nothing beside the moral principle of duty which could have been powerful enough to move us to this or that action and to so great a sacrifice; yet we cannot from this infer with certainty that it was not really some secret impulse of self-love, under the false appearance of duty, that was the actual determining cause of the will. We like then to flatter ourselves by falsely taking credit for a more noble motive; whereas in fact we can never, even by the strictest examination, get completely behind the secret springs of action; since when the question is of moral worth, it is not with the actions which we see that we are concerned, but with those inward principles of them which we do not see.

Moreover, we cannot better serve the wishes of those who ridicule all morality as a mere chimera of human imagination overstepping itself from vanity, than by conceding to them that notions of duty must be drawn only from experience (as, from indolence, people are ready to think is also the case with all other notions); for this is to prepare for them a certain triumph. I am willing to admit out of love of humanity that even most of our actions are correct, but if we look closer at them we everywhere come upon the dear self which is always prominent, and it is this they have in view, and not the strict command of duty which would often require self-denial. Without being an enemy of virtue, a cool observer, one that does not mistake the wish for good, however lively, for its reality, may sometimes doubt whether true virtue is actually found anywhere in the world, and this especially as years increase and the judgment is partly made wiser by experience, and partly also more acute in observation. This being so, nothing can secure us from falling away altogether from our ideas of duty, or maintain in the soul a well-grounded respect for its law, but the clear conviction that although there should never have been actions which really sprang from such pure sources, yet whether this or that takes place is not at all the question; but that reason of itself, independent on all experience, ordains what ought to take place, that accordingly actions of which perhaps the world has hitherto never given an example, the feasibility even of which might be very much doubted by one who founds everything on experience, are nevertheless inflexibly commanded by reason; that, *ex. gr.* even though there might never yet have been a sincere friend, yet not a whit the less is pure sincerity in friendship required of every man, because, prior to all experience, this duty is involved as duty in the idea of a reason determining the will by *à priori* principles.

When we add further that, unless we deny that the notion of morality has any truth or reference to any possible object, we must admit that its law must be valid, not merely for men, but for all *rational creatures generally*, not merely under certain contingent conditions or with exceptions, but *with absolute necessity,* then it is clear that no experience could enable us to infer even the possibility of such apodictic laws. For with what right could we bring into unbounded respect as a universal precept for every rational nature that which perhaps holds only under the contingent conditions of humanity? Or how could laws of the determination of *our* will be regarded as laws of the determination of the will of rational beings generally, and for us only as such, if they were merely empirical, and did not take their origin wholly *à priori* from pure but practical reason?

Nor could anything be more fatal to morality than that we should wish to derive it from examples. For every example of it that is set before me must be first itself tested by principles of morality, whether it is worthy to serve as an original example, *i.e.* as a pattern, but by no means can it authoritatively furnish the conception of morality. Even the Holy One of the Gospels must first be compared with our ideal of moral perfection before we can recognise Him as such; and so He says of Himself, "Why call ye Me (whom you see) good; none is good (the model of good) but God only (whom ye do not see)?" But whence have we the conception of God as the supreme good? Simply from the *idea* of moral perfection, which reason frames *à priori,* and connects inseparably with the notion of a free-will. Imitation finds no place at all in morality, and examples serve only for encouragement, *i.e.* they put beyond doubt the feasibility of what the law commands, they make visible that which the practical rule expresses more generally, but they can never authorize us to set aside the true original which lies in reason, and to guide ourselves by examples.

If then there is no genuine supreme principle of morality but what must rest simply on pure reason, independent on all experience, I think it is not necessary even to put the question, whether it is good to exhibit these concepts in their generality (*in abstracto*) as they are established *à priori* along with the principles belonging to them, if our knowledge is to be distinguished from the *vulgar,* and to be called philosophical. In our times indeed this might perhaps be necessary; for if we collected votes, whether pure rational knowledge separated from everything empirical, that is to say, metaphysic of morals, or whether popular practical philosophy is to be preferred, it is easy to guess which side would preponderate.

This descending to popular notions is certainly very commendable, if the ascent to the principles of pure reason has first taken place and been satisfactorily accomplished. This implies that we first *found* Ethics on Metaphysics, and then, when it is firmly established, procure a *hearing* for it by giving it a popular character. But it is quite absurd to try to be popular in the first inquiry, on which the soundness of the principles depends. It is not only that this proceeding can never lay claim to the very rare merit of a true *philosophical popularity,* since there is no art in being intelligible if one renounces all thoroughness of insight; but also it produces a disgusting medley of compiled observations and half-reasoned principles. Shallow pates enjoy this because it can be used for every-day chat, but the sagacious find in it only confusion, and being unsatisfied and unable to help themselves, they turn away their eyes, while philosophers, who see quite well through this delusion, are little listened to when they call men off for a time from this pretended popularity, in order that they might be rightfully popular after they have attained a definite insight.

We need only look at the attempts of moralists in that favourite fashion, and we shall find at one time the special constitution of human nature (including, however, the idea of a rational nature generally), at one time perfection, at another happiness, here moral sense, there fear of God, a little of this, and a little of that, in marvellous mixture without its occurring to them to ask whether the principles of morality are to be sought in the knowledge of human nature at all (which we can have only from experience); and, if this is not so, if these principles are to be found altogether *à priori* free from everything empirical, in pure rational concepts only, and nowhere else, not even in the smallest degree; then rather to adopt the method of making this a separate inquiry, as pure practical philosophy, or (if one may use a name so decried) as metaphysic of morals,[1] to bring it by itself to completeness, and to require the public, which wishes for popular treatment, to await the issue of this undertaking.

Such a metaphysic of morals, completely isolated, not mixed with any anthropology, theology, physics, or hyperphysics, and still less with occult qualities (which we might call hypophysical), is not only an indispensable substratum of all sound theoretical knowledge of duties, but is at the same time a desideratum of the highest importance to the actual fulfilment of their precepts. For the pure conception of duty, unmixed with any foreign addition of empirical attractions, and, in a word, the conception of the moral law, exercises on the human heart, by way of reason alone(which first becomes aware with this that it can of itself be practical), an influence so much more powerful than all other springs[2] which may be derived from the field of experience, that in the consciousness of its worth, it despises the latter, and can by degrees become their master; whereas a mixed ethics, compounded partly of motives drawn from feelings and inclinations, and partly also of conceptions of reason, must make the mind waver between motives which cannot be brought under any principle, which lead to good only by mere accident, and very often also to evil.

From what has been said, it is clear that all moral conceptions have their seat and origin completely *à priori* in the reason, and that, moreover, in the commonest reason just as truly as in that which is in the highest degree speculative; that they cannot be obtained by abstraction from any empirical, and therefore merely contingent knowledge; that it is just this purity of their origin that makes them worthy to serve as our supreme practical principle, and that just in proportion as we add anything empirical, we detract from their genuine influence, and from the absolute value of actions; that it is not only of the greatest necessity, in a purely speculative point of view, but is also of the greatest practical importance to derive these notions and laws from pure reason, to present them pure and unmixed, and even to determine the compass of this practical or pure rational knowledge, *i.e.* to determine the whole faculty of pure practical reason; and, in doing so, we must not make its principles dependent on the particular nature of human reason, though in speculative philosophy this may be permitted, or may even at times be necessary; but since moral laws ought to hold good for every rational creature, we must derive them from the general concept of a rational being. In this way, although for its *application* to man morality has need of anthropology, yet, in the first instance, we

---

1. Just as pure mathematics are distinguished from applied, pure logic from applied, so if we choose we may also distinguish pure philosophy of morals (metaphysic) from applied (viz. applied to human nature). By this designation we are also at once reminded that moral principles are not based on properties of human nature, but must subsist *à priori* of themselves, while from such principles practical rules must be capable of being deduced for every rational nature, and accordingly for that of man.

2. I have a letter from the late excellent Sulzer, in which he asks me what can be the reason that moral instruction, although containing much that is convincing for the reason, yet accomplishes so little? My answer was postponed in order that I might make it complete. But it is simply this that the teachers themselves have not got their own notions clear, and when they endeavour to make up for this by raking up motives of moral goodness from every quarter, trying to make their physic right strong, they spoil it. For the commonest understanding shows that if we imagine, on the one hand, an act of honesty done with steadfast mind, apart from every view to advantage of any kind in this world or another, and even under the greatest temptations of necessity or allurement, and, on the other hand, a similar act which was affected, in however low a degree, by a foreign motive, the former leaves far behind and eclipses the second; it elevates the soul, and inspires the wish to be able to act in like manner oneself; Even moderately young children feel this impression, and one should never represent duties to them in any other light.

must treat it independently as pure philosophy, *i.e.* as metaphysic, complete in itself (a thing which in such distinct branches of science is easily done); knowing well that unless we are in possession of this, it would not only be vain to determine the moral element of duty in right actions for purposes of speculative criticism, but it would be impossible to base morals on their genuine principles, even for common practical purposes, especially of moral instruction, so as to produce pure moral dispositions, and to engraft them on men's minds to the promotion of the greatest possible good in the world.

But in order that in this study we may not merely advance by the natural steps from the common moral judgment (in this case very worthy of respect) to the philosophical, as has been already done, but also from a popular philosophy, which goes no further than it can reach by groping with the help of examples, to metaphysic (which does not allow itself to be checked by anything empirical, and as it must measure the whole extent of this kind of rational knowledge, goes as far as ideal conceptions, where even examples fail us), we must follow and clearly describe the practical faculty of reason, from the general rules of its determination to the point where the notion of duty springs from it.

Everything in nature works according to laws. Rational beings alone have the faculty of acting according *to the conception* of laws, that is according to principles, *i.e.* have a *will*. Since the deduction of actions from principles requires *reason*, the will is nothing but practical reason. If reason infallibly determines the will, then the actions of such a being which are recognised as objectively necessary are subjectively necessary also, *i.e.* the will is a faculty to choose *that only* which reason independent on inclination recognises as practically necessary, *i.e.* as good. But if reason of itself does not sufficiently determine the will, if the latter is subject also to subjective conditions (particular impulses) which do not always coincide with the objective conditions; in a word, if the will does not *in itself* completely accord with reason (which is actually the case with men), then the actions which objectively are recognised as necessary are subjectively contingent, and the determination of such a will according to objective laws is *obligation,* that is to say, the relation of the objective laws to a will that is not thoroughly good is conceived as the determination of the will of a rational being by principles of reason, but which the will from its nature does not of necessity follow.

The conception of an objective principle, in so far as it is obligatory for a will, is called a command (of reason), and the formula of the command is called an Imperative.

All imperatives are expressed by the word *ought* [or *shall*], and thereby indicate the relation of an objective law of reason to a will, which from its subjective constitution is not necessarily determined by it (an obligation). They say that something would be good to do or to forbear, but they say it to a will which does not always do a thing because it is conceived to be good to do it. That is practically *good,* however, which determines the will by means of the conceptions of reason, and consequently not from subjective causes, but objectively, that is on principles which are valid for every rational being as such. It is distinguished from the *pleasant,* as that which influences the will only by means of sensation from merely subjective causes, valid only for the sense of this or that one, and not as a principle of reason, which holds for every one.[1]

A perfectly good will would therefore be equally subject to objective laws (viz. laws of good), but could not be conceived as *obliged* thereby to act lawfully, because of itself from its subjective constitution it can only be determined by the conception of good. Therefore no imperatives hold for the Divine will, or in general for a *holy* will; *ought* is here out of place, because the volition is already of itself necessarily in

---

1. The dependence of the desires on sensations is called inclination, and this accordingly always indicates a *want*. The dependence of a contingently determinable will on principles of reason is called an *interest*. This therefore is found only in the case of a dependent will, which does not always of itself conform to reason; in the Divine will we cannot conceive any interest. But the human will can also *take an interest* in a thing without therefore acting *from* interest. The former signifies the *practical* interest in the action, the latter the *pathological* in the object of the action. The former indicates only dependence of the will on principles of reason in themselves; the second, dependence on principles of reason for the sake of inclination, reason supplying only the practical rules how the requirement of the inclination may be satisfied. In the first case the action interests me in the second the object of the action (because it is pleasant to me). We have seen in the first section that in an action done from duty we must look not to the interest in the object, but only to that in the action itself, and in its rational principle (viz. the law).

unison with the law. Therefore imperatives are only formulæ to express the relation of objective laws of all volition to the subjective imperfection of the will of this or that rational being, *e.g.* the human will.

Now all *imperatives* command either *hypothetically* or *categorically.* The former represent the practical necessity of a possible action as means to something else that is willed (or at least which one might possibly will). The categorical imperative would be that which represented an action as necessary of itself without reference to another end, *i.e.* as objectively necessary.

Since every practical law represents a possible action as good, and on this account, for a subject who is practically determinable by reason, necessary, all imperatives are formulae determining an action which is necessary according to the principle of a will good in some respects. If now the action is good only as a means *to something else,* then the imperative is *hypothetical;* if it is conceived as good *in itself* and consequently as being necessarily the principle of a will which of itself conforms to reason, then it is *categorical.*

Thus the imperative declares what action possible by me would be good, and presents the practical rule in relation to a will which does not forthwith perform an action simply because it is good, whether because the subject does not always know that it is good, or because, even if it know this, yet its maxims might be opposed to the objective principles of practical reason.

Accordingly the hypothetical imperative only says that the action is good for some purpose, *possible* or *actual.* In the first case it is a Problematical, in the second an Assertorial practical principle. The categorical imperative which declares an action to be objectively necessary in itself without reference to any purpose, *i.e.* without any other end, is valid as a (practical) Apodictic principle.

Whatever is possible only by the power of some rational being may also be conceived as a possible purpose of some will; and therefore the principles of action as regards the means necessary to attain some possible purpose are in fact infinitely numerous. All sciences have a practical part, consisting of problems expressing that some end is possible for us, and of imperatives directing how it may be attained. These may, therefore, be called in general imperatives of skill. Here there is no question whether the end is ra-

tional and good, but only what one must do in order to attain it. The precepts for the physician to make his patient thoroughly healthy, and for a poisoner to ensure certain death, are of equal value in this respect, that each serves to effect its purpose perfectly. Since in early youth it cannot be known what ends are likely to occur to us in the course of life, parents seek to have their children taught a *great many things,* and provide for their *skill* in the use of means for all sorts of arbitrary ends, of none of which can they determine whether it may not perhaps hereafter be an object to their pupil, but which it is at all events *possible* that he might aim at; and this anxiety is so great that they commonly neglect to form and correct their judgment on the value of the things which may be chosen as ends.

There is *one* end, however, which may be assumed to be actually such to all rational beings (so far as imperatives apply to them, viz. as dependent beings), and therefore, one purpose which they not merely *may* have, but which we may with certainty assume that they all actually *have* by a natural necessity, and this is *happiness.* The hypothetical imperative which expresses the practical necessity of an action as means to the advancement of happiness is Assertorial. We are not to present it as necessary for an uncertain and merely possible purpose, but for a purpose which we may presuppose with certainty and *à priori* in every man, because it belongs to his being. Now skill in the choice of means to his own great well-being may be called *prudence,*[1] in the narrowest sense. And thus the imperative which refers to the choice of means to one's own happiness, *i.e.* the precept of prudence, is still always *hypothetical;* the action is not commanded absolutely, but only as means to another purpose.

Finally, there is an imperative which commands a certain conduct immediately, without having as its condition any other purpose to be attained by it. This imperative is Categorical. It concerns not the

---

1. The word prudence is taken in two senses: in the one it may bear the name of knowledge of the world, in the other that of private prudence. The former is a man's ability to influence others so as to use them for his own purposes. The latter is the sagacity to combine all these purposes for his own lasting benefit. This latter is properly that to which the value even of the former is reduced, and when a man is prudent in the former sense, but not in the latter, we might better say of him that he is clever and cunning, but, on the whole, imprudent.

matter of the action, or its intended result, but its form and the principle of which it is itself a result; and what is essentially good in it consists in the mental disposition, let the consequence be what it may. This imperative may be called that of Morality.

There is a marked distinction also between the volitions on these three sorts of principles in the *dissimilarity* of the obligation of the will. In order to mark this difference more clearly, I think they would be most suitably named in their order if we said they are either *rules* of skill, or *counsels* of prudence, or *commands* (*laws*) of morality. For it is *law* only that involves the conception of an *unconditional* and objective necessity, which is consequently universally valid; and commands are laws which must be obeyed, that is, must be followed, even in opposition to inclination. *Counsels,* indeed, involve necessity, but one which can only hold under a contingent subjective condition, viz. they depend on whether this or that man reckons this or that as part of his happiness; the categorical imperative, on the contrary, is not limited by any condition, and as being absolutely, although practically, necessary, may be quite properly called a command. We might also call the first kind of imperatives *technical* (belonging to art), the second *pragmatic*[1] (to welfare), the third *moral* (belonging to free conduct generally, that is, to morals).

Now arises the question, how are all these imperatives possible? This question does not seek to know how we can conceive the accomplishment of the action which the imperative ordains, but merely how we can conceive the obligation of the will which the imperative expresses. No special explanation is needed to show how an imperative of skill is possible. Whoever wills the end, wills also (so far as reason decides his conduct) the means in his power which are indispensably necessary thereto. This proposition is, as regards the volition, analytical; for, in willing an object as my effect, there is already thought the causality of myself as an acting cause, that is to say, the use of the means; and the impera-

tive educes from the conception of volition of an end the conception of actions necessary to this end. Synthetical propositions must no doubt be employed in defining the means to a proposed end; but they do not concern the principle, the act of the will, but the object and its realization. *Ex. gr.,* that in order to bisect a line on an unerring principle I must draw from its extremities two intersecting arcs; this no doubt is taught by mathematics only in synthetical propositions; but if I know that it is only by this process that the intended operation can be performed, then to say that if I fully will the operation, I also will the action required for it, is an analytical proposition; for it is one and the same thing to conceive something as an effect which I can produce in a certain way, and to conceive myself as acting in this way.

If it were only equally easy to give a definite conception of happiness, the imperatives of prudence would correspond exactly with those of skill, and would like-wise be analytical. For in this case as in that, it could be said, whoever wills the end, wills also (according to the dictate of reason necessarily) the indispensable means thereto which are in his power. But, unfortunately, the notion of happiness is so indefinite that although every man wishes to attain it, yet he never can say definitely and consistently what it is that he really wishes and wills. The reason of this is that all the elements which belong to the notion of happiness are altogether empirical, *i.e.* they must be borrowed from experience, and nevertheless the idea of happiness requires an absolute whole, a maximum of welfare in my present and all future circumstances. Now it is impossible that the most clear-sighted, and at the same time most powerful being (supposed finite) should frame to himself a definite conception of what he really wills in this. Does he will riches, how much anxiety, envy, and snares might he not thereby draw upon his shoulders? Does he will knowledge and discernment, perhaps it might prove to be only an eye so much the sharper to show him so much the more fearfully the evils that are now concealed from him and that cannot be avoided, or to impose more wants on his desires, which already give him concern enough. Would he have long life, who guarantees to him that it would not be a long misery? Would he at least have health? how often has uneasiness of the body restrained from excesses into which perfect health would have allowed one to fall? and so on. In short

---

1. It seems to me that the proper signification of the word *pragmatic* may be most accurately defined in this way. For *sanctions* are called pragmatic which flow properly not from the law of the states as necessary enactments, but from *precaution* for the general welfare. A history is composed pragmatically when it teaches *prudence,* i.e. instructs the world how it can provide for its interests better, or at least as well, as the men of former time.

he is unable, on any principle, to determine with certainty what would make him truly happy; because to do so he would need to be omniscient. We cannot therefore act on any definite principles to secure happiness, but only on empirical counsels, *ex. gr.* of regimen, frugality, courtesy, reserve, &c., which experience teaches do, on the average, most promote well-being. Hence it follows that the imperatives of prudence do not, strictly speaking, command at all, that is, they cannot present actions objectively as practically *necessary;* that they are rather to be regarded as counsels (*consilia*) than precepts (*præcepta*) of reason, that the problem to determine certainly and universally what action would promote the happiness of a rational being is completely insoluble, and consequently no imperative respecting it is possible which should, in the strict sense, command to do what makes happy; because happiness is not an ideal of reason but of imagination, resting solely on empirical grounds, and it is vain to expect that these should define an action by which one could attain the totality of a series of consequences which is really endless. This imperative of prudence would however be an analytical proposition if we assume that the means to happiness could be certainly assigned; for it is distinguished from the imperative of skill only by this, that in the latter the end is merely possible, in the former it is given; as however both only ordain the means to that which we suppose to be willed as an end, it follows that the imperative which ordains the willing of the means to him who wills the end is in both cases analytical. Thus there is no difficulty in regard to the possibility of an imperative of this kind either.

On the other hand the question, how the imperative of *morality* is possible, is undoubtedly one, the only one, demanding a solution, as this is not at all hypothetical, and the objective necessity which it presents cannot rest on any hypothesis, as is the case with the hypothetical imperatives. Only here we must never leave out of consideration that we *cannot* make out *by any example,* in other words empirically, whether there is such an imperative at all; but it is rather to be feared that all those which seem to be categorical may yet be at bottom hypothetical. For instance, when the precept is: Thou shalt not promise deceitfully; and it is assumed that the necessity of this is not a mere counsel to avoid some other evil, so that it should mean: thou shalt not

make a lying promise, lest if it become known thou shouldst destroy thy credit, but that an action of this kind must be regarded as evil in itself, so that the imperative of the prohibition is categorical; then we cannot show with certainty in any example that the will was determined merely by the law, without any other spring of action, although it may appear to be so. For it is always possible that fear of disgrace, perhaps also obscure dread of other dangers, may have a secret influence on the will. Who can prove by experience the non-existence of a cause when all that experience tells us is that we do not perceive it? But in such a case the so-called moral imperative, which as such appears to be categorical and unconditional, would in reality be only a pragmatic precept, drawing our attention to our own interests, and merely teaching us to take these into consideration.

We shall therefore have to investigate *à priori* the possibility of a categorical imperative, as we have not in this case the advantage of its reality being given in experience, so that its possibility should be requisite only for its explanation, not for its establishment. In the meantime it may be discerned beforehand that the categorical imperative alone has the purport of a practical law: all the rest may indeed be called *principles* of the will but not laws, since whatever is only necessary for the attainment of some arbitrary purpose may be considered as in itself contingent, and we can at any time be free from the precept if we give up the purpose: on the contrary, the unconditional command leaves the will no liberty to choose the opposite; consequently it alone carries with it that necessity which we require in a law.

Secondly, in the case of this categorical imperative or law of morality, the difficulty (of discerning its possibility) is a very profound one. It is an *à priori* synthetical practical proposition;[1] and as there is so much difficulty in discerning the possibility of speculative propositions of this kind, it may readily be

---

1. I connect the act with the will without presupposing any condition resulting from any inclination, but *à priori,* and therefore necessarily (though only objectively, *i.e.* assuming the idea of a reason possessing full power over all subjective motives). This is accordingly a practical proposition which does not deduce the willing of an action by mere analysis from another already presupposed (for we have not such a perfect will), but connects it immediately with the conception of the will of a rational being, as something not contained in it.

supposed that the difficulty will be no less with the practical.

In this problem we will first inquire whether the mere conception of a categorical imperative may not perhaps supply us also with the formula of it, containing the proposition which alone can be a categorical imperative; for even if we know the tenor of such an absolute command, yet how it is possible will require further special and laborious study, which we postpone to the last section.

When I conceive a hypothetical imperative in general, I do not know beforehand what it will contain until I am given the condition. But when I conceive a categorical imperative I know at once what it contains. For as the imperative contains besides the law only the necessity that the maxims[1] shall conform to this law, while the law contains no conditions restricting it, there remains nothing but the general statement that the maxim of the action should conform to a universal law, and it is this conformity alone that the imperative properly represents as necessary.

There is therefore but one categorical imperative, namely this: *Act only on that maxim whereby thou canst at the same time will that it should become a universal law.*

Now if all imperatives of duty can be deduced from this one imperative as from their principle, then, although it should remain undecided whether what is called duty is not merely a vain notion, yet at least we shall be able to show what we understand by it and what this notion means.

Since the universality of the law according to which effects are produced constitutes what is properly called *nature* in the most general sense (as to form), that is, the existence of things so far as it is determined by general laws, the imperative of duty may be expressed thus: *Act as if the maxim of thy action were to become by thy will a Universal Law of Nature.*

We will now enumerate a few duties, adopting the usual division of them into duties to ourselves and to others, and into perfect and imperfect duties.[2]

1. A man reduced to despair by a series of misfortunes feels wearied of life, but is still so far in possession of his reason that he can ask himself whether it would not be contrary to his duty to himself to take his own life. Now he inquires whether the maxim of his action could become a universal law of nature. His maxim is: From self-love I adopt it as a principle to shorten my life when its longer duration is likely to bring more evil than satisfaction. It is asked then simply whether this principle founded on self-love can become a universal law of nature. Now we see at once that a system of nature of which it should be a law to destroy life by means of the very feeling whose special nature it is to impel to the improvement of life would contradict itself, and therefore could not exist as a system of nature; hence that maxim cannot possibly exist as a universal law of nature, and consequently would be wholly inconsistent with the supreme principle of all duty.

2. Another finds himself forced by necessity to borrow money. He knows that he will not be able to repay it, but sees also that nothing will be lent to him, unless he promises stoutly to repay it in a definite time. He desires to make this promise, but he has still so much conscience as to ask himself: Is it not unlawful and inconsistent with duty to get out of a difficulty in this way? Suppose however that he resolves to do so, then the maxim of his action would be expressed thus: When I think myself in want of money, I will borrow money and promise to repay it, although I know that I never can do so. Now this principle of self-love or of one's own advantage may perhaps be consistent with my whole future welfare; but the question now is, is it right? I change then the suggestion of self-love into a universal law, and state the question thus: How would it be if my maxim were a universal law? Then I see at once that it could

---

1. A MAXIM is a subjective principle of action, and must be distinguished from the *objective principle*, namely, practical law. The former contains the practical rule set by reason according to the conditions of the subject (often its ignorance or its inclinations), so that it is the principle on which the subject *acts;* but the law is the objective principle valid for every rational being, and is the principle on which it *ought to act,* that is, an imperative.

---

2. It must be noted here that I reserve the division of duties for a future *metaphysic of morals;* so that I give it here only as an arbitrary one (in order to arrange my examples). For the rest, I understand by a perfect duty one that admits no exception in favour of inclination, and then I have not merely external, but also internal perfect duties. This is contrary to the use of the word adopted in the schools; but I do not intend to justify it here, as it is all one for my purpose whether it is admitted or not.

never hold as a universal law of nature but would necessarily contradict itself. For supposing it to be a universal law that everyone when he thinks himself in a difficulty should be able to promise whatever he pleases, with the purpose of not keeping his promise, the promise itself would become impossible, as well as the end that one might have in view in it, since no one would consider that anything was promised to him, but would ridicule all such statements as vain pretences.

3. A third finds in himself a talent which with the help of some culture might make him a useful man in many respects. But he finds himself in comfortable circumstances, and prefers to indulge in pleasure rather than to take pains in enlarging and improving his happy natural capacities. He asks, however, whether his maxim of neglect of his natural gifts, besides agreeing with his inclination to indulgence, agrees also with what is called duty. He sees then that a system of nature could indeed subsist with such a universal law although men (like the South Sea islanders) should let their talents rust, and resolve to devote their lives merely to idleness, amusement, and propagation of their species—in a word, to enjoyment; but he cannot possibly *will* that this should be a universal law of nature, or be implanted in us as such by a natural instinct. For, as a rational being, he necessarily wills that his faculties be developed, since they serve him, and have been given him, for all sorts of possible purposes.

4. A fourth, who is in prosperity, while he sees that others have to contend with great wretchedness and that he could help them, thinks: What concern is it of mine? Let everyone be as happy as heaven pleases, or as he can make himself; I will take nothing from him nor even envy him, only I do not wish to contribute anything to his welfare or to his assistance in distress Now no doubt if such a mode of thinking were a universal law, the human race might very well subsist, and doubtless even better than in a state in which every one talks of sympathy and good-will, or even takes care occasionally to put it into practice, but on the other side, also cheats when he can, betrays the rights of men, or otherwise violates them. But although it is possible that a universal law of nature might exist in accordance with that maxim, it is impossible to *will* that such a principle should have the universal validity of a law of nature. For a will

which resolved this would contradict itself, inasmuch as many cases might occur in which one would have need of the love and sympathy of others, and in which, by such a law of nature, sprung from his own will, he would deprive himself of all hope of the aid he desires.

These are a few of the many actual duties, or at least what we regard as such, which obviously fall into two classes on the one principle that we have laid down. We must be *able to will* that a maxim of our action should be a universal law. This is the canon of the moral appreciation of the action generally. Some actions are of such a character that their maxim cannot without contradiction be even *conceived* as a universal law of nature, far from it being possible that we should *will* that it *should* be so. In others this intrinsic impossibility is not found, but still it is impossible to *will* that their maxim should be raised to the universality of a law of nature, since such a will would contradict itself. It is easily seen that the former violate strict or rigorous (inflexible) duty; the latter only laxer (meritorious) duty. Thus it has been completely shown by these examples how all duties depend as regards the nature of the obligation (not the object of the action) on the same principle.

If now we attend to ourselves on occasion of any transgression of duty, we shall find that we in fact do not will that our maxim should be a universal law, for that is impossible for us; on the contrary we will that the opposite should remain a universal law, only we assume the liberty of making an *exception* in our own favour or (just for this time only) in favour of our inclination. Consequently if we considered all cases from one and the same point of view, namely, that of reason, we should find a contradiction in our own will, namely, that a certain principle should be objectively necessary as a universal law, and yet subjectively should not be universal, but admit of exceptions. As however we at one moment regard our action from the point of view of a will wholly conformed to reason, and then again look at the same action from the point of view of a will affected by inclination, there is not really any contradiction, but an antagonism of inclination to the precept of reason, whereby the universality of the principle is changed into a mere generality, so that the practical principle of reason shall meet the maxim half way. Now, although this cannot be justified in our own impartial judgment, yet it proves that we do really recognise the validity of the categorical imperative and (with all respect for it) only allow ourselves a few exceptions, which we think unimportant and forced from us.

We have thus established at least this much, that if duty is a conception which is to have any import and real legislative authority for our actions, it can only be expressed in categorical, and not at all in hypothetical imperatives. We have also, which is of great importance, exhibited clearly and definitely for every practical application the content of the categorical imperative, which must contain the principle of all duty if there is such a thing at all. We have not yet, however, advanced so far as to prove *à priori* that there actually is such an imperative, that there is a practical law which commands absolutely of itself and without any other impulse, and that the following of this law is duty.

With the view of attaining to this it is of extreme importance to remember that we must not allow ourselves to think of deducing the reality of this principle from the *particular attributes of human nature*. For duty is to be a practical, unconditional necessity of action; it must therefore hold for all rational beings (to whom an imperative can apply at all) and *for this reason only* be also a law for all human wills. On the contrary, whatever is deduced from the particular natural characteristics of humanity, from certain feelings and propensions, nay even, if possible, from any particular tendency proper to human reason, and which need not necessarily hold for the will of every rational being; this may indeed supply us with a maxim, but not with a law; with a subjective principle on which we may have a propension and inclination to act, but not with an objective principle on which we should be *enjoined* to act, even though all our propensions, inclinations, and natural dispositions were opposed to it. In fact the sublimity and intrinsic dignity of the command in duty are so much the more evident, the less the subjective impulses favour it and the more they oppose it, without being able in the slightest degree to weaken the obligation of the law or to diminish its validity.

Here then we see philosophy brought to a critical position, since it has to be firmly fixed, notwithstanding that it has nothing to support it either in heaven or earth. Here it must show its purity as absolute dictator of its own laws, not the herald of those which are whispered to it by an implanted sense or who knows what tutelary nature. Although these may be better than nothing, yet they can never afford principles dictated by reason, which must have their source wholly *à priori* and thence their commanding authority, expecting everything from the supremacy of the law and the due respect for it, nothing from inclination, or else condemning the man to self-contempt and inward abhorrence.

Thus every empirical element is not only quite incapable of being an aid to the principle of morality, but is even highly prejudicial to the purity of morals, for the proper and inestimable worth of an absolutely good will consists just in this, that the principle of action is free from all influence of contingent grounds, which alone experience can furnish. We cannot too much or too often repeat our warning against this lax and even mean habit of thought which seeks for its principle amongst empirical motives and laws; for human reason in its weariness is glad to rest on this pillow, and in a dream of sweet illusions (in which, instead of Juno, it embraces a cloud) it substitutes for morality a bastard patched up from limbs of various derivation, which looks like anything one chooses to see in it; only not like virtue to one who has once beheld her in her true form.[1]

The question then is this: Is it a necessary law *for all rational beings* that they should always judge of their actions by maxims of which they can themselves will that they should serve as universal laws? If it is so, then it must be connected (altogether *à priori*) with the very conception of the will of a rational being generally. But in order to discover this connexion we must, however reluctantly, take a step into metaphysic, although into a domain of it which is distinct from speculative philosophy, namely, the metaphysic of morals. In a practical philosophy, where it is not the reasons of what *happens* that we have to ascertain, but the laws of what *ought to happen*, even although it never does, *i.e.* objective practical laws, there it is not necessary to inquire into the reasons why anything pleases or displeases, how the pleasure of mere sensation differs from taste, and whether the latter is distinct from a general sat-

---

1. To behold virtue in her proper form is nothing else but to contemplate morality stripped of all admixture of sensible things and of every spurious ornament of reward or self-love. How much she then eclipses everything else that appears charming to the affections, every one may readily perceive with the least exertion of his reason, if it be not wholly spoiled for abstraction.

isfaction of reason; on what the feeling of pleasure or pain rests, and how from it desires and inclinations arise, and from these again maxims by the co-operation of reason: for all this belongs to an empirical psychology, which would constitute the second part of physics, if we regard physics as the *philosophy of nature,* so far as it is based on *empirical laws.* But here we are concerned with objective practical laws, and consequently with the relation of the will to itself so far as it is determined by reason alone, in which case whatever has reference to anything empirical is necessarily excluded; since if *reason of itself alone* determines the conduct (and it is the possibility of this that we are now investigating), it must necessarily do so *à priori.*

The will is conceived as a faculty of determining oneself to action *in accordance with the conception of certain laws.* And such a faculty can be found only in rational beings. Now that which serves the will as the objective ground of its self-determination is the *end,* and if this is assigned by reason alone, it must hold for all rational beings. On the other hand, that which merely contains the ground of possibility of the action of which the effect is the end, this is called the *means.* The subjective ground of the desire is the *spring,* the objective ground of the volition is the *motive;* hence the distinction between subjective ends which rest on springs, and objective ends which depend on motives valid for every rational being. Practical principles are *formal* when they abstract from all subjective ends, they are *material* when they assume these, and therefore particular springs of action. The ends which a rational being proposes to himself at pleasure as *effects* of his actions (material ends) are all only relative, for it is only their relation to the particular desires of the subject that gives them their worth, which therefore cannot furnish principles universal and necessary for all rational beings and for every volition, that is to say practical laws. Hence all these relative ends can give rise only to hypothetical imperatives.

Supposing, however, that there were something *whose existence* has *in itself* an absolute worth, something which, being *an end in itself,* could be a source of definite laws, then in this and this alone would lie the source of a possible categorical imperative, *i.e.* a practical law.

Now I say: man and generally any rational being *exists* as an end in himself, *not merely as a means* to be arbitrarily used by this or that will, but in all his actions, whether they concern himself or other ratio-

nal beings, must be always regarded at the same time as an end. All objects of the inclinations have only a conditional worth, for if the inclinations and the wants founded on them did not exist, then their object would be without value. But the inclinations themselves being sources of want, are so far from having an absolute worth for which they should be desired, that on the contrary it must be the universal wish of every rational being to be wholly free from them. Thus the worth of any object which is *to be acquired* by our action is always conditional. Beings whose existence depends not on our will but on nature's, have nevertheless, if they are irrational beings, only a relative value as means, and are therefore called *things;* rational beings, on the contrary, are called *persons,* because their very nature points them out as ends in themselves, that is as something which must not be used merely as means, and so far therefore restricts freedom of action (and is an object of respect). These, therefore, are not merely subjective ends whose existence has a worth *for us* as an effect of our action, but *objective ends,* that is things whose existence is an end in itself: an end moreover for which no other can be substituted, which they should subserve *merely* as means, for otherwise nothing whatever would possess *absolute worth;* but if all worth were conditioned and therefore contingent, then there would be no supreme practical principle of reason whatever.

If then there is a supreme practical principle or, in respect of the human will, a categorical imperative, it must be one which, being drawn from the conception of that which is necessarily an end for every one because it is *an end in itself,* constitutes an *objective* principle of will, and can therefore serve as a universal practical law. The foundation of this principle is: *rational nature exists as an end in itself.* Man necessarily conceives his own existence as being so: so far then this is a *subjective* principle of human actions. But every other rational being regards its existence similarly, just on the same rational principle that holds for me:[1] so that it is at the same time an objective principle, from which as a supreme practical law all laws of the will must be capable of being deduced. Accordingly the practical imperative will be

---

1. This proposition is here stated as a postulate. The grounds of it will be found in the concluding section.

as follows: *So act as to treat humanity, whether in thine own person or in that of any other, in every case as an end withal, never as means only*. We will now inquire whether this can be practically carried out.

To abide by the previous examples:

Firstly, under the head of necessary duty to oneself: He who contemplates suicide should ask himself whether his action can be consistent with the idea of humanity *as an end in itself*. If he destroys himself in order to escape from painful circumstances, he uses a person merely as a *mean* to maintain a tolerable condition up to the end of life. But a man is not a thing, that is to say, something which can be used merely as means, but must in all his actions be always considered as an end in himself. I cannot, therefore, dispose in any way of a man in my own person so as to mutilate him, to damage or kill him. (It belongs to ethics proper to define this principle more precisely so as to avoid all misunderstanding, *e.g.* as to the amputation of the limbs in order to preserve myself; as to exposing my life to danger with a view to preserve it, &c. This question is therefore omitted here.)

Secondly, as regards necessary duties, or those of strict obligation, towards others; he who is thinking of making a lying promise to others will see at once that he would be using another man *merely as a mean,* without the latter containing at the same time the end in himself. For he whom I propose by such a promise to use for my own purposes cannot possibly assent to my mode of acting towards him, and therefore cannot himself contain the end of this action. This violation of the principle of humanity in other men is more obvious if we take in examples of attacks on the freedom and property of others. For then it is clear that he who trangresses the rights of men, intends to use the person of others merely as means, without considering that as rational beings they ought always to be esteemed also as ends, that is, as beings who must be capable of containing in themselves the end of the very same action.[1]

Thirdly, as regards contingent (meritorious) duties to oneself; is not enough that the action does not vi-

olate humanity in our own person as an end in itself, it must also *harmonize with* it. Now there are in humanity capacities of greater perfection, which belong to the end that nature has in view in regard to humanity in ourselves as the subject: to neglect these might perhaps be consistent with the *maintenance* of humanity as an end in itself; but not with the *advancement* of this end.

Fourthly, as regards meritorious duties towards others: the natural end which all men have is their own happiness. Now humanity might indeed subsist, although no one should contribute anything to the happiness of others, provided he did not intentionally withdraw anything from it; but after all this would only harmonise negatively not positively with *humanity as an end in itself,* if every one does not also endeavour, as far as in him lies, to forward the ends of others. For the ends of any subject which is an end in himself, ought as far as possible to be *my* ends also, if that conception is to have its *full* effect with me.

This principle, that humanity and generally every rational nature is *an end in itself* (which is the supreme limiting condition of every man's freedom of action), is not borrowed from experience, *firstly,* because it is universal, applying as it does to all rational beings whatever, and experience is not capable of determining anything about them; *secondly,* because it does not present humanity as an end to men (subjectively), that is as an object which men do of themselves actually adopt as an end; but as an objective end, which must as a law constitute the supreme limiting condition of all our subjective ends, let them be what we will; it must therefore spring from pure reason. In fact the objective principle of all practical legislation lies (according to the first principle) in *the rule* and its form of universality which makes it capable of being a law (say *e.g.,* a law of nature); but the *subjective* principle is in the *end;* now by the second principle the subject of all ends is each rational being, inasmuch as it is in end in itself. Hence follows the third practical principle of the will, which is the ultimate condition of its harmony with the universal practical

---

1. Let it not be thought that the common: *quod tibi non vis fieri, &c.,* could serve here as the rule or principle. For it is only a deduction from the former, though with several limitations; it cannot be a universal law, for it does not contain the principle of duties to oneself, nor of the duties of benevolence to others (for many a one would gladly consent that others should not benefit him, provided only that he might be excused from showing benevolence to them), nor finally that of duties of strict obligation to one another, for on this principle the criminal might argue against the judge who punishes him, and so on.

reason, viz.: the idea of *the will of every rational being as a universally legislative will.*

On this principle all maxims are rejected which are inconsistent with the will being itself universal legislator. Thus the will is not subject simply to the law, but so subject that it must be regarded *as itself giving the law,* and on this ground only, subject to the law (of which it can regard itself as the author).

In the previous imperatives, namely, that based on the conception of the conformity of actions to general laws, as in a *physical system of nature,* and that based on the universal *prerogative* of rational beings as *ends* in themselves—these imperatives just because they were conceived as categorical, excluded from any share in their authority all admixture of any interest as a spring of action; they were however only *assumed* to be categorical, because such an assumption was necessary to explain the conception of duty. But we could not prove independently that there are practical propositions which command categorically, nor can it be proved in this section; one thing however could be done, namely, to indicate in the imperative itself by some determinate expression, that in the case of volition from duty all interest is renounced, which is the specific criterion of categorical as distinguished from hypothetical imperatives. This is done in the present (third) formula of the principle, namely, in the idea of the will of every rational being as a *universally legislating will.*

For although a will *which is subject to laws* may be attached to this law by means of an interest, yet a will which is itself a supreme law given so far as it is such cannot possibly depend on any interest, since a will so dependent would itself still need another law restricting the interest of its self-love by the condition that it should be valid as universal law.

Thus the *principle* that every human will is *a will which in all its maxims gives universal laws,*[1] provided it be otherwise justified, would be very *well adapted* to be the categorical imperative, in this respect, namely, that just because of the idea of universal legislation it is *not based on any interest,* and therefore it alone among all possible imperatives can be *unconditional.* Or still better, converting the proposition, if

there is a categorical imperative (*i.e.,* a law for the will of every rational being), it can only command that everything be done from maxims of one's will regarded as a will which could at the same time will that it should itself give universal laws, for in that case only the practical principle and the imperative which it obeys are unconditional, since they cannot be based on any interest.

Looking back now on all previous attempts to discover the principle of morality, we need not wonder why they all failed. It was seen that man was bound to laws by duty, but it was not observed that the laws to which he is subject are *only those of his own giving,* though at the same time they are *universal,* and that he is only bound to act in conformity with his own will; a will, however, which is designed by nature to give universal laws. For when one has conceived man only as subject to a law (no matter what), then this law required some interest, either by way of attraction or constraint, since it did not originate as a law from *his own* will, but this will was according to a law obliged by *something else* to act in a certain manner. Now by this necessary consequence all the labour spent in finding a supreme principle of *duty* was irrevocably lost. For men never elicited duty, but only a necessity of acting from a certain interest. Whether this interest was private or otherwise, in any case the imperative must be conditional, and could not by any means be capable of being a moral command. I will therefore call this the principle of *Autonomy* of the will, in contrast with every other which I accordingly reckon as *Heteronomy.*

The conception of every rational being as one which must consider itself as giving in all the maxims of its will universal laws, so as to judge itself and its actions from this point of view—this conception leads to another which depends on it and is very fruitful, namely, that of *a kingdom of ends.*

By a *kingdom* I understand the union of different rational beings in a system by common laws. Now since it is by laws that ends are determined as regards their universal validity, hence, if we abstract from the personal differences of rational beings, and likewise from all the content of their private ends, we shall be able to conceive all ends combined in a systematic whole (including both rational beings as ends in themselves, and also the special ends which each may propose to himself), that is to say, we can

---

1. I may be excused from adducing examples to elucidate this principle, as those which have already been used to elucidate the categorical imperative and its formula would all serve for the like purpose here.

conceive a kingdom of ends, which on the preceding principles is possible.

For all rational beings come under the *law* that each of them must treat itself and all others *never merely as means,* but in every case *at the same time as ends in themselves.* Hence results a systematic union of rational beings by common objective laws, *i.e.,* a kingdom which may be called a kingdom of ends, since what these laws have in view is just the relation of these beings to one another as ends and means. It is certainly only an ideal.

A rational being belongs as a *member* to the kingdom of ends when, although giving universal laws in it, he is also himself subject to these laws. He belongs to it *as sovereign* when, while giving laws, he is not subject to the will of any other.

A rational being must always regard himself as giving laws either as member or as sovereign in a kingdom of ends which is rendered possible by the freedom of will. He cannot, however, maintain the latter position merely by the maxims of his will, but only in case he is a completely independent being without wants and with unrestricted power adequate to his will.

Morality consists then in the reference of all action to the legislation which alone can render a kingdom of ends possible. This legislation must be capable of existing in every rational being, and of emanating from his will, so that the principle of this will is, never to act on any maxim which could not without contradiction be also a universal law, and accordingly always so to act *that the will could at the same time regard itself as giving in its maxims universal laws.* If now the maxims of rational beings are not by their own nature coincident with this objective principle, then the necessity of acting on it is called practical necessitation, *i.e.,* duty. Duty does not apply to the sovereign in the kingdom of ends, but it does to every member of it and to all in the same degree.

The practical necessity of acting on this principle, *i.e.,* duty, does not rest at all on feelings, impulses, or inclinations, but solely on the relation of rational beings to one another, a relation in which the will of a rational being must always be regarded as *legislative,* since otherwise it could not be conceived as *an end in itself.* Reason then refers every maxim of the will, regarding it as legislating universally, to every other will and also to every action towards oneself; and this not on account of any other practical motive or

any future advantage, but from the idea of the *dignity* of a rational being, obeying no law but that which he himself also gives.

In the kingdom of ends everything has either Value or Dignity. Whatever has a value can be replaced by something else which is *equivalent;* whatever, on the other hand, is above all value, and therefore admits of no equivalent, has a dignity.

Whatever has reference to the general inclinations and wants of mankind has a *market value;* whatever, without presupposing a want, corresponds to a certain taste, that is to a satisfaction in the mere purposeless play of our faculties, has a *fancy value;* but that which constitutes the condition under which alone anything can be an end in itself, this has not merely a relative worth, *i.e.,* value, but an intrinsic worth, that is *dignity.*

Now morality is the condition under which alone a rational being can be an end in himself, since by this alone is it possible that he should be a legislating member in the kingdom of ends. Thus morality, and humanity as capable of it, is that which alone has dignity. Skill and diligence in labour have a market value; wit, lively imagination, and humour, have fancy value; on the other hand, fidelity to promises, benevolence from principle (not from instinct), have an intrinsic worth. Neither nature nor art contains anything which in default of these it could put in their place, for their worth consists not in the effects which spring from them, not in the use and advantage which they secure, but in the disposition of mind, that is, the maxims of the will which are ready to manifest themselves in such actions, even though they should not have the desired effect. These actions also need no recommendation from any subjective taste or sentiment, that they may be looked on with immediate favour and satisfaction: they need no immediate propension or feeling for them; they exhibit the will that performs them as an object of an immediate respect, and nothing but reason is required to *impose* them on the will, not to *flatter* it into them, which, in the case of duties, would be a contradiction. This estimation therefore shows that the worth of such a disposition is dignity, and places it infinitely above all value, with which it cannot for a moment be brought into comparison or competition without as it were violating its sanctity.

What then is it which justifies virtue or the morally good disposition, in making such lofty claims? It is nothing less than the privilege it secures to the rational being of participating in the giving of universal laws, by which it qualifies him to be a member of a possible kingdom of ends, a privilege to which he was already destined by his own nature as being an end in himself; and on that account legislating in the kingdom of ends; free as regards all laws of physical nature, and obeying those only which he himself gives, and by which his maxims can belong to a system of universal law, to which at the same time he submits himself. For nothing has any worth except what the law assigns it. Now the legislation itself which assigns the worth of everything, must for that very reason possess dignity, that is an unconditional incomparable worth, and the word *respect* alone supplies a becoming expression for the esteem which a rational being must have for it. *Autonomy* then is the basis of the dignity of human and of every rational nature.

The three modes of presenting the principle of morality that have been adduced are at bottom only so many formulæ of the very same law, and each of itself involves the other two. There is, however, a difference in them, but it is rather subjectively than objectively practical, intended namely to bring an idea of the reason nearer to intuition (by means of a certain analogy), and thereby nearer to feeling. All maxims, in fact, have—

1. A *form,* consisting in universality; and in this view the formula of the moral imperative is expressed thus, that the maxims must be so chosen as if they were to serve as universal laws of nature.

2. A *matter,* namely, an end, and here the formula says that the rational being, as it is an end by its own nature and therefore an end in itself, must in every maxim serve as the condition limiting all merely relative and arbitrary ends.

3. A *complete characterisation* of all maxims by means of that formula, namely, that all maxims ought by their own legislation to harmonise with a possible kingdom of ends as with a kingdom of nature.[1] There

is a progress here in the order of the categories of *unity* of the form of the will (its universality), *plurality* of the matter (the objects, *i.e.,* the ends), and *totality* of the system of these. In forming our moral *judgment* of actions it is better to proceed always on the strict method, and start from the general formula of the categorical imperative: *Act according to a maxim which can at the same time make itself a universal law.* If, however, we wish to gain an *entrance* for the moral law, it is very useful to bring one and the same action under the three specified conceptions, and thereby as far as possible to bring it nearer to intuition.

We can now end where we started at the beginning, namely, with the conception of a will unconditionally good. *That will is absolutely good* which cannot be evil, in other words, whose maxim, if made a universal law, could never contradict itself. This principle then is its supreme law: Act always on such a maxim as thou canst at the same time will to be a universal law; this is the sole condition under which a will can never contradict itself; and such an imperative is categorical. Since the validity of the will as a universal law for possible actions is analogous to the universal connexion of the existence of things by general laws, which is the formal notion of nature in general, the categorical imperative can also be expressed thus: *Act on maxims which can at the same time have for their object themselves as universal laws of nature.* Such then is the formula of an absolutely good will.

Rational nature is distinguished from the rest of nature by this, that it sets before itself an end. This end would be the matter of every good will. But since in the idea of a will that is absolutely good without being limited by any condition (of attaining this or that end) we must abstract wholly from every end *to be effected* (since this would make every will only relatively good), it follows that in this case the end must be conceived, not as an end to be effected, but as an *independently* existing end. Consequently it is conceived only negatively, *i.e.,* as that which we must never act against, and which, therefore, must never be regarded merely as means, but must in every volition be esteemed as an end likewise. Now this end can be nothing but the subject of all possible ends, since this is also the subject of a possible absolutely good will; for such a will cannot without contradiction be postponed to any other object. The

---

1. Teleology considers nature as a kingdom of ends; Ethics regards a possible kingdom of ends as a kingdom of nature. In the first case, the kingdom of ends is a theoretical idea, adopted to explain what actually is. In the latter it is a practical idea, adopted to bring about that which is not yet, but which can be realised by our conduct, namely, if it conforms to this idea.

principle: So act in regard to every rational being (thyself and others), that he may always have place in thy maxim as an end in himself, is accordingly essentially identical with this other: Act upon a maxim which, at the same time, involves its own universal validity for every rational being. For that in using means for every end I should limit my maxim by the condition of its holding good as a law for every subject, this comes to the same thing as that the fundamental principle of all maxims of action must be that the subject of all ends, i.e., the rational being himself, be never employed merely as means, but as the supreme condition restricting the use of all means, that is in every case as an end likewise.

It follows incontestably that, to whatever laws any rational being may be subject, he being an end in himself must be able to regard himself as also legislating universally in respect of these same laws, since it is just this fitness of his maxims for universal legislation that distinguishes him as an end in himself; also it follows that this implies his dignity (prerogative) above all mere physical beings, that he must always take his maxims from the point of view which regards himself, and likewise every other rational being, as lawgiving beings (on which account they are called persons). In this way a world of rational beings (*mundus intelligibilis*) is possible as a kingdom of ends, and this by virtue of the legislation proper to all persons as members. Therefore every rational being must so act as if he were by his maxims in every case a legislating member in the universal kingdom of ends. The formal principle of these maxims is: So act as if thy maxim were to serve likewise as the universal law (of all rational beings). A kingdom of ends is thus only possible on the analogy of a kingdom of nature, the former however only by maxims, that is self-imposed rules, the latter only by the laws of efficient causes acting under necessitation from without. Nevertheless, although the system of nature is looked upon as a machine, yet so far as it has reference to rational beings as its ends, it is given on this account the name of a kingdom of nature. Now such a kingdom of ends would be actually realised by means of maxims conforming to the canon which the categorical imperative prescribes to all rational beings, *if they were universally followed*. But although a rational being, even if he punctually follows this maxim himself, cannot reckon upon all others being therefore true to the same, nor expect that the kingdom of nature and its orderly arrangements shall be in harmony with him as a fitting member, so as to form a kingdom of ends to which he himself contributes, that is to say, that it shall favour his expectation of happiness, still that law: Act according to the maxims of a member of a merely possible kingdom of ends legislating in it universally, remains in its full force, inasmuch as it commands categorically. And it is just in this that the paradox lies; that the mere dignity of man as a rational creature, without any other end or advantage to be attained thereby, in other words, respect for a mere idea, should yet serve as an inflexible precept of the will, and that it is precisely in this independence of the maxim on all such springs of action that its sublimity consists; and it is this that makes every rational subject worthy to be a legislative member in the kingdom of ends: for otherwise he would have to be conceived only as subject to the physical law of his wants. And although we should suppose the kingdom of nature and the kingdom of ends to be united under one sovereign, so that the latter kingdom thereby ceased to be a mere idea and acquired true reality, then it would no doubt gain the accession of a strong spring, but by no means any increase of its intrinsic worth. For this sole absolute lawgiver must, notwithstanding this, be always conceived as estimating the worth of rational beings only by their disinterested behaviour, as prescribed to themselves from that idea [the dignity of man] alone. The essence of things is not altered by their external relations, and that which abstracting from these, alone constitutes the absolute worth of man, is also that by which he must be judged, whoever the judge may be, and even by the Supreme Being. *Morality* then is the relation of actions to the autonomy of the will, that is, to the potential universal legislation by its maxims. An action that is consistent with the autonomy of the will is *permitted;* one that does not agree therewith is *forbidden.* A will whose maxims necessarily coincide with the laws of autonomy is a *holy* will, good absolutely. The dependence of a will not absolutely good on the principle of autonomy (moral necessitation) is obligation. This then cannot be applied to a holy being. The objective necessity of actions from obligation is called *duty.*

From what has just been said, it is easy to see how it happens that although the conception of duty implies subjection to the law, we yet ascribe a certain *dignity* and sublimity to the person who fulfils all his duties. There is not, indeed, any sublimity in him, so far as he is *subject* to the moral law; but inasmuch as in regard to that very law he is likewise a *legislator,* and on that account alone subject to it, he has sublimity. We have also shown above that neither fear nor inclination, but simply respect for the law, is the spring which can give actions a moral worth. Our own will, so far as we suppose it to act only under the condition that its maxims are potentially universal laws, this ideal will which is possible to us is the proper object of respect, and the dignity of humanity consists just in this capacity of being universally legislative, though with the condition that it is itself subject to this same legislation.

The Autonomy of the Will as the Supreme Principle of Morality.

Autonomy of the will is that property of it by which it is a law to itself (independently on any property of the objects of volition). The principle of autonomy then is: Always so to choose that the same volition shall comprehend the maxims of our choice as a universal law. We cannot prove that this practical rule is an imperative, *i.e.,* that the will of every rational being is necessarily bound to it as a condition, by a mere analysis of the conceptions which occur in it, since it is a synthetical proposition; we must advance beyond the cognition of the objects to a critical examination of the subject, that is of the pure practical reason, for this synthetic proposition which commands apodictically must be capable of being cognised wholly *à priori*. This matter, however, does not belong to the present section. But that the principle of autonomy in question is the sole principle of morals can be readily shown by mere analysis of the conceptions of morality. For by this analysis we find that its principle must be a categorical imperative, and that what this commands is neither more nor less than this very autonomy.

Heteronomy of the Will as the Source of All Spurious Principles of Morality.

If the will seeks the law which is to determine it *anywhere else* than in the fitness of its maxims to be universal laws of its own dictation, consequently if it goes out of itself and seeks this law in the character of any of its objects, there always results *heteronomy.*

The will in that case does not give itself the law, but it is given by the object through its relation to the will. This relation whether it rests on inclination or on conceptions of reason only admits of hypothetical imperatives: I ought to do something *because I wish for something else.* On the contrary, the moral, and therefore categorical, imperative says: I ought to do so and so, even though I should not wish for anything else. *Ex. gr.,* the former says: I ought not to lie if I would retain my reputation; the latter says: I ought not to lie although it should not bring me the least discredit. The latter therefore must so far abstract from all objects that they shall have no *influence* on the will, in order that practical reason (will) may not be restricted to administering an interest not belonging to it, but may simply show its own commanding authority as the supreme legislation. Thus, *ex. gr.,* I ought to endeavour to promote the happiness of others, not as if its realization involved any concern of mine (whether by immediate inclination or by any satisfaction indirectly gained through reason), but simply because a maxim which excludes it cannot be comprehended as a universal law in one and the same volition.

Classification
Of All Principles of Morality Which can be Founded on the Conception of Heteronomy.

Here as elsewhere human reason in its pure use, so long as it was not critically examined, has first tried all possible wrong ways before it succeeded in finding the one true way.

All principles which can be taken from this point of view are either *empirical* or *rational.* The *former,* drawn from the principle of *happiness,* are built on physical or moral feelings; the *latter,* drawn from the principle of *perfection,* are built either on the rational conception of perfection as a possible effect, or on that of an independent perfection (the will of God) as the determining cause of our will.

Empirical principles are wholly incapable of serving as a foundation for moral laws. For the universality with which these should hold for all rational beings without distinction, the unconditional practical necessity which is thereby imposed on them is lost when their foundation is taken from the *particular constitution of human nature,* or the accidental circumstances in which it is placed. The principle of *private happi-*

ness, however, is the most objectionable, not merely because it is false, and experience contradicts the supposition that prosperity is always proportioned to good conduct, nor yet merely because it contributes nothing to the establishment of morality—since it is quite a different thing to make a prosperous man and a good man, or to make one prudent and sharp-sighted for his own interests, and to make him virtuous—but because the springs it provides for morality are such as rather undermine it and destroy its sublimity, since they put the motives to virtue and to vice in the same class, and only teach us to make a better calculation, the specific difference between virtue and vice being entirely extinguished. On the other hand, as to moral feeling, this supposed special sense,[1] the appeal to it is indeed superficial when those who cannot *think* believe that *feeling* will help them out, even in what concerns general laws: and besides, feelings which naturally differ infinitely in degree cannot furnish a uniform standard of good and evil, nor has any one a right to form judgments for others by his own feelings: nevertheless this moral feeling is nearer to morality and its dignity in this respect, that it pays virtue the honour of ascribing to her *immediately* the satisfaction and esteem we have for her, and does not, as it were, tell her to her face that we are not attached to her by her beauty but by profit.

Amongst the *rational* principles of morality, the ontological conception of *perfection,* notwithstanding its defects, is better than the theological conception which derives morality from a Divine absolutely perfect will. The former is, no doubt, empty and indefinite, and consequently useless for finding in the boundless field of possible reality the greatest amount suitable for us; moreover, in attempting to distinguish specifically the reality of which we are now speaking from every other, it inevitably tends to turn in a circle, and cannot avoid tacitly presupposing the morality which it is to explain; it is nevertheless preferable to the theological view, first, because we have no intuition of the Divine perfection, and

can only deduce it from our own conceptions, the most important of which is that of morality, and our explanation would thus be involved in a gross circle; and, in the next place, if we avoid this, the only notion of the Divine will remaining to us is a conception made up of the attributes of desire of glory and dominion, combined with the awful conceptions of might and vengeance, and any system of morals erected on this foundation would be directly opposed to morality.

However, if I had to choose between the notion of the moral sense and that of perfection in general (two systems which at least do not weaken morality, although they are totally incapable of serving as its foundation), then I should decide for the latter, because it at least withdraws the decision of the question from the sensibility and brings it to the court of pure reason; and although even here it decides nothing, it at all events preserves the indefinite idea (of a will good in itself) free from corruption, until it shall be more precisely defined.

For the rest I think I may be excused here from a detailed refutation of all these doctrines; that would only be superfluous labour, since it is so easy, and is probably so well seen even by those whose office requires them to decide for one of these theories (because their hearers would not tolerate suspension of judgment). But what interests us more here is to know that the prime foundation of morality laid down by all these principles is nothing but heteronomy of the will, and for this reason they must necessarily miss their aim.

In every case where an object of the will has to be supposed, in order that the rule may be prescribed which is to determine the will, there the rule is simply heteronomy; the imperative is conditional, namely, *if* or *because* one wishes for this object, one should act so and so: hence it can never command morally, that is categorically. Whether the object determines the will by means of inclination, as in the principle of private happiness, or by means of reason directed to objects of our possible volition generally, as in the principle of perfection, in either case the will never determines itself *immediately* by the conception of the action, but only by the influence which the foreseen effect of the action has on the will; *I ought to do something, on this account, because I wish for something else;* and here there must be yet another law assumed in me as its subject, by which I necessarily will this other

---

1. I class the principle of moral feeling under that of happiness, because every empirical interest promises to contribute to our well-being by the agreeableness that a thing affords, whether it be immediately and without a view to profit, or whether profit be regarded. We must likewise, with Hutcheson, class the principle of sympathy with the happiness of others under his assumed moral sense.

thing, and this law again requires an imperative to restrict this maxim. For the influence which the conception of an object within the reach of our faculties can exercise on the will of the subject in consequence of its natural properties, depends on the nature of the subject, either the sensibility (inclination and taste), or the understanding and reason, the employment of which is by the peculiar constitution of their nature attended with satisfaction. It follows that the law would be, properly speaking, given by nature, and as such, it must be known and proved by experience, and would consequently be contingent, and therefore incapable of being an apodictic practical rule, such as the moral rule must be. Not only so, but it is *inevitably only heteronomy;* the will does not give itself the law, but it is given by a foreign impulse by means of a particular natural constitution of the subject adapted to receive it. An absolutely good will then, the principle of which must be a categorical imperative, will be indeterminate as regards all objects, and will contain merely the *form of volition* generally, and that as autonomy, that is to say, the capability of the maxims of every good will to make themselves a universal law, is itself the only law which the will of every rational being imposes on itself, without needing to assume any spring or interest as a foundation.

How such a synthetical practical à priori *proposition is possible* and why it is necessary, is a problem whose solution does not lie within the bounds of the metaphysic of morals; and we have not here affirmed its truth, much less professed to have a proof of it in our power. We simply showed by the development of the universally received notion of morality that an autonomy of the will is inevitably connected with it, or rather is its foundation. Whoever then holds morality to be anything real, and not a chimerical idea without any truth, must likewise admit the principle of it that is here assigned. This section then, like the first, was merely analytical. Now to prove that morality is no creation of the brain, which it cannot be if the categorical imperative and with it the autonomy of the will is true, and as an *à priori* principle absolutely necessary, this supposes the *possibility of a synthetic use of pure practical reason,* which however we cannot venture on without first giving a critical examination of this faculty of reason. In the concluding section we shall give the principal outlines of this critical examination as far as is sufficient for our purpose.

Third Section.
Transition from the Metaphysic of Morals to the Critique of Pure Practical Reason.

The Concept of Freedom Is the Key That Explains the Autonomy of the Will.

The *will* is a kind of causality belonging to living beings in so far as they are rational, and *freedom* would be this property of such causality that it can be efficient, independently on foreign causes *determining* it; just as *physical necessity* is the property that the causality of all irrational beings has of being determined to activity by the influence of foreign causes.

The preceding definition of freedom is *negative,* and therefore unfruitful for the discovery of its essence; but it leads to a *positive* conception which is so much the more full and fruitful. Since the conception of causality involves that of laws, according to which, by something that we call cause, something else, namely, the effect, must be produced [laid down]; hence, although freedom is not a property of the will depending on physical laws, yet it is not for that reason lawless; on the contrary it must be a causality acting according to immutable laws, but of a peculiar kind; otherwise a free will would be an absurdity. Physical necessity is a heteronomy of the efficient causes, for every effect is possible only according to this law, that something else determines the efficient cause to exert its causality. What else then can freedom of the will be but autonomy, that is the property of the will to be a law to itself? But the proposition: The will is in every action a law to itself, only expresses the principle, to act on no other maxim than that which can also have as an object itself as a universal law. Now this is precisely the formula of the categorical imperative and is the principle of morality, so that a free will and a will subject to moral laws are one and the same.

On the hypothesis then of freedom of the will, morality together with its principle follows from it by mere analysis of the conception. However the latter is still a synthetic proposition; viz., an absolutely good will is that whose maxim can always include itself regarded as a universal law; for this property of its maxim can never be discovered by analysing the conception of an absolutely good will. Now such synthetic propositions are only possible in this way: that the two cognitions are connected together by their union with a third in which they are both to be found. The *positive* concept of freedom furnishes this third cognition, which cannot, as with physical causes, be the nature of the sensible world (in the concept of which we find conjoined the concept of something in relation as cause to *something else* as effect). We cannot now at once show what this third is to which freedom points us, and of which we have an idea *à priori,* nor can we make intelligible how the concept of freedom is shown to be legitimate from principles of pure practical reason, and with it the possibility of a categorical imperative; but some further preparation is required.

Freedom
Must Be Presupposed as a Property of the Will of All Rational Beings.

It is not enough to predicate freedom of our own will, from whatever reason, if we have not sufficient grounds for predicating the same of all rational beings. For as morality serves as a law for us only because we are *rational beings,* it must also hold for all rational beings; and as it must be deduced simply from the property of freedom, it must be shown that freedom also is a property of all rational beings. It is not enough then to prove it from certain supposed experiences of human nature (which indeed is quite impossible, and it can only be shown *à priori*), but we must show that it belongs to the activity of all rational beings endowed with a will. Now I say every being that cannot act except *under the idea of freedom* is just for that reason in a practical point of view really free, that is to say, all laws which are inseparably connected with freedom have the same force for him as if his will had been shown to be free in itself by a proof theoretically conclusive.[1] Now I affirm that we must attribute to every rational being which has a will that it has also the idea of freedom and acts entirely under this idea. For in such a being we conceive a reason that is practical, that is, has causality in reference to its objects. Now we cannot possibly conceive a reason consciously receiving a bias

from any other quarter with respect to its judgments, for then the subject would ascribe the determination of its judgment not to its own reason, but to an impulse. It must regard itself as the author of its principles independent on foreign influences. Consequently as practical reason or as the will of a rational being it must regard itself as free, that is to say, the will of such a being cannot be a will of its own except under the idea of freedom. This idea must therefore in a practical point of view be ascribed to every rational being.

Of the Interest Attaching to the Ideas of Morality.

We have finally reduced the definite conception of morality to the idea of freedom. This latter, however, we could not prove to be actually a property of ourselves or of human nature; only we saw that it must be presupposed if we would conceive a being as rational and conscious of its causality in respect of its actions, i.e., as endowed with a will; and so we find that on just the same grounds we must ascribe to every being endowed with reason and will this attribute of determining itself to action under the idea of its freedom.

Now it resulted also from the presupposition of this idea that we became aware of a law that the subjective principles of action, *i.e.,* maxims, must always be so assumed that they can also hold as objective, that is, universal principles, and so serve as universal laws of our own dictation. But why then should I subject myself to this principle and that simply as a rational being, thus also subjecting to it all other beings endowed with reason? I will allow that no interest *urges* me to this, for that would not give a categorical imperative, but I must *take* an interest in it and discern how this comes to pass; for this 'I ought' is properly an 'I would,' valid for every rational being, provided only that reason determined his actions without any hindrance. But for beings that are in addition affected as we are by springs of a different kind, namely, sensibility, and in whose case that is not always done which reason alone would do, for these that necessity is expressed only as an 'ought,' and the subjective necessity is different from the objective.

It seems then as if the moral law, that is, the principle of autonomy of the will, were properly speaking only presupposed in the idea of freedom, and as if we could not prove its reality and objective necessity independently. In that case we should still have gained something considerable by at least determining the

---

1. I adopt this method of assuming freedom merely *as an idea* which rational beings suppose in their actions, in order to avoid the necessity of proving it in its theoretical aspect also. The former is sufficient for my purpose; for even though the speculative proof should not be made out, yet a being that cannot act except with the idea of freedom is bound by the same laws that would oblige a being who was actually free. Thus we can escape here from the onus which presses on the theory.

true principle more exactly than had previously been done; but as regards its validity and the practical necessity of subjecting oneself to it, we should not have advanced a step. For if we were asked why the universal validity of our maxim as a law must be the condition restricting our actions, and on what we ground the worth which we assign to this manner of acting— a worth so great that there cannot be any higher interest; and if we were asked further how it happens that it is by this alone a man believes he feels his own personal worth, in comparison with which that of an agreeable or disagreeable condition is to be regarded as nothing, to these questions we could give no satisfactory answer.

We find indeed sometimes that we can take an interest in a personal quality which does not involve any interest of external condition, provided this quality makes us capable of participating in the condition in case reason were to effect the allotment; that is to say, the mere being worthy of happiness can interest of itself even without the motive of participating in this happiness. This judgment, however, is in fact only the effect of the importance of the moral law which we before presupposed (when by the idea of freedom we detach ourselves from every empirical interest); but that we ought to detach ourselves from these interests, *i.e.,* to consider ourselves as free in action and yet as subject to certain laws, so as to find a worth simply in our own person which can compensate us for the loss of everything that gives worth to our condition; this we are not yet able to discern in this way, nor do we see how it is possible so to act—in other words, *whence the moral law derives its obligation.*

It must be freely admitted that there is a sort of circle here from which it seems impossible to escape. In the order of efficient causes we assume ourselves free, in order that in the order of ends we may conceive ourselves as subject to moral laws: and we afterwards conceive ourselves as subject to these laws, because we have attributed to ourselves freedom of will: for freedom and self-legislation of will are both autonomy, and therefore are reciprocal conceptions, and for this very reason one must not be used to explain the other or give the reason of it, but at most only for logical purposes to reduce apparently different notions of the same object to one single concept (as we reduce different fractions of the same value to the lowest terms).

One resource remains to us, namely, to inquire whether we do not occupy different points of view when by means of freedom we think ourselves as causes efficient *à priori*, and when we form our conception of ourselves from our actions as effects which we see before our eyes.

It is a remark which needs no subtle reflection to make, but which we may assume that even the commonest understanding can make, although it be after its fashion by an obscure discernment of judgment which it calls feeling, that all the 'ideas'[1] that come to us involuntarily (as those of the senses) do not enable us to know objects otherwise than as they affect us; so that what they may be in themselves remains unknown to us, and consequently that as regards 'ideas' of this kind even with the closest attention and clearness that the understanding can apply to them, we can by them only attain to the knowledge of *appearances,* never to that of *things in themselves.* As soon as this distinction has once been made (perhaps merely in consequence of the difference observed between the ideas given us from without, and in which we are passive, and those that we produce simply from ourselves, and in which we show our own activity), then it follows of itself that we must admit and assume behind the appearance something else that is not an appearance, namely, the things in themselves, although we must admit that as they can never be known to us except as they affect us, we can come no nearer to them, nor can we ever know what they are in themselves. This must furnish a distinction, however crude, between a *world of sense* and the *world of understanding,* of which the former may be different according to the difference of the sensuous impressions in various observers, while the second which is its basis always remains the same. Even as to himself, a man cannot pretend to know what he is in himself from the knowledge he has by internal sensation. For as he does not as it were create himself, and does not come by the conception of himself *à priori* but empirically, it naturally follows that he can obtain his knowledge even of himself only by the inner sense, and consequently only through the appearances of his nature and the way in which his consciousness is affected. At the same time beyond these characteristics of his own subject, made up of mere appear-

---

1. [The common understanding being here spoken of, I use the word 'idea' in its popular sense.]

ances, he must necessarily suppose something else as their basis, namely, his *ego,* whatever its characteristics in itself may be. Thus in respect to mere perception and receptivity of sensations he must reckon himself as belonging to the *world of sense,* but in respect of whatever there may be of pure activity in him (that which reaches consciousness immediately and not through affecting the senses) he must reckon himself as belonging to the *intellectual world,* of which however he has no further knowledge. To such a conclusion the reflecting man must come with respect to all the things which can be presented to him: it is probably to be met with even in persons of the commonest understanding, who, as is well known, are very much inclined to suppose behind the objects of the senses something else invisible and acting of itself. They spoil it however by presently sensualizing this invisible again; that is to say, wanting to make it an object of intuition, so that they do not become a whit the wiser.

Now man really finds in himself a faculty by which he distinguishes himself from everything else, even from himself as affected by objects, and that is *Reason.* This being pure spontaneity is even elevated above the *understanding.* For although the latter is a spontaneity and does not, like sense, merely contain intuitions that arise when we are affected by things (and are therefore passive), yet it cannot produce from its activity any other conceptions than those which merely serve *to bring the intuitions of sense under rules,* and thereby to unite them in one consciousness, and without this use of the sensibility it could not think at all, whereas, on the contrary, Reason shows so pure a spontaneity in the case of what I call Ideas [Ideal Conceptions] that it thereby far transcends everything that the sensibility can give it, and exhibits its most important function in distinguishing the world of sense from that of understanding, and thereby prescribing the limits of the understanding itself.

For this reason a rational being must regard himself *qua* intelligence (not from the side of his lower faculties) as belonging not to the world of sense, but to that of understanding; hence he has two points of view from which he can regard himself, and recognise laws of the exercise of his faculties, and consequently of all his actions: *first,* so far as he belongs to the world of sense, he finds himself subject to laws of nature (heteronomy); *secondly,* as belonging to the intelligible world, under laws which being independent on nature have their foundation not in experience but in reason alone.

As a rational being, and consequently belonging to the intelligible world, man can never conceive the causality of his own will otherwise than on condition of the idea of freedom, for independence on the determining causes of the sensible world (an independence which Reason must always ascribe to itself) is freedom. Now the idea of freedom is inseparably connected with the conception of *autonomy,* and this again with the universal principle of morality which is ideally the foundation of all actions of *rational* beings, just as the law of nature is of all phenomena.

Now the suspicion is removed which we raised above, that there was a latent circle involved in our reasoning from freedom to autonomy, and from this to the moral law, viz., that we lay down the idea of freedom because of the moral law only that we might afterwards in turn infer the latter from freedom, and that consequently we could assign no reason at all for this law, but could only [present][1] it as a *petitio principii* which well disposed minds would gladly concede to us, but which we could never put forward as a provable proposition. For now we see that when we conceive ourselves as free we transfer ourselves into the world of understanding as members of it, and recognise the autonomy of the will with its consequence, morality; whereas, if we conceive ourselves as under obligation we consider ourselves as belonging to the world of sense, and at the same time to the world of understanding.

How Is a Categorical Imperative Possible?

Every rational being reckons himself qua intelligence as belonging to the world of understanding, and it is simply as an efficient cause belonging to that world that he calls his causality a will. On the other side he is also conscious of himself as a part of the world of sense in which his actions which are mere appearances [phenomena] of that causality are displayed; we cannot however discern how they are possible from this causality which we do not know; but instead of that, these actions as belonging to the sensible world must be viewed as determined by other phenomena, namely, desires and inclinations. If

---

1. [The verb is wanting in the original.]

therefore I were only a member of the world of understanding, then all my actions would perfectly conform to the principle of autonomy of the pure will; if I were only a part of the world of sense they would necessarily be assumed to conform wholly to the natural law of desires and inclinations, in other words, to the heteronomy of nature. (The former would rest on morality as the supreme principle, the latter on happiness.) Since however the world of understanding contains the foundation of the world of sense, and consequently of its laws also, and accordingly gives the law to my will (which belongs wholly to the world of understanding) directly, and must be conceived as doing so, it follows that, although on the one side I must regard myself as a being belonging to the world of sense, yet on the other side I must recognise myself as subject as an intelligence to the law of the world of understanding, i.e., to reason, which contains this law in the idea of freedom, and therefore as subject to the autonomy of the will: consequently I must regard the laws of the world of understanding as imperatives for me, and the actions which conform to them as duties.

And thus what makes categorical imperatives possible is this, that the idea of freedom makes me a member of an intelligible world, in consequence of which if I were nothing else all my actions *would* always conform to the autonomy of the will: but as I at the same time intuite myself as a member of the world of sense, they *ought* so to conform, and this *categorical* 'ought' implies a synthetic *à priori* proposition, inasmuch as besides my will as affected by sensible desires there is added further the idea of the same will but as belonging to the world of the understanding, pure and practical of itself, which contains the supreme condition according to Reason of the former will; precisely as to the intuitions of sense there are added concepts of the understanding which of themselves signify nothing but regular form in general, and in this way synthetic *à priori* propositions became possible, on which all knowledge of physical nature rests.

The practical use of common human reason confirms this reasoning. There is no one, not even the most consummate villain, provided only that he is otherwise accustomed to the use of reason, who, when we set before him examples of honesty of purpose, of steadfastness in following good maxims, of sympathy and general benevolence (even combined with great sacrifices of advantages and comfort), does not wish that he might also possess these qualities. Only on account of his inclinations and impulses he cannot attain this in himself, but at the same time he wishes to be free from such inclinations which are burdensome to himself. He proves by this that he transfers himself in thought with a will free from the impulses of the sensibility into an order of things wholly different from that of his desires in the field of the sensibility, since he cannot expect to obtain by that wish any gratification of his desires, nor any position which would satisfy any of his actual or supposable inclinations (for this would destroy the pre-eminence of the very idea which wrests that wish from him): he can only expect a greater intrinsic worth of his own person. This better person, however, he imagines himself to be when he transfers himself to the point of view of a member of the world of the understanding, to which he is involuntarily forced by the idea of freedom, *i.e.*, of independence on *determining* causes of the world of sense; and from this point of view he is conscious of a good will, which by his own confession constitutes the law for the bad will that he possesses as a member of the world of sense—a law whose authority he recognises while transgressing it. What he morally 'ought' is then what he necessarily 'would' as a member of the world of the understanding, and is conceived by him as an 'ought' only inasmuch as he likewise considers himself as a member of the world of sense.

On the Extreme Limits of All Practical Philosophy.

All men attribute to themselves freedom of will. Hence come all judgments upon actions as being such as *ought to have been done,* although they *have not been* done. However this freedom is not a conception of experience, nor can it be so, since it still remains, even though experience shows the contrary of what on supposition of freedom are conceived as its necessary consequences. On the other side it is equally necessary that everything that takes place should be fixedly determined according to laws of nature. This necessity of nature is likewise not an empirical conception, just for this reason, that it involves the motion of necessity and consequently of *à priori* cognition. But this conception of a system of nature is confirmed by experience, and it must even be inevitably presupposed if experience itself is to be possible, that is, a connected knowledge of the objects of sense resting on general laws. Therefore freedom is only an Idea [Ideal Conception] of Reason, and its objective reality in itself is doubtful, while nature is a *concept* of the *understanding* which proves, and must necessarily prove, its reality in examples of experience.

There arises from this a dialectic of Reason, since the freedom attributed to the will appears to contradict the necessity of nature, and placed between these two ways Reason for *speculative purposes* finds the road of physical necessity much more beaten and more appropriate than that of freedom; yet for *practical purposes* the narrow footpath of freedom is the only one on which it is possible to make use of reason in our conduct; hence it is just as impossible for the subtlest philosophy as for the commonest reason of men to argue away freedom. Philosophy must then assume that no real contradiction will be found between freedom and physical necessity of the same human actions, for it cannot give up the conception of nature any more than that of freedom.

Nevertheless, even though we should never be able to comprehend how freedom is possible, we must at least remove this apparent contradiction in a convincing manner. For if the thought of freedom contradicts either itself or nature, which is equally necessary, it must in competition with physical necessity be entirely given up.

It would, however, be impossible to escape this contradiction if the thinking subject, which seems to itself free, conceived itself *in the same sense* or in *the very same relation* when it calls itself free as when in respect of the same action it assumes itself to be subject to the law of nature. Hence it is an indispensable problem of speculative philosophy to show that its illusion respecting the contradiction rests on this, that we think of man in a different sense and relation when we call him free, and when we regard him as subject to the laws of nature as being part and parcel of nature. It must therefore show that not only *can* both these very well co-exist, but that both must be thought *as necessarily united* in the same subject, since otherwise no reason could be given why we should burden reason with an idea which, though it may possibly *without contradiction* be reconciled with another that is sufficiently established, yet entangles us in a perplexity which sorely embarrasses Reason

in its theoretic employment. This duty, however, belongs only to speculative philosophy, in order that it may clear the way for practical philosophy. The philosopher then has no option whether he will remove the apparent contradiction or leave it untouched; for in the latter case the theory respecting this would be *bonum vacans* into the possession of which the fatalist would have a right to enter, and chase all morality out of its supposed domain as occupying it without title.

We cannot, however, as yet say that we are touching the bounds of practical philosophy. For the settlement of that controversy does not belong to it; it only demands from speculative reason that it should put an end to the discord in which it entangles itself in theoretical questions, so that practical reason may have rest and security from external attacks which might make the ground debatable on which it desires to build.

The claims to freedom of will made even by common reason are founded on the consciousness and the admitted supposition that reason is independent on merely subjectively determined causes which together constitute what belongs to sensation only, and which consequently come under the general designation of sensibility. Man considering himself in this way as an intelligence, places himself thereby in a different order of things and in a relation to determining grounds of a wholly different kind when on the one hand he thinks of himself as an intelligence endowed with a will, and consequently with causality, and when on the other he perceives himself as a phenomenon in the world of sense (as he really is also), and affirms that his causality is subject to external determination according to laws of nature. Now he soon becomes aware that both can hold good, nay, must hold good at the same time. For there is not the smallest contradiction in saying that a *thing in appearance* (belonging to the world of sense) is subject to certain laws, on which the very same *as a thing* or being *in itself* is independent; and that he must conceive and think of himself in this two-fold way, rests as to the first on the consciousness of himself as an object affected through the senses, and as to the second on the consciousness of himself as an intelligence, *i.e.,* as independent on sensible impressions in the employment of his reason (in other words as belonging to the world of understanding).

Hence it comes to pass that man claims the possession of a will which takes no account of anything that comes under the head of desires and inclinations, and on the contrary conceives actions as possible to him, nay, even as necessary, which can only be done by disregarding all desires and sensible inclinations. The causality of such actions lies in him as an intelligence and in the laws of effects and actions [which depend] on the principles of an intelligible world, of which indeed he knows nothing more than that in it pure reason alone independent on sensibility gives the law; moreover since it is only in that world, as an intelligence, that he is his proper self (being as man only the appearance of himself) those laws apply to him directly and categorically, so that the incitements of inclinations and appetites (in other words the whole nature of the world of sense) cannot impair the laws of his volition as an intelligence. Nay, he does not even hold himself responsible for the former or ascribe them to his proper self, *i.e.,* his will: he only ascribes to his will any indulgence which he might yield them if he allowed them to influence his maxims to the prejudice of the rational laws of the will.

When practical Reason *thinks* itself into a world of understanding it does not thereby transcend its own limits, as it would if it tried to enter it by *intuition* or *sensation*. The former is only a negative thought in respect of the world of sense, which does not give any laws to reason in determining the will, and is positive only in this single point that this freedom as a negative characteristic is at the same time conjoined with a (positive) faculty and even with a causality of reason, which we designate a will, namely, a faculty of so acting that the principle of the actions shall conform to the essential character of a rational motive, *i.e.,* the condition that the maxim have universal validity as a law. But were it to borrow an *object of will,* that is, a motive, from the world of understanding, then it would overstep its bounds and pretend to be acquainted with something of which it knows nothing. The conception of a world of the understanding is then only a *point of view* which Reason finds itself compelled to take outside the appearances in order to *conceive itself as practical,* which would not be possible if the influences of the sensibility had a determining power on man, but which is necessary unless he is to be denied the consciousness of himself as an intelligence, and consequently as a rational cause, energizing by reason, that is, operating freely. This thought certainly involves the idea of an order and a system of laws different from that of the mechanism of nature which belongs to the sensible world, and it makes the conception of an intelligible world necessary (that is to say, the whole system of rational beings as things in themselves). But it does not in the least authorise us to think of it further than as to its *formal* condition only, that is, the universality of the maxims of the will as laws, and consequently the autonomy of the latter, which alone is consistent with its freedom, whereas, on the contrary, all laws that refer to a definite object give heteronomy, which only belongs to laws of nature, and can only apply to the sensible world.

But Reason would overstep all its bounds if it undertook to *explain how* pure reason can be practical, which would be exactly the same problem as to explain how *freedom is possible.*

For we can explain nothing but that which we can reduce to laws, the object of which can be given in some possible experience. But freedom is a mere Idea [Ideal Conception], the objective reality of which can in no wise be shown according to laws of nature, and consequently not in any possible experience; and for this reason it can never be comprehended or understood, because we cannot support it by any sort of example or analogy. It holds good only as a necessary hypothesis of reason in a being that believes itself conscious of a will, that is, of a faculty distinct from mere desire (namely a faculty of determining itself to action as an intelligence, in other words, by laws of reason independently on natural instincts). Now where determination according to laws of nature ceases, there all *explanation* ceases also, and nothing remains but *defence, i.e.,* the removal of the objections of those who pretend to have seen deeper into the nature of things, and thereupon boldly declare freedom impossible. We can only point out to them that the supposed contradiction that they have discovered in it arises only from this, that in order to be able to apply the law of nature to human actions, they must necessarily consider man as an appearance: then when we demand of them that they should also think of him *qua* intelligence as a thing in itself, they still persist in considering him in this respect also as an appearance. In this view it would no doubt be a contradiction to suppose the causality of the same subject (that is, his will) to be withdrawn from all the natural laws of the sensible world. But this contradiction disappears, if they would only bethink themselves and admit, as is reasonable, that behind the appearances there must also lie at their root (although hidden) the things in themselves, and that we cannot expect the laws of these to be the same as those that govern their appearances.

The subjective impossibility of explaining the freedom of the will is identical with the impossibility of discovering and explaining an interest[1] which man can take in the moral law. Nevertheless he does actually take an interest in it, the basis of which in us we call the moral feeling, which some have falsely assigned as the standard of our moral judgment, whereas it must rather be viewed as the *subjective* effect that the law exercises on the will, the objective principle of which is furnished by Reason alone.

In order indeed that a rational being who is also affected through the senses should will what Reason alone directs such beings that they ought to will, it is no doubt requisite that reason should have a power *to infuse a feeling of pleasure* or satisfaction in the fulfilment of duty, that is to say, that it should have a causality, by which it determines the sensibility according to its own principles. But it is quite impossible to discern, *i.e.* to make it intelligible *à priori*, how a mere thought, which itself contains nothing sensible, can itself produce a sensation of pleasure or pain; for this is a particular kind of causality of which as of every other causality we can determine nothing whatever *à priori;* we must only consult experience about it. But as this cannot supply us with

any relation of cause and effect except between two objects of experience, whereas in this case, although indeed the effect produced lies within experience, yet the cause is supposed to be pure reason acting through mere ideas which offer no object to experience, it follows that for us men it is quite impossible to explain how and why the *universality of the maxim as a law,* that is, morality, interests. This only is certain, that it is not *because it interests* us that it has validity for us (for that would be heteronomy and dependence of practical reason on sensibility, namely, on a feeling as its principle, in which case it could never give moral laws), but that it interests us because it is valid for us as men, inasmuch as it had its source in our will as intelligences, in other words in our proper self, *and what belongs to mere appearance is necessarily subordinated by reason to the nature of the thing in itself.*

The question then: How a categorical imperative is possible can be answered to this extent that we can assign the only hypothesis on which it is possible, namely, the idea of freedom; and we can also discern the necessity of this hypothesis, and this is sufficient for the *practical exercise* of reason, that is, for the conviction of the *validity of this imperative,* and hence of the moral law; but how this hypothesis itself is possible can never be discerned by any human reason. On the hypothesis, however, that the will of an intelligence is free, its *autonomy,* as the essential formal condition of its determination, is a necessary consequence. Moreover, this freedom of will is not merely quite *possible* as a hypothesis (not involving any contradiction to the principle of physical necessity in the connexion of the phenomena of the sensible world) as speculative philosophy can show: but further, a rational being who is conscious of a causality through reason, that is to say, of a will (distinct from desires), must *of necessity* make it practically, that is, in idea, the condition of all his voluntary actions. But to explain how pure reason can be of itself practical without the aid of any spring of action that could be derived from any other source, *i.e.* how the mere principle of the *universal validity of all its maxims as laws* (which would certainly be the form of a pure practical reason) can of itself supply a spring, without any matter (object) of the will in which one could antecedently take any interest; and how it can produce an interest which would be called purely *moral;* or in other words, *how pure reason can be practical*—to explain this is beyond the power of human

---

1. Interest is that by which reason becomes practical, *i.e.,* a cause determining the will. Hence we say of rational beings only that they take an interest in a thing; irrational beings only feel sensual appetites. Reason takes a direct interest in action then only when the universal validity of its maxims is alone sufficient to determine the will. Such an interest alone is pure. But if it can determine the will only by means of another object of desire or on the suggestion of a particular feeling of the subject, then Reason takes only an indirect interest in the action, and as Reason by itself without experience cannot discover either objects of the will or a special feeling actuating it, this latter interest would only be empirical, and not a pure rational interest. The logical interest of Reason (namely, to extend its insight) is never direct, but presupposes purposes for which reason is employed.

reason, and all the labour and pains of seeking an explanation of it are lost.

It is just the same as if I sought to find out how freedom itself is possible as the causality of a will. For then I quit the ground of philosophical explanation, and I have no other to go upon. I might indeed revel in the world of intelligences which still remains to me, but although I have an *idea* of it which is well founded, yet I have not the least *knowledge* of it, nor can I ever attain to such knowledge with all the efforts of my natural faculty of reason. It signifies only a something that remains over when I have eliminated everything belonging to the world of sense from the actuating principles of my will, serving merely to keep in bounds the principle of motives taken from the field of sensibility; fixing its limits and showing that it does not contain all in all within itself, but that there is more beyond it; but this something more I know no further. Of pure reason which frames this ideal, there remains after the abstraction of all matter, *i.e.,* knowledge of objects, nothing but the form, namely, the practical law of the universality of the maxims, and in conformity with this the conception of reason in reference to a pure world of understanding as a possible efficient cause, that is a cause determining the will. There must here be a total absence of springs; unless this idea of an intelligible world is itself the spring, or that in which reason primarily takes an interest; but to make this intelligible is precisely the problem that we cannot solve.

Here now is the extreme limit of all moral inquiry, and it is of great importance to determine it even on this account, in order that reason may not on the one hand, to the prejudice of morals, seek about in the world of sense for the supreme motive and an interest comprehensible but empirical; and on the other hand, that it may not impotently flap its wings without being able to move in the (for it) empty space of transcendent concepts which we call the intelligible world, and so lose itself amidst chimeras. For the rest, the idea of a pure world of understanding as a system of all intelligences, and to which we ourselves as rational beings belong (although we are likewise on the other side members of the sensible world), this remains always a useful and legitimate idea for the purposes of rational belief, although all knowledge stops at its threshold, useful, namely, to produce in us a lively interest in the moral law by means of the noble ideal of a universal kingdom of *ends in themselves* (rational beings), to which we can belong as members then only when we carefully conduct ourselves according to the maxims of freedom as if they were laws of nature.

Concluding Remark.

The speculative employment of reason *with respect to nature* leads to the absolute necessity of some supreme cause of *the world:* the practical employment of reason *with a view to freedom* leads also to absolute necessity, but only *of the laws of the actions* of a rational being as such. Now it is an essential *principle* of reason, however employed, to push its knowledge to a consciousness of its *necessity* (without which it would not be rational knowledge). it is however an equally essential *restriction* of the same reason that it can neither discern the *necessity* of what is or what happens, nor of what ought to happen, unless a condition is supposed on which it is or happens or ought to happen. In this way, however, by the constant inquiry for the condition, the satisfaction of reason is only further and further postponed. Hence it unceasingly seeks the unconditionally necessary, and finds itself forced to assume it, although without any means of making it comprehensible to itself, happy enough if only it can discover a conception which agrees with this assumption. It is therefore no fault in our deduction of the supreme principle of morality, but an objection that should be made to human reason in general, that it cannot enable us to conceive the absolute necessity of an unconditional practical law (such as the categorical imperative must be). It cannot be blamed for refusing to explain this necessity by a condition, that is to say, by means of some interest assumed as a basis, since the law would then cease to be a moral law, *i.e.* a supreme law of freedom. And thus while we do not comprehend the practical unconditional necessity of the moral imperative, we yet comprehend its *incomprehensibility,* and this is all that can be fairly demanded of a philosophy which strives to carry its principles up to the very limit of human reason.

JEREMY BENTHAM

FROM *An Introduction to the Principles of Morals and Legislation*

Utilitarianism, one of the main moral theories throughout the last two centuries, has its foundation in the work of such towering figures as John Locke and David Hume. But it was through the efforts of Jeremy Bentham that this theory first began to make a significant impact on society. Bentham, born in London in 1748, entered Queen's College, Oxford, at the age of twelve to study law. He spent his life in the effort to develop a new system of jurisprudence, the motivation for which began with his experiences as a law student; to his dismay, Bentham discovered that the English business of law was brutal, costly, and, even to its practitioners, horribly obscure. These failures he attributed to what he called the prevailing "intuitionism" of his time. Actions that revolted the sensibilities of legislators or judges were punished severely, whether or not any harmful consequences followed from the act, yet many actions with horrid consequences were punished lightly or not at all. Actions, he argued, should be considered right or wrong based on the consequences they bring about rather than being considered thus in and of themselves. In order to construct a legal system that would be less costly, more efficient, humane, and simpler than what currently passed for justice, Bentham proposed a utilitarian theory of individual and societal morality.

In his work, Bentham attempted to make ethics and politics scientifically verifiable disciplines by formulating quantitative standards of evaluation. He began with the psychological generalization that all actions are motivated by the desire for pleasure and the fear of pain. From the equation between ethical obligation and psychological necessity, Bentham then derived the general principle of utility, which approves or disapproves every action according to the tendency of that action to augment or diminish happiness. His most characteristic, original, yet controversial contribution to ethical theory is the "hedonic calculus" for measuring pleasures and pains.

Utilitarianism presupposes one overriding moral principle: that one ought to aim at the greatest happiness of the greatest number. He was not unaware that this principle lacked a foundation, noting that it could not be proved. Instead, it is used to prove, in his words, "everything else." Bentham and his followers formed a political movement that helped bring about legislative reforms that judged existing social institutions in terms of their utility: their tendency to produce the greatest happiness for the greatest number. Bentham's utilitarianism was more socially oriented than that of Locke and Hume, and it resulted in improved social legislation and institutions.

The only major theoretical work he published himself was An Introduction to the Principles of Morals and Legislation *(Oxford, 1789), the first four chapters of which are included here. The remaining work published in his lifetime consisted of political tracts and pamphlets. His influence ranged over various parts of Europe, but reached its height in*

England, where Benthamites attained a powerful political influence and attracted such extraordinary men as James Mill and his son John Stuart Mill (whose work we shall read in the next chapter). Even long after Mill's death, utilitarians brought about legal reforms in his native country.

Even though Bentham's influence on politics and social institutions was widely felt, the most powerful advocate of utilitarianism in philosophy was the great John Stuart Mill. It is mostly due to Mill's improvements on the theory of Bentham that Utilitarianism remains a powerful voice within moral philosophy to this day. It is a theory that provokes impassioned argument from both its supporters and critics. As an example of the controversy it elicits, we have included in this volume a spirited debate between a leading exponent of utilitarianism, J. J. C. Smart, and one of its most ardent critics, Bernard Williams.

Chapter I. Of the Principle of Utility.

I. *Mankind governed by pain and pleasure.* Nature has placed mankind under the governance of two sovereign masters, *pain* and *pleasure.* It is for them alone to point out what we ought to do, as well as to determine what we shall do. On the one hand the standard of right and wrong, on the other the chain of causes and effects, are fastened to their throne. They govern us in all we do, in all we say, in all we think: every effort we can make to throw off our subjection, will serve but to demonstrate and confirm it. In words a man may pretend to abjure their empire: but in reality he will remain subject to it all the while. The *principle of utility* recognises this subjection, and assumes it for the foundation of that system, the object of which is to rear the fabric of felicity by the hands of reason and of law. Systems which attempt to question it, deal in sounds instead of sense, in caprice instead of reason, in darkness instead of light.

But enough of metaphor and declamation: it is not by such means that moral science is to be improved.

II. *Principle of utility, what.* The principle of utility is the foundation of the present work: it will be proper therefore at the outset to give an explicit and determinate account of what is meant by it. By the principle of utility is meant that principle which approves or disapproves of every action whatsoever, according to the tendency which it appears to have to augment or diminish the happiness of the party whose interest is in question: or, what is the same thing in other words, to promote or to oppose that

happiness. I say of every action whatsoever; and therefore not only of every action of a private individual but of every measure of government.

III. *Utility, what.* By utility is meant that property in any object, whereby it tends to produce benefit, advantage, pleasure, good, or happiness, (all this in the present case comes to the same thing) or (what comes again to the same thing) to prevent the happening of mischief, pain, evil, or unhappiness to the party whose interest is considered: if that party be the community in general, then the happiness of the community: if a particular individual, then the happiness of that individual.

IV. *Interest of the community, what.* The interest of the community is one of the most general expressions that can occur in the phraseology of morals: no wonder that the meaning of it is often lost. When it has a meaning, it is this. The community is a fictitious *body,* composed of the individual persons who are considered as constituting as it were its *members.* The interest of the community then is, what?—the sum of the interests of the several members who compose it.

V. It is in vain to talk of the interest of the community, without understanding what is the interest of the individual. A thing is said to promote the interest, or to be *for* the interest, of an individual, when it tends to add to the sum total of his pleasures: or, what comes to the same thing, to diminish the sum total of his pains.

VI. *An action conformable to the principle of utility, what.* An action then may be said to be conformable to the principle of utility, or, for shortness sake, to utility, (meaning with respect to the community at large) when the tendency it has to augment the happiness of the community is greater than any it has to diminish it.

VII. *A measure of government conformable to the principle of utility, what.* A measure of government (which is but a particular kind of action, performed by a particular person or persons) may be said to be conformable to or dictated by the principle of utility, when in like manner the tendency which it has to augment the happiness of the community is greater than any which it has to diminish it.

VIII. *Laws or dictates of utility, what.* When an action, or in particular a measure of government, is supposed by a man to be conformable to the principle of utility, it may be convenient, for the purposes of discourse, to imagine a kind of law or dictate, called a law or dictate of utility: and to speak of the action in question, as being conformable to such law or dictate.

IX. *A partizan of the principle of utility, who.* A man may be said to be a partizan of the principle of utility, when the approbation or disapprobation he annexes to any action, or to any measure, is determined by and proportioned to the tendency which he conceives it to have to augment or to diminish the happiness of the community: or in other words, to its conformity or unconformity to the laws or dictates of utility.

X. *Ought, ought not, right and wrong, etc. how to be understood.* Of an action that is conformable to the principle of utility one may always say either that it is one that ought to be done, or at least that it is not one that ought not to be done. One may say also, that it is right it should be done; at least that it is not wrong it should be done: that it is a right action; at least that it is not a wrong action. When thus interpreted, the words *ought,* and *right* and *wrong,* and others of that stamp, have a meaning: when otherwise, they have none.

XI. *To prove the rectitude of this principle is at once unnecessary and impossible.* Has the rectitude of this principle been ever formally contested? It should seem that it had, by those who have not known what they have been meaning. Is it susceptible of any direct proof? it should seem not: for that which is used to prove every thing else, cannot itself be proved: a chain of proofs must have their commencement somewhere. To give such proof is as impossible as it is needless.

XII. *It has seldom, however, as yet been consistently pursued.* Not that there is or ever has been that human creature breathing, however stupid or perverse, who has not on many, perhaps on most occasions of his life, deferred to it. By the natural constitution of the human frame, on most occasions of their lives men in general embrace this principle, without thinking of it: if not for the ordering of their own actions, yet for the trying of their own actions, as well as of those of other men. There have been, at the same time, not many, perhaps, even of the most intelligent, who have been disposed to embrace it purely and without reserve. There are even few who have not taken some occasion or other to quarrel with it, either on account of their not understanding always how to apply it, or on account of some prejudice or other which they were afraid to examine into, or could not bear to part with. For such is the stuff that man is made of: in principle and in practice, in a right track and in a wrong one, the rarest of all human qualities is consistency.

XIII. *It can never be consistently combated.* When a man attempts to combat the principle of utility, it is with reasons drawn, without his being aware of it, from that very principle itself. His arguments, if they prove any thing, prove not that the principle is *wrong,* but that, according to the applications he supposes to be made of it, it is *misapplied.* Is it possible for a man to move the earth? Yes; but he must first find out another earth to stand upon.

XIV. *Course to be taken for surmounting prejudices that may have been entertained against it.* To disprove the propriety of it by arguments is impossible; but, from the causes that have been mentioned, or from some confused or partial view of it, a man may happen to be disposed not to relish it. Where this is the case, if he thinks the settling of his opinions on such a subject worth the trouble, let him take the following steps, and at length, perhaps, he may come to reconcile himself to it.

1. Let him settle with himself, whether he would wish to discard this principle altogether; if so, let him consider what it is that all his reasonings (in matters of politics especially) can amount to?

2. If he would, let him settle with himself, whether he would judge an act without any principle, or whether there is any other he would judge and act by?

3. If there be, let him examine and satisfy himself whether the principle he thinks he has found is really any separate intelligible principle; or whether it be not a mere principle in words, a kind of phrase, which at bottom expresses neither more nor less than the mere averment of his own unfounded sentiments; that is, what in another person he might be apt to call caprice?

4. If he is inclined to think that his own approbation or disapprobation, annexed to the idea of an act, without any regard to its consequences, is a sufficient foundation for him to judge and act upon, let him ask himself whether his sentiment is to be a standard of right and wrong, with respect to every other man, or whether every man's sentiment has the same privilege of being a standard to itself?

5. In the first case, let him ask himself whether his principle is not despotical, and hostile to all the rest of human race?

6. In the second case, whether it is not anarchial, and whether at this rate there are not as many different standards of right and wrong as there are men? and whether even to the same man, the same thing, which is right to-day, may not (without the least change in its nature) be wrong to-morrow? and whether the same thing is not right and wrong in the same place at the same time? and in either case, whether all argument is not at an end? and whether, when two men have said, 'I like this,' and 'I don't like it,' they can (upon such a principle) have any thing more to say?

7. If he should have said to himself, No: for that the sentiment which he proposes as a standard must be grounded on reflection, let him say on what particulars the reflection is to turn? if on particulars having relation to the utility of the act, then let him say whether this is not deserting his own principle, and borrowing assistance from that very one in opposition to which he sets it up: or if not on those particulars, on what other particulars?

8. If he should be for compounding the matter, and adopting his own principle in part, and the principle of utility in part, let him say how far he will adopt it?

9. When he has settled with himself where he will stop, then let him ask himself how he justifies to himself the adopting it so far? and why he will not adopt it any farther?

10. Admitting any other principle than the principle of utility to be a right principle, a principle that it is right for a man to pursue; admitting (what is not true) that the word *right* can have a meaning without reference to utility, let him say whether there is any such thing as a *motive* that a man can have to pursue the dictates of it: if there is let him say what that motive is, and how it is to be distinguished from those which enforce the dictates of utility: if not, then lastly let him say what it is this other principle can be good for?

Chapter II. Of Principles Adverse to That of Utility.

I. *All other principles then that of utility must be wrong.* If the principle of utility be a right principle to be governed by, and that in all cases, it follows from what has been just observed, that whatever principle differs from it in any case must necessarily be a wrong one. To prove any other principle, therefore, to be a wrong one, there needs no more than just to show it to be what it is, a principle of which the dictates are in some point or other different from those of the principle of utility: to state it is to confute it.

II. *Ways in which a principle may be wrong.* A principle may be different from that of utility in two ways: 1. By being constantly opposed to it: this is the case with a principle which may be termed the principle of *asceticism.* 2. By being sometimes opposed to it, and sometimes not, as it may happen: this is the case with another, which may be termed the principle of *sympathy* and *antipathy.*

III. *Principle of asceticism, what.* By the principle of asceticism I mean that principle, which, like the principle of utility, approves or disapproves of any action, according to the tendency which it appears to have to augment or diminish the happiness of the party whose interest is in question; but in an inverse manner: approving of actions in as far as they tend to diminish his happiness; disapproving of them in as far as they tend to augment it.

IV. *A partizan of the principle of asceticism, who.* It is evident that any one who reprobates any the least particle of pleasure, as such, from whatever source derived, is *pro tanto* a partizan of the principle of asceticism. It is only upon that principle, and not from the principle of utility, that the most abominable pleasure which the vilest of malefactors ever reaped from his crime would be to be reprobated, if it stood alone. The case is, that it never does stand alone; but is necessarily followed by such a quantity of pain (or, what comes to the same thing, such a chance for a certain quantity of pain) that the pleasure in comparison of it, is as nothing: and this is the true and sole, but perfectly sufficient, reason for making it a ground for punishment.

V. *This principle has had in some a philosophical, in others a religious origin.* There are two classes of men of very different complexions, by whom the principle of asceticism appears to have been embraced; the one a set of moralists, the other a set of religionists. Different accordingly have been the motives which appear to have recommended it to the notice of these different parties. Hope, that is the prospect of pleasure, seems to have animated the former: hope, the aliment of philosophic pride: the hope of honour and reputation at the hands of men. Fear, that is the prospect of pain, the latter: fear, the offspring of superstitious fancy: the fear of future punishment at the hands of a splenetic and revengeful Deity. I say in this case fear: for of the invisible future, fear is more powerful than hope. These circumstances characterize the two different parties among the partizans of the principle of asceticism; the parties and their motives different, the principle the same.

VI. *It has been carried farther by the religious party than by the philosophical.* The religious party, however, appear to have carried it farther than the philosophical: they have acted more consistently and less wisely. The philosophical party have scarcely gone farther than to reprobate pleasure: the religious party have frequently gone so far as to make it a matter of merit and of duty to court pain. The philosophical party have hardly gone farther than the making pain a matter of indifference. It is no evil, they have said: they have not said, it is a good. They have not so much as reprobated all pleasure in the lump. They have discarded only what they have called the gross; that is, such as are organical, or of which the origin is easily traced up to such as are organical: they have even cherished and magnified the refined. Yet this, however, not under the name of pleasure: to cleanse itself from the sordes of its impure original, it was necessary it should change its name: the honourable, the glorious, the reputable, the becoming, the *honestum,* the *decorum,* it was to be called: in short, any thing but pleasure.

VII. *The philosophical branch of it has had most influence among persons of education, the religious among the vulgar.* From these two sources have flowed the doctrines from which the sentiments of the bulk of mankind have all along received a tincture of this principle; some from the philosophical, some from the religious, some from both. Men of education more frequently from the philosophical, as more suited to the elevation of their sentiments: the vulgar more frequently from the superstitious, as more suited to the narrowness of their intellect, undilated by knowledge: and to the abjectness of their condition, continually open to the attacks of fear. The tinctures, however, derived from the two sources, would naturally intermingle, insomuch that a man would not always know by which of them he was most influenced: and they would often serve to corroborate and enliven one another. It was this conformity that made a kind of alliance between parties of a complexion otherwise so dissimilar: and disposed them to unite upon various occasions against the common enemy, the partizan of the principle of utility, whom they joined in branding with the odious name of Epicurean.

VIII. *The principle of asceticism has never been steadily applied by either party to the Business of Government.* The principle of asceticism, however, with whatever warmth it may have been embraced by its partizans as a rule of private conduct, seems not to have been carried to any considerable length, when applied to the business of government. In a few instances it has been carried a little way by the philosophical party: witness the Spartan regimen. Though then, perhaps, it may be considered as having been a measure of security: and an application, though a precipitate and perverse application, of the principle of utility. Scarcely in any instances, to any considerable length, by the religious: for the various monastic orders, and the societies of the Quakers, Dumplers, Moravians, and other religionists, have been free societies, whose regimen no man has been astricted to without the intervention of his own consent. Whatever merit a man may have thought there would be in making himself miserable, no such notion seems ever to have occurred to any of them, that it may be a merit, much less a duty, to make others miserable: although it should seem, that if a certain quantity of misery were a thing so desirable, it would not matter much whether it were brought by each man upon himself, or by one man upon another. It is true, that from the same source from whence, among the religionists, the attachment to the principle of asceticism took its rise, flowed other doctrines and practices, from which misery in abundance was produced in one man by the instrumentality of another: witness the holy wars, and the persecutions for religion. But the passion for producing misery in these cases proceeded upon some special ground: the exercise of it was confined to persons of particular descriptions: they were tormented, not as men, but as heretics and infidels. To have inflicted the same miseries on their fellow-believers and fellow-sectaries, would have been as blameable in the eyes even of these religionists, as in those of a partizan of the principle of utility. For a man to give himself a certain number of stripes was indeed meritorious: but to give the same number of stripes to another man, not consenting, would have been a sin. We read of saints, who for the good of their souls, and the mortification of their bodies, have voluntarily yielded themselves a prey to vermin: but though many persons of this class have wielded the reins of empire, we read of none who have set themselves to work, and made laws on purpose, with a view of stocking the body politic with the breed of highwaymen, housebreakers, or incendiaries. If at any time they have suffered the nation to be preyed upon by swarms of idle pensioners, or useless placemen, it has rather been from negligence and imbecility, than from any settled plan for oppressing and plundering of the people. If at any time they have sapped the sources of national wealth, by cramping commerce, and driving the inhabitants into emigration, it has been with other views, and in pursuit of other ends. If they have declaimed against the pursuit of pleasure, and the use of wealth, they have commonly stopped at declamation: they have not, like Lycurgus, made express ordinances for the purpose of banishing the precious metals. If they have established idleness by a law, it has been not because idleness, the mother of vice and misery, is itself a virtue, but because idleness (say they) is the road to holiness. If under the notion of fasting, they have joined in the plan of confining their subjects to a diet, thought by some to be of the most nourishing and

prolific nature, it has been not for the sake of making them tributaries to the nations by whom that diet was to be supplied, but for the sake of manifesting their own power, and exercising the obedience of the people. If they have established, or suffered to be established, punishments for the breach of celibacy, they have done no more than comply with the petitions of those deluded rigorists, who, dupes to the ambitious and deep-laid policy of their rulers, first laid themselves under that idle obligation by a vow.

IX. *The principle of asceticism, in its origin, was but that of utility misapplied.* The principle of asceticism seems originally to have been the reverie of certain hasty speculators, who having perceived, or fancied, that certain pleasures, when reaped in certain circumstances, have, at the long run, been attended with pains more than equivalent to them, took occasion to quarrel with every thing that offered itself under the name of pleasure. Having then got thus far, and having forgot the point which they set out from, they pushed on, and went so much further as to think it meritorious to fall in love with pain. Even this, we see, is at bottom but the principle of utility misapplied.

X. *It can never be consistently pursued.* The principle of utility is capable of being consistently pursued; and it is but tautology to say, that the more consistently it is pursued, the better it must ever be for humankind. The principle of asceticism never was, nor ever can be, consistently pursued by any living creature. Let but one tenth part of the inhabitants of this earth pursue it consistently, and in a day's time they will have turned it into a hell.

XI. *The principle of sympathy and antipathy, what.* Among principles adverse to that of utility, that which at this day seems to have most influence in matters of government, is what may be called the principle of sympathy and antipathy. By the principle of sympathy and antipathy, I mean that principle which approves or disapproves of certain actions, not on account of their tending to augment the happiness, nor yet on account of their tending to diminish the happiness of the party whose interest is in question, but merely because a man finds himself disposed to approve or disapprove of them: holding up that approbation or disapprobation as a sufficient reason for itself, and disclaiming the necessity of looking out for any extrinsic ground. Thus far in the general department of morals: and in the particular department of politics, measuring out the quantum (as well as determining the ground) of punishment, by the degree of the disapprobation.

XII. *This is rather the negation of all principle, then any thing positive.* It is manifest, that this is rather a principle in name than in reality: it is not a positive principle of itself, so much as a term employed to signify the negation of all principle. What one expects to find in a principle is something that points out some external consideration, as a means of warranting and guiding the internal sentiments of approbation and disapprobation: this expectation is but ill fulfilled by a proposition, which does neither more nor less than hold up each of those sentiments as a ground and standard for itself.

XIII. *Sentiments of a partizan of the principle of antipathy.* In looking over the catalogue of human actions (says a partizan of this principle) in order to determine which of them are to be marked with the seal of disapprobation, you need but to take counsel of your own feelings: whatever you find in yourself a propensity to condemn, is wrong for that very reason. For the same reason it is also meet for punishment: in what proportion it is adverse to utility, or whether it be adverse to utility at all, is a matter that makes no difference. In that same *proportion* also is it meet for punishment: if you hate much, punish much: if you hate little, punish little: punish as you hate. If you hate not at all, punish not at all: the fine feelings of the soul are not to be overborne and tyrannized by the harsh and rugged dictates of political utility.

XIV. *The systems that have been formed concerning the standard of right and wrong, are all reducible to this principle.* The various systems that have been formed concerning the standard of right and wrong, may all be reduced to the principle of sympathy and antipathy. One account may serve for all of them. They consist all of them in so many contrivances for avoiding the obligation of appealing to any external standard, and for prevailing upon the reader to accept of the author's sentiment or opinion as a reason for itself. The phrases different, but the principle the same.

XV. *This principle will frequently coincide with that of utility.* It is manifest, that the dictates of this principle will frequently coincide with those of utility, though perhaps without intending any such thing. Probably more frequently than not: and hence it is

that the business of penal justice is carried on upon that tolerable sort of footing upon which we see it carried on in common at this day. For what more natural or more general ground of hatred to a practice can there be, than the mischievousness of such practice? What all men are exposed to suffer by, all men will be disposed to hate. It is far yet, however, from being a constant ground: for when a man suffers, it is not always that he knows what it is he suffers by. A man may suffer grievously, for instance, by a new tax, without being able to trace up the cause of his sufferings to the injustice of some neighbour, who has eluded the payment of an old one.

XVI. *This principle is most apt to err on the side of severity.* The principle of sympathy and antipathy is most apt to err on the side of severity. It is for applying punishment in many cases which deserve none: in many cases which deserve some, it is for applying more than they deserve. There is no incident imaginable, be it ever so trivial, and so remote from mischief, from which this principle may not extract a ground of punishment. Any difference in taste: any difference in opinion: upon one subject as well as upon another. No disagreement so trifling which perseverance and altercation will not render serious. Each becomes in the other's eyes an enemy, and, if laws permit, a criminal. This is one of the circumstances by which the human race is distinguished (not much indeed to its advantage) from the brute creation.

XVII. *But errs, in some instances, on the side of lenity.* It is not, however, by any means unexampled for this principle to err on the side of lenity. A near and perceptible mischief moves antipathy. A remote and imperceptible mischief, though not less real, has no effect. Instances in proof of this will occur in numbers in the course of the work. It would be breaking in upon the order of it to give them here.

XVIII. *The theological principle, what—not a separate principle.* It may be wondered, perhaps, that in all this while no mention has been made of the *theological* principle; meaning that principle which professes to recur for the standard of right and wrong to the will of God. But the case is, this is not in fact a distinct principle. It is never any thing more or less than one or other of the three before-mentioned principles presenting itself under another shape. The *will* of God here meant cannot be his revealed will, as contained in the sacred writings: for that is a system which nobody ever thinks of recurring to at this time of day, for the details of political administration: and even before it can be applied to the details of private conduct, it is universally allowed, by the most eminent divines of all persuasions, to stand in need of pretty ample interpretations; else to what use are the works of those divines? And for the guidance of these interpretations, it is also allowed, that some other standard must be assumed. The will then which is meant on this occasion, is that which may be called the *presumptive* will: that is to say, that which is presumed to be his will on account of the conformity of its dictates to those of some other principle. What then may be this other principle? it must be one or other of the three mentioned above: for there cannot, as we have seen, be any more. It is plain, therefore, that, setting revelation out of the question, no light can ever be thrown upon the standard of right and wrong, by any thing that can be said upon the question, what is God's will. We may be perfectly sure, indeed, that whatever is right is conformable to the will of God: but so far is that from answering the purpose of showing us what is right, that it is necessary to know first whether a thing is right, in order to know from thence whether it be conformable to the will of God.

XIX. *Antipathy, let the actions it dictates be ever so right, is never of itself a right ground of action.* There are two things which are very apt to be confounded, but which it imports us carefully to distinguish:——the motive or cause, which, by operating on the mind of an individual, is productive of any act: and the ground or reason which warrants a legislator, or other by-stander, in regarding that act with an eye of approbation. When the act happens, in the particular instance in question, to be productive of effects which we approve of, much more if we happen to observe that the same motive may frequently be productive, in other instances, of the like effects, we are apt to transfer our approbation to the motive itself, and to assume, as the just ground for the approbation we bestow on the act, the circumstance of its originating from that motive. It is in this way that the sentiment of antipathy has often been considered as a just ground of action. Antipathy, for instance, in such or such a case, is the cause of an action which is attended with good effects: but this does not make it a right ground of action in that case, any more than in any other. Still farther. Not only the effects are

good, but the agent sees beforehand that they will be so. This may make the action indeed a perfectly right action: but it does not make antipathy a right ground of action. For the same sentiment of antipathy, if implicitly deferred to, may be, and very frequently is, productive of the very worst effects. Antipathy, therefore, can never be a right ground of action. No more, therefore, can resentment, which, as will be seen more particularly hereafter, is but a modification of antipathy. The only right ground of action, that can possibly subsist, is, after all, the consideration of utility, which, if it is a right principle of action, and of approbation, in any one case, is so in every other. Other principles in abundance, that is, other motives, may be the reasons why such and such an act *has* been done: that is, the reasons or causes of its being done: but it is this alone that can be the reason why it might or ought to have been done. Antipathy or resentment requires always to be regulated, to prevent its doing mischief: to be regulated by what? always by the principle of utility. The principle of utility neither requires nor admits of any other regulator than itself.

Chapter III. Of the Four Sanctions or Sources of Pain and Pleasure.

I. *Connexion of this chapter with preceding.* It has been shown that the happiness of the individuals, of whom a community is composed, that is their pleasures and their security, is the end and the sole end which the legislator ought to have in view: the sole standard in conformity to which each individual ought, as far as depends upon the legislator to be *made* to fashion his behaviour. But whether it be this or any thing else that is to be *done*, there is nothing by which a man can ultimately be *made* to do it, but either pain or pleasure. Having taken a general view of these two grand objects (*viz.* pleasure, and what comes to the same thing, immunity from pain) in the character of *final* causes; it will be necessary to take a view of pleasure and pain itself, in the character of *efficient* causes or means.

II. *Four sanctions or sources of pleasure and pain.* There are four distinguishable sources from which pleasure and pain are in use to flow: considered separately, they may be termed the *physical*, the *political*, the *moral*, and the *religious*: and inasmuch as the pleasures and pains belonging to each of them are capable of giving a binding force to any law or rule of conduct, they may all of them be termed *sanctions*.

III. *The physical sanction.* If it be in the present life, and from the ordinary course of nature, not purposely modified by the interposition of the will of any human being, nor by any extraordinary interposition of any superior invisible being, that the pleasure or the pain takes place or is expected, it may be said to issue from or to belong to the *physical sanction.*

IV. *The political.* If at the hands of a *particular* person or set of persons in the community, who under names correspondent to that of *judge*, are chosen for the particular purpose of dispensing it, according to the will of the sovereign or supreme ruling power in the state, it may be said to issue from the *political sanction.*

V. *The moral or popular.* If at the hands of such *chance* persons in the community, as the party in question may happen in the course of his life to have concerns with, according to each man's spontaneous disposition, and not according to any settled or concerted rule, it may be said to issue from the *moral* or *popular sanction.*

VI. *The religious.* If from the immediate hand of a superior invisible being, either in the present life, or in a future, it may be said to issue from the *religious sanction.*

VII. *The pleasures and pains which belong to the religious sanction, may regard either the present life or a future.* Pleasures or pains which may be expected to issue from the *physical, political,* or *moral* sanctions, must all of them be expected to be experienced, if ever, in the *present* life: those which may be expected to issue from the *religious* sanction, may be expected to be experienced either in the *present* life or in a *future.*

VIII. *Those which regard the present life, from which soever source they flow, differ only in the circumstances of their production.* Those which can be experienced in the present life, can of course be no others than such as human nature in the course of the present life is susceptible of: and from each of these sources may flow all the pleasures or pains of which, in the course of the present life, human nature is susceptible. With regard to these then (with which alone we have in this place any concern) those of them which belong to any one of those sanctións, differ not ultimately in kind from those which belong to any one

of the other three: the only difference there is among them lies in the circumstances that accompany their production. A suffering which befalls a man in the natural and spontaneous course of things, shall be styled, for instance, a *calamity*; in which case, if it be supposed to befall him through any imprudence of his, it may be styled a punishment issuing from the physical sanction. Now this same suffering, if inflicted by the law, will be what is commonly called a *punishment*; if incurred for want of any friendly assistance, which the misconduct, or supposed misconduct, of the sufferer has occasioned to be withholden, a punishment issuing from the *moral* sanction; if through the immediate interposition of a particular providence, a punishment issuing from the religious sanction.

IX. *Example.* A man's goods, or his person, are consumed by fire. If this happened to him by what is called an accident, it was a calamity: if by reason of his own imprudence (for instance, from his neglecting to put his candle out) it may be styled a punishment of the physical sanction: if it happened to him by the sentence of the political magistrate, a punishment belonging to the political sanction; that is, what is commonly called a punishment: if for want of any assistance which his *neighbour* withheld from him out of some dislike to his *moral* character, a punishment of the *moral* sanction: if by an immediate act of *God's* displeasure, manifested on account of some *sin* committed by him, or through any distraction of mind, occasioned by the dread of such displeasure, a punishment of the *religious* sanction.

X. *Those which regard a future life are not specifically known.* As to such of the pleasures and pains belonging to the religious sanction, as regard a future life, of what kind these may be we cannot know. These lie not open to our observation. During the present life they are matter only of expectation: and, whether that expectation be derived from natural or revealed religion, the particular kind of pleasure or pain, if it be different from all those which lie open to our observation, is what we can have no idea of. The best ideas we can obtain of such pains and pleasures are altogether unliquidated in point of quality. In what other respects our ideas of them may be liquidated will be considered in another place.

XI. *The physical sanction included in each of the other three.* Of these four sanctions the physical is altogether, we may observe, the ground-work of the political and the moral: so is it also of the religious, in as far as the latter bears relation to the present life. It is included in each of those other three. This may operate in any case, (that is, any of the pains or pleasures belonging to it may operate) independently of *them*: none of *them* can operate but by means of this. In a word, the powers of nature may operate of themselves; but neither the magistrate, nor men at large, *can* operate, nor is God in the case in question *supposed* to operate, but through the powers of nature.

XII. *Use of this chapter.* For these four objects, which in their nature have so much in common, it seemed of use to find a common name. It seemed of use, in the first place, for the convenience of giving a name to certain pleasures and pains, for which a name equally characteristic could hardly otherwise have been found: in the second place, for the sake of holding up the efficacy of certain moral forces, the influence of which is apt not to be sufficiently attended to. Does the political Sanction exert an influence over the conduct of mankind? The moral, the religious sanctions do so too. In every inch of his career are the operations of the political magistrate liable to be aided or impeded by these two foreign powers: who, one or other of them, or both, are sure to be either his rivals or his allies. Does it happen to him to leave them out in his calculations? he will be sure almost to find himself mistaken in the result. Of all this we shall find abundant proofs in the sequel of this work. It behoves him, therefore, to have them continually before his eyes; and that under such a name as exhibits the relation they bear to his own purposes and designs.

Chapter IV. Value of a Lot of Pleasure or Pain, How to Be Measured.

I. *Use of this chapter.* Pleasures then, and the avoidance of pains, are the *ends* which the legislator has in view: it behoves him therefore to understand their *value*. Pleasures and pains are the *instruments* he has to work with: it behoves him therefore to understand their force, which is again, in other words, their value.

II. *Circumstances to be taken into the account in esti-mating the value of a pleasure or pain considered with reference to a single person, and by itself.* To a person

considered by *himself*, the value of a pleasure or pain considered by *itself*, will be greater or less, according to the four following circumstances:

1. Its *intensity*.
2. Its *duration*.
3. Its *certainty* or *uncertainty*.
4. Its *propinquity* or *remoteness*.

III. —*considered as connected with other pleasures or pains.* These are the circumstances which are to be considered in estimating a pleasure or a pain considered each of them by itself. But when the value of any pleasure or pain is considered for the purpose of estimating the tendency of any *act* by which it is produced, there are two other circumstances to be taken into the account; these are,

5. Its *fecundity*, or the chance it has of being followed by sensations of the *same* kind: that is, pleasures, if it be a pleasure: pains, if it be a pain.
6. Its *purity*, or the chance it has of *not* being followed by sensations of the *opposite* kind: that is, pains, if it be a pleasure: pleasures, if it be a pain.

These two last, however, are in strictness scarcely to be deemed properties of the pleasure or the pain itself; they are not, therefore, in strictness to be taken into the account of the value of that pleasure or that pain. They are in strictness to be deemed properties only of the act, or other event, by which such pleasure or pain has been produced; and accordingly are only to be taken into the account of the tendency of such act or such event.

IV. —*considered with reference to a number of persons.* To a *number* of persons, with reference to each of whom the value of a pleasure or a pain is considered, it will be greater or less, according to seven circumstances: to wit, the six preceding ones; *viz.*

1. Its *intensity*.
2. Its *duration*.
3. Its *certainty* or *uncertainty*.
4. Its *propinquity* or *remoteness*.
5. Its *fecundity*.
6. Its *purity*.

And one other; to wit:

7. Its *extent*; that is, the number of persons to whom it *extends*; or (in other words) who are affected by it.

V. *Process for estimating the tendency of any act or event.* To take an exact account then of the general tendency of any act, by which the interests of a community are affected, proceed as follows. Begin with any one person of those whose interests seem most immediately to be affected by it: and take an account,

1. Of the value of each distinguishable *pleasure* which appears to be produced by it in the *first* instance.

2. Of the value of each *pain* which appears to be produced by it in the *first* instance.

3. Of the value of each pleasure which appears to be produced by it *after* the first. This constitutes the *fecundity* of the first *pleasure* and the *impurity* of the first *pain*.

4. Of the value of each *pain* which appears to be produced by it after the first. This constitutes the *fecundity* of the first *pain*, and the *impurity* of the first pleasure.

5. Sum up all the values of all the *pleasures* on the one side, and those of all the pains on the other. The balance, if it be on the side of pleasure, will give the *good* tendency of the act upon the whole, with respect to the interests of that *individual* person; if on the side of pain, the *bad* tendency of it upon the whole.

6. Take an account of the *number* of persons whose interests appear to be concerned; and repeat the above process with respect to each. *Sum up* the numbers expressive of the degrees of *good* tendency, which the act has, with respect to each individual, in regard to whom the tendency of it is *good* upon the whole: do this again with respect to each individual, in regard to whom the tendency of it is *good* upon the whole: do this again with respect to each individual, in regard to whom the tendency of it is bad upon the whole. Take the *balance*; which, if on the side of *pleasure*, will give the general *good tendency* of the act, with respect to the total number or community of individuals concerned; if on the side of pain, the general *evil tendency*, with respect to the same community.

VI. *Use of the foregoing process.* It is not to be expected that this process should be strictly pursued previously to every moral judgment, or to every legislative or judicial operation. It may, however, be always kept in view: and as near as the process actually pursued on these occasions approaches to it, so near will such process approach to the character of an exact one.

VII. *The same process applicable to good and evil, profit and mischief, and all other modifications of pleasure and pain.* The same process is alike applicable to pleasure and pain, in whatever shape they appear: and by whatever denomination they are distinguished: to pleasure, whether it be called *good* (which is properly the cause or instrument of pleasure) or *profit* (which is distant pleasure, or the cause or instrument of distant pleasure,) or *convenience*, or *advantage*, *benefit*, *emolument*, *happiness*, and so forth: to pain, whether it be called *evil*, (which corresponds to *good*) or *mischief*, or *inconvenience*, or *disadvantage*, or *loss*, or *unhappiness*, and so forth.

VIII. *Conformity of men's practice to this theory.* Nor is this a novel and unwarranted, any more than it is a useless theory. In all this there is nothing but what the practice of mankind, wheresoever they have a clear view of their own interest, is perfectly conformable to. An article of property, an estate in land, for instance, is valuable, on what account? On account of the pleasures of all kinds which it enables a man to produce, and what comes to the same thing the pains of all kinds which it enables him to avert. But the value of such an article of property is universally understood to rise or fall according to the length or shortness of the time which a man has in it: the certainty or uncertainty of its coming into possession: and the nearness or remoteness of the time at which, if at all, it is to come into possession. As to the *intensity* of the pleasures which a man may derive from it, this is never thought of, because it depends upon the use which each particular person may come to make of it; which cannot be estimated till the particular pleasures he may come to derive from it, or the particular pains he may come to exclude by means of it, are brought to view. For the same reason, neither does he think of the *fecundity* or *purity* of those pleasures. . . .

JOHN STUART MILL

Utilitarianism

John Stuart Mill (1806–1873), philosopher, economist, and social reformer, was born in London, the son of the Scottish philosopher James Mill. The young Mill never attended school but instead was given an extraordinary education by his father. By the age of three he had begun reading Greek and had taken up Latin by the age of eight. Mill had read most of the Greek and Latin classics, had read widely in history, and had done extensive work in logic and mathematics by the time he was fourteen. However, it was to the reading of a treatise by Jeremy Bentham at the age of fifteen that he attributed his recognition of his life's work. With the power of a religious revelation, Bentham's essay produced in John Stuart Mill the goal of reforming the world.

With the assistance of his father, Mill became an active radical in the Benthamite movement. He thought that progress in reforming society and its institutions would be achieved most quickly by making the ideas of the reforms appealing to a wide population. Thus, he is often criticized by subsequent philosophers for being a mediocre thinker who offered few new thoughts of his own. But this perception resulted from Mill's efforts to provide a philosophy that was inclusive rather than exclusive, one that was constructive rather than destructive, not a weakness of thinking. He thought it necessary for social reform to offer a philosophical alternative that would attract a larger audience.

Mill wrote many articles, essays, and tracts on a wide variety of subjects, but his System of Logic, *published in 1843, achieved a rapid and wide success, being adopted as a text at both Oxford and Cambridge. His book* On Liberty *(1859) he felt to be his work of most enduring value. But it is in his essay* Utilitarianism *(1863) that his ethical views are most clearly elaborated.*

Mill believed that society would be cohesive only if the moral values underlying society were widely accepted. Lacking such acceptance, society would never be unified. Mill saw in his own time the first signs of the widespread weakening of the Christian moral view. He saw his task as that of providing an alternative system of moral value that would be acceptable to both those who still clung to the institutions and values of Christianity as well as to those who would be willing to embrace new ideas. The moral system that was to unify society under the banner of shared moral values was utilitarianism

In his essay Utilitarianism, *Mill attempts to remedy defects in Bentham's version of utilitarianism .Two of his contributions have received a great deal of criticism. First, Mill correctly saw that Bentham's view that pleasures were all equal in quality, that "pushpin was as good as philosophy," lead to a reduction of the notion of pleasure to mere bodily feelings. As a reproof, Mill argued that some pleasures were more valuable than others. "It is better to be Socrates dissatisfied than a fool satisfied." Additionally, it is Mill's attempt to provide support for the utilitarian principle against charges of dogmatism that enabled G. E. Moore to accuse Mill of committing the "naturalistic fallacy." (See Moore's* Principia Ethica).

Mill was largely successful in his efforts to make the moral theory of utilitarianism appeal to a wide audience. Schneewind calls Mill "the most influential philosopher in the English-speaking world in the nineteenth century."[1] It is largely due to his efforts that utilitarianism has continued to have a powerful influence to this day.

Chapter I General Remarks

There are few circumstances among those which make up the present condition of human knowledge more unlike what might have been expected, or more significant of the backward state in which speculation on the most important subjects still lingers, than the little progress which has been made in the decision of the controversy respecting the criterion of right and wrong. From the dawn of philosophy, the question concerning the *summum bonum,* or, what is the same thing, concerning the foundation of morality, has been accounted the main problem in speculative thought, has occupied the most gifted intellects and divided them into sects and schools, carrying on a vigorous warfare against one another. And after more than two thousand years the same discussions continue, philosophers are still ranged under the same contending banners, and neither thinkers nor mankind at large seem nearer to being unanimous on the subject than when the youth Socrates listened to the old Protagoras, and asserted (if Plato's dialogue be grounded on a real conversation) the theory of utilitarianism against the popular morality of the so-called sophist.

It is true that similar confusion and uncertainty and, in some cases, similar discordance exist respecting the first principles of all the sciences, not excepting that which is deemed the most certain of them—mathematics, without much impairing, generally indeed without impairing at all, the trustworthiness of the conclusions of those sciences. An apparent anomaly, the explanation of which is that the detailed doctrines of a science are not usually deduced from, nor depend for their evidence upon, what are called its first principles. Were it not so, there would be no science more precarious, or

whose conclusions were more insufficiently made out, than algebra, which derives none of its certainty from what are commonly taught to learners as its elements, since these, as laid down by some of its most eminent teachers, are as full of fictions as English law, and of mysteries as theology. The truths which are ultimately accepted as the first principles of a science are really the last results of metaphysical analysis, practised on the elementary notions with which the science is conversant; and their relation to the science is not that of foundations to an edifice, but of roots to a tree, which may perform their office equally well though they be never dug down to and exposed to light. But though in science the particular truths precede the general theory, the contrary might be expected to be the case with a practical art, such as morals or legislation. All action is for the sake of some end, and rules of action, it seems natural to suppose, must take their whole character and color from the end to which they are subservient. When we engage in a pursuit, a clear and precise conception of what we are pursuing would seem to be the first thing we need, instead of the last we are to look forward to. A test of right and wrong must be the means, one would think, of ascertaining what is right or wrong, and not a consequence of having already ascertained it.

The difficulty is not avoided by having recourse to the popular theory of a natural faculty, a sense or instinct, informing us of right and wrong. For—besides that the existence of such a moral instinct is itself one of the matters in dispute—those believers in it who have any pretensions to philosophy have been obliged to abandon the idea that it discerns what is right or wrong in the particular case in hand, as our other senses discern the sight or sound actually present. Our moral faculty, according to all those of its interpreters who are entitled to the name of thinkers, supplies us only with the general principles of moral judgments; it is a branch of our reason, not of our sensitive faculty; and must be looked to for the abstract doctrines of morality, not for perception of it in the

---

1. J. B. Schneewind, "John Stuart Mill," in *The Encyclopedia of Philosophy,* Vol. 5, New York: Macmillan and The Free Press, 1967.

concrete. The intuitive, no less than what may be termed the inductive, school of ethics insists on the necessity of general laws. They both agree that the morality of an individual action is not a question of direct perception, but of the application of a law to an individual case. They recognize also, to a great extent, the same moral laws, but differ as to their evidence and the source from which they derive their authority. According to the one opinion, the principles of morals are evident *à priori,* requiring nothing to command assent except that the meaning of the terms be understood. According to the other doctrine, right and wrong, as well as truth and falsehood, are questions of observation and experience. But both hold equally that morality must be deduced from principles; and the intuitive school affirm as strongly as the inductive that there is a science of morals. Yet they seldom attempt to make out a list of the *à priori* principles which are to serve as the premises of the science; still more rarely do they make any effort to reduce those various principles to one first principle, or common ground of obligation. They either assume the ordinary precepts of morals as of *a priori* authority, or they lay down as the common groundwork of those maxims, some generality much less obviously authoritative than the maxims themselves, and which has never succeeded in gaining popular acceptance. Yet to support their pretensions there ought either to be some one fundamental principle or law at the root of all morality, or, if there be several, there should be a determinate order of precedence among them; and the one principle, or the rule for deciding between the various principles when they conflict, ought to be self-evident.

To inquire how far the bad effects of this deficiency have been mitigated in practice, or to what extent the moral beliefs of mankind have been vitiated or made uncertain by the absence of any distinct recognition of an ultimate standard, would imply a complete survey and criticism of past and present ethical doctrine. It would, however, be easy to show that whatever steadiness or consistency these moral beliefs have attained has been mainly due to the tacit influence of a standard not recognized. Although the non-existence of an acknowledged first principle has made ethics not so much a guide as a consecration of men's actual sentiments, still, as men's sentiments, both in favor and of aversion, are greatly influenced by what they suppose to be the effect of things upon their happiness, the principle of utility, or, as Bentham latterly called it, the greatest happiness principle, has had a large share in forming the moral doctrines even of those who most scornfully reject its authority. Nor is there any school of thought which refuses to admit that the influence of actions on happiness is a most material and even predominant consideration in many of the details of morals, however unwilling to acknowledge it as the fundamental principle of morality and the source of moral obligation. I might go much further and say that to all those *a priori* moralists who deem it necessary to argue at all, utilitarian arguments are indispensable. It is not my present purpose to criticize these thinkers; but I cannot help referring, for illustration, to a systematic treatise by one of the most illustrious of them, the *Metaphysics of Ethics* by Kant. This remarkable man, whose system of thought will long remain one of the landmarks in the history of philosophical speculation, does, in the treatise in question, lay down a universal first principle as the origin and ground of moral obligation; it is this: "So act that the rule on which thou actest would admit of being adopted as a law by all rational beings." But when he begins to deduce from this precept any of the actual duties of morality, he fails, almost grotesquely, to show that there would be any contradiction, any logical (not to say physical) impossibility, in the adoption by all rational beings of the most outrageously immoral rules of conduct. All he knows is that the *consequences* of their universal adoption would be such as no one would choose to incur.

On the present occasion, I shall, without further discussion of the other theories, attempt to contribute something towards the understanding and appreciation of the "utilitarian" or "happiness" theory, and towards such proof as it is susceptible of. It is evident that this cannot be proof in the ordinary and popular meaning of the term. Questions of ultimate ends are not amenable to direct proof. Whatever can be proved to be good must be so by being shown to be a means to something admitted to be good without proof. The medical art is proved to be good by its conducing to health; but how is it possible to prove that health is good? The art of music is good, for the reason, among others, that it produces pleasure; but what proof is it possible to give that pleasure is good? If, then, it is asserted that there is a comprehensive formula, including all things which are in themselves good, and that whatever else is good is not so as an end but as a means, the formula may be accepted or rejected, but is not a subject of what is commonly understood by proof. We are not, however, to infer that its acceptance or rejection must depend on blind impulse, or arbitrary choice. There is a larger meaning of the word "proof," in which this question is as amenable to it as any other of the disputed questions of philosophy. The subject is within the cognizance of the rational faculty; and neither does that faculty deal with it solely in the way of intuition. Considerations may be presented capable of determining the intellect either to give or withhold its assent to the doctrine; and this is equivalent to proof.

We shall examine presently of what nature are these considerations; in what manner they apply to the case, and what rational grounds, therefore, can be given for accepting or rejecting the utilitarian formula. But it is a preliminary condition of rational acceptance or rejection that the formula should be correctly understood. I believe that the very imperfect notion ordinarily formed of its meaning is the chief obstacle which impedes its reception, and that, could it be cleared even from only the grosser misconceptions the question would be greatly simplified and a large proportion of its difficulties removed. Before, therefore, I attempt to enter into the philosophical grounds which can be given for assenting to the utilitarian standard, I shall offer some illustrations of the doctrine itself, with the view of showing more clearly what it is, distinguishing it from what it is not, and disposing of such of the practical objections to it as either originate in, or are closely connected with, mistaken interpretation of its meaning. Having thus prepared the ground, I shall afterwards endeavor to throw such light as I can call upon the question considered as one of philosophical theory.

Chapter II What Utilitarianism Is

A passing remark is all that needs be given to the ignorant blunder of supposing that those who stand up for utility as the test of right and wrong use the term in that restricted and merely colloquial sense in which utility is opposed to pleasure. An apology is due to the philosophical opponents of utilitarianism, for even the momentary appearance of confounding them with anyone capable of so absurd a misconception; which is the more extraordinary, inasmuch as the contrary accusation, of referring everything to pleasure, and that, too, in its grossest form, is another of the common charges against utilitarianism: and, as has been pointedly remarked by an able writer, the same sort of persons, and often the very same persons, denounce the theory "as impracticably dry when the word 'utility' precedes the word 'pleasure', and as too practically voluptuous when the word 'pleasure' precedes the word 'utility'." Those who know anything about the matter are aware that every writer, from Epicurus to Bentham, who maintained the theory of utility, meant by it, not something to be contradistinguished from pleasure, but pleasure itself, together with exemption from pain; and instead of opposing the useful to the agreeable or the ornamental, have always declared that the useful means these, among other things. Yet the common herd, including the herd of writers, not only in newspapers and periodicals, but in books of weight and pretension, are perpetually falling into this shallow mistake. Having caught up the word "utilitarian," while knowing nothing whatever about it but its sound, they habitually express by it the rejection or the neglect of pleasure in some of its forms: of beauty, of ornament, or of amusement. Nor is the term thus ignorantly misapplied solely in disparagement, but occasionally in compliment, as though it implied superiority to frivolity and the mere pleasures of the moment. And this perverted use is the only one in which the word is popularly known, and the one from which the new generation are acquiring their sole notion of its meaning. Those who introduced the word, but who had for many years discontinued it as a distinctive appellation, may well feel themselves called upon to resume it if by doing so they can hope to contribute anything towards rescuing it from this utter degradation.[1]

---

1. The author of this essay has reason for believing himself to be the first person who brought the word "utilitarian" into use. He did not invent it, but adopted it from a passing expression in Mr. Galt's *Annals of the Parish*. After using it as a designation for several years, he and others abandoned it from a growing dislike to anything resembling a badge or watchword of sectarian distinction. But as a name for one single opinion, not a set of opinions—to denote the recognition of utility as a standard, not any particular way of applying it—the term supplies a want in the language, and offers, in many cases, a convenient mode of avoiding tiresome circumlocution.

The creed which accepts as the foundation of morals "utility" or the "greatest happiness principle" holds that actions are right in proportion as they tend to promote happiness, wrong as they tend to produce the reverse of happiness. By happiness is intended pleasure, and the absence of pain; by unhappiness, pain, and the privation of pleasure. To give a clear view of the moral standard set up by the theory, much more requires to be said; in particular, what things it includes in the ideas of pain and pleasure; and to what extent this is left an open question. But these supplementary explanations do not affect the theory of life on which this theory of morality is grounded—namely, that pleasure and freedom from pain are the only things desirable as ends; and that all desirable things (which are as numerous in the utilitarian as in any other scheme) are desirable either for the pleasure inherent in themselves, or as means to the promotion of pleasure and the prevention of pain.

Now such a theory of life excites in many minds, and among them in some of the most estimable in feeling and purpose, inveterate dislike. To suppose that life has (as they express it) no higher end than pleasure—no better and nobler object of desire and pursuit—they designate as utterly mean and groveling; as a doctrine worthy only of swine, to whom the followers of Epicurus were, at a very early period, contemptuously likened; and modern holders of the doctrine are occasionally made the subject of equally polite comparisons by its German, French, and English assailants.

When thus attacked, the Epicureans have always answered that it is not they, but their accusers, who represent human nature in a degrading light, since the accusation supposes human beings to be capable of no pleasures except those of which swine are capable. If this supposition were true, the charge could not be gainsaid, but would then be no longer an imputation; for if the sources of pleasure were precisely the same to human beings and to swine, the rule of life which is good enough for the one would be good enough for the other. The comparison of the Epicurean life to that of beasts is felt as degrading, precisely because a beast's pleasures do not satisfy a human being's conceptions of happiness. Human beings have faculties more elevated than the animal appetites and, when once made conscious of them, do not regard anything as happiness which does not in-clude their gratification. I do not, indeed, consider the Epicureans to have been by any means faultless in drawing out their scheme of consequences from the utilitarian principle. To do this in any sufficient manner, many Stoic, as well as Christian, elements require to be included. But there is no known Epicurean theory of life which does not assign to the pleasures of the intellect, of the feelings and imagination, and of the moral sentiments, a much higher value of pleasures than to those of mere sensation. It must be admitted, however, that utilitarian writers in general have placed the superiority of mental over bodily pleasures chiefly in the greater permanency, safety, uncostliness, etc., of the former—that is, in their circumstantial advantages rather than in their intrinsic nature. And on all these points utilitarians have fully proved their case; but they might have taken the other and, as it may be called, higher ground with entire consistency. It is quite compatible with the principle of utility to recognize the fact that some kinds of pleasure are more desirable and more valuable than others. It would be absurd that, while, in estimating all other things, quality is considered as well as quantity, the estimation of pleasures should be supposed to depend on quantity alone.

If I am asked what I mean by difference of quality in pleasures, or what makes one pleasure more valuable than another, merely as a pleasure, except its being greater in amount, there is but one possible answer. Of two pleasures, if there be one to which all or almost all who have experience of both give a decided preference, irrespective of a feeling of moral obligation to prefer it, that is the more desirable pleasure. If one of the two is, by those who are competently acquainted with both, placed so far above the other that they prefer it, even though knowing it to be attended with a greater amount of discontent, and would not resign it for any quantity of the other pleasure which their nature is capable of, we are justified in ascribing to the preferred enjoyment a superiority in quality so far outweighing quantity as to render it, in comparison, of small account.

Now it is an unquestionable fact that those who are equally acquainted with and equally capable of appreciating and enjoying both, do give a most marked preference to the manner of existence which employs their higher faculties. Few human creatures would consent to be changed into any of the lower animals for a promise of the fullest allowance of a beast's pleasures; no intelligent human being would consent to be a fool, no instructed person would be an ignoramus, no person of feeling and conscience would be selfish and base, even though they should be persuaded that the fool, the dunce, or the rascal is better satisfied with his lot than they are with theirs. They would not resign what they possess more than he for the most complete satisfaction of all the desires which they have in common with him. If they ever fancy they would, it is only in cases of unhappiness so extreme that to escape from it they would exchange their lot for almost any other, however undesirable in their own eyes. A being of higher faculties requires more to make him happy, is capable probably of more acute suffering, and certainly accessible to it at more points, than one of an inferior type; but in spite of these liabilities, he can never really wish to sink into what he feels to be a lower grade of existence. We may give what explanation we please of this unwillingness; we may attribute it to pride, a name which is given indiscriminately to some of the most and to some of the least estimable feelings of which mankind are capable: we may refer it to the love of liberty and personal independence, an appeal to which was with the Stoics one of the most effective means for the inculcation of it; to the love of power or to the love of excitement, both of which do really enter into and contribute to it; but its most appropriate appellation is a sense of dignity, which all human beings possess in one form or other, and in some, though by no means in exact, proportion to their higher faculties, and which is so essential a part of the happiness of those in whom it is strong that nothing which conflicts with it could be otherwise than momentarily an object of desire to them. Whoever supposes that this preference takes place at a sacrifice of happiness—that the superior being, in anything like equal circumstances, is not happier than the inferior—confounds the two very different ideas of happiness and content. It is indisputable that the being whose capacities of enjoyment are low has the greatest chance of having them fully satisfied; and a highly endowed being will always feel that any happiness which he can look for, as the world is constituted, is imperfect. But he can learn to bear its imperfections, if they are at all bearable; and they will not make him envy the being who is indeed unconscious of the imperfections, but only because he feels not at all the good which those imperfec-

tions qualify. It is better to be a human being dissatisfied than a pig satisfied; better to be Socrates dissatisfied than a fool satisfied. And if the fool, or the pig, are of a different opinion, it is because they only know their own side of the question. The other party to the comparison knows both sides.

It may be objected that many who are capable of the higher pleasures occasionally, under the influence of temptation, postpone them to the lower. But this is quite compatible with a full appreciation of the intrinsic superiority of the higher. Men often, from infirmity of character, make their election for the nearer good, though they know it to be the less valuable; and this no less when the choice is between two bodily pleasures than when it is between bodily and mental. They pursue sensual indulgences to the injury of health, though perfectly aware that health is the greater good. It may be further objected that many who begin with youthful enthusiasm for everything noble, as they advance in years, sink into indolence and selfishness. But I do not believe that those who undergo this very common change voluntarily choose the lower description of pleasures in preference to the higher. I believe that, before they devote themselves exclusively to the one, they have already become incapable of the other. Capacity for the nobler feelings is in most natures a very tender plant, easily killed, not only by hostile influences, but by mere want of sustenance; and in the majority of young persons it speedily dies away if the occupations to which their position in life has devoted them, and the society into which it has thrown them, are not favorable to keeping that higher capacity in exercise. Men lose their high aspirations as they lose their intellectual tastes, because they have not time or opportunity for indulging them; and they addict themselves to inferior pleasures, not because they deliberately prefer them, but because they are either the only ones to which they have access, or the only ones which they are any longer capable of enjoying. It may be questioned whether any one who has remained equally susceptible to both classes of pleasures, ever knowingly and calmly preferred the lower, though many, in all ages, have broken down in an ineffectual attempt to combine both.

From this verdict of the only competent judges, I apprehend there can be no appeal. On a question which is the best worth having of two pleasures, or which of two modes of existence is the most grateful to the feelings, apart from its moral attributes and from its consequences, the judgment of those who are qualified by knowledge of both, or, if they differ, that of the majority of them, must be admitted as final. And there needs be the less hesitation to accept this judgment respecting the quality of pleasures, since there is no other tribunal to be referred to even on the question of quantity. What means are there of determining which is the acutest of two pains, or the intensest of two pleasurable sensations, except the general suffrage of those who are familiar with both? Neither pains nor pleasures are homogeneous, and pain is always heterogeneous with pleasure. What is there to decide whether a particular pleasure is worth purchasing at the cost of a particular pain, except the feelings and judgment of the experienced? When, therefore, those feelings and judgment declare the pleasures derived from the higher faculties to be preferable *in kind,* apart from the question of intensity, to those of which the animal nature disjoined from the higher faculties, is susceptible, they are entitled on this subject to the same regard.

I have dwelt on this point, as being a necessary part of a perfectly just conception of utility or happiness considered as the directive rule of human conduct. But it is by no means an indispensable condition to the acceptance of the utilitarian standard; for that standard is not the agent's own greatest happiness, but the greatest amount of happiness altogether; and if it may possibly be doubted whether a noble character is always the happier for its nobleness, there can be no doubt that it makes other people happier, and that the world in general is immensely a gainer by it. Utilitarianism, therefore, could only attain its end by the general cultivation of nobleness of character, even if each individual were only benefited by the nobleness of others, and his own, so far as happiness is concerned, were a sheer deduction from the benefit. But the bare enunciation of such an absurdity as this last renders refutation superfluous.

According to the greatest happiness principle, as above explained, the ultimate end, with reference to and for the sake of which all other things are desirable—whether we are considering our own good or that of other people—is an existence exempt as far as possible from pain, and as rich as possible in enjoyments, both in point of quantity and quality; the test of quality and the rule for measuring it against quan-

tity being the preference felt by those who, in their opportunities of experience, to which must be added their habits of self-consciousness and self-observation, are best furnished with the means of comparison. This, being, according to the utilitarian opinion, the end of human action, is necessarily also the standard of morality, which may accordingly be defined "the rules and precepts for human conduct," by the observance of which an existence such as has been described might be, to the greatest extent possible, secured to all mankind; and not to them only, but, so far as the nature of things admits, to the whole sentient creation.

Against this doctrine, however, arises another class of objectors who say that happiness, in any form, cannot be the rational purpose of human life and action; because, in the first place, it is unattainable; and they contemptuously ask, What right hast thou to be happy?—a question which Mr. Carlyle clenches by the addition, What right, a short time ago, hadst thou even *to be*? Next they say that men can do *without* happiness; that all noble human beings have felt this, and could not have become noble but by learning the lesson of *Entsagen,* or renunciation; which lesson, thoroughly learnt and submitted to, they affirm to be the beginning and necessary condition of all virtue.

The first of these objections would go to the root of the matter were it well founded; for if no happiness is to be had at all by human beings, the attainment of it cannot be the end of morality or of any rational conduct. Though, even in that case, something might still be said for the utilitarian theory, since utility includes not solely the pursuit of happiness, but the prevention or mitigation of unhappiness; and if the former aim be chimerical, there will be all the greater scope and more imperative need for the latter, so long at least as mankind think fit to live, and do not take refuge in the simultaneous act of suicide recommended under certain conditions by Novalis. When, however, it is thus positively asserted to be impossible that human life should be happy, the assertion, if not something like a verbal quibble, is at least an exaggeration. If by happiness be meant a continuity of highly pleasurable excitement, it is evident enough that this is impossible. A state of exalted pleasure lasts only moments or in some cases, and with some intermissions, hours or days, and is the occasional brilliant flash of enjoyment, not its permanent and steady flame. Of this the philosophers who have taught that happiness is the end of life were as fully aware as those who taunt them. The happiness which they meant was not a life of rapture; but moments of such, in an existence made up of few and transitory pains, many and various pleasures, with a decided predominance of the active over the passive, and having as the foundation of the whole not to expect more from life than it is capable of bestowing. A life thus composed, to those who have been fortunate enough to obtain it, has always appeared worthy of the name of happiness. And such an existence is even now the lot of many, during some considerable portion of their lives. The present wretched education and wretched social arrangements are the only real hindrance to its being attainable by almost all.

The objectors perhaps may doubt whether human beings, if taught to consider happiness as the end of life, would be satisfied with such a moderate share of it. But great numbers of mankind have been satisfied with much less. The main constituents of a satisfied life appear to be two, either of which by itself is often found sufficient for the purpose: tranquility and excitement. With much tranquility, many find that they can be content with very little pleasure; with much excitement, many can reconcile themselves to a considerable quantity of pain. There is assuredly no inherent impossibility of enabling even the mass of mankind to unite both, since the two are so far from being incompatible that they are in natural alliance, the prolongation of either being a preparation for, and exciting a wish for, the other. It is only those in whom indolence amounts to a vice that do not desire excitement after an interval of repose; it is only those in whom the need of excitement is a disease that feel the tranquility which follows excitement dull and insipid, instead of pleasurable in direct proportion to the excitement which preceded it. When people who are tolerably fortunate in their outward lot do not find in life sufficient enjoyment to make it valuable to them, the cause generally is caring for nobody but themselves. To those who have neither public nor private affections, the excitements of life are much curtailed, and in any case dwindle in value as the time approaches when all selfish interests must be terminated by death; while those who leave after them objects of personal affection, and especially those who have also culti-

vated a fellow-feeling with the collective interests of mankind, retain as lively an interest in life on the eve of death as in the vigor of youth and health. Next to selfishness, the principal cause which makes life unsatisfactory is want of mental cultivation. A cultivated mind — I do not mean that of a philosopher, but any mind to which the fountains of knowledge have been opened, and which has been taught, in any tolerable degree, to exercise its faculties—finds sources of inexhaustible interest in all that surrounds it: in the objects of nature, the achievements of art, the imaginations of poetry, the incidents of history, the ways of mankind, past and present, and their prospects in the future. It is possible, indeed, to become indifferent to all this, and that too without having exhausted a thousandth part of it, but only when one has had from the beginning no moral or human interest in these things, and has sought in them only the gratification of curiosity.

Now there is absolutely no reason in the nature of things why an amount of mental culture sufficient to give an intelligent interest in these objects of contemplation should not be the inheritance of 'every one born in a civilized country. As little is there an inherent necessity that any human being should be a selfish egotist, devoid of every feeling or care but those which center in his own miserable individuality. Something far superior to this is sufficiently common even now, to give ample earnest of what the human species may be made. Genuine private affections and a sincere interest in the public good are possible, though in unequal degrees, to every rightly brought up human being. In a world in which there is so much to interest, so much to enjoy, and so much also to correct and improve, every one who has this moderate amount of moral and intellectual requisites is capable of an existence which may be called enviable; and unless such a person, through bad laws or subjection to the will of others, is denied the liberty to use the sources of happiness within his reach, he will not fail to find this enviable existence, if he escape the positive evils of life, the great sources of physical and mental suffering—such as indigence, disease, and the unkindness, worthlessness, or premature loss of objects of affection. The main stress of the problem lies, therefore, in the contest with these calamities from which it is a rare good fortune entirely to escape; which, as things now are, cannot be obviated, and often cannot be in any material degree mitigated. Yet no one whose opinion deserves a moment's consideration can doubt that most of the great positive evils of the world are in themselves removable, and will, if human affairs continue to improve, be in the end reduced within narrow limits. Poverty, in any sense implying suffering, may be completely extinguished by the wisdom of society combined with the good sense and providence of individuals. Even that most intractable of enemies, disease, may be indefinitely reduced in dimensions by good physical and moral education and proper control of noxious influences, while the progress of science holds out a promise for the future of still more direct conquests over this detestable foe. And every advance in that direction relieves us from some, not only of the chances which cut short our own lives, but, what concerns us still more, which deprive us of those in whom our happiness is wrapt up. As for vicissitudes of fortune and other disappointments connected with worldly circumstances, these are principally the effect either of gross imprudence, of ill-regulated desires, or of bad or imperfect social institutions. All the grand sources, in short, of human suffering are in a great degree, many of them almost entirely, conquerable by human care and effort; and though their removal is grievously slow—though a long succession of generations will perish in the breach before the conquest is completed, and this world becomes all that, if will and knowledge were not wanting, it might easily be made—yet every mind sufficiently intelligent and generous to bear a part, however small and inconspicuous, in the endeavour will draw a noble enjoyment from the contest itself, which he would not for any bribe in the form of selfish indulgence consent to be without.

And this leads to the true estimation of what is said by the objectors concerning the possibility and the obligation of learning to do without happiness. Unquestionably it is possible to do without happiness; it is done involuntarily by nineteen-twentieths of mankind, even in those parts of our present world which are least deep in barbarism; and it often has to be done voluntarily by the hero or the martyr, for the sake of something which he prizes more than his individual happiness. But this something, what is it, unless the happiness of others or some of the requisites of happiness? It is noble to be capable of resigning entirely one's own portion of happiness, or chances of it; but, after all, this self-sacrifice must be

for some end; it is not its own end; and if we are told that its end is not happiness but virtue, which is better than happiness, I ask, would the sacrifice be made if the hero or martyr did not believe that it would earn for others immunity from similar sacrifices? Would it be made if he thought that his renunciation of happiness for himself would produce no fruit for any of his fellow creatures, but to make their lot like his, and place them also in the condition of persons who have renounced happiness? All honor to those who can abnegate for themselves the personal enjoyment of life when by such renunciation they contribute worthily to increase the amount of happiness in the world; but he who does it or professes to do it for any other purpose is no more deserving of admiration than the ascetic mounted on his pillar. He may be an inspiriting proof of what men *can* do, but assuredly not an example of what they *should*.

Though it is only in a very imperfect state of the world's arrangements that any one can best serve the happiness of others by the absolute sacrifice of his own, yet, so long as the world is in that imperfect state, I fully acknowledge that the readiness to make such a sacrifice is the highest virtue which can be found in man. I will add that in this condition of the world, paradoxical as the assertion may be, the conscious ability to do without happiness gives the best prospect of realizing such happiness as is attainable. For nothing except that consciousness can raise a person above the chances of life, by making him feel that, let fate and fortune do their worst, they have not power to subdue him; which, once felt, frees him from excess of anxiety concerning the evils of life, and enables him, like many a Stoic in the worst times of the Roman Empire, to cultivate in tranquility the sources of satisfaction accessible to him, without concerning himself about the uncertainty of their duration any more than about their inevitable end.

Meanwhile, let utilitarians never cease to claim the morality of self-devotion as a possession which belongs by as good a right to them as either to the Stoic or to the Transcendentalist. The utilitarian morality does recognize in human beings the power of sacrificing their own greatest good for the good of others. It only refuses to admit that the sacrifice is itself a good. A sacrifice which does not increase or tend to increase the sum total of happiness, it considers as wasted. The only self-renunciation which it applauds is devotion to the happiness, or to some of the means of happiness, of others, either of mankind collectively or of individuals within the limits imposed by the collective interests of mankind.

I must again repeat what the assailants of utilitarianism seldom have the justice to acknowledge, that the happiness which forms the utilitarian standard of what is right in conduct is not the agent's own happiness but that of all concerned. As between his own happiness and that of others, utilitarianism requires him to be as strictly impartial as a disinterested and benevolent spectator. In the golden rule of Jesus of Nazareth, we read the complete spirit of the ethics of utility. "To do as you would be done by," and "to love your neighbor as yourself," constitute the ideal perfection of utilitarian morality. As the means of making the nearest approach to this ideal, utility would enjoin, first, that laws and social arrangements should place the happiness or (as, speaking practically, it may be called) the interest of every individual as nearly as possible in harmony with the interest of the whole; and, secondly, that education and opinion, which have so vast a power over human character, should so use that power as to establish in the mind of every individual an indissoluble association between his own happiness and the good of the whole, especially between his own happiness and the practice of such modes of conduct, negative and positive, as regard for the universal happiness prescribes; so that not only he may be able to conceive the possibility of happiness to himself, consistently with conduct opposed to the general good, but also that a direct impulse to promote the general good may be in every individual one of the habitual motives of action, and the sentiments connected therewith may fill a large and prominent place in every human being's sentient existence. If the impugners of the utilitarian morality represented it to their own minds in this its true character, I know not what recommendation possessed by any other morality they could possibly affirm to be wanting to it; what more beautiful or more exalted developments of human nature any other ethical system can be supposed to foster, or what springs of action, not accessible to the utilitarian, such systems rely on for giving effect to their mandates.

The objectors to utilitarianism cannot always be charged with representing it in a discreditable light. On the contrary, those among them who entertain anything like a just idea of its disinterested character sometimes find fault with its standard as being too high for humanity. They say it is exacting too much to require that people shall always act from the inducement of promoting the general interests of society. But this is to mistake the very meaning of a standard of morals, and confound the rule of action with the motive of it. It is the business of ethics to tell us what are our duties, or by what test we may know them; but no system of ethics requires that the sole motive of all we do shall be a feeling of duty; on the contrary, ninety-nine hundredths of all our actions are done from other motives, and rightly so done if the rule of duty does not condemn them. It is the more unjust to utilitarianism that this particular misapprehension should be made a ground of objection to it, inasmuch as utilitarian moralists have gone beyond almost all others in affirming that the motive has nothing to do with the morality of the action, though much with the worth of the agent. He who saves a fellow creature from drowning does what is morally right, whether his motive be duty or the hope of being paid for his trouble; he who betrays the friend that trusts him is guilty of a crime, even if his object be to serve another friend to whom he is under greater obligations. But to speak only of actions done from the motive of duty, and in direct obedience to principle: it is a misapprehension of the utilitarian mode of thought to conceive it as implying that people should fix their minds upon so wide a generality as the world, or society at large. The great majority of good actions are intended not for the benefit of the world, but for that of individuals, of which the good of the world is made up; and the thoughts of the most virtuous man need not on these occasions travel beyond the particular persons concerned, except so far as is necessary to assure himself that in benefiting them he is not violating the rights, that is, the legitimate and authorized expectations, of any one else. The multiplication of happiness is, according to the utilitarian ethics, the object of virtue: the occasions on which any person (except one in a thousand) has it in his power to do this on an extended scale, in other words, to be a public benefactor, are but exceptional; and on these occasions alone is he called on to consider public utility; in every other case, private utility, the interest or happiness of some few persons, is all he has to attend to.

Those alone the influence of whose actions extends to society in general need concern themselves habitually about so large an object. In the case of abstinences indeed—of things which people forbear to do from moral considerations, though the consequences in the particular case might be beneficial—it would be unworthy of an intelligent agent not to be consciously aware that the action is of a class which, if practiced generally, would be generally injurious, and that this is the ground of the obligation to abstain from it. The amount of regard for the public interest implied in this recognition is no greater than is demanded by every system of morals, for they all enjoin to abstain from whatever is manifestly pernicious to society.

The same considerations dispose of another reproach against the doctrine of utility, founded on a still grosser misconception of the purpose of a standard of morality, and of the very meaning of the words "right" and "wrong." It is often affirmed that utilitarianism renders men cold and unsympathizing; that it chills their moral feelings towards individuals; that it makes them regard only the dry and hard consideration of the consequences of actions, not taking into their moral estimate the qualities from which those actions emanate. If the assertion means that they do not allow their judgment respecting the rightness or wrongness of an action to be influenced by their opinion of the qualities of the person who does it, this is a complaint not against utilitarianism, but against any standard of morality at all; for certainly no known ethical standard decides an action to be good or bad because it is done by a good or a bad man, still less because done by an amiable, a brave, or a benevolent man, or the contrary. These considerations are relevant, not to the estimation of actions, but of persons; and there is nothing in the utilitarian theory inconsistent with the fact that there are other things which interest us in persons besides the rightness and wrongness of their actions. The Stoics, indeed, with the paradoxical misuse of language which was part of their system, and by which they strove to raise themselves above all concern about anything but virtue, were fond of saying that he who has that has everything; that he, and only he, is rich, is beautiful, is a king. But no claim of this description is made for the virtuous man by the utilitarian doctrine. Utilitarians are quite aware that there are other desirable possessions and qualities besides virtue, and are perfectly willing to allow to all of them their full worth. They are also aware that a right action does not necessarily indicate a virtuous character, and that actions which are blamable often proceed from qualities entitled to praise. When this is apparent in any particular case, it modifies their estimation, not certainly of the act, but of the agent. I grant that they are, notwithstanding, of opinion that in the long run the best proof of a good character is good actions; and resolutely refuse to consider any mental disposition as good of which the predominant tendency is to produce bad conduct. This makes them unpopular with many people; but it is an unpopularity which they must share with every one who regards the distinction between right and wrong in a serious light; and the reproach is not one which a conscientious utilitarian need be anxious to repel.

If no more be meant by the objection than that many utilitarians look on the morality of actions, as measured by the utilitarian standards, with too exclusive a regard, and do not lay sufficient stress upon the other beauties of character which go towards making a human being lovable or admirable, this may be admitted. Utilitarians who have cultivated their moral feelings, but not their sympathies, nor their artistic perceptions, do fall into this mistake; and so do all other moralists under the same conditions. What can be said in excuse for other moralists is equally available for them, namely, that, if there is to be any error, it is better that it should be on that side. As a matter of fact, we may affirm that among utilitarians, as among adherents of other systems, there is every imaginable degree of rigidity and of laxity in the application of their standard; some are even puritanically rigorous, while others are as indulgent as can possibly be desired by sinner or by sentimentalist. But on the whole, a doctrine which brings prominently forward the interest that mankind have in the repression and prevention of conduct which violates the moral law, is likely to be inferior to no other in turning the sanctions of opinion against such violations. It is true, the question, "What does violate the moral law?" is one on which those who recognize different standards of morality are likely now and then to differ. But difference of opinion on moral questions was not first introduced into the world by utilitarianism, while that doctrine does supply, if not always an easy, at all events a tangible and intelligible, mode of deciding such differences.

It may not be superfluous to notice a few more of the common misapprehensions of utilitarian ethics, even those which are so obvious and gross that it might appear impossible for any person of candor and intelligence to fall into them; since persons, even of considerable mental endowment, often give themselves so little trouble to understand the bearings of any opinion against which they entertain a prejudice, and men are in general so little conscious of this voluntary ignorance as a defect, that the vulgarest misunderstandings of ethical doctrines are continually met with in the deliberate writings of persons of the greatest pretensions both to high principle and to philosophy. We not uncommonly hear the doctrine of utility inveighed against as a godless doctrine. If it be necessary to say anything at all against so mere an assumption, we may say that the question depends upon what idea we have formed of the moral character of the Deity. If it be a true belief that God desires, above all things, the happiness of his creatures, and that this 'was his purpose in their creation, utility is not only not a godless doctrine, but more profoundly religious than any other. If it be meant that utilitarianism does not recognize the revealed will of God as the supreme law of morals, I answer that a utilitarian who believes in the perfect goodness and wisdom of God necessarily believes that whatever God has thought fit to reveal on the subject of morals must fulfil the requirements of utility in a supreme degree. But others besides utilitarians have been of opinion that the Christian revelation was intended, and is fitted, to inform the hearts and minds of mankind with a spirit which should enable them to find for themselves what is right, and incline them to do it when found, rather than to tell them, except in a very general way, what it is; and that we need a doctrine of ethics, carefully followed out, to *interpret* to us the will of God. Whether this opinion is correct or not, it is superfluous here to discuss; since whatever aid religion, either natural or revealed, can afford to ethical investigation, is as open to the utilitarian moralist as to any other. He can use it as the testimony of God to the usefulness or hurtfulness of any given course of action, by as good a right as others can use it for the inculcation of a transcendental law, having no connection with usefulness or with happiness.

Again, utility is often summarily stigmatized as an immoral doctrine by giving it the name of "expediency," and taking advantage of the popular use of that term to contrast it with principle. But the expedient, in the sense in which it is opposed to the right, generally means that which is expedient for the particular interest of the agent himself; as when a minister sacrifices the interests of his country to keep himself in place. When it means anything better than this, it means that which is expedient for some immediate object, some temporary purpose, but which violates a rule whose observance is expedient in a much higher degree. The expedient, in this sense, instead of being the same thing with the useful, is a branch of the hurtful. Thus it would often be expedient, for the purpose of getting over some momentary embarrassment, or attaining some object immediately useful to ourselves or others, to tell a lie. But inasmuch as the cultivation in ourselves of a sensitive feeling on the subject of veracity is one of the most useful, and the enfeeblement of that feeling one of the most hurtful, things to which our conduct can be instrumental; and inasmuch as any, even unintentional, deviation from truth does that much towards weakening the trustworthiness of human assertion, which is not only the principal support of all present social well-being but the insufficiency of which does more than any one thing that can be named to keep back civilization, virtue, everything on which human happiness on the largest scale depends—we feel that the violation, for a present advantage, of a rule of such transcendent expediency is not expedient, and that he who, for the sake of convenience to himself or to some other individual, does what depends on him to deprive mankind of the good, and inflict upon them the evil, involved in the greater or less reliance which they can place in each other's word, acts the part of one of their worst enemies. Yet that even this rule, sacred as it is, admits of possible exceptions is acknowledged by all moralists; the chief of which is when the withholding of some fact (as of information from a malefactor, or of bad news from a person dangerously ill) would save an individual (especially an individual other than oneself) from great and unmerited evil, and when the withholding can only be effected by denial. But in order that the exception may not extend itself beyond the need, and may have the least possible effect in weakening reliance on veracity, it ought to be recognized and, if possible, its limits defined; and, if the principle of utility is good for anything, it must be good for weighing these conflicting utilities against one another, and marking out the region within which one or the other preponderates.

Again, defenders of utility often find themselves called upon to reply to such objections as this—that there is not time, previous to action, for calculating and weighing the effects of any line of conduct on the general happiness. This is exactly as if any one were to say that it is impossible to guide our conduct by Christianity because there is not time, on every occasion on which anything has to be done, to read through the Old and New Testaments. The answer to the objection is that there has been ample time, namely, the whole past duration of the human species. During all that time, mankind have been learning by experience the tendencies of actions; on which experience all the prudence, as well as all the morality, of life are dependent. People talk as if the commencement of this course of experience had hitherto been put off, and as if, at the moment when some man feels tempted to meddle with the property or life of another, he had to begin considering for the first time whether murder and theft are injurious to human happiness. Even then I do not think that he would find the question very puzzling; but, at all events, the matter is now done to his hand. It is truly a whimsical supposition that, if mankind were agreed in considering utility to be the test of morality, they would remain without any agreement as to what *is* useful, and would take no measures for having their notions on the subject taught to the young, and enforced by law and opinion. There is no difficulty in proving any ethical standard whatever to work ill if we suppose universal idiocy to be conjoined with it; but on any hypothesis short of that, mankind must by this time have acquired positive beliefs as to the effects of some actions on their happiness; and the beliefs which have thus come down are the rules of morality for the multitude, and for the philosopher until he has succeeded in finding better. That philosophers might easily do this, even now, on many subjects; that the received code of ethics is by no means of divine right; and that mankind have still much to learn as to the effects of actions on the general happiness, I admit or rather earnestly maintain. The corollaries from the principle of utility, like the precepts of every practical art, admit of indefinite improvement, and, in a progressive state of the human mind, their improvement is perpetually going on. But to consider the rules of morality as improvable is one thing; to pass over the intermediate generalization entirely and endeavor to test each individual action directly by the first principle is another. It is a strange notion that the acknowledgment of a first principle is inconsistent with the admission of secondary ones. To inform a traveller respecting the place of his ultimate destination is not to forbid the use of landmarks and direction-posts on the way. The proposition that happiness is the end and aim of morality does not mean that no road ought to be laid down to that goal, or that persons going thither should not be advised to take one direction rather than another. Men really ought to leave off talking a kind of nonsense on this subject, which they would neither talk nor listen to on other matters of practical concernment. Nobody argues that the art of navigation is not founded on astronomy because sailors cannot wait to calculate the Nautical Almanac. Being rational creatures, they go to sea with it ready calculated; and all rational creatures go out upon the sea of life with their minds made up on the common questions of right and wrong, as well as on many of the far more difficult questions of wise and foolish. And this, as long as foresight is a human quality, it is to be presumed they will continue to do. Whatever we adopt as the fundamental principle of morality, we require subordinate principles to apply it by; the impossibility of doing without them, being common to all systems, can afford no argument against any one in particular; but gravely to argue as if no such secondary principles could be had, and as if mankind had remained till now, and always must remain, without drawing any general conclusions from the experience of human life, is as high a pitch, I think, as absurdity has ever reached in philosophical controversy.

The remainder of the stock arguments against utilitarianism mostly consist in laying to its charge the common infirmities of human nature, and the general difficulties which embarrass conscientious persons in shaping their course through life. We are told that a utilitarian will be apt to make his own particular case an exception to moral rules, and, when under temptation, will see a utility in the breach of a rule, greater than he will see in its observance. But is utility the only creed which is able to furnish us with excuses for evil doing, and means of cheating our own conscience? They are afforded in abundance by all doctrines which recognize as a fact in morals the existence of conflicting considerations, which all doctrines do that have been believed by sane persons. It is not the fault of any creed, but of the complicated nature of human affairs, that rules of conduct cannot be so framed as to require no exceptions, and that hardly any kind of action can safely be laid down as either always obligatory or always condemnable. There is no ethical creed which does not temper the rigidity of its laws by giving a certain latitude, under the moral responsibility of the agent, for accommodation to peculiarities of circumstances; and under every creed, at the opening thus made, self-deception and dishonest casuistry get in. There exists no moral system under which there do not arise unequivocal cases of conflicting obligation. These are the real difficulties, the knotty points both in the theory of ethics and in the conscientious guidance of personal conduct. They are overcome practically, with greater or with less success, according to the intellect and virtue of the individual; but it can hardly be pretended than anyone will be the less qualified for dealing with them, from possessing an ultimate standard to which conflicting rights and duties can be referred. If utility is the ultimate source of moral obligations, utility may be invoked to decide between them when their demands are incompatible. Though the application of the standard may be difficult, it is better than none at all; while in other systems the moral laws all claiming independent authority, there is no common umpire entitled to interfere between them; their claims to precedence one over another rest on little better than sophistry, and, unless determined, as they generally are, by the unacknowledged influence of consideration of utility, afford a free scope for the action of personal desires and partialities. We must remember that only in these cases of conflict between secondary principles is it requisite that first principles should be appealed to. There is no case of moral obligation in which some secondary principle is not involved; and if only one, there can seldom be any real doubt which one it is, in the mind of any person by whom the principle itself is recognized.

Chapter III Of the Ultimate Sanction of the Principle of Utility

The question is often asked, and properly so, in regard to any supposed moral standard—What is its sanction? what are the motives to obey? or more specifically, what is the source of its obligation? whence does it derive its binding force? It is a necessary part of moral philosophy to provide the answer to this question, which, though frequently assuming the shape of an objection to the utilitarian morality, as if it had some special applicability to that above others, really arises in regard to all standards. It arises, in fact, whenever a person is called on to *adopt* a standard, or refer morality to any basis on which he has not been accustomed to rest it. For the customary morality, that which education and opinion have consecrated is the only one which presents itself to the mind with the feeling of being *in itself* obligatory; and when a person is asked to believe that this morality *derives* its obligation from some general principle round which custom has not thrown the same halo, the assertion is to him a paradox; the supposed corollaries seem to have a more binding force than the original theorem; the superstructure seems to stand better without than with what is represented as its foundation. He says to himself, I feel that I am bound not to rob or murder, betray or deceive; but why am I bound to promote the general happiness? If my own happiness lies in something else, why may I not give that the preference?

If the view adopted by the utilitarian philosophy of the nature of the moral sense be correct, this difficulty will always present itself until the influences which form moral character have taken the same hold of the principle which they have taken of some of the consequences—until, by the improvement of education, the feeling of unity with our fellow creatures shall be (what it cannot be denied that Christ intended it to be) as deeply rooted in our character, and to our own consciousness as completely a part of our nature, as the horror of crime is in an ordinarily well brought up young person. In the meantime, however, the difficulty has no peculiar application to the doctrine of utility, but is inherent in every attempt to analyze morality and reduce it to principles; which, unless the principle is already in men's minds invested with as much sacredness as any of its applications, always seems to divest them of a part of their sanctity.

The principle of utility either has, or there is no reason why it might not have, all the sanctions which belong to any other system of morals. Those sanctions are either external or internal. Of the external sanctions it is not necessary to speak at any length. They are the hope of favor and the fear of displeasure from our fellow creatures or from the Ruler of the universe, along with whatever we may have of sympathy or affection for them, or of love and awe of Him, inclining us to do His will independently of selfish consequences. There is evidently no reason why all these motives for observance should not attach themselves to the utilitarian morality as completely and as powerfully as to any other. Indeed, those of them which refer to our fellow creatures are sure to do so, in proportion to the amount of general intelligence; for whether there be any other ground of moral obligation than the general happiness or not, men do desire happiness; and however imperfect may be their own practice, they desire and commend all conduct in others towards themselves by which they think their happiness is promoted. With regard to the religious motive, if men believe, as most profess to do, in the goodness of God, those who think that conduciveness to the general happiness is the essence or even only the criterion of good must necessarily believe that it is also that which God approves. The whole force therefore of external reward and punishment, whether physical or moral, and whether proceeding from God or from our fellow men, together with all that the capacities of human nature admit of disinterested devotion to either, become available to enforce the utilitarian morality, in proportion as that morality is recognized; and the more powerfully, the more the appliances of education and general cultivation are bent to the purpose.

So far as to external sanctions. The internal sanction of duty, whatever our standard of duty may be, is one and the same—a feeling in our own mind; a pain, more or less intense, attendant on violation of duty, which in properly cultivated moral natures rises, in the more serious cases, into shrinking from it as an impossibility. This feeling, when disinterested and connecting itself with the pure idea of duty, and not with some particular form of it, or with

any of the merely accessory circumstances, is the essence of conscience; though in that complex phenomenon as it actually exists, the simple fact is in general all encrusted over with collateral associations derived from sympathy, from love, and still more from fear; from all the forms of religious feeling; from the recollections of childhood and of all our past life; from self-esteem, desire of the esteem of others, and occasionally even self-abasement. This extreme complication is, I apprehend, the origin of the sort of mystical character which, by a tendency of the human mind of which there are many other examples, is apt to be attributed to the idea of moral obligation, and which leads people to believe that the idea cannot possibly attach itself to any other objects than those which, by a supposed mysterious law, are found in our present experience to excite it. Its binding force, however, consists in the existence of a mass of feeling which must be broken through in order to do what violates our standard of right, and which, if we do nevertheless violate that standard, will probably have to be encountered afterwards in the form of remorse. Whatever theory we have of the nature or origin of conscience, this is what essentially constitutes it.

The ultimate sanction, therefore, of all morality (external motives apart) being a subjective feeling in our own minds, I see nothing embarrassing to those whose standard is utility in the question, What is the sanction of that particular standard? We may answer, the same as of all other moral standards—the conscientious feelings of mankind. Undoubtedly this sanction has no binding efficacy on those who do not possess the feelings it appeals to; but neither will these persons be more obedient to any other moral principle than to the utilitarian one. On them morality of any kind has no hold but through the external sanctions. Meanwhile the feelings exist, a fact in human nature, the reality of which, and the great power with which they are capable of acting on those in whom they have been duly cultivated, are proved by experience. No reason has ever been shown why they may not be cultivated to as great intensity in connection with the utilitarian, as with any other rule of morals.

There is, I am aware, a disposition to believe that a person who sees in moral obligation a transcendental fact, an objective reality belonging to the province of "things in themselves," is likely to be more obedient to it than one who believes it to be entirely subjective, having its seat in human consciousness only. But whatever a person's opinion may be on this point of ontology, the force he is really urged by is his own subjective feeling, and is exactly measured by its strength. No one's belief that duty is an objective reality is stronger than the belief that God is so; yet the belief in God, apart from the expectation of actual reward and punishment, only operates on conduct through, and in proportion to, the subjective religious feeling. The sanction, so far as it is disinterested, is always in the mind itself; and the notion, therefore, of the transcendental moralists must be that this sanction will not exist in the mind unless it is believed to have its root out of the mind; and that if a person is able to say to himself, "This which is restraining me and which is called my conscience is only a feeling in my own mind," he may possibly draw the conclusion that when the feeling ceases the obligation ceases, and that if he find the feeling inconvenient, he may disregard it and endeavor to get rid of it. But is this danger confined to the utilitarian morality? Does the belief that moral obligation has its seat outside the mind make the feeling of it too strong to be got rid of? The fact is so far otherwise that all moralists admit and lament the ease with which, in the generality of minds, conscience can be silenced or stifled. The question, "Need I obey my conscience?" is quite as often put to themselves by persons who never heard of the principle of utility, as by its adherents. Those whose conscientious feelings are so weak as to allow of their asking this question, if they answer it affirmatively, will not do so because they believe in the transcendental theory, but because of the external sanctions.

It is not necessary, for the present purpose, to decide whether the feeling of duty is innate or implanted. Assuming it to be innate, it is an open question to what objects it naturally attaches itself; for the philosophic supporters of that theory are now agreed that the intuitive perception is of principles of morality and not of the details. If there be anything innate in the matter, I see no reason why the feeling which is innate shoud not be that of regard to the pleasures and pains of others. If there is any principle of morals which is intuitively obligatory, I should say it must be that. If so, the intuitive ethics would coincide with the utilitarian, and there would be no further quarrel between them. Even as it is, the intu-

itive moralists, though they believe that there are other intuitive moral obligations, do already believe this to be one; for they unanimously hold that a large *portion* of morality turns upon the consideration due to the interests of our fellow creatures. Therefore, if the belief in the transcendental origin of moral obligation gives any additional efficacy to the internal sanction, it appears to me that the utilitarian principle has already the benefit of it.

On the other hand, if, as is my own belief, the moral feelings are not innate but acquired, they are not for that reason the less natural. It is natural to man to speak, to reason, to build cities, to cultivate the ground, though these are acquired faculties. The moral feelings are not indeed a part of our nature, in the sense of being in any perceptible degree present in all of us; but this, unhappily, is a fact admitted by those who believe the most strenuously in their transcendental origin. Like the other acquired capacities above referred to, the moral faculty, if not a part of our nature, is a natural outgrowth from it; capable, like them, in a certain, small degree, of springing up spontaneously; and susceptible of being brought by cultivation to a high degree of development. Unhappily it is also susceptible, by a sufficient use of the external sanctions and of the force of early impressions, of being cultivated in almost any direction, so that there is hardly anything so absurd or so mischievous that it may not, by means of these influences, be made to act on the human mind with all the authority of conscience. To doubt that the same potency might be given by the same means to the principle of utility, even if it had no foundation in human nature, would be flying in the face of all experience.

But moral associations which are wholly of artificial creation, when intellectual culture goes on, yield by degrees to the dissolving force of analysis; and if the feeling of duty when associated with utility, would appear equally arbitrary; if there were no leading department of our nature, no powerful class of sentiments, with which that association would harmonize, which would make us feel it congenial and incline us not only to foster it in others (for which we have abundant interested motives), but also to cherish it in ourselves — if there were not, in short, a natural basis of sentiment for utilitarian morality, it might well happen that this association also, even after it had been implanted by education, might be analyzed away.

But there *is* this basis of powerful natural sentiment; and this it is which, when once the general happiness is recognized as the ethical standard, will constitute the strength of the utilitarian morality. This firm foundation is that of the social feelings of mankind; the desire to be in unity with our fellow creatures, which is already a powerful principle in human nature, and happily one of those which tend to become stronger, even without express inculcation, from the influences of advancing civilization. The social state is at once so natural, so necessary, and so habitual to man, that, except in some unusual circumstances or by an effort of voluntary abstraction, he never conceives himself otherwise than as a member of a body; and this association is riveted more and more, as mankind are further removed from the state of savage independence. Any condition, therefore, which is essential to a state of society, becomes more and more an inseparable part of every person's conception of the state of things which he is born into, and which is the destiny of a human being. Now society between human beings, except in the relation of master and slave, is manifestly impossible on any other footing than that the interests of all are to be consulted. Society between equals can only exist on the understanding that the interests of all are to be regarded equally. And since in all states of civilization, every person, except an absolute monarch, has equals, everyone is obliged to live on these terms with somebody; and in every age some advance is made towards a state in which it will be impossible to live permanently on other terms with anybody. In this way people grow up unable to conceive as possible to them a state of total disregard of other people's interests. They are under a necessity of conceiving themselves as at least abstaining from all the grosser injuries, and (if only for their own protection) living in a state of constant protest against them. They are also familiar with the fact of co-operating with others, and proposing to themselves a collective, not an individual, interest as the aim (at least for the time being) of their actions. So long as they are co-operating, their ends are identified with those of others; there is at least a temporary feeling that the interests of others are their own interests. Not only does all strengthening of social ties, and all healthy growth of society, give to each individual a stronger personal interest in practically consulting the welfare of others, it also leads him to identify his *feelings*

more and more with their good, or at least with an even greater degree of practical consideration for it. He comes, as though instinctively, to be conscious of himself as a being who *of course* pays regard to others. The good of others becomes to him a thing naturally and necessarily to be attended to, like any of the physical conditions of our existence. Now, whatever amount of this feeling a person has, he is urged by the strongest motive both of interest and of sympathy to demonstrate it, and to the utmost of his power encourage it in others; and even if he has none of it himself, he is as greatly interested as any one else that others should have it. Consequently the smallest germs of the feeling are laid hold of and nourished by the contagion of sympathy and the influences of education; and a complete web of corroborative association is woven round it, by the powerful agency of the external sanctions. This mode of conceiving ourselves and human life, as civilization goes on, is felt to be more and more natural. Every step in political improvement renders it more so, by removing the sources of opposition of interest and levelling those inequalities of legal privilege between individuals or classes, owing to which there are large portions of mankind whose happiness it is still practicable to disregard. In an improving state of the human mind, the influences are constantly on the increase which tend to generate in each individual a feeling of unity with all the rest; which, if perfect, would make him never think of, or desire, any beneficial condition for himself, in the benefits of which they are not included. If we now suppose this feeling of unity to be taught as a religion, and the whole force of education, of institutions, and of opinion, directed, as it once was in the case of religion, to make every person grow up from infancy surrounded on all sides both by the profession and the practice of it, I think that no one who can realize this conception will feel any misgiving about the sufficiency of the ultimate sanction for the happiness morality. To any ethical student who finds the realization difficult, I recommend, as a means of facilitating it, the second of M. Comte's two principal works, the *Traité de politique positive*. I entertain the strongest objections to the system of politics and morals set forth in that treatise; but I think it has superabundantly shown the possibility of giving to the service of humanity, even without the aid of belief in a Providence, both the psychological power and the social efficacy of a religion, making it take hold of human life, and color all thought, feeling, and action, in a manner of which the greatest ascendancy ever exercised by any religion may be but a type and foretaste; and of which the danger is, not that it should be insufficient, but that it should be so excessive as to interfere unduly with human freedom and individuality.

Neither is it necessary to the feeling which constitutes the binding force of the utilitarian morality on those who recognize it, to wait for those social influences which would make its obligation felt by mankind at large. In the comparatively early state of human advancement in which we now live, a person cannot, indeed, feel that entireness of sympathy with all others, which would make any real discordance in the general direction of their conduct in life impossible, but already a person in whom the social feeling is at all developed cannot bring himself to think of the rest of his fellow creatures as struggling rivals with him for the means of happiness, whom he must desire to see defeated in their object in order that he may succeed in his. The deeply rooted conception which every individual even now has of himself as a social being tends to make him feel it one of his natural wants that there should be harmony between his feelings and aims and those of his fellow creatures. If differences of opinion and of mental culture make it impossible for him to share many of their actual feelings—perhaps make him denounce and defy those feelings—he still needs to be conscious that his real aim and theirs do not conflict; that he is not opposing himself to what they really wish for, namely, their own good, but is, on the contrary, promoting it. This feeling in most individuals is much inferior in strength to their selfish feelings, and is often wanting altogether. But to those who have it, it possesses all the characters of a natural feeling. It does not present itself to their minds as a superstition of education, or a law despotically imposed by the power of society, but as an attribute which it would not be well for them to be without. This conviction is the ultimate sanction of the greatest happiness morality. This it is which makes any mind of well-developed feelings work with, and not against, the outward motives to care for others, afforded by what I have called the external sanctions; and, when those sanctions are wanting, or act in an opposite direction, constitutes in itself a powerful internal binding force, in proportion to the sensitiveness and thoughtfulness of the character; since few but those whose mind is a moral blank could bear to lay out their course of life on the plan of paying no regard to others except so far as their own private interest compels.

Chapter IV Of What Sort of Proof the Principle of Utility is Susceptible

It has already been remarked that questions of ultimate ends do not admit of proof, in the ordinary acceptation of the term. To be incapable of proof by reasoning is common to all first principles, to the first premises of our knowledge, as well as to those of our conduct. But the former, being matters of fact, may be the subject of a direct appeal to the faculties which judge of fact—namely, our senses and our internal consciousness. Can an appeal be made to the same faculties on questions of practical ends? Or by what other faculty is cognizance taken of them?

Questions about ends are, in other words, questions what things are desirable. The utilitarian doctrine is that happiness is desirable, and the only thing desirable, as an end; all other things being only desirable as means to that end. What ought to be required of this doctrine, what conditions is it requisite that the doctrine should fulfill—to make good its claim to be believed?

The only proof capable of being given that an object is visible is that people actually see it. The only proof that a sound is audible is that people hear it; and so of the other sources of our experience. In like manner, I apprehend, the sole evidence it is possible to produce that anything is desirable is that people do actually desire it. If the end which the utilitarian doctrine proposes to itself were not, in theory and in practice, acknowledged to be an end, nothing could ever convince any person that it was so. No reason can be given why the general happiness is desirable, except that each person, so far as he believes it to be attainable, desires his own happiness. This, however, being a fact, we have not only all the proof which the case admits of, but all which it is possible to require, that happiness is a good; that each person's happiness is a good to that person, and the general happiness, therefore, a good to the aggregate of all persons. Happiness has made out its title as *one* of the ends of conduct, and consequently one of the criteria of morality.

But it has not by this alone, proved itself to be the sole criterion. To do that, it would seem, by the same rule, necessary to show, not only that people desire happiness, but that they never desire anything else. Now it is palpable that they do desire things which, in common language, are decidedly distinguished from happiness. They desire, for example, virtue and the absence of vice, no less really than pleasure and the absence of pain. The desire of virtue is not as universal, but it is as authentic a fact as the desire of happiness. And hence the opponents of the utilitarian standard deem that they have a right to infer that there are other ends of human action besides happiness, and that happiness is not the standard of approbation and disapprobation.

But does the utilitarian doctrine deny that people desire virtue, or maintain that virtue is not a thing to be desired? The very reverse. It maintains not only that virtue is to be desired, but that it is to be desired disinterestedly, for itself. Whatever may be the opinion of utilitarian moralists as to the original conditions by which virtue is made virtue, however they may believe (as they do) that actions and dispositions are only virtuous because they promote another end than virtue, yet this being granted, and it having been decided, from considerations of this description, what is virtuous, they not only place virtue at the very head of the things which are good as means to the ultimate end, but they also recognize as a psychological fact the possibility of its being, to the individual, a good in itself, without looking to any end beyond it; and hold that the mind is not in a right state, not in a state conformable to utility, not in the state most conducive to the general happiness, unless it does love virtue in this manner—as a thing desirable in itself, even although, in the individual instance, it should not produce those other desirable consequences which it tends to produce, and on account of which it is held to be virtue. This opinion is not, in the smallest degree, a departure from the happiness principle. The ingredients of happiness are very various, and each of them is desirable in itself, and not merely when considered as swelling an aggregate. The principle of utility does not mean that any given pleasure, as music, for instance, or any given exemption from pain, as for example health, is to be looked upon as means to a collective something termed happiness, and to be desired on that account. They are desired and desirable in and for themselves; besides being means, they are a part of the end. Virtue, according to the utilitarian doctrine, is not naturally and originally part of the end, but it is capable of becoming so; and in those who love it disinterestedly it has become so, and is desired and cherished, not as a means to happiness, but as a part of their happiness.

To illustrate this further, we may remember that virtue is not the only thing originally a means, and which if it were not a means to anything else would be and remain indifferent, but which by association with what it is a means to comes to be desired for itself, and that too with the utmost intensity. What, for example, shall we say of the love of money? There is nothing originally more desirable about money than about any heap of glittering pebbles. Its worth is solely that of the things which it will buy; the desires for other things than itself, which it is a means of gratifying. Yet the love of money is not only one of the strongest moving forces of human life, but money is, in many cases, desired in and for itself; the desire to possess it is often stronger than the desire to use it, and goes on increasing when all the desires which point to ends beyond it, to be compassed by it, are falling off. It may, then, be said truly that money is desired not for the sake of an end, but as part of the end. From being a means to happiness, it has come to be itself a principal ingredient of the individual's conception of happiness. The same may be said of the majority of the great objects of human life: power, for example, or fame, except that to each of these there is a certain amount of immediate pleasure annexed, which has at least the semblance of being naturally inherent in them—a thing which cannot be said of money. Still, however, the strongest natural attraction, both of power and of fame, is the immense aid they give to the attainment of our other wishes; and it is the strong association thus generated between them and all our objects of desire which gives to the direct desire of them the intensity it often assumes, so as in some characters to surpass in strength all other desires. In these cases the means have become a part of the end, and a more important part of it than any of the things which they are means to. What was once desired as an instrument for the attainment of happiness has come to be desired for its own sake. In being desired for its own sake it is, however, desired as *part* of happiness. The person is made, or thinks he would be made, happy by its mere possession; and is made unhappy by failure to obtain it. The desire of it is not a different thing from the desire of happiness any more than the love of music or the desire of health. They are included in happiness. They are some of the elements of which the desire of happiness is made up. Happiness is not an abstract idea but a concrete whole; and these are some of its parts. And the utilitarian standard sanctions and approves their being so. Life would be a poor thing, very ill provided with sources of happiness, if there were not this provision of nature by which things originally indifferent, but conducive to, or otherwise associated with, the satisfaction of our primitive desires, become in themselves sources of pleasure more valuable than the primitive pleasures, both in permanency, in the space of human existence that they are capable of covering, and even in intensity.

Virtue, according to the utilitarian conception, is a good of this description. There was no original desire of it, or motive to it, save its conduciveness to pleasure, and especially to protection from pain. But through the association thus formed it may be felt a good in itself, and desired as such with as great intensity as any other good; and with this difference between it and the love of money, of power, or of fame, that all of these may, and often do, render the individual noxious to the other members of the society to which he belongs, whereas there is nothing which makes him so much a blessing to them as the cultivation of the disinterested love of virtue. And consequently, the utilitarian standard, while it tolerates and approves those other acquired desires, up to the point beyond which they would be more injurious to the general happiness than promotive of it, enjoins and requires the cultivation of the love of virtue up to the greatest strength possible, as being above all things important to the general happiness.

It results from the preceding considerations that there is in reality nothing desired except happiness. Whatever is desired otherwise than as a means to some end beyond itself, and ultimately to happiness, is desired as itself a part of happiness, and is not desired for itself until it has become so. Those who desire virtue for its own sake desire it either because the consciousness of it is a pleasure, or because the consciousness of being without it is a pain, or for both reasons united; as in truth the pleasure and pain seldom exist separately, but almost always together—the same person feeling pleasure in the degree of virtue attained, and pain in not having attained more. If one of these gave him no pleasure, and the other no pain, he would not love or desire virtue, or would desire it only for the other benefits which it might produce to himself or to persons whom he cared for.

We have now, then, an answer to the question, of what sort of proof the principle of utility is susceptible. If the opinion which I have now stated is psychologically true—if human nature is so constituted as to desire nothing which is not either a part of happiness or a means of happiness, we can have no other proof, and we require no other, that these are the only things desirable. If so, happiness is the sole end of human action, and the promotion of it the test by which to judge of all human conduct; from whence it necessarily follows that it must be the criterion of morality, since a part is included in the whole.

And now to decide whether this is really so, whether mankind do desire nothing for itself but that which is a pleasure to them, or of which the absence is a pain, we have evidently arrived at a question of fact and experience, dependent, like all similar questions, upon evidence. It can only be determined by practised self-consciousness and self-observation, assisted by observation of others. I believe that these sources of evidence, impartially consulted, will declare that desiring a thing and finding it pleasant, aversion to it and thinking of it as painful, are phenomena entirely inseparable or rather two parts of the same phenomenon; in strictness of language, two different modes of naming the same psychological fact; that to think of an object as desirable (unless for the sake of its consequences) and to think of it as pleasant are one and the same thing; and that to desire anything except in proportion as the idea of it is pleasant, is a physical and metaphysical impossibility.

So obvious does this appear to me that I expect it will hardly be disputed; and the objection made will be, not that desire can possibly be directed to anything ultimately except pleasure and exemption from pain, but that the will is a different thing from desire; that a person of confirmed virtue or any other person whose purposes are fixed carries out his purposes without any thought of the pleasure he has in contemplating them or expects to derive from their fulfilment, and persists in acting on them, even though these pleasures are much diminished by changes in his character or decay of his passive sensibilities, or are outweighed by the pains which the pursuit of the purposes may bring upon him. All this I fully admit and have stated it elsewhere as positively and emphatically as anyone. Will, the active phenomenon is a different thing from desire, the seat of passive sensibility and though originally an offshoot from it, may in time take root and detach itself from the parent stock, so much so that in the case of an habitual purpose, instead of willing the thing because we desire it, we often desire it only because we will it. This, however, is but an instance of that familiar fact, the power of habit, and is nowise confined to the case of virtuous actions. Many indifferent things which men originally did from a motive of some sort, they continue to do from habit. Sometimes this is done unconsciously; the consciousness coming only after the action; at other times with conscious volition, but volition which has become habitual and is put in operation by the force of habit, in opposition perhaps to the deliberate preference, as often happens with those who have contracted habits of vicious or hurtful indulgence. Third and last comes the case in which the habitual act of will in the individual instance is not in contradiction to the general intention prevailing at other times, but in fulfilment of it; as in the case of the person of confirmed virtue and of all who pursue deliberately and consistently any determinate end. The distinction between will and desire thus understood is an authentic and highly important psychological fact; but the fact consists solely in this—that will, like all other parts of our constitution, is amenable to habit, and that we may will from habit what we no longer desire for itself, or desire only because we will it. It is not the less true that will, in the beginning, is entirely produced by desire; including in that term the repelling influence of pain as well as the attractive one of pleasure. Let us take into consideration no longer the person who has a confirmed will to do right, but him in whom that virtuous will is still feeble, conquerable by temptation, and not to be fully relied on; by what means can it be strengthened? How can the will to be virtuous, where it does not exist in sufficient force, be implanted or awakened? Only by making the person *desire* virtue—by making him think of it in a pleasurable light, or of its ab-

sence in a painful one. It is by associating the doing right with pleasure, or the doing wrong with pain, or by eliciting and impressing and bringing home to the person's experience the pleasure naturally involved in the one or the pain in the other, that it is possible to call forth that will to be virtuous which, when confirmed, acts without any thought of either pleasure or pain. Will is the child of desire, and passes out of the dominion of its parent only to come under that of habit. That which is the result of habit affords no presumption of being intrinsically good; and there would be no reason for wishing that the purpose of virtue should become independent of pleasure and pain were it not that the influence of the pleasurable and painful associations which prompt to virtue is not sufficiently to be depended on for unerring constancy of action until it has acquired the support of habit. Both in feeling and in conduct, habit is the only thing which imparts certainty; and it is because of the importance to others of being able to rely absolutely on one's feelings and conduct, and to oneself of being able to rely on one's own, that the will to do right ought to be cultivated into this habitual independence. In other words, this state of the will is a means to good, not intrinsically a good; and does not contradict the doctrine that nothing is a good to human beings but in so far as it is either itself pleasurable or a means of attaining pleasure or averting pain.

But if this doctrine be true, the principle of utility is proved. Whether it is so or not, must now be left to the consideration of the thoughtful reader.

On the Connection Between Justice and Utility

In all ages of speculation one of the strongest obstacles to the reception of the doctrine that utility or happiness is the criterion of right and wrong has been drawn from the idea of justice. The powerful sentiment and apparently clear perception which that word recalls with a rapidity and certainty resembling an instinct have seemed to the majority of thinkers to point to an inherent quality in things; to show that the just must have an existence in nature as something absolute, generically distinct from every variety of the expedient and, in idea, opposed to it, though (as is commonly acknowledged) never, in the long run, disjoined from it in fact.

In the case of this, as of our other moral sentiments, there is no necessary connection between the question of its origin and that of its binding force. That a feeling is bestowed on us by nature does not necessarily legitimate all its promptings. The feeling of justice might be a peculiar instinct, and might yet require, like our other instincts, to be controlled and enlightened by a higher reason. If we have intellectual instincts leading us to judge in a particular way, as well as animal instincts that prompt us to act in a particular way, there is no necessity that the former should be more infallible in their sphere than the latter in theirs; it may as well happen that wrong judgments are occasionally suggested by those, as wrong actions by these. But though it is one thing to believe that we have natural feelings of justice, and another to acknowledge them as an ultimate criterion of conduct, these two opinions are very closely connected in point of fact. Mankind are always predisposed to believe that any subjective feeling, not otherwise accounted for, is a revelation of some objective reality. Our present object is to determine whether the reality to which the feeling of justice corresponds is one which needs any such special revelation, whether the justice or injustice of an action is a thing intrinsically peculiar and distinct from all its other qualities or only a combination of certain of those qualities presented under a peculiar aspect. For the purpose of this inquiry it is practically important to consider whether the feeling itself, of justice and injustice, is *sui generis* like our sensations of color and taste or a derivative feeling formed by a combination of others. And this it is the more essential to examine, as people are in general willing enough to allow that objectively the dictates of justice coincide with a part of the field of general expediency; but inasmuch as the subjective mental feeling of justice is different from that which commonly attaches to simple expediency, and, except in the extreme cases of the latter, is far more imperative in its demands, people find it difficult to see in justice only a particular kind or branch of general utility, and think that its superior binding force requires a totally different origin.

To throw light upon this question, it is necessary to attempt to ascertain what is the distinguishing character of justice, or of injustice; what is the quality, or whether there is any quality, attributed in common to all modes of conduct designated as unjust (for justice, like many other moral attributes, is best defined by its opposite), and distinguishing them from such modes of conduct as are disapproved, but without having that particular epithet of disapprobation applied to them. If in everything which men are accustomed to characterize as just or unjust some one common attribute or collection of attributes is always present, we may judge whether this particular attribute or combination of attributes would he capable of gathering round it a sentiment of that peculiar character and intensity by virtue of the general laws of our emotional constitution, or whether the sentiment is inexplicable and requires to be regarded as a special provision of nature. If we find the former to be the case, we shall, in resolving this question, have resolved also the main problem; if the latter, we shall have to seek for some other mode of investigating it.

To find the common attributes of a variety of objects, it is necessary to begin by surveying the objects themselves in the concrete. Let us therefore advert successively to the various modes of action and arrangements of human affairs which are classed, by universal or widely spread opinion, as just or as unjust. The things well known to excite the sentiments associated with those names are of a very multifarious character. I shall pass them rapidly in review, without studying any particular arrangement.

In the first place, it is mostly considered unjust to deny anyone of his personal liberty, his property, or any other thing which belongs to him by law. Here, therefore, is one instance of the application of the terms "just" and "unjust" in a perfectly definite sense, namely, that it is just to respect, unjust to violate, the *legal rights* of anyone. But this judgment admits of several exceptions, arising from the other forms in which the notions of justice and injustice present themselves. For example, the person who suffers the deprivation may (as the phrase is) have *forfeited* the rights which he is so deprived of—a case to which we shall return presently. But also—

Secondly, the legal rights of which he is deprived may be rights which *ought* not to have belonged to him; in other words, the law which confers on him these rights may be a bad law. When it is so or when (which is the same thing for our purpose) it is supposed to be so, opinions will differ as to the justice or injustice of infringing it. Some maintain that no law, however bad, ought to be disobeyed by an individual citizen; that his opposition to it, if shown at all, should only be shown in endeavoring to get it altered by competent authority. This opinion (which condemns many of the most illustrious benefactors of mankind, and would often protect pernicious institutions against the only weapons which, in the state of things existing at the time, have any chance of succeeding against them) is defended by those who hold it on grounds of expediency, principally on that of the importance to the common interest of mankind, of maintaining inviolate the sentiment of submission to law. Other persons, again, hold the directly contrary opinion that any law, judged to be bad, may blamelessly be disobeyed, even though it be not judged to be unjust but only inexpedient, while others would confine the license of disobedience to the case of unjust laws; but, again, some say that all laws which are inexpedient are unjust, since every law imposes some restriction on the natural liberty of mankind, which restriction is an injustice unless legitimated by tending to their good. Among these diversities of opinion it seems to be universally admitted that there may be unjust laws, and that law, consequently, is not the ultimate criterion of justice, but may give to one person a benefit, or impose on another an evil, which justice condemns. When, however, a law is thought to be unjust, it seems always to be regarded as being so in the same way in which a breach of law is unjust, namely, by infringing somebody's right, which, as it cannot in this case be a legal right, receives a different appellation and is called a moral right. We may say, therefore, that a second case of injustice consists in taking or withholding from any person that to which he has a *moral right.*

Thirdly, it is universally considered just that each person should obtain that (whether good or evil) which he *deserves,* and unjust that he should obtain a good or be made to undergo an evil which he does not deserve. This is, perhaps, the clearest and most emphatic form in which the idea of justice is conceived by the general mind. As it involves the notion of desert, the question arises what constitutes desert? Speaking in a general way, a person is understood to deserve good if he does right, evil if he does wrong; and in a more particular sense, to deserve good from those to whom he does or has done good, and evil from those to whom he does or has done evil. The precept of returning good for evil has never been regarded as a case of the fulfillment of justice, but as one in which the claims of justice are waived, in obedience to other considerations.

Fourthly, it is confessedly unjust to *break faith* with anyone: to violate an engagement, either express or implied, or disappoint expectations raised by our own conduct, at least if we have raised those expectations knowingly and voluntarily. Like the other obligations of justice already spoken of, this one is not regarded as absolute, but as capable of being overruled by a stronger obligation of justice on the other side, or by such conduct on the part of the person concerned as is deemed to absolve us from our obligation to him and to constitute a *forfeiture* of the benefit which he has been led to expect.

Fifthly, it is, by universal admission, inconsistent with justice to be *partial*—to show favor or preference to one person over another in matters to which favor and preference do not properly apply. Impartiality, however, does not seem to be regarded as a duty in itself, but rather as instrumental to some other duty; for it is admitted that favor and preference are not always censurable, and, indeed, the cases in which they are condemned are rather the exception than the rule. A person would be more likely to be blamed than applauded for giving his family or friends no superiority in good offices over strangers when he could do so without violating any other duty; and no one thinks it unjust to seek one person in preference to another as a friend, connection, or companion. Impartiality where rights are concerned is of course obligatory, but this is involved in the more general obligation of giving to everyone his right. A tribunal, for example, must be impartial because it is bound to award, without regard to any other consideration, a disputed object to the one of two parties who has the right to it. There are other cases in which impartiality means being solely influenced by desert, as with those who, in the capacity of judges, preceptors, or parents, administer reward and punishment as such. There are cases, again, in which it means being solely influenced by consideration for the public interest, as in making a selection among candidates for a government employment. Impartiality, in short, as an obligation of justice, may be said to mean being exclusively influenced by the considerations which it is supposed ought to influence the particular case in hand, and resisting solicitation of any motives which prompt to conduct different from what those considerations would dictate.

Nearly allied to the idea of impartiality is that of *equality,* which often enters as a component part both into the conception of justice and into the practice of it, and, in the eyes of many persons, constitutes its essence. But in this, still more than in any other case, the notion of justice varies in different persons, and always conforms in its variations to their notion of utility. Each person maintains that equality is the dictate of justice, except where he thinks that expediency requires inequality. The justice of giving equal protection to the rights of all is mainly tamed by those who support the most outrageous inequality in the rights themselves. Even in slave countries it is theoretically admitted that the rights of the slave, such as they are, ought to be as sacred as those of the master, and that a tribunal which fails to enforce them with equal strictness is wanting in justice; while, at the same time, institutions which leave to the slave scarcely any rights to enforce are not deemed unjust because they are not deemed inexpedient. Those who think that utility requires distinctions of rank do not consider it unjust that riches and social privileges should be unequally dispensed; but those who think this inequality inexpedient think it unjust also. Whoever thinks that government is necessary sees no injustice in as much inequality as is constituted by giving to the magistrate powers not granted to other people. Even among those who hold leveling doctrines, there are differences of opinion about expediency. Some communists consider it unjust that the produce of the labor of the community should be shared on any other principle than that of exact equality; others think it just that those should receive most whose wants are greatest; while others hold that those who work harder, or who produce more, or whose services are more valuable to the community, may justly claim a larger quota in the division of the produce. And the sense of natural justice may be plausibly appealed to in behalf of everyone of these opinions.

Among so many diverse applications of the term "justice," which yet is not regarded as ambiguous, it is a matter of some difficulty to seize the mental link which holds them together, and on which the moral sentiment adhering to the term essentially depends. Perhaps, in this embarrassment, some help may be derived from the history of the word, as indicated by its etymology.

In most if not in all languages, the etymology of the word which corresponds to "just" points distinctly to an origin connected with the ordinances of law. *Justum* is a form of *jussum*, that which has been ordered. *Dikaion* comes directly from *dike*, a suit at law. *Recht*, from which came *right* and *righteous*, is synonymous with law. The courts of justice, the administration of justice, are the courts and the administration of law. *La justice*, in French, is the established term for judicature. I am not committing the fallacy, imputed with some show of truth to Horne Tooke, of assuming that a word must still continue to mean what it originally meant. Etymology is slight evidence of what the idea now signified is, but the very best evidence of how it sprang up. There can, I think, be no doubt that the *idée mère*, the primitive element, in the formation of the notion of justice was conformity to law. It constituted the entire idea among the Hebrews, up to the birth of Christianity; as might be expected in the case of a people whose laws attempted to embrace all subjects on which precepts were required, and who believed those laws to be a direct emanation from the Supreme Being. But other nations, and in particular the Greeks and Romans, who knew that their laws had been made originally, and still continued to be made, by men, were not afraid to admit that those men might make bad laws; might do, by law, the same things, and from the same motives, which if done by individuals without the sanction of law would be called unjust. And hence the sentiment of injustice came to be attached, not to all violations of law, but only to violations of such laws as *ought* to exist, including such as ought to exist but do not, and to laws themselves if supposed to be contrary to what ought to be law. In this manner the idea of law and of its injunctions was still predominant in the notion of justice, even when the laws actually in force ceased to be accepted as the standard of it.

It is true that mankind consider the idea of justice and its obligations as applicable to many things which neither are, nor is it desired that they should be, regulated by law. Nobody desires that laws should interfere with the whole detail of private life; yet everyone allows that in all daily conduct a person may and does show himself to be either just or unjust. But even here, the idea of the breach of what ought to be law still lingers in a modified shape. It would always give us pleasure, and chime in with our feelings of fitness, that acts which we deem unjust should be punished, though we do not always think it expedient that this should be done by the tribunals. We forego that gratification on account of incidental inconveniences. We should be glad to see just conduct enforced and injustice repressed, even in the minutest details, if we were not, with reason, afraid of trusting the magistrate with so unlimited an amount of power over individuals. When we think that a person is bound in justice to do a thing, it is an ordinary form of language to say that he ought to be compelled to do it. We should be gratified to see the obligation enforced by anybody who had the power. If we see that its enforcement by law would be inexpedient, we lament the impossibility, we consider the impunity given to injustice as an evil, and strive to make amends for it by bringing a strong expression of our own and the public disapprobation to bear upon the offender. Thus the idea of legal constraint is still the generating idea of the notion of justice, though undergoing several transformations before that notion as it exists in an advanced state of society becomes complete.

The above is, I think, a true account, as far as it goes, of the origin and progressive growth of the idea of justice. But we must observe that it contains as yet nothing to distinguish that obligation from moral obligation in general. For the truth is that the idea of penal sanction, which is the essence of law, enters not only into the conception of injustice, but into that of any kind of wrong. We do not call anything wrong unless we mean to imply that a person ought to be punished in some way or other for doing it—if not by law, by the opinion of his fellow creatures; if not by opinion, by the reproaches of his own conscience. This seems the real turning point of the distinction between morality and simple expediency. It is a part of the notion of duty in every one of its forms that a person may rightfully be compelled to fulfill it. Duty is a thing which may be *exacted* from a person, as one exacts a debt. Unless we think that it may be exacted from him, we do not call it his duty. Reasons of prudence, or the interest of other people, may militate against actually exacting it, but the person himself, it is clearly understood, would not be entitled to complain. There are other things, on the contrary, which we wish that people should do, which we like or admire them for doing, perhaps dislike or despise them for not doing, but yet admit that they are not bound to do; it is not a case of moral obligation; we do not blame them, that is, we do not think that they are proper

objects of punishment. How we come by these ideas of deserving and not deserving punishment will appear, perhaps, in the sequel; but I think there is no doubt that this distinction lies at the bottom of the notions of right and wrong; that we call any conduct wrong, or employ, instead, some other term of dislike or disparagement, according as we think that the person ought, or ought not, to be punished for it; and we say it would be right to do so and so, or merely that it would be desirable or laudable, according as we would wish to see the person whom it concerns compelled, or only persuaded and exhorted, to act in that manner.[1]

This, therefore, being the characteristic difference which marks off, not justice, but morality in general from the remaining provinces of expediency and worthiness, the character is still to be sought which distinguishes justice from other branches of morality. Now it is known that ethical writers divide moral duties into two classes, denoted by the ill-chosen expressions, duties of perfect and of imperfect obligation; the latter being those in which, though the act is obligatory, the particular occasions of performing it are left to our choice, as in the case of charity or beneficence, which we are indeed bound to practice but not toward any definite person, nor at any prescribed time. In the more precise language of philosophic jurists, duties of perfect obligation are those duties in virtue of which a correlative *right* resides in some person or persons; duties of imperfect obligation are those moral obligations which do not give birth to any right. I think it will be found that this distinction exactly coincides with that which exists between justice and the other obligations of morality. In our survey of the various popular acceptations of justice, the term appeared generally to involve the idea of a personal right—a claim on the part of one or more individuals, like that which the law gives when it confers a proprietary or other legal right. Whether the injustice consists in depriving a person of a possession, or in breaking faith with him, or in treating him worse than he deserves, or worse than other people who have no greater claims—in each

---

1. See this point enforced and illustrated by Professor Bain, in an admirable chapter (entitled "The Ethical Emotions, or the Moral Sense"), of the second of the two treatises composing his elaborate and profound work on the Mind.

case the supposition implies two things: a wrong done, and some assignable person who is wronged. Injustice may also be done by treating a person better than others; but the wrong in this case is to his competitors, who are also assignable persons. It seems to me that this feature in the case—a right in some person, correlative to the moral obligation—constitutes the specific difference between justice and generosity or beneficence. Justice implies something which it is not only right to do, and wrong not to do, but which some individual person can claim from us as his moral right. No one has a moral right to our generosity or beneficence because we are not morally bound to practice those virtues toward any given individual. And it will be found with respect to this as to every correct definition that the instances which seem to conflict with it are those which most confirm it. For if a moralist attempts, as some have done, to make out that mankind generally, though not any given individual, have a right to all the good we can do them, he at once, by that thesis, includes generosity and beneficence within the category of justice. He is obliged to say that our utmost exertions are *due* to our fellow creatures, thus assimilating them to a debt; or that nothing less can be a sufficient *return* for what society does for us, thus classing the case as one of gratitude; both of which are acknowledged cases of justice, and not of the virtue of beneficence; and whoever does not place the distinction between justice and morality in general, where we have now placed it, will be found to make no distinction between them at all, but to merge all morality in justice.

Having thus endeavored to determine the distinctive elements which enter into the composition of the idea of justice, we are ready to enter on the inquiry whether the feeling which accompanies the idea is attached to it by a special dispensation of nature, or whether it could have grown up, by any known laws, out of the idea itself; and, in particular, whether it can have originated in considerations of general expediency.

I conceive that the sentiment itself does not arise from anything which would commonly or correctly be termed an idea of expediency, but that, though the sentiment does not, whatever is moral in it does.

We have seen that the two essential ingredients in the sentiment of justice are the desire to punish a person who has done harm and the knowledge or belief that there is some definite individual or individuals to whom harm has been done.

Now it appears to me that the desire to punish a person who has done harm to some individual is a spontaneous outgrowth from two sentiments, both in the highest degree natural and which either are or resemble instincts: the impulse of self-defense and the feeling of sympathy.

It is natural to resent and to repel or retaliate any harm done or attempted against ourselves or against those with whom we sympathize. The origin of this sentiment it is not necessary here to discuss. Whether it be an instinct or a result of intelligence, it is, we know, common to all animal nature; for every animal tries to hurt those who have hurt, or who it thinks are about to hurt, itself or its young. Human beings, on this point, only differ from other animals in two particulars. First, in being capable of sympathizing, not solely with their offspring, or, like some of the more noble animals, with some superior animal who is kind to them, but with all human, and even with all sentient, beings; secondly, in having a more developed intelligence, which gives a wider range to the whole of their sentiments, whether self-regarding or sympathetic. By virtue of his superior intelligence, even apart from his superior range of sympathy, a human being is capable of apprehending a community of interest between himself and the human society of which he forms a part, such that any conduct which threatens the security of the society generally is threatening to his own, and calls forth his instinct (if instinct it be) of self-defense. The same superiority of intelligence, joined to the power of sympathizing with human beings generally, enables him to attach himself to the collective idea of his tribe, his country, or mankind in such a manner that any act hurtful to them raises his instinct of sympathy and urges him to resistance.

The sentiment of justice, in that one of its elements which consists of the desire to punish, is thus, I conceive, the natural feeling of retaliation or vengeance, rendered by intellect and sympathy applicable to those injuries, that is, to those hurts, which wound us through, or in common with, society at large. This sentiment, in itself, has nothing moral in it; what is moral is the exclusive subordination of it to the social sympathies, so as to wait on and obey their call. For the natural feeling would make us resent indiscriminately whatever anyone does that is disagreeable to us; but, when moralized by the social feeling, it only acts in the directions conformable to the general good: just persons resenting a hurt to society, though not otherwise a hurt to themselves, and not resenting a hurt to themselves, however painful, unless it be of the kind which society has a common interest with them in the repression of.

It is no objection against this doctrine to say that, when we feel our sentiment of justice outraged, we are not thinking of society at large or of any collective interest, but only of the individual case. It is common enough, certainly, though the reverse of commendable, to feel resentment merely because we have suffered pain; but a person whose resentment is really a moral feeling, that is, who considers whether an act is blamable before he allows himself to resent it—such a person, though he may not say expressly to himself that he is standing up for the interest of society, certainly does feel that he is asserting a rule which is for the benefit of others as well as for his own. If he is not feeling this, if he is regarding the act solely as it affects him individually, he is not consciously just; he is not concerning himself about the justice of his actions. This is admitted even by anti-utilitarian moralists. When Kant (as before remarked) propounds as the fundamental principle of morals, "So act that thy rule of conduct might be adopted as a law by all rational beings," he virtually acknowledges that the interest of mankind collectively, or at least of mankind indiscriminately, must be in the mind of the agent when conscientiously deciding on the morality of the act. Otherwise he uses words without a meaning; for that a rule even of utter selfishness could not *possibly* be adopted by all rational beings—that there is any insuperable obstacle in the nature of things to its adoption—cannot be even plausibly maintained. To give any meaning to Kant's principle, the sense put upon it must be that we ought to shape our conduct by a rule which all rational beings might adopt *with benefit to their collective interest.*

To recapitulate: the idea of justice supposes two things—a rule of conduct and a sentiment which sanctions the rule. The first must be supposed common to all mankind and intended for their good. The other (the sentiment) is a desire that punishment may be suffered by those who infringe the rule. There is involved, in addition, the conception of some definite person who suffers by the infringement, whose rights (to use the expression appropriated to the case) are violated by it. And the sentiment of justice appears to me to be the animal desire to repel or retaliate a hurt or damage to oneself or to those with whom one sympathizes, widened so as to include all persons, by the human capacity of enlarged sympathy and the human conception of intelligent self-interest. From the latter elements the feeling derives its morality; from the former, its peculiar impressiveness and energy of self-assertion.

I have, throughout, treated the idea of a *right* residing in the injured person and violated by the injury, not as a separate element in the composition of the idea and sentiment, but as one of the forms in which the other two elements clothe themselves. These elements are a hurt to some assignable person or persons, on the one hand, and a demand for punishment, on the other. An examination of our own minds, I think, will show that these two things include all that we mean when we speak of violation of a right. When we call anything a person's right, we mean that he has a valid claim on society to protect him in the possession of it, either by the force of law or by that of education and opinion. If he has what we consider a sufficient claim, on whatever account, to have something guaranteed to him by society, we say that he has a right to it. If we desire to prove that anything does not belong to him by right, we think this done as soon as it is admitted that society ought not to take measures for securing it to him, but should leave him to chance or to his own exertions. Thus a person is said to have a right to what he can earn in fair professional competition, because society ought not to allow any other person to hinder him from endeavoring to earn in that manner as much as he can. But he has not a right to three hundred a year, though he may happen to be earning it; because society is not called on to provide that he shall earn that sum On the contrary, if he owns ten thousand pounds three-per-cent stock, he *has* a right to three hundred a year because society has come under an obligation to provide him with an income of that amount.

To have a right, then, is, I conceive, to have something which society ought to defend me in the possession of. If the objector goes on to ask why it ought, I can give him no other reason than general utility. If that expression does not seem to convey a sufficient feeling of the strength of the obligation, nor to account for the peculiar energy of the feeling, it is because there goes to the composition of the sentiment, not a rational only but also an animal element—the thirst for retaliation; and this thirst derives its intensity, as well as its moral justification, from the extraordinarily important and impressive kind of utility which is concerned. The interest involved is that of security, to everyone's feelings the most vital of all interests. All other earthly benefits are needed by one person, not needed by another; and many of era can, if necessary, be cheerfully foregone or replaced by something else; but security no human being can possibly do without; on it we depend for all our immunity from evil and for the whole value of all and every good, beyond the passing moment, since nothing but the gratification of the instant could be of any worth to us if we could be deprived of everything the next instant by whoever was momentarily stronger than ourselves. Now this most indispensable of all necessaries, after physical nutriment, cannot be had unless the machinery for providing it is kept unintermittedly in active play. Our notion, therefore, of the claim we have on our fellow creatures to join in making safe for us the very groundwork of our existence gathers feelings around it so much more intense than those concerned in any of the more common cases of utility that the difference in degree (as is often the case in psychology) becomes a real difference in kind. The claim assumes that character of absoluteness, that apparent infinity and incommensurability with all other considerations which constitute the distinction between the feeling of right and wrong and that of ordinary expediency and inexpediency. The feelings concerned are so powerful and we count so positively on finding a responsive feeling in others (all being alike interested) that *ought* and *should* grow into *must,* and recognized indispensability becomes a moral necessity, analogous to physical, and often not inferior to it in binding force.

If the preceding analysis, or something resembling it, be not the correct account of the notion of justice—if justice be totally independent of utility, and be a standard *per se,* which the mind can recognize by simple introspection of itself—it is hard to understand why that internal oracle is so ambiguous, and why so many things appear either just or unjust, according to the light in which they are regarded.

We are continually informed that utility is an uncertain standard, which every different person interprets differently, and that there is no safety but in the immutable, ineffaceable, and unmistakable dictates of justice, which carry their evidence in themselves and are independent of the fluctuations of opinion. One would suppose from this that on questions of justice there could be no controversy; that, if we take that for our rule, its application to any given case could leave us in as little doubt as a mathematical demonstration. So far is this from being the fact that there is as much difference of opinion, and as much discussion, about what is just as about what is useful to society. Not only have different nations and individuals different notions of justice, but in the mind of one and the same individual, justice is not some one rule, principle, or maxim, but many which do not always coincide in their dictates, and, in choosing between which, he is guided either by some extraneous standard or by his own personal predilections.

For instance, there are some who say that is it unjust to punish anyone for the sake of example to others, that punishment is just only when intended for the good of the sufferer himself. Others maintain the extreme reverse, contending that to punish persons who have attained years of discretion, for their own benefit, is despotism and injustice, since, if the matter at issue is solely their own good, no one has a right to control their own judgment of it; but that they may justly be punished to prevent evil to others, this being the exercise of the legitimate right of self-defense. Mr. Owen, again, affirms that it is unjust to punish at all, for the criminal did not make his own character; his education and the circumstances which surrounded him have made him a criminal, and for these he is not responsible. All these opinions are extremely plausible; and so long as the question is argued as one of justice simply, without going down to the principles which lie under justice and are the source of its authority, I am unable to see how any of these reasoners can be refuted. For in truth every one of the three builds upon rules of justice confessedly true. The first appeals to the acknowledged injustice of singling out an individual and making him a sacrifice, without his consent, for other people's benefit. The second relies on the acknowledged justice of self-defense and the admitted injustice of forcing one person to conform to another's notions of what constitutes his good. The

Owenite invokes the admitted principle that it is unjust to punish anyone for what he cannot help. Each is triumphant so long as he is not compelled to take into consideration any other maxims of justice than the one he has selected; but as soon as their several maxims are brought face to face, each disputant seems to have exactly as much to say for himself as the others. No one of them can carry but his own notion of justice without trampling upon another equally binding. These are difficulties; they have always been felt to be such; and many devices have been invented to turn rather than to overcome them. As a refuge from the last of the three, men imagined what they called the freedom of the will—fancying that they could not justify punishing a man whose will is in a thoroughly hateful state unless it be supposed to have come into that state through no influence of anterior circumstances. To escape from the other difficulties, a favorite contrivance has been the fiction of a contract whereby at some unknown period all the members of society engaged to obey the laws and consented to be punished for any disobedience to them, thereby giving to their legislators the right, which it is assumed they would not otherwise have had, of punishing them, either for their own good or for that of society. This happy thought was considered to get rid of the whole difficulty and to legitimate the infliction of punishment, in virtue of another received maxim of justice, *volenti non fit injuria*—that is not unjust which is done with the consent of the person who is supposed to be hurt by it. I need hardly remark that, even if the consent were not a mere fiction, this maxim is not superior in authority to the others which it is brought in to supersede. It is, on the contrary, an instructive specimen of the loose and irregular manner in which supposed principles of justice grow up. This particular one evidently came into use as a help to the coarse exigencies of courts of law, which are sometimes obliged to be content with very uncertain presumptions, on account of the greater evils which would often arise from any attempt on their part to cut finer. But even courts of law are not able to adhere consistently to the maxim, for they allow voluntary engagements to be set aside on the ground of fraud, and sometimes on that of mere mistake or misinformation.

Again, when the legitimacy of inflicting punishment is admitted, how many conflicting conceptions of justice come to light in discussing the proper apportionment of punishments to offenses. No rule on the subject recommends itself so strongly to the primitive and spontaneous sentiment of justice as the *lex talionis*, an eye for an eye and a tooth for a tooth. Though this principle of the Jewish and of the Mohammedan law has been generally abandoned in Europe as a practical maxim, there is, I suspect, in most minds, a secret hankering after it; and when retribution accidentally falls on an offender in that precise shape, the general feeling of satisfaction evinced bears witness how natural is the sentiment to which this repayment in kind is acceptable. With many, the test of justice in penal infliction is that the punishment should be proportioned to the offense, meaning that it should he exactly measured by the moral guilt of the culprit (whatever be their standard for measuring moral guilt), the consideration what amount of punishment is necessary to deter from the offense having nothing to do with the question of justice, in their estimation; while there are others to whom that consideration is all in all, who maintain that it is not just, at least for man, to inflict on a fellow creature, whatever may be his offenses, any amount of suffering beyond the least that will suffice to prevent him from repeating, and others from imitating, his misconduct.

To take another example from a subject already once referred to. In co-operative industrial association, is it just or not that talent or skill should give a title to superior remuneration? On the negative side of the question it is argued that whoever does the best he can deserves equally well, and ought not in justice to be put in a position of inferiority for no fault of his own; that superior abilities have already advantages more than enough, in the admiration they excite, the personal influence they command, and the internal sources of satisfaction attending them, without adding to these a superior share of the world's goods; and that society is bound in justice rather to make compensation to the less favored for this unmerited inequality of advantages than to aggravate it. On the contrary side it is contended that society receives more from the more efficient laborer; that, his services being more useful, society owes him a larger return for them; that a greater share of the joint result is actually his work, and not to allow his claim to it is a kind of robbery; that, if he is only to receive as much as others, he can only be justly required to produce as much, and to give a smaller amount of time and exertion, proportioned to his superior efficiency. Who shall decide between these appeals to conflicting principles of justice? Justice has in this case two sides to it, which it is impossible to bring into harmony, and the two disputants have chosen opposite sides; the one looks to what it is just that the individual should receive, the other to what it is just that the community should give. Each, from his own point of view, is unanswerable; and any choice between them, on grounds of justice, must be perfectly arbitrary. Social utility alone can decide the preference.

How many, again, and how irreconcilable are the standards of justice to which reference is made in discussing the repartition of taxation. One opinion is that payment to the state should be in numerical proportion to pecuniary means. Others think that justice dictates what they term graduated taxation— taking a higher percentage from those who have more to spare. In point of natural justice a strong case might be made for disregarding means altogether, and taking the same absolute sum (whenever it could be got) from everyone; as the subscribers to a mess or to a club all pay the same sum for the same privileges, whether they can all equally afford it or not. Since the protection (it might be said) of law and government is afforded to and is equally required by all, there is no injustice in making all buy it at the same price. It is reckoned justice, not injustice, that a dealer should charge to all customers the same price for the same article, not a price varying according to their means of payment. This doctrine, as applied to taxation, finds no advocates because it conflicts so strongly with man's feelings of humanity and of social expediency; but the principle of justice which it invokes is as true and as binding as those which can be appealed to against it. Accordingly it exerts a tacit influence on the line of defense employed for other modes of assessing taxation. People feel obliged to argue that the state does more for the rich man than for the poor, as a justification for its taking more from them, though this is in reality not true, for the rich would be far better able to protect themselves, in the absence of law or government, than the poor, and indeed would probably be successful in converting the poor into their slaves. Others, again, so far defer to the same conception of justice as to maintain that all should pay an equal capitation tax for the protection of their persons (these being of equal value to all), and an unequal tax for the protection of their property, which is unequal. To this others reply that the all of one man is as valuable to him as the all of another. From these confusions there is no other mode of extrication than the utilitarian.

Is, then, the difference between the just and the expedient a merely imaginary distinction? Have mankind been under a delusion in thinking that justice is a more sacred thing than policy, and that the latter ought only to be listened to after the former has been satisfied? By no means. The exposition we have given of the nature and origin of the sentiment recognizes a real distinction; and no one of those who profess the most sublime contempt for the consequences of actions as an element in their morality attaches more importance to the distinction than I do. While I dispute the pretensions of any theory which sets up an imaginary standard of justice not grounded on utility, I account the justice which is grounded on utility to be the chief part, and incomparably the most sacred and binding part, of all morality. Justice is a name for certain classes of moral rules which concern the essentials of human well-being more nearly, and are therefore of more absolute obligation, than any other rules for the guidance of life; and the notion which we have found to be of the essence of the idea of justice—that of a right residing in an individual—implies and testifies to this more binding obligation.

The moral rules which forbid mankind to hurt one another (in which we must never forget to include wrongful interference with each other's freedom) are more vital to human well-being than any maxims, however important, which only point out the best mode of managing some department of human affairs. They have also the peculiarity that they are the main element in determining the whole of the social feelings of mankind. It is their observance which alone preserves peace among human beings; if obedience to them were not the rule, and disobedience the exception, everyone would see in everyone else an enemy against whom he must be perpetually guarding himself. What is hardly less important, these are the precepts which mankind have the strongest and the most direct inducements for impressing upon one another. By merely giving to each other prudential instruction or exhortation, they may gain, or think they gain, nothing; in inculcating on each other the duty of, positive beneficence, they have an unmistakable interest, but far less in degree; a person may possibly not need the benefits of others, but he always needs that they should not do him hurt. Thus the moralities which protect every individual from being harmed by others, either directly or by being hindered in his freedom of pursuing his own good, are at once those which he himself has most at heart and those which he has the strongest interest in publishing and enforcing by word and deed. It is by a person's observance of these that his fitness to exist as one of the fellowship of human beings is tested and decided; for on that depends his being a nuisance or not to those with whom he is in contact. Now it is these moralities primarily which compose the obligations of justice. The most marked cases of injustice, and those which give the tone to the feeling of repugnance which characterizes the sentiment, are acts of wrongful aggression or wrongful exercise of power over someone; the next are those which consist in wrongfully withholding from him something which is his due—in both cases inflicting on him a positive hurt, either in the form of direct suffering or of the privation of some good which he had reasonable ground, either of a physical or of a social kind, for counting upon.

The same powerful motives which command the observance of these primary moralities enjoin the punishment of those who violate them; and as the impulses of self-defense, of defense of others, and of vengeance are all called forth against such persons, retribution, or evil for evil, becomes closely connected with the sentiment of justice, and is universally included in the idea. Good for good is also one of the dictates of justice; and this, though its social utility is evident, and though it carries with it a natural human feeling, has not at first sight that obvious connection with hurt or injury which, existing in the most elementary cases of just and unjust, is the source of the characteristic intensity of the sentiment. But the connection, though less obvious, is not less real. He who accepts benefits and denies a return of them when needed inflicts a real hurt by disappointing one of the most natural and reasonable of expectations, and one which he must at least tacitly have encouraged, otherwise the benefits would seldom have been conferred. The important rank, among human evils and wrongs, of the disappointment of expectation is shown in the

fact that it constitutes the principal criminality of two such highly immoral acts as a breach of friendship and a breach of promise. Few hurts which human beings can sustain are greater, and none wound more, then when that on which they habitually and with full assurance relied fails them in the hour of need; and few wrongs are greater than this mere withholding of good; none excite more resentment, either in the person suffering or in a sympathizing spectator. The principle, therefore, of giving to each what they deserve, that is, good for good as well as evil for evil, is not only included within the idea of justice as we have defined it, but is a proper object of that intensity of sentiment which places the just in human estimation above the simply expedient.

Most of the maxims of justice current in the world, and commonly appealed to in its transactions, are simply instrumental to carrying into effect the principles of justice which we have now spoken of. That a person is only responsible for what he has done voluntarily, or could voluntarily have avoided, that it is unjust to condemn any person unheard; that the punishment ought to be proportioned to the offense, and the like, are maxims intended to prevent the just principle of evil for evil from being perverted to the infliction of evil without that justification. The greater part of these common maxims have come into use from the practice of courts of justice, which have been naturally led to a more complete recognition and elaboration than was likely to suggest itself to others, of the rules necessary to enable them to fulfill their double function—of inflicting punishment when due, and of awarding to each person his right.

That first of judicial virtues, impartiality, is an obligation of justice, partly for the reason last mentioned, as being a necessary condition of the fulfillment of other obligations of justice. But this is not the only source of the exalted rank, among human obligations, of those maxims of equality and impartiality, which, both in popular estimation and in that of the most enlightened, are included among the precepts of justice. In one point of view, they may be considered as corollaries from the principles already laid down. If it is a duty to do to each according to his deserts, returning good for good, as well as repressing evil by evil, it necessarily follows that we should treat all equally well (when no higher duty forbids) who have deserved equally well of us, and that society should treat all equally well who have deserved equally well of *it,* that is, who have deserved equally well absolutely. This is the highest abstract standard of social and distributive justice, toward which all institutions and the efforts of all virtuous citizens should be made in the utmost possible degree to converge. But this great moral duty rests upon a still deeper foundation, being a direct emanation from the first principle of morals, and not a mere logical corollary from secondary or derivative doctrines. It is involved in the very meaning of utility, or the greatest happiness principle. That principle is a mere form of words without rational signification unless one person's happiness, supposed equal in degree (with the proper allowance made for kind), is counted for exactly as much as another's. Those conditions being supplied, Bentham's dictum, "everybody to count for one, nobody for more than one," might be written under the principle of utility as an explanatory commentary.[1] The equal claim of everybody to happiness, in the estimation of the moralist and of the legislator, involves an equal claim to all the means of happiness except in so far as the inevitable conditions of human life and the general interest in which that of every individual is included set limits to the maxim; and those limits ought to be strictly construed. As every other maxim of justice, so this is by no means applied or held applicable universally; on the contrary, as I have already remarked, it bends to every person's ideas of social expediency. But in whatever case it is deemed applicable at all, it is held to be the dictate of justice. All persons are deemed to have a *right* to equality of treatment, except when some recognized social expediency requires the reverse. And hence all social inequalities which have ceased to be considered expedient assume the character, not of simple inexpediency, but of injustice, and appear so tyrannical that people are apt to wonder how they ever could have been tolerated—forgetful that they themselves, perhaps, tolerate other inequalities under an equally mistaken notion of expediency, the correction of which would make that which they approve seem quite as monstrous as what they have at last learned to condemn. The entire history of social improvement has been a series of transitions by which one custom or institution after another, from being a supposed primary necessity of social existence, has passed into the rank of a universally stigmatized injustice and tyranny. So it has been with the distinctions of slaves and freemen, nobles and serfs, patricians and plebeians; and so it will be, and in part already is, with the aristocracies of color, race, and sex.

It appears from what has been said that justice is a name for certain moral requirements which, regarded collectively, stand higher in the scale of social utility, and are therefore of more paramount obligation, than any others, though particular cases may occur in which some other social duty is so important as to overrule any one of the general maxims of

---

1. This implication, in the first principle of the utilitarian scheme, of perfect impartiality between persons is regarded by Mr. Herbert Spencer (in his *Social Statics*) as a disproof of the pretensions of utility to be a sufficient guide to right; since (he says) the principle of utility presupposes the anterior principle that everybody has an equal right to happiness. It may be more correctly described as supposing that equal amounts of happiness are equally desirable, whether felt by the same or different persons. This, however, is not a *pre*supposition, not a premise needful to support the principle of utility, but the very principle itself; for what is the principle of utility if it he not that "happiness" and "desirable" are synonymous terms? If there is any anterior principle implied, it can be no other than this, that the truths of arithmetic are applicable to the valuation of happiness, as of all other measurable quantities.

(Mr. Herbert Spencer, in a private communication on the subject of the preceding note, objects to being considered an opponent of utilitarianism and states that he regards happiness as the ultimate end of morality; but deems that end only partially attainable by empirical generalizations from the observed results of con-

duct, and completely attainable only by deducing, from the laws of life and the conditions of existence, what kinds of action necessarily tend to produce happiness, and what kinds to produce unhappiness. With the exception of the word "necessarily," I have no dissent to express from this doctrine; and (omitting that word) I am not aware that any modern advocate of utilitarianism is of a different opinion. Bentham, certainly, to whom in the *Social Statics* Mr. Spencer particularly referred, is, least of all writers, chargeable with unwillingness to deduce the effect of actions on happiness from the laws of human nature and the universal conditions of human life. The common charge against him is of relying too exclusively upon such deductions and declining altogether to be bound by the generalizations from specific experience which Mr. Spencer thinks that utilitarians generally confine themselves to. My own opinion (and, as I collect, Mr. Spencer's) is that in ethics, as in all other branches of scientific study, the consilience of the results of both these processes, each corroborating and verifying the other, is requisite to give to any general proposition the kind and degree of evidence which constitutes scientific proof.)

justice. Thus, to save a life, it may not only be allowable, but a duty, to steal or take by force the necessary food or medicine, or to kidnap and compel to officiate the only qualified medical practitioner. In such cases, as we do not call anything justice which is not a virtue, we usually say, not that justice must give way to some other moral principle, but that what is just in ordinary cases is, by reason of that other principle, not just in the particular case. By this useful accommodation of language, the character of indefeasibility attributed to justice is kept up, and we are saved from the necessity of maintaining that there can be laudable injustice.

The considerations which have now been adduced resolve, I conceive, the only real difficulty in the utilitarian theory of morals. It has always been evident that all cases of justice are also cases of expediency; the difference is in the peculiar sentiment which attaches to the former, as contradistinguished from the latter. If this characteristic sentiment has been sufficiently accounted for; if there is no necessity to assume for it any peculiarity of origin; if it is simply the natural feeling of resentment, moralized by being made co-extensive with the demands of social good; and if this feeling not only does but ought to exist in all the classes of cases to which the idea of justice corresponds—that idea no longer presents itself as a stumbling block to the utilitarian ethics. Justice remains the appropriate name for certain social utilities which are vastly more important, and therefore more absolute and imperative, than any others are as a class (though not more so than others may be in particular cases); and which, therefore, ought to be, as well as naturally are, guarded by a sentiment, not only different in degree, but also in kind; distinguished from the milder feeling which attaches to the mere idea of promoting human pleasure or convenience at once by the more definite nature of its commands and by the sterner character of its sanctions.

FRIEDRICH NIETZSCHE

FROM *Beyond Good and Evil* and *A Genealogy of Morals*

Friedrich Nietzsche, one of the most influential and notorious philosophers of modern times, was born in Rocken, Prussia, in 1844. Both his maternal and paternal grandfathers were Lutheran ministers, as was his father. Later, Nietzsche was to become one of his century's most vocal critics of the Christian faith into which he was born. Although he abandoned the religion and the patriotism of his family, he and his father shared a similar fate—both men died insane.

As a young man, Nietzsche excelled in his studies. He began his university education studying theology and classical philology at the University of Bonn, but he later withdrew from theology and followed his favorite professor to the University of Leipzig. While enrolled at Leipzig, he published some pamphlets that drew the attention of the classics department at the University of Basil, in Switzerland. When, in 1868, they queried Nietzsche's mentor at Leipzig as to the suitability of the author of the pamphlets for a professor's position in their department, Nietzsche was recommended so unhesitatingly that Basil appointed him to a chair in their university even though he had not yet received his doctorate. In 1869 Leipzig awarded him his doctorate, without his writing a thesis or taking an examination.

Nietzsche's first published book, The Birth of Tragedy (1872), upset the world of classical studies by arguing that the culture and spirit of ancient Greece was more complex than prevailing wisdom acknowledged. He identified two contrary tendencies, what he called the Apollonian and the Dionysian, which together made up the Greek spirit. As was to occur with his following books, this initial work was met with scorn and disparagement from other classical scholars, yet his ideas were to outshine and outlive those of his critics.

The will to power, the most prominent and central concept in Nietzsche's philosophy, developed out of his study of classical Greece. What all people want is power and that is the end for which all else is done. Like Hobbes, Nietzsche regarded altruism as contrary to natural impulse. Although his concept of the will to power was, and still is, often regarded as the prototype of fascism, most serious interpreters of his thought resist such a conclusion. But this charge, along with accusations of anti-Semitism, the infamous pronouncement that God is dead, and his promotion of a new, superior man—the Superman—have all contributed to a certain mystique surrounding the philosophy of Nietzsche, even to this day.

Adding to this aura of menace and mystery is the manner in which he presented his ideas. Much of his work is in the form of aphorisms. As he declared in a subtitle to one of his later works, he "philosophized with a hammer." In this text are excerpts from two books, Beyond Good and Evil (1886), two hundred pages of numbered aphorisms, and A Genealogy of Morals (1887), a collection of three essays. These two works are usually considered by British and American philosophers to be his most philosophical.

It is in Beyond Good and Evil that he famously articulates his idea of master- and slave-morality. Morality is a mixture of both master and slave types, yet it is important to understand their differences. In the morality of the master, or aristocratic morality, "good" and "bad" mean "noble" and "ignoble." But slave morality praises that which is beneficial to the weak and powerless. By the standards of slave-morality, the man who is good by the standards of master-morality is regarded as evil. Slave-morality, according to Nietzsche, is the morality of the herd. In A Genealogy of Morals, he continues on the same theme, but takes up the concept of resentment. Because the weak and powerless fear the powerful, resentment becomes their weapon. The history of morality is the conflict between these two moralities.

Nietzsche's works exerted the most influence on twentieth-century existentialists such as Albert Camus, Jean-Paul Sartre, Paul Tillich, and Max Scheler. Yet even his detractors have to acknowledge the power of his ideas which went largely unrecognized until after his death. This rebellious philosopher went insane in January of 1889. Nietzsche spent his last years in a vegetative state, unaware of the approach of the tumultuous modern era about which he was so prophetic. He died in 1900.

Chapter V
The Natural History of Morals

186

The moral sentiment in Europe at present is perhaps as subtle, belated, diverse, sensitive, and refined, as the "Science of Morals" belonging thereto is recent, initial, awkward, and coarse-fingered:—an interesting contrast, which sometimes becomes incarnate and obvious in the very person of a moralist. Indeed, the expression, "Science of Morals" is, in respect to what is designated thereby, far too presumptuous and counter to *good* taste,—which is always a foretaste of more modest expressions. One ought to avow with the utmost fairness *what* is still necessary here for a long time, *what* is alone proper for the present:

namely, the collection of material, the comprehensive survey and classification of an immense domain of delicate sentiments of worth, and distinctions of worth, which live, grow, propagate, and perish—and perhaps attempts to give a clear idea of the recurring and more common forms of these living crystallisations—as preparation for a *theory of types* of morality. To be sure, people have not hitherto been so modest. All the philosophers, with a pedantic and ridiculous seriousness, demanded of themselves something very much higher, more pretentious, and ceremonious, when they concerned themselves with morality as a science: they wanted to *give a basis* to morality—and every philosopher hitherto has believed that he has given it a basis; morality itself, however, has been regarded as something "given." How far from their awkward pride was the seemingly insignificant problem—left in dust and decay—of a description of forms of morality, notwithstanding that the finest hands and senses could hardly be fine enough for it! It was precisely owing to moral philosophers knowing the moral facts imperfectly, in an arbitrary epitome, or an accidental abridgement—perhaps as the morality of their environment, their position, their church, their *Zeitgeist*, their climate and zone—it was precisely because they were badly instructed with regard to nations, eras, and past ages, and were by no means eager to know about these matters, that they did not even come in sight of the real problems of morals—problems which only disclose themselves by a comparison of *many* kinds of morality. In every "Science of Morals" hitherto, strange as it may sound, the problem of morality itself has been *omitted*; there has been no suspicion that there was anything problematic there! That which philosophers called "giving a basis to morality," and endeavoured to realise, has, when seen in a right light, proved merely a learned form of good *faith* in prevailing morality, a new means of its *expression*, consequently just a matter-of-fact within the sphere of a definite morality, yea, in its ultimate motive, a sort of denial that it is *lawful* for this morality to be called in question—and in any case the reverse of the testing, analysing, doubting, and vivisecting of this very faith. Hear, for instance, with what innocence—almost worthy of honour—Schopenhauer represents his own task, and draw your conclusions concerning the scientificness of a "Science" whose latest master still talks in the strain of children and old wives: "The principle," he says (page 136 of the *Grundprobleme der Ethik**), "the axiom about the purport of which all moralists are *practically* agreed: *neminem laede, immo omnes quantum potes juva*—is *really* the proposition which all moral teachers strive to establish, . . . the *real* basis of ethics which has been sought, like the philosopher's stone, for centuries."—The difficulty of establishing the proposition referred to may indeed be great—it is well known that Schopenhauer also was unsuccessful in his efforts; and whoever has thoroughly realised how absurdly false and sentimental this proposition is, in a world whose essence is Will to Power, may be reminded that Schopenhauer, although a pessimist, *actually*—played the flute . . . daily after dinner: one may read about the matter in his biography. A question by the way: a pessimist, a repudiator of God and of the world, who *makes a halt* at morality—who assents to morality, and plays the flute to *laede-neminem* morals, what? Is that really—a pessimist?

187

Apart from the value of such assertions as "there is a categorical imperative in us," one can always ask: What does such an assertion indicate about him who makes it? There are systems of morals which are meant to justify their author in the eyes of other people; other systems of morals are meant to tranquillise him, and make him self-satisfied; with other systems he wants to crucify and humble himself; with others he wishes to take revenge; with others to conceal himself; with others to glorify himself and gain superiority and distinction;—this system of morals helps its author to forget, that system makes him, or something of him, forgotten; many a moralist would like to exercise power and creative arbitrariness over mankind; many another, perhaps, Kant especially, gives us to understand by his morals that "what is estimable in me, is that I know how to obey—and with you it *shall* not be otherwise than with me!" In short, systems of morals are only a *sign-language of the emotions.*

188

In contrast to *laisser-aller*, every system of morals is a sort of tyranny against "nature" and also against "reason"; that is, however, no objection, unless one should

---

* Pages 54-55 of Schopenhauer's *Basis of Morality*, translated by Arthur B. Bullock, M.A. (1903).

again decree by some system of morals, that all kinds of tyranny and unreasonableness are unlawful. What is essential and invaluable in every system of morals, is that it is a long constraint. In order to understand Stoicism, or Port-Royal, or Puritanism, one should remember the constraint under which every language has attained to strength and freedom—the metrical constraint, the tyranny of rhyme and rhythm. How much trouble have the poets and orators of every nation given themselves!—not excepting some of the prose writers of to-day, in whose ear dwells an inexorable conscientiousness—"for the sake of a folly," as utilitarian bunglers say, and thereby deem themselves wise—"from submission to arbitrary laws," as the anarchists say, and thereby fancy themselves "free", even free-spirited. The singular fact remains, however, that everything of the nature of freedom, elegance, boldness, dance, and masterly certainty, which exists or has existed, whether it be in thought itself, or in administration, or in speaking and persuading, in art just as in conduct, has only developed by means of the tyranny of such arbitrary law; and in all seriousness, it is not at all improbable that precisely this is "nature" and "natural"—and not *laisse-aller*! Every artist knows how different from the state of letting himself go, is his "most natural" condition, the free arranging, locating, disposing, and constructing in the moments of "inspiration"—and how strictly and delicately he then obeys a thousand laws, which, by their very rigidness and precision, defy all formulation by means of ideas (even the most stable idea has, in comparison therewith, something floating, manifold, and ambiguous in it). The essential thing "in heaven and in earth" is, apparently (to repeat it once more), that there should be long *obedience* in the same direction; there thereby results, and has always resulted in the long run, something which has made life worth living; for instance, virtue, art, music, dancing, reason, spirituality—anything whatever that is transfiguring, refined, foolish, or divine. The long bondage of the spirit, the distrustful constraint in the communicability of ideas, the discipline which the thinker imposed on himself to think in accordance with the rules of a church or a court, or conformable to Aristotelian premises, the persistent spiritual will to interpret everything that happened according to a Christian scheme, and in every occurrence to rediscover and justify the Christian God:ᵗ—all this violence, arbitrariness, severity, dreadfulness, and unreasonableness, has proved itself the disciplinary

means whereby the European spirit has attained its strength, its remorseless curiosity and subtle mobility; granted also that much irrecoverable strength and spirit had to be stifled, suffocated, and spoilt in the process (for here, as everywhere, "nature" shows herself as she is, in all her extravagant and *indifferent* magnificence, which is shocking, but nevertheless noble). That for centuries European thinkers only thought in order to prove something—nowadays, on the contrary, we are suspicious of every thinker who "wishes to prove something"—that it was always settled beforehand what was to be the result of their strictest thinking, as it was perhaps in the Asiatic astrology of former times, or as it is still at the present day in the innocent, Christian-moral explanation of immediate personal events "for the glory of God," or "for the good of the soul":—this tyranny, this arbitrariness, this severe and magnificent stupidity, has *educated* the spirit; slavery, both in the coarser and the finer sense, is apparently an indispensable means even of spiritual education and discipline. One may look at every system of morals in this light: it is "nature" therein which teaches to hate the *laisser-aller*, the too great freedom, and implants the need for limited horizons, for immediate duties— it teaches the *narrowing of perspectives*, and thus, in a certain sense, that stupidity is a condition of life and development. "Thou must obey some one, and for a long time; *otherwise* thou wilt come to grief, and lose all respect for thyself"—this seems to me to be the moral imperative of nature, which is certainly neither "categorical," as old Kant wished (consequently the "otherwise"), nor does it address itself to the individual (what does nature care for the individual!), but to nations, races, ages, and ranks, above all, however, to the animal "man" generally, to *mankind*.

189

Industrious races find it a great hardship to be idle: it was a master stroke of *English* instinct to hallow and begloom Sunday to such an extent that the Englishman unconsciously hankers for his week- and work-day again: —as a kind of cleverly devised, cleverly intercalated *fast*, such as is also frequently found in the ancient world (although, as is appropriate in southern nations, not precisely with respect to work). Many kinds of fasts are necessary; and wherever powerful influences and habits prevail, legislators have to see that intercalary days are appointed, on which such impulses are fettered, and learn to hunger anew.

Viewed from a higher standpoint, whole generations and epochs, when they show themselves infected with any moral fanaticism, seem like those intercalated periods of restraint and fasting, during which an impulse learns to humble and submit itself—at the same time also to *purify* and *sharpen* itself; certain philosophical sects likewise admit of a similar interpretation (for instance, the Stoa, in the midst of Hellenic culture, with the atmosphere rank and overcharged with Aphrodisiacal odours).—Here also is a hint for the explanation of the paradox, why it was precisely in the most Christian period of European history, and in general only under the pressure of Christian sentiments, that the sexual impulse sublimated into love (*amour-passion*).

190

There is something in the morality of Plato which does not really belong to Plato, but which only appears in his philosophy, one might say, in spite of him: namely, Socratism, for which he himself was too noble. "No one desires to injure himself, hence all evil is done unwittingly. The evil man inflicts injury on himself; he would not do so, however, if he knew that evil is evil. The evil man, therefore, is only evil through error; if one free him from error one will necessarily make him—good."—This mode of reasoning savours of the *populace*, who perceive only the unpleasant consequences of evil-doing, and practically judge that "it is *stupid* to do wrong"; while they accept "good" as identical with "useful and pleasant," without further thought. As regards every system of utilitarianism, one may at once assume that it has the same origin, and follow the scent: one will seldom err.—Plato did all he could to interpret something refined and noble into the tenets of his teacher, and above all to interpret himself into them—he, the most daring of all interpreters, who lifted the entire Socrates out of the street, as a popular theme and song, to exhibit him in endless and impossible modifications—namely, in all his own disguises and multiplicities. In jest, and in Homeric language as well, what is the Platonic Socrates, if not—

πρόσθε Πλάτων ὄπισθέν τε Πλάτων μέσση τε Χίμαιρα.

191

The old theological problem of "Faith" and "Knowledge," or more plainly, of instinct and reason—the question whether, in respect to the valuation of

things, instinct deserves more authority than rationality, which wants to appreciate and act according to motives, according to a "Why," that is to say, in conformity to purpose and utility—it is always the old moral problem that first appeared in the person of Socrates, and had divided men's minds long before Christianity. Socrates himself, following, of course, the taste of his talent—that of a surpassing dialectician—took first the side of reason; and, in fact, what did he do all his life but laugh at the awkward incapacity of the noble Athenians, who were men of instinct, like all noble men, and could never give satisfactory answers concerning the motives of their actions? In the end, however, though silently and secretly, he laughed also at himself: with his finer conscience and introspection, he found in himself the same difficulty and incapacity. "But why"—he said to himself—"should one on that account separate oneself from the instincts! One must set them right and the reason *also*—one must follow the instincts, but at the same time persuade the reason to support them with good arguments." This was the real *falseness* of that great and mysterious ironist; he brought his conscience up to the point that he was satisfied with a kind of self-outwitting: in fact, he perceived the irrationality in the moral judgment. —Plato, more innocent in such matters, and without the craftiness of the plebeian, wished to prove to himself, at the expenditure of all his strength—the greatest strength a philosopher had ever expended—that reason and instinct lead spontaneously to one goal, to the good, to "God"; and since Plato, all theologians and philosophers have followed the same path—which means that in matters of morality, instinct (or as Christians call it, "Faith," or as I call it, "the herd") has hitherto triumphed. Unless one should make an exception in the case of Descartes, the father of rationalism (and consequently the grandfather of the Revolution), who recognised only the authority of reason: but reason is only a tool, and Descartes was superficial.

192

Whoever has followed the history of a single science, finds in its development a clue to the understanding of the oldest and commonest processes of all "knowledge and cognisance": there, as here, the premature hypotheses, the fictions, the good stupid will to "belief," and the lack of distrust and patience are first developed—our senses learn late, and never learn completely, to be subtle, reliable, and cautious organs of knowledge. Our eyes find it easier on a given occasion to produce a picture already often produced, than to seize upon the divergence and novelty of an impression: the latter requires more force, more "morality." It is difficult and painful for the ear to listen to anything new; we hear strange music badly. When we hear another language spoken, we involuntarily attempt to form the sounds into words with which we are more familiar and conversant—it was thus, for example, that the Germans modified the spoken word *arcubalista* into *armbrust* (crossbow). Our senses are also hostile and averse to the new; and generally, even in the "simplest" processes of sensation, the emotions *dominate*—such as fear, love, hatred, and the passive emotion of indolence.—As little as a reader nowadays reads all the single words (not to speak of syllables) of a page—he rather takes about five out of every twenty words at random, and "guesses" the probably appropriate sense to them—just as little do we see a tree correctly and completely in respect to its leaves, branches, colour, and shape; we find it so much easier to fancy the chance of a tree. Even in the midst of the most remarkable experiences, we still do just the same; we fabricate the greater part of the experience, and can hardly be made to contemplate any event, *except* as "inventors" thereof. All this goes to prove that from our fundamental nature and from remote ages we have been—*accustomed to lying.* Or, to express it more politely and hypocritically, in short, more pleasantly—one is much more of an artist than one is aware of.—In an animated conversation, I often see the face of the person with whom I am speaking so clearly and sharply defined before me, according to the thought he expresses, or which I believe to be evoked in his mind, that the degree of distinctness far exceeds the *strength* of my visual faculty—the delicacy of the play of the muscles and of the expression of the eyes *must* therefore be imagined by me. Probably the person put on quite a different expression, or none at all.

193

Quidquid luce fuit, tenebris agit: but also contrariwise. What we experience in dreams, provided we experience it often, pertains at last just as much to the general belongings of our soul as anything "actually" experienced; by virtue thereof we are richer or poorer, we have a requirement more or less, and finally, in broad daylight, and even in the brightest moments of our waking life, we are ruled to some extent by the nature of our dreams. Supposing that some one has often flown in his dreams, and that at last, as soon as he dreams, he is conscious of the power and art of flying as his privilege and his peculiarly enviable happiness; such a person, who believes that on the slightest impulse, he can actualise all sorts of curves and angles, who knows the sensation of a certain divine levity, an "upwards" without effort or constraint, a "downwards" without descending or lowering—without *trouble!*—how could the man with such dream-experiences and dream-habits fail to find "happiness" differently coloured and defined, even in his waking hours! How could he fail—to long *differently* for happiness? "Flight," such as is described by poets, must, when compared with his own "flying," be far too earthly, muscular, violent, far too "troublesome" for him.

194

The difference among men does not manifest itself only in the difference of their lists of desirable things—in their regarding different good things as worth striving for, and being disagreed as to the greater or less value, the order of rank, of the commonly recognised desirable things:—it manifests itself much more in what they regard as actually *having* and *possessing* a desirable thing. As regards a woman, for instance, the control over her body and her sexual gratification serves as an amply sufficient sign of ownership and possession to the more modest man; another with a more suspicious and ambitious thirst for possession, sees the "questionableness," the mere apparentness of such ownership, and wishes to have finer tests in order to know especially whether the woman not only gives herself to him, but also gives up for his sake what she has or would like to have—only *then* does he look upon her as "possessed." A third, however, has not even here got to the limit of his distrust and his desire for possession: he asks himself whether the woman, when she gives up everything for him, does not perhaps do so for a phantom of him; he wishes first to be thoroughly, indeed, profoundly well known; in order to be loved at all he ventures to let himself be found out. Only then does he feel the beloved one fully in his possession, when she no longer deceives herself about him, when she loves him just as much for the sake of his devilry and concealed insatiability, as for his goodness, patience, and spirituality. One man would like to possess a nation, and he finds all the higher arts of Cagliostro and Catalina suitable for his purpose. Another, with a more refined thirst for possession, says to himself; "One may not deceive where one desires to possess"—he is irritated and impatient at the idea that a mask of him should rule in the hearts of the people: "I must, therefore, *make* myself known, and first of all learn to know myself!" Amongst helpful and charitable people, one almost always finds the awkward craftiness which first gets up suitably him who has to be helped, as though, for instance, he should "merit" help, seek just *their* help, and would show himself deeply grateful, attached, and subservient to them for all help. With these conceits, they take control of the needy as a property, just as in general they are charitable and helpful out of a desire for property. One finds them jealous when they are crossed or forestalled in their charity. Parents involuntarily make something like themselves out of their children—they call that "education"; no mother doubts at the bottom of her heart that the child she has born is thereby her property, no father hesitates about his right to *his own* ideas and notions of worth. Indeed, in former times fathers deemed it right to use their discretion concerning the life or death of the newly born (as amongst the ancient Germans). And like the father, so also do the teacher, the class, the priest, and the prince still see in every new individual an unobjectionable opportunity for a new possession. The consequence is . . .

195

The Jews—a people "born for slavery," as Tacitus and the whole ancient world say of them; "the chosen people among the nations," as they themselves say and believe—the Jews performed the miracle of the inversion of valuations, by means of which life on earth obtained a new and dangerous charm for a couple of millenniums. Their prophets fused into one the expressions "rich," "godless," "wicked," "violent," "sensual," and for the first time coined the word "world" as a term of reproach. In this inversion of valuations (in which is also included the use of the word "poor" as synonymous with "saint" and "friend") the significance of the Jewish people is to be found; it is with *them* that the *slave-insurrection in morals* commences.

196

It is to be *inferred* that there are countless dark bodies near the sun—such as we shall never see. Amongst ourselves, this is an allegory; and the psychologist of morals reads the whole star-writing merely as an allegorical and symbolic language in which much may be unexpressed.

197

The beast of prey and the man of prey (for instance, Cæsar Borgia) are fundamentally misunderstood, "nature" is misunderstood, so long as one seeks a "morbidness" in the constitution of these healthiest of all tropical monsters and growths, or even an innate "hell" in them—as almost all moralists have done hitherto. Does it not seem that there is a hatred of the virgin forest and of the tropics among moralists? And that the "tropical man" must be discredited at all costs, whether as disease and deterioration of mankind, or as his own hell and self-torture? And why? In favour of the "temperate zones"? In favour of the temperate men? The "moral"? The mediocre? —This for the chapter: "Morals as Timidity."

198

All the systems of morals which address themselves with a view to their "happiness," as it is called—what else are they but suggestions for behaviour adapted to the degree of *danger* from themselves in which the individuals live; recipes for their passions, their good and bad propensities, in so far as such have the Will to Power and would like to play the master; small and great expediencies and elaborations, permeated with the musty odour of old family medicines and old-wife wisdom; all of them grotesque and absurd in their form—because they address themselves to "all," because they generalise where generalisation is not authorised; all of them speaking unconditionally, and taking themselves unconditionally; all of them flavoured not merely with one grain of salt, but rather endurable only, and sometimes even seductive, when they are over-spiced and begin to smell dangerously, especially of "the other world." That is all of little value when estimated intellectually, and is far from being "science," much less "wisdom"; but, repeated once more, and three times repeated, it is expediency, expediency, expediency, mixed with stupidity, stupidity, stupidity—whether it be the indifference and statuesque coldness towards the heated folly of the emotions, which the Stoics advised and fostered; or the no-more-laughing and no-more-weeping of Spinoza, the destruction of the emotions by their analysis and vivisection, which he recommended so naïvely; or the lowering of the emotions to an innocent mean at which they may be satisfied, the Aristotelianism of morals; or even morality as the enjoyment of the emotions in a voluntary attenuation and spiritualisation by the symbolism of art, perhaps as music, or as love of God, and of mankind for God's sake—for in religion the passions are once more enfranchised, provided that . . . ; or, finally, even the complaisant and wanton surrender to the emotions, as has been taught by Hafis and Goethe, the bold letting-go of the reins, the spiritual and corporeal *licentia morum* in the exceptional cases of wise old codgers and drunkards, with whom it "no longer has much danger." —This also for the chapter: "Morals as Timidity."

199

Inasmuch as in all ages, as long as mankind has existed, there have also been human herds (family alliances, communities, tribes, peoples, states, churches), and always a great number who obey in proportion to the small number who command—in view, therefore, of the fact that obedience has been most practised and fostered among mankind hitherto, one may reasonably suppose that, generally speaking, the need thereof is now innate in every one, as a kind of *formal conscience* which gives the command: "Thou shalt unconditionally do something, unconditionally refrain from something"; in short, "Thou shalt." This need tries to satisfy itself and to fill its form with a content; according to its strength, impatience, and eagerness, it at once seizes as an omnivorous appetite with little selection, and accepts whatever is shouted into its ear by all sorts of commanders—parents, teachers, laws, class prejudices, or public opinion. The extraordinary limitation of human development, the hesitation, protractedness, frequent retrogression, and turning thereof, is attributable to the fact that the herd-instinct of obedience is transmitted best, and at the cost of the art of command. If one imagine this instinct increasing to its greatest extent, commanders and independent individuals will finally be lacking altogether; or they will suffer inwardly from a bad conscience, and will have to impose a deception on themselves in the first place in order to be able to command: just as if they also were only obeying. This condition of things actually exists in Europe at present—I call it the moral hypocrisy of the commanding class. They know no other way of protecting themselves from their bad conscience than by playing the role of executors of older and higher orders (of predecessors, of the constitution, of justice, of the law, or of God himself), or they even justify themselves by maxims from the current opinions of the herd, as "first servants of their people," or "instruments of the public weal." On the other hand, the gregarious European man nowadays assumes an air as if he were the only kind of man that is allowable; he glorifies his qualities, such as public spirit, kindness, deference, industry, temperance, modesty, indulgence, sympathy, by virtue of which he is gentle, endurable, and useful to the herd, as the peculiarly human virtues. In cases, however, where it is believed that the leader and bell-wether cannot be dispensed with, attempt after attempt is made nowadays to replace commanders by the summing together of clever gregarious men: all representative constitutions, for example, are of this origin. In spite of all, what a blessing, what a deliverance from a weight becoming unendurable, is the appearance of an absolute ruler for these gregarious Europeans—of this fact the effect of the appearance of Napoleon was the last great proof: the history of the influence of Napoleon is almost the history of the higher happiness to which the entire century has attained in its worthiest individuals and periods.

200

The man of an age of dissolution which mixes the races with one another, who has the inheritance of a diversified descent in his body—that is to say, contrary, and often not only contrary, instincts and standards of value, which struggle with one another and are seldom at peace—such a man of late culture and broken lights, will, on an average, be a weak man. His fundamental desire is that the war which is *in him* should come to an end; happiness appears to him in the character of a soothing medicine and mode of thought (for instance, Epicurean or Christian); it is above all things the happiness of repose, of undisturbedness, of repletion, of final unity—it is the "Sabbath of Sabbaths," to use the expression of the holy rhetorician, St. Augustine, who was himself such a man.—Should, however, the contrariety and conflict in such natures operate as an *additional* incentive and stimulus to life—and if, on the other hand, in addition to their powerful and irreconcilable instincts, they have also inherited and indoctrinated into them a proper mastery and subtlety for carrying on the conflict with themselves (that is to say, the faculty of self-control and self-deception), there then arise those marvellously incomprehensible, and inexplicable beings, those enigmatical men, predestined for conquering and circumventing others, the finest examples of which are Alcibiades and Cæsar (with whom I should like to associate the *first* of Europeans according to my taste, the Hohenstaufen, Frederick the Second), and amongst artists, perhaps Lionardo da Vinci. They appear precisely in the same periods when that weaker type, with its longing for repose, comes to the front; the two types are complementary to each other, and spring from the same causes.

201

As long as the utility which determines moral estimates is only gregarious utility, as long as the preservation of the community is only kept in view, and the immoral is sought precisely and exclusively in what seems dangerous to the maintenance of the community, there can be no "morality of love to one's neighbour." Granted even that there is already a little constant exercise of consideration, sympathy, fairness, gentleness, and mutual assistance, granted that even in this condition of society all those instincts are already active which are latterly distinguished by honourable names as "virtues," and eventually almost coincide with the conception "morality": in that period they do not as yet belong to the domain of moral valuations—they are still ultra-moral. A sympathetic action, for instance, is neither called good nor bad, moral nor immoral, in the best period of the Romans; and should it be praised, a sort of resentful disdain is compatible with this praise, even at the best, directly the sympathetic action is compared with one which contributes to the welfare of the whole, to the *res publica*. After all, "love to our neighbour" is always a secondary matter, partly conventional and arbitrarily manifested in relation to our *fear of our neighbour*. After the fabric of society seems on the whole established and secured against external dangers, it is this fear of our neighbour which again creates new perspectives of moral valuation. Certain strong and dangerous instincts, such as the love of enterprise, foolhardiness, revengefulness, astuteness, rapacity, and love of power, which up till then had not only to be honoured from

the point of view of general utility—under other names, of course, than those here given—but had to be fostered and cultivated (because they were perpetually required in the common danger against the common enemies), are now felt in their dangerousness to be doubly strong—when the outlets for them are lacking—and are gradually branded as immoral and given over to calumny. The contrary instincts and inclinations now attain to moral honour; the gregarious instinct gradually draws its conclusions. How much or how little dangerousness to the community or to equality is contained in an opinion, a condition, an emotion, a disposition, or an endowment—that is now the moral perspective; here again fear is the mother of morals. It is by the loftiest and strongest instincts, when they break out passionately and carry the individual far above and beyond the average, and the low level of the gregarious conscience, that the self-reliance of the community is destroyed; its belief in itself, its backbone, as it were, breaks; consequently these very instincts will be most branded and defamed. The lofty independent spirituality, the will to stand alone, and even the cogent reason, are felt to be dangers; everything that elevates the individual above the herd, and is a source of fear to the neighbour, is henceforth called *evil*; the tolerant, unassuming, self-adapting, self-equalising disposition, the *mediocrity* of desires, attains to moral distinction and honour. Finally, under very peaceful circumstances, there is always less opportunity and necessity for training the feelings to severity and rigour; and now every form of severity, even in justice, begins to disturb the conscience; a lofty and rigourous nobleness and self-responsibility almost offends, and awakens distrust, "the lamb," and still more "the sheep," wins respect. There is a point of diseased mellowness and effeminacy in the history of society, at which society itself takes the part of him who injures it, the part of the *criminal*, and does so, in fact, seriously and honestly. To punish, appears to it to be somehow unfair—it is certain that the idea of "punishment" and "the obligation to punish" are then painful and alarming to people. "Is it not sufficient if the criminal be rendered *harmless*? Why should we still punish? Punishment itself is terrible!"—with these questions gregarious morality, the morality of fear, draws its ultimate conclusion. If one could at all do away with danger, the cause of fear, one would have done away with this morality at the same time, it would no longer be necessary, it *would not consider itself* any longer necessary!—Whoever examines the conscience of the present-day European, will always elicit the same imperative from its thousand moral folds and hidden recesses, the imperative of the timidity of the herd: "we wish that some time or other there may be *nothing more to fear*!" Some time or other—the will and the way *thereto* is nowadays called "progress" all over Europe.

202 ·

Let us at once say again what we have already said a hundred times, for people's ears nowadays are unwilling to hear such truths—*our* truths. We know well enough how offensively it sounds when any one plainly, and without metaphor, counts man amongst the animals; but it will be accounted to us almost a *crime*, that it is precisely in respect to men of "modern ideas" that we have constantly applied the terms "herd," "herd-instincts," and such like expressions. What avail is it? We cannot do otherwise, for it is precisely here that our new insight is. We have found that in all the principal moral judgments Europe has become unanimous, including likewise the countries where European influence prevails: in Europe people evidently *know* what Socrates thought he did not know, and what the famous serpent of old once promised to teach—they "know" to-day what is good and evil. It must then sound hard and be distasteful to the ear, when we always insist that that which here thinks it knows, that which here glorifies itself with praise and blame, and calls itself good, is the instinct of the herding human animal: the instinct which has come and is ever coming more and more to the front, to preponderance and supremacy over other instincts, according to the increasing physiological approximation and resemblance of which it is the symptom. *Morality in Europe at present is herding-animal morality*; and therefore, as we understand the matter, only one kind of human morality, beside which, before which, and after which many other moralities, and above all *higher* moralities, are or should be possible. Against such a "possibility," against such a "should be," however, this morality defends itself with all its strength; it says obstinately and inexorably: "I am morality itself and nothing else is morality!" Indeed, with the help of a religion which has humoured and flattered the sublimest desires of the herding-animal, things have reached such a point that we always find a more visible expression of this morality even in political and social arrangements: the *democratic* movement is the inheritance of the Christian movement. That its *tempo*, however, is much too slow and sleepy for the more impatient ones, for those who are sick and distracted by the herding-instinct, is indicated by the increasingly furious howling, and always less disguised teeth-gnashing of the anarchist dogs, who are now roving through the highways of European culture. Apparently in opposition to the peacefully industrious democrats and Revolution-ideologues, and still more so to the awkward philosophasters and fraternity-visionaries who call themselves Socialists and want a "free society," those are really at one with them all in their thorough and instinctive hostility to every form of society other than that of the *autonomous* herd (to the extent even of repudiating the notions "master" and "servant"—*ni dieu ni maître*, says a socialist formula); at one in their tenacious opposition to every special claim, every special right and privilege (this means ultimately opposition to *every* right, for when all are equal, no one needs "rights" any longer); at one in their distrust of punitive justice (as though it were a violation of the weak, unfair to the *necessary* consequences of all former society); but equally at one in their religion of sympathy, in their compassion for all that feels, lives, and suffers (down to the very animals, up even to "God"—the extravagance of "sympathy for God" belongs to a democratic age); altogether at one in the cry and impatience of their sympathy, in their deadly hatred of suffering generally, in their almost feminine incapacity for witnessing it or *allowing* it; at one in their involuntary beglooming and heart-softening, under the spell of which Europe seems to be threatened with a new Buddhism; at one in their belief in the morality of *mutual* sympathy, as though it were morality in itself, the climax, the *attained* climax of mankind, the sole hope of the future, the consolation of the present, the great discharge from all the obligations of the past; altogether at one in their belief in the community as the *deliverer*, in the herd, and therefore in "themselves."

203 ·

We, who hold a different belief—we, who regard the democratic movement, not only as a degenerating form of political organisation, but as equivalent to a degenerating, a waning type of man, as involving his mediocrising and depreciation: where have *we* to fix our hopes? In *new philosophers*—there is no other alternative: in minds strong and original enough to initiate opposite estimates of value, to transvalue and invert "eternal valuations"; in forerunners, in men of the future, who in the present shall fix the constraints and fasten the knots which will compel millenniums to take *new* paths. To teach man the future of humanity as his *will*, as depending on human will, and to make preparation for vast hazardous enterprises and collective attempts in rearing and educating, in order thereby to put an end to the frightful rule of folly and chance which has hitherto gone by the name of "history" (the folly of the "greatest number" is only its last form)—for that purpose a new type of philosophers and commanders will some time or other be needed, at the very idea of which everything that has existed in the way of occult, terrible, and benevolent beings might look pale and dwarfed. The image of such leaders hovers before *our* eyes: —is it lawful for me to say it aloud, ye free spirits? The conditions which one would partly have to create and partly utilise for their genesis; the presumptive methods and tests by virtue of which a soul should grow up to such an elevation and power as to feel a *constraint* to these tasks; a transvaluation of values, under the new pressure and hammer of which a conscience should be steeled and a heart transformed into brass, so as to bear the weight of such responsibility; and on the other hand the necessity for such leaders, the dreadful danger that they might be lacking, or miscarry and degenerate: —these are *our* real anxieties and glooms, ye know it well, ye free spirits! these are the heavy distant thoughts and storms which sweep across the heaven of *our* life. There are few pains so grievous as to have seen, divined, or experienced how an exceptional man has missed his way and deteriorated; but he who has the rare eye for the universal danger of "man" himself *deteriorating*, he who like us has recognised the extraordinary fortuitousness which has hitherto played its game in respect to the future of mankind—a game in which neither the hand, nor even a "finger of God" has participated! —he who divines the fate that is hidden under the idiotic unwariness and blind confidence of "modern ideas," and still more under the whole of Christo-European morality—suffers from an anguish with which no other is to be compared. He sees at a glance all that could still *be made out of man* through a favourable accumulation and augmentation of human powers and arrangements; he knows with all the knowledge of his conviction how unexhausted man still is for the greatest possibilities, and how often in the past the type man has stood in presence of mysterious decisions and new paths:—he knows still better from his painfulest recollections on what wretched obstacles promising developments of the highest rank have hitherto usually gone to pieces, broken down, sunk, and become contemptible. The *universal degeneracy of mankind* to the level of the "man of the future"—as idealised by the socialistic fools and shallow-pates—this degeneracy and dwarfing of man to an absolutely gregarious animal (or as they call it, to a man of "free society"), this brutalising of man into a pigmy with equal rights and claims, is undoubtedly *possible*! He who has thought out this possibility to its ultimate conclusion knows *another* loathing unknown to the rest of mankind—and perhaps also a new *mission*!

. . .

Chapter VII Our Virtues

214 •

Our Virtues? —It is probable that we, too, have still our virtues, although naturally they are not those sincere and massive virtues on account of which we hold our grandfathers in esteem and also at a little distance from us. We Europeans of the day after to-morrow, we firstlings of the twentieth century—with all our dangerous curiosity, our multifariousness and art of disguising, our mellow and seemingly sweetened cruelty in sense and spirit—we shall presumably, *if* we must have virtues, have those only which have come to agreement with our most secret and heartfelt inclinations, with our most ardent requirements: well, then, let us look for them in our labyrinths!—where, as we know, so many things lose themselves, so many things get quite lost! And is there anything finer than to *search* for one's own virtues? Is it not almost to *believe* in one's own virtues? But this "believing in one's own virtues"—is it not practically the same as what was formerly called one's "good conscience," that long, respectable pigtail of an idea, which our grandfathers used to hang behind their heads, and often enough also behind their understandings? It seems, therefore, that however little we may imagine ourselves to be old-fashioned and grandfatherly respectable in other respects, in one thing we are nevertheless the worthy grandchildren of our grandfathers, we last Europeans with good consciences: we also still wear their pigtail.—Ah! if you only knew how soon, so very soon—it will be different!

215

As in the stellar firmament there are sometimes two suns which determine the path of one planet, and in certain cases suns of different colours shine around a single planet, now with red light, now with green, and then simultaneously illumine and flood it with motley colours: so we modern men, owing to the complicated mechanism of our "firmament," are determined by *different* moralities; cur actions shine alternately in different colours, and are seldom unequivocal—and there are often cases, also, in which our actions are *motley-coloured*.

216 .

To love one's enemies? I think that has been well learnt: it takes place thousands of times at present on a large and small scale; indeed, at times the higher and sublimer thing takes place:—we learn to *despise* when we love, and precisely when we love best; all of it, however, unconsciously, without noise, without ostentation, with the shame and secrecy of goodness, which forbids the utterance of the pompous word and the formula of virtue. Morality as attitude—is opposed to our taste nowadays. This is also an advance, as it was an advance in our fathers that religion as an attitude finally became opposed to their taste, including the enmity and Voltairean bitterness against religion (and all that formerly belonged to freethinker-pantomime). It is the music in our conscience, the dance in our spirit, to which Puritan litanies, moral sermons, and goody goodness won't chime.

217

Let us be careful in dealing with those who attach great importance to being credited with moral tact and subtlety in moral discernment! They never forgive us if they have once made a mistake *before* us (or even with *regard to* us)—they inevitably become our instinctive calumniators and detractors, even when they still remain our "friends." —Blessed are the forgetful: for they "get the better" even of their blunders.

218

The psychologists of France—and where else are there still psychologists nowadays?—have never yet exhausted their bitter and manifold enjoyment of the *betise bourgeoise*, just as though . . . in short, they betray something thereby. Flaubert, for instance, the honest citizen of Rouen, neither saw, heard, nor tasted anything else in the end; it was his mode of self-torment and refined cruelty. As this is growing wearisome, I would now recommend for a change something else for a pleasure—namely, the unconscious astuteness with which good, fat, honest mediocrity always behaves towards loftier spirits and the tasks they have to perform, the subtle, barbed, Jesuitical astuteness, which is a thousand times subtler than the taste and understanding of the middle-class in its best moments—subtler even than the understanding of its victims: —a repeated proof that "instinct" is the most intelligent of all kinds of intelligence which have hitherto been discovered. In short, you psychologists, study the philosophy of the "rule" in its struggle with the "exception": there you have a spectacle fit for Gods and godlike malignity! Or, in plainer words, practise vivisection on "good people," on the *"homo bonae voluntatis,"* . . . on *yourselves*!

219 .

The practice of judging and condemning morally, is the favourite revenge of the intellectually shallow on those who are less so; it is also a kind of indemnity for their being badly endowed by nature; and finally, it is an opportunity for acquiring spirit and *becoming* subtle:—malice spiritualises. They are glad in their inmost heart that there is a standard according to which those who are over-endowed with intellectual goods and privileges, are equal to them; they contend for the "equality of all before God," and almost *need* the belief in God for this purpose. It is among them that the most powerful antagonists of atheism are found. If any one were to say to them: "a lofty spirituality is beyond all comparison with the honesty and respectability of a merely moral man"—it would make them furious; I shall take care not to say so. I would rather flatter them with my theory that lofty spirituality itself exists only as the ultimate product of moral qualities; that it is a synthesis of all qualities attributed to the "merely moral" man, after they have been acquired singly through long training and practice, perhaps during a whole series of generations; that lofty spirituality is precisely the spiritualising of justice, and the beneficent severity which knows that it is authorised to maintain *gradations of rank* in the world, even among things—and not only among men.

220

Now that the praise of the "disinterested person" is so popular one must—probably not without some danger—get an idea of *what* people actually take an interest in, and what are the things generally which fundamentally and profoundly concern ordinary men—including the cultured, even the learned, and perhaps philosophers also, if appearances do not deceive. The fact thereby becomes obvious that the greater part of what interests and charms higher natures, and more refined and fastidious tastes, seems absolutely "uninteresting" to the average man:—if, notwithstanding, he perceive devotion to these interests, he calls it *désintéressé*, and wonders how it is possible to act "disinterestedly." There have been philosophers who could give this popular astonishment a seductive and mystical, other-world expression (perhaps because they did not know the higher nature by experience?), instead of stating the naked and candidly reasonable truth that "disinterested" action is very interesting and "interested" action, provided that . . . "And love?"—What! Even an action for love's sake shall be "unegoistic"? But you fools—! "And the praise of the self-sacrificer?" —But whoever has really offered sacrifice knows that he wanted and obtained something for it—perhaps something from himself for something from himself; that he relinquished here in order to have more there, perhaps in general to be more, or even feel himself "more". But this is a realm of questions and answers in which a more fastidious spirit does not like to stay: for here truth has to stifle her yawns so much when she is obliged to answer. And after all, truth is a woman; one must not use force with her.

221

"It sometimes happens," said a moralistic pedant and trifle-retailer, "that I honour and respect an unselfish man: not, however, because he is unselfish, but because I think he has a right to be useful to another man at his own expense. In short, the question is always who *he* is, and who *the other* is. For instance, in a person created and destined for command, self-denial and modest retirement, instead of being virtues would be the waste of virtues: so it seems to me. Every system of unegoistic morality which takes itself unconditionally and appeals to every one, not only sins against good taste, but is also an incentive to sins of omission, an *ad-*

ditional seduction under the mask of philanthropy—and precisely a seduction and injury to the higher, rarer, and more privileged types of men. Moral systems must be compelled first of all to bow before the *gradations of rank*; their presumption must be driven home to their conscience—until they thoroughly understand at last that it is *immoral* to say that "what is right for one is proper for another."—So said my moralistic pedant and *bonhomme*. Did he perhaps deserve to be laughed at when he thus exhorted systems of morals to practise morality? But one should not be too much in the right if one wishes to have the laughers on *one's own* side; a grain of wrong pertains even to good taste.

222

Wherever sympathy (fellow-suffering) is preached nowadays—and, if I gather rightly, no other religion is any longer preached—let the psychologist have his ears open through all the vanity, through all the noise which is natural to these preachers (as to all preachers), he will hear a hoarse, groaning, genuine note of *self-contempt*. It belongs to the overshadowing and uglifying of Europe, which has been on the increase for a century (the first symptoms of which are already specified documentarily in a thoughtful letter of Galiani to Madame d'Epinay)—*if it is not really the cause thereof*! The man of "modern ideas," the conceited ape, is excessively dissatisfied with himself—this is perfectly certain. He suffers, and his vanity wants him only "to suffer with his fellows."

223

The hybrid European—a tolerably ugly plebeian, taken all in all—absolutely requires a costume: he needs history as a storeroom of costumes. To be sure, he notices that none of the costumes fit him properly—he changes and changes. Let us look at the nineteenth century with respect to these hasty preferences and changes in its masquerades of style, and also with respect to its moments of desperation on account of "nothing suiting" us. It is in vain to get ourselves up as romantic, or classical, or Christian, or Florentine, or *barocco*, or "national," *in moribus et artibus*: it does not "clothe us"! But the "spirit," especially the "historical spirit," profits even by this desperation: once and again a new sample of the past or of the foreign is tested, put on, taken off, packed up, and above all *studied*—we are the first studious age *in puncto* of "costumes," I mean as concerns morals, articles of belief, artistic tastes, and religions; we are prepared as no other age has ever been for a carnival in the grand style, for the most spiritual festival-laughter and arrogance, for the transcendental height of supreme folly and Aristophanic ridicule of the world. Perhaps we are still discovering the domain of our *invention* just here, the domain where even we can still be original, probably as parodists of the world's history and as God's Merry-Andrews,—perhaps, though nothing else of the present have a future, our *laughter* itself may have a future!

224

The *historical sense* (or the capacity for divining quickly the order of rank of the valuations according to which a people, a community, or an individual has lived, the "divining instinct" for the relationships of these valuations, for the relation of the authority of the valuations to the authority of the operating forces),—this historical sense, which we Europeans claim as our specialty, has come to us in the train of the enchanting and mad *semi-barbarity* into which Europe has been plunged by the democratic mingling of classes and races—it is only the nineteenth century that has recognised this faculty as its sixth sense. Owing to this mingling the past of every form and mode of life, and of cultures which were formerly closely contiguous and superimposed on one another, flows forth into us "modern souls"; our instincts now run back in all directions, we ourselves are a kind of chaos: in the end, as we have said, the spirit perceives its advantage therein. By means of our semi-barbarity in body and in desire, we have secret access everywhere, such as a noble age never had; we have access above all to the labyrinth of imperfect civilisations, and to every form of semi-barbarity that has at any time existed on earth; and so far as the most considerable part of human civilisation hitherto has just been semi-barbarity, the "historical sense" implies almost the sense and instinct for everything, the taste and tongue for everything: whereby it immediately proves itself to be an *ignoble* sense. For instance, we enjoy Homer once more: it is perhaps our happiest acquisition that we know how to appreciate Homer, whom men of distinguished culture (as the French of the seventeenth century, like Saint-Evremond, who reproached him for his *esprit vaste*, and even Voltaire, the last echo of the century) cannot

and could not so easily appropriate—whom they scarcely permitted themselves to enjoy. The very decided Yea and Nay of their palate, their promptly ready disgust, their hesitating reluctance with regard to everything strange, their horror of the bad taste even of lively curiosity, and in general the averseness of every distinguished and self-sufficing culture to avow a new desire, a dissatisfaction with its own condition, or an admiration of what is strange: all this determines and disposes them unfavourably even towards the best things of the world which are not their property or *could not* become their prey—and no faculty is more unintelligible to such men than just this historical sense, with its truckling, plebeian curiosity. The case is not different with Shakespeare, that marvellous Spanish-Moorish-Saxon synthesis of taste, over whom an ancient Athenian of the circle of Æschylus would have half-killed himself with laughter or irritation: but we—accept precisely this wild motleyness, this medley of the most delicate, the most coarse, and the most artificial, with a secret confidence and cordiality; we enjoy it as a refinement of art reserved expressly for us, and allow ourselves to be as little disturbed by the repulsive fumes and the proximity of the English populace in which Shakespeare's art and taste lives, as perhaps on the Chiaja of Naples, where, with all our senses awake, we go our way enchanted and voluntarily, in spite of the drain-odour of the lower quarters of the town. That as men of the "historical sense" we have our virtues, is not to be disputed:—we are unpretentious, unselfish, modest, brave, habituated to self-control and self-renunciation, very grateful, very patient, very complaisant—but with all this we are perhaps not very "tasteful" Let us finally confess it, that what is most difficult for us men of the "historical sense" to grasp, feel, taste, and love, what finds us fundamentally prejudiced and almost hostile, is precisely the perfection and ultimate maturity in every culture and art, the essentially noble in works and men, their moment of smooth sea and halcyon self-sufficiency, the goldenness and coldness which all things show that have perfected themselves. Perhaps our great virtue of the historical sense is in necessary contrast to *good* taste, at least to the very bad taste; and we can only evoke in ourselves imperfectly, hesitatingly, and with compulsion the small, short, and happy godsends and glorifications of human life as they shine here and there: those moments and marvellous experiences when a great power has voluntarily come to a halt before the boundless and infinite,—when a superabundance of refined delight has been enjoyed by a sudden checking and petrifying, by standing firmly and planting oneself fixedly on still trembling ground. *Proportionateness* is strange to us, let us confess it to ourselves; our itching is really the itching for the infinite, the immeasurable. Like the rider on his forward panting horse, we let the reins fall before the infinite, we modern men, we semi-barbarians—and are only in *our* highest bliss when we—*are in most danger*.

225

Whether it be hedonism, pessimism, utilitarianism, or eudæmonism, all those modes of thinking which measure the worth of things according to *pleasure* and *pain,* that is, according to accompanying circumstances and secondary considerations, are plausible modes of thought and naïvetés, which every one conscious of *creative* powers and an artist's conscience will look down upon with scorn, though not without sympathy. Sympathy for *you!*—to be sure, that is not sympathy as you understand it: it is not sympathy for social "distress," for "society" with its sick and misfortuned, for the hereditarily vicious and defective who lie on the ground around us; still less is it sympathy for the grumbling, vexed, revolutionary slave-classes who strive after power—they call it "freedom." *Our* sympathy is a loftier and further-sighted sympathy:—we see how *man* dwarfs himself, how *you* dwarf him! and there are moments when we view *your* sympathy with an indescribable anguish, when we resist it,—when we regard your seriousness as more dangerous than any kind of levity. You want, if possible—and there is not a more foolish "if possible"—*to do away with suffering;* and we?—it really seems that *we* would rather have it increased and made worse than it has ever been! Well-being, as you understand it—is certainly not a goal; it seems to us an *end;* a condition which at once renders man ludicrous and contemptible—and makes his destruction *desirable!* The discipline of suffering, of *great* suffering—know ye not that it is only *this* discipline that has produced all the elevations of humanity hitherto? The tension of soul in misfortune which communicates to it its energy, its shuddering in view of rack and ruin, its inventiveness and bravery in undergoing, enduring, interpreting, and exploiting misfortune, and whatever depth, mystery, disguise, spirit, artifice, or greatness has been bestowed upon the soul—has it not been bestowed

through suffering, through the discipline of great suffering? In man *creature* and *creator* are united: in man there is not only matter, shred, excess, clay, mire, folly, chaos; but there is also the creator, the sculptor, the hardness of the hammer, the divinity of the spectator, and the seventh day—do ye understand this contrast? And that *your* sympathy for the "creature in man" applies to that which has to be fashioned, bruised, forged, stretched, roasted, annealed, refined—to that which must necessarily *suffer,* and *is meant* to suffer? And *our* sympathy—do ye not understand what our *reverse* sympathy applies to, when it resists your sympathy as the worst of all pampering and enervation?—So it is sympathy *against* sympathy!—But to repeat it once more, there are higher problems than the problems of pleasure and pain and sympathy; and all systems of philosophy which deal only with these are naïvetés.

226 ·

We Immoralists.—This world with which *we* are concerned, in which *we* have to fear and love, this almost invisible, inaudible world of delicate command and delicate obedience, a world of "almost" in every respect, captious, insidious, sharp, and tender—yes, it is well protected from clumsy spectators and familiar curiosity! We are woven into a strong net and garment of duties, and *cannot* disengage ourselves—precisely here, we are "men of duty," even we! Occasionally it is true we dance in our "chains" and betwixt our "swords"; it is none the less true that more often we gnash our teeth under the circumstances, and are impatient at the secret hardship of our lot. But do what we will, fools and appearances say of us: "these are men *without* duty,"—we have always fools and appearances against us!

227

Honesty, granting that it is the virtue from which we cannot rid ourselves, we free spirits—well, we will labour at it with all our perversity and love, and not tire of "perfecting" ourselves in *our* virtue, which alone remains: may its glance some day overspread like a gilded, blue, mocking twilight this aging civilisation with its dull gloomy seriousness! And if, nevertheless, our honesty should one day grow weary, and sigh, and stretch its limbs, and find us too hard, and would fain have it pleasanter, easier, and gentler, like an agreeable vice, let us remain *hard,* we latest Stoics, and let us send to its help whatever devilry we have in us:—our disgust at the clumsy and undefined, our *"nitimur in vetitum,"* our love of adventure, our sharpened and fastidious curiosity, our most subtle, disguised, intellectual Will to Power and universal conquest, which rambles and roves avidiously around all the realms of the future—let us go with all our "devils" to the help of our "God"! It is probable that people will misunderstand and mistake us on that account: what does it matter! They will say: "Their 'honesty'—that is their devilry, and nothing else!" What does it matter! And even if they were right—have not all Gods hitherto been such sanctified, re-baptized devils? And after all, what do we know of ourselves? And what the spirit that leads us wants *to be called?* (It is a question of names.) And how many spirits we harbour? Our honesty, we free spirits—let us be careful lest it become our vanity, our ornament and ostentation, our limitation, our stupidity! Every virtue inclines to stupidity, every stupidity to virtue; "stupid to the point of sanctity," they say in Russia,—let us be careful lest out of pure honesty we do not eventually become saints and bores! Is not life a hundred times too short for us—to bore ourselves? One would have to believe in eternal life in order to. . ..

228.

I hope to be forgiven for discovering that all moral philosophy hitherto has been tedious and has belonged to the soporific appliances—and that "virtue," in my opinion, has been *more* injured by the *tediousness* of its advocates than by anything else; at the same time, however, I would not wish to overlook their general usefulness. It is desirable that as few people as possible should reflect upon morals, and consequently it is *very* desirable that morals should not some day become interesting! But let us not be afraid! Things still remain to-day as they have always been: I see no one in Europe who has (or *discloses*) an idea of the fact that philosophising concerning morals might be conducted in a dangerous, captious, and ensnaring manner—that *calamity* might be involved therein. Observe, for example, the indefatigable, inevitable English utilitarians: how ponderously and respectably they stalk on, stalk along (a Homeric metaphor expresses it better) in the footsteps of Bentham, just as he had already

stalked in the footsteps of the respectable Helvétius! (no, he was not a dangerous man, Helvétius, *ce sénateur Pococurante,* to use an expression of Galiani). No new thought, nothing of the nature of a finer turning or better expression of an old thought, not even a proper history of what has been previously thought on the subject: an *impossible* literature, taking it all in all, unless one knows how to leaven it with some mischief. In effect, the old English vice called *cant,* which is *moral Tartuffism,* has insinuated itself also into these moralists (whom one must certainly read with an eye to their motives if one *must* read them), concealed this time under the new form of the scientific spirit; moreover, there is not absent from them a secret struggle with the pangs of conscience, from which a race of former Puritans must naturally suffer, in all their scientific tinkering with morals. (Is not a moralist the opposite of a Puritan? That is to say, as a thinker who regards morality as questionable, as worthy of interrogation, in short, as a problem? Is moralising not—immoral?) In the end, they all want *English* morality to be recognised as authoritative, inasmuch as mankind, or the "general utility," or "the happiness of the greatest number," —no! the happiness of *England,* will be best served thereby. They would like, by all means, to convince themselves that the striving after *English* happiness, I mean after *comfort* and *fashion* (and in the highest instance, a seat in Parliament), is at the same time the true path of virtue; in fact, that in so far as there has been virtue in the world hitherto, it has just consisted in such striving. Not one of those ponderous, conscience-stricken herding-animals (who undertake to advocate the cause of egoism as conducive to the general welfare) wants to have any knowledge or inkling of the facts that the "general welfare" is no ideal, no goal, no notion that can be at all grasped, but is only a nostrum,—that what is fair to one *may not* at all be fair to another, that the requirement of one morality for all is really a detriment to higher men, in short, that there is a *distinction of rank* between man and man, and consequently between morality and morality. They are an unassuming and fundamentally mediocre species of men, these utilitarian Englishmen, and, as already remarked, in so far as they are tedious, one cannot think highly enough of their utility. One ought even to *encourage* them, as has been partially attempted in the following rhymes:—

Hail, ye worthies, barrow-wheeling,
"Longer—better," aye revealing,
    Stiffer aye in head and knee;
Unenraptured, never jesting,
Mediocre everlasting,
    Sans genie et sans esprit!

229

In these later ages, which may be proud of their humanity, there still remains so much fear, so much *superstition* of the fear, of the "cruel wild beast," the mastering of which constitutes the very pride of these humaner ages—that even obvious truths, as if by the agreement of centuries, have long remained unuttered, because they have the appearance of helping the finally slain wild beast back to life again. I perhaps risk something when I allow such a truth to escape; let others capture it again and give it so much "milk of pious sentiment"* to drink, that it will lie down quiet and forgotten, in its old corner.—One ought to learn anew about cruelty, and open one's eyes; one ought at last to learn impatience, in order that such immodest gross errors—as, for instance, have been fostered by ancient and modern philosophers with regard to tragedy—may no longer wander about virtuously and boldly. Almost everything that we call "higher culture" is based upon the spiritualising and intensifying of *cruelty*—this is my thesis; the "wild beast" has not been slain at all, it lives, it flourishes, it has only been—transfigured. That which constitutes the painful delight of tragedy is cruelty; that which operates agreeably in so-called tragic sympathy, and at the basis even of everything sublime, up to the highest and most delicate thrills of metaphysics, obtains its sweetness solely from the intermingled ingredient of cruelty. What the Roman enjoys in the arena, the Christian in the ecstasies of the cross, the Spaniard at the sight of the faggot and stake, or of the bull-fight, the present-day Japanese who presses his way to the tragedy, the workman of the Parisian suburbs who has a homesickness for bloody revolutions, the Wagnerienne who, with unhinged will, "undergoes" the performance of "Tristan and Isolde"—what all these enjoy, and strive with mysterious ardour to drink in, is the philtre of the great Circe "cruelty." Here, to be sure, we must put aside entirely the blun-

dering psychology of former times, which could only teach with regard to cruelty that it originated at the sight of the suffering of *others*: there is an abundant, superabundant enjoyment even in one's own suffering, in causing one's own suffering—and wherever man has allowed himself to be persuaded to self-denial in the *religious* sense, or to self-mutilation, as among the Phoenicians and ascetics, or in general, to desensualisation, decarnalisation, and contrition, to Puritanical repentance-spasms, to vivisection of conscience and to Pascal-like *sacrifizia dell' intelleto,* he is secretly allured and impelled forwards by his cruelty, by the dangerous thrill of cruelty *towards himself.*— Finally, let us consider that even the seeker of knowledge operates as an artist and glorifier of cruelty, in that he compels his spirit to perceive *against* its own inclination, and often enough against the wishes of his heart:—he forces it to say Nay, where he would like to affirm, love, and adore; indeed, every instance of taking a thing profoundly and fundamentally, is a violation, an intentional injuring of the fundamental will of the spirit, which instinctively aims at appearance and superficiality,—even in every desire for knowledge there is a drop of cruelty.

230 ·

Perhaps what I have said here about a "fundamental will of the spirit" may not be understood without further details; I may be allowed a word of explanation.— That imperious something which is popularly called "the spirit," wishes to be master internally and externally, and to feel itself master; it has the will of a multiplicity for a simplicity, a binding, taming, imperious, and essentially ruling will. Its requirements and capacities here, are the same as those assigned by physiologists to everything that lives, grows, and multiplies. The power of the spirit to appropriate foreign elements reveals itself in a strong tendency to assimilate the new to the old, to simplify the manifold, to overlook or repudiate the absolutely contradictory; just as it arbitrarily re-underlines, makes prominent, and falsifies for itself certain traits and lines in the foreign elements, in every portion of the "outside world." Its object thereby is the incorporation of new "experiences," the assortment of new things in the old arrangements—in short, growth; or more properly, the *feeling* of growth, the feeling of increased power—is its object. This same will has at its service an apparently opposed impulse of the spirit, a suddenly adopted preference of ignorance,

---

*An expression from Schiller's *William Tell,* Act 1V, Scene 3.

of arbitrary shutting out, a closing of windows, an inner denial of this or that, a prohibition to approach, a sort of defensive attitude against much that is knowable, a contentment with obscurity, with the shutting-in horizon, an acceptance and approval of ignorance: as that which is all necessary according to the degree of its appropriating power, its "digestive power," to speak figuratively (and in fact "the spirit" resembles a stomach more than anything else). Here also belong an occasional propensity of the spirit to let itself be deceived (perhaps with a waggish suspicion that it is *not* so and so, but is only allowed to pass as such), a delight in uncertainty and ambiguity, an exulting enjoyment of arbitrary, out-of-the-way narrowness and mystery, of the too-near, of the foreground, of the magnified, the diminished, the misshapen, the beautified—an enjoyment of the arbitrariness of all these manifestations of power. Finally, in this connection, there is the not unscrupulous readiness of the spirit to deceive other spirits and dissemble before them—the constant pressing and straining of a creating, shaping, changeable power: the spirit enjoys therein its craftiness and its variety of disguises, it enjoys also its feeling of security therein—it is precisely by its Protean arts that it is best protected and concealed!—*Counter to* this propensity for appearance, for simplification, for a disguise, for a cloak, in short, for an outside—for every outside is a cloak—there operates the sublime tendency of the man of knowledge, which takes, and *insists* on taking things profoundly, variously, and thoroughly; as a kind of cruelty of the intellectual conscience and taste, which every courageous thinker will acknowledge in himself, provided, as it ought to be, that he has sharpened and hardened his eye sufficiently long for introspection, and is accustomed to severe discipline and even severe words. He will say: "There is something cruel in the tendency of my spirit": let the virtuous and amiable try to convince him that it is not so! In fact, it would sound nicer, if, instead of our cruelty, perhaps our "extravagant honesty" were talked about, whispered about and glorified—we free, *very* free spirits—and some day perhaps *such* will actually be our—posthumous glory! Meanwhile—for there is plenty of time until then—we should be least inclined to deck ourselves out in such florid and fringed moral verbiage; our whole former work has just made us sick of this taste and its sprightly exuberance. They are beautiful, glistening, jingling, festive words: honesty, love of truth, love of wisdom, sacrifice for knowledge, heroism of the truthful—there is something in them that makes one's heart swell with pride. But we anchorites and marmots have long ago persuaded ourselves in all the secrecy of an anchorite's conscience, that this worthy parade of verbiage also belongs to the old false adornment, frippery, and gold-dust of unconscious human vanity, and that even under such flattering colour and repainting, the terrible original text homo natura must again be recognised. In effect, to translate man back again into nature; to master the many vain and visionary interpretations and subordinate meanings which have hitherto been scratched and daubed over the eternal original text, *homo natura;* to bring it about that man shall henceforth stand before man as he now, hardened by the discipline of science, stands before the *other* forms of nature, with fearless Œdipus-eyes, and stopped Ulysses-ears, deaf to the enticements of old metaphysical bird-catchers, who have piped to him far too long: "Thou art more! thou art higher! thou hast a different origin!"—this may be a strange and foolish task, but that it is a *task,* who can deny! Why did we choose it, this foolish task? Or, to put the question differently: "Why knowledge at all?" Every one will ask us about this. And thus pressed, we, who have asked ourselves the question a hundred times, have not found, and cannot find any better answer. . . .

231

Learning alters us, it does what all nourishment does that does not merely "conserve"—as the physiologist knows. But at the bottom of our souls, quite "down below," there is certainly something unteachable, a granite of spiritual fate, of predetermined decision and answer to predetermined, chosen questions. In each cardinal problem there speaks an unchangeable "I am this"; a thinker cannot learn anew about man and woman, for instance, but can only learn fully—he can only follow to the end what is "fixed" about them in himself. Occasionally we find certain solutions of problems which make strong beliefs for *us;* perhaps they are henceforth called "convictions." Later on—one sees in them only footsteps to self-knowledge, guide-posts to the problem which we ourselves *are*—or more correctly to the great stupidity which we embody, our spiritual fate, the *unteachable* in us, quite "down below."—In view of this liberal compliment which I have just paid myself, permission will perhaps be more readily allowed me to utter some truths about "woman as she is," provided that it is known at the outset how literally they are merely—*my* truths.

232

Woman wishes to be independent, and therefore she begins to enlighten men about "woman as she is"—*this* is one of the worst developments of the general *uglifying* of Europe. For what must these clumsy attempts of feminine scientificality and self-exposure bring to light! Woman has so much cause for shame; in woman there is so much pedantry, superficiality, schoolmasterliness, petty presumption, unbridledness, and indiscretion concealed—study only woman's behaviour towards children!—which has really been best restrained and dominated hitherto by the *fear* of man. Alas, if ever the "eternally tedious in woman"—she has plenty of it!—is allowed to venture forth! if she begins radically and on principle to unlearn her wisdom and art—of charming, of playing, of frightening away sorrow, of alleviating and taking easily; if she forgets her delicate aptitude for agreeable desires! Female voices are already raised, which, by Saint Aristophanes! make one afraid:—with medical explicitness it is stated in a threatening manner what woman first and last *requires* from man. Is it not in the very worst taste that woman thus sets herself up to be scientific? Enlightenment hitherto has fortunately been men's affair, men's gift—we remained therewith "among ourselves"; and in the end, in view of all that women write about "woman," we may well have considerable doubt as to whether woman really *desires* enlightenment about herself—and *can* desire it. If woman does not thereby seek a new *ornament* for herself—I believe ornamentation belongs to the eternally feminine?—why, then, she wishes to make herself feared: perhaps she thereby wishes to get the mastery. But she does not *want* truth—what does woman care for truth? From the very first nothing is more foreign, more repugnant, or more hostile to woman than truth—her great art is falsehood, her chief concern is appearance and beauty. Let us confess it, we men: we honour and love *this* very art and *this* very instinct in woman: we who have the hard task, and for our recreation gladly seek the company of beings under whose hands, glances, and delicate follies, our seriousness, our gravity, and profundity appear almost like follies to us. Finally, I ask the question: Did a woman herself ever acknowledge profundity in a woman's mind, or justice in a woman's heart? And is it not true that on the whole "woman" has hitherto been most despised by woman herself, and not at all by us?—We men desire that woman should not continue to compromise herself by enlightening us; just as it was man's care and the consideration for woman, when the church decreed: *mulier taceat in ecclesia.* It was to the benefit of woman when Napoleon gave the too eloquent Madame de Staël to understand: *mulier taceat in politicis!*—and in my opinion, he is a true friend of woman who calls out to women to-day: *mulier taceat de muliere!*

233

It betrays corruption of the instincts—apart from the fact that it betrays bad taste—when a woman refers to Madame Roland, or Madame de Staël, or Monsieur George Sand, as though something were proved thereby in *favour* of "woman as she is." Among men, these are the three *comical* women as they are—nothing more!—and just the best involuntary *counter-arguments* against feminine emancipation and autonomy.

234

Stupidity in the kitchen; woman as cook; the terrible thoughtlessness with which the feeding of the family and the master of the house is managed! Woman does not understand what food *means,* and she insists on being cook! If woman had been a thinking creature, she should certainly, as cook for thousands of years, have discovered the most important physiological facts, and should likewise have got possession of the healing art! Through bad female cooks—through the entire lack of reason in the kitchen—the development of mankind has been longest retarded and most interfered with: even to-day matters are very little better.—A word to High School girls.

235

There are turns and casts of fancy, there are sentences, little handfuls of words, in which a whole culture, a whole society suddenly crystallises itself. Among these is the incidental remark of Madame de Lambert to her son: "*Mon ami, ne vous permettez jamais que des folies, qui vous feront grand plaisir*"—the motherliest and wisest remark, by the way, that was ever addressed to a son.

236

I have no doubt that every noble woman will oppose what Dante and Goethe believed about woman—the former when he sang, *"ella guardava suso, ed io in lei,"* and the latter when he interpreted it, "the eternally feminine draws us *aloft*"; for *this* is just what she believes of the eternally masculine.

237

Seven Apophthegms for Women

How the longest ennui flees,
When a man comes to our knees!

Age, alas! and science staid,
Furnish even weak virtue aid.

Sombre garb and silence meet:
Dress for every dame—discreet.

Whom I thank when in my bliss?
God!—and my good tailoress!

Young, a flower-decked cavern home;
Old, a dragon thence doth roam.

Noble title, leg that's fine,
Man as well: Oh, were *he* mine!

Speech in brief and sense in mass—
Slippery for the jenny-ass!

237A

Woman has hitherto been treated by men like birds, which, losing their way, have come down among them from an elevation: as something delicate, fragile, wild, strange, sweet, and animating—but as something also which must be cooped up to prevent it flying away.

238

To be mistaken in the fundamental problem of "man and woman," to deny here the profoundest antagonism and the necessity for an eternally hostile tension, to dream here perhaps of equal rights, equal training, equal claims and obligations: that is a *typical* sign of shallow-mindedness; and a thinker who has proved himself shallow at this dangerous spot—shallow in instinct!—may generally be regarded as suspicious, nay more, as betrayed, as discovered; he will probably prove too "short" for all fundamental questions of life, future as well as present, and will be unable to descend into *any* of the depths. On the other hand, a man who has depth of spirit as well as of desires, and has also the depth of benevolence which is capable of severity and harshness, and easily confounded with them, can only think of woman as

Orientals do: he must conceive of her as a possession, as confinable property, as a being predestined for service and accomplishing her mission therein—he must take his stand in this matter upon the immense rationality of Asia, upon the superiority of the instinct of Asia, as the Greeks did formerly; those best heirs and scholars of Asia—who, as is well known, with their *increasing* culture and amplitude of power, from Homer to the time of Pericles, became gradually *stricter* towards woman, in short, more oriental. *How* necessary, *how* logical, even *how* humanely desirable this was, let us consider for ourselves!

239

The weaker sex has in no previous age been treated with so much respect by men as at present—this belongs to the tendency and fundamental taste of democracy, in the same way as disrespectfulness to old age—what wonder is it that abuse should be immediately made of this respect? They want more, they learn to make claims, the tribute of respect is at last felt to be well-nigh galling: rivalry for rights, indeed actual strife itself, would be preferred: in a word, woman is losing modesty. And let us immediately add that she is also losing taste. She is unlearning to *fear* man: but the woman who "unlearns to fear" sacrifices her most womanly instincts. That woman should venture forward when the fear-inspiring quality in man—or more definitely, the *man* in man—is no longer either desired or fully developed, is reasonable enough and also intelligible enough; what is more difficult to understand is that precisely thereby—woman deteriorates. This is what is happening nowadays: let us not deceive ourselves about it! Wherever the industrial spirit has triumphed over the military and aristocratic spirit, woman strives for the economic and legal independence of a clerk: "woman as clerkess" is inscribed on the portal of the modern society which is in course of formation. While she thus appropriates new rights, aspires to be "master," and inscribes "progress" of woman on her flags and banners, the very opposite realises itself with terrible obviousness: *woman retrogrades*. Since the French Revolution the influence of woman in Europe has *declined* in proportion as she has increased her rights and claims; and the "emancipation of woman," in so far as it is desired and demanded by women themselves (and not only by masculine shallowpates), thus proves to be a remarkable symptom of the increased weakening and deadening of the most womanly instincts. There is *stupidity* in this movement, an almost masculine stupidity, of which a well-reared woman—who is always a sensible woman—might be heartily ashamed. To lose the intuition as to the ground upon which she can most surely achieve victory; to neglect exercise in the use of her proper weapons; to let-herself-go before man, perhaps even "to the book," where formerly she kept herself in control and in refined, artful humility; to neutralise with her virtuous audacity man's faith in a *veiled,* fundamentally different ideal in woman, something eternally, necessarily feminine: to emphatically and loquaciously dissuade man from the idea that woman must be preserved, cared for, protected, and indulged, like some delicate, strangely wild, and often pleasant domestic animal; the clumsy and indignant collection of everything of the nature of servitude and bondage which the position of woman in the hitherto existing order of society has entailed and still entails (as though slavery were a counter-argument, and not rather a condition of every higher culture, of every elevation of culture):—what does all this betoken, if not a disintegration of womanly instincts, a de-feminising? Certainly, there are enough of idiotic friends and corrupters of woman amongst the learned asses of the masculine sex, who advise woman to de-feminise herself in this manner, and to imitate all the stupidities from which "man" in Europe, European "manliness," suffers,—who would like to lower woman to "general culture," indeed even to newspaper reading and meddling with politics. Here and there they wish even to make women into free spirits and literary workers: as though a woman without piety would not be something perfectly obnoxious or ludicrous to a profound and godless man; —almost everywhere her nerves are being ruined by the most morbid and dangerous kind of music (our latest German music), and she is daily being made more hysterical and more incapable of fulfilling her first and last function, that of bearing robust children. They wish to "cultivate" her in general still more, and intend, as they say, to make the "weaker sex" *strong* by culture: as if history did not teach in the most emphatic manner that the "cultivating" of mankind and his weakening—that is to say, the weakening, dissipating, and languishing of his *force of will*—have always kept pace with one another, and that the most powerful and influential women in the world (and lastly, the mother of Napoleon) had just to thank their force of will—and not their schoolmasters!—for their power and ascendency over men. That which inspires respect in woman, and often enough fear also, is her *nature,* which is more "natural" than that of man, her gen-

uine, carnivora-like, cunning flexibility, her tiger-claws beneath the glove, her *naïveté* in egoism, her untrainableness and innate wildness, the incomprehensibleness, extent and deviation of her desires and virtues. . . . That which, in spite of fear, excites one's sympathy for the dangerous and beautiful cat, "woman," is that she seems more afflicted, more vulnerable, more necessitous of love and more condemned to disillusionment than any other creature. Fear and sympathy: it is with these feelings that man has hitherto stood in the presence of woman, always with one foot already in tragedy, which rends while it delights.—What? And all that is now to be at an end? And the *disenchantment* of woman is in progress? The tediousness of woman is slowly evolving? Oh Europe! Europe! We know the horned animal which was always most attractive to thee, from which danger is ever again threatening thee! Thy old fable might once more become "history"—an immense stupidity might once again overmaster thee and carry thee away! And no God concealed beneath it—no! only an "idea," a "modern idea"! . . .

First Essay
"Good and Evil," "Good and Bad"

1.

Those English psychologists, who up to the present are the only philosophers who are to be thanked for any endeavour to get as far as a history of the origin of morality—these men, I say, offer us in their own personalities no paltry problem;—they even have, if I am to be quite frank about it, in their capacity of living riddles, an advantage over their books—*they themselves are interesting!* These English psychologists—what do they really mean? We always find them voluntarily or involuntarily at the same task of pushing to the front the *partie honteuse* of our inner world, and looking for the efficient, governing, and decisive principle in that precise quarter where the intellectual self-respect of the race would be the most reluctant to find it (for example, in the *vis inertiæ* of habit, or in forgetfulness, or in a blind and fortuitous mechanism and association of ideas, or in some factor that is purely passive, reflex, molecular, or fundamentally stupid)—what is the real motive power which always impels these psychologists in precisely *this* direction? Is it an instinct for human disparagement somewhat sinister, vulgar, and malignant, or perhaps incomprehensible even to itself? or perhaps a touch of pessimistic jealousy, the mistrust of disillusioned idealists who have become gloomy, poisoned, and bitter? or a petty subconscious enmity and rancour against Christianity (and Plato), that has conceivably never crossed the threshold of consciousness? or just a vicious taste for those elements of life which are bizarre, painfully paradoxical, mystical, and illogical? or, as a final alternative, a dash of each of these motives—a little vulgarity, a little gloominess, a little anti-Christianity, a little craving for the necessary piquancy?

But I am told that it is simply a case of old frigid and tedious frogs crawling and hopping around men and inside men, as if they were as thoroughly at home there, as they would be in a *swamp*.

I am opposed to this statement, nay, I do not believe it; and if, in the impossibility of knowledge, one is permitted to wish, so do I wish from my heart that just the converse metaphor should apply, and that these analysts with their psychological microscopes should be, at bottom, brave, proud, and magnanimous animals who know how to bridle both their hearts and their smarts, and have specifically trained themselves to sacrifice what is desirable to what is true, *any* truth in fact, even the simple, bitter, ugly, repulsive, unchristian, and immoral truths—for there are truths of that description.

2.

All honour, then, to the noble spirits who would fain dominate these historians of morality. But it is certainly a pity that they lack the *historical sense* itself, that they themselves are quite deserted by all the beneficent spirits of history. The whole train of their thought runs, as was always the way of old-fashioned philosophers, on *thoroughly* unhistorical lines: there is no doubt on this point. The crass ineptitude of their genealogy of morals is immediately apparent when the question arises of ascertaining the origin of the idea and judgment of "good." "Man had originally," so speaks their decree, "praised and called 'good' altruistic acts from the standpoint of those on whom they were conferred, that is, those to whom they were *useful;* subsequently the origin of this praise was *forgotten,* and altruistic acts, simply because, as a sheer matter of habit, they were praised as good, came also to be felt as good—as though they contained in themselves some intrinsic goodness."

The thing is obvious:—this initial derivation contains already all the typical and idiosyncratic traits of the English psychologists—we have "utility," "forgetting," "habit," and finally "error," the whole assemblage forming the basis of a system of values, on which the higher man has up to the present prided himself as though it were a kind of privilege of man in general. This pride *must* be brought low, this system of values *must* lose its values: is that attained?

Now the first argument that comes ready to my hand is that the real homestead of the concept "good" is sought and located in the wrong place: the judgment "good" did *not* originate among those to whom goodness was shown. Much rather has it been the good themselves, that is, the aristocratic, the powerful, the high-stationed, the high-minded, who have felt that they themselves were good, and that their actions were good, that is to say of the first order, in contradistinction to all the low, the low-minded, the vulgar, and the plebeian. It was out of this pathos of distance that they first arrogated the right to create values for their own profit, and to coin the names of such values: what had they to do with utility? The standpoint of utility is as alien and as inapplicable as it could possibly be, when we have to deal with so volcanic an effervescence of supreme values, creating and demarcating as they do a hierarchy within themselves: it is at this juncture that one arrives at an appreciation of the contrast to that tepid temperature, which is the presupposition on which every combination of worldly wisdom and every calculation of practical expediency is always based—and not for one occasional, not for one exceptional instance, but chronically. The pathos of nobility and distance, as I have said, the chronic and despotic *esprit de corps* and fundamental instinct of a higher dominant race coming into association with a meaner race, an "under race," this is the origin of the antithesis of good and bad.

(The masters' right of giving names goes so far that it is permissible to look upon language itself as the expression of the power of the masters: they say "this *is* that, and that," they seal finally every object and every event with a sound, and thereby at the same time take possession of it.) It is because of this origin that the word "good" is far from having any necessary connection with altruistic acts, in accordance with the superstitious belief of these moral philosophers. On the contrary, it is on the occasion of the *decay* of aristocratic values, that the antitheses between "egoistic" and "altruistic" presses more and more heavily on the human conscience—it is, to use my own language, the *herd instinct* which finds in this antithesis an expression in many ways. And even then it takes a considerable time for this instinct to become sufficiently dominant, for the valuation to be inextricably dependent on this antithesis (as is the case in contemporary Europe); for to-day the prejudice is predominant, which, acting even now with all the intensity of an obsession and brain disease, holds that "moral," "altruistic," and *"désintéressé"* are concepts of equal value.

3.

In the second place, quite apart from the fact that this hypothesis as to the genesis of the value "good" cannot be historically upheld, it suffers from an inherent psychological contradiction. The utility of altruistic conduct has presumably been the origin of its being praised, and this origin has become *forgotten:*—But in what conceivable way is this forgetting *possible?* Has perchance the utility of such conduct ceased at some given moment? The contrary is the case. This utility has rather been experienced every day at all times, and is consequently a feature that obtains a new and regular emphasis with every fresh day; it follows that, so far from vanishing from the consciousness, so far indeed from being forgotten, it must necessarily become impressed on the consciousness with ever-increasing distinctness. How much more logical is that contrary theory (it is not the truer for that) which is represented, for instance, by Herbert Spencer, who places the concept "good" as essentially similar to the concept "useful," "purposive," so that in the judgments "good" and "bad" mankind is simply summarising and investing with a sanction its *unforgotten* and *unforgettable experiences* concerning the "useful-purposive" and the "mischievous-non-purposive." According to this theory, "good" is the attribute of that which has previously shown itself useful; and so is able to claim to be considered "valuable in the highest degree," "valuable in itself." This method of explanation is also, as I have said, wrong, but at any rate the explanation itself is coherent, and psychologically tenable.

4.

The guide-post which first put me on the *right* track was this question—what is the true etymological significance of the various symbols for the idea "good" which have been coined in the various languages? I then found that they all led back to *the same evolution of the same idea*—that everywhere "aristocrat," "noble" (in the social sense), is the root idea, out of which have necessarily developed "good" in the sense of "with aristocratic soul," "noble," in the sense of "with a soul of high calibre," "with a privileged soul"—a development which invariably runs parallel with that other evolution by which "vulgar," "plebeian," "low," are made to change finally into "bad." The most eloquent proof of this last contention is the German word *"schlecht"* itself: this word is identical with *"schlicht"*—(compare *"schlechtweg"* and *"schlechterdings"*)—which, originally and as yet without any sinister innuendo, simply denoted the plebeian man in contrast to the aristocratic man. It is at the sufficiently late period of the Thirty Years' War that this sense becomes changed to the sense now current. From the standpoint of the Genealogy of Morals this discovery seems to be substantial: the lateness of it is to be attributed to the retarding influence exercised in the modern world by democratic prejudice in the sphere of all questions of origin. This extends, as will shortly be shown, even to the province of natural science and physiology, which *prima facie* is the most objective. The extent of the mischief which is caused by this prejudice (once it is free of all trammels except those of its own malice), particularly to Ethics and History, is shown by the notorious case of Buckle: it was in Buckle that that *plebeianism* of the modern spirit, which is of English origin, broke out once again from its malignant soil with all the violence of a slimy volcano, and with that salted, rampant, and vulgar eloquence with which up to the present time all volcanoes have spoken.

5.

With regard to *our* problem, which can justly be called an *intimate* problem, and which elects to appeal to only a limited number of ears: it is of no small interest to ascertain that in those words and roots which denote "good" we catch glimpses of that arch-trait, on the strength of which the aristocrats feel themselves to be beings of a higher order than their fellows. Indeed, they call themselves in perhaps the most frequent instances simply after their superiority in power (*e.g.* "the powerful," "the lords," "the commanders"), or after the most obvious sign of their superiority, as for example "the rich," "the possessors" (that is the meaning of *arya;* and the Iranian and Slav languages correspond). But they also call themselves after some *characteristic idio-syncrasy;* and this is the case which now concerns us. They name themselves, for instance, "the truthful": this is first done by the Greek nobility whose mouthpiece is found in Theognis, the Megarian poet. The word ἐσθλός, which is coined for the purpose, signifies etymologically "one who *is*," who has reality, who is real, who is true; and then with a subjective twist, the "true," as the "truthful": at this stage in the evolution of the idea, it becomes the motto and party cry of the nobility, and quite completes the transition to the meaning "noble," so as to place outside the pale the lying, vulgar man, as Theognis conceives and portrays him—till finally the word after the decay of the nobility is left to delineate psychological *noblesse,* and becomes as it were ripe and mellow. In the word κακός as in δειλός (the plebeian in contrast to the ἀγαθός) the cowardice is emphasised. This affords perhaps an inkling on what lines the etymological origin of the very ambiguous ἀγαθός is to be investigated. In the Latin *malus* (which I place side by side with μέλας) the vulgar man can be distinguished as the dark-coloured, and above all as the black-haired (*"hic niger est"*), as the pre-Aryan inhabitants of the Italian soil, whose complexion formed the clearest feature of distinction from the dominant blondes, namely, the Aryan conquering race:—at any rate Gaelic has afforded me the exact analogue—*Fin* (for instance, in the name *Fin-Gal*), the distinctive word of the nobility, finally—good, noble, clean, but originally the blonde-haired man in contrast to the dark black-haired aboriginals. The Celts, if I may make a parenthetic statement, were throughout a blonde race; and it is wrong to connect, as Virchow still connects, those traces of an essentially dark-haired population which are to be seen on the more elaborate ethnographical maps of Germany with any Celtic ancestry or with any admixture of Celtic blood: in this context it is rather the *pre-Aryan* population of Germany which surges up to these districts. (The same is true substantially of the whole of Europe: in point of fact, the subject race has finally again obtained the upper hand, in complexion and the shortness of the skull, and perhaps in the intellectual and social qualities. Who can guarantee that modern democracy, still more modern anarchy, and indeed that tendency to the "Commune," the most primitive form of society, which is now common to all the Socialists in Europe, does not in its real essence signify a monstrous reversion—and that the conquering and *master* race—the Aryan

race, is not also becoming inferior physiologically?) I believe that I can explain the Latin *bonus* as the "warrior": my hypothesis is that I am right in deriving *bonus* from an older *duonus* (compare *bellum-duellum* = *duenlum,* in which the word *duonus* appears to me to be contained). *Bonus* accordingly as the man of discord, of variance, "entzweiung" (*duo*), as the warrior: one sees what in ancient Rome "the good" meant for a man. Must not our actual German word *gut* mean *"the godlike,* the man of godlike race"? and be identical with the national name (originally the nobles' name) of the *Goths?*

The grounds for this supposition do not appertain to this work.

6.

Above all, there is no exception (though there are opportunities for exceptions) to this rule, that the idea of political superiority always resolves itself into the idea of psychological superiority, in those cases where the highest caste is at the same time the *priestly* caste, and in accordance with its general characteristics confers on itself the privilege of a title which alludes specifically to its priestly function. It is in these cases, for instances, that "clean" and "unclean" confront each other for the first time as badges of class distinction; here again there develops a "good" and a "bad," in a sense which has ceased to be merely social. Moreover, care should be taken not to take these ideas of "clean" and "unclean" too seriously, too broadly, or too symbolically: all the ideas of ancient man have, on the contrary, got to be understood in their initial stages, in a sense which is, to an almost inconceivable extent, crude, coarse, physical, and narrow, and above all essentially *unsymbolical.* The "clean man" is originally only a man who washes himself, who abstains from certain foods which are conducive to skin diseases, who does not sleep with the unclean women of the lower classes, who has a horror of blood—not more, not much more! On the other hand, the very nature of a priestly aristocracy shows the reasons why just at such an early juncture there should ensue a really dangerous sharpening and intensification of opposed values: it is, in fact, through these opposed values that gulfs are cleft in the social plane, which a veritable Achilles of free thought would shudder to cross. There is from the outset a certain *diseased taint* in such sacerdotal aristocracies, and in the habits which prevail in such societies—habits which, *averse* as they are to action, constitute a compound of introspection and explosive emotionalism, as a result of which there appears that introspective morbidity and neurasthenia, which adheres almost inevitably to all priests at all times: with regard, however, to the remedy which they themselves have invented for this disease—the philosopher has no option but to state, that it has proved itself in its effects a hundred times more dangerous than the disease, from which it should have been the deliverer. Humanity itself is still diseased from the effects of the naïvetés of this priestly cure. Take, for instance, certain kinds of diet (abstention from flesh), fasts, sexual continence, flight into the wilderness (a kind of Weir-Mitchell isolation, though of course without that system of excessive feeding and fattening which is the most efficient antidote to all the hysteria of the ascetic ideal); consider too the whole metaphysic of the priests, with its war on the senses, its enervation, its hair-splitting; consider its self-hypnotism on the fakir and Brahman principles (it uses Brahman as a glass disc and obsession), and that climax which we can understand only too well of an unusual satiety with its panacea of *nothingness* (or God:—the demand for a *unio mystica* with God is the demand of the Buddhist for nothingness, Nirvana—and nothing else!). In sacerdotal societies *every* element is on a more dangerous scale, not merely cures and remedies, but also pride, revenge, cunning, exaltation, love, ambition, virtue, morbidity:—further, it can fairly be stated that it is on the soil of this *essentially dangerous* form of human society, the sacerdotal form, that man really becomes for the first time an *interesting animal*, that it is in this form that the soul of man has in a higher sense attained *depths* and become *evil*—and those are the two fundamental forms of the superiority which up to the present man has exhibited over every other animal.

7.

The reader will have already surmised with what ease the priestly mode of valuation can branch off from the knightly aristocratic mode, and then develop into the very antithesis of the latter: special impetus is given to this opposition, by every occasion when the castes of the priests and warriors confront each other with mutual jealousy and cannot agree over the prize. The knightly aristocratic "values" are based on a careful cult of the physical, on a flowering, rich, and even effervescing healthiness, that goes considerably beyond what is necessary for maintaining life, on war, adventure, the chase, the dance, the tourney—on everything, in fact, which is contained in strong, free, and joyous action. The priestly-aristocratic mode of valuation is—we have seen—based on other hypotheses: it is bad enough for this class when it is a question of war! Yet the priests are, as is notorious, *the worst enemies*—why? Because they are the weakest. Their weakness causes their hate to expand into a monstrous and sinister shape, a shape which is most crafty and most poisonous. The really great haters in the history of the world have always been priests, who are also the cleverest haters—in comparison with the cleverness of priestly revenge, every other piece of cleverness is practically negligible. Human history would be too fatuous for anything were it not for the cleverness imported into it by the weak—take at once the most important instance. All the world's efforts against the "aristocrats," the "mighty," the "masters," the "holders of power," are negligible by comparison with what has been accomplished against those classes by *the Jews*—the Jews, that priestly nation which eventually realised that the one method of effecting satisfaction on its enemies and tyrants was by means of a radical transvaluation of values, which was at the same time an act of the *cleverest revenge*. Yet the method was only appropriate to a nation of priests, to a nation of the most jealously nursed priestly revengefulness. It was the Jews who, in opposition to the aristocratic equation (good = aristocratic = beautiful = happy = loved by the gods), dared with a terrifying logic to suggest the contrary equation, and indeed to maintain with the teeth of the most profound hatred (the hatred of weakness) this contrary equation, namely, "the wretched are alone the good; the poor, the weak, the lowly, are alone the good; the suffering, the needy, the sick, the loathsome, are the only ones who are pious, the only ones who are blessed, for them alone is salvation—but you, on the other hand, you aristocrats, you men of power, you are to all eternity the evil, the horrible, the covetous, the insatiate, the godless; eternally also shall you be the unblessed, the cursed, the damned!" We know who it was who reaped the heritage of this Jewish transvaluation. In the context of the monstrous and inordinately fateful initiative which the Jews have exhibited in connection with this most fundamental of all declarations of war, I remember the passage which came to my pen on another occasion (*Beyond Good and Evil*, Aph. 195)—that it was, in fact, with the Jews that the *revolt of the slaves* begins in the sphere *of morals;* that revolt which has behind it a history of two millennia, and which at the present day has only moved out of our sight, because it—has achieved victory.

8.

But you understand this not? You have no eyes for a force which has taken two thousand years to achieve victory?—There is nothing wonderful in this: all *lengthy* processes are hard to see and to realise. But *this* is what took place: from the trunk of that tree of revenge and hate, Jewish hate,—that most profound and sublime hate, which creates ideals and changes old values to new creations, the like of which has never been on earth,—there grew a phenomenon which was equally incomparable, *a new love,* the most profound and sublime of all kinds of love;—and from what other trunk could it have grown? But beware of supposing that this love has soared on its upward growth, as in any way a real negation of that thirst for revenge, as an antithesis to the Jewish hate! No, the contrary is the truth! This love grew out of that hate, as its crown, as its triumphant crown, circling wider and wider amid the clarity and fulness of the sun, and pursuing in the very kingdom of light and height its goal of hatred, its victory, its spoil, its strategy, with the same intensity with which the roots of that tree of hate sank into everything which was deep and evil with increasing stability and increasing desire. This Jesus of Nazareth, the incarnate gospel of love, this "Redeemer" bringing salvation and victory to the poor, the sick, the sinful— was he not really temptation in its most sinister and irresistible form, temptation to take the tortuous path to those very *Jewish* values and those very Jewish ideals? Has not Israel really obtained the final goal of its sublime revenge, by the tortuous paths of this "Redeemer," for all that he might pose as Israel's adversary and Israel's destroyer? Is it not due to the black magic of a really *great* policy of revenge, of a far-seeing, burrowing revenge, both acting and calculating with slowness, that Israel himself must repudiate before all the world the actual instrument of his own revenge and nail it to the cross, so that all the world—that is, all the enemies of Israel—-could nibble without suspicion at this very bait? Could, moreover, any human mind with all its elaborate ingenuity invent a bait that was more truly *dangerous*? Anything that was even equivalent in the power of its seductive, intoxicating, defiling, and corrupting influence to that symbol of the holy cross, to that awful paradox of a "god on the cross," to that mys-

tery of the unthinkable, supreme, and utter horror of the self-crucifixion of a god for the *salvation of man*? It is at least certain that *sub hoc signo* Israel, with its revenge and transvaluation of all values, has up to the present always triumphed again over all other ideals, over all more aristocratic ideals.

9.

"But why do you talk of nobler ideals? Let us submit to the facts; that the people have triumphed—or the slaves, or the populace, or the herd, or whatever name you care to give them—if this has happened through the Jews, so be it! In that case no nation ever had a greater mission in the world's history. The 'masters' have been done away with; the morality of the vulgar man has triumphed. This triumph may also be called a blood-poisoning (it has mutually fused the races)— I do not dispute it; but there is no doubt but that this intoxication has succeeded. The 'redemption' of the human race (that is, from the masters) is progressing swimmingly; everything is obviously becoming Judaised, or Christianised, or vulgarised (what is there in the words?). It seems impossible to stop the course of this poisoning through the whole body politic of mankind—but its tempo and pace may from the present time be slower, more delicate, quieter, more discreet—there is time enough. In view of this context has the Church nowadays any necessary purpose? Has it, in fact, a right to live? Or could man get on without it? *Quæritur.* It seems that it fetters and retards this tendency, instead of accelerating it. Well, even that might be its utility. The Church certainly is a crude and boorish institution, that is repugnant to an intelligence with any pretence at delicacy, to a really modern taste. Should it not at any rate learn to be somewhat more subtle? It alienates nowadays, more than it allures. Which of us would, forsooth, be a freethinker if there were no Church? It is the Church which repels us, *not* its poison—apart from the Church we like the poison." This is the epilogue of a freethinker to my discourse, of an honourable animal (as he has given abundant proof), and a democrat to boot; he had up to that time listened to me, and could not endure my silence, but for me, indeed, with regard to this topic there is much on which to be silent.

10.

The revolt of the slaves in morals begins in the very principle of *resentment* becoming creative and giving birth to values—a resentment experienced by creatures who, deprived as they are of the proper outlet of action, are forced to find their compensation in an imaginary revenge. While every aristocratic morality springs from a triumphant affirmation of its own demands, the slave morality says "no" from the very outset to what is "outside itself," "different from itself," and "not itself": and this "no" is its creative deed. This volte-face of the valuing standpoint—this *inevitable* gravitation to the objective instead of back to the subjective—is typical of "resentment": the slave-morality requires as the condition of its existence an external and objective world, to employ physiological terminology, it requires objective stimuli to be capable of action at all—its action is fundamentally a reaction. The contrary is the case when we come to the aristocrat's system of values: it acts and grows spontaneously, it merely seeks its antithesis in order to pronounce a more grateful and exultant "yes" to its own self;—its negative conception, "low," "vulgar," "bad," is merely a pale late-born foil in comparison with its positive and fundamental conception (saturated as it is with life and passion), of "we aristocrats, we good ones, we beautiful ones, we happy ones."

When the aristocratic morality goes astray and commits sacrilege on reality, this is limited to that particular sphere with which it is *not* sufficiently acquainted—a sphere, in fact, from the real knowledge of which it disdainfully defends itself. It misjudges, in some cases, the sphere which it despises, the sphere of the common vulgar man and the low people: on the other hand, due weight should be given to the consideration that in any case the mood of contempt, of disdain, of superciliousness, even on the supposition that it *falsely* portrays the object of its contempt, will always be far removed from that degree of falsity which will always characterise the attacks—in effigy, of course—of the vindictive hatred and revengefulness of the weak in onslaughts on their enemies. In point of fact, there is in contempt too strong an admixture of nonchalance, of casualness, of boredom, of impatience, even of personal exultation, for it to be capable of distorting its victim into a real caricature or a real monstrosity. Attention again should be paid to the almost benevolent *nuances* which, for instance, the Greek nobility imports into all the words by which it distinguishes the common people from itself; note how continuously a kind of pity, care, and consideration imparts its hon-

eyed *flavour,* until at last almost all the words which are applied to the vulgar man survive finally as expressions for "unhappy," "worthy of pity" (compare δειλός, δείλαιος, πονηρός, μοχθηρός; the latter two names really denoting the vulgar man as labour-slave and beast of burden)—and how, conversely, "bad," "low," "unhappy" have never ceased to ring in the Greek ear with a tone in which "unhappy" is the predominant note: this is a heritage of the old noble aristocratic morality, which remains true to itself even in contempt (let philologists remember the sense in which ὀτζυρός, ἄνολδος, τλήμων, δυστχεῖν, ξυμφορά used to be employed. The "well-born" simply *felt* themselves the "happy"; they did not have to manufacture their happiness artificially through looking at their enemies, or in cases to talk and lie themselves into happiness (as is the custom with all resentful men); and similarly, complete men as they were, exuberant with strength, and consequently *necessarily* energetic, they were too wise to dissociate happiness from action—activity becomes in their minds necessarily counted as happiness (that is the etymology of εὖπράττειν)—all in sharp contrast to the "happiness" of the weak and the oppressed, with their festering venom and malignity, among whom happiness appears essentially as a narcotic, a deadening, a quietude, a peace, a "Sabbath," an enervation of the mind and relaxation of the limbs,—in short, a purely *passive* phenomenon. While the aristocratic man lived in confidence and openness with himself (γενναῖος, "noble-born," emphasises the nuance "sincere," and perhaps also "naïf"), the resentful man, on the other hand, is neither sincere nor naïf, nor honest and candid with himself. His soul *squints;* his mind loves hidden crannies, tortuous paths and backdoors, everything secret appeals to him as *his* world, *his* safety, *his* balm; he is past master in silence, in not forgetting, in waiting, in provisional self-depreciation and self-abasement. A race of such *resentful* men will of necessity eventually prove more *prudent* than any aristocratic race, it will honour prudence on quite a distinct scale, as, in fact, a paramount condition of existence, while prudence among aristocratic men is apt to be tinged with a delicate flavour of luxury and refinement; so among them it plays nothing like so integral a part as that complete certainty of function of the governing *un-conscious* instincts, or as indeed a certain lack of prudence, such as a vehement and valiant charge, whether against danger or the enemy, or as those ecstatic bursts of rage, love, reverence, gratitude, by which at all times noble souls have recognised each other. When the resentment of the aristocratic man manifests itself, it fulfils and exhausts itself in an immediate reaction, and consequently instills no *venom:* on the other hand, it never manifests itself at all in countless instances, when in the case of the feeble and weak it would be inevitable. An inability to take seriously for any length of time their enemies, their disasters, their *misdeeds*—that is the sign of the full strong natures who possess a superfluity of moulding plastic force, that heals completely and produces forgetfulness: a good example of this in the modern world is Mirabeau, who had no memory for any insults and meannesses which were practised on him, and who was only incapable of forgiving because he forgot. Such a man indeed shakes off with a shrug many a worm which would have buried itself in another; it is only in characters like these that we see the possibility (supposing, of course, that there is such a possibility in the world) of the real *"love* of one's enemies." What respect for his enemies is found, forsooth, in an aristocratic man—and such a reverence is already a bridge to love! He insists on having his enemy to himself as his distinction. He tolerates no other enemy but a man in whose character there is nothing to despise and *much* to honour! On the other hand, imagine the "enemy" as the resentful man conceives him—and it is here exactly that we see his work, his creativeness; he has conceived "the evil enemy," the "evil one," and indeed that is the root idea from which he now evolves as a contrasting and corresponding figure a "good one," himself—his very self!

11.

The method of this man is quite contrary to that of the aristocratic man, who conceives the root idea "good" spontaneously and straight away, that is to say, out of himself, and from that material then creates for himself a concept of "bad"! This "bad" of aristocratic origin and that "evil" out of the cauldron of unsatisfied hatred—the former an imitation, an "extra," an additional nuance; the latter, on the other hand, the original, the beginning, the essential act in the conception of a slave morality—these two words "bad" and "evil," how great a difference do they mark, in spite of the fact that they have an identical contrary in the idea "good." But the idea "good" is *not* the same: much rather let the question be asked, "Who is really evil according to the meaning of the morality of resentment?" In all sternness let it be answered thus:—*just* the good man of the other morality, just the aristocrat, the powerful one, the one who rules, but who is distorted by the venomous eye of resentfulness, into a new colour, a new signification, a new appearance. This particular point we would be the last to deny: the man who learnt to know those "good" ones only as enemies, learnt at the same time not to know them only as *"evil enemies,"* and the same men who *inter pares* were kept so rigorously in bounds through convention, respect, custom, and gratitude, though much more through mutual vigilance and jealousy *inter pares*, these men who in their relations with each other find so many new ways of manifesting consideration, self-control, delicacy, loyalty, pride, and friendship, these men are in reference to what is outside their circle (where the foreign element, a *foreign* country, begins), not much better than beasts of prey, which have been let loose. They enjoy there freedom from all social control, they feel that in the wilderness they can give vent with impunity to that tension which is produced by enclosure and imprisonment in the peace of society, they *revert* to the innocence of the beast-of-prey conscience, like jubilant monsters, who perhaps come from a ghostly bout of murder, arson, rape, and torture, with bravado and a moral equanimity, as though merely some wild student's prank had been played, perfectly convinced that the poets have now an ample theme to sing and celebrate. It is impossible not to recognise at the core of all these aristocratic races the beast of prey; the magnificent *blonde brute*, avidly rampant for spoil and victory; this hidden core needed an outlet from time to time, the beast must get loose again, must return into the wilderness—the Roman, Arabic, German, and Japanese nobility, the Homeric heroes, the Scandinavian Vikings, are all alike in this need. It is the aristocratic races who have left the idea "Barbarian" on all the tracks in which they have marched; nay, a consciousness of this very barbarianism, and even a pride in it, manifests itself even in their highest civilisation (for example, when Pericles says to his Athenians in that celebrated funeral oration, "Our audacity has forced a way over every land and sea, rearing everywhere imperishable memorials of itself for *good* and for *evil*"). This audacity of aristocratic races, mad, absurd, and spasmodic as may be its expression; the incalculable and fantastic nature of their enterprises,—Pericles sets in special relief and glory the ραθυμία of the Athenians, their nonchalance and contempt for safety, body, life, and comfort, their awful joy and intense delight in all destruction, in all the ecstasies of victory and cruelty,—all these features become crystallised, for those who suffered thereby in the picture of the "barbarian," of the "evil enemy," perhaps of the "Goth" and of the "Vandal." The profound, icy mistrust which the German provokes, as soon as he arrives at power,—even at the present time,—is always still an aftermath of that inextinguishable horror with which for whole centuries Europe has regarded the wrath of the blonde Teuton beast (although between the old Germans and ourselves there exists scarcely a psychological, let alone a physical, relationship). I have once called attention to the embarrassment of Hesiod, when he conceived the series of social ages, and endeavoured to express them in gold, silver, and bronze. He could only dispose of the contradiction, with which he was confronted, by the Homeric world, an age magnificent indeed, but at the same time so awful and so violent, by making two ages out of one, which he henceforth placed one behind the other—first, the age of the heroes and demigods, as that world had remained in the memories of the aristocratic families, who found therein their own ancestors; secondly, the bronze age, as that corresponding age appeared to the descendants of the oppressed, spoiled, ill-treated, exiled, enslaved; namely, as an age of bronze, as I have said, hard, cold, terrible, without feelings and without conscience, crushing everything, and bespattering everything with blood. Granted the truth of the theory now believed to be true, that the very *essence of all civilisation* is to *train* out of man, the beast of prey, a tame and civilised animal, a domesticated animal, it follows indubitably that we must regard as the real *tools of civilisation* all those instincts of reaction and resentment, by the help of which the aristocratic races, together with their ideals, were finally degraded and overpowered; though that has not yet come to be synonymous with saying that the bearers of those tools also *represented* the civilisation. It is rather the contrary that is not only probable–nay, it is *palpable* to-day; these bearers of vindictive instincts that have to be bottled up, these descendants of all European and non-European slavery, especially of the pre-Aryan population—these people, I say, represent the *decline* of humanity! These "tools of civilisation" are a disgrace to humanity, and constitute in reality more of an argument against civilisation, more of a reason why civilisation should be suspected. One

may be perfectly justified in being always afraid of the blonde beast that lies at the core of all aristocratic races, and in being on one's guard: but who would not a hundred times prefer to be afraid, when one at the same time admires, than to be immune from fear, at the cost of being perpetually obsessed with the loathsome spectacle of the distorted, the dwarfed, the stunted, the envenomed? And is that not our fate? What produces to-day our repulsion towards "man"?—for we suffer from "man," there is no doubt about it. It is not fear; it is rather that we have nothing more to fear from men; it is that the worm "man" is in the foreground and pullulates; it is that the "tame man," the wretched mediocre and unedifying creature, has learnt to consider himself a goal and a pinnacle, an inner meaning, an historic principle, a "higher man"; yes, it is that he has a certain right so to consider himself, in so far as he feels that in contrast to that excess of deformity, disease, exhaustion, and effeteness whose odour is beginning to pollute present-day Europe, he at any rate has achieved a relative success, he at any rate still says "yes" to life.

12.

I cannot refrain at this juncture from uttering a sigh and one last hope. What is it precisely which I find intolerable? That which I alone cannot get rid of, which makes me choke and faint? Bad air! Bad air! That something misbegotten comes near me; that I must inhale the odour of the entrails of a misbegotten soul!—That excepted, what can one not endure in the way of need, privation, bad weather, sickness, toil, solitude? In point of fact, one manages to get over everything, born as one is to a burrowing and battling existence; one always returns once again to the light, one always lives again one's golden hour of victory—and then one stands as one was born, unbreakable, tense, ready for something more difficult, for something more distant, like a bow stretched but the tauter by every strain. But from time to time do ye grant me—assuming that "beyond good and evil" there are goddesses who can grant—one glimpse, grant me but one glimpse only, of something perfect, fully realised, happy, mighty, triumphant, of something that still gives cause for fear! A glimpse of a man that justifies the existence of man, a glimpse of an incarnate human happiness that realises and redeems, for the sake of which one may hold fast to *the belief in man*! For the position is this: in the dwarfing and levelling of the European man lurks *our* greatest peril, for it is this outlook which fatigues—we see to-day nothing which wishes to be greater, we surmise that the process is always still backwards, still backwards towards something more attentuated, more inoffensive, more cunning, more comfortable, more mediocre, more indifferent, more Chinese, more Christian—man, there is no doubt about it, grows always "better"—the destiny of Europe lies even in this—that in losing the fear of man, we have also lost the hope in man, yea, the will to be man. The sight of man now fatigues.—What is present-day Nihilism if it is not *that?*—We are tired of *man.*

13.

But let us come back to it; the problem of *another* origin of the good—of the good, as the resentful man thought it out—demands its solution. It is not surprising that the lambs should bear a grudge against the great birds of prey, but that is no reason for blaming the great birds of prey for taking the little lambs. And when the lambs say among themselves, "Those birds of prey are evil, and he who is as far removed from being a bird of prey, who is rather its opposite, a lamb,—is he not good?" then there is nothing to cavil at in the setting up of this ideal, though it may also be that the birds of prey will regard it a little sneeringly, and perchance say to themselves, "*We* bear no grudge against them, these good lambs, we even like them: nothing is tastier than a tender lamb." To require of strength that it should *not* express itself as strength, that it should not be a wish to overpower, a wish to overthrow, a wish to become master, a thirst for enemies and antagonisms and triumphs, is just as absurd as to require of weakness that it should express itself as strength. A quantum of force is just such a quantum of movement, will, action—rather it is nothing else than just those very phenomena of moving, willing, acting, and can only appear otherwise in the misleading errors of language (and the fundamental fallacies of reason which have become petrified therein), which understands, and understands wrongly, all working as conditioned by a worker, by a "subject." And just exactly as the people separate the lightning from its flash, and interpret the latter as a thing done, as the working of a subject which is called lightning, so also does the popular morality separate strength from the expression of strength, as though behind the strong man there existed some indifferent neutral *substratum*, which enjoyed a *caprice and option*

as to whether or not it should express strength. But there is no such *substratum*, there is no "being" behind doing, working, becoming; "the doer" is a mere appanage to the action. The action is everything. In point of fact, the people duplicate the doing, when they make the lightning lighten, that is a "doing-doing"; they make the same phenomenon first a cause, and then, secondly, the effect of that cause. The scientists fail to improve matters when they say, "Force moves, force causes," and so on. Our whole science is still, in spite of all its coldness, of all its freedom from passion, a dupe of the tricks of language, and has never succeeded in getting rid of that superstitious changeling "the subject" (the atom, to give another instance, is such a changeling, just as the Kantian "Thing-in-itself"). What wonder, if the suppressed and stealthily simmering passions of revenge and hatred exploit for their own advantage their belief, and indeed hold no belief with a more steadfast enthusiasm than this— "that the strong has the *option* of being weak, and the bird of prey of being a lamb." Thereby do they win for themselves the right of attributing to the birds of prey the *responsibility* for being birds of prey: when the oppressed, downtrodden, and overpowered say to themselves with the vindictive guile of weakness, "Let us be otherwise than the evil, namely, good! and good is every one who does not oppress, who hurts no one, who does not attack, who does not pay back, who hands over revenge to God, who holds himself, as we do, in hiding; who goes out of the way of evil, and demands, in short, little from life; like ourselves the patient, the meek, the just,"—yet all this, in its cold and unprejudiced interpretation, means nothing more than "once for all, the weak are weak; it is good to do *nothing for which we are not strong enough*"; but this dismal state of affairs, this prudence of the lowest order, which even insects possess (which in a great danger are fain to sham death so as to avoid doing "too much"), has, thanks to the counterfeiting and self-deception of weakness, come to masquerade in the pomp of an ascetic, mute, and expectant virtue, just as though the *very* weakness of the weak—that is, forsooth, its *being*, its working, its whole unique inevitable inseparable reality—were a voluntary result, something wished, chosen, a deed, an act of *merit.* This kind of man finds the belief in a neutral, free-choosing "subject" *necessary* from an instinct of self-preservation, of self-assertion, in which every lie is fain to sanctify itself. The subject (or, to use popular language, the *soul*) has perhaps proved itself the best dogma in the world simply because it rendered possible to the horde of mortal, weak, and oppressed individuals of every kind, that most sublime specimen of self-deception, the interpretation of weakness as freedom, of being this, or being that, as *merit*.

14.

Will any one look a little into—right into—the mystery of how *ideals* are *manufactured* in this world? Who has the courage to do it? Come!

Here we have a vista opened into these grimy workshops. Wait just a moment, dear Mr. Inquisitive and Foolhardy; your eye must first grow accustomed to this false changing light—Yes! Enough! Now speak! What is happening below down yonder? Speak out! Tell what you see, man of the most dangerous curiosity—for now *I* am the listener.

"I see nothing, I hear the more. It is a cautious, spiteful, gentle whispering and muttering together in all the corners and crannies. It seems to me that they are lying; a sugary softness adheres to every sound. Weakness is turned to *merit*, there is no doubt about it—it is just as you say."

Further!

"And the impotence which requites not, is turned to 'goodness,' craven baseness to meekness, submission to those whom one hates, to obedience (namely, obedience to one of whom they say that he ordered this submission—they call him God). The inoffensive character of the weak, the very cowardice in which he is rich, his standing at the door, his forced necessity of waiting, gain here fine names, such as 'patience,' which is also called 'virtue'; not being able to avenge one's self, is called not wishing to avenge one's self, perhaps even forgiveness (for *they* know not what they do—we alone know what they do). They also talk of the 'love of their enemies' and sweat thereby."

Further!

"They are miserable, there is no doubt about it, all these whisperers and counterfeiters in the corners, although they try to get warm by crouching close to each other, but they tell me that their misery is a favour and distinction given to them by God, just as one beats the dogs one likes best; that perhaps this misery is also a preparation, a probation, a training; that perhaps it is still more something which will one day be compensated and paid back with a tremendous interest in gold, nay in happiness. This they call 'Blessedness.' "

Further!

"They are now giving me to understand, that not only are they better men than the mighty, the lords of the earth, whose spittle they have got to lick (*not* out of fear, not at all out of fear! But because God ordains that one should honour all authority)—not only are they better men, but that they also have a 'better time,' at any rate, will one day have a 'better time.' But enough! Enough! I can endure it no longer. Bad air! Bad air! These workshops *where ideals are manufactured*—verily they reek with the crassest lies."

Nay. Just one minute! You are saying nothing about the masterpieces of these virtuosos of black magic, who can produce whiteness, milk, and innocence out of any black you like: have you not noticed what a pitch of refinement is attained by their *chef d'œuvre*, their most audacious, subtle, ingenious, and lying artist-trick? Take care! These cellar-beasts, full of revenge and hate—what do they make, forsooth, out of their revenge and hate? Do you hear these words? Would you suspect, if you trusted only their words, that you are among men of resentment and nothing else?

"I understand, I prick my ears up again (ah! ah! ah! and I hold my nose). Now do I hear for the first time that which they have said so often: 'We good, *we are the righteous*'—what they demand they call not revenge but 'the triumph of *righteousness*'; what they hate is not their enemy, no, they hate 'unrighteousness,' 'godlessness'; what they believe in and hope is not the hope of revenge, the intoxication of sweet revenge (—"sweeter than honey," did Homer call it?), but the victory of God, of the *righteous God* over the 'godless'; what is left for them to love in this world is not their brothers in hate, but their 'brothers in love,' as they say, all the good and righteous on the earth."

And how do they name that which serves them as a solace against all the troubles of life—their phantasmagoria of their anticipated future blessedness?

"How? Do I hear right? They call it 'the last judgment,' the advent of *their* kingdom, 'the kingdom of God'—but *in the meanwhile* they live 'in faith,' 'in love,' 'in hope.' "

Enough! Enough!

15.

In the faith in what? In the love for what? In the hope of what? These weaklings!—they also, forsooth, wish to be strong some time; there is no doubt about it, some time *their* kingdom also must come— "the kingdom of God" is their name for it, as has been mentioned:—they are so meek in everything! Yet in order to experience *that* kingdom it is necessary to live long, to live beyond death,—yes, *eternal* life is necessary so that one can make up for ever for that earthly life "in faith," "in love," "in hope." Make up for what? Make up by what? Dante, as it seems to me, made a crass mistake when with awe-inspiring ingenuity he placed that inscription over the gate of his hell, "Me too made eternal love": at any rate the following inscription would have a much better right to stand over the gate of the Christian Paradise and its "eternal blessedness"—"Me too made eternal hate"— granted of course that a truth may rightly stand over the gate to a lie! For what is the blessedness of that Paradise? Possibly we could quickly surmise it; but it is better that it should be explicitly attested by an authority who in such matters is not to be disparaged, Thomas of Aquinas, the great teacher and saint. "*Beati in regno celesti,*" says he, as gently as a lamb, "*videbunt poenas damnatorum, ut beatitudo illis magis complaceat.*" . . .

16.

Let us come to a conclusion. The *two opposing values,* "good and bad," "good and evil," have fought a dreadful, thousand-year fight in the world, and though indubitably the second value has been for a long time in the preponderance, there are not wanting places where the fortune of the fight is still undecisive. It can almost be said that in the meanwhile the fight reaches a higher and higher level, and that in the meanwhile it has become more and more intense; and always more and more psychological; so that nowadays there is perhaps no more decisive mark of the *higher nature,* of the more psychological nature, than to be in that sense self-contradictory, and to be actually still a battleground for those two opposites. The symbol of this fight, written in a writing which has remained worthy of perusal throughout the course of history up to the present time, is called "Rome against Judæa, Judæa against Rome." Hitherto there has been no greater event *than* that fight, the putting of *that* question, *that* deadly antagonism. Rome found in the Jew the incarnation of the unnatural, as though it were its diametrically opposed monstrosity, and in Rome the Jew was held to be *convicted of hatred* of the whole human race:

and rightly so, in so far as it is right to link the well-being and the future of the human race to the unconditional mastery of the aristocratic values, of the Roman values. What, conversely, did the Jews feel against Rome? One can surmise it from a thousand symptoms, but it is sufficient to carry one's mind back to the Johannian Apocalypse, that most obscene of all the written outbursts, which has revenge on its conscience. (One should also appraise at its full value the profound logic of the Christian instinct, when over this very book of hate it wrote the name of the Disciple of Love, that self-same disciple to whom it attributed that impassioned and ecstatic Gospel— therein lurks a portion of truth, however much literary forging may have been necessary for this purpose.) The Romans were the strong and aristocratic; a nation stronger and more aristocratic has never existed in the world, has never even been dreamed of; every relic of them, every inscription enraptures, granted that one can divine *what* it is that writes the inscription. The Jews, conversely, were that priestly nation of resentment *par excellence,* possessed by a unique genius for popular morals: just compare with the Jews the nations with analogous gifts, such as the Chinese or the Germans, so as to realise afterwards what is first rate, and what is fifth rate.

Which of them has been provisionally victorious, Rome or Judæa? but there is not a shadow of doubt; just consider to whom in Rome itself nowadays you bow down, as though before the quintessence of all the highest values—and not only in Rome, but almost over half the world, everywhere where man has been tamed or is about to be tamed—to *three Jews,* as we know, and *one Jewess* (to Jesus of Nazareth, to Peter the fisher, to Paul the tent-maker, and to the mother of the aforesaid Jesus, named Mary). This is very remarkable: Rome is undoubtedly defeated. At any rate there took place in the Renaissance a brilliantly sinister revival of the classical ideal, of the aristocratic valuation of all things: Rome herself, like a man waking up from a trance, stirred beneath the burden of the new Judaised Rome that had been built over her, which presented the appearance of an œcumenical synagogue and was called the "Church": but immediately Judæa triumphed again, thanks to that fundamentally popular (German and English) movement of revenge, which is called the Reformation, and taking also into account its inevitable corollary, the restoration of the Church—the restoration also of the ancient graveyard peace of classical Rome. Judæa proved yet once more victorious over the classical ideal in the French Revolution, and in a sense which was even more crucial and even more profound: the last political aristocracy that existed in Europe, that of the *French* seventeenth and eighteenth centuries, broke into pieces beneath the instincts of a resentful populace—never had the world heard a greater jubilation, a more uproarious enthusiasm: indeed, there took place in the midst of it the most monstrous and unexpected phenomenon; the ancient ideal *itself* swept before the eyes and conscience of humanity with all its life and with unheard-of splendour, and in opposition to resentment's lying war-cry of *the prerogative of the most*, in opposition to the will to lowliness, abasement, and equalisation, the will to a retrogression and twilight of humanity, there rang out once again, stronger, simpler, more penetrating than ever, the terrible and enchanting counter-war-cry of *the prerogative of the few*! Like a final sign-post to other ways, there appeared Napoleon, the most unique and violent anachronism that ever existed, and in him the incarnate problem *of the aristocratic ideal in itself*—consider well what a problem it is:—Napoleon, that synthesis of Monster and Superman.

17.

Was it therewith over? Was that greatest of all antitheses of ideals thereby relegated *ad acta* for all time? Or only postponed, postponed for a long time? May there not take place at some time or other a much more awful, much more carefully prepared flaring up of the old conflagration? Further! Should not one wish *that* consummation with all one's strength?—will it one's self? demand it one's self? He who at this juncture begins, like my readers, to reflect, to think further, will have difficulty in coming quickly to a conclusion,—ground enough for me to come myself to a conclusion, taking it for granted

that for some time past what I mean has been sufficiently clear, what I exactly *mean* by that dangerous motto which is inscribed on the body of my last book: *Beyond Good and Evil*—at any rate that is not the same as "Beyond Good and Bad."

NOTE.—I avail myself of the opportunity offered by this treatise to express, openly and formally, a wish which up to the present has only been expressed in occasional conversations with scholars, namely, that some Faculty of philosophy should, by means of a series of prize essays, gain the glory of having promoted the further study of the *history of morals*—perhaps this book may serve to give a forcible impetus in such a direction. With regard to a possibility of this character, the following question deserves consideration. It merits quite as much the attention of philologists and historians as of actual professional philosophers.

"What indication of the history of the evolution of the moral ideas is afforded by philology, and especially by etymological investigation?"

On the other hand, it is, of course, equally necessary to induce physiologists and doctors to be interested in these problems (*of the value of the valuations* which have prevailed up to the present): in this connection the professional philosophers may be trusted to act as the spokesmen and intermediaries in these particular instances, after, of course, they have quite succeeded in transforming the relationship between philosophy and physiology and medicine, which is originally one of coldness and suspicion, into the most friendly and fruitful reciprocity. In point of fact, all tables of values, all the "thou shalts" known to history and ethnology, need primarily a *physiological*, at any rate in preference to a psychological, elucidation and interpretation; all equally require a critique from medical science. The question, "What is the *value* of this or that table of 'values' and morality?" will be asked from the most varied standpoints. For instance, the question of "valuable *for what*" can never be analysed with sufficient nicety. That, for instance, which would evidently have value with regard to promoting in a race the greatest possible powers of endurance (or with regard to increasing its adaptability to a specific climate, or with regard to the preservation of the greatest number) would have nothing like the same value, if it were a question of evolving a stronger species. In gauging values, the good of the majority and the good of the minority are opposed standpoints: we leave it to the naïveté of English biologists to regard the former standpoint as *intrinsically* superior. *All* the sciences have now to pave the way for the future task of the philosopher; this task being understood to mean, that he must solve the problem of *value*, that he has to fix the *hierarchy of values*.

HENRY SIDGWICK

FROM *The Methods of Ethics*

No philosopher better exemplifies moral philosophy in the mid-nineteenth century than does Henry Sidgwick. Born in 1838 in Yorkshire, England, Sidgwick derived an abiding interest in philosophy during his youth as a result of his deep concern over the loss of his Christian faith. After a superior undergraduate career at Trinity College, Cambridge, he was appointed to a lectureship there in 1859 and was elected to the chair of moral philosophy in 1883. Aside from an interest in ethics, he wrote on education, political theory, the history of political institutions, and literature. He was an active supporter of the movement for women's education at his university, devoting a considerable amount of time and money to the establishment of Newnham College for women at Cambridge. Psychical phenomena were also a great interest of Sidgwick's: He helped found the Society for Psychical Research and served two terms as its president.

Sidgwick's reputation rests primarily on three works: The Methods of Ethics *(1874),* Outlines of the History of Ethics *(1886), and* Lectures on the Ethics of Green, Spencer, and Martineau *(1902, published posthumously). The Methods, excerpted in this volume, were considered by C. D. Broad to be the best single work in moral philosophy in the English language. Unfortunately, the density and painstaking detail of his philosophical writing style, devoid of the humor that characterized his normal character, hindered the appreciation of the importance and originality of his ideas. Nonetheless, one can appreciate in his attention to detail the attributes of the analytical style of philosophy, which was to predominate in Anglo-American philosophy in our own century.*

In The Methods, *Sidgwick attempts to reconcile perhaps the greatest controversy in moral philosophy in his century—the dispute between intuitionism and utilitarianism. Sidgwick set down four moral principles he believed to be self-evident. Two of these—that the good of each person is equally important and that the rational person must aim for the good—he used to deduce the abstract principle of benevolence. He believed this principle was accepted by intuitionists as the foundation of their own rules, and thus, he had shown that intuitionism was fundamentally utilitarian. Also, the foundations of utilitarianism rest on truths known, according to Sidgwick, not by inference but by intuition. Therefore, the two methods of ethics can be completely synthesized.*

Sidgwick is usually considered a utilitarian, albeit one with an intuitionist bent, but he disagreed with several aspects of the orthodox view of utilitarianism established by Bentham and, later, J. S. Mill. For example, he rejected the empiricist epistemology of Mill and Bentham and the metaphysical materialism and reductive sensationalism to which he thought the empiricist epistemology led. Likewise, he rejected the utilitarian attempt to define ethical terms such as "good" in terms of nonethical terms such as "pleasant" and the motivational theories of Bentham and Mill. Further, Sidgwick held that utilitarianism did not necessarily lead to radical political views like those of Mill. Additionally, Sidgwick disputed Mill's attempt to provide a philosophical basis for utilitarianism upon the psychological fact that people act to maximize pleasure. A psychological thesis, according to Sidgwick, can never be the foundation for a philosophical thesis. In his denial that one can derive the moral "ought" from the psychological "is," Sidgwick anticipates the "naturalistic fallacy" that his student, G. E. Moore, was to make famous at the beginning of the new century. The naturalistic fallacy condemned as fallacious all attempts to define "good" and led to sweeping changes in moral philosophy.

Book I Chapter I

Introduction

§ 1. The boundaries of the study called Ethics are variously and often vaguely conceived: but they will perhaps be sufficiently defined, at the outset, for the purposes of the present treatise, if a 'Method of Ethics' is explained to mean any rational procedure by which we determine what individual human beings 'ought'—or what it is 'right' for them—to do, or to seek to realise by voluntary action.[1] By using the word "individual" I provisionally distinguish the study of Ethics from that of Politics,[2] which seeks to determine the proper constitution and the right public conduct of governed societies: both Ethics and Politics being, in my view, distinguished from positive sciences by having as their special and primary object to determine what ought to be, and not to ascertain what merely is, has been, or will be.

The student of Ethics seeks to attain systematic and precise general knowledge of what ought to be, and in this sense his aims and methods may properly be termed 'scientific': but I have preferred to call Ethics a study rather than a science, because it is widely thought that a Science must necessarily have some department of actual existence for its subject-matter. And in fact the term 'Ethical Science' might, without violation of usage, denote either the department of Psychology that deals with voluntary action

and its springs, and with moral sentiments and judgments, as actual phenomena of individual human minds; or the department of Sociology dealing with similar phenomena, as manifested by normal members of the organised groups of human beings which we call societies. We observe, however, that most persons do not pursue either of these studies merely from curiosity, in order to ascertain what actually exists, has existed, or will exist in time. They commonly wish not only to understand human action, but also to regulate it; in this view they apply the ideas 'good' and 'bad,' 'right, and 'wrong,' to the conduct or institutions which they describe; and thus pass, as I should say, from the point of view of Psychology or Sociology to that of Ethics or Politics. My definition of Ethics is designed to mark clearly the fundamental importance of this transition. It is true that the mutual implication of the two kinds of study—the positive and the practical—is, on any theory, very close and complete. On any theory, our view of what ought to be must be largely derived, in details, from our apprehension of what is; the means of realising our ideal can only be thoroughly learnt by a careful study of actual phenomena; and to any individual asking himself 'What ought I to do or aim at?' it is important to examine the answers which his fellow-men have actually given to similar questions. Still it seems clear that an attempt to ascertain the general laws or uniformities by which the varieties of human conduct, and of men's sentiments and judgments respecting conduct, may be *explained,* is essentially different from an attempt to determine which among these varieties of conduct is *right* and which of these divergent judgments *valid*. It is, then, the systematic consideration of these latter questions which constitutes, in my view, the special and distinct aim of Ethics and Politics.

---

1. [T]he terms 'right' and 'what ought to be' . . . may be used as convertible, for most purposes.

2. I use 'Politics' in what I take to be its most ordinary signification, to denote the science or study of Right or Good Legislation and Government. There is a wider possible sense of the term, according to which it would include the greater part of Ethics: *i.e.* if understood to be the Theory of Right Social Relations.

§ 2. In the language of the preceding section I could not avoid taking account of two different forms in which the fundamental problem of Ethics is stated; the difference between which leads, as we shall presently see, to rather important consequences. Ethics is sometimes considered as an investigation of the true Moral laws or rational precepts of Conduct; sometimes as an inquiry into the nature of the Ultimate End of reasonable human action—the Good or 'True Good' of man—and the method of attaining it. Both these views are familiar, and will have to be carefully considered: but the former seems most prominent in modern ethical thought, and most easily applicable to modern ethical systems generally. For the Good investigated in Ethics is limited to Good in some degree attainable by human effort; accordingly knowledge of the end is sought in order to ascertain what actions are the right means to its attainment. Thus however prominent the notion of an Ultimate Good—other than voluntary action of any kind—may be in an ethical system, and whatever interpretation may be given to this notion, we must still arrive finally, if it is to be practically useful, at some determination of precepts or directive rules of conduct.

On the other hand, the conception of Ethics as essentially an investigation of the 'Ultimate Good' of Man and the means of attaining it is not universally applicable, without straining, to the view of Morality which we may conveniently distinguish as the Intuitional view; according to which conduct is held to be right when conformed to certain precepts or principles of Duty, intuitively known to be unconditionally binding. In this view the conception of Ultimate Good is not necessarily of fundamental importance in the determination of Right conduct except on the assumption that Right conduct itself—or the character realised in and developed through Right conduct—is the sole Ultimate Good for man. But this assumption is not implied in the Intuitional view of Ethics: nor would it, I conceive, accord with the moral common sense of modern Christian communities. For we commonly think that the complete notion of human Good or Well-being must include the attainment of Happiness as well as the performance of Duty; even if we hold with Butler that "the happiness of the world is the concern of Him who is the Lord and the Proprietor of it," and that, accordingly, it is not right for men to make their performance of Duty conditional on their knowledge of its conduciveness to their Happiness. For those

who hold this, what men ought to take as the *practically* ultimate end of their action and standard of Right conduct, may in some cases have no logical connexion with the conception of Ultimate Good for man: so that, in such cases, however indispensable this latter conception may be to the completeness of an ethical system, it would still not be important for the methodical determination of Right conduct.

It is on account of the prevalence of the Intuitional view just mentioned, and the prominent place which it consequently occupies in my discussion, that in defining Ethics I have avoided the term 'Art of Conduct' which some would regard as its more appropriate designation. For the term 'Art'—when applied to the contents of a treatise—seems to signify systematic express knowledge (as distinguished from the implicit knowledge or organised habit which we call skill) of the right means to a given end. Now if we assume that the rightness of action depends on its conduciveness to some ulterior end, then no doubt—when this end has been clearly ascertained—the process of determining the right rules of conduct for human beings in different relations and circumstances would naturally come under the notion of Art. But on the view that the practically ultimate end of moral action is often the Rightness of the action itself—or the Virtue realised in and confirmed by such action—and that this is known intuitively in each case or class of cases, we can hardly regard the term 'Art' as properly applicable to the systematisation of such knowledge. Hence, as I do not wish to start with any assumption incompatible with this latter view, I prefer to consider Ethics as the science or study of what is right or what ought to be, so far as this depends upon the voluntary action of individuals.[1]

§ 3. If, however, this view of the scope of Ethics is accepted, the question arises why it is commonly taken to consist, to a great extent, of psychological discussion as to the 'nature of the moral faculty'; especially as I have myself thought it right to include some discussion of this kind in the present treatise. For it does not at first appear why this should belong to Ethics, any more than discussions about the mathematical faculty or the faculty of sense-perception

---

1. The relation of the notion of 'Good' to that of 'Right' or 'what ought to be' will be further considered . . .

belong to mathematics and physics respectively. Why do we not simply start with certain premises, stating what ought to be done or sought, without considering the faculty by which we apprehend their truth?

One answer is that the moralist has a practical aim: we desire knowledge of right conduct in order to act on it. Now we cannot help believing what we see to be true, but we can help doing what we see to be right or wise, and in fact often do what we know to be wrong or unwise: thus we are forced to notice the existence in us of irrational springs of action, conflicting with our knowledge and preventing its practical realisation: and the very imperfectness of the connexion between our practical judgment and our will impels us to seek for more precise knowledge as to the nature of that connexion.

But this is not all. Men never ask, 'Why should I believe what I see to be true?' but they frequently ask, 'Why should I do what I see to be right?' It is easy to reply that the question is futile, since it could only be answered by a reference to some other recognised principle of right conduct, and the question might just as well be asked as regards that again, and so on. But still we do ask the question widely and continually, and therefore this demonstration of its futility is not completely satisfactory: we require besides some explanation of its persistency.

One explanation that may be offered is that, since we are moved to action not by moral judgment alone, but also by desires and inclinations that operate independently of moral judgment, the answer which we really want to the question 'Why should I do it?' is one which does not merely prove a certain action to be right, but also stirs in us a predominant inclination to do the action.

That this explanation is true for some minds in some moods I would not deny. Still I think that when a man seriously asks 'why he should do' anything, he commonly assumes in himself a determination to pursue whatever conduct may be shown by argument to be reasonable, even though it be very different from that to which his non-rational inclinations may prompt. And we are generally agreed that reasonable conduct in any case has to be determined on principles, in applying which the agent's inclination—as it exists apart from such determination—is only one element among several that have to be considered, and commonly not the most important element. But when we ask what these principles are, the diversity of answers which we find manifestly declared in the systems and fundamental formulæ of professed moralists seems to be really present in the common practical reasoning of men generally; with this difference, that whereas the philosopher seeks unity of principle, and consistency of method at the risk of paradox, the unphilosophic man is apt to hold different principles at once, and to apply different methods in more or less confused combination. If this be so, we can offer another explanation of the persistent unsatisfied demand for an ultimate reason, above noticed. For if there are different views of the ultimate reasonableness of conduct, implicit in the thought of ordinary men, though not brought into clear relation to each other,—it is easy to see that any single answer to the question 'why' will not be completely satisfactory, as it will be given only from one of these points of view, and will always leave room to ask the question from some other.

I am myself convinced that this is the main explanation of the phenomenon: and it is on this conviction that the plan of the present treatise is based. We cannot, of course, regard as valid reasonings that lead to conflicting conclusions; and I therefore assume as a fundamental postulate of Ethics, that so far as two methods conflict, one or other of them must be modified or rejected. But I think it fundamentally important to recognise, at the outset of Ethical inquiry, that there is a diversity of methods applied in ordinary practical thought.

§ 4. What then are these different methods? what are the different practical principles which the common sense of mankind is *prima facie* prepared to accept as ultimate? Some care is needed in answering this question: because we frequently prescribe that this or that 'ought' to be done or aimed at without any express reference to an ulterior end, while yet such an end is tacitly presupposed. It is obvious that such prescriptions are merely, what Kant calls them, Hypothetical Imperatives; they are not addressed to any one who has not first accepted the end.

For instance: a teacher of any art assumes that his pupil wants to produce the product of the art, or to produce it excellent in quality: he tells him that he *ought* to hold the awl, the hammer, the brush differently. A physician assumes that his patient wants health: he tells him that he *ought* to rise early, to live plainly, to take hard exercise. If the patient deliberately prefers ease and good living to health, the physician's precepts fall to the ground: they are no longer addressed to him. So, again, a man of the world assumes that his hearers wish to get on in society, when he lays down rules of dress, manner, conversation, habits of life. A similar view may be plausibly taken of many rules prescribing what are sometimes called "duties to oneself": it may be said that they are given on the assumption that a man regards his own Happiness as an ultimate end: that if any one should be so exceptional as to disregard it, he does not come within their scope: in short, that the *'ought'* in such formulæ is still implicitly relative to an *optional* end.

It does not, however, seem to me that this account of the matter is exhaustive. We do not all look with simple indifference on a man who declines to take the right means to attain his own happiness, on no other ground than that he does not care about happiness. Most men would regard such a refusal as irrational, with a certain disapprobation; they would thus implicitly assent to Butler's statement[1] that "interest, one's own happiness, is a manifest obligation." In other words, they would think that a man *ought* to care for his own happiness. The word 'ought' thus used is no longer relative: happiness now appears as an ultimate end, the pursuit of which—at least within the limits imposed by other duties—appears to be prescribed by reason 'categorically,' as Kant would say, *i.e.* without any tacit assumption of a still ulterior end. And it has been widely held by even orthodox moralists that all morality rests ultimately on the basis of "reasonable self-love";[2] *i.e.* that its rules are ultimately binding on any individual only so far as it is his interest on the whole to observe them.

Still, common moral opinion certainly regards the duty or virtue of Prudence as only a part—and not the most important part—of duty or virtue in general. Common moral opinion recognises and inculcates other fundamental rules—*e.g.* those of Justice, Good Faith, Veracity—which, in its ordinary judgments on particular cases, it is inclined to treat as binding without qualification and without regard to ulterior consequences. And, in the ordinary form of the Intuitional view of Ethics, the "categorical" prescription of such rules is maintained explicitly and definitely, as a result of philosophical reflection: and the realisation of Virtue in act—at least in the case of

the virtues just mentioned—is held to consist in strict and unswerving conformity to such rules.

On the other hand it is contended by many Utilitarians that all the rules of conduct which men prescribe to one another as moral rules are really—though in part unconsciously—prescribed as means to the general happiness of mankind, or of the whole aggregate of sentient beings; and it is still more widely held by Utilitarian thinkers that such rules, however they may originate, are only valid so far as their observance is conducive to the general happiness. This contention I shall hereafter examine with due care. Here I wish only to point out that, if the duty of aiming at the general happiness is thus taken to include all other duties, as subordinate applications of it, we seem to be again led to the notion of Happiness as an ultimate end categorically prescribed,—only it is now General Happiness and not the private happiness of any individual. And this is the view that I myself take of the Utilitarian principle.

At the same time, it is not necessary, in the methodical investigation of right conduct, considered relatively to the end either of private or of general happiness, to assume that the end itself is determined or prescribed by reason: we only require to assume, in reasoning to cogent practical conclusions, that it is adopted as ultimate and paramount. For if a man accepts any end as ultimate and paramount, he accepts implicitly as his "method of ethics" whatever process of reasoning enables him to determine the actions most conducive to this end. Since, however, to every difference in the end accepted at least some difference in method will generally correspond: if all the ends which men are found practically to adopt as ultimate (subordinating everything else to the attainment of them under the influence of 'ruling passions'), were taken as principles for which the student of Ethics is called upon to construct rational methods, his task would be very complex and extensive. But if we confine ourselves to such ends as the common sense of mankind appears to accept as rational ultimate ends, the task is reduced, I think, within manageable limits; since this criterion will exclude at least many of the objects which men practically seem to regard as paramount. Thus many men sacrifice health, fortune, happiness, to Fame; but no one, so far as I know, has deliberately maintained that Fame is an object which it is reasonable for men to seek for its own sake. It only commends itself to reflective minds either (1) as a source of

---

1. See the Preface to Butler's *Sermons on Human Nature.*

2. The phrase is Butler's.

Happiness to the person who gains it, or (2) a sign of his Excellence, moral or intellectual, or (3) because it attests the achievement by him of some important benefit to society, and at the same time stimulates him and others to further achievement in the future: and the conception of "benefit" would, when examined in its turn, lead us again to Happiness or Excellence of human nature,—since a man is commonly thought to benefit others either by making them happier or by making them wiser and more virtuous.

Whether there are any ends besides these two, which can be reasonably regarded as ultimate, it will hereafter be part of our business to investigate: but we may perhaps say that *prima facie* the only two ends which have a strongly and widely supported claim to be regarded as rational ultimate ends are the two just mentioned, Happiness and Perfection or Excellence of human nature—meaning here by 'Excellence' not primarily superiority to others, but a partial realisation of, or approximation to, an ideal type of human Perfection. And we must observe that the adoption of the former of these ends leads us to two *prima facie* distinct methods, according as it is sought to be realised universally, or by each individual for himself alone. For though doubtless a man may often best promote his own happiness by labouring and abstaining for the sake of others, it seems to be implied in our common notion of self-sacrifice that actions most conducive to the general happiness do not—in this world at least—always tend also to the greatest happiness of the agent. And among those who hold that "happiness is our being's end and aim" we seem to find a fundamental difference of opinion as to whose happiness it is that it is ultimately reasonable to aim at. For to some it seems that "the constantly proper end of action on the part of any individual at the moment of action is his real greatest happiness from that moment to the end of his life";[1] whereas others hold that the view of reason is essentially universal, and that it cannot be reasonable to take as an ultimate and paramount end the happiness of any one individual rather than that of any other—at any rate if equally deserving and susceptible of it—so that general happiness must be the "true standard of right and wrong, in the field of

morals" no less than of politics.[2] It is, of course, possible to adopt an end intermediate between the two, and to aim at the happiness of some limited portion of mankind, such as one's family or nation or race: but any such limitation seems arbitrary, and probably few would maintain it to be reasonable *per se*, except as the most practicable way of aiming at the general happiness, or of indirectly securing one's own.

The case seems to be otherwise with Excellence or Perfection.[3] At first sight, indeed, the same alternatives present themselves:[4] it seems that the Excellence aimed at may be taken either individually or universally; and circumstances are conceivable in which a man is not unlikely to think that he could best promote the Excellence of others by sacrificing his own. But no moralist who takes Excellence as an ultimate end has ever approved of such sacrifice, at least so far as Moral Excellence is concerned; no one has ever directed an individual to promote the virtue of others except in so far as this promotion is compatible with, or rather involved in, the complete realisation of Virtue in himself.[5] So far, then, there seems to be no need of separating the method of determining right conduct which takes the Excellence or Perfection of the individual as the ultimate aim from that which aims at the Excellence or Perfection of the human community. And since Virtue is commonly conceived as the most valuable element of human Excellence—and an element essentially

---

1. Bentham, *Memoirs* (vol. x. of Bowring's edition), p. 560.

2. Bentham again, Memoirs, p.79 . . . The Utilitarians since Bentham have sometimes adopted one, sometimes the other, of these two principles as paramount.

3. I use the terms 'Excellence' and 'Perfection' to denote the same ultimate end regarded in somewhat different aspects: meaning by either an ideal complex of mental qualities, of which we admire and approve the manifestation in human life: but using 'Perfection' to denote the ideal as such, while 'Excellence' denotes such partial realisation of or approximation to the ideal as we actually find in human experience.

4. It may be said that even more divergent views of the reasonable end are possible here than in the case of happiness: for we are not necessarily limited (as in that case) to the consideration of sentient beings: inanimate things also seem to have a perfection and excellence of their own and to be capable of being made better or worse in their kind; and this perfection, or one species of it, appears to be the end of the Fine Arts. But reflection I think shows that neither beauty nor any other quality of inanimate objects can be regarded as good or desirable in itself, out of relation to the perfection or happiness of sentient beings.

5. Kant roundly denies that it can be my duty to take the Perfection of others for my end: but his argument is not, I think, valid.

preferable to any other element that can come into competition with it as an alternative for rational choice—any method which takes Perfection or Excellence of human nature as ultimate End will *prima facie* coincide to a great extent with that based on what I called the Intuitional view: and I have accordingly decided to treat it as a special form of this latter. The two methods which take happiness as an ultimate end it will be convenient to distinguish as Egoistic and Universalistic Hedonism: and as it is the latter of these, as taught by Bentham and his successors, that is more generally understood under the term 'Utilitarianism,' I shall always restrict that word to this signification. For Egoistic Hedonism it is somewhat hard to find a single perfectly appropriate term. I shall often call this simply Egoism: but it may sometimes be convenient to call it Epicureanism: for though this name more properly denotes a particular historical system, it has come to be commonly used in the wider sense in which I wish to employ it.

§ 5. The last sentence suggests one more explanation, which, for clearness' sake, it seems desirable to make: an explanation, however, rather of the plan and purpose of the present treatise than of the nature and boundaries of the subject of Ethics as generally understood.

There are several recognised ways of treating this subject, none of which I have thought it desirable to adopt. We may start with existing systems, and either study them historically, tracing the changes in thought through the centuries, or compare and classify them according to relations of resemblance, or criticise their internal coherence. Or we may seek to add to the number of these systems: and claim after so many unsuccessful efforts to have at last attained the one true theory of the subject, by which all others may be tested. The present book contains neither the exposition of a system nor a natural or critical history of systems. I have attempted to define and unfold not one Method of Ethics, but several: at the same time these are not here studied historically, as methods that have actually been used or proposed for the regulation of practice; but rather as alternatives between which—so far as they cannot be reconciled—the human mind seems to me necessarily forced to choose, when it attempts to frame a complete synthesis of practical maxims and to act in a perfectly consistent manner. Thus, they might perhaps be called natural methods rationalised; because men commonly seem to guide them-

selves by a mixture of different methods, more or less disguised under ambiguities of language. The impulses or principles from which the different methods take their rise, the different claims of different ends to be rational, are admitted, to some extent, by all minds: and as along with these claims is felt the need of harmonising them—since it is, as was said, a postulate of the Practical Reason, that two conflicting rules of action cannot both be reasonable—the result is ordinarily either a confused blending, or a forced and premature reconciliation, of different principles and methods. Nor have the systems framed by professed moralists been free from similar defects. The writers have usually proceeded to synthesis without adequate analysis; the practical demand for the former being more urgently felt than the theoretical need of the latter. For here as in other points the development of the theory of Ethics would seem to be somewhat impeded by the preponderance of practical considerations; and perhaps a more complete detachment of the theoretical study of right conduct from its practical application is to be desired for the sake even of the latter itself: since a treatment which is a compound between the scientific and the hortatory is apt to miss both the results that it would combine; the mixture is bewildering to the brain and not stimulating to the heart. So again, I am inclined to think that here, as in other sciences, it would be an advantage to draw as distinct a line as possible between the known and the unknown; as the clear indication of an unsolved problem is at any rate a step to its solution. In ethical treatises, however, there has been a continual tendency to ignore and keep out of sight the difficulties of the subject; either unconsciously, from a latent conviction that the questions which the writer cannot answer satisfactorily must be questions which ought not to be asked; or consciously, that he may not shake the sway of morality over the minds of his readers. This last well-meant precaution frequently defeats itself: the difficulties thus concealed in exposition are liable to reappear in controversy: and then they appear not carefully limited, but magnified for polemical purposes. Thus we get on the one hand vague and hazy reconciliation, on the other loose and random exaggeration of discrepancies; and neither process is effective to dispel the original vagueness and ambiguity which lurks in the fundamental notions of our common practical reasonings. To eliminate or reduce this indefiniteness and confusion is the sole immediate end that I have proposed to myself in the present work. In order better to execute this task, I have refrained from expressly attempting any such complete and final solution of the chief ethical difficulties and controversies as would convert this exposition of various methods into the development of a harmonious system. At the same time I hope to afford aid towards the construction of such a system; because it seems easier to judge of the mutual relations and conflicting claims of different modes of thought, after an impartial and rigorous investigation of the conclusions to which they logically lead. It is not uncommon to find in reflecting on practical principles, that—however unhesitatingly they seem to command our assent at first sight, and however familiar and apparently clear the notions of which they are composed—nevertheless when we have carefully examined the consequences of adopting them they wear a changed and somewhat dubious aspect. The truth seems to be that most of the practical principles that have been seriously put forward are more or less satisfactory to the common sense of mankind, so long as they have the field to themselves. They all find a response in our nature: their fundamental assumptions are all such as we are disposed to accept, and such as we find to govern to a certain extent our habitual conduct. When I am asked, "Do you not consider it ultimately reasonable to seek pleasure and avoid pain for yourself?" "Have you not a moral sense?" "Do you not intuitively pronounce some actions to be right and others wrong?" "Do you not acknowledge the general happiness to be

a paramount end?" I answer 'yes' to all these questions. My difficulty begins when I have to choose between the different principles or inferences drawn from them. We admit the necessity, when they conflict, of making this choice, and that it is irrational to let sometimes one principle prevail and sometimes another; but the necessity is a painful one. We cannot but hope that all methods may ultimately coincide: and at any rate, before making our election we may reasonably wish to have the completest possible knowledge of each.

My object, then, in the present work, is to expound as clearly and as fully as my limits will allow the different methods of Ethics that I find implicit in our common moral reasoning; to point out their mutual relations; and where they seem to conflict, to define the issue as much as possible. In the course of this endeavour I am led to discuss the considerations which should, in my opinion, be decisive in determining the adoption of ethical first principles: but it is not my primary aim to establish such principles; nor, again, is it my primary aim to supply a set of practical directions for conduct. I have wished to keep the reader's attention throughout directed to the processes rather than the results of ethical thought: and have therefore never stated as my own any positive practical conclusions unless by way of illustration: and have never ventured to decide dogmatically any controverted points, except where the controversy seemed to arise from want of precision or clearness in the definition of principles, or want of consistency in reasoning.

G.E. MOORE

FROM *Principia Ethica*

George Edward Moore (1873–1958) is a transitional figure in the history of moral philosophy in most of the English speaking world. Even though other philosophers were more influential on the continent and in America, in the analytic tradition of philosophy it is usual to use the 1903 publication of Moore's major work, the Principia Ethica, *to indicate the beginning of contemporary ethical theory.*

Moore was born near London in 1873. His family was relatively prosperous: his father was a physician, and his mother's family were prominent Quaker merchants. In 1892 he enrolled in Trinity College, Cambridge, to study classics; however, after two years, he turned his attention to philosophy where he studied under Sidgwick. After completing a dissertation on Kant's ethics, he earned a fellowship at Cambridge and taught there from 1898–1904 amid lively philosophical discussion with his colleague Bertrand Russell. When his fellowship expired, he continued to write philosophy, living on an inheritance until, in 1911, he was invited back to Cambridge. There he remained until 1939 when he reached the mandatory age of retirement. Even after his retirement from the university, Moore continued his philosophical activities, writing and discussing problems with students and friends until his death at the age of 85. His life outside of philosophy was relatively uneventful, but his effect on moral philosophy was profound.

While Moore was on his fellowship at Cambridge, he published several articles and what became a most important book, the Principia Ethica. *It is in this work that Moore famously charges previous moral philosophers with a failure to begin their work in ethics at the beginning. If moral philosophers only undertake to discover what is good conduct, says Moore, they fail to acknowledge the necessity of first determining what is good. Moore claims that previous philosophers failed to make a distinction between two important questions in ethics: What kind of actions ought we to perform? and, What kind of things ought to exist for their own sake? The answer to the first question for Moore is simply those actions that bring about the most good. But attempts to answer the second question, that is, attempts to define "good," commit what Moore labeled the "naturalistic fallacy." Moore makes the radical claim that good, like the property yellow, is a simple, unanalyzable non-natural characteristic. We may know it when we see it, but we cannot define it.*

The primary object of Moore's attack is ethical naturalism, the view that moral judgments are just a special subset of facts about the world. Two theories representative of ethical naturalism singled out by Moore are those of John Stuart Mill and Herbert Spencer. For utilitarians such as Mill, good is defined in terms of happiness. But, says Moore, happiness cannot be identical with good because one can always ask whether happiness itself is good. Mill has provided an example of something that is good, not a definition of good. Likewise Moore charges Spencer, whom he sees as defining the good as "more evolved," with committing the naturalistic fallacy. Even though it is proper now to question whether Moore's characterization of these two eminent philosophers was fair to either of them, Moore's influence in ethical theory was, and remains, widely felt.

Moore's arguments against ethical naturalism have contributed to much of the controversy in contemporary ethical theory. On the one hand, many philosophers lined up under Moore's banner of nonnaturalism but did not support his alternative, ideal utilitarianisim. Intuitionists such as Prichard, Ross, and Carritt carried forward the Moorean criticisms of ethical naturalism yet offered deontological theories as an alternative to utilitarianisim. On the other hand, while both naturalism and nonnaturalism are cognitive theories, even some noncognitivist ethical theories, such as those of the emotivists Stevenson and Ayer, may owe their origins to the work of Moore.

Chapter I. The Subject-Matter of Ethics.

1. It is very easy to point out some among our every-day judgments, with the truth of which Ethics is undoubtedly concerned. Whenever we say, 'So and so is a good man,' or 'That fellow is a villain'; whenever we ask, 'What ought I to do?' or 'Is it wrong for me to do like this?'; whenever we hazard such remarks as 'Temperance is a virtue and drunkenness a vice'—it is undoubtedly the business of Ethics to discuss such questions and such statements; to argue what is the true answer when we ask what it is right to do, and to give reasons for thinking that our statements about the character of persons or the morality of actions are true or false. In the vast majority of cases, where we make statements involving any of the terms 'virtue', 'vice,' 'duty,' 'right,' 'ought,' 'good,' 'bad,' we are making ethical judgments; and if we wish to discuss their truth, we shall be discussing a point of Ethics.

So much as this is not disputed; but it falls very far short of defining the province of Ethics. That province may indeed be defined as the whole truth about that which is at the same time common to all such judgments and peculiar to them. But we have still to ask the question: What is it that is thus common and peculiar? And this is a question to which very different answers have been given by ethical philosophers of acknowledged reputation, and none of them, perhaps, completely satisfactory.

2. If we take such examples as those given above, we shall not be far wrong in saying that they are all of them concerned with the question of 'conduct'—with the question, what, in the conduct of us, human beings, is good, and what is bad, what is right, and what is wrong. For when we say that a man is good, we commonly mean that he acts rightly; when we say

that drunkenness is a vice, we commonly mean that to get drunk is a wrong or wicked action. And this discussion of human con- duct is, in fact, that with which the name 'Ethics' is most intimately associated. It is so associated by derivation; and conduct is undoubtedly by far the commonest and most generally interesting object of ethical judgments.

Accordingly, we find that many ethical philosophers are disposed to accept as an adequate definition of 'Ethics' the statement that it deals with the question what is good or bad in human conduct. They hold that its enquiries are properly confined to 'conduct' or to 'practice'; they hold that the name 'practical philosophy' covers all the matter with which it has to do. Now, without discussing the proper meaning of the word (for verbal questions are properly left to the writers of dictionaries and other persons interested in literature; philosophy, as we shall see, has no concern with them), I may say that I intend to use 'Ethics' to cover more than this—a usage, for which there is, I think, quite sufficient authority. I am using it to cover an enquiry for which, at all events, there is no other word: the general enquiry into what is good.

Ethics is undoubtedly concerned with the question what good conduct is; but, being concerned with this, it obviously does not start at the beginning, unless it is prepared to tell us what is good as well as what is conduct. For 'good conduct' is a complex notion: all conduct is not good; for some is certainly bad and some may be indifferent. And on the other hand, other things, beside conduct, may be good; and if they are so, then, 'good' denotes some property, that is common to them and conduct; and if we examine good conduct alone of all good things, then we shall be in danger of mistaking for this property, some property which is not shared by those other things: and thus we shall have made a mistake about Ethics even in this limited sense; for we shall not know what good conduct really is. This is a mistake which many writers have actually made, from limiting their enquiry to conduct. And hence I shall try to avoid it by considering first what is good in general; hoping, that if we can arrive at any certainty about this, it will be much easier to settle the question of good conduct: for we all know pretty well what 'conduct' is. This, then, is our first question: What is good? and What is bad? and to the discussion of this question (or these questions) I give the name of Ethics, since that science must, at all events, include it.

3. But this is a question which may have many meanings. If, for example, each of us were to say 'I am doing good now' or 'I had a good dinner yesterday,' these statements would each of them be some sort of answer to our question, although perhaps a false one. So, too, when A asks B what school he ought to send his son to, B's answer will certainly be an ethical judgment. And similarly all distribution of praise or blame to any personage or thing that has existed, now exists, or will exist, does give some answer to the question 'What is good?' In all such cases some particular thing is judged to be good or bad: the question 'What?' is answered by 'This.' But this is not the sense in which a scientific Ethics asks the question. Not one, of all the many million answers of this kind, which must be true, can form a part of an ethical system; although that science must contain reasons and principles sufficient for deciding on the truth of all of them. There are far too many persons, things and events in the world, past, present, or to come, for a discussion of their individual merits to be embraced in any science. Ethics, therefore, does not deal at all with facts of this nature, facts that are unique, individual, absolutely particular; facts with which such studies as history, geography, astronomy, are compelled, in part at least, to deal. And, for this reason, it is not the business of the ethical philosopher to give personal advice or exhortation.

4. But there is another meaning which may be given to the question 'What is good?' 'Books are good' would be an answer to it, though an answer obviously false; for some books are very bad indeed. And ethical judgment of this kind do indeed belong to Ethics; though I shall not deal with many of them.

Such is the judgment 'Pleasure is good'—a judgment, of which Ethics should discuss the truth, although it is not nearly as important as that other judgment, with which we shall be much occupied presently—'Pleasure *alone* is good.' It is judgments of this sort, which are made in such books on Ethics as contain a list of 'virtues'—in Aristotle's 'Ethics' for example. But it is judgments of precisely the same kind, which form the substance of what is commonly supposed to be a study different from Ethics, and one much less respectable—the study of Casuistry. We may be told that Casuistry differs from Ethics, in that it is much more detailed and particular, Ethics much more general. But it is most important to notice that Casuistry does not deal with anything that is absolutely particular—particular in the only sense in which a perfectly precise line can be drawn between it and what is general. It is not particular in the sense just noticed, the sense in which this book is a particular book, and A's friend's advice particular advice. Casuistry may indeed be *more* particular and Ethics *more* general; but that means that they differ only in degree and not in kind. And this is universally true of 'particular' and 'general,' when used in this common, but inaccurate, sense. So far as Ethics allows itself to give lists of virtues or even to name constituents of the Ideal, it is indistinguishable from Casuistry. Both alike deal with what is general, in the sense in which physics and chemistry deal with what is general. Just as chemistry aims at discovering what are the properties of oxygen, *wherever it occurs*, and not only of this or that particular specimen of oxygen; so Casuistry aims at discovering what actions are good, *whenever they occur*. In this respect Ethics and Casuistry alike are to be classed with such sciences as physics, chemistry and physiology, in their absolute distinction from those of which history and geography are instances. And it is to be noted that, owing to their detailed nature, casuistical investigations are actually nearer to physics and to chemistry than are the investigations usually assigned to Ethics. For just as physics cannot rest content with the discovery that light is propagated by waves of ether, but must go on to discover the particular nature of the ether-waves corresponding to each several colour; so Casuistry, not content with the general law that charity is a virtue must attempt to discover the relative merits of every different form of charity. Casuistry forms, therefore, part of the ideal of ethical science: Ethics cannot be complete without it. The defects of Casuistry are not defects of principle; no objection can be taken to its aim and object. It has failed only because it is far too difficult a subject to be treated adequately in our present state of knowledge. The casuist has been unable to distinguish, in the cases which he treats, those elements upon which their value depends. Hence he often thinks two cases to be alike in respect of value, when in reality they are alike only in some other respect. It is to mistakes of this kind that the pernicious influence of such investigations has been due. For Casuistry is the goal of ethical investigation. It cannot be safely attempted at the beginning of our studies, but only at the end.

5. But our question 'What is good?' may have still another meaning. We may, in the third place, mean to ask, not what thing or things are good, but how 'good' is to be defined. This is an enquiry which belongs only to Ethics, not to Casuistry; and this is the enquiry which will occupy us first.

It is an enquiry to which most special attention should be directed; since this question, how 'good' is to be defined, is the most fundamental question in all Ethics. That which is meant by 'good' is, in fact, except its converse 'bad,' the *only* simple object of thought which is peculiar to Ethics. Its definition is, therefore, the most essential point in the definition of Ethics; and moreover a mistake with regard to it entails a far larger number of erroneous ethical judgments than any other. Unless this first question be fully understood, and its true answer clearly recognised, the rest of Ethics is as good as useless from the point of view of systematic knowledge. True ethical judgments, of the two kinds last dealt with, may indeed be made by those who do not know the answer to this question as well as by those who do; and it goes without saying that the two classes of people may lead equally good lives. But it is extremely unlikely that the *most general* ethical judgments will be equally valid, in the absence of a true answer to this question: I shall presently try to shew that the gravest errors have been largely due to beliefs in a false answer. And, in any case, it is impossible that, till the answer to this question be known, any one should know *what is the evidence* for any ethical judgment whatsoever. But the main object of Ethics, as a systematic science, is to give correct *reasons* for thinking that this or that is good; and, unless this

question be answered, such reasons cannot be given. Even, therefore, apart from the fact that a false answer leads to false conclusions, the present enquiry is a most necessary and important part of the science of Ethics.

6. What, then, is good? How is good to be defined? Now, it may be thought that this is a verbal question. A definition does indeed often mean the expressing of one word's meaning in other words. But this is not the sort of definition I am asking for. Such a definition can never be of ultimate importance in any study except lexicography. If I wanted that kind of definition I should have to consider in the first place how people generally used the word 'good'; but my business is not with its proper usage, as established by custom. I should, indeed, be foolish, if I tried to use it for something which it did not usually denote: if, for instance, I were to announce that, whenever I used the word 'good,' I must be understood to be thinking of that object which is usually denoted by the word 'table.' I shall, therefore, use the word in the sense in which I think it is ordinarily used; but at the same time I am not anxious to discuss whether I am right in thinking that it is so used. My business is solely with that object or idea, which I hold, rightly or wrongly, that the word is generally used to stand for. What I want to discover is the nature of that object or idea, and about this I am extremely anxious to arrive at an agreement.

But, if we understand the question in this sense, my answer to it may seem a very disappointing one. If I am asked 'What is good?' my answer is that good is good, and that is the end of the matter. Or if I am asked 'How is good to be defined?' my answer is that it cannot be defined, and that is all I have to say about it. But disappointing as these answers may appear, they are of the very last importance. To readers who are familiar with philosophic terminology, I can express their importance by saying that they amount to this: That propositions about the good are all of them in synthetic and never analytic; and that is plainly no trivial matter. And the same thing may be expressed more popularly, by saying that, if I am right, then nobody can foist upon us such an axiom as that 'Pleasure is the only good' or that 'The good is the desired' on the pretence that this is 'the very meaning of the word.'

7. Let us, then, consider this position. My point is that 'good' is a simple notion, just as 'yellow' is a

simple notion; that, just as you cannot, by any manner of means, explain to any one who does not already know it, what yellow is, so you cannot explain what good is. Definitions of the kind that I was asking for, definitions which describe the real nature of the object or notion denoted by a word, and which do not merely tell us what the word is used to mean, are only possible when the object or notion in question is something complex. You can give a definition of a horse, because a horse has many different properties and qualities, all of which you can enumerate. But when you have enumerated them all, when you have reduced a horse to his simplest terms, then you can no longer define those terms. They are simply something which you think of or perceive, and to any one who cannot think of or perceive them, you can never, by any definition, make their nature known. It may perhaps be objected to this that we are able to describe to others, objects which they have never seen or thought of. We can, for instance, make a man understand what a chimaera is, although he has never heard of one or seen one. You can tell him that it is an animal with a lioness's head and body, with a goat's head growing from the middle of its back, and with a snake in place of a tail. But here the object which you are describing is a complex object; it is entirely composed of parts, with which we are all perfectly familiar—a snake, a goat, a lioness; and we know, too, the manner in which those parts are to be put together, because we know what is meant by the middle of a lioness's back, and where her tail is wont to grow. And so it is with all objects, not previously known, which we are able to define: they are all complex; all composed of parts, which may themselves, in the first instance, be capable of similar definition, but which must in the end be reducible to simplest parts, which can no longer be defined. But yellow and good, we say, are not complex: they are notions of that simple kind, out of which definitions are composed and with which the power of further defining ceases.

8. When we say, as Webster says, 'The definition of horse is "A hoofed quadruped of the genus Equus,"' we may, in fact, mean three different things. (1) We may mean merely: 'When I say "horse," you are to understand that I am talking about a hoofed quadruped of the genus Equus.' This might be called the arbitrary verbal definition: and I do not mean that good is in-

definable in that sense. (2) We may mean, as Webster ought to mean: 'When most English people say "horse," they mean a hoofed quadruped of the genus Equus.' This may be called the verbal definition proper, and I do not say that good is indefinable in this sense either; for it is certainly possible to discover how people use a word: otherwise, we could never have known that 'good' may be translated by 'gut' in German and by 'bon' in French. But (3) we may, when we define horse, mean something much more important. We may mean that a certain object, which we all of us know, is composed in a certain manner: that it has four legs, a head, a heart, a liver, etc., etc., all of them arranged in definite relations to one another. It is in this sense that I deny good to be definable. I say that it is not composed of any parts, which we can substitute for it in our minds when we are thinking of it. We might think just as clearly and correctly about a horse, if we thought of all its parts and their arrangement instead of thinking of the whole: we could, I say, think how a horse differed from a donkey just as well, just as truly, in this way, as now we do, only not so easily; but there is nothing whatsoever which we could so substitute for good; and that is what I mean, when I say that good is indefinable.

9. But I am afraid I have still not removed the chief difficulty which may prevent acceptance of the proposition that good is indefinable. I do not mean to say that *the* good, that which is good, is thus indefinable; if I did think so, I should not be writing on Ethics, for my main object is to help towards discovering that definition. It is just because I think there will be less risk of error in our search for a definition of 'the good,' that I am now insisting that *good* is indefinable. I must try to explain the difference between these two. I suppose it may be granted that 'good' is an adjective. Well 'the good, that which is good,' must therefore be the substantive to which the adjective 'good' will apply: it must be the whole of that to which the adjective will apply, and the adjective must *always* truly apply to it. But if it is that to which the adjective will apply, it must be something different from that adjective itself; and the whole of that something different, whatever it is, will be our definition of *the* good. Now it may be that this something will have other adjectives, beside 'good,' that will apply to it. It may be full of pleasure, for example; it may be intelligent: and if these two adjectives are really part of its

definition, then it will certainly be true, that pleasure and intelligence are good. And many people appear to think that, if we say 'Pleasure and intelligence are good,' or if we say 'Only pleasure and intelligence are good,' we are defining 'good.' Well, I cannot deny that propositions of this nature may sometimes be called definitions; I do not know well enough how the word is generally used to decide upon this point. I only wish it to be understood that that is not what I mean when I say there is no possible definition of good, and that I shall not mean this if I use the word again. I do most fully believe that some true proposition of the form 'Intelligence is good and intelligence alone is good' can be found; if none could be found, our definition of *the* good would be impossible. As it is, I believe *the* good to be definable; and yet I still say that good itself is indefinable.

10. 'Good,' then, if we mean by it that quality which we assert to belong to a thing, when we say that the thing is good, is incapable of any definition, in the most important sense of that word. The most important sense of 'definition' is that in which a definition states what are the parts which invariably compose a certain whole; and in this sense 'good' has no definition because it is simple and has no parts. It is one of those innumerable objects of thought which are themselves incapable of definition, because they are the ultimate terms by reference to which whatever *is* capable of definition must be defined. That there must be an indefinite number of such terms is obvious, on reflection; since we cannot define anything except by an analysis, which, when carried as far as it will go, refers us to something, which is simply different from anything else, and which by that ultimate difference explains the peculiarity of the whole which we are defining: for every whole contains some parts which are common to other wholes also. There is, therefore, no intrinsic difficulty in the contention that 'good' denotes a simple and indefinable quality. There are many other instances of such qualities.

Consider yellow, for example. We may try to define it, by describing its physical equivalent; we may state what kind of light vibrations must stimulate the normal eye, in order that we may perceive it. But a moment's reflection is sufficient to shew that those light-vibrations are not themselves what we mean by yellow. *They* are not what we perceive. Indeed we

should never have been able to discover their existence, unless we had first been struck by the patent difference of quality between the different colours. The most we can be entitled to say of those vibrations is that they are what corresponds in space to the yellow which we actually perceive.

Yet a mistake of this simple kind has commonly been made about 'good.' It may be true that all things which are good are *also* something else, just as it is true that all things which are yellow produce a certain kind of vibration in the light. And it is a fact, that Ethics aims at discovering what are those other properties belonging to all things which are good. But far too many philosophers have thought that when they named those other properties they were actually defining good; that these properties, in fact, were simply not 'other,' but absolutely and entirely the same with goodness. This view I propose to call the 'naturalistic fallacy' and of it I shall now endeavour to dispose.

11. Let us consider what it is such philosophers say. And first it is to be noticed that they do not agree among themselves. They not only say that they are right as to what good is, but they endeavour to prove that other people who say that it is something else, are wrong. One, for instance, will affirm that good is pleasure, another, perhaps, that good is that which is desired; and each of these will argue eagerly to prove that the other is wrong. But how is that possible? One of them says that good is nothing but the object of desire, and at the same time tries to prove that it is not pleasure. But from his first assertion, that good just means the object of desire, one of two things must follow as regards his proof:

(1) He may be trying to prove that the object of desire is not pleasure. But, if this be all, where is his Ethics? The position he is maintaining is merely a psychological one. Desire is something which occurs in our minds, and pleasure is something else which so occurs; and our would-be ethical philosopher is merely holding that the latter is not the object of the former. But what has that to do with the question in dispute? His opponent held the ethical proposition that pleasure was the good, and although he should prove a million times over the psychological proposition that pleasure is not the object of desire, he is no nearer proving his opponent to be wrong. The position is like this. One man says a triangle is a circle: another replies 'A triangle is a straight line, and I will

prove to you that I am right: *for*' (this is the only argument) 'a straight line is not a circle.' 'That is quite true,' the other may reply; 'but nevertheless a triangle is a circle, and you have said nothing whatever to prove the contrary. What is proved is that one of us is wrong, for we agree that a triangle cannot be both a straight line and a circle: but which is wrong, there can be no earthly means of proving, since you define triangle as straight line and I define it as circle.'— Well, that is one alternative which any naturalistic Ethics has to face; if good is *defined* as something else, it is then impossible either to prove that any other definition is wrong or even to deny such definition.

(2) The other alternative will scarcely be more welcome. It is that the discussion is after all a verbal one. When A says 'Good means pleasant' and B says 'Good means desired,' they may merely wish to assert that most people have used the word for what is pleasant and for what is desired respectively. And this is quite an interesting subject for discussion: only it is not a whit more an ethical discussion than the last was. Nor do I think that any exponent of naturalistic Ethics would be willing to allow that this was all he meant. They are all so anxious to persuade us that what they call the good is what we really *ought* to do. 'Do, pray, act so, because the word "good" is generally used to denote actions of this nature': such, on this view, would be the substance of their teaching. And in so far as they tell us how we ought to act, their teaching is truly ethical, as they mean it to be. But how perfectly absurd is the reason they would give for it! 'You are to do this, because most people use a certain word to denote conduct such as this.' 'You are to say the thing which is not, because most people call it lying.' That is an argument just as good!—My dear sirs, what we want to know from you as ethical teachers, is not how people use a word; it is not even, what kind of actions they approve, which the use of this word 'good' may certainly imply: what we want to know is simply what *is* good. We may indeed agree that what most people do think good, is actually so; we shall at all events be glad to know their opinions: but when we say their opinions about what *is* good, we do mean what we say; we do not care whether they call that thing which they mean 'horse' or 'table' or 'chair,' 'gut' or 'bon' or 'ἀγαθός'; we want to know what it is that they so call. When they say 'Pleasure is good,' we cannot believe that they merely mean 'Pleasure is pleasure' and nothing more than that.

12. Suppose a man says 'I am pleased'; and suppose that is not a lie or a mistake but the truth. Well, if it is true, what does that mean? It means that his mind, a certain definite mind, distinguished by certain definite marks from all others, has at this moment a certain definite feeling called pleasure. 'Pleased' *means* nothing but having pleasure, and though we may be more pleased or less pleased, and even, we may admit for the present, have one or another kind of pleasure; yet in so far as it is pleasure we have, whether there be more or less of it, and whether it be of one kind or another, what we have is one definite thing, absolutely indefinable, some one thing that is the same in all the various degrees and in all the various kinds of it that there may be. We may be able to say how it is related to other things: that, for example, it is in the mind, that it causes desire, that we are conscious of it, etc., etc. We can, I say, describe its relations to other things, but define it we can *not*. And if anybody tried to define pleasure for us as being any other natural object; if anybody were to say, for instance, that pleasure *means* the sensation of red, and were to proceed to deduce from that that pleasure is a colour, we should be entitled to laugh at him and to distrust his future statements about pleasure. Well, that would be the same fallacy which I have called the naturalistic fallacy. That 'pleased' does not mean 'having the sensation of red,' or anything else whatever, does not prevent us from understanding what it does mean. It is enough for us to know that 'pleased' does mean 'having the sensation of pleasure,' and though pleasure is absolutely indefinable, though pleasure is pleasure and nothing else whatever, yet we feel no difficulty in saying that we are pleased. The reason is, of course, that when I say 'I am pleased,' I do not mean that 'I' am the same thing as 'having pleasure.' And similarly no difficulty need be found in my saying that 'pleasure is good' and yet not meaning that 'pleasure' is the same thing as 'good,' that pleasure *means* good, and that good *means* pleasure. If I were to imagine that when I said 'I am pleased,' I meant that I was exactly the same thing as 'pleased,' I should not indeed call that a naturalistic fallacy, although it would be the same fallacy as I have called naturalistic with reference to Ethics. The reason of this is obvious enough. When a man confuses two natural objects with one another, defining the one by the other, if for instance, he confuses himself, who is

one natural object, with 'pleased' or with 'pleasure' which are others, then there is no reason to call the fallacy naturalistic. But if he confuses 'good,' which is not in the same sense a natural object, with any natural object whatever, then there is a reason for calling that a naturalistic fallacy; its being made with regard to 'good' marks it as something quite specific, and this specific mistake deserves a name because it is so common. As for the reasons why good is not to be considered a natural object, they may be reserved for discussion in another place. But, for the present, it is sufficient to notice this: Even if it were a natural object, that would not alter the nature of the fallacy nor diminish its importance one whit. All that I have said about it would remain quite equally true: only the name which I have called it would not be so appropriate as I think it is. And I do not care about the name: what I do care about is the fallacy. It does not matter what we call it, provided we recognise it when we meet with it. It is to be met with in almost every book on Ethics; and yet it is not recognised: and that is why it is necessary to multiply illustrations of it, and convenient to give it a name. It is a very simple fallacy indeed. When we say that an orange is yellow, we do not think our statement binds us to hold that 'orange' means nothing else than 'yellow,' or that nothing can be yellow but an orange. Supposing the orange is also sweet! Does that bind us to say that 'sweet' is exactly the same thing as 'yellow,' that 'sweet' must be defined as 'yellow'? And supposing it be recognised that 'yellow' just means 'yellow' and nothing else whatever, does that make it any more difficult to hold that oranges are yellow? Most certainly it does not: on the contrary, it would be absolutely meaningless to say that oranges were yellow, unless yellow did in the end mean just 'yellow' and nothing else whatever—unless it was absolutely indefinable. We should not get any very clear notion about things, which are yellow—we should not get very far with our science, if we were bound to hold that everything which was yellow, *meant* exactly the same thing as yellow. We should find we had to hold that an orange was exactly the same thing as a stool, a piece of paper, a lemon, anything you like. We could prove any number of absurdities; but should we be the nearer to the truth? Why, then, should it be different with 'good'? Why, if good is good and indefinable, should I be held to deny that pleasure is good? Is there any difficulty in holding both to be true at once? On the contrary, there is no meaning in saying that pleasure is good, unless good is something different from pleasure. It is absolutely useless, so far as Ethics is concerned, to prove, as Mr Spencer tries to do, that increase of pleasure coincides with increase of life, unless good *means* something different from either life or pleasure. He might just as well try to prove that an orange is yellow by shewing that it always is wrapped up in paper.

13. In fact, if it is not the case that 'good' denotes something simple and indefinable, only two alternatives are possible: either it is a complex, a given whole, about the correct analysis of which there may be disagreement; or else it means nothing at all, and there is no such subject as Ethics. In general, however, ethical philosophers have attempted to define good, without recognising what such an attempt must mean. They actually use arguments which involve one or both of the absurdities considered in § 11. We are, therefore, justified in concluding that the attempt to define good is chiefly due to want of clearness as to the possible nature of definition. There are, in fact, only two serious alternatives to be considered, in order to establish the conclusion that 'good' does denote a simple and indefinable notion. It might possibly denote a complex, as 'horse' does; or it might have no meaning at all. Neither of these possibilities has, however, been clearly conceived and seriously maintained, as such, by those who presume to define good; and both may be dismissed by a simple appeal to facts.

(1) The hypothesis that disagreement about the meaning of good is disagreement with regard to the correct analysis of a given whole, may be most plainly seen to be incorrect by consideration of the fact that, whatever definition be offered, it may be always asked, with significance, of the complex so defined, whether it is itself good. To take, for instance, one of the more plausible, because one of the more complicated, of such proposed definitions, it may easily be thought, at first sight, that to be good may mean to be that which we desire to desire. Thus if we apply this definition to a particular instance and say 'When we think that A is good, we are thinking that A is one of the things which we desire to desire,' our proposition may seem quite plausible. But, if we carry the investigation further, and ask ourselves 'Is it good to desire to desire A?' it is

apparent, on a little reflection, that this question is itself as intelligible; as the original question 'Is A good'—that we are, in fact, now asking for exactly the same information about the desire to desire A, for which we formerly asked with regard to A itself. But it is also apparent that the meaning of this second question cannot be correctly analysed into 'Is the desire to desire A one of the things which we desire to desire?': we have not before our minds anything so complicated as the question 'Do we desire to desire to desire to desire A?' Moreover any one can easily convince himself by inspection that the predicate of this proposition— 'good'—is positively different from the notion of 'desiring to desire' which enters into its subject: 'That we should desire to desire A is good' is *not* merely equivalent to 'That A should be good is good.' It may indeed be true that what we desire to desire is always also good; perhaps, even the converse may be true: but it is very doubtful whether this is the case, and the mere fact that we understand very well what is meant by doubting it, shews clearly that we have two different notions before our minds.

(2) And the same consideration is sufficient to dismiss the hypothesis that 'good' has no meaning whatsoever. It is very natural to make the mistake of supposing that what is universally true is of such a nature that its negation would be self-contradictory: the importance which has been assigned to analytic propositions in the history of philosophy shews how easy such a mistake is. And thus it is very easy to conclude that what seems to be a universal ethical principle is in fact an identical proposition; that, if, for example, whatever is called 'good' seems to be pleasant, the proposition 'Pleasure is the good' does not assert a connection between two different notions, but involves only one, that of pleasure, which is easily recognised as a distinct entity. But whoever will attentively consider with himself what is actually before his mind when he asks the question 'Is pleasure (or whatever it may be) after all good?' can easily satisfy himself that he is not merely wondering whether pleasure is pleasant. And if he will try this experiment with each suggested definition in succession, he may become expert enough to recognise that in every case he has before his mind a unique object, with regard to the connection of which with any other object, a distinct question may be asked. Every one does in fact understand the question 'Is

this good?' When he thinks of it, his state of mind is different from what it would be, were he asked 'Is this pleasant, or desired, or approved?' It has a distinct meaning for him, even though he may not recognise in what respect it is distinct. Whenever he thinks of 'intrinsic value,' or 'intrinsic worth,' or says that a thing 'ought to exist,' he has before his mind the unique object—the unique property of things—which I mean by 'good.' Everybody is constantly aware of this notion, although he may never become aware at all that it is different from other notions of which he is also aware. But, for correct ethical reasoning, it is extremely important that he should become aware of this fact; and, as soon as the nature of the problem is clearly understood, there should be little difficulty in advancing so far in analysis.

14. 'Good,' then, is indefinable; and yet, so far as I know, there is only one ethical writer, Prof. Henry Sidgwick, who has clearly recognised and stated this fact. We shall see, indeed, how far many of the most reputed ethical systems fall short of drawing the conclusions which follow from such a recognition. At present I will only quote one instance, which will serve to illustrate the meaning and importance of this principle that 'good' is indefinable, or, as Prof. Sidgwick says, an 'unanalysable notion.' It is an instance to which Prof. Sidgwick himself refers in a note on the passage, in which he argues that 'ought' is unanalysable.[1]

'Bentham,' says Sidgwick, 'explains that his fundamental principle "states the greatest happiness of all those whose interest is in question as being the right and proper end of human action"'; and yet 'his language in other passages of the same chapter would seem to imply' that he *means* by the word "right" "conducive to the general happiness." Prof. Sidgwick sees that, if you take these two statements together, you get the absurd result that 'greatest happiness is the end of human action, which is conducive to the general happiness'; and so absurd does it seem to him to call this result, as Bentham calls it, 'the fundamental principle of a moral system,' that he suggests that Bentham cannot have meant it. Yet Prof. Sidgwick himself states elsewhere[2] that Psychological Hedonism is 'not seldom confounded with Egoistic Hedonism';

---

1. *Methods of Ethics*, Bk. 1, Chap. iii, § 1 (6th edition).

2. *Methods of Ethics*, Bk. 1, Chap. iv, § 1.

and that confusion, as we shall see, rests chiefly on that same fallacy, the naturalistic fallacy, which is implied in Bentham's statements. Prof. Sidgwick admits therefore that this fallacy is sometimes committed, absurd as it is; and I am inclined to think that Bentham may really have been one of those who committed it. Mill, as we shall see, certainly did commit it. In any case, whether Bentham committed it or not, his doctrine, as above quoted, will serve as a very good illustration of this fallacy, and of the importance of the contrary proposition that good is indefinable.

Let us consider this doctrine. Bentham seems to imply, so Prof. Sidgwick says, that the word 'right' *means* 'conducive to general happiness.' Now this, by itself, need not necessarily involve the naturalistic fallacy. For the word 'right' is very commonly appropriated to actions which lead to the attainment of what is good; which are regarded as *means* to the ideal and not as ends-in-themselves. This use of 'right,' as denoting what is good as a means, whether or not it be also good as an end, is indeed the use to which I shall confine the word. Had Bentham been using 'right' in this sense, it might be perfectly consistent for him to *define* right as 'conducive to the general happiness,' *provided only* (and notice this proviso) he had already proved, or laid down as an axiom, that general happiness was *the* good, or (what is equivalent to this) that general happiness alone was good. For in that case he would have already defined *the* good as general happiness (a position perfectly consistent, as we have seen, with the contention that 'good' is indefinable), and, since right was to be defined as 'conducive to *the* good,' it would actually *mean* 'conducive to general happiness.' But this method of escape from the charge of having committed the naturalistic fallacy has been closed by Bentham himself. For his fundamental principle is, we see, that the greatest happiness of all concerned is the *right* and proper *end* of human action. He applies the word 'right,' therefore, to the end, as such, not only to the means which are conducive to it; and, that being so, right can no longer be defined as 'conducive to the general happiness,' without involving the fallacy in question. For now it is obvious that the definition of right as conducive to general happiness can be used by him in support of the fundamental principle that general happiness is the right end; instead of being itself derived from that principle. If right, by definition, means conducive to general happiness, then it is obvious that general happiness is the right end. It is not

necessary now first to prove or assert that general happiness is the right end, before right is defined as conducive to general happiness—a perfectly valid procedure; but on the contrary the definition of right as conducive to general happiness proves general happiness to be the right end—a perfectly invalid procedure, since in this case the statement that 'general happiness is the right end of human action' is not an ethical principle at all, but either, as we have seen, a proposition about the meaning of words, or else a proposition about the *nature* of general happiness, not about its rightness or goodness.

Now, I do not wish the importance I assign to this fallacy to be misunderstood. The discovery of it does not at all refute Bentham's contention that greatest happiness is the proper end of human action, if that be understood as an ethical proposition, as he undoubtedly intended it. That principle may be true all the same; we shall consider whether it is so in succeeding chapters. Bentham might have maintained it, as Prof. Sidgwick does, even if the fallacy had been pointed out to him. What I am maintaining is that the *reasons* which he actually gives for his ethical proposition are fallacious ones so far as they consist in a definition of right. What I suggest is that he did not perceive them to be fallacious; that, if he had done so, he would have been led to seek for other reasons in support of his Utilitarianism; and that, had he sought for other reasons, he *might* have found none which he thought to be sufficient. In that case he would have changed his whole system—a most important consequence. It is undoubtedly also possible that he would have thought other reasons to be sufficient, and in that case his ethical system, in its main results, would still have stood. But, even in this latter case, his use of the fallacy would be a serious objection to him as an ethical philosopher. For it is the business of Ethics, I must insist, not only to obtain true results, but also to find valid reasons for them. The direct object of Ethics is knowledge and not practice; and any one who uses the naturalistic fallacy has certainly not fulfilled this first object, however correct his practical principles may be.

My objections to Naturalism are then, in the first place, that it offers no reason at all, far less any valid reason, for any ethical principle whatever; and in this it already fails to satisfy the requirements of Ethics, as a scientific study. But in the second place I contend that, though it gives a reason for no ethical principle, it is a *cause* of the acceptance of false principles—it deludes the mind into accepting ethical principles, which are false; and in this it is contrary to every aim of Ethics. It is easy to see that if we start with a definition of right conduct as conduct conducive to general happiness; then, knowing that right conduct is universally conduct conducive to the good, we very easily arrive at the result that the good is general happiness. If, on the other hand, we once recognise that we must start our Ethics without a definition, we shall be much more apt to look about us, before we adopt any ethical principle whatever; and the more we look about us, the less likely are we to adopt a false one. It may be replied to this: Yes, but we shall look about us just as much, before we settle on our definition, and are therefore just as likely to be right. But I will try to shew that this is not the case. If we start with the conviction that a definition of good can be found, we start with the conviction that good *can mean* nothing else than some one property of things; and our only business will then be to discover what that property is. But if we recognise that, so far as the meaning of good goes, anything whatever may be good, we start with a much more open mind. Moreover, apart from the fact that, when we think we have a definition, we cannot logically defend our ethical principles in any way whatever, we shall also be much less apt to defend them well, even if illogically. For we shall start with the conviction that good must mean so and so, and shall therefore be inclined either to misunderstand our opponent's arguments or to cut them short with the reply, 'This is not an open question: the very meaning of the word decides it; no one can think otherwise except through confusion.'

15. Our first conclusion as to the subject-matter of Ethics is, then, that there is a simple, indefinable, unanalysable object of thought by reference to which it must be defined. By what name we call this unique object is a matter of indifference, so long as we clearly recognise what it is and that it does differ from other objects. The words which are commonly taken as the signs of ethical judgments all do refer to it; and they are expressions of ethical judgments solely because they do so refer. But they may refer to it in two different ways, which it is very important to distinguish, if we are to have a complete definition of the range of ethical judgments. Before I proceeded to argue that there was such an indefinable

notion involved in ethical notions, I stated (§ 4) that it was necessary for Ethics to enumerate all true universal judgments, asserting that such and such a thing was good, whenever it occurred. But, although all such judgments do refer to that unique notion which I have called 'good,' they do not all refer to it in the same way. They may either assert that this unique property does always attach to the thing in question, or else they may assert only that the thing in question is *a cause or necessary condition* for the existence of other things to which this unique property does attach. The nature of these two species of universal ethical judgments is extremely different; and a great part of the difficulties, which are met with in ordinary ethical speculation, are due to the failure to distinguish them clearly. Their difference has, indeed, received expression in ordinary language by the contrast between the terms 'good as means' and 'good in itself,' 'value as a means' and 'intrinsic value.' But these terms are apt to be applied correctly only in the more obvious instances; and this seems to be due to the fact that the distinction between the conceptions which they denote has not been made a separate object of investigation. This distinction may be briefly pointed out as follows.

16. Whenever we judge that a thing is 'good as a means,' we are making a judgment with regard to its causal relations: we judge *both* that it will have a particular kind of effect, *and* that that effect will be good in itself. But to find causal judgments that are universally true is notoriously a matter of extreme difficulty. The late date at which most of the physical sciences became exact, and the comparative fewness of the laws which they have succeeded in establishing even now, are sufficient proofs of this difficulty. With regard, then, to what are the most frequent objects of ethical judgments, namely actions, it is obvious that we cannot be satisfied that any of our universal causal judgments are true, even in the sense in which scientific laws are so. We cannot even discover hypothetical laws of the form 'Exactly this action will always, under these conditions, produce exactly that effect.' But for a correct ethical judgment with regard to the effects of certain actions we require more than this in two respects. (1) We require to know that a given action will produce a certain effect, *under whatever circumstances it occurs*. But this is certainly impossible. It is certain

that in different circumstances the same action may produce effects which are utterly different in all respects upon which the value of the effects depends. Hence we can never be entitled to more than a *generalisation*—to a proposition of the form 'This result *generally* follows this kind of action'; and even this generalisation will only be true, if the circumstances under which the action occurs are generally the same. This is in fact the case, to a great extent, within any one particular age and state of society. But, when we take other ages into account, in many most important cases the normal circumstances of a given kind of action will be so different, that the generalisation which is true for one will not be true for another. With regard then to ethical judgments which assert that a certain kind of action is good as a means to a certain kind of effect, none will be *universally* true; and many, though *generally* true at one period, will be generally false at others. But (2) we require to know not only that *one* good effect will be produced, but that, among all subsequent events affected by the action in question, the balance of good will be greater than if any other possible action had been performed. In other words, to judge that an action is generally a means to good is to judge not only that it generally does *some* good, but that it generally does the greatest good of which the circumstances admit. In this respect ethical judgments about the effects of action involve a difficulty and a complication far greater than that involved in the establishment of scientific laws. For the latter we need only consider a single effect; for the former it is essential to consider not only this, but the effects of that effect, and so on as far as our view into the future can reach. It is, indeed, obvious that our view can never reach far enough for us to be certain that any action will produce the best possible effects. We must be content, if the greatest possible balance of good seems to be produced within a limited period. But it is important to notice that the whole series of effects within a period of considerable length is actually taken account of in our common judgments that an action is good as a means; and that hence this additional complication, which makes ethical generalisations so far more difficult to establish than scientific laws, is one which is involved in actual ethical discussions, and is of practical importance. The commonest rules of conduct involve such considerations as the balancing of future bad health

against immediate gains; and even if we can never settle with any certainty how we shall secure the greatest possible total of good, we try at least to assure ourselves that probable future evils will not be greater than the immediate good.

17. There are, then, judgments which state that certain kinds of things have good effects; and such judgments, for the reasons just given, have the important characteristics (1) that they are unlikely to be true, if they state that the kind of thing in question *always* has good effects, and (2) that, even if they only state that it *generally* has good effects, many of them will only be true of certain periods in the world's history. On the other hand there are judgments which state that certain kinds of things are themselves good; and these differ from the last in that, if true at all, they are all of them universally true. It is, therefore, extremely important to distinguish these two kinds of possible judgments. Both may be expressed in the same language: in both cases we commonly say 'Such and such a thing is good.' But in the one case 'good' will mean 'good as means' *i.e.* merely that the thing is a means to good—will have good effects: in the other case it will mean 'good as end'—we shall be judging that the thing itself has the property which, in the first case, we asserted only to belong to its effects. It is plain that these are very different assertions to make about a thing; it is plain that either or both of them may be made, both truly and falsely, about all manner of things; and it is certain that unless we are clear as to which of the two we mean to assert, we shall have a very poor chance of deciding rightly whether our assertion is true or false. It is precisely this clearness as to the meaning of the question asked which has hitherto been almost entirely lacking in ethical speculation. Ethics has always been predominantly concerned with the investigation of a limited class of actions. With regard to these we may ask *both* how far they are good in themselves *and* how far they have a general tendency to produce good results. And the arguments brought forward in ethical discussion have always been of both classes—both such as would prove the conduct in question to be good in itself and such as would prove it to be good as a means. But that these are the only questions which any ethical discussion can have to settle, and that to settle the one is *not* the same thing as to settle the other—these two fundamental facts have in general

escaped the notice of ethical philosophers. Ethical questions are commonly asked in an ambiguous form. It is asked 'What is a man's duty under these circumstances?' or 'Is it right to act in this way?' or 'What ought we to aim at securing?' But all these questions are capable of further analysis; a correct answer to any of them involves both judgments of what is good in itself and causal judgments. This is implied even by those who maintain that we have a direct and immediate judgment of absolute rights and duties. Such a judgment can only mean that the course of action in question is *the* best thing to do; that, by acting so, every good that *can* be secured will have been secured. Now we are not concerned with the question whether such a judgment will ever be true. The question is: What does it imply, if it is true? And the only possible answer is that, whether true or false, it implies both a proposition as to the degree of goodness of the action in question, as compared with other things, and a number of causal propositions. For it cannot be denied that the action will have consequences: and to deny that the consequences matter is to make a judgment of their intrinsic value, as compared with the action itself. In asserting that the action is *the* best thing to do, we assert that it together with its consequences presents a greater sum of intrinsic value than any possible alternative. And this condition may be realised by any of the three cases:—(a) If the action itself has greater intrinsic value than any alternative, whereas both its consequences and those of the alternatives are absolutely devoid either of intrinsic merit or intrinsic demerit; or (b) if, though its consequences are intrinsically bad, the balance of intrinsic value is greater than would be produced by any alternative; or (c) if, its consequences being intrinsically good, the degree of value belonging to them and it conjointly is greater than that of any alternative series. In short, to assert that a certain line of conduct is, at a given time, absolutely right or obligatory, is obviously to assert that more good or less evil will exist in the world, if it be adopted than if anything else be done instead. But this implies a judgment as to the value both of its own consequences and of those of any possible alternative. And that an action will have such and such consequences involves a number of causal judgments.

Similarly, in answering the question 'What ought we to aim at securing?' causal judgments are again involved, but in a somewhat different way. We are liable to forget, because it is so obvious, that this question can never be answered correctly except by naming something which *can* be secured. Not everything can be secured; and, even if we judge that nothing which cannot be obtained would be of equal value with that which can, the possibility of the latter, as well as its value, is essential to its being a proper end of action. Accordingly neither our judgments as to what actions we ought to perform, nor even our judgments as to the ends which they ought to produce, are pure judgments of intrinsic value. With regard to the former, an action which is absolutely obligatory *may* have no intrinsic value whatsoever; that it is perfectly virtuous may mean merely that it causes the best possible effects. And with regard to the latter, these best possible results which justify our action can, in any case, have only so much of intrinsic value as the laws of nature allow us to secure; and they in their turn *may* have no intrinsic value whatsoever, but may merely be a means to the attainment (in a still further future) of something that has such value. Whenever, therefore, we ask 'What ought we to do?' or 'What ought we to try to get?' we are asking questions which involve a correct answer to two others, completely different in kind from one another. We must know *both* what degree of intrinsic value different things have, *and* how these different things may be obtained. But the vast majority of questions which have actually been discussed in Ethics—*all* practical questions, indeed—involve this double knowledge; and they have been discussed without any clear separation of the two distinct questions involved. A great part of the vast disagreements prevalent in Ethics is to be attributed to this failure in analysis. By the use of conceptions which involve both that of intrinsic value and that of causal relation, as if they involved intrinsic value only, two different errors have been rendered almost universal. Either it is assumed that nothing has intrinsic value which is not possible, or else it is assumed that what is necessary must have intrinsic value. Hence the primary and peculiar business of Ethics, the determination what things have intrinsic value and in what degrees, has received no adequate treatment at all. And on the other hand a *thorough* discussion of means has been also largely neglected, owing to an obscure perception of the truth that it is perfectly irrelevant to the question of intrinsic values. But however this may be, and however strongly any particular reader may be convinced that some one of the mutually contradictory systems which hold the field has given a correct answer either to the question what has intrinsic value, or to the question what we ought to do, or to both, it must at least be admitted that the questions what is best in itself and what will bring about the best possible, are utterly distinct; that both belong to the actual subject-matter of Ethics; and that the more clearly distinct questions are distinguished, the better is our chance of answering both correctly.

18. There remains one point which must not be omitted in a complete description of the kind of questions which Ethics has to answer. The main division of those questions is, as I have said, into two; the question what things are good in themselves, and the question to what other things these are related as effects. The first of these, which is the primary ethical question and is presupposed by the other, includes a correct comparison of the various things which have intrinsic value (if there are many such) in respect of the degree of value which they have; and such comparison involves a difficulty of principle which has greatly aided the confusion of intrinsic value with mere 'goodness as a means.' It has been pointed out that one difference between a judgment which asserts that a thing is good in itself, and a judgment which asserts that it is a means to good, consists in the fact that the first, if true of one instance of the thing in question, is necessarily true of all; whereas a thing which has good effects under some circumstances may have bad ones under others. Now it is certainly true that all judgments of intrinsic value are in this sense universal; but the principle which I have now to enunciate may easily make it appear as if they were not so but resembled the judgment of means in being merely general. There is, as will presently be maintained, a vast number of different things, each of which has intrinsic value; there are also very many which are positively bad; and there is a still larger class of things, which appear to be indifferent. But a thing belonging to any of these three classes may occur as part of a whole, which includes among its other parts other things belonging both to the same and to the other two classes; and these wholes, as such, may also have intrinsic value. The paradox, to which it is necessary to call attention, is that *the value of such a whole bears no regular proportion to the sum of the values of its parts*. It

is certain that a good thing may exist in such a relation to another good thing that the value of the whole thus formed is immensely greater than the sum of the values of the two good things. It is certain that a whole formed of a good thing and an indifferent thing may have immensely greater value than that good thing itself possesses. It is certain that two bad things or a bad thing and an indifferent thing may form a whole much worse than the sum of badness of its parts. And it seems as if indifferent things may also be the sole constituents of a whole which has great value, either positive or negative. Whether the addition of a bad thing to a good whole may increase the positive value of the whole, or the addition of a bad thing to a bad may produce a whole having positive value, may seem more doubtful; but it is, at least, possible, and this possibility must be taken into account in our ethical investigations. However we may decide particular questions, the principle is clear. *The value of a whole must not be assumed to be the same as the sum of the values of its parts.*

A single instance will suffice to illustrate the kind of relation in question. It seems to be true that to be conscious of a beautiful object is a thing of great intrinsic value; whereas the same object, if no one be conscious of it, has certainly comparatively little value, and is commonly held to have none at all. But the consciousness of a beautiful object is certainly a whole of some sort in which we can distinguish as parts the object on the one hand and the being conscious on the other. Now this latter factor occurs as part of a different whole, whenever we are conscious of anything; and it would seem that some of these wholes have at all events very little value, and may even be indifferent or positively bad. Yet we cannot always attribute the slightness of their value to any positive demerit in the object which differentiates them from the consciousness of beauty; the object itself may approach as near as possible to absolute neutrality. Since, therefore, mere consciousness does not always confer great value upon the whole of which it forms a part, even though its object may have no great demerit, we cannot attribute the great superiority of the consciousness of a beautiful thing over the beautiful thing itself to the mere addition of the value of consciousness to that of the beautiful thing. Whatever the intrinsic value of consciousness may be, it does not give to the whole of which it forms a part a value proportioned to the sum of its value and that of its object. If this be so, we have here an instance of a whole possessing a different intrinsic value from the sum of that of its parts; and whether it be so or not, what is meant by such a difference is illustrated by this case.

19. There are, then, wholes which possess the property that their value is different from the sum of the values of their parts; and the relations which subsist between such parts and the whole of which they form a part have not hitherto been distinctly recognised or received a separate name. Two points are especially worthy of notice. (1) It is plain that the existence of any such part is a necessary condition for the existence of that good which is constituted by the whole. And exactly the same language will also express the relation between a means and the good thing which is its effect. But yet there is a most important difference between the two cases, constituted by the fact that the part is, whereas the means is not, a part of the good thing for the existence of which its existence is a necessary condition. The necessity by which, if the good in question is to exist, the means to it must exist is merely a natural or causal necessity. If the laws of nature were different, exactly the same good might exist, although what is now a necessary condition of its existence did not exist. The existence of the means has no intrinsic value; and its utter annihilation would leave the value of that which it is now necessary to secure entirely unchanged. But in the case of a part of such a whole as we are now considering, it is otherwise. In this case the good in question cannot conceivably exist, unless the part exist also. The necessity which connects the two is quite independent of natural law. What is asserted to have intrinsic value is the existence of the whole; and the existence of the whole includes the existence of its part. Suppose the part removed, and what remains is *not* what was asserted to have intrinsic value; but if we suppose a means removed, what remains is just what *was* asserted to have intrinsic value. And yet (2) the existence of the part may *itself* have no more intrinsic value than that of the means. It is this fact which constitutes the paradox of the relation which we are discussing. It has just been said that what has intrinsic value is the existence of the whole, and that this includes the existence of the part; and from this it would seem a natural inference that the existence of the part has intrinsic value. But the inference would be as false as if we were to con-

clude that, because the number of two stones was two, each of the stones was also two. The part of a valuable whole retains exactly the same value when it is, as when it is not, a part of that whole. If it had value under other circumstances, its value is not any greater, when it is part of a far more valuable whole; and if it had no value by itself, it has none still, however great be that of the whole of which it now forms a part. We are not then justified in asserting that one and the same thing is under some circumstances intrinsically good, and under others not so; as we are justified in asserting of a means that it sometimes does and sometimes does not produce good results. And yet we are justified in asserting that it is far more desirable that a certain thing should exist under some circumstances than under others; namely when other things will exist in such relations to it as to form a more valuable whole. *It* will not have more intrinsic value under these circumstances than under others; *it* will not necessarily even be a means to the existence of things having more intrinsic value: but it will, like a means, be a necessary condition for the existence of that which *has* greater intrinsic value, although, unlike a means, it will itself form a part of this more valuable existent.

20. I have said that the peculiar relation between part and whole which I have just been trying to define is one which has received no separate name. It would, however, be useful that it should have one; and there is a name, which might well be appropriated to it, if only it could be divorced from its present unfortunate usage. Philosophers, especially those who profess to have derived great benefit from the writings of Hegel, have latterly made much use of the terms 'organic whole,' 'organic unity,' 'organic relation.' The reason why these terms might well be appropriated to the use suggested is that the peculiar relation of parts to whole, just defined, is one of the properties which distinguishes the wholes to which they are actually applied with the greatest frequency. And the reason why it is desirable that they should be divorced from their present usage is that, as at present used, they have no distinct sense and, on the contrary, both imply and propagate errors of confusion.

To say that a thing is an 'organic whole' is generally understood to imply that its parts are related to one another and to itself as means to end; it is also understood to imply that they have a property described in some such phrase as that they have 'no meaning or significance apart from the whole'; and finally such a whole is also treated as if it had the property to which I am proposing that the name should be confined. But those who use the term give us, in general, no hint as to how they suppose these three properties to be related to one another. It seems generally to be assumed that they are identical; and always, at least, that they are necessarily connected with one another. That they are not identical I have already tried to shew; to suppose them so is to neglect the very distinctions pointed out in the last paragraph; and the usage might well be discontinued merely because it encourages such neglect. But a still more cogent reason for its discontinuance is that, so far from being necessarily connected, the second is a property which can attach to nothing, being a self-contradictory conception; whereas the first, if we insist on its most important sense, applies to many cases, to which we have no reason to think that the third applies also, and the third certainly applies to many to which the first does not apply.

21. These relations between the three properties just distinguished may be illustrated by reference to a whole of the kind from which the name 'organic' was derived—a whole which is an organism in the scientific sense—namely the human body.

(1) There exists between many parts of our body (though not between all) a relation which has been familiarised by the fable, attributed to Menenius Agrippa, concerning the belly and its members. We can find in it parts such that the continued existence of the one is a necessary condition for the continued existence of the other; while the continued existence of this latter is also a necessary condition for the continued existence of the former. This amounts to no more than saying that in the body we have instances of two things, both enduring for some time, which have a relation of mutual causal dependence on one another—a relation of 'reciprocity.' Frequently no more than this is meant by saying that the parts of the body form an 'organic unity,' or that they are mutually means and ends to one another. And we certainly have here a striking characteristic of living things. But it would be extremely rash to assert that this relation of mutual causal dependence was only exhibited by living things and hence was sufficient to define their peculiarity. And it is obvious that of two things which have this relation of mutual dependence, neither may have intrinsic value, or one may

have it and the other lack it. They are not necessarily 'ends' to one another in any sense except that in which 'end' means 'effect.' And moreover it is plain that in this sense the whole cannot be an end to any of its parts. We are apt to talk of 'the whole' in contrast to one of its parts, when in fact we mean only *the rest* of the parts. But strictly the whole must include all its parts and no part can be a cause of the whole, because it cannot be a cause of itself. It is plain, therefore, that this relation of mutual causal dependence implies nothing with regard to the value of either of the objects which have it; and that, even if both of them happen also to have value, this relation between them is one which cannot hold between part and whole.

But (2) it may also be the case that our body as a whole has a value greater than the sum of values of its parts; and this may be what is meant when it is said that the parts are means to the whole. It is obvious that if we ask the question 'Why *should* the parts be such as they are?' a proper answer may be 'Because the whole they form has so much value.' But it is equally obvious that the relation which we thus assert to exist between part and whole is quite different from that which we assert to exist between part and part when we say 'This part exists, because that one could not exist without it.' In the latter case we assert the two parts to be causally connected; but, in the former, part and whole cannot be causally connected, and the relation which we assert to exist between them may exist even though the parts are not causally connected either. All the parts of a picture do not have that relation of mutual causal dependence, which certain parts of the body have, and yet the existence of those which do not have it may be absolutely essential to the value of the whole. The two relations are quite distinct in kind, and we cannot infer the existence of the one from that of the other. It can, therefore, serve no useful purpose to include them both under the same name; and if we are to say that a whole is organic because its parts are (in this sense) 'means' to the whole, we must *not* say that it is organic because its parts are causally dependent on one another.

22. But finally (3) the sense which has been most prominent in recent uses of the term 'organic whole' is one whereby it asserts the parts of such a whole to have a property which the parts of no whole can possibly have. It is supposed that just as the whole

would not be what it is but for the existence of the parts, so the parts would not be what they are but for the existence of the whole; and this is understood to mean not merely that any particular part could not exist unless the others existed too (which is the case where relation (1) exists between the parts), but actually that the part is no distinct object of thought—that the whole, of which it is a part, is in its turn a part of it. That this supposition is self-contradictory a very little reflection should be sufficient to shew. We may admit, indeed, that when a particular thing is a part of a whole, it does possess a predicate which it would not otherwise possess— namely that it is a part of that whole. But what cannot be admitted is that this predicate alters the nature or enters into the definition of the thing which has it. When we think of the part *itself,* we mean just *that which* we assert, in this case, to *have* the predicate that it is part of the whole; and the mere assertion that *it* is a part of the whole involves that it should itself be distinct from that which we assert of it. Otherwise we contradict ourselves since we assert that, not *it,* but something else—namely it together with that which we assert of it—has the predicate which we assert of it. In short, it is obvious that no part contains analytically the whole to which it belongs, or any other parts of that whole. The relation of part to whole is *not* the same as that of whole to part; and the very definition of the latter is that it does contain analytically that which is said to be its part. And yet this very self-contradictory doctrine is the chief mark which shews the influence of Hegel upon modern philosophy—an influence which pervades almost the whole of orthodox philosophy. This is what is generally implied by the cry against falsification by abstraction: that a whole is always a part of its part! 'If you want to know the truth about a part,' we are told, 'you must consider *not* that part, but something else—namely the whole: *nothing* is true of the part, but only of the whole.' Yet plainly it must be true of the part at least that it is a part of the whole; and it is obvious that when we say it is, we do *not* mean merely that the whole is a part of itself. This doctrine, therefore, that a part can have 'no meaning or significance apart from its whole' must be utterly rejected. It implies itself that the statement 'This is a part of that whole' has a meaning; and in order that this may have one, both subject and predicate must have a distinct

meaning. And it is easy to see how this false doctrine has arisen by confusion with the two relations (1) and (2) which may really be properties of wholes.

(*a*) The *existence* of a part may be connected by a natural or causal necessity with the existence of the other parts of its whole; and further what is a part of a whole and what has ceased to be such a part, although differing intrinsically from one another, may be called by one and the same name. Thus, to take a typical example, if an arm be cut off from the human body, we still call it an arm. Yet an arm, when it is a part of the body, undoubtedly differs from a dead arm: and hence we may easily be led to say 'The arm which is a part of the body would not be what it is, if it were not such a part,' and to think that the contradiction thus expressed is in reality a characteristic of things. But, in fact, the dead arm never was a part of the body; it is only *partially* identical with the living arm. Those parts of it which are identical with parts of the living arm are exactly the same, whether they belong to the body or not; and in them we have an undeniable instance of one and the same thing at one time forming a part, and at another not forming a part of the presumed 'organic whole.' On the other hand those properties which *are* possessed by the living, and *not* by the dead, arm, do not exist in a changed form in the latter: they simply do not exist there *at all.* By a causal necessity their existence depends on their having that relation to the other parts of the body which we express by saying that they form part of it. Yet, most certainly, *if* they ever did not form part of the body, they *would* be exactly what they are when they do. That they differ intrinsically from the properties of the dead arm and that they form part of the body are propositions not analytically related to one another. There is no contradiction in supposing them to retain such intrinsic differences and yet not to form part of the body.

But (*b*) when we are told that a living arm has no *meaning* or *significance* apart from the body to which it belongs, a different fallacy is also suggested. 'To have meaning or significance' is commonly used in the sense of 'to have importance'; and this again means 'to have value either as a means or as an end.' Now it is quite possible that even a living arm, apart from its body, would have no intrinsic value whatever; although the whole of which it is a part has great intrinsic value owing to its presence. Thus we may easily come to say that, *as* a part of the body, it has great value, whereas *by itself* it would have none; and thus that its whole 'meaning' lies in its relation to the body. But in fact the value in question obviously does not belong to *it* at all. To have value merely as a part is equivalent to having no value at all, but merely being a part of that which has it. Owing, however, to neglect of this distinction, the assertion that a part has value, *as a part*, which it would not otherwise have, easily leads to the assumption that it is also different, as a part, from what it would otherwise be; for it is, in fact, true that two things which have a different value must also differ in other respects. Hence the assumption that one and the same thing, because it is a part of a more valuable whole at one time than at another, therefore has more intrinsic value at one time than at another, has encouraged the self-contradictory belief that one and the same thing may be two different things, and that only in one of its forms is it truly what it is.

For these reasons, I shall, where it seems convenient, take the liberty to use the term 'organic' with a special sense. I shall use it to denote the fact that a whole has an intrinsic value different in amount from the sum of the values of its parts. I shall use it to denote this and only this. The term will not imply any causal relation whatever between the parts of the whole in question. And it will not imply either, that the parts are inconceivable except as parts of that whole, or that, when they form parts of such a whole, they have a value different from that which they would have if they did not. Understood in this special and perfectly definite sense the relation of an organic whole to its parts is one of the most important which Ethics has to recognise. A chief part of that science should be occupied in comparing the relative values of various goods; and the grossest errors will be committed in such comparison if it be assumed that wherever two things form a whole, the value of that whole is merely the sum of the values of those two things. With this question of 'organic wholes,' then, we complete the enumeration of the kind of problems, with which it is the business of Ethics to deal.

23. In this chapter I have endeavoured to enforce the following conclusions. (1) The peculiarity of Ethics is not that it investigates assertions about human conduct, but that it investigates assertions about that property of things which is denoted by the term 'good,' and the converse property denoted by the term 'bad.' It must, in order to establish its con-

clusions, investigate the truth of *all* such assertions, *except* those which assert the relation of this property only to a single existent (1–4). (2) This property, by reference to which the subject-matter of Ethics must be defined, is itself simple and indefinable (5–14). And (3) all assertions about its relation to other things are of two, and only two, kinds: they either assert in what degree things themselves possess this property, or else they assert causal relations between other things and those which possess it (15–17). Finally, (4) in considering the different degrees in which things themselves possess this property, we have to take account of the fact that a whole may possess it in a degree different from that which is obtained by summing the degrees in which its parts possess it (18–22).

Chapter II. Naturalistic Ethics.

24. It results from the conclusions of Chapter I, that all ethical questions fall under one or other of three classes. The first class contains but one question—the question What is the nature of that peculiar predicate, the relation of which to other things constitutes the object of all other ethical investigations? or, in other words, What is *meant* by good? This first question I have already attempted to answer. The peculiar predicate, by reference to which the sphere of Ethics must be defined, is simple, unanalysable, indefinable. There remain two classes of questions with regard to the relation of this predicate to other things. We may ask either (1) To what things and in what degree does this predicate directly attach? What things are good in themselves? or (2) By what means shall we be able to make what exists in the world as good as possible? What causal relations hold between what is best in itself and other things?

In this and the two following chapters, I propose to discuss certain theories, which offer us an answer to the question What is good in itself? I say advisedly—*an* answer: for these theories are all characterised by the fact that, if true, they would simplify the study of Ethics very much. They all hold that there is only *one* kind of fact, of which the existence has any value at all. But they all also possess another characteristic, which is my reason for grouping them together and treating them first: namely that the main reason why the single kind of fact they name has been held to define the sole good, is that it has been held to define what is meant by 'good' itself. In other words they are all theories of the end or ideal, the adoption of which has been chiefly caused by the commission of what I have called the naturalistic fallacy: they all confuse the first and second of the three possible questions which Ethics can ask. It is, indeed, this fact which explains their contention that only a single kind of thing is good. That a thing should be good, it has been thought, *means* that it possesses this single property: and hence (it is thought) only what possesses this property is good. The inference seems very natural; and yet what is meant by it is self-contradictory. For those who make it fail to perceive that their conclusion 'what possesses this property is good' is a significant proposition: that it does not mean either 'what possesses this property, possesses this property' or 'the word "good" denotes that a thing possesses this property.' And yet, if it does *not* mean one or other of these two things, the inference contradicts its own premise.

I propose, therefore, to discuss certain theories of what is good in itself, which are *based* on the naturalistic fallacy, in the sense that the commission of this fallacy has been the main cause of their wide acceptance. The discussion will be designed both (1) further to illustrate the fact that the naturalistic fallacy is a fallacy, or, in other words, that we are all aware of a certain simple quality, which (and not anything else) is what we mainly mean by the term 'good'; and (2) to shew that not one, but many different things, possess this property. For I cannot hope to recommend the doctrine that things which are good do not owe their goodness to their common possession of any other property, without a criticism of the main doctrines, opposed to this, whose power to recommend themselves is proved by their wide prevalence.

25. The theories I propose to discuss may be conveniently divided into two groups. The naturalistic fallacy always implies that when we think 'This is good,' what we are thinking is that the thing in question bears a definite relation to some one other thing. But this one thing, by reference to which good is defined, may be either what I may call a natural object—something of which the existence is admittedly an object of experience—or else it may be an object which is only inferred to exist in a supersensible real world. These two types of ethical theory I propose to treat separately. Theories of the second type may conveniently be called 'metaphysical,' and I shall postpone consideration of them till Chapter IV. In this and the following chapter, on the other hand, I shall deal with theories which owe their prevalence to the supposition that good can be defined by reference to a *natural object*; and these are what I mean by the name, which gives the title to this chapter, 'Naturalistic Ethics.' It should be observed that the fallacy, by reference to which I define 'Metaphysical Ethics,' is the same in kind; and I give it but one name, the naturalistic fallacy. But when we regard the ethical theories recommended by this fallacy, it seems convenient to distinguish those which consider goodness to consist in a relation to something which exists here and now, from those which do not. According to the former, Ethics is an empirical or positive science: its conclusions could be all established by means of empirical observation and induction. But this is not the case with Metaphysical Ethics. There is, therefore, a marked distinction between these two groups of ethical theories based on the same fallacy. And within Naturalistic theories, too, a convenient division may also be made. There is one natural object, namely pleasure, which has perhaps been as frequently held to be the sole good as all the rest put together. And there is, moreover, a further reason for treating Hedonism separately. That doctrine has, I think, as plainly as any other, owed its prevalence to the naturalistic fallacy; but it has had a singular fate in that the writer, who first clearly exposed the fallacy of the naturalistic arguments by which it had been attempted to *prove* that pleasure was the sole good, has maintained that nevertheless it *is* the sole good. I propose, therefore, to divide my discussion of Hedonism from that of other Naturalistic theories; treating of Naturalistic Ethics in general in this chapter, and of Hedonism, in particular, in the next.

26. The subject of the present chapter is, then, ethical theories which declare that no intrinsic value is to be found except in the possession of some one *natural* property, other than pleasure; and which declare this because it is supposed that to be 'good' *means* to possess the property in question. Such theories I call 'Naturalistic.' I have thus appropriated the name Naturalism to a particular method of approaching Ethics—a method which, strictly understood, is inconsistent with the possibility of any Ethics whatsoever. This method consists in substituting for 'good'

some one property of a natural object or of a collection of natural objects; and in thus replacing Ethics by some one of the natural sciences. In general, the science thus substituted is one of the sciences specially concerned with man, owing to the general mistake (for such I hold it to be) of regarding the matter of Ethics as confined to human conduct. In general, Psychology has been the science substituted, as by J. S. Mill; or Sociology, as by Professor Clifford, and other modern writers. But any other science might equally well be substituted. It is the same fallacy which is implied, when Professor Tyndall recommends us to 'conform to the laws of matter': and here the science which it is proposed to substitute for Ethics is simply Physics. The name then is perfectly general; for, no matter what the something is that good is held to mean, the theory is still Naturalism. Whether good be defined as yellow or green or blue, as loud or soft, as round or square, as sweet or bitter, as productive of life or productive of pleasure, as willed or desired or felt: whichever of these or of any other object in the world, good may be held to *mean*, the theory, which holds it to *mean* them, will be a naturalistic theory. I have called such theories naturalistic because all of these terms denote properties, simple or complex, of some simple or complex natural object; and, before I proceed to consider them, it will be well to define what is meant by 'nature' and by 'natural objects.'

By 'nature,' then, I do mean and have meant that which is the subject-matter of the natural sciences and also of psychology. It may be said to include all that has existed, does exist, or will exist in time. If we consider whether any object is of such a nature that it may be said to exist now, to have existed, or to be about to exist, then we may know that that object is a natural object, and that nothing, of which this is not true, is a natural object. Thus, for instance, of our minds we should say that they did exist yesterday, that they do exist to-day, and probably will exist in a minute or two. We shall say that we had thoughts yesterday, which have ceased to exist now, although their effects may remain: and in so far as those thoughts did exist, they too are natural objects.

There is, indeed, no difficulty about the 'objects' themselves, in the sense in which I have just used the term. It is easy to say which of them are natural, and which (if any) are not natural. But when we begin to consider the properties of objects, then I fear the problem is more difficult. Which among the properties of natural objects are natural properties and which are not? For I do not deny that good is a property of certain natural objects: certain of them, I think, *are* good; and yet I have said that 'good' itself is not a natural property. Well, my test for these too also concerns their existence in time. Can we imagine 'good' as existing *by itself* in time, and not merely as a property of some natural object? For myself, I cannot so imagine it, whereas with the greater number of properties of objects—those which I call the natural properties—their existence does seem to me to be independent of the existence of those objects. They are, in fact, rather parts of which the object is made up than mere predicates which attach to it. If they were all taken away, no object would be left, not even a bare substance: for they are in themselves substantial and give to the object all the substance that it has. But this is not so with good. If indeed good were a feeling, as some would have us believe, then it would exist in time. But that is why to call it so is to commit the naturalistic fallacy. It will always remain pertinent to ask, whether the feeling itself is good; and if so, then good cannot itself be identical with any feeling.

27. Those theories of Ethics, then, are 'naturalistic' which declare the sole good to consist in some one property of things, which exists in time; and which do so because they suppose that 'good' itself can be defined by reference to such a property. And we may now proceed to consider such theories.

And, first of all, one of the most famous of ethical maxims is that which recommends a 'life according to nature.' That was the principle of the Stoic Ethics; but, since their Ethics has some claim to be called metaphysical, I shall not attempt to deal with it here. But the same phrase reappears in Rousseau; and it is not unfrequently maintained even now that what we ought to do is to live naturally. Now let us examine this contention in its general form. It is obvious, in the first place, that we cannot say that everything natural is good, except perhaps in virtue of some metaphysical theory, such as I shall deal with later. If everything natural is equally good, then certainly Ethics, as it is ordinarily understood, disappears: for nothing is more certain, from an ethical point of view, than that some things are bad and others good; the object of Ethics is, indeed, in chief part, to give you general rules whereby you may avoid the one and secure the other. What, then, does 'natural' mean, in this advice to live naturally, since it obviously cannot apply to everything that is natural?

The phrase seems to point to a vague notion that there is some such thing as natural good; to a belief that Nature may be said to fix and decide what shall be good, just as she fixes and decides what shall exist. For instance, it may be supposed that 'health' is susceptible of a natural definition, that Nature has fixed what health shall be: and health, it may be said, is obviously good; hence in this case Nature has decided the matter; we have only to go to her and ask her what health is, and we shall know what is good: we shall have based an ethics upon science. But what is this natural definition of health? I can only conceive that health should be defined in natural terms as the *normal* state of an organism; for undoubtedly disease is also a natural product. To say that health is what is preserved by evolution, and what itself tends to preserve, in the struggle for existence, the organism which possesses it, comes to the same thing: for the point of evolution is that it pretends to give a causal explanation of why some forms of life are normal and others are abnormal; it explains the origin of species. When therefore we are told that health is natural, we may presume that what is meant is that it is normal; and that when we are told to pursue health as a natural end, what is implied is that the normal must be good. But is it so obvious that the normal must be good? Is it really obvious that health, for instance, is good? Was the excellence of Socrates or of Shakespeare normal? Was it not rather abnormal, extraordinary? It is, I think, obvious in the first place, that not all that is good is normal; that, on the contrary, the abnormal is often better than the normal: peculiar excellence, as well as peculiar viciousness, must obviously be not normal but abnormal. Yet it may be said that nevertheless the normal is good; and I myself am not prepared to dispute that health is good. What I contend is that this must not be taken to be obvious; that it must be regarded as an open question. To declare it to be obvious is to suggest the naturalistic fallacy: just as, in some recent books, a proof that genius is diseased, abnormal, has been used in order to suggest that genius ought not to be encouraged. Such reasoning is fallacious, and dangerously fallacious. The fact is that in the very words 'health' and 'disease' we do commonly include the notion that the one is good and the other bad. But, when a so-called scientific definition of them is attempted, a definition in natural terms, the only one possible is that by way of 'normal' and 'abnormal.' Now, it is easy to prove that some things commonly thought excellent are abnormal; and it follows that they are diseased. But it does not follow, except by virtue of the naturalistic fallacy, that those things, commonly thought good, are therefore bad. All that has really been shewn is that in some cases there is a conflict between the common judgment that genius is good, and the common judgment that health is good. It is not sufficiently recognised that the latter judgment has not a whit more warrant for its truth than the former; that both are perfectly open questions. It may be true, indeed, that by 'healthy' we do commonly imply 'good'; but that only shews that when we so use the word, we do not mean the same thing by it as the thing which is meant in medical science. That *health, when* the word is used to denote something good, is good, goes no way at all to shew that health, when the word is used to denote something normal, is also good. We might as well say that, because 'bull' denotes an Irish joke and also a certain animal, the joke and the animal must be the same thing. We must not, therefore, be frightened by the assertion that a thing is natural into the admission that it is good; good does not, by definition, mean anything that is natural; and it is therefore always an open question whether anything that is natural is good.

28. But there is another slightly different sense in which the word 'natural' is used with an implication that it denotes something good. This is when we speak of natural affections, or unnatural crimes and vices. Here the meaning seems to be, not so much that the action or feeling in question is normal or abnormal, as that it is necessary. It is in this connection that we are advised to imitate savages and beasts. Curious advice certainly; but, of course, there may be something in it. I am not here concerned to enquire under what circumstances some of us might with advantage take a lesson from the cow. I have really no doubt that such exist. What I am concerned with is a certain kind of reason, which I think is sometimes used to support this doctrine—a naturalistic reason. The notion sometimes lying at the bottom of the minds of preachers of this gospel is that we cannot improve on nature. This notion is certainly true, in the sense that anything we can do, that may be better than the present state of things, will be a natural product. But that is not what is meant by this phrase; nature is again used to mean a mere part

of nature; only this time the part meant is not so much the normal as an arbitrary minimum of what is necessary for life. And when this minimum is recommended as 'natural'—as the way of life to which Nature points her finger—then the naturalistic fallacy is used. Against this position I wish only to point out that though the performance of certain acts, not in themselves desirable, may be *excused* as necessary means to the preservation of life, that is no reason for *praising* them, or advising us to limit ourselves to those simple actions which are necessary, if it is possible for us to improve our condition even at the expense of doing what is in this sense unnecessary. Nature does indeed set limits to what is possible; she does control the means we have at our disposal for obtaining what is good; and of this fact, practical Ethics, as we shall see later, must certainly take account: but when she is supposed to have a preference for what is necessary, what is necessary means only what is necessary to obtain a certain end, presupposed as the highest good; and what the highest good is Nature cannot determine. Why should we suppose that what is merely necessary to life is *ipso facto* better than what is necessary to the study of metaphysics, useless as that study may appear? It may be that life is only worth living, because it enables us to study metaphysics—is a necessary means thereto. The fallacy of this argument from nature has been discovered as long ago as Lucian. 'I was almost inclined to laugh,' says Callicratidas, in one of the dialogues imputed to him, 'just now, when Charicles was praising irrational brutes and the savagery of the Scythians: in the heat of his argument he was almost repenting that he was born a Greek. What wonder if lions and bears and pigs do not act as I was proposing? That which reasoning would fairly lead a man to choose, cannot be had by creatures that do not reason, simply because they are so stupid. If Prometheus or some other god had given each of them the intelligence of a man, then they would not have lived in deserts and mountains nor fed on one another. They would have built temples just as we do, each would have lived in the centre of his family, and they would have formed a nation bound by mutual laws. Is it anything surprising that brutes, who have had the misfortune to be unable to obtain by forethought any of the goods, with which reasoning provides us, should have missed love too? Lions do not love; but neither do they philosophise; bears do

not love; but the reason is they do not know the sweets of friendship. It is only men, who, by their wisdom and their knowledge, after many trials, have chosen what is best.'

29. To argue that a thing is good *because* it is 'natural,' or bad *because* it is 'unnatural,' in these common senses of the term, is therefore certainly fallacious: and yet such arguments are very frequently used. But they do not commonly pretend to give a systematic theory of Ethics. Among attempts to *systematise* an appeal to nature, that which is now most prevalent is to be found in the application to ethical questions of the term 'Evolution'—in the ethical doctrines which have been called 'Evolutionistic.' These doctrines are those which maintain that the course of 'evolution,' while it shews us the direction in which we *are* developing, thereby and for that reason shews us the direction in which we *ought* to develop. Writers, who maintain such a doctrine, are at present very numerous and very popular; and I propose to take as my example the writer, who is perhaps the best known of them all—Mr Herbert Spencer. Mr Spencer's doctrine, it must be owned, does not offer the *clearest* example of the naturalistic fallacy as used in support of Evolutionistic Ethics. A clearer example might be found in the doctrine of Guyau,[1] a writer who has lately had considerable vogue in France, but who is not so well known as Spencer. Guyau might almost be called a disciple of Spencer; he is frankly evolutionistic, and frankly naturalistic; and I may mention that he does not seem to think that he differs from Spencer by reason of his naturalism. The point in which he has criticised Spencer concerns the question how far the ends of 'pleasure' and of 'increased life' coincide as motives and means to the attainment of the ideal: he does not seem to think that he differs from Spencer in the fundamental principle that the ideal is 'Quantity of life, measured in breadth as well as in length,' or, as Guyau says, 'Expansion and intensity of life'; nor in the naturalistic reason which he gives for this principle. And I am not sure that he does differ from Spencer in these points. Spencer does, as I shall shew, use the naturalistic fallacy in details; but with regard to his fundamental principles, the following doubts occur: Is he funda-

---

1. See *Esquisse d'une Morale sans Obligation ni Sanction,* par M. Guyau. 4me edition. Paris: F. Alcan, 1896.

mentally a Hedonist? And, if so, is he a naturalistic Hedonist? In that case he would better have been treated in my next chapter. Does he hold that a tendency to increase quantity of life is merely a *criterion* of good conduct? Or does he hold that such increase of life is marked out by nature as an end at which we ought to aim?

I think his language in various places would give colour to all these hypotheses; though some of them are mutually inconsistent. I will try to discuss the main points.

30. The modern vogue of 'Evolution' is chiefly owing to Darwin's investigations as to the origin of species. Darwin formed a strictly biological hypothesis as to the manner in which certain forms of animal life became established, while others died out and disappeared. His theory was that this might be accounted for, partly at least, in the following way. When certain varieties occurred (the cause of their occurrence is still, in the main, unknown), it might be that some of the points, in which they varied from their parent species or from other species then existing, made them better able to persist in the environment in which they found themselves—less liable to be killed off. They might, for instance, be better able to endure the cold or heat or changes of the climate; better able to find nourishment from what surrounded them; better able to escape from or resist other species which fed upon them; better fitted to attract or to master the other sex. Being thus less liable to die, their numbers relatively to other species would increase; and that very increase in their numbers might tend towards the extinction of those other species. This theory, to which Darwin gave the name 'Natural Selection,' was also called the theory of survival of the fittest. The natural process which it thus described was called evolution. It was very natural to suppose that evolution meant evolution from what was lower into what was higher; in fact it was observed that at least one species, commonly called higher—the species man—had so survived, and among men again it was supposed that the higher races, ourselves for example, had shewn a tendency to survive the lower, such as the North American Indians. We can kill them more easily than they can kill us. The doctrine of evolution was then represented as an explanation of how the higher species survives the lower. Spencer, for example, constantly uses 'more evolved' as equivalent to 'higher.' But it is

to be noted that this forms no part of Darwin's scientific theory. That theory will explain, equally well, how by an alteration in the environment (the gradual cooling of the earth, for example) quite a different species from man, a species which we think infinitely lower, might survive us. The survival of the fittest does *not* mean, as one might suppose, the survival of what is fittest to fulfil a good purpose—best adapted to a good end: at the last, it means merely the survival of the fittest to survive; and the value of the scientific theory, and it is a theory of great value, just consists in shewing what are the causes which produce certain biological effects. Whether these effects are good or bad, it cannot pretend to judge.

31. But now let us hear what Mr Spencer says about the application of Evolution to Ethics.

'I recur, he says,[1] 'to the main proposition set forth in these two chapters, which has, I think, been fully justified. Guided by the truth that as the conduct with which Ethics deals is part of conduct at large, conduct at large must be generally understood before this part can be specially understood; and guided by the further truth that to understand conduct at large we must understand the evolution of conduct; we have been led to see that Ethics has for its subject-matter, that form which universal conduct assumes during the last stages of its evolution. We have also concluded that these last stages in the evolution of conduct are those displayed by the *highest*[2] type of being when he is forced, by increase of numbers, to live more and more in presence of his fellows. And there has followed *the corollary that conduct gains ethical sanction*[2] in proportion as the activities, becoming less and less militant and more and more industrial, are such as do not necessitate mutual injury or hindrance, but consist with, and are furthered by, co-operation and mutual aid.

'These implications of the Evolution-Hypothesis, we shall now see harmonize with the leading moral ideas men have otherwise reached.'

Now, if we are to take the last sentence strictly—if the propositions which precede it are really thought by Mr Spencer to be *implications* of the Evolution-Hypothesis—there can be no doubt that Mr Spencer has committed the naturalistic fallacy.

---

1. *Data Of Ethics,* Chap. II, § 7, *ad fin.*

2. The italics are mine.

All that the Evolution-Hypothesis tells us is that certain kinds of conduct are more evolved than others; and this is, in fact, all that Mr Spencer has attempted to prove in the two chapters concerned. Yet he tells us that one of the things it has proved is that *conduct gains ethical sanction* in proportion as it displays certain characteristics. What he has tried to prove is only that, in proportion as it displays those characteristics, it is *more evolved.* It is plain, then, that Mr Spencer *identifies* the gaining of ethical sanction with the being more evolved: this follows strictly from his words. But Mr Spencer's language is extremely loose; and we shall presently see that he seems to regard the view it here implies as false. We cannot, therefore, take it as Mr Spencer's definite view that 'better' means nothing but 'more evolved'; or even that what is 'more evolved' is *therefore* 'better.' But we are entitled to urge that he is influenced by these views, and therefore by the naturalistic fallacy. It is only by the assumption of such influence that we can explain his confusion as to what he has really proved, and the absence of any attempt to prove, what he says he has proved, that conduct which is more evolved is better. We shall look in vain for any attempt to shew that 'ethical sanction' is in proportion to 'evolution,' or that it is the 'highest' type of being which displays the most evolved conduct; yet Mr Spencer concludes that this is the case. It is only fair to assume that he is not sufficiently conscious how much these propositions stand in need of proof—what a very different thing is being 'more evolved' from being 'higher' or 'better.' It may, of course, be true that what is more evolved is also higher and better. But Mr Spencer does not seem aware that to assert the one is in any case not the same thing as to assert the other. He argues at length that certain kinds of conduct are 'more evolved,' and then informs us that he has proved them to gain ethical sanction in proportion, without any warning that he has omitted the most essential step in such a proof. Surely this is sufficient evidence that he does not see how essential that step is.

32. Whatever be the degree of Mr Spencer's own guilt, what has just been said will serve to illustrate the kind of fallacy which is constantly committed by those who profess to 'base' Ethics on Evolution. But we must hasten to add that the view which Mr Spencer elsewhere most emphatically recommends is an utterly different one. It will be useful briefly to deal with this, in order that no injustice may be done

to Mr Spencer. The discussion will be instructive partly from the lack of clearness, which Mr Spencer displays, as to the relation of this view to the 'evolutionistic' one just described; and partly because there is reason to suspect that in this view also he is influenced by the naturalistic fallacy.

We have seen that, at the end of his second chapter, Mr Spencer seems to announce that he has already proved certain characteristics of conduct to be a measure of its ethical value. He seems to think that he has proved this merely by considering the evolution of conduct; and he has certainly not given any such proof, unless we are to understand that 'more evolved' is a mere synonym for 'ethically better.' He now promises merely to *confirm* this certain conclusion by shewing that it 'harmonizes with the leading moral ideas men have otherwise reached.' But, when we turn to his third chapter, we find that what he actually does is something quite different. He here asserts that to establish the conclusion 'Conduct is better in proportion as it is more evolved' an entirely new proof is necessary. That conclusion will be *false,* unless a certain proposition, of which we have heard nothing so far, is true—unless it be true that life is *pleasant* on the whole. And the ethical proposition, for which he claims the support of the 'leading moral ideas' of mankind, turns out to be that 'life is good or bad, according as it does, or does not, bring a surplus of agreeable feeling' (§ 10). Here, then, Mr Spencer appears, not as an Evolutionist, but as a Hedonist, in Ethics. No conduct is better, *because* it is more evolved. Degree of evolution can at most be a *criterion* of ethical value; and it will only be that, if we can prove the extremely difficult generalisation that the more evolved is always, on the whole, the pleasanter. It is plain that Mr Spencer here rejects the naturalistic identification of 'better' with 'more evolved'; but it is possible that he is influenced by another naturalistic identification—that of 'good' with 'pleasant.' It is possible that Mr Spencer is a naturalistic Hedonist.

33. Let us examine Mr Spencer's own words. He begins this third chapter by an attempt to shew that *we call* 'good the acts conducive to life, in self or others, and bad those which directly or indirectly tend towards death, special or general' (§ 9). And then he asks: 'Is there any assumption made' in so calling them? 'Yes'; he answers, 'an assumption of extreme significance has been made—an assumption underlying all moral estimates. The question to

be definitely raised and answered before entering on any ethical discussion, is the question of late much agitated—Is life worth living? Shall we take the pessimist view? or shall we take the optimist view? . . . On the answer to this question depends every decision concerning the goodness or badness of conduct.' But Mr Spencer does not immediately proceed to give the answer. Instead of this, he asks another question: 'But now, have these irreconcilable opinions [pessimist and optimist] anything in common ?' And this question he immediately answers by the statement: 'Yes, there is one postulate in which pessimists and optimists agree. Both their arguments assume it to be self-evident that life is good or bad, according as it does, or does not, bring a surplus of agreeable feeling' (§ 10). It is to the defence of this statement that the rest of the chapter is devoted; and at the end Mr Spencer formulates his conclusion in the following words: 'No school can avoid taking for the ultimate moral aim a desirable state of feeling called by whatever name—gratification, enjoyment, happiness. Pleasure somewhere, at some time, to some being or beings, is an inexpugnable element of the conception' (§ 16 *ad fin.*).

Now in all this, there are two points to which I wish to call attention. The first is that Mr Spencer does not, after all, tell us clearly what he takes to be the relation of Pleasure and Evolution in ethical theory. Obviously he should mean that pleasure is the *only* intrinsically desirable thing; that other good things are 'good' only in the sense that they are means to its existence. Nothing but this can properly be meant by asserting it to be 'the ultimate moral aim,' or, as he subsequently says (§ 62 *ad fin.*), 'the ultimately supreme end.' And, if this were so, it would follow that the more evolved conduct was better than the less evolved, only because, and in proportion as, it gave more pleasure. But Mr Spencer tells us that two conditions are, taken together, *sufficient* to prove the more evolved conduct better: (1) That it should tend to produce more life; (2) That life should be worth living or contain a balance of pleasure. And the point I wish to emphasise is that if these conditions are sufficient, then pleasure cannot be the sole good. For though to produce more life is, if the second of Mr Spencer's propositions be correct, *one way* of producing more pleasure, it is not the only way. It is quite possible that a small quantity of life, which was more intensely and uniformly pre-

sent, should give a greater quantity of pleasure than the greatest possible quantity of life that was only just 'worth living.' And in that case, on the hedonistic supposition that pleasure is the only thing worth having, we should have to prefer the smaller quantity of life and therefore, according to Mr Spencer, the less evolved conduct. Accordingly, if Mr Spencer is a true Hedonist, the fact that life gives a balance of pleasure is *not,* as he seems to think, sufficient to prove that the more evolved conduct is the better. If Mr Spencer means us to understand that it *is* sufficient, then his view about pleasure can only be, not that it is the sole good or 'ultimately supreme end,' but that a balance of it is a necessary constituent of the supreme end. In short, Mr Spencer seems to maintain that more life is decidedly better than less, *if only* it give a balance of pleasure: and that contention is inconsistent with the position that pleasure is 'the ultimate moral aim.' Mr Spencer implies that of two quantities of life, which gave an equal amount of pleasure, the larger would nevertheless be preferable to the less. And if this be so, then he must maintain that quantity of life or degree of evolution is itself an ultimate condition of value. He leaves us, therefore, in doubt whether he is not still retaining the Evolutionistic proposition, that the more evolved is better, simply because it is more evolved, alongside of the Hedonistic proposition, that the more pleasant is better, simply because it is more pleasant.

But the second question which we have to ask is: What reasons has Mr Spencer for assigning to pleasure the position which he does assign to it? He tells us, we saw, that the 'arguments' both of pessimists and of optimists 'assume it to be self-evident that life is good or bad, according as it does, or does not, bring a surplus of agreeable feeling'; and he betters this later by telling us that 'since avowed or implied pessimists, and optimists of one or other shade, taken together constitute all men, it results that this postulate is universally accepted' (§ 16). That these statements are absolutely false is, of course, quite obvious: but why does Mr Spencer think them true? and, what is more important (a question which Mr Spencer does not distinguish too clearly from the last), why does he think the postulate itself to be true? Mr Spencer himself tells us his 'proof is' that 'reversing the application of the words' good and bad—applying the word 'good' to conduct, the 'aggregate results' of which are painful, and the word 'bad' to conduct, of which the 'aggregate results' are pleasurable—'creates absurdities' (§ 16). He does not say whether this is because it is absurd to think that the quality, which we *mean by the word* 'good,' really applies to what is painful. Even, however, if we assume him to mean this, and if we assume that absurdities are thus created, it is plain he would only prove that what is painful is properly thought to be *so far* bad, and what is pleasant to be *so far* good: it would not prove at all that pleasure is '*the* supreme end.' There is, however, reason to think that part of what Mr Spencer means is the naturalistic fallacy: that he imagines 'pleasant' or 'productive of pleasure' is the very meaning of the word 'good,' and that 'the absurdity' is due to this. It is at all events certain that he does not distinguish this possible meaning from that which would admit that 'good' denotes an unique indefinable quality. The doctrine of naturalistic Hedonism is, indeed, quite strictly implied in his statement that 'virtue' cannot '*be defined* otherwise than in terms of happiness' (§ 13); and, though, as I remarked above, we cannot insist upon Mr Spencer's words as a certain clue to any definite meaning, that is only because he generally expresses by them several inconsistent alternatives—the naturalistic fallacy being, in this case, one such alternative. It is certainly impossible to find any further reasons given by Mr Spencer for his conviction that pleasure both is the supreme end, and is universally admitted to be so. He seems to assume throughout that we *must* mean by good conduct what is productive of pleasure, and by bad what is productive of pain. So far, then, as he is a Hedonist, he would seem to be a naturalistic Hedonist.

So much for Mr Spencer. It is, of course, quite possible that his treatment of Ethics contains many interesting and instructive remarks. It would seem, indeed, that Mr Spencer's main view, that of which he is most clearly and most often conscious, is that pleasure is the sole good, and that to consider the direction of evolution is by far the best *criterion* of the way in which we shall get most of it: and this theory, *if* he could establish that amount of pleasure is always in direct proportion to amount of evolution *and also* that it was plain what conduct was more evolved, *would* be a very valuable contribution to the science of Sociology; it would even, if pleasure were the sole good, be a valuable contribution to Ethics. But the above discussion should have made it plain that, if

what we want from an ethical philosopher is a scientific and systematic Ethics, not merely an Ethics professedly 'based on science'; if what we want is a clear discussion of the fundamental principles of Ethics, and a statement of the ultimate reasons why one way of acting should be considered better than another— then Mr Spencer's 'Data of Ethics' is immeasurably far from satisfying these demands.

34. It remains only to state clearly what is definitely fallacious in prevalent views as to the relation of Evolution to Ethics—in those views with regard to which it seems so uncertain how far Mr Spencer intends to encourage them. I propose to confine the term 'Evolutionistic Ethics' to the view that we need only to consider the tendency of 'evolution' in order to discover the direction in which we *ought* to go. This view must be carefully distinguished from certain others, which may be commonly confused with it. (1) It might, for instance, be held that the direction in which living things have hitherto developed is, as a matter of fact, the direction of progress. It might be held that the 'more evolved' is, as a matter of fact, also better. And in such a view no fallacy is involved. But, if it is to give us any guidance as to how we ought to act in the future, it does involve a long and painful investigation of the exact points in which the superiority of the more evolved consists. We cannot assume that, because evolution is progress *on the whole,* therefore every point in which the more evolved differs from the less is a point in which it is better than the less. A simple consideration of the course of evolution will therefore, on this view, by no means suffice to inform us of the course we ought to pursue. We shall have to employ all the resources of a strictly ethical discussion in order to arrive at a correct valuation of the different results of evolution—to distinguish the more valuable from the less valuable, and both from those which are no better than their causes, or perhaps even worse. In fact it is difficult to see how, on this view—if all that be meant is that evolution has *on the whole* been a progress—the theory of evolution can give any assistance to Ethics at all. The judgment that evolution has been a progress is itself an independent ethical judgment; and even if we take it to be more certain and obvious than any of the detailed judgments upon which it must logically depend for confirmation, we certainly cannot use it as a datum from which to infer details. It is, at all events, certain that,

if this had been the *only* relation held to exist between Evolution and Ethics, no such importance would have been attached to the bearing of Evolution on Ethics as we actually find claimed for it. (2) The view, which, as I have said, seems to be Mr Spencers main view, may also be held without fallacy. It may be held that the more evolved, though not itself the better, is a *criterion,* because a concomitant, of the better. But this view also obviously involves an exhaustive preliminary discussion of the fundamental ethical question what, after all, is better. That Mr Spencer entirely dispenses with such a discussion in support of his contention that pleasure is the sole good, I have pointed out; and that, if we attempt such a discussion, we shall arrive at no such simple result, I shall presently try to shew. If however the good is not simple, it is by no means likely that we shall be able to discover Evolution to be a criterion of it. We shall have to establish a relation between two highly complicated sets of data; and, moreover, if we had once settled what were goods, and what their comparative values, it is extremely unlikely that we should need to call in the aid of Evolution as a criterion of how to get the most. It is plain, then, again, that if this were the only relation imagined to exist between Evolution and Ethics, it could hardly have been thought to justify the assignment of any importance in Ethics to the theory of Evolution. Finally, (3) it may be held that, though Evolution gives us no help in discovering what results of our efforts will be best, it does give some help in discovering what it is *possible* to attain and what are the means to its attainment. That the theory really may be of service to Ethics in this way cannot be denied. But it is certainly not common to find this humble, ancillary bearing clearly and exclusively assigned to it. In the mere fact, then, that these non-fallacious views of the relation of Evolution to Ethics would give so very little importance to that relation, we have evidence that what is typical in the coupling of the two names is the fallacious view to which I propose to restrict the name 'Evolutionistic Ethics.' This is the view that we ought to move in the direction of evolution simply *because* it is the direction of evolution. That the forces of Nature are working on that side is taken as a presumption that it is the right side. That such a view, apart from metaphysical presuppositions, with which I shall presently deal, is simply fallacious, I have tried to shew. It can only rest on a confused belief that somehow the good simply *means* the side on which Nature is working. And it thus involves another confused belief which is very marked in Mr Spencer's whole treatment of Evolution. For, after all, is Evolution the side on which Nature is working? In the sense, which Mr Spencer gives to the term, and in any sense in which it can be regarded as a fact that the more evolved is higher, Evolution denotes only a *temporary* historical process. That things will permanently continue to evolve in the future, or that they have always evolved in the past, we have not the smallest reason to believe. For Evolution does not, in this sense, denote a natural *law,* like the law of gravity. Darwin's theory of natural selection does indeed state a natural law: it states that, given certain conditions, certain results will always happen. But Evolution, as Mr Spencer understands it and as it is commonly understood, denotes something very different. It denotes only a process which has actually occurred at a given time, because the conditions at the beginning of that time happened to be of a certain nature. That such conditions will always be given, or have always been given, cannot be assumed; and it is only the process which, according to natural law, must follow from *these* conditions and no others, that appears to be also on the whole a progress. Precisely the same natural laws—Darwin's, for instance—would under other conditions render inevitable not Evolution—not a development from lower to higher—but the converse process, which has been called Involution. Yet Mr Spencer constantly speaks of the process which is exemplified in the development of man as if it had all the augustness of a universal Law of Nature: whereas we have no reason to believe it other than a temporary accident, requiring not only certain universal natural laws, but also the existence of a certain state of things at a certain time. The only *laws* concerned in the matter are certainly such as, under other circumstances, would allow us to infer, not the development, but the extinction of man. And that circumstances will always be favourable to further development, that Nature will always work on the side of Evolution, we have no reason whatever to believe. Thus the idea that Evolution throws important light on Ethics seems to be due to a double confusion. Our respect for the process is enlisted by the representation of it as the Law of Nature. But, on the other hand, our respect for Laws of Nature would be speedily diminished, did we not imagine that this desirable process was one of them. To suppose that a Law of Nature is *therefore* respectable, is to commit the naturalistic fallacy; but no one, probably, would be tempted to commit it, unless something which *is* respectable, were represented as a Law of Nature. If it were clearly recognised that there is no evidence for supposing Nature to be on the side of the Good, there would probably be less tendency to hold the opinion, which on other grounds is demonstrably false, that no such evidence is required. And if both false opinions were clearly seen to be false, it would be plain that Evolution has very little indeed to say to Ethics.

35. In this chapter I have begun the criticism of certain ethical views, which seem to owe their influence mainly to the naturalistic fallacy—the fallacy which consists in identifying the simple notion which we mean by 'good' with some other notion. They are views which profess to tell us what is good in itself; and my criticism of them is mainly directed (1) to bring out the negative result, that we have no reason to suppose that which they declare to be the sole good, really to be so, (2) to illustrate further the positive result, already established in Chapter I, that the fundamental principles of Ethics must be *synthetic* propositions, declaring what things, and in what degree, possess a simple and unanalysable property which may be called 'intrinsic value' or 'goodness.' The chapter began (1) by dividing the views to be criticised into (*a*) those which, supposing 'good' to be defined by reference to some super-sensible reality, conclude that the sole good is to be found in such a reality, and may therefore be called 'Metaphysical,' (*b*) those which assign a similar position to some natural object, and may therefore be called 'Naturalistic.' Of naturalistic views, that which regards 'pleasure' as the sole good has received far the fullest and most serious treatment and was therefore reserved for Chapter III: all other forms of Naturalism may be first dismissed, by taking typical examples (24–26). (2) As typical of naturalistic views, other than Hedonism, there was first taken the popular commendation of what is 'natural': it was pointed out that by 'natural' there might here be meant either 'normal' or 'necessary,' and that neither the 'normal' nor the 'necessary' could be seriously supposed to be either always good or the only good things (27–28). (3) But a more important type, because one which claims to be capable of system, is to be found in 'Evolutionistic Ethics.' The influence of the fallacious

opinion that to be 'better' *means* to be 'more evolved' was illustrated by an examination of Mr Herbert Spencer's Ethics; and it was pointed out that, but for the influence of this opinion, Evolution could hardly have been supposed to have any important bearing upon Ethics (29–34).

Chapter III. Hedonism.

36. In this chapter we have to deal with what is perhaps the most famous and the most widely held of all ethical principles—the principle that nothing is good but pleasure. My chief reason for treating of this principle in this place is, as I said, that Hedonism appears in the main to be a form of Naturalistic Ethics: in other words, that pleasure has been so generally held to be the sole good, is almost entirely due to the fact that it has seemed to be somehow involved in the *definition* of 'good'—to be pointed out by the very meaning of the word. If this is so, then the prevalence of Hedonism has been mainly due to what I have called the naturalistic fallacy—the failure to distinguish clearly that unique and indefinable quality which we mean by good. And that it is so, we have very strong evidence in the fact that, of all hedonistic writers, Prof. Sidgwick alone has clearly recognised that by 'good' we do mean something unanalysable, and has alone been led thereby to emphasise the fact that, if Hedonism be true, its claims to be so must be rested solely on its self-evidence—that we must maintain 'Pleasure is the sole good' to be a mere *intuition*. It appeared to Prof. Sidgwick as a new discovery that what he calls the 'method' of Intuitionism must be retained as valid alongside of, and indeed as the foundation of, what he calls the alternative 'methods' of Utilitarianism and Egoism. And that it was a new discovery can hardly be doubted. In previous Hedonists we find no clear and consistent recognition of the fact that their fundamental proposition involves the assumption that a certain unique predicate can be directly seen to belong to pleasure alone among existents: they do not emphasise, as they could hardly have failed to have done had they perceived it, how utterly independent of all other truths this truth must be.

Moreover it is easy to see how this unique position should have been assigned to pleasure without any clear consciousness of the assumption involved.

Hedonism is, for a sufficiently obvious reason, the first conclusion at which any one who begins to reflect upon Ethics naturally arrives. It is very easy to notice the fact that we are pleased with things. The things we enjoy and the things we do not, form two unmistakable classes, to which our attention is constantly directed. But it is comparatively difficult to distinguish the fact that we *approve* a thing from the fact that we are pleased with it. Although, if we look at the two states of mind, we must see that they are different, even though they generally go together, it is very difficult to see in *what respect* they are different, or that the difference can in any connection be of more importance than the many other differences, which are so patent and yet so difficult to analyse, between one *kind* of enjoyment and another. It is very difficult to see that by 'approving' of a thing we mean *feeling that it has a certain predicate*—the predicate, namely, which defines the peculiar sphere of Ethics; whereas in the enjoyment of a thing no such unique object of thought is involved. Nothing is more natural than the vulgar mistake, which we find expressed in a recent book on Ethics:[1] 'The primary ethical fact is, we have said, that something is approved or disapproved: that is, in other words, the ideal representation of certain events in the way of sensation, perception, or idea, is attended with a feeling of pleasure or of pain.' In ordinary speech, 'I want this,' 'I like this,' 'I care about this' are constantly used as equivalents for 'I think this good.' And in this way it is very natural to be led to suppose that there is no distinct class of ethical judgments, but only the class 'things enjoyed'; in spite of the fact, which is very clear, if not very common, that we do not always approve what we enjoy. It is, of course, very obvious that from the supposition that 'I think this good' is identical with 'I am pleased with this,' it cannot be *logically* inferred that pleasure alone is good. But, on the other hand, it is very difficult to see what could be logically inferred from such a supposition; and it seems *natural* enough that such an inference should suggest itself. A very little examination of what is commonly written on the subject will suffice to shew that a logical confusion of this nature is very common. Moreover the very commission of the nat-

uralistic fallacy involves that those who commit it should not recognise clearly the meaning of the proposition 'This is good'—that they should not be able to distinguish this from other propositions which seem to resemble it; and, where this is so, it is, of course, impossible that its logical relations should be clearly perceived.

37. There is, therefore, ample reason to suppose that Hedonism is in general a form of Naturalism— that its acceptance is generally due to the naturalistic fallacy. It is, indeed, only when we have detected this fallacy, when we have become clearly aware of the unique object which is meant by 'good,' that we are able to give to Hedonism the precise definition used above, 'Nothing is good but pleasure': and it may, therefore, be objected that, in attacking this doctrine under the name of Hedonism, I am attacking a doctrine which has never really been held. But it is very common to hold a doctrine, without being clearly aware what it is you hold; and though, when Hedonists argue in favour of what they call Hedonism, I admit that, in order to suppose their arguments valid, they must have before their minds something *other* than the doctrine I have defined, yet, in order to draw the conclusions that they draw, it is necessary that they should *also* have before their minds this doctrine. In fact, my justification for supposing that I shall have refuted *historical* Hedonism, if I refute the proposition 'Nothing is good but pleasure,' is, that although Hedonists have rarely stated their principle in this form and though its truth, in this form, will certainly not follow from their arguments, yet their ethical *method* will follow logically from nothing else. Any pretence of the hedonistic method, to discover to us practical truths which we should not otherwise have known, is founded on the principle that the course of action which will bring the greatest balance of pleasure is certainly the right one; and, failing an absolute proof that the greatest balance of pleasure *always* coincides with the greatest balance of other goods, which it is not generally attempted to give, this principle can only be justified if pleasure be the sole good. Indeed it can hardly be doubted that Hedonists are distinguished by arguing, in disputed practical questions, *as if* pleasure were the sole good; and that it is justifiable, for this among other reasons, to take this as *the* ethical principle of Hedonism will, I hope, be made further evident by the whole discussion of this chapter.

---

1. A. E. Taylor's *Problem of Conduct*, p.120.

By Hedonism, then, I mean the doctrine that pleasure *alone* is good as an end—'good' in the sense which I have tried to point out as indefinable. The doctrine that pleasure, *among other things,* is good as an end, is not Hedonism; and I shall not dispute its truth. Nor again is the doctrine that other things, beside pleasure, are good as means, at all inconsistent with Hedonism: the Hedonist is not bound to maintain that 'Pleasure alone is good,' if under good he includes, as we generally do, what is good as means to an end, *as well as* the end itself. In attacking Hedonism, I am therefore simply and solely attacking the doctrine that 'Pleasure *alone* is good as an end or in itself': I am not attacking the doctrine that 'Pleasure *is* good as an end or in itself,' nor am I attacking any doctrine whatever as to what are the best means we can take in order to obtain pleasure or any other end. Hedonists do, in general, recommend a course of conduct which is very similar to that which I should recommend. I do not quarrel with them about most of their practical conclusions, I quarrel only with the reasons by which they seem to think their conclusions can be supported; and I do emphatically deny that the correctness of their conclusions is any ground for inferring the correctness of their principles. A correct conclusion may always be obtained by fallacious reasoning; and the good life or virtuous maxims of a Hedonist afford absolutely no presumption that his ethical philosophy is also good. It is his ethical philosophy alone with which I am concerned: what I dispute is the excellence of his reasoning, not the excellence of his character as a man or even as moral teacher. It may be thought that my contention is unimportant, but that is no ground for thinking that I am not in the right. What I am concerned with is knowledge only—that we should think correctly and so far arrive at some truth, however unimportant: I do not say that such knowledge will make us more useful members of society. If any one does not care for knowledge for its own sake, then I have nothing to say to him: only it should not be thought that a lack of interest in what I have to say is any ground for holding it untrue.

38. Hedonists, then, hold that all other things but pleasure, whether conduct or virtue or knowledge, whether life or nature or beauty, are only good as means to pleasure or for the sake of pleasure, never for their own sakes or as ends in themselves. This view was held by Aristippus, the disciple of Socrates, and by the Cyrenaic school which he founded; it is associated with Epicurus and the Epicureans; and it has been held in modern times, chiefly by those philosophers who call themselves 'Utilitarians'—by Bentham, and by Mill, for instance. Herbert Spencer, as we have seen, also says he holds it; and Professor Sidgwick, as we shall see, holds it too.

Yet all these philosophers, as has been said, differ from one another more or less, both as to what they mean by Hedonism, and as to the reasons for which it is to be accepted as a true doctrine. The matter is therefore obviously not quite so simple as it might at first appear. My own object will be to shew quite clearly what the theory must imply, if it is made precise, if all confusions and inconsistencies are removed from the conception of it; and, when this is done, I think it will appear that all the various reasons given for holding it to be true, are really quite inadequate; that they are not reasons for holding Hedonism, but only for holding some other doctrine which is confused therewith. In order to attain this object I propose to take first Mill's doctrine, as set forth in his book called *Utilitarianism*: we shall find in Mill a conception of Hedonism, and arguments in its favour, which fairly represent those of a large class of hedonistic writers. To these representative conceptions and arguments grave objections, objections which appear to me to be conclusive, have been urged by Professor Sidgwick. These I shall try to give in my own words; and shall then proceed to consider and refute Professor Sidgwick's own much more precise conceptions and arguments. With this, I think, we shall have traversed the whole field of Hedonistic doctrine. It will appear, from the discussion, that the task of deciding what is or is not good in itself is by no means an easy one; and in this way the discussion will afford a good example of the method which it is necessary to pursue in attempting to arrive at the truth with regard to this primary class of ethical principles. In particular it will appear that two principles of method must be constantly kept in mind: (1) that the naturalistic fallacy must not be committed; (2) that the distinction between means and ends must be observed.

39. I propose, then, to begin by an examination of Mill's *Utilitarianism*. That is a book which contains an admirably clear and fair discussion of many ethical principles and methods. Mill exposes not a few simple mistakes which are very likely to be made by

those who approach ethical problems without much previous reflection. But what I am concerned with is the mistakes which Mill himself appears to have made, and these only so far as they concern the Hedonistic principle. Let me repeat what that principle is. It is, I said, that pleasure is the only thing at which we ought to aim, the only thing that is good as an end and for its own sake. And now let us turn to Mill and see whether he accepts this description of the question at issue. 'Pleasure,' he says at the outset, 'and freedom from pain, are the only things desirable as ends' (p. 10[1]); and again, at the end of his argument, 'To think of an object as desirable (unless for the sake of its consequences) and to think of it as pleasant are one and the same thing' (p. 58). These statements, taken together, and apart from certain confusions which are obvious in them, seem to imply the principle I have stated; and if I succeed in shewing that Mill's reasons for them do not prove them, it must at least be admitted that I have not been fighting with shadows or demolishing a man of straw.

It will be observed that Mill adds 'absence of pain' to 'pleasure' in his first statement, though not in his second. There is, in this, a confusion, with which, however, we need not deal. I shall talk of 'pleasure' alone, for the sake of conciseness; but all my arguments will apply *à fortiori* to 'absence of pain': it is easy to make the necessary substitutions.

Mill holds, then, that 'happiness is desirable, and *the only thing desirable*,[2] as an end; all other things being only desirable as means to that end' (p. 52). Happiness he has already defined as 'pleasure, and the absence of pain' (p.10); he does not pretend that this is more than an arbitrary verbal definition; and, *as such*, I have not a word to say against it. His principle, then, is 'pleasure is the only thing desirable,' if I may be allowed, when I say 'pleasure,' to include in that word (so far as necessary) absence of pain. And now what are his reasons for holding that principle to be true? He has already told us (p. 6) that 'Questions of ultimate ends are not amenable to direct proof. Whatever can be proved to be good, must be so by being shewn to be a means to something *admitted to be good without proof.*' With this, I perfectly

agree: indeed the chief object of my first chapter was to shew that this is so. Anything which is good as an end must be admitted to be good without proof. We are agreed so far. Mill even uses the same examples which I used in my second chapter. 'How,' he says, 'is it possible to prove that health is good?' 'What proof is it possible to give that pleasure is good?' Well, in Chapter IV, in which he deals with the proof of his Utilitarian principle, Mill repeats the above statement in these words: 'It has already,' he says, 'been remarked, that questions of ultimate ends do not admit of proof, in the ordinary acceptation of the term' (p. 52). 'Questions about ends,' he goes on in this same passage, 'are, in other words, questions what things are desirable.' I am quoting these repetitions, because they make it plain what otherwise might have been doubted, that Mill is using the words 'desirable' or 'desirable as an end' as absolutely and precisely equivalent to the words 'good as an end.' We are, then, now to hear, what reasons he advances for this doctrine that pleasure alone is good as an end.

40. 'Questions about ends,' he says (pp. 52–3), 'are, in other words, questions what things are desirable. The utilitarian doctrine is, that happiness is desirable, and the only thing desirable, as an end; all other things being only desirable as means to that end. What ought to be required of this doctrine—what conditions is it requisite that the doctrine should fulfil—to make good its claim to be believed?

'The only proof capable of being given that a thing is visible, is that people actually see it. The only proof that a sound is audible, is that people hear it; and so of the other sources of our experience. In like manner, I apprehend, the sole evidence it is possible to produce that anything is desirable, is that people do actually desire it. If the end which the utilitarian doctrine proposes to itself were not, in theory and in practice, acknowledged to be an end, nothing could ever convince any person that it was so. No reason can be given why the general happiness is desirable, except that each person, so far as he believes it to be attainable, desires his own happiness. This, however, being the fact, we have not only all the proof which the case admits of, but all which it is possible to require, that happiness is a good: that each person's happiness is a good to that person, and the general happiness, therefore, a good to the aggregate of all persons. Happiness has made out its title as *one* of the ends of conduct, and consequently one of the criteria of morality.'

There, that is enough. That is my first point. Mill has made as naïve and artless a use of the naturalistic fallacy as anybody could desire. 'Good,' he tells us, means 'desirable,' and you can only find out what is desirable by seeking to find out what is actually desired. This is, of course, only one step towards the proof of Hedonism; for it may be, as Mill goes on to say, that other things beside pleasure are desired. Whether or not pleasure is the only thing desired is, as Mill himself admits (p. 58), a psychological question, to which we shall presently proceed. The important step for Ethics is this one just taken, the step which pretends to prove that 'good' means 'desired.'

Well, the fallacy in this step is so obvious, that it is quite wonderful how Mill failed to see it. The fact is that 'desirable' does not mean 'able to be desired' as 'visible' means 'able to be seen.' The desirable means simply what *ought* to be desired or *deserves* to be desired; just as the detestable means not what can be but what ought to be detested and the damnable what deserves to be damned. Mill has, then, smuggled in, under cover of the word 'desirable,' the very notion about which he ought to be quite clear. 'Desirable' does indeed mean 'what it is good to desire'; but when this is understood, it is no longer plausible to say that our only test of *that,* is what is actually desired. Is it merely a tautology when the Prayer Book talks of *good* desires? Are not *bad* desires also possible? Nay, we find Mill himself talking of a 'better and nobler object of desire' (p. 10), as if, after all, what is desired were not *ipso facto* good, and good in proportion to the amount it is desired. Moreover, if the desired is *ipso facto* the good; then the good is *ipso facto* the motive of our actions, and there can be no question of finding motives for doing it, as Mill is at such pains to do. If Mill's explanation of 'desirable' be *true,* then his statement (p. 26) that the rule of action may be *confounded* with the motive of it is untrue: for the motive of action will then be according to him *ipso facto* its rule; there can be no distinction between the two, and therefore no confusion, and thus he has contradicted himself flatly. These are specimens of the contradictions, which, as I have tried to shew, must always follow from the use of the naturalistic fallacy; and I hope I need now say no more about the matter.

41. Well, then, the first step by which Mill has attempted to establish his Hedonism is simply fallacious. He has attempted to establish the identity of the good with the desired, by confusing the proper sense of 'desirable,' in which it denotes that which it is good to desire, with the sense which it would bear if it were analogous to such words as 'visible.' If 'desirable' is to be identical with 'good,' then it must bear one sense; and if it is to be identical with 'desired,' then it must bear quite another sense. And yet to Mill's contention that the desired is necessarily good, it is quite essential that these two senses of 'desirable' should be the same. If he holds they are the same, then he has contradicted himself elsewhere; if he holds they are not the same, then the first step in his proof of Hedonism is absolutely worthless.

But now we must deal with the second step. Having proved, as he thinks, that the good means the desired, Mill recognises that, if he is further to maintain that pleasure alone is good, he must prove that pleasure alone is really desired. This doctrine that 'pleasure alone is the object of all our desires' is the doctrine which Prof. Sidgwick has called Psychological Hedonism: and it is a doctrine which most eminent psychologists are now agreed in rejecting. But it is a necessary step in the proof of any such Naturalistic Hedonism as Mill's; and it is so commonly held, by people not expert either in psychology or in philosophy, that I wish to treat it at some length. It will be seen that Mill does not hold it in this bare form. He admits that other things than pleasure are desired; and this admission is at once a contradiction of his Hedonism. One of the shifts by which he seeks to evade this contradiction we shall afterwards consider. But some may think that no such shifts are needed: they may say of Mill, what Callicles says of Polus in the *Gorgias*,[1] that he has made this fatal admission through a most unworthy fear of appearing paradoxical; that they, on the other hand, will have the courage of their convictions, and will not be ashamed to go to any lengths of paradox, in defence of what they hold to be the truth.

42. Well, then, we are supposing it held that pleasure is the object of all desire, that it is the universal end of all human activity. Now I suppose it will not be denied that people are commonly said to desire other things: for instance, we usually talk of desiring

---

1. 481 c–487 B.

food and drink, of desiring money, approbation, fame. The question, then, must be of what is meant by desire, and by the object of desire. There is obviously asserted some sort of necessary or universal relation between something which is called desire, and another thing which is called pleasure. The question is of what sort this relation is; whether in conjunction with the naturalistic fallacy above mentioned, it will justify Hedonism. Now I am not prepared to deny that there is some universal relation between pleasure and desire; but I hope to shew, that, if there is, it is of such sort as will rather make against than for Hedonism. It is urged that pleasure is always the object of desire, and I am ready to admit that pleasure is always, in part at least, the *cause* of desire. But this distinction is very important. Both views might be expressed in the same language; both might be said to hold that whenever we desire, we always desire *because of* some pleasure: if I asked my supposed Hedonist, 'Why do you desire that?' he might answer, quite consistently with his contention, 'Because there is pleasure there,' and if he asked me the same question, I might answer, equally consistently with my contention, 'Because there is pleasure here.' Only our two answers would not mean the same thing. It is this use of the same language to denote quite different facts, which I believe to be the chief cause why Psychological Hedonism is so often held, just as it was also the cause of Mill's naturalistic fallacy.

Let us try to analyse the psychological state which is called 'desire.' That name is usually confined to a state of mind in which the idea of some object or event, not yet existing, is present to us. Suppose, for instance, I am desiring a glass of port wine. I have the idea of drinking such a glass before my mind, although I am not yet drinking it. Well, how does pleasure enter in to this relation? My theory is that it enters in, in this way. The *idea* of the drinking causes a feeling of pleasure in my mind, which helps to produce that state of incipient activity, which is called 'desire.' It is, therefore, because of a pleasure, which I already have—the pleasure excited by a mere idea—that I desire the wine, which I have not. And I am ready to admit that a pleasure of this kind, an actual pleasure, is always among the causes of every desire, and not only of every desire, but of every mental activity, whether conscious or sub-conscious. I am ready to *admit* this, I say: I cannot vouch that it is the true psychological doctrine; but, at all events,

it is not *primâ facie* quite absurd. And now, what is the other doctrine, the doctrine which I am supposing held, and which is at all events essential to Mill's argument? It is this. That when I desire the wine, it is not the wine which I desire but the pleasure which I expect to get from it. In other words, the doctrine is that the idea of a pleasure *not actual* is always necessary to cause desire; whereas my doctrine was that the *actual* pleasure caused by the idea of something else was always necessary to cause desire. It is these two different theories which I suppose the Psychological Hedonists to confuse: the confusion is, as Mr Bradley puts it,[1] between 'a pleasant thought' and 'the thought of a pleasure.' It is in fact only where the latter, the 'thought of a pleasure,' is present, that pleasure can be said to be the *object* of desire, or the *motive* to action. On the other hand, when only a pleasant thought is present, as, I admit, *may* always be the case, then it is the object of the thought—that which we are thinking about—which is the object of desire and the motive to action; and the pleasure, which that thought excites, may, indeed, cause our desire or move us to action, but it is not our end or object nor our motive.

Well, I hope this distinction is sufficiently clear. Now let us see how it bears upon Ethical Hedonism. I assume it to be perfectly obvious that the idea of the object of desire is not always and only the idea of a pleasure. In the first place, plainly, we are not always conscious of expecting pleasure, when we desire a thing. We may be only conscious of the thing which we desire, and may be impelled to make for it at once, without any calculation as to whether it will bring us pleasure or pain. And, in the second place, even when we do expect pleasure, it can certainly be very rarely pleasure *only* which we desire. For instance, granted that, when I desire my glass of port wine, I have also an idea of the pleasure I expect from it, plainly that pleasure cannot be the only object of my desire; the port wine must be included in my object, else I might be led by my desire to take wormwood instead of wine. If the desire were directed *solely* towards the pleasure, it could not lead me to take the wine; if it is to take a definite direction, it is absolutely necessary that the idea of the object, from which the pleasure is expected, should also be present and should control

_____

1. *Ethical Studies*, p. 232.

my activity. The theory then that what is desired is always and only pleasure must break down: it is impossible to prove that pleasure alone is good, by that line of argument. But, if we substitute for this theory, that other, possibly true, theory, that pleasure is always the cause of desire, then all the plausibility of our ethical doctrine that pleasure alone is good straightway disappears. For in this case, pleasure is not what I desire, it is not what I want: it is something which I already have, before I can want anything. And can any one feel inclined to maintain, that that which I already have, while I am still desiring something else, is always and alone the good?

43. But now let us return to consider another of Mill's arguments for his position that 'happiness is the sole end of human action.' Mill admits, as I have said, that pleasure is not the only thing we actually desire. 'The desire of virtue,' he says, 'is not as universal, but it is as authentic a fact, as the desire of happiness.'[1] And again, 'Money is, in many cases, desired in and for itself.'[2] These admissions are, of course, in naked and glaring contradiction with his argument that pleasure is the only thing desirable, because it is the only thing desired. How then does Mill even attempt to avoid this contradiction? His chief argument seems to be that 'virtue,' 'money' and other such objects, when they are thus desired in and for themselves, are desired only as 'a part of happiness.'[3] Now what does this mean? Happiness, as we saw, has been defined by Mill, as 'pleasure and the absence of pain.' Does Mill mean to say that 'money,' these actual coins, which he admits to be desired in and for themselves, are a part either of pleasure or of the absence of pain? Will he maintain that those coins themselves are in my mind, and actually a part of my pleasant feelings?. If this is to be said, all words are useless: nothing can possibly be distinguished from anything else; if these two things are not distinct, what on earth is? We shall hear next that this table is really and truly the same thing as this room; that a cab-horse is in fact indistinguishable from St Paul's Cathedral; that this book of Mill's which I hold in my hand, because it was his pleasure to produce it, is now and at this moment a part of

the happiness which he felt many years ago and which has so long ceased to be. Pray consider a moment what this contemptible nonsense really means. 'Money,' says Mill, 'is only desirable as a means to happiness.' Perhaps so; but what then? 'Why,' says Mill, 'money is undoubtedly desired for its own sake.' 'Yes, go on, say we. 'Well,' says Mill, 'if money is desired for its own sake, it must be desirable as an end-in-itself: I have said so myself.' 'Oh,' say we, 'but you also said just now that it was only desirable as a means.' 'I own I did,' says Mill, 'but I will try to patch up matters, by saying that what is only a means to an end, is the same thing as a part of that end. I daresay the public won't notice.' And the public haven't noticed. Yet this is certainly what Mill has done. He has broken down the distinction between means and ends, upon the precise observance of which his Hedonism rests. And he has been compelled to do this, because he has failed to distinguish 'end' in the sense of what is desirable, from 'end' in the sense of what is desired: a distinction which, nevertheless, both the present argument and his whole book presupposes. This is a consequence of the naturalistic fallacy.

44. Mill, then, has nothing better to say for himself than this. His two fundamental propositions are, in his own words, 'that to think of an object as desirable (unless for the sake of its consequences), and to think of it as pleasant, are one and the same thing; and that to desire anything except in proportion as the idea of it is pleasant, is a physical and metaphysical impossibility.'[4] Both of these statements are, we have seen, merely supported by fallacies. The first seems to rest on the naturalistic fallacy; the second rests partly on this, partly on the fallacy of confusing ends and means, and partly on the fallacy of confusing a pleasant thought with the thought of a pleasure. His very language shews this. For that the idea of a thing is pleasant, in his second clause, is obviously meant to be the same fact which he denotes by 'thinking of it as pleasant,' in his first.

Accordingly, Mill's arguments for the proposition that pleasure is the sole good, and our refutation of those arguments, may be summed up as follows:

First of all, he takes 'the desirable,' which he uses as a synonym for 'the good,' to *mean* what *can* be de-

---

1. p. 53.

2. p. 55.

3. pp. 56–7.

4. p. 58.

sired. The test, again, of what can be desired, is, according to him, what actually is desired: if, therefore, he says, we can find some one thing which is always and alone desired, that thing will necessarily be the only thing that is desirable, the only thing that is good as an end. In this argument the naturalistic fallacy is plainly involved. That fallacy, I explained, consists in the contention that good *means* nothing but some simple or complex notion, that can be defined in terms of natural qualities. In Mill's case, good is thus supposed to *mean* simply what is desired; and what is desired is something which can thus be defined in natural terms. Mill tells us that we ought to desire something (an ethical proposition), because we actually do desire it; but if his contention that 'I ought to desire' means nothing but 'I do desire' were true, then he is only entitled to say, 'We do desire so and so, because we do desire it'; and that is not an ethical proposition at all; it is a mere tautology. The whole object of Mill's book is to help us to discover what we ought to do; but, in fact, by attempting to define the meaning of this 'ought,' he has completely debarred himself from ever fulfilling that object: he has confined himself to telling us what we do do.

Mill's first argument then is that, because good means desired, therefore the desired is good; but having thus arrived at an ethical conclusion, by denying that any ethical conclusion is possible, he still needs another argument to make his conclusion a basis for Hedonism. He has to prove that we always do desire pleasure or freedom from pain, and that we never desire anything else whatever. This second doctrine, which Professor Sidgwick has called Psychological Hedonism, I accordingly discussed. I pointed out how obviously untrue it is that we never desire anything but pleasure; and how there is not a shadow of ground for saying even that, whenever we desire anything, we always desire pleasure *as well as* that thing. I attributed the obstinate belief in these untruths partly to a confusion between the cause of desire and the object of desire. It may, I said, be true that desire can never occur unless it be preceded by some *actual* pleasure; but even if this is true, it obviously gives no ground for saying that the object of desire is always some *future* pleasure. By the object of desire is meant that, of which the idea causes desire in us; it is some pleasure, which we anticipate, some pleasure which we

have not got, which is the object of desire, whenever we do desire pleasure. And any actual pleasure, which may be excited by the idea of this anticipated pleasure, is obviously not the same pleasure as that anticipated pleasure, of which only the idea is actual. This actual pleasure is not what we want; what we want is always something which we have not got; and to say that pleasure always causes us to want is quite a different thing from saying that what we want is always pleasure.

Finally, we saw, Mill admits all this. He insists that we do *actually* desire other things than pleasure, and yet he says we do *really* desire nothing else. He tries to explain away this contradiction, by confusing together two notions, which he has before carefully distinguished—the notions of means and of end. He now says that a means to an end is the same thing as a part of that end. To this last fallacy special attention should be given, as our ultimate decision with regard to Hedonism will largely turn upon it.

45. It is this ultimate decision with regard to Hedonism at which we must now try to arrive. So far I have been only occupied with refuting Mill's naturalistic arguments for Hedonism; but the doctrine that pleasure alone is desirable may still be true, although Mill's fallacies cannot prove it so. This is the question which we have now to face. This proposition, 'pleasure alone is good or desirable,' belongs undoubtedly to that class of propositions, to which Mill at first rightly pretended it belonged, the class of first principles, which are not amenable to direct proof. But in this case, as he also rightly says, 'considerations may be presented capable of determining the intellect either to give or withhold its assent to the doctrine' (p. 7). It is such considerations that Professor Sidgwick presents, and such also that I shall try to present for the opposite view. This proposition that 'pleasure alone is good as an end,' the fundamental proposition of Ethical Hedonism, will then appear, in Professor Sidgwick's language, as an object of intuition. I shall try to shew you why my intuition denies it, just as his intuition affirms it. It *may* always be true notwithstanding; neither intuition can *prove* whether it is true or not; I am bound to be satisfied, if I can 'present considerations capable of determining the intellect' to reject it.

Now it may be said that this is a very unsatisfactory state of things. It is indeed; but it is important to make a distinction between two different reasons, which may be given for calling it unsatisfactory. Is it unsatisfactory because our principle cannot be proved? or is it unsatisfactory merely because we do not agree with one another about it? I am inclined to think that the latter is the chief reason. For the mere fact that in certain cases proof is impossible does not usually give us the least uneasiness. For instance, nobody can prove that this is a chair beside me; yet I do not suppose that any one is much dissatisfied for that reason. We all agree that it is a chair, and that is enough to content us, although it is quite possible we may be wrong. A madman, of course, might come in and say that it is not a chair but an elephant. We could not prove that he was wrong, and the fact that he did not agree with us might then begin to make us uneasy. Much more, then, shall we be uneasy, if some one, whom we do not think to be mad, disagrees with us. We shall try to argue with him, and we shall probably be content if we lead him to agree with us, although we shall not have proved our point. We can only persuade him by shewing him that our view is consistent with something else which he holds to be true, whereas his original view is contradictory to it. But it will be impossible to prove that that something else, which we both agree to be true, is really so; we shall be satisfied to have settled the matter in dispute by means of it, merely because we are agreed on it. In short, our dissatisfaction in these cases is almost always of the type felt by the poor lunatic in the story. 'I said the world was mad,' says he, 'and the world said that I was mad; and, confound it, they outvoted me.' It is, I say, almost always such a disagreement, and not the impossibility of proof, which makes us call the state of things unsatisfactory. For, indeed, who can prove that proof itself is a warrant of truth ? We are all agreed that the laws of logic are true and therefore we accept a result which is proved by their means; but such a proof is satisfactory to us only because we are all so fully agreed that it is a warrant of truth. And yet we cannot, by the nature of the case, prove that we are right in being so agreed.

Accordingly, I do not think we need be much distressed by our admission that we cannot prove whether pleasure alone is good or not. We may be able to arrive at an agreement notwithstanding; and if so, I think it will be satisfactory. And yet I am not very sanguine about our prospects of such satisfaction. Ethics, and philosophy in general, have always been in a peculiarly unsatisfactory state. There has been no agreement about them, as there is about the existence of chairs and lights and benches. I should therefore be a fool if I hoped to settle one great point of controversy, now and once for all. It is extremely improbable I shall convince. It would be highly presumptuous even to hope that in the end, say two or three centuries hence, it will be agreed that pleasure is not the sole good. Philosophical questions are so difficult, the problems they raise are so complex, that no one can fairly expect, now, any more than in the past, to win more than a very limited assent. And yet I confess that the considerations which I am about to present appear to me to be absolutely convincing. I do think that they *ought* to convince, if only I can put them well. In any case, I can but try. I *shall* try now to put an end to that unsatisfactory state of things, of which I have been speaking. I shall try to produce an agreement that the fundamental principle of Hedonism is very like an absurdity, by shewing what it must mean, if it is clearly thought out, and how that clear meaning is in conflict with other beliefs, which will, I hope, not be so easily given up.

46. Well, then, we now proceed to discuss Intuitionistic Hedonism. And the beginning of this discussion marks, it is to be observed, a turning-point in my ethical method. The point I have been labouring hitherto, the point that 'good is indefinable,' and that to deny this involves a fallacy, is a point capable of strict proof: for to deny it involves contradictions. But now we are coming to the question, for the sake of answering which Ethics exists, the question what things or qualities are good. Of any answer to *this* question no direct proof is possible, and that, just because of our former answer, as to the meaning of good, direct proof *was* possible. We are now confined to the hope of what Mill calls 'indirect proof,' the hope of determining one another's intellect; and we are now so confined, just because, in the matter of the former question we are not so confined. Here, then, is an intuition to be submitted to our verdict—the intuition that 'pleasure alone is good as an end—good in and for itself.'

47. Well, in this connection it seems first desirable to touch on another doctrine of Mill's—another doctrine which, in the interest of Hedonism, Professor Sidgwick has done very wisely to reject. This is the doctrine of 'difference of quality in plea-

sures.' 'If I am asked,' says Mill,[1] 'what I mean by difference of quality in pleasures, or what makes one pleasure more valuable than another, merely as a pleasure, except its being greater in amount, there is but one possible answer. Of two pleasures, if there be one to which all or almost all who have experience of both give a decided preference, irrespective of any feeling of moral obligation to prefer it, that is the more desirable pleasure. If one of the two is, by those who are competently acquainted with both, placed so far above the other that they prefer it, even though knowing it to be attended with a greater amount of discontent, and would not resign it for any quantity of the other pleasure which their nature is capable of, we are justified in ascribing to the preferred enjoyment a superiority in quality, so far outweighing quantity as to render it, in comparison, of small account.'

Now it is well known that Bentham rested his case for Hedonism on 'quantity of pleasure' alone. It was his maxim, that 'quantity of pleasure being equal, pushpin is as good as poetry.' And Mill apparently considers Bentham to have proved that nevertheless poetry is better than pushpin; that poetry does produce a greater quantity of pleasure. But yet, says Mill, the Utilitarians 'might have taken the other and, as it may be called, higher ground, with entire consistency' (p. 11). Now we see from this that Mill acknowledges 'quality of pleasure' to be another or different ground for estimating pleasures, than Bentham's quantity; and moreover, by that question-begging 'higher,' which he afterwards translates into 'superior,' he seems to betray an uncomfortable feeling, that, after all, if you take quantity of pleasure for your only standard, something may be wrong and you may deserve to be called a pig. And it may presently appear that you very likely would deserve that name. But, meanwhile, I only wish to shew that Mill's admissions as to quality of pleasure are either inconsistent with his Hedonism, or else afford no other ground for it than would be given by mere quantity of pleasure.

It will be seen that Mill's test for one pleasure's superiority in quality over another is the preference of most people who have experienced both. A pleasure so preferred, he holds, is more desirable. But then, as

we have seen, he holds that 'to think of an object as desirable and to think of it as pleasant are one and the same thing' (p. 58). He holds, therefore, that the preference of experts merely proves that one pleasure is pleasanter than another. But if that is so, how can he distinguish this standard from the standard of quantity of pleasure? Can one pleasure be pleasanter than another, except in the sense that it gives *more* pleasure? 'Pleasant' must, if words are to have any meaning at all, denote some one quality common to all the things that are pleasant; and, if so, then one thing can only be more pleasant than another, according as it has more or less of this one quality. But, then, let us try the other alternative, and suppose that Mill does not seriously mean that this preference of experts merely proves one pleasure to be pleasanter than another. Well, in this case what does 'preferred' mean? It cannot mean 'more desired,' since, as we know, the degree of desire is always, according to Mill, in exact proportion to the degree of pleasantness. But, in that case, the basis of Mill's Hedonism collapses, for he is admitting that one thing may be preferred over another, and thus proved more desirable, although it is not more desired. In this case Mill's judgment of preference is just a judgment of that intuitional kind which I have been contending to be necessary to establish the hedonistic or any other principle. It is a direct judgment that one thing is more desirable, or better than another; a judgment utterly independent of all considerations as to whether one thing is more desired or pleasanter than another. This is to admit that good is good and indefinable.

48. And note another point that is brought out by this discussion. Mill's judgment of preference, so far from establishing the principle that pleasure alone is good, is obviously inconsistent with it. He admits that experts can judge whether one pleasure is more desirable than another, because pleasures differ in quality. But what does this mean? If one pleasure can differ from another in quality, that means, that *a* pleasure is something complex, something composed, in fact, of pleasure *in addition to* that which produces pleasure. For instance, Mill speaks of 'sensual indulgences' as 'lower pleasures.' But what is a sensual indulgence? It is surely a certain excitement of some sense *together with* the pleasure caused by such excitement. Mill, therefore, in admitting that a sensual indulgence can be directly judged to be lower than another pleasure, in which the degree of pleasure involved may be the

---

1. p. 12.

same, is admitting that other things may be good, or bad, quite independently of the pleasure which accompanies them. *A pleasure is, in fact, merely a misleading term which conceals the fact that what we are dealing with is not pleasure but something else, which may indeed necessarily produce pleasure, but is nevertheless quite distinct from it.*

Mill, therefore, in thinking that to estimate quality of pleasure is quite consistent with his hedonistic principle that pleasure and absence of pain alone are desirable as ends, has again committed the fallacy of confusing ends and means. For take even the most favourable supposition of his meaning; let us suppose that by a pleasure he does not mean, as his words imply, that which produces pleasure and the pleasure produced. Let us suppose him to mean that there are various kinds of pleasure, in the sense in which there are various kinds of colour—blue, red, green, etc. Even in this case, if we are to say that our end is colour alone, then, although it is impossible we should have colour without having some particular colour, yet the particular colour we must have, is only a *means* to our having colour, if colour is really our end. And if colour is our only possible end, as Mill says pleasure is, then there can be no possible reason for preferring one colour to another, red, for instance, to blue, except that the one is more of a colour than the other. Yet the opposite of this is what Mill is attempting to hold with regard to pleasures.

Accordingly a consideration of Mill's view that some pleasures are superior to others *in quality* brings out one point which may 'help to determine the intellect' with regard to the intuition 'Pleasure is the only good.' For it brings out the fact that if you say 'pleasure,' you must mean 'pleasure': you must mean some one thing common to all different 'pleasures,' some one thing, which may exist in different degrees, but which cannot differ in *kind*. I have pointed out that, if you say, as Mill does, that quality of pleasure is to be taken into account, then you are no longer holding that pleasure *alone* is good as an end, since you imply that something else, something which is *not* present in all pleasures, is *also* good as an end. The illustration I have given from colour expresses this point in its most acute form. It is plain that if you say 'Colour alone is good as an end,' then you can give no possible reason for preferring one colour to another. Your only standard of good and

bad will then be 'colour'; and since red and blue both conform equally to this, the only standard, you can have no other whereby to judge whether red is better than blue. It is true that you cannot have colour unless you also have one or all of the particular colours: they, therefore, if colour is the end, will all be good as means, but none of them can be better than another even as a means, far less can any one of them be regarded as an end in itself. Just so with pleasure: If we do really mean 'Pleasure alone is good as an end,' then we must agree with Bentham that 'Quantity of pleasure being equal, pushpin is as good as poetry.' To have thus dismissed Mill's reference to quality of pleasure, is therefore to have made one step in the desired direction. The reader will now no longer be prevented from agreeing with me, by any idea that the hedonistic principle 'Pleasure alone is good as an end' is consistent with the view that one pleasure may be of a better quality than another. These two views, we have seen, are contradictory to one another. We must choose between them: and if we choose the latter, then we must give up the principle of Hedonism.

49. But, as I said, Professor Sidgwick has seen that they are inconsistent. He has seen that he must choose between them. He has chosen. He has rejected the test by quality of pleasure, and has accepted the hedonistic principle. He still maintains that 'Pleasure alone is good as an end.' I propose therefore to discuss the considerations which he has offered in order to convince us. I shall hope by that discussion to remove some more of such prejudices and misunderstandings as might prevent agreement with me. If I can shew that some of the considerations which Professor Sidgwick urges are such as we need by no means agree with, and that others are actually rather in my favour than in his, we may have again advanced a few steps nearer to the unanimity which we desire.

50. The passages in the *Methods of Ethics* to which I shall now invite attention are to be found in I. IX. 4 and in III. XIV. 4–5.

The first of these two passages runs as follows:

"I think that if we consider carefully such permanent results as are commonly judged to be good, other than qualities of human beings, we can find nothing that, on reflection, appears to possess this quality of goodness out of relation to human existence, or at least to some consciousness or feeling.

"For example, we commonly judge some inanimate objects, scenes, etc. to be good as possessing beauty, and others bad from ugliness: still no one would consider it rational to aim at the production of beauty in external nature, apart from any possible contemplation of it by human beings. In fact when beauty is maintained to be objective, it is not commonly meant that it exists as beauty out of relation to any mind whatsoever: but only that there is some standard of beauty valid for all minds.

"It may, however, be said that beauty and other results commonly judged to be good, though we do not conceive them to exist out of relation to human beings (or at least minds of some kind), are yet so far separable as ends from the human beings on whom their existence depends, that their realization may conceivably come into competition with the perfection or happiness of these beings. Thus, though beautiful things cannot be thought worth producing except as possible objects of contemplation, still a man may devote himself to their production without any consideration of the persons who are to contemplate them. Similarly knowledge is a good which cannot exist except in minds; and yet one may be more interested in the development of knowledge than in its possession by any particular minds; and may take the former as an ultimate end without regarding the latter.

"Still, as soon as the alternatives are clearly apprehended, it will, I think, be generally held that beauty, knowledge, and other ideal goods, as well as all external material things, are only reasonably to be sought by men in so far as they conduce (1) to Happiness or (2) to the Perfection or Excellence of human existence. I say 'human,' for though most utilitarians consider the pleasure (and freedom from pain) of the inferior animals to be included in the Happiness which they take as the right and proper end of conduct, no one seems to contend that we ought to aim at perfecting brutes except as a means to our ends, or at least as objects of scientific or aesthetic contemplation for us. Nor, again, can we include, as a practical end, the existence of beings above the human. We certainly apply the idea of Good to the Divine Existence, just as we do to His work, and indeed in a preeminent manner: and when it is said that, 'we should do all things to the glory of God,' it may seem to be implied that the existence of God is made better by our glorifying Him. Still this inference when explicitly drawn appears somewhat impious; and theologians generally recoil from it, and refrain from using the notion of a possible addition to the Goodness of the Divine Existence as a ground of human duty. Nor can the influence of our actions on other extra-human intelligences besides the Divine be at present made matter of scientific discussion.

"I shall therefore confidently lay down, that if there be any Good other than Happiness to be sought by man, as an ultimate practical end, it can only be the Goodness, Perfection, or Excellence of Human Existence. How far this notion includes more than Virtue, what its precise relation to Pleasure is, and to what method we shall be logically led if we accept it as fundamental, are questions which we shall more conveniently discuss after the detailed examination of these two other notions, Pleasure and Virtue, in which we shall be engaged in the two following Books."

It will be observed that in this passage Prof. Sidgwick tries to limit the range of objects among which the ultimate end may be found. He does not yet say what that end is, but he does exclude from it everything but certain characters of Human Existence. And the possible ends, which he thus excludes, do not again come up for consideration. They are put out of court once for all by this passage and by this passage only. Now is this exclusion justified?

I cannot think it is. 'No one,' says Prof. Sidgwick, 'would consider it rational to aim at the production of beauty in external nature, apart from any possible contemplation of it by human beings.' Well, I may say at once, that I, for one, do consider this rational; and let us see if I cannot get any one to agree with me. Consider what this admission really means. It entitles us to put the following case. Let us imagine one world exceedingly beautiful. Imagine it as beautiful as you can; put into it whatever on this earth you most admire— mountains, rivers, the sea; trees, and sunsets, stars and moon. Imagine these all combined in the most exquisite proportions, so that no one thing jars against another, but each contributes to increase the beauty of the whole. And then imagine the ugliest world you can possibly conceive. Imagine it simply one heap of filth, containing everything that is most disgusting to us, for whatever reason, and the whole, as far as may be, without one redeeming feature. Such a pair of worlds we are entitled to compare: they fall within Prof. Sidgwick's meaning, and the comparison is highly relevant to it. The only thing we are not entitled to imagine is that any human being ever has or ever, by any possibility, *can,* live in either, can ever see and enjoy the beauty of the one or hate the foulness of the other. Well, even so, supposing them quite apart from any possible contemplation by human beings; still, is it irrational to hold that it is better that the beautiful world should exist, than the one which is ugly? Would it not be well, in any case, to do what we could to produce it rather than the other? Certainly I cannot help thinking that it would; and I hope that some may agree with me in this extreme instance. The instance is extreme. It is highly improbable, not to say, impossible, we should ever have such a choice before us. In any actual choice we should have to consider the possible effects of our action upon conscious beings, and among these possible effects there are always some, I think, which ought to be preferred to the existence of mere beauty. But this only means that in our present state, in which but a very small portion of the good is attainable, the pursuit of beauty for its own sake must always be postponed to the pursuit of some greater good, which is equally attainable. But it is enough for my purpose, if it be admitted that, *supposing* no greater good were at all attainable, then beauty must in itself be regarded as a greater good than ugliness; if it be admitted that, in that case, we should not be left without any reason for preferring one course of action to another, we should not be left without any duty whatever, but that it would then be our positive duty to make the world more beautiful, so far as we were able, since nothing better than beauty could then result from our efforts. If this be once admitted, if in any imaginable case you do admit that the existence of a more beautiful thing is better in itself than that of one more ugly, quite apart from its effects on any human feeling, then Prof. Sidgwick's principle has broken down. Then we shall have to include in our ultimate end something beyond the limits of human existence. I admit, of course, that our beautiful world would be better still, if there were human beings in it to contemplate and enjoy its beauty. But that admission makes nothing against my point. If it be once admitted that the beautiful world *in itself* is better than the ugly, then it follows, that however many beings may enjoy it, and however much better their enjoyment may be than it is itself, yet its mere existence adds *something* to the goodness of the whole: it is not only a means to our end, but also itself a part thereof.

51. In the second passage to which I referred above, Prof. Sidgwick returns from the discussion of Virtue and Pleasure, with which he has meanwhile been engaged, to consider what among the parts of Human Existence to which, as we saw, he has limited the ultimate end, can really be considered as such end. What I have just said, of course, appears to me to destroy the force of this part of his argument too. If, as I think, other things than any part of Human Existence can be ends-in-themselves, then Prof. Sidgwick cannot claim to have discovered the Summum Bonum, when he has merely determined what parts of Human Existence are in themselves desirable. But this error may be admitted to be utterly insignificant in comparison with that which we are now about to discuss.

"It may be said," says Prof. Sidgwick (III. xiv. §§4–5), "that we may...regard cognition of Truth, contemplation of Beauty, Free or Virtuous action, as in some measure preferable alternatives to Pleasure or Happiness—even though we admit that Happiness must be included as a part of Ultimate Good. . . . I think, however, that this view ought not to commend itself to the sober judgment of reflective persons. In order to shew this, I must ask the reader to use the same twofold procedure that I before requested him to employ in considering the absolute and independent validity of common moral precepts. I appeal firstly to his intuitive judgment after due consideration of the question when fairly placed before it: and secondly to a comprehensive comparison of the ordinary judgments of mankind. As regards the first argument, to me at least it seems clear after reflection that these objective relations of the conscious subject, when distinguished from the consciousness accompanying and resulting from them, are not ultimately and intrinsically desirable; any more than material or other objects are, when considered apart from any relation to conscious existence. Admitting that we have actual experience of such preferences as have just been described, of which the ultimate object is something that is not merely consciousness: it still seems to me that when (to use Butler's phrase) we 'sit down in a cool hour,' we can only justify to ourselves the importance that we attach to any of these objects by considering its conduciveness, in one way or another, to the happiness of sentient beings.

"The second argument, that refers to the common sense of mankind, obviously cannot be made completely cogent; since, as above stated, several cultivated persons do habitually judge that knowledge, art, etc.,—not to speak of Virtue—are ends independently of the pleasure derived from them. But we may urge not only that all these elements of 'ideal good' are productive of pleasure in various ways; but also that they seem to obtain the commendation of Common Sense, roughly speaking, in proportion to the degree of this productiveness. This seems obviously true of Beauty; and will hardly be denied in respect of any kind of social ideal: it is paradoxical to maintain that any degree of Freedom, or any form of social order, would still be commonly regarded as desirable even if we were certain that it had no tendency to promote the general happiness. The case of Knowledge is rather more complex; but certainly Common Sense is most impressed with the value of knowledge, when its 'fruitfulness' has been demonstrated. It is, however, aware that experience has frequently shewn how knowledge, long fruitless, may become unexpectedly fruitful, and how light may be shed on one part of the field of knowledge from another apparently remote: and even if any particular branch of scientific pursuit could be shewn to be devoid of even this indirect utility, it would still deserve some respect on utilitarian grounds; both as furnishing to the inquirer the refined and innocent pleasures of curiosity, and because the intellectual disposition which it exhibits and sustains is likely on the whole to produce fruitful knowledge. Still in cases approximating to this last, Common Sense is somewhat disposed to complain of the mis-direction of valuable effort; so that the meed of honour commonly paid to Science seems to be graduated, though perhaps unconsciously, by a tolerably exact utilitarian scale. Certainly the moment the legitimacy of any branch of scientific inquiry is seriously disputed, as in the recent case of vivisection, the controversy on both sides is generally conducted on an avowedly utilitarian basis.

"The case of Virtue requires special consideration: since the encouragement in each other of virtuous impulses and dispositions is a main aim of men's ordinary moral discourse; so that even to raise the question whether this encouragement can go too far has a paradoxical air. Still, our experience includes rare and exceptional cases in which the concentration of effort on the cultivation of virtue has seemed to have effects adverse to general happiness, through being intensified to the point of moral fanaticism, and so involving a neglect of other conditions of happiness. If, then, we admit as actual or possible such 'infelicific' effects of the cultivation of Virtue, I think we shall also generally admit that, in the case supposed, conduciveness to general happiness should be the criterion for deciding how far the cultivation of Virtue should be carried."

There we have Prof Sidgwick's argument completed. We ought not, he thinks, to aim at knowing the Truth, or at contemplating Beauty, except in so far as such knowledge or such contemplation contributes to increase the pleasure or to diminish the pain of sentient beings. Pleasure alone is good for its own sake: knowledge of the Truth is good only as a means to pleasure.

52. Let us consider what this means. What is pleasure? It is certainly something of which we may be conscious, and which, therefore, may be distinguished from our consciousness of it. What I wish first to ask is this: Can it really be said that we value pleasure, except in so far as we are conscious of it? Should we think that the attainment of pleasure, of which we never were and never could be conscious, was something to be aimed at for its own sake? It may be impossible that such pleasure should ever exist, that it should ever be thus divorced from consciousness; although there is certainly much reason to believe that it is not only possible but very common. But, even supposing that it were impossible, that is quite irrelevant. Our question is: Is it the pleasure, as distinct from the consciousness of it, that we set value on? Do we think the pleasure valuable in itself, or must we insist that, if we are to think the pleasure good, we must have consciousness of it too?

This consideration is very well put by Socrates in Plato's dialogue *Philebus* (21 A).

'Would *you* accept, Protarchus,' says Socrates, 'to live your whole life in the enjoyment of the greatest pleasures?' 'Of course I would,' says Protarchus.

Socrates. Then would you think you needed anything else besides, if you possessed this one blessing in completeness?

Protarchus. Certainly not.

Socrates. Consider what you are saying. You would not need to be wise and intelligent and reasonable, nor anything like this? Would you not even care to keep your sight?

Protarchus. Why should I? I suppose I should have all I want, if I was pleased.

Socrates. Well, then, supposing you lived so, you would enjoy always throughout your life the greatest pleasure?

Protarchus. Of course.

Socrates. But, on the other hand, inasmuch as you would not possess intelligence and memory and knowledge and true opinion, you would, in the first place, necessarily be without the knowledge whether you were pleased or not. For you would be devoid of any kind of wisdom. You admit this?

Protarchus. I do. The consequence is absolutely necessary.

Socrates. Well, then, besides this, not having memory, you must also be unable to remember even that you ever were pleased; of the pleasure which falls upon you at the moment not the least vestige must afterwards remain. And again, not having true opinion, you cannot think that you are pleased when you are; and, being bereft of your reasoning faculties, you cannot even have the power to reckon that you will be pleased in future. You must live the life of an oyster, or of some other of those living creatures, whose home is the seas and whose souls are concealed in shelly bodies. Is all this so, or can we think otherwise than this?

Protarchus. How can we?

Socrates. Well, then, can we think such a life desirable?

Protarchus. Socrates, your reasoning has left me utterly dumb.

Socrates, we see, persuades Protarchus that Hedonism is absurd. If we are really going to maintain that pleasure alone is good as an end, we must maintain that it is good, whether we are conscious of it or not. We must declare it reasonable to take as our ideal (an unattainable ideal it may be) that we should be as happy as possible, even on condition that we never know and never can know that we are happy. We must be willing to sell in exchange for the mere happiness every vestige of knowledge, both in ourselves and in others, both of happiness itself and of every other thing. Can we really still disagree? Can any one still declare it obvious that this is reasonable? That pleasure alone is good as an end?

The case, it is plain, is just like that of the colours,[1] only, as yet, not nearly so strong. It is far more possible that we should some day be able to produce the intensest pleasure, without any consciousness that it is there, than that we should be able to produce mere

colour, without its being any particular colour. Pleasure and consciousness can be far more easily distinguished from one another, than colour from the particular colours. And yet even if this were not so, we should be bound to distinguish them if we really wished to declare pleasure alone to be our ultimate end. Even if consciousness were an inseparable accompaniment of pleasure, a *sine quâ non* of its existence, yet, if pleasure is the only end, we are bound to call consciousness a mere *means* to it, in any intelligible sense that can be given to the word *means*. And if, on the other hand, as I hope is now plain, the pleasure would be comparatively valueless without the consciousness, then we are bound to say that pleasure is *not* the only end, that some consciousness at least must be included with it as a veritable part of the end.

For our question now is solely what the end is: it is quite another question how far that end may be attainable *by itself,* or must involve the simultaneous attainment of other things. It may well be that the *practical* conclusions at which Utilitarians do arrive, and even those at which they ought logically to arrive, are not far from the truth. But in so far as their *reason* for holding these conclusions to be true is that 'Pleasure alone is good as an end,' they are *absolutely* wrong: and it is with *reasons* that we are chiefly concerned in any scientific Ethics.

53. It seems, then, clear that Hedonism is in error, so far as it maintains that pleasure alone, and not the consciousness of pleasure, is the sole good. And this error seems largely due to the fallacy which I pointed out above in Mill—the fallacy of confusing means and end. It is falsely supposed that, since pleasure must always be accompanied by consciousness (which is, itself, extremely doubtful), therefore it is indifferent whether we say that pleasure or the consciousness of pleasure is the sole good. *Practically,* of course, it would be indifferent at which we aimed, if it were certain that we could not get the one without the other; but where the question is of what is good in itself—where we ask: For the sake of what is it desirable to get that which we aim at ?—the distinction is by no means unimportant. Here we are placed before an exclusive alternative. *Either* pleasure by itself (even though we can't get it) would be all that is desirable, *or* a consciousness of it would be more desirable still. Both these propositions cannot be true; and I think it is plain that the latter is true; whence it follows that pleasure is *not* the sole good.

---

1. § 48.

Still it may be said that, even if consciousness of pleasure, and not pleasure alone, is the sole good, this conclusion is not very damaging to Hedonism. It may be said that Hedonists have always meant by pleasure the consciousness of pleasure, though they have not been at pains to say so; and this, I think is, in the main, true. To correct their formula in this respect could, therefore, only be a matter of practical importance, if it is possible to produce pleasure without producing consciousness of it. But even this importance, which I think our conclusion so far really has, is, I admit, comparatively slight. What I wish to maintain is that even consciousness of pleasure is not the sole good: that, indeed, it is absurd so to regard it. And the chief importance of what has been said so far lies in the fact that the same method, which shews that consciousness of pleasure is more valuable than pleasure, seems also to shew that consciousness of pleasure is itself far less valuable than other things. The supposition that consciousness of pleasure is the sole good is due to a neglect of the same distinctions which have encouraged the careless assertion that pleasure is the sole good.

The method which I employed in order to shew that pleasure itself was not the sole good, was that of considering what value we should attach to it, if it existed in absolute isolation, stripped of all its usual accompaniments. And this is, in fact, the only method that can be safely used, when we wish to discover what degree of value a thing has in itself. The necessity of employing this method will be best exhibited by a discussion of the arguments used by Prof. Sidgwick in the passage last quoted, and by an exposure of the manner in which they are calculated to mislead.

54. With regard to the second of them, it only maintains that other things, which might be supposed to share with pleasure the attribute of goodness, 'seem to obtain the commendation of Common Sense, roughly speaking, in proportion to the degree' of their productiveness of pleasure. Whether even this rough proportion holds between the commendation of Common Sense and the felicific effects of that which it commends is a question extremely difficult to determine; and we need not enter into it here. For, even assuming it to be true, and assuming the judgments of Common Sense to be on the whole correct, what would it shew? It would shew, cer-

tainly, that pleasure was a good *criterion* of right action—that the same conduct which produced most pleasure would also produce most good on the whole. But this would by no means entitle us to the conclusion that the greatest pleasure *constituted* what was best on the whole: it would still leave open the alternative that the greatest quantity of pleasure was as a matter of fact, *under actual conditions,* generally accompanied by the greatest quantity of *other goods,* and that it therefore was *not* the sole good. It might indeed seem to be a strange coincidence that these two things should always, even in this world, be in proportion to one another. But the strangeness of this coincidence will certainly not entitle us to argue directly that it does not exist—that it is an illusion, due to the fact that pleasure is really the sole good. The coincidence may be susceptible of other explanations; and it would even be our duty to accept it unexplained, if direct intuition seemed to declare that pleasure was not the sole good. Moreover it must be remembered that the need for assuming such a coincidence rests in any case upon the extremely doubtful proposition that felicific effects *are* roughly in proportion to the approval of Common Sense. And it should be observed that, though Prof. Sidgwick maintains this to be the case, his detailed illustrations only tend to shew the very different proposition that a thing is not held to be good, unless it gives a balance of pleasure; not that the degree of commendation is in proportion to the quantity of pleasure.

55. The decision, then, must rest upon Prof. Sidgwick's first argument—'the appeal' to our 'intuitive judgment after due consideration of the question when fairly placed before it.' And here it seems to me plain that Prof. Sidgwick has failed, in two essential respects, to place the question fairly before either himself or his reader.

(1) What he has to shew is, as he says himself, not merely that 'Happiness must be included as a part of Ultimate Good.' This view, he says, 'ought not to commend itself to the sober judgment of reflective persons.' And why? Because 'these objective relations, when distinguished from the consciousness accompanying and resulting from them, are not ultimately and intrinsically desirable.' Now, this reason, which is offered as shewing that to consider Happiness as a mere part of Ultimate Good does not meet the facts of intuition, is, on the contrary, only sufficient to

shew that it *is* a part of Ultimate Good. For from the fact that no value resides in one part of a whole, considered by itself, we cannot infer that all the value belonging to the whole does reside in the other part, considered by itself. Even if we admit that there is much value in the enjoyment of Beauty, and none in the mere contemplation of it, which is one of the constituents of that complex fact, it does not follow that all the value belongs to the other constituent, namely the pleasure which we take in contemplating it. It is quite possible that this constituent also has no value in itself; that the value belongs to the whole state, and to that only: so that *both* the pleasure *and* the contemplation are mere parts of the good, and both of them equally necessary parts. In short, Prof. Sidgwick's argument here depends upon the neglect of that principle, which I tried to explain in my first chapter and which I said I should call the principle of 'organic relations.'[1] The argument is calculated to mislead, because it supposes that, if we see a whole state to be valuable, and also see that one element of that state has no value *by itself,* then the other element, *by itself,* must have all the value which belongs to the whole state. The fact is, on the contrary, that, since the whole may be organic, the other element need have no value whatever, and that even if it have some, the value of the whole may be very much greater. For this reason, as well as to avoid confusion between means and end, it is absolutely essential to consider each distinguishable quality, *in isolation,* in order to decide what value it possesses. Prof. Sidgwick, on the other hand, applies this method of isolation only to *one* element in the wholes he is considering. He does not ask the question: If consciousness of pleasure existed absolutely by itself, would a sober judgment be able to attribute much value to it? It is, in fact, always misleading to take a whole, that is valuable (or the reverse), and then to ask simply: To which of its constituents does this whole owe its value or its vileness? It may well be that it owes it to *none;* and, if one of them does appear to have some value in itself, we shall be led into the grave error of supposing that all the value of the whole belongs to it alone. It seems to me that this error has commonly been committed with regard to pleasure. Pleasure does seem to be a necessary constituent of most valu-

able wholes; and, since the other constituents, into which we may analyse them, may easily seem not to have any value, it is natural to suppose that all the value belongs to pleasure. That this natural supposition does not follow from the premises is certain; and that it is, on the contrary, ridiculously far from the truth appears evident to my 'reflective judgment.' If we apply either to pleasure or to consciousness of pleasure the only safe method, that of isolation, and ask ourselves: Could we accept, as a very good thing, that mere consciousness of pleasure, and absolutely nothing else, should exist, even in the greatest quantities? I think we can have no doubt about answering: No. Far less can we accept this as the *sole* good. Even if we accept Prof. Sidgwick's implication (which yet appears to me extremely doubtful) that consciousness of pleasure has a greater value by itself than Contemplation of Beauty, it seems to me that a pleasurable Contemplation of Beauty has certainly an immeasurably greater value than mere Consciousness of Pleasure. In favour of this conclusion I can appeal with confidence to the 'sober judgment of reflective persons.'

56. (2) That the value of a pleasurable whole does not belong solely to the pleasure which it contains, may, I think, be made still plainer by consideration of another point in which Prof. Sidgwick's argument is defective. Prof. Sidgwick maintains, as we saw, the doubtful proposition, that the *conduciveness* to pleasure of a thing is in rough proportion to its commendation by Common Sense. But he does not maintain, what would be undoubtedly false, that the pleasantness of every state is in proportion to the commendation of that state. In other words, it is only when you take into account *the whole consequences of any state,* that he is able to maintain the coincidence of quantity of pleasure with the objects approved by Common Sense. If we consider each state by itself, and ask what is the judgment of Common Sense as to its goodness *as an end,* quite apart from its goodness as a means, there can be no doubt that Common Sense holds many much less pleasant states to be better than many far more pleasant: that it holds, with Mill, that there are higher pleasures, which are more valuable, though less pleasant, than those which are lower. Prof Sidgwick might, of course, maintain that in this Common Sense is merely confusing means and ends: that what it holds to be better as an end, is in reality only better as a means. But I think his argu-

1. pp. 27–30, 36.

ment is defective in that he does not seem to see sufficiently plainly that, as far as intuitions of goodness *as an end* are concerned, he is running grossly counter to Common Sense; that he does not emphasise sufficiently the distinction between *immediate* pleasantness and *conduciveness* to pleasure. In order to place fairly before us the question what is good as an end we must take states that are immediately pleasant and ask if the more pleasant are always also the better; and whether, if some that are less pleasant appear to be so, it is only because we think they are likely to increase the number of the more pleasant. That Common Sense would deny both these suppositions, and rightly so, appears to me indubitable. It is commonly held that certain of what would be called the lowest forms of sexual enjoyment, for instance, are positively bad, although it is by no means clear that they are not the most pleasant states we ever experience. Common Sense would certainly not think it a sufficient justification for the pursuit of what Prof. Sidgwick calls the 'refined pleasures' here and now, that they are the best means to the future attainment of a heaven, in which there would be no more refined pleasures—no contemplation of beauty, no personal affections—but in which the greatest possible pleasure would be obtained by a perpetual indulgence in bestiality. Yet Prof. Sidgwick would be bound to hold that, if the greatest possible pleasure could be obtained in this way, and if it were attainable, such a state of things would be a heaven indeed, and that all human endeavours should be devoted to its realisation. I venture to think that this view is as false as it is paradoxical.

57. It seems to me, then, that if we place fairly before us the question: Is consciousness of pleasure the sole good? the answer must be: No. And with this the last defence of Hedonism has been broken down. In order to put the question fairly we must isolate consciousness of pleasure. We must ask: Suppose we *were* conscious of pleasure only, and of nothing else, not even that we were conscious, would that state of things, however great the quantity, be very desirable? No one, I think, can suppose it so. On the other hand, it seems quite plain, that we do regard as very desirable, many complicated states of mind in which the consciousness of pleasure is combined with consciousness of other things—states which we call 'enjoyment of' so and so. If this is correct, then it follows that consciousness of pleasure is not the sole

good, and that many other states, in which it is included as a part, are much better than it. Once we recognise the principle of organic unities, any objection to this conclusion, founded on the supposed fact that the other elements of such states have no value in themselves, must disappear. And I do not know that I need say any more in refutation of Hedonism.

58. It only remains to say something of the two forms in which a hedonistic doctrine is commonly held—Egoism and Utilitarianism.

Egoism, as a form of Hedonism, is the doctrine which holds that we ought each of us to pursue our own greatest happiness as our ultimate end. The doctrine will, of course, admit that sometimes the best means to this end will be to give pleasure to others; we shall, for instance, by so doing, procure for ourselves the pleasures of sympathy, of freedom from interference, and of self-esteem; and these pleasures, which we may procure by sometimes aiming directly at the happiness of other persons, may be greater than any we could otherwise get. Egoism in this sense must therefore be carefully distinguished from Egoism in another sense, the sense in which Altruism is its proper opposite. Egoism, as commonly opposed to Altruism, is apt to denote merely selfishness. In this sense, a man is an egoist, if all his actions are actually directed towards gaining pleasure for himself; whether he holds that he ought to act so, because he will thereby obtain for himself the greatest possible happiness on the whole, or not. Egoism may accordingly be used to denote the theory that we should always aim at getting pleasure for ourselves, because that is the best *means* to the ultimate end, whether the ultimate end be our own greatest pleasure or not. Altruism, on the other hand, may denote the theory that we ought always to aim at other people's happiness, on the ground that this is the best *means* of securing our own as well as theirs. Accordingly an Egoist, in the sense in which I am now going to talk of Egoism, an Egoist, who holds that his own greatest happiness is the ultimate end, may at the same time be an Altruist: he may hold that he ought to 'love his neighbour,' as the best means to being happy himself. And conversely an Egoist, in the other sense, may at the same time be a Utilitarian. He may hold that he ought always to direct his efforts towards getting pleasure for himself on the ground that he is thereby most likely to increase the general sum of happiness.

59. I shall say more later about this second kind of Egoism, this anti-altruistic Egoism, this Egoism as a doctrine of means. What I am now concerned with is that utterly distinct kind of Egoism, which holds that each man ought rationally to hold: My own greatest happiness is the only good thing there is: my actions can only be good as means, in so far as they help to win me this. This is a doctrine which is not much held by writers now-a-days. It is a doctrine that was largely held by English Hedonists in the 17th and 18th centuries: it is, for example, at the bottom of Hobbes' Ethics. But even the English school appear to have made one step forward in the present century: they are most of them now-a-days Utilitarians. They do recognise that if my own happiness is good, it would be strange that other people's happiness should not be good too.

In order fully to expose the absurdity of this kind of Egoism, it is necessary to examine certain confusions upon which its plausibility depends.

The chief of these is the confusion involved in the conception of 'my own good' as distinguished from 'the good of others.' This is a conception which we all use every day; it is one of the first to which the plain man is apt to appeal in discussing any question of Ethics: and Egoism is commonly advocated chiefly because its meaning is not clearly perceived. It is plain, indeed, that the name 'Egoism' more properly applies to the theory that 'my own good' is the sole good, than that my own pleasure is so. A man may quite well be an Egoist, even if he be not a Hedonist. The conception which is, perhaps, most closely associated with Egoism is that denoted by the words 'my own interest.' The Egoist is the man who holds that a tendency to promote his own interest is the sole possible, and sufficient, justification of all his actions. But this conception of 'my own interest' plainly includes, in general, very much more than my own pleasure. It is, indeed, only because and in so far as 'my own interest' has been thought to consist solely in my own pleasure, that Egoists have been led to hold that my own pleasure is the sole good. Their course of reasoning is as follows: The only thing I ought to secure is my own interest; but my own interest consists in my greatest possible pleasure; and therefore the only thing I ought to pursue is my own pleasure. That it is very natural, *on*

reflection, thus to identify my own pleasure with my own interest; and that it has been generally done by modern *moralists,* may be admitted. But, when Prof. Sidgwick points this out (III. XIV. § 5, Div. III.), he should have also pointed out that this identification has by no means been made in ordinary thought. When the plain man says 'my own interest, he does *not* mean 'my own pleasure'—he does not commonly even include this—he means my own advancement, my own reputation, the getting of a better income etc., etc. That Prof. Sidgwick should not have noticed this, and that he should give the reason he gives for the fact that the ancient *moralists* did not identify 'my own interest' with my own pleasure, seems to be due to his having failed to notice that very confusion in the conception of 'my own good' which I am now to point out. That confusion has, perhaps, been more clearly perceived by Plato than by any other moralist, and to point it out suffices to refute Prof. Sidgwick's own view that Egoism is rational.

What, then, is meant by 'my own good'? In what sense can a thing be good *for me*? It is obvious, if we reflect, that the only thing which can belong to me, which can be *mine,* is something which is good, and not the fact that it is good. When therefore, I talk of anything I get as 'my own good,' I must mean either that the thing I get is good, or that my possessing it is good. In both cases it is only the thing or the possession of it which is *mine,* and not *the goodness* of that thing or that possession. There is no longer any meaning in attaching the 'my' to our predicate and saying: The possession of this *by me* is *my* good. Even if we interpret this by 'My possession of this is what *I* think good,' the same still holds: for *what* I think is that my possession of it is good *simply;* and, if I think rightly, then the truth is that my possession of it *is* good simply—not, in any sense, *my* good; and, if I think wrongly, it is not good at all. In short, when I talk of a thing as 'my own good' all that I can mean is that something which will be exclusively mine, as my own pleasure is mine (whatever be the various senses of this relation denoted by 'possession'), is also *good absolutely;* or rather that my possession of it is *good absolutely.* The *good* of it can in no possible sense be 'private' or belong to me; any more than a thing can *exist* privately or *for* one person only. The only reason I can have for aiming at 'my own good,' is that it is *good absolutely* that what I so call should belong to me—*good absolutely* that I should *have* something, which, if I have it, others cannot have. But if it is *good absolutely* that I should have it, then everyone else has as much reason for aiming at *my* having it, as I have myself. If, therefore, it is true of *any* single man's 'interest' or 'happiness' that it ought to be his sole ultimate end, this can only mean that *that* man's 'interest' or 'happiness' is *the sole good, the* Universal Good, and the only thing that anybody ought to aim at. What Egoism holds, therefore, is that *each* man's happiness is the sole good—that a number of different things are *each* of them the only good thing there is—an absolute contradiction! No more complete and thorough refutation of any theory could be desired

60. Yet Prof. Sidgwick holds that Egoism is rational; and it will be useful briefly to consider the reasons which he gives for this absurd conclusion. 'The Egoist,' he says (last Chap. § 1), 'may avoid the proof of Utilitarianism by declining to affirm,' either 'implicitly or explicitly, that his own greatest happiness is not merely the ultimate rational end for himself, but a part of Universal Good,' And in the passage to which he here refers us, as having there 'seen' this, he says: 'It cannot be proved that the difference between his own happiness and another's happiness is not *for him* all-important' (IV. ii. § 1). What does Prof. Sidgwick mean by these phrases 'the ultimate rational end for himself,' and '*for him* all-important'? He does not attempt to define them; and it is largely the use of such undefined phrases which causes absurdities to be committed in philosophy.

Is there any sense in which a thing can be an ultimate rational end for one person and not for another? By 'ultimate' must be meant at least that the end is good-in-itself—good in our undefinable sense; and by 'rational,' at least, that it is truly good. That a thing should be an ultimate rational end means, then, that it is truly good in itself; and that it is truly good in itself means that it is a part of Universal Good. Can we assign any meaning to that qualification 'for himself,' which will make it cease to be a part of Universal Good? The thing is impossible: for the Egoist's happiness must *either* be good in itself, and so a part of Universal Good, *or else* it cannot be good in itself at all: there is no escaping this dilemma. And if it is not good at all, what reason can he have for aiming at it? how can it be a rational end for him? That qualification 'for himself' has no

meaning unless it implies '*not* for others'; and if it implies 'not for others,' then it cannot be a rational end for him, since it cannot be truly good in itself: the phrase 'an ultimate rational end for himself' is a contradiction in terms. By saying that a thing is an end for one particular person, or good for him, can only be meant one of four things. Either (1) it may be meant that the end in question is something which will belong exclusively to him; but in that case, if it is to be rational for him to aim at it, that he should exclusively possess it must be a part of Universal Good. Or (2) it may be meant that it is the only thing at which he ought to aim; but this can only be, because, by so doing, he will do the most he can towards realising Universal Good: and this, in our case, will only give Egoism as a doctrine of *means.* Or (3) it may be meant that the thing is what he desires or thinks good; and then, if he thinks wrongly, it is not a rational end at all, and, if *he* thinks rightly, it is a part of Universal Good. Or (4) it may be meant that it is peculiarly appropriate that a thing which will belong exclusively to him should also by him be approved or aimed at; but, in this case, both that it should belong to him and that he should aim at it must be parts of Universal Good: by saying that a certain relation between two things is fitting or appropriate, we can only mean that the existence of that relation is absolutely good in itself (unless it be so as a means, which gives case (2)). By no possible meaning, then, that can be given to the phrase that his own happiness is the ultimate rational end for himself can the Egoist escape the implication that his own happiness is absolutely good; and by saying that it is *the* ultimate rational end, he must mean that it is the only good thing—the whole of Universal Good: and, if he further maintains, that each man's happiness is the ultimate rational end for *him,* we have the fundamental contradiction of Egoism—that an immense number of different things are, *each* of them, *the sole good.*—And it is easy to see that the same considerations apply to the phrase that 'the difference between his own happiness and another's is *for him* all-important.' This can only mean either (1) that his own happiness is the only end which will affect him, or (2) that the only important thing for him (as a means) is to look to his own happiness, or (3) that it is only his own happiness which he cares about, or (4) that it is good that each man's happiness should be the only concern of that man.

And none of these propositions, true as they may be, have the smallest tendency to shew that if his own happiness is desirable at all, it is not a part of Universal Good. Either his own happiness is a good thing or it is not; and, in whatever sense it may be all-important for him, it must be true that, if it is not good, he is not justified in pursuing it, and that, if it is good, everyone else has an equal reason to pursue it, so far as they are able and so far as it does not exclude their attainment of other more valuable parts of Universal Good. In short it is plain that the addition of 'for him' 'for me' to such words as 'ultimate rational end,' 'good,' 'important' can introduce nothing but confusion. The only possible reason that can justify any action is that by it the greatest possible amount of what is good absolutely should be realised. And if anyone says that the attainment of his own happiness justifies his actions, he must mean that this is the greatest possible amount of Universal Good which he can realise. And this again can only be true either because *he* has no power to realise more, in which case he only holds Egoism as a doctrine of means; or else because his own happiness is the greatest amount of Universal Good which can be realised at all, in which case we have Egoism proper, and the flagrant contradiction that every person's happiness is singly the greatest amount of Universal Good which can be realised at all.

61. It should be observed that, since this is so, 'the relation of Rational Egoism to Rational Benevolence,' which Prof. Sidgwick regards 'as the profoundest problem of Ethics' (III. xiii. § 5, *n*. 1), appears in quite a different light to that in which he presents it. 'Even if a man,' he says, 'admits the self-evidence of the principle of Rational Benevolence, he may still hold that his own happiness is an end which it is irrational for him to sacrifice to any other; and that therefore a harmony between the maxim of Prudence and the maxim of Rational Benevolence must be somehow demonstrated, if morality is to be made completely rational. This latter view is that which I myself hold' (last Chap. § 1). Prof. Sidgwick then goes on to shew 'that the inseparable connection between Utilitarian Duty and the greatest happiness of the individual who conforms to it cannot be satisfactorily demonstrated on empirical grounds' (Ib. § 3). And the final paragraph of his book tells us that, since 'the reconciliation of duty and self-interest is to be regarded as a hypothesis logically necessary to avoid a fundamental *contradiction* in one chief

department of our thought, it remains to ask how far this necessity constitutes a sufficient reason for accepting this hypothesis'[1] (Ib. § 3). To 'assume the existence of such a Being, as God, by the *consensus* of theologians, is conceived to be' would, he has already argued, ensure the required reconciliation; since the Divine Sanctions of such a God 'would, of course, suffice to make it always every one's interest to promote universal happiness to the best of his knowledge' (Ib. § 3).

Now what is this 'reconciliation of duty and self-interest,' which Divine Sanctions could ensure? It would consist in the mere fact that the same conduct which produced the greatest possible happiness of the greatest number would always also produce the greatest possible happiness of the agent. If this were the case (and our empirical knowledge shews that it is not the case in this world), 'morality' would, Prof. Sidgwick thinks, be 'completely rational': we should avoid 'an ultimate and fundamental contradiction in our apparent intuitions of what is Reasonable in conduct.' That is to say, we should avoid the necessity of thinking that it is as manifest an obligation to secure our own greatest Happiness (maxim of Prudence), as to secure the greatest Happiness on the whole (maxim of Benevolence). But it is perfectly obvious we should not. Prof. Sidgwick here commits the characteristic fallacy of Empiricism —the fallacy of thinking that an alteration in *facts* could make a contradiction cease to be a contradiction. That a single man's happiness should be *the sole good,* and that also everybody's happiness should be *the sole good,* is a contradiction which cannot be solved by the assumption that the same conduct will secure both: it would be equally contradictory, however certain we were that that assumption was justified. Prof. Sidgwick strains at a gnat and swallows a camel. He thinks the Divine Omnipotence must be called into play to secure that what gives other people pleasure should also give it to him—that only so can Ethics be made rational; while he overlooks the fact that even this exercise of Divine Omnipotence would leave in Ethics a contradiction, in comparison with which his difficulty is a trifle—a contradiction, which would reduce all Ethics to mere nonsense, and before which the Divine Omnipotence must be powerless to all eternity. That *each* man's happiness should be the *sole*

---

1. The italics are mine.

good, which we have seen to be the principle of Egoism, is in itself a contradiction: and that it should also be true that the Happiness of all is the *sole good,* which is the principle of Universalistic Hedonism, would introduce another contradiction. And that these propositions should all be true might well be called 'the profoundest problem in Ethics': it would be a problem necessarily insoluble. But they *cannot* all be true, and there is no reason, but confusion, for the supposition that they are. Prof. Sidgwick confuses this contradiction with the mere fact (in which there is no contradiction) that our own greatest happiness and that of all do not seem always attainable by the same means. This fact, if Happiness were the sole good, would indeed be of some importance; and, on any view, similar facts are of importance. But they are nothing but instances of the one important fact that in this world the quantity of good which is attainable is ridiculously small compared to that which is imaginable. That I cannot get the most possible pleasure for myself, if I produce the most possible pleasure on the whole, is no more *the* profoundest problem of Ethics, than that in any case I cannot get as much pleasure altogether as would be desirable. It only states that, if we get as much good as possible in one place, we may get less on the whole, because the quantity of attainable good is limited. To say that I have to choose between my own good and that of *all* is a false antithesis: the only rational question is how to choose between my own and that of *others,* and the principle on which this must be answered is exactly the same as that on which I must choose whether to give pleasure to this other person or to that.

62. It is plain, then, that the doctrine of Egoism is self-contradictory; and that one reason why this is not perceived, is a confusion with regard to the meaning of the phrase 'my own good.' And it may be observed that this confusion and the neglect of this contradiction are necessarily involved in the transition from Naturalistic Hedonism, as ordinarily held, to Utilitarianism. Mill, for instance, as we saw, declares: 'Each person, so far as he believes it to be attainable, desires his own happiness.' And he offers this as a reason why the general happiness is desirable. We have seen that to regard it as such, involves, in the first place, the naturalistic fallacy. But moreover, even if that fallacy were not a fallacy, it could only be a reason for Egoism and not for Utilitarianism. Mill's argument is as follows: A man de-

sires his own happiness; therefore his own happiness is desirable. Further: A man desires nothing but his own happiness; therefore his own happiness is alone desirable. We have next to remember, that everybody, according to Mill, so desires his own happiness: and then it will follow that everybody's happiness is alone desirable. And this is simply a contradiction in terms. Just consider what it means. Each man's happiness is the only thing desirable: several different things are *each* of them the *only* thing desirable. This is the fundamental contradiction of Egoism. In order to think that what his arguments tend to prove is not Egoism but Utilitarianism, Mill must think that he can infer from the proposition 'Each man's happiness is his own good,' the proposition 'The happiness of all is the good of all'; whereas in fact, if we understand what 'his own good' means, it is plain that the latter can only be inferred from 'The happiness of all is the good of each.' Naturalistic Hedonism, then, logically leads only to Egoism. Of course, a Naturalist might hold that what we aimed at was simply 'pleasure' not our own pleasure; and *that,* always assuming the naturalistic fallacy, would give an unobjectionable ground for Utilitarianism. But more commonly he will hold that it is his own pleasure he desires, or at least will confuse this with the other; and then he must logically be led to adopt Egoism and not Utilitarianism.

63. The second cause I have to give why Egoism should be thought reasonable, is simply its confusion with that other kind of Egoism—Egoism as a doctrine of means. This second Egoism has a right to say: You ought to pursue your own happiness, sometimes at all events; it may even say: Always. And when we find it saying this we are apt to forget its proviso: But only as a means to something else. The fact is we are in an imperfect state; we cannot get the ideal all at once. And hence it is often our bounden duty, we often *absolutely* 'ought,' to do things which are good only or chiefly as means: we have to do the best we can, what is absolutely 'right,' but not what is absolutely good. Of this I shall say more hereafter. I only mention it here because I think it is much more plausible to say that we ought to pursue our own pleasure as a means than as an end, and that this doctrine, through confusion, lends some of its plausibility to the utterly different doctrine of Egoism proper: My own greatest pleasure is the only good thing.

64. So much for Egoism. Of Utilitarianism not much need be said; but two points may seem deserving of notice.

The first is that this name, like that of Egoism, does not naturally suggest that all our actions are to be judged according to the degree in which they are a means to *pleasure*. Its natural meaning is that the standard of right and wrong in conduct is its tendency to promote the *interest* of everybody. And by *interest* is commonly meant a variety of different goods, classed together only because they are what a man commonly desires for himself, so far as his desires have not that psychological quality which is meant by 'moral.' The 'useful' thus means, and was in ancient Ethics systematically used to mean, what is a means to the attainment of goods other than moral goods. It is quite an unjustifiable assumption that these goods are only good as means to pleasure or that they are commonly so regarded. The chief reason for adopting the name 'Utilitarianism' was, indeed, merely to emphasize the fact that right and wrong conduct must be judged by its results—as a means, in opposition to the strictly Intuitionistic view that certain ways of acting were right and others wrong, whatever their results might be. In thus insisting that what is right must mean what produces the best possible results Utilitarianism is fully justified. But with this correct contention there has been historically, and very naturally, associated a double error. (1) The best possible results were assumed to consist only in a limited class of goods, roughly coinciding with those which were popularly distinguished as the results of merely 'useful' or 'interested' actions; and these again were hastily assumed to be good only as means to pleasure. (2) The Utilitarians tend to regard everything as a mere means, neglecting the fact that some things which are good as means are also good as ends. Thus, for instance, assuming pleasure to be a good, there is a tendency to value present pleasure only as a means to future pleasure, and not, as is strictly necessary if pleasure is good as an end, also to *weigh it against* possible future pleasures. Much utilitarian argument involves the logical absurdity that what is here and now, never has any value in itself, but is only to be judged by its consequences; which again, of course, when they are realised, would have no value in themselves, but would be mere means to a still further future, and so on *ad infinitum.*

The second point deserving notice with regard to Utilitarianism is that, when the name is used for a form of Hedonism, it does not commonly, even in its description of its *end,* accurately distinguish between means and end. Its best-known formula is that the result by which actions are to be judged is 'the greatest happiness of the greatest number.' But it is plain that, if pleasure is the sole good, provided the quantity be equally great, an equally desirable result will have been obtained whether it be enjoyed by many or by few, or even if it be enjoyed by nobody. It is plain that, if we ought to aim at the greatest happiness of the greatest number, this can only, on the hedonistic principle, be because the existence of pleasure in a great number of persons seems to be the best *means* available for attaining the existence of the greatest quantity of pleasure. This may actually be the case; but it is fair to suspect that Utilitarians have been influenced, in their adoption of the hedonistic principle, by this failure to distinguish clearly between pleasure or consciousness of pleasure and its possession by a person. It is far easier to regard the possession of pleasure by a number of persons as the sole good, than so to regard the mere existence of an equally great quantity of pleasure. If, indeed, we were to take the Utilitarian principle strictly, and to assume them to mean that the possession of pleasure by many persons was good in itself, the principle is not hedonistic: it includes as a necessary part of the ultimate end, the existence of a number of persons, and this will include very much more than mere pleasure.

Utilitarianism, however, as commonly held, must be understood to maintain that either mere consciousness of pleasure, or consciousness of pleasure together with the minimum adjunct which may be meant by the existence of such consciousness in at least one *person,* is the *sole good.* This is its significance as an ethical doctrine; and as such it has already been refuted in my refutation of Hedonism. The most that can be said for it is that it does not seriously mislead in its practical conclusions, on the ground that, as an empirical fact, the method of acting which brings most good on the whole does also bring most pleasure. Utilitarians do indeed generally devote most of their arguments to shewing that the course of action which will bring most pleasure is in general such as common sense would approve. We have seen that Prof. Sidgwick appeals to this fact as tending to shew that pleasure is the sole good; and we have also seen that it does not tend to shew this. We have seen how very flimsy the other arguments advanced for this proposition are; and that, if it be fairly considered by itself, it appears to be quite ridiculous. And, moreover, that the actions which produce most good on the whole do also produce most pleasure is extremely doubtful. The arguments tending to shew it are all more or less vitiated by the assumption that what appear to be necessary conditions for the attainment of most pleasure in the near future, will always continue so to be. And, even with this vicious assumption, they only succeed in making out a highly problematical case. How, therefore, this fact is to be explained, if it be a fact, need not concern us. It is sufficient to have shewn that many complex states of mind are much more valuable than the pleasure they contain. If this be so, *no form of Hedonism can be true*. And, since the practical guidance afforded by pleasure as a criterion is small in proportion as the calculation attempts to be accurate, we can well afford to await further investigation, before adopting a guide, whose utility is very doubtful and whose trustworthiness we have grave reason to suspect.

65. The most important points which I have endeavoured to establish in this chapter are as follows. (1) Hedonism must be strictly defined as the doctrine that 'Pleasure is the only thing which is good in itself': this view seems to owe its prevalence mainly to the naturalistic fallacy, and Mill's arguments may be taken as a type of those which are fallacious in this respect; Sidgwick alone has defended it without committing this fallacy, and its final refutation must therefore point out the errors in his arguments (36–38). (2) Mill's 'Utilitarianism' is criticised: it being shewn (a) that he commits the naturalistic fallacy in identifying 'desirable' with 'desired'; (b) that pleasure is not the only object of desire. The common arguments for Hedonism seem to rest on these two errors (39–44). (3) Hedonism is considered as an 'Intuition,' and it is pointed out (a) that Mill's allowance that some pleasures are inferior in quality to others implies both that it is an Intuition and that it is a false one (46–48); (b) that Sidgwick fails to distinguish 'pleasure' from 'consciousness of pleasure,' and that it is absurd to regard the former, at all events, as the sole good (49–52); (c) that it seems equally absurd to regard 'consciousness of pleasure' as the sole good, since, if it were so, a world in which nothing else existed might be absolutely perfect: Sidgwick fails to put to himself this question, which is the only clear and decisive one (53–57). (4) What are commonly considered to be the two main types of Hedonism, namely, Egoism and Utilitarianism, are not only different from, but strictly contradictory of, one another; since the former asserts 'My own greatest pleasure is the *sole* good,' the latter 'The greatest pleasure of all is the *sole* good.' Egoism seems to owe its plausibility partly to the failure to observe this contradiction—a failure which is exemplified by Sidgwick; partly to a confusion of Egoism as doctrine of end, with the same as doctrine of means. If Hedonism is true, Egoism cannot be so; still less can it be so, if Hedonism is false. The end of Utilitarianism, on the other hand, would, if Hedonism were true, be, not indeed the best conceivable, but the best possible for us to promote; but it is refuted by the refutation of Hedonism (58–64).

JOHN DEWEY

FROM *The Quest for Certainty*

As might be expected, not all moral philosophers were deterred by Moore's attacks on ethical naturalism. John Dewey (1859–1952), the first American philosopher in our readings, represents an ethical naturalism undeterred by Moore's criticism. Born in Burlington, Vermont, the young Dewey was an adequate, although not brilliant, student who gave little indication that he would become one of America's premier philosophers and a champion of social reform. He entered the University of Vermont in 1875 and taught high school upon graduation. After a time, he pursued his interest in philosophy by enrolling in the graduate program at Johns Hopkins University. Among his teachers at Johns Hopkins was Charles S. Peirce, the great pragmatist.

Dewey's career was spent teaching and writing in a variety of areas of philosophy, including moral philosophy, aesthetics, philosophy of education, and social criticism. His first teaching appointment was at the University of Michigan where he stayed for ten years. In 1894, he left Michigan for the University of Chicago, where he founded the laboratory school known as the Dewey School. Because of problems with the administration, he left Chicago in 1904 to take an appointment at Columbia, where he stayed until his retirement in 1930. Although Dewey was a seminal figure in American twentieth-century philosophy, his influence is primarily confined to America. His only real importance abroad was indirect, in his response to problems in ethics generated by G.E. Moore.

In ethical theory, Dewey advocated a form of ethical naturalism, a view of moral philosophy quite contrary to that of Moore. While Moore makes a sharp separation between the good as a means and the good as an end, Dewey emphasizes their interrelated character. Moore emphasizes the distinction between judgments of fact and judgments of value while Dewey denies the distinction altogether. For Dewey, all knowledge is practical knowledge. And the methodology of all knowledge should be the same. That is, it should employ the experimental method of science.

Along with his work in moral philosophy, Dewey wrote and did extensive research in the philosophy of education and social theory. He is probably best known for his work in the philosophy of education, but he held that all philosophy could be conceived of as the philosophy of education. His social theory does not stand alone either; rather it is entwined with his ethics. For Dewey, the purpose of social philosophy was to point the way to the societal conditions that would bring about the kind of life wherein people could make the intelligent decisions that morality required. Although many of his ideas were innovative—even radical—his role throughout his life was that of reformer, not revolutionary. Despite a youthful zeal for Hegelian idealism, he became, and remained, skeptical of utopian ideals and panaceas. The work reprinted here, Chapter X of Quest for Certainty, was published in 1929 and helped point the way for current biological, sociobiological, evolutionary, and other naturalist theories of ethics.

Chapter X The Construction of Good

We saw at the outset of our discussion that insecurity generates the quest for certainty. Consequences issue from every experience, and they are the source of our interest in what is present. Absence of arts of regulation diverted the search for security into irrelevant modes of practice, into rite and cult; thought was devoted to discovery of omens rather than of signs of what is to occur. Gradually there was differentiation of two realms, one higher, consisting of the powers which determine human destiny in all important affairs. With this religion was concerned. The other consisted of the prosaic matters in which man relied upon his own skill and his matter-of-fact insight. Philosophy inherited the idea of this division. Meanwhile in Greece many of the arts had attained a state of development which raised them above a merely routine state; there were intimations of measure, order and regularity in materials dealt with which give intimations of underlying rationality. Because of the growth of mathematics, there arose also the ideal of a purely rational knowledge, intrinsically solid and worthy and the means by which the intimations of rationality within changing phenomena could be comprehended within science. For the intellectual class the stay and consolation, the warrant of certainty, provided by religion was henceforth found in intellectual demonstration of the reality of the objects of an ideal realm.

With the expansion of Christianity, ethico-religious traits came to dominate the purely rational ones. The ultimate authoritative standards for regulation of the dispositions and purposes of the human will were fused with those which satisfied the demands for necessary and universal truth. The authority of ultimate Being was, moreover, represented on earth by the Church; that which in its nature transcended intellect was made known by a revelation of which the Church was the interpreter and guardian. The system endured for centuries. While it endured, it provided an integration of belief and conduct for the western world. Unity of thought and practice extended down to every detail of the management of life; efficacy of its operation did not depend upon thought. It was guaranteed by the most powerful and authoritative of all social institutions.

Its seemingly solid foundation was, however, undermined by the conclusions of modern science.

They effected, both in themselves and even more in the new interests and activities they generated, a breach between what man is concerned with here and now and the faith concerning ultimate reality which, in determining his ultimate and eternal destiny, had previously given regulation to his present life. The problem of restoring integration and cooperation between man's beliefs about the world in which he lives and his beliefs about the values and purposes that should direct his conduct is the deepest problem of modern life. It is the problem of any philosophy that is not isolated from that life.

The attention which has been given to the fact that in its experimental procedure science has surrendered the separation between knowing and doing has its source in the fact that there is now provided within a limited, specialized and technical field the possibility and earnest, as far as theory is concerned, of effecting the needed integration in the wider field of collective human experience. Philosophy is called upon to be the theory of the practice, through ideas sufficiently definite to be operative in experimental endeavor, by which the integration may be made secure in actual experience. Its central problem is the relation that exists between the beliefs about the nature of things due to natural science to beliefs about values—using that word to designate whatever is taken to have rightful authority in the direction of conduct. A philosophy which should take up this problem is struck first of all by the fact that beliefs about values are pretty much in the position in which beliefs about nature were before the scientific revolution. There is either a basic distrust of the capacity of experience to develop its own regulative standards, and an appeal to what philosophers call eternal values, in order to ensure regulation of belief and action; or there is acceptance of enjoyments actually experienced irrespective of the method or operation by which they are brought into existence. Complete bifurcation between rationalistic method and an empirical method has its final and most deeply human significance in the ways in which good and bad are thought of and acted for and upon.

As far as technical philosophy reflects this situation, there is division of theories of values into two kinds. On the one hand, goods and evils, in every region of life, as they are concretely experienced, are regarded as characteristic of an inferior order of Being—intrinsically inferior. Just because they are things of human experience, their worth must be estimated by reference to standards and ideals derived from ultimate reality. Their defects and perversion are attributed to the same fact; they are to be corrected and controlled through adoption of methods of conduct derived from loyalty to the requirements of Supreme Being. This philosophic formulation gets actuality and force from the fact that it is a rendering of the beliefs of men in general as far as they have come under the influence of institutional religion. Just as rational conceptions were once superimposed upon observed and temporal phenomena, so eternal values are superimposed upon experienced goods. In one case as in the other, the alternative is supposed to be confusion and lawlessness. Philosophers suppose these eternal values are known by reason; the mass of persons that they are divinely revealed.

Nevertheless, with the expansion of secular interests, temporal values have enormously multiplied; they absorb more and more attention and energy. The sense of transcendent values has become enfeebled; instead of permeating all things in life, it is more and more restricted to special times and acts. The authority of the church to declare and impose divine will and purpose has narrowed. Whatever men say and profess, their tendency in the presence of actual evils is to resort to natural and empirical means to remedy them. But in formal belief, the old doctrine of the inherently disturbed and unworthy character of the goods and standards of ordinary experience persists. This divergence between what men do and what they nominally profess is closely connected with the confusions and conflicts of modern thought.

It is not meant to assert that no attempts have been made to replace the older theory regarding the authority of immutable and transcendent values by conceptions more congruous with the practices of daily life. The contrary is the case. The utilitarian theory, to take one instance, has had great power. The idealistic school is the only one in contemporary philosophies, with the exception of one form of neorealism, that makes much of the notion of a reality which is all one with ultimate moral and religious values. But this school is also the one most concerned with the conservation of "spiritual" life. Equally significant is the fact that empirical theories retain the notion that thought and judgment are concerned with values that are experienced independently of them. For these theories, emotional satisfactions occupy the same place that sensations hold in traditional empiricism. Values are constituted by liking and enjoyment; to be enjoyed and to be a value are two names for one and the same fact. Since science has extruded values from its objects, these empirical theories do everything possible to emphasize their purely subjective character of value. A psychological theory of desire and liking is supposed to cover the whole ground of the theory of values; in it, immediate feeling is the counterpart of immediate sensation.

I shall not object to this empirical theory as far as it connects the theory of values with concrete experiences of desire and satisfaction. The idea that there is such a connection is the only way known to me by which the pallid remoteness of the rationalistic theory, and the only too glaring presence of the institutional theory of transcendental values can be escaped. The objection is that the theory in question holds down value to objects *antecedently* enjoyed, apart from reference to the method by which they come into existence; it takes enjoyments which are casual because unregulated by intelligent operations to be values in and of themselves. Operational thinking needs to be applied to the judgment of values just as it has now finally been applied in conceptions of physical objects. Experimental empiricism in the field of ideas of good and bad is demanded to meet the conditions of the present situation.

The scientific revolution came about when material of direct and uncontrolled experience was taken as problematic; as supplying material to be transformed by reflective operations into known objects. The contrast between experienced and known objects was found to be a temporal one; namely, one between empirical subject matters which were had or "given" prior to the acts of experimental variation and redisposition and those which succeeded these acts and issued from them. The notion of an act whether of sense or thought which supplied a valid measure of thought in immediate knowledge was discredited. Consequences of operations became the important thing. The suggestion almost imperatively follows that escape from the defects of transcendental absolutism is not to be had by setting up as values enjoyments that happen anyhow, but in defining value by enjoyments which are the consequences of intelligent action. Without the intervention of thought, enjoyments are not values but problematic goods, becoming values when they re-issue in a changed form from intelligent behavior. The fundamental trouble with the current empirical theory of values is that it merely formulates and justifies the socially prevailing habit of regarding enjoyments as they are actually experienced as values in and of themselves. It completely side-steps the question of regulation of these enjoyments. This issue involves nothing less than the problem of the directed reconstruction of economic, political and religious institutions.

There was seemingly a paradox involved in the notion that if we turned our backs upon the immediately perceived qualities of things, we should be enabled to form valid conceptions of objects, and that these conceptions could be used to bring about a more secure and more significant experience of them. But the method terminated in disclosing the connections or interactions upon which perceived objects, viewed as events, depend. Formal analogy suggests that we regard our direct and original experience of things liked and enjoyed as only *possibilities* of values to be achieved; that enjoyment becomes a value when we discover the relations upon which its presence depends. Such a causal and operational definition gives only a conception of a value, not a value itself. But the utilization of the conception in action results in an object having secure and significant value.

The formal statement may be given concrete content by pointing to the difference between the enjoyed and the enjoyable, the desired and the desirable, the satis*fying* and the satis*factory*. To say that something is enjoyed is to make a statement about a fact, something already in existence; it is not to judge the value of that fact. There is no difference between such a proposition and one which says that something is sweet or sour, red or black. It is just correct or incorrect and that is the end of the matter. But to call an object a value is to assert that it satisfies or fulfills certain conditions. Function and status in meeting conditions is a different matter from bare existence. The fact that something is desired only raises the *question* of its desirability; it does not settle it. Only a child in the degree of his immaturity thinks to settle the question of desirability by reiterated proclamation: "I want it, I want it, I want it." What is objected to in the current empirical theory

of values is not connection of them with desire and enjoyment but failure to distinguish between enjoyments of radically different sorts. There are many common expressions in which the difference of the two kinds is clearly recognized. Take for example the difference between the ideas of "satisfying" and "satisfactory." To say that something satisfies is to report something as an isolated finality. To assert that it is satis*factory* is to define it in its connections and interactions. The fact that it pleases or is immediately congenial poses a problem to judgment. How shall the satisfaction be rated? Is it a value or is it not? Is it something to be prized and cherished, *to be* enjoyed? Not stern moralists alone but every day experience informs us that finding satisfaction in a thing may be a warning, a summons to be on the lookout for consequences. To declare something satis*factory* is to assert that it meets specifiable conditions. It is in effect, a judgment that the thing "will do." It involves a prediction; it contemplates a future in which the thing will continue to serve; it *will* do. It asserts a consequence the thing will actively institute; it will *do*. That it is satisfying is the content of a proposition of fact; that it is satisfactory is a judgment, an estimate, an appraisal. It denotes an attitude *to be* taken, that of striving to perpetuate and to make secure.

It is worth notice that besides the instances given, there are many other recognitions in ordinary speech of the distinction. The endings "able," "worthy," and "ful" are cases in point. Noted and notable, noteworthy; remarked and remarkable; advised and advisable; wondered at and wonderful; pleasing and beautiful; loved and lovable; blamed and blameable, blameworthy; objected to and objectionable; esteemed and estimable; admired and admirable; shamed and shameful; honored and honorable; approved and approvable, worthy of approbation, etc. The multiplication of words adds nothing to the force of the distinction. But it aids in conveying a sense of the fundamental character of the distinction; of the difference between mere report of an already existent fact and judgment as to the importance and need of bringing a fact into existence; or, if it is already there, of sustaining it in existence. The latter is a genuine practical judgment, and marks the only type of judgment that has to do with the direction of action. Whether or no we reserve the term "value" for the latter, (as seems to me proper) is a minor matter; that the distinction be acknowledged as the key to understanding the relation of values to the direction of conduct is the important thing.

This element of direction by an idea of value applies to science as well as anywhere else. For in every scientific undertaking, there is passed a constant succession of estimates; such as "it is worth treating these facts as data or evidence; it is advisable to try this experiment; to make that observation; to entertain such and such a hypothesis; to perform this calculation," etc.

The word "taste" has perhaps got too completely associated with arbitrary liking to express the nature of judgments of value. But if the word be used in the sense of an appreciation at once cultivated and active one may say that the formation of taste is the chief matter wherever values enter in, whether intellectual, esthetic or moral. Relatively immediate judgments, which we call tact or to which we give the name of intuition, do not precede reflective inquiry, but are the funded products of much thoughtful experience. Expertness of taste is at once the result and the reward of constant exercise of thinking. Instead of there being no disputing about tastes, they are the one thing worth disputing about, if by "dispute" is signified discussion involving reflective inquiry. Taste, if we use the word in its best sense is the outcome of experience brought cumulatively to bear on the intelligent appreciation of the real worth of likings and enjoyments. There is nothing in which a person so completely reveals himself as in the things which he judges enjoyable and desirable. Such judgments are the sole alternative to the domination of belief by impulse, chance, blind habit and self-interest. The formation of a cultivated and effectively operative good judgment or taste with respect to what is esthetically admirable, intellectually acceptable and morally approvable is the supreme task set to human beings by the incidents of experience.

Propositions about what is or has been liked are of instrumental value in reaching judgments of value, in as far as the conditions and consequences of the thing liked are thought about. In themselves they make no claims; they put forth no demand upon subsequent attitudes and acts; they profess no authority to direct. If one likes a thing he likes it; that *is* a point about which there can be no dispute:—although it is not so easy to state just *what* is liked as is frequently assumed. A judgment about what is *to be* desired and enjoyed is, on the other hand, a claim

on future action; it possesses *de jure* and not merely *de facto* quality. It is a matter of frequent experience that likings and enjoyments are of all kinds, and that many are such as reflective judgments condemn. By way of self-justification and "rationalization," an enjoyment creates a tendency to assert that the thing enjoyed is a value. This assertion of validity adds authority to the fact. It is a decision that the object has a right to exist and hence a claim upon action to further its existence.

The analogy between the status of the theory of values and the theory of ideas about natural objects before the rise of experimental inquiry may be carried further. The sensationalistic theory of the origin and test of thought evoked, by way of reaction, the transcendental theory of *a priori* ideas. For it failed utterly to account for objective connection, order and regularity in objects observed. Similarly, any doctrine that identifies the mere fact of being liked with the value of the object liked so fails to give direction to conduct when direction is needed that it automatically calls forth the assertion that there are values eternally in Being that are the standards of all judgments and the obligatory ends of all action. Without the introduction of operational thinking, we oscillate between a theory that, in order to save the objectivity of judgments of values, isolates them from experience and nature, and a theory that, in order to save their concrete and human significance, reduces them to mere statements about our own feelings.

Not even the most devoted adherents of the notion that enjoyment and value are equivalent facts would venture to assert that because we have once liked a thing we should go on liking it; they are compelled to introduce the idea that *some* tastes are to be cultivated. Logically, there is no ground for introducing the idea of cultivation; liking is liking and one is as good as another. If enjoyments *are* values, the judgment of value cannot regulate the form which liking takes; it cannot regulate its own conditions. Desire and purpose, and hence action, are left without guidance, although the question of regulation of their formation is the supreme problem of practical life. Values (to sum up) may be connected inherently with liking, and yet not with *every* liking but only with those that judgment has approved, after examination of the relation upon which the object liked depends. A casual liking is one that happens without knowledge of how it occurs nor to what effect. The difference between it and one which is sought because of a judgment that it is worth having and is to be striven for, makes just the difference between enjoyments which are accidental and enjoyments that have value and hence a claim upon our attitude and conduct.

In any case, the alternative rationalistic theory does not afford the guidance for the sake of which eternal and immutable norms are appealed to. The scientist finds no help in determining the probable truth of some proposed theory by comparing it with a standard of absolute truth and immutable being. He has to rely upon definite operations undertaken under definite conditions—upon method. We can hardly imagine an architect getting aid in the construction of a building from an ideal at large, though we can understand his framing an ideal on the basis of knowledge of actual conditions and needs. Nor does the ideal of perfect beauty in antecedent Being give direction to a painter in producing a particular work of art. In morals, absolute perfection does not seem to be more than a generalized hypostatization of the recognition that there is a good to be sought, an obligation to be met—both being concrete matters. Nor is the defect in this respect merely negative. An examination of history would reveal, I am confident, that these general and remote schemes of value actually obtain a content definite enough and near enough to concrete situations as to afford guidance in action only by consecrating some institution or dogma already having social currency. Concreteness is gained, but it is by protecting from inquiry some accepted standard which perhaps is outworn and in need of criticism.

When theories of values do not afford intellectual assistance in framing ideas and beliefs about values that are adequate to direct action, the gap must be filled by other means. If intelligent method is lacking, prejudice, the pressure of immediate circumstance, self-interest and class-interest, traditional customs, institutions of accidental historic origin, are *not* lacking, and they tend to take the place of intelligence. Thus we are led to our main proposition: *Judgments about values are judgments about the conditions and the results of experienced objects; judgments about that which should regulate the formation of our desires, affections and enjoyments.* For whatever decides their formation will determine the main course of our conduct, personal and social.

If it sounds strange to hear that we should frame our judgments as to what has value by considering the connections in existence of what we like and enjoy, the reply is not far to seek. As long as we do not engage in this inquiry enjoyments (values if we choose to apply that term) are casual; they are given by "nature," not constructed by art. Like natural objects in their qualitative existence, they at most only supply material for elaboration in rational discourse. A *feeling* of good or excellence is as far removed from goodness in fact as a feeling that objects are intellectually thus and so is removed from their being actually so. To recognize that the truth of natural objects can be reached only by the greatest care in selecting and arranging directed operations, and then to suppose that values can be truly determined by the mere fact of liking seems to leave us in an incredible position. All the serious perplexities of life come back to the genuine difficulty of forming a judgment as to the values of the situation; they come back to a conflict of goods. Only dogmatism can suppose that serious moral conflict is between something clearly bad and something known to be good, and that uncertainty lies wholly in the will of the one choosing. Most conflicts of importance are conflicts between things which are or have been satisfying, not between good and evil. And to suppose that we can make a hierarchical table of values at large once for all, a kind of catalogue in which they are arranged in an order of ascending or descending worth, is to indulge in a gloss on our inability to frame intelligent judgments in the concrete. Or else it is to dignify customary choice and prejudice by a title of honor.

The alternative to definition, classification and systematization of satisfactions just as they happen to occur is judgment of them by means of the relations under which they occur. If we know the conditions under which the act of liking, of desire and enjoyment, takes place, we are in a position to know what are the consequences of that act. The difference between the desired and the desirable, admired and the admirable, becomes effective at just this point. Consider the difference between the proposition "That thing has been eaten," and the judgment "That thing is edible." The former statement involves no knowledge of any relation except the one stated; while we are able to judge of the edibility of anything only when we have a knowledge of its interactions with other things sufficient to enable us to foresee its probable effects when it is taken into the organism and produces effects there.

To assume that anything can be known in isolation from its connections with other things is to identify knowing with merely having some object before perception or in feeling, and is thus to lose the key to the traits that distinguish an object as known. It is futile, even silly, to suppose that some quality that is directly present constitutes the whole of the thing presenting the quality. It does not do so when the quality is that of being hot or fluid or heavy, and it does not when the quality is that of giving pleasure, or being enjoyed. Such qualities are, once more, effects, ends in the sense of closing termini of processes involving causal connections. They are something to be investigated, challenges to inquiry and judgment. The more connections and interactions we ascertain, the more we *know* the object in question. Thinking is search for these connections. Heat experienced as a consequence of directed operations has a meaning quite different from the heat that is casually experienced without knowledge of how it came about. The same is true of enjoyments. Enjoyments that issue from conduct directed by insight into relations have a meaning and a validity due to the way in which they are experienced. Such enjoyments are not repented of; they generate no after-taste of bitterness. Even in the midst of direct enjoyment, there is a sense of validity, of authorization, which intensifies the enjoyment. There is solicitude for perpetuation of the *object* having value which is radically different from mere anxiety to perpetuate the *feeling* of enjoyment.

Such statements as we have been making are, therefore, far from implying that there are values apart from things actually enjoyed as good. To find a thing enjoy*able* is, so to say, a *plus* enjoyment. We saw that it was foolish to treat the scientific object as a rival to or substitute for the perceived object, since the former is intermediate between uncertain and settled situations and those experienced under conditions of greater control. In the same way, judgment of the value of an object to be experienced is instrumental to appreciation of it when it is realized. But the notion that every object that happens to satisfy has an equal claim with every other to be a value is like supposing that every object of perception has the same cognitive force as every other. There is no knowledge without perception; but objects perceived are *known* only when they are determined as consequences of connective operations. There is no value except where there is satisfaction, but there have to be certain conditions fulfilled to transform a satisfaction into a value.

The time will come when it will be found passing strange that we of this age should take such pains to control by every means at command the formation of ideas of physical things, even those most remote from human concern, and yet are content with haphazard beliefs about the qualities of objects that regulate our deepest interests; that we are scrupulous as to methods of forming ideas of natural objects, and either dogmatic or else driven by immediate conditions in framing those about values. There is, by implication, if not explicitly, a prevalent notion that values are already well known and that all which is lacking is the will to cultivate them in the order of their worth. In fact the most profound lack is not the will to act upon goods already known but the will to know what they are.

It is not a dream that it is possible to exercise some degree of regulation of the occurrence of enjoyments which are of value. Realization of the possibility is exemplified, for example, in the technologies and arts of industrial life—that is, up to a definite limit. Men desired heat, light, and speed of transit and of communication beyond what nature provides of itself. These things have been attained not by lauding the enjoyment of these things and preaching their desirability, but by study of the conditions of their manifestation. Knowledge of relations having been obtained, ability to produce followed, and enjoyment ensued as a matter of course. It is, however, an old story that enjoyment of these things as goods is no warrant of their bringing only good in their train. As Plato was given to pointing out, the physician knows how to heal and the orator to persuade, but the ulterior knowledge of whether it is better for a man to be healed or to be persuaded to the orator's opinion remains unsettled. Here there appears the split between what are traditionally and conventionally called the values of the baser arts and the higher values of the truly personal and humane arts.

With respect to the former, there is no assumption that they can be had and enjoyed without definite operative knowledge. With respect to them it is also clear that the degree in which we value them is measurable by the pains taken to control the conditions of their occurrence. With respect to the latter, it is assumed that no one who is honest can be in doubt what they are; that by revelation, or conscience, or the instruction of others, or immediate feeling, they are clear beyond question. And instead of action in their behalf being taken to be a measure of the extent to which things *are* values to us, it is assumed that the difficulty is to persuade men to act upon what they already know to be good. Knowledge of conditions and consequences is regarded as wholly indifferent to judging what is of serious value, though it is useful in a prudential way in trying to actualize it. In consequence, the existence of values that are by common consent of a secondary and technical sort are under a fair degree of control, while those denominated supreme and imperative are subject to all the winds of impulse, custom and arbitrary authority.

This distinction between higher and lower types of value is itself something to be looked into. Why should there be a sharp division made between some goods as physical and material and others as ideal and "spiritual"? The question touches the whole dualism of the material and the ideal at its root. To denominate anything "matter" or "material" is not in truth to disparage it. It is, if the designation is correctly applied, a way of indicating that the thing in question is a condition or means of the existence of something else. And disparagement of effective means is practically synonymous with disregard of the things that are termed, in eulogistic fashion, ideal and spiritual. For the latter terms if they have any concrete application at all signify something which is a desirable consummation of conditions, a cherished fulfillment of means. The sharp separation between material and ideal good thus deprives the latter of the underpinning of effective support while it opens the way for treating things which should be employed as means as ends in themselves. For since men cannot after all live without some measure of possession of such matters as health and wealth, the latter things will be viewed as values and ends in isolation unless they are treated as integral constituents of the goods that are deemed supreme and final.

The relations that determine the occurrence of what human beings experience, especially when social connections are taken into account, are indefinitely wider and more complex than those that determine the events termed physical; the latter are the outcome of definite selective operations. This is the reason why we know something about remote objects like the stars better than we know significantly characteristic things about our own bodies and minds. We forget the infinite number of things we do not know about the stars, or rather that what we call a star is itself the product of the elimination, enforced and deliberate, of most of the traits that belong to an actual existence. The amount of knowledge we possess about stars would not seem very great or very important if it were carried over to human beings and exhausted our knowledge of them. It is inevitable that genuine knowledge of man and society should lag far behind physical knowledge.

But this difference is not a ground for making a sharp division between the two, nor does it account for the fact that we make so little use of the experimental method of forming our ideas and beliefs about the concerns of man in his characteristic social relations. For this separation religions and philosophies must admit some responsibility. They have erected a distinction between a narrower scope of relations and a wider and fuller one into a difference of kind, naming one kind material, and the other mental and moral. They have charged themselves gratuitously with the office of diffusing belief in the necessity of the division, and with instilling contempt for the material as something inferior in kind in its intrinsic nature and worth. Formal philosophies undergo evaporation of their technical solid contents; in a thinner and more viable form they find their way into the minds of those who know nothing of their original forms. When these diffuse and, so to say, airy emanations re-crystallize in the popular mind they form a hard deposit of opinion that alters slowly and with great difficulty.

What difference would it actually make in the arts of conduct, personal and social, if the experimental theory were adopted not as a mere theory, but as a part of the working equipment of habitual attitudes on the part of everyone? It would be impossible, even were time given, to answer the question in adequate detail, just as men could not foretell in advance the consequences for knowledge of adopting the experimental method. It is the nature of the method that it has to be tried. But there are generic lines of difference which, within the limits of time at disposal, may be sketched.

Change from forming ideas and judgments of value on the basis of conformity to antecedent objects, to constructing enjoyable objects directed by knowledge of consequences, is a change from looking to the past to looking to the future. I do not for a moment suppose that the experiences of the past, personal and social, are of no importance. For without them we should not be able to frame any ideas whatever of the conditions under which objects are enjoyed nor any estimate of the consequences of esteeming and liking them. But past experiences are significant in giving us intellectual instrumentalities of judging just these points. They are tools, not finalities. Reflection upon what we have liked and have enjoyed is a necessity. But it tells us nothing about the *value* of these things until enjoyments are themselves reflectively controlled, or, until, as they are recalled, we form the best judgment possible about what led us to like this sort of thing and what has issued from the fact that we liked it.

We are not, then, to get away from enjoyments experienced in the past and from recall of them, but from the notion that they are the arbiters of things to be further enjoyed. At present, the arbiter is found in the past, although there are many ways of interpreting what in the past is authoritative. Nominally, the most influential conception doubtless is that of a revelation once had or a perfect life once lived. Reliance upon precedent, upon institutions created in the past, especially in law, upon rules of morals that have come to us through unexamined customs, upon uncriticized tradition, are other forms of dependence. It is not for a moment suggested that we can get away from customs and established institutions. A mere break would doubtless result simply in chaos. But there is no danger of such a break. Mankind is too inertly conservative both by constitution and by education to give the idea of this danger actuality. What there is genuine danger of is that the force of new conditions will produce disruption externally and mechanically: this is an ever present danger. The prospect is increased, not mitigated, by that conservatism which insists upon the adequacy of old standards to meet new conditions. What is needed is intelligent examination of the consequences that are actually effected by inherited institutions and customs, in order that there may be intelligent consideration of the ways in which they are to be intentionally modified in behalf of generation of different consequences.

This is the significant meaning of transfer of experimental method from the technical field of physical experience to the wider field of human life. We trust the method in forming our beliefs about things not directly connected with human life. In effect, we distrust it in moral, political and economic affairs. In the fine arts, there are many signs of a change. In the past, such a change has often been an omen and precursor of changes in other human attitudes. But, generally speaking, the idea of actively adopting experimental method in social affairs, in the matters deemed of most enduring and ultimate worth, strikes most persons as a surrender of all standards and regulative authority. But in principle, experimental method does not signify random and aimless action; it implies direction by ideas and knowledge. The question at issue is a practical one. Are there in existence the ideas and the knowledge that permit experimental method to be effectively used in social interests and affairs?

Where will regulation come from if we surrender familiar and traditionally prized values as our directive standards? Very largely from the findings of the natural sciences. For one of the effects of the separation drawn between knowledge and action is to deprive scientific knowledge of its proper service as a guide of conduct—except once more in those technological fields which have been degraded to an inferior rank. Of course, the complexity of the conditions upon which objects of human and liberal value depend is a great obstacle, and it would be too optimistic to say that we have as yet enough knowledge of the scientific type to enable us to regulate our judgments of value very extensively. But we have more knowledge than we try to put to use, and until we try more systematically we shall not know what are the important gaps in our sciences judged from the point of view of their moral and humane use.

For moralists usually draw a sharp line between the field of the natural sciences and the conduct that is regarded as moral. But a moral that frames its judgments of value on the basis of consequences must depend in a most intimate manner upon the conclusions of science. For the knowledge of the relations between changes which enable us to connect things as antecedents and consequences *is* science. The narrow scope which moralists often give to morals, their isolation of some conduct as virtuous and vicious from other large ranges of conduct, those having to do with health and vigor, business, education, with all the affairs in which desires and affection are implicated, is perpetuated by this habit of exclusion of the subject-matter of natural science from a rôle in formation of moral standards and ideals. The same attitude operates in the other direction to keep natural science a technical specialty, and it works unconsciously to encourage its use exclusively in regions where it can be turned to personal and class advantage, as in war and trade.

Another great difference to be made by carrying the experimental habit into all matter of practice is that it cuts the roots of what is often called subjectivism, but which is better termed egoism. The subjective attitude is much more widespread than would be inferred from the philosophies which have that label attached. It is as rampant in realistic philosophies as in any others, sometimes even more so, although disguised from those who hold these philosophies under the cover of reverence for and enjoyment of ultimate values. For the implication of placing the standard of thought and knowledge in antecedent existence is that our thought makes no difference in what is significantly real. It then affects only our own attitude toward it.

This constant throwing of emphasis back upon a change made in ourselves instead of one made in the world in which we live seems to me the essence of what is objectionable in "subjectivism." Its taint hangs about even Platonic realism with its insistent evangelical dwelling upon the change made within the mind by contemplation of the realm of essence, and its depreciation of action as transient and all but sordid—a concession to the necessities of organic existence. All the theories which put conversion "of the eye of the soul" in the place of a conversion of natural and social objects that modifies goods actually experienced, is a retreat and escape from existence—and this retraction into self is, once more, the heart of subjective egoisms. The typical example is perhaps the other-worldliness found in religions whose chief concern is with the salvation of the personal soul. But other-worldliness is found as well in estheticism and in all seclusion within ivory towers.

It is not in the least implied that change in personal attitudes, in the disposition of the "subject," is not of great importance. Such change, on the contrary, is involved in any attempt to modify the conditions of the environment. But there is a radical difference between a change in the self that is cultivated and valued as an end, and one that is a means to alteration, through action, of objective conditions. The Aristotelian-medieval conviction that highest bliss is found in contemplative possession of ultimate Being presents an ideal attractive to some types of mind; it sets forth a refined sort of enjoyment. It is a doctrine congenial to minds that despair of the effort involved in creation of a better world of daily experience. It is, apart from theological attachments, a doctrine sure to recur when social conditions are so troubled as to make actual endeavor seem hopeless. But the subjectivism so externally marked in modern thought as compared with ancient is either a development of the old doctrine under new conditions or is of merely technical import. The medieval version of the doctrine at least had the active support of a great social institution by means of which man could be brought into the state of mind that prepared him for ultimate enjoyment of eternal Being. It had a certain solidity and depth which is lacking in modern theories that would attain the result by merely emotional or speculative procedures, or by any means not demanding a change in objective existence so as to render objects of value more empirically secure.

The nature in detail of the revolution that would be wrought by carrying into the region of values the principle now embodied in scientific practice cannot be told; to attempt it would violate the fundamental idea that we know only after we have acted and in consequences of the outcome of action. But it would surely effect a transfer of attention and energy from the subjective to the objective. Men would think of themselves as agents not as ends; ends would be found in experienced enjoyment of the fruits of a transforming activity. In as far as the subjectivity of modern thought represents a discovery of the part played by personal responses, organic and acquired, in the causal production of the qualities and values of objects, it marks the possibility of a decisive gain. It puts us in possession of some of the conditions that control the occurrence of experienced objects, and thereby it supplies us with an instrument of regulation. There is something querulous in the sweeping denial that things as experienced, as perceived and enjoyed, in any way depend upon interaction with human selves. The error of doctrines that have exploited the part played by personal and subjective reactions in determining what is perceived and enjoyed lies either in exaggerating this factor of constitution into the sole condition—as happens in subjective idealism—or else in treating it as a finality instead of, as with all knowledge, an instrument in direction of further action.

A third significant change that would issue from carrying over experimental method from physics to man concerns the import of standards, principles, rules. With the transfer, these, and all tenets and creeds about good and goods, would be recognized to be hypotheses. Instead of being rigidly fixed, they would be treated as intellectual instruments to be tested and confirmed—and altered—through consequences effected by acting upon them. They would lose all pretense of finality—the ulterior source of dogmatism. It is both astonishing and depressing that so much of the energy of mankind has gone into fighting for (with weapons of the flesh as well as of the spirit) the truth of creeds, religious, moral and political, as distinct from what has gone into effort to try creeds by putting them to the test of acting upon them. The change would do away with the intolerance and fanaticism that attend the notion that beliefs and judgments are capable of inherent truth and authority; inherent in the sense of being independent of what they lead to when used as directive principles. The transformation does not imply merely that men are responsible for acting upon what they profess to believe; that is an old doctrine. It goes much further. Any belief as such is tentative, hypothetical; it is not just to be acted upon, but is to be *framed* with reference to its office as a guide to action. Consequently, it should be the last thing in the world to be picked up casually and then clung to rigidly. When it is apprehended as a tool and only a tool, an instrumentality of direction, the same scrupulous attention will go to its formation as now goes into the making of instruments of precision in technical fields. Men, instead of being proud of accepting and asserting beliefs and "principles" on the ground of loyalty, will be as ashamed of that procedure as they would now be to confess their assent to a scientific theory out of reverence for Newton or Helmholz or whomever, without regard to evidence.

If one stops to consider the matter, is there not something strange in the fact that men should consider loyalty to "laws," principles, standards, ideals to be an inherent virtue, accounted unto them for righteousness? It is as if they were making up for some secret sense of weakness by rigidity and intensity of insistent attachment. A moral law, like a law in physics, is not something to swear by and stick to at all hazards; it is a formula of the way to respond when specified conditions present themselves. Its soundness and pertinence are tested by what happens when it is acted upon. Its claim or authority rests finally upon the imperativeness of the situation that has to be dealt with, not upon its own intrinsic nature—as any tool achieves dignity in the measure of needs served by it. The idea that adherence to standards external to experienced objects is the only alternative to confusion and lawlessness was once held in science. But knowledge became steadily progressive when it was abandoned, and clews and tests found within concrete acts and objects were employed. The test of consequences is more exacting than that afforded by fixed general rules. In addition, it secures constant development, for when new acts are tried new results are experienced, while the lauded immutability of eternal ideals and norms is in itself a denial of the possibility of development and improvement.

The various modifications that would result from adoption in social and humane subjects of the experimental way of thinking are perhaps summed up in saying that it would place *method and means* upon the level of importance that has, in the past, been imputed exclusively to ends. Means have been regarded as menial, and the useful as the servile. Means have been treated as poor relations to be endured, but not inherently welcome. The very meaning of the word "ideals" is significant of the divorce which has obtained between means and ends. "Ideals" are thought to be remote and inaccessible of attainment; they are too high and fine to be sullied by realization. They serve vaguely to arouse "aspiration," but they do not evoke and direct strivings for embodiment in actual existence. They hover in an indefinite way over the actual scene; they are expiring ghosts of a once significant kingdom of divine reality whose rule penetrated to every detail of life.

It is impossible to form a just estimate of the paralysis of effort that has been produced by indifference to means. Logically, it is truistic that lack of consideration for means signifies that so-called ends are not taken seriously. It is as if one professed devotion to painting pictures conjoined with contempt for canvas, brush and paints; or love of music on condition that no instruments, whether the voice or something external, be used to make sounds. The good workman in the arts is known by his respect for his tools and by his interest in perfecting his technique. The glorification in the arts of ends at the expense of means would be taken to be a sign of complete insincerity or even insanity. Ends separated from means are either sentimental indulgences or if they happen to exist are merely accidental. The ineffectiveness in action of "ideals" is due precisely to the supposition that means and ends are not on exactly the same level with respect to the attention and care they demand.

It is, however, much easier to point out the formal contradiction implied in ideals that are professed without equal regard for the instruments and techniques of their realization, than it is to appreciate the concrete ways in which belief in their separation has found its way into life and borne corrupt and poisonous fruits. The separation marks the form in which the traditional divorce of theory and practice has expressed itself in actual life. It accounts for the relative impotency of arts concerned with enduring human welfare. Sentimental attachment and subjective eulogy take the place of action. For there is no art without tools and instrumental agencies. But it also explains the fact that in actual behavior, energies devoted to matters nominally thought to be inferior, material and sordid, engross attention and interest. After a polite and pious deference has been paid to "ideals," men feel free to devote themselves to matters which are more immediate and pressing.

It is usual to condemn the amount of attention paid by people in general to material ease, comfort, wealth, and success gained by competition, on the ground that they give to mere means the attention that ought to be given to ends, or that they have taken for ends things which in reality are only means. Criticisms of the place which economic interest and action occupy in present life are full of complaints that men allow lower aims to usurp the place that belongs to higher and ideal values. The final source of the trouble is, however, that moral and spiritual "leaders" have propagated the notion that ideal ends may be cultivated in isolation from "material" means, as if means and material were not synonymous. While they condemn men for giving to means the thought and energy that ought to go to

ends, the condemnation should go to them. For they have not taught their followers to think of material and economic activities as *really* means. They have been unwilling to frame their conception of the values that should be regulative of human conduct on the basis of the actual conditions and operations by which alone values can be actualized.

Practical needs are imminent; with the mass of mankind they are imperative. Moreover, speaking generally, men are formed to act rather than to theorize. Since the ideal ends are so remotely and accidentally connected with immediate and urgent conditions that need attention, after lip service is given to them, men naturally devote themselves to the latter. If a bird in the hand is worth two in a neighboring bush, an actuality in hand is worth, for the direction of conduct, many ideals that are so remote as to be invisible and inaccessible. Men hoist the banner of the ideal, and then march in the direction that concrete conditions suggest and reward.

Deliberate insincerity and hypocrisy are rare. But the notion that action and sentiment are inherently unified in the constitution of human nature has nothing to justify it. Integration is something to be achieved. Division of attitudes and responses, compartmentalizing of interests, is easily acquired. It goes deep just because the acquisition is unconscious, a matter of habitual adaptation to conditions. Theory separated from concrete doing and making is empty and futile; practice then becomes an immediate seizure of opportunities and enjoyments which conditions afford without the direction which theory—knowledge and ideas—has power to supply. The problem of the relation of theory and practice is not a problem of theory alone; it is that, but it is also the most practical problem of life. For it is the question of how intelligence may inform action, and how action may bear the fruit of increased insight into meaning: a clear view of the values that are worth while and of the means by which they are to be made secure in experienced objects. Construction of ideals in general and their sentimental glorification are easy; the responsibilities both of studious thought and of action are shirked. Persons having the advantage of positions of leisure and who find pleasure in abstract theorizing—a most delightful indulgence to those to whom it appeals—have a large measure of liability for a cultivated diffusion of ideals and aims that are separated from the conditions which are the means of actualization. Then other persons who find themselves in positions of social power and authority readily claim to be the bearers and defenders of ideal ends in church and state. They then use the prestige and authority their representative capacity as guardians of the highest ends confers on them to cover actions taken in behalf of the harshest and narrowest of material ends.

The present state of industrial life seems to give a fair index of the existing separation of means and ends. Isolation of economics from ideal ends, whether of morals or of organized social life, was proclaimed by Aristotle. Certain things, he said, are conditions of a worthy life, personal and social, but are not constituents of it. The economic life of man, concerned with satisfaction of wants, is of this nature. Men have wants and they must be satisfied. But they are only prerequisites of a good life, not intrinsic elements in it. Most philosophers have not been so frank nor perhaps so logical. But upon the whole, economics has been treated as on a lower level than either morals or politics. Yet the life which men, women and children actually lead, the opportunities open to them, the values they are capable of enjoying, their education, their share in all the things of art and science, are mainly determined by economic conditions. Hence we can hardly expect a moral system which ignores economic conditions to be other than remote and empty.

Industrial life is correspondingly brutalized by failure to equate it as the means by which social and cultural values are realized. That the economic life, thus exiled from the pale of higher values, takes revenge by declaring that it is the only social reality, and by means of the doctrine of materialistic determination of institutions and conduct in all fields, denies to deliberate morals and politics any share of causal regulation, is not surprising.

When economists were told that their subject-matter was merely material, they naturally thought they could be "scientific" only by excluding all reference to distinctively human values. Material wants, efforts to satisfy them, even the scientifically regulated technologies highly developed in industrial activity, are then taken to form a complete and closed field. If any reference to social ends and values is introduced it is by way of an external addition, mainly hortatory. That economic life largely determines the conditions under which mankind has access to concrete values may be recognized or it may not be. In either case, the notion that it is the means to be utilized in order to secure significant values as the common and shared possession of mankind is alien and inoperative. To many persons, the idea that the ends professed by morals are impotent save as they are connected with the working machinery of economic life seems like deflowering the purity of moral values and obligations.

The social and moral effects of the separation of theory and practice have been merely hinted at. They are so manifold and so pervasive that an adequate consideration of them would involve nothing less than a survey of the whole field of morals, economics and politics. It cannot be justly stated that these effects are in fact direct consequences of the quest for certainty by thought and knowledge isolated from action. For, as we have seen, this quest was itself a reflex product of actual conditions. But it may be truly asserted that this quest, undertaken in religion and philosophy, has had results which have reinforced the conditions which originally brought it about. Moreover, search for safety and consolation amid the perils of life by means other than intelligent action, by feeling and thought alone, began when actual means of control were lacking, when arts were undeveloped. It had then a relative historic justification that is now lacking. The primary problem for thinking which lays claim to be philosophic in its breadth and depth is to assist in bringing about a reconstruction of all beliefs rooted in a basic separation of knowledge and action; to develop a system of operative ideas congruous with present knowledge and with present facilities of control over natural events and energies.

We have noted more than once how modern philosophy has been absorbed in the problem of affecting an adjustment between the conclusions of natural science and the beliefs and values that have authority in the direction of life. The genuine and poignant issue does not reside where philosophers for the most part have placed it. It does not consist in accommodation to each other of two realms, one physical and the other ideal and spiritual, nor in the reconciliation of the "categories" of theoretical and practical reason. It is found in that isolation of executive means and ideal interests which has grown up under the influence of the separation of theory and practice. For this, by nature, involves the separation of the material and the spiritual. Its solution, therefore, can be found only in action wherein the phenomena of material and economic life are equated with the purposes that command the loyalties of affection and purpose, and in which ends and ideals are framed in terms of the possibilities of actually experienced situations. But while the solution cannot be found in "thought" alone, it can be furthered by thinking which is operative—which frames and defines ideas in terms of what may be done, and which uses the conclusions of science as instrumentalities. William James was well within the bounds of moderation when he said that looking forward instead of backward, looking to what the world and life might become instead of to what they have been, is an alteration in the "seat of authority."

It was incidentally remarked earlier in our discussion that the serious defect in the current empirical philosophy of values, the one which identifies them with things actually enjoyed irrespective of the conditions upon which they depend, is that it formulates and in so far consecrates the conditions of our present social experience. Throughout these chapters, primary attention has perforce been given to the methods and statements of philosophic theories. But these statements are technical and specialized in formulation only. In origin, content and import they are reflections of some condition or some phase of concrete human experience. Just as the theory of the separation of theory and practice has a practical origin and a momentous practical consequence, so the empirical theory that values are identical with whatever men actually enjoy, no matter how or what, formulates an aspect, and an undesirable one, of the present social situation.

For while our discussion has given more attention to the other type of philosophical doctrine, that which holds that regulative and authoritative standards are found in transcendent eternal values, it has not passed in silence over the fact that actually the greater part of the activities of the greater number of human beings is spent in effort to seize upon and hold onto such enjoyments as the actual scene permits. Their energies and their enjoyments are controlled in fact, but they are controlled by external conditions rather than by intelligent judgment and endeavor. If philosophies have any influence over the thoughts and acts of men, it is a serious matter that the most widely held empirical theory should in effect justify this state of things by identifying values with the objects of any interest as such. As long as the only theories of value placed before us for intellectual assent alternate between sending us to a realm of eternal and fixed values and sending us to enjoyments such as actually obtain, the formulation, even as only a theory, of an experimental empiricism which finds values to be identical with goods that are the fruit of intelligently directed activity has its measure of practical significance.

W. D. ROSS

FROM *The Right and the Good*

Some of those who followed Moore in his attack on naturalism were, like Moore, broadly categorized as intuitionists. Yet many were intuitionists of a different stripe. In general, intuitionists hold that it is futile to produce an ethical theory from the facts of reality. However, whereas Moore advocated an ideal form of utilitarianism, albeit a nonnatural one, other intuitionists put forward theories that were nonnaturalist and deontological.

(A deontological theory holds that the value of an act is intrinsic to some feature of the act itself, not to the consequences of the act.) The most extreme of these deontological nonnaturalists was H. A. Prichard, who argued in his landmark article "Does Moral Philosophy Rest on a Mistake?" that arguments are out of place in the determination of what we are obliged to do. In a situation requiring a moral decision, we are either immediately aware of our obligations or we are not. The philosopher who we will read in this chapter, Sir David Ross, used the work of Prichard as a starting point and became the most influential of the deontological nonnaturalists.

William David Ross, Aristotle scholar and moral philosopher, was born in Scotland in 1877. Educated at Edinburgh University and Balliol College, Oxford, Ross became professor and later provost at Oriel College, Oxford. Ross was prominent in both academic and public life; he was awarded the Order of the British Empire for his contributions in World War I and knighted in 1938. He died in 1971.

It is as an Aristotle scholar that Ross first made a significant contribution to philosophy. Ross edited the Oxford translations of Aristotle, published between 1908 and 1931, translating the Metaphysics *and the* Ethics *himself. Outside of Aristotelian scholarship, his main contribution to philosophy was in moral philosophy. He argued the case for a deontological version of intuitionism in his classic work,* The Right and the Good *(1930). In the* Foundations of Ethics *(1939), he restated his case and replied to criticisms.*

Ross accepted Prichard's view that we have an intuitive understanding of our obligations. Our duties, he went on, are of a special kind, what he called prima facie *duties. A* prima facie *duty is, as the name implies, self-evident. When we examine our* prima facie *duties, argued Ross, we will see that we do not always reason as the utilitarian recommends. By virtue of special obligations we have, such as beneficence and fidelity, we should not always act to maximize good. Ross' theory is deontological, yet he disputes the position of the premier deontologist, Immanuel Kant, claiming that Kant errs when he declares that our moral obligations are absolute. Our* prima facie *duties often conflict.*

Even though Ross' ethical theory received harsh criticism from those who would criticize either deontological theories or intuitionist theories, his work has had a lasting impact on subsequent moral philosophy. The Right and the Good *has come to be considered a classic work of moral philosophy after having been the center of controversy for many years. Even at the end of the twentieth century, Ross' theory of* prima facie *duties has many adherents who consider it a viable theory.*

I. The Meaning of 'Right'

The purpose of this inquiry is to examine the nature, relations, and implications of three conceptions which appear to be fundamental in ethics—those of 'right', 'good' in general, and 'morally good.' The inquiry will have much in common with the inquiries, of which there have been many in recent years, into the nature of value, and I shall have occasion to discuss some of the more important theories of value; but my object is a more limited one. I offer no discussion, except at most a purely incidental and illustrative one, of certain forms of value, such as economic value and

beauty. My interest will throughout be ethical, and value will be discussed only so far as it seems to be relevant to this interest.

I propose to begin with the term 'right.' A considerable ambiguity attaches to any attempt to discuss the meaning of any term. Professor G. E. Moore has well indicated three main objects that such an attempt at definition may have. 'When we say, as Webster says, "The definition of horse is, 'A hoofed quadruped of the genus Equus,'" we may, in fact, mean three different things. (1) We may mean merely: "When l say 'horse,' you are to understand that I am talking about a hoofed quadruped of the genus Equus." This might be called the arbitrary verbal definition.... (2) We may mean, as Webster ought to mean: When most English people say 'horse', they mean a hoofed quadruped of the genus Equus." This may be called the verbal definition proper. . . . But (3) we may, when we define horse, mean something much more important. We may mean that a certain object, which we all of us know, is composed in a certain manner: that it has four legs, a head, a heart, a liver, etc., etc., all of them arranged in definite relations to one another.'[1]

We must ask ourselves whether, in discussing the meaning of 'right,' we are attempting any one of these kinds of definition, or something different from them all. I certainly do not wish *merely* to indicate a sense in which I propose to use the term 'right.' I wish to keep in touch with the general usage of the word. While other things may be called 'right' (as in the phrases 'the right road,' 'the right solution'), the word is specially applied to acts, and it is the sense (by general consent a very important one) in which it is so applied that I wish to discuss. But we must be prepared to find that the general usage of the word is not entirely consistent with itself. Most of the words in any language have a certain amount of ambiguity; and there is special danger of ambiguity in the case of a word like 'right,' which does not stand for anything we can point out to one another or apprehend by one of the senses. Even with words that do stand for such things there is this danger. Even if two people find that the things the one calls red are just the things the other calls red, it is by no means certain that they mean the same quality. There is only a general presumption that since the structure of their eyes (if neither is colour-blind) is pretty much the same, the same object acting on the eyes of the two men produces pretty much the same kind of sensation. And in the case of a term like 'right,' there is nothing parallel to the highly similar organization of different people's eyes, to create a presumption that when they call the same act right, they mean to refer to the same quality of it. In point of fact, there is a serious difference of view as to the *application* of the term 'right.' Suppose, for instance, that a man pays a particular debt simply from fear of the legal consequences of not doing so, some people would say he had done

what was right, and others would deny this: they would say that no moral value attaches to such an act, and that since 'right' is meant to imply moral value, the act cannot be right. They might generalize and say that no act is right unless it is done from a sense of duty, or if they shrank from so rigorous a doctrine, they might at least say that no act is right unless done from *some* good motive, such as either sense of duty or benevolence.

This difference of view may be due to either of two uses. Both parties may be using 'right' in the same sense, the sense of 'morally obligatory,' and differing as to the further character an act must have in order to have this quality. *Or* the first party may be using 'right' in this sense, and the second in the sense of 'morally good.' It is not clear to me which of these two things is usually happening when this difference of view arises. But it seems probable that both things really happen—that some people fail to notice the distinction between 'right' and 'morally good,' and that others, while distinguishing the meaning of these terms, think that only what is morally good is right. A discussion of the first of these positions only is strictly in point here, where we are discussing the *meaning* of 'right.' It seems to me clear that 'right' does not mean the same as 'morally good'; and we can test this by trying to substitute one for the other. If they meant the same thing we should be able to substitute, for instance, 'he is a right man' for 'he is a morally good man'; nor is our inability to do this merely a matter of English idiom, for if we turn to the sort of moral judgement in which we do use the word 'right,' such as 'this is the right act,' it is clear that by this we mean 'this act is the act *that ought to be done,*' 'this act is *morally obligatory*'; and to substitute either of these phrases for 'morally good' in 'he is a morally good man' would obviously be not merely unidiomatic, but absurd. It should be obvious, then, that 'right' and 'morally good' mean different things. But some one might say that while 'morally good' has a wider application than 'right,' in that it can be applied to agents as well as to acts, yet when applied to acts they mean the same thing. I should like therefore to convince him that 'right act' cannot mean the same as 'act that ought to be done' and *also* the same as 'morally good act.' If I can convince him of this, I think he will see the propriety of not using 'right act' in the sense of 'morally good act.'

---

1. *Principia Ethica*, 8.

But we ought first to note a minor difference between the meaning of 'right' and the meaning of 'something that ought to be done' or 'that is my duty' or 'that is incumbent on me.' It may sometimes happen that there is a set of two or more acts one or other of which ought to be done by me rather than any act not belonging to this set. In such a case any act of this set is right, but none is my duty; my duty is to do 'one or other' of them. Thus 'right' has a somewhat wider possible application than 'something that ought to be done' or any of its equivalents. But we want an adjective to express the same meaning as 'something that ought to be done,' and though we have 'obligatory' at our disposal, that also has its ambiguity, since it sometimes means 'compulsory.' We should have to say 'morally obligatory' to make our meaning quite clear; and to obviate the necessity of using this rather cumbrous expression, I will use 'right' in this sense. I hope that this paragraph will prevent any confusion arising from this slightly inaccurate usage.

Some might deny the correctness of the distinction just drawn. They might say that when there are two or more acts one or other of which, as we say, we ought to do (it not being our duty to do one rather than another), the truth is that these are simply alternative ways of producing a single result, and that our duty is, strictly, not to do 'one or other' of the acts, but to produce the result; this alone is our duty, and this alone is right. This answer does, I think, fairly apply to many cases in which it is the production of a certain result that we think obligatory, the means being optional: e.g. to a case in which it is our duty to convey information to some one, but morally immaterial whether we do so orally or in writing. But in principle, at any rate, there may be other cases in which it is our duty to produce one or other of two or more *different* states of affairs, without its being our duty to produce one of them rather than another; in such a case each of these acts will be right, and none will be our duty.

If it can be shown that nothing that ought to be done is ever morally good, it will be clear *a fortiori* that 'morally good' does not *mean* the same as 'that ought to be done.' Now it is, I think, quite clear that the only acts that are morally good are those that proceed from a good motive; this is maintained by those whom I am now trying to convince, and I entirely agree. If, then, we can show that action from a good motive is never morally obligatory, we shall have established that what is morally good is never right, and *a fortiori* that 'right' does not *mean* the same as 'morally good.' That action from a good motive is never morally obligatory follows (1) from the Kantian principle, which is generally admitted, that 'I ought' implies 'I can.' It is not the case that I can by choice produce a certain motive (whether this be an ordinary desire or the sense of obligation) in myself at a moment's notice, still less that I can at a moment's notice make it effective in stimulating me to act. I can act from a certain motive only if I have the motive; if not, the most I can do is to cultivate it by suitably directing my attention or by acting in certain appropriate ways so that on some future occasion it *will* be present in me, and I shall be able to act from it. My *present* duty, therefore, cannot be to act here and now from it.

(2) A similar conclusion may be reached by a *reductio ad absurdum*. Those who hold that our duty is to act from a certain motive usually (Kant is the great exemplar) hold that the motive from which we ought to act is the sense of duty. Now if the sense of duty is to be my motive for doing a certain act, it must be the sense that it is my duty to do that act. If, therefore, we say 'it is my duty to do act *A* from the sense of duty,' this means 'it is my duty to do act *A* from the sense that it is my duty to do act *A*.' And here the whole expression is in contradiction with a part of itself. The whole sentence says 'it is my duty to-do-act-*A*-from-the-sense-that-it-is-my-duty-to-do-act-*A*.' But the latter part of the sentence implies that what I think is that it is my duty to-do-act-*A* simply. And if, as the theory in question requires, we try to amend the latter part of the expression to bring it into accord with the whole expression, we get the result 'it is my duty to do act *A* from the sense that it is my duty to do act *A* from the sense that it is my duty to do act *A*,' where again the last part of the expression is in conflict with the theory, and with the sentence as a whole. It is clear that a further similar amendment, and a further, and in the end an infinite series of amendments would be necessary in the attempt to bring the last part of the expression into accordance with the theory, and that even then we should not have succeeded in doing so.

Again, suppose that I say to you 'it is your duty to do act *A* from the sense of duty'; that means 'it is your duty to do act *A* from the sense that it is your duty to do act *A*.' Then *I* think that it is your duty to act from a certain motive, but I suggest that *you* should act under the supposition that it is your duty to do a certain thing, irrespective of motive, i.e. under a supposition which I must think false since it contradicts my own.

The only conclusion that can be drawn is that our duty is to do certain things, not to do them from the sense of duty.[1]

The latter of these two arguments ((1) and (2)) cannot be used against those who hold that it is our duty to act from some other motive than the sense of duty; the sense of duty is the only motive that leads to the infinite series in question. But the first of the two arguments seems in itself sufficient against *any* theory which holds that motive of any kind is included in the content of duty. And though the second argument does not refute the view that we ought to act from some other motive, it would be paradoxical to hold that we ought to act from some other motive but never ought to act from a sense of duty, which is the highest motive.

Let us now return to the three senses in which Professor Moore points out that we may understand an attempt to define a certain term. So far, the position we have taken up with regard to 'right' includes something of each of the first two attitudes he distinguishes. In using 'right' as synonymous (but for the minor distinction already pointed out) with 'what is my duty,' and as distinct from 'morally good,' I believe I am conforming to what most men (if not all men) usually mean when they use the word. But I could not maintain that they always use the word in this way. I am, therefore, to some extent adopting the first of the attitudes he distinguishes, and expressing my own intention to use 'right' in this sense only. And this is justified by the great confusion that has been introduced into ethics by the phrase 'a right action' being used sometimes of the initiation of a certain change in the state of affairs irrespective of motive, and at other times of such initiation from some particular motive, such as sense of duty or benevolence. I would further suggest that additional

clearness would be gained if we used 'act' of the thing done, the initiation of change, and 'action' of the doing of it, the initiating of change, from a certain motive. We should then talk of a right act but not of a right action, of a morally good action but not of a morally good act. And it may be added that the doing of a right act may be a morally bad action, and that the doing of a wrong act may be a morally good action; for 'right' and 'wrong' refer entirely to the thing done, 'morally good' and 'morally bad' entirely to the motive from which it is done. A firm grasp of this distinction will do much to remove some of the perplexities of our moral thought.

The question remains, what attitude we are to take up towards Professor Moore's third sense of 'definition.' Are we to hold that 'right' can be defined in the sense of being reduced to elements simpler than itself? At first sight it might appear that egoism and utilitarianism are attempts to define 'right'—to define it as 'productive of the greatest possible pleasure to the agent' or as 'productive of the greatest possible pleasure to mankind'; and I think these theories have often been so understood by some of those who accept them. But the leaders of the school are not unanimous in so understanding their theory. Bentham seems to understand it so. He says[2] that 'when thus interpreted' (i.e. as meaning 'conformable to the principle of utility'), 'the words *ought* and *right*... and others of that stamp, have a meaning; when otherwise, they have none.' And elsewhere[3] he says 'admitting (what is not true) that the word *right* can have a meaning without reference to utility.' Yet, as Sidgwick points out,[4] 'when Bentham explains (*Principles of Morals and Legislation*, Chap I, 5 § I, note) that his fundamental principle "states the greatest happiness of all those whose interest is in question as being the right and proper end of human action," we cannot understand him really to mean by the word "right" "conducive to the general happiness"; for the proposition that it is conducive to general happiness to take general happiness as an end of action, though not exactly a tautology, can hardly serve as the fundamental principle of a moral system.' Bentham has evidently not made up his

---

1. It should be added, however, that one, and an important one, of our duties is to cultivate in ourselves the sense of duty. But then this is the duty of cultivating in ourselves the sense of duty, and not of cultivating in ourselves, from the sense of duty, the sense of duty.

2. *Principles of Morals and Legislation*, Ch. 1,§ 10.

3. *Methods of Ethics*, ed. 7, 26 n.

4. ib. § 14. 10.

mind clearly whether he thinks that 'right' *means* 'productive of the general happiness,' *or* that being productive of the general happiness is what makes right acts right; and would very likely have thought the difference unimportant. Mill does not so far as I know discuss the question whether right is definable. He states his creed in the form 'actions are right in proportion as they tend to promote happiness,'[1] where the claim that is made is not that this is what 'right' means, but that this is the other characteristic in virtue of which actions that are right are right. And Sidgwick says[2] that the meaning of 'right' or 'ought' is too elementary to admit of any formal definition,' and expressly repudiates[3] the view that 'right' means 'productive of any particular sort of result.'

The most deliberate claim that 'right' is definable as 'productive of so and so' is made by Prof. G. E. Moore, who claims in *Principia Ethica* that 'right' means 'productive of the greatest possible good.' Now it has often been pointed out against hedonism, and by no one more clearly than by Professor Moore, that the claim that 'good' just means 'pleasant' cannot seriously be maintained; that while it may or may not be true that the only things that are good are pleasant, the statement that the good is just the pleasant is a synthetic, not an analytic proposition; that the words 'good' and 'pleasant' stand for distinct qualities, even if the things that possess the one are precisely the things that possess the other. If this were not so, it would not be intelligible that the proposition 'the good is just the pleasant' should have been maintained on the one hand, and denied on the other, with so much fervour; for we do not fight for or against analytic propositions; we take them for granted. Must not the same claim be made about the statement 'being right means being an act productive of the greatest good producible in the circumstances'? Is it not plain on reflection that this is not what we *mean* by right, even if it be a true statement about what *is* right? It seems clear for instance that when an ordinary man says it is right to fulfil promises he is not in the least thinking of the total consequences of such an act, about which he knows

and cares little or nothing. 'Ideal utilitarianism'[4] is, it would appear, plausible only when it is understood not as an analysis or definition of the notion of 'right' but as a statement that all acts that are right, and only these, possess the further characteristic of being productive of the best possible consequences, and are right because they possess this other characteristic.

If I am not mistaken, Professor Moore has moved to this position, from the position that 'right' is *analysable* into 'productive of the greatest possible good.' In *Principia Ethica* the latter position is adopted: e.g. 'This use of "right," as denoting what is good as a means, whether or not it is also good as an end, is indeed the use to which I shall confine the word'.[5] 'To assert that a certain line of conduct is, at a given time, absolutely right or obligatory, is obviously to assert that more good or less evil will exist in the world, if it be adopted, than if anything else be done instead.'[6] 'To ask what kind of actions one ought to perform, or what kind of conduct is right, is to ask what kind of effects such action and conduct will produce... What I wish first to point out is that "right" does and can mean nothing but "cause of a good result," and is thus always identical with "useful"... That the assertion "I am morally bound to perform this action" is identical with the assertion "this action will produce the greatest possible amount of good in the Universe" has already been briefly shewn...; but it is important to insist that this fundamental point is demonstrably certain.... Our "duty," therefore, can only be defined as that action, which will cause more good to exist in the Universe than any possible alternative. And what is "right" or "morally permissible" only differs from this, as what will *not* cause *less* good than any possible alternative.'[7]

In his later book, *Ethics,* Professor Moore seems to have come to adopt the other position, though perhaps not quite unequivocally. On page 8 he names as one of the 'more fundamental questions' of ethics the question 'what, after all, is it that we mean

---

1. *Utilitarianism,* copyright eds., 9.

3. *Methods of Ethics,* ed. 7, 32.

2. ib. 25–6.

4. I use this as a well known way of referring to Professor Moore's view. 'Agathistic utilitarianism' would indicate more distinctly the difference between it and hedonistic utilitarianism.

5. p. 18.

6. p. 25.

7. pp. 146–8. Cf. also pp. 167, 169, 180–1.

to say of an action when we say that it is right or ought to be done?' Here it is still suggested that 'right' is perhaps analysable or definable. But to this question *Ethics* nowhere distinctly offers an answer, and on page 9 we find, 'Can we discover any single reason, applicable to all right actions equally, which is, in every case, *the* reason why an action is right, when it is right?' This is the question which Professor Moore in fact sets himself to answer. But the *reason* for an action's being right is evidently not the same thing as its *rightness,* and Professor Moore seems already to have passed to the view that productivity of maximum good is not the definition of 'right' but another characteristic which underlies and accounts for the rightness of right acts. Again, he describes hedonistic utilitarianism as asking, 'can we discover any characteristic, over and above the mere fact that they are right, which belongs to absolutely *all* voluntary actions which are right, and which at the same time does not belong to any except those which are right?'[1] This is the question which he describes hedonism as essentially answering, and since his own view differs from hedonism not in logical form but just by the substitution of 'good' for 'pleasure,' his theory also seems to be essentially an answer to this question, i.e. not to the question what is rightness but to the question what is the universal accompaniment and, as he is careful to add,[2] the necessitating ground of rightness. Again, he describes hedonistic utilitarianism as giving us 'a criterion, or test, or standard by which we could discern with regard to any action whether it is right or wrong.'[3] And similarly, I suppose, he regards his own theory as offering a different criterion of rightness. But obviously a criterion of rightness is not rightness itself. And, most plainly of all, he says, 'It is indeed quite plain, I think, that the meaning of the two words' ('duty' and 'expediency,' the latter being equivalent to 'tendency to produce the maximum good') 'is *not* the same; for, if it were, then it would be a mere tautology to say that it is always our duty to do what will have the best possible consequences.'[4] If we contrast this with *Principia Ethica,*

page 169, 'if I ask whether an action is *really* my duty or *really* expedient, the predicate of which I question the applicability to the action in question is precisely the same,' we see how much Professor Moore has changed his position, and changed it in the direction in which, as I have been urging, it must be changed if it is to be made plausible. And if it is clear that 'right' does not mean 'productive of the greatest possible good,' it is *a fortiori* clear that it does not *mean* 'productive of the greatest possible pleasure, for the agent or for mankind,' but that productivity of the greatest possible pleasure for the agent or for mankind is at most the ground of the rightness of acts, rightness itself being admitted to be a distinct characteristic, and one which utilitarianism does not claim to define.

But there are theories other than utilitarianism which claim to define 'right.' It would be tedious to try to refute all such theories. With regard to many of them[5] it seems to be enough to ask one's readers whether it is not clear to them on reflection that the proposed definition of 'right' bears in fact no resemblance to what they mean by 'right.' But there is one group of theories to which some reference should be made, viz. those that give what may be called a subjective theory of 'right,' that identify the rightness of an act with its tendency to produce either some feeling or some opinion in the mind of some one who contemplates it. This type of theory has been dealt with very thoroughly by Professor Moore,[6] and I should have little or nothing to add to his convincing refutation. But such theories are perhaps even more prevalent with regard to 'good' than to 'right,' and in my fourth chapter I discuss them at some length. I would ask my readers to read the argument there offered, and to reflect whether the refutation I offer[7] of subjective accounts of 'good' does not apply with equal force to subjective accounts of 'right.'

Any one who is satisfied that neither the subjective theories of the meaning of 'right,' nor what is far the most attractive of the attempts to reduce it to simpler objective elements, is correct, will probably be prepared to agree that 'right' is an irreducible notion.

---

1. p 17.

2. pp. 44, 54.

3. p.43.

4. p. 173

---

5. e.g. the evolutionary theory which identifies 'right' with 'conducive to life.'

6. *Ethics,* Chs. 3, 4.

7. pp. 80–104.

Nor is this result impugned by inquiries into the historical development of our present moral notions from an earlier state of things in which 'what is right' was hardly disentangled from 'what the tribe ordains.' The point is that we can now see clearly that 'right' does not mean 'ordained by any given society.' And it may be doubted whether even primitive men thought that it did. Their thoughts about what in particular was right were to a large extent limited by the customs and sanctions of their race and age. But this is not the same as to say that they thought that 'right' just meant 'what my race and age ordains.' Moral progress has been possible just because there have been men in all ages who have seen the difference and have practised, or at least preached, a morality in some respects higher than that of their race and age. And even the supporters of the lower morality held, we may suspect, that their laws and customs were in accordance with a 'right' other than themselves. 'It is the custom' has been accompanied by 'the custom is right,' or 'the custom is ordained by some one who has the right to command.' And if human consciousness is continuous, by descent, with a lower consciousness which had no notion of right at all, that need not make us doubt that the notion is an ultimate and irreducible one, or that the rightness (*prima facie*) of certain types of act is self-evident; for the nature of the self-evident is not to be evident to every mind however undeveloped, but to be apprehended directly by minds which have reached a certain degree of maturity, and for minds to reach the necessary degree of maturity the development that takes place from generation to generation is as much needed as that which takes place from infancy to adult life.

In this connexion it may be well to refer briefly to a theory which has enjoyed much popularity, particularly in France—the theory of the sociological school of Durkheim and Lévy-Bruhl, which seeks to replace moral philosophy by the 'science des mœurs,' the historical and comparative study of the moral beliefs and practices of mankind. It would be foolish to deny the value of such a study, or the interest of many of the facts it has brought to light with regard to the historical origin of many such beliefs and practices. It has shown with success that many of the most strongly felt repulsions towards certain types of conduct are relics of a bygone system of totems and fetishes, their connexion with which is little suspected by those who feel them. What must be denied is the capacity of any such inquiry to take the place of moral philosophy. The attitude of the sociological school towards the systems of moral belief that they find current in various ages and races is a curiously inconsistent one. On the one hand we are urged to accept an existing code as something analogous to an existing law of nature, something not to be questioned or criticized but to be accepted and conformed to as part of the given scheme of things; and on this side the school is able sincerely to proclaim itself conservative of moral values, and is indeed conservative to the point of advocating the acceptance in full of conventional morality. On the other hand, by showing that any given code is the product partly of bygone superstitions and partly of out-of-date utilities, it is bound to create in the mind of any one who accepts its teaching (as it presupposes in the mind of the teacher) a sceptical attitude towards any and every given code. In fact the analogy which it draws between a moral code and a natural system like the human body (a favourite comparison) is an entirely fallacious one. By analysing the constituents of the human body you do nothing to diminish the reality of the human body as a given fact, and you learn much which will enable you to deal effectively with its diseases. But beliefs have the characteristics which bodies have not, of being true or false, of resting on knowledge or of being the product of wishes, hopes, and fears; and in so far as you can exhibit them as being the product of purely psychological and nonlogical causes of this sort, while you leave intact the fact that many people hold such opinions you remove their authority and their claim to be carried out in practice.

It is often said, in criticism of views such as those of the sociological school, that the question of the validity of a moral code is quite independent of the question of its origin. This does not seem to me to be true. An inquiry into the origin of a judgement may have the effect of establishing its validity. Take, for instance, the judgement that the angles of a triangle are equal to two right angles. We find that the historical origin of this judgement lies in certain pre-existing judgements which are its premises, plus the exercise of a certain activity of inferring. Now if we find that these pre-existing judgements were really instances of knowing, and that the inferring was also really knowing—was the apprehension of a necessary connexion—our inquiry into the origin of the judgement in question will have established its validity. On the other hand, if any one can show that *A* holds actions of type *B* to be wrong simply because (for instance) he knows such actions to be forbidden by the society he lives in, he shows that *A* has no real reason for believing that such actions have the specific quality of wrongness, since between being forbidden by the community and being wrong there is no necessary connexion. He does not, indeed, show the belief to be untrue, but he shows that *A* has no sufficient reason for holding it true; and in this sense he undermines its validity.

This is, in principle, what the sociological school attempts to do. According to this school, or rather according to its principles if consistently carried out, no one moral code is any truer, any nearer to the apprehension of an objective moral truth, than any other; each is simply the code that is necessitated by the conditions of its time and place, and is that which most completely conduces to the preservation of the society that accepts it. But the human mind will not rest content with such a view. It is not in the least bound to say that there has been constant progress in morality, or in moral belief. But it is competent to see that the moral code of one race or age is in certain respects inferior to that of another. It has in fact an *a priori* insight into certain broad principles of morality, and it can distinguish between a more and a less adequate recognition of these principles. There are not merely so many moral codes which can be described and whose vagaries can be traced to historical causes; there is a system of moral truth, as objective as all truth must be, which, and whose implications, we are interested in discovering; and from the point of view of this, the genuinely ethical problem, the sociological inquiry is simply beside the mark. It does not touch the questions to which we most desire answers.[1]

II. What Makes Right Acts Right?

The real point at issue between hedonism and utilitarianism on the one hand and their opponents on the other is not whether 'right' means 'productive of so and so'; for it cannot with any plausibility be maintained that it does. The point at issue is that to which we now pass, viz. whether there is any general character which makes right acts right, and if so, what it is. Among the main historical attempts to state a single characteristic of all right actions which is the foundation of their rightness are those made by egoism and utilitarianism. But I do not propose to discuss these, not because the subject is unimportant, but because it has been dealt with so often and so well already, and because there has come to be so much agreement among moral philosophers that neither of these theories is satisfactory. A much more attractive theory has been put forward by Professor Moore: that what makes actions right is that they are productive of more *good* than could have been produced by any other action open to the agent.[2]

This theory is in fact the culmination of all the attempts to base rightness on productivity of some sort of result. The first form this attempt takes is the attempt to base rightness on conduciveness to the advantage or pleasure of the agent. This theory comes to grief over the fact, which stares us in the face, that a great part of duty consists in an observance of the rights and a furtherance of the interests of others, whatever the cost to ourselves may be. Plato and others may be right in holding that a regard for the rights of others never in the long run involves a loss of happiness for the agent, that 'the just life profits a man.' But this, even if true, is irrelevant to the rightness of the act. As soon as a man does an action *because* he thinks he will promote his own interests thereby, he is acting not from a sense of its rightness but from self-interest.

To the egoistic theory hedonistic utilitarianism supplies a much-needed amendment. It points out correctly that the fact that a certain pleasure will be enjoyed by the agent is no reason why he *ought* to bring it into being rather than an equal or greater

---

1. For a lucid and up to a point appreciative account of the sociological school, and a penetrating criticism of its deficiencies, see ch. 2 of M. D. Parodi's *La Problème Morale et la Pensée Contemporaine*.

2. I take the theory which, as I have tried to show, seems to be put forward in *Ethics* rather than the earlier and less plausible theory put forward in *Principia Ethica*. . . .

pleasure to be enjoyed by another, though, human nature being what it is, it makes it not unlikely that he *will* try to bring it into being. But hedonistic utilitarianism in its turn needs a correction. On reflection it seems clear that pleasure is not the only thing in life that we think good in itself, that for instance we think the possession of a good character, or an intelligent understanding of the world, as good or better. A great advance is made by the substitution of 'productive of the greatest good' for 'productive of the greatest pleasure.'

Not only is this theory more attractive than hedonistic utilitarianism, but its logical relation to that theory is such that the latter could not be true unless *it* were true, while it might be true though hedonistic utilitarianism were not. It is in fact one of the logical bases of hedonistic utilitarianism. For the view that what produces the maximum pleasure is right has for its bases the views (1) that what produces the maximum good is right, and (2) that pleasure is the only thing good in itself. If they were not assuming that what produces the maximum *good* is right, the utilitarians' attempt to show that pleasure is the only thing good in itself, which is in fact the point they take most pains to establish, would have been quite irrelevant to their attempt to prove that only what produces the maximum *pleasure* is right. If, therefore, it can be shown that productivity of the maximum good is not what makes all right actions right, we shall *a fortiori* have refuted hedonistic utilitarianism.

When a plain man fulfils a promise because he thinks he ought to do so, it seems clear that he does so with no thought of its total consequences, still less with any opinion that these are likely to be the best possible. He thinks in fact much more of the past than of the future. What makes him think it right to act in a certain way is the fact that he has promised to do so—that and, usually, nothing more. That his act will produce the best possible consequences is not his reason for calling it right. What lends colour to the theory we are examining, then, is not the actions (which form probably a great majority of our actions) in which some such reflection as 'I have promised' is the only reason we give ourselves for thinking a certain action right, but the exceptional cases in which the consequences of fulfilling a promise (for instance) would be so disastrous to others that we judge it right not to do so. It must of course be admitted that such cases exist. If I have promised to meet a friend at a particular time for some trivial purpose, I should certainly think myself justified in breaking my engagement if by doing so I could prevent a serious accident or bring relief to the victims of one. And the supporters of the view we are examining hold that my thinking so is due to my thinking that I shall bring more good into existence by the one action than by the other. A different account may, however, be given of the matter, an account which will, I believe, show itself to be the true one. It may be said that besides the duty of fulfilling promises I have and recognize a duty of relieving distress,[1] and that when I think it right to do the latter at the cost of not doing the former, it is not because I think I shall produce more good thereby but because I think it the duty which is in the circumstances more of a duty. This account surely corresponds much more closely with what we really think in such a situation. If, so far as I can see, I could bring equal amounts of good into being by fulfilling my promise and by helping some one to whom I had made no promise, I should not hesitate to regard the former as my duty. Yet on the view that what is right is right because it is productive of the most good I should not so regard it.

There are two theories, each in its way simple, that offer a solution of such cases of conscience. One is the view of Kant, that there are certain duties of perfect obligation, such as those of fulfilling promises, of paying debts, of telling the truth, which admit of no exception whatever in favour of duties of imperfect obligation, such as that of relieving distress. The other is the view of, for instance, Professor Moore and Dr. Rashdall, that there is only the duty of producing good, and that all 'conflicts of duties' should be resolved by asking 'by which action will most good be produced?' But it is more important that our theory fit the facts than that it be simple, and the account we have given above corresponds (it seems to me) better than either of the simpler theories with what we really think, viz. that normally promise-keeping, for example, should come before benevolence, but that when and only when the good to be produced by the benevolent act is very great and the promise comparatively trivial, the act of benevolence becomes our duty.

---

1. These are not strictly speaking duties, but things that tend to be our duty, or *prima facie* duties.

In fact the theory of 'ideal utilitarianism,' if I may for brevity refer so to the theory of Professor Moore, seems to simplify unduly our relations to our fellows. It says, in effect, that the only morally significant relation in which my neighbours stand to me is that of being possible beneficiaries by my action.[1] They do stand in this relation to me, and this relation is morally significant. But they may also stand to me in the relation of promisee to promiser, of creditor to debtor, of wife to husband, of child to parent, of friend to friend, of fellow countryman to fellow countryman, and the like; and each of these relations is the foundation of a *prima facie* duty, which is more or less incumbent on me according to the circumstances of the case. When I am in a situation, as perhaps I always am, in which more than one of these *prima facie* duties is incumbent on me, what I have to do is to study the situation as fully as I can until I form the considered opinion (it is never more) that in the circumstances one of them is more incumbent than any other; then I am bound to think that to do this *prima facie* duty is my duty *sans phrase* in the situation.

I suggest '*prima facie* duty' or 'conditional duty' as a brief way of referring to the characteristic (quite distinct from that of being a duty proper) which an act has, in virtue of being of a certain kind (e.g. the keeping of a promise), of being an act which would be a duty proper if it were not at the same time of another kind which is morally significant. Whether an act is a duty proper or actual duty depends on *all* the morally significant kinds it is an instance of. The phrase '*prima facie* duty' must be apologized for, since (1) it suggests that what we are speaking of is a certain kind of duty, whereas it is in fact not a duty, but something related in a special way to duty. Strictly speaking, we want not a phrase in which duty is qualified by an adjective, but a separate noun. (2) '*Prima*' *facie* suggests that one is speaking only of an appearance which a moral situation presents at first sight, and which may turn out to be illusory; whereas what I am speaking of is an objective fact involved in the nature of the situation, or more strictly in an element of its nature, though not, as duty proper does, arising from its *whole* nature. I can, however, think of no term which fully meets the case. 'Claim' has been suggested by Professor Prichard. The word 'claim' has the advantage of being quite a familiar one in this connexion, and it seems to cover much of the ground. It would be quite natural to say, 'a person to whom I have made a promise has a claim on me,' and also, 'a person whose distress I could relieve (at the cost of breaking the promise) has a claim on me.' But (1) while 'claim' is appropriate from *their* point of view, we want a word to express the corresponding fact from the agent's point of view—the fact of his being subject to claims that can be made against him; and ordinary language provides us with no such correlative to 'claim.' And (2) (what is more important) 'claim' seems inevitably to suggest two persons, one of whom might make a claim on the other; and while this covers the ground of social duty, it is inappropriate in the case of that important part of duty which is the duty of cultivating a certain kind of character in oneself. It would be artificial, I think, and at any rate metaphorical, to say that one's character has a claim on oneself.

There is nothing arbitrary about these *prima facie* duties. Each rests on a definite circumstance which cannot seriously be held to be without moral significance. Of *prima facie* duties I suggest, without claiming completeness or finality for it, the following division.[2]

(1) Some duties rest on previous acts of my own. These duties seem to include two kinds, (*a*) those resting on a promise or what may fairly be called an

---

1. Some will think it, apart from other considerations, a sufficient refutation of this view to point out that I also stand in that relation to myself, so that for this view the distinction of oneself from others is morally insignificant.

2. I should make it plain at this stage that I am assuming the correctness of some of our main convictions as to *prima facie* duties, or, more strictly, am claiming that we *know* them to be true. To me it seems as self-evident as anything could be, that to make a promise, for instance, is to create a moral claim on us in someone else. Many readers will perhaps say that they do *not* know this to be true. If so, I certainly cannot prove it to them; I can only ask them to reflect again, in the hope that they will ultimately agree that they also know it to be true. The main moral convictions of the plain man seem to me to be, not opinions which it is for philosophy to prove or disprove, but knowledge from the start; and in my own case I seem to find little difficulty in distinguishing these essential convictions from other moral convictions which L also have, which are merely fallible opinions based on an imperfect study of the working for good or evil of certain institutions or types of action.

implicit promise, such as the implicit undertaking not to tell lies which seems to be implied in the act of entering into conversation (at any rate by civilized men), or of writing books that purport to be history and not fiction. These may be called the duties of fidelity. *(b)* Those resting on a previous wrongful act. These may be called the duties of reparation. (2) Some rest on previous acts of other men, i.e. services done by them to me. These may be loosely described as the duties of gratitude. (3) Some rest on the fact or possibility of a distribution of pleasure or happiness (or of the means thereto) which is not in accordance with the merit of the persons concerned; in such cases there arises a duty to upset or prevent such a distribution. These are the duties of justice. (4) Some rest on the mere fact that there are other beings in the world whose condition we can make better in respect of virtue, or of intelligence, or of pleasure. These are the duties of beneficence. (5) Some rest on the fact that we can improve our own condition in respect of virtue or of intelligence. These are the duties of self-improvement. (6) I think that we should distinguish from (4) the duties that may be summed up under the title of 'not injuring others.' No doubt to injure others is incidentally to fail to do them good; but it seems to me clear that non-maleficence is apprehended as a duty distinct from that of beneficence, and as a duty of a more stringent character. It will be noticed that this alone among the types of duty has been stated in a negative way. An attempt might no doubt be made to state this duty, like the others, in a positive way. It might be said that it is really the duty to prevent ourselves from acting either from an inclination to harm others or from an inclination to seek our own pleasure, in doing which we should incidentally harm them. But on reflection it seems clear that the primary duty here is the duty not to harm others, this being a duty whether or not we have an inclination that if followed would lead to our harming them; and that when we have such an inclination the primary duty not to harm others gives rise to a consequential duty to resist the inclination. The recognition of this duty of non-maleficence is the first step on the way to the recognition of the duty of beneficence; and that accounts for the prominence of the commands 'thou shalt not kill,' 'thou shalt not commit adultery,' 'thou shalt not steal,' 'thou shalt not bear false witness,' in so early a code as the Decalogue. But even when we have come to recognize the duty of beneficence, it appears to me that the duty of non-maleficence is recognized as a distinct one, and as *prima facie* more binding. We should not in general consider it justifiable to kill one person in order to keep another alive, or to steal from one in order to give alms to another.

The essential defect of the 'ideal utilitarian' theory is that it ignores, or at least does not do full justice to, the highly personal character of duty. If the only duty is to produce the maximum of good, the question who is to have the good—whether it is myself, or my benefactor, or a person to whom I have made a promise to confer that good on him, or a mere fellow man to whom I stand in no such special relation—should make no difference to my having a duty to produce that good. But we are all in fact sure that it makes a vast difference.

One or two other comments must be made on this provisional list of the provisions of duty. (1) The nomenclature is not strictly correct. For by 'fidelity' or 'gratitude' we mean, strictly, certain states of motivation; and, as I have urged, it is not our duty to have certain motives, but to do certain acts. By 'fidelity,' for instance, is meant, strictly, the disposition to fulfil promises and implicit promises *because we have made them.* We have no general word to cover the actual fulfilment of promises and implicit promises *irrespective of motive;* and I use 'fidelity,' loosely but perhaps conveniently, to fill this gap. So too I use 'gratitude' for the returning of services, irrespective of motive. The term 'justice' is not so much confined, in ordinary usage, to a certain state of motivation, for we should often talk of a man as acting justly even when we did not think his motive was the wish to do what was just simply for the sake of doing so. Less apology is therefore needed for our use of 'justice' in this sense. And I have used the word 'beneficence' rather than 'benevolence,' in order to emphasize the fact that it is our duty to do certain things, and not to do them from certain motives.

(2) If the objection be made, that this catalogue of the main types of duty is an unsystematic one resting on no logical principle, it may be replied, first, that it makes no claim to being ultimate. It is a *prima facie* classification of the duties which reflection on our moral convictions seems actually to reveal. And if these convictions are, as I would claim that they

are, of the nature of knowledge, and if I have not misstated them, the list will be a list of authentic conditional duties, correct as far as it goes though not necessarily complete. The list of *goods* put forward by the rival theory is reached by exactly the same method—the only sound one in the circumstances—viz. that of direct reflection on what we really think. Loyalty to the facts is worth more than a symmetrical architectonic or a hastily reached simplicity. If further reflection discovers a perfect logical basis for this or for a better classification, so much the better.

(3) It may, again, be objected that our theory that there are these various and often conflicting types of *prima facie* duty leaves us with no principle upon which to discern what is our actual duty in particular circumstances. But this objection is not one which the rival theory is in a position to bring forward. For when we have to choose between the production of two heterogeneous goods, say knowledge and pleasure, the 'ideal utilitarian' theory can only fall back on an opinion, for which no logical basis can be offered, that one of the goods is the greater; and this is no better than a similar opinion that one of two duties is the more urgent. And again, when we consider the infinite variety of the effects of our actions in the way of pleasure, it must surely be admitted that the claim which *hedonism* sometimes makes, that it offers a readily applicable criterion of right conduct, is quite illusory.

I am unwilling, however, to content myself with an *argumentum ad hominem,* and I would contend that in principle there is no reason to anticipate that every act that is our duty is so for one and the same reason. Why should two sets of circumstances, or one set of circumstances, *not* possess different characteristics, any one of which makes a certain act our *prima facie* duty? When I ask what it is that makes me in certain cases sure that I have a *prima facie* duty to do so and so, I find that it lies in the fact that I have made a promise; when I ask the same question in another case, I find the answer lies in the fact that I have done a wrong. And if on reflection I find (as I think I do) that neither of these reasons is reducible to the other, I must not on any *a priori* ground assume that such a reduction is possible.

An attempt may be made to arrange in a more systematic way the main types of duty which we have indicated. In the first place it seems self-evident that if there are things that are intrinsically good, it is *prima facie* a duty to bring them into existence rather than not to do so, and to bring as much of them into existence as possible. It will be argued in our fifth chapter that there are three main things that are intrinsically good—virtue, knowledge, and, with certain limitations, pleasure. And since a given virtuous disposition, for instance, is equally good whether it is realized in myself or in another, it seems to be my duty to bring it into existence whether in myself or in another. So too with a given piece of knowledge.

The case of pleasure is difficult; for while we clearly recognize a duty to produce pleasure for others, it is by no means so clear that we recognize a duty to produce pleasure for ourselves. This appears to arise from the following facts. The thought of an act as our duty is one that presupposes a certain amount of reflection about the act; and for that reason does not normally arise in connexion with acts towards which we are already impelled by another strong impulse. So far, the cause of our not thinking of the promotion of our own pleasure as a duty is analogous to the cause which usually prevents a highly sympathetic person from thinking of the promotion of the pleasure of others as a duty. He is impelled so strongly by direct interest in the well-being of others towards promoting their pleasure that he does not stop to ask whether it is his duty to promote it; and we are all impelled so strongly towards the promotion of our own pleasure that we do not stop to ask whether it is a duty or not. But there is a further reason why even when we stop to think about the matter it does not usually present itself as a duty: viz. that, since the performance of most of our duties involves the giving up of some pleasure that we desire, the doing of duty and the getting of pleasure for ourselves come by a natural association of ideas to be thought of as incompatible things. This association of ideas is in the main salutary in its operation, since it puts a check on what but for it would be much too strong, the tendency to pursue one's own pleasure without thought of other considerations. Yet if pleasure is good, it seems in the long run clear that it is right to get it for ourselves as well as to produce it for others, when this does not involve the failure to discharge some more stringent *prima facie* duty. The question is a very difficult one, but it seems that this conclusion can be denied only on one or other of three grounds: (1) that pleasure is not *prima facie* good (i.e. good when it is neither the actualization of a bad disposition nor undeserved), (2) that there is no *prima facie* duty to produce as much that is good as we can, or (3) that though there is a *prima facie* duty to produce other things that are good, there is no *prima facie* duty to produce pleasure which will be enjoyed by ourselves. I give reasons later for not accepting the first contention. The second hardly admits of argument but seems to me plainly false. The third seems plausible only if we hold that an act that is pleasant or brings pleasure to ourselves must for that reason not be a duty; and this would lead to paradoxical consequences, such as that if a man enjoys giving pleasure to others or working for their moral improvement, it cannot be his duty to do so. Yet it seems to be a very stubborn fact, that in our ordinary consciousness we are not aware of a duty to get pleasure for ourselves; and by way of partial explanation of this I may add that though, as I think, one's own pleasure is a good and there is a duty to produce it, it is only if we *think* of our own pleasure not as simply our own pleasure, but as an objective good, something that an impartial spectator would approve, that we can think of the getting it as a duty; and we do not habitually think of it in this way.

If these contentions are right, what we have called the duty of beneficence and the duty of self-improvement rest on the same ground. No different principles of duty are involved in the two cases. If we feel a special responsibility for improving our own character rather than that of others, it is not because a special principle is involved, but because we are aware that the one is more under our control than the other. It was on this ground that Kant expressed the practical law of duty in the form 'seek to make yourself good and other people happy.' He was so persuaded of the internality of virtue that he regarded any attempt by one person to produce virtue in another as bound to produce, at most, only a counterfeit of virtue, the doing of externally right acts not from the true principle of virtuous action but out of regard to another person. It must be admitted that one man cannot compel another to be virtuous; compulsory virtue would just not be virtue. But experience clearly shows that Kant overshoots the mark when he contends that one man cannot do anything to *promote* virtue in another, to

bring such influences to bear upon him that his own response to them is more likely to be virtuous than his response to other influences would have been. And our duty to do this is not different in kind from our duty to improve our own characters.

It is equally clear, and clear at an earlier stage of moral development, that if there are things that are bad in themselves we ought, *prima facie,* not to bring them upon others; and on this fact rests the duty of non-maleficence.

The duty of justice is particularly complicated, and the word is used to cover things which are really very different—things such as the payment of debts, the reparation of injuries done by oneself to another, and the bringing about of a distribution of happiness between other people in proportion to merit. I use the word to denote only the last of these three. In the fifth chapter I shall try to show that besides the three (comparatively) simple goods, virtue, knowledge, and pleasure, there is a more complex good, not reducible to these, consisting in the proportionment of happiness to virtue. The bringing of this about is a duty which we owe to all men alike, though it may be reinforced by special responsibilities that we have undertaken to particular men. This, therefore, with beneficence and self-improvement, comes under the general principle that we should produce as much good as possible, though the good here involved is different in kind from any other.

But besides this general obligation, there are special obligations. These may arise, in the first place, incidentally, from acts which were not essentially meant to create such an obligation, but which nevertheless create it. From the nature of the case such acts may be of two kinds—the infliction of injuries on others, and the acceptance of benefits from them. It seems clear that these put us under a special obligation to other men, and that only these acts can do so incidentally. From these arise the twin duties of reparation and gratitude.

And finally there are special obligations arising from acts the very intention of which, when they were done, was to put us under such an obligation. The name for such acts is 'promises'; the name is wide enough if we are willing to include under it implicit promises, i.e. modes of behaviour in which without explicit verbal promise we intentionally create an expectation that we can be counted on to behave in a certain way in the interest of another person.

These seem to be, in principle, all the ways in which *prima facie* duties arise. In actual experience they are compounded together in highly complex ways. Thus, for example, the duty of obeying the laws of one's country arises partly (as Socrates contends in the *Crito*) from the duty of gratitude for the benefits one has received from it; partly from the implicit promise to obey which seems to be involved in permanent residence in a country whose laws we know we are *expected* to obey, and still more clearly involved when we ourselves invoke the protection of its laws (this is the truth underlying the doctrine of the social contract); and partly (if we are fortunate in our country) from the fact that its laws are potent instruments for the general good.

Or again, the sense of a general obligation to bring about (so far as we can) a just apportionment of happiness to merit is often greatly reinforced by the fact that many of the existing injustices are due to a social and economic system which we have, not indeed created, but taken part in and assented to; the duty of justice is then reinforced by the duty of reparation.

It is necessary to say something by way of clearing up the relation between *prima facie* duties and the actual or absolute duty to do one particular act in particular circumstances. If, as almost all moralists except Kant are agreed, and as most plain men think, it is sometimes right to tell a lie or to break a promise, it must be maintained that there is a difference between *prima facie* duty and actual or absolute duty. When we think ourselves justified in breaking, and indeed morally obliged to break, a promise in order to relieve some one's distress, we do not for a moment cease to recognize a *prima facie* duty to keep our promise, and this leads us to feel, not indeed shame or repentance, but certainly compunction, for behaving as we do; we recognize, further, that it is our duty to make up somehow to the promisee for the breaking of the promise. We have to distinguish from the characteristic of being our duty that of tending to be our duty. Any act that we do contains various elements in virtue of which it falls under various categories. In virtue of being the breaking of a promise, for instance, it tends to be wrong; in virtue of being an instance of relieving distress it tends to be right. Tendency to be one's duty may be called a parti-resultant, attribute, i.e. one which belongs to an act in virtue of some one component in its nature.

Being one's duty is a toti-resultant attribute, one which belongs to an act in virtue of its whole nature and of nothing less than this. This distinction between parti-resultant and toti-resultant attributes is one which we shall meet in another context also.

Another instance of the same distinction may be found in the operation of natural laws. *Qua* subject to the force of gravitation towards some other body, each body tends to move in a particular direction with a particular velocity; but its actual movement depends on *all* the forces to which it is subject. It is only by recognizing this distinction that we can preserve the absoluteness of laws of nature, and only by recognizing a corresponding distinction that we can preserve the absoluteness of the general principles of morality. But an important difference between the two cases must be pointed out. When we say that in virtue of gravitation a body tends to move in a certain way, we are referring to a causal influence actually exercised on it by another body or other bodies. When we say that in virtue of being deliberately untrue a certain remark tends to be wrong, we are referring to no causal relation, to no relation that involves succession in time, but to such a relation as connects the various attributes of a mathematical figure. And if the word 'tendency' is thought to suggest too much a causal relation, it is better to talk of certain types of act as being *prima facie* right or wrong (or of different persons as having different and possibly conflicting claims upon us), than of their tending to be right or wrong.

Something should be said of the relation between our apprehension of the *prima facie* rightness of certain types of act and our mental attitude towards particular acts. It is proper to use the word 'apprehension' in the former case and not in the latter. That an act, *qua* fulfilling a promise, or *qua* effecting a just distribution of good, or *qua* returning services rendered, or *qua* promoting the good of others, or *qua* promoting the virtue or insight of the agent, is *prima facie* right, is self-evident; not in the sense that it is evident from the beginning of our lives, or as soon as we attend to the proposition for the first time, but in the sense that when we have reached sufficient mental maturity and have given sufficient attention to the proposition it is evident without any need of proof, or of evidence beyond itself. It is self-evident just as a mathematical axiom, or the validity of a form of inference, is evident. The moral order expressed in these propositions is just as much part of the fundamental nature of the universe (and, we may add, of any possible universe in which there were moral agents at all) as is the spatial or numerical structure expressed in the axioms of geometry or arithmetic. In our confidence that these propositions are true there is involved the same trust in our reason that is involved in our confidence in mathematics; and we should have no justification for trusting it in the latter sphere and distrusting it in the former. In both cases we are dealing with propositions that cannot be proved, but that just as certainly need no proof.

Some of these general principles of *prima facie* duty may appear to be open to criticism. It may be thought, for example, that the principle of returning good for good is a falling off from the Christian principle, generally and rightly recognized as expressing the highest morality, of returning good for evil. To this it may be replied that I do not suggest that there is a principle commanding us to return good for good and forbidding us to return good for evil, and that I do suggest that there is a positive duty to seek the good of all men. What I maintain is that an act in which good is returned for good is recognized as *specially* binding on us just because it is of that character, and that *ceteris paribus* any one would think it his duty to help his benefactors rather than his enemies, if he could not do both; just as it is generally recognized that *ceteris paribus* we should pay our debts rather than give our money in charity, when we cannot do both. A benefactor is not only a man, calling for our effort on his behalf on that ground, but also our benefactor, calling for our *special* effort on *that* ground.

Our judgements about our actual duty in concrete situations have none of the certainty that attaches to our recognition of the general principles of duty. A statement is certain, i.e. is an expression of knowledge, only in one or other of two cases: when it is either self-evident, or a valid conclusion from self-evident premises. And our judgements about our particular duties have neither of these characters. (1) They are not self-evident. Where a possible act is seen to have two characteristics, in virtue of one of which it is *prima facie* right, and in virtue of the other *prima facie* wrong, we are (I think) well aware that we are not certain whether we ought or ought not to do it; that whether we do it or not, we are taking a moral risk. We come in the long run,

after consideration, to think one duty more pressing than the other, but we do not feel certain that it is so. And though we do not always recognize that a possible act has two such characteristics, and though there *may* be cases in which it has not, we are never certain that any particular possible act has not, and therefore never certain that it is right, nor certain that it is wrong. For, to go no further in the analysis, it is enough to point out that any particular act will in all probability in the course of time contribute to the bringing about of good or of evil for many human beings, and thus have a *prima facie* rightness or wrongness of which we know nothing. (2) Again, our judgements about our particular duties are not logical conclusions from self-evident premises. The only possible premises would be the general principles stating their *prima facie* rightness or wrongness *qua* having the different characteristics they do have; and even if we could (as we cannot) apprehend the extent to which an act will tend on the one hand, for example, to bring about advantages for our benefactors, and on the other hand to bring about disadvantages for fellow men who are not our benefactors, there is no principle by which we can draw the conclusion that it is on the whole right or on the whole wrong. In this respect the judgement as to the rightness of a particular act is just like the judgement as to the beauty of a particular natural object or work of art. A poem is, for instance, in respect of certain qualities beautiful and in respect of certain others not beautiful; and our judgement as to the degree of beauty it possesses on the whole is never reached by logical reasoning from the apprehension of its particular beauties or particular defects. Both in this and in the moral case we have more or less probable opinions which are not logically justified conclusions from the general principles that are recognized as self-evident.

There is therefore much truth in the description of the right act as a fortunate act. If we cannot be certain that it is right, it is our good fortune if the act we do is the right act. This consideration does not, however, make the doing of our duty a mere matter of chance. There is a parallel here between the doing of duty and the doing of what will be to our personal advantage. We never *know* what act will in the long run be to our advantage. Yet it is certain that we are more likely in general to secure our advantage if we estimate to the best of our ability the probable tendencies of our actions in this respect, than if we act on caprice. And similarly we are more likely to do our duty if we reflect to the best of our ability on the *prima facie* rightness or wrongness of various possible acts in virtue of the characteristics we perceive them to have, than if we act without reflection. With this greater likelihood we must be content.

Many people would be inclined to say that the right act for me is not that whose general nature I have been describing, viz. that which if I were omniscient I should see to be my duty, but that which on all the evidence available to me I should think to be my duty. But suppose that from the state of partial knowledge in which I think act *A* to be my duty, I could pass to a state of perfect knowledge in which I saw act *B* to be my duty, should I not say 'act *B* was the right act for me to do?' I should no doubt add 'though I am not to be blamed for doing act *A*.' But in adding this, am I not passing from the question 'what is right' to the question 'what is morally good?' At the same time I am not making the *full* passage from the one notion to the other; for in order that the act should be morally good, or an act I am not to be blamed for doing, it must not merely be the act which it is reasonable for me to think my duty; it must also be done for that reason, or from some other morally good motive. Thus the conception of the right act as the act which it is reasonable for me to think my duty is an unsatisfactory compromise between the true notion of the right act and the notion of the morally good action.

The general principles of duty are obviously not self-evident from the beginning of our lives. How do they come to be so? The answer is, that they come to be self-evident to us just as mathematical axioms do. We find by experience that this couple of matches and that couple make four matches, that this couple of balls on a wire and that couple make four balls: and by reflection on these and similar discoveries we come to see that it is of the nature of two and two to make four. In a precisely similar way, we see the *prima facie* rightness of an act which would be the fulfilment of a particular promise, and of another which would be the fulfilment of another promise, and when we have reached sufficient maturity to think in general terms, we apprehend *prima facie* rightness to belong to the nature of any fulfilment of promise. What comes first in time is the apprehension of the self-evident *prima facie* rightness of an in-

dividual act of a particular type. From this we come by reflection to apprehend the self-evident general principle of *prima facie* duty. From this, too, perhaps along with the apprehension of the self-evident *prima facie* rightness of the same act in virtue of its having another characteristic as well, and perhaps in spite of the apprehension of its *prima facie* wrongness in virtue of its having some third characteristic, we come to believe something not self-evident at all, but an object of probable opinion, viz. that this particular act is (not *prima facie* but) actually right.

In this respect there is an important difference between rightness and mathematical properties. A triangle which is isosceles necessarily has two of its angles equal, whatever other characteristics the triangle may have—whatever, for instance, be its area, or the size of its third angle. The equality of the two angles is a parti-resultant attribute. And the same is true of all mathematical attributes. It is true, I may add, of *prima facie* rightness. But no act is ever, in virtue of falling under some general description, necessarily actually right; its rightness depends on its whole nature[1] and not on any element in it. The reason is that no mathematical object (no figure, for instance, or angle) ever has two characteristics that tend to give it opposite resultant characteristics, while moral acts often (as every one knows) and indeed always (as on reflection we must admit) have different characteristics that tend to make them at the same time *prima facie* right and *prima facie* wrong; there is probably no act, for instance, which does good to any one without doing harm to some one else, and *vice versa*.

Supposing it to be agreed, as I think on reflection it must, that no one *means* by 'right' just 'productive of the best possible consequences,' or 'optimific,' the attributes 'right' and 'optimific' might stand in either of two kinds of relation to each other. (1) They might be so related that we could apprehend *a priori* either immediately or deductively, that any act that is optimific is right and any act that is right is optimific, as

---

1. To avoid complicating unduly the statement of the general view I am putting forward, I have here rather overstated it. Any act is the origination of a great variety of things many of which make no difference to its rightness or wrongness. But there are always many elements in its nature (i.e. in what it is the origination of) that make a difference to its rightness or wrongness, and no element in its nature can he dismissed without consideration as indifferent.

we can apprehend that any triangle that is equilateral is equiangular and *vice versa*. Professor Moore's view is, I think, that the coextensiveness of 'right' and 'optimific' is apprehended immediately.[1] He rejects the possibility of any proof of it. Or (2) the two attributes might be such that the question whether they are invariably connected had to be answered by means of an inductive inquiry. Now at first sight it might seem as if the constant connexion of the two attributes could be immediately apprehended. It might seem absurd to suggest that it could be right for any one to do an act which would produce consequences less good than those which would be produced by some other act in his power. Yet a little thought will convince us that this is not absurd. The type of case in which it is easiest to see that this is so is, perhaps, that in which one has made a promise. In such a case we all think that *prima facie* it is our duty to fulfil the promise irrespective of the precise goodness of the total consequences. And though we do not think it is necessarily our actual or absolute duty to do so, we are far from thinking that any, even the slightest, gain in the value of the total consequences will necessarily justify us in doing something else instead. Suppose, to simplify the case by abstraction, that the fulfilment of a promise to A would produce 1,000 units of good[2] for him, but that by doing some other act I could produce 1,001 units of good for B, to whom I have made no promise, the other consequences of the two acts being of equal value; should we really think it self-evident that it was our duty to do the second act and not the first? I think not. We should, I fancy, hold that only a much greater disparity of value between the total consequences would justify us in failing to discharge our *prima facie* duty to A. After all, a promise is a promise, and is not to be treated so lightly as the theory we are examining would imply. What, exactly, a promise is, is not so easy to determine, but we are surely agreed that it constitutes a serious moral limitation to our freedom of action. To produce the 1,001 units of good for B rather than

fulfil our promise to A would be to take, not perhaps our duty as philanthropists too seriously, but certainly our duty as makers of promises too lightly.

Or consider another phase of the same problem. If I have promised to confer on A a particular benefit containing 1,000 units of good, is it self-evident that if by doing some different act I could produce 1,001 units of good for A himself (the other consequences of the two acts being supposed equal in value), it would be right for me to do so? Again, I think not. Apart from my general *prima facie* duty to do A what good I can, I have another *prima facie* duty to do him the particular service I have promised to do him, and this is not to be set aside in consequence of a disparity of good of the order of 1,001 to 1,000, though a much greater disparity might justify me in so doing.

Or again, suppose that A is a very good and B a very bad man, should I then, even when I have made no promise, think it self-evidently right to produce 1,001 units of good for B rather than 1,000 for A? Surely not. I should be sensible of a *prima facie* duty of justice, i.e. of producing a distribution of goods in proportion to merit, which is not outweighed by such a slight disparity in the total goods to be produced.

Such instances—and they might easily be added to—make it clear that there is no self-evident connexion between the attributes 'right' and 'optimific.' The theory we are examining has a certain attractiveness when applied to our decision that a particular act is our duty (though I have tried to show that it does not agree with our actual moral judgements even here). But it is not even plausible when applied to our recognition of *prima facie* duty. For if it were self-evident that the right coincides with the optimific, it should be self-evident that what is *prima facie* right is *prima facie* optimific. But whereas we are certain that keeping a promise is *prima facie* right, we are not certain that it is *prima facie* optimific (though we are perhaps certain that it is *prima facie* bonific). Our certainty that it is *prima facie* right depends not on its consequences but on its being the fulfilment of a promise. The theory we are examining involves too much difference between the evident ground of our conviction about *prima facie* duty and the alleged ground of our conviction about actual duty.

The coextensiveness of the right and the optimific is, then, not self-evident. And I can see no way of

---

1. *Ethics,* 181.

2. I am assuming that good is objectively quantitative... , but not that we can accurately assign an exact quantitative measure to it. Since it is of a definite amount, we can make the *supposition* that its amount is so-and-so, though we cannot with any confidence *assert* that it is.

proving it deductively; nor, so far as I know, has any one tried to do so. There remains the question whether it can be established inductively. Such an inquiry, to be conclusive, would have to be very thorough and extensive. We should have to take a large variety of the acts which we, to the best of our ability, judge to be right. We should have to trace as far as possible their consequences, not only for the persons directly affected but also for those indirectly affected, and to these no limit can be set. To make our inquiry thoroughly conclusive, we should have to do what we cannot do, viz. trace these consequences into an unending future. And even to make it reasonably conclusive, we should have to trace them far into the future. It is clear that the most we could possibly say is that a large variety of typical acts that are judged right appear, so far as we can trace their consequences, to produce more good than any other acts possible to the agents in the circumstances. And such a result falls far short of proving the constant connexion of the two attributes. But it is surely clear that no inductive inquiry justifying even this result has ever been carried through. The advocates of utilitarian systems have been so much persuaded either of the identity or of the self-evident connexion of the attributes 'right' and 'optimific' (or 'felicific') that they have not attempted even such an inductive inquiry as is possible. And in view of the enormous complexity of the task and the inevitable inconclusiveness of the result, it is worth no one's while to make the attempt. What, after all, would be gained by it? If, as I have tried to show, for an act to be right and to be optimific are not the same thing, and an act's being optimific is not even the ground of its being right, then if we could ask ourselves (though the question is really unmeaning) which we ought to do, right acts because they are right or optimific acts because they are optimific, our answer must be 'the former.' If they are optimific as well as right, that is interesting but not morally important; if not, we still ought to do them (which is only another way of saying that they *are* the right acts), and the question whether they are optimific has no importance for moral theory.

There is one direction in which a fairly serious attempt has been made to show the connexion of the attributes 'right' and 'optimific.' One of the most evident facts of our moral consciousness is the sense which we have of the sanctity of promises, a sense which does not, on the face of it, involve the thought that one will be bringing more good into existence by fulfilling the promise than by breaking it. It is plain, I think, that in our normal thought we consider that the fact that we have made a promise is in itself sufficient to create a duty of keeping it, the sense of duty resting on remembrance of the past promise and not on thoughts of the future consequences of its fulfilment. Utilitarianism tries to show that this is not so, that the sanctity of promises rests on the good consequences of the fulfilment of them and the bad consequences of their non-fulfilment. It does so in this way: it points out that when you break a promise you not only fail to confer a certain advantage on your promisee but you diminish his confidence, and indirectly the confidence of others, in the fulfilment of promises. You thus strike a blow at one of the devices that have been found most useful in the relations between man and man—the device on which, for example, the whole system of commercial credit rests—and you tend to bring about a state of things wherein each man, being entirely unable to rely on the keeping of promises by others, will have to do everything for himself, to the enormous impoverishment of human well-being.

To put the matter otherwise, utilitarians say that when a promise ought to be kept it is because the total good to be produced by keeping it is greater than the total good to be produced by breaking it, the former including as its main element the maintenance and strengthening of general mutual confidence, and the latter being greatly diminished by a weakening of this confidence. They say, in fact, that the case I put some pages back never arises—the case in which by fulfilling a promise I shall bring into being 1,000 units of good for my promisee, and by breaking it 1,001 units of good for some one else, the other effects of the two acts being of equal value. The other effects, they say, never are of equal value. By keeping my promise I am helping to strengthen the system of mutual confidence; by breaking it I am helping to weaken this; so that really the first act produces $1,000+x$ units of good, and the second $1,001-y$ units, and the difference between $+x$ and $-y$ is enough to outweigh the slight superiority in the *immediate* effects of the second act. In answer to this it may be pointed out that there must be some amount of good that exceeds the difference between $+x$ and

$-y$ (i.e. exceeds $x+y$); say, $x+y+z$. Let us suppose the *immediate* good effects of the second act to be assessed not at 1,001 but at $1,000+x+y+z$. Then its *net* good effects are $1,000+x+z$, i.e. greater than those of the fulfilment of the promise; and the utilitarian is bound to say forthwith that the promise should be broken. Now, we may ask whether that is really the way we think about promises? Do we really think that the production of the slightest balance of good, no matter who will enjoy it, by the breach of a promise frees us from the obligation to keep our promise? We need not doubt that a system by which promises are made and kept is one that has great advantages for the general well-being. But that is not the whole truth. To make a promise is not merely to adapt an ingenious device for promoting the general well-being; it is to put oneself in a new relation to one person in particular, a relation which creates a specifically new *prima facie* duty to him, not reducible to the duty of promoting the general well-being of society. By all means let us try to foresee the net good effects of keeping one's promise and the net good effects of breaking it, but even if we assess the first at $1,000+x$ and the second at $1,000+x+z$, the question still remains whether it is not our duty to fulfil the promise. It may be suspected, too, that the effect of a single keeping or breaking of a promise in strengthening or weakening the fabric of mutual confidence is greatly exaggerated by the theory we are examining. And if we suppose two men dying together alone, do we think that the duty of one to fulfil before he dies a promise he has made to the other would be extinguished by the fact that neither act would have any effect on the general confidence? Any one who holds this may be suspected of not having reflected on what a promise is.

I conclude that the attributes 'right' and 'optimific' are not identical, and that we do not know either by intuition, by deduction, or by induction that they coincide in their application, still less that the latter is the foundation of the former. It must be added, however, that if we are ever under no special obligation such as that of fidelity to a promisee or of gratitude to a benefactor, we ought to do what will produce most good; and that even when we are under a special obligation the tendency of acts to promote general good is one of the main factors in determining whether they are right.

In what has preceded, a good deal of use has been made of 'what we really think' about moral questions; a certain theory has been rejected because it does not agree with what we really think. It might be said that this is in principle wrong; that we should not be content to expound what our present moral consciousness tells us but should aim at a criticism of our existing moral consciousness in the light of theory. Now I do not doubt that the moral consciousness of men has in detail undergone a good deal of modification as regards the things we think right, at the hands of moral theory. But if we are told, for instance, that we should give up our view that there is a special obligatoriness attaching to the keeping of promises because it is self-evident that the only duty is to produce as much good as possible, we have to ask ourselves whether we really, when we reflect, *are* convinced that this is self-evident, and whether we really *can* get rid of our view that promise-keeping has a bindingness independent of productiveness of maximum good. In my own experience I find that I cannot, in spite of a very genuine attempt to do so; and I venture to think that most people will find the same, and that just because they cannot lose the sense of special obligation, they cannot accept as self-evident, or even as true, the theory which would require them to do so. In fact it seems, on reflection, self-evident that a promise, simply as such, is something that *prima facie* ought to be kept, and it does *not,* on reflection, seem self-evident that production of maximum good is the only thing that makes an act obligatory. And to ask us to give up at the bidding of a theory our actual apprehension of what is right and what is wrong seems like asking people to repudiate their actual experience of beauty, at the bidding of a theory which says 'only that which satisfies such and such conditions can be beautiful.' If what I have called our actual apprehension is (as I would maintain that it is) truly an apprehension, i.e. an instance of knowledge, the request is nothing less than absurd.

I would maintain, in fact, that what we are apt to describe as 'what we think' about moral questions contains a considerable amount that we do not think but know, and that this forms the standard by reference to which the truth of any moral theory has to be tested, instead of having itself to be tested by reference to any theory. I hope that I have in what precedes indicated what in my view these elements of knowledge are that are involved in our ordinary moral consciousness.

It would be a mistake to found a natural science on 'what we really think,' i.e. on what reasonably thoughtful and well-educated people think about the subjects of the science before they have studied them scientifically. For such opinions are interpretations, and often misinterpretations, of sense-experience; and the man of science must appeal from these to sense-experience itself, which furnishes his real data. In ethics no such appeal is possible. We have no more direct way of access to the facts about rightness and goodness and about what things are right or good, than by thinking about them; the moral convictions of thoughtful and well-educated people are the data of ethics just as sense-perceptions are the data of a natural science. Just as some of the latter have to be rejected as illusory, so have some of the former; but as the latter are rejected only when they are in conflict with other more accurate sense-perceptions, the former are rejected only when they are in conflict with other convictions which stand better the test of reflection. The existing body of moral convictions of the best people is the cumulative product of the moral reflection of many generations, which has developed an extremely delicate power of appreciation of moral distinctions; and this the theorist cannot afford to treat with anything other than the greatest respect. The verdicts of the moral consciousness of the best people are the foundation on which he must build; though he must first compare them with one another and eliminate any contradictions they may contain.

It is worth while to try to state more definitely the nature of the acts that are right. We may try to state first what (if anything) is the universal nature of *all* acts that are right. It is obvious that any of the acts that we do has countless effects, directly or indirectly, on countless people, and the probability is that any act, however right it be, will have adverse effects (though these may be very trivial) on some innocent people. Similarly, any wrong act will probably have beneficial effects on some deserving people. Every act therefore, viewed in some aspects, will be *prima facie* right, and viewed in others, *prima facie* wrong, and right acts can be distinguished from wrong acts only as being those which, of all those possible for the agent in the circumstances, have the greatest balance of *prima facie* rightness, in those respects in which they are *prima facie* right, over their *prima facie* wrongness, in those respects in which they are *prima facie* wrong—*prima facie* rightness and wrongness being understood in the sense previously explained. For the estimation of the comparative stringency of these *prima facie* obligations no general rules can, so far as I can see, be laid down. We can only say that a great deal of stringency belongs to the duties of 'perfect obligation'—the duties of keeping our promises, of repairing wrongs we have done, and of returning the equivalent of services we have received. For the rest, ἐν τῇ αἰσθήσει ἡ κρίσις.[1] This sense of our particular duty in particular circumstances, preceded and informed by the fullest reflection we can bestow on the act in all its bearings, is highly fallible, but it is the only guide we have to our duty.

When we turn to consider the nature of individual right acts, the first point to which attention should be called is that any act may be correctly described in an indefinite, and in principle infinite, number of ways. An act is the production of a change in the state of affairs (if we ignore, for simplicity's sake, the comparatively few cases in which it is the maintenance of an existing state of affairs; cases which, I think, raise no special difficulty). Now the only changes we can *directly* produce are changes in our own bodies or in our own minds. But these are not, as such, what as a rule we think it our duty to produce. Consider some comparatively simple act, such as telling the truth or fulfilling a promise. In the first case what I produce directly is movements of my vocal organs. But what I think it my duty to produce is a true view in some one else's mind about some fact, and between my movement of my vocal organs and this result there intervenes a series of physical events and events in his mind. Again, in the second case, I may have promised, for instance, to return a book to a friend. I may be able, by a series of movements of my legs and hands, to place it in his hands. But what I am just as likely to do, and to think I have done my duty in doing, is to send it by a messenger or to hand it to his

---

1. 'The decision rests with perception.' *Arist. Nic. Eth.* 1109 b 23, 1126 b 4.

servant or to send it by post; and in each of these cases what I *do* directly is worthless in itself and is connected by a series of intermediate links with what I do think it is my duty to bring about, viz. his receiving what I have promised to return to him. This being so, it *seems* as if what I *do* has no obligatoriness in itself and as if one or other of three accounts should be given of the matter, each of which makes rightness not belong to what I do, considered in its own nature.

(1) One of them would be that what is obligatory is not *doing* anything in the natural sense of producing any change in the state of affairs, but *aiming* at something—at, for instance, my friend's reception of the book. But this account will not do. For (*a*) to aim at something is to act from a motive consisting of the wish to bring that thing about. But we have seen that motive never forms part of the content of our duty; if anything is certain about morals, that, I think, is certain. And (*b*) if I have promised to return the book to my friend, I obviously do not fulfil my promise and do my duty merely by aiming at his receiving the book; I must see that he actually receives it. (2) A more plausible account is that which says I must do that which is likely to produce the result. But this account is open to the second of these objections, and probably also to the first. For in the first place, however likely my act may seem, even on careful consideration, and even however likely it may in fact be, to produce the result, if it does not produce it I have not done what I promised to do, i.e. have not done my duty. And secondly, when it is said that I ought to do what is likely to produce the result, what is *probably* meant is that I ought to do a certain thing as a result of the wish to produce a certain result, and of the thought that my act is likely to produce it; and this again introduces motive into the content of duty. (3) Much the most plausible of the three accounts is that which says, 'I ought to do that which will actually produce a certain result.' This escapes objection (*b*). Whether it escapes objection (*a*) or not depends on what exactly is meant. If it is meant that I ought to do a certain thing from the wish to produce a certain result and the thought that it will do so, the account is still open to objection (*a*). But if it is meant simply that I ought to do a certain thing, and that the reason why I ought to do it is that it will produce a certain result, objection (*a*) is avoided. Now this account in its second form is that which

utilitarianism gives. It says what is right is certain acts, not certain acts motivated in a certain way; and it says that acts are never right by their own nature but by virtue of the goodness of their actual results. And this account is, I think, clearly nearer the truth than one which makes the rightness of an act depend on the goodness of either the *intended* or the *likely* results.

Nevertheless, this account appears not to be the true one. For it implies that what we consider right or our duty is what we do *directly*. It is this, e.g. the packing up and posting of the book, that derives its moral significance not from its own nature but from its consequences. But this is *not* what we should describe, strictly, as our duty; our duty is to fulfil our promise, i.e. to put the book into our friend's possession. This we consider obligatory in its own nature, just because it is a fulfilment of promise, and not because of *its* consequences. But, it might be replied by the utilitarian, I do not do this; I only do something that leads up to this, and what I do has no moral significance in itself but only because of its consequences. In answer to this, however, we may point out that a cause produces not only its immediate, but also its remote consequences, and the latter no less than the former. I, therefore, not only produce the immediate movements of parts of my body but also my friend's reception of the book, which results from these. Or, if this be objected to on the grounds that I can hardly be said to have produced my friend's reception of the book when I have packed and posted it, owing to the time that has still to elapse before he receives it, and that to say I have produced the result hardly does justice to the part played by the Post Office, we may at least say that I have *secured* my friend's reception of the book. What I do is as truly describable in this way as by saying that it is the packing and posting of a book. (It is equally truly describable in many other ways; e.g. I have provided a few moments' employment for Post Office officials. But this is irrelevant to the argument.) And if we ask ourselves whether it is *qua* the packing and posting of a book, or *qua* the securing of my friend's getting what I have promised to return to him, that my action is right, it is clear that it is in the second capacity that it is right; and in this capacity, the only capacity in which it is right, it is right by its own nature and not because of its consequences.

This account may no doubt be objected to, on the ground that we are ignoring the freedom of will of the other agents—the sorter and the postman, for instance—who are equally responsible for the result. Society, it may be said, is not like a machine, in which event follows event by rigorous necessity. Some one may, for instance, in the exercise of his freedom of will, steal the book on the way. But it is to be observed that I have excluded that case, and any similar case. I am dealing with the case in which I secure my friend's receiving the book; and if he does not receive it I have not secured his receiving it. If on the other hand the book reaches its destination, that alone shows that, the system of things being what it is, the trains by which the book travels and the railway lines along which it travels being such as they are and subject to the laws they are subject to, the postal officials who handle it being such as they are, having the motives they have and being subject to the psychological laws they are subject to, my posting the book was the one further thing which was sufficient to procure my friend's receiving it. If it had not been sufficient, the result would not have followed. The attainment of the result proves the sufficiency of the means. The objection in fact rests on the supposition that there can be unmotived action, i.e. an event without a cause, and may be refuted by reflection on the universality of the law of causation.

It is equally true that non-attainment of the result proves the insufficiency of the means. If the book had been destroyed in a railway accident or stolen by a dishonest postman, that would prove that my immediate act was not sufficient to produce the desired result. We get the curious consequence that however carelessly I pack or dispatch the book, if it comes to hand I have done my duty, and however carefully I have acted, if the book does not come to hand I have not done my duty. Success and failure are the only test, and a sufficient test, of the performance of duty. Of course, I should deserve more praise in the second case than in the first; but that is an entirely different question; we must not mix up the question of right and wrong with that of the morally good and the morally bad. And that our conclusion is not as strange as at first sight it might seem is shown by the fact that if the carelessly dispatched book comes to hand, it is not my duty to send another copy, while if the carefully dispatched book does not come to hand I must send another copy to replace it. In the first case I have not my duty still to do, which shows that I have done it; in the second I have it still to do, which shows that I have not done it.

We have reached the result that my act is right *qua* being an ensuring of one of the particular states of affairs of which it is an ensuring, viz., in the case we have taken, of my friend's receiving the book I have promised to return to him. But this answer requires some correction; for it refers only to the *prima facie* rightness of my act. If to be a fulfilment of promise were a sufficient ground of the rightness of an act, all fulfilments of promises would be right, whereas it seems clear that there are cases in which some other *prima facie* duty overrides the *prima facie* duty of fulfilling a promise. The more correct answer would be that the ground of the actual rightness of the act is that, of all acts possible for the agent in the circumstances, it is that whose *prima facie* rightness in the respects in which it is *prima facie* right most outweighs its *prima facie* wrongness in any respects in which it is *prima facie* wrong. But since its *prima facie* rightness is mainly due to its being a fulfilment of promise, we may call its being so the salient element in the ground of its rightness.

Subject to this qualification, then, it is as being the production (or if we prefer the word, the securing or ensuring) of the reception by my friend of what I have promised him (or in other words as the fulfilment of my promise) that my act is right. It is not right as a packing and posting of a book. The packing and posting of the book is only incidentally right, right only because it is a fulfilment of promise, which is what is directly or essentially right.

Our duty, then, is not to do certain things which will produce certain results. Our acts, at any rate our acts of special obligation, are not right because they will produce certain results—which is the view common to all forms of utilitarianism. To say that is to say that in the case in question what is essentially right is to pack and post a book, whereas what is essentially right is to secure the possession by my friend of what I have promised to return to him. An act is not right because it, being one thing, produces good results different from itself; it is right because it is itself the production of a certain state of affairs. Such production is right in itself, apart from any consequence.

But, it might be said, this analysis applies only to acts of special obligation; the utilitarian account still holds good for the acts in which we are not under a special obligation to any person or set of persons but only under that of augmenting the general good. Now merely to have established that there are special obligations to do certain things irrespective of their consequences would be already to have made a considerable breach in the utilitarian walls; for according to utilitarianism there is no such thing, there is only the single obligation to promote the general good. But, further, on reflection it is clear that just as (in the case we have taken) my act is not only the packing and posting of a book but the fulfilling of a promise, and just as it is in the latter capacity and not in the former that it is my duty, so an act whereby I augment the general good is not only, let us say, the writing of a begging letter on behalf of a hospital, but the

producing (or ensuring) of whatever good ensues therefrom, and it is in the latter capacity and not in the former that it is right, if it is right. That which is right is right not because it is an act, one thing, which will produce another thing, an increase of the general welfare, but because it is itself the producing of an increase in the general welfare. Or, to qualify this in the necessary way, its being the production of an increase in the general welfare is the salient element in the ground of its rightness. Just as before we were led to recognize the prima facie rightness of the fulfilment of promises, we are now led to recognize the prima facie rightness of promoting the general welfare. In both cases we have to recognize the intrinsic rightness of a certain type of act, not depending on its consequences but on its own nature.

A. J. AYER

FROM *Language, Truth and Logic*

Both ethical naturalism and ethical nonnaturalism are considered cognitive theories. In other words, both kinds of theories consider moral judgments to be statements of fact that are either true or false. However, a most influential ethical theory arose in the early part of this century that was a noncognitivist theory. This theory, now known as emotive theory (or emotivism), held that moral judgments were not factual statements and, thus, were neither true nor false. Words like "good," "right," and "ought" are emotive terms, terms that are used either to indicate the attitude of the speaker (or writer) or to evoke a response in the hearer (or reader). The first formulation of this theory came from Axel Hagerstrom, a Swedish philosopher who outlined the terms of the theory in a paper published in 1911. Later, I. A. Richards and Bertrand Russell introduced the Swedish theory to the English-speaking world. It was the development of emotive theory by A. J. Ayer and C. L. Stevenson, however, that made it a force to be reckoned with in moral philosophy. An excerpt from Ayer represents emotivism in this text.

Alfred Jules Ayer was born in England in 1910 and educated at Eton and Christ Church, Oxford. He began his teaching career in 1933 at Oxford, teaching first at Christ Church and later at Wadham. In 1946, he was appointed to a position at University College, London, where he remained until being returned to Wadham in 1959.

Ayer wrote, as a young man, one of the most influential philosophical books of this century, Language, Truth and Logic. *Published in 1936, this book set out the radical theory of the emotivists in clear and vigorous prose. Ayer argued that since there are no moral facts, there can be no moral knowledge. Moral utterances are not used to state facts or assert truths. Instead their role is noncognitive: they are used to express or evoke attitudes and emotions. The role of moral philosophy, then, is not the search for the rational foundations of morality or the systematic formulation of an ethical theory, but rather an investigation of moral language.*

Ayer's revolutionary book had an enormous impact, but he did not claim that the ideas it contained were original. Ayer declared that his work was profoundly influenced by the ethical views of the historical British empiricists Berkeley and Hume (Hume could be considered an early emotivist). Yet Ayer's work also reflects the contemporary extension of that view expounded by the Vienna circle, a group of scientifically-minded philosophers who favored an anti-metaphysical movement known as logical positivism.

Emotivism became an extremely powerful and popular ethical theory, soon eclipsing Moore's intuitionism. For many of its proponents, this theory seemed to mark the culmination of work in moral philosophy. It appeared to explain why moral philosophy was destined to be marked by dispute, controversy, and a lack of agreement about all principle matters. After all, if people are merely expressing their attitudes when they make moral judgments, the prospect of bringing an opponent over to your side in a moral dispute seems futile. Yet despite its popularity, many moral philosophers eventually came to believe that something was inherently wrong in this theory. Since emotivism denied the possibility of moral reasoning, its proponents were accused of trying to discredit ethics. Eventually emotivism was repudiated by most subsequent writers on moral philosophy.

Chapter I The Elimination of Metaphysics

The traditional disputes of philosophers are, for the most part, as unwarranted as they are unfruitful. The surest way to end them is to establish beyond question what should be the purpose and method of a philosophical enquiry. And this is by no means so difficult a task as the history of philosophy would lead one to suppose. For if there are any questions which science leaves it to philosophy to answer, a straightforward process of elimination must lead to their discovery.

We may begin by criticising the metaphysical thesis that philosophy affords us knowledge of a reality transcending the world of science and common sense. Later on, when we come to define metaphysics and account for its existence, we shall find that it is possible to be a metaphysician without believing in a transcendent reality; for we shall see that many metaphysical utterances are due to the commission of logical errors, rather than to a conscious desire on the part of their authors to go beyond the limits of experience. But it is convenient for us to take the case of those who believe that it is possible to have knowledge of a transcendent reality as a starting-point for our discussion. The arguments which we use to refute them will subsequently be found to apply to the whole of metaphysics.

One way of attacking a metaphysician who claimed to have knowledge of a reality which transcended the phenomenal world would be to enquire from what premises his propositions were deduced. Must he not begin, as other men do, with the evidence of his senses? And if so, what valid process of reasoning can possibly lead him to the conception of a transcendent reality? Surely from empirical premises nothing whatsoever concerning the properties, or even the existence, of anything super-empirical can legitimately be inferred. But this objection would be met by a denial on the part of the metaphysician that his assertions were ultimately based on the evidence of his senses. He would say that he was endowed with a faculty of intellectual intuition which enabled him to know facts that could not be known through sense-experience. And even if it could be shown that he was relying on empirical premises, and that his venture into a nonempirical world was therefore logically unjustified, it would not follow that the assertions which he made concerning this nonempirical world could not be true. For the fact that a conclusion does not follow from its putative premise is not sufficient to show that it is false. Consequently one cannot overthrow a system of transcendent metaphysics merely by criticising the way in which it comes into being. What is required is rather a criticism of the nature of the actual statements which comprise it. And this is the line of argument which we shall, in fact, pursue. For we shall maintain that no statement which refers to a "reality" transcending the limits of all possible sense-experience can possibly have any literal significance; from which it must follow that the labours of those who have striven to describe such a reality have all been devoted to the production of nonsense.

It may be suggested that this is a proposition which has already been proved by Kant. But although Kant also condemned transcendent metaphysics, he did so on different grounds. For he said that the human understanding was so constituted that it lost itself in contradictions when it ventured out beyond the limits of possible experience and attempted to deal with things in themselves. And thus he made the impossibility of a transcendent metaphysic not, as we do, a matter of logic, but a matter of fact. He asserted, not that our minds could not conceivably have had the power of penetrating beyond the phenomenal world, but merely that they were in fact devoid of it. And this leads the critic to ask how, if it is possible to know only what lies within the bounds of sense-experience, the author can be justified in asserting that real things do exist beyond, and how he can tell what are the boundaries beyond which the human understanding may not venture, unless he succeeds in passing them himself. As Wittgenstein says, "in order to draw a limit to thinking, we should have to think both sides of this limit,"[1] a truth to which Bradley gives a special twist in maintaining that the man who is ready to prove that metaphysics is impossible is a brother metaphysician with a rival theory of his own.[2]

Whatever force these objections may have against the Kantian doctrine, they have none whatsoever against the thesis that I am about to set forth. It cannot here be said that the author is himself overstepping the barrier he maintains to be impassable. For the fruitlessness of attempting to transcend the limits of possible sense-experience will be deduced, not from a psychological hypothesis concerning the actual constitution of the human mind, but from the rule which determines the literal significance of language. Our charge against the metaphysician is not that he attempts to employ the understanding in a field where it cannot profitably venture, but that he produces sentences which fail to conform to the conditions under which alone a sentence can be literally significant. Nor are we ourselves obliged to talk nonsense in order to show that all sentences of a certain type are necessarily devoid of literal significance. We need only formulate the criterion which enables us to test whether a sentence expresses a genuine proposition about a matter of fact, and then point out that the sentences under consideration fail to satisfy it. And this we shall now proceed to do. We shall first of all formulate the criterion in somewhat vague terms, and then give the explanations which are necessary to render it precise.

The criterion which we use to test the genuineness of apparent statements of fact is the criterion of verifiability. We say that a sentence is factually significant to any given person, if, and only if, he knows how to verify the proposition which it purports to express—that is, if he knows what observations would lead him, under certain conditions, to accept the proposition as being true, or reject it as being false. If, on the other hand, the putative proposition is of such a character that the assumption of its truth, or falsehood, is consistent with any assumption whatsoever concerning the nature of his future experience, then, as far as he is concerned, it is, if not a tautology, a mere pseudo-proposition. The sentence expressing it may be emotionally significant to him; but it is not literally significant. And with regard to questions the procedure is the same. We enquire in every case what observations would lead us to answer the question, one way or the other; and, if none can be discovered, we must conclude that the sentence under consideration does not, as far as we are concerned, express a genuine question, however strongly its grammatical appearance may suggest that it does.

---

1. *Tractatus Logico-Philosophicus*, Preface.

2. Bradley, *Appearance and Reality*, 2nd ed., p. 1.

As the adoption of this procedure is an essential factor in the argument of this book, it needs to be examined in detail.

In the first place, it is necessary to draw a distinction between practical verifiability, and verifiability in principle. Plainly we all understand, in many cases believe, propositions which we have not in fact taken steps to verify. Many of these are propositions which we could verify if we took enough trouble. But there remain a number of significant propositions, concerning matters of fact, which we could not verify even if we chose; simply because we lack the practical means of placing ourselves in the situation where the relevant observations could be made. A simple and familiar example of such a proposition is the proposition that there are mountains on the farther side of the moon.[1] No rocket has yet been invented which would enable me to go and look at the farther side of the moon, so that I am unable to decide the matter by actual observation. But I do know what observations would decide it for me, if, as is theoretically conceivable, I were once in a position to make them. And therefore I say that the proposition is verifiable in principle, if not in practice, and is accordingly significant. On the other hand, such a metaphysical pseudo-proposition as "the Absolute enters into, but is itself incapable of, evolution and progress,"[2] is not even in principle verifiable. For one cannot conceive of an observation which would enable one to determine whether the Absolute did, or did not, enter into evolution and progress. Of course it is possible that the author of such a remark is using English words in a way in which they are not commonly used by English-speaking people, and that he does, in fact, intend to assert something which could be empirically verified. But until he makes us understand how the proposition that he wishes to express would be verified, he fails to communicate anything to us. And if he admits, as I think the author of the remark in question would have admitted, that his words were not intended to express either a tautology or a proposition which was capable, at least in principle, of being verified, then it follows that he has made an utterance which has no literal significance even for himself.

A further distinction which we must make is the distinction between the "strong" and the "weak" sense of the term "verifiable." A proposition is said to be verifiable, in the strong sense of the term, if, and only if, its truth could be conclusively established in experience. But it is verifiable, in the weak sense, if it is possible for experience to render it probable. In which sense are we using the term when we say that a putative proposition is genuine only if it is verifiable?

It seems to me that if we adopt conclusive verifiability as our criterion of significance, as some positivists have proposed,[3] our argument will prove too much. Consider, for example, the case of general propositions of law—such propositions, namely, as "arsenic is poisonous"; "all men are mortal"; "a body tends to expand when it is heated." It is of the very nature of these propositions that their truth cannot be established with certainty by any finite series of observations. But if it is recognised that such general propositions of law are designed to cover an infinite number of cases, then it must be admitted that they cannot, even in principle, be verified conclusively. And then, if we adopt conclusive verifiability as our criterion of significance, we are logically obliged to treat these general propositions of law in the same fashion as we treat the statements of the metaphysician.

In face of this difficulty, some positivists[4] have adopted the heroic course of saying that these general propositions are indeed pieces of nonsense, albeit an essentially important type of nonsense. But here the introduction of the term "important" is simply an attempt to hedge. It serves only to mark the authors' recognition that their view is somewhat too paradoxical, without in any way removing the paradox. Besides, the difficulty is not confined to the case of general propositions of law, though it is there revealed most plainly. It is hardly less obvious in the case of propositions about the remote past. For it must surely be admitted that, however strong the evidence in favour of historical statements may be, their truth can

---

1. This example has been used by Professor Schlick to illustrate the same point.

2. A remark taken at random from *Appearance and Reality*, by F. H. Bradley.

3. e.g. M. Schlick, "Positivismus und Realismus," *Erkenntnis*, Vol. I, 1930. F. Waismann, "Logische Analyse des Warscheinlichkeitsbegriffs," *Erkenntnis*, Vol. 1, 1930.

4. e.g. M. Schlick, "Die Kausalität in der gegenwärtigen Physik," *Naturwissenschaft*, Vol. 19, 1931.

never become more than highly probable. And to maintain that they also constituted an important, or unimportant, type of nonsense would be unplausible, to say the very least. Indeed, it will be our contention that no proposition, other than a tautology, can possibly be anything more than a probable hypothesis. And if this is correct, the principle that a sentence can be factually significant only if it expresses what is conclusively verifiable is self-stultifying as a criterion of significance. For it leads to the conclusion that it is impossible to make a significant statement of fact at all.

Nor can we accept the suggestion that a sentence should be allowed to be factually significant if, and only if, it expresses something which is definitely confutable by experience.[1] Those who adopt this course assume that, although no finite series of observations is ever sufficient to establish the truth of a hypothesis beyond all possibility of doubt, there are crucial cases in which a single observation, or series of observations, can definitely confute it. But, as we shall show later on, this assumption is false. A hypothesis cannot be conclusively confuted any more than it can be conclusively verified. For when we take the occurrence of certain observations as proof that a given hypothesis is false, we presuppose the existence of certain conditions. And though, in any given case, it may be extremely improbable that this assumption is false, it is not logically impossible. We shall see that there need be no self-contradiction in holding that some of the relevant circumstances are other than we have taken them to be, and consequently that the hypothesis has not really broken down. And if it is not the case that any hypothesis can be definitely confuted, we cannot hold that the genuineness of a proposition depends on the possibility of its definite confutation.

Accordingly, we fall back on the weaker sense of verification. We say that the question that must be asked about any putative statement of fact is not, Would any observations make its truth or falsehood logically certain? but simply, Would any observations be relevant to the determination of its truth or falsehood? And it is only if a negative answer is given to this second question that we conclude that the statement under consideration is nonsensical.

To make our position clearer, we may formulate it in another way. Let us call a proposition which records an actual or possible observation an experiential proposition. Then we may say that it is the mark of a genuine factual proposition, not that it should be equivalent to an experiential proposition, or any finite number of experiential propositions, but simply that some experiential propositions can be deduced from it in conjunction with certain other premises without being deducible from those other premises alone.[2]

This criterion seems liberal enough. In contrast to the principle of conclusive verifiability, it clearly does not deny significance to general propositions or to propositions about the past. Let us see what kinds of assertion it rules out.

A good example of the kind of utterance that is condemned by our criterion as being not even false but nonsensical would be the assertion that the world of sense-experience was altogether unreal. It must, of course, be admitted that our senses do sometimes deceive us. We may, as the result of having certain sensations, expect certain other sensations to be obtainable which are, in fact, not obtainable. But, in all such cases, it is further sense-experience that informs us of the mistakes that arise out of sense-experience. We say that the senses sometimes deceive us, just because the expectations to which our sense-experiences give rise do not always accord with what we subsequently experience. That is, we rely on our senses to substantiate or confute the judgements which are based on our sensations. And therefore the fact that our perceptual judgements are sometimes found to be erroneous has not the slightest tendency to show that the world of sense-experience is unreal. And, indeed, it is plain that no conceivable observation, or series of observations, could have any tendency to show that the world revealed to us by sense-experience was unreal. Consequently, anyone who condemns the sensible world as a world of mere appearance, as opposed to reality, is saying something which, according to our criterion of significance, is literally nonsensical.

---

1. This has been proposed by Karl Popper in his *Logik der Forschung*.

2. This is an over-simplified statement, which is not literally correct. I give what I believe to be the correct formulation in the Introduction.

An example of a controversy which the application of our criterion obliges us to condemn as fictitious is provided by those who dispute concerning the number of substances that there are in the world. For it is admitted both by monists, who maintain that reality is one substance, and by pluralists, who maintain that reality is many, that it is impossible to imagine any empirical situation which would be relevant to the solution of their dispute. But if we are told that no possible observation could give any probability either to the assertion that reality was one substance or to the assertion that it was many, then we must conclude that neither assertion is significant. We shall see later on[1] that there are genuine logical and empirical questions involved in the dispute between monists and pluralists. But the metaphysical question concerning "substance" is ruled out by our criterion as spurious.

A similar treatment must be accorded to the controversy between realists and idealists, in its metaphysical aspect. A simple illustration, which I have made use of in a similar argument elsewhere,[2] will help to demonstrate this. Let us suppose that a picture is discovered and the suggestion made that it was painted by Goya. There is a definite procedure for dealing with such a question. The experts examine the picture to see in what way it resembles the accredited works of Goya, and to see if it bears any marks which are characteristic of a forgery; they look up contemporary records for evidence of the existence of such a picture, and so on. In the end, they may still disagree, but each one knows what empirical evidence would go to confirm or discredit his opinion. Suppose, now, that these men have studied philosophy, and some of them proceed to maintain that this picture is a set of ideas in the perceiver's mind, or in God's mind, others that it is objectively real. What possible experience could any of them have which would be relevant to the solution of this dispute one way or the other? In the ordinary sense of the term "real," in which it is opposed to "illusory," the reality of the picture is not in doubt. The disputants have satisfied themselves that the picture is real, in this sense, by obtaining a correlated series of sensations of sight and sensations of touch. Is there any similar process by which they could discover whether the picture was real, in the sense in which the term "real" is opposed to "ideal"? Clearly there is none. But, if that is so, the problem is fictitious according to our criterion. This does not mean that the realist-idealist controversy may be dismissed without further ado. For it can legitimately be regarded as a dispute concerning the analysis of existential propositions, and so as involving a logical problem which, as we shall see, can be definitively solved.[3] What we have just shown is that the question at issue between idealists and realists becomes fictitious when, as is often the case, it is given a metaphysical interpretation.

There is no need for us to give further examples of the operation of our criterion of significance. For our object is merely to show that philosophy, as a genuine branch of knowledge, must be distinguished from metaphysics. We are not now concerned with the historical question how much of what has traditionally passed for philosophy is actually metaphysical. We shall, however, point out later on that the majority of the "great philosophers" of the past were not essentially metaphysicians, and thus reassure those who would otherwise be prevented from adopting our criterion by considerations of piety.

As to the validity of the verification principle, in the form in which we have stated it, a demonstration will be given in the course of this book. For it will be shown that all propositions which have factual content are empirical hypotheses; and that the function of an empirical hypothesis is to provide a rule for the anticipation of experience.[4] And this means that every empirical hypothesis must be relevant to some actual, or possible, experience, so that a statement which is not relevant to any experience is not an empirical hypothesis, and accordingly has no factual content. But this is precisely what the principle of verifiability asserts.

It should be mentioned here that the fact that the utterances of the metaphysician are nonsensical does not follow simply from the fact that they are devoid of factual content. It follows from that fact, together with the fact that they are not *a priori* propositions.

1. In Chapter VIII.

2. Vide "Demonstration of the Impossibility of Metaphysics," *Mind,* 1934, p. 339.

3. Vide Chapter VIII.

4. Vide Chapter V.

And in assuming that they are not *a priori* propositions, we are once again anticipating the conclusions of a later chapter in this book.[1] For it will be shown there that *a priori* propositions, which have always been attractive to philosophers on account of their certainty, owe this certainty to the fact that they are tautologies. We may accordingly define a metaphysical sentence as a sentence which purports to express a genuine proposition, but does, in fact, express neither a tautology nor an empirical hypothesis. And as tautologies and empirical hypotheses form the entire class of significant propositions, we are justified in concluding that all metaphysical assertions are nonsensical. Our next task is to show how they come to be made.

The use of the term "substance," to which we have already referred, provides us with a good example of the way in which metaphysics mostly comes to be written. It happens to be the case that we cannot, in our language, refer to the sensible properties of a thing without introducing a word or phrase which appears to stand for the thing itself as opposed to anything which may be said about it. And, as a result of this, those who are infected by the primitive superstition that to every name a single real entity must correspond assume that it is necessary to distinguish logically between the thing itself and any, or all, of its sensible properties. And so they employ the term "substance" to refer to the thing itself. But from the fact that we happen to employ a single word to refer to a thing, and make that word the grammatical subject of the sentences in which we refer to the sensible appearances of the thing, it does not by any means follow that the thing itself is a "simple entity," or that it cannot be defined in terms of the totality of its appearances. It is true that in talking of "its" appearances we appear to distinguish the thing from the appearances, but that is simply an accident of linguistic usage. Logical analysis shows that what makes these "appearances" the "appearances of" the same thing is not their relationship to an entity other than themselves, but their relationship to one another. The metaphysician fails to see this because he is misled by a superficial grammatical feature of his language.

A simpler and clearer instance of the way in which a consideration of grammar leads to meta-

physics is the case of the metaphysical concept of Being. The origin of our temptation to raise questions about Being, which no conceivable experience would enable us to answer, lies in the fact that, in our language, sentences which express existential propositions and sentences which express attributive propositions may be of the same grammatical form. For instance, the sentences "Martyrs exist" and "Martyrs suffer" both consist of a noun followed by an intransitive verb, and the fact that they have grammatically the same appearance leads one to assume that they are of the same logical type. It is seen that in the proposition "Martyrs suffer," the members of a certain species are credited with a certain attribute, and it is sometimes assumed that the same thing is true of such a proposition as "Martyrs exist." If this were actually the case, it would, indeed, be as legitimate to speculate about the Being of martyrs as it is to speculate about their suffering. But, as Kant pointed out,[2] existence is not an attribute. For, when we ascribe an attribute to a thing, we covertly assert that it exists: so that if existence were itself an attribute, it would follow that all positive existential propositions were tautologies, and all negative existential propositions self-contradictory; and this is not the case.[3] So that those who raise questions about Being which are based on the assumption that existence is an attribute are guilty of following grammar beyond the boundaries of sense.

A similar mistake has been made in connection with such propositions as "Unicorns are fictitious." Here again the fact that there is a superficial grammatical resemblance between the English sentences "Dogs are faithful" and "Unicorns are fictitious," and between the corresponding sentences in other languages, creates the assumption that they are of the same logical type. Dogs must exist in order to have the property of being faithful, and so it is held that unless unicorns in some way existed they could not have the property of being fictitious. But, as it is plainly self-contradictory to say that fictitious objects exist, the device is adopted of saying that they are real in some non-empirical sense—that they have a

---

1. Chapter IV.

2. Vide *The Critique of Pure Reason,* "Transcendental Dialectic," Book II, Chapter iii, section 4.

3. This argument is well stated by John Wisdom, *Interpretation and Analysis,* pp. 62, 63.

mode of real being which is different from the mode of being of existent things. But since there is no way of testing whether an object is real in this sense, as there is for testing whether it is real in the ordinary sense, the assertion that fictitious objects have a special non-empirical mode of real being is devoid of all literal significance. It comes to be made as a result of the assumption that being fictitious is an attribute. And this is a fallacy of the same order as the fallacy of supposing that existence is an attribute, and it can be exposed in the same way.

In general, the postulation of real non-existent entities results from the superstition, just now referred to, that, to every word or phrase that can be the grammatical subject of a sentence, there must somewhere be a real entity corresponding. For as there is no place in the empirical world for many of these "entities," a special non-empirical world is invoked to house them. To this error must be attributed, not only the utterances of a Heidegger, who bases his metaphysics on the assumption that "Nothing" is a name which is used to denote something peculiarly mysterious,[1] but also the prevalence of such problems as those concerning the reality of propositions and universals whose senselessness, though less obvious, is no less complete.

These few examples afford a sufficient indication of the way in which most metaphysical assertions come to be formulated. They show how easy it is to write sentences which are literally nonsensical without seeing that they are nonsensical. And thus we see that the view that a number of the traditional "problems of philosophy" are metaphysical, and consequently fictitious, does not involve any incredible assumptions about the psychology of philosophers.

Among those who recognise that if philosophy is to be accounted a genuine branch of knowledge it must be defined in such a way as to distinguish it from metaphysics, it is fashionable to speak of the metaphysician as a kind of misplaced poet. As his statements have no literal meaning, they are not subject to any criteria of truth or falsehood: but they may still serve to express, or arouse, emotion, and thus be subject to ethical or aesthetic standards. And

it is suggested that they may have considerable value, as means of moral inspiration, or even as works of art. In this way, an attempt is made to compensate the metaphysician for his extrusion from philosophy.[2]

I am afraid that this compensation is hardly in accordance with his deserts. The view that the metaphysician is to be reckoned among the poets appears to rest on the assumption that both talk nonsense. But this assumption is false. In the vast majority of cases the sentences which are produced by poets do have literal meaning. The difference between the man who uses language scientifically and the man who uses it emotively is not that the one produces sentences which are incapable of arousing emotion, and the other sentences which have no sense, but that the one is primarily concerned with the expression of true propositions, the other with the creation of a work of art. Thus, if a work of science contains true and important propositions, its value as a work of science will hardly be diminished by the fact that they are inelegantly expressed. And similarly, a work of art is not necessarily the worse for the fact that all the propositions comprising it are literally false. But to say that many literary works are largely composed of falsehoods, is not to say that they are composed of pseudo-propositions. It is, in fact, very rare for a literary artist to produce sentences which have no literal meaning. And where this does occur, the sentences are carefully chosen for their rhythm and balance. If the author writes nonsense, it is because he considers it most suitable for bringing about the effects for which his writing is designed.

The metaphysician, on the other hand, does not intend to write nonsense. He lapses into it through being deceived by grammar, or through committing errors of reasoning, such as that which leads to the view that the sensible world is unreal. But it is not the mark of a poet simply to make mistakes of this sort. There are some, indeed, who would see in the fact that the metaphysician's utterances are senseless a reason against the view that they have aesthetic value. And, without going so far as this, we may safely say that it does not constitute a reason for it.

---

1. Vide *Was ist Metaphysik,* by Heidegger: criticised by Rudolf Carnap in his "Uberwindung der Metaphysik durch logische Analyse der Sprache," *Erkenntnis,* Vol. II, 1932.

2. For a discussion of this point, see also C. A. Mace, "Representation and Expression," *Analysis,* Vol. I, No. 3; and "Metaphysics and Emotive Language," *Analysis,* Vol. II, Nos. 1 and 2.

It is true, however, that although the greater part of metaphysics is merely the embodiment of humdrum errors, there remain a number of metaphysical passages which are the work of genuine mystical feeling; and they may more plausibly be held to have moral or aesthetic value. But, as far as we are concerned, the distinction between the kind of metaphysics that is produced by a philosopher who has been duped by grammar, and the kind that is produced by a mystic who is trying to express the in-expressible, is of no great importance: what is important to us is to realise that even the utterances of the metaphysician who is attempting to expound a vision are literally senseless; so that henceforth we may pursue our philosophical researches with as little regard for them as for the more inglorious kind of metaphysics which comes from a failure to understand the workings of our language.

Chapter VI Critique of Ethics and Theology

There is still one objection to be met before we can claim to have justified our view that all synthetic propositions are empirical hypotheses. This objection is based on the common supposition that our speculative knowledge is of two distinct kinds—that which relates to questions of empirical fact, and that which relates to questions of value. It will be said that "statements of value" are genuine synthetic propositions, but that they cannot with any show of justice be represented as hypotheses, which are used to predict the course of our sensations; and, accordingly, that the existence of ethics and æsthetics as branches of speculative knowledge presents an insuperable objection to our radical empiricist thesis.

In face of this objection, it is our business to give an account of "judgements of value" which is both satisfactory in itself and consistent with our general empiricist principles. We shall set ourselves to show that in so far as statements of value are significant, they are ordinary "scientific" statements; and that in so far as they are not scientific, they are not in the literal sense significant, but are simply expressions of emotion which can be neither true nor false. In maintaining this view, we may confine ourselves for the present to the case of ethical statements. What is said about them will be found to apply, *mutatis mutandis,* to the case of æsthetic statements also.[1]

The ordinary system of ethics, as elaborated in the works of ethical philosophers, is very far from being a homogeneous whole. Not only is it apt to contain pieces of metaphysics, and analyses of non-ethical concepts: its actual ethical contents are themselves of very different kinds. We may divide them, indeed, into four main classes. There are, first of all, propositions which express definitions of ethical terms, or judgements about the legitimacy or possibility of certain definitions. Secondly, there are propositions describing the phenomena of moral experience, and their causes. Thirdly, there are exhortations to moral virtue. And, lastly, there are actual ethical judgements. It is unfortunately the case that the distinction between these four classes, plain as it is, is commonly ignored by ethical philosophers; with the result that it is often very difficult to tell from their works what it is that they are seeking to discover or prove.

In fact, it is easy to see that only the first of our four classes, namely that which comprises the propositions relating to the definitions of ethical terms, can be said to constitute ethical philosophy. The propositions which describe the phenomena of moral experience, and their causes, must be assigned to the science of psychology, or sociology. The exhortations to moral virtue are not propositions at all, but ejaculations or commands which are designed to provoke the reader to action of a certain sort. Accordingly, they do not belong to any branch of philosophy or science. As for the expressions of ethical judgements, we have not yet determined how they should be classified. But inasmuch as they are certainly neither definitions nor comments upon definitions, nor quotations, we may say decisively that they do not belong to ethical philosophy. A strictly philosophical treatise on ethics should therefore make no ethical pronouncements. But it should, by giving an analysis of ethical terms, show what is the category to which all such pronouncements belong. And this is what we are now about to do.

A question which is often discussed by ethical philosophers is whether it is possible to find definitions which would reduce all ethical terms to one or

---

1. The argument that follows should be read in conjunction with the Introduction.

two fundamental terms. But this question, though it undeniably belongs to ethical philosophy, is not relevant to our present enquiry. We are not now concerned to discover which term, within the sphere of ethical terms, is to be taken as fundamental; whether, for example, "good" can be defined in terms of "right" or "right" in terms of "good," or both in terms of "value." What we are interested in is the possibility of reducing the whole sphere of ethical terms to non-ethical terms. We are enquiring whether statements of ethical value can be translated into statements of empirical fact.

That they can be so translated is the contention of those ethical philosophers who are commonly called subjectivists, and of those who are known as utilitarians. For the utilitarian defines the rightness of actions, and the goodness of ends, in terms of the pleasure, or happiness, or satisfaction, to which they give rise; the subjectivist, in terms of the feelings of approval which a certain person, or group of people, has towards them. Each of these types of definition makes moral judgements into a sub-class of psychological or sociological judgements; and for this reason they are very attractive to us. For, if either was correct, it would follow that ethical assertions were not generically different from the factual assertions which are ordinarily contrasted with them; and the account which we have already given of empirical hypotheses would apply to them also.

Nevertheless we shall not adopt either a subjectivist or a utilitarian analysis of ethical terms. We reject the subjectivist view that to call an action right, or a thing good, is to say that it is generally approved of, because it is not self-contradictory to assert that some actions which are generally approved of are not right, or that some things which are generally approved of are not good. And we reject the alternative subjectivist view that a man who asserts that a certain action is right, or that a certain thing is good, is saying that he himself approves of it, on the ground that a man who confessed that he sometimes approved of what was bad or wrong would not be contradicting himself. And a similar argument is fatal to utilitarianism. We cannot agree that to call an action right is to say that of all the actions possible in the circumstances it would cause, or be likely to cause, the greatest happiness, or the greatest balance of pleasure over pain, or the greatest balance of satisfied over unsatisfied desire, because we find that it is

not self-contradictory to say that it is sometimes wrong to perform the action which would actually or probably cause the greatest happiness, or the greatest balance of pleasure over pain, or of satisfied over unsatisfied desire. And since it is not self-contradictory to say that some pleasant things are not good, or that some bad things are desired, it cannot be the case that the sentence "x is good" is equivalent to "x is pleasant," or to "x is desired." And to every other variant of utilitarianism with which I am acquainted the same objection can be made. And therefore we should, I think, conclude that the validity of ethical judgements is not determined by the felific tendencies of actions, any more than by the nature of people's feelings; but that it must be regarded as "absolute" or "intrinsic," and not empirically calculable.

If we say this, we are not, of course, denying that it is possible to invent a language in which all ethical symbols are definable in non-ethical terms, or even that it is desirable to invent such a language and adopt it in place of our own; what we are denying is that the suggested reduction of ethical to non-ethical statements is consistent with the conventions of our actual language. That is, we reject utilitarianism and subjectivism, not as proposals to replace our existing ethical notions by new ones, but as analyses of our existing ethical notions. Our contention is simply that, in our language, sentences which contain normative ethical symbols are not equivalent to sentences which express psychological propositions, or indeed empirical propositions of any kind.

It is advisable here to make it plain that it is only normative ethical symbols, and not descriptive ethical symbols, that are held by us to be indefinable in factual terms. There is a danger of confusing these two types of symbols, because they are commonly constituted by signs of the same sensible form. Thus a complex sign of the form "x is wrong" may constitute a sentence which expresses a moral judgement concerning a certain type of conduct, or it may constitute a sentence which states that a certain type of conduct is repugnant to the moral sense of a particular society. In the latter case, the symbol "wrong" is a descriptive ethical symbol, and the sentence in which it occurs expresses an ordinary sociological proposition; in the former case, the symbol "wrong" is a normative ethical symbol, and the sentence in which it occurs does not, we maintain, express an empirical proposition at all. It is only with normative ethics that we are at present concerned; so that whenever ethical symbols are used in the course of this argument without qualification, they are always to be interpreted as symbols of the normative type.

In admitting that normative ethical concepts are irreducible to empirical concepts, we seem to be leaving the way clear for the "absolutist" view of ethics—that is, the view that statements of value are not controlled by observation, as ordinary empirical propositions are, but only by a "mysterious intellectual intuition." A feature of this theory, which is seldom recognized by its advocates, is that it makes statements of value unverifiable. For it is notorious that what seems intuitively certain to one person may seem doubtful, or even false, to another. So that unless it is possible to provide some criterion by which one may decide between conflicting intuitions, a mere appeal to intuition is worthless as a test of a proposition's validity. But in the case of moral judgements, no such criterion can be given. Some moralists claim to settle the matter by saying that they "know" that their own moral judgements are correct. But such an assertion is of purely psychological interest, and has not the slightest tendency to prove the validity of any moral judgement. For dissentient moralists may equally well "know" that their ethical views are correct. And, as far as subjective certainty goes, there will be nothing to choose between them. When such differences of opinion arise in connection with an ordinary empirical proposition, one may attempt to resolve them by referring to, or actually carrying out, some relevant empirical test. But with regard to ethical statements, there is, on the "absolutist" or "intuitionist" theory, no relevant empirical test. We are therefore justified in saying that on this theory ethical statements are held to be unverifiable. They are, of course, also held to be genuine synthetic propositions.

Considering the use which we have made of the principle that a synthetic proposition is significant only if it is empirically verifiable, it is clear that the acceptance of an "absolutist" theory of ethics would undermine the whole of our main argument. And as we have already rejected the "naturalistic" theories which are commonly supposed to provide the only alternative to "absolutism" in ethics, we seem to have reached a difficult position. We shall meet the difficulty by showing that the correct treatment of ethical statements is afforded by a third theory, which is wholly compatible with our radical empiricism.

We begin by admitting that the fundamental ethical concepts are unanalysable, inasmuch as there is no criterion by which one can test the validity of the judgements in which they occur. So far we are in agreement with the absolutists. But, unlike the absolutists, we are able to give an explanation of this fact about ethical concepts. We say that the reason why they are unanalysable is that they are mere pseudo-concepts. The presence of an ethical symbol in a proposition adds nothing to its factual content. Thus if I say to someone, "You acted wrongly in stealing that money," I am not stating anything more than if I had simply said, "You stole that money." In adding that this action is wrong I am not making any further statement about it. I am simply evincing my moral disapproval of it. It is as if I had said, "You stole that money," in a peculiar tone of horror, or written it with the addition of some special exclamation marks. The tone, or the exclamation marks, adds nothing to the literal meaning of the sentence. It merely serves to show that the expression of it is attended by certain feelings in the speaker.

If now I generalise my previous statement and say, "Stealing money is wrong," I produce a sentence which has no factual meaning—that is, expresses no proposition which can be either true or false. It is as if I had written "Stealing money!!"—where the shape and thickness of the exclamation marks show, by a suitable convention, that a special sort of moral disapproval is the feeling which is being expressed. It is clear that there is nothing said here which can be true or false. Another man may disagree with me about the wrongness of stealing, in the sense that he may not have the same feelings about stealing as I have, and he may quarrel with me on account of my moral sentiments. But he cannot, strictly speaking, contradict me. For in saying that a certain type of action is right or wrong, I am not making any factual statement, not even a statement about my own state of mind. I am merely expressing certain moral sentiments. And the man who is ostensibly contradicting me is merely expressing his moral sentiments. So that there is plainly no sense in asking which of us is in the right. For neither of us is asserting a genuine proposition.

What we have just been saying about the symbol "wrong" applies to all normative ethical symbols.

Sometimes they occur in sentences which record ordinary empirical facts besides expressing ethical feeling about those facts: sometimes they occur in sentences which simply express ethical feeling about a certain type of action, or situation, without making any statement of fact. But in every case in which one would commonly be said to be making an ethical judgement, the function of the relevant ethical word is purely "emotive." It is used to express feeling about certain objects, but not to make any assertion about them.

It is worth mentioning that ethical terms do not serve only to express feeling. They are calculated also to arouse feeling, and so to stimulate action. Indeed some of them are used in such a way as to give the sentences in which they occur the effect of commands. Thus the sentence "It is your duty to tell the truth" may be regarded both as the expression of a certain sort of ethical feeling about truthfulness and as the expression of the command "Tell the truth." The sentence "You ought to tell the truth" also involves the command "Tell the truth," but here the tone of the command is less emphatic. In the sentence "It is good to tell the truth" the command has become little more than a suggestion. And thus the "meaning" of the word "good," in its ethical usage, is differentiated from that of the word "duty" or the word "ought." In fact we may define the meaning of the various ethical words in terms both of the different feelings they are ordinarily taken to express, and also the different responses which they are calculated to provoke.

We can now see why it is impossible to find a criterion for determining the validity of ethical judgements. It is not because they have an "absolute" validity which is mysteriously independent of ordinary sense-experience, but because they have no objective validity whatsoever. If a sentence makes no statement at all, there is obviously no sense in asking whether what it says is true or false. And we have seen that sentences which simply express moral judgements do not say anything. They are pure expressions of feeling and as such do not come under the category of truth and falsehood. They are unverifiable for the same reason as a cry of pain or a word of command is unverifiable—because they do not express genuine propositions.

Thus, although our theory of ethics might fairly be said to be radically subjectivist, it differs in a very important respect from the orthodox subjectivist theory. For the orthodox subjectivist does not deny, as we do, that the sentences of a moralizer express genuine propositions. All he denies is that they express propositions of a unique non-empirical character. His own view is that they express propositions about the speaker's feelings. If this were so, ethical judgements clearly would be capable of being true or false. They would be true if the speaker had the relevant feelings, and false if he had not. And this is a matter which is, in principle, empirically verifiable. Furthermore they could be significantly contradicted. For if I say, "Tolerance is a virtue," and someone answers, "You don't approve of it," he would, on the ordinary subjectivist theory, be contradicting me. On our theory, he would not be contradicting me, because, in saying that tolerance was a virtue, I should not be making any statement about my own feelings or about anything else. I should simply be evincing my feelings, which is not at all the same thing as saying that I have them.

The distinction between the expression of feeling and the assertion of feeling is complicated by the fact that the assertion that one has a certain feeling often accompanies the expression of that feeling, and is then, indeed, a factor in the expression of that feeling. Thus I may simultaneously express boredom and say that I am bored, and in that case my utterance of the words, "I am bored," is one of the circumstances which make it true to say that I am expressing or evincing boredom. But I can express boredom without actually saying that I am bored. I can express it by my tone and gestures, while making a statement about something wholly unconnected with it, or by an ejaculation, or without uttering any words at all. So that even if the assertion that one has a certain feeling always involves the expression of that feeling, the expression of a feeling assuredly does not always involve the assertion that one has it. And this is the important point to grasp in considering the distinction between our theory and the ordinary subjectivist theory. For whereas the subjectivist holds that ethical statements actually assert the existence of certain feelings, we hold that ethical statements are expressions and excitants of feeling which do not necessarily involve any assertions.

We have already remarked that the main objection to the ordinary subjectivist theory is that the validity of ethical judgements is not determined by the nature of their author's feelings. And this is an objection which our theory escapes. For it does not imply that the existence of any feelings is a necessary and sufficient condition of the validity of an ethical judgement. It implies, on the contrary, that ethical judgements have no validity.

There is, however, a celebrated argument against subjectivist theories which our theory does not escape. It has been pointed out by Moore that if ethical statements were simply statements about the speaker's feelings, it would be impossible to argue about questions of value.[1] To take a typical example: if a man said that thrift was a virtue, and another replied that it was a vice, they would not, on this theory, be disputing with one another. One would be saying that he approved of thrift, and the other that *he* didn't; and there is no reason why both these statements should not be true. Now Moore held it to be obvious that we do dispute about questions of value, and accordingly concluded that the particular form of subjectivism which he was discussing was false.

It is plain that the conclusion that it is impossible to dispute about questions of value follows from our theory also. For as we hold that such sentences as "Thrift is a virtue" and "Thrift is a vice" do not express propositions at all, we clearly cannot hold that they express incompatible propositions. We must therefore admit that if Moore's argument really refutes the ordinary subjectivist theory, it also refutes ours. But, in fact, we deny that it does refute even the ordinary subjectivist theory. For we hold that one really never does dispute about questions of value.

This may seem, at first sight, to be a very paradoxical assertion. For we certainly do engage in disputes which are ordinarily regarded as disputes about questions of value. But, in all such cases, we find, if we consider the matter closely, that the dispute is not really about a question of value, but about a question of fact. When someone disagrees with us about the moral value of a certain action or type of action, we do admittedly resort to argument in order to win him over to our way of thinking. But we do not attempt to show by our arguments that he has the "wrong" ethical feeling towards a situation whose nature he has correctly apprehended. What we attempt to show is that he is mistaken about the facts of the case. We argue that he has misconceived the agent's motive: or that he has misjudged the effects of the action, or its probable effects in view of the agent's knowledge; or that he has failed to take into account the special circumstances in which the agent was placed. Or else we employ more general arguments about the effects which actions of a certain type tend to produce, or the qualities which are usually manifested in their performance. We do this in the hope that we have only to get our opponent to agree with us about the nature of the empirical facts for him to adopt the same moral attitude towards them as we do. And as the people with whom we argue have generally received the same moral education as ourselves, and live in the same social order, our expectation is usually justified. But if our opponent happens to have undergone a different process of moral "conditioning" from ourselves, so that, even when he acknowledges all the facts, he still disagrees with us about the moral value of the actions under discussion, then we abandon the attempt to convince him by argument. We say that it is impossible to argue with him because he has a distorted or undeveloped moral sense; which signifies merely that he employs a different set of values from our own. We feel that our own system of values is superior, and therefore speak in such derogatory terms of his. But we cannot bring forward any arguments to show that our system is superior. For our judgement that it is so is itself a judgement of value, and accordingly outside the scope of argument. It is because argument fails us when we come to deal with pure questions of value, as distinct from questions of fact, that we finally resort to mere abuse.

In short, we find that argument is possible on moral questions only if some system of values is presupposed. If our opponent concurs with us in expressing moral disapproval of all actions of a given type *t*, then we may get him to condemn a particular action A, by bringing forward arguments to show that A is of type *t*. For the question whether A does or does not belong to that type is a plain question of fact. Given that a man has certain moral principles, we argue that he must, in order to be consistent, react morally to certain things in a certain way. What we do not and cannot argue about is the validity of these moral principles. We merely praise or condemn them in the light of our own feelings.

---

1. cf. *Philosophical Studies*, "The Nature of Moral Philosophy."

If anyone doubts the accuracy of this account of moral disputes, let him try to construct even an imaginary argument on a question of value which does not reduce itself to an argument about a question of logic or about an empirical matter of fact. I am confident that he will not succeed in producing a single example. And if that is the case, he must allow that its involving the impossibility of purely ethical arguments is not, as Moore thought, a ground of objection to our theory, but rather a point in favour of it.

Having upheld our theory against the only criticism which appeared to threaten it, we may now use it to define the nature of all ethical enquiries. We find that ethical philosophy consists simply in saying that ethical concepts are pseudo-concepts and therefore unanalysable. The further task of describing the different feelings that the different ethical terms are used to express, and the different reactions that they customarily provoke, is a task for the psychologist. There cannot be such a thing as ethical science, if by ethical science one means the elaboration of a "true" system of morals. For we have seen that, as ethical judgements are mere expressions of feeling, there can be no way of determining the validity of any ethical system, and, indeed, no sense in asking whether any such system is true. All that one may legitimately enquire in this connection is, What are the moral habits of a given person or group of people, and what causes them to have precisely those habits and feelings? And this enquiry falls wholly within the scope of the existing social sciences.

It appears, then, that ethics, as a branch of knowledge, is nothing more than a department of psychology and sociology. And in case anyone thinks that we are overlooking the existence of casuistry, we may remark that casuistry is not a science, but is a purely analytical investigation of the structure of a given moral system. In other words, it is an exercise in formal logic.

When one comes to pursue the psychological enquiries which constitute ethical science, one is immediately enabled to account for the Kantian and hedonistic theories of morals. For one finds that one of the chief causes of moral behaviour is fear, both conscious and unconscious, of a god's displeasure, and fear of the enmity of society. And this, indeed, is the reason why moral precepts present themselves to some people as "categorical" commands. And one finds, also, that the moral code of a society is partly determined by the beliefs of that society concerning the conditions of its own happiness—or, in other words, that a society tends to encourage or discourage a given type of conduct by the use of moral sanctions according as it appears to promote or detract from the contentment of the society as a whole. And this is the reason why altruism is recommended in most moral codes and egotism condemned. It is from the observation of this connection between morality and happiness that hedonistic or eudæmonistic theories of morals ultimately spring, just as the moral theory of Kant is based on the fact, previously explained, that moral precepts have for some people the force of inexorable commands. As each of these theories ignores the fact which lies at the root of the other, both may be criticized as being one-sided; but this is not the main objection to either of them. Their essential defect is that they treat propositions which refer to the causes and attributes of our ethical feelings as if they were definitions of ethical concepts. And thus they fail to recognise that ethical concepts are pseudo-concepts and consequently indefinable.

As we have already said, our conclusions about the nature of ethics apply to æsthetics also. Æsthetic terms are used in exactly the same way as ethical terms. Such æsthetic words as "beautiful" and "hideous" are employed, as ethical words are employed, not to make statements of fact, but simply to express certain feelings and evoke a certain response. It follows, as in ethics, that there is no sense in attributing objective validity to æsthetic judgements, and no possibility of arguing about questions of value in æsthetics, but only about questions of fact. A scientific treatment of aesthetics would show us what in general were the causes of æsthetic feeling, why various societies produced and admired the works of art they did, why taste varies as it does within a given society, and so forth. And these are ordinary psychological or sociological questions. They have, of course, little or nothing to do with aesthetic criticism as we understand it. But that is because the purpose of æsthetic criticism is not so much to give knowledge as to communicate emotion. The critic, by calling attention to certain features of the work under review, and expressing his own feelings about them, endeavours to make us share his attitude towards the work as a whole. The only relevant propositions that he formulates are propositions describing the nature of the work. And these are plain records of fact. We conclude, therefore, that there is nothing in æsthetics, any more than there is in ethics, to justify the view that it embodies a unique type of knowledge.

It should now be clear that the only information which we can legitimately derive from the study of our æsthetic and moral experiences is information about our own mental and physical make-up. We take note of these experiences as providing data for our psychological and sociological generalisations. And this is the only way in which they serve to increase our knowledge. It follows that any attempt to make our use of ethical and æsthetic concepts the basis of a metaphysical theory concerning the existence of a world of values, as distinct from the world of facts, involves a false analysis of these concepts. Our own analysis has shown that the phenomena of moral experience cannot fairly be used to support any rationalist or metaphysical doctrine whatsoever. In particular, they cannot, as Kant hoped, be used to establish the existence of a transcendent god.

This mention of God brings us to the question of the possibility of religious knowledge. We shall see that this possibility has already been ruled out by our treatment of metaphysics. But, as this is a point of considerable interest, we may be permitted to discuss it at some length.

It is now generally admitted, at any rate by philosophers, that the existence of a being having the attributes which define the god of any non-animistic religion cannot be demonstratively proved. To see that this is so, we have only to ask ourselves what are the premises from which the existence of such a god could be deduced. If the conclusion that a god exists is to be demonstratively certain, then these premises must be certain; for, as the conclusion of a deductive argument is already contained in the premises, any uncertainty there may be about the truth of the premises is necessarily shared by it. But we know that no empirical proposition can ever be anything more than probable. It is only *a priori* propositions that are logically certain. But we cannot deduce the existence of a god from an *a priori* proposition. For we know that the reason why *a priori* propositions are certain is that they are tautologies. And from a set of tautologies nothing but a further tautology can be validly deduced. It follows that there is no possibility of demonstrating the existence of a god.

What is not so generally recognised is that there can be no way of proving that the existence of a god, such as the God of Christianity, is even probable. Yet this also is easily shown. For if the existence of such a god were probable, then the proposition that he existed would be an empirical hypothesis. And in that case it would be possible to deduce from it, and other empirical hypotheses, certain experiential propositions which were not deducible from those other hypotheses alone. But in fact this is not possible. It is sometimes claimed, indeed, that the existence of a certain sort of regularity in nature constitutes sufficient evidence for the existence of a god. But if the sentence "God exists" entails no more than that certain types of phenomena occur in certain sequences, then to assert the existence of a god will be simply equivalent to asserting that there is the requisite regularity in nature; and no religious man would admit that this was all he intended to assert in asserting the existence of a god. He would say that in talking about God, he was talking about a transcendent being who might be known through certain empirical manifestations, but certainly could not be defined in terms of those manifestations. But in that case the term "god" is a metaphysical term. And if "god" is a metaphysical term, then it cannot be even probable that a god exists. For to say that "God exists" is to make a metaphysical utterance which cannot be either true or false. And by the same criterion, no sentence which purports to describe the nature of a transcendent god can possess any literal significance.

It is important not to confuse this view of religious assertions with the view that is adopted by atheists, or agnostics.[1] For it is characteristic of an agnostic to hold that the existence of a god is a possibility in which there is no good reason either to believe or disbelieve; and it is characteristic of an atheist to hold that it is at least probable that no god exists. And our view that all utterances about the nature of God are nonsensical, so far from being identical with, or even lending any support to, either of these familiar contentions, is actually incompatible with them. For if the assertion that there is a god is nonsensical, then the atheist's assertion that there is no god is equally nonsensical, since it is only a significant proposition that can be significantly contradicted. As for the agnostic, although he refrains from

---

1. This point was suggested to me by Professor H. H. Price.

saying either that there is or that there is not a god, he does not deny that the question whether a transcendent god exists is a genuine question. He does not deny that the two sentences "There is a transcendent god" and "There is no transcendent god" express propositions one of which is actually true and the other false. All he says is that we have no means of telling which of them is true, and therefore ought not to commit ourselves to either. But we have seen that the sentences in question do not express propositions at all. And this means that agnosticism also is ruled out.

Thus we offer the theist the same comfort as we gave to the moralist. His assertions cannot possibly be valid, but they cannot be invalid either. As he says nothing at all about the world, he cannot justly be accused of saying anything false, or anything for which he has insufficient grounds. It is only when the theist claims that in asserting the existence of a transcendent god he is expressing a genuine proposition that we are entitled to disagree with him.

It is to be remarked that in cases where deities are identified with natural objects, assertions concerning them may be allowed to be significant. If, for example, a man tells me that the occurrence of thunder is alone both necessary and sufficient to establish the truth of the proposition that Jehovah is angry, I may conclude that, in his usage of words, the sentence "Jehovah is angry" is equivalent to "It is thundering." But in sophisticated religions, though they may be to some extent based on men's awe of natural process which they cannot sufficiently understand, the "person" who is supposed to control the empirical world is not himself located in it; he is held to be superior to the empirical world, and so outside it; and he is endowed with super-empirical attributes. But the notion of a person whose essential attributes are non-empirical is not an intelligible notion at all. We may have a word which is used as if it named this "person," but, unless the sentences in which it occurs express propositions which are empirically verifiable, it cannot be said to symbolize anything. And this is the case with regard to the word "god," in the usage in which it is intended to refer to a transcendent object. The mere existence of the noun is enough to foster the illusion that there is a real, or at any rate a possible entity corresponding to it. It is only when we enquire what God's attributes are that we discover that "God," in this usage, is not a genuine name.

It is common to find belief in a transcendent god conjoined with belief in an after-life. But, in the form which it usually takes, the content of this belief is not a genuine hypothesis. To say that men do not ever die, or that the state of death is merely a state of prolonged insensibility, is indeed to express a significant proposition, though all the available evidence goes to show that it is false. But to say that there is something imperceptible inside a man, which is his soul or his real self, and that it goes on living after he is dead, is to make a metaphysical assertion which has no more factual content than the assertion that there is a transcendent god.

It is worth mentioning that, according to the account which we have given of religious assertions, there is no logical ground for antagonism between religion and natural science. As far as the question of truth or falsehood is concerned, there is no opposition between the natural scientist and the theist who believes in a transcendent god. For since the religious utterances of the theist are not genuine propositions at all, they cannot stand in any logical relation to the propositions of science. Such antagonism as there is between religion and science appears to consist in the fact that science takes away one of the motives which make men religious. For it is acknowledged that one of the ultimate sources of religious feeling lies in the inability of men to determine their own destiny; and science tends to destroy the feeling of awe with which men regard an alien world, by making them believe that they can understand and anticipate the course of natural phenomena, and even to some extent control it. The fact that it has recently become fashionable for physicists themselves to be sympathetic towards religion is a point in favour of this hypothesis. For this sympathy towards religion marks the physicists' own lack of confidence in the validity of their hypotheses, which is a reaction on their part from the anti-religious dogmatism of nineteenth-century scientists, and a natural outcome of the crisis through which physics has just passed.

It is not within the scope of this enquiry to enter more deeply into the causes of religious feeling, or to discuss the probability of the continuance of religious belief. We are concerned only to answer those questions which arise out of our discussion of the possibility of religious knowledge. The point which we wish to establish is that there cannot be any transcendent truths of religion. For the sentences which the theist uses to express such "truths" are not literally significant.

An interesting feature of this conclusion is that it accords with what many theists are accustomed to say themselves. For we are often told that the nature of God is a mystery which transcends the human understanding. But to say that something transcends the human understanding is to say that it is unintelligible. And what is unintelligible cannot significantly be described. Again, we are told that God is not an object of reason but an object of faith. This may be nothing more than an admission that the existence of God must be taken on trust, since it cannot be proved. But it may also be an assertion that God is the object of a purely mystical intuition, and cannot therefore be defined in terms which are intelligible to the reason. And I think there are many theists who would assert this. But if one allows that it is impossible to define God in intelligible terms, then one is allowing that it is impossible for a sentence both to be significant and to be about God. If a mystic admits that the object of his vision is something which cannot be described, then he must also admit that he is bound to talk nonsense when he describes it.

For his part, the mystic may protest that his intuition does reveal truths to him, even though he cannot explain to others what these truths are; and that we who do not possess this faculty of intuition can have no ground for denying that it is a cognitive faculty. For we can hardly maintain *a priori* that there are no ways of discovering true propositions except those which we ourselves employ. The answer is that we set no limit to the number of ways in which one may come to formulate a true proposition. We do not in any way deny that a synthetic truth may be discovered by purely intuitive methods as well as by the rational method of induction. But we do say that every synthetic proposition, however it may have been arrived at, must be subject to the test of actual experience. We do not deny *a priori* that the mystic is able to discover truths by his own special methods. We wait to hear what are the propositions which embody his discoveries, in order to see whether they are verified or confuted by our empirical observations. But the mystic, so far from producing propositions which are empirically verified, is unable to produce any intelligible propositions at all. And therefore we say that his intuition has not revealed to him any facts. It is no use his saying that

he has apprehended facts but is unable to express them. For we know that if he really had acquired any information, he would be able to express it. He would be able to indicate in some way or other how the genuineness of his discovery might be empirically determined. The fact that he cannot reveal what he "knows," or even himself devise an empirical test to validate his "knowledge," shows that his state of mystical intuition is not a genuinely cognitive state. So that in describing his vision the mystic does not give us any information about the external world; he merely gives us indirect information about the condition of his own mind.

These considerations dispose of the argument from religious experience, which many philosophers still regard as a valid argument in favour of the existence of a god. They say that it is logically possible for men to be immediately acquainted with God, as they are immediately acquainted with a sense-content, and that there is no reason why one should be prepared to believe a man when he says that he is seeing a yellow patch, and refuse to believe him when he says that he is seeing God. The answer to this is that if the man who asserts that he is seeing God is merely asserting that he is experiencing a peculiar kind of sense-content, then we do not for a moment deny that his assertion may be true. But, ordinarily, the man who says that he is seeing God is saying not merely that he is experiencing a religious emotion, but also that there exists a transcendent being who is the object of this emotion; just as the man who says that he sees a yellow patch is ordinarily saying not merely that his visual sense-field contains a yellow sense-content, but also that there exists a yellow object to which the sense-content belongs. And it is not irrational to be prepared to believe a man when he asserts the existence of a yellow object, and to refuse to believe him when he asserts the existence of a transcendent god. For whereas the sentence "There exists here a yellow-coloured material thing" expresses a genuine synthetic proposition which could be empirically verified, the sentence "There exists a transcendent god" has, as we have seen, no literal significance.

We conclude, therefore, that the argument from religious experience is altogether fallacious. The fact that people have religious experiences is interesting from the psychological point of view, but it does not in any way imply that there is such a thing as religious knowledge, edge, any more than our having moral experiences implies that there is such a thing as moral knowledge. The theist, like the moralist, may believe that his experiences are cognitive experiences, but, unless he can formulate his "knowledge" in propositions that are empirically verifiable, we may be sure that he is deceiving himself. It follows that those philosophers who fill their books with assertions that they intuitively "know" this or that moral or religious "truth" are merely providing material for the psycho-analyst. For no act of intuition can be said to reveal a truth about any matter of fact unless it issues in verifiable propositions. And all such propositions are to be incorporated in the system of empirical propositions which constitutes science.

JEAN-PAUL SARTRE

Existentialism

The contemporary ethical writings collected in this book reflect almost exclusively the philosophy that predominated in the English-speaking world—the tradition of English empiricism. During the early twentieth century in England and the United States, metaphysics was declared dead and the great systems of the past, ethical theories included, appeared more and more to lack any justifiable foundation. However, in this reading we encounter a representative of another tradition, one in which metaphysics and grand systematizing is very much alive. This is the movement in Continental philosophy known as existentialism.

Although a variety of disparate philosophical voices are usually broadly assigned the title of existentialist—Kierkegaard, Nietzsche, Camus, Merleau-Ponty, and Jaspers, for example—here we read a philosopher who labeled himself an existentialist—Jean-Paul Sartre. Born in Paris in 1905, Sartre studied, taught, and wrote both philosophy and literature, beginning prior to World War II. During the war, he was active in the French resistance. After the war, Sartre emerged as the dominant figure in the existentialism movement, which included his friends (and intellectual adversaries) Albert Camus and Maurice Merleau-Ponty.

Sartre wrote a great variety of material, including serious philosophy, reviews, plays, and stories. Some of his successful literary works are No Exit *(1947),* The Flies *(1947), and* Nausea *(1938). His most important philosophical work, completed during the German occupation of Paris, was* Being and Nothingness *(1943).* Existentialism as a Humanism *(1946), given here in its entirety, originated as a lecture in which Sartre attempted to lay out in a clear and unambiguous way what he advocated in the larger work.*

Although much of Sartre's writings cover a variety of philosophical concerns, such as epistemology and ontology, everything Sartre wrote can be considered primarily about ethics. His work is profoundly moral and humanistic because of the nature of the existentialist movement, especially the atheistic existentialism of Sartre. Existentialism, as defined by Sartre, is the philosophical movement that insists that for human beings, existence precedes essence. That is, unique among creation, humans have no innate purpose or function. Instead, each person unavoidably defines herself through her choices. It is through one's choices that values are created, since the fact that there is no God means that the universe and everything in it has no objective value. Because values arise only out of individual choices and have no external source, the ethical theory of Sartre, like those of Ayer and Hare, can be considered a noncognitive theory, one that denies that moral statements assert moral facts.

In opposition to the ethical theories that follow the empiricist tradition predominant in England and the United States, the work of Sartre develops out of Continental rationalism and idealism. This is the tradition that begins with Descartes and moves through Kant, Hegel, and the phenomenologists such as Husserl and Heidegger. Historically, the Continental tradition has had a minimal effect in England and the United States but has been predominant in Europe and South America.

I should like on this occasion to defend existentialism against some charges which have been brought against it.

First, it has been charged with inviting people to remain in a kind of desperate quietism because, since no solutions are possible, we should have to consider action in this world as quite impossible. We should then end up in a philosophy of contemplation; and since contemplation is a luxury, we come in the end to a bourgeois philosophy. The communists in particular have made these charges.

On the other hand, we have been charged with dwelling on human degradation, with pointing up everywhere the sordid, shady, and slimy, and neglecting the gracious and beautiful, the bright side of human nature; for example, according to Mlle. Mercier, a Catholic critic, with forgetting the smile of the child. Both sides charge us with having ignored human solidarity, with considering man as an isolated being. The communists say that the main reason for this is that we take pure subjectivity, the *Cartesian I think*, as our starting point; in other words, the moment in which man becomes fully aware of what it means to him to be an isolated being; as a result, we are unable to return to a state of solidarity with the men who are not ourselves, a state which we can never reach in the *cogito*.

From the Christian standpoint, we are charged with denying the reality and seriousness of human undertakings, since, if we reject God's commandments and the eternal verities, there no longer remains anything but pure caprice, with everyone permitted to do as he pleases and incapable, from his own point of view, of condemning the points of view and acts of others.

I shall try today to answer these different charges. Many people are going to be surprised at what is said here about humanism. We shall try to see in what sense it is to be understood. In any case, what can be said from the very beginning is that by existentialism we mean a doctrine which makes human life possible and, in addition, declares that every truth and every action implies a human setting and a human subjectivity.

As is generally known, the basic charge against us is that we put the emphasis on the dark side of human life. Someone recently told me of a lady who, when she let slip a vulgar word in a moment of irritation, excused herself by saying, "I guess I'm becoming an existentialist." Consequently, existentialism is regarded as something ugly; that is why we are said to be naturalists; and if we are, it is rather surprising that in this day and age we cause so much more alarm and scandal than does naturalism, properly so called. The kind of person who can take in his stride such a novel as Zola's *The Earth* is disgusted as soon as he starts reading an existentialist novel; the kind of person who is resigned to the wisdom of the ages—which is pretty sad—finds us even sadder. Yet, what can be more disillusioning than saying "true charity begins at home" or "a scoundrel will always return evil for good?"

We know the commonplace remarks made when this subject comes up, remarks which always add up to the same thing: we shouldn't struggle against the powers-that-be; we shouldn't resist authority; we shouldn't try to rise above our station; any action which doesn't conform to authority is romantic; any effort not based on past experience is doomed to failure; experience shows that man's bent is always toward trouble, that there must be a strong hand to hold him in check, if not, there will be anarchy. There are still people who go on mumbling these melancholy old saws, the people who say, "It's only human!" whenever a more or less repugnant act is pointed out to them, the people who glut themselves on *chansons réalistes;* these are the people who accuse existentialism of being too gloomy, and to such an extent that I wonder whether they are complaining about it, not for its pessimism, but much rather its optimism. Can it be that what really scares them in the doctrine I shall try to present here is that it leaves to man a possibility of choice? To answer this question, we must re-examine it on a strictly philosophical plane. What is meant by the term *existentialism*?

Most people who use the word would be rather embarrassed if they had to explain it, since, now that the word is all the rage, even the work of a musician or painter is being called existentialist. A gossip columnist in *Clartés* signs himself *The Existentialist,* so that by this time the word has been so stretched and has taken on so broad a meaning, that it no longer means anything at all. It seems that for want of an advance-guard doctrine analogous to surrealism, the kind of people who are eager for scandal and flurry turn to this philosophy which in other respects does not at all serve their purposes in this sphere.

Actually, it is the least scandalous, the most austere of doctrines. It is intended strictly for specialists and philosophers. Yet it can be defined easily. What complicates matters is that there are two kinds of existentialist; first, those who are Christian, among whom I would include Jaspers and Gabriel Marcel, both Catholic; and on the other hand the atheistic existentialist, among whom I class Heidegger, and then the French existentialists and myself. What they have in common is that they think that existence precedes essence, or, if you prefer, that subjectivity must be the starting point.

Just what does that mean? Let us consider some object that is manufactured, for example, a book or a paper-cutter: here is an object which has been made by an artisan whose inspiration came from a concept. He referred to the concept of what a paper-cutter is and likewise to a known method of production, which is part of the concept, something which is, by and large, a routine. Thus, the paper-cutter is at once an object produced in a certain way and, on the other hand, one having a specific use; and one can not postulate a man who produces a paper-cutter but does not know what it is used for. Therefore, let us say that, for the paper-cutter, essence—that is, the ensemble of both the production routines and the properties which enable it to be both produced and defined—precedes existence. Thus, the presence of the paper-cutter or book in front of me is determined. Therefore, we have here a technical view of the world whereby it can be said that production precedes existence.

When we conceive God as the Creator, He is generally thought of as a superior sort of artisan. Whatever doctrine we may be considering, whether one like that of Descartes or that of Leibnitz, we always grant that will more or less follows understanding or, at the very least, accompanies it, and that when God creates He knows exactly what He is creating. Thus, the concept of man in the mind of God is comparable to the concept of paper-cutter in the mind of the manufacturer, and, following certain techniques and a conception, God produces man, just as the artisan, following a definition and a technique, makes a paper-cutter. Thus, the individual man is the realisation of a certain concept in the divine intelligence.

In the eighteenth century, the atheism of the *philosophes* discarded the idea of God, but not so much for the notion that essence precedes existence. To a certain extent, this idea is found everywhere; we find it in Diderot, in Voltaire, and even in Kant. Man has a human nature; this human nature, which is the concept of the human, is found in all men, which means that each man is a particular example of a universal concept, man. In Kant, the result of this universality is that the wild-man, the natural man, as well as the bourgeois, are circumscribed by the same definition and have the same basic qualities. Thus, here too the essence of man precedes the historical existence that we find in nature.

Atheistic existentialism, which I represent, is more coherent. It states that if God does not exist, there is at least one being in whom existence precedes essence, a being who exists before he can be defined by any concept, and that this being is man, or, as Heidegger says, human reality. What is meant here by saying that existence precedes essence? It means that, first of all, man exists, turns up, appears on the scene, and, only afterwards, defines himself. If man, as the existentialist conceives him, is indefinable, it is because at first he is nothing. Only afterward will he be something, and he himself will have made what he will be. Thus, there is no human nature, since there is no God to conceive it. Not only is man what he conceives himself to be, but he is also only what he wills himself to be after this thrust toward existence.

Man is nothing else but what he makes of himself. Such is the first principle of existentialism. It is also what is called subjectivity, the name we are labeled with when charges are brought against us. But what do we mean by this, if not that man has a greater dignity than a stone or table? For we mean that man first exists, that is, that man first of all is the being who hurls himself toward a future and who is conscious of imagining himself as being in the future. Man is at the start a plan which is aware of itself, rather than a patch of moss, a piece of garbage, or a cauliflower; nothing exists prior to this plan; there is nothing in heaven; man will be what he will have planned to be. Not what he will want to be. Because by the word "will" we generally mean a conscious decision, which is subsequent to what we have already made of ourselves. I may want to belong to a political party, write a book, get married; but all that is only a manifestation of an earlier, more spontaneous choice that is called "will." But if existence really does precede essence, man is responsible for what he is. Thus, existentialism's first move is to make every man aware of what he is and to make the full responsibility of his existence rest on him. And when we say that a man is responsible for himself, we do not only mean that he is responsible for his own individuality, but that he is responsible for all men.

The word subjectivism has two meanings, and our opponents play on the two. Subjectivism means, on the one hand, that an individual chooses and makes himself; and, on the other, that it is impossible for man to transcend human subjectivity. The second of these is the essential meaning of existentialism. When we say that man chooses his own self, we mean that every one of us does likewise; but we also mean by that that in making this choice he also

chooses all men. In fact, in creating the man that we want to be, there is not a single one of our acts which does not at the same time create an image of man as we think he ought to be. To choose to be this or that is to affirm at the same time the value of what we choose, because we can never choose evil. We always choose the good, and nothing can be good for us without being good for all.

If, on the other hand, existence precedes essence, and if we grant that we exist and fashion our image at one and the same time, the image is valid for everybody and for our whole age. Thus, our responsibility is much greater than we might have supposed, because it involves all mankind. If I am a workingman and choose to join a Christian trade-union rather than be a communist, and if by being a member I want to show that the best thing for man is resignation, that the kingdom of man is not of this world, I am not only involving my own case—I want to be resigned for everyone. As a result, my action has involved all humanity. To take a more individual matter, if I want to marry, to have children; even if this marriage depends solely on my own circumstances or passion or wish, I am involving all humanity in monogamy and not merely myself. Therefore, I am responsible for myself and for everyone else. I am creating a certain image of man of my own choosing. In choosing myself, I choose man.

This helps us understand what the actual content is of such rather grandiloquent words as anguish, forlornness, despair. As you will see, it's all quite simple.

First, what is meant by anguish? The existentialists say at once that man is anguish. What that means is this: the man who involves himself and who realizes that he is not only the person he chooses to be, but also a law-maker who is, at the same time, choosing all mankind as well as himself, can not help escape the feeling of his total and deep responsibility. Of course, there are many people who are not anxious; but we claim that they are hiding their anxiety, that they are fleeing from it. Certainly, many people believe that when they do something, they themselves are the only ones involved, and when someone says to them, "What if everyone acted that way?" they shrug their shoulders and answer, "Everyone doesn't act that way." But really, one should always ask himself, "What would happen if everybody looked at things that way?" There is no escaping this disturbing thought except by a kind of double-dealing. A man who lies and makes excuses for himself by saying "not everybody does that," is someone with an uneasy conscience, because the act of lying implies that a universal value is conferred upon the lie.

Anguish is evident even when it conceals itself. This is the anguish that Kierkegaard called the anguish of Abraham. You know the story: an angel has ordered Abraham to sacrifice his son; if it really were an angel who has come and said, "You are Abraham, you shall sacrifice your son," everything would be all right. But everyone might first wonder, "Is it really an angel, and am I really Abraham? What proof do I have?"

There was a madwoman who had hallucinations; someone used to speak to her on the telephone and give her orders. Her doctor asked her, "Who is it who talks to you?" She answered, "He says it's God." What proof did she really have that it was God? If an angel comes to me, what proof is there that it's an angel? And if I hear voices, what proof is there that they come from heaven and not from hell, or from the subconscious, or a pathological condition? What proves that they are addressed to me? What proof is there that I have been appointed to impose my choice and my conception of man on humanity? I'll never find any proof or sign to convince me of that. If a voice addresses me, it is always for me to decide that this is the angel's voice; if I consider that such an act is a good one, it is I who will choose to say that it is good rather than bad.

Now, I'm not being singled out as an Abraham, and yet at every moment I'm obliged to perform exemplary acts. For every man, everything happens as if all mankind had its eyes fixed on him and were guiding itself by what he does. And every man ought to say to himself, "Am I really the kind of man who has the right to act in such a way that humanity might guide itself by my actions?" And if he does not say that to himself, he is masking his anguish.

There is no question here of the kind of anguish which would lead to quietism, to inaction. It is a matter of a simple sort of anguish that anybody who has had responsibilities is familiar with. For example, when a military officer takes the responsibility for an attack and sends a certain number of men to death, he chooses to do so, and in the main he alone makes the choice. Doubtless, orders come from above, but they are too broad; he interprets them,

and on this interpretation depend the lives of ten or fourteen or twenty men. In making a decision he can not help having a certain anguish. All leaders know this anguish. That doesn't keep them from acting; on the contrary, it is the very condition of their action. For it implies that they envisage a number of possibilities, and when they choose one, they realize that it has value only because it is chosen. We shall see that this kind of anguish, which is the kind that existentialism describes, is explained, in addition, by a direct responsibility to the other men whom it involves. It is not a curtain separating us from action, but is part of action itself.

When we speak of forlornness, a term Heidegger was fond of, we mean only that God does not exist and that we have to face all the consequences of this. The existentialist is strongly opposed to a certain kind of secular ethics which would like to abolish God with the least possible expense. About 1880, some French teachers tried to set up a secular ethics which went something like this: God is a useless and costly hypothesis; we are discarding it; but, meanwhile, in order for there to be an ethics, a society, a civilization, it is essential that certain values be taken seriously and that they be considered as having an *a priori* existence. It must be obligatory, *a priori*, to be honest, not to lie, not to beat your wife, to have children, etc., etc. So we're going to try a little device which will make it possible to show that values exist all the same, inscribed in a heaven of ideas, though otherwise God does not exist. In other words—and this, I believe, is the tendency of everything called reformism in France—nothing will be changed if God does not exist. We shall find ourselves with the same norms of honesty, progress, and humanism, and we shall have made of God an outdated hypothesis which will peacefully die off by itself.

The existentialist, on the contrary, thinks it very distressing that God does not exist, because all possibility of finding values in a heaven of ideas disappears along with Him; there can no longer be an *a priori* Good, since there is no infinite and perfect consciousness to think it. Nowhere is it written that the Good exists, that we must be honest, that we must not lie; because the fact is we are on a plane where there are only men. Dostoievsky said, "If God didn't exist, everything would be possible." That is the very starting point of existentialism. Indeed, everything is permissible if God does not exist, and as a result man is forlorn, because neither within him nor without does he find anything to cling to. He can't start making excuses for himself.

If existence really does precede essence, there is no explaining things away by reference to a fixed and given human nature. In other words, there is no determinism, man is free, man is freedom. On the other hand, if God does not exist, we find no values or commands to turn to which legitimize our conduct. So, in the bright realm of values, we have no excuse behind us, nor justification before us. We are alone, with no excuses.

That is the idea I shall try to convey when I say that man is condemned to be free. Condemned, because he did not create himself, yet, in other respects is free; because, once thrown into the world, he is responsible for everything he does. The existentialist does not believe in the power of passion. He will never agree that a sweeping passion is a ravaging torrent which fatally leads a man to certain acts and is therefore an excuse. He thinks that man is responsible for his passion.

The existentialist does not think that man is going to help himself by finding in the world some omen by which to orient himself. Because he thinks that man will interpret the omen to suit himself. Therefore, he thinks that man, with no support and no aid, is condemned every moment to invent man. Ponge, in a very fine article, has said, "Man is the future of man." That's exactly it. But if it is taken to mean that this future is recorded in heaven, that God sees it, then it is false, because it would really no longer be a future. If it is taken to mean that, whatever a man may be, there is a future to be forged, a virgin future before him, then this remark is sound. But then we are forlorn.

To give you an example which will enable you to understand forlornness better, I shall cite the case of one of my students who came to see me under the following circumstances: his father was on bad terms with his mother, and, moreover, was inclined to be a collaborationist; his older brother had been killed in the German offensive of 1940, and the young man, with somewhat immature but generous feelings, wanted to avenge him. His mother lived alone with him, very much upset by the half-treason of her husband and the death of her older son; the boy was her only consolation.

The boy was faced with the choice of leaving for England and joining the Free French Forces—that is, leaving his mother behind—or remaining with his mother and helping her to carry on. He was fully aware that the woman lived only for him and that his going-off—and perhaps his death—would plunge her into despair. He was also aware that every act that he did for his mother's sake was a sure thing, in the sense that it was helping her to carry on, whereas every effort he made toward going off and fighting was an uncertain move which might run aground and prove completely useless; for example, on his way to England he might, while passing through Spain, be detained indefinitely in a Spanish camp; he might reach England or Algiers and be stuck in an office at a desk job. As a result, he was faced with two very different kinds of action: one, concrete, immediate, but concerning only one individual; the other concerned an incomparably vaster group, a national collectivity, but for that very reason was dubious, and might be interrupted en route. And, at the same time, he was wavering between two kinds of ethics. On the one hand, an ethics of sympathy, of personal devotion; on the other, a broader ethics, but one whose efficacy was more dubious. He had to choose between the two.

Who could help him choose? Christian doctrine? No. Christian doctrine says, "Be charitable, love your neighbor, take the more rugged path, etc., etc." But which is the more rugged path? Whom should he love as a brother? The fighting man or his mother? Which does the greater good, the vague act of fighting in a group, or the concrete one of helping a particular human being to go on living? Who can decide *a priori*? Nobody. No book of ethics can tell him. The Kantian ethics says, "Never treat any person as a means, but as an end." Very well, if I stay with my mother, I'll treat her as an end and not as a means; but by virtue of this very fact, I'm running the risk of treating the people around me who are fighting, as means; and, conversely, if I go to join those who are fighting, I'll be treating them as an end, and, by doing that, I run the risk of treating my mother as a means.

If values are vague, and if they are always too broad for the concrete and specific case that we are considering, the only thing left for us is to trust our instincts. That's what this young man tried to do; and when I saw him, he said, "In the end, feeling is what counts. I ought to choose whichever pushes me in one direction. If I feel that I love my mother enough to sacrifice everything else for her—my desire for vengeance, for action, for adventure—then I'll stay with her. If, on the contrary, I feel that my love for my mother isn't enough, I'll leave."

But how is the value of a feeling determined? What gives his feeling for his mother value? Precisely the fact that he remained with her. I may say that I like so-and-so well enough to sacrifice a certain amount of money for him, but I may say so only if I've done it. I may say "I love my mother well enough to remain with her" if I have remained with her. The only way to determine the value of this affection is, precisely, to perform an act which confirms and defines it. But, since I require this affection to justify my act, I find myself caught in a vicious circle.

On the other hand, Gide has well said that a mock feeling and a true feeling are almost indistinguishable; to decide that I love my mother and will remain with her, or to remain with her by putting on an act, amount somewhat to the same thing. In other words, the feeling is formed by the acts one performs; so, I can not refer to it in order to act upon it. Which means that I can neither seek within myself the true condition which will impel me to act, nor apply to a system of ethics for concepts which will permit me to act. You will say, "At least, he did go to a teacher for advice." But if you seek advice from a priest, for example, you have chosen this priest; you already knew, more or less, just about what advice he was going to give you. In other words, choosing your adviser is involving yourself. The proof of this is that if you are a Christian, you will say, "Consult a priest." But some priests are collaborating, some are just marking time, some are resisting. Which to choose? If the young man chooses a priest who is resisting or collaborating, he has already decided on the kind of advice he's going to get. Therefore, in coming to see me he knew the answer I was going to give him, and I had only one answer to give: "You're free, choose, that is, invent." No general ethics can show you what is to be done; there are no omens in the world. The Catholics will reply, "But there are." Granted—but, in any case, I myself choose the meaning they have.

When I was a prisoner, I knew a rather remarkable young man who was a Jesuit. He had entered the Jesuit order in the following way: he had had a number of very bad breaks; in childhood, his father died, leaving him in poverty, and he was a scholarship student at a religious institution where he was constantly made to feel that he was being kept out of charity; then, he failed to get any of the honors and distinctions that children like; later on, at about eighteen, he bungled a love affair; finally, at twenty-two, he failed in military training, a childish enough matter, but it was the last straw.

This young fellow might well have felt that he had botched everything. It was a sign of something, but of what? He might have taken refuge in bitterness or despair. But he very wisely looked upon all this as a sign that he was not made for secular triumphs, and that only the triumphs of religion, holiness, and faith were open to him. He saw the hand of God in all this, and so he entered the order. Who can help seeing that he alone decided what the sign meant?

Some other interpretation might have been drawn from this series of setbacks; for example, that he might have done better to turn carpenter or revolutionist. Therefore, he is fully responsible for the interpretation. Forlornness implies that we ourselves choose our being. Forlornness and anguish go together.

As for despair, the term has a very simple meaning. It means that we shall confine ourselves to reckoning only with what depends upon our will, or on the ensemble of probabilities which make our action possible. When we want something, we always have to reckon with probabilities. I may be counting on the arrival of a friend. The friend is coming by rail or street-car; this supposes that the train will arrive on schedule, or that the street-car will not jump the track. I am left in the realm of possibility; but possibilities are to be reckoned with only to the point where my action comports with the ensemble of these possibilities, and no further. The moment the possibilities I am considering are not rigorously involved by my action, I ought to disengage myself from them, because no God, no scheme, can adapt the world and its possibilities to my will. When Descartes said, "Conquer yourself rather than the world," he meant essentially the same thing.

The Marxists to whom I have spoken reply, "You can rely on the support of others in your action, which obviously has certain limits because you're not going to live forever. That means: rely on both what others are doing elsewhere to help you, in China, in Russia, and what they will do later on, after your death, to carry on the action and lead it to its fulfillment, which will be the revolution. You even *have* to rely upon that, otherwise you're immoral." I reply at once that I will always rely on fellow-fighters insofar as these comrades are involved with me in a common struggle, in the unity of a party or a group in which I can more or less make my weight felt; that is, one whose ranks I am in as a fighter and whose movements I am aware of at every moment. In such a situation, relying on the unity and will of the party is exactly like counting on the fact that the train will arrive on time or that the car won't jump the track. But, given that man is free and that there is no human nature for me to depend on, I can not count on men whom I do not know by relying on human goodness or man's concern for the good of society. I don't know what will become of the Russian revolution; I may make an example of it to the extent that at the present time it is apparent that the proletariat plays a part in Russia that it plays in no other nation. But I can't swear that this will inevitably lead to a triumph of the proletariat. I've got to limit myself to what I see.

Given that men are free and that tomorrow they will freely decide what man will be, I can not be sure that, after my death, fellow-fighters will carry on my work to bring it to its maximum perfection. Tomorrow, after my death, some men may decide to set up Fascism, and the others may be cowardly and muddled enough to let them do it. Fascism will then be the human reality, so much the worse for us.

Actually, things will be as man will have decided they are to be. Does that mean that I should abandon myself to quietism? No. First, I should involve myself; then, act on the old saw, "Nothing ventured, nothing gained." Nor does it mean that I shouldn't belong to a party, but rather that I shall have no illusions and shall do what I can. For example, suppose I ask myself, "Will socialization, as such, ever come about?" I know nothing about it. All I know is that I'm going to do everything in my power to bring it about. Beyond that, I can't count on anything. Quietism is the attitude of people who say, "Let others do what I can't do." The doctrine I am presenting is the very opposite of quietism, since it declares, "There is no reality except in action." Moreover, it goes further, since it adds, "Man is nothing else than his plan; he exists only to the extent that he fulfills himself; he is therefore nothing else than the ensemble of his acts, nothing else than his life."

According to this, we can understand why our doctrine horrifies certain people. Because often the only way they can bear their wretchedness is to think, "Circumstances have been against me. What I've been and done doesn't show my true worth. To be sure, I've had no great love, no great friendship, but that's because I haven't met a man or woman who was worthy. The books I've written haven't been very good because I haven't had the proper leisure. I haven't had children to devote myself to because I didn't find a man with whom I could have spent my life. So there remains within me, unused and quite viable, a host of propensities, inclinations, possibilities, that one wouldn't guess from, the mere series of things I've done."

Now, for the existentialist there is really no love other than one which manifests itself in a person's being in love. There is no genius other than one which is expressed in works of art; the genius of Proust is the sum of Proust's works; the genius of Racine is his series of tragedies. Outside of that, there is nothing. Why say that Racine could have written another tragedy, when he didn't write it? A man is involved in life, leaves his impress on it, and outside of that there is nothing. To be sure, this may seem a harsh thought to someone whose life hasn't been a success. But, on the other hand, it prompts people to understand that reality alone is what counts, that dreams, expectations, and hopes warrant no more than to define a man as a disappointed dream, as miscarried hopes, as vain expectations. In other words, to define him negatively and not positively. However, when we say, "You are nothing else than your life," that does not imply that the artist will be judged solely on the basis of his works of art; a thousand other things will contribute toward summing him up. What we mean is that a man is nothing else than a series of undertakings, that he is the sum, the organization, the ensemble of the relationships which make up these undertakings.

When all is said and done, what we are accused of, at bottom, is not our pessimism, but an optimistic toughness. If people throw up to us our works of fiction in which we write about people who are soft, weak, cowardly, and sometimes even downright bad, it's not because these people are soft, weak, cowardly, or bad; because if we were to say, as Zola did, that they are that way because of heredity, the workings of environment, society, because of biological or psychological determinism, people would be reassured. They would say, "Well, that's what we're like, no one can do anything about it." But when the existentialist writes about a coward, he says that this coward is responsible for his cowardice. He's not like that because he has a cowardly heart or lung or brain; he's not like that on account of his physiological makeup; but he's like that because he has made himself a coward by his acts. There's no such thing as a cowardly constitution; there are nervous constitutions; there is poor blood, as the common people say, or strong constitutions. But the man whose blood is poor is not a coward on that account, for what makes cowardice is the act of renouncing or yielding. A constitution is not an act; the coward is defined on the basis of the acts he performs. People feel, in a vague sort of way, that this coward we're talking about is guilty of being a coward, and the thought frightens them. What people would like is that a coward or a hero be born that way.

One of the complaints most frequently made about *The Ways of Freedom* can be summed up as follows: "After all, these people are so spineless, how are you going to make heroes out of them?" This objection almost makes me laugh, for it assumes that people are born heroes. That's what people really want to think. If you're born cowardly, you may set your mind perfectly at rest; there's nothing you can do about it; you'll be cowardly all your life, whatever you may do. If you're born a hero, you may set your mind just as much at rest; you'll be a hero all your life; you'll drink like a hero and eat like a hero. What the existentialist says is that the coward makes himself cowardly, that the hero makes himself heroic. There's always a possibility for the coward not to be cowardly any more and for the hero to stop being heroic. What counts is total involvement; some one particular action or set of circumstances is not total involvement.

Thus, I think we have answered a number of the charges concerning existentialism. You see that it can not be taken for a philosophy of quietism, since it defines man in terms of action; nor for a pessimistic description of man— there is no doctrine more optimistic, since man's destiny is within himself; nor for an attempt to discourage man from acting, since it tells him that the only hope is in his acting and that action is the only thing that enables a man to live. Consequently, we are dealing here with an ethics of action and involvement.

Nevertheless, on the basis of a few notions like these, we are still charged with immuring man in his private subjectivity. There again we're very much misunderstood. Subjectivity of the individual is indeed our point of departure, and this for strictly philosophic reasons. Not because we are bourgeois, but because we want a doctrine based on truth and not a lot of fine theories, full of hope but with no real basis. There can be no other truth to take off from than this: *I think; therefore, I exist.* There we have the absolute truth of consciousness becoming aware of itself. Every theory which takes man out of the moment in which he becomes aware of himself is, at its very beginning, a theory which confounds truth, for outside the Cartesian *cogito*, all views are only probable, and a doctrine of probability which is not bound to a truth dissolves into thin air. In order to describe the probable, you must have a firm hold on the true. Therefore, before there can be any truth whatsoever, there must be an absolute truth; and this one is simple and easily arrived at; it's on everyone's doorstep; it's a matter of grasping it directly.

Secondly, this theory is the only one which gives man dignity, the only one which does not reduce him to an object. The effect of all materialism is to treat all men, including the one philosophizing, as objects, that is, as an ensemble of determined reactions in no way distinguished from the ensemble of qualities and phenomena which constitute a table or a chair or a stone. We definitely wish to establish the human realm as an ensemble of values distinct from the material realm. But the subjectivity that we have thus arrived at, and which we have claimed to be truth, is not a strictly individual subjectivity, for we have demonstrated that one discovers in the *cogito* not only himself, but others as well.

The philosophies of Descartes and Kant to the contrary, through the *I think* we reach our own self in the presence of others, and the others are just as real to us as our own self. Thus, the man who becomes aware of himself through the *cogito* also perceives all others, and he perceives them as the condition of his own existence. He realizes that he can not be anything (in the sense that we say that someone is witty or nasty or jealous) unless others recognize it as such. In order to get any truth about myself, I must have contact with another person. The other is indispensable to my own existence, as well as to my knowledge about myself. This being so, in discovering my inner being I discover the other person at the same time, like a freedom placed in front of me which thinks and wills only for or against me. Hence, let us at once announce the discovery of a world which we shall call inter-subjectivity; this is the world in which man decides what he is and what others are.

Besides, if it is impossible to find in every man some universal essence which would be human nature, yet there does exist a universal human condition. It's not by chance that today's thinkers speak more readily of man's condition than of his nature. By condition they mean, more or less definitely, the *a priori* limits which outline man's fundamental situation in the universe. Historical situations vary; a man may be born a slave in a pagan society or a feudal lord or a proletarian. What does not vary is the necessity for him to exist in the world, to be at work there, to be there in the midst of other people, and to be mortal there. The limits are neither subjective or objective, or, rather, they have an objective and a subjective side. Objective because they are to be found everywhere and are recognizable everywhere; subjective because they are *lived* and are nothing if man does not live them, that is, freely determine his existence with reference to them. And though the configurations may differ, at least none of them are completely strange to me, because they all appear as attempts either to pass beyond these limits or recede from them or deny them or adapt to them. Consequently, every configuration, however individual it may be, has a universal value.

Every configuration, even the Chinese, the Indian, or the Negro, can be understood by a Westerner. "Can be understood" means that by virtue of a situation that he can imagine, a European of 1945 can, in like manner, push himself to his limits and reconstitute within himself the configuration of the Chinese, the Indian, or the African. Every configuration has universality in the sense that every configuration can be understood by every man. This does not at all mean that this configuration defines man forever, but that it can be met with again. There is always a way to understand the idiot, the child, the savage, the foreigner, provided one has the necessary information.

In this sense we may say that there is a universality of man; but it is not given, it is perpetually being made. I build the universal in choosing myself; I build it in understanding the configuration of every other man, whatever age he might have lived in. This absoluteness of choice does not do away with the relativeness of each epoch. At heart, what existentialism shows is the connection between the absolute character of free involvement, by virtue of which every man realizes himself in realizing a type of mankind, an involvement always comprehensible in any age whatsoever and by any person whosoever, and the relativeness of the cultural ensemble which may result from such a choice; it must be stressed that the relativity of Cartesianism and the absolute character of Cartesian involvement go together. In this sense, you may, if you like, say that each of us performs an absolute act in breathing, eating, sleeping, or behaving in any way whatever. There is no difference between being free, like a configuration, like an existence which chooses its essence, and being absolute. There is no difference between being an absolute temporarily localised, that is, localised in history, and being universally comprehensible.

This does not entirely settle the objection to subjectivism. In fact, the objection still takes several forms. First, there is the following: we are told, "So you're able to do anything, no matter what!" This is expressed in various ways. First we are accused of anarchy; then they say, "You're unable to pass judgment on others, because there's no reason to prefer one configuration to another"; finally they tell us, "Everything is arbitrary in this choosing of yours. You take something from one pocket and pretend you're putting it into the other."

These three objections aren't very serious. Take the first objection. "You're able to do anything, no matter what" is not to the point. In one sense choice is possible, but what is not possible is not to choose. I can always choose, but I ought to know that if I do not choose, I am still choosing. Though this may seem purely formal, it is highly important for keeping fantasy and caprice within bounds. If it is true that in facing a situation, for example, one in which, as a person capable of having sexual relations, of having children, I am obliged to choose an attitude, and if I in any way assume responsibility for a choice which, in involving myself, also involves all mankind, this has nothing to do with caprice, even if no *a priori* value determines my choice.

If anybody thinks that he recognizes here Gide's theory of the arbitrary act, he fails to see the enormous difference between this doctrine and Gide's. Gide does not know what a situation is. He acts out of pure caprice. For us, on the contrary, man is in an organized situation in which he himself is involved. Through his choice, he involves all mankind, and he can not avoid making a choice: either he will remain chaste, or he will marry without having children, or he will marry and have children; anyhow, whatever he may do, it is impossible for him not to take full responsibility for the way he handles this problem. Doubtless he chooses without referring to pre-established values, but it is unfair to accuse him of caprice. Instead, let us say that moral choice is to be compared to the making of a work of art. And before going any further, let it be said at once that we are not dealing here with an aesthetic ethics, because our opponents are so dishonest that they even accuse us of that. The example I've chosen is a comparison only.

Having said that, may I ask whether anyone has ever accused an artist who has painted a picture of not having drawn his inspiration from rules set up *a priori*? Has anyone ever asked, "What painting ought he to make?" It is clearly understood that there is no definite painting to be made, that the artist is engaged in the making of his painting, and that the painting to be made is precisely the painting he will have made. It is clearly understood that there are no *a priori* aesthetic values, but that there are values which appear subsequently in the coherence of the painting, in the correspondence between what the artist intended and the result. Nobody can tell what the painting of tomorrow will be like. Painting can be judged only after it has once been made. What connection does that have with ethics? We are in the same creative situation. We never say that a work of art is arbitrary. When we speak of a canvas of Picasso, we never say that it is arbitrary; we understand quite well that he was making himself what he is at the very time he was painting, that the ensemble of his work is embodied in his life.

The same holds on the ethical plane. What art and ethics have in common is that we have creation and invention in both cases. We can not decide *a priori* what there is to be done. I think that I pointed that out quite sufficiently when I mentioned the case of the student who came to see me, and who might have applied to all the ethical systems, Kantian or otherwise, without getting any sort of guidance. He was obliged to devise his law himself. Never let it be said by us that this man—who, taking affection, individual action, and kind-heartedness toward a specific person as his ethical first principle, chooses to remain with his mother, or who, preferring to make a sacrifice, chooses to go to England—has made an arbitrary choice. Man makes himself. He isn't ready made at the start. In choosing his ethics, he makes himself, and force of circumstances is such that he can not abstain from choosing one. We define man only in relationship to involvement. It is therefore absurd to charge us with arbitrariness of choice.

In the second place, it is said that we are unable to pass judgment on others. In a way this is true, and in another way, false. It is true in this sense, that, whenever a man sanely and sincerely involves himself and chooses his configuration, it is impossible for him to prefer another configuration, regardless of what his own may be in other respects. It is true in this sense, that we do not believe in progress. Progress is betterment. Man is always the same. The situation confronting him varies. Choice always remains a choice in a situation. The problem has not changed since the time one could choose between those for and those against slavery, for example, at the time of the Civil War, and the present time, when one can side with the Maquis Resistance Party, or with the Communists.

But, nevertheless, one can still pass judgment, for, as I have said, one makes a choice in relationship to others. First, one can judge (and this is perhaps not a judgment of value, but a logical judgment) that certain choices are based on error and others on truth. If we have defined man's situation as a free choice, with no excuses and no recourse, every man who takes refuge behind the excuse of his passions, every man who sets up a determinism, is a dishonest man.

The objection may be raised, "But why mayn't he choose himself dishonestly?" I reply that I am not obliged to pass moral judgment on him, but that I do define his dishonesty as an error. One can not help considering the truth of the matter. Dishonesty is obviously a falsehood because it belies the complete freedom of involvement. On the same grounds, I maintain that there is also dishonesty if I choose to state that certain values exist prior to me; it is self-contradictory for me to want them and at the same state that they are imposed on me. Suppose someone says to me, "What if I want to be dishonest?" I'll answer, "There's no reason for you not to be, but I'm saying that that's what you are, and that the strictly coherent attitude is that of honesty."

Besides, I can bring moral judgment to bear. When I declare that freedom in every concrete circumstance can have no other aim than to want itself, if man has once become aware that in his forlornness he imposes values, he can no longer want but one thing, and that is freedom, as the basis of all values. That doesn't mean that he wants it in the abstract. It means simply that the ultimate meaning of the acts of honest men is the quest for freedom as such. A man who belongs to a communist or revolutionary union wants concrete goals; these goals imply an abstract desire for freedom; but this freedom is wanted in something concrete. We want freedom for freedom's sake and in every particular circumstance. And in wanting freedom we discover that it depends entirely on the freedom of others, and that the freedom of others depends on ours. Of course, freedom as the definition of man does not depend on others, but as soon as there is involvement, I am obliged to want others to have freedom at the same time that I want my own freedom. I can take freedom as my goal only if I take that of others as a goal as well. Consequently, when, in all honesty, I've recognized that man is a being in whom existence precedes essence, that he is a free being who, in various circumstances, can want only his freedom, I have at the same time recognized that I can want only the freedom of others.

Therefore, in the name of this will for freedom, which freedom itself implies, I may pass judgment on those who seek to hide from themselves the complete arbitrariness and the complete freedom of their existence. Those who hide their complete freedom from themselves out of a spirit of seriousness or by means of deterministic excuses, I shall call cowards; those who try to show that their existence was necessary when it is the very contingency of man's appearance on earth, I shall call stinkers. But cowards or stinkers can be judged only from a strictly unbiased point of view.

Therefore though the content of ethics is variable, a certain form of it is universal. Kant says that freedom desires both itself and the freedom of others. Granted. But he believes that the formal and the universal are enough to constitute an ethics. We, on the other hand, think that principles which are too abstract run aground in trying to decide action. Once again, take the case of the student. In the name of what, in the name of what great moral maxim do you

think he could have decided, in perfect peace of mind, to abandon his mother or to stay with her? There is no way of judging. The content is always concrete and thereby unforeseeable; there is always the element of invention. The one thing that counts is knowing whether the inventing that has been done, has been done in the name of freedom.

For example, let us look at the following two cases. You will see to what extent they correspond, yet differ. Take *The Mill on the Floss*. We find a certain young girl, Maggie Tulliver, who is an embodiment of the value of passion and who is aware of it. She is in love with a young man, Stephen, who is engaged to an insignificant young girl. This Maggie Tulliver, instead of heedlessly preferring her own happiness, chooses, in the name of human solidarity, to sacrifice herself and give up the man she loves. On the other hand, Sanseverina, in *The Charterhouse of Parma*, believing that passion is man's true value, would say that a great love deserves sacrifices; that it is to be preferred to the banality of the conjugal love that would tie Stephen to the young ninny he had to marry. She would choose to sacrifice the girl and fulfill her happiness; and, as Stendhal shows, she is even ready to sacrifice herself for the sake of passion, if this life demands it. Here we are in the presence of two strictly opposed moralities. I claim that they are much the same thing; in both cases what has been set up as the goal is freedom.

You can imagine two highly similar attitudes: one girl prefers to renounce her love out of resignation; another prefers to disregard the prior attachment of the man she loves out of sexual desire. On the surface these two actions resemble those we've just described. However, they are completely different. Sanseverina's attitude is much nearer that of Maggie Tulliver, one of heedless rapacity.

Thus, you see that the second charge is true and, at the same time, false. One may choose anything if it is on the grounds of free involvement.

The third objection is the following: "You take something from one pocket and put it into the other. That is, fundamentally, values aren't serious, since you choose them." My answer to this is that I'm quite vexed that that's the way it is; but if I've discarded God the Father, there has to be someone to invent values. You've got to take things as they are. Moreover, to say that we invent values means nothing else but this: life has no meaning *a priori*. Before you come alive, life is nothing; it's up to you to give it a meaning, and value is nothing else but the meaning that you choose. In that way, you see, there is a possibility of creating a human community.

I've been reproached for asking whether existentialism is humanistic. It's been said, "But you said in *Nausea* that the humanists were all wrong. You made fun of a certain kind of humanist. Why come back to it now?" Actually, the word humanism has two very different meanings. By humanism one can mean a theory which takes man as an end and as a higher value. Humanism in this sense can be found in Cocteau's tale *Around the World in Eighty Hours* when a character, because he is flying over some mountains in an airplane, declares, "Man is simply amazing." That means that I, who did who did not build the airplanes, shall personally benefit from these particular inventions, and that I, as man, shall personally consider myself responsible for, and honored by, acts of a few particular men. This would imply that we ascribe a value to man on the basis of the highest deeds of certain men. This humanism is absurd, because only the dog or the horse would be able to make such an over-all judgment about man, which they are careful not to do, at least to my knowledge.

But it can not be granted that a man may make a judgment about man. Existentialism spares him from any such judgment. The existentialist will never consider man as an end because he is always in the making. Nor should we believe that there is a mankind to which we might set up a cult in the manner of Auguste Comte. The cult of mankind ends in the self-enclosed humanism of Comte, and, let it be said, of fascism. This kind of humanism we can do without.

But there is another meaning of humanism. Fundamentally it is this: man is constantly outside of himself; in projecting himself, in losing himself outside of himself, he makes for man's existing; and, on the other hand, it is by pursuing transcendent goals that he is able to exist; man, being this state of passing-beyond, and seizing upon things only as they bear upon this passing-beyond, is at the heart, at the center of this passing-beyond. There is no universe other than a human universe, the universe of human subjectivity. This connection between transcendency, as a constituent element of man—not in the sense that God is transcendent, but in the sense of passing beyond—and subjectivity, in the sense that man is not closed in on himself but is always present in a human universe, is what we call existentialist humanism. Humanism, because we remind man that there is no law-maker other than himself, and that in his forlornness he will decide by himself; because we point out that man will fulfill himself as man, not in turning toward himself, but in seeking outside of himself a goal which is just this liberation, just this particular fulfillment.

From these few reflections it is evident that nothing is more unjust than the objections that have been raised against us. Existentialism is nothing else than an attempt to draw all the consequences of a coherent atheistic position. It isn't trying to plunge man into despair at all. But if one calls every attitude of unbelief despair, like the Christians, then the word is not being used in its original sense. Existentialism isn't so atheistic that it wears itself out showing that God doesn't exist. Rather, it declares that even if God did exist, that would change nothing. There you've got our point of view. Not that we believe that God exists, but we think that the problem of His existence is not the issue. In this sense existentialism is optimistic, a doctrine of action, and it is plain dishonesty for Christians to make no distinction between their own despair and ours and then to call us despairing.

R. M. HARE

FROM *Freedom and Reason*

A further theoretical development in ethics that takes Moore's criticism of naturalism as its starting point is the linguistic theory of R. M. Hare (1919–). Hare, professor of philosophy at the University of Florida, produced two influential books on the meaning of ethical discourse, The Language of Morals *(1952) and* Freedom and Reason *(1963). In these works, Hare contended that the emotivists were correct to condemn cognitivist ethical theories, both naturalist and nonnaturalist. But where they went wrong, said Hare, was in their claim that the language of morals tries to get people to act in a certain way. Hare argued that moral language tells people how to act because moral language is prescriptive. And since it is prescriptive, it shares traits with the other major type of prescriptive statements—imperatives (commands).*

Hare saw as his task the logical study of the language of morals. Morality is a matter of using language in a particular way. A weakness of the emotivist view was that it seemed to allow a person to advocate or condemn virtually any activity that is physically or conceptually possible, no matter how bizarre or wrong by commonsense standards. Hare's theory overcomes this weakness. Since moral statements are prescriptive claims rather than mere declarations of personal preference, they must conform to the logical requirement that they be universalizable. Although one can evaluate any particular course of action as morally good or bad, to be consistent, that moral evaluation must apply to any situation in which the subject of the moral judgment is relevantly similar to the current situation. This means that if I prescribe some action for someone else, I must be willing to act in that same way, or follow the same prohibitions, when I am in a similar situation. If moral statements must be universalizable, then a moral statement is actually a moral principle.

Hare's "universal prescriptivism," as he called it, appeared to offer an alternative to emotivism that corresponded to the commonsense view that morality should not be able to justify an action simply because someone happens to favor it. Yet critics pointed out that universalizability was not necessarily as effective as Hare had contended. After all, people could still prescribe acts that appeared either silly or evil, just as long as they were willing to act in that way themselves.

The emphasis in moral philosophy on the logic of moral language reached its peak by the mid-twentieth century. Although ethical work continued in this vein, attention began to turn once again to the need for a theory of morality that addressed more pressing practical concerns. The final section of this text presents representative work from the second half of the twentieth century that reflects this growing interest in normative ethical theories.

Part II Moral Reasoning

And as ye would that men should do to you, do ye also to them
likewise.   ST. LUKE, VI 31

6 . A Moral Argument

6.1. Historically, one of the chief incentives to the
study of ethics has been the hope that its findings
might be of help to those faced with difficult moral
problems. That this is still a principal incentive for
many people is shown by the fact that modern
philosophers are often reproached for failing to make
ethics relevant to morals.[1] This is because one of the
main tenets of many recent moral philosophers has
been that the most popular method by which it was
sought to bring ethics to bear on moral problems was
not feasible—namely the method followed by the
group of theories loosely known as 'naturalist.'

The method of naturalism is so to characterize the
meanings of the key moral terms that, given certain
factual premises, not themselves moral judgements,
moral conclusions can be deduced from them. If this
could be done, it was thought that it would be of
great assistance to us in making moral decisions; we
should only have to find out the non-moral facts,
and the moral conclusion as to what we ought to do
would follow. Those who say that it cannot be done
leave themselves the task of giving an alternative account of moral reasoning.

Naturalism seeks to make the findings of ethics
relevant to moral decisions by making the former
not morally *neutral*. It is a very natural assumption
that if a statement of ethics is relevant to morals,
then it cannot be neutral as between different moral
judgements; and naturalism is a tempting view for
those who make this assumption. Naturalistic definitions are not morally neutral, because with their
aid we could show that statements of non-moral
facts *entailed* moral conclusions. And some have
thought that unless such an entailment can be
shown to hold, the moral philosopher has not made
moral reasoning possible.

One way of escaping this conclusion is to say that
the relation linking a set of non-moral premises with
a moral conclusion is not one of entailment, but that
some other logical relation, peculiar to morals, justifies the inference. This is the view put forward, for
example, by Mr. Toulmin.[2] Since I have argued elsewhere against this approach, I shall not discuss it
here. Its advocates have, however, hit upon an important insight that moral reasoning does not necessarily proceed by way of *deduction* of moral
conclusions from non-moral premises. Their further
suggestion, that therefore it makes this transition by
means of some other, peculiar, non-deductive kind of
inference, is not the only possibility. It may be that
moral reasoning is not, typically, any kind of 'straight-
line' or 'linear' reasoning from premises to conclusion.

6.2. A parallel from the philosophy of science will
perhaps make this point clear. It is natural to suppose that what the scientist does is to reason from
premises, which are the data of observation, to conclusions, which are his 'scientific laws', by means of
a special sort of inference called 'inductive'. Against
this view, Professor Popper has forcibly argued that
in science there are no inferences other than deductive; the typical procedure of scientists is to propound hypotheses, and then look for ways of testing
them—i.e. experiments which, if they are false, will
show them to be so. A hypothesis which, try as we
may, we fail to falsify, we accept provisionally, though
ready to abandon it if, after all, further experiment
refutes it; and of those that are so accepted we rate
highest the ones which say most, and which would,
therefore, be most likely to have been falsified if they
were false. The only inferences which occur in this
process are deductive ones, from the truth of certain
observations to the falsity of a hypothesis. There is no
reasoning which proceeds from the data of observation to the *truth* of a hypothesis. Scientific inquiry is
rather a kind of *exploration*, or looking for hypotheses which will stand up to the test of experiment.[3]

We must ask whether moral reasoning exhibits
any similar features. I want to suggest that it too is a
kind of exploration, and not a kind of linear inference, and that the only inferences which take place

---

1. I have tried to fill in some of the historical background of these
reproaches, and to assess the justification for them, in my article
in *The Philosophy of C. D. Broad*, ed. P. Schilpp.

2. S.E. Toulmin, *The Place of Reason in Ethics,* esp pp.38–60. See
my review in *Philosophical Quarterly,* i (1950/1), 372, and LM 3.4.

3. K.R. Popper, *The Logic of Scientific Discovery* (esp. pp. 32 f.). See
also his article in C. A. Mace (ed.), *British Philosophy in the Mid-
Century,* p.155.

in it are deductive. What we are doing in moral reasoning is to look for moral judgements and moral principles which, when we have considered their logical consequences and the facts of the case, we can still accept. As we shall see, this approach to the problem enables us to reject the assumption, which seemed so natural, that ethics cannot be relevant to moral decisions without ceasing to be neutral. This is because we are not going to demand any inferences in our reasoning other than deductive ones, and because none of these deductive inferences rely for their validity upon naturalistic definitions of moral terms.

Two further parallels may help to make clear the sense in which ethics is morally neutral. In the kind of scientific reasoning just described, mathematics plays a major part, for many of the deductive inferences that occur are mathematical in character. So we are bound to admit that mathematics is relevant to scientific inquiry. Nevertheless, it is also neutral, in the sense that no discoveries about matters of physical fact can be made with the aid of mathematics alone, and that no mathematical inference can have a conclusion which says more, in the way of prediction of observations, than its premises implicitly do.

An even simpler parallel is provided by the rules of games. The rules of a game are neutral as between the players, in the sense that they do not, by themselves, determine which player is going to win. In order to decide who wins, the players have to play the game in accordance with the rules, which involves their making, themselves, a great many individual decisions. On the other hand, the 'neutrality' of the rules of a game does not turn it into a game of chance, in which the bad player is as likely to win as the good.

Ethical theory, which determines the meanings and functions of the moral words, and thus the 'rules' of the moral 'game,' provides only a clarification of the conceptual framework within which moral reasoning takes place; it is therefore, in the required sense, neutral as between different moral opinions. But it is highly relevant to moral reasoning because, as with the rules of a game, there could be no such thing as moral reasoning without this framework, and the framework dictates the form of the reasoning. It follows that naturalism is not the only way of providing for the possibility of moral reason-ing; and this may, perhaps, induce those who have espoused naturalism as a way of making moral thought a rational activity to consider other possibilities.

The rules of moral reasoning are, basically, two, corresponding to the two features of moral judgements which I argued for in the first half of this book, prescriptivity and universalizability. When we are trying, in a concrete case, to decide what we ought to do, what we are looking for (as I have already said) is an action to which we can commit ourselves (prescriptivity) but which we are at the same time prepared to accept as exemplifying a principle of action to be prescribed for others in like circumstances (universalizability). If, when we consider some proposed action, we find that, when universalized, it yields prescriptions which we cannot accept, we reject this action as a solution to our moral problem—if we cannot universalize the prescription, it cannot become an 'ought.'

It is to be noticed that, troublesome as was the problem of moral weakness when we were dealing theoretically with the logical character of the moral concepts, it cannot trouble us here. For if a person is going to reason seriously at all about a moral question, he has to presuppose that the moral concepts are going, in his reasoning, to be used prescriptively. One cannot start a moral argument about a certain proposal on the basis that, whatever the conclusion of it, it makes no difference to what anybody is to do. When one has arrived at a conclusion, one may then be too weak to put it into practice. But *in arguing* one has to discount this possibility; for, as we shall see, to abandon the prescriptivity of one's moral judgements is to unscrew an essential part of the logical mechanism on which such arguments rely. This is why, if a person were to say 'Let's have an argument about this grave moral question which faces us, but let's not think of any conclusion we may come to as requiring anybody to *do* one thing rather than another,' we should be likely to accuse him of flippancy, or worse.

6.3. I will now try to exhibit the bare bones of the theory of moral reasoning that I wish to advocate by considering a very simple (indeed over-simplified) example. As we shall see, even this very simple case generates the most baffling complexities; and so we may be pardoned for not attempting anything more difficult to start with.

The example is adapted from a well-known parable.[1] *A* owes money to *B*, and *B* owes money to *C*, and it is the law that creditors may exact their debts by putting their debtors into prison. *B* asks himself, 'Can I say that I ought to take this measure against *A* in order to make him pay?' He is no doubt *inclined* to do this, or *wants* to do it. Therefore, if there were no question of universalizing his prescriptions, he would assent readily to the *singular* prescription 'Let me put *A* into prison' (4.3). But when he seeks to turn this prescription into a moral judgement, and say, 'I *ought* to put *A* into prison because he will not pay me what he owes,' he reflects that this would involve accepting the principle 'Anyone who is in my position ought to put his debtor into prison if he does not pay.' But then he reflects that *C* is in the same position of unpaid creditor with regard to himself (*B*), and that the cases are otherwise identical; and that if anyone in this position ought to put his debtors into prison, then so ought *C* to put him (*B*) into prison. And to accept the moral prescription '*C* ought to put me into prison' would commit him (since, as we have seen, he must be using the word 'ought' prescriptively) to accepting the singular prescription 'Let *C* put me into prison'; and this he is not ready to accept. But if he is not, then neither can he accept the original judgement that he (*B*) ought to put *A* into prison for debt. Notice that the whole of this argument would break down if 'ought' were not being used both universalizably *and prescriptively;* for if it were not being used prescriptively, the step from '*C* ought to put me into prison' to 'Let *C* put me into prison' would not be valid.

The structure and ingredients of this argument must now be examined. We must first notice an analogy between it and the Popperian theory of scientific method. What has happened is that a provisional or suggested moral principle has been rejected because one of its particular consequences proved unacceptable. But an important difference between the two kinds of reasoning must also be noted; it is what we should expect, given that the data of scientific observation are recorded in descriptive statements, whereas we are here dealing with prescriptions. What knocks out a suggested hypothesis, on Popper's theory, is a singular statement of fact: the hypothesis has

the consequence that *p;* but not-*p*. Here the logic is just the same, except that in place of the observation—statements '*p*' and 'not-*p*' we have the singular *prescriptions* 'Let *C* put *B* into prison for debt' and its contradictory. Nevertheless, given that *B* is disposed to reject the first of these prescriptions, the argument against him is just as cogent as in the scientific case.

We may carry the parallel further. Just as science, seriously pursued, is the search for hypotheses and the testing of them by the attempt to falsify their particular consequences, so morals, as a serious endeavour, consists in the search for principles and the testing of them against particular cases. Any rational activity has its discipline, and this is the discipline of moral thought: to test the moral principles that suggest themselves to us by following out their consequences and seeing whether we can accept *them*.

No argument, however, starts from nothing. We must therefore ask what we have to have before moral arguments of the sort of which I have given a simple example can proceed. The first requisite is that the facts of the case should be given; for all moral discussion is about some particular set of facts, whether actual or supposed. Secondly we have the logical framework provided by the meaning of the word 'ought' (i.e. prescriptivity and universalizability, both of which we saw to be necessary). Because moral judgements have to be universalizable, *B* cannot say that he ought to put *A* into prison for debt without committing himself to the view that *C*, who is *ex hypothesi* in the same position *vis-à-vis* himself, ought to put *him* into prison; and because moral judgements are prescriptive, this would be, in effect, prescribing to *C* to put him into prison; and this he is unwilling to do, since he has a strong inclination not to go to prison. This inclination gives us the third necessary ingredient in the argument: if *B* were a completely apathetic person, who literally did not mind what happened to himself or to anybody else, the argument would not touch him. The three necessary ingredients which we have noticed, then, are (1) facts; (2) logic; (3) inclinations. These ingredients enable us, not indeed to arrive at an evaluative conclusion, but to *reject* an evaluative proposition. We shall see later that these are not, in all cases, the only necessary ingredients.

6.4. In the example which we have been using, the position was deliberately made simpler by supposing that *B* actually stood to some other person in

---

1. Matthew xviii. 23.

exactly the same relation as A does to him. Such cases are unlikely to arise in practice. But it is not necessary for the force of the argument that *B* should *in fact* stand in this relation to anyone; it is sufficient that he should consider hypothetically such a case, and see what would be the consequences in it of those moral principles between whose acceptance and rejection he has to decide. Here we have an important point of difference from the parallel scientific argument, in that the crucial case which leads to rejection of the principle can itself be a supposed, not an observed, one. That hypothetical cases will do as well as actual ones is important, since it enables us to guard against a possible misinterpretation of the argument which I have outlined. It might be thought that what moves *B* is the *fear* that *C* will actually do to him as he does to A—as happens in the gospel parable. But this fear is not only irrelevant to the moral argument; it does not even provide a particularly strong non-moral motive unless the circumstances are somewhat exceptional. *C* may, after all, not find out what *B* has done to *A*; or *C*'s moral principles may be different from *B*'s, and independent of them, so that what moral principle *B* accepts makes no difference to the moral principles on which *C* acts.

Even, therefore, if *C* did not exist, it would be no answer to the argument for *B* to say 'But in my case there is no fear that anybody will ever be in a position to do to me what I am proposing to do to A.' For the argument does not rest on any such fear. All that is essential to it is that *B* should disregard the fact that he plays the particular role in the situation which he does, without disregarding the inclinations which people have in situations of this sort. In other words, he must be prepared to give weight to *A*'s inclinations and interests as if they were his own. This is what turns selfish prudential reasoning into moral reasoning. It is much easier, psychologically, for *B* to do this if he is actually placed in a situation like *A*'s vis-à-vis somebody else; but this is not necessary, provided that he has sufficient imagination to envisage what it is like to be *A*. For our first example, a case was deliberately chosen in which little imagination was necessary; but in most normal cases a certain power of imagination and readiness to use it is a fourth necessary ingredient in moral arguments, alongside those already mentioned, viz. logic (in the shape of universalizability and prescriptivity), the facts, and the inclinations or interests of the people concerned.

It must be pointed out that the absence of even one of these ingredients may render the rest ineffective. For example, impartiality by itself is not enough. If, in becoming impartial, *B* became also completely dispassionate and apathetic, and moved as little by other people's interests as by his own, then, as we have seen, there would be nothing to make him accept or reject one moral principle rather than another. That is why those who, like Adam Smith and Professor Kneale, advocate what have been called 'Ideal Observer Theories' of ethics, sometimes postulate as their imaginary ideal observer not merely an impartial spectator, but an impartially *sympathetic* spectator.[1] To take another example, if the person who faces the moral decision has no imagination, then even the fact that someone can do the very same thing to him may pass him by. If, again, he lacks the readiness to universalize, then the vivid imagination of the sufferings which he is inflicting on others may only spur him on to intensify them, to increase his own vindictive enjoyment. And if he is ignorant of the material facts (for example about what is likely to happen to a person if one takes out a writ against him), then there is nothing to tie the moral argument to particular choices.

6.5. The best way of testing the argument which we have outlined will be to consider various ways in which somebody in *B*'s position might seek to escape from it. There are indeed a number of such ways; and all of them may be successful, at a price. It is important to understand what the price is in each case. We may classify these manœuvres which are open to *B* into two kinds. There are first of all the moves which depend on his using the moral words in a different way from that on which the argument relied. We saw that for the success of the argument it was necessary that 'ought' should be used universalizably

---

1. It will be plain that there are affinities, though there are also differences, between this type of theory and my own. For such theories see W. C. Kneale, *Philosophy,* xxv (1950), 162; R. Firth and R. B. Brandt, *Philosophy and Phenomenological Research,* xii (1951/2), 317, and xv (1954/5), 407, 414, 422; and J. Harrison, *Aristotelian Society* supp. vol. xxviii (1954), 132. Firth, unlike Kneale, says that the observer must be 'dispassionate,' but see Brandt, op. cit., p. 411 n. For a shorter discussion see Brandt, *Ethical Theory,* p.173. Since for many Christians God occupies the role of 'ideal observer,' the moral judgements which they make may be expected to coincide with those arrived at by the method of reasoning which I am advocating.

and prescriptively. If *B* uses it in a way that is either not prescriptive or not universalizable, then he can escape the force of the argument, at the cost of resigning from the kind of discussion that we thought we were having with him. We shall discuss these two possibilities separately. Secondly, there are moves which can still be made by *B,* even though he is using the moral words in the same way as we are. We shall examine three different sub-classes of these.

Before dealing with what I shall call the *verbal* manœuvers in detail, it may be helpful to make a general remark. Suppose that we are having a simple mathematical argument with somebody, and he admits, for example, that there are five eggs in this basket, and six in the other, but maintains that there are a dozen eggs in the two baskets taken together; and suppose that this is because he is using the expression a 'dozen' to mean 'eleven.' It is obvious that we cannot compel him logically to admit that there are not a dozen eggs, in *his* sense of 'dozen.' But it is equally obvious that this should not disturb us. For such a man only appears to be dissenting from us. His dissent is only apparent, because the proposition which his words express is actually consistent with the conclusion which we wish to draw; he *says* 'There are a dozen eggs'; but he *means* what we should express by saying 'There are eleven eggs'; and this we are not disputing. It is important to remember that in the moral case also the dissent may be only apparent, if the words are being used in different ways, and that it is no defect in a method of argument if it does not make it possible to prove a conclusion to a person when he is using words in such a way that the conclusion does not follow.

It must be pointed out, further (since this is a common source of confusion), that in this argument nothing whatever hangs upon our *actual* use of words in common speech, any more than it does in the arithmetical case. That we use the sound 'dozen' to express the meaning that we customarily do use it to express is of no consequence for the argument about the eggs; and the same may be said of the sound 'ought.' There is, however, something which I, at any rate, customarily express by the sound 'ought,' whose character is correctly described by saying that it is a universal or universalizable prescription. I hope that what I customarily express by the sound 'ought' is the same as what most people customarily express by it; but if I am mistaken in this assump-

tion, I shall still have given a correct account, so far as I am able, of that which I express by this sound.[1] Nevertheless, this account will interest other people mainly in so far as my hope that they understand the same thing as I do by 'ought' is fulfilled; and since I am moderately sure that this is indeed the case with many people, I hope that I may be of use to them in elucidating the logical properties of the concept which they thus express.

At this point, however, it is of the utmost importance to stress that the fact that two people express the same thing by 'ought' does not entail that they share the same moral opinions. For the formal, logical properties of the word 'ought' (those which are determined by its *meaning*) are only one of the four factors (listed earlier) whose combination governs a man's moral opinion on a given matter. Thus ethics, the study of the logical properties of the moral words, remains morally neutral (its conclusions neither are substantial moral judgements, nor entail them, even in conjunction with factual premises); its bearing upon moral questions lies in this, that it makes logically impossible certain combinations of moral and other prescriptions. Two people who are using the word 'ought' in the same way may yet disagree about what ought to be done in a certain situation, either because they differ about the facts, or because one or other of them lacks imagination, or because their different inclinations make one reject some singular prescription which the other can accept. For all that, ethics (i.e. the logic of moral language) is an immensely powerful engine for producing moral agreement; for if two people are willing to use the moral word 'ought,' and to use it in the same way (viz. the way that I have been describing), the other possible sources of moral disagreement are all eliminable. People's inclinations about most of the important matters in life tend to be the same (very few people, for example, like being starved or run over by motorcars); and, even when they are not, there is a way of generalizing the argument, to be described in the next chapter, which enables us to make allowance for differences in inclinations. The facts are often, given sufficient patience, ascertainable. Imagination can be cultivated. If these three factors are looked after, as they can be, agreement on the use of 'ought' is the

---

1. Cf. Moore, *Principia Ethica,* p.6.

only other necessary condition for producing moral agreement, at any rate in typical cases. And, if I am not mistaken, this agreement in use is already there in the discourse of anybody with whom we are at all likely to find ourselves arguing; all that is needed is to think clearly, and so make it evident.

After this methodological digression, let us consider what is to be done with the man who professes to be using 'ought' in some different way from that which I have described—because he is not using it prescriptively, or not universalizably. For the reasons that I have given, if he takes either of these courses, he is no longer in substantial moral disagreement with us. Our apparent moral disagreement is really only verbal; for although, as we shall see shortly, there may be a residuum of substantial disagreement, this cannot be moral.

Let us take first the man who is using the word 'ought' prescriptively, but not universalizably. He can say that he ought to put his debtor into prison, although he is not prepared to agree that his creditor ought to put *him* into prison. We, on the other hand, since we are not prepared to admit that our creditors in these circumstances ought to put us into prison, cannot say that we ought to put our debtors into prison. So there is an appearance of substantial moral disagreement, which is intensified by the fact that, since we are both using the word 'ought' prescriptively, our respective views will lead to different particular actions. Different *singular* prescriptions about what to do are (since both our judgements are prescriptive) derivable from what we are respectively saying. But this is not enough to constitute a moral disagreement. For that, we should have to differ, not only about what *is* to be done in some particular case, but about some universal principle concerning what *ought* to be done in cases of a certain sort; and since B is (on the hypothesis considered) advocating no such universal principle, he is saying nothing with which we can be in moral or evaluative disagreement. Considered purely as prescriptions, indeed, our two views are in substantial disagreement; but the moral, evaluative (i.e. the *universal* prescriptive) disagreement is only verbal, because, when the expression of B's view is understood as he means it, the view turns out not to be a view about the morality of the action at all. So B, by this manœuvre, can go on prescribing to himself to put A into prison, but has to abandon the claim that he is justifying the action morally, as we

understand the word 'morally.' One may, of course, use any word as one pleases, at a price. But he can no longer claim to be giving that sort of justification of his action for which, as I think, the common expression is 'moral justification' (10.7).

I need not deal at length with the second way in which B might be differing from us in his use of 'ought,' viz. by not using it prescriptively. If he were not using it prescriptively, it will be remembered, he could assent to the singular prescription 'Let not C put me into prison for debt,' and yet assent also to the non-prescriptive moral judgement 'C ought to put me into prison for debt.' And so his disinclination to be put into prison for debt by C would furnish no obstacle to his saying that he (B) ought to put A into prison for debt. And thus he could carry out his own inclination to put A into prison with apparent moral justification. The justification would be, however, only apparent. For if B is using the word 'ought' non-prescriptively, then 'I ought to put A into prison for debt' does not entail the singular prescription 'Let me put A into prison for debt'; the 'moral' judgement becomes quite irrelevant to the choice of what to do. There would also be the same lack of substantial moral disagreement as we noticed in the preceding case. B would not be disagreeing with us other than verbally, so far as the moral question is concerned (though there might be points of *factual* disagreement between us, arising from the *descriptive* meaning of our judgements). The 'moral' disagreement could be only verbal, because whereas we should be dissenting from the universalizable prescription 'B ought to put A into prison for debt,' *this* would not be what B was expressing, though the words he would be using would be the same. For B would not, by these words, be expressing a prescription at all.

6.6. So much for the ways (of which my list may well be incomplete) in which B can escape from our argument by using the word 'ought' in a different way from us. The remaining ways of escape are open to him even if he is using 'ought' in the same way as we are, viz. to express a universalizable prescription.

We must first consider that class of escape-routes whose distinguishing feature is that B, while using the moral words in the same way as we are, refuses to make positive moral judgements at all in certain cases. There are two main variations of this manœuvre. B may either say that it is indifferent, morally, whether he imprisons A or not; or he may refuse to make any moral judgement at all, even one of indifference, about the case. It will be obvious that if he adopts either of these moves, he can evade the argument as so far set out. For that argument only forced him to *reject* the moral judgement 'I ought to imprison *A* for debt.' It did not force him to assent to any moral judgement; in particular, he remained free to assent, either to the judgement that he ought not to imprison *A* for debt (which is the one that we want him to accept) or to the judgement that it is neither the case that he ought, nor the case that he ought not (that it is, in short, indifferent); and he remained free, also, to say 'I am just not making any moral judgements at all about this case.'

We have not yet, however, exhausted the arguments generated by the demand for universalizability, provided that the moral words are being used in a way which allows this demand. For it is evident that these manœuvres could, in principle, be practised in any case whatever in which the morality of an act is in question. And this enables us to place *B* in a dilemma. Either he practises this manœuver in *every* situation in which he is faced with a moral decision; or else he practises it only *sometimes*. The first alternative, however, has to be sub-divided; for 'every situation' might mean 'every situation in which he himself has to face a moral decision regarding one of his own actions,' or it might mean 'every situation in which a moral question arises for him, whether about his own actions or about somebody else's.' So there are three courses that he can adopt: (1) He either refrains altogether from making moral judgements, or makes none except judgements of indifference (that is to say, he either observes a complete moral silence, or says 'Nothing matters morally'; either of these two positions might be called a sort of amoralism); (2) He makes moral judgements in the normal way about other people's actions, but adopts one or other of the kinds of amoralism, just mentioned, with regard to his own; (3) He expresses moral indifference, or will make no moral judgement at all, with regard to *some* of his own actions and those of other people, but makes moral judgements in the normal way about others.

Now it will be obvious that in the first case there is nothing that we can do, and that this should not disturb us. Just as one cannot win a game of chess against an opponent who will not make any moves—and just as one cannot argue mathematically with a person who will not commit himself to

any mathematical statements—so moral argument is impossible with a man who will make no moral judgements at all, or—which for practical purposes comes to the same thing—makes only judgements of indifference. Such a person is not entering the arena of moral dispute, and therefore it is impossible to contest with him. He is compelled also—and this is important—to abjure the protection of morality for his own interests.

In the other two cases, however, we have an argument left. If a man is prepared to make positive moral judgements about other people's actions, but not about his own, or if he is prepared to make them about some of his own decisions, but not about others, then we can ask him on what principle he makes the distinction between these various cases. This is a particular application of the demand for universalizability. He will still have left to him the ways of escape from this demand which are available in all its applications, and which we shall consider later. But there is no way of escape which is available in this application, but not in others. He must either produce (or at least admit the existence of) some principle which makes him hold different moral opinions about apparently similar cases, or else admit that the judgements he is making are not moral ones. But in the latter case, he is in the same position, in the present dispute, as the man who will not make any moral judgements at all; he has resigned from the contest.

In the particular example which we have been considering, we supposed that the cases of *B* and of *C*, his own creditor, were identical. The demand for universalization therefore compels *B* to make the same moral judgement, whatever it is, about both cases. He has therefore, unless he is going to give up the claim to be arguing morally, either to say that neither he nor *C* ought to exercise their legal rights to imprison their debtors; or that both ought (a possibility to which we shall recur in the next section); or that it is indifferent whether they do. But the last alternative leaves it open to *B* and *C* to do what they like in the matter; and we may suppose that, though *B* himself would like to have this freedom, he will be unwilling to allow it to *C*. It is as unlikely that he will *permit C* to put him (*B*) into prison as that he will *prescribe* it (10.5). We may say, therefore, that while move (1), described above, constitutes an abandonment of the dispute, moves (2) and (3) really add nothing new to it.

6.7. We must next consider a way of escape which may seem much more respectable than those which I have so far mentioned. Let us suppose that *B* is a firm believer in the rights of property and the sanctity of contracts. In this case he may say roundly that debtors ought to be imprisoned by their creditors whoever they are, and that, specifically, *C* ought to imprison him (*B*), and he (*B*) ought to imprison *A*. And he may, unlike the superficially similar person described earlier, be meaning by 'ought' just what we usually mean by it—i.e. he may be using the word prescriptively, realizing that in saying that *C* ought to put him into prison, he is prescribing that *C* put him in prison. *B*, in this case, is perfectly ready to go to prison for his principles, in order that the sanctity of contracts may be enforced. In real life, *B* would be much more likely to take this line if the situation in which he himself played the role of debtor were not actual but only hypothetical; but this, as we saw earlier, ought not to make any difference to the argument.

We are not yet, however, in a position to deal with this escape-route. All we can do is to say why we cannot now deal with it, and leave this loose end to be picked up later. *B*, if he is sincere in holding the principle about the sanctity of contracts (or any other universal moral principle which has the same effect in this particular case), may have two sorts of grounds for it. He may hold it on utilitarian grounds, thinking that, unless contracts are rigorously enforced, the results will be so disastrous as to outweigh any benefits that *A*, or *B* himself, may get from being let off. This could, in certain circumstances, be a good argument. But we cannot tell whether it is, until we have generalized the type of moral argument which has been set out in this chapter, to cover cases in which the interests of more than two parties are involved. As we saw, it is only the interests of *A* and *B* that come into the argument as so far considered (the interests of the third party, *C*, do not need separate consideration, since *C* was introduced only in order to show *B*, if necessary fictionally, a situation in which the roles were reversed; therefore *C*'s interests, being a mere replica of *B*'s, will vanish, as a separate factor, once the *A/B* situation, and the moral judgements made on it, are universalized). But if utilitarian grounds of the sort suggested are to be adduced, they will bring with them a reference to all the other people whose interests would be harmed by laxity in the enforcement of contracts. This es-

cape-route, therefore, if this is its basis, introduces considerations which cannot be assessed until we have generalized our form of argument to cover 'multilateral' moral situations (7.2 ff.). At present, it can only be said that if *B* can show that leniency in the enforcement of contracts would really have the results he claims for the community at large, he might be justified in taking the severer course. This will be apparent after we have considered in some detail an example (that of the judge and the criminal) which brings out these considerations even more clearly.

On the other hand, *B* might have a quite different, non-utilitarian kind of reason for adhering to his principle. He might be moved, not by any weight which he might attach to the interests of other people, but by the thought that to enforce contracts of this sort is necessary in order to conform to some moral or other *ideal* that he has espoused. Such ideals might be of various sorts. He might be moved; for example, by an ideal of abstract justice, of the *fiat justitia, ruat caelum* variety. We have to distinguish such an ideal of justice, which pays no regard to people's interests, from that which is concerned merely to do justice *between* people's interests. It is very important, if considerations of justice are introduced into a moral argument, to know of which sort they are. Justice of the second kind can perhaps be accommodated within a moral view which it is not misleading to call utilitarian (7.4). But this is not true of an ideal of the first kind. It is characteristic of this sort of non-utilitarian ideals that, when they are introduced into moral arguments, they render ineffective the appeal to universalized self-interest which is the foundation of the argument that we have been considering. This is because the person who has whole-heartedly espoused such an ideal (we shall call him the 'fanatic') does not mind if people's interests—even his own—are harmed in the pursuit of it. (8.6, 9.1).

It need not be justice which provides the basis of such an escape-route as we are considering. Any moral ideal would do, provided that it were pursued regardless of other people's interests. For example, *B* might be a believer in the survival of the fittest, and think that, in order to promote this, he (and everyone else) ought to pursue their own interests by all means in their power and regardless of everyone else's interests. This ideal might lead him, in this particular case, to put *A* in prison, and he might agree that *C* ought to do the same to him, if he were not clever enough to avoid this fate. He might think that universal obedience to such a principle would maximize the production of supermen and so make the world a better place. If these were his grounds, it is possible that we might argue with him factually, showing that the universal observance of the principle would not have the results he claimed. But we might be defeated in this factual argument if he had an ideal which made him call the world 'a better place' when the jungle law prevailed; he could then agree to our factual statements, but still maintain that the condition of the world described by us as resulting from the observance of his principle would be better than its present condition. In this case, the argument might take two courses. If we could get him to imagine himself in the position of the weak, who went to the wall in such a state of the world, we might bring him to realize that to hold his principle involved prescribing that things should be done to him, in hypothetical situations, which he could not sincerely prescribe. If so, then argument would be on the rails again, and could proceed on lines which we have already sketched. But he might stick to his principle and say 'If I were weak, then I ought to go to the wall'. If he did this, he would be putting himself beyond the reach of what we shall call 'golden-rule' or 'utilitarian' arguments by becoming what we shall call a 'fanatic.' Since a great part of the rest of this book will be concerned with people who take this sort of line, it is unnecessary to pursue their case further at this point.

6.8. The remaining manœuvre that *B* might seek to practise is probably the commonest. It is certainly the one which is most frequently brought up in philosophical controversies on this topic. This consists in a fresh appeal to the facts—i.e. in asserting that there are in fact morally relevant differences between his case and that of others. In the example which we have been considering, we have artificially ruled out this way of escape by assuming that the case of *B* and *C* is exactly similar to that of *A* and *B*; from this it follows *a fortiori* that there are no morally relevant differences. Since the *B/C* case may be a hypothetical one, this condition of exact similarity can always be fulfilled, and therefore this manœuvre is based on a misconception of the type of argument against which it is directed. Nevertheless it may be

useful, since this objection is so commonly raised, to deal with it at this point, although nothing further will be added thereby to what has been said already.

It may be claimed that no two actual cases would ever be exactly similar; there would always be some differences, and *B* might allege that some of these were morally relevant. He might allege, for example, that, whereas his family would starve if *C* put him into prison, this would not be the case if he put *A* into prison, because *A*'s family would be looked after by *A*'s relatives. If such a difference existed, there might be nothing logically disreputable in calling it morally relevant, and such arguments are in fact often put forward and accepted.

The difficulty, however, lies in drawing the line between those arguments of this sort which are legitimate, and those which are not. Suppose that *B* alleges that the fact that *A* has a hooked nose or a black skin entitles him, *B*, to put him in prison, but that *C* ought not to do the same thing to him, *B*, because his nose is straight and his skin white. Is this an argument of equal logical respectability? Can I say that the fact that I have a mole in a particular place on my chin entitles me to further my own interests at others' expense, but that they are forbidden to do this by the fact that they lack this mark of natural pre-eminence?

The answer to this manœuvre is implicit in what has been said already about the relevance, in moral arguments, of hypothetical as well as of actual cases. The fact that no two actual cases are ever identical has no bearing on the problem. For all we have to do is to imagine an identical case in which the roles are reversed. Suppose that my mole disappears, and that my neighbour grows one in the very same spot on his chin. Or, to use our other example, what does *B* say about a hypothetical case in which he has a black skin or a hooked nose, and *A* and *C* are both straight-nosed and white-skinned (9.4; 11.7)? Since this is the same argument, in essentials, as we used at the very beginning, it need not be repeated here. *B* is in fact faced with a dilemma. Either the property of his own case, which he claims to be morally relevant, is a properly universal property (i.e. one describable without reference to individuals), or it is not. If it is a universal property, then, because of the meaning of the word 'universal,' it is a property which might be possessed by another case in which he played a different role (though in fact it may not be); and we can therefore ask him to ignore the fact that it is he himself who plays the role which he does in this case. This will force him to count as morally relevant only those properties which he is prepared to allow to be relevant even when other people have them. And this rules out all the attractive kinds of special pleading. On the other hand, if the property in question is not a properly universal one, then he has not met the demand for universalizability, and cannot claim to be putting forward a moral argument at all.

6.9. It is necessary, in order to avoid misunderstanding, to add two notes to the foregoing discussion. The misunderstanding arises through a too literal interpretation of the common forms of expression—which constantly recur in arguments of this type—'How would you like it if...?' and 'Do as you would be done by.' Though I shall later, for convenience, refer to the type of arguments here discussed as 'golden-rule' arguments, we must not be misled by these forms of expression.

First of all, we shall make the nature of the argument clearer if, when we are asking B to imagine himself in the position of his victim, we phrase our question, never in the form 'What *would* you say, or feel, or think, or how *would* you like it, if you were he?', but always in the form 'What *do* you say (*in propria persona*) about a hypothetical case in which you are in your victim's position?' The importance of this way of phrasing the question is that, if the question were put in the first way, B might reply 'Well, of course, if anybody did this to me I should resent it very much and make all sorts of adverse moral judgements about the act; but this has absolutely no bearing on the validity of the moral opinion which I am *now* expressing.' To involve him in contradiction, we have to show that he *now* holds an opinion about the hypothetical case which is inconsistent with his opinion about the actual case.

The second thing which has to be noticed is that the argument, as set out, does not involve any sort of deduction of a moral judgement, or even of the negation of a moral judgement, from a factual statement about people's inclinations, interests, &c. We are not saying to B 'You are as a matter of fact averse to this being done to you in a hypothetical case; and from this it follows logically that you ought not to do it to another.' Such a deduction would be a breach of Hume's Law ('No "ought" from an "is"'), to which I have repeatedly declared my adherence (*LM* 2.5).

The point is, rather, that because of his aversion to its being done to him in the hypothetical case, he cannot accept the singular *prescription* that in the hypothetical case it should be done to him; and this, because of the logic of 'ought,' precludes him from accepting the moral judgement that he ought to do likewise to another in the actual case. It is not a question of a factual statement about a person's inclinations being inconsistent with a moral judgement; rather, his inclinations being what they are, he cannot assent sincerely to a certain singular prescription, and if he cannot do this, he cannot assent to a certain universal prescription which entails it, when conjoined with factual statements about the circumstances whose truth he admits. Because of this entailment, if he assented to the factual statements and to the universal prescription, but refused (as he must, his inclinations being what they are) to assent to the singular prescription, he would be guilty of a logical inconsistency.

If it be asked what the relation is between his aversion to being put in prison in the hypothetical case, and his inability to accept the hypothetical singular prescription that if he were in such a situation he should be put into prison, it would seem that the relation is not unlike that between a belief that the cat is on the mat, and an inability to accept the proposition that the cat is not on the mat. Further attention to this parallel will perhaps make the position clearer. Suppose that somebody advances the hypothesis that cats never sit on mats, and that we refute him by pointing to a cat on a mat. The logic of our refutation proceeds in two stages. Of these, the second is: 'Here is a cat sitting on a mat, so it is not the case that cats never sit on mats.' This is a piece of logical deduction; and to it, in the moral case, corresponds the step from 'Let this not be done to me' to 'It is not the case that I ought to do it to another in similar circumstances.' But in both cases there is a first stage whose nature is more obscure, and different in the two cases, though there is an analogy between them.

In the 'cat' case, it is logically possible for a man to look straight at the cat on the mat, and yet believe that there is no cat on the mat. But if a person with normal eyesight and no psychological aberrations does this, we say that he does not understand the meaning of the words, 'The cat is on the mat.' And even if he does not have normal eyesight, or suffers from some psychological aberration (such a phobia of cats, say, that he just *cannot* admit to himself that he is face to face with one), yet, if we can convince him that everyone else can see a cat there, he will have to admit that there is a cat there, or be accused of misusing the language.

If, on the other hand, a man says 'But I *want* to be put in prison, if ever I am in that situation,' we can, indeed, get as far as accusing him of having eccentric desires; but we cannot, when we have proved to him that nobody else has such a desire, face him with the choice of either saying, with the rest, 'Let this not be done to me,' or else being open to the accusation of not understanding what he is saying. For it is not an incorrect use of words to want eccentric things. Logic does not prevent me wanting to be put in a gas chamber if a Jew. It is perhaps true that I logically cannot want for its own sake an experience which I think of as *unpleasant;* for to say that I think of it as unpleasant may be logically inconsistent with saying that I want it for its own sake. If this is so, it is because 'unpleasant' is a prescriptive expression. But 'to be put in prison' and 'to be put in a gas chamber if a Jew,' are not prescriptive expressions; and therefore these things can be wanted without offence to logic. It is, indeed, in the logical possibility of wanting *anything* (neutrally described) that the 'freedom' which is alluded to in my title essentially consists. And it is this, as we shall see, that lets by the person whom I shall call the 'fanatic' (9.1 ff.).

There is not, then, a complete analogy between the man who says 'There is no cat on the mat' when there is, and the man who wants things which others do not. But there is a partial analogy, which, having noticed this difference, we may be able to isolate. The analogy is between two relations; the relations between, in both cases, the 'mental state' of these men and what they say. If I believe that there is a cat on the mat I cannot sincerely say that there is not; and, if I want not to be put into prison more than I want anything else, I cannot sincerely say 'Let me be put into prison.' When, therefore, I

said above 'His inclinations being what they are, he cannot assent sincerely to a certain singular prescription,' I was making an analytic statement (although the 'cannot' is not a logical 'cannot'); for if he were to assent sincerely to the prescription, that would entail *ex vi terminorum* that his inclinations had changed—in the very same way that it is analytically true that, if the other man were to say sincerely that there was a cat on the mat, when before he had sincerely denied this, he must have changed his belief.

If, however, instead of writing 'His inclinations being what they are, he cannot . . .,' we leave out the first clause and write simply 'He cannot . . .,' the statement is no longer analytic; we are making a statement about his psychology which might be false. For it is logically possible for inclinations to change; hence it is possible for a man to come sincerely to hold an ideal which requires that he himself should be sent to a gas chamber if a Jew. That is the price we have to pay for our freedom. But, as we shall see, in order for reason to have a place in morals it is not necessary for us to close this way of escape by means of a logical barrier; it is sufficient that, men and the world being what they are, we can be very sure that hardly anybody is going to take it with his eyes open. And when we are arguing with one of the vast majority who are not going to take it, the reply that somebody else *might* take it does not help his case against us. In this respect, all moral arguments are *ad hominem*.[1]

_____

1. The above discussion may help to atone for what is confused or even wrong in *LM* 3.3 (p.42). The remarks there about the possibility or impossibility of accepting certain moral principles gave the impression of creating an impasse; I can, however, plead that in *LM* 4.4 (p.69) there appeared a hint of the way out which is developed in this book.

G. E. M. ANSCOMBE

Modern Moral Philosophy

Moral philosophy in England and the United States in the first half of the twentieth century was primarily concerned with metaethical issues—the language and logic of ethics. Since Moore's Principia Ethica in 1903, the ability of philosophers to provide a rationally justified moral system (or normative ethical theory) had been seriously called into question. As a result, moral philosophers increasingly turned their attention to the meaning of moral terms and the logical status of moral judgments. By the middle of the century, however, a renewed interest in normative ethics began to emerge. Although many metaethical issues are still of great interest to moral philosophers, the final section of this text highlights some representative samples of recent important work in normative ethics that build upon and push forward the work of the great philosophers of the past.

This first article, "Modern Moral Philosophy" by G. E. M. Anscombe, has helped to initiate an interest in an approach to ethical theory that had not received much attention for, literally, millennia. Many moral philosophers, already grown dissatisfied with both the prevalent utilitarian and deontological theories, heeded Anscombe's call in this article to turn moral philosophy away from a discourse of moral oughts—moral right and moral wrong. These concepts, Anscombe charged, belong to an ethical theory built upon an earlier conception of ethics that required a divine moral law that no longer applies. Discussing what one ought to do—what is right and what is wrong—no longer has any benefit in moral philosophy. As an alternative, moral philosophers should turn their attention to a discourse about virtues, moral norms, and character.

Thus began an ever-increasing interest in the ethical writings of Aristotle, whose ethical focus, as we discovered earlier, was on virtues, norms, and character. The theory that has developed from this change in philosophical direction—virtue ethics—emphasizes the character of the moral person rather than the rightness or wrongness of actions. The question to be answered in virtue ethics is, What kind of person should I be? rather than, What kind of acts should I do? For another reading that addresses concerns about the virtues and character, see "Moral Saints" by Susan Wolf.

Modern Moral Philosophy[1]

I will begin by stating three theses which I present in this paper. The first is that it is not profitable for us at present to do moral philosophy; that should be laid aside at any rate until we have an adequate philosophy of psychology, in which we are conspicuously lacking. The second is that the concepts of obligation, and duty—*moral* obligation and *moral* duty, that is to say—and of what is *morally* right and wrong, and of the *moral* sense of "ought," ought to be jettisoned if this is psychologically possible; because they are survivals, or derivatives from survivals, from an earlier conception of ethics which no longer generally survives, and are only harmful without it. My third thesis is that the differences between the well-known English writers on moral philosophy from Sidgwick to the present day are of little importance.

Anyone who has read Aristotle's *Ethics* and has also read modern moral philosophy must have been struck by the great contrasts between them. The concepts which are prominent among the moderns seem to be lacking, or at any rate buried or far in the background, in Aristotle. Most noticeably, the term "moral" itself, which we have by direct inheritance from Aristotle, just doesn't seem to fit, in its modern sense, into an account of Aristotelian ethics. Aristotle distinguishes virtues as moral and intellectual. Have some of what he calls "intellectual" virtues what *we* should call a "moral" aspect? It would seem so; the criterion is presumably that a failure in an "intellectual" virtue—like that of having good judgment in calculating how to bring about something useful, say in municipal government—may be *blameworthy*. But—it may reasonably be asked—cannot *any* failure be made a matter of blame or reproach? Any derogatory criticism, say of the workmanship of a product or the design of a machine, can be called blame or reproach. So we want to put in the word "morally" again: sometimes such a failure may be *morally* blameworthy, sometimes not. Now has Aristotle got this idea of *moral* blame, as opposed to any other? If he has, why isn't it more central? There are some mistakes, he says, which are causes, not of involuntariness in actions, but of scoundrelism, and

for which a man is blamed. Does this mean that there is a *moral* obligation not to make certain intellectual mistakes? Why doesn't he discuss obligation in general, and this obligation in particular? If someone professes to be expounding Aristotle and talks in a modern fashion about "moral" such-and-such, he must be very imperceptive if he does not constantly feel like someone whose jaws have somehow got out of alignment: the teeth don't come together in a proper bite.

We cannot, then, look to Aristotle for any elucidation of the modern way of talking about "moral" goodness, obligation, etc. And all the best-known writers on ethics in modern times, from Butler to Mill, appear to me to have faults as thinkers on the subject which make it impossible to hope for any direct light on it from them. I will state these objections with the brevity which their character makes possible.

Butler exalts conscience, but appears ignorant that a man's conscience may tell him to do the vilest things.

Hume defines "truth" in such a way as to exclude ethical judgments from it, and professes that he has proved that they are so excluded. He also implicitly defines "passion" in such a way that aiming at anything is having a passion. His objection to passing from "is" to "ought" would apply equally to passing from "is" to "owes" or from "is" to "needs." (However, because of the historical situation, he has a point here, which I shall return to.)

Kant introduces the idea of "legislating for oneself," which is as absurd as if in these days, when majority votes command great respect, one were to call each reflective decision a man made a *vote* resulting in a majority, which as a matter of proportion is overwhelming, for it is always 1–0. The concept of legislation requires superior power in the legislator. His own rigoristic convictions on the subject of lying were so intense that it never occurred to him that a lie could be relevantly described as anything but just a lie (e.g. as "a lie in such-and-such circumstances"). His rule about universalizable maxims is useless without stipulations as to what shall count as a relevant description of an action with a view to constructing a maxim about it.

Bentham and Mill do not notice the difficulty of the concept "pleasure." They are often said to have gone wrong through committing the "naturalistic fallacy";

1 This paper was originally read to the Voltaire Society in Oxford.

but this charge does not impress me because I do not find accounts of it coherent. But the other point—about pleasure—seems to me a fatal objection from the very outset. The ancients found this concept pretty baffling. It reduced Aristotle to sheer babble about "the bloom on the cheek of youth" because, for good reasons, he wanted to make it out both identical with and different from the pleasurable activity. Generations of modern philosophers found this concept quite unperplexing, and it reappeared in the literature as a problematic one only a year or two ago when Ryle wrote about it. The reason is simple: since Locke, pleasure was taken to be some sort of internal impression. But it was superficial, if that was the right account of it, to make it the point of actions. One might adapt something Wittgenstein said about "meaning" and say "Pleasure cannot be an internal impression, for no internal impression could have the consequences of pleasure."

Mill also, like Kant, fails to realize the necessity for stipulation as to relevant descriptions, if his theory is to have content. It did not occur to him that acts of murder and theft could be otherwise described. He holds that where a proposed action is of such a kind as to fall under some one principle established on grounds of utility, one must go by that; where it falls under none or several, the several suggesting contrary views of the action, the thing to do is to calculate particular consequences. But pretty well any action can be so described as to make it fall under a variety of principles of utility (as I shall say for short) if it falls under any.

I will now return to Hume. The features of Hume's philosophy which I have mentioned, like many other features of it, would incline me to think that Hume was a mere—brilliant—sophist; and his procedures are certainly sophistical. But I am forced, not to reverse, but to add to, this judgment by a peculiarity of Hume's philosophizing: namely that although he reaches his conclusions—with which he is in love—by sophistical methods, his considerations constantly open up very deep and important problems. It is often the case that in the act of exhibiting the sophistry one finds oneself noticing matters which deserve a lot of exploring: the obvious stands in need of investigation as a result of the points that Hume pretends to have made. In this, he is unlike, say, Butler. It was already well known that conscience could dictate vile actions; for Butler to

have written disregarding this does not open up any new topics for us. But with Hume it is otherwise: hence he is a very profound and great philosopher, in spite of his sophistry. For example:

Suppose that I say to my grocer "Truth consists in *either* relations of ideas, as that 20s.=£1, or matters of fact, as that I ordered potatoes, you supplied them, and you sent me a bill. So it doesn't apply to such a proposition as that I *owe* you such-and-such a sum."

Now if one makes this comparison, it comes to light that the relation of the facts mentioned to the description "X owes Y so much money" is an interesting one, which I will call that of being "brute relative to" that description. Further, the "brute" facts mentioned here themselves have descriptions relatively to which *other* facts are "brute"—as, e.g., *he had potatoes carted to my house* and *they were left there* are brute facts relative to "he supplied me with potatoes." And the fact *X owes Y money* is in turn "brute" relative to other descriptions—e.g. "X is solvent." Now the relation of "relative bruteness" is a complicated one. To mention a few points: if xyz is a set of facts brute relative to a description A, then xyz is a set out of a range some set among which holds if A holds; but the holding of some set among these does not necessarily entail A, because exceptional circumstances can always make a difference; and what are exceptional circumstances relatively to A can generally only be explained by giving a few diverse examples, and *no* theoretically adequate provision can be made for exceptional circumstances, since a further special context can theoretically always be imagined that would reinterpret any special context. Further, though in normal circumstances, xyz would be a justification for A, that is not to say that A just comes to the same as "xyz"; and also there is apt to be an institutional context which gives its point to the description A, of which institution A is of course not itself a description. (E.g. the statement that I give someone a shilling is not a description of the institution of money or of the currency of this country.) Thus, though it would be ludicrous to pretend that there can be no such thing as a transition from, e.g., "is" to "owes," the character of the transition is in fact rather interesting and comes to light as a result of reflecting on Hume's arguments.[1]

---

1. The above two paragraphs are an abstract of a paper "On Brute Facts" forthcoming in *Analysis*.

That I owe the grocer such-and-such a sum would be one of a set of facts which would be "brute" in relation to the description "I am a bilker." "Bilking" is of course a species of "dishonesty" or "injustice." (Naturally the consideration will not have any effect on my actions unless I want to commit or avoid acts of injustice.)

So far, in spite of their strong associations, I conceive "bilking," "injustice" and "dishonesty" in a merely "factual" way. That I can do this for "bilking" is obvious enough; "justice" I have no idea how to define, except that its sphere is that of actions which relate to someone else, but "injustice," its defect, can for the moment be offered as a generic name covering various species. E.g.: "bilking," "theft" (which is relative to whatever property institutions exist), "slander," "adultery," "punishment of the innocent."

In present-day philosophy an explanation is required how an unjust man is a bad man, or an unjust action a bad one; to give such an explanation belongs to ethics; but it cannot even be begun until we are equipped with a sound philosophy of psychology. For the proof that an unjust man is a bad man would require a positive account of justice as a "virtue." This part of the subject-matter of ethics is, however, completely closed to us until we have an account of what *type of characteristic* a virtue is—a problem, not of ethics, but of conceptual analysis—and how it relates to the actions in which it is instanced: a matter which I think Aristotle did not succeed in really making clear. For this we certainly need an account at least of what a human action is at all, and how its description as "doing such-and-such" is affected by its motive and by the intention or intentions in it; and for this an account of such concepts is required.

The terms "should" or "ought" or "needs" relate to good and bad: e.g. machinery needs oil, or should or ought to be oiled, in that running without oil is bad for it, or it runs badly without oil. According to this conception, of course, "should" and "ought" are not used in a special "moral" sense when one says that a man should not bilk. (In Aristotle's sense of the term "moral" (ἠθικός), they are being used in connection with a *moral* subject-matter: namely that of human passions and (non-technical) actions.) But they have now acquired a special so-called "moral" sense—i.e. a sense in which they imply some absolute verdict (like one of guilty / not guilty on a man) on what is described in the "ought" sentences used in certain types of context: not merely the contexts that *Aristotle* would call "moral"—passions and actions—but also some of the contexts that he would call "intellectual."

The ordinary (and quite indispensable) terms "should," "needs," "ought," "must"—acquired this special sense by being equated in the relevant contexts with "is obliged," or "is bound," or "is required to," in the sense in which one can be obliged or bound by law, or something can be required by law.

How did this come about? The answer is in history: between Aristotle and us came Christianity, with its *law* conception of ethics. For Christianity derived its ethical notions from the Torah. (One might be inclined to think that a law conception of ethics could arise only among people who accepted an allegedly divine positive law; that this is not so is shown by the example of the Stoics, who also thought that whatever was involved in conformity to human virtues was required by divine law.)

In consequence of the dominance of Christianity for many centuries, the concepts of being bound, permitted, or excused became deeply embedded in our language and thought. The Greek word "ἁμαρτάνειν," the aptest to be turned to that use, acquired the sense "sin," from having meant "mistake," "missing the mark," "going wrong." The Latin *peccatum* which roughly corresponded to ἁμάρτημα was even apter for the sense "sin," because it was already associated with "culpa"—"guilt"—a juridical notion. The blanket term "illicit," "unlawful," meaning much the same as our blanket term "wrong," explains itself. It is interesting that Aristotle did not have such a blanket term. He has blanket terms for wickedness—"villain," "scoundrel"; but of course a man is not a villain or a scoundrel by the performance of one bad action, or a few bad actions. And he has terms like "disgraceful," "impious"; and specific terms signifying defect of the relevant virtue, like "unjust"; but no term corresponding to "illicit." The extension of this term (i.e. the range of its application) could be indicated in his terminology only by a quite lengthy sentence: that is "illicit" which, whether it is a thought or a consented-to passion or an action or an omission in thought or action, is something contrary to one of the virtues the lack of which shows a man to be bad *qua* man. That formulation would yield a concept co-extensive with the concept "illicit."

To have a *law* conception of ethics is to hold that what is needed for conformity with the virtues failure in which is the mark of being bad *qua* man (and not merely, say, *qua* craftsman or logician)—that what is needed for *this*, is required by divine law. Naturally it is not possible to have such a conception unless you believe in God as a lawgiver; like Jews, Stoics, and Christians. But if such a conception is dominant for many centuries, and then is given up, it is a natural result that the concepts of "obligation," of being bound or required as by a law, should remain though they had lost their root; and if the word "ought" has become invested in certain contexts with the sense of "obligation," it too will remain to be spoken with a special emphasis and a special feeling in these contexts.

It is as if the notion "criminal" were to remain when criminal law and criminal courts had been abolished and forgotten. A Hume discovering this situation might conclude that there was a special sentiment, expressed by "criminal," which alone gave the word its sense. So Hume discovered the situation in which the notion "obligation" survived, and the notion "ought" was invested with that peculiar force having which it is said to be used in a "moral" sense, but in which the belief in divine law had long since been abandoned: for it was substantially given up among Protestants at the time of the Reformation.[1] The situation, if I am right, was the interesting one of the survival of a concept outside the framework of thought that made it a really intelligible one.

When Hume produced his famous remarks about the transition from "is" to "ought," he was, then, bringing together several quite different points. One I have tried to bring out by my remarks on the transition from "is" to "owes" and on the relative "bruteness" of facts. It would be possible to bring out a different point by enquiring about the transition from "is" to "needs"; from the characteristics of an organism to the environment that it needs,

for example. To say that it needs that environment is not to say, e.g., that you want it to have that environment, but that it won't flourish unless it has it. Certainly, it all depends whether you *want* it to flourish! as Hume would say. But what "all depends" on whether you want it to flourish is whether the fact that it needs that environment, or won't flourish without it, has the slightest influence on your actions. Now *that* such-and-such "ought" to be or "is needed" is supposed to have an influence on your actions: from which it seemed natural to infer that to judge that it "ought to be" was in fact to grant what you judged "ought to be" influence on your actions. And no amount of truth as to what *is* the case could possibly have a logical claim to have influence on your actions. (It is not judgment as such that sets us in motion; but our judgment on how to get or do something we *want*.) Hence it *must* be impossible to infer "needs" or "ought to be" from "is." But in the case of a plant, let us say, the inference from "is" to "needs" is certainly not in the least dubious. It is interesting and worth examining; but not at all fishy. Its interest is similar to the interest of the relation between brute and less brute facts: these relations have been very little considered. And while you can contrast "what it needs" with "what it's got"—like contrasting *de facto* and *de jure*—that does not make its needing this environment less of a "truth."

Certainly in the case of what the plant needs, the thought of a need will only affect action if you want the plant to flourish. Here, then, there is no necessary connection between what you can judge the plant "needs" and what you want. But there is some sort of necessary connection between what you think *you* need, and what you want. The connection is a complicated one; it is possible *not* to want something that you judge you need. But, e.g., it is not possible never to want *anything* that you judge you need. This, however, is not a fact about the meaning of the word "to need," but about the phenomenon of *wanting*. Hume's reasoning, we might say, in effect, leads one to think it must be about the word "to need," or "to be good for."

Thus we find two problems already wrapped up in the remark about a transition from "is" to "ought"; now supposing that we had clarified the "relative bruteness" of facts on the one hand, and the notions involved in "needing," and "flourishing" on the other—there would *still* remain a third point. For, following Hume,

---

1. They did not deny the existence of divine law; but their most characteristic doctrine was that it was given, not to be obeyed, but to show man's incapacity to obey it, even by grace; and this applied not merely to the ramified prescriptions of the Torah, but to the requirements of "natural divine law." Cf. in this connection the decree of Trent against the teaching that Christ was only to be trusted in as mediator, not obeyed as legislator.

someone might say: Perhaps you have made out your point about a transition from "is" to "owes" and from "is" to "needs": but only at the cost of showing "owes" and "needs" sentences to express a *kind* of truths, a *kind* of facts. And it remains impossible to infer *"morally ought"* from "is" sentences.

This comment, it seems to me, would be correct. This word "ought," having become a word of mere mesmeric force, could not, in the character of having that force, be inferred from anything whatever. It may be objected that it could be inferred from other "morally ought" sentences: but that cannot be true. The appearance that this is so is produced by the fact that we say "All men are φ" and "Socrates is a man" implies "Socrates is φ." But here "φ" is a dummy predicate. We mean that if you substitute a real predicate for "φ" the implication is valid. A real predicate is required; not just a word containing no intelligible thought: a word retaining the suggestion force, and apt to have a strong psychological effect, but which no longer signifies a real concept at all.

For its suggestion is one of a *verdict* on my action, according as agrees or disagrees with the description in the "ought" sentence. And where one does not think there is a judge or a law, the notion of verdict may retain its psychological effect, but not its meaning. Now imagine that just this word "verdict" *were* so used—with a characteristically solemn emphasis—as to retain its atmosphere but not its meaning, and someone were to say: "For a *verdict*, after all, you need a law and a judge." The reply might be made: "Not at all, for if there were a law and a judge who gave a verdict, the question for us would be whether accepting that verdict is something that there is a *Verdict* on." This is an analogue of an argument which is so frequently referred to as decisive: If someone does have a divine law conception of ethics, all the same, he has to agree that he has to have a judgment that he *ought* (morally ought) to obey the divine law; so his ethic is in exactly the same position as any other: he merely has a "practical major premise":[1] "Divine law ought to be obeyed" where someone else has, e.g., "The greatest happiness principle ought to be employed in all decisions."

I should judge that Hume and our present-day ethicists had done a considerable service by showing that no content could be found in the notion "morally ought"; if it were not that the latter philosophers try to find an alternative (very fishy) content and to retain the psychological force of the term. It would be most reasonable to drop it. It has no reasonable sense outside a law conception of ethics; they are not going to maintain such a conception; and you can do ethics without it, as is shown by the example of Aristotle. It would be a great improvement if, instead of "morally wrong," one always named a genus such as "untruthful," "unchaste," "unjust." We should no longer ask whether doing something was "wrong," passing directly from some description of an action to this notion; we should ask whether, e.g., it was unjust; and the answer would sometimes be clear at once.

I now come to the epoch in modern English moral philosophy marked by Sidgwick. There is a startling change that seems to have taken place between Mill and Moore. Mill assumes, as we saw, that there is no question of calculating the particular consequences of an action such as murder or theft; and we saw too that his position was stupid, because it is not at all clear how an action *can* fall under just one principle of utility. In Moore and in subsequent academic moralists of England we find it taken to be pretty obvious that "the right action" is the action which produces the best possible consequences (reckoning among consequences the intrinsic values ascribed to certain kinds of act by some "Objectivists"[2]). Now it follows from this that a man does well, subjectively speaking, if he acts for the best in the particular circumstances according to his judgment of the total consequences of this particular action. I say that this follows, not that any philosopher has said precisely that. For discussion of these questions can of course get extremely complicated: e.g. it can be doubted whether "such-and-such is the right action" is a satisfactory formulation, on the grounds that things have to exist to have predicates—so perhaps the best formulation is "I am obliged"; or again, a

---

1. As it is absurdly called. Since major premise=premise containing the term which is predicate in the conclusion, it is a solecism to speak of it in the connection with practical reasoning.

2. Oxford Objectivists of course distinguish between "consequences" and "intrinsic values" and so produce a misleading appearance of not being "consequentialists." But they do not hold—and Ross explicitly denies—that the gravity of, e.g., procuring the condemnation of the innocent is such that it cannot be outweighed by, e.g., national interest. Hence their distinction is of no importance.

philosopher may deny that "right" is a "descriptive" term, and then take a roundabout route through linguistic analysis to reach a view which comes to the same thing as "the right action is the one productive of the best consequences" (e.g. the view that you frame your "principles" to effect the end you choose to pursue, the connexion between "choice" and "best" being supposedly such that choosing reflectively means that you choose how to act so as to produce the best consequences); further, the roles of what are called "moral principles" and of the "motive of duty" have to be described; the differences between "good" and "morally good" and "right" need to be explored, the special characteristics of "ought" sentences investigated. Such discussions generate an appearance of significant diversity of views where what is really significant is an overall similarity. The overall similarity is made clear if you consider that every one of the best known English academic moral philosophers has put out a philosophy according to which, e.g., it is not possible to hold that it cannot be right to kill the innocent as a means to any end whatsoever and that someone who thinks otherwise is in error. (I have to mention both points; because Mr. Hare, for example, while teaching a philosophy which would encourage a person to judge that killing the innocent would be what he "ought" to choose for overriding purposes, would also teach, I think, that if a man chooses to make avoiding killing the innocent for any purpose his "supreme practical principle," he cannot be impugned for error: that just is his "principle." But with that qualification, I think it can be seen that the point I have mentioned holds good of every single English academic moral philosopher since Sidgwick.) Now this is a significant thing: for it means that all these philosophies are quite incompatible with the Hebrew-Christian ethic. For it has been characteristic of that ethic to teach that there are certain things forbidden whatever *consequences* threaten, such as: choosing to kill the innocent for any purpose, however good; vicarious punishment; treachery (by which I mean obtaining a man's confidence in a grave matter by promises of trustworthy friendship and then betraying him to his enemies); idolatry; sodomy; adultery; making a false profession of faith. The prohibition of certain things simply in virtue of their description as such-and-such identifiable kinds of action, regardless of any further consequences, is certainly not the whole of the Hebrew-Christian ethic; but it is a noteworthy feature of it; and if every academic philosopher since Sidgwick has written in such a way as to exclude this ethic, it would argue a certain provinciality of mind not to see this incompatibility as the most important fact about these philosophers, and the differences between them as somewhat trifling by comparison.

It is noticeable that none of these philosophers displays any consciousness that there is such an ethic, which he is contradicting: it is pretty well taken for obvious among them all that a prohibition such as that on murder does not operate in face of some consequences. But of course the strictness of the prohibition has as its point *that you are not to be tempted by fear or hope of consequences.*

If you notice the transition from Mill to Moore, you will suspect that it was made somewhere by someone; Sidgwick will come to mind as a likely name; and you will in fact find it going on, almost casually, in him. He is rather a dull author; and the important things in him occur in asides and footnotes and small bits of argument which are not concerned with his grand classification of the "methods of ethics." A divine law theory of ethics is reduced to an insignificant variety by a footnote telling us that "the best theologians" (God knows whom he meant) tell us that God is to be obeyed in his capacity of a *moral* being. ἢ φορτικὸς ὁ ἔπαινος; one seems to hear Aristotle saying: "Isn't the praise vulgar?"[1]—But Sidgwick *is* vulgar in that kind of way: he thinks, for example, that humility consists in underestimating your own merits—i.e. in a species of untruthfulness; and that the ground for having laws against blasphemy was that it was offensive to believers; and that to go accurately into the virtue of purity is to offend against its canons, a thing he reproves "medieval theologians" for not realizing.

From the point of view of the present enquiry, the most important thing about Sidgwick was his definition of intention. He defines intention in such a way that one must be said to intend any foreseen consequences of one's voluntary action. This definition is obviously incorrect, and I dare say that no one would be found to defend it now. He uses it to put forward an ethical thesis which would now be accepted by many people: the thesis that it does not make any difference to a man's responsibility for something that he foresaw, that he felt no desire for it, either as an end

---

1. E.N. [*Ethica Nicomachea*] 1178b16.

or as a means to an end. Using the language of intention more correctly, and avoiding Sidgwick's faulty conception, we may state the thesis thus: it does not make any difference to a man's responsibility for an effect of his action which he can foresee, that he does not intend it. Now this sounds rather edifying; it is I think quite characteristic of very bad degenerations of thought on such questions that they sound edifying. We can see what it amounts to by considering an example. Let us suppose that a man has a responsibility for the maintenance of some child. Therefore deliberately to withdraw support from it is a bad sort of thing for him to do. It would be bad for him to withdraw its maintenance because he didn't want to maintain it any longer; *and* also bad for him to withdraw it because by doing so he would, let us say, compel someone else to do something. (We may suppose for the sake of argument that compelling that person to do that thing is in itself quite admirable.) But now he has to choose between doing something disgraceful and going to prison; if he goes to prison, it will follow that he withdraws support from the child. By Sidgwick's doctrine, there is no difference in his responsibility for ceasing to maintain the child, between the case where he does it for its own sake or as a means to some other purpose, and when it happens as a foreseen and unavoidable consequence of his going to prison rather than do something disgraceful. It follows that he must weigh up the relative badness of withdrawing support from the child and of doing the disgraceful thing; and it may easily be that the disgraceful thing is in fact a less vicious action than intentionally withdrawing support from the child would be; if then the fact that withdrawing support from the child is a side effect of his going to prison does not make any difference to his responsibility, this consideration will incline him to do the disgraceful thing; which can still be pretty bad. And of course, once he has started to look at the matter in this light, the only reasonable thing for him to consider will be the consequences and not the intrinsic badness of this or that action. So that, given that he judges reasonably that no *great* harm will come of it, he can do a much more disgraceful thing than deliberately withdrawing support from the child. And if his calculations turn out in fact wrong, it will appear that he was not responsible for the consequences, because he did not foresee them. For in fact Sidgwick's thesis leads to its being quite impossible to estimate the badness of an action except in the light of *expected* consequences. But if so, then *you* must estimate the badness in the light of the consequences *you* expect; and so it will follow that you can exculpate yourself from the *actual* consequences of the most disgraceful actions, so long as you can make out a case for not having foreseen them. Whereas I should contend that a man is responsible for the bad consequences of his bad actions, but gets no credit for the good ones; and contrariwise is not responsible for the bad consequences of good actions.

The denial of *any* distinction between foreseen and intended consequences, as far as responsibility is concerned, was not made by Sidgwick in developing any one "method of ethics"; he made this important move on behalf of everybody and just on its own account; and I think it plausible to suggest that *this* move on the part of Sidgwick explains the difference between old-fashioned Utilitarianism and that *consequentialism,* as I name it, which marks him and every English academic moral philosopher since him. By it, the kind of consideration which would formerly have been regarded as a temptation, the kind of consideration urged upon men by wives and flattering friends, was given a status by moral philosophers in their theories.

It is a necessary feature of consequentialism that it is a shallow philosophy. For there are always borderline cases in ethics. Now if you are either an Aristotelian, or a believer in divine law, you will deal with a borderline case by considering whether doing such-and-such in such-and-such circumstances is, say, murder, or is an act of injustice; and according as you decide it is or it isn't, you judge it to be a thing to do or not. This would be the method of casuistry; and while it may lead you to stretch a point on the circumference, it will not permit you to destroy the centre. But if you are a consequentialist, the question "What is it right to do in such-and-such circumstances?" is a stupid one to raise. The casuist raises such a question only to ask "Would it be *permissible* to do so-and-so?" or "Would it be permissible *not* to do so-and-so?" Only if it would *not* be permissible *not* to do so-and-so could he say "*This* would be *the* thing to do."[1] Otherwise, though he may speak

---

1. Necessarily a rare case: for the positive precepts, e.g. "Honour your parents," hardly ever prescribe, and seldom even necessitate, any particular action.

against some action, he cannot prescribe any—for in an *actual* case, the circumstances (beyond the ones imagined) might suggest all sorts of possibilities, and you can't know in advance what the possibilities are going to be. Now the consequentialist has no footing on which to say "This would be permissible, this not"; because by his own hypothesis, it is the consequences that are to decide, and he has no business to pretend that he can lay it down what possible twists a man could give doing this or that; the most he can say is: a man must not *bring about* this or that; he has no right to say he will, in an actual case, bring about such-and-such unless he does so-and-so. Further, the consequentialist, in order to be imagining borderline cases at all, has of course to assume some sort of law or standard according to which this is a borderline case, Where then does he get the standard from? In practice the answer invariably is: from the standards current in his society or his circle. And it has in fact been the mark of all these philosophers that they have been extremely conventional; they have nothing in them by which to revolt against the conventional standards of their sort of people; it is impossible that they should be profound. But the chance that a whole range of conventional standards will be decent is small.—Finally, the point of considering hypothetical situations, perhaps very improbable ones, *seems* to be to elicit from yourself or someone else a hypothetical decision to do something of a bad kind. I don't doubt this has the effect of predisposing people—who will never get into the situations for which they have made hypothetical choices—to consent to similar bad actions, or to praise and flatter those who do them, so long as their crowd does so too, when the desperate circumstances imagined don't hold at all.

Those who recognize the origins of the notions of "obligation" and of the emphatic, "moral," *ought,* in the divine law conception of ethics, but who reject the notion of a divine legislator, sometimes look about for the possibility of retaining a law conception without a divine legislator. This search, I think, has some interest in it. Perhaps the first thing that suggests itself is the "norms" of a society. But just as one cannot be impressed by Butler when one reflects what conscience can tell people to do, so, I think, one cannot be impressed by this idea if one reflects what the "norms" of a society can be like. That legislation can be "for oneself" I reject as absurd; whatever you do "for yourself"

may be admirable; but is not legislating. Once one sees this, one may say: I have to frame my own rules, and these are the best I can frame, and I shall go by them until I know something better: as a man might say "I shall go by the customs of my ancestors." Whether this leads to good or evil will depend on the *content* of the rules or of the customs of one's ancestors. If one is lucky it will lead to good. Such an attitude would be hopeful in this at any rate: it seems to have in it some Socratic doubt where, from having to fall back on such expedients, it should be clear that Socratic doubt is good; in fact rather generally it must be good for anyone to think "Perhaps in some way I can't see, I may be on a bad path, perhaps I am hopelessly wrong in some essential way".—The search for "norms" might lead someone to look for laws of nature, as if the universe were a legislator; but in the present day this is not likely to lead to good results: it might lead one to eat the weaker according to the laws of nature, but would hardly lead anyone nowadays to notions of justice; the pre-Socratic feeling about justice as comparable to the balance or harmony which kept things going is very remote to us.

There is another possibility here: "obligation" may be contractual. Just as we look at the law to find out what a man subject to it is required by it to do, so we look at a contract to find out what the man who has made it is required by it to do. Thinkers, admittedly remote from us, might have the idea of a *foedus rerum,* of the universe not as a legislator but as the embodiment of a contract. Then if you could find out what the contract was, you would learn your obligations under it. Now, you cannot be under a law unless it has been promulgated to you; and the thinkers who believed in "natural divine law" held that it was promulgated to every grown man in his knowledge of good and evil. Similarly you cannot be in a contract without having contracted, i.e. given signs of entering upon the contract. Just possibly, it might be argued that the use of language which one makes in the ordinary conduct of life amounts in some sense to giving the signs of entering into various contracts. If anyone had this theory, we should want to see it worked out. I suspect that it would be largely formal; it might be possible to construct a system embodying the law (whose status might be compared to that of "laws" of logic): "what's sauce for the goose is sauce for the gander," but hardly one descending to such particularities as the prohibition on murder or sodomy. Also, while it is clear that you can be subject to a law that you do not acknowledge and have not thought of as law, it does not seem reasonable to say that you can enter upon a contract without knowing that you are doing so; such ignorance is usually held to be destructive of the nature of a contract.

It might remain to look for "norms" in human virtues: just as *man* has so many teeth, which is certainly not the average number of teeth men have, but is the number of teeth for the species, so perhaps the species *man,* regarded not just biologically, but from the point of view of the activity of thought and choice in regard to the various departments of life— powers and faculties and use of things needed— "has" such-and-such virtues: and this "man" with the complete set of virtues is the "norm," as "man" with, e.g., a complete set of teeth is a norm. But in *this* sense "norm" has ceased to be roughly equivalent to "law." In *this* sense the notion of a "norm" brings us nearer to an Aristotelian than a law conception of ethics. There is, I think, no harm in that; but if someone looked in this direction to give "norm" a sense, then he ought to recognize what has happened to the notion "norm," which he wanted to mean "law— without bringing God in"—it has ceased to mean "law" at all; and *so* the notions of "moral obligation," "the moral ought," and "duty" are best put on the Index, if he can manage it.

But meanwhile—is it not clear that there are several concepts that need investigating simply as part of the philosophy of psychology and,—as I should recommend—*banishing ethics totally* from our minds? Namely—to begin with: "action," "intention," "pleasure," "wanting." More will probably turn up if we start with these. Eventually it might be possible to advance to considering the concept 'virtue"; with which, I suppose, we should be beginning some sort of a study of ethics.

I will end by describing the advantages of using the word "ought" in a non-emphatic fashion, and not in a special "moral" sense; of discarding the term "wrong" in a "moral" sense, and using such notions as "unjust."

It is possible, if one is allowed to proceed just by giving examples, to distinguish between the intrinsically unjust, and what is unjust given the circumstances. To arrange to get a man judicially punished for something which it can be clearly seen he has not done is intrinsically unjust. This might be done, of course, and often has been done, in all sorts of ways;

by suborning false witnesses, by a rule of law by which something is "deemed" to be the case which is admittedly not the case as a matter of fact, and by open insolence on the part of the judges and powerful people when they more or less openly say: "A fig for the fact that you did not do it; we mean to sentence you for it all the same." What is unjust given, e.g., normal circumstances is to deprive people of their ostensible property without legal procedure, not to pay debts, not to keep contracts, and a host of other things of the kind. Now, the circumstances can clearly make a great deal of difference in estimating the justice or injustice of such procedures as these; and these circumstances may *sometimes* include expected consequences; for example, a man's claim to a bit of property can become a nullity when its seizure and use can avert some obvious disaster: as, e.g., if you could use a machine of his to produce an explosion in which it would be destroyed, but by means of which you could divert a flood or make a gap which a fire could not jump. Now this certainly does not mean that what would ordinarily be an act of injustice, but is not intrinsically unjust, can always be rendered just by a reasonable calculation of better consequences; far from it; but the problems that would be raised in an attempt to draw a boundary line (or boundary area) here are obviously complicated. And while there are certainly some general remarks which ought to be made here, and some boundaries that can be drawn, the decision on particular cases would for the most part be determined κατὰ τὸν ὀρθὸν λόγον "according to what's reasonable."—E.g. that *such-and-such* a delay of payment of a *such-and-such* debt to a person *so* circumstanced, on the part of a person *so* circumstanced, would or would not be unjust, is really only to be decided "according to what's reasonable"; and for this there can *in principle* be no canon other than giving a few examples. That is to say, while it is because of a big gap in philosophy that we can give no general account of the concept of virtue and of the concept of justice, but have to proceed, using the concepts, only by giving examples; still there is an area where it is not because of any gap, but is in principle the case, that there is no account except by way of examples: and that is where the canon is "what's reasonable": which of course is *not* a canon.

That is all I wish to say about what is just in some circumstances, unjust in others; and about the way in which expected consequences can play a part in determining what is just. Returning to my example of the intrinsically unjust: if a procedure *is* one of judicially punishing a man for what he is clearly understood not to have done, there can be absolutely no argument about the description of this as unjust. No circumstances, and no expected consequences, which do *not* modify the description of the procedure as one of judicially punishing a man for what he is known not to have done can modify the description of it as unjust. Someone who attempted to dispute this would only be pretending not to know what "unjust" means: for this is a paradigm case of injustice.

And here we see the superiority of the term "unjust" over the terms "morally right" and "morally wrong." For in the context of English moral philosophy since Sidgwick it appears legitimate to discuss whether it *might* be "morally right" in some circumstances to adopt that procedure; but it cannot be argued that the procedure would in any circumstances be just.

Now I am not able to do the philosophy involved— and I think that no one in the present situation of English philosophy *can* do the philosophy involved— but it is clear that a good man is a just man; and a just man is a man who habitually refuses to commit or participate in any unjust actions for fear of any consequences, or to obtain any advantage, for himself or anyone else. Perhaps no one will disagree. But, it will be said, what *is* unjust is sometimes determined by expected consequences; and certainly that is true. But there are cases where it is not: now if someone says, "I agree, but all this wants a lot of explaining," then he is right, and, what is more, the situation at present is that we can't do the explaining; we lack the philosophic equipment. But if someone really thinks, *in advance,*[1] that it is open to question whether such an action as

procuring the judicial execution of the innocent should be quite excluded from consideration—I do not want to argue with him; he shows a corrupt mind.

In such cases our moral philosophers seek to impose a dilemma upon us. "If we have a case where the term 'unjust' applies purely in virtue of a factual description, can't one raise the question whether one sometimes conceivably ought to do injustice? If 'what is unjust' is determined by consideration of whether it is *right* to do so-and-so in such-and-such circumstances, then the question whether it is 'right' to commit injustice can't arise, just because 'wrong' has been built into the definition of injustice. But if we have a case where the description 'unjust' applies purely in virtue of the facts, without bringing 'wrong' in, then the question can arise whether one 'ought' perhaps to commit an injustice, whether it might not be 'right' to? And of course 'ought' and 'right' are being used in their *moral* senses here. Now either you must decide what is 'morally right' in the light of certain *other* 'principles,' or you make a 'principle' about *this* and decide that an injustice is never 'right'; but even if you do the latter you are going beyond the facts; you are making a decision that you will not, or that it is wrong to, commit injustice. But in either case, *if* the term 'unjust' is determined simply by the facts, it is not the term 'unjust' that determines that the term 'wrong' applies, but a decision that injustice is *wrong,* together with the diagnosis of the 'factual' description as entailing injustice. But the man who makes an absolute decision that injustice is 'wrong' has no footing on which to criticize someone who does *not* make that decision as judging falsely."

In this argument "wrong" of course is explained as meaning "morally wrong," and all the atmosphere of the term is retained while its substance is guaranteed quite null. Now let us remember that "morally wrong" is the term which is the heir of the notion "illicit," or "what there is an obligation *not* to do"; which belongs in a divine law theory or ethics. Here it really does add something to the description "unjust" to say there is an obligation not to do it; for what obliges is the divine law—as rules oblige in a game. So if the divine law obliges not to commit injustice by forbidding injustice, it really does add something to the description "unjust" to say there is an obligation not to do it, And it is because "morally wrong" is the heir of this concept, but an heir that is cut off from the family of concepts from which it

---

[1]. If he thinks it in the concrete situation, he is of course merely a normally tempted human being. In discussion when this paper was read, as was perhaps to be expected, this case was produced: a government is required to have an innocent man tried, sentenced and executed under threat of a "hydrogen bomb war." It would seem strange to me to have much hope of so averting a war threatened by such men as made this demand. But the most important thing about the way in which cases like this are invented in discussions, is the assumption that only two courses are open: here, compliance and open defiance. No one can say in advance of such a situation what the possibilities are going to be—e.g. that there is none of stalling by a feigned willingness to comply, accompanied by a skillfully arranged "escape" of the victim.

sprang, that "morally wrong" *both* goes beyond the mere factual description "unjust" *and* seems to have no discernible content except a certain compelling force, which I should call purely psychological. And such is the force of the term that philosophers actually suppose that the divine law notion can be dismissed as making no essential difference even if it is held—*because* they think that a "practical principle" running "I *ought* (i.e. am morally obliged) to obey divine laws" is required for the man who believes in divine laws. But actually this notion of obligation is a notion which only operates in the context of law. And I should be inclined to congratulate the present-day moral philosophers on depriving "morally ought" of its now delusive appearance of content, if only they did not manifest a detestable desire to retain the atmosphere of the term.

It may be possible, if we are resolute, to discard the notion "morally ought," and simply return to the ordinary "ought," which, we ought to notice, is such an extremely frequent term of human language that it is difficult to imagine getting on without it. Now if we do return to it, can't it reasonably be asked whether one might ever need to commit injustice, or whether it won't be the best thing to do? Of course it can. And the answers will be various. One man—a philosopher—may say that since justice is a virtue, and injustice a vice, and virtues and vices are built up by the performances of the action in which they are instanced, an act of injustice will tend to make a man bad; and essentially the flourishing of a man *qua* man consists in his being good (e.g. in virtues); but for any X to which such terms apply, X needs what makes it flourish, so a man needs, or ought to perform, only virtuous actions; and even if, as it must be admitted may happen, he flourishes less, or not at all, in inessentials, by avoiding injustice, his life is spoiled in essentials by not avoiding injustice—so he still needs to perform only just actions. That is roughly how Plato and Aristotle talk; but it can be seen that philosophically there is a huge gap, at present unfillable as far as we are concerned, which needs to be filled by an account of human nature, human action, the type of characteristic a virtue is, and above all of human "flourishing." And it is the last concept that appears the most doubtful. For it is a bit much to swallow that a man in pain and hunger and poor and friendless is "flourishing," as Aristotle himself admitted. Further, someone might say that one at least needed to stay alive to "flourish." Another man unim-

pressed by all that will say in a hard case "What we need is such-and-such, which we won't get without doing this (which is unjust)—so this is what we ought to do." Another man, who does not follow the rather elaborate reasoning of the philosophers, simply says "I know it is in any case a disgraceful thing to say that one had better commit this unjust action." The man who believes in divine laws will say perhaps "It is forbidden, and however it looks, it cannot be to anyone's profit to commit injustice"; he like the Greek philosophers can think in terms of "flourishing." If he is a Stoic, he is apt to have a decidedly strained notion of what "flourishing consists in"; if he is a Jew or Christian, he need not have any very distinct notion: the way it will profit him to abstain from injustice is something that he leaves it to God to determine, himself only saying "It can't do me any good to go against his law." (But he also hopes for a great reward in a new life later on, e.g. at the coming of Messiah; but in this he is relying on special promises.)

It is left to modern moral philosophy—the moral philosophy of all the well-known English ethicists since Sidgwick—to construct systems according to which the man who says "We need such-and-such, and will only get it this way" *may* be a virtuous character: that is to say, it is left open to debate whether such a procedure as the judicial punishment of the innocent may not in some circumstances be the "right" one to adopt; and though the present Oxford moral philosophers would accord a man *permission* to "make it his principle" not to do such a thing, they teach a philosophy according to which the particular consequences of such an action *could* "morally" be taken into account by a man who was debating what to do; and if they were such as to conflict with his "ends," it might be a step in his moral education to frame a moral principle under which he "managed" (to use Mr. Nowell-Smith's phrase[1]) to bring the action; or it might be a new "decision of principle," making which was an advance in the formation of his moral thinking (to adopt Mr. Hare's conception), to decide: in such-and-such circumstances one ought to procure the judicial condemnation of the innocent. And that is my complaint.

Somerville College, Oxford.

---

1. *Ethics.*

JOHN RAWLS

FROM *A Theory of Justice*

It is difficult to overestimate the effect that John Rawls' A Theory of Justice (1971) has had on contemporary moral philosophy. With this book, by now a contemporary classic, Rawls has helped direct attention in ethics to the notions of justice and rights. What are the conditions for a just society and just social institutions? How should we balance the concerns of individual rights and equality within society? Answering these kinds of questions has taken on a new importance for moral philosophers as a result of Rawls' influential book.

In this book, the rules of a just society are determined, in a now-famous manner, by negotiation with the other members of the society in special circumstances. Social rules are just if they are agreed to by all negotiators who are in what Rawls calls the "original position." In this position, the participants must negotiate behind a "veil of ignorance," unaware of their own status within the society that is being formed. Rawls argues that, in these circumstances, people will choose rules that will benefit all members of the society, since they themselves do not know who they will be when they lift the veil. They will want to negotiate a society in which all are well-off.

Rawls' theory is an original, systematic ethical theory that attempts to set out the conditions for a just society, yet draws upon a Hobbesian social contract theory. Social contract theory, or contractarianism, traces its main historical root to the work of Thomas Hobbes in the seventeenth century. For social contract theory, morality results from following the rules necessary for a functioning society. Therefore, the theory analyzes the interplay of social forces that could produce a justifiable system of rules within society. (9.4; 11.7)

The interest in contractarianism generated in the last three decades shows no sign of diminishing. The theory has taken its place alongside utilitarianism, Kantian deontology, and virtue ethics as one of the prominent ethical theories of the latter half of this century. Additional issues associated with social contract theory are found in "Morality and Advantage" by David Gauthier.

. . .

3. The Main Idea of the Theory of Justice

My aim is to present a conception of justice which generalizes and carries to a higher level of abstraction the familiar theory of the social contract as found, say, in Locke, Rousseau, and Kant.[1] In order to do this we are not to think of the original contract as one to enter a particular society or to set up a particular form of government. Rather, the guiding idea is that the principles of justice for the basic structure of society are the object of the original agreement. They are the principles that free and rational persons concerned to further their own interests would accept in an initial position of equality as defining the fundamental terms of their association. These principles are to regulate all further agreements; they specify the kinds of social cooperation that can be entered into and the forms of government that can be established. This way of regarding the principles of justice I shall call justice as fairness.

Thus we are to imagine that those who engage in social cooperation choose together, in one joint act, the principles which are to assign basic rights and duties and to determine the division of social benefits. Men are to decide in advance how they are to regulate their claims against one another and what is to be the foundation charter of their society. Just as each person must decide by rational reflection what constitutes his good, that is, the system of ends which it is rational for him to pursue, so a group of persons must decide once and for all what is to count among them as just and unjust. The choice which rational men would make in this hypothetical situation of equal liberty, assuming for the present that this choice problem has a solution, determines the principles of justice.

In justice as fairness the original position of equality corresponds to the state of nature in the traditional theory of the social contract. This original position is not, of course, thought of as an actual historical state of affairs, much less as a primitive condition of culture. It is understood as a purely hypothetical situation characterized so as to lead to a certain conception of justice.[2] Among the essential features of this situation is that no one knows his place in society, his class position or social status, nor does any one know his fortune in the distribution of natural assets and abilities, his intelligence, strength, and the like. I shall even assume that the parties do not know their conceptions of the good or their special psychological propensities. The principles of justice are chosen behind a veil of ignorance. This ensures that no one is advantaged or disadvantaged in the choice of principles by the outcome of natural chance or the contingency of social circumstances. Since all are similarly situated and no one is able to design principles to favor his particular condition, the principles of justice are the result of a fair agreement or bargain. For given the circumstances of the original position, the symmetry of everyone's relations to each other, this initial situation is fair between individuals as moral persons, that is, as rational beings with their own ends and capable, I shall assume, of a sense of justice. The original position is, one might say, the appropriate initial status quo, and thus the fundamental agreements reached in it are fair. This explains the propriety of the name "justice as fairness": it conveys the idea that the principles of justice are agreed to in an initial situation that is fair. The name does not mean that the concepts of justice and fairness are the same, any more than the phrase "poetry as metaphor" means that the concepts of poetry and metaphor are the same.

---

1. As the text suggests, I shall regard Locke's *Second Treatise of Government,* Rousseau's *The Social Contract,* and Kant's ethical works beginning with *The Foundations of the Metaphysics of Morals* as definitive of the contract tradition. For all of its greatness, Hobbes's *Leviathan* raises special problems. A general historical survey is provided by J. W. Gough, *The Social Contract,* 2nd ed. (Oxford, The Clarendon Press, 1957), and Otto Gierke, *Natural Law and the Theory of Society,* trans. with an introduction by Ernest Barker (Cambridge, The University Press, 1934). A presentation of the contract view as primarily an ethical theory is to be found in G. R. Grice, *The Grounds of Moral Judgment* (Cambridge, The University Press, 1967). See also §19, note 30.

---

2. Kant is clear that the original agreement is hypothetical. See *The Metaphysics of Morals,* pt. I (*Rechtslehre*), especially §§47, 52; and pt. II of the essay "Concerning the Common Saying: This May Be True in Theory but It Does Not Apply in Practice," in *Kant's Political Writings,* ed. Hans Reiss and trans. by H. B. Nisbet (Cambridge, The University Press, 1970), pp.73–87. See Georges Vlachos, *La Pensée politique de Kant* (Paris, Presses Universitaires de France, 1962), pp. 326–335; and J. G. Murphy, *Kant: The Philosophy of Right* (London, Macmillan, 1970), pp. 109–112, 133–136, for a further discussion.

Justice as fairness begins, as I have said, with one of the most general of all choices which persons might make together, namely, with the choice of the first principles of a conception of justice which is to regulate all subsequent criticism and reform of institutions. Then, having chosen a conception of justice, we can suppose that they are to choose a constitution and a legislature to enact laws, and so on, all in accordance with the principles of justice initially agreed upon. Our social situation is just if it is such that by this sequence of hypothetical agreements we would have contracted into the general system of rules which defines it. Moreover, assuming that the original position does determine a set of principles (that is, that a particular conception of justice would be chosen), it will then be true that whenever social institutions satisfy these principles those engaged in them can say to one another that they are cooperating on terms to which they would agree if they were free and equal persons whose relations with respect to one another were fair. They could all view their arrangements as meeting the stipulations which they would acknowledge in an initial situation that embodies widely accepted and reasonable constraints on the choice of principles. The general recognition of this fact would provide the basis for a public acceptance of the corresponding principles of justice. No society can, of course, be a scheme of cooperation which men enter voluntarily in a literal sense; each person finds himself placed at birth in some particular position in some particular society, and the nature of this position materially affects his life prospects. Yet a society satisfying the principles of justice as fairness comes as close as a society can to being a voluntary scheme, for it meets the principles which free and equal persons would assent to under circumstances that are fair. In this sense its members are autonomous and the obligations they recognize self-imposed.

One feature of justice as fairness is to think of the parties in the initial situation as rational and mutually disinterested. This does not mean that the parties are egoists, that is, individuals with only certain kinds of interests, say in wealth, prestige, and domination. But they are conceived as not taking an interest in one another's interests. They are to presume that even their spiritual aims may be opposed, in the way that the aims of those of different religions may be opposed. Moreover, the concept of rationality must be interpreted as far as possible in the narrow sense, standard in economic theory, of taking the most effective means to given ends. I shall modify this concept to some extent, as explained later (§ 25), but one must try to avoid introducing into it any controversial ethical elements. The initial situation must be characterized by stipulations that are widely accepted.

In working out the conception of justice as fairness one main task clearly is to determine which principles of justice would be chosen in the original position. To do this we must describe this situation in some detail and formulate with care the problem of choice which it presents. These matters I shall take up in the immediately succeeding chapters. It may be observed, however, that once the principles of justice are thought of as arising from an original agreement in a situation of equality, it is an open question whether the principle of utility would be acknowledged. Offhand it hardly seems likely that persons who view themselves as equals, entitled to press their claims upon one another, would agree to a principle which may require lesser life prospects for some simply for the sake of a greater sum of advantages enjoyed by others. Since each desires to protect his interests, his capacity to advance his conception of the good, no one has a reason to acquiesce in an enduring loss for himself in order to bring about a greater net balance of satisfaction. In the absence of strong and lasting benevolent impulses, a rational man would not accept a basic structure merely because it maximized the algebraic sum of advantages irrespective of its permanent effects on his own basic rights and interests. Thus it seems that the principle of utility is incompatible with the conception of social cooperation among equals for mutual advantage. It appears to be inconsistent with the idea of reciprocity implicit in the notion of a well-ordered society. Or, at any rate, so I shall argue.

I shall maintain instead that the persons in the initial situation would choose two rather different principles: the first requires equality in the assignment of basic rights and duties, while the second holds that social and economic inequalities, for example inequalities of wealth and authority, are just only if they result in compensating benefits for everyone, and in particular for the least advantaged members of society. These principles rule out justifying institutions on the grounds that the hardships of some are offset by a greater good in the aggregate. It may be expedient but it is not just that some should have less in order that others may prosper. But there is no injustice in the greater benefits earned by a few provided that the situation of persons not so fortunate is thereby improved. The intuitive idea is that since everyone's well-being depends upon a scheme of cooperation without which no one could have a satisfactory life, the division of advantages should be such as to draw forth the willing cooperation of everyone taking part in it, including those less well situated. Yet this can be expected only if reasonable terms are proposed. The two principles mentioned seem to be a fair agreement on the basis of which those better endowed, or more fortunate in their social position, neither of which we can be said to deserve, could expect the willing cooperation of others when some workable scheme is a necessary condition of the welfare of all.[3] Once we decide to look for a conception of justice that nullifies the accidents of natural endowment and the contingencies of social circumstance as counters in quest for political and economic advantage, we are led to these principles. They express the result of leaving aside those aspects of the social world that seem arbitrary from a moral point of view.

The problem of the choice of principles, however, is extremely difficult. I do not expect the answer I shall suggest to be convincing to everyone. It is, therefore, worth noting from the outset that justice as fairness, like other contract views, consists of two parts: (1) an interpretation of the initial situation and of the problem of choice posed there, and (2) a set of principles which, it is argued, would be agreed to. One may accept the first part of the theory (or some variant thereof), but not the other, and conversely. The concept of the initial contractual situation may seem reasonable although the particular principles proposed are rejected. To be sure, I want to maintain that the most appropriate conception of this situation does lead to principles of justice contrary to utilitarianism and perfectionism, and therefore that the contract doctrine provides an alternative to these views. Still, one may dispute this contention even though one grants that the contractarian method is a useful way of studying ethical theories and of setting forth their underlying assumptions.

Justice as fairness is an example of what I have called a contract theory. Now there may be an objection to the term "contract" and related expressions, but I think it will serve reasonably well. Many words have misleading connotations which at first are likely to confuse. The terms "utility" and "utilitarianism" are surely no exception. They too have unfortunate suggestions which hostile critics have been willing to exploit; yet they are clear enough for those prepared to study utilitarian doctrine. The same should be true of the term "contract" applied to moral theories. As I have mentioned, to understand it one has to keep in mind that it implies a certain level of abstraction. In particular, the content of the relevant agreement is not to enter a given society or to adopt a given form of government, but to accept certain moral principles. Moreover, the undertakings referred to are purely hypothetical: a contract view holds that certain principles would be accepted in a well-defined initial situation.

The merit of the contract terminology is that it conveys the idea that principles of justice may be conceived as principles that would be chosen by rational persons, and that in this way conceptions of justice may be explained and justified. The theory of justice is a part, perhaps the most significant part, of the theory of rational choice. Furthermore, principles of justice deal with conflicting claims upon the advantages won by social cooperation; they apply to the relations among several persons or groups. The word "contract" suggests this plurality as well as the condition that the appropriate division of advantages must be in accordance with principles acceptable to all parties. The condition of publicity for principles of justice is also connoted by the contract phraseology. Thus, if these principles are the outcome of an agreement, citizens have a knowledge of the principles that others follow. It is characteristic of contract theories to stress the public nature of political principles. Finally there is the long tradition of the contract doctrine. Expressing the tie with this line of thought helps to define ideas and accords with natural piety. There are then several advantages in the use of the term "contract." With due precautions taken, it should not be misleading.

A final remark. Justice as fairness is not a complete contract theory. For it is clear that the contractarian

---

3. For the formulation of this intuitive idea I am indebted to Allan Gibbard.

idea can be extended to the choice of more or less an entire ethical system, that is, to a system including principles for all the virtues and not only for justice. Now for the most part I shall consider only principles of justice and others closely related to them; I make no attempt to discuss the virtues in a systematic way. Obviously if justice as fairness succeeds reasonably well, a next step would be to study the more general view suggested by the name "rightness as fairness." But even this wider theory fails to embrace all moral relationships, since it would seem to include only our relations with other persons and to leave out of account how we are to conduct ourselves toward animals and the rest of nature. I do not contend that the contract notion offers a way to approach these questions which are certainly of the first importance; and I shall have to put them aside. We must recognize the limited scope of justice as fairness and of the general type of view that it exemplifies. How far its conclusions must be revised once these other matters are understood cannot be decided in advance.

4. The Original Position and Justification

I have said that the original position is the appropriate initial status quo which insures that the fundamental agreements reached in it are fair. This fact yields the name "justice as fairness." It is clear, then, that I want to say that one conception of justice is more reasonable than another, or justifiable with respect to it, if rational persons in the initial situation would choose its principles over those of the other for the role of justice. Conceptions of justice are to be ranked by their acceptability to persons so circumstanced. Understood in this way the question of justification is settled by working out a problem of deliberation: we have to ascertain which principles it would be rational to adopt given the contractual situation. This connects the theory of justice with the theory of rational choice.

If this view of the problem of justification is to succeed, we must, of course, describe in some detail the nature of this choice problem. A problem of rational decision has a definite answer only if we know the beliefs and interests of the parties, their relations with respect to one another, the alternatives between which they are to choose, the procedure whereby they make up their minds, and so on. As the cir-

cumstances are presented in different ways, correspondingly different principles are accepted. The concept of the original position, as I shall refer to it, is that of the most philosophically favored interpretation of this initial choice situation for the purposes of a theory of justice.

But how are we to decide what is the most favored interpretation? I assume, for one thing, that there is a broad measure of agreement that principles of justice should be chosen under certain conditions. To justify a particular description of the initial situation one shows that it incorporates these commonly shared presumptions. One argues from widely accepted but weak premises to more specific conclusions. Each of the presumptions should by itself be natural and plausible; some of them may seem innocuous or even trivial. The aim of the contract approach is to establish that taken together they impose significant bounds on acceptable principles of justice. The ideal outcome would be that these conditions determine a unique set of principles; but I shall be satisfied if they suffice to rank the main traditional conceptions of social justice.

One should not be misled, then, by the somewhat unusual conditions which characterize the original position. The idea here is simply to make vivid to ourselves the restrictions that it seems reasonable to impose on arguments for principles of justice, and therefore on these principles themselves. Thus it seems reasonable and generally acceptable that no one should be advantaged or disadvantaged by natural fortune or social circumstances in the choice of principles. It also seems widely agreed that it should be impossible to tailor principles to the circumstances of one's own case. We should insure further that particular inclinations and aspirations, and persons' conceptions of their good do not affect the principles adopted. The aim is to rule out those principles that it would be rational to propose for acceptance, however little the chance of success, only if one knew certain things that are irrelevant from the standpoint of justice. For example, if a man knew that he was wealthy, he might find it rational to advance the principle that various taxes for welfare measures be counted unjust; if he knew that he was poor, he would most likely propose the contrary principle. To represent the desired restrictions one imagines a situation in which everyone is deprived of this sort of information. One excludes the knowledge of those contingencies which sets men at odds and allows them to be guided by their prejudices. In this manner the veil of ignorance is arrived at in a natural way. This concept should cause no difficulty if we keep in mind the constraints on arguments that it is meant to express. At any time we can enter the original position, so to speak, simply by following a certain procedure, namely, by arguing for principles of justice in accordance with these restrictions.

It seems reasonable to suppose that the parties in the original position are equal. That is, all have the same rights in the procedure for choosing principles; each can make proposals, submit reasons for their acceptance, and so on. Obviously the purpose of these conditions is to represent equality between human beings as moral persons, as creatures having a conception of their good and capable of a sense of justice. The basis of equality is taken to be similarity in these two respects. Systems of ends are not ranked in value; and each man is presumed to have the requisite ability to understand and to act upon whatever principles are adopted. Together with the veil of ignorance, these conditions define the principles of justice as those which rational persons concerned to advance their interests would consent to as equals when none are known to be advantaged or disadvantaged by social and natural contingencies.

There is, however, another side to justifying a particular description of the original position. This is to see if the principles which would be chosen match our considered convictions of justice or extend them in an acceptable way. We can note whether applying these principles would lead us to make the same judgments about the basic structure of society which we now make intuitively and in which we have the greatest confidence; or whether, in cases where our present judgments are in doubt and given with hesitation, these principles offer a resolution which we can affirm on reflection. There are questions which we feel sure must be answered in a certain way. For example, we are confident that religious intolerance and racial discrimination are unjust. We think that we have examined these things with care and have reached what we believe is an impartial judgment not likely to be distorted by an excessive attention to our own interests. These convictions are provisional fixed points which we presume any conception of

justice must fit. But we have much less assurance as to what is the correct distribution of wealth and authority. Here we may be looking for a way to remove our doubts. We can check an interpretation of the initial situation, then, by the capacity of its principles to accommodate our firmest convictions and to provide guidance where guidance is needed.

In searching for the most favored description of this situation we work from both ends. We begin by describing it so that it represents generally shared and preferably weak conditions. We then see if these conditions are strong enough to yield a significant set of principles. If not, we look for further premises equally reasonable. But if so, and these principles match our considered convictions of justice, then so far well and good. But presumably there will be discrepancies. In this case we have a choice. We can either modify the account of the initial situation or we can revise our existing judgments, for even the judgments we take provisionally as fixed points are liable to revision. By going back and forth, sometimes altering the conditions of the contractual circumstances, at others withdrawing our judgments and conforming them to principle, I assume that eventually we shall find a description of the initial situation that both expresses reasonable conditions and yields principles which match our considered judgments duly pruned and adjusted. This state of affairs I refer to as reflective equilibrium.[4] It is an equilibrium because at last our principles and judgments coincide; and it is reflective since we know to what principles our judgments conform and the premises of their derivation. At the moment everything is in order. But this equilibrium is not necessarily stable. It is liable to be upset by further examination of the conditions which should be imposed on the contractual situation and by particular cases which may lead us to revise our judgments. Yet for the time being we have done what we can to render coherent and to justify our convictions of social justice. We have reached a conception of the original position.

---

4. The process of mutual adjustment of principles and considered judgments is not peculiar to moral philosophy. See Nelson Goodman, *Fact, Fiction, and Forecast* (Cambridge, Mass., Harvard University Press, 1955), pp. 65–68, for parallel remarks concerning the justification of the principles of deductive and inductive inference.

. . .

11. Two Principles of Justice

I shall now state in a provisional form the two principles of justice that I believe would be chosen in the original position. In this section I wish to make only the most general comments, and therefore the first formulation of these principles is tentative. As we go on I shall run through several formulations and approximate step by step the final statement to be given much later. I believe that doing this allows the exposition to proceed in a natural way.

The first statement of the two principles reads as follows.

First: each person is to have an equal right to the most extensive basic liberty compatible with a similar liberty for others.

Second: social and economic inequalities are to be arranged so that they are both (a) reasonably expected to be to everyone's advantage, and (b) attached to positions and offices open to all. There are two ambiguous phrases in the second principle, namely "everyone's advantage" and "equally open to all." Determining their sense more exactly will lead to a second formulation of the principle in §13. The final version of the two principles is given in §45; §39 considers the rendering of the first principle.

By way of general comment, these principles primarily apply, as I have said, to the basic structure of society. They are to govern the assignment of rights and duties and to regulate the distribution of social and economic advantages. As their formulation suggests, these principles presuppose that the social structure can be divided into two more or less distinct parts, the first principle applying to the one, the second to the other. They distinguish between those aspects of the social system that define and secure the equal liberties of citizenship and those that specify and establish social and economic inequalities. The basic liberties of citizens are, roughly speaking, political liberty (the right to vote and to be eligible for public office) together with freedom of speech and assembly; liberty of conscience and freedom of thought; freedom of the person along with the right to hold (personal) property; and freedom from arbitrary arrest and seizure as defined by the concept of the rule of law. These liberties are all required to be equal by the first principle, since citizens of a just society are to have the same basic rights.

The second principle applies, in the first approximation, to the distribution of income and wealth and to the design of organizations that make use of differences in authority and responsibility, or chains of command. While the distribution of wealth and income need not be equal, it must be to everyone's advantage, and at the same time, positions of authority and offices of command must be accessible to all. One applies the second principle by holding positions open, and then, subject to this constraint, arranges social and economic inequalities so that everyone benefits.

These principles are to be arranged in a serial order with the first principle prior to the second. This ordering means that a departure from the institutions of equal liberty required by the first principle cannot be justified by, or compensated for, by greater social and economic advantages. The distribution of wealth and income, and the hierarchies of authority, must be consistent with both the liberties of equal citizenship and equality of opportunity.

It is clear that these principles are rather specific in their content, and their acceptance rests on certain assumptions that I must eventually try to explain and justify. A theory of justice depends upon a theory of society in ways that will become evident as we proceed. For the present, it should be observed that the two principles (and this holds for all formulations) are a special case of a more general conception of justice that can be expressed as follows.

> All social values—liberty and opportunity, income and wealth, and the bases of self-respect—are to be distributed equally unless an unequal distribution of any, or all, of these values is to everyone's advantage.

Injustice, then, is simply inequalities that are not to the benefit of all. Of course, this conception is extremely vague and requires interpretation.

As a first step, suppose that the basic structure of society distributes certain primary goods, that is, things that every rational man is presumed to want. These goods normally have a use whatever a person's rational plan of life. For simplicity, assume that the chief primary goods at the disposition of society are rights and liberties, powers and opportunities, income and wealth. (Later on in Part Three the primary good of self-respect has a central place.) These are the social primary goods. Other primary goods such as health and vigor, intelligence and imagination, are natural goods; although their possession is influenced by the basic structure, they are not so directly under its control. Imagine, then, a hypothetical initial arrangement in which all the social primary goods are equally distributed: everyone has similar rights and duties, and income and wealth are evenly shared. This state of affairs provides a benchmark for judging improvements. If certain inequalities of wealth and organizational powers would make everyone better off than in this hypothetical starting situation, then they accord with the general conception.

Now it is possible, at least theoretically, that by giving up some of their fundamental liberties men are sufficiently compensated by the resulting social and economic gains. The general conception of justice imposes no restrictions on what sort of inequalities are permissible; it only requires that everyone's position be improved. We need not suppose anything so drastic as consenting to a condition of slavery. Imagine instead that men forego certain political rights when the economic returns are significant and their capacity to influence the course of policy by the exercise of these rights would be marginal in any case. It is this kind of exchange which the two principles as stated rule out; being arranged in serial order they do not permit exchanges between basic liberties and economic and social gains. The serial ordering of principles expresses an underlying preference among primary social goods. When this preference is rational so likewise is the choice of these principles in this order.

In developing justice as fairness I shall, for the most part, leave aside the general conception of justice and examine instead the special case of the two principles in serial order. The advantage of this procedure is that from the first the matter of priorities is recognized and an effort made to find principles to deal with it. One is led to attend throughout to the conditions under which the acknowledgment of the absolute weight of liberty with respect to social and economic advantages, as defined by the lexical order of the two principles, would be reasonable. Offhand, this ranking appears extreme and too special a case to be of much interest; but there is more justification

for it than would appear at first sight. Or at any rate, so I shall maintain (§82). Furthermore, the distinction between fundamental rights and liberties and economic and social benefits marks a difference among primary social goods that one should try to exploit. It suggests an important division in the social system. Of course, the distinctions drawn and the ordering proposed are bound to be at best only approximations. There are surely circumstances in which they fail. But it is essential to depict clearly the main lines of a reasonable conception of justice; and under many conditions anyway, the two principles in serial order may serve well enough. When necessary we can fall back on the more general conception.

The fact that the two principles apply to institutions has certain consequences. Several points illustrate this. First of all, the rights and liberties referred to by these principles are those which are defined by the public rules of the basic structure. Whether men are free is determined by the rights and duties established by the major institutions of society. Liberty is a certain pattern of social forms. The first principle simply requires that certain sorts of rules, those defining basic liberties, apply to everyone equally and that they allow the most extensive liberty compatible with a like liberty for all. The only reason for circumscribing the rights defining liberty and making men's freedom less extensive than it might otherwise be is that these equal rights as institutionally defined would interfere with one another.

Another thing to bear in mind is that when principles mention persons, or require that everyone gain from an inequality, the reference is to representative persons holding the various social positions, or offices, or whatever, established by the basic structure. Thus in applying the second principle I assume that it is possible to assign an expectation of well-being to representative individuals holding these positions. This expectation indicates their life prospects as viewed from their social station. In general, the expectations of representative persons depend upon the distribution of rights and duties throughout the basic structure. When this changes, expectations change. I assume, then, that expectations are connected: by raising the prospects of the representative man in one position we presumably increase or decrease the prospects of representative men in other positions. Since it applies to institutional forms, the second principle (or rather the first part of it) refers to the expectations of representative individuals. As I shall discuss below, neither principle applies to distributions of particular goods to particular individuals who may be identified by their proper names. The situation where someone is considering how to allocate certain commodities to needy persons who are known to him is not within the scope of the principles. They are meant to regulate basic institutional arrangements. We must not assume that there is much similarity from the standpoint of justice between an administrative allotment of goods to specific persons and the appropriate design of society. Our common-sense intuitions for the former may be a poor guide to the latter.

Now the second principle insists that each person benefit from permissible inequalities in the basic structure. This means that it must be reasonable for each relevant representative man defined by this structure, when he views it as a going concern, to prefer his prospects with the inequality to his prospects without it. One is not allowed to justify differences in income or organizational powers on the ground that the disadvantages of those in one position are outweighed by the greater advantages of those in another. Much less can infringements of liberty be counterbalanced in this way. Applied to the basic structure, the principle of utility would have us maximize the sum of expectations of representative men (weighted by the number of persons they represent, on the classical view); and this would permit us to compensate for the losses of some by the gains of others. Instead, the two principles require that every one benefit from economic and social inequalities.

. . .

18. Principles for Individuals: The Principles of Fairness

In the discussion so far I have considered the principles which apply to institutions or, more exactly, to the basic structure of society. It is clear, however, that principles of another kind must also be chosen, since a complete theory of right includes principles for individuals as well. In fact, as the accompanying diagram indicates, one needs in addition principles for the law of nations and of course priority rules for assigning weights when principles conflict. I shall not take up the principles for the law of nations, except in passing (§58); nor shall I attempt any systematic discussion of the principles for individuals. But certain principles of this type are an essential part of any theory of justice. In this and the next section the meaning of several of these principles is explained, although the examination of the reasons for choosing them is postponed until later (§§51–52).

The accompanying diagram is purely schematic. It is not suggested that the principles associated with the concepts lower down in the tree are deduced from the higher ones. The diagram simply indicates the kinds of principles that must be chosen before a full conception of right is on hand. The Roman numerals express the order in which the various sorts of principles are to be acknowledged in the original position. Thus the principles for the basic structure of society are to be agreed to first, principles for individuals next, followed by those for the law of nations. Last of all the priority rules are adopted, although we may tentatively choose these earlier contingent on subsequent revision.

Now the order in which principles are chosen raises a number of questions which I shall skip over. The important thing is that the various principles are to be adopted in a definite sequence and the reasons for this ordering are connected with the more difficult parts of the theory of justice. To illustrate: while it would be possible to choose many of the natural duties before those for the basic structure without changing the principles in any substantial way, the sequence in either case reflects the fact that obligations presuppose principles for social forms. And some natural duties also presuppose such principles, for example, the duty to support just institutions. For this reason it seems simpler to adopt all principles for individuals after those for the basic structure. That principles for institutions are chosen first shows the social nature of the virtue of justice, its intimate connection with social practices so often noted by idealists. When Bradley says that the individual is a bare abstraction, he can be interpreted to say, without too much distortion, that a person's obligations and duties presuppose a moral conception of institutions and therefore that the content of just institutions must be defined before the requirements

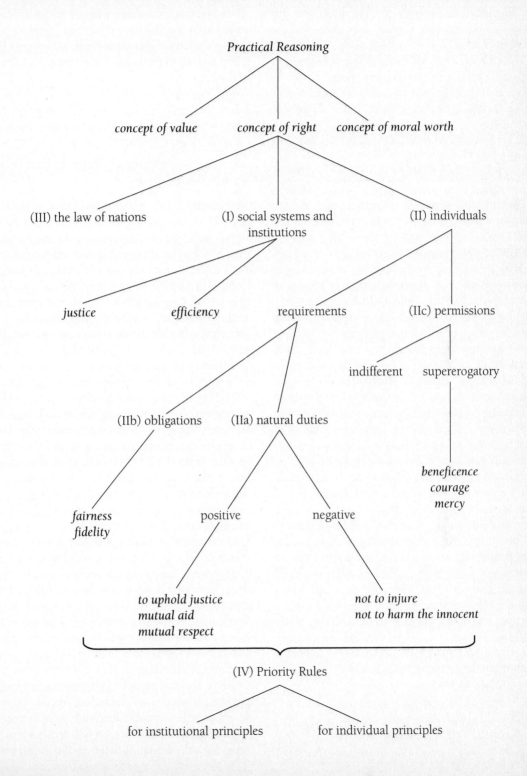

Practical Reasoning

concept of value   *concept of right*   *concept of moral worth*

(III) the law of nations   (I) social systems and institutions   (II) individuals

justice   *efficiency*   requirements   (IIc) permissions

indifferent   supererogatory

(IIb) obligations   (IIa) natural duties

beneficence
courage
mercy

fairness
fidelity

positive   negative

to uphold justice
mutual aid
mutual respect

not to injure
not to harm the innocent

(IV) Priority Rules

for institutional principles   for individual principles

for individuals can be set out.[5] And this is to say that, in most cases, the principles for obligations and duties should be settled upon after those for the basic structure.

Therefore, to establish a complete conception of right, the parties in the original position are to choose in a definite order not only a conception of justice but also principles to go with each major concept falling under the concept of right. These concepts are I assume relatively few in number and have a determinate relation to each other. Thus, in addition to principles for institutions there must be an agreement on principles for such notions as fairness and fidelity, mutual respect and beneficence as these apply to individuals, as well as on principles for the conduct of states. The intuitive idea is this: the concept of something's being right is the same as, or better, may be replaced by, the concept of its being in accordance with the principles that in the original position would be acknowledged to apply to things of its kind. I do not interpret this concept of right as providing an analysis of the meaning of the term "right" as normally used in moral contexts. It is not meant as an analysis of the concept of right in the traditional sense. Rather, the broader notion of rightness as fairness is to be understood as a replacement for existing conceptions. There is no necessity to say that sameness of meaning holds between the word "right" (and its relatives) in its ordinary use and the more elaborate locutions needed to express this ideal contractarian concept of right. For our purposes here I accept the view that a sound analysis is best understood as providing a satisfactory substitute, one that meets certain desiderata while avoiding certain obscurities and confusions. In other words, explication is elimination: we start with a concept the expression for which is somehow troublesome; but it serves certain ends that cannot be given up. An explication achieves these ends in other ways that are relatively free of difficulty.[6] Thus if the theory of justice as fairness, or more generally of rightness as fairness, fits our considered judgments in reflective equilibrium, and if it enables us to say all that on due

examination we want to say, then it provides a way of eliminating customary phrases in favor of other expressions. So understood one may think of justice as fairness and rightness as fairness as providing a definition or explication of the concepts of justice and right.

. . .

26. The Reasoning Leading to the Two Principles of Justice

In this and the next two sections I take up the choice between the two principles of justice and the principle of average utility. Determining the rational preference between these two options is perhaps the central problem in developing the conception of justice as fairness as a viable alternative to the utilitarian tradition. I shall begin in this section by presenting some intuitive remarks favoring the two principles. I shall also discuss briefly the qualitative structure of the argument that needs to be made if the case for these principles is to be conclusive.

It will be recalled that the general conception of justice as fairness requires that all primary social goods be distributed equally unless an unequal distribution would be to everyone's advantage. No restrictions are placed on exchanges of these goods and therefore a lesser liberty can be compensated for by greater social and economic benefits. Now looking at the situation from the standpoint of one person selected arbitrarily, there is no way for him to win special advantages for himself. Nor, on the other hand, are there grounds for his acquiescing in special disadvantages. Since it is not reasonable for him to expect more than an equal share in the division of social goods, and since it is not rational for him to agree to less, the sensible thing for him to do is to acknowledge as the first principle of justice one requiring an equal distribution. Indeed, this principle is so obvious that we would expect it to occur to anyone immediately.

Thus, the parties start with a principle establishing equal liberty for all, including equality of opportunity, as well as an equal distribution of income and wealth. But there is no reason why this acknowledgment should be final. If there are inequalities in the basic structure that work to make everyone better off

---

5. See F. H. Bradley, *Ethical Studies,* 2nd ed. (Oxford, The Clarendon Press, 1927), pp. 163–189.

6. See W. V. Quine, *Word and Object* (Cambridge, Mass., M.I.T. Press, 1960), pp. 257–262, whom I follow here.

in comparison with the benchmark of initial equality, why not permit them? The immediate gain which a greater equality might allow can be regarded as intelligently invested in view of its future return. If, for example, these inequalities set up various incentives which succeed in eliciting more productive efforts, a person in the original position may look upon them as necessary to cover the costs of training and to encourage effective performance. One might think that ideally individuals should want to serve one another. But since the parties are assumed not to take an interest in one another's interests, their acceptance of these inequalities is only the acceptance of the relations in which men stand in the circumstances of justice. They have no grounds for complaining of one another's motives. A person in the original position would, therefore, concede the justice of these inequalities. Indeed, it would be shortsighted of him not to do so. He would hesitate to agree to these regularities only if he would be dejected by the bare knowledge or perception that others were better situated; and I have assumed that the parties decide as if they are not moved by envy. In order to make the principle regulating inequalities determinate, one looks at the system from the standpoint of the least advantaged representative man. Inequalities are permissible when they maximize, or at least all contribute to, the long-term expectations of the least fortunate group in society.

Now this general conception imposes no constraints on what sorts of inequalities are allowed, whereas the special conception, by putting the two principles in serial order (with the necessary adjustments in meaning) forbids exchanges between basic liberties and economic and social benefits. I shall not try to justify this ordering here. From time to time in later chapters this problem will be considered (§§39, 82). But roughly, the idea underlying this ordering is that if the parties assume that their basic liberties can be effectively exercised, they will not exchange a lesser liberty for an improvement in economic well-being. It is only when social conditions do not allow the effective establishment of these rights that one can concede their limitation; and these restrictions can be granted only to the extent that they are necessary to prepare the way for a free society. The denial of equal liberty can be defended only if it is necessary to raise the level of civilization so that in due course these freedoms can be enjoyed. Thus in

adopting a serial order we are in effect making a special assumption in the original position, namely, that the parties know that the conditions of their society, whatever they are, admit the effective realization of the equal liberties. The serial ordering of the two principles of justice eventually comes to be reasonable if the general conception is consistently followed. This lexical ranking is the long-run tendency of the general view. For the most part I shall assume that the requisite circumstances for the serial order obtain.

It seems clear from these remarks that the two principles are at least a plausible conception of justice. The question, though, is how one is to argue for them more systematically. Now there are several things to do. One can work out their consequences for institutions and note their implications for fundamental social policy. In this way they are tested by a comparison with our considered judgments of justice. Part II is devoted to this. But one can also try to find arguments in their favor that are decisive from the standpoint of the original position. In order to see how this might be done, it is useful as a heuristic device to think of the two principles as the maximin solution to the problem of social justice. There is an analogy between the two principles and the maximin rule for choice under uncertainty.[7] This is evident from the fact that the two principles are those a person would choose for the design of a society in which his enemy is to assign him his place. The maximin rule tells us to rank alternatives by their worst possible outcomes: we are to adopt the alternative the worst outcome of which is superior to the worst outcomes of the others. The persons in the original position do not, of course, assume that their initial place in society is decided by a malevolent opponent. As I note below, they should not reason from false premises. The veil of ignorance does not violate this idea, since an absence of information is

---

7. An accessible discussion of this and other rules of choice under uncertainty can be found in W. J. Baumol, *Economic Theory and Operations Analysis,* 2nd ed. (Englewood Cliffs, N.J., Prentice-Hall Inc., 1965), ch. 24. Baumol gives a geometric interpretation of these rules, including the diagram used in §13 to illustrate the difference principle. See pp. 558–562. See also R. D. Luce and Howard Raiffa, *Games and Decisions* (New York, John Wiley and Sons, Inc., 1957), ch. XIII, for a fuller account.

not misinformation. But that the two principles of justice would be chosen if the parties were forced to protect themselves against such a contingency explains the sense in which this conception is the maximin solution. And this analogy suggests that if the original position has been described so that it is rational for the parties to adopt the conservative attitude expressed by this rule, a conclusive argument can indeed be constructed for these principles. Clearly the maximin rule is not, in general, a suitable guide for choices under uncertainty. But it is attractive in situations marked by certain special features. My aim, then, is to show that a good case can be made for the two principles based on the fact that the original position manifests these features to the fullest possible degree, carrying them to the limit, so to speak.

Consider the gain-and-loss table below. It represents the gains and losses for a situation which is not a game of strategy. There is no one playing against the person making the decision; instead he is faced with several possible circumstances which may or may not obtain. Which circumstances happen to exist does not depend upon what the person choosing decides or whether he announces his moves in advance. The numbers in the table are monetary values (in hundreds of dollars) in comparison with some initial situation. The gain (g) depends upon the individual's decision (d) and the circumstances (c). Thus $g = f(d, c)$. Assuming that there are three possible decisions and three possible circumstances, we might have this gain-and-loss table.

Decisions	Circumstances		
	C_1	C_2	C_3
d_1	−7	8	12
d_2	−8	7	14
d_3	5	6	8

The maximin rule requires that we make the third decision. For in this case the worst that can happen is that one gains five hundred dollars, which is better than the worst for the other actions. If we adopt one of these we may lose either eight or seven hundred dollars. Thus, the choice of d_3 maximizes $f(d,c)$ for that value of c, which for a given d, minimizes f. The term "maximin" means the *maximum minimorum,* and the rule directs our attention to the worst that can happen under any proposed course of action, and to decide in the light of that.

Now there appear to be three chief features of situations that give plausibility to this unusual rule.[8] First, since the rule takes no account of the likelihoods of the possible circumstances, there must be some reason for sharply discounting estimates of these probabilities. Offhand, the most natural rule of choice would seem to be to compute the expectation of monetary gain for each decision and then to adopt the course of action with the highest prospect. (This expectation is defined as follows: let g_{ij} represent the numbers in the numbers in the gain-and-loss table, where i is the row index and j is the column index; and let p_j, j = 1, 2, 3, be the likelihoods of the circumstances, with $\Sigma p_j = 1$. Then the expectation for the ith decision is equal to $\Sigma p_j g_{ij}$.) Thus it must be, for example, that the situation is one in which a knowledge of likelihoods is impossible, or at best extremely insecure. In this case it is unreasonable not to be skeptical of probabilistic calculations unless there is no other way out, particularly if the decision is a fundamental one that needs to be justified to others.

The second feature that suggests the maximin rule is the following: the person choosing has a conception of the good such that he cares very little, if anything, for what he might gain above the minimum stipend that he can, in fact, be sure of by following the maximin rule. It is not worthwhile for him to take a chance for the sake of a further advantage, especially when it may turn out that he loses much that is important to him. This last provision brings in the third feature, namely, that the rejected alternatives have outcomes that one can hardly accept. The situation involves grave risks. Of course these features work most effectively in combination. The paradigm situation for following the maximin rule is when all three features are realized to the highest degree. This rule does not, then, generally apply, nor of course is it self-evident. Rather, it is a maxim, a rule of thumb, that comes into its own in special circumstances. Its application depends upon the qualitative structure of the possible gains and losses in relation to one's conception of the good, all this against a background in which it is reasonable to discount conjectural estimates of likelihoods.

---

8. Here I borrow from William Fellner, *Probability and Profit* (Homewood, Ill., R. D. Irwin, Inc., 1965), pp. 140–142, where these features are noted.

It should be noted, as the comments on the gain-and-loss table say, that the entries in the table represent monetary values and not utilities. This difference is significant since for one thing computing expectations on the basis of such objective values is not the same thing as computing expected utility and may lead to different results. The essential point though is that in justice as fairness the parties do not know their conception of the good and cannot estimate their utility in the ordinary sense. In any case, we want to go behind de facto preferences generated by given conditions. Therefore expectations are based upon an index of primary goods and the parties make their choice accordingly. The entries in the example are in terms of money and not utility to indicate this aspect of the contract doctrine.

Now, as I have suggested, the original position has been defined so that it is a situation in which the maximin rule applies. In order to see this, let us review briefly the nature of this situation with these three special features in mind. To begin with, the veil of ignorance excludes all but the vaguest knowledge of likelihoods. The parties have no basis for determining the probable nature of their society, or their place in it. Thus they have strong reasons for being wary of probability calculations if any other course is open to them. They must also take in account the fact that their choice of principles should seem reasonable to others, in particular their descendants, whose rights will be deeply affected by it. There are further grounds for discounting that I shall mention as we go along. For the present it suffices to note that these considerations are strengthened by the fact that the parties know very little about the gain-and-loss table. Not only are they unable to conjecture the likelihoods of the various possible circumstances, they cannot say much about what the possible circumstances are, much less enumerate them and foresee the outcome of each alternative available. Those deciding are much more in the dark than the illustration by a numerical table suggests. It is for this reason that I have spoken of an analogy with the maximin rule.

Several kinds of arguments for the two principles of justice illustrate the second feature. Thus, if we can maintain that these principles provide a workable theory of social justice, and that they are compatible with reasonable demands of efficiency, then

this conception guarantees a satisfactory minimum. There may be, on reflection, little reason for trying to do better. Thus much of the argument, especially in Part Two, is to show, by their application to the main questions of social justice, that the two principles are a satisfactory conception. These details have a philosophical purpose. Moreover, this line of thought is practically decisive if we can establish the priority of liberty, the lexical ordering of the two principles. For this priority implies that the persons in the original position have no desire to try for greater gains at the expense of the equal liberties. The minimum assured by the two principles in lexical order is not one that the parties wish to jeopardize for the sake of greater economic and social advantages. In parts of Chapters IV and IX I present the case for this ordering.

Finally, the third feature holds if we can assume that other conceptions of justice may lead to institutions that the parties would find intolerable. For example, it has sometimes been held that under some conditions the utility principle (in either form) justifies, if not slavery or serfdom, at any rate serious infractions of liberty for the sake of greater social benefits. We need not consider here the truth of this claim, or the likelihood that the requisite conditions obtain. For the moment, this contention is only to illustrate the way in which conceptions of justice may allow for outcomes which the parties may not be able to accept. And having the ready alternative of the two principles of justice which secure a satisfactory minimum, it seems unwise, if not irrational, for them to take a chance that these outcomes are not realized.

. . .

40. The Kantian Interpretation of Justice as Fairness

For the most part I have considered the content of the principle of equal liberty and the meaning of the priority of the rights that it defines. It seems appropriate at this point to note that there is a Kantian interpretation of the conception of justice from which this principle derives. This interpretation is based upon Kant's notion of autonomy. It is a mistake, I believe, to emphasize the place of generality and universality in Kant's ethics. That moral principles are general and universal is hardly new with him; and as we have seen these conditions do not in any case take us very far. It is impossible to construct a moral theory on so slender a basis, and therefore to limit the discussion of Kant's doctrine to these notions is to reduce it to triviality. The real force of his view lies elsewhere.[9]

For one thing, he begins with the idea that moral principles are the object of rational choice. They define the moral law that men can rationally will to govern their conduct in an ethical commonwealth. Moral philosophy becomes the study of the conception and outcome of a suitably defined rational decision. This idea has immediate consequences. For once we think of moral principles as legislation for a kingdom of ends, it is clear that these principles must not only be acceptable to all but public as well. Finally Kant supposes that this moral legislation is to be agreed to under conditions that characterize men as free and equal rational beings. The description of the original position is an attempt to interpret this conception. I do not wish to argue here for this interpretation on the basis of Kant's text. Certainly some will want to read him differently. Perhaps the remarks to follow are best taken as suggestions for relating justice as fairness to the high point of the contractarian tradition in Kant and Rousseau.

Kant held, I believe, that a person is acting autonomously when the principles of his action are chosen by him as the most adequate possible expression of his nature as a free and equal rational being. The principles he acts upon are not adopted because of his social position or natural endowments, or in view of the particular kind of society in which he lives or the specific things that he happens to want. To act on such principles is to act heteronomously. Now the veil of ignorance deprives the persons in the original position of the knowledge that would enable them to choose heteronomous principles. The parties arrive at their choice together as free and equal rational persons knowing only that those circumstances obtain which give rise to the need for principles of justice.

To be sure, the argument for these principles does add in various ways to Kant's conception. For example, it adds the feature that the principles chosen are to apply to the basic structure of society; and premises characterizing this structure are used in deriving the principles of justice. But I believe that this and other additions are natural enough and remain fairly close to Kant's doctrine, at least when all of his ethical writings are viewed together. Assuming, then, that the reasoning in favor of the principles of justice is correct, we can say that when persons act on these principles they are acting in accordance with principles that they would choose as rational and independent persons in an original position of equality. The principles of their actions do not depend upon social or natural contingencies, nor do they reflect the bias of the particulars of their plan of life or the aspirations that motivate them. By acting from these principles persons express their nature as free and equal rational beings subject to the general conditions of human life. For to express one's nature as a being of a particular kind is to act on the principles that would be chosen if this nature were the decisive determining element. Of course, the choice of the parties in the original position is subject to the restrictions of that situation. But when we knowingly act on the principles of justice in the ordinary course of events, we deliberately assume the limitations of the original position. One reason for doing this, for persons who can do so and want to, is to express their nature as free and equal rational beings.

The principles of justice are also categorical imperatives in Kant's sense. For by a categorical imperative Kant understands a principle of conduct that applies to a person in virtue of his nature as a free and equal rational being. The validity of the princi-

---

9. To be avoided at all costs is the idea that Kant's doctrine simply provides the general, or formal, elements for a utilitarian (or indeed for any other) theory. See, for example, R. M. Hare, *Freedom and Reason* (Oxford, The Clarendon Press, 1963), pp. 123f. One must not lose sight of the full scope of his view, one must take the later works into consideration. Unfortunately, there is no commentary on Kant's moral theory as a whole; perhaps it would prove impossible to write. But the standard works of H. J. Paton, *The Categorical Imperative* (Chicago, University of Chicago Press, 1948), and L. W. Beck, *A Commentary on Kant's Critique of Practical Reason* (Chicago, University of Chicago Press, 1960), and others need to be further complemented by studies of the other writings. See here M. J. Gregor's *Laws of Freedom* (Oxford, Basil Blackwell, 1963), an account of *The Metaphysics of Morals,* and J. G. Murphy's brief *Kant: The Philosophy of Right* (London, Macmillan, 1970). Beyond this, *The Critique of Judgment, Religion within the Limits of Reason,* and the political writings cannot be neglected without distorting his doctrine. For the last, see *Kant's Political Writings,* ed. Hans Reiss and trans. H. B. Nisbet (Cambridge, The University Press, 1970).

ple does not presuppose that one has a particular desire or aim. Whereas a hypothetical imperative by contrast does assume this: it directs us to take certain steps as effective means to achieve a specific end. Whether the desire is for a particular thing, or whether it is for something more general, such as certain kinds of agreeable feelings or pleasures, the corresponding imperative is hypothetical. Its applicability depends upon one's having an aim which one need not have as a condition of being a rational human individual. The argument for the two principles of justice does not assume that the parties have particular ends, but only that they desire certain primary goods. These are things that it is rational to want whatever else one wants. Thus given human nature, wanting them is part of being rational; and while each is presumed to have some conception of the good, nothing is known about his final ends. The preference for primary goods is derived, then, from only the most general assumptions about rationality and the conditions of human life. To act from the principles of justice is to act from categorical imperatives in the sense that they apply to us whatever in particular our aims are. This simply reflects the fact that no such contingencies appear as premises in their derivation.

We may note also that the motivational assumption of mutual disinterest accords with Kant's notion of autonomy, and gives another reason for this condition. So far this assumption has been used to characterize the circumstances of justice and to provide a clear concept to guide the deliberation of the parties. We have also seen that the concept of benevolence, being a second-order notion, would not work out well. Now we can add that the assumption of mutual disinterest is to allow for freedom in the choice of a system of final ends.[10] Liberty in adopting a conception of the good is limited only by principles that are deduced from a doctrine which imposes no prior constraints on these conceptions. Presuming mutual disinterest in the original position carries out this idea. We postulate that the parties have opposing claims in a suitably general sense. If their ends were restricted in some specific way, this would appear at the outset as an arbitrary restriction on freedom. Moreover, if the parties were conceived as altruists, or

as pursuing certain kinds of pleasures, then the principles chosen would apply, as far as the argument would have shown, only to persons whose freedom was restricted to choices compatible with altruism or hedonism. As the argument now runs, the principles of justice cover all persons with rational plans of life, whatever their content, and these principles represent the appropriate restrictions on freedom. Thus it is possible to say that the constraints on conceptions of the good are the result of an interpretation of the contractual situation that puts no prior limitations on what men may desire. There are a variety of reasons, then, for the motivational premise of mutual disinterest. This premise is not only a matter of realism about the circumstances of justice or a way to make the theory manageable. It also connects up with the Kantian idea of autonomy.

There is, however, a difficulty that should be clarified. It is well expressed by Sidgwick.[11] He remarks that nothing in Kant's ethics is more striking than the idea that a man realizes his true self when he acts from the moral law, whereas if he permits his actions to be determined by sensuous desires or contingent aims, he becomes subject to the law of nature. Yet in Sidgwick's opinion this idea comes to naught. It seems to him that on Kant's view the lives of the saint and the scoundrel are equally the outcome of a free choice (on the part of the noumenal self) and equally the subject of causal laws (as a phenomenal self). Kant never explains why the scoundrel does not express in a bad life his characteristic and freely chosen selfhood in the same way that a saint expresses his characteristic and freely chosen selfhood in a good one. Sidgwick's objection is decisive, I think, as long as one assumes, as Kant's exposition may seem to allow, both that the noumenal self can choose any consistent set of principles and that acting from such principles, whatever they are, is sufficient to express one's choice as that of a free and equal rational being. Kant's reply must be that though acting on any consistent set of principles could be the outcome of a decision on the part of the noumenal self, not all such action by the phenomenal self expresses this decision as that of a free and equal rational being.

---

10. For this point I am indebted to Charles Fried.

11. See *The Methods of Ethics,* 7th ed. (London, Macmillan, 1907), Appendix, "The Kantian Conception of Free Will" (reprinted from *Mind,* vol. 13, 1888), pp. 511–516, esp. p. 516.

Thus if a person realizes his true self by expressing it in his actions, and if he desires above all else to realize this self, then he will choose to act from principles that manifest his nature as a free and equal rational being. The missing part of the argument concerns the concept of expression. Kant did not show that acting from the moral law expresses our nature in identifiable ways that acting from contrary principles does not.

This defect is made good, I believe, by the conception of the original position. The essential point is that we need an argument showing which principles, if any, free and equal rational persons would choose and these principles must be applicable in practice. A definite answer to this question is required to meet Sidgwick's objection. My suggestion is that we think of the original position as the point of view from which noumenal selves see the world. The parties qua noumenal selves have complete freedom to choose whatever principles they wish; but they also have a desire to express their nature as rational and equal members of the intelligible realm with precisely this liberty to choose, that is, as beings who can look at the world in this way and express this perspective in their life as members of society. They must decide, then, which principles when consciously followed and acted upon in everyday life will best manifest this freedom in their community, most fully reveal their independence from natural contingencies and social accident. Now if the argument of the contract doctrine is correct, these principles are indeed those defining the moral law, or more exactly, the principles of justice for institutions and individuals. The description of the original position interprets the point of view of noumenal selves, of what it means to be a free and equal rational being. Our nature as such beings is displayed when we act from the principles we would choose when this nature is reflected in the conditions determining the choice. Thus men exhibit their freedom, their independence from the contingencies of nature and society, by acting in ways they would acknowledge in the original position.

Properly understood, then, the desire to act justly derives in part from the desire to express most fully what we are or can be, namely free and equal rational beings with a liberty to choose. It is for this reason, I believe, that Kant speaks of the failure to act on the moral law as giving rise to shame and not to feelings of guilt. And this is appropriate, since for him acting unjustly is acting in a manner that fails to express our nature as a free and equal rational being. Such actions therefore strike at our self-respect, our sense of our own worth, and the experience of this loss is shame (§67). We have acted as though we belonged to a lower order, as though we were a creature whose first principles are decided by natural contingencies. Those who think of Kant's moral doctrine as one of law and guilt badly misunderstand him. Kant's main aim is to deepen and to justify Rousseau's idea that liberty is acting in accordance with a law that we give to ourselves. And this leads not to a morality of austere command but to an ethic of mutual respect and self-esteem.[12]

The original position may be viewed, then, as a procedural interpretation of Kant's conception of autonomy and the categorical imperative. The principles regulative of the kingdom of ends are those that would be chosen in this position, and the description of this situation enables us to explain the sense in which acting from these principles expresses our nature as free and equal rational persons. No longer are these notions purely transcendent and lacking explicable connections with human conduct, for the procedural conception of the original position allows us to make these ties. It is true that I have departed from Kant's views in several respects. I shall not discuss these matters here; but two points should be noted. The person's choice as a noumenal self I have assumed to be a collective one. The force of the self's being equal is that the principles chosen must be acceptable to other selves. Since all are similarly free and rational, each must have an equal say in adopting the public principles of the ethical commonwealth. This means that as noumenal selves, everyone is to consent to these principles. Unless the scoundrel's principles would be chosen, they cannot express this free choice, however much a single self might be of a mind to opt for them. Later I shall try to define a clear sense in which this unanimous agreement is best expressive of the nature of even a single self (§85). It in no way overrides a person's

---

12. See B. A. O. Williams, "The Idea of Equality," in *Philosophy, Politics and Society,* Second Series, ed. Peter Laslett and W. G. Runciman (Oxford, Basil Blackwell, 1962), pp. 115f. For confirmation of this interpretation, see Kant's remarks on moral education in *The Critique of Practical Reason,* pt. II. See also Beck, *Commentary on Kant's Critique of Practical Reason,* pp. 233–236.

interests as the collective nature of the choice might seem to imply. But I leave this aside for the present.

Secondly, I have assumed all along that the parties know that they are subject to the conditions of human life. Being in the circumstances of justice, they are situated in the world with other men who likewise face limitations of moderate scarcity and competing claims. Human freedom is to be regulated by principles chosen in the light of these natural restrictions. Thus justice as fairness is a theory of human justice and among its premises are the elementary facts about persons and their place in nature. The freedom of pure intelligences not subject to these constraints, and the freedom of God, is outside the scope of the theory. It might appear that Kant meant his doctrine to apply to all rational beings as such and therefore to God and the angels as well. Men's social situation in the world may seem to have no role in his theory in determining the first principles of justice. I do not believe that Kant held this view, but I cannot discuss this question here. It suffices to say that if I am mistaken, the Kantian interpretation of justice as fairness is less faithful to Kant's intentions than I am presently inclined to suppose.

THOMAS E. HILL, JR.

Servility and Self-Respect

Kantian deontology has experienced a revitalization in the latter half of the twentieth century. Kant's ethical theory is considered deontological because it does not judge the rightness or wrongness of an action by considering the act's consequences, as does utilitarianism. Instead, for Kantian deontology, morality is founded on absolute moral rules, and these could be determined by reason alone. The moral individual acts in accord with these absolute rules out of regard for duty. While it is Kantian deontology that is experiencing renewed interest, Kant's is not the only deontological ethical theory. The prima facie duty theory of Ross, introduced earlier in this century, is also a deontological theory. But unlike Kant, Ross did not believe that our duties, known "at first glance," are absolute, that is, unconditional and without exception. Sometimes other considerations outweigh our prima facie duty, and sometimes our duties conflict with one another.

Among the authors who have written extensively in support of a Kantian ethical system is Thomas E. Hill, Jr., professor of philosophy at the University of North Carolina, Chapel Hill. In his 1973 article, Hill gives examples of servile characters—those who lack a certain kind of self-respect—and argues that utilitarianism fails to identify what is morally wrong about servility. For the utilitarian, servility is wrong if it leads to bad consequences, and we would expect the servile person to be less happy. Yet this need not be the case. The harm that accrues to the servile wife, postulates Hill, may be overbalanced by the pleasure given the domineering husband. By utilitarian standards, servility in this case would be good, not bad. To account for the wrongness of servility, contends Hill, one must appeal to Kantian concerns, not utilitarian ones. What is wrong with servility is that the servile person fails to treat him or her self in a morally appropriate way because, according to Kantian theory, to respect the moral law one must respect oneself. For another article that takes a Kantian perspective, see "Between Consenting Adults" by Onora O'Neill.

Servility and Self-Respect

Several motives underlie this paper.[1] In the first place, I am curious to see if there is a legitimate source for the increasingly common feeling that servility can be as much a vice as arrogance. There seems to be something morally defective about the Uncle Tom and the submissive housewife; and yet, on the other hand, if the only interests they sacrifice are their own, it seems that we should have no right to complain. Secondly, I have some sympathy for the now unfashionable view that each person has duties to himself as well as to others. It does seem absurd to say that a person could literally violate his own rights or owe himself a debt of gratitude, but I suspect that the classic defenders of duties to oneself had something different in mind. If there are duties to oneself, it is natural to expect that a duty to avoid being servile would have a prominent place among them. Thirdly, I am interested in making sense of Kant's puzzling, but suggestive, remarks about respect for persons and respect for the moral law. On the usual reading, these remarks seem unduly moralistic; but, viewed in another way, they suggest an argument for a kind of self-respect which is incompatible with a servile attitude.

My procedure will not be to explicate Kant directly. Instead I shall try to isolate the defect of servility and sketch an argument to show why it is objectionable, noting only in passing how this relates to Kant and the controversy about duties to oneself. What I say about self-respect is far from the whole story. In particular, it is not concerned with esteem for one's special abilities and achievements or with the self-confidence which characterizes the especially autonomous person. Nor is my concern with the psychological antecedents and effects of self-respect. Nevertheless, my conclusions, if correct, should be of interest; for they imply that, given a common view of morality, there are nonutilitarian moral reasons for each person, regardless of his merits, to respect himself. To avoid servility to the extent that one can is not simply a right but a duty, not simply a duty to others but a duty to oneself.

_____

1. An earlier version of this paper was presented at the meetings of the American Philosophical Association, Pacific Division. A number of revisions have been made as a result of the helpful comments of others, especially Norman Dahl, Sharon Hill, Herbert Morris, and Mary Mothersill.

I

Three examples may give a preliminary idea of what I mean by *servility*. Consider, first, an extremely deferential black, whom I shall call the *Uncle Tom*. He always steps aside for white men; he does not complain when less qualified whites take over his job; he gratefully accepts whatever benefits his all-white government and employers allot him, and he would not think of protesting its insufficiency. He displays the symbols of deference to whites, and of contempt towards blacks: he faces the former with bowed stance and a ready 'sir' and 'Ma'am'; he reserves his strongest obscenities for the latter. Imagine, too, that he is not playing a game. He is not the shrewdly prudent calculator, who knows how to make the best of a bad lot and mocks his masters behind their backs. He accepts without question the idea that, as a black, he is owed less than whites. He may believe that blacks are mentally inferior and of less social utility, but that is not the crucial point. The attitude which he displays is that what he values, aspires for, and can demand is of less importance than what whites value, aspire for, and can demand. He is far from the picture book's carefree, happy servant, but he does not feel that he has a right to expect anything better.

Another pattern of servility is illustrated by a person I shall call the Self-Deprecator. Like the Uncle Tom, he is reluctant to make demands. He says nothing when others take unfair advantage of him. When asked for his preferences or opinions, he tends to shrink away as if what he said should make no difference. His problem, however, is not a sense of racial inferiority but rather an acute awareness of his own inadequacies and failures as an individual. These defects are not imaginary: he has in fact done poorly by his own standards and others'. But, unlike many of us in the same situation, he acts as if his failings warrant quite unrelated maltreatment even by strangers. His sense of shame and self-contempt make him content to be the instrument of others. He feels that nothing is owed him until he has earned it and that he has earned very little. He is not simply playing a masochist's game of winning sympathy by disparaging himself. On the contrary, he assesses his individual merits with painful accuracy.

A rather different case is that of the *Deferential Wife*. This is a woman who is utterly devoted to serving her husband. She buys the clothes *he* prefers, invites the guests *he* wants to entertain, and makes love whenever *he* is in the mood. She willingly moves to a new city in order for him to have a more attractive job, counting her own friendships and geographical preferences insignificant by comparison. She loves her husband, but her conduct is not simply an expression of love. She is happy, but she does not subordinate herself as a means to happiness. She does not simply defer to her husband in certain spheres as a trade-off for his deference in other spheres. On the contrary, she tends not to form her own interests, values, and ideals; and, when she does, she counts them as less important than her husband's. She readily responds to appeals from Women's Liberation that she agrees that women are mentally and physically equal, if not superior, to men. She just believes that the proper role for a woman is to serve her family. As a matter of fact, much of her happiness derives from her belief that she fulfills this role very well. No one is trampling on her rights, she says; for she is quite glad, and proud, to serve her husband as she does.

Each one of these cases reflects the attitude which I call servility.[2] It betrays the absence of a certain kind of self-respect. What I take this attitude to be, more specifically, will become clearer later on. It is important at the outset, however, not to confuse the three cases sketched above with other, superficially similar cases. In particular, the cases I have sketched are not simply cases in which someone refuses to press his rights, speaks disparagingly of himself, or devotes himself to another. A black, for example, is not necessarily servile because he does not demand a just wage; for, seeing that such a demand would result in his being fired, he might forbear for the sake of his children. A self-critical person is not necessarily servile by virtue of bemoaning his faults in public; for his behavior may be merely a complex way of

satisfying his own inner needs quite independent of a willingness to accept abuse from others. A woman need not be servile whenever she works to make her husband happy and prosperous; for she might freely and knowingly choose to do so from love or from a desire to share the rewards of his success. If the effort did not require her to submit to humiliation or maltreatment, her choice would not mark her as servile. There may, of course, be grounds for objecting to the attitudes in these cases; but the defect is not servility of the sort I want to consider. It should also be noted that my cases of servility are not simply instances of deference to superior knowledge or judgment. To defer to an expert's judgment on matters of fact is not to be servile; to defer to his every wish and whim is. Similarly, the belief that one's talents and achievements are comparatively low does not, by itself, make one servile. It is no vice to acknowledge the truth, and one may in fact have achieved less, and have less ability, than others. To be servile is not simply to hold certain empirical beliefs but to have a certain attitude concerning one's rightful place in a moral community.

II

Are there grounds for regarding the attitudes of the Uncle Tom, the Self-Deprecator, and the Deferential Wife as morally objectionable? Are there moral arguments we could give them to show that they ought to have more self-respect? None of the more obvious replies is entirely satisfactory.

One might, in the first place, adduce utilitarian considerations. Typically the servile person will be less happy than he might be. Moreover, he may be less prone to make the best of his own socially useful abilities. He may become a nuisance to others by being overly dependent. He will, in any case, lose the special contentment that comes from standing up for one's rights. A submissive attitude encourages exploitation, and exploitation spreads misery in a variety of ways. These considerations provide a prima facie case against the attitudes of the Uncle Tom, the Deferential Wife, and the Self-Deprecator, but they are hardly conclusive. Other utilities tend to counterbalance the ones just mentioned. When people refuse to press their rights, there are usually ,others who profit. There are undeniable pleasures in associating with those who are devoted, understanding, and

2. Each of the cases is intended to represent only one possible pattern of servility. I make no claims about how often these patterns are exemplified, nor do I mean to imply that only these patterns could warrant the labels "Deferential Wife," "Uncle Tom," etc. All the more, I do not mean to imply any comparative judgments about the causes or relative magnitude of the problems of racial and sexual discrimination. One person, e.g. a self-contemptuous woman with a sense of racial inferiority, might exemplify features of several patterns at once; and, of course, a person might view her being a woman the way an Uncle Tom views his being black, etc.

grateful for whatever we see fit to give them—as our fondness for dogs attests. Even the servile person may find his attitude a source of happiness, as the case of the Deferential Wife illustrates. There may be comfort and security in thinking that the hard choices must be made by others, that what I would say has little to do with what ought to be done. Self-condemnation may bring relief from the pangs of guilt even if it is not deliberately used for that purpose. On balance, then, utilitarian considerations may turn out to favor servility as much as they oppose it.

For those who share my moral intuitions, there is another sort of reason for not trying to rest a case against servility on utilitarian considerations. Certain utilities seem irrelevant to the issue. The utilitarian must weigh them along with others, but to do so seems morally inappropriate. Suppose, for example, that the submissive attitudes of the Uncle Tom and the Deferential Wife result in positive utilities for those who dominate and exploit them. Do we need to tabulate *these* utilities before conceding that servility is objectionable? The Uncle Tom, it seems, is making an error, a moral error, quite apart from consideration of how much others in fact profit from his attitude. The Deferential Wife may be quite happy; but if her happiness turns out to be contingent on her distorted view of her own rights and worth as a person, then it carries little moral weight against the contention that she ought to change that view. Suppose I could cause a woman to find her happiness in denying all her rights and serving my every wish. No doubt I could do so only by nonrational manipulative techniques, which I ought not to use. But is this the only objection? My efforts would be wrong, it seems, not only because of the techniques they require but also because the resultant attitude is itself objectionable. When a person's happiness stems from a morally objectionable attitude, it ought to be discounted. That a sadist gets pleasure from seeing others suffer should not count even as a partial justification for his attitude. That a servile person derives pleasure from denying her moral status, for similar reasons, cannot make her attitude acceptable. These brief intuitive remarks are not intended as a refutation of utilitarianism, with all its many varieties; but they do suggest that it is well to look elsewhere for adequate grounds for rejecting the attitudes of the Uncle Tom, the Self-Deprecator, and the Deferential Wife.

One might try to appeal to meritarian considerations. That is, one might argue that the servile person *deserves* more than he allows himself. This line of argument, however, is no more adequate than the utilitarian one. It may be wrong to deny others what they deserve, but it is not so obviously wrong to demand less for oneself than one deserves. In any case, the Self-Deprecator's problem is not that he underestimates his merits. By hypothesis, he assesses his merits quite accurately. We cannot reasonably tell him to have more respect for himself because he *deserves* more respect; he knows that he has not *earned* better treatment. His problem, in fact, is that he thinks of his moral status with regard to others as entirely dependent upon his merits. His interests and choices are important, he feels, only if he has earned the right to make demands; or if he had rights by birth, they were forfeited by his subsequent failures and misdeeds. My Self-Deprecator is no doubt an atypical person, but nevertheless he illustrates an important point. Normally when we find a self-contemptuous person, we can plausibly argue that he is not so bad as he thinks, that his self-contempt is an overreaction prompted more by inner needs than by objective assessment of his merits. Because this argument cannot work with the Self-Deprecator, his case draws attention to a distinction, applicable in other cases as well, between saying that someone deserves respect for his merits and saying that he is owed respect as a person. On meritarian grounds we can only say 'You deserve better than this,' but the defect of the servile person is not merely failure to recognize his merits.

Other common arguments against the Uncle Tom, et al, may have some force but seem not to strike to the heart of the problem. For example, philosophers sometimes appeal to the value of human potentialities. As a human being, it is said, one at least has a capacity for rationality, morality, excellence, or autonomy, and this capacity is worthy of respect. Although such arguments have the merit of making respect independent of a person's actual deserts, they seem quite misplaced in some cases. There comes a time when we have sufficient evidence that a person is not ever going to *be* rational, moral, excellent, or autonomous even if he still has a capacity, in some sense, for being so. As a person approaches death with an atrocious record so far, the chances of his realizing his diminishing capacities become increasingly slim. To make these capacities the basis of his self-respect is to rest it on a shifting and unstable ground. We do, of course, respect persons for capacities which they are not exercising at the moment; for example, I might respect a person as a good philosopher even though he is just now blundering into gross confusion. In these cases, however, we respect the person for an active capacity, a ready disposition, which he has displayed on many occasions. On this analogy, a person should have respect for himself only when his capacities are developed and ready, needing only to be triggered by an appropriate occasion or the removal of some temporary obstacle. The Uncle Tom and the Deferential Wife, however, may in fact have quite limited capacities of this sort, and, since the Self-Deprecator is already overly concerned with his own inadequacies, drawing attention to his capacities seems a poor way to increase his self-respect. In any case, setting aside the Kantian nonempirical capacity for autonomy, the capacities of different persons vary widely; but what the servile person seems to overlook is something by virtue of which he is equal with every other person.

III

Why, then, is servility a moral defect? There is, I think, another sort of answer which is worth exploring. The first part of this answer must be an attempt to isolate the objectionable features of the servile person; later we can ask why these features are objectionable. As a step in this direction, let us examine again our three paradigm cases. The moral defect in each case, I suggest, is a failure to understand and acknowledge one's own moral rights. I assume, without argument here, that each person has moral rights.[3] Some of these rights may be basic human rights; that is, rights for which a person needs only to be human to qualify. Other rights will be derivative and contingent upon his special commitments, institutional affiliations, etc. Most rights will be prima facie ones; some may be absolute. Most can be waived under ap-

propriate conditions; perhaps some cannot. Many rights can be forfeited; but some, presumably, cannot. The servile person does not, strictly speaking, violate his own rights. At least in our paradigm cases he fails to acknowledge fully his own moral status because he does not fully understand what his rights are, how they can be waived, and when they can be forfeited.

The defect of the Uncle Tom, for example, is that he displays an attitude that denies his moral equality with whites. He does not realize, or apprehend in an effective way, that he has as much right to a decent wage and a share of political power as any comparable white. His gratitude is misplaced; he accepts benefits which are his by right as if they were gifts. The Self-Deprecator is servile in a more complex way. He acts as if he has forfeited many important rights which in fact he has not. He does not understand, or fully realize in his own case, that certain rights to fair and decent treatment do not have to be earned. He sees his merits clearly enough, but he fails to see that what he can expect from others is not merely a function of his merits. The Deferential Wife *says* that she understands her rights vis-à-vis her husband, but what she fails to appreciate is that her consent to serve him is a valid waiver of her rights only under certain conditions. If her consent is coerced, say, by the lack of viable options for women in her society, then her consent is worth little. If socially fostered ignorance of her own talents and alternatives is responsible for her consent, then her consent should not count as a fully legitimate waiver of her right to equal consideration within the marriage. All the more, her consent to defer constantly to her husband is not a legitimate setting aside of her rights if it results from her mistaken belief that she has a moral duty to do so. (Recall: "The *proper* role for a woman is to serve her family.") If she believes that she has a *duty* to defer to her husband, then, whatever she may say, she cannot fully understand that she has a *right* not to defer to him. When she says that she freely gives up such a right, she is confused. Her confusion is rather like that of a person who has been persuaded by an unscrupulous lawyer that it is legally incumbent on him to refuse a jury trial but who nevertheless tells the judge that he understands that he has a right to a jury trial and freely waives it. He does not really understand what it is to have and freely give up the right if he thinks that it would be an offense for him to exercise it.

---

3. As will become evident, I am also presupposing some form of cognitive or "naturalistic" interpretation of rights. If, to accommodate an emotivist or prescriptivist, we set aside talk of moral knowledge and ignorance, we might construct a somewhat analogous case against servility from the point of view of those who adopt principles ascribing rights to all; but the argument, I suspect, would be more complex and less persuasive.

Insofar as servility results from moral ignorance or confusion, it need not be something for which a person is to blame. Even self-reproach may be inappropriate; for at the time a person is in ignorance he cannot feel guilty about his servility, and later he may conclude that his ignorance was unavoidable. In some cases, however, a person might reasonably believe that he should have known better. If, for example, the Deferential Wife's confusion about her rights resulted from a motivated resistance to drawing the implications of her own basic moral principles, then later she might find some ground for self-reproach. Whether blameworthy or not, servility could still be morally objectionable at least in the sense that it ought to be discouraged, that social conditions which nourish it should be reformed, and the like. Not all morally undesirable features of a person are ones for which he is responsible, but that does not mean that they are defects merely from an esthetic or prudential point of view.

In our paradigm cases, I have suggested, servility is a kind of deferential attitude towards others resulting from ignorance or misunderstanding of one's moral rights. A sufficient remedy, one might think, would be moral enlightenment. Suppose, however, that our servile persons come to know their rights but do not substantially alter their behavior. Are they not still servile in an objectionable way? One might even think that reproach is more appropriate now because they know what they are doing.

The problem, unfortunately, is not as simple as it may appear. Much depends on what they tolerate and why. Let us set aside cases in which a person merely refuses to *fight* for his rights, chooses not to exercise certain rights, or freely waives many rights which he might have insisted upon. Our problem concerns the previously servile person who continues to display the same marks of deference even after he fully knows his rights. Imagine, for example, that even after enlightenment our Uncle Tom persists in his old pattern behavior, giving all the typical signs of believing that the injustices done to him are not really wrong. Suppose, too, that the newly enlightened Deferential Wife continues to defer to her husband, refusing to disturb the old way of life by introducing her new ideas. She acts as if she accepts the idea that she is merely doing her duty though actually she no longer believes it. Let us suppose, further, that the Uncle Tom and the Deferential Wife are

not merely generous with their time and property; they also accept without protest, and even appear to sanction, treatment which is humiliating and degrading. That is, they do not simply consent to waive mutually acknowledged rights; they tolerate violations of their rights with apparent approval. They pretend to give their permission for subtle humiliations which they really believe no permission can make legitimate. Are such persons still servile despite their moral knowledge?

The answer, I think, should depend upon why the deferential role is played. If the motive is a morally commendable one, or a desire to avert dire consequences to oneself, or even an ambition to set an oppressor up for a later fall, then I would not count the role player as servile. The Uncle Tom, for instance, is not servile in my sense if he shuffles and bows to keep the Klan from killing his children, to save his own skin, or even to buy time while he plans the revolution. Similarly, the Deferential Wife is not servile if she tolerates an abusive husband because he is so ill that further strain would kill him, because protesting would deprive her of her only means of survival, or because she is collecting atrocity stories for her book against marriage. If there is fault in these situations, it seems inappropriate to call it *servility*. The story is quite different, however, if a person continues in his deferential role just from laziness, timidity, or a desire for some minor advantage. He shows too little concern for his moral status as a person, one is tempted to say, if he is willing to deny it for a small profit or simply because it requires some effort and courage to affirm it openly. A black who plays the Uncle Tom merely to gain an advantage over other blacks is harming them, of course; but he is also displaying disregard for his own moral position as an equal among human beings. Similarly a woman throws away her rights too lightly if she continues to play the subservient role because she is used to it or is too timid to risk a change. A Self-Deprecator who readily accepts what he knows are violations of his rights may be indulging his peculiar need for punishment at the expense of denying something more valuable. In these cases, I suggest, we have a kind of servility independent of any ignorance or confusion about one's rights. The person who has it may or may not be blameworthy, depending on many factors; and the line between servile and nonservile role playing will often be hard to draw. Nevertheless, the objectionable feature is perhaps clear enough for present purposes: it is a willingness to disavow one's moral status, publicly and systematically, in the absence of any strong reason to do so.

My proposal, then, is that there are at least two types of servility: one resulting from misunderstanding of one's rights and the other from placing a comparatively low value on them. In either case, servility manifests the absence of a certain kind of self-respect. The respect which is missing is not respect for one's merits but respect for one's rights. The servile person displays this absence of respect not directly by acting contrary to his own rights but indirectly by acting as if his rights were nonexistent or insignificant. An arrogant person ignores the rights of others, thereby arrogating for himself a higher status than he is entitled to; a servile person denies his own rights, thereby assuming a lower position than he is entitled to. Whether rooted in ignorance or simply lack of concern for moral rights, the attitudes in both cases may be incompatible with a proper regard for morality. That this is so is obvious in the case of arrogance; but to see it in the case of servility requires some further argument.

IV

The objectionable feature of the servile person, as I have described him, is his tendency to disavow his own moral rights either because he misunderstands them or because he cares little for them. The question remains: why should anyone regard this as a moral defect? After all, the rights which he denies are his own. He may be unfortunate, foolish, or even distasteful; but why *morally* deficient? One sort of answer, quite different from those reviewed earlier, is suggested by some of Kant's remarks. Kant held that servility is contrary to a perfect nonjuridical duty to oneself.[4] To say that the duty is perfect is roughly to say that it is stringent, never overridden by other considerations (e.g. beneficence). To say that the duty is nonjuridical is to say that a person cannot legitimately be coerced to comply. Although Kant did not develop an explicit argument for this view, an argument can easily be constructed from materials which reflect the spirit, if not the letter, of his moral theory. The argument which I have in mind is prompted by Kant's contention that respect for persons, strictly speaking, is respect for moral law.[5] If taken as a claim about all sorts of respect, this seems quite implausible. If it means that we respect persons only for their moral character, their capacity for moral conduct, or their status as "authors" of the moral law, then it seems unduly moralistic. My strategy is to construe the remark as saying that at least one sort of respect for persons is respect for the rights which the moral law accords them. If one respects the moral law, then one must respect one's own moral rights; and this amounts to having a kind of self-respect incompatible with servility.

The premises for the Kantian argument, which are all admittedly vague, can be sketched as follows:

First, let us assume, as Kant did, that all human beings have equal basic human rights. Specific rights vary with different conditions, but all must be justified from a point of view under which all are equal. Not all rights need to be earned, and some cannot be forfeited. Many rights can be waived but only under certain conditions of knowledge and freedom. These conditions are complex and difficult to state; but they include something like the condition that a person's consent releases others from obligation only if it is autonomously given, and consent resulting from underestimation of one's moral status is not autonomously given. Rights can be objects of knowledge, but also of ignorance, misunderstanding, deception, and the like.

Second, let us assume that my account of servility is correct; or, if one prefers, we can take it as a definition. That is, in brief, a servile person is one who tends to deny or disavow his own moral rights because he does not understand them or has little concern for the status they give him.

Third, we need one formal premise concerning moral duty, namely, that each person ought, as far as

---

4. See Immanuel Kant, *The Doctrine of Virtue,* Part II of *The Metaphysics of Morals,* ed. by M. J. Gregor (New York: Harper & Row, 1964), 99-103; Prussian Academy edition, Vol. VI, pp. 434-37.

5. Immanuel Kant, *Groundwork of the Metaphysics of Morals,* ed. by H. J. Paton (New York: Harper & Row, 1964), p. 69; Prussian Academy edition, Vol. IV, p.401; *The Critique of Practical Reason,* ed. by Lewis W. Beck (New York: Bobbs-Merrill, 1956), pp. 81, 84; Prussian Academy edition, Vol. V, pp. 78, 81. My purpose here is not to interpret what Kant meant but to give a sense to his remark.

possible, to respect the moral law. In less Kantian language, the point is that everyone should approximate, to the extent that he can, the ideal of a person who fully adopts the moral point of view. Roughly, this means not only that each person ought to do what is morally required and refrain from what is morally wrong but also that each person should treat all the provisions of morality as valuable—worth preserving and prizing as well as obeying. One must, so to speak, take up the spirit of morality as well as meet the letter of its requirements. To keep one's promises, avoid hurting others, and the like, is not sufficient; one should also take an attitude of respect towards the principles, ideals, and goals of morality. A respectful attitude towards a system of rights and duties consists of more than a disposition to conform to its definite rules of behavior; it also involves holding the system in esteem, being unwilling to ridicule it, and being reluctant to give up one's place in it. The essentially Kantian idea here is that morality, as a system of equal fundamental rights and duties, is worthy of respect, and hence a completely moral person would respect it in word and manner as well as in deed. And what a completely moral person would do, in Kant's view, is our duty to do so far as we can.

The assumptions here are, of course, strong ones, and I make no attempt to justify them. They are, I suspect, widely held though rarely articulated. In any case, my present purpose is not to evaluate them but to see how, if granted, they constitute a case against servility. The objection to the servile person, given our premises, is that he does not satisfy the basic requirement to respect morality. A person who fully respected a system of moral rights would be disposed to learn his proper place in it, to affirm it proudly, and not to tolerate abuses of it lightly. This is just the sort of disposition that the servile person lacks. If he does not understand the system, he is in no position to respect it adequately. This lack of respect may be no fault of his own, but it is still a way in which he falls short of a moral ideal. If, on the other hand, the servile person knowingly disavows his moral rights by pretending to approve of violations of them, then, barring special explanations, he shows an indifference to whether the provisions of morality are honored and publicly acknowledged. This avoidable display of indifference, by our Kantian premises, is contrary to the duty to respect morality. The disre-

spect in this second case is somewhat like the disrespect a religious believer might show towards his religion if, to avoid embarrassment, he laughed congenially while nonbelievers were mocking the beliefs which he secretly held. In any case, the servile person, as such, does not express disrespect for the system of moral rights in the obvious way by violating the rights of others. His lack of respect is more subtly manifested by his acting before others as if he did not know or care about his position of equality under that system.

The central idea here may be illustrated by an analogy. Imagine a club, say, an old German dueling fraternity. By the rules of the club, each member has certain rights and responsibilities. These are the same for each member regardless of what titles he may hold outside the club. Each has, for example, a right to be heard at meetings, a right not to be shouted down by the others. Some rights cannot be forfeited: for example, each may vote regardless of whether he has paid his dues and satisfied other rules. Some rights cannot be waived: for example, the right to be defended when attacked by several members of the rival fraternity. The members show respect for each other by respecting the status which the rules confer on each member. Now one new member is careful always to allow the others to speak at meetings; but when they shout him down, he does nothing. He just shrugs as if to say, 'Who am I to complain?' When he fails to stand up in defense of a fellow member, he feels ashamed and refuses to vote. He does not deserve to vote, he says. As the only commoner among illustrious barons, he feels that it is his place to serve them and defer to their decisions. When attackers from the rival fraternity come at him with swords drawn, he tells his companions to run and save themselves. When they defend him, he expresses immense gratitude—as if they had done him a gratuitous favor. Now one might argue that our new member fails to show respect for the fraternity and its rules. He does not actually violate any of the rules by refusing to vote, asking others not to defend him, and deferring to the barons, but he symbolically disavows the equal status which the rules confer on him. If he ought to have respect for the fraternity, he ought to change his attitude. Our servile person, then, is like the new member of the dueling fraternity in having insufficient respect for a system of rules and ideals. The difference is that everyone ought to respect morality whereas there is no comparable moral requirement to respect the fraternity.

The conclusion here is, of course, a limited one. Self-sacrifice is not always a sign of servility. It is not a duty always to press one's rights. Whether a given act is evidence of servility will depend not only on the attitude of the agent but also on the specific nature of his moral rights, a matter not considered here. Moreover, the extent to which a person is responsible, or blameworthy, for his defect remains an open question. Nevertheless, the conclusion should not be minimized. In order to avoid servility, a person who gives up his rights must do so with a full appreciation for what they are. A woman, for example, may devote herself to her husband if she is uncoerced, knows what she is doing, and does not pretend that she has no decent alternative. A self-contemptuous person may decide not to press various unforfeited rights but only if he does not take the attitude that he is too rotten to deserve them. A black may demand less than is due to him provided he is prepared to acknowledge that no one has a right to expect this of him. Sacrifices of this sort, I suspect, are extremely rare. Most people, if they fully acknowledge their rights, would not autonomously refuse to press them.

An even stronger conclusion would emerge if we could assume that some basic rights cannot be waived. That is, if there are some rights that others are bound to respect regardless of what we say, then, barring special explanation, we would be obliged not only to acknowledge these rights but also to avoid any appearance of consenting to give them up. To act as if we could release others from their obligation to grant these rights, apart from special circumstances, would be to fail to respect morality. Rousseau, held, for example, that at least a minimal right to liberty cannot be waived. A man who consents to be enslaved, giving up liberty without *quid pro quo,* thereby displays a conditioned slavish mentality that renders his consent worthless. Similarly, a Kantian might argue that a person cannot release others from the obligation to refrain from killing him: consent is no defense against the charge of murder. To accept principles of this sort is to hold that rights to life and liberty are, as Kant believed, rather like a trustee's rights to preserve something valuable entrusted to him: he has not only a right but a duty to preserve it.

Even if there are no specific rights which cannot be waived, there might be at least one formal right of this sort. This is the right to some minimum degree of respect from others. No matter how willing a person is to submit to humiliation by others, they ought to show him some respect as a person. By analogy with self-respect, as presented here, this respect owed by others would consist of a willingness to acknowledge fully, in word as well as action, the person's basically equal moral status as defined by his other rights. To the extent that a person gives even tacit consent to humiliations incompatible with this respect, he will be acting as if he waives a right which he cannot in fact give up. To do this, barring special explanations, would mark one as servile.

V

Kant held that the avoidance of servility is a duty to oneself rather than a duty to others. Recent philosophers, however, tend to discard the idea of a duty to oneself as a conceptual confusion. Although admittedly the analogy between a duty to oneself and a duty to others is not perfect, I suggest that something important is reflected in Kant's contention.

Let us consider briefly the function of saying that a duty is *to* someone. *First,* to say that a duty is *to* a given person sometimes merely indicates who is the object of that duty. That is, it tells us that the duty is concerned with how that person is to be treated, how his interests and wishes are to be taken into account, and the like. Here we might as well say that we have a duty *towards,* or *regarding* that person. Typically the person in question is the beneficiary of the fulfillment of the duty. For example, in this sense I have a duty to my children and even a duty to a distant stranger if I promised a third party that I would help that stranger. Clearly a duty to avoid servility would be a duty to oneself at least in this minimal sense, for it is a duty to avoid, so far as possible, the denial of one's own moral status. The duty is concerned with understanding and affirming one's rights, which are, at least as a rule, for one's own benefit.

Second, when we say that a duty is *to* a certain person, we often indicate thereby the person especially entitled to complain in case the duty is not fulfilled. For example, if I fail in my duty to my colleagues, then it is they who can most appropriately reproach me. Others may sometimes speak up on their behalf, but, for the most part, it is not the business of strangers to set me straight. Analogously, to say that the duty to avoid servility is a duty to oneself would indicate that, though sometimes a person may justifiably reproach himself for being servile, others are not generally in the appropriate position to complain. Outside encouragement is sometimes necessary, but, if any blame is called for, it is primarily self-recrimination and not the censure of others.

Third, mention of the person to whom a duty is owed often tells us something about the source of that duty. For example, to say that I have a duty to another person may indicate that the argument to show that I have such a duty turns upon a promise to that person, his authority over me, my having accepted special benefits from him, or, more generally, his rights. Accordingly, to say that the duty to avoid servility is a duty to oneself would at least imply that it is not entirely based upon promises to others, their authority, their beneficence, or an obligation to respect their rights. More positively, the assertion might serve to indicate that the source of the duty is one's own rights rather than the rights of others, etc. That is, one ought not to be servile because, in some broad sense, one ought to respect one's own rights as a person. There is, to be sure, an asymmetry: one has certain duties to others because one ought not to violate their rights, and one has a duty to oneself because one ought to affirm one's own rights. Nevertheless, to dismiss duties to oneself out of hand is to overlook significant similarities.

Some familiar objections to duties to oneself, moreover, seem irrelevant in the case of servility. For example, some place much stock in the idea that a person would have no duties if alone on a desert island. This can be doubted, but in any case is irrelevant here. The duty to avoid servility is a duty to take a certain stance towards others and hence would be inapplicable if one were isolated on a desert island. Again, some suggest that if there were duties to oneself then one could make promises to oneself or owe oneself a debt of gratitude. Their paradigms are familiar ones. Someone remarks, 'I promised myself a vacation this year' or 'I have been such a good boy I owe myself a treat.' Concentration on these facetious cases tends to confuse the issue. In any case the duty to avoid servility, as presented here, does not pre-

suppose promises to oneself or debts of gratitude to oneself. Other objections stem from the intuition that a person has no duty to promote his own happiness. A duty to oneself, it is sometimes assumed, must be a duty to promote one's own happiness. From a utilitarian point of view, in fact, this is what a duty to oneself would most likely be. The problems with such alleged duties, however, are irrelevant to the duty to avoid servility. This is a duty to understand and affirm one's rights, not to promote one's own welfare. While it is usually in the interest of a person to affirm his rights, our Kantian argument against servility was not based upon this premise. Finally, a more subtle line of objection turns on the idea that, given that rights and duties are correlative, a person who acted contrary to a duty to oneself would have to be violating his own rights, which seems absurd.[6] This objection raises issues too complex to examine here. One should note, however, that I have tried to give a sense to saying that servility is contrary to a duty to oneself without presupposing that the servile person violates his own rights. If acts contrary to duties to others are always violations of their rights, then duties to oneself are not parallel with duties to others to that extent. But this does not mean that it is empty or pointless to say that a duty is to oneself.

My argument against servility may prompt some to say that the duty is "to morality" rather than "to oneself." All this means, however, is that the duty is derived from a basic requirement to respect the provisions of morality; and in this sense every duty is a duty "to morality." My duties to my children are also derivative from a general requirement to respect moral principles, but they are still duties *to* them.

Kant suggests that duties to oneself are a precondition of duties to others. On our account of servility, there is at least one sense in which this is so. Insofar as the servile person is ignorant of his own rights, he is not in an adequate position to appreciate the rights of others. Misunderstanding the moral basis for his equal status with others, he is necessarily liable to

---

6. This, I take it, is part of M. G. Singer's objection to duties to oneself in *Generalization in Ethics* (New York: Alfred A. Knopf, 1961), pp. 311–18. I have attempted to examine Singer's arguments in detail elsewhere.

underestimate the rights of those with whom he classifies himself. On the other hand, if he plays the servile role knowingly, then, barring special explanation, he displays a lack of concern to see the principles of morality acknowledged and respected and thus the absence of one motive which can move a moral person to respect the rights of others. In either case, the servile person's lack of self-respect necessarily puts him in a less than ideal position to respect others. Failure to fulfill one duty to oneself, then, renders a person liable to violate duties to others. This, however, is a consequence of our argument against servility, not a presupposition of it.

THOMAS E. HILL, JR.
UNIVERSITY OF CALIFORNIA,
LOS ANGELES

J. J. C. SMART

FROM *Utilitarianism: For and Against*

Utilitarianism, the dominant ethical theory in the nineteenth century, continues to be a central ethical theory in late twentieth-century moral philosophy. Utilitarianism insists that the rightness or wrongness of an act is determined by the good or bad consequences of that act. Typically, the goodness or badness of the consequences of the act is determined by the amount of pleasure or happiness that the act brings about for all concerned. An action is right if it brings about the greatest amount of happiness (or pleasure) and the least amount of unhappiness (or pain) for the greatest number compared to any alternative action.

The historical roots of utilitarianism lie in Greece and in England. In Greece, and later Rome, Epicureanism, like utilitarianism, was hedonistic—pleasure was the only intrinsic good. In England, David Hume and John Locke were often classified as early utilitarians. But with Jeremy Bentham and then John Stuart Mill, a definitive formulation of the utilitarian ethical theory was put forward. Other prominent British ethicists in the utilitarian tradition are Henry Sidgwick and G.E. Moore.

Despite its prominent position among moral philosophers, utilitarianism has generated a host of dissenters who criticize the flaws they find inherent in the theory. Yet no matter how often the theory is criticized, a spirited defense arises from supporters. This chapter is an excerpt from a work that has received a great deal of attention since its publication in 1973—a book J. J. C. Smart co-authored with the famous critic of utilitarianism, Bernard Williams. Here, Smart defends act-utilitarianism, one variety of utilitarianisim. The act-utilitarian, among whom Smart counts himself, holds that a person ought to perform the action that maximizes happiness and minimizes unhappiness.

The rule-utilitarian, on the other hand, says that we ought to follow the rules that tend to maximize happiness and minimize unhappiness. In his defense of act-utilitarianism, Smart brings up several issues central to the theory. Among these are concerns about higher and lower pleasures, increasing average happiness versus total happiness, and the remote consequences of our actions. For a critical perspective on utilitarianism, see the excerpt from Smart's co-author, Bernard Williams.

Hedonistic and Non-Hedonistic Utilitarianism

An act-utilitarian judges the rightness or wrongness of actions by the goodness and badness of their consequences. But is he to judge the goodness and badness of the consequences of an action solely by their pleasantness and unpleasantness? Bentham,[1] who thought that quantity of pleasure being equal, the experience of playing pushpin was as good as that of reading poetry, could be classified as a hedonistic act-utilitarian. Moore,[2] who believed that some states of mind, such as those of acquiring knowledge, had intrinsic value quite independent of their pleasantness, can be called an ideal utilitarian. Mill seemed to occupy an intermediate position.[3] He held that there are higher and lower pleasures. This seems to imply that pleasure is a necessary condition for goodness but that goodness depends on other qualities of experience than pleasantness and unpleasantness. I propose to call Mill a quasi-ideal utilitarian. For Mill, pleasantness functions like x in the algebraic product, $x \times y \times z$. If $x = 0$ the product is zero. For Moore pleasantness functions more like x in $(x + 1) \times y \times z$. If $x = 0$ the product need not be zero. Of course this is only a very rough analogy.

What Bentham, Mill and Moore are all agreed on is that the rightness of an action is to be judged solely by consequences, states of affairs brought about by the action. Of course we shall have to be careful here not to construe 'state of affairs' so widely that any ethical doctrine becomes utilitarian. For if we did so we would not be saying anything at all in advocating utilitarianism. If, for example, we allowed 'the state of having just kept a promise,' then a deontologist who said we should keep promises simply because they are promises would be a utilitarian. And we do not wish to allow this.

According to the type of non-cognitivist (or subjectivist) ethics that I am assuming, the function of the words 'ought' and 'good' is primarily to express approval, or in other words, to commend. With 'ought' we commend actions. With 'good' we may commend all sorts of things, but here I am concerned with 'good' as used to commend states of affairs or consequences of actions. Suppose we could know with certainty the total consequences of two alternative actions A and B, and suppose that A and B are the only possible actions open to us. Then in deciding whether we ought to do A or B, the act-utilitarian would ask whether the total consequences of A are better than those of B, or vice versa, or whether the total consequences are equal. That is, he commends A rather than B if he thinks that the total consequences of A are better than those of B. But to say 'better' is itself to commend. So the act-utilitarian has to do a double evaluation or piece of commending. First of all he has to evaluate consequences. Then on the basis of his evaluation of consequences he has to evaluate the actions A and B which would lead to these two sets of consequences. It is easy to fail to notice that this second evaluation is needed, but we can see that it is necessary if we remind ourselves of the following fact. This is that a non-utilitarian, say a philosopher of the type of Sir David Ross, might agree with us in the evaluation of the relative merits of the total sets of consequences of the actions A and B and yet disagree with us about whether we ought to

1. Jeremy Bentham's most important ethical work is 'An Introduction to the Principles of Morals and Legislation,' in *A Fragment on Government and an Introduction to the Principles of Morals and Legislation*, ed. Wilfrid Harrison (Blackwell, Oxford, 1948). For the remark on poetry and pushpin see Bentham's *Works* (Tait, Edinburgh, 1843), vol. 2, pp. 253–4.

2. G. E. Moore, *Principia Ethica* (Cambridge University Press, London, 1962).

3. J. S. Mill, *Utilitarianism*, ed. Mary Warnock (Collins, London, 1962).

do *A* or *B*. He might agree with us in the evaluation of total consequences but disagree with us in the evaluation of possible actions. He might say: "The total consequences of *A* are better than the total consequences of *B,* but it would be *unjust* to do *A,* for you *promised* to do *B.*"

My chief concern in this study is with the *second* type of evaluation: the evaluation of actions. The utilitarian addresses himself to people who very likely agree with him as to what consequences are good ones, but who disagree with him about the principle that what we ought to do is to produce the best consequences. For a reason, which will appear presently, the difference between ideal and hedonistic utilitarianism in most cases will not usually lead to a serious disagreement about what ought to be done in practice. In this section, however, I wish to clear the ground by saying something about the *first* type of evaluation, the evaluation of consequences. It is with respect to this evaluation that Bentham, Mill and Moore differ from one another. Let us consider Mill's contention that it is 'better to be Socrates dissatisfied than a fool satisfied'.[1] Mill holds that pleasure is not to be our sole criterion for evaluating consequences: the state of mind of Socrates might be less pleasurable than that of the fool, but, according to Mill, Socrates would be happier than the fool.

It is necessary to observe, first of all, that a purely hedonistic utilitarian, like Bentham, might agree with Mill in preferring the experiences of discontented philosophers to those of contented fools. His preference for the philosopher's state of mind, however, would not be an *intrinsic* one. He would say that the discontented philosopher is a useful agent in society and that the existence of Socrates is responsible for an improvement in the lot of humanity generally. Consider two brothers. One may be of a docile and easy temperament: he may lead a supremely contented and unambitious life, enjoying himself hugely. The other brother may be ambitious, may stretch his talents to the full, may strive for scientific success and academic honours, and may discover

some invention or some remedy for disease or improvement in agriculture which will enable innumerable men of easy temperament to lead a contented life, whereas otherwise they would have been thwarted by poverty, disease or hunger. Or he may make some advance in pure science which will later have beneficial practical applications. Or, again, he may write poetry which will solace the leisure hours and stimulate the brains of practical men or scientists, thus indirectly leading to an improvement in society. That is, the pleasures of poetry or mathematics may be *extrinsically* valuable in a way in which those of pushpin or sun-bathing may not be. Though the poet or mathematician may be discontented, society as a whole may be the more contented for his presence.

Again, a man who enjoys pushpin is likely eventually to become bored with it, whereas the man who enjoys poetry is likely to retain this interest throughout his life. Moreover the reading of poetry may develop imagination and sensitivity, and so as a result of his interest in poetry a man may be able to do more for the happiness of others than if he had played pushpin and let his brain deteriorate. In short, both for the man immediately concerned and for others, the pleasures of poetry are, to use Bentham's word, more *fecund* than those of pushpin.

Perhaps, then, our preference for poetry over pushpin not one of intrinsic value, but is merely one of extrinsic value. Perhaps strictly in itself and at a particular moment, a contented sheep is as good as a contented philosopher. However it is hard to agree to this. If we did we should have to agree that the human population ought ideally to be reduced by contraceptive methods and the sheep population more than correspondingly increased. Perhaps just so many humans should be left as could keep innumerable million of placid sheep in contented idleness and immunity from depredations by ferocious animals. Indeed if a contented idiot is as good as a contented philosopher, and if a contented sheep is as good as a contented idiot, then a contented fish is as good as a contented sheep, and a contented beetle is as good as a contented fish. Where shall we stop?

Maybe we have gone wrong in talking of pleasure as though it were no more than contentment. Contentment consists roughly in relative absence of unsatisfied desires; pleasure is perhaps something more positive and consists in a balance between

---

1. *Utilitarianism,* p. 9. The problem of the unhappy sage and the happy fool is cleverly stated in Voltaire's 'Histoire d'un bon Bramin,' *Choix de Contes,* edited with an introduction and notes by F. C. Green (Cambridge University Press, London, 1951), pp. 245–7.

absence of unsatisfied desires and presence of satisfied desires. We might put the difference in this way: pure unconsciousness would be a limiting case of contentment, but not of pleasure. A stone has no unsatisfied desires, but then it just has no desires. Nevertheless, this consideration will not resolve the disagreement between Bentham and Mill. No doubt a dog has as intense a desire to discover rats as the philosopher has to discover the mysteries of the universe. Mill would wish to say that the pleasures of the philosopher were more valuable intrinsically than those of the dog, however intense these last might be.

It appears, then, that many of us may well have a preference not only for enjoyment as such but for certain sorts of enjoyment. And this goes for many of the humane and beneficent readers whom I am addressing. I suspect that they too have an intrinsic preference for the more complex and intellectual pleasures. This is not surprising. We must not underrate the mere brute strength of a hard and fit human being: by any standards man is a large and strong animal. Nevertheless above all else man owes his survival to his superior intelligence. If man were not a species which was inclined above all else to think and strive, we should not be where we are now. No wonder that men have a liking for intelligence and complexity, and this may become increasingly so in future. Perhaps some people may feel that my remarks here are somewhat too complacent, in view of the liking of so many people for low-grade entertainments, such as certain popular television programmes. But even the most avid television addict probably enjoys solving practical problems connected with his car, his furniture, or his garden. However unintellectual he might be, he would certainly resent the suggestion that he should, if it were possible, change places with a contented sheep, or even a lively and happy dog. Nevertheless, when all is said and done, we must not disguise the fact that disagreements in ultimate attitude are possible between those who like Mill have, and those who like Bentham have not, an intrinsic preference for the 'higher' pleasures. However it is possible for two people to disagree about ultimate ends and yet agree in practice about what ought to be done. It is worth while enquiring how much practical ethics is likely to be affected by the possibility of disagreement over the question of Socrates dissatisfied versus the fool satisfied.

'Not very much,' one feels like saying at first. We noted that the most complex and intellectual pleasures are also the most fecund. Poetry elevates the mind, makes one more sensitive, and so harmonizes with various intellectual pursuits, some of which are of practical value. Delight in mathematics is even more obviously, on Benthamite views, a pleasure worth encouraging, for on the progress of mathematics depends the progress of mankind. Even the most hedonistic schoolmaster would prefer to see his boys enjoying poetry and mathematics rather than neglecting these arts for the pleasures of marbles or the tuckshop. Indeed many of the brutish pleasures not only lack fecundity but are actually the reverse of fecund. To enjoy food too much is to end up fat, unhealthy and without zest or vigour. To enjoy drink too much is even worse. In most circumstances of ordinary life the pure hedonist will agree in his practical recommendations with the quasi-ideal utilitarian.

This need not always be so. Some years ago two psychologists, Olds and Milner, carried out some experiments with rats.[1] Through the skull of each rat they inserted an electrode. These electrodes penetrated to various regions of the brain. In the case of some of these regions the rat showed behaviour characteristics of pleasure when a current was passed from the electrode, in others they seemed to show pain, and in others the stimulus seemed neutral. That a stimulus was pleasure-giving was shown by the fact that the rat would learn to pass the current himself by pressing a lever. He would neglect food and make straight for this lever and start stimulating himself. In some cases he would sit there pressing the lever every few seconds for hours on end. This calls up a pleasant picture of the voluptuary of the future, a bald-headed man with a number of electrodes protruding from his skull, one to give the physical pleasure of sex, one for that of eating, one

---

1. James Olds and Peter Milner, 'Positive reinforcement produced by electrical stimulation of the septal area and other regions of the rat brain,' *Journal of Comparative and Physiological Psychology* 47 (1954) 19–27. James Olds, 'A preliminary mapping of electrical reinforcing effect in the rat brain,' *ibid.* 49 (1956) 281–5. I. J. Good has also used these results of Olds and Milner in order to discuss ethical hedonism. See his 'A problem for the hedonist,' in I. J. Good (ed.), *The Scientist Speculates* (Heinemann London, 1962). Good takes the possibility of this sort of thing to provide a *reductio ad absurdum* of hedonism.

for that of drinking, and so on. Now is this the sort of life that all our ethical planning should culminate in? A few hours' work a week, automatic factories, comfort and security from disease, and hours spent at a switch, continually electrifying various regions of one's brain? Surely not. Men were made for higher things, one can't help wanting to say, even though one knows that men weren't made for anything, but are the product of evolution by natural selection.

It might be said that the objection to continual sensual stimulation of the above sort is that though it would be pleasant in itself it would be infecund of future pleasures. This is often so with the ordinary sensual pleasures. Excessive indulgence in the physical pleasures of sex may possibly have a debilitating effect and may perhaps interfere with the deeper feelings of romantic love. But whether stimulation by the electrode method would have this weakening effect and whether it would impair the possibility of future pleasures of the same sort is another matter. For example, there would be no excessive secretion of hormones. The whole biochemical mechanism would, almost literally, be short-circuited. Maybe, however, a person who stimulated himself by the electrode method would find it so enjoyable that he would neglect all other pursuits. Maybe if everyone became an electrode operator people would lose interest in everything else and the human race would die out.

Suppose, however, that the facts turned out otherwise: that a man could (and would) do his full share of work in the office or the factory and come back in the evening to a few hours contented electrode work, without bad after-effects. This would be his greatest pleasure, and the pleasure would be so great intrinsically and so easily repeatable that its lack of fecundity would not matter. Indeed perhaps by this time human arts, such as medicine, engineering, agriculture and architecture will have been brought to a pitch of perfection sufficient to enable most of the human race to spend most of its time electrode operating, without compensating pains of starvation, disease and squalor. Would this be a satisfactory state of society? Would this be the millennium towards which we have been striving? Surely the pure hedonist would have to say that it was.

It is time, therefore, that we had another look at the concept of happiness. Should we say that the electrode operator was really happy? This is a diffi-

cult question to be clear about, because the concept of happiness is a tricky one. But whether we should call the electrode operator 'happy' or not, there is no doubt (a) that he would be *contented* and (b) that he would be *enjoying himself.*

Perhaps a possible reluctance to call the electrode operator 'happy' might come from the following circumstance. The electrode operator might be perfectly contented, might perfectly enjoy his electrode operating, and might not be willing to exchange his lot for any other. And we ourselves, perhaps, once we became electrode operators too, could become perfectly contented and satisfied. But nevertheless, as we are now, we just do not want to become electrode operators. We want other things, perhaps to write a book or get into a cricket team. If someone said 'from tomorrow onwards you are going to be forced to be an electrode operator' we should not be pleased. Maybe from tomorrow onwards, once the electrode work had started, we should be perfectly contented, but we are not contented now at the prospect. We are not satisfied at being told that we would be in a certain state from tomorrow onwards, even though we may know that from tomorrow onwards we should be perfectly satisfied. All this is psychologically possible. It is just the obverse of a situation which we often find. I remember an occasion on which I was suspended by cable car half-way up a precipitous mountain. As the cable car creaked upwards, apparently so flimsily held above the yawning chasm below, I fervently wished that I had never come in it. When I bought the ticket for the cable car I knew that I should shortly be wishing that I had never bought it. And yet I should have been annoyed if I had been refused it. Again, a man may be very anxious to catch a bus, so as to be in time for a dental appointment, and yet a few minutes later, while the drill is boring into his tooth, may wish that he had missed that bus. It is, contrariwise, perfectly possible that I should be annoyed today if told that from tomorrow onwards I should be an electrode addict, even though I knew that from tomorrow onwards I should be perfectly contented.

This, I think, explains part of our hesitancy about whether to call the electrode operator 'happy.' The notion of happiness ties up with that of contentment: to be fairly happy at least involves being fairly contented, though it involves something more as well. Though we should be contented when we became electrode operators, we are not contented now with the prospect that we should become electrode operators. Similarly if Socrates had become a fool he might thereafter have been perfectly contented. Nevertheless if beforehand he had been told that he would in the future become a fool he would have been even more dissatisfied than in fact he was. This is part of the trouble about the dispute between Bentham and Mill. The case involves the possibility of (a) our being contented if we are in a certain state, and (b) our being contented at the prospect of being so contented. Normally situations in which we should be contented go along with our being contented at the prospect of our getting into such situations. In the case of the electrode operator and in that of Socrates and the fool we are pulled two ways at once.

Now to call a person 'happy' is to say more than that he is contented for most of the time, or even that he frequently enjoys himself and is rarely discontented or in pain. It is, I think, in part to express a favourable attitude to the idea of such a form of contentment and enjoyment. That is, for *A* to call *B* 'happy,' *A* must be contented at the prospect of *B* being in his present state of mind and at the prospect of *A* himself, should the opportunity arise, enjoying that sort of state of mind. That is, 'happy' is a word which is mainly descriptive (tied to the concepts of contentment and enjoyment) but which is also partly evaluative. It is because Mill approves of the 'higher' pleasures,. e.g. intellectual pleasures, so much more than he approves of the more simple and brutish pleasures, that, quite apart from consequences and side effects, he can pronounce the man who enjoys the pleasures of philosophical discourse as 'more happy' than the man who gets enjoyment from pushpin or beer drinking.

The word 'happy' is not wholly evaluative, for there would be something absurd, as opposed to merely unusual, in calling a man who was in pain, or who was not enjoying himself, or who hardly ever enjoyed himself, or who was in a more or less permanent state of intense dissatisfaction, a 'happy' man. For a man to be happy he must, as a minimal condition, be fairly contented and moderately enjoying himself for much of the time. Once this minimal condition is satisfied we can go on to evaluate various types of contentment and enjoyment and to grade them in terms of happiness. Happiness is, of course, a long-term concept in a way that enjoyment is not. We can talk of a man enjoying himself at a quarter past two precisely, but hardly of a man being happy at a quarter past two precisely. Similarly we can talk of it raining at a quarter past two precisely, but hardly about it being a wet climate at a quarter past two precisely. But happiness involves enjoyment at various times, just as a wet climate involves rain at various times.

To be enjoying oneself, Ryle once suggested, is to be doing what you want to be doing and not to be wanting to do anything else,[1] or, more accurately, we might say that one enjoys oneself the more one wants to be doing what one is in fact doing and the less one wants to be doing anything else. A man will not enjoy a round of golf if (a) he does not particularly want to play golf, or (b) though he wants to play golf there is something else he wishes he were doing at the same time, such as buying the vegetables for his wife, filling in his income tax forms, or listening to a lecture on philosophy. Even sensual pleasures come under the same description. For example the pleasure of eating an ice-cream involves having a certain physical sensation, in a way in which the pleasure of golf or of symbolic logic does not, but the man who is enjoying an ice-cream can still be said to be doing what he wants to do (have a certain physical sensation) and not to be wanting to do anything else. If his mind is preoccupied with work or if he is conscious of a pressing engagement somewhere else, he will not enjoy the physical sensation, however intense it be, or will not enjoy it very much.

The hedonistic ideal would then appear to reduce to a state of affairs in which each person is enjoying himself. Since, as we noted, a dog may, as far as we can tell, enjoy chasing a rat as much as a philosopher or a mathematician may enjoy solving a problem, we must, if we adopt the purely hedonistic position, defend the higher pleasures on account of their fecundity. And that might not turn out to be a workable defence in a world made safe for electrode operators.

To sum up so far, happiness is partly an evaluative concept, and so the utilitarian maxim 'You ought to maximize happiness' is doubly evaluative. There is

---

1. Gilbert Ryle, *The Concept of Mind* (Hutchison, London, 1949), p. 108.

the possibility of an ultimate disagreement between two utilitarians who differ over the question of push-pin versus poetry, or Socrates dissatisfied versus the fool satisfied. The case of the electrode operator shows that two utilitarians might come to advocate very different courses of actions if they differed about what constituted happiness, and this difference between them would be simply an ultimate difference in attitude. Some other possibilities of the 'science fiction' type will be mentioned briefly below. So I do not wish to say that the difference in ultimate valuation between a hedonistic and a non-hedonistic utilitarian will *never* lead to difference in practice.

Leaving these more remote possibilities out of account, however, and considering the decisions we have to make at present, the question of whether the 'higher' pleasures should be preferred to the 'lower' ones does seem to be of slight practical importance. There are already perfectly good hedonistic arguments for poetry as against pushpin. As has been pointed out, the more complex pleasures are incomparably more fecund than the less complex ones: not only are they enjoyable in themselves but they are a means to further enjoyment. Still less, on the whole, do they lead to disillusionment, physical deterioration or social disharmony. The connoisseur of poetry may enjoy himself no more than the connoisseur of whisky, but he runs no danger of a headache on the following morning. Moreover the question of whether the general happiness would be increased by replacing most of the human population by a bigger population of contented sheep and pigs is not one which by any stretch of the imagination could become a live issue. Even if we thought, on abstract grounds, that such a replacement would be desirable, we should not have the slightest chance of having our ideas generally adopted.

So much for the issue between Bentham and Mill. What about that between Mill and Moore? Could a pleasurable state of mind have no intrinsic value at all, or perhaps even a negative intrinsic value?[1] Are there pleasurable states of mind towards which we have an unfavourable attitude, even though we disregard their consequences? In order to decide this question let us imagine a universe consisting of one sentient being only, who falsely believes that there

are other sentient beings and that they are undergoing exquisite torment. So far from being distressed by the thought, he takes a great delight in these imagined sufferings. Is this better or worse than a universe containing no sentient being at all? Is it worse, again, than a universe containing only one sentient being with the same beliefs as before but who sorrows at the imagined tortures of his fellow creatures? I suggest, as against Moore, that the universe containing the deluded sadist is the preferable one. After all he is happy, and since there is no other sentient being, what harm can he do? Moore would nevertheless agree that the sadist was happy, and this shows how happiness, though partly an evaluative concept, is also partly not an evaluative concept.

It is difficult, I admit, not to feel an immediate repugnance at the thought of the deluded sadist. If throughout our childhood we have been given an electric shock whenever we had tasted cheese, then cheese would have become immediately distasteful to us. Our repugnance to the sadist arises, naturally enough, because in our universe sadists invariably do harm. If we lived in a universe in which by some extraordinary laws of psychology a sadist was always confounded by his own knavish tricks and invariably did a great deal of good, then we should feel better disposed towards the sadistic mentality. Even if we could de-condition ourselves from feeling an immediate repugnance to a sadist (as we could de-condition ourselves from a repugnance to cheese by going through a course in which the taste of cheese was invariably associated with a pleasurable stimulus) language might make it difficult for us to distinguish an extrinsic distaste for sadism, founded on our distaste for the consequences of sadism, from an immediate distaste for sadism as such. Normally when we call a thing 'bad' we mean indifferently to express a dislike for it in itself or to express a dislike for what it leads to. When a state of mind is sometimes extrinsically good and sometimes extrinsically bad, we find it easy to distinguish between our intrinsic and extrinsic preferences for instances of it, but when a state of mind is always, or almost always, extrinsically bad, it is easy for us to confuse an extrinsic distaste for it with an intrinsic one. If we allow for this, it does not seem so absurd to hold that there are no pleasures which are intrinsically bad. Pleasures are bad only because they cause harm to the person who has them or to other people. But if

---

1. Cf G.E. Moore, *Principia Ethica*, pp. 209–10.

anyone likes to disagree with me about this I do not feel very moved to argue the point. Such a disagreement about ultimate ends is not likely to lead to any disagreement in practice. For in all actual cases there are sufficient extrinsic reasons for abhorring sadism and similar states of mind. *Approximate* agreement about ultimate ends is often quite enough for rational and co-operative moral discourse. In practical cases the possibility of factual disagreement about what causes produce what effects is likely to be overwhelmingly more important than disagreement in ultimate ends between hedonistic and ideal utilitarians.

There are of course many valuations other than that of the intrinsic goodness of sadistic pleasures which divide the ideal from the hedonistic utilitarian. For example the ideal utilitarian would hold that an intellectual experience, even though not pleasurable, would be intrinsically good. Once more, however, I think we can convince ourselves that in most cases this disagreement about ends will not lead to disagreement about means. Intellectual experiences are in the hedonistic view extrinsically good. Of course there may be wider issues dividing the hedonistic from the ideal utilitarian, if Moore is the ideal utilitarian. I would argue that Moore's principle of organic unities destroys the essential utilitarianism of his doctrine. He need never disagree in practice as a utilitarian ought to, with Sir David Ross. Every trick that Ross can play with his *prima facie* duties, Moore can play, in a different way, with his organic unities.[1]

. . .

Rightness and Wrongness of Actions

I shall now state the act-utilitarian doctrine. Purely for simplicity of exposition I shall put it forward in a broadly hedonistic form. If anyone values states of mind such as knowledge independently of their pleasurableness he can make appropriate verbal alterations to convert it from hedonistic to ideal utilitarianism. And I shall not here take sides on the issue between hedonistic and quasi-ideal utilitarianism. I shall concern myself with the evaluation signified by 'ought' in 'one ought to do that which will produce the best consequences,' and leave to one side the evaluation signified by the word 'best.'

Let us say, then, that the only reason for performing an action A rather than an alternative action B is that doing A will make mankind (or, perhaps, all sentient beings) happier than will doing B. (Here I put aside the consideration that in fact we can have only probable belief about the effects of our actions, and so our reason should be more precisely stated as that doing A will produce more probable benefit than will doing B. For convenience of exposition I shelve this question of probability for a page or two.) This is so simple and natural a doctrine that we can surely expect that many of my readers will have at least some propensity to agree. For I am talking, as I said earlier, to sympathetic and benevolent men, that is, to men who desire the happiness of mankind. Since they have a favourable attitude to the general happiness, surely they will have a tendency to submit to an ultimate moral principle which does no more than express this attitude. It is true that these men, being human, will also have purely selfish attitudes. Either these attitudes will be in harmony with the general happiness (in cases where everyone's looking after his own interests promotes the maximum general happiness) or they will not be in harmony with the general happiness, in which case they will largely cancel one another out, and so could not be made the basis of an interpersonal discussion anyway. It is possible, then, that many sympathetic and benevolent people depart from or fail to attain a utilitarian ethical principle only under the stress of tradition, of superstition, or of unsound philosophical reasoning. If this hypothesis should turn out to be correct, at least as far as these readers are concerned, then the utilitarian may contend that there is no need for him to defend his position directly, save by stating it in a consistent manner, and by showing that common objections to it are unsound. After all, it expresses an ultimate attitude, not a liking for something merely as a means to something else. Save for attempting to remove confusions and discredit superstitions which may get in the way of clear moral thinking, he cannot, of course, appeal to argument and must rest his hopes on the good feeling

---

1. A similar point is made by A. C. Ewing in his article 'Recent developments in British ethical thought,' in C. A. Mace (ed.), *British Philosophy in the Mid-Century* (Allen and Unwin, London, 1957: second edition 1966). Ewing sees it not as I have done as showing that the principle of organic unities destroys the utilitarian character of a theory, but as a way of reconciling utilitarianism with Rossian principles.

of his readers. If any reader is not a sympathetic and benevolent man, then of course it cannot be expected that he will have an ultimate pro-attitude to human happiness in general. Also some good-hearted readers may reject the utilitarian position because of certain considerations relating to justice. I postpone discussion of these.

The utilitarian's ultimate moral principle, let it be remembered, expresses the sentiment not of altruism but of benevolence, the agent counting himself neither more nor less than any other person. Pure altruism cannot be made the basis of a universal moral discussion because it might lead different people to different and perhaps incompatible courses of action, even though the circumstances were identical. When two men each try to let the other through a door first a deadlock results. Altruism could hardly commend itself to those of a scientific, and hence universalistic, frame of mind. If you count in my calculations why should I not count in your calculations? And why should I pay more attention to my calculations than to yours? Of course we often tend to praise and honour altruism even more than generalized benevolence. This is because people too often err on the side of selfishness, and so altruism is a fault on the right side. If we can make a man try to be an altruist he may succeed as far as acquiring a generalized benevolence.

Suppose we could predict the future consequences of actions with certainty. Then it would be possible to say that the total future consequences of action *A* are such-and-such and that the total future consequences of action *B* are so-and-so. In order to help someone to decide whether to do *A* or to do *B* we could say to him: 'Envisage the total consequences of *A*, and think them over carefully and imaginatively. Now envisage the total consequences of *B*, and think them over carefully. As a benevolent and humane man, and thinking of yourself just as one man among others, would you prefer the consequences of *A* or those of *B*?' That is, we are asking for a comparison of one (present and future) *total* situation with another (present and future) *total* situation. So far we are not asking for a *summation* or *calculation* of pleasures or happiness. We are asking only for a comparison of total situations. And it seems clear that we can frequently make such a comparison and say that one total situation is better than another. For example few people would not prefer a total situa-

tion in which a million people are well-fed, well-clothed, free of pain, doing interesting and enjoyable work, and enjoying the pleasures of conversation, study, business, art, humour, and so on, to a total situation where there are ten thousand such people only, or perhaps 999,999 such people plus one man with toothache, or neurotic, or shivering with cold. In general, we can sum things up by saying that if we are humane, kindly, benevolent people, we want as many people as possible now and in the future to be as happy as possible. Someone might object that we cannot envisage the total future situation, because this stretches into infinity. In reply to this we may say that it does not stretch into infinity, as all sentient life on earth will ultimately be extinguished, and furthermore we do not normally in practice need to consider very remote consequences, as these in the end approximate rapidly to zero like the furthermost ripples on a pond after a stone has been dropped into it.

But do the remote consequences of an action diminish to zero? Suppose that two people decide whether to have a child or remain childless. Let us suppose that they decide to have the child, and that they have a limitless succession of happy descendants. The remote consequences do not seem to get less. Not at any rate if these people are Adam and Eve. The difference would be between the end of the human race and a limitless accretion of human happiness, generation by generation. The Adam and Eve example shows that the 'ripples on the pond' postulate is not needed in every case for a rational utilitarian decision. If we had some reason for thinking that every generation would be more happy than not we would not (in the Adam and Eve sort of case) need to be worried that the remote consequences of our action would be in detail unknown. The necessity for the 'ripples in the pond' postulate comes from the fact that usually we do not know whether remote consequences will be good or bad. Therefore we cannot know what to do unless we can assume that remote consequences can be left out of account. This can often be done. Thus if we consider two actual parents, instead of Adam and Eve, then they need not worry about thousands of years hence. Not, at least, if we assume that there will be ecological forces determining the future population of the world. If these parents do not have remote descendants, then other people will presumably have more than they would otherwise. And there is no reason to suppose that my descendants would be more or less happy than yours. We must note, then, that unless we are dealing with 'all or nothing' situations (such as the Adam and Eve one, or that of someone in a position to end human life altogether) we need some sort of 'ripples in the pond' postulate to make utilitarianism workable in practice. I do not know how to prove such a postulate, though it seems plausible enough. If it is not accepted, not only utilitarianism, but also deontological systems like that of Sir David Ross, who at least admits beneficence as one *prima facie* duty among the others, will be fatally affected.

Sometimes, of course, more needs to be said. For example one course of action may make some people very happy and leave the rest as they are or perhaps slightly less happy. Another course of action may make all men rather more happy than before but no one very happy. Which course of action makes mankind happier on the whole? Again, one course of action may make it highly probable that everyone will be made a little happier whereas another course of action may give us a much smaller probability that everyone will be made very much happier. In the third place, one course of action may make everyone happy in a pig-like way, whereas another course of action may make a few people happy in a highly complex and intellectual way.

It seems therefore that we have to weigh the maximizing of happiness against equitable distribution, to weigh probabilities with happiness, and to weigh the intellectual and other qualities of states of mind with their pleasurableness. Are we not therefore driven back to the necessity of some calculus of happiness? Can we just say: "envisage two total situations and tell me which you prefer"? If this were possible, of course there would be no need to talk of summing happiness or of a calculus. All we should have to do would be to put total situations in an order of preference. Since this is not always possible there is a difficulty, to which I shall return shortly.

We have already considered the question of intellectual versus non-intellectual pleasures and activities. This is irrelevant to the present issue because there seems to be no reason why the ideal or quasi-ideal utilitarian cannot use the method of envisaging total situations just as much as the hedonistic utilitarian. It is just a matter of envisaging various alternative total situations, stretching out into the future, and saying which situation one prefers. The non-

hedonistic utilitarian may evaluate the total situations differently from the hedonistic utilitarian, in which case there will be an ultimate ethical disagreement. This possibility of ultimate disagreement is always there, though we have given reasons for suspecting that it will not frequently lead to important disagreement in practice.

Let us now consider the question of equity. Suppose that we have the choice of sending four equally worthy and intelligent boys to a medium-grade public school or of leaving three in an adequate but uninspiring grammar school and sending one to Eton. (For sake of the example I am making the almost certainly incorrect assumption that Etonians are happier than other public-school boys and that these other public-school boys are happier than grammar-school boys.) Which course of action makes the most for the happiness of the four boys? Let us suppose that we can neglect complicating factors, such as that the superior Etonian education might lead one boy to develop his talents so much that he will have an extraordinary influence on the well-being of mankind, or that the unequal treatment of the boys might cause jealousy and rift in the family. Let us suppose that the Etonian will be as happy as (we may hope) Etonians usually are, and similarly for the other boys, and let us suppose that remote effects can be neglected. Should we prefer the greater happiness of one boy to the moderate happiness of all four? Clearly one parent may prefer one total situation (one boy at Eton and three at the grammar school) while another may prefer the other total situation (all four at the medium-grade public school). Surely both parents have an equal claim to being sympathetic and benevolent, and yet their difference of opinion here is not founded on an empirical disagreement about facts. I suggest, however, that there are not in fact many cases in which such a disagreement could arise. Probably the parent who wished to send one son to Eton would draw the line at sending one son to Eton plus giving him expensive private tuition during the holidays plus giving his other sons no secondary education at all. It is only within rather small limits that this sort of disagreement about equity can arise. Furthermore the cases in which we can make one person *very* much happier without increasing *general* happiness are rare ones. The law of diminishing returns comes in here. So, in most practical cases, a disagreement about what should be done will be an empirical disagreement about what total situation is likely to be brought about by an action, and will not be a disagreement about which total situation is preferable. For example the inequalitarian parent might get the other to agree with him if he could convince him that there was a much higher probability of an Etonian benefiting the human race, such as by inventing a valuable drug or opening up the mineral riches of Antarctica, than there is of a non-Etonian doing so. (Once more I should like to say that I do not myself take such a possibility very seriously!) I must again stress that since disagreement about what causes produce what effects is in practice so much the most important sort of disagreement, to have intelligent moral discussion with a person we do not in fact need complete agreement with him about ultimate ends: an approximate agreement is sufficient.

Rawls[1] has suggested that we must maximize the general happiness only if we do so in a *fair* way. An *unfair* way of maximizing the general happiness would be to do so by a method which involved making some people less happy than they might be otherwise. As against this suggestion a utilitarian might make the following rhetorical objection: if it is rational for me to choose the pain of a visit to the dentist in order to prevent the pain of toothache, why is it not rational of me to choose a pain for Jones, similar to that of my visit to the dentist, if that is the only way in which I can prevent a pain, equal to that of my toothache, for Robinson? Such situations continually occur in war, in mining, and in the fight against disease, when we may often find ourselves in the position of having in the general interest to inflict suffering on good and happy men. However it must be conceded that these objections against fairness as an *ultimate* principle must be rhetorical only, and that Rawls's principle could perhaps be incorporated in a restrained system of deontological ethics, which would avoid the artificiality of the usual forms of deontology. There are in any case plenty of good utilitarian reasons for adopting the principle of fairness as an important, but not inviolable, rule of thumb.

We must now deal with the difficulty about probability. We have so far avoided the common objection to utilitarianism that it involves the allegedly

absurd notion of a summation or calculus of happiness or goodness. We have done this by using the method of comparing total situations. All we have to do is to envisage two or more total situations and say which we prefer. A purely ordinal, not a quantitative, judgement is all we require. However in taking this position we have oversimplified the matter. Unfortunately we cannot say with certainty what would be the various total situations which could result from our actions. Worse still, we cannot even assign rough probabilities to the total situations as a whole. All we can do is to assign various probabilities to the various possible effects of an action. For example, one course of action may almost certainly lead to a fairly good result next year together with a high probability of a slightly good result the year after, while another action may give a very small probability of a moderately good result the year after and a very small but not negligible probability of a rather bad result the year after that. (I am assuming that in both cases the still more remote results become negligible or such as to cancel one another out.) If we had to weight total situations with probabilities, this would give us enough conceptual difficulty, but it now appears that we have to go within total situations and weight different elements within them according to different probabilities. We seem to be driven back towards a calculus.

If it were possible to assign numerical probabilities to the various effects of our actions we could devise a way of applying the method of total situations. Suppose that we could say that an action X would either give Smith the pleasure of eating ice-cream with probability 4/5 or the pain of toothache with probability 1/5 and that it would give Jones the pleasure of sympathy with probability 3/5 or the displeasure of envy with probability 2/5 and that no other important results (direct or indirect) would accrue. Suppose that the only alternative action to X is Y and that this has no effect on Smith but causes Jones to go to sleep with probability 3/5 or to go for a walk with probability 2/5 and that no other important results (direct or indirect) would accrue. Then we could say that the total situations we have to imagine and to compare are (a) (for X): four people (just like Smith) eating ice-cream plus one (just like Smith) with toothache plus three sympathetic people (just like Jones) plus two envious people (just like Jones), and (b) (for Y): three people (just like Jones) who are asleep plus two (just like Jones) going

1. 'Justice as fairness,' *Philosophical Review* 67 (1958) 164–94.

for a walk. In the example I have, for convenience, taken all probabilities to be multiples of 1/5. If they did not have common denominators we should have to make them such, by expressing them as multiples of a denominator which is the lowest common multiple of the original denominators.

However it is not usually possible to assign a numerical probability to a particular event. No doubt we could use actuarial tables to ascertain the probability that a friend of ours, who is of a certain age, a certain carefully specified medical history, and a certain occupation, will die within the next year. But can we give a numerical value to the probability that a new war will break out, that a proof of Fermat's last theorem will be found, or that our knowledge of genetical linkage in human chromosomes will be much improved in the next five years? Surely it is meaningless to talk of a numerical value for these probabilities, and it is probabilities of this sort with which we have to deal in our moral life.

When, however, we look at the way in which in fact we take some of our ordinary practical decisions we see that there is a sense in which most people think that we can weigh up probabilities and advantages. A man deciding whether to migrate to a tropical country may well say to himself, for example, that he can expect a pleasanter life for himself and his family in that country, unless there is a change in the system of government there, which is not very likely, or unless one of his children catches an epidemic disease, which is perhaps rather more likely, and so on, and thinking over all these advantages and disadvantages and probabilities and improbabilities he may come out with the statement that on the whole it seems preferable for him to go there or with the statement that on the whole it seems preferable for him to stay at home.

If we are able to take account of probabilities in our ordinary prudential decisions it seems idle to say that in the field of ethics, the field of our universal and humane attitudes, we cannot do the same thing, but must rely on some dogmatic morality, in short on some set of rules or rigid criteria. Maybe sometimes we just will be unable to say whether we prefer for humanity an improbable great advantage or a probable small advantage, and in these cases perhaps we shall have to toss a penny to decide what to do. Maybe we have not any precise methods for deciding what to do, but then our imprecise methods

must just serve their turn. We need not on that account be driven into authoritarianism, dogmatism or romanticism.

So, at any rate, it appears at first sight. But if I cannot say any more the utilitarian position as it is here presented has a serious weakness. The suggested method of developing normative ethics is to appeal to feelings, namely of benevolence, and to reason, in the sense of conceptual clarification and also of empirical enquiry, but not, as so many moralists do, to what the ordinary man says or thinks. The ordinary man is frequently irrational in his moral thinking. And if he can be irrational about morals why cannot he be irrational about probabilities? The fact that the ordinary man thinks that he can weigh up probabilities in making prudential decisions does not mean that there is really any sense in what he is doing. What utilitarianism badly needs, in order to make its theoretical foundations secure, is some method according to which numerical probabilities, even approximate ones, could in theory, though not necessarily always in practice, be assigned to any imagined future event.

D. Davidson and P. Suppes have proposed a method whereby, at any rate in simplified situations, *subjective* probabilities can be given a numerical value.[1] Their theory was to some extent anticipated in an essay by F. P. Ramsey,[2] in which he tries to show how numbers can be assigned to probabilities in the sense of degrees of belief. This allows us to give a theory of rational, in the sense of *self-consistent,* utilitarian choice, but to make utilitarianism thoroughly satisfactory we need something more. We need a method of assigning numbers to *objective,* not subjective, probabilities. Perhaps one method might be to accept the Davidson-Suppes method of assigning subjective probabilities, and define objective probabilities as the subjective probabilities of an unbiased and far-sighted man. This, however, would require independent criteria for lack of bias and for far-sightedness. I do not know how to do this, but I suspect, from the work that is at present being done on

---

1. D. Davidson, P. Suppes, and S. Siegel, *Decision Making: An Experimental Approach* (Stanford University Press, Stanford, California, 1957).

2. F. P. Ramsey, *The Foundations of Mathematics* (Routledge and Kegan Paul, London, 1931), ch. 7, 'Truth and Probability.'

decision-making, that the situation may not be hopeless. But until we have an adequate theory of *objective* probability utilitarianism is not on a secure theoretical basis.[1] Nor, for that matter, is ordinary prudence; nor are deontological systems of ethics, like that of Sir David Ross, which assign some weight to beneficence. And any system of deontological ethics implies some method of weighing up the claims of conflicting *prima facie* duties, for it is impossible that deontological rules of conduct should *never* conflict, and the rationale of this is perhaps even more insecure than is the theory of objective probability.

_____

1. R. McNaughton's interesting article 'A metrical concept of happiness,' *Philosophy and Phenomenological Research* 14 (1953–4) 171–83, does not enable us to propose a complete utilitarian calculus, because it neglects probability considerations.

BERNARD WILLIAMS

FROM *Utilitarianism: For and Against*

In this reading excerpted from Utilitarianism: For and Against *(1973), Bernard Williams puts forward a hard-hitting criticism of utilitarianism, the ethical theory proposed by Bentham and Mill in which the rightness or wrongness of an act is determined by the good or bad consequences of that act. Williams argues that utilitarianism lacks an adequate account of personal integrity; consequently, utilitarians can sometimes be in situations where they must compromise their integrity or give up what Williams calls their "deeply held projects" in order to do what their theory deems is right. Williams gives as an example a case that has become famous in recent moral philosophy. Imagine a situation, says Williams, where a tourist in South America accidently comes upon soldiers preparing to execute twenty Indians in a small village. The Indians are being executed as a lesson to the other inhabitants following some anti-government protests. The captain of the soldiers offers this unfortunate tourist an "honored guest's" privilege: if he personally kills one of the Indians, the other nineteen will be set free. If the tourist refuses, all twenty will be shot.*

    Williams charges that the moral decision is clear for the utilitarian. If the tourist kills one Indian, less misery occurs than if the soldiers kill twenty. Therefore, clearly the tourist should kill the Indian. Yet even when the tourist's revulsion to killing is brought into the calculation, his resistance to carrying out the murder suggests some form of moral cowardice. Here is the point Williams wants to isolate: utilitarianism does not place a value on integrity or a person's personal projects. To demand that the tourist kill an innocent man, even to save nineteen others, is to attack his integrity, to alienate him from his own actions and convictions.

    Even though Williams believes that the flaws inherent in utilitarianism should be enough to condemn it as a viable theory, not all moral philosophers are critical of utilitarianism. For a defense of utilitarianism, see the excerpt from Williams' co-author on this book, J. J. C. Smart. For other perspectives on utilitarianism, see the readings from Bentham, Mill, Sidgwick, and Moore.

Negative responsibility: and two examples

Although I have defined a state of affairs being *accessible* to an agent in terms of the actions which are *available* to him,[1] nevertheless it is the former notion which is really more important for consequentialism. Consequentialism is basically indifferent to whether a state of affairs consists in what I do, or is produced by what I do, where that notion is itself wide enough to include, for instance, situations in which other people do things which I have made them do, or allowed them to do, or encouraged them to do, or given them a chance to do. All that consequentialism is interested in is the idea of these doings being *consequences* of what I do, and that is a relation broad enough to include the relations just mentioned, and many others.

Just what the relation is, is a different question, and at least as obscure as the nature of its relative, cause and effect. It is not a question I shall try to pursue; I will rely on cases where I suppose that any consequentialist would be bound to regard the situations in question as consequences of what the agent does. There are cases where the supposed consequences stand in a rather remote relation to the action, which are sometimes difficult to assess from a practical point of view, but which raise no very interesting question for the present enquiry. The more interesting points about consequentialism lie rather elsewhere. There are certain situations in which the causation of the situation, the relation it has to what I do, is in no way remote or problematic in itself, and entirely justifies the claim that the situation is a consequence of what I do: for instance, it is quite clear, or reasonably clear, that if I do a certain thing, this situation will come about, and if I do not, it will not. So from a consequentialist point of view it goes into the calculation of consequences along with any other state of affairs accessible to me. Yet from some, at least, non-consequentialist points of view, there is a vital difference between some such situations and others: namely, that in some a vital link in the production of the eventual outcome is provided by *someone else's* doing something. But for consequentialism, all causal connexions are on the same level, and it makes no difference, so far as that goes, whether the causation of a given state of affairs lies through another agent, or not.

Correspondingly, there is no relevant difference which consists *just* in one state of affairs being brought about by me, without intervention of other agents, and another being brought about through the intervention of other agents; although some genuinely causal differences involving a difference of value may correspond to that (as when, for instance, the other agents derive pleasure or pain from the transaction), that kind of difference will already be included in the specification of the state of affairs to be produced. Granted that the states of affairs have been adequately described in causally and evaluatively relevant terms, it makes no further comprehensible difference who produces them. It is because consequentialism attaches value ultimately to states of affairs, and its concern is with what states of affairs the world contains, that it essentially involves the notion of *negative responsibility*: that if I am ever responsible for anything, then I must be just as much responsible for things that I allow or fail to prevent, as I am for things that I myself, in the more everyday restricted sense, bring about.[2] Those things also must enter my deliberations, as a responsible moral agent, on the same footing. What matters is what states of affairs the world contains, and so what matters with respect to a given action is what comes about if it is done, and what comes about if it is not done, and those are questions not intrinsically affected by the nature of the causal linkage, in particular by whether the outcome is partly produced by other agents.

The strong doctrine of negative responsibility flows directly from consequentialism's assignment of ultimate value to states of affairs. Looked at from another point of view, it can be seen also as a special application of something that is favoured in many moral outlooks not themselves consequentialist—something which, indeed, some thinkers have been disposed to regard as the essence of morality itself: a principle of impartiality. Such a principle will claim

---

1. See last section.

2. This is a fairly modest sense of 'responsibility,' introduced merely by one's ability to reflect on, and decide, what one ought to do. This presumably escapes Smart's ban on the notion of 'the responsibility' as 'a piece of metaphysical nonsense'—his remarks seem to be concerned solely with situations of inter-personal blame. For the limitations of that, see below, section 6.

that there can be no relevant difference from a moral point of view which consists just in the fact, not further explicable in general terms, that benefits or harms accrue to one person rather than to another— 'it's me' can never in itself be a morally comprehensible reason.[1] This principle, familiar with regard to the reception of harms and benefits, we can see consequentialism as extending to their production: from the moral point of view, there is no comprehensible difference which consists just in my bringing about a certain outcome rather than someone else's producing it. That the doctrine of negative responsibility represents in this way the extreme of impartiality, and abstracts from the identity of the agent, leaving just a locus of causal intervention in the world—that fact is not merely a surface paradox. It helps to explain why consequentialism can seem to some to express a more serious attitude than non-consequentialist views, why part of its appeal is to a certain kind of high-mindedness. Indeed, that is part of what is wrong with it.

For a lot of the time so far we have been operating at an exceedingly abstract level. This has been necessary in order to get clearer in general terms about the differences between consequentialist and other outlooks, an aim which is important if we want to know what features of them lead to what results for our thought. Now, however, let us look more concretely at two examples, to see what utilitarianism might say about them, what we might say about utilitarianism and, most importantly of all, what would be implied by certain ways of thinking about the situations. The examples are inevitably schematized, and they are open to the objection that they beg as many questions as they illuminate. There are two ways in particular in which examples in moral philosophy tend to beg important questions. One is that, as presented, they arbitrarily cut off and restrict the range of alternative courses of action—this objection might particularly be made against the first of my two examples. The second is that they inevitably present one with the situation as a going concern, and cut off questions about how the agent got into it,

and correspondingly about moral considerations which might flow from that: this objection might perhaps specially arise with regard to the second of my two situations. These difficulties, however, just have to be accepted, and if anyone finds these examples cripplingly defective in this sort of respect, then he must in his own thought rework them in richer and less question-begging form. If he feels that no presentation of any imagined situation can ever be other than misleading in morality, and that there can never be any substitute for the concrete experienced complexity of actual moral situations, then this discussion, with him, must certainly grind to a halt: but then one may legitimately wonder whether every discussion with him about conduct will not grind to a halt, including any discussion about the actual situations, since discussion about how one would think and feel about situations somewhat different from the actual (that is to say, situations to that extent imaginary) plays an important role in discussion of the actual.

(1) George, who has just taken his Ph.D. in chemistry, finds it extremely difficult to get a job. He is not very robust in health, which cuts down the number of jobs he might be able to do satisfactorily. His wife has to go out to work to keep them, which itself causes a great deal of strain, since they have small children and there are severe problems about looking after them. The results of all this, especially on the children, are damaging. An older chemist, who knows about this situation, says that he can get George a decently paid job in a certain laboratory, which pursues research into chemical and biological warfare. George says that he cannot accept this, since he is opposed to chemical and biological warfare. The older man replies that he is not too keen on it himself, come to that, but after all George's refusal is not going to make the job or the laboratory go away; what is more, he happens to know that if George refuses the job, it will certainly go to a contemporary of George's who is not inhibited by any such scruples and is likely if appointed to push along the research with greater zeal than George would. Indeed, it is not merely concern for George and his family, but (to speak frankly and in confidence) some alarm about this other man's excess of zeal, which has led the older man to offer to use his influence to get George the job. . . . George's wife, to whom he is deeply attached, has views (the details of which need not

---

1. There is a tendency in some writers to suggest that it is not a comprehensible reason at all. But this, I suspect, is due to the overwhelming importance those writers ascribe to the moral point of view.

concern us) from which it follows that at least there is nothing particularly wrong with research into CBW. What should he do?

(2) Jim finds himself in the central square of a small South American town. Tied up against the wall are a row of twenty Indians, most terrified, a few defiant, in front of them several armed men in uniform. A heavy man in a sweat-stained khaki shirt turns out to be the captain in charge and, after a good deal of questioning of Jim which establishes that he got there by accident while on a botanical expedition, explains that the Indians are a random group of the inhabitants who, after recent acts of protest against the government, are just about to be killed to remind other possible protestors of the advantages of not protesting. However, since Jim is an honoured visitor from another land, the captain is happy to offer him a guest's privilege of killing one of the Indians himself. If Jim accepts, then as a special mark of the occasion, the other Indians will be let off. Of course, if Jim refuses, then there is no special occasion, and Pedro here will do what he was about to do when Jim arrived, and kill them all. Jim, with some desperate recollection of schoolboy fiction, wonders whether if he got hold of a gun, he could hold the captain, Pedro and the rest of the soldiers to threat, but it is quite clear from the set-up that nothing of that kind is going to work: any attempt at that sort of thing will mean that all the Indians will be killed, and himself. The men against the wall, and the other villagers, understand the situation, and are obviously begging him to accept. What should he do?

To these dilemmas, it seems to me that utilitarianism replies, in the first case, that George should accept the job, and in the second, that Jim should kill the Indian. Not only does utilitarianism give these answers but, if the situations are essentially as described and there are no further special factors, it regards them, it seems to me, as *obviously* the right answers. But many of us would certainly wonder whether, in (1), that could possibly be the right answer at all; and in the case of (2), even one who came to think that perhaps that was the answer, might well wonder whether it was obviously the answer. Nor is it just a question of the rightness or obviousness of these answers. It is also a question of what sort of considerations come into finding the answer. A feature of utilitarianism is that it cuts out a kind of consideration which for some others makes a difference to what they feel about such cases: a consideration involving the idea, as we might first and very simply put it, that each of us is specially responsible for what *he* does, rather than for what other people do. This is an idea closely connected with the value of integrity. It is often suspected that utilitarianism, at least in its direct forms, makes integrity as a value more or less unintelligible. I shall try to show that this suspicion is correct. Of course, even if that is correct, it would not necessarily follow that we should reject utilitarianism; perhaps, as utilitarians sometimes suggest, we should just forget about integrity, in favour of such things as a concern for the general good. However, if I am right, we cannot merely do that, since the reason why utilitarianism cannot understand integrity is that it cannot coherently describe the relations between a man's projects and his actions.

Two Kinds of Remoter Effect

A lot of what we have to say about this question will be about the relations between my projects and other people's projects. But before we get on to that, we should first ask whether we are assuming too hastily what the utilitarian answers to the dilemmas will be. In terms of more direct effects of the possible decisions, there does not indeed seem much doubt about the answer in either case; but it might be said that in terms of more remote or less evident effects counterweights might be found to enter the utilitarian scales. Thus the effect on George of a decision to take the job might be invoked, or its effect on others who might know of his decision. The possibility of there being more beneficent labours in the future from which he might be barred or disqualified, might be mentioned; and so forth. Such effects—in particular, possible effects on the agent's character, and effects on the public at large—are often invoked by utilitarian writers dealing with problems about lying or promise-breaking, and some similar considerations might be invoked here.

There is one very general remark that is worth making about arguments of this sort. The certainty that attaches to these hypotheses about possible effects is usually pretty low; in some cases, indeed, the hypothesis invoked is so implausible that it would scarcely pass if it were not being used to deliver the respectable moral answer, as in the standard fantasy that one of the effects of one's telling a particular lie is to weaken the disposition of the world at large to tell the truth. The demands on the certainty or probability of these beliefs as beliefs about particular actions are much milder than they would be on beliefs favouring the unconventional course. It may be said that this is as it should be, since the presumption must be in favour of the conventional course: but that scarcely seems a *utilitarian* answer, unless utilitarianism has already taken off in the direction of not applying the consequences to the particular act at all.

Leaving aside that very general point, I want to consider now two types of effect that are often invoked by utilitarians, and which might be invoked in connexion with these imaginary cases. The attitude or tone involved in invoking these effects may sometimes seem peculiar; but that sort of peculiarity soon becomes familiar in utilitarian discussions, and indeed it can be something of an achievement to retain a sense of it.

First, there is the psychological effect on the agent. Our descriptions of these situations have not so far taken account of how George or Jim will be after they have taken the one course or the other; and it might be said that if they take the course which seemed at first the utilitarian one, the effects on them will be in fact bad enough and extensive enough to cancel out the initial utilitarian advantages of that course. Now there is one version of this effect in which, for a utilitarian, some confusion must be involved, namely that in which the agent feels bad, his subsequent conduct and relations are crippled and so on, *because he thinks that he has done the wrong thing*—for if the balance of outcomes was as it appeared to be *before* invoking this effect, then he has not (from the utilitarian point of view) done the wrong thing. So that version of the effect, for a rational and utilitarian agent, could not possibly make any difference to the assessment of right and wrong. However, perhaps he is not a thoroughly rational agent, and is disposed to have bad feelings, whichever he decided to do. Now such feelings, which are from a strictly utilitarian point of view irrational—nothing, a utilitarian can point out, is advanced by having them—cannot, consistently, have any great weight in a utilitarian calculation. I shall consider in a moment an argument to suggest that they should have no weight at all in it. But short of that, the utilitarian could reasonably say that such

feelings should not be encouraged, even if we accept their existence, and that to give them a lot of weight is to encourage them. Or, at the very best, even if they are straightforwardly and without any discount to be put into the calculation, their weight must be small: they are after all (and at best) one man's feelings.

That consideration might seem to have particular force in Jim's case. In George's case, his feelings represent a larger proportion of what is to be weighed, and are more commensurate in character with other items in the calculation. In Jim's case, however, his feelings might seem to be of very little weight compared with other things that are at stake. There is a powerful and recognizable appeal that can be made on this point: as that a refusal by Jim to do what he has been invited to do would be a kind of self-indulgent squeamishness. That is an appeal which can be made by other than utilitarians—indeed, there are some uses of it which cannot be consistently made by utilitarians, as when it essentially involves the idea that there is something dishonourable about such self-indulgence. But in some versions it is a familiar, and it must be said a powerful, weapon of utilitarianism. One must be clear, though, about what it can and cannot accomplish. The most it can do, so far as I can see, is to invite one to consider how seriously, and for what reasons, one feels that what one is invited to do is (in these circumstances) wrong, and in particular, to consider that question from the utilitarian point of view. When the agent is not seeing the situation from a utilitarian point of view, the appeal cannot force him to do so; and if he does come round to seeing it from a utilitarian point of view, there is virtually nothing left for the appeal to do. If he does not see it from a utilitarian point of view, he will not see his resistance to the invitation, and the unpleasant feelings he associates with accepting it, *just* as disagreeable experiences of his; they figure rather as emotional expressions of a thought that to accept would be wrong. He may be asked, as by the appeal, to consider whether he is right, and indeed whether he is fully serious, in thinking that. But the assertion of the appeal, that he is being self-indulgently squeamish, will not itself answer that question, or even help to answer it, since it essentially tells him to regard his feelings just as unpleasant experiences of his, and he cannot, by doing that, answer the question they pose when they are precisely not so regarded, but are regarded as indications[1] of what he thinks is right and wrong. If he does come round fully to the utilitarian point of view then of course he will regard these feelings just as unpleasant experiences of his. And once Jim—at least—has come to see them in that light, there is nothing left for the appeal to do, since *of course* his feelings, so regarded, are of virtually no weight at all in relation to the other things at stake. The 'squeamishness' appeal is not an argument which adds in a hitherto neglected consideration. Rather, it is an invitation to consider the situation, and one's own feelings, from a utilitarian point of view.

The reason why the squeamishness appeal can be very unsettling, and one can be unnerved by the suggestion of self-indulgence in going against utilitarian considerations, is not that we are utilitarians who are uncertain what utilitarian value to attach to our moral feelings, but that we are partially at least not utilitarians, and cannot regard our moral feelings merely as objects of utilitarian value. Because our moral relation to the world is partly given by such feelings, and by a sense of what we can or cannot 'live with,' to come to regard those feelings from a purely utilitarian point of view, that is to say, as happenings outside one's moral self; is to lose a sense of one's moral identity; to lose, in the most literal way, one's integrity. At this point utilitarianism alienates one from one's moral feelings; we shall see a little later how, more basically, it alienates one from one's actions as well.

If, then, one is really going to regard one's feelings from a strictly utilitarian point of view, Jim should give very little weight at all to his; it seems almost indecent, in fact, once one has taken that point of view, to suppose that he should give any at all. In George's case one might feel that things were slightly different. It is interesting, though, that one reason why one might think that—namely that one person principally affected is his wife—is very dubiously available to a utilitarian. George's wife has some reason to be interested in George's integrity and his sense of it; the Indians, quite properly, have no interest in Jim's. But it is not at all clear how utilitarianism would describe that difference.

There is an argument, and a strong one, that a strict utilitarian should give not merely small extra weight, in calculations of right and wrong, to feelings of this kind, but that he should give absolutely no weight to them at all. This is based on the point, which we have already seen, that if a course of action is, before taking these sorts of feelings into account, utilitarianly preferable, then bad feelings about that kind of action will be from a utilitarian point of view irrational. Now it might be thought that even if that is so, it would not mean that in a utilitarian calculation such feelings should not be taken into account; it is after all a well-known boast of utilitarianism that it is a realistic outlook which seeks the best in the world as it is, and takes any form of happiness or unhappiness into account. While a utilitarian will no doubt seek to diminish the incidence of feelings which are utilitarianly irrational—or at least of disagreeable feelings which are so—he might be expected to take them into account while they exist. This is without doubt classical utilitarian doctrine, but there is good reason to think that utilitarianism cannot stick to it without embracing results which are startlingly unacceptable and perhaps self-defeating.

Suppose that there is in a certain society a racial minority. Considering merely the ordinary interests of the other citizens, as opposed to their sentiments, this minority does no particular harm; we may suppose that it does not confer any very great benefits either. Its presence is in those terms neutral or mildly beneficial. However, the other citizens have such prejudices that they find the sight of this group, even the knowledge of its presence, very disagreeable. Proposals are made for removing in some way this minority. If we assume various quite plausible things (as that programmes to change the majority sentiment are likely to be protracted and ineffective) then even if the removal would be unpleasant for the minority, a utilitarian calculation might well end up favouring this step, especially if the minority were a rather small minority and the majority were very severely prejudiced, that is to say, were made very severely uncomfortable by the presence of the minority.

A utilitarian might find that conclusion embarrassing; and not merely because of its nature, but because of the grounds on which it is reached. While a

---

utilitarian might be expected to take into account certain other sorts of consequences of the prejudice, as that a majority prejudice is likely to be displayed in conduct disagreeable to the minority, and so forth, he might be made to wonder whether the unpleasant experiences of the prejudiced people should be allowed, *merely as such,* to count. If he does count them, merely as such, then he has once more separated himself from a body of ordinary moral thought which he might have hoped to accommodate; he may also have started on the path of defeating his own view of things. For one feature of these sentiments is that they are from the utilitarian point of view itself irrational, and a thoroughly utilitarian person would either not have them, or if he found that he did tend to have them, would himself seek to discount them. Since the sentiments in question are such that a rational utilitarian would discount them in himself, it is reasonable to suppose that he should discount them in his calculations about society; it does seem quite unreasonable for him to give just as much weight to feelings—considered just in themselves, one must recall, as experiences of those that have them—which are essentially based on views which are from a utilitarian point of view irrational, as to those which accord with utilitarian principles. Granted this idea, it seems reasonable for him to rejoin a body of moral thought in other respects congenial to him, and discount those sentiments, just considered in themselves, totally, on the principle that no pains or discomforts are to count in the utilitarian sum which their subjects have just because they hold views which are by utilitarian standards irrational. But if he accepts that, then in the cases we are at present considering no extra weight at all can be put in for bad feelings of George or Jim about their choices, if those choices are, leaving out those feelings, on the first round utilitarianly rational.

The psychological effect on the agent was the first of two general effects considered by utilitarians, which had to be discussed. The second is in general a more substantial item, but it need not take so long, since it is both clearer and has little application to the present cases. This is the *precedent effect.* As Burke rightly emphasized, this effect can be important: that one morally *can* do what someone has actually done, is a psychologically effective principle, if not a deontically valid one. For the effect to operate, obviously some conditions must hold on the public-

ity of the act and on such things as the status of the agent (such considerations weighed importantly with Sir Thomas More); what these may be will vary evidently with circumstances.

In order for the precedent effect to make a difference to a utilitarian calculation, it must be based upon a confusion. For suppose that there is an act which would be the best in the circumstances, except that doing it will encourage by. precedent other people to do things which will not be the best things to do. Then the situation of those other people must be relevantly different from that of the original agent; if it were not, then in doing the same as what would be the best course for the original agent, they would necessarily do the best thing themselves. But if the situations are in this way relevantly different, it must be a confused perception which takes the first situation, and the agent's course in it, as an adequate precedent for the second.

However, the fact that the precedent effect, if it really makes a difference, is in this sense based on a confusion, does not mean that it is not perfectly real, nor that it is to be discounted: social effects are by their nature confused in this sort of way. What it does emphasize is that calculations of the precedent effect have got to be realistic, involving considerations of how people are actually likely to be influenced. In the present examples, however, it is very implausible to think that the precedent effect could be invoked to make any difference to the calculation. Jim's case is extraordinary enough, and it is hard to imagine who the recipients of the effect might be supposed to be; while George is not in a sufficiently public situation or role for the question to arise in that form, and in any case one might suppose that the motivations of others on such an issue were quite likely to be fixed one way or another already.

No appeal, then, to these other effects is going to make a difference to what the utilitarian will decide about our examples. Let us now look more closely at the structure of those decisions.

Integrity

The situations have in common that if the agent does not do a certain disagreeable thing, someone else will, and in Jim's situation at least the result, the state of affairs after the other man has acted, if he does, will be worse than after Jim has acted, if Jim does. The same, on a smaller scale, is true of George's case. I have already suggested that it is inherent in consequentialism that it offers a strong doctrine of negative responsibility: if I know that if I do X, O_1 will eventuate, and if I refrain from doing X, O_2 will, and that O_2 is worse than O_1, then I am responsible for O_2 if I refrain voluntarily from doing X. 'You could have prevented it,' as will be said, and truly, to Jim, if he refuses, by the relatives of the other Indians. (I shall leave the important question, which is to the side of the present issue, of the obligations, if any, that nest round the word 'know': how far does one, under utilitarianism, have to research into the possibilities of maximally beneficent action, including prevention?)

In the present cases, the situation of O_2 includes another agent bringing about results worse than O_1. So far as O_2 has been identified up to this point—merely as the worse outcome which will eventuate if I refrain from doing X—we might equally have said that what that other brings about is O_2; but that would be to underdescribe the situation. For what occurs if Jim refrains from action is not solely twenty Indians dead, but *Pedro's killing twenty Indians,* and that is not a result which Pedro brings about, though the death of the Indians is. We can say: what one does is not included in the outcome of what one does, while what another does can be included in the outcome of what one does. For that to be so, as the terms are now being used, only a very weak condition has to be satisfied: for Pedro's killing the Indians to be the outcome of Jim's refusal, it only has to be causally true that if Jim had not refused, Pedro would not have done it.

That may be enough for us to speak, in some sense, of Jim's responsibility for that outcome, if it occurs; but it is certainly not enough, it is worth noticing, for us to speak of Jim's *making* those things happen. For granted this way of their coming about, he could have made them happen only by making Pedro shoot, and there is no acceptable sense in which his refusal makes Pedro shoot. If the captain had said on Jim's refusal, 'you leave me with no alternative,' he would have been lying, like most who use that phrase. While the deaths, and the killing, may be the outcome of Jim's refusal, it is misleading to think, in such a case, of Jim having an *effect* on the world through the medium (as it happens) of Pedro's acts; for this is to leave Pedro out of the picture in his

essential role of one who has intentions and projects, projects for realizing which Jim's refusal would leave an opportunity. Instead of thinking in terms of supposed effects of Jim's projects on Pedro, it is more revealing to think in terms of the effects of Pedro's projects on Jim's decision. This is the direction from which I want to criticize the notion of negative responsibility.

There are of course other ways in which this notion can be criticized. Many have hoped to discredit it by insisting on the basic moral relevance of the distinction between action and inaction, between intervening and letting things take their course. The distinction is certainly of great moral significance, and indeed it is not easy to think of any moral outlook which could get along without making some use of it. But it is unclear, both in itself and in its moral applications, and the unclarities are of a kind which precisely cause it to give way when, in very difficult cases, weight has to be put on it. There is much to be said in this area, but I doubt whether the sort of dilemma we are considering is going to be resolved by a simple use of this distinction. Again, the issue of negative responsibility can be pressed on the question of how limits are to be placed on one's apparently boundless obligation, implied by utilitarianism, to improve the world. Some answers are needed to that, too—and answers which stop short of relapsing into the bad faith of supposing that one's responsibilities could be adequately characterized just by appeal to one's roles.[1] But, once again, while that is a real question, it cannot be brought to bear directly on the present kind of case, since it is hard to think of anyone supposing that in Jim's case it would be an adequate response for him to say that it was none of his business.

What projects does a utilitarian agent have? As a utilitarian, he has the general project of bringing about maximally desirable outcomes; how he is to do this at any given moment is a question of what causal levers, so to speak, are at that moment within reach. The desirable outcomes, however, do not just consist of agents carrying out *that* project; there must be other more basic or lower-order projects which he and other agents have, and the desirable outcomes

---

1. For some remarks bearing on this, see *Morality,* the section on 'Goodness and roles,' and Cohen's article there cited.

are going to consist, in part, of the maximally harmonious realization of those projects ('in part,' because one component of a utilitarianly desirable outcome may be the occurrence of agreeable experiences which are not the satisfaction of anybody's projects). Unless there were first-order projects, the general utilitarian project would have nothing to work on, and would be vacuous. What do the more basic or lower-order projects comprise? Many will be the obvious kinds of desires for things for oneself, one's family, one's friends, including basic necessities of life, and in more relaxed circumstances, objects of taste. Or there may be pursuits and interests of an intellectual, cultural or creative character. I introduce those as a separate class not because the objects of them lie in a separate class, and provide—as some utilitarians, in their churchy way, are fond of saying—'higher' pleasures. I introduce them separately because the agent's identification with them may be of a different order. It does not have to be: cultural and aesthetic interests just belong, for many, along with any other taste; but some people's commitment to these kinds of interests just is at once more thoroughgoing and serious than their pursuit of various objects of taste, while it is more individual and permeated with character than the desire for the necessities of life.

Beyond these, someone may have projects connected with his support of some cause: Zionism, for instance, or the abolition of chemical and biological warfare. Or there may be projects which flow from some more general disposition towards human conduct and character, such as a hatred of injustice, or of cruelty, or of killing.

It may be said that this last sort of disposition and its associated project do not count as (logically) 'lower-order' relative to the higher-order project of maximizing desirable outcomes; rather, it may be said, it is itself a 'higher-order' project. The vital question is not, however, how it is to be classified, but whether it and similar projects are to count among the projects whose satisfaction is to be included in the maximizing sum, and, correspondingly, as contributing to the agent's happiness. If the utilitarian says 'no' to that, then he is almost certainly committed to a version of utilitarianism as absurdly superficial and shallow as Benthamite versions have often been accused of being. For this project will be discounted, presumably, on the ground that it involves,

in the specification of its object, the mention of other people's happiness or interests: thus it is the kind of project which (unlike the pursuit of food for myself) presupposes a reference to other people's projects. But that criterion would eliminate any desire at all which was not blankly and in the most straightforward sense egoistic.[1] Thus we should be reduced to frankly egoistic first-order projects, and—for all essential purposes—the one second-order utilitarian project of maximally satisfying first-order projects. Utilitarianism has a tendency to slide in this direction, and to leave a vast hole in the range of human desires, between egoistic inclinations and necessities at one end, and impersonally benevolent happiness-management at the other. But the utilitarianism which has to leave this hole is the most primitive form, which offers a quite rudimentary account of desire. Modern versions of the theory are supposed to be neutral with regard to what sorts of things make people happy or what their projects are. Utilitarianism would do well then to acknowledge the evident fact that among the things that make people happy is not only making other people happy, but being taken up or involved in any of a vast range of projects, or—if we waive the evangelical and moralizing associations of the word—commitments. One can be committed to such things as a person, a cause, an institution, a career, one's own genius, or the pursuit of danger.

Now none of these is itself the *pursuit of happiness:* by an exceedingly ancient platitude, it is not at all clear that there could be anything which was just that, or at least anything that had the slightest chance of being successful. Happiness, rather, requires being involved in, or at least content with, something else.[2] It is not impossible for utilitarian-

---

1. On the subject of egoistic and non-egoistic desires, see 'Egoism and altruism,' in *Problems of the Self* (Cambridge University Press, London, 1973).

2. This does not imply that there is no such thing as the project of pursuing pleasure. Some writers who have correctly resisted the view that all desires are desires for pleasure, have given an account of pleasure so thoroughly adverbial as to leave it quite unclear how there could be a distinctively hedonist way of life at all. Some room has to be left for that, though there are important difficulties both in defining it and living it. Thus (particularly in the case of the very rich) it often has highly ritual aspects, apparently part of a strategy to counter boredom.

ism to accept that point: it does not have to be saddled with a naïve and absurd philosophy of mind about the relation between desire and happiness. What it does have to say is that if such commitments are worth while, then pursuing the projects that flow from them, and realizing some of those projects, will make the person for whom they are worth while, happy. It may be that to claim that is still wrong: it may well be that a commitment can make sense to a man (can make sense of his life) without his supposing that it will make him *happy*.[1] But that is not the present point; let us grant to utilitarianism that all worthwhile human projects must conduce, one way or another, to happiness. The point is that even if that is true, it does not follow, nor could it possibly be true, that those projects are themselves projects of pursuing happiness. One has to believe in, or at least want, or quite minimally, be content with, other things, for there to be anywhere that happiness can come from.

Utilitarianism, then, should be willing to agree that its general aim of maximizing happiness does not imply that what everyone is doing is just pursuing happiness. On the contrary, people have to be pursuing other things. What those other things may be, utilitarianism, sticking to its professed empirical stance, should be prepared just to find out. No doubt some possible projects it will want to discourage, on the grounds that their being pursued involves a negative balance of happiness to others: though even there, the unblinking accountant's eye of the strict utilitarian will have something to put in the positive column, the satisfactions of the destructive agent. Beyond that, there will be a vast variety of generally beneficent or at least harmless projects; and some no doubt, will take the form not just of tastes or fancies, but of what I have called 'commitments.' It may even be that the utilitarian researcher will find that many of those with commitments, who have really identified themselves with objects outside themselves, who are thoroughly involved with other persons, or institutions, or activities or causes, are actually happier than those whose projects and wants are not like that. If so, that is an important piece of utilitarian empirical lore.

When I say 'happier' here, I have in mind the sort of consideration which any utilitarian would be committed to accepting: as for instance that such people are less likely to have a break-down or commit suicide. Of course that is not all that is actually involved, but the point in this argument is to use to the maximum degree utilitarian notions, in order to locate a breaking point in utilitarian thought. In appealing to this strictly utilitarian notion, I am being more consistent with utilitarianism than Smart is. In his struggles with the problem of the brain-electrode man, Smart commends the idea that 'happy' is a partly evaluative term, in the sense that we call 'happiness' those kinds of satisfaction which, as things are, we approve of. But *by what standard* is this surplus element of approval supposed, from a utilitarian point of view, to be allocated? There is no source for it, on a strictly utilitarian view, except further degrees of satisfaction, but there are none of those available, or the problem would not arise. Nor does it help to appeal to the fact that we dislike in prospect things which we like when we get there, for from a utilitarian point of view it would seem that the original dislike was merely irrational or based on an error. Smart's argument at this point seems to be embarrassed by a well-known utilitarian uneasiness, which comes from a feeling that it is not respectable to ignore the 'deep,' while not having anywhere left in human life to locate it.[2]

Let us now go back to the agent as utilitarian, and his higher-order project of maximizing desirable outcomes. At this level, he is committed only to that: what the outcome will actually consist of will depend entirely on the facts, on what persons with what projects and what potential satisfactions there are within calculable reach of the causal levers near which he finds himself. His own substantial projects and commitments come into it, but only as one lot among others—they potentially provide one set of satisfactions among those which he may be able to assist from where he happens to be. He is the agent of the satisfaction system who happens to be at a particular point at a particular time: in Jim's case, our man in South America. His own decisions as a utilitarian agent are a function of all the satisfactions which he can affect from where he is: and this means that the projects of others, to an indeterminately great extent, determine his decision.

---

1. For some remarks on this possibility, see *Morality,* section on 'What is morality about?'

2. One of many resemblances in spirit between utilitarianism and high-minded evangelical Christianity.

This may be so either positively or negatively. It will be so positively if agents within the causal field of his decision have projects which are at any rate harmless, and so should be assisted. It will equally be so, but negatively, if there is an agent within the causal field whose projects are harmful, and have to be frustrated to maximize desirable outcomes. So it is with Jim and the soldier Pedro. On the utilitarian view, the undesirable projects of other people as much determine, in this negative way, one's decisions as the desirable ones do positively: if those people were not there, or had different projects, the causal nexus would be different, and it is the actual state of the causal nexus which determines the decision. The determination to an indefinite degree of my decisions by other people's projects is just another aspect of my unlimited responsibility to act for the best in a casual framework formed to a considerable extent by their projects.

The decision so determined is, for utilitarianism, the right decision. But what if it conflicts with some project of mine? This, the utilitarian will say, has already been dealt with: the satisfaction to you of fulfilling your project, and any satisfactions to others of your so doing, have already been through the calculating device and have been found inadequate. Now in the case of many sorts of projects, that is a perfectly reasonable sort of answer. But in the case of projects of the sort I have called 'commitments,' those with which one is more deeply and extensively involved and identified, this cannot just by itself be an adequate answer, and there may be no adequate answer at all. For, to take the extreme sort of case, how can a man, as a utilitarian agent, come to regard as one satisfaction among others, and a dispensable one, a project or attitude round which he has built his life, just because someone else's projects have so structured the causal scene that that is how the utilitarian sum comes out?

The point here is not, as utilitarians may hasten to say, that if the project or attitude is that central to his life, then to abandon it will be very disagreeable to him and great loss of utility will be involved. I have already argued in section 4 that it is not like that; on the contrary, once he is prepared to look at it like that, the argument in any serious case is over anyway. The point is that he is identified with his actions as flowing from projects and attitudes which in some cases he takes seriously at the deepest level, as what

his life is about (or, in some cases, this section of his life—seriousness is not necessarily the same as persistence). It is absurd to demand of such a man, when the sums come in from the utility network which the projects of others have in part determined, that he should just step aside from his own project and decision and acknowledge the decision which utilitarian calculation requires. It is to alienate him in a real sense from his actions and the source of his action in his own convictions. It is to make him into a channel between the input of everyone's projects, including his own, and an output of optimific decision; but this is to neglect the extent to which *his* actions and *his* decisions have to be seen as the actions and decisions which flow from the projects and attitudes with which he is most closely identified. It is thus, in the most literal sense, an attack on his integrity.[1]

These sorts of considerations do not in themselves give solutions to practical dilemmas such as those provided by our examples; but I hope they help to provide other ways of thinking about them. In fact, it is not hard to see that in George's case, viewed from this perspective, the utilitarian solution would be wrong. Jim's case is different, and harder. But if (as I suppose) the utilitarian is probably right in this case, that is not to be found out just by asking the utilitarian's questions. Discussions of it—and I am not going to try to carry it further here—will have to take seriously the distinction between my killing someone, and its coming about because of what I do that someone else kills them: a distinction based, not so much on the distinction between action and inaction, as on the distinction between my projects and someone else's projects. At least it will have to start by taking that seriously, as utilitarianism does not; but then it will have to build out from there by asking why that distinction seems to have less, or a different, force in this case than it has in George's. One question here would be how far one's powerful objection to killing people just is, in fact,

---

1. Interestingly related to these notions is the Socratic idea that courage is a virtue particularly connected with keeping a clear sense of what one regards as most important. They do centrally raise questions about the value of pride. Humility, as something beyond the real demand of correct self-appraisal, was specially a Christian virtue because it involved subservience to God. In a secular context it can only represent subservience to other men and their projects.

an application of a powerful objection to their being killed. Another dimension of that is the issue of how much it matters that the people at risk are actual, and there, as opposed to hypothetical, or future, or merely elsewhere.1

There are many other considerations that could come into such a question, but the immediate point of all this is to draw one particular contrast with utilitarianism: that to reach a grounded decision in such a case should not be regarded as a matter of just discounting one's reactions, impulses and deeply held projects in the face of the pattern of utilities, nor yet merely adding them in—but in the first instance of trying to understand them.

Of course, time and circumstances are unlikely to make a grounded decision, in Jim's case at least, pos-

sible. It might not even be decent. Instead of thinking in a rational and systematic way either about utilities or about the value of human life, the relevance of the people at risk being present, and so forth, the presence of the people at risk may just have its effect. The significance of the immediate should not be underestimated. Philosophers, not only utilitarian ones, repeatedly urge one to view the world *sub specie aeternitatis*,[2] but for most human purposes that is not a good *species* to view it under. If we are not agents of the universal satisfaction system, we are not primarily janitors of any system of values, even our own: very often, we just act, as a possibly confused result of the situation in which we are engaged. That, I suspect, is very often an exceedingly good thing. To what extent utilitarians regard it as a good thing is an obscure question. To that sort of question I now turn.

---

1. For a more general discussion of this issue see Charles Fried, *An Anatomy of Values* (Harvard University Press, Cambridge, Mass., 1970), Part Three.

---

2. Cf. Smart.

DAVID GAUTHIER

Morality and Advantage

David Gauthier, professor of philosophy at the University of Pittsburgh, defends a social contract theory in his 1986 book Morals by Agreement. *For social contract theory, morality results from following the rules necessary for a well-functioning society. Therefore, the theory is interested in the interplay of social forces that could produce a justifiable system of rules. Social contract theory has its primary historical foundation in the work of Thomas Hobbes.*

The work of Hobbes provides the starting point for Gauthier's article "Morality and Advantage" published in 1976. Here, Gauthier explores the seemingly paradoxical relationship of morality to the true interest of the individual: a paradox, says Gauthier, that Hobbes noticed but failed to resolve. Employing a version of the Prisoner's Dilemma, a hypothetical situation used in decision theory, Gauthier demonstrates that acting in our best interests sometimes requires acting immorally.

"Morality and Advantage" demonstrates one of the ways that contributions in other fields can be useful for ethical theory. Decision theory, the result of joint efforts by economists, philosophers, mathematicians, and social scientists, examines decision-making in both its descriptive and normative aspects. As a descriptive endeavor, decision theory studies how people make decisions. As a normative study, decision theory explores the kinds of decisions rational people ought to make. It is particularly as a normative study that decision theory has many applications to ethics.

For another article relevant to social contract theory, see the excerpt from A Theory of Justice *by John Rawls.*

I

Hume asks, rhetorically, "what theory of morals can ever serve any useful purpose, unless it can show, by a particular detail, that all the duties which it recommends, are also the true interest of each individual?"[1] But there are many to whom this question does not seem rhetorical. Why, they ask, do we speak the language of morality, impressing upon our fellows their duties and obligations, urging them with appeals to what is right and good, if we could speak to the same effect in the language of prudence, appealing to considerations of interest and advantage? When the poet, Ogden Nash, is moved by the muse to cry out:

O Duty,
Why hast thou not the visage of a sweetie or a cutie ?[2]

we do not anticipate the reply:

O Poet,
I really am a cutie and I think you ought to know it.

The belief that duty cannot be reduced to interest, or that morality may require the agent to subordinate all considerations of advantage, is one which has withstood the assaults of contrary-minded philosophers from Plato to the present. Indeed, were it not for the conviction that only interest and advantage can motivate human actions, it would be difficult to understand philosophers contending so vigorously for the identity, or at least compatibility, of morality with prudence.

Yet if morality is not true prudence it would be wrong to suppose that those philosophers who have sought some connection between morality and advantage have been merely misguided. For it is a truism that we should all expect to be worse off if men were to substitute prudence, even of the most enlightened kind, for morality in all of their deliberations. And this truism demands not only some connection between morality and advantage, but a seemingly paradoxical connection. For if we should all expect to suffer, were men to be prudent instead of moral, then morality must contribute to advantage in a unique way, a way in which prudence—following reasons of advantage—cannot.

Thomas Hobbes is perhaps the first philosopher who tried to develop this seemingly paradoxical connection between morality and advantage. But since he could not admit that a man might ever reasonably subordinate considerations of advantage to the dictates of obligation, he was led to deny the possibility of real conflict between morality and prudence. So his argument fails to clarify the distinction between the view that claims of obligation reduce to considerations of interest and the view that claims of obligation promote advantage in a way in which considerations of interest cannot.

---

1. David Hume, *An Enquiry Concerning the Principles of Morals,* sec. ix, pt. ii.

2. Ogden Nash, "Kind of an Ode to Duty."

More recently, Kurt Baier has argued that "being moral is following rules designed to overrule self-interest whenever it is in the interest of everyone alike that everyone should set aside his interest."[3] Since prudence is following rules of (enlightened) self-interest, Baier is arguing that morality is designed to overrule prudence when it is to everyone's advantage that it do so—or, in other words, that morality contributes to advantage in a way in which prudence cannot.[4]

Baier does not actually demonstrate that morality contributes to advantage in this unique and seemingly paradoxical way. Indeed, he does not ask how it is possible that morality should do this. It is this possibility which I propose to demonstrate.

II

Let us examine the following proposition, which will be referred to as "the thesis": *Morality is a system of principles such that it is advantageous for everyone if everyone accepts and acts on it, yet acting on the system of principles requires that some persons perform disadvantageous acts.*[5]

What I wish to show is that this thesis *could be true,* that morality could possess those characteristics attributed to it by the thesis. I shall not try to show that the thesis is true-indeed, I shall argue in Section V that it presents at best an inadequate conception of morality. But it is plausible to suppose that a modified form of the thesis states a necessary, although not a sufficient, condition for a moral system.

Two phrases in the thesis require elucidation. The first is "advantageous for everyone." I use this phrase to mean that *each* person will do better if the system is accepted and acted on than if *either* no system is accepted and acted on *or* a system is accepted and

acted on which is similar, save that it never requires any person to perform disadvantageous acts.

Clearly, then, the claim that it is advantageous for everyone to accept and act on the system is a very strong one; it may be so strong that no system of principles which might be generally adopted could meet it. But I shall consider in Section V one among the possible ways of weakening the claim.

The second phrase requiring elucidation is "disadvantageous acts." I use this phrase to refer to acts which, in the context of their performance, would be less advantageous to the performer than some other act open to him in the same context. The phrase does not refer to acts which merely impose on the performer some short-term disadvantage that is recouped or outweighed in the long run. Rather it refers to acts which impose a disadvantage that is never recouped. It follows that the performer may say to himself, when confronted with the requirement to perform such an act, that it would be better *for him* not to perform it.

It is essential to note that the thesis, as elucidated, does not maintain that morality is advantageous for everyone in the sense that each person will do *best* if the system of principles is accepted and acted on. Each person will do better than if no system is adopted, or than if the one particular alternative mentioned above is adopted, but not than if any alternative is adopted.

Indeed, for each person required by the system to perform some disadvantageous act, it is easy to specify a better alternative—namely, the system modified so that it does not require *him* to perform any act disadvantageous to himself. Of course, there is no reason to expect such an alternative to be better than the moral system for everyone, or in fact for anyone other than the person granted the special exemption.

A second point to note is that each person must gain more from the disadvantageous acts performed by others than he loses from the disadvantageous acts performed by himself. If this were not the case, then some person would do better if a system were adopted exactly like the moral system save that it never requires *any* person to perform disadvantageous acts. This is ruled out by the force of "advantageous for everyone."

This point may be clarified by an example. Suppose that the system contains exactly one principle. Everyone is always to tell the truth. It follows

---

3. Kurt Baier, *The Moral Point of View: A Rational Basis of Ethics* (Ithaca, 1958), p. 314.

4. That this, and only this, is what he is entitled to claim may not be clear to Baier, for he supposes his account of morality to answer the question "Why should we be moral?," interpreting "we" distributively. This, I shall argue in Sec. IV, is quite mistaken.

5. The thesis is not intended to state Baier's view of morality. I shall suggest in Sec. V that Baier's view would require substituting "everyone can expect to benefit" for ' it is advantageous to everyone." The thesis is stronger and easier to discuss.

from the thesis that each person gains more from those occasions on which others tell the truth, even though it is disadvantageous to them to do so, than he loses from those occasions on which he tells the truth even though it is disadvantageous to him to do so.

Now this is not to say that each person gains by telling others the truth in order to ensure that in return they tell him the truth. Such gains would merely be the result of accepting certain short-term disadvantages (those associated with truth-telling) in order to reap long-term benefits (those associated with being told the truth). Rather, what is required by the thesis is that those disadvantages which a person incurs in telling the truth, when he can expect neither short-term nor long-term benefits to accrue to him from truth-telling, are outweighed by those advantages he receives when others tell him the truth when they can expect no benefits to accrue to them from truth-telling.

The principle enjoins truth-telling in those cases in which whether one tells the truth or not will have no effect on whether others tell the truth. Such cases include those in which others have no way of knowing whether or not they are being told the truth. The thesis requires that the disadvantages one incurs in telling the truth in these cases are less than the advantages one receives in being told the truth by others in parallel cases; and the thesis requires that this holds for everyone.

Thus we see that although the disadvantages imposed by the system on any person are less than the advantages secured him through the imposition of disadvantages on others, yet the disadvantages are real in that incurring them is *unrelated* to receiving the advantages. The argument of long-term prudence, that I ought to incur some immediate disadvantage *so that* I shall receive compensating advantages later on, is entirely inapplicable here.

III

It will be useful to examine in some detail an example of a system which possesses those characteristics ascribed by the thesis to morality. This example, abstracted from the field of international relations, will enable us more clearly to distinguish, first, conduct based on immediate interest; second, conduct which is truly prudent; and third, conduct which promotes mutual advantage but is not prudent.

A and *B* are two nations with substantially opposed interests, who find themselves engaged in an arms race against each other. Both possess the latest in weaponry, so that each recognizes that the actual outbreak of full-scale war between them would be mutually disastrous. This recognition leads *A* and *B* to agree that each would be better off if they were mutually disarming instead of mutually arming. For mutual disarmament would preserve the balance of power between them while reducing the risk of war.

Hence *A* and *B* enter into a disarmament pact. The pact is advantageous for both if both accept and act on it, although clearly it is not advantageous for either to act on it if the other does not.

Let *A* be considering whether or not to adhere to the pact in some particular situation, whether or not actually to perform some act of disarmament. *A* will quite likely consider the act to have disadvantageous consequences. *A* expects to benefit, not by its own acts of disarmament, but by *B*'s acts. Hence if *A* were to reason simply in terms of immediate interest, *A* might well decide to violate the pact.

But *A*'s decision need be neither prudent nor reasonable. For suppose first that *B* is able to determine whether or not *A* adheres to the pact. If *A* violates, then *B* will detect the violation and will then consider what to do in the light of *A*'s behavior. It is not to *B*'s advantage to disarm alone; *B* expects to gain, not by its own acts of disarmament, but by *A*'s acts. Hence *A*'s violation, if known to *B*, leads naturally to *B*'s counter-violation. If this continues, the effect of the pact is entirely undone, and *A* and *B* return to their mutually disadvantageous arms race. *A*, foreseeing this when considering whether or not to adhere to the pact in the given situation, must therefore conclude that the truly prudent course of action is to adhere.

Now suppose that *B* is unable to determine whether or not *A* adheres to the pact in the particular situation under consideration. If *A* judges adherence to be in itself disadvantageous, then it will decide, both on the basis of immediate interest and on the basis of prudence, to violate the pact. Since *A*'s decision is unknown to *B*, it cannot affect whether or not *B* adheres to the pact, and so the advantage gained by *A*'s violation is not outweighed by any consequent loss.

Therefore if *A* and *B* are prudent they will adhere to their disarmament pact whenever violation would be detectable by the other, and violate the pact whenever violation would not be detectable by the other. In other words, they will adhere openly and violate secretly. The disarmament pact between *A* and *B* thus possesses two of the characteristics ascribed by the thesis to morality. First, accepting the pact and acting on it is more advantageous for each than making no pact at all. Second, in so far as the pact stipulates that each must disarm even when disarming is undetectable by the other, it requires each to perform disadvantageous acts—acts which run counter to considerations of prudence.

One further condition must be met if the disarmament pact is to possess those characteristics ascribed by the thesis to a system of morality. It must be the case that the requirement that each party perform disadvantageous acts be essential to the advantage conferred by the pact; or, to put the matter in the way in which we expressed it earlier, both *A* and *B* must do better to adhere to this pact than to a pact which is similar save that it requires no disadvantageous acts. In terms of the example, *A* and *B* must do better to adhere to the pact than to a pact which stipulates that each must disarm only when disarming is detectable by the other.

We may plausibly suppose this condition to be met. Although *A* will gain by secretly retaining arms itself, it will lose by *B*'s similar acts, and its losses may well outweigh its gains. *B* may equally lose more by *A*'s secret violations than it gains by its own. So, despite the fact that prudence requires each to violate secretly, each may well do better if both adhere secretly than if both violate secretly. Supposing this to be the case, the disarmament pact is formally analogous to a moral system, as characterized by the thesis. That is, acceptance of and adherence to the pact by *A* and *B* is more advantageous for each, either than making no pact at all or than acceptance of and adherence to a pact requiring only open disarmament, and the pact requires each to perform acts of secret disarmament which are disadvantageous.

Some elementary notation, adapted for our purposes from the mathematical theory of games, may make the example even more perspicuous. Given a disarmament pact between *A* and *B*, each may pursue two pure strategies—adherence and violation. There are, then, four possible combinations of strategies, each determining a particular outcome. These outcomes can be ranked preferentially for each na-

tion; we shall let the numerals 1 to 4 represent the ranking from first to fourth preference. Thus we construct a simple matrix,[6] in which *A*'s preferences are stated first:

		B	
		adheres	*violates*
	adheres	2, 2	4, 1
A			
	violates	1, 4	3, 3

The matrix does not itself show that agreement is advantageous to both, for it gives only the rankings of outcomes given the agreement. But it is plausible to assume that *A* and *B* would rank mutual violation on a par with no agreement. If we assume this, we can then indicate the value to each of making and adhering to the pact by reference to the matrix.

The matrix shows immediately that adherence to the pact is not the most advantageous possibility for either, since each prefers the outcome, if it alone violates, to the outcome of mutual adherence. It shows also that each gains less from its own violations than it loses from the other's, since each ranks mutual adherence above mutual violation.

Let us now use the matrix to show that, as we argued previously, public adherence to the pact is prudent and mutually advantageous, whereas private adherence is not prudent although mutually advantageous. Consider first the case when adherence—and so violation—are open and public.

If adherence and violation are open, then each knows the strategy chosen by the other, and can adjust its own strategy in the light of this knowledge—or, in other words, the strategies are interdependent. Suppose that each initially chooses the strategy of adherence. *A* notices that if it switches to violation it gains moving from 2 to 1 in terms of preference ranking. Hence immediate interest dictates such a switch. But it notices further that if it switches, then *B* can also be expected to switch—moving from 4 to 3 on its preference scale. The eventual outcome

---

6. Those familiar with the theory of games will recognize the matrix as a variant of the Prisoner's Dilemma. In a more formal treatment, it would be appropriate to develop the relation between morality and advantage by reference to the Prisoner's Dilemma. This would require reconstructing the disarmament pact and the moral system as proper games. Here I wish only to suggest the bearing of game theory on our enterprise.

would be stable, in that neither could benefit from switching from violation back to adherence. But the eventual outcome would represent not a gain for A but a loss—moving from 2 to 3 on its preference scale. Hence prudence dictates no change from the strategy of adherence. This adherence is mutually advantageous; A and B are in precisely similar positions in terms of their pact.

Consider now the case when adherence and violation are secret and private. Neither nation knows the strategy chosen by the other, so the two strategies are independent. Suppose A is trying to decide which strategy to follow. It does not know B's choice. But it notices that if B adheres, then it pays A to violate, attaining 1 rather than 2 in terms of preference ranking. If B violates, then again it pays A to violate, attaining 3 rather than 4 on its preference scale. Hence, no matter which strategy B chooses, A will do better to violate, and so prudence dictates violation.

B of course reasons in just the same way. Hence each is moved by considerations of prudence to violate the pact, and the outcome assigns each rank 3 on its preference scale. This outcome is mutually disadvantageous to A and B, since mutual adherence would assign each rank 2 on its preference scale.

If A and B are both capable only of rational prudence, they find themselves at an impasse. The advantage of mutual adherence to the agreement when violations would be secret is not available to them, since neither can find it in his own over-all interest not to violate secretly. Hence, strictly prudent nations cannot reap the maximum advantage possible from a pact of the type under examination.

Of course, what A and B will no doubt endeavor to do is eliminate the possibility of secret violations of their pact. Indeed, barring additional complications, each must find it to his advantage to make it possible for the other to detect his own violations. In other words, each must find it advantageous to ensure that their choice of strategies is interdependent, so that the pact will always be prudent for each to keep. But it may not be possible for them to ensure this, and to the extent that they cannot, prudence will prevent them from maximizing mutual advantage.

IV

We may now return to the connection of morality with advantage. Morality, if it is a system of principles of the type characterized in the thesis, requires that some persons perform acts genuinely disadvantageous to themselves, as a means to greater mutual advantage. Our example shows sufficiently that such a system is possible, and indicates more precisely its character. In particular, by an argument strictly parallel to that which we have pursued, we may show that men who are merely prudent will not perform the required disadvantageous acts. But in so violating the principles of morality, they will disadvantage themselves. Each will lose more by the violations of others than he will gain by his own violations.

Now this conclusion would be unsurprising if it were only that no man can gain if he alone is moral rather than prudent. Obviously such a man loses, for he adheres to moral principles to his own disadvantage, while others violate them also to his disadvantage. The benefit of the moral system is not one which any individual can secure for himself, since each man gains from the sacrifices of others.

What is surprising in our conclusion is that no man can ever gain if he is moral. Not only does he not gain by being moral if others are prudent, but he also does not gain by being moral if others are moral. For although he now receives the advantage of others' adherence to moral principles, he reaps the disadvantage of his own adherence. As long as his own adherence to morality is independent of what others do (and this is required to distinguish morality from prudence), he must do better to be prudent.

If all men are moral, all will do better than if all are prudent. But any one man will always do better if he is prudent than if he is moral. There is no real paradox in supposing that morality is advantageous, even though it requires the performance of disadvantageous acts.

On the supposition that morality has the characteristics ascribed to it by the thesis, is it possible to answer the question "Why should we be moral?" where "we" is taken distributively, so that the question is a compendious way of asking, for each person, "Why should I be moral?" More simply, is it possible to answer the question "Why should I be moral?"

I take it that this question, if asked seriously, demands a reason for being moral other than moral reasons themselves. It demands that moral reasons be shown to be reasons for acting by a noncircular argument. Those who would answer it, like Baier, endeavor to do so by the introduction of considerations of advantage.

Two such considerations have emerged from our discussion. The first is that if all are moral, all will do better than if all are prudent. This will serve to answer the question "Why should we be moral?" if this question is interpreted rather as "Why should we all be moral—rather than all being something else?" If we must all be the same, then each person has a reason—a prudential reason—to prefer that we all be moral.

But, so interpreted, "Why should we be moral?" is not a compendious way of asking, for each person, "Why should I be moral?" Of course, if everyone is to be whatever I am, then I should be moral. But a general answer to the question "Why should I be moral?" cannot presuppose this.

The second consideration is that any individual always does better to be prudent rather than moral, provided his choice does not determine other choices. But in so far as this answers the question "Why should I be moral?" it leads to the conclusion "I should not be moral." One feels that this is not the answer which is wanted.

We may put the matter otherwise. The individual who needs a reason for being moral which is not itself a moral reason cannot have it. There is nothing surprising about this; it would be much more surprising if such reasons could be found. For it is more than apparently paradoxical to suppose that considerations of advantage could ever of themselves justify accepting a real disadvantage.

V

I suggested in Section II that the thesis, in modified form, might provide a necessary, although not a sufficient, condition for a moral system. I want now to consider how one might characterize the man who would qualify as moral according to the thesis—I shall call him the "moral" man—and then ask what would be lacking from this characterization, in terms of some of our commonplace moral views.

The rationally prudent man is incapable of moral behavior, in even the limited sense defined by the thesis. What difference must there be between the prudent man and the "moral" man? Most simply, the "moral" man is the prudent but trustworthy man. I treat trustworthiness as the capacity which enables its possessor to adhere, and to judge that he ought to adhere, to a commitment which he has made, without regard to considerations of advantage.

The prudent but trustworthy man does not possess this capacity completely. He is capable of trustworthy behavior only in so far as he regards his *commitment* as advantageous. Thus he differs from the prudent man just in the relevant respect; he accepts arguments of the form "If it is advantageous for me to agree[7] to do x, and I do agree to do x, then I ought to do x, whether or not it then proves advantageous for me to do x."

Suppose that A and B, the parties to the disarmament pact, are prudent but trustworthy. A, considering whether or not secretly to violate the agreement, reasons that its advantage in making and keeping the agreement, provided B does so as well, is greater than its advantage in not making it. If it can assume that B reasons in the same way, then it is in a position to conclude that it ought not to violate the pact. Although violation would be advantageous, consideration of this advantage is ruled out by A's trustworthiness, given the advantage in agreeing to the pact.

The prudent but trustworthy man meets the requirements implicitly imposed by the thesis for the "moral" man. But how far does this "moral" man display two characteristics commonly associated with morality—first, a willingness to make sacrifices, and second, a concern with fairness?

Whenever a man ignores his own advantage for reasons other than those of greater advantage, he may be said to make some sacrifice. The "moral" man, in being trustworthy, is thus required to make certain sacrifices. But these are extremely limited. And—not surprisingly, given the general direction of our argument—it is quite possible that they limit the advantages which the "moral" man can secure.

Once more let us turn to our example. A and B have entered into a disarmament agreement and,

---

7. The word "agree" requires elucidation. It is essential not to confuse an advantage in agreeing to do x with an advantage in saying that one will do x. If it is advantageous for me to agree to do x, then there is some set of actions open to me which includes both saying that I will do x and doing x, and which is more advantageous to me than any set of actions open to me which does not include saying that I will do x. On the other hand, if it is advantageous for me to say that I will do x, then there is some set of actions open to me which includes saying that I will do x, and which is more advantageous to me than any set which does not include saying that I will do x. But this set need not include doing x.

being prudent but trustworthy, are faithfully carrying it out. The government of *A* is now informed by its scientists, however, that they have developed an effective missile defense, which will render *A* invulnerable to attack by any of the weapons actually or potentially at *B*'s disposal, barring unforeseen technological developments. Furthermore, this defense can be installed secretly. The government is now called upon to decide whether to violate its agreement with *B*, install the new defense, and, with the arms it has retained through its violation, establish its dominance over *B*.

A is in a type of situation quite different from that previously considered. For it is not just that *A* will do better by secretly violating its agreement. *A* reasons not only that it will do better to violate no matter what *B* does, but that it will do better if both violate than if both continue to adhere to the pact. *A* is now in a position to gain from abandoning the agreement; it no longer finds mutual adherence advantageous.

We may represent this new situation in another matrix:

		B	
		adheres	*violates*
	adheres	3, 2	4, 1
A			
	violates	1, 4	2, 3

We assume again that the ranking of mutual violation is the same as that of no agreement. Now had this situation obtained at the outset, no agreement would have been made, for *A* would have had no reason to enter into a disarmament pact. And of course had *A* expected this situation to come about, no agreement—or only a temporary agreement—would have been made; *A* would no doubt have risked the short-term dangers of the continuing arms race in the hope of securing the long-run benefit of predominance over *B* once its missile defense was completed. On the contrary, *A* expected to benefit from the agreement, but now finds that, because of its unexpected development of a missile defense, the agreement is not in fact advantageous to it.

The prudent but trustworthy man is willing to carry out his agreements, and judges that he ought to carry them out, in so far as he considers them advantageous. *A* is prudent but trustworthy. But is *A* willing to carry out its agreement to disarm, now that it no longer considers the agreement advantageous?

If *A* adheres to its agreement in this situation, it makes a sacrifice greater than any advantage it receives from the similar sacrifices of others. It makes a sacrifice greater in kind than any which can be required by a mutually advantageous agreement. It must, then, possess a capacity for trustworthy behavior greater than that ascribed to the merely prudent but trustworthy man (or nation). This capacity need not be unlimited; it need not extend to a willingness to adhere to any commitment no matter what sacrifice is involved. But it must involve a willingness to adhere to a commitment made in the expectation of advantage, should that expectation be disappointed.

I shall call the man (or nation) who is willing to adhere, and judges that he ought to adhere, to his prudentially undertaken agreements even if they prove disadvantageous to him, the trustworthy man. It is likely that there are advantages available to trustworthy men which are not available to merely prudent but trustworthy men. For there may be situations in which men can make agreements which each expects to be advantageous to him, provided he can count on the others' adhering to it whether or not their expectation of advantage is realized. But each can count on this only if all have the capacity to adhere to commitments regardless of whether the commitment actually proves advantageous. Hence, only trustworthy men who know each other to be such will be able rationally to enter into, and so to benefit from, such agreements.

Baier's view of morality departs from that stated in the thesis in that it requires trustworthy, and not merely prudent but trustworthy, men. Baier admits that "a person might do better for himself by following enlightened self-interest rather than morality."[8] This admission seems to require that morality be a system of principles which each person may expect, initially, to be advantageous to him, if adopted and adhered to by everyone, but not a system which actually is advantageous to everyone.

Our commonplace moral views do, I think, support the view that the moral man must be trustworthy. Hence, we have established one modification required in the thesis, if it is to provide a more adequate set of conditions for a moral system.

---

8. Baier, *op. cit.*, p. 314.

But there is a much more basic respect in which the "moral" man falls short of our expectations. He is willing to temper his single-minded pursuit of advantage only by accepting the obligation to adhere to prudentially undertaken commitments. He has no real concern for the advantage of others, which would lead him to modify his pursuit of advantage when it conflicted with the similar pursuits of others. Unless he expects to gain, he is unwilling to accept restrictions on the pursuit of advantage which are intended to equalize the opportunities open to all. In other words, he has no concern with fairness.

We tend to think of the moral man as one who does not seek his own well-being by means which would deny equal well-being to his fellows. This marks him off clearly from the "moral" man, who differs from the prudent man only in that he can overcome the apparent paradox of prudence and obtain those advantages which are available only to those who can display real restraint in their pursuit of advantage.

Thus a system of principles might meet the conditions laid down in the thesis without taking any account of considerations of fairness. Such a system would contain principles for ensuring increased advantage (or expectation of advantage) to everyone, but no further principle need be present to determine the distribution of this increase.

It is possible that there are systems of principles which, if adopted and adhered to, provide advantages which strictly prudent men, however rational, cannot attain. These advantages are a function of the sacrifices which the principles impose on their adherents.

Morality may be such a system. If it is, this would explain our expectation that we should all be worse off were we to substitute prudence for morality in our deliberations. But to characterize morality as a system of principles advantageous to all is not to answer the question "Why should I be moral?" nor is it to provide for those considerations of fairness which are equally essential to our moral understanding.

David P. Gauthier
University of Toronto

SUSAN WOLF

Moral Saints

Should people strive for moral perfection? In "Moral Saints," Susan Wolf, professor of philosophy at Johns Hopkins University, criticizes the supposition that the ideally moral person—the moral saint—provides an appropriate moral model. The moral saint, according to Wolf, is the person "whose every action is as morally good as possible." While the continual sacrifice of one's own interests to the interests of others appears commendable, the moral saint may fail to develop those nonmoral interests, skills, and relationships necessary for a healthy human life. Wolf contends that close analysis of the life of the moral saint calls into question the common assumption that it is "always better to be morally better."

Published in 1983, "Moral Saints" has special relevance to virtue ethics, the ethical theory that has its historical foundation in the ethics of Plato and Aristotle. Virtue ethics offers an alternative to the action-based ethical theories of utilitarianism and Kantian de-

ontology. Whereas action-based theories focus on the kinds of actions that the ethical person should take, virtue- or character-based theories such as virtue ethics focus on the character of the moral person. The question to be answered in virtue ethics is, What kind of person should I be? rather than, What kind of acts should I do? For an article that was instrumental in directing philosophical attention to the value of a virtue-based ethical theory in this century, see "Modern Moral Philosophy" by G. E. M. Anscombe. For an introduction to the historical basis for this approach to ethics, see the readings from Plato and Aristotle.

I DON'T know whether there are any moral saints. But if there are, I am glad that neither I nor those about whom I care most are among them. By *moral saint* I mean a person whose every action is as morally good as possible, a person, that is, who is as morally worthy as can be. Though I shall in a moment acknowledge the variety of types of person that might be thought to satisfy this description, it seems to me that none of these types serve as unequivocally compelling personal ideals. In other words, I believe that moral perfection, in the sense of moral saintliness, does not constitute a model of personal well-being toward which it would be particularly rational or good or desirable for a human being to strive.

Outside the context of moral discussion, this will strike many as an obvious point. But, within that context, the point, if it be granted, will be granted with some discomfort. For within that context it is generally assumed that one ought to be as morally good as possible and that what limits there are to morality's hold on us are set by features of human nature of which we ought not to be proud. If, as I believe, the ideals that are derivable from common sense and philosophically popular moral theories do not support these assumptions, then something has to change. Either we must change our moral theories in ways that will make them yield more palatable ideals, or, as I shall argue, we must change our conception of what is involved in affirming a moral theory.

In this paper, I wish to examine the notion of a moral saint, first, to understand what a moral saint would be like and why such a being would be unat-

tractive, and, second, to raise some questions about the significance of this paradoxical figure for moral philosophy. I shall look first at the model(s) of moral sainthood that might be extrapolated from the morality or moralities of common sense. Then I shall consider what relations these have to conclusions that can be drawn from utilitarian and Kantian moral theories. Finally, I shall speculate on the implications of these considerations for moral philosophy.

Moral Saints and Common Sense

Consider first what, pretheoretically, would count for us—contemporary members of Western culture—as a moral saint. A necessary condition of moral sainthood would be that one's life be dominated by a commitment to improving the welfare of others or of society as a whole. As to what role this commitment must play in the individual's motivational system, two contrasting accounts suggest themselves to me which might equally be thought to qualify a person for moral sainthood.

First, a moral saint might be someone whose concern for others plays the role that is played in most of our lives by more selfish, or, at any rate, less morally worthy concerns. For the moral saint, the promotion of the welfare of others might play the role that is played for most of us by the enjoyment of material comforts, the opportunity to engage in the intellectual and physical activities of our choice, and the love, respect, and companionship of people whom we love, respect, and enjoy. The happiness of the moral saint, then, would truly lie in the happiness of others, and so he would devote himself to others gladly, and with a whole and open heart.

On the other hand, a moral saint might be someone for whom the basic ingredients of happiness are not unlike those of most of the rest of us. What

I have benefited from the comments of many people who have heard or read an earlier draft of this paper. I wish particularly to thank Douglas MacLean, Robert Nozick, Martha Nussbaum, and the Society for Ethics and Legal Philosophy.

makes him a moral saint is rather that he pays little or no attention to his own happiness in light of the overriding importance he gives to the wider concerns of morality. In other words, this person sacrifices his own interests to the interests of others, and feels the sacrifice as such.

Roughly, these two models may be distinguished according to whether one thinks of the moral saint as being a saint out of love or one thinks of the moral saint as being a saint out of duty (or some other intellectual appreciation and recognition of moral principles). We may refer to the first model as the model of the Loving Saint; to the second, as the model of the Rational Saint.

The two models differ considerably with respect to the qualities of the motives of the individuals who conform to them. But this difference would have limited effect on the saints' respective public personalities. The shared content of what these individuals are motivated to be—namely, as morally good as possible—would play the dominant role in the determination of their characters. Of course, just as a variety of large-scale projects, from tending the sick to political campaigning, may be equally and maximally morally worthy, so a variety of characters are compatible with the ideal of moral sainthood. One moral saint may be more or less jovial, more or less garrulous, more or less athletic than another. But, above all, a moral saint must have and cultivate those qualities which are apt to allow him to treat others as justly and kindly as possible. He will have the standard moral virtues to a nonstandard degree. He will be patient, considerate, even-tempered, hospitable, charitable in thought as well as in deed. He will be very reluctant to make negative judgments of other people. He will be careful not to favor some people over others on the basis of properties they could not help but have.

Perhaps what I have already said is enough to make some people begin to regard the absence of moral saints in their lives as a blessing. For there comes a point in the listing of virtues that a moral saint is likely to have where one might naturally begin to wonder whether the moral saint isn't, after all, too good—if not too good for his own good, at least too good for his own well-being. For the moral virtues, given that they are, by hypothesis, *all* present in the same individual, and to an extreme degree, are apt to crowd out the nonmoral virtues, as

well as many of the interests and personal characteristics that we generally think contribute to a healthy, well-rounded, richly developed character.

In other words, if the moral saint is devoting all his time to feeding the hungry or healing the sick or raising money for Oxfam, then necessarily he is not reading Victorian novels, playing the oboe, or improving his backhand. Although no one of the interests or tastes in the category containing these latter activities could be claimed to be a necessary element in a life well lived, a life in which *none* of these possible aspects of character are developed may seem to be a life strangely barren.

The reasons why a moral saint cannot, in general, encourage the discovery and development of significant nonmoral interests and skills are not logical but practical reasons. There are, in addition, a class of nonmoral characteristics that a moral saint cannot encourage in himself for reasons that are not just practical. There is a more substantial tension between having any of these qualities unashamedly and being a moral saint. These qualities might be described as going against the moral grain. For example, a cynical or sarcastic wit, or a sense of humor that appreciates this kind of wit in others, requires that one take an attitude of resignation and pessimism toward the flaws and vices to be found in the world. A moral saint, on the other hand, has reason to take an attitude in opposition to this—he should try to look for the best in people, give them the benefit of the doubt as long as possible, try to improve regrettable situations as long as there is any hope of success. This suggests that, although a moral saint might well enjoy a good episode of *Father Knows Best*, he may not in good conscience be able to laugh at a Marx Brothers movie or enjoy a play by George Bernard Shaw.

An interest in something like gourmet cooking will be, for different reasons, difficult for a moral saint to rest easy with. For it seems to me that no plausible argument can justify the use of human resources involved in producing a *paté de canard en croute* against possible alternative beneficent ends to which these resources might be put. If there is a justification for the institution of haute cuisine, it is one which rests on the decision *not* to justify every activity against morally beneficial alternatives, and this is a decision a moral saint will never make. Presumably, an interest in high fashion or interior design will fare much the same, as will, very possibly, a cultivation of the finer arts as well.

A moral saint will have to be very, very nice. It is important that he not be offensive. The worry is that, as a result, he will have to be dull-witted or humorless or bland.

This worry is confirmed when we consider what sorts of characters, taken and refined both from life and from fiction, typically form our ideals. One would hope they would be figures who are morally good—and by this I mean more than just not morally bad—but one would hope, too, that they are not *just* morally good, but talented or accomplished or attractive in nonmoral ways as well. We may make ideals out of athletes, scholars, artists—more frivolously, out of cowboys, private eyes, and rock stars. We may strive for Katharine Hepburn's grace, Paul Newman's "cool"; we are attracted to the high-spirited passionate nature of Natasha Rostov; we admire the keen perceptiveness of Lambert Strether. Though there is certainly nothing immoral about the ideal characters or traits I have in mind, they cannot be superimposed upon the ideal of a moral saint. For although it is a part of many of these ideals that the characters set high, and not merely acceptable, moral standards for themselves, it is also essential to their power and attractiveness that the moral strengths go, so to speak, alongside of specific, independently admirable, nonmoral ground projects and dominant personal traits.

When one does finally turn one's eyes toward lives that are dominated by explicitly moral commitments, moreover, one finds oneself relieved at the discovery of idiosyncrasies or eccentricities not quite in line with the picture of moral perfection. One prefers the blunt, tactless, and opinionated Betsy Trotwood to the unfailingly kind and patient Agnes Copperfield; one prefers the mischievousness and the sense of irony in Chesterton's Father Brown to the innocence and undiscriminating love of St. Francis.

It seems that, as we look in our ideals for people who achieve nonmoral varieties of personal excellence in conjunction with or colored by some version of high moral tone, we look in our paragons of moral excellence for people whose moral achievements occur in conjunction with or colored by some interests or traits that have low moral tone. In other words, there seems to be a limit to how much morality we can stand.

One might suspect that the essence of the problem is simply that there is a limit to how much of *any* single value, or any single type of value, we can stand. Our objection then would not be specific to a life in which one's dominant concern is morality, but would apply to any life that can be so completely characterized by an extraordinarily dominant concern. The objection in that case would reduce to the recognition that such a life is incompatible with well-roundedness. If that were the objection, one could fairly reply that well-roundedness is no more supreme a virtue than the totality of moral virtues embodied by the ideal it is being used to criticize. But I think this misidentifies the objection. For the way in which a concern for morality may dominate a life, or, more to the point, the way in which it may dominate an ideal of life, is not easily imagined by analogy to the dominance an aspiration to become an Olympic swimmer or a concert pianist might have.

A person who is passionately committed to one of these latter concerns might decide that her attachment to it is strong enough to be worth the sacrifice of her ability to maintain and pursue a significant portion of what else life might offer which a proper devotion to her dominant passion would require. But a desire to be as morally good as possible is not likely to take the form of one desire among others which, because of its peculiar psychological strength, requires one to forego the pursuit of other weaker and separately less demanding desires. Rather, the desire to be as morally good as possible is apt to have the character not just of a stronger, but of a higher desire, which does not merely successfully compete with one's other desires but which rather subsumes or demotes them. The sacrifice of other interests for the interest in morality, then, will have the character, not of a choice, but of an imperative.

Moreover, there is something odd about the idea of morality itself, or moral goodness, serving as the object of a dominant passion in the way that a more concrete and specific vision of a goal (even a concrete *moral* goal) might be imagined to serve. Morality itself does not seem to be a suitable object of passion. Thus, when one reflects, for example, on the Loving Saint easily and gladly giving up his fishing trip or his stereo or his hot fudge sundae at the drop of the moral hat, one is apt to wonder not at how much he loves morality, but at how little he loves these other things. One thinks that, if he can give these up so easily, he does not know what it *is* to truly love them. There seems, in other words, to be a kind of joy which the Loving Saint, either by nature or by practice, is incapable of experiencing. The Rational Saint, on the other hand, might retain strong nonmoral and concrete desires—he simply denies himself the opportunity to act on them. But this is no less troubling. The Loving Saint one might suspect of missing a piece of perceptual machinery, of being blind to some of what the world has to offer. The Rational Saint, who sees it but foregoes it, one suspects of having a different problem—a pathological fear of damnation, perhaps, or an extreme form of self-hatred that interferes with his ability to enjoy the enjoyable in life.

In other words, the ideal of a life of moral sainthood disturbs not simply because it is an ideal of a life in which morality unduly dominates. The normal person's direct and specific desires for objects, activities, and events that conflict with the attainment of moral perfection are not simply sacrificed but removed, suppressed, or subsumed. The way in which morality, unlike other possible goals, is apt to dominate is particularly disturbing, for it seems to require either the lack or the denial of the existence of an identifiable, personal self.

This distinctively troubling feature is not, I think, absolutely unique to the ideal of the moral saint, as I have been using that phrase. It is shared by the conception of the pure aesthete, by a certain kind of religious ideal, and, somewhat paradoxically, by the model of the thorough-going, self-conscious egoist. It is not a coincidence that the ways of comprehending the world of which these ideals are the extreme embodiments are sometimes described as "moralities" themselves. At any rate, they compete with what we ordinarily mean by 'morality.' Nor is it a coincidence that these ideals are naturally described as fanatical. But it is easy to see that these other types of perfection cannot serve as satisfactory personal ideals; for the realization of these ideals would be straightforwardly immoral. It may come as a surprise to some that there may in addition be such a thing as a *moral* fanatic.

Some will object that I am being unfair to "common-sense morality"—that it does not really require a moral saint to be either a disgusting goody-goody or an obsessive ascetic. Admittedly, there is no logical inconsistency between having any of the personal characteristics I have mentioned and being a moral saint. It is not morally wrong to notice the faults and shortcomings of others or to recognize and appreciate nonmoral talents and skills. Nor is it immoral to be an avid Celtics fan or to have a passion for caviar or to be an excellent cellist. With enough imagination, we can always contrive a suitable history and set of circumstances that will embrace such characteristics in one or another specific fictional story of a perfect moral saint.

If one turned onto the path of moral sainthood relatively late in life, one may have already developed interests that can be turned to moral purposes. It may be that a good golf game is just what is needed to secure that big donation to Oxfam. Perhaps the cultivation of one's exceptional artistic talent will turn out to be the way one can make one's greatest contribution to society. Furthermore, one might stumble upon joys and skills in the very service of morality. If, because the children are short a ninth player for the team, one's generous offer to serve reveals a natural fielding arm or if one's part in the campaign against nuclear power requires accepting a lobbyist's invitation to lunch at Le Lion d'Or, there is no moral gain in denying the satisfaction one gets from these activities. The moral saint, then, may, by happy accident, find himself with nonmoral virtues on which he can capitalize morally or which make psychological demands to which he has no choice but to attend. The point is that, for a moral saint, the existence of these interests and skills can be given at best the status of happy accidents—they cannot be encouraged for their own sakes as distinct, independent aspects of the realization of human good.

It must be remembered that from the fact that there is a tension between having any of these qualities and being a moral saint it does not follow that having any of these qualities is immoral. For it is not part of common-sense morality that one ought to be a moral saint. Still, if someone just happened to want to be a moral saint, he or she would not have or encourage these qualities, and, on the basis of our common-sense values, this counts as a reason *not* to want to be a moral saint.

One might still wonder what kind of reason this is, and what kind of conclusion this properly allows us to draw. For the fact that the models of moral saints are unattractive does not necessarily mean that they are unsuitable ideals. Perhaps they are unattractive because they make us feel uncomfortable—they highlight our own weaknesses, vices, and flaws. If so, the fault lies not in the characters of the saints, but in those of our unsaintly selves.

To be sure, some of the reasons behind the disaffection we feel for the model of moral sainthood have to do with a reluctance to criticize ourselves and a reluctance to committing ourselves to trying to give up activities and interests that we heartily enjoy. These considerations might provide an *excuse* for the fact that we are not moral saints, but they do not provide a basis for criticizing sainthood as a possible ideal. Since these considerations rely on an appeal to the egoistic, hedonistic side of our natures, to use them as a basis for criticizing the ideal of the moral saint would be at best to beg the question and at worst to glorify features of ourselves that ought to be condemned.

The fact that the moral saint would be without qualities which we have and which, indeed, we like to have, does not in itself provide reason to condemn the ideal of the moral saint. The fact that some of these qualities are good qualities, however, and that they are qualities we *ought* to like, does provide reason to discourage this ideal and to offer other ideals in its place. In other words, some of the qualities the moral saint necessarily lacks are virtues, albeit nonmoral virtues, in the unsaintly characters who have them. The feats of Groucho Marx, Reggie Jackson, and the head chef at Lutece are impressive accomplishments that it is not only permissible but positively appropriate to recognize as such. In general, the admiration of and striving toward achieving any of a great variety of forms of personal excellence are character traits it is valuable and desirable for people to have. In advocating the development of these varieties of excellence, we advocate nonmoral reasons for acting, and in thinking that it is good for a person to strive for an ideal that gives a substantial role to the interests and values that correspond to these virtues, we implicitly acknowledge the goodness of ideals incompatible with that of the moral saint. Finally, if we think that it is *as* good, or even better for a person to strive for one of these ideals than it is for him or her to strive for and realize the ideal of the moral saint, we express a conviction that it is good not to be a moral saint.

Moral Saints and Moral Theories

I have tried so far to paint a picture—or, rather, two pictures—of what a moral saint might be like, drawing on what I take to be the attitudes and beliefs about morality prevalent in contemporary, common-sense thought. To my suggestion that common-sense morality generates conceptions of moral saints that are unattractive or otherwise unacceptable, it is open to someone to reply, "so much the worse for common-sense morality." After all, it is often claimed that the goal of moral philosophy is to correct and improve upon common-sense morality, and I have as yet given no attention to the question of what conceptions of moral sainthood, if any, are generated from the leading moral theories of our time.

A quick, breezy reading of utilitarian and Kantian writings will suggest the images, respectively, of the Loving Saint and the Rational Saint. A utilitarian, with his emphasis on happiness, will certainly prefer the Loving Saint to the Rational one, since the Loving Saint will himself be a happier person than the Rational Saint. A Kantian, with his emphasis on reason, on the other hand, will find at least as much to praise in the latter as in the former. Still, both models, drawn as they are from common sense, appeal to an impure mixture of utilitarian and Kantian intuitions. A more careful examination of these moral theories raises questions about whether either model of moral sainthood would really be advocated by a believer in the explicit doctrines associated with either of these views.

Certainly, the utilitarian in no way denies the value of self-realization. He in no way disparages the development of interests, talents, and other personally attractive traits that I have claimed the moral saint would be without. Indeed, since just these features enhance the happiness both of the individuals who possess them and of those with whom they associate, the ability to promote these features both in oneself and in others will have considerable positive weight in utilitarian calculations.

This implies that the utilitarian would not support moral sainthood as a universal ideal. A world in which everyone, or even a large number of people, achieved moral sainthood—even a world in which they *strove* to achieve it—would probably contain less happiness than a world in which people realized a diversity of ideals involving a variety of personal and perfectionist values. More pragmatic considerations also suggest that, if the utilitarian wants to influence more people to achieve more good, then he would do better to encourage them to pursue happiness-producing goals that are more attractive and more within a normal person's reach.

These considerations still leave open, however, the question of what kind of an ideal the committed utilitarian should privately aspire to himself. Utilitarianism requires him to want to achieve the greatest general happiness, and this would seem to commit him to the ideal of the moral saint.

One might try to use the claims I made earlier as a basis for an argument that a utilitarian should choose to give up utilitarianism. If, as I have said, a moral saint would be a less happy person both to be and to be around than many other possible ideals, perhaps one could create more total happiness by not trying too hard to promote the total happiness. But this argument is simply unconvincing in light of the empirical circumstances of our world. The gain in happiness that would accrue to oneself and one's neighbors by a more well-rounded, richer life than that of the moral saint would be pathetically small in comparison to the amount by which one could increase the general happiness if one devoted oneself explicitly to the care of the sick, the downtrodden, the starving, and the homeless. Of course, there may be psychological limits to the extent to which a person can devote himself to such things without going crazy. But the utilitarian's individual limitations would not thereby become a positive feature of his personal ideals.

The unattractiveness of the moral saint, then, ought not rationally convince the utilitarian to abandon his utilitarianism. It may, however, convince him to take efforts not to wear his saintly moral aspirations on his sleeve. If it is not too difficult, the utilitarian will try not to make those around him uncomfortable. He will not want to appear "holier than thou"; he will not want to inhibit others' ability to enjoy themselves. In practice, this might make the perfect utilitarian a less nauseating companion than the moral saint I earlier portrayed. But insofar as this kind of reasoning produces a more bearable public personality, it is at the cost of giving him a personality that must be evaluated as hypocritical and condescending when his private thoughts and attitudes are taken into account.

Still, the criticisms I have raised against the saint of common-sense morality should make some difference to the utilitarian's conception of an ideal which neither requires him to abandon his utilitarian principles nor forces him to fake an interest he does not have or a judgment he does not make. For it may be that a limited and carefully monitored allotment of time and energy to be devoted to the pursuit of some nonmoral interests or to the development of some nonmoral talents would make a person a better contributor to the general welfare than he would be if he allowed himself no indulgences of this sort. The enjoyment of such activities in no way compromises a commitment to utilitarian principles as long as the involvement with these activities is conditioned by a willingness to give them up whenever it is recognized that they cease to be in the general interest.

This will go some way in mitigating the picture of the loving saint that an understanding of utilitarianism will on first impression suggest. But I think it will not go very far. For the limitations on time and energy will have to be rather severe, and the need to monitor will restrict not only the extent but also the quality of one's attachment to these interests and traits. They are only weak and somewhat peculiar sorts of passions to which one can consciously remain so conditionally committed. Moreover, the way in which the utilitarian can enjoy these "extra-curricular" aspects of his life is simply not the way in which these aspects are to be enjoyed insofar as they figure into our less saintly ideals.

The problem is not exactly that the utilitarian values these aspects of his life only as a means to an end, for the enjoyment he and others get from these aspects are not a means to, but a part of, the general happiness. Nonetheless, he values these things only because of and insofar as they *are* a part of the general happiness. He values them, as it were, under the description 'a contribution to the general happiness.' This is to be contrasted with the various ways in which these aspects of life may be valued by nonutilitarians. A person might love literature because of the insights into human nature literature affords. Another might love the cultivation of roses because roses are things of great beauty and delicacy. It may be true that these features of the respective activities also explain why these activities are happiness-producing. But, to the nonutilitarian, this may not be to the point. For if one values these activities in these more direct ways, one may not be willing to exchange them for others that produce an equal, or even a greater amount of happiness. From that point of view, it is not because they produce happiness that these activities are valuable; it is because these activities are valuable in more direct and specific ways that they produce happiness.

To adopt a phrase of Bernard Williams', the utilitarian's manner of valuing the not explicitly moral aspects of his life "provides (him) with one thought too many".[1] The requirement that the utilitarian have this thought—periodically, at least—is indicative of not only a weakness but a shallowness in his appreciation of the aspects in question. Thus, the ideals toward which a utilitarian could acceptably strive would remain too close to the model of the common-sense moral saint to escape the criticisms of that model which I earlier suggested. Whether a Kantian would be similarly committed to so restrictive and unattractive a range of possible ideals is a somewhat more difficult question.

The Kantian believes that being morally worthy consists in always acting from maxims that one could will to be universal law, and doing this not out of any pathological desire but out of reverence for the moral law as such. Or, to take a different formulation of the categorical imperative, the Kantian believes that moral action consists in treating other persons always as ends and never as means only. Presumably, and according to Kant himself, the Kantian thereby commits himself to some degree of benevolence as well as to the rules of fair play. But we surely would not will that *every* person become a moral saint, and treating others as ends hardly requires bending over backwards to protect and promote their interests. On one interpretation of Kantian doctrine, then, moral perfection would be achieved simply by unerring obedience to a limited set of side-constraints. On this interpretation, Kantian theory simply does not yield an ideal conception of a person of any fullness comparable to that of the moral saints I have so far been portraying.

On the other hand, Kant does say explicitly that we have a duty of benevolence, a duty not only to allow others to pursue their ends, but to take up their ends as our own. In addition, we have positive duties to ourselves, duties to increase our natural as well as our moral perfection. These duties are unlimited in the degree to which they *may* dominate a life. If action in accordance with and motivated by the thought of these duties is considered virtuous, it is natural to assume that the more one performs such actions, the more virtuous one is. Moreover, of virtue in general Kant says, "it is an ideal which is unattainable while yet our duty is constantly to approximate to it".[2] On this interpretation, then, the Kantian moral saint, like the other moral saints I have been considering, is dominated by the motivation to be moral.

Which of these interpretations of Kant one prefers will depend on the interpretation and the importance one gives to the role of the imperfect duties in Kant's over-all system. Rather than choose between them here, I shall consider each briefly in turn.

On the second interpretation of Kant, the Kantian moral saint is, not surprisingly, subject to many of the same objections I have been raising against other versions of moral sainthood. Though the Kantian saint may differ from the utilitarian saint as to *which* actions he is bound to perform and which he is bound to refrain from performing, I suspect that the range of activities acceptable to the Kantian saint will remain objectionably restrictive. Moreover, the manner in which the Kantian saint must think about and justify the activities he pursues and the character traits he develops will strike us, as it did with the utilitarian saint, as containing "one thought too many." As the utilitarian could value his activities and character traits only insofar as they fell under the description of 'contributions to the general happiness,' the Kantian would have to value his activities and character traits insofar as they were manifestations of respect for the moral law. If the development of our powers to achieve physical, intellectual, or artistic excellence, or the activities directed toward making others happy are to have any moral worth, they must arise from a reverence for the dignity that members of our species have as a result of being endowed with pure practical reason. This is a good and noble motivation, to be

---

1. "Persons, Character and Morality" in Amelie Rorty, ed., *The Identities of Persons* (Berkeley: Univ. of California Press, 1976), p. 214.

2. Immanuel Kant, *The Doctrine of Virtue*, Mary J. Gregor, trans. (New York: Harper & Row, 1964), p. 71.

sure. But it is hardly what one expects to be dominantly behind a person's aspirations to dance as well as Fred Astaire, to paint as well as Picasso, or to solve some outstanding problem in abstract algebra, and it is hardly what one hopes to find lying dominantly behind a father's action on behalf of his son or a lover's on behalf of her beloved.

Since the basic problem with any of the models of moral sainthood we have been considering is that they are dominated by a single, all-important value under which all other possible values must be subsumed, it may seem that the alternative interpretation of Kant, as providing a stringent but finite set of obligations and constraints, might provide a more acceptable morality. According to this interpretation of Kant, one is as morally good as can be so long as one devotes some limited portion of one's energies toward altruism and the maintenance of one's physical and spiritual health, and otherwise pursues one's independently motivated interests and values in such a way as to avoid overstepping certain bounds. Certainly, if it be a requirement of an acceptable moral theory that perfect obedience to its laws and maximal devotion to its interests and concerns be something we can wholeheartedly strive for in ourselves and wish for in those around us, it will count in favor of this brand of Kantianism that its commands can be fulfilled without swallowing up the perfect moral agent's entire personality.

Even this more limited understanding of morality, if its connection to Kant's views is to be taken at all seriously, is not likely to give an unqualified seal of approval to the nonmorally directed ideals I have been advocating. For Kant is explicit about what he calls "duties of apathy and self-mastery" (69/70)—duties to ensure that our passions are never so strong as to interfere with calm, practical deliberation, or so deep as to wrest control from the more disinterested, rational part of ourselves. The tight and self-conscious rein we are thus obliged to keep on our commitments to specific individuals and causes will doubtless restrict our value in these things, assigning them a necessarily attenuated place.

A more interesting objection to this brand of Kantianism, however, comes when we consider the implications of placing the kind of upper bound on moral worthiness which seemed to count in favor of this conception of morality. For to put such a limit on one's capacity to be moral is effectively to deny, not just the moral necessity, but the moral goodness of a devotion to benevolence and the maintenance of justice that passes beyond a certain, required point. It is to deny the possibility of going morally above and beyond the call of a restricted set of duties. Despite my claim that all-consuming moral saintliness is not a particularly healthy and desirable ideal, it seems perverse to insist that, were moral saints to exist, they would not, in their way, be remarkably noble and admirable figures. Despite my conviction that it is as rational and as good for a person to take Katharine Hepburn or Jane Austen as her role model instead of Mother Theresa, it would be absurd to deny that Mother Theresa is a morally better person.

I can think of two ways of viewing morality as having an upper bound. First, we can think that altruism and impartiality are indeed positive moral interests, but that they are moral only if the degree to which these interests are actively pursued remains within certain fixed limits. Second, we can think that these positive interests are only incidentally related to morality and that the essence of morality lies elsewhere, in, say, an implicit social contract or in the recognition of our own dignified rationality. According to the first conception of morality, there is a cut-off line to the amount of altruism or to the extent of devotion to justice and fairness that is worthy of moral praise. But to draw this line earlier than the line that brings the altruist in question into a worse-off position than all those to whom he devotes himself seems unacceptably artificial and gratuitous. According to the second conception, these positive interests are not essentially related to morality at all. But then we are unable to regard a more affectionate and generous expression of good will toward others as a natural and reasonable extension of morality, and we encourage a cold and unduly self-centered approach to the development and evaluation of our motivations and concerns.

A moral theory that does not contain the seeds of an all-consuming ideal of moral sainthood thus seems to place false and unnatural limits on our opportunity to do moral good and our potential to deserve moral praise. Yet the main thrust of the arguments of this paper has been leading to the conclusion that, when such ideals are present, they are not ideals to which it is particularly reasonable or healthy or desirable for human beings to aspire. These claims, taken together, have the appearance of a dilemma from which there is no obvious escape. In a moment, I shall argue that, despite appearances, these claims should not be understood as constituting a dilemma. But, before I do, let me briefly describe another path which those who are convinced by my above remarks may feel inclined to take.

If the above remarks are understood to be implicitly critical of the views on the content of morality which seem most popular today, an alternative that naturally suggests itself is that we revise our views about the content of morality. More specifically, my remarks may be taken to support a more Aristotelian, or even a more Nietzschean, approach to moral philosophy. Such a change in approach involves substantially broadening or replacing our contemporary intuitions about which character traits constitute moral virtues and vices and which interests constitute moral interests. If, for example, we include personal bearing, or creativity, or sense of style, as features that contribute to one's *moral* personality, then we can create moral ideals which are incompatible with and probably more attractive than the Kantian and utilitarian ideals I have discussed. Given such an alteration of our conception of morality, the figures with which I have been concerned above might, far from being considered to be moral saints, be seen as morally inferior to other more appealing or more interesting models of individuals.

This approach seems unlikely to succeed, if for no other reason, because it is doubtful that any single, or even any reasonably small number of substantial personal ideals could capture the full range of possible ways of realizing human potential or achieving human good which deserve encouragement and praise. Even if we could provide a sufficiently broad characterization of the range of positive ways for human beings to live, however, I think there are strong reasons not to want to incorporate such a characterization more centrally into the framework of morality itself. For, in claiming that a character trait or activity is morally good, one claims that there is a certain kind of reason for developing that trait or engaging in that activity. Yet, lying behind our criticism of more conventional conceptions of moral

sainthood, there seems to be a recognition that among the immensely valuable traits and activities that a human life might positively embrace are some of which we hope that, if a person does embrace them, he does so *not* for moral reasons. In other words, no matter how flexible we make the guide to conduct which we choose to label "morality," no matter how rich we make the life in which perfect obedience to this guide would result, we will have reason to hope that a person does not wholly rule and direct his life by the abstract and impersonal consideration that such a life would be morally good.

Once it is recognized that morality itself should not serve as a comprehensive guide to conduct, moreover, we can see reasons to retain the admittedly vague contemporary intuitions about what the classification of moral and nonmoral virtues, interests, and the like should be. That is, there seem to be important differences between the aspects of a person's life which are currently considered appropriate objects of moral evaluation and the aspects that might be included under the altered conception of morality we are now considering, which the latter approach would tend wrongly to blur or to neglect. Moral evaluation now is focused primarily on features of a person's life over which that person has control; it is largely restricted to aspects of his life which are likely to have considerable effect on other people. These restrictions seem as they should be. Even if responsible people could reach agreement as to what constituted good taste or a healthy degree of well-roundedness, for example, it seems wrong to insist that everyone try to achieve these things or to blame someone who fails or refuses to conform.

If we are not to respond to the unattractiveness of the moral ideals that contemporary theories yield either by offering alternative theories with more palatable ideals or by understanding these theories in such a way as to prevent them from yielding ideals at all, how, then, are we to respond? Simply, I think, by admitting that moral ideals do not, and need not, make the best personal ideals. Earlier, I mentioned one of the consequences of regarding as a test of an adequate moral theory that perfect obedience to its laws and maximal devotion to its interests be something we can wholeheartedly strive for in ourselves and wish for in those around us. Drawing out the consequences somewhat further should, I think, make us more doubtful of the proposed test than of the theories which, on this test, would fail. Given the empirical circumstances of our world, it seems to be an ethical fact that we have unlimited potential to be morally good, and endless opportunity to promote moral interests. But this is not incompatible with the not-so-ethical fact that we have sound, compelling, and not particularly selfish reasons to choose not to devote ourselves univocally to realizing this potential or to taking up this opportunity.

Thus, in one sense at least, I am not really criticizing either Kantianism or utilitarianism. Insofar as the point of view I am offering bears directly on recent work in moral philosophy, in fact, it bears on critics of these theories who, in a spirit not unlike the spirit of most of this paper, point out that the perfect utilitarian would be flawed in this way or the perfect Kantian flawed in that.[1] The assumption lying behind these claims, implicitly or explicitly, has been that the recognition of these flaws shows us something wrong with utilitarianism as opposed to Kantianism, or something wrong with Kantianism as opposed to utilitarianism, or something wrong with both of these theories as opposed to some nameless third alternative. The claims of this paper suggest, however, that this assumption is unwarranted. The flaws of a perfect master of a moral theory need not reflect flaws in the intramoral content of the theory itself.

Moral Saints and Moral Philosophy

In pointing out the regrettable features and the necessary absence of some desirable features in a moral saint, I have not meant to condemn the moral saint or the person who aspires to become one. Rather, I have meant to insist that the ideal of moral sainthood should not be held as a standard against which any

other ideal must be judged or justified, and that the posture we take in response to the recognition that our lives are not as morally good as they might be need not be defensive.[2] It is misleading to insist that one is *permitted* to live a life in which the goals, relationships, activities, and interests that one pursues are not maximally morally good. For our lives are not so comprehensively subject to the requirement that we apply for permission, and our nonmoral reasons for the goals we set ourselves are not excuses, but may rather be positive, good reasons which do not exist *despite* any reasons that might threaten to outweigh them. In other words, a person may be *perfectly wonderful* without being *perfectly moral.*

Recognizing this requires a perspective which contemporary moral philosophy has generally ignored. This perspective yields judgments of a type that is neither moral nor egoistic. Like moral judgments, judgments about what it would be good for a person to be are made from a point of view outside the limits set by the values, interests, and desires that the person might actually have. And, like moral judgments, these judgments claim for themselves a kind of objectivity or a grounding in a perspective which any rational and perceptive being can take up. Unlike moral judgments, however, the good with which these judgments are concerned is not the good of anyone or any group other than the individual himself.

Nonetheless, it would be equally misleading to say that these judgments are made for the sake of the individual himself. For these judgments are not concerned with what kind of life it is in a person's interest to lead, but with what kind of interests it would be good for a person to have, and it need not be in a person's interest that he acquire or maintain objectively good interests. Indeed, the model of the Loving Saint, whose interests are identified with the interests of

---

1. See, e.g., Williams, *op. cit.* and J. J. C. Smart and Bernard Williams, *Utilitarianism: For and Against* (New York: Cambridge, 1973). Also, Michael Stocker, "The Schizophrenia of Modern Ethical Theories," this JOURNAL. LXIII, 14 (Aug. 12, 1976): 453–466.

2. George Orwell makes a similar point in "Reflections on Gandhi," in *A Collection of Essays by George Orwell* (New York: Harcourt Brace Jovanovich, 1945), p. 176: "sainthood is . . . a thing that human beings must avoid. . . . It is too readily assumed that . . . the ordinary man only rejects it because it is too difficult; in other words, that the average human being is a failed saint. It is doubtful whether this is true. Many people genuinely do not wish to be saints, and it is probable that some who achieve or aspire to sainthood have never felt much temptation to be human beings."

morality, is a model of a person for whom the dictates of rational self-interest and the dictates of morality coincide. Yet, I have urged that we have reason not to aspire to this ideal and that some of us would have reason to be sorry if our children aspired to and achieved it.

The moral point of view, we might say, is the point of view one takes up insofar as one takes the recognition of the fact that one is just one person among others equally real and deserving of the good things in life as a fact with practical consequences, a fact the recognition of which demands expression in one's actions and in the form of one's practical deliberations. Competing moral theories offer alternative answers to the question of what the most correct or the best way to express this fact is. In doing so, they offer alternative ways to evaluate and to compare the variety of actions, states of affairs, and so on that appear good and bad to agents from other, nonmoral points of view. But it seems that alternative interpretations of the moral point of view do not exhaust the ways in which our actions, characters, and their consequences can be comprehensively and objectively evaluated. Let us call the point of view from which we consider what kinds of lives are good lives, and what kinds of persons it would be good for ourselves and others to be, the *point of view of individual perfection.*

Since either point of view provides a way of comprehensively evaluating a person's life, each point of view takes account of, and, in a sense, subsumes the other. From the moral point of view, the perfection of an individual life will have some, but limited, value—for each individual remains, after all, just one person among others. From the perfectionist point of view, the moral worth of an individual's relation to his world will likewise have some, but limited, value—for, as I have argued, the (perfectionist) goodness of an individual's life does not vary proportionally with the degree to which it exemplifies moral goodness.

It may not be the case that the perfectionist point of view is like the moral point of view in being a point of view we are ever *obliged* to take up and express in our actions. Nonetheless, it provides us with reasons that are independent of moral reasons for wanting ourselves and others to develop our characters and live our lives in certain ways. When we take up this point of view and ask how much it would be

good for an individual to act from the moral point of view, we do not find an obvious answer.[1]

The considerations of this paper suggest, at any rate, that the answer is not "as much as possible." This has implications both for the continued development of moral theories and for the development of metamoral views and for our conception of moral philosophy more generally. From the moral point of view, we have reasons to want people to live lives that seem good from outside that point of view. If, as I have argued, this means that we have reason to want people to live lives that are not morally perfect, then any plausible moral theory must make use of some conception of supererogation.[2]

If moral philosophers are to address themselves at the most basic level to the question of how people should live, however, they must do more than adjust the content of their moral theories in ways that leave room for the affirmation of nonmoral values. They must examine explicitly the range and nature of these nonmoral values, and, in light of this examination, they must ask how the acceptance of a moral theory is to be understood and acted upon. For the claims of this paper do not so much conflict with the content of any particular currently popular moral

---

1. A similar view, which has strongly influenced mine, is expressed by Thomas Nagel in "The Fragmentation of Value," in *Mortal Questions* (New York: Cambridge, 1979), pp. 128–141. Nagel focuses on the difficulties such apparently incommensurable points of view create for specific, isolable practical decisions that must be made both by individuals and by societies. In focusing on the way in which these points of view figure into the development of individual personal ideals, the questions with which I am concerned are more likely to lurk in the background of any individual's life.

2. The variety of forms that a conception of supererogation might take, however, has not generally been noticed. Moral theories that make use of this notion typically do so by identifying some specific set of principles as universal moral requirements and supplement this list with a further set of directives which it is morally praiseworthy but not required for an agent to follow. [See, e.g., Charles Fried, *Right and Wrong* (Cambridge, Mass.: Harvard, 1979).] But it is possible that the ability to live a morally blameless life cannot be so easily or definitely secured as this type of theory would suggest. The fact that there are some situations in which an agent is morally required to do something and other situations in which it would be good but not required for an agent to do something does not imply that there are specific principles such that, in any situation, an agent is required to act in accordance with these principles and other specific principles such that, in any situation, it would be good but not required for an agent to act in accordance with those principles.

theory as they call into question a metamoral assumption that implicitly surrounds discussions of moral theory more generally. Specifically, they call into question the assumption that it is always better to be morally better.

The role morality plays in the development of our characters and the shape of our practical deliberations need be neither that of a universal medium into which all other values must be translated nor that of an ever-present filter through which all other values must pass. This is not to say that moral value should not be an important, even the most important, kind of value we attend to in evaluating and improving ourselves and our world. It is to say that our values cannot be fully comprehended on the model of a hierarchical system with morality at the top.

The philosophical temperament will naturally incline, at this point, toward asking, "What, then, *is* at the top—or, if there is no top, how *are* we to decide when and how much to be moral?" In other words, there is a temptation to seek a metamoral—though not, in the standard sense, metaethical—theory that will give us principles, or, at least, informal directives on the basis of which we can develop and evaluate more comprehensive personal ideals. Perhaps a theory that distinguishes among the various roles a person is expected to play within a life—as professional, as citizen, as friend, and so on—might give us some

rules that would offer us, if nothing else, a better framework in which to think about and discuss these questions. I am pessimistic, however, about the chances of such a theory to yield substantial and satisfying results. For I do not see how a metamoral theory could be constructed which would not be subject to considerations parallel to those which seem inherently to limit the appropriateness of regarding moral theories as ultimate comprehensive guides for action.

This suggests that, at some point, both in our philosophizing and in our lives, we must be willing to raise normative questions from a perspective that is unattached to a commitment to any particular well-ordered system of values. It must be admitted that, in doing so, we run the risk of finding normative answers that diverge from the answers given by whatever moral theory one accepts. This, I take it, is the grain of truth in G. E. Moore's "open question" argument. In the background of this paper, then, there lurks a commitment to what seems to me to be a healthy form of intuitionism. It is a form of intuitionism which is not intended to take the place of more rigorous, systematically developed, moral theories—rather, it is intended to put these more rigorous and systematic moral theories in their place.

UNIVERSITY of MARYLAND
SUSAN WOLF

ONORA O'NEILL

Between Consenting Adults

Many people, including moral philosophers, have become increasingly interested in what it means to be a human. Our society has experienced great leaps in technological innovation: almost endlessly prolonged life, in vitro fertilization, and the possibility of human cloning are just a few examples of the ways in which technology has forced a need to find answers to the questions of what it means to be a human.

An example of work on the ethical issues of personhood is the 1985 essay by Onora O'Neill given here. Although most people would agree that it is wrong to treat any person as less than human, what kind of treatment is proper is less clear. O'Neill brings a Kantian perspective to bear in an effort to better understand how people ought to be treated. She considers proper treatment in two contexts: the proper treatment of persons within an intimate relationship and the proper treatment of people at work.

Unlike utilitarianism, Kant's ethical theory does not judge the rightness or wrongness of an action by considering the consequences of the action. Instead, Kant argued that absolute moral rules could be determined by reason alone, and the moral individual was one who followed those rules out of regard for duty. A Kantian perspective is particularly appropriate for issues of personhood: one formulation of Kant's Categorical Imperative—the means by which our moral maxims are evaluated—is that one can never morally treat another as merely a means to an end. For another essay on Kantian concerns, see Thomas E. Hill, Jr.'s, "Servility and Self-Respect."

Much of Kant's ethics is distant from the ordinary moral consciousness of our day. But one pair of Kantian notions is still widely current. Few moral criticisms strike deeper than the allegation that somebody has used another; and few ideals gain more praise than that of treating others as persons.

But this consensus is often shallow, since there is little agreement about what it takes to use others in morally problematic ways or to treat them as persons. I shall look here at three common conceptions of these ideals, which make little distinction between the two of them. I shall then outline interpretations of both which seem to me more convincing and richer than the commonly accepted ones. On the interpretations I offer the two ideals are distinct, though related. Merely not to be used is not enough for being treated as a person. Making another into a tool or instrument in my project is one way of failing to treat that other as a person: but only one way.

At a certain point I shall return to the Kantian texts to suggest that the sort of understanding of these ideals that I have outlined is at stake there. But the exegetical ambitions are limited. I shall say nothing about Kant's conception of a person and its metaphysical background. I shall not spell out all the textual considerations that lie behind this reading of the Formula of the End in Itself. I merely state and

will not try to show that one of these reasons is that this interpretation can make sense of Kant's puzzling claims about the equivalence of the various formulations of the Categorical Imperative. I shall not explore Kant's thoughts about using oneself and treating oneself as a person. I shall try only to make plausible a certain understanding of what it is to use others and to treat them as persons. I shall therefore use illustrations from areas of life where we often fear that others are used or not treated as persons, and in particular from presumed sexual and economic uses of others. I shall argue that an adequate understanding of what it is to treat others as persons must view them not abstractly as possibly consenting adults, but as particular men and women with limited and determinate capacities to understand or to consent to proposals for action. Unless we take one another's limitations seriously we risk acting in ways which would be enough to treat "ideal" rational beings as persons, but are not enough for treating finitely rational, human beings as persons.

A second aim is to provide a reading of some central claims of Kant's ethics which does not depend on an inflated view of human cognitive and volitional capacities, does not generate implications which are rigorously insensitive to variations of circumstances, and is not tied to a strongly individualistic conception of agency.

The Personal Touch

One view of treating another as a person rather than using him or her is that it demands a certain tone and manner. If we show indifference to others, we do

Earlier versions of this article were helped by a number of discussions. I am particularly grateful to Thomas Hill, Sally Ruddick, Arnold Zweig, R. R. Rockingham Gill, Raaman Gillon, Adam Morton, Patricia Greenspan, Heinz Lubasz, David Krell, Diana Bell, Lenn Goodman, and William Ruddick.

not treat them as persons; if our interactions are personal in tone, whether sympathetic or hostile, we treat them as persons. On this view employers who are cold or distant with their employees do not treat them as persons, but involved employers do so. A prostitute who does her or his job with uninvolved perfunctoriness is using the clients, and if their manner is similar they use her or him; but if each had a personal manner, the relationship would be personal and neither would use the other.

If this is what it is to treat others as persons and not to use them, neither notion can be fundamental for moral or political thought. We are familiar with uses of others which are cloaked by an involved and concerned manner. A planned seduction of someone less experienced treats him or her as means even when charmingly done. Employers who take paternalistic interest in employees' lives may yet both use them and fail to treat them as persons. Yet relationships without a personal tone may neither use others nor fail to treat them as persons. An impersonal relationship with a sales assistant may not use him or her in any morally objectionable way, nor fail in treating him or her as other than a person. A personal touch may, we shall see, be an important aspect of treating others as persons. But the notion entirely fails to capture the requirements for avoiding using others and provides a scanty account of treating others as persons.

ACTUAL CONSENT

A deeper and historically more important understanding of the idea of treating others as persons sees their consent to actions which affect them as morally significant. On this view it is morally objectionable to treat others in ways to which they do not consent. To do so treats another as a thing or tool, which cannot, so does not, consent to the ways in which it is used; so fails to treat others as persons, who can choose, so may withhold consent from actions which affect them.

On this understanding of treating others as persons, rape and seduction are decisively unacceptable. The rapist's victim is coerced rather than consenting; and the seducer's victim lacks insight into what is proposed, so neither can nor does consent to it. But many relationships between prostitutes and their clients are not, on this view, morally objectionable, since they are relationships between consenting adults. Similarly, slavery and forced labor and various forms of economic fraud use others and don't treat them as persons, but a contractual relationship like that between employer and employee does not use others or fail to treat them as persons.

This liberal understanding of avoiding using others and of treating them as persons encounters difficulties of various sorts when we consider what consent is.

An initial difficulty is that it is unclear what constitutes consent. In legal and institutional contexts the criteria are supposedly clearest. Here formal procedures supposedly show who consents to which actions by which others. But here too presumptions of consent are defeasible. Even the clearest formulas of consent, such as signatures and formal oaths, may not indicate consent when there is ignorance, duress, misrepresentation, pressure, or the like.[1] Such circumstances may void contracts and even nullify marriages. Formal procedures for consenting may reveal only spurious consent, so cannot guarantee that everyone is treated as a person in this second sense.

Where formal procedures are lacking, the problem of determining what has been consented to is greater. Various debates about express and tacit consent reflect these difficulties. But the real problem here is not that consent is sometimes given in ways that are implicit rather than explicit, but that it is unclear where consent—even the most explicit consent—stops. A nod to the auctioneer, though "implicit," conveys a quite precise consent to offering a price increased by a specified amount for a particular lot. At other times the boundaries of explicit consent are unclear. Like other propositional attitudes, consent is opaque. Consent may not extend to the logical implications, likely results, or the indispensable presuppositions of that which is explicitly consented to. A classical and instructive example of this range of difficulties occurs in liberal political debates over how far consent to a

---

1. Excessive reliance on formal indicators of "consent" suggests doubt whether the consent is genuine. Consider the widespread European use of "treaties" to "legitimize" acquisition of land or sovereignty by seeking the signatures of barely literate native peoples with no understanding of European moral and legal traditions. Cf. D. F. McKenzie's discussion of the treaty of Waitangi in "The Sociology of a Text: Orality, and Print Literacy in Early New Zealand," *The Library*, ser. VI, vol. 6, no. 4 (1984): 333–65.

particular constitution (explicitly or implicitly given) signifies consent to particular governments formed under that constitution, and how far consent to a particular government or party constitutes consent to various components of government or party policy. The notion of loyal opposition is never more than contextually determinate.

A second range of difficulties arises when the consent given does not match the activities it supposedly legitimates. Marxist critics of capitalist economic forms suggest that workers do not consent to their employment despite its outwardly contractual form. For workers, unlike capitalists, cannot (at least in "ideal" capitalism) choose to be without work, on pain of starvation. Hence the outward contractual form masks an underlying coercion. Workers choose between employers (in boom times) and cannot choose or consent to nonemployment. Analogously, women in most societies hitherto have not really consented to their restricted life possibilities. A choice between marriage partners does not show that the married life has been chosen. The outward form of market economies and of unarranged marriages mask how trivial the range of dissent and consent is. In a Marxist view bourgeois freedom is not the real thing, and men and women in bourgeois societies are still often treated as things rather than as persons. Bourgeois ideologies offer a fiction of freedom. They structure a false consciousness which obscures the extent to which human beings are used and not treated as persons.

A third range of difficulties with taking actual consent as pivotal for treating others as persons emerges when abilities to consent and dissent are impaired. Discussions in medical ethics show how hard it is to ensure that the consent that patients provide to their treatment is genuine. It is not genuine whenever they don't understand what they are supposedly consenting to or lack the autonomy to do anything other than "consent" to what they think the doctor wants or requires. Patients cannot easily understand complex medical procedures; yet if they consent only to a simplified account, they may not consent to the treatment proposed. And their peculiar dependence makes it hard even for those who are informed to make autonomous decisions about proposed treatment. Paradoxically, the case of severely impaired patients may seem easiest to handle. Patients too impaired to give informed consent evi-

dently cannot be treated as persons in this sense. Paternalism may then seem permissible, even required, for those who are, if temporarily, *only* patients. But with less impaired patients we are not so ready to set aside the ideal of treating others as persons. The difficult case is raised by those who are, as Mill would have put it, "in the maturity of their faculties." Even when we are mature we are seldom ideal rational patients. Here we confront the possibility that consent may be spurious even when based on average understanding and a standard ability to make decisions.

It is not only when we are subjects or employees or patients that we have a partial understanding of ways in which others propose to act toward us and an incomplete ability to make decisions for ourselves. Others' apparent consent, even their apparently informed consent, may *standardly* be insufficient to show that we treat them as persons when we interact with them. The problems of the defeasibility and indeterminacy of consent, of ideological distortions and self-deception, and of impaired capacities to consent, are all forms of one underlying problem. The deeper problem in this area is simply a corollary of the opacity of intentionality. When we consent to another's proposals we consent, even when "fully" informed, only to some specific formulation of what the other has it in mind to do. We may remain ignorant of further, perhaps equally pertinent, accounts of what is proposed, including some to which we would not consent. ("I didn't know I was letting myself in for that!" we may protest.) Even when further descriptions are inferable from the one consented to, the inference may not be made; and often we cannot infer which determinate action will enact some proposal. If we want to give an account of genuine, morally significant, consent, we need to explain *which* aspects of actions must be consented to if nobody is to be used or treated as less than a person. An account of genuine consent must then show how the morally significant aspects of plans, proposals, and intentions are picked out as candidates for consent.

Hypothetical Consent

Before considering how this might be done, I shall look at an account of treating others as persons which doesn't require us to know what they consent to. This strategy explains treating others as persons not in terms of the consent actually given, but in terms of the hypothetical consent fully rational beings would give to the same proposal. The strategy has obvious merits.

One merit is that it suggests that at least sometimes actual consent is not morally decisive, even if well informed. Hence it allows for our strong intuitions that even a consensus may be iniquitous or irrelevant (perhaps it reflects false consciousness), and that not everything done between consenting adults treats the other as a person. This approach also deals readily with cases of impaired capacities to consent. Since it appeals to capacities that are standardly lacking, there is, in a way, no difference in its approach to those in "the maturity of their faculties" and to those more gravely impaired. By the standards of full rationality we are all impaired. But we can always ask whether the fully rational would consent.

But these merits are the acceptable face of a serious deficiency in this strategy. If treating others as persons requires only hypothetical rational consent, we may, as Berlin long ago pointed out, find ourselves overriding the actual dissent of others, coercing them in the name of higher and more rational selves who would consent to what is proposed. It seems implausible that treating others as persons should even sometimes be a matter of overriding what others as we know them actually choose.

Other difficulties with this strategy arise from the varied conceptions of rationality invoked. Many conceptions of rationality presuppose a given set of desires. If these are the actual desires of the consenter, appeal to hypothetical consent will not overcome the worry that a consensus may be iniquitous or reflect local ideology. Yet if there is no appeal to the consenter's actual desires, but only to some hypothetical set of rationally structured desires, then the theory may be too weak to determine what would rationally be consented to. Given that there are many rationally structured sets of hypothetical desires, rational structure alone cannot determine what would rationally be consented to. But there are difficulties in spelling out the content and grounds of a stronger (e.g., quasi-Platonic) account of rational desires that might determine hypothetical consent.

The appeal of hypothetical consent criteria of treating others as persons is to overcome the limitations of actual consent criteria by endowing hypo-thetical agents with cognitive capacities that extend their understanding of what is proposed. But it is just not clear how far the insight of even the ideally rational reaches. Do they, for example, have a more determinate insight into proposals addressed to them than do those who make the proposals? What do they make of internally incoherent proposals? Which aspects of others' proposals are pivotal for the consent or dissent of the fully rational? A convincing account of hypothetical rational consent has to explain *which* aspects of others' actions must be hypothetically consented to if those actions are not to use others or fail to treat them as persons. This approach cannot exempt us from the need to discover the morally significant aspects of plans, proposals, and intentions that are candidates for consent.

Significant and Spurious Consent

If the notion of consent is to help explicate what it is to treat others as persons, we need an account of genuine, morally significant consent, and to distinguish this from spurious or morally trivial consent. Three preliminary points seem to me significant.

First, morally significant consent cannot be consent to all aspects of another's proposals which may affect me. Any complicated action will be done under many descriptions; but most of these will be without moral significance. Morally significant consent will, I suggest, be consent to the deeper or more fundamental aspects of another's proposals. If I consent to be the subject for a medical experiment which drags on longer than expected, I may have been inconvenienced, but not gravely misled. But my consent will have been spurious, and I will not have been treated as a person, but indeed used, if I consented to a seriously misleading account of the experiment and its risks.

Second, if another's consent is to be morally significant, it must indeed be his or her consent. To treat others as persons we must allow them *the possibility either to consent to or to dissent from what is proposed.* The initiator of action can ensure this; but the consenting cannot be up to him or her. The morally significant aspect of treating others as persons may lie in making their consent or dissent *possible*, rather than in what they actually consent to or would hypothetically consent to if fully rational. A requirement that we ensure that others have this possibility cuts deep whenever they will be much affected by what we propose. There isn't much difficulty in ensuring that those who will in any case be no more than spectators have a genuine possibility of dissent from their minimal part in a project. They need only be allowed to absent themselves or to express disagreement, distaste, or the like. But those closely involved in or affected by a proposal have no genuine possibility of dissent unless they can avert or modify the action by withholding consent and collaboration. If those closely affected have the possibility of dissent, they will be able to require an initiator of action either to modify the action, or to desist or to override the dissent. But an initiator who presses on in the face of actively expressed dissent undercuts any genuine possibility of refusing the proposal and rather chooses to enforce it on others. Any "consent" the proposal then receives will be spurious, and will not show that others have not been used, let alone that they have been treated as persons.

Third, we need to understand what makes genuine consent to the more fundamental aspects of action possible. But there is no guarantee that any one set of requirements makes genuine consent possible in all circumstances. There may be some necessary conditions, whose absence always makes genuine consent or dissent impossible, and other conditions which are needed to make consent possible only in some circumstances. It is plausible to think that when we act in ways that would *always* preclude genuine consent or dissent, we will have used others. For example, if we coerce or deceive others, their dissent, and so their genuine consent, is in principle ruled out. Here we do indeed use others, treating them as mere props or tools in our own projects. Even the most autonomous cannot genuinely consent to proposals about which they are deceived or with which they are compelled to comply. Even if a proposal would have been welcomed, and coercion or deception is otiose, its enforcement or surreptitious imposition precludes consent.

In other cases a proposal for action may not in principle preclude consent and dissent, but the particular others affected may be unable to dissent from it, or genuinely to consent to it. A full understanding of treating others as persons should, I suggest, take some account of the particularities of persons. It must allow that we take seriously the possibility of dissent and consent for others who, far from being abstractly autonomous beings, have their particular cognitive limitations and partial autonomy, which affect their abilities to dissent and to consent variously in varying circumstances. We are concerned not only to be treated as a person—any person—but to some extent as the particular persons we are. We are not merely possibly consenting adults, but particular friends, colleagues, clients, rivals, relations, lovers, neighbors; we have each of us a particular history, character, set of abilities and weaknesses, interests and desires. Even when others do not deceive or coerce us, or treat us in any way as tools, we may yet feel that they do not treat us as persons either. There is some point to the thought that being treated as a person needs a personal touch. Not being used may be enough for being treated as a person when our particular identity and specific character are irrelevant, for example in commercial or other transactions with anonymous members of the public. (Even here we may think standards of courtesy must be met.) Still, in public contexts not being used may be the major part of being treated as a person: for if consent and dissent are in principle possible, we can refuse the opportunities, offers, or activities that do not suit us. But where we have specific relations with particular others, being treated as a person may require far more. It may demand that we treat others not impersonally, but to some extent as the persons they are.

POSSIBLE CONSENT: A KANTIAN READING

A shift of focus to possible consent has deep implications. When we see morally required actions as those to which others either actually or hypothetically consent, we implicitly view morality as closely connected to desires. Another's actual consent will usually reflect his or her wants or preferences; and standard modern views of hypothetical consent construe it in terms of actual preferences on which a rational ordering is hypothetically imposed. Yet it seems implausible that treating others as persons can be of *prime* moral importance if it amounts only to avoiding what they don't want or wouldn't rationally want. In a moral theory in which wants are basic, the notion of treating others as persons carries no independent weight. In Kantian terms we might say that the notion of a person doesn't matter in a heteronomous moral theory. If wants or rationalized preferences are morally fundamental, consent is of derivative concern. It is only within moral theories for beings who can sometimes act independently of desires—who are to that extent autonomous—that the notion of consent carries independent weight. In such theories it is important that consent be possible for others, but of less concern whether what they consent to is what they want.

An account of using others and treating them as persons which starts from the notions of possible consent and dissent reveals the Kantian origins of these notions. The Kantian texts also provide suggestions for explicating, elaborating, and differentiating the two notions.[2]

Kant's theory of action sees each act as done on a *maxim*, an underlying principle (often, but not necessarily, an agent's fundamental intention) used to guide and orchestrate more specific, ancillary aspects of action.[3] The Formula of the End in Itself enjoins action on maxims that

> treat humanity whether in your own person or in the person of any other never simply as a means, but always at the same time as an end (*Groundwork*, p. 429).

Here there are two separate aspects to treating others as persons: the maxim must not use them (negatively) as mere means, but must also (positively) treat them as ends in themselves (cf. ibid., p. 430).

Kant describes the first sort of failure as action on maxims to which no other could possibly consent, and the second as pursuit of ends another cannot share. He writes of such a case:

> The man whom I seek to use for my purposes by such a (false) promise cannot possibly agree with my way of behaving to him, and so cannot himself share the end of action (ibid., p. 429).

The failure is dual: the victim of deceit *cannot agree* to the initiator's maxim, so is used, and *a fortiori cannot share* the initiator's end, so is not treated as a person. Similarly with a maxim of coercion: victims cannot agree with a coercer's fundamental principle or maxim (which denies them the choice between consent and dissent), and further cannot share a coercer's ends. (Victims may *want* the same ends as their coercers; but that is not the same as sharing those ends, for one who is coerced, even if pointlessly, is not pursuing, nor therefore sharing, ends at all.) Those who are either deceived or coerced are then *both* used *and* not treated as persons.

It does not follow from this that nothing done in acting on a maxim of deception or coercion can be agreed to or shared by those deceived or coerced. On the contrary, deception standardly works by revealing subsidiary intentions or aspects of action, which misleadingly point to some underlying maxim to which consent can be given. Deception only works when the underlying intention or proposal is kept

---

2. References to Kantian texts will be parenthetical, using the following editions: *Groundwork*, trans. H. J. Paton, as *The Moral Law* (London: Hutchinson), 1953, Prussian Academy pagination; *The Doctrine of Virtue*, trans. M. Gregor (New York: Harper & Row), 1964, Prussian Academy pagination; "Perpetual Peace" in *Kant's Political Writings*, ed. Hans Reiss, trans H. B. Nisbet (Cambridge: Cambridge University Press, 1971).

3. For more detailed discussion of Kant's maxims see also Otfried Höffe, "Kant's kategorischer Imperativ als Kriterium des Sittlichen," *Zeitschrift für Philosophische Forschung*, Vol. 31, 1977, pp. 254–84 and O. O'Neill, "Consistency In Action," in *Morality and Universality: Essays on Ethical Universalizability*, ed. N. Potter and M. Timmons (Reidel, forthcoming). The most basic consideration is that maxims are underlying principles, by which subsidiary aspects of action are governed and orchestrated. They must often be inferred from these subsidiary aspects. Even when they are the maxims of individual action, they are not always accessible to consciousness. And some maxims are not maxims of individual agents, but the maxims of institutions or practices.

Hence not all maxims are intentions. Nor are all intentions maxims, since trivial and superficial aspects of action are often intended. The Categorical Imperative provides only a test of maxims; but it doesn't follow that anything is permissible provided it is a nonfundamental aspect of action. Since maxims guide subsidiary aspects of action, the latter will be morally required (or forbidden) when they are indispensable (or incompatible) with what is needed to enact and embody a morally worthy maxim in a particular context. Only in drastic conditions will what would otherwise be deeply wrong be legitimated because needed to enact a morally worthy maxim. In wartime Poland Schindler could act on a maxim of protecting some Jews only by enslaving them and collaborating with the Nazis. Cf. Thomas Keneally, *Schindler's Ark* (Hodder & Stoughton, 1982). In prerevolutionary St. Petersburg Sonya Marmeladovna could support and sustain her family only by prostitution. It does not follow that such actions would be either permissible or required to enact fundamental principles of justice or of love outside such very special circumstances.

obscure. The deceiver's actual maxim therefore cannot be consented to. A maxim of coercion does not have to be obscure—it may be brutally plain—but clearly denies victims the choice between consent and dissent.

While the boundaries of coercive action are often unclear, we can agree on central cases involving physical force, dire and credible threats and institutionalized forms of domination such as slavery. But here too victims can and do consent to many of the coercer's subsidiary intentions. It is always hard to know when "going along with" what is coercively proposed becomes collaboration with the coercer. (Rape trials are instructive.[4]) And it is hard to tell just when an ostensibly deceived party becomes a conniving party. But while such complexities make judgment of actual cases hard, they don't alter the point that a maxim of deception or coercion treats another as mere means and not as a person, even if the victim becomes so involved in the initiator's action that we judge that he or she has become a collaborator or accessory.

The second part of Kant's account of treating others as persons urges us not merely not to use them as means, but to treat them as "ends in themselves." By this he doesn't mean that others should be our goals or purposes. Only what we aim for, including what we desire, can be a goal or purpose. This sort of subjective end depends on us for its existence. Others who exist independently of our action can't be subjective ends, but only ends in themselves. Ends in themselves may provide us with grounds of action not by being the *aim* or *effect* of action, but by constituting *limits* to our actions (*Groundwork*, p. 428).[5]

Others may limit my action by being autonomous beings whose maxims guide their projects and activities to their varied ends. To respect a limit of this sort cannot be thought of on a spatial analogy of avoiding certain areas, for the varying activities of others take place in the world that we share, and not in discrete spatial capsules (as libertarians might prefer). Not to treat others as mere means introduces minimal, but indispensable, requirements for coordinating action in a world shared by autonomous beings, namely that nobody act in ways others cannot possibly consent to, so in principle precluding their autonomous action. To treat others as ends may also require action when dissent is in principle possible, but those who are actually involved have limited capacities to dissent.

The negative requirement of not using others can be stated in some (no doubt incomplete) abstraction from the particular features of other rational beings ("the problem of justice can be solved even for a 'nation of devils'" [*Kant's Political Writings*, p. 112]), but we can give only an indeterminate account of the "positive" requirements for treating others as ends in themselves. Whenever treating others as persons goes beyond not using them, we must take into account "humanity in their person," i.e., their *particular* capacities for rational and autonomous action.[6] This can be done with vacuous ease for abstractly rational beings. But human beings, while they are creatures of reason rather than instinct, are yet only limitedly rational beings, of whose capacities for autonomous action we can give no determinate account in the abstract. Hence the only abstract account we can give of the "positive" maxims on which we must act in treating other men and women as persons are very general policies. But these "wide"

---

4. In more than one way. In this area remarkably exacting, but varied, conceptions of what constitutes evidence of dissent are put forward. Cf. Carole Pateman, "Women and Consent," *Political Theory*, Vol. 8 (1980): 149–68. Cf. also her discussion of some inadequacies of "consenting adult" accounts of prostitution, in "Defending Prostitution: Charges Against Ericsson," *Ethics* 93 (1983): 561–65.

5. See Thomas Hill, "Humanity as an End in Itself," *Ethics* 91 (1980–81): 84–99. Hill's analysis of the Formula of the End in Itself is acute and instructive. However, he suggests that it has the advantage that it needs no interpretation of the notion of a maxim (p. 91). But the question of whether we are using others, or treating them as persons, is as sensitive to how we describe what we are doing as the question whether what we propose could be universally done.

6. Hill construes "humanity" as "including only those powers necessarily associated with rationality and the 'power to set ends,'" ibid., p. 86. The reading offered here takes this point of departure but also stresses, as we must for instructive consideration of "wide" duties, that human rationality and autonomy are quite limited. Only so can we understand why Kant thinks both that others are limits, ends which are to be "conceived only negatively—that is, as an end against which we should never act" (*Groundwork*, p. 437), and that there are positive duties to such ends. Where rationality and autonomy are patently incomplete we act against them if we assume that they are not and fail to support them. Cf. O. O'Neill, "Paternalism and Partial Autonomy," *Journal of Medical Ethics* 10 (1984): 173–78.

duties to share others' ends (and develop talents) can have determinate implications in particular contexts.

The "positive" aspects of treating others as ends in themselves require action on maxims of sharing others' ends. It is not enough when we deal with other human beings (as opposed to abstract rational beings) to act on maxims with which they can possibly agree, whatever their ends. It is also necessary to adopt maxims which "endeavour to further the ends of others" (*Groundwork*, p. 430). To treat human beings as persons, rather than as "ideal" rational beings, we must not only not use them, but must take their particular capacities for autonomy and rationality into account. Since other humans have varied ends, are precariously autonomous and rational, and far from self-sufficient in other ways, sharing even some of their ends may make varied demands. Kant claims that these demands can be grouped under the headings of respect and love (or beneficence). He repeatedly uses physical metaphors to express the ways in which these two sorts of demands differ:

> The principle of *mutual love* admonishes men constantly to *come nearer* to each other; that of the *respect* which they owe each other to keep themselves at a *distance* from one another (*The Doctrine of Virtue*, p. 447).

Policies of respect must recognize that others' maxims and projects are their maxims and projects. They must avoid merely taking over or achieving the aims of these maxims and projects, and allow others the "space" in which to pursue them for themselves. Respect for others requires, Kant thinks, that we avoid contempt, mockery, disdain, detraction, and the like and that we show others recognition (ibid., pp. 461–68). Policies of practical love or beneficence require us to recognize the needs particular others have for assistance in acting on their maxims and achieving their ends. Love requires us to adopt maxims of "active practical benevolence (beneficence) which consists in making another's happiness my own" (ibid., p. 451). To do this is to make the other's ends, whose achievement would constitute his or her happiness, in part my own. Such beneficence includes assistance to others, generosity, active sympathy, and conciliatoriness and the avoidance of envy and malicious joy (ibid., pp. 451–60).

However, the Kantian conception of beneficence is from the start antipaternalistic. The duty to seek others' happiness is always a duty to promote and share others' ends *without* taking them over, rather than duty to provide determinate goods and services or to meet others' needs, or to see that their ends are achieved. Beneficence of this sort presupposes others who are at least partly autonomous and have their own ends. The tension between beneficence and treating others as persons, which is central to many discussions of paternalism, is absent from Kant's account:

> I cannot do good to anyone according to *my* conception of happiness (except to young children and the insane) but only according to that of the one I intend to benefit (ibid., p. 453).

What remains is, as Kant indicates, the unavoidable tension between love and respect. We experience it every time we try to work out how to share others' ends without taking them over.[7] It is a tension that has no general solution, but can be resolved in particular contexts. Kant's wide duties specify no rules of action for all rational beings, for the ways in which sharing others' ends can perhaps be exemplified would differ wholly for other sorts of rational beings (imagine beings who are psychological impervious to one another, or less dependent on the physical world than we are), and will in any case differ greatly for human beings with varied ends.

The overall picture which this reading of the Formula of the End in Itself generates is that a morally worthy life must be based on maxims of justice (including noncoercion and nondeceit), of respect, and of love. Such a life neither uses others (by acting on maxims which preempt consent or dissent), nor fails to share others' ends (by acting on maxims which either disregard or take over those ends or lend them no support). In each case it is our *fundamental* proposals, principles, or basic intentions that must meet these conditions. We neither do nor can make it possible for others, even for others closely affected, to consent to

---

7. But what will count as a good resolution? One guideline might be this: the underlying principle of action should be one that subordinates sharing ends to leaving another with ends that can be shared. Hence only nonfundamental failures of respect may be part of loving action (e.g., presuming to make a minor arrangement or commitment for another which he or she will likely want made; Sonya Marmeladovna's sacrifice of self-respect out of love for her brothers and sisters); but where lack of respect is fundamental the supposedly loving action will cease to be so.

or dissent from *every* aspect (or even every intentional aspect) of what we propose; nor can we lead lives in which we at all times help all others achieve their ends. Justice and respect vary with circumstances, and beneficence is in addition unavoidably selective. Nevertheless there are occasions when action of a specific sort is required: there are contexts and relationships to others in which to do nothing would be sufficient evidence that the underlying maxim or principle is unjust or lacking in respect or nonbeneficent. Although love and beneficence are unavoidably select this does not mean that when we act on these maxims we can neglect all the central projects of lives with which ours are closely involved.

Morally Worthy Maxims and Consenting Adults

If this reading of the Formula of the End in Itself is to be more than Kantian exegesis, it should help us to think about using others and failing to treat them as persons. The classical examples of presumed sexual and economic use of others, in particular, should be illuminated. But there is one further difficulty in pursuing this thought.

Kant's analysis of treating others as persons leads him, in the first instance, to claims about maxims of morally worthy action. His fundamental moral categories are those of moral worth and lack of moral worth rather than those of right and wrong. Right and wrong, the categories of "legality," are, in his eyes, derivative from those of morality.[8] Right action conforms in outward respects, but perhaps only in outward respects, with what is morally worthy. Specifically obligatory action not merely conforms outwardly to what moral worth requires, but is mandated (in those circumstances) by some maxim of moral worth.

Yet we have seen that no determinate outward performance either conforms to or is prescribed by maxims of sharing others' ends. "Wide" duties do not have determinate outward manifestations. Even "strict" duties may be performed in outwardly varying ways. For any underlying principle or maxim will have to be enacted or embodied in different ancillary aspects of action in differing situations. How

then can we get from a Kantian account of not using others and sharing their ends—of morally worthy action—to a view of what is right or wrong to do? How, in particular, can a Kantian account help us to think about particular sexual or economic problems? Isn't it likely that there is no timeless sexual or economic morality for abstractly autonomous beings? (And no sex and no economics.)

Yet we may have got a great deal of what we are likely to need. For we need to understand what would be right or wrong in actual, determinate situations. Kantian maxims do not entail rules or prescriptions for all possible contexts. Since a maxim is the *maxima propositio* or major premise of a piece of practical reasoning, it is not there that we should look for details about determinate situations. But when a maxim is supplemented by an account of a particular situation—the minor premise of practical reasoning[9]—we may discover which sorts of outward performance are required, compatible, or proscribed in that situation. We may, for example, find that in *these* circumstances there is no way in which *that* sort of action could be compatible with justice; or on the other hand, that in *this* situation we must, if fundamentally committed to a maxim of love or respect, include something of *that* sort. The conclusions of such reasoning will not be unrestricted; they will hold good not for rational beings as such, nor even for the human condition, but for quite specific human conditions. But when we act this is just what we need to know. We do not need to know what it would be to refrain from detraction or to be generous in all possible worlds, but only how to discern what would be respectful or generous in particular situations. Casuistry is indispensable in all movements from major premise to decision, and all claims about what is obligatory, permissible, and forbidden hold only for determinate contexts. Even when we have reasons for thinking that the maxim of some action was itself not morally worthy, judgments of what is obligatory (or

---

8. Cf. *Groundwork*, 397ff.; *The Doctrine of Virtue*, 218–20 and O. O'Neill, "Kant After Virtue," *Inquiry* 26 (1984): 387–405.

9. Contrary to a whole tradition of Kant commentary, Kant has a lot to say about the minor premise in practical reasoning, especially in *The Critique of Judgement*. For recent discussions see Hannah Arendt, *Lectures on Kant's Political Philosophy*, ed. Ronald Beiner (Chicago: University of Chicago Press, 1982); Beiner's interpretive essay in the same volume and his *Political Judgment* (London: Methuen, 1983); O. O'Neill, "The Power of Example," *Philosophy,* forthcoming.

merely permissible or forbidden) are made by reference to the outward aspects of action that would have been required (or compatible or ruled out) by acting on a morally worthy maxim in that situation.

Treating Others as Persons in Sexual Relationships

If this account of using others and treating them as persons is plausible, it should throw light on areas of life where such failures are thought common. One such area is sexual relationships and encounters. We might also hope to gain some understanding of *why* sexual relationships are thought peculiarly vulnerable to these sorts of failure.

Some sexual coercion is relatively straightforward. It isn't hard to see why the victim of rape or of lesser sexual assault is used. However, rape differs from other forms of coercion in that, because of the implicit nature of much sexual communication and social traditions which encourage forms of sexual duplicity, it is unusually hard to be sure when there has been coercion. Also coercion of less straightforward sorts may occur in some sexual relationships and transactions, including in relationships between prostitutes and their clients. Here the outward transaction may be an agreement between consenting adults. But when we remember the institutional context of much (at least contemporary, western) prostitution, including the practices of pimping, brothel keeping, and various forms of social ostracism and consequent dependence on a harsh subculture, we may come to think that not all transactions between prostitutes and clients are uncoerced: but it may not be the client who coerces.

Deception is a pervasive possibility in sexual encounters and relationships. Not only are there well-known deceptions, such as seduction and breach of promise, but varied further possibilities. Many of these reflect the peculiarly implicit nature of sexual communication. Commercial and various distanced sexual encounters standardly use the very means of expression which deeper and longer lasting attachments use. But when the endearments and gestures of intimacy are not used to convey what they standardly convey, miscommunication is peculiarly likely. Endearments standardly express not just momentary enthusiasm but affection; the contact of eyes, lips, skin conveys some openness, acceptance,

and trust (often enough much more); embrace conveys a commitment which goes beyond a momentary clinging. These are potent gestures of human emotional life. If insufficient trust and commitment are present to warrant such expression, then those who use these endearments and gestures risk giving false messages about feelings, desires, and even commitments. But perhaps, we may think, at least in sexual relationships which are commercial or very casual or largely formal, it is well understood by all concerned that these expressions have been decontextualized and no longer express the underlying intentions or attitudes or principles that they might express in a more wholehearted relationship. But if such expressions are fully decontextualized, what part are they playing in an entirely casual or commercial or formalized encounter? If the expressions are taken at face value, yet what they would standardly express is lacking, each is likely to deceive the other. Relationship of prostitution, casual sexual encounters, and the sexual aspect of faded marriages are not invariably deceptive. Such sexual relations may be either too crudely mechanical to use or misuse expressions of intimacy, or sufficiently informed by trust and concern for the language of intimacy to be appropriate. But relationships and encounters which standardly combine superficial expression of commitment with its underlying absence are peculiarly vulnerable to deception. Where too much is unexpressed, or misleadingly expressed, each risks duping the other and using him or her as means.

Avoiding deceit and coercion are only the core of treating others as persons in sexual relationships. In avoiding these we avoid clear and obvious ways of using as (mere) means. But to treat another as a person in an intimate, and especially an intimate sexual, relationship requires far more. These further requirements reflect the intimacy rather than the specifically sexual character of a relationship. However, if sexual relationships cannot easily be merely relationships between consenting adults, further requirements for treating another as a person are likely to arise in any sexual relationship. Intimate bodies cannot easily have separate lives.

Intimacy, sexual or not, alters relationships in two ways that are relevant here. First, those who are intimate acquire deep and detailed (but incomplete) knowledge of one another's life, character, and desires. Secondly, each forms some desires which incorporate or refer to the other's desires, and consequently finds his or her happiness in some ways contingent upon the fulfillment of the other's desires.[10] Intimacy is not a merely cognitive relationship, but one where special possibilities for respecting and sharing (alternatively for disrespecting and frustrating) another's ends and desires develop. It is in intimate relationships that we are most able to treat others as persons—and most able to fail to do so.

Intimacy makes failures of respect and of love more possible. Lack of respect in intimate relationships may, for example, take both manipulative and paternalistic forms. The manipulator trades on the fact that the other is not just a possibly consenting adult, but one whose particular desires are known and may depend in part on the manipulator's desires. One who succumbs to so-called "moral" blackmail could have refused without suffering coercion and was not deceived, but was confronted with the dilemma of sacrificing something central to his or her life—perhaps career or integrity or relationships with others, or perhaps mainly the desire to accommodate the manipulator's desires—unless willing to comply. In intimate relationships it is all too easy to make the other an offer he or she cannot refuse; when we are close to others we can undercut their pursuit of ends without coercion or deceit. Modes of bargaining and negotiating with others which do not make dissent impossible for consenting adults in the abstract, and might be acceptable in public contexts, may yet undercut others' pursuit of their ends in intimate relationships. Here it is peculiarly demanding to leave the other "space" for his or her pursuit of ends. To do so, and so maintain respect for those with whom we are intimate, requires us to take account not only of the particular interlock of desires, dependencies, and vulnerabilities that have arisen in a given relationship, but also that we heed any wider social context whose modes of discourse and received opinions may systematically undermine or belittle the other's ends and capacities to pursue them. Respect for others—the most basic aspect of sharing

their ends—requires the greatest tact and insight when we are most aware of ways in which others' capacities to pursue ends autonomously are vulnerable.

Contexts which make manipulation hard to avoid also offer opportunities for paternalistic failures of respect. Unlike the manipulator, the paternalist does not deploy knowledge of the other and the other's ends to reduce his or her "space" for pursuit of those ends. The paternalist rather begins from a failure to acknowledge either *what* the other's ends are, or that they are the *other's* ends. This failure of respect entails failures to share those ends, for to the paternalist they are either invisible or else not the other's ends but rather the ends to be sought for the other. The paternalist tries to express beneficence or love by imposing a conception of others' ends or interests. Lack of respect is then compounded by lack of love. Those who try to remake or control the lives of others with whom they are intimate do not merely fail in respect, however sincerely they may claim to seek the other's good. Paternalism towards those who have their own ends is not a form of love. However, since it is only fundamental principles of actions (whether plans, proposals, policies, or intentions) that must meet these standards, superficial departure from them when acting on morally acceptable fundamental principles may be acceptable, or even required. The jokes and surprises in which friendship may be expressed do not count as deceptions; but if they were incident to action on other maxims might constitute fraud or serious disrespect or unacceptable paternalism.[11]

---

10. By this I don't mean merely that sexual desire may include desires that refer to the other's sexual desires, but more broadly that at least some desires in intimate relationships are altruistic in the strict sense that they can be specified only by reference to the other's desires. This allows for hostile intimacy where desire may be for frustration rather than the fulfillment of the other's desires.

11. A sensitive element of the pattern of casuistry outlined here is determining which principles are the maxim(s) of a given action, and which ancillary. Here counterfactual considerations must always be introduced. We can reject claims that some principle of action is the maxim of a given act when we have reason to believe that, without fundamental changes either in circumstance or in moral outlook, that principle would not have been acted on. A claim to be acting out of friendship rather than disrespect in throwing a surprise party would be rebutted if the party would be thrown even when friendship would require other implementations (the friend is exhausted or ill or bereaved or shy). A claim that demands on another are not coercive but benevolent could be rebutted only if there are good reasons for thinking the actual refusal wholly neurotic, as well as that disregard of the refusal would benefit the refuser. Imposition of, for example, medical treatment or sexual attentions in the face of refusal could be fundamentally respectful and benevolent only if the coercion would be dropped given some evidence that the refusal is not entirely neurotic.

Even in intimate relationships not all failures of love are consequent upon failures of respect. It is not only in manipulative and paternalistic action, where others' ends are respectively used and overlooked, that we may fail to share the ends of those with whom we are intimate. Failures of love also occur when the other's ends are indeed respected, and he or she is left the "space" in which to pursue them, yet no positive encouragement, assistance, or support for their pursuit is given. Vulnerable, finite beings do not treat one another as ends *merely* by leaving each other an appropriate "space." Here again detailed knowledge of others and their desires, strengths, and weaknesses offers wider possibilities. The support, concern, and generosity we need from particular others if our pursuit of ends is to be not merely unprevented but sufficiently shared to be a genuine possibility are quite specific. If we are to treat others with whom we are intimate with love as well as respect, we must both see and (to some extent) support their ends.

Avoiding using others and treating them as persons both demand a lot in intimate relationships. Only the avoidance of coercion demands no more than usual here, perhaps because coercion tends to destroy intimacy. Deception remains a possibility in any relationship, and more so where much is conveyed elliptically or by gesture. In brief sexual encounters as well as in commercial and formalized sexual relations the discrepancy of expression and underlying attitude offers many footholds for deception; even in sustained intimate relationships underlying attitudes and outlook can become, as it were, decoupled from the expression and gesture which convey them to the other, so that the language of intimacy is used deceptively. Intimate relationships also provide appropriate settings for manipulative and paternalistic failures of respect and consequent and other failures of love. But the other side of these gloomy thoughts is that intimacy also offers the best chances for treating others as the persons they are.

Treating Others as Persons in Work and Employment

It is odd that working life is also often thought to involve uses of others and failures to treat them as persons. Here we do not find the features that open sexual and intimate relationships to these failures. In modern employment relations, communication is usually explicit; employers and employees must have some coinciding desires, but need and often have no desires whose content is determined by the other's desires, and may be quite ignorant of one another's specific desires and capacities. Yet there are reasons why this area of life too makes it hard to ensure that nobody is either used or treated as less than a person.

To begin with there are straightforward ways in which we can be used by those for whom we work. Coercion is as vivid a possibility here as in sexual contexts. Sporadic forms include pressganging and underpayment of wages; institutionalized forms evidently include slavery and forced labor. Straightforward deception is also well entrenched in many forms of employment, and includes fraud and trickery of enormous variety. Hence some ways of being used in working contexts are obvious enough. But these are the working relationships that developed economic forms, including specifically capitalism, preclude. Yet it is widely claimed that capitalist and (perhaps) other modern economic forms not merely do not treat workers as persons, but use them.

This claim can be sustained only if there are unstraightforward ways in which workers are used, in which no maxims of coercion or deception can be attributed to any individual. When individuals act on maxims of coercion or deception we have straightforward failures, with which the legal system of capitalist or other developed economic forms can deal, and which the Kantian perspective, even in its standard interpretations, is well designed to detect. But unobvious forms of coercion or deception are harder to grasp.

A principal source of this problem is that the Kantian approach, like the legal frameworks with which it tallies, is standardly interpreted as individualistic. The interpretation of maxims adopted here is, however, too broad to entail individualism; it does not require that maxims be consciously entertained, nor therefore see only the fundamental intentions of individuals as maxims. On this account the guiding principle of any endeavor or practice or institution is its maxim. In many capitalist economic relations, including employment, all individual intentions may be morally acceptable. The capitalist employer may have fundamental conscious intentions to which his employees can indeed consent or dissent, so appears on this score not to treat them in any morally objectionable way. What could be more paradigmatic of an offer that can be refused than an offer of employment that is, as they say in wage negotiations, "on the table"? If we argue that such offers are either coercive or deceptive, we must take a broader view of maxims, and judge not the principles which particular would-be employers have in mind, but the principles which guide the institution of employment in a capitalist system. The underlying principle of capitalist employment, whatever that may be, may perhaps use some as means or to fail to treat them as persons, even where individuals' intentions fail in neither way.

The extension of ethical reasoning beyond individual concerns must then use the results of social inquiry. If, for example, we take an idealized Marxist account of capitalist employment, the Kantian approach would generate clear ethical results. On that account capitalist employers, whatever their individual intentions, base their action on a maxim of extracting surplus value (if they did not, employing others would be pointless). Since capitalism aims at profit, it must pay workers less than the value they produce. But this essential feature of capitalism is obscured from workers, who accept deceptive accounts of the terms of their employment to which consent and dissent are possible. But if the principle to which consent is possible (and actually given) is not the underlying maxim of capitalist employment, then this consent cannot show that there has been no deception at a fundamental level. What it can, however, show is that if there has been such deception, then it is, as in the case of the institutionalized coercion of organized prostitution, a deception without an individual deceiver.

Whether the underlying principle of capitalist employment *in fact* has the structure Marxists claim and so makes consent impossible is a further question. Might there not be a nondeceptive form of capitalism, in which the possibility of dissent is ensured by framing offers of employment in terms of the principles which really underlie capitalist employment relations? On this hypothesis workers with fully raised consciousness would have a genuine possibility to dissent from or consent to a maxim of employment which was not ideologically masked, and so would not be used. They would understand that profits would be made off their labor, but could

still accept the terms offered. If deceptive forms were all that is wrong with a capitalist maxim of employment, it might be remediable. But on a Marxist analysis coercion lurks behind the deception. When the underlying form of the capitalist maxim of employment is disclosed we supposedly discover that the deception served a purpose (or many purposes), and in particular that it makes an activity that workers (under "ideal" capitalism) cannot choose to avoid except on pain of the coercion of starvation, appear to them as one which they could choose or refuse. Employees will then invariably be used, since they have the possibility of dissenting or consenting only to a principle that isn't really the underlying principle of their employment at all. Either they will be both deceived and coerced, if they do not see through this offer, or if they see through it, they will not be deceived, but only coerced. In either case they will be used. The underlying maxim of "ideal" capitalist employment requires workers to choose between unemployment without welfare benefit and a wage "bargain" which is backed by this threat.

This argument, of course, depends on accepting a Marxist account of the fundamental maxim of capitalist employment and rejecting ideologically opposed accounts, such as those which view all maxims as specific to individual agents and deny that the market itself can be thought of as grounded in maxims. The argument neither supposes nor shows that the claims made about employment relations in "ideal" capitalism apply accurately to employment relations in actual capitalist economies, where for example, welfare payments may mitigate or remove the coercive character of threatened unemployment. For present purposes the interest the sketch is to show *one* way in which workers may be used in the Kantian sense even under systems of employment that ostensibly enshrine the principle of free, hence of possible, consent, and more generally how Kantian ethical reasoning might be extended beyond the private sphere.

In employment, as in other activities, being used is only one way of being treated as less than a person. A great many complaints that workers are not being treated as persons can be traced not to the ways in which they may be straightforwardly or unstraightforwardly used, but to the degree to which contemporary employment practices make a point of treating workers uniformly, and so not as the particular persons that they are.[12] In this matter modern employment practices are wholly different from intimate relationships. Workers in modern (not only capitalist) economies are treated in standard and uniform ways which take little account of differences in ends and capacities to seek them. Where work is "rationalized" and there is a "rate for the job," and hours and qualifications are standardized, there are few ways in which employees' particular ends and abilities to pursue them are taken into account on the job. If doing a job well amounts to doing it like the robot who may replace you, the maxim of such organization of work cannot go far to treat employees as the particular persons they are. In such employment it is not misuse of information about others' ends or capacities for autonomy, nor intentional failure to share ends, but rather systematic disregard of all particular characteristics that lies behind failure to respect or to share ends. Rationalized work practices treat all workers as persons (qualms about exploitation of employees apart), but take little account of their specific characteristics. This may be partly remedied in the practices of some workplaces, or eased by management or work practices which allow more worker involvement or self-management. But if such arrangements are only a matter of introducing "a personal touch," they impose outward forms of respect and beneficence without underlying changes that would treat workers as the particular persons they are, and may only introduce paternalistic and manipulative practices into working life.

A larger question in this area is whether working life should be like this. Shouldn't working life be impersonal? Isn't this our guarantee against nepotism, favoritism, and other types of personal bias and patronage? Is not justice the sole relevant standard in employment relations? The career open to talents has to be based on maxims of impersonal fairness. But the career open to talents is also the career closed to lack of talent and conducted without concern for the fact that we are not abstractly consenting adults. Perhaps the underlying issue is whether and when the lives of those who work with or for one another can be sufficiently separate for justice to be the only consideration. Mutual respect, solidarity, and assistance that go beyond what the job requires may not be dispensable whenever work is collaborative. Our working relations too are relations with determinate others and not with abstractly rational economic men and women.

Conclusions

The popular view that we can readily be used or treated as less than persons both in intimate relationships and at work can be sustained in a Kantian framework. In each context we may be faced with proposals to which we *cannot* (whether because deceived or because coerced) give our consent. But the characteristic ways in which we may be treated as less than persons even when not used are quite different in the two contexts. In intimate relationships everything is there which would make it possible to treat the other as the particular person he or she is, by respecting and sharing his or her pursuit of ends. Here if we fail to respect or to share the other's ends the failure is imputable to us. But contemporary employment relations are set up on principles that are impersonal. Employer and employee have only "relevant" information about one another, and need only slightly coinciding ends. Hence when employees are not treated as the particular persons they are, the failure does not standardly rest with a particular employer, who may correctly think that he or she has done all that an employer should. The demand that employees be treated as ends in themselves and shown respect and beneficence is a political demand for new economic structures, whose "maxim of employment" acknowledges our desire, and perhaps need, to be treated more as the persons we are, and less impersonally. It is a demand which we must take seriously if we doubt that we are, even in the maturity of our faculties, merely consenting adults.

---

12. For an account of the nature of working life under modern "scientific" management practices, see, for example, Harry Bravennan, *Labor and Monopoly Capital* (New York Monthly Review Press, 1974). The changes he chronicles are not unique to capitalism.

VIRGINIA HELD

Feminism and Moral Theory

Feminism in the late twentieth century has had an impact on all areas of philosophy, including moral philosophy. While the traditional ethical theories—utilitarianism, Kantian deontology, virtue ethics, and social contract theory—remain prominent, the development of a feminist ethics has garnered significant attention and interest. While the traditional theories have strong historical roots—Mill, Kant, Aristotle, and Hobbes would probably all recognize the modern versions of their theories—feminist ethics is a thoroughly modern phenomenon. Even though it lacks historical roots, feminist ethics deserves a place in a historical anthology of ethical theories because it is tightly linked to historical theories in that it is a reaction to them. The need for a feminist theory has arisen from a weakness of the historical theories, specifically a failure to appreciate and value the distinctive experience of women. In "Feminism and Moral Theory," representative of work in feminist ethics, Virginia Held of the City University of New York explains the need for a feminist theory in moral philosophy.

Held questions whether any single moral theory can adequately account for the different contexts of human activity. Just as a moral theory developed for the courtroom may not be adequate in the context of political bargaining, the reigning traditional moral theories are not adequate in the context of women's moral lives because they fail to take into account the special concerns that make up women's experiences. Women typically have roles different from those of men and until recently, their experience has mostly been confined to the context of the family. Women's experience, therefore, provides a different perspective on the constitution of a moral theory. Only when women's unique experience is taken into account can it be determined whether a feminist ethical theory serves the contexts of women's lives better than the traditional models. A feminist moral theory is necessary, argues Held, to determine how to evaluate women's moral experience.

The development of a feminist ethics remains an ongoing quest. For another sample of work being done in feminist ethics, see Annette Baier's "Whom Can Women Trust?"

The tasks of moral inquiry and moral practice are such that different moral approaches may be appropriate for different domains of human activity. I have argued in a recent book that we need a division of moral labor.[1] In *Rights and Goods*, I suggest that we ought to try to develop moral inquiries that will be as satisfactory as possible for the actual contexts in which we live and in which our experience is located. Such a division of moral labor can be expected to yield different moral theories for different contexts of human activity, at least for the foreseeable future. In my view, the moral approaches most suitable for the courtroom are not those most suitable for political bargaining; the moral approaches suitable for economic activity are not those suitable for relations within the family, and so on. The task of achieving a unified moral field theory covering all domains is one we may do well to postpone, while we do our best to devise and to "test" various moral theories in actual contexts and in light of our actual moral experience.

What are the implications of such a view for women? Traditionally, the experience of women has been located to a large extent in the context of the family. In recent centuries, the family has been thought of as a "private" domain distinct not only from that of the "public" domain of the polis, but also from the domain of production and of the marketplace. Women (and men) certainly need to develop moral inquiries appropriate to the context of mothering and of family relations, rather than accepting the application to this context of theories developed for the marketplace or the polis. We can certainly show that the moral guidelines appropriate to mothering are different from those that now seem suitable for various other domains of activity as presently constituted. But we need to do more as well: we need to consider whether distinctively feminist moral theories, suitable for the contexts in which the experience of women has or will continue

to be located, are better moral theories than those already available, and better for other domains as well.

The Experience of Women

We need a theory about how to count the experience of women. It is not obvious that it should count equally in the construction or validation of moral theory. To merely survey the moral views of women will not necessarily lead to better moral theories. In the Greek thought that developed into the Western philosophical tradition,[2] reason was associated with the public domain from which women were largely excluded. If the development of adequate moral theory is best based on experience in the public domain, the experience of women so far is less relevant. But that the public domain is the appropriate locus for the development of moral theory is among the tacit assumptions of existing moral theory being effectively challenged by feminist scholars. We cannot escape the need for theory in confronting these issues.

We need to take a stand on what moral experience is. As I see it, moral experience is "the experience of consciously choosing, of voluntarily accepting or rejecting, of willingly approving or disapproving, of living with these choices, and above all of acting and of living with these actions and their outcomes. . . . Action is as much a part of experience as is perception."[3] Then we need to take a stand on whether the moral experience of women is as valid a source or test of moral theory as is the experience of men, or on whether it is more valid.

Certainly, engaging in the process of moral inquiry is as open to women as it is to men, although the domains in which the process has occurred has been open to men and women in different ways. Women have had fewer occasions to experience for themselves the moral problems of governing, leading, exercising power over others (except children), and engaging in physically violent conflict. Men, on the other hand, have had fewer occasions to experience

I am especially grateful to my daughter Julia Held for the suggestions she made concerning a draft of this paper and for the many insights she provided; she had given birth to Alexander Held White shortly before I began the paper. I am also grateful to many others who have expressed their thoughts about the issues involved. I especially thank Annette Baier, Brian Barry, Sandra Bartky, Larry Blum, Nancy Fraser, Marilyn Friedman, Ann Garry, Carol Gilligan. Jeffrie Murphy, Lucius Outlaw, and Carole Pateman for their early comments, and Marcia Baron, Louise De

Salvo, Dorothy Helly, Nancy Holmstrom, Amélie Rorty, Sara Ruddick, Christina Hoff Sommers, Joan Tronto, and the editors of this volume for additional later comments.

For financial support, I am grateful to the Center for Advanced Study in the Behavioral Sciences at Stanford, where I was a Fellow while writing the paper, to the Andrew Mellon Foundation, and to Hunter College of the City University of New York.

the moral problems of family life and the relations between adults and children. Although vast amounts of moral experience are open to all human beings who make the effort to become conscientious moral inquirers, the contexts in which experience is obtained may make a difference. It is essential that we avoid taking a given moral theory, such as a Kantian one, and deciding that those who fail to develop toward it are deficient, for this procedure imposes a theory on experience, rather than letting experience determine the fate of theories, moral and otherwise.

We can assert that as long as women and men experience different problems, moral theory ought to reflect the experience of women as fully as it reflects the experience of men. The insights and judgments and decisions of women as they engage in the process of moral inquiry should be presumed to be as valid as those of men. In the development of moral theory, men ought to have no privileged position to have their experience count for more. If anything, their privileged position in society should make their experience more suspect rather than more worthy of being counted, for they have good reasons to rationalize their privileged positions by moral arguments that will obscure or purport to justify these privileges.[4]

If the differences between men and women in confronting moral problems are due to biological factors that will continue to provide women and men with different experiences, the experience of women should still count for at least as much as the experience of men. There is no justification for discounting the experience of women as deficient or underdeveloped on biological grounds. Biological "moral inferiority" makes no sense.

The empirical question of whether and to what extent women think differently from men about moral problems is being investigated.[5] If, in fact, women approach moral problems in characteristic ways, these approaches should be reflected in moral theories as fully as are those of men. If the differing approaches to morality that seem to be displayed by women and by men are the result of historical conditions and not biological ones, we could assume that in nonsexist societies, the differences would disappear, and the experience of either gender might adequately substitute for the experience of the other.[6] Then feminist moral theory might be the same as moral theory of any kind. But since we can hardly imagine what a nonsexist society would be

like, and surely should not wait for one before evaluating the experience of women, we can say that we need feminist moral theory to deal with the differences of which we are now aware and to contribute to the development of the nonsexist society that might make the need for a distinctively feminist moral theory obsolete. Specifically, we need feminist moral theory to deal with the regions of experience that have been central to women's experience and neglected by traditional moral theory. If the resulting moral theory would be suitable for all humans in all contexts, and thus could be thought of as a human moral theory or a universal moral theory, it would be a feminist moral theory as well if it adequately reflected the experience and standpoint of women.

That the available empirical evidence for differences between men and women with respect to morality is tentative and often based on reportage and interpretation, rather than on something more "scientific,"[7] is no problem at all for the claim that we need feminist moral theory. If such differences turn out to be further substantiated, we will need theory to evaluate their implications, and we should be prepared now for this possibility (or, as many think, probability). If the differences turn out to be insignificant, we still need feminist moral theory to make the moral claim that the experience of women is of equal worth to the experience of men, and even more important, that women themselves are of equal worth as human beings. If it is true that the only differences between women and men are anatomical, it still does not follow that women are the moral equals of men. Moral equality has to be based on moral claims. Since the devaluation of women is a constant in human society as so far developed, and has been accepted by those holding a wide variety of traditional moral theories, it is apparent that feminist moral theory is needed to provide the basis for women's claims to equality.

We should never forget the horrors that have resulted from acceptance of the idea that women think differently from men, or that men are rational beings, women emotional ones. We should be constantly on guard for misuses of such ideas, as in social roles that determine that women belong in the home or in educational programs that discourage women from becoming, for example, mathematicians. Yet, excessive fear of such misuses should not stifle exploration of the ways in which such claims may, in some measure, be true. As philosophers, we can be careful not to conclude that whatever tendencies exist ought to be reinforced. And if we succeed in making social scientists more alert to the naturalistic fallacy than they would otherwise be, that would be a side benefit to the development of feminist moral theory.

Mothering and Markets

When we bring women's experience fully into the domain of moral consciousness, we can see how questionable it is to imagine contractual relationships as central or fundamental to society and morality. They seem, instead, the relationships of only very particular regions of human activity.[8]

The most central and fundamental social relationship seems to be that between mother or mothering person and child. It is this relationship that creates and recreates society. It is the activity of mothering which transforms biological entities into human social beings. Mothers and mothering persons produce children and empower them with language and symbolic representations. Mothers and mothering persons thus produce and create human culture.

Despite its implausibility, the assumption is often made that human mothering is like the mothering of other animals rather than being distinctively human. In accordance with the traditional distinction between the family and the polis, and the assumption that what occurs in the public sphere of the polis is distinctively human, it is assumed that what human mothers do within the family belongs to the "natural" rather than to the "distinctively human" domain. Or, if it is recognized that the activities of human mothers do not resemble the activities of the mothers of other mammals, it is assumed that, at least, the difference is far narrower than the difference between what animals do and what humans who take part in government and industry and art do. But, in fact, mothering is among the most human of human activities.

Consider the reality. A human birth is thoroughly different from the birth of other animals, because a human mother can choose not to give birth. However extreme the alternative, even when abortion is not a possibility, a woman can choose suicide early enough in her pregnancy to consciously prevent the birth. A human mother comprehends that she brings about the birth of another human being. A human mother is then responsible, at least in an existentialist sense, for the creation of a new human life. The event is essentially different from what is possible for other animals.

Human mothering is utterly different from the mothering of animals without language. The human mother or nurturing person constructs with and for the child a human social reality. The child's understanding of language and of symbols, and of all that they create and make real, occurs in interactions between child and caretakers. Nothing seems more distinctively human than this. In comparison, government can be thought to resemble the governing of ant colonies, industrial production to be similar to the building of beaver dams, a market exchange to be like the relation between a large fish that protects and a small fish that grooms, and the conquest by force of arms that characterizes so much of human history to be like the aggression of packs of animals. But the imparting of language and the creation within and for each individual of a human social reality, and often a new human social reality, seems utterly human.

An argument is often made that art and industry and government create new human reality, while mothering merely "reproduces" human beings, their cultures, and social structures. But consider a more accurate view: in bringing up children, those who mother create new human *persons*. They change persons, the culture, and the social structures that depend on them, by creating the kinds of persons who can continue to transform themselves and their surroundings. Creating new and better persons is surely as "creative" as creating new and better objects or institutions. It is not only bodies that do not spring into being unaided and fully formed; neither do imaginations, personalities, and minds.

Perhaps morality should make room first for the human experience reflected in the social bond between mothering person and child, and for the human projects of nurturing and of growth apparent for both persons in the relationship. In comparison, the transactions of the marketplace seem peripheral; the authority of weapons and the laws they uphold, beside the point.

The relation between buyer and seller has often been taken as the model of all human interactions.[9] Most of the social contract tradition has seen this relation of contractual exchange as fundamental to law and political authority as well as to economic activity. And some contemporary moral philosophers see the contractual relation as the relation on which even morality itself should be based. The marketplace, as a model for relationships, has become so firmly entrenched in our normative theories that it is rarely questioned as a proper foundation for recommendations extending beyond the marketplace. Consequently, much moral thinking is built on the concept of rational economic man. Relationships between human beings are seen as arising, and as justified, when they serve the interests of individual rational contractors.

In the society imagined in the model based on assumptions about rational economic man, connections between people become no more than instrumental. Nancy Hartsock effectively characterizes the worldview of these assumptions, and shows how misguided it is to suppose that the relationship between buyer and seller can serve as a model for all human relations: "the paradigmatic connections between people [on this view of the social world] are instrumental or extrinsic and conflictual, and in a world populated by these isolated individuals, relations of competition and domination come to be substitutes for a more substantial and encompassing community."[10]

Whether the relationship between nurturing person (who need not be a biological mother) and child should be taken as itself paradigmatic, in place of the contractual paradigm, or whether it should be seen only as an obviously important relationship that does not fit into the contractual framework and should not be overlooked, remains to be seen. It is certainly instructive to consider it, at least tentatively, as paradigmatic. If this were done, the competition and desire for domination thought of as acceptable for rational economic man might appear as a very particular and limited human connection, suitable perhaps, if at all, only for a restricted marketplace. Such a relation of conflict and competition can be seen to be unacceptable for establishing the social trust on which public institutions must rest,[11] or for upholding the bonds on which caring, regard, friendship, or love must be based.[12]

The social map would be fundamentally altered by adoption of the point of view here suggested. Possibly, the relationship between "mother" and child

would be recognized as a much more promising source of trust and concern than any other, for reasons to be explored later. In addition, social relations would be seen as dynamic rather than as fixed-point exchanges. And assumptions that human beings are equally capable of entering or not entering into the contractual relations taken to characterize social relations generally would be seen for the distortions they are. Although human mothers could do other than give birth, their choices to do so or not are usually highly constrained. And children, even human children, cannot choose at all whether to be born.

It may be that no human relationship should be thought of as paradigmatic for all the others. Relations between mothering persons and children can become oppressive for both, and relations between equals who can decide whether to enter into agreements may seem attractive in contrast. But no mapping of the social and moral landscape can possibly be satisfactory if it does not adequately take into account and provide appropriate guidance for relationships between mothering persons and children.

Between the Self and the Universal

Perhaps the most important legacy of the new insights will be the recognition that more attention must be paid to the domain *between* the self—the ego, the self-interested individual—on the one hand, and the universal—everyone, others in general—on the other hand. Ethics traditionally has dealt with these poles, trying to reconcile their conflicting claims. It has called for impartiality against the partiality of the egoistic self, or it has defended the claims of egoism against such demands for a universal perspective.

In seeing the problems of ethics as problems of reconciling the interests of the self with what would be right or best for everyone, moral theory has neglected the intermediate region of family relations and relations of friendship, and has neglected the sympathy and concern people actually feel for particular others. As Larry Blum has shown, "contemporary moral philosophy in the Anglo-American tradition has paid little attention to [the] morally significant phenomena" of sympathy, compassion, human concern, and friendship.[13]

Standard moral philosophy has construed personal relationships as aspects of the self-interested feelings of individuals, as when a person might favor those he loves over those distant because it satisfies his own desires to do so. Or it has let those close others stand in for the universal "other," as when an analysis might be offered of how the conflict between self and others is to be resolved in something like "enlightened self-interest" or "acting out of respect for the moral law," and seeing this as what should guide us in our relations with those close, particular others with whom we interact.

Owen Flanagan and Jonathan Adler provide useful criticism of what they see as Kohlberg's "adequacy thesis"—the assumption that the more formal the moral reasoning, the better.[14] But they themselves continue to construe the tension in ethics as that between the particular self and the universal. What feminist moral theory will emphasize, in contrast, will be the domain of particular others in relations with one another.

The region of "particular others" is a distinct domain, where it can be seen that what becomes artificial and problematic are the very "self" and "all others" of standard moral theory. In the domain of particular others, the self is already closely entwined in relations with others, and the relation may be much more real, salient, and important than the interests of any individual self in isolation. But the "others" in the picture are not "all others," or everyone," or what a universal point of view could provide. They are particular flesh and blood others for whom we have actual feelings in our insides and in our skin, not the others of rational constructs and universal principles.

Relationships can be characterized as trusting or mistrustful, mutually considerate or selfish, and so forth. Where trust and consideration are appropriate, we can find ways to foster them. But doing so will depend on aspects of what can be understood only if we look at relations between persons. To focus on either self-interested individuals or the totality of all persons is to miss the qualities of actual relations between actual human beings.

Moral theories must pay attention to the neglected realm of particular others in actual contexts. In doing so, problems of egoism vs. the universal moral point of view appear very different, and may recede to the region of background insolubility or relative unimportance. The important problems may then be seen to be how we ought to guide or maintain or reshape the relationships, both close and more distant, that we have or might have with actual human beings.

Particular others can, I think, be actual starving children in Africa with whom one feels empathy or even the anticipated children of future generations, not just those we are close to in any traditional context of family, neighbors, or friends. But particular others are still not "all rational beings" or "the greatest number."

In recognizing the component of feeling and relatedness between self and particular others, motivation is addressed as an inherent part of moral inquiry. Caring between parent and child is a good example.[15] We should not glamorize parental care. Many mothers and fathers dominate their children in harmful or inappropriate ways, or fail to care adequately for them. But when the relationship between "mother" and child is as it should be, the caretaker does not care for the child (nor the child for the caretaker) because of universal moral rules. The love and concern one feels for the child already motivate much of what one does. This is not to say that morality is irrelevant. One must still decide what one ought to do. But the process of addressing the moral questions in mothering and of trying to arrive at answers one can find acceptable involves motivated acting, not just thinking. And neither egoism nor a morality of universal rules will be of much help.

Mothering is, of course, not the only context in which the salient moral problems concern relations between particular others rather than conflicts between egoistic self and universal moral laws; all actual human contexts may be more like this than like those depicted by Hobbes or Kant. But mothering may be one of the best contexts in which to make explicit why familiar moral theories are so deficient in offering guidance for action. And the variety of contexts within mothering, with the different excellences appropriate for dealing with infants, young children, or adolescents, provide rich sources of insight for moral inquiry

The feelings characteristic of mothering—that there are too many demands on us, that we cannot do everything that we ought to do—are highly instructive. They give rise to problems different from those of universal rule vs. self-interest. They require us to weigh the claims of one self-other relationship against the claims of other self-other relationships, to try to bring about some harmony between them, to see the issues in an actual temporal context, and to act rather than merely reflect.

For instance, we have limited resources for caring. We cannot care for everyone or do everything a caring approach suggests. We need moral guidelines for ordering our priorities. The hunger of our own children comes before the hunger of children we do not know. But the hunger of children in Africa ought to come before some of the expensive amusements we may wish to provide for our own children. These are moral problems calling to some extent for principled answers. But we have to figure out what we ought to do when actually buying groceries, cooking meals, refusing the requests of our children for the latest toy they have seen advertised, and sending money to UNICEF. The context is one of real action, not of ideal thought.

Principles and Particulars

When we take the context of mothering as central, rather than peripheral, for moral theory, we run the risk of excessively discounting other contexts. It is a commendable risk, given the enormously more prevalent one of excessively discounting mothering. But I think that the attack on principles has sometimes been carried too far by critics of traditional moral theory.

Noddings, for instance, writes that "To say, 'It is wrong to cause pain needlessly,' contributes nothing by way of knowledge and can hardly be thought likely to change the attitude or behavior of one who might ask, 'Why is it wrong?' . . . Ethical caring. . . depends not upon rule or principle" but upon the development of a self "in congruence with one's best remembrance of caring and being cared-for. "[16]

We should not forget that an absence of principles can be an invitation to capriciousness. Caring may be a weak defense against arbitrary decisions, and the person cared for may find the relation more satisfactory if both persons, but especially the person caring, are guided, to some extent, principles concerning obligations and rights. To argue that no two cases are ever alike is to invite moral chaos. Furthermore, for one person to be in a position of caretaker means that that person has the power to withhold care, to leave the other without it. The person cared for is usually in a position of vulnerability. The moral significance of this needs to be addressed along with other aspects of the caring relationship. Principles may remind a giver of care to avoid being capricious or domineering. While most of the moral problems involved in mothering contexts may deal with issues above and beyond the moral minimums that can be covered by principles concerning rights and obligations, that does not mean that these minimums can be dispensed with.

Noddings's discussion is unsatisfactory also in dealing with certain types of questions, for instance those of economic justice. Such issues cry out for relevant principles. Although caring may be needed to motivate us to act on such principles, the principles are not dispensable. Noddings questions the concern people may have for starving persons in distant countries, because she sees universal love and universal justice as masculine illusions. She refrains from judging that the rich deserve less or the poor more, because caring for individuals cannot yield such judgments. But this may amount to taking a given economic stratification as given, rather than as the appropriate object of critical scrutiny that it should be. It may lead to accepting that the rich will care for the rich and the poor for the poor, with the gap between them, however unjustifiably wide, remaining what it is. Some important moral issues seem beyond the reach of an ethic of caring, once caring leads us, perhaps through empathy, to be concerned with them.

On ethical views that renounce principles as excessively abstract, we might have few arguments to uphold the equality of women. After all, as parents can care for children recognized as weaker, less knowledgeable, less capable, and with appropriately restricted rights, so men could care for women deemed inferior in every way. On a view that ethics could satisfactorily be founded on caring alone, men could care for women considered undeserving of equal rights in all the significant areas in which women have been struggling to have their equality recognized. So an ethic of care, essential as a component of morality, seems deficient if taken as an exclusive preoccupation.

That aspect of the attack on principles which seems entirely correct is the view that not all ethical problems can be solved by appeal to one or a very few simple principles. It is often argued that all more particular moral rules or principles can be derived from such underlying ones as the Categorical Imperative or the Principle of Utility, and that these can be applied to all moral problems. The call for an ethic of care may be a call, which I share, for a more pluralistic view of ethics, recognizing that we need a division of moral labor employing different moral approaches for different domains, at least for the time being.[17] Satisfactory intermediate principles for areas such as those of international affairs, or family relations, cannot be derived from simple universal principles, but must be arrived at in conjunction with experience within the domains in question.

Attention to particular others will always require that we respect the particularity of the context, and arrive at solutions to moral problems that will not give moral principles more weight than their due. But their due may remain considerable. And we will need principles concerning relationships, not only concerning the actions of individuals, as we will need evaluations of kinds of relationships, not only of the character traits of individuals.

Birth and Valuing

To a large extent, the activity of mothering is potentially open to men as well as to women. Fathers can conceivably come to be as emotionally close, or as close through caretaking, to children as are mothers. The experience of relatedness, of resonsibility for the growth and empowerment of new life, and of responsiveness to particular others, ought to be incorporated into moral theory, and will have to be so incorporated for moral theory to be adequate. At present, in this domain, it is primarily the experience of women (and of children) that has not been sufficiently reflected in moral theory and that ought to be so reflected. But this is not to say that it must remain experience available only to women. If men came to share fully and equitably in the care of all persons who need care—especially children, the sick, the old—the moral values that now arise for women in the context of caring might arise as fully for men.

There are some experiences, however, that are open only to women: menstruating, having an abortion, giving birth, suckling. We need to consider their possible significance or lack of significance for moral experience and theory. I will consider here only one kind of experience not open to men but of obviously great importance to women: the experience of giving birth or of deciding not to. Does the very experience of giving birth, or of deciding not to exercise the capacity to do so, make a significant difference for moral experience and moral theory? I think the answer must be: perhaps.

Of course birthing is a social as well as a personal or biological event. It takes place in a social context structured by attitudes and arrangements that deeply affect how women experience it: whether it will be accepted as "natural," whether it will be welcomed and celebrated, or whether it will be fraught with fear or shame. But I wish to focus briefly on the conscious awareness women can have of what they are doing in giving birth, and on the specifically personal and biological aspects of human birthing.

It is women who give birth to other persons. Women are responsible for the existence of new persons in ways far more fundamental than are men. It is not bizarre to recognize that women can, through abortion or suicide, choose not to give birth. A woman can be aware of the possibility that she can act to prevent a new person from existing, and can be aware that if this new person exists, it is because of what she has done and made possible.

In the past we have called attention to the extent to which women do not control their capacity to give birth. They are under extreme economic and social pressure to engage in intercourse, to marry, and to have children. Legal permission to undergo abortion is a recent, restricted, and threatened capacity. When the choice not to give birth requires grave risk to life, health, or well-being, or requires suicide, we should be careful not to misrepresent the situation when we speak of a woman's "choice" to become a mother, or of how she "could have done other" than have a child, or that since she chose to become a mother, she is responsible for her child." It does not follow that because women are responsible for creating human beings, they should be held responsible by society for caring for them, either alone, primarily, or even at all. These two kinds of responsibility should not be confused, and I am speaking here only of the first. As conscious human beings, women can do other than give birth, and if they do give birth, they are responsible for the creation of other human beings. Though it may be very difficult for women to avoid giving birth, the very familiarity of the literary image of the woman who drowns herself or throws herself from a cliff rather than bear an illegitimate child should remind us that such eventualities are not altogether remote from consciousness.

Women have every reason to be justifiably angry with men who refuse to take responsibility for their share of the events of pregnancy and birth, or for the care children require. Because, for so long, we have wanted to increase the extent to which men would recognize their responsibilities for causing pregnancy, and would share in the long years of care needed to bring a child to independence, we have tended to emphasize the ways in which the responsibilities for creating a new human being are equal between women and men.[18] But in fact, men produce sperm and women produce babies, and the difference is enormous. Excellent arguments can be made that boys and men suffer "womb envy"; indeed, men lack a wondrous capacity that women possess.[19]

Of all the human capacities, it is probably the capacity to create new human beings that is most worth celebrating. We can expect that a woman will care about and feel concern for a child she has created as the child grows and develops, and that she feels responsible for having given the child life. But her concern is more than something to be expected. It is, perhaps, justifiable in certain ways unique to women.

Children are born into actual situations. A mother cannot escape ultimate responsibility for having given birth to this particular child in these particular circumstances. She can be aware that she could have avoided intercourse, or used more effective contraception, or waited to get pregnant until her circumstances were different; that she could have aborted this child and had another later; or that she could have killed herself and prevented this child from facing the suffering or hardship of this particular life. The momentousness of all these decisions about giving or not giving life can hardly fail to affect what she experiences in relation to the child.

Perhaps it might be thought that many of these issues arise in connection with infanticide, and that if one refrains from killing an infant, one is responsible for giving the infant life. Infanticide is as open to men as to women. But to kill or refrain from killing a child, once the child is capable of life with caretakers different from the person who is responsible

for having given birth to the child, is a quite different matter from creating or not creating this possibility, and I am concerned in this discussion with the moral significance of giving birth.

It might also be thought that those, including the father, who refrain from killing the mother, or from forcing her to have an abortion, are also responsible for not preventing the birth of the child.[20] But unless the distinction between suicide and murder, and between having an abortion and forcing a woman to have an abortion against her will, are collapsed completely, the issues would be very different. To refrain from murdering someone else is not the same as deciding not to kill oneself. And to decide not to force someone else to have an abortion is different from deciding not to have an abortion when one could. The person capable of giving birth who decides not to prevent the birth is the person responsible, in the sense of "responsible" I am discussing, for creating another human being. To create a new human being is not the same as to refrain from ending the life of a human being who already exists.

Perhaps there is a tendency to want to approve of or to justify what one has decided with respect to giving life. In deciding to give birth, perhaps a woman has a natural tendency to approve of the birth, to believe that the child ought to have been born. Perhaps this inclines her to believe whatever may follow from this: that the child is entitled to care, and that feelings of love for the child are appropriate and justified. The conscious decision to create a new human being may provide women with an inclination to value the child and to have hope for the child's future. Since, in her view, the child ought to have been born, a woman may feel that the world ought to be hospitable to the child. And if the child ought to have been born, the child ought to grow into an admirable human adult. The child's life has, and should continue to have, value that is recognized.

Consider next the phenomenon of sacrifice. In giving birth, women suffer severe pain for the sake of new life. Having suffered for the child in giving the child life, women may have a natural tendency to value what they have endured pain for. There is a tendency, often noted in connection with war, for people to feel that because sacrifices have been made, the sacrifice should have been "worth it," and if necessary, other things ought to be done so that the sacrifice "shall not have been in vain." There may be a similar tendency for those who have suffered to give birth to assure themselves that the pain was for the good reason of creating a new life that is valuable and that will be valued.

Certainly, this is not to say that there is anything good or noble about suffering, or that merely because people want to believe that what they suffered for was worthwhile, it was. A vast amount of human suffering has been in vain, and could and should have been avoided. The point is that once suffering has already occurred and the "price," if we resort to such calculations, has already been paid, it will be worse if the result is a further cost, and better if the result is a clear benefit that can make the price, when it is necessary for the result, validly "worth it."

The suffering of the mother who has given birth will more easily have been worthwhile if the child's life has value. The chance that the suffering will be outweighed by future happiness is much greater if the child is valued by the society and the family into which the child is born. If the mother's suffering yields nothing but further suffering and a being deemed to be of no value, her suffering may truly have been in vain. Anyone can have reasons to value children. But the person who has already undergone the suffering needed to create one has a special reason to recognize that the child is valuable and to want the child to be valued so that the suffering she has already borne will have been, truly, worthwhile.

These arguments can be repeated for the burdens of work and anxiety normally expended in bringing up a child. Those who have already borne these burdens have special reasons for wanting to see the grown human being for whom they have cared as valuable and valued. Traditionally, women have not only borne the burdens of childbirth, but, with little help, the much greater burdens of child rearing. Of course, the burdens of child rearing could be shared fully by men, as they have been partially shared by women other than natural mothers. Although the concerns involved in bringing up a child may greatly outweigh the suffering of childbirth itself, this does not mean that giving birth is incidental.

The decision not to have children is often influenced by a comparable tendency to value the potential child.[21] Knowing how much care the child would deserve and how highly, as a mother, she would value the child, a woman who gives up the prospect of motherhood can recognize how much she is losing. For such reasons, a woman may feel overwhelming ambivalence concerning the choice.

Consider, finally, how biology can affect our ways of valuing children. Although men and women may share a desire or an instinctive tendency to wish to reproduce, and although these feelings may be equally strong for both men and women, such feelings might affect their attitudes toward a given child very differently. In terms of biological capacity, a mother has a relatively greater stake in a child to which she has given birth. This child is about one-twentieth or one twenty-fifth of all the children she could possibly have, whereas a man could potentially have hundreds or thousands of other children. In giving birth, a woman has already contributed a large amount of energy and effort toward the production of this particular child, while a man has, biologically, contributed only a few minutes. To the extent that such biological facts may influence attitudes, the attitudes of the mother and father toward the "worth" or "value" of a particular child may be different. The father might consider the child more easily replaceable in the sense that the father's biological contribution can so easily and so painlessly be repeated on another occasion or with another woman; for the mother to repeat her biological contribution would be highly exhausting and painful. The mother, having already contributed so much more to the creation of this particular child than the father, might value the result of her effort in proportion. And her pride at what she has accomplished in giving birth can be appropriately that much greater. She has indeed "accomplished" far more than has the father.

So even if instincts or desires to reproduce oneself or one's genes, or to create another human being, are equally powerful among men and women, a given child is, from the father's biological standpoint, much more incidental and interchangeable: any child out of the potential thousands he might sire would do. For the mother, on the other hand, if this particular child does not survive and grow, her chances for biological reproduction are reduced to a much greater degree. To suggest that men may think of their children as replaceable is offensive to many men, and women. Whether such biological facts as those I have mentioned have any significant effect on parental attitudes is not known. But arguments from biological facts to social attitudes, and even to moral norms, have a very long history and are still highly popular; we should be willing to examine the sorts of unfamiliar arguments I have suggested that can be drawn from biological facts. *If* anatomy is destiny, men may be "naturally" more indifferent toward particular children than has been thought.

Since men, then, do not give birth, and do not experience the responsibility, the pain, and momentousness of childbirth, they lack the particular motives to value the child that may spring from this capacity and this fact. Of course, many other reasons for valuing a child are felt by both parents, by caretakers of either gender, and by those who are not parents, but the motives discussed, and others arising from giving birth, may be morally significant. The long years of child care may provide stronger motives for valuing a child than do the relatively short months of pregnancy and hours of childbirth. The decisions and sacrifices involved in bringing up a child can be more affecting than those normally experienced in giving birth to a child. So the possibility for men to acquire such motives through child care may outweigh any long-term differences in motivation between women and men. But it might yet remain that the person responsible for giving birth would continue to have a greater sense of responsibility for how the child develops, and stronger feelings of care and concern for the child.

That adoptive parents can feel as great concern for and attachment to their children as can biological parents may indicate that the biological components in valuing children are relatively modest in importance. However, to the extent that biological components are significant, they would seem to affect men and women in different ways.

Morality and Human Tendencies

So far, I have been describing possible feelings rather than attaching any moral value to them. That children are valued does not mean that they are valuable, and if mothers have a natural tendency to value their children, it does not follow that they ought to. But if feelings are taken to be relevant to moral theory, the feelings of valuing the child, like the feelings of empathy for other persons in pain, may be of moral significance.

To the extent that a moral theory takes natural male tendencies into account, it would at least be reasonable to take natural female tendencies into account. Traditional moral theories often suppose it is legitimate for individuals to maximize self-interest, or satisfy their preferences, within certain constraints based on the equal rights of others. If it can be shown that the tendency to want to pursue individual self-interest is a stronger tendency among men than among women, this would certainly be relevant to an evaluation of such theory. And if it could be shown that a tendency to value children and a desire to foster the developing capabilities of the particular others for whom we care is a stronger tendency among women than among men, this too would be relevant in evaluating moral theories.

The assertion that women have a tendency to value children is still different from the assertion that they ought to. Noddings speaks often of the "natural" caring of mothers for children.[22] I do not intend to deal here with the disputed empirical question of whether human mothers do or do not have a strong natural tendency to love their children. And I am certainly not claiming that natural mothers have greater skills or excellences in raising children than have others, including, perhaps, men. I am trying, rather, to explore possible "reasons" for mothers to value children, reasons that might be different for mothers and potential mothers than they would be for anyone else asking the question: why should we value human beings? And it does seem that certain possible reasons for valuing living human beings are present for mothers in ways that are different from what they would be for others. The reason, if it is one, that the child should be valued because I have suffered to give the child life is different from the reason, if it is one, that the child should be valued because someone unlike me suffered to give the child life. And both of these reasons are different from the reason, if it is one, that the child should be valued because the continued existence of the child satisfies a preference of a parent, or because the child is a bearer of universal rights, or has the capacity to experience pleasure.

Many moral theories, and fields dependent on them such as economics, employ the assumption that to increase the utility of individuals is a good thing to do. But if asked *why* it is a good thing to increase utility, or satisfy desire, or produce pleasure, or *why* doing so counts as a good reason for something, it is very difficult to answer. The claim is taken as a kind of starting assumption for which no *further* reason can be given. It seems to rest on a view that people seek pleasure, or that we can recognize pleasure as having intrinsic value. But if women recognize quite different assumptions as more likely to be valid, that would certainly be of importance to ethics. We might then take it as one of our starting assumptions that creating good relations of care and concern and trust between ourselves and our children, and creating social arrangements in which children will be valued and well cared for, are more important than maximizing individual utilities. And the moral theories that might be compatible with such assumptions might be very different from those with which we are familiar.

A number of feminists have independently declared their rejection of the Abraham myth.[23] We do not approve the sacrifice of children out of religious duty. Perhaps, for those capable of giving birth, reasons to value the actual life of the born will, in general, seem to be better than reasons justifying the sacrifice of such life.[24] This may reflect an accordance of priority to caring for particular others over abstract principle. From the perspectives of Rousseau, of Kant, of Hegel, and of Kohlberg, this is a deficiency of women. But from a perspective of what is needed for late twentieth century survival, it may suggest a superior morality. Only feminist moral theory can offer a satisfactory evaluation of such suggestions, because only feminist moral theory can adequately understand the alternatives to traditional moral theory that the experience of women requires.

Notes

1. See Virginia Held, *Rights and Goods: Justifying Social Action* (New York: Free Press, Macmillan, 1984).

2. See Genevieve Lloyd, *The Man of Reason: "Male" and "Female" in Western Philosophy* (Minneapolis: University of Minnesota Press, 1984).

3. Virginia Held, *Rights and Goods,* p. 272. See also V. Held, "The Political 'Testing' of Moral Theories," *Midwest Studies in Philosophy* 7 (1982): 343–63.

4. For discussion, see especially Nancy Hartsock, *Money, Sex, and Power* (New York: Longman, 1983), chaps. 10, 11.

5. Lawrence Kohlberg's studies of what he claimed to be developmental stages in moral reasoning suggested that girls progress less well and less far than boys through these stages. See his *The Philosophy of Moral Development* (San Francisco: Harper & Row, 1981); and

L. Kohlberg and R. Kramer, "Continuities and Discontinuities in Child and Adult Moral Development," *Human Development* 12 (1969): 93–120. James R. Rest, on the other hand, claims in his study of adolescents in 1972 and 1974 that "none of the male-female differences on the Defining Issues Test . . . and on the Comprehension or Attitudes tests were significant." See his "Longitudinal Study of the Defining Issues Test of Moral Judgment: A Strategy for Analyzing Developmental Change," *Developmental Psychology* (Nov. 1975): 738–48; quotation at 741. Carol Gilligan's In *A Different Voice* (Cambridge: Harvard University Press, 1982) suggests that girls and women tend to organize their thinking about moral problems somewhat differently from boys and men; her subsequent work supports the view that whether people tend to construe moral problems in terms of rules of justice or in terms of caring relationships is at present somewhat associated with gender (Carol Gilligan, address at Conference on Women and Moral Thought, SUNY Stony Brook, March 21, 1985). Other studies have shown that females are significantly more inclined than males to cite compassion and sympathy as reasons for their moral positions; see Constance Boucher Holstein, "Irreversible, Stepwise Sequence in the Development of Moral Judgment: A Longitudinal Study of Males and Females." *Child Development* 47, no.1 (March 1976): 51–61.

6. For suggestions on how Gilligan's stages, like Kohlberg's, might be thought to be historically and culturally, rather than more universally, based, see Linda Nicholson, "Women, Morality, and History," *Social Research* 50, no. 3 (Autumn 1983): 514–36.

7. See, e.g., Debra Nails, "Social-Scientific Sexism: Gilligan's Mismeasure of Man," *Social Research* 50, no.3 (Autumn 1983): 643–64.

8. I have discussed this in a paper that has gone through several major revisions and changes of title, from its presentation at a conference at Loyola University on April 18, 1983, to its discussion at Dartmouth College, April 2, 1984. I will refer to it as "Non-Contractual Society: A Feminist Interpretation." See also Carole Pateman, "The Fraternal Social Contract: Some Observations on Patriarchy," paper presented at American Political Science Association meeting, Aug. 30–Sept. 2, 1984, and "The Shame of the Marriage Contract," in *Women's Views of the Political World of Men,* edited by Judith Hicks Stiehm (Dobbs Ferry, N.Y: Transnational Publishers, 1984).

9. For discussion, see especially Nancy Hartsock, *Money, Sex, and Power.*

10. Ibid., p.39.

11. See Held, *Rights and Goods,* chap. 5.

12. Ibid., chap. 11.

13. Lawrence A. Blum, *Friendship, Altruism and Morality* (London: Routledge and Kegan Paul, 1980), p.1.

14. Owen J. Flanagan, Jr., and Jonathan E. Adler, "Impartiality and Particularity," *Social Research* 50, no.3 (Autumn 1983): 576–96.

15. See, e.g., Nell Noddings, *Caring: A Feminine Approach to Ethics and Moral Education* (Berkeley: University of California Press, 1984) pp.91–94.

16. Ibid., pp. 91–94.

17. Participants in the conference on Women and Moral Theory offered the helpful term "domain relativism" for the version of this view that I defended.

18. See, e.g., Virginia Held, "The Obligations of Mothers and Fathers," repr. in *Mothering: Essays in Feminist Theory,* edited by Joyce Trebilcot (Totowa, N.J.: Rowman and Allanheld, 1984).

19. See Eva Kittay, "Womb Envy: An Explanatory Concept," in *Mothering,* edited by Joyce Trebilcot. To overcome the pernicious aspects of the "womb envy" she skillfully identifies and describes, Kittay argues that boys should be taught that their "procreative contribution is of equal significance" (p.123). While boys should certainly be told the truth, the truth may remain that, as she states elsewhere, "there is the. . .

awesome quality of creation itself—the transmutation performed by the parturient woman" (p.99).

20. This point was made by Marcia Baron in correspondence with me.

21. In exploring the values involved in birth and mothering, we need to develop views that include women who do not give birth. As Margaret Simons writes, "we must define a feminist maternal ethic that supports a woman's right not to have children." See Margaret A. Simons, "Motherhood, Feminism, and Identity," *Hypatia, Women's Studies International Forum* 7, 5 (1984): 353.

22. E.g., Noddings, *Caring,* pp. 31, 43, 49.

23. See Gilligan, *In a Different Voice,* p.104; Held, "Non-Contractual Society: A Feminist Interpretation;" and Noddings, *Caring,* p. 43.

24. That some women enthusiastically send their sons off to war may be indicative of a greater than usual acceptance of male myths rather than evidence against this claim, since the enthusiasm seems most frequent in societies where women have the least influence in the formation of prevailing religious and other beliefs.

MARTHA NUSSBAUM

The Stoics on the Extirpation of the Passions

As the ethical writings of Aristotle and Plato have been receiving renewed attention in the last few decades, the ethics of two other ancient movements—Epicureanism and Stoicism—are also arousing curiosity. These movements were the two dominant philosophical schools between the death of Aristotle and the emergence of Christianity. Epicurean ethics are hedonistic: the sole standard of good is pleasure. For the Epicurean, therefore, the right acts are those that lead to pleasure. Yet the Epicureans did not advocate a life of indulgence. They distinguished between healthy "natural pleasures" (e.g., eating) and unhealthy "unnatural pleasures" (e.g., eating caviar).

The ethical goal for the Stoics was indifference to pleasure and pain. In order to live such a life, they proposed that one should live according to nature. Since the distinctive nature of humans is reason, one should live according to rational principles. The Stoic emphasis was on rationality and self-control, an important aspect of which was mastery over the emotions.

Martha Nussbaum of the Law School at the University of Chicago focuses on the Stoic view of emotions in "The Stoics on the Extirpation of the Passions." Although

Stoicism has been influential throughout the history of moral philosophy, in this essay Nussbaum demonstrates that we may still have much to learn from these ancient philosophers, especially in their treatment of human emotions. For more on the Stoics and Epicureans, see the readings from Epicurus and Epictetus.

'There is, I assure you, a medical art for the soul. It is philosophy, whose aid need not be sought, as in bodily diseases, from outside ourselves. We must endeavor with all our resources and all our strength to become capable of doctoring ourselves' (Cic *TD* III.6). 'There are certain healthful practical arguments that may be compared to the prescriptions of useful drugs; these I am writing down, having found them effective in healing my own sores, which, even if not thoroughly cured, have at least ceased to spread' (Sen *Ep* 8.2). So first Cicero, then Seneca, display the Stoic use of the medical analogy, which is more pervasive and more highly developed in Stoic texts than it is in those of any other Hellenistic school-so pervasive, in fact, that Cicero declares he is tired of their 'excessive attention' to such analogies (*TD* IV.23). The analogy can be traced back to the greatest of the Stoic philosophers, Chrysippus, who wrote, in his book on the therapeutic treatment of the passions:

> It is not true that there exists an art called medicine, concerned with the diseased body, but no corresponding art concerned with the diseased soul. Nor is it true that the latter is inferior to the former, in its theoretical grasp and therapeutic treatment of individual cases. (*PHP* V.2.22, 298D = *SVF* 111.471)

The analogy, Chrysippus continues, has value in guiding our search for philosophical cures: 'For the correlative affinity of the two will reveal to us, I think, the similarity of therapeutic treatments and the analogical relationship of the two modes of doctoring' (*PHP* V.2.24). In this way a study of the medical analogy will help Stoic philosophy to reach its practical goal.

The Stoics, like their Hellenistic rivals, both Epicurean and Skeptic, employ an analogy between philosophy and medicine, both to illustrate the proper function of philosophy in relation to human problems and to discover and justify a concrete ac-

count of philosophy's content, methods, and procedures. And it is clear that the Stoics, like the other two schools, wish to claim that a philosophical art of soul-healing, correctly developed and duly applied, is both necessary and sufficient for attaining the highest ends of human life. 'Be convinced at least of this,' Cicero's interlocutor declares, 'that unless the soul is cured, which cannot be done without philosophy there will be no end to our miseries. Therefore let us, now that we have made a beginning, put ourselves in the hands of philosophy for treatment; we shall be cured, if we want to be' (*TD* 111.13). What are these philosophical treatments? What arguments do they use? And—above—all-what forms of human sickness do they claim to heal?

In order to see the power of the Stoic conception of therapy we need to focus on their account of the emotions or passions and on its consequences for their reply to Aristotelian and ordinary conceptions of the worth of external goods, in private and in public life.[1] Beginning from a very brief summary of some essential elements in the Stoic account of good,

---

1. In what follows, I shall use these two words more or less interchangeably, making no salient distinction between them. 'Emotions' is the more common modern generic term, while 'passions' is both etymologically closer to the most common Greek and Latin terms and more firmly entrenched in the Western philosophical tradition. In any case, what I mean to designate by these terms is a genus of which phenomena such as fear, love, grief, anger, envy, jealousy, and other relatives—but not bodily appetites such as hunger and thirst—are the species. (This corresponds to the Stoic use of Greek πἀθη, though other Greek writers use πἀθη more broadly, preserving the connection with the verb πἀσχειν.) This family of experiences, which we call emotions as opposed to appetites, is grouped together by many Greek writers, beginning at least with Plato, and his account of the soul's middle part. The Stoics and Plato recognize the same family grouping, though they differ on the family's analysis and definition, and also on the question whether these experiences are properly ascribed to animals and children. We must remember throughout that a πἀθοζ is a concrete episode, stemming from, but not identical with, an underlying dispositional condition (cf. § IV).

we shall go on to investigate the notorious thesis of Chrysippus that the passions are forms of false belief or judgment. This thesis has, as I think we shall see, considerably more philosophical and intuitive power than might at first be evident. We shall then ask why, according to the Stoics, the passions are to be not moderated, but completely extirpated from the good life, and what arguments the Stoics can use to convince a non-Stoic that this extirpation is required. The aim of this essay will be to reconstruct Chrysippus' views; we shall use other sources (for example Cicero and Seneca) as sources for those views.

I

We must begin by setting down, somewhat dogmatically and without detailed textual argument, certain features of the Stoic conception of the human end or good that will play a role in their diagnosis and treatment of the passions. (This will not prevent us from asking, later on, how the diagnosis and this conception of health are interrelated.) According to Stoicism, only virtue is worth choosing for its own sake; and virtue all by itself suffices for a completely good human life, that is, for εὐδαιμονία. Virtue is something unaffected by external contingency—both (apparently) as to its acquisition and as to its maintenance once acquired.[1] Items that are not fully under the control of the agent—such as health, wealth, freedom from pain, the good functioning of the bodily faculties—have no intrinsic worth, nor is their causal relationship to εὐδαιμονία even that of an instrumental necessary condition. In short, if we take all these things away, if we imagine the wise man living in the worst possible natural circumstances, so long "as he is good—and once good he cannot be corrupted—his εὐδαιμονία will still be complete. He

will be living as valuable and choiceworthy and enviable a life as a human being possibly could.

At this point we enter an area of considerable controversy and obscurity. For the Stoics (in order, apparently, to explain why and how the wise person will actually act in any way at all out there in the world) also insist that these external goods are appropriately *preferred*, in many circumstances, to their opposites. The wise person will in many cases, and rightly (for the wise person never errs) pursue health and not sickness, freedom from pain rather than pain, and so forth. There are some texts that seem to suggest that these items may therefore be correctly said to have some worth, even if only a derivative or second-grade worth. It is extremely difficult to tell exactly what worth (ἀξία) is, and how it is related to goodness (τὸ ἀγαθόν), which is consistently denied to all indifferents. I do not intend to get enmeshed in this difficult problem of interpretation here. I shall simply record certain facts that seem to me uncontroversial, sketch several available routes out of the interpretative dilemma, and then show the significance of these observations for the issues that will concern us most.

It is quite clear, then, that for the Stoics virtue admits of no tradeoffs in terms of any other good; indeed it is not even commensurable with any other good. This ultimate good, Cicero insists, has a unique quality that is not reducible to degrees or quantities of anything else (*Fin* III-33-4). For this reason we cannot speak of adding other goods to virtue to get a larger total: 'It is not the case that wisdom plus health is worth more than wisdom by itself separately' (*Fin* III.44). And given that the other goods and virtue are not commensurable with one another, and given that virtue alone has the highest worth, we then cannot speak of exchanging a piece or part of virtue, however 'small,' for even the largest possible amount of any other good or goods. No such trade-off would ever be justified. Furthermore, it is equally clear that for the Stoics external goods are neither parts of εὐδαιμονία nor necessary for εὐδαιμονία. They are 'things that are of no importance for living happily or miserably' (*Fin* III.50). Virtue by itself is self-sufficient, sufficient for εὐδαιμονία. But the Stoics, like Aristotle, also hold that εὐδαιμονία is, by definition, inclusive of everything that has intrinsic value, everything that is choiceworthy for its own sake. Putting these claims together, we are forced to

---

1. There are actually difficulties surrounding both of these claims. For since the Stoics, beginning at least with Chrysippus, did not claim to *be* wise men, and clearly thought the appearance of a wise man a rare and remarkable event, for which decent effort alone is not sufficient, they might appear to be placing this most important matter in the control of forces beyond the agent. They would certainly resist this inference; but it is not entirely clear what account they give in reply. As for the losing of virtue, numerous texts insist that the Stoic position (in contrast to that of the Peripatetics) is that virtue once acquired cannot be lost.

conclude, what a large number of texts in fact assert, that external goods, all goods other than virtue, have no intrinsic value at all.

At this point we might try various interpretative strategies. We might say that the preferred indifferents have a kind of second-class worth and are ordered below virtue in the sort of hierarchy that is known in contemporary philosophy as a 'lexical ordering': we satisfy all the claims of virtue first, but at any time when we have satisfied them we may go on to consider the claims of the indifferents. Or we might claim that the worth of the indifferents derives from the productive relation in which they stand to virtue in the career of the child, whose natural orientation to these externals plays a crucial positive role in the process of development. When the child's reason matures and he or she develops virtue, she does not cease to be a natural being, and she still appropriately follows the animal aspects of her natural constitution, when and as virtue permits. Various other similar solutions have been suggested. But I think it is clear that what we must absolutely avoid doing, if we are faithful to the spirit of the Stoic conception, is to attach to the indifferents, to external good, the sort of value that most ordinary people are seen to attach to them and that Aristotle explicitly accords them. That is, we must neither ascribe to them any intrinsic worth as constituent parts of the agent's εὐδαιμονία nor view them as absolutely indispensable necessary conditions for the εὐδαίμων life. But most ordinary people, and Aristotle with them, do ascribe intrinsic worth to love and friendship, which are in their nature relations with unstable and uncontrolled external items. Most people, again, see themselves as social beings, for whom the loss of a country or of political privileges is the loss of an intrinsic value. Most people believe that the good human life cannot be pursued and realized without a certain amount of food, shelter, and bodily health. The Stoic is committed to denying all of this.

It is particularly important to understand that when the Stoics deny all value to items other than virtue they are including here *all* the items to whose presence or absence the contingencies of the external world can make a difference. This means that they are committed to denying the intrinsic worth of external worldly action, and even, as they explicitly assert, the

intrinsic worth of life itself (D.L. VII.102). Not only 'external goods' like wealth and honor, not only 'relational goods' like the love of children, friendship, erotic love, political attachment, but also individual forms of virtuous activity, such as acting courageously, justly, and moderately, are held to be strictly speaking, worthless, on the grounds that they can, as Aristotle has argued and as anyone knows, be cut off or impeded by accidents beyond our control. But the wise man must be self-sufficient; his life is *always* εὐδαίμων, no matter what happens (*TD* 5.85). The virtues are held to be *states* of soul (διαθέσεις—cf. D.L. VII.89, 98). Cicero's interlocutor tells us that it is as if we said that in spear throwing the ultimate end was to 'do all one could to aim straight'—and the actual hitting of the target, even, presumably, the actual throwing action, will be no part of what is esteemed (*Fin* III.22). Virtue, then, is not an *inert* inner condition: it is imagined as a striving or straining: indeed, as Diogenes Laertius tells us, 'the good man is always using his soul, which is perfect' (VII.128). But, first, these inner activities are explicitly said to be unaffected by worldly contingency (D.L. VII.128); second, they are held to be complete in themselves, quite apart from their emergence into the world. They are complete in themselves, from the very moment they begin. The worldly performance is for this reason called a mere 'aftergrowth' (ἐπιγεννηματικόν, Cic *Fin* III.32). The wise man does not need to stride out into the world at all, to open up his soul to the world, to press the exigencies of his soul upon the world. He can, as Seneca so frequently says, simply stay at home; for at home, inside himself, he has whatever he needs. In this way the Stoics not only repudiate the value of the usual list of 'external goods,' to which (with the exception of φιλία) even Aristotle does not ascribe *intrinsic* worth. They go further and break with one of the claims about human good to which, as Aristotle tells us, ordinary people will most readily give their agreement: namely, that the good life consists in activity and that this activity goes on out in the world.

We are beginning to get a picture of the radical detachment of the Stoic sage, the detachment that greets slavery and even torture with equanimity, the detachment that receives the news of a child's death with the remarkable words, 'I was already aware that I had begotten a mortal' (Cic. *TD* III.30). Of this detachment and the view of the self it implies, we shall speak more in what follows.[1]

II

Among the most notorious and paradoxical theses in the history of philosophy is Chrysippus' thesis that the passions are forms of false judgment or false belief. On its face this claim seems bizarre indeed. For emotions such as fear, grief, anger, pity, and erotic love seem to us (and seem to the Stoics too, when they write about them concretely) to be (as their name implies) violent motions or upheavals in the soul, quite unlike the calm graspings and placings of reason. To equate passion with belief or judgment seems, furthermore, to ignore the element of passivity that installed the term 'passion' as another generic name. For judgments seem to be things that we actively make or do, not things that we suffer. In short: to feel love or fear or grief or anger is to be in a condition of tumult, violent movement, and vulnerability. How can this condition possibly be equivalent to judging that such and such is the case?

We can readily see why the Stoics might have *wished* to defend this strange claim. For it helps them in no small measure to establish the necessity and efficacy of philosophy as the art of life. If passions are not sub-rational stirrings coming from our animal nature, but modifications of the rational faculty, then, to be moderated and eventually cured they must be approached by a therapeutic technique that uses the arts of reason. And if judgments are *all* that the passions are, if there is no part of them that lies outside the rational faculty, then a rational art that sufficiently modifies judgments, seeking out the correct ones and installing them in place of the false, will actually be sufficient for curing human beings of

the ills that are caused by the passions.[2] False beliefs can be altogether removed, leaving no troublesome trace behind them. If, in addition, the curing of the passions (which, as we shall see, means their total extirpation) is the central task for which we require an art of life, then philosophy, in showing that it can cure them, will establish its own practical sovereignty. So the analysis of the passions and the description of a philosophical therapy go hand in hand. Chrysippus wrote, we are told, four books on the passions. In the first three he argued for his analysis of passion and gave his accounts and definitions of the particular passions. The fourth book turned from this theoretical basis to the practice of curing. It was called the θεραπευτικόν, the therapeutic book, and also the ηθικόν, the one concerned with ethical practice. Clearly this book required and rested on the analysis for which the first three books had argued.

But it is one thing to see why a certain thesis is important to a philosopher, quite another to assess its truth. A closer analysis shows, however, that the apparently strange thesis is not merely a handy theoretical tool imposed by force upon the experience of life. It is one the most powerful candidates for truth in this area; and it is also far less counterintuitive than we might at first think.

These two issues—intuitive acceptability and truth—are closely linked in most contemporary ethical thought. They were also closely linked in the thought of Chrysippus. It would be surprising indeed if he had completely missed the mark where ordinary belief and experience are concerned. For more than any other ancient philosopher, with the possible exception of Aristotle, he is constantly, deeply, and almost obsessively concerned with the close investigation of ordinary thought and language. It is clear that his book on the emotions is no exception to this general policy. Aristotle characteristically begins an inquiry with a brief dialectical summary of ordinary beliefs and sayings on a topic.

---

1. At this point, in the longer manuscript from which this article is drawn, there follows a section examining the Stoic view that all inner activities—thoughts, feelings, intentions—are morally assessible, are, indeed, good or bad acts in themselves, straight from their conception in the heart, whether or not they ever make their way out into the world. (See esp. Cic *Fin* III.32.) This supplies Stoics with a further motivation for wishing to treat the passions: for passions are pollutions of an agent's moral being, even if they do not lead to bad external action.

2. Later Stoics who reject Chrysippus' view and posit a natural irrational part of the soul are led to the view that philosophy must be supplemented by music (understood in a rather non-cognitive way) which alone can tame this animal part. See esp. the fragments of Diogenes of Babylon *On Music* in *SVF* III, pp. 221-35. Early Stoics value poetry, but on cognitive grounds.

Chrysippus goes further, filling much of his four-book work with scores of observations on ordinary usage, on common expressions, on literary passages used as evidence for ordinary belief, and even on our gestures as evidence of our common conceptions. He clearly thinks that our language and our daily practices reveal truth, and that philosophical theory ignores these data at its peril. Some of the examples recorded by Galen seem tendentious or naive; many more seem, to me at least, to reveal a subtle and careful attention to the nuance of what we say and the conceptual structure revealed in what we say. And it is very clear indeed that Chrysippus thought that his theory of the passions was the one to which everyday intuitions gave strongest support. Galen sometimes objects to his arguments on the grounds that experience refutes them. But more often, and revealingly, he mocks Chrysippus for spending too much time on what non-experts and poets say, too little on the theories of the philosophical experts. This all indicates that we cannot claim to have understood Chrysippus' theory unless we have seen not only how it coheres with his other theories, but also how it might be defended on intuitive and experiential grounds.

There is in Greek thought about the emotions, from Plato and Aristotle straight on through Epicurus, an agreement that the emotions are not simply blind surges of affect, stirrings or sensations that are identified, and distinguished from one another, by their felt quality alone. Unlike appetites such as thirst and hunger, they have an important cognitive element: they embody ways of interpreting the world. The feelings that go with the experience of emotion are hooked up with and rest upon beliefs or judgments that are their basis or ground, in such a way that the emotion as a whole can appropriately be evaluated as true and false, and also as rational or irrational, according to our evaluation of the grounding belief. Since the belief is the ground of the feeling, the feeling, and therefore the emotion as a whole, can be modified by a modification of belief. These ideas provided Aristotle with the basis of his accounts of emotions like anger and pity; they were also put to work in Epicurean therapy. Two further elements of continuity in the tradition prepare the way for Chrysippus' move. First, the beliefs on which emotions are based prominently include our evaluative beliefs, our beliefs about what is good and bad, worthwhile and worthless, helpful and noxious.

To cherish something, to ascribe to it a certain high value, is to give oneself a basis for the response of profound joy when it is present; of fear when it is threatened; of grief when it is lost; of anger when someone else damages it; of envy when someone else has it and you don't; of pity when someone else loses such a thing through no fault of his or her own. Second, the evaluative beliefs on which the major emotions rest all have something in common. They all involve the ascription of a high value to vulnerable 'external goods'—to items that are to some extent not in the full control of the agent, items that can be affected by happenings in the world. They presuppose, then, the non-self-sufficiency of the most valuable things (or some of them). They embody conception of the agent's good according to which the good is not simply 'at home' inside of him, but consists, instead, in a complex web of connections between the agent and unstable worldly items such as loved friends, city, possessions, the conditions of action. They presuppose that we have hostages to fortune. In this sense, we notice that there is a remarkable unity among the emotions. They share a common basis, and appear to be distinguished from one another more by circumstantial and perspectival considerations than by their grounding beliefs. What we fear for ourselves we pity when it happens to another; what we love and rejoice in today engenders fear lest fortune should remove it tomorrow; we grieve when what we fear has come to pass. When others promote the vulnerable elements of our good we feel gratitude; the same relation to an external good gives rise to anger, should the action of others prove maleficent.

In all these cases the emotion will not, as Aristotle stresses, get off the ground unless an evaluative belief ascribes not only worth, but also serious or high worth, to the uncontrolled external item. Fear requires the thought that *important* damages can happen to us through no fault of our own; anger, again, requires the thought that the item slighted by another is of serious value. I do not go around fearing that my coffee cup will break; I am not angry if someone takes a paper-clip. I do not pity someone who has lost a toothbrush. My breakfast cereal does not fill me with joy and delight; even my morning coffee is not an object of love.

These examples suggest a further thought, one that will be exploited by Stoic therapy. The damages of fortune, when they are seen as trivial or light, and thus prove insufficient to ground an emotion, are frequently seen this way because the object damaged or promoted is itself seen, with respect to its value, as replaceable. Coffee cups and paper-clips are rarely reasons for grief, because we don't care which one we use. There is a readily renewable supply, and all alike serve the function for which we value the item. If we try to imagine a case where the loss of a coffee cup would be an occasion for grief, we find ourselves imagining a case in which the particular item is endowed by the owner with a historical or sentimental value that makes it a unique particular. This suggests that the removal of the sense of particularity and specialness, in big things as well as small, might contribute to the eradication of fear, anger, and even love, should we wish to effect their eradication.

This tradition of Greek thought about the emotions seems, so far, to be not bizarre, but intuitively quite plausible. If Chrysippus does indeed end up in a counterintuitive position, he starts from a basis that seems to articulate our intuitions about the emotions as well as any philosophical reflection on this topic ever has. Chrysippus places himself within this tradition; but he also makes a radical departure from it. To see what he has done, we need to distinguish four theses that are defended within this tradition about the relationship between belief or judgment and passion.

(1) A P-belief is necessary for passion P.

(2) A P-belief is a constituent element in passion P.

(3) A P-belief is sufficient for passion P

(4) A P-belief is identical with passion P.

To be precise enough, this classification would need several refinements. First, we would need to distinguish occurrent passions from entrenched dispositional states. Stoic theory does this well, as we shall later see (§ IV). Second, we would need to get clear in each case about exactly what level of belief we are working with, and about how the different levels interact. Generic beliefs that at least some external uncontrolled items have high value; more concrete beliefs that there are serious damages that I may suffer by another's agency, through no fault of my own; the very concrete belief that X has wronged me in such and such a way just now—all of these are at work in the passion of anger; they need to be distinguished and their role in the passion assessed. The Stoics thought carefully about this. For now,

however, I shall speak only of 'a P-belief,' thinking of the highly specific occurrent evaluative belief (for example, 'X has seriously damaged an important element of my good life just now') that is the basis for a concrete episode of passion; this specific belief of course presupposes the more general ones, and would be removed with their removal.

To put things roughly and somewhat crudely: Plato and Epicurus hold (1) and probably none of the other theses—though their position on (2) is unclear, and Epicurus might be prepared to grant (3). Aristotle clearly holds both (1) and (2). ([1] is compatible with [2], unless we stipulate that the *way* the belief operates as necessary condition is to be an external independently specifiable *cause* of the passion.) He does not hold (3), because he insists that another element, the feeling of pleasure and pain, must also be there in order for the passion to be there. This element is not itself a belief, and it seems to be Aristotle's view that the presence of the belief does not, by itself, guarantee the presence of that added element. For he talks of people who believe they are wronged but don't get angry; instead they allow themselves to be 'trampled on.' This, he believes, is not a good response to a wrong, but it is perfectly possible. Again, he speaks of people whose experience with danger is so routine, so entrenched, that they believe that danger is there but experience no fear. Zeno, Chrysippus' predecessor, seems to have held (1), in a causal form that is incompatible with (2), and also (3). He says that the belief reliably causes a fluttering feeling, and that this feeling, not the belief, is what the passion itself *is*. He appears to deny (2); and yet there is need for caution here. For it appears that he individuates and defines passions at least partially via their causes, the beliefs; and it seems to be his view that the very same feeling not only could not be caused in another manner, but would not, if it were otherwise caused, count as that πάθος. All of these people, then, defend a close and intimate connection between passion and belief; but this connection stops short of identity.

III

Now we want to know: what leads Chrysippus to take the final step? We might have thought that the Zenonian and/or the Aristotelian position would have been sufficient to defend whatever picture of philosophical therapy the Stoics wish to defend.

Now clearly Chrysippus does not ignore or deny the affective and kinetic aspects of passion—for he says that the judgment that is identical with the passion is itself a πλεονάζουσα ὁρμή, an excessive inclination. But he wants to say that the sort of tumultuous movement it is, is a judgment; and that its seat is the rational soul. Why does he want to say this?

Here we frequently get a superficial answer. The Stoics, we are reminded, recognize only a single part to the soul, namely the rational part. They reject Plato's division of the soul into three distinct elements. Hence they *have* to make all psychological conditions conditions of this one element, no matter how odd or implausible this might seem. This seems to me quite inadequate as an answer. It was not an item of unargued dogma for the Stoics that the soul has just one part; it was a conclusion, and a conclusion of arguments in moral psychology, prominently including arguments about the passions. Galen tells us that Chrysippus argued first for the existence of some ἄλογος δύναμις, some irrational capability, in the soul, and *then* went on to consider the relative merits of a view that separates passion from judgment and the view he finally adopted, arguing against a pluralist psychology and in favor of his own one-part account of passion, as the view that best explained human irrationality. Posidonius, a perfectly good Stoic, takes the opposite course, restoring the three parts of the soul and placing emotion in an irrational part, because he felt that *this* gave Stoicism its best account of human irrationality. So what needs explaining is precisely the fact that is being invoked as an explanation-namely, why Chrysippus decides to make all passional states the conditions of a single part or faculty, and the same faculty that does our practical reasoning. Why does he think this the best and most plausible account?

We must begin by noting that a judgment, for the Stoics, is defined as an assent to an appearance. In other words, it is a process that has two stages. First, it occurs to me, or strikes me, that such and such is the case. (Stoic appearances are usually propositional.) It looks to me that way, I see things that way—but so far I haven't really accepted it. I can now go on to accept or embrace the appearance, commit myself to it; in that case, it has become my judgment. I can also deny or repudiate it: in that case, I am judging the contradictory. Or, like the

skeptic, I can live with it without committing myself one way or the other. Aristotle already uses a similar analysis. He gives the following example. The sun strikes me as being about a foot across. (That's the way it looks to me, that's what I see it *as*.) But if I have acquired a belief, to which I'm committed, that the sun is larger than the inhabited world, I will reject the appearance. I distance myself from it, I do not accept or embrace it—though of course it may go on looking that way to me. I say to myself, 'That's the way it looks to me, but of course that's not the way things really are.' In this simple perceptual case there seems to be nothing odd about saying both that the appearance presents itself to my cognitive faculties and that its acceptance or rejection is the work of those very faculties. Embracing or acknowledging an appearance, committing oneself to it as true, seems to be a task that *requires* the discriminating power of cognition. And unless we have an anachronistic Humean picture of cognition, according to which it is motionless, performing calculations without commitment, it seems in no way strange to say that it is reason itself that reaches out and takes that appearance to itself, saying, to to speak, 'Yes, that's the one I'll have. That's the way things are.' The classic way of distinguishing humans from other animals, from Aristotle on, is, in fact, to point to the fact that animals just move in the way appearances cause them, without making judgments. They move the way things strike them, without commitment. The extra element of selection, recognition, and commitment that sets us apart from the beasts is taken to be the contribution of reason. In fact, we might say that this is paradigmatically what reason *is*: that faculty in virtue of which we commit ourselves to a view of the way things are.

Let us now examine a different case. A person I love very much has died. It strikes me, it appears to me, that an item of enormous and irreplaceable value that was there a short time ago is there in my life no longer. If we want to display the appearance pictorially—a conception of appearing that some Stoic texts occasionally suggest—we might think of a stretch of daily life with a big empty space in it, the space that the loved person used to fill by his presence. In fact, the representation of this evaluative proposition, properly done, might require a whole series of picturings, as I would notice the person's absence in every corner of my existence,[1] notice the breaking of a thousand delicate and barely perceptible threads. Another sort of picturing would also be possible: I could see that wonderful beloved face, and see it both *as* enormously beloved and as irretrievably cut off from me. What we must insist on, however, is that the appearance is propositional: its content is *that* such and such is the case; and it is evaluative. Whether pictorially displayed or not, it represents the dead person as of enormous importance, as unlike anything or anyone else in the world.[2]

So far, we are still at the stage of appearing. Now several things might happen. I might reject or repudiate the appearance, push it away from me—if, for example, I decide that it is a nightmare or a morbid imagining. I might, like the skeptic, get myself into an attitude of complete neutrality about it, so that I neither commit myself to it nor reject it. But suppose that I embrace it, really accept or assent to it, commit myself to it as the way things are. Is a full assent to the idea that someone tremendously beloved is forever lost to me compatible with emotional equanimity? Chrysippus' claim is that it is not. I cannot really perform that act of recognition without profound upheaval. Not if what I am recognizing is that proposition with all its evaluative elements. Suppose I say, quite calmly, 'Yes, I know that the person I love most is dead and I'll never see him again. But I feel nothing; it does not disturb me at all.' (Remember Cicero's story about the father who says, on learning of his son's death, 'I was already aware that I had begotten a mortal.') Chrysippus will say, This person is in a state of denial. She is not *really* assenting to that proposition. She may be saying the words, but there is something in her that is resisting it. Or if she is assenting to something, it is not to that same proposi-

tion. She may be assenting to the proposition that a mortal human being has died: even (just possibly) to the proposition that X (the man she loves) has died; what she has not assented to is the proposition, that the person whom she loves and values above all others,[3] has died. For to recognize *this* is to be violently disturbed.

Notice the crucial importance of getting clear about which proposition we have in mind here. Some of the literature about Chrysippus' view makes the salient proposition one without any evaluative element, say, 'Socrates is dead.' We have already seen that the beliefs or judgments that are hooked up with emotion in the pre-Stoic tradition are judgments about value: cherishings and disvaluings of external uncontrolled items. We should now insist that the appearances that the Stoic agent either acknowledges or does not are, similarly, appearances with a marked evaluative element. To be more precise, in order to be equivalent to a passion they must have three features. First, they must make a claim about what, from the point of view of that agent, is valuable and fine, or the contrary. The texts speak always of the 'opinion of good and bad,' the 'supposition of good and bad'—both in giving the general theory and in defining particular passions (e.g. *SVF* III.385, 386, 387, 391, 393, 394). And we should insist here that the propositions express not simply the agent's desires and preferences, but his or her values: the scheme of ends believed choiceworthy, by which she chooses to live. Thus several texts insist that the agent not only believes that something bad is at hand, but believes that it is the sort of bad thing about which it would be right to be upset. This added element of affirmation shows us that we are not talking about mere desiderative whim and caprice.

Second, the propositions ascribe to the item in question not only some value, but a serious or very high value (or disvalue). Chrysippus tells us explicitly that the mistake—and the passion—come not in thinking the things in question to be good, but in thinking them to be much better than they are—in fact, to be the most important things (cf. *PHP* IV.5

---

1. I have depicted the grief as self-referential: strictly speaking, there are two aspects here. I mourn the dead person both as a part of my existence and experience, and also for his own sake, morning the loss of life and activity to him.

2. Strictly speaking, the recognition of qualitative uniqueness does not seem to be necessary—for I might believe that each and every human life is of enormous importance and value, no matter how like or unlike humans are to one another in both intrinsic and historical/relational characteristics. But the ascription of an extremely high value to a particular object is frequently connected with, and also nourished by, the thought that the object is irreplaceable.

---

3. I do not intend to suggest that loving implies high *moral* evaluation; I mean only to say that it implies thinking of the object as of tremendous *importance,* however that importance is to be understood.

20-22, 262D = *SVF* III.480; compare Galen's paraphrase, which adds the word μέγιστα—264D). Similarly, accounts of the dispositional conditions that underlie particular episodes of passion make them equivalent to a belief that something is very very worth pursuing (*valde expetenda,* Cic *TD* IV.26 = *SVF* III.427, Sen *Ep* 75,11 = *SVF* III.428; the Greek has σφόδρα, cf. *SVF* III.421), although that thing is in fact either only slightly choiceworthy or not choiceworthy at all. Again, a passage of Posidonius, reporting Chrysippus, speaks of a conviction that a thing contains a 'great benefit' (fr. 164 E-K). The belief that money is a good thing is said to turn into a chronic infirmity only 'when one holds that money is the greatest good and even supposes that life is not worth living for the man who has lost it' (*PHP* IV.5.25, 264D).

Finally, the belief must have a certain content: it must be concerned with vulnerable external things, things that can fail to be present, that can arrive by surprise, that are not fully under our control. This is common ground between Chrysippus and the pre-Stoic tradition. The Stoics do not explicitly include this in their definitions, though they repeatedly underline the connection between passion and a concern with external goods, and emphasize that a person who ceases to be concerned with externals will be free of passion. For this failure to be explicit they are reproached by Posidonius, who points out that the wise man ascribes the highest possible value to his wisdom, and yet does not feel fear for its loss, longing for its presence, and so forth (fr. 164 E-K, 266D). Again, sometimes the texts speak as if the relevant group of judgments was identified by its falsity, relative to Stoic moral theory. This seems to be a strategic error too, since the Stoics claim to be able to persuade opponents who have another conception of good (see below, §V). The passion-beliefs all share, as the more concrete definitions make clear, a subject matter; and they can and should be identified and defined with reference to that subject matter. This would answer Posidonius' worry, and make more perspicuous the motivations behind the theory and the call for extirpation.

So far we have gotten only to thesis (3) on our list. We have argued that a judgment is an embracing of an appearing proposition; and that the real embracing of or assent to a certain sort of evaluative proposition is sufficient for being moved emotion-ally. It entails the emotion; if emotion is not there then we are entitled to say that real acknowledgment of the proposition is not (or not yet) there. But all of this—though it goes against Aristotle's claim that the belief-component of the emotion is independent of the feeling—could, apparently, be satisfied by a causal picture like Zeno's, in which the belief of necessity produces the passion, which is still seen as a distinct item. We still need to know, then, what leads Chrysippus to make the emotion itself a function of reason, and to make it identical with the assent which is the judgment.

First, then, why should the upheaval be seen as a state of reason? Well, what *is* it that gets the terrible shock of grief? I think of the person I love—I embrace in my mind the fact that that extraordinary person will never be with me again—and I am shaken. Where? Is the grief a fluttering off in my ear, or a trembling in my stomach? Is it a movement in some animal appetitive nature that I share with dogs and cats? No, these answers seem wrong. It seems clear that we don't want to relegate the grief itself to such trivial and undignified seats as these. We want to give it a seat that is specifically human, and discerning enough, complex enough, to house such a complex and evaluatively discriminating response. What part of me is worthy of grieving for the person I love? Perhaps we could invent a special emotional part of the soul to house it. But in order to be capable of housing it, this part would have to be capable of conceiving of the beloved person in all his beauty and specialness; of comprehending and responding to the evaluative proposition on which the grief is based, even of accepting it. It would have to be able to know and properly estimate the richness of our love for each other; to insist on the tremendous importance of that love, even in the face of Stoic arguments belittling it; and so forth. But then it will need to be very much like reason: capable of the same acts of selection, evaluation, and vision that are usually taken to be the works of reason. It then begins to seem peculiar to redouble faculties. If we have a faculty on hand that can perform this job, we surely would do best to make the grief a state of that same faculty. The point is, once we make the emotions as cognitive and selective as Chrysippus, building on his tradition, argued that they must be, then it makes no sense to have an irrational part of the soul. Reason looks like just the place to house them.

But, we object, this is not yet clear. For if it is true that emotion's seat must be capable of many cognitive operations, there also seems to be an affective side to emotion that we have difficulty housing in the soul's rational part. We have already begun to respond to this point by stressing the fact that Stoic reason is dynamic, not static. It moves, embraces, refuses. It can move rapidly or slowly; it can move directly or with hesitation. We have imagined it entertaining the appearance of the loved person's death and then, so to speak, rushing towards it, opening itself to take it in. So why would a faculty this dynamic, this versatile, be unable to house, as well, the disorderly motions of the ensuing grief? Sophocles' Creon, confronted by the death of his only son, says, 'I accept this knowledge and am shaken in my reason' (*Antigone* 1095). What Chrysippus wants us to see is that this *can* happen; reason is capable of that. But if this is so, why push off the affect into some corner of the soul more brutish, less discriminating, less closely connected with the cognitive and receptive processes that we have seen to be involved in grieving? 'I recognize this and (incidentally) I am shaken in my gut.' Here we lose the close connection between the recognition and the being shaken that Chrysippus' analysis, and Creon's speech, give us. No, we want to say, the recognizing and the upheaval belong to one and the same part of me, the part with which I make sense of the world.

I have spoken of the recognition and the 'ensuing' upheaval. The final stage in Chrysippus' argument is to tell us that this distinction is wrong and misleading. When I grieve, I do not first of all coolly embrace the proposition, 'My wonderful lover is dead,' and then set about grieving. No, the real, full recognition of that dreadful event *is* the upheaval. It is like putting your hand straight down on the sharp point of a nail. The baneful appearance sits there, asking me what I am going to do about it. If I go up to embrace it, if I take it into myself, open myself to receive it, I am at that very moment putting the world's knife into my own insides. That's not preparation for upheaval, that's upheaval itself. That very act of assent is itself a wrenching, tearing violation of my self-sufficiency and my undisturbed condition. The passion is a 'very violent motion' that carries us along, 'pushing us violently' towards action (*SVF* 390). But this does not imply that it is not a form of recognition. For, as Chrysippus insists, 'it is belief it-self that contains the disorderly kinetic element' (*SVF* 394). Knowing can itself be violent.

Seneca adds a useful distinction. Sometimes, he says, the presence an appearance might evoke a reaction even when the appearance itself is not accepted or taken in, but, so to speak, just strikes against your surface. Sudden pallor, a leap of the heart, sexual excitation—all of these bodily movements may be caused by the appearance alone, without assent or judgment. (In saying this he is following a tradition hat goes straight back to Aristotle's *De Motu Animalium*, which uses the very same examples.) But these are not passions: these are mere bodily movements. It is only when the appearance has been allowed in, that we get—in the very act of recognition—the tumult of the mind that is the passion (*Ir* II.3).

In short: we have here a dynamic conception of practical knowing or judging, in which a judgment is not a cool inert act of intellect set over against a proposition, but an acknowledgment, with the core of my being, that such and such is the case. To acknowledge a proposition is to realize in one's being its full significance, to take it in and be changed by it. On this conception—which seems to me to be a powerful one—there is every reason to insist that passion and judgment do not come apart: rather, the passion is itself a certain sort of assent or acknowledgment: an acknowledgment of the tremendously high importance of something beyond my control, an acknowledgment appropriately called 'excessive' because it transgresses the limits prescribed by right reason for our relation to things external.

Chrysippus adds one further significant element to his account. The judgment, to be equivalent to a passion, must be πρόσφατον: not yet spoiled or digested, 'fresh.' This word, used frequently of food, and also of corpses newly dead, implies that no decomposition has yet set in—the item in question still has its pristine character. The point of this seems to be to allow for certain sorts of affective distancing, especially over time, compatibly with the retention of the same belief or judgment. When the person I am mourning has been dead for a long time, I will no longer have the violent recognition of his death that is identical with grief. Without the supplement, Chrysippus would then have been required to say that I no longer judge or believe that he is dead; or, equally implausible, that this cool and distant recognition is itself identical with grief. He does not wish to say either of these things. For there are many ways to acknowledge an irreplaceable loss, and over time those ways naturally transform themselves. When, like food, the loss has been assimilated or digested, I will still have the same judgment and the same recognition, but it seems wrong to say that I still have the passion. Loss of 'freshness' is usually portrayed in the texts as a temporal matter; though we might be able to imagine other factors that might distance me from passion without entailing a refusal to recognize or admit the proposition.

It may seem that here Chrysippus gives the game away. For isn't he admitting after all that there is something more to grieving than believing that . . . ? And isn't this something, this 'freshness,' an irrational element that has nothing to do itself with grieving? Yes, and no. Yes, having a certain belief is not, we now see, sufficient for grieving. (Though we should remember that Chrysippus advances this point with uncharacteristic tentativeness, saying that the phenomenon is 'hard to understand' [ἀσυλλόγιστον].) No, because the difference is itself a cognitive difference—a difference in the way that proposition is active in, received by, the self; above all, a difference in its relation to other propositions. The 'fresh' acceptance is something tearing and wrenching. Since it concerns my deepest values, it upsets everything in me, all the cognitive structures of hope, cherishing, and expectation that I have built up around those values. But when the proposition has been there for a long time, when the element of surprise and tearing is gone, it has lost its extreme sharpness, its intrusive cutting-edge, since I have by that time adjusted my life and the rest of my beliefs to fit with it. It does not assault my other beliefs, it sits alongside of them. For example, I don't any longer look forward to happy times that I will share with my lover. I don't have the belief that he will be with me tonight, or expect to see his face when I open the door. These, however, are cognitive changes. It was the discrepancy of the death-proposition with so many others that gave grief its bite, and time removes this discrepancy: not because the grief-proposition changes, but because other related propositions change. As Chrysippus says in this very passage, 'things don't present the same appearances.'

Chrysippus' picture has interesting implications for the analysis of ethical conflict. On the parts-of-the-soul view, conflict is viewed as struggle between two forces, different in character, and simultaneously active within the soul. Reason leads this way, desire pushes that way. The outcome may or may not be a matter of sheer strength; what is crucial is that both forces are active together, until one wins. Suppose that I am mourning for the person I love; suppose I am also, at the same time, striving to be a good Stoic, distancing myself from my grief with the thought that virtue is sufficient for happiness. The parts view will say that my irrational element is doing the grieving, while the rational part is thinking philosophical thoughts and endeavoring to restrain me from grief. Chrysippus would urge us, instead, to regard the conflict as an oscillation of the whole soul between recognition and denial. He speaks of the soul 'turning and shifting as a whole,' 'not the conflict and civil war of two parts, but the turning of a single reason in two different directions, which escapes our notice on account of the sharpness and swiftness of the change' (*SVF* III.459 = Plut *Virt Mor* 441C, 441F). At one moment, I assent (my whole being assents) to the idea that an irreplaceable wonderful person has departed from my life. At another moment, I distance myself from that knowledge, saying, 'No, you will find someone' else.' Or, 'that is just one person like many others.' Or, in the words of Seneca: 'You have buried the one you love; look about for someone to love. It is more prudent to replace your love than to weep for him' (*Ep* 63,11). Then the thought of my lover, with his particular eyes, his ways of moving and talking, overwhelms me, and I assent once again, to the thought that something has gone from my life that I can never replace. Chrysippus claims that this story of oscillation and shifting perspective is a more accurate account of the inner life of mourning than the story of battle and struggle. The oscillation may of course be extremely rapid; his point is that in this rhythm of embracing and denial, this uneven intermittence of vision, we have a more accurate analysis of the struggle of mourning than the parts model can provide. When I deny the evaluative proposition about my lover's specialness, at that moment I really am not grieving. When I am fully acknowledging that irreplaceability, I am not at the same time committing myself to a Stoic view of the good. We cannot fully comprehend the complex agony of these conflicts if we downplay their cognitive content, thinking in terms of contending forces. They must be seen as urgent struggles of reason with itself concerning what is valuable and fine in the universe, concerning nothing less than how to imagine the world. To struggle against grief is to strive towards a different view of the universe, in which that face does not appear, luminous and wonderful, on every path; in which places, no longer seen as habitations for that particular form, flatten out and lose their agonizing sharpness.

The picture of oscillation can explain one further feature of the experience of mourning that the parts model fails to notice. In my example, the thought of the Stoic attitude towards loss and the relapse into grief were not accidentally connected; one can be seen to have been, in a strange way, the cause of the other. It was the fact that I noticed myself looking for someone else to love, I caught myself saying Seneca's cold words about replacing, that threw me back, so to speak, into the arms of my grief. It was the cognitive content of one picture that reminded me violently of the opposing picture: the very suggestion of other replacements that prompted the return of that one face—as the ebbing tide is followed inexorably by the flood. The parts model cannot explain this rhythm, except to say that sometimes one force, sometimes the other, wins the upper hand. Chrysippus' view strikingly anticipates the account of mourning in Proust, when it suggests that the explanatory connections are tighter, and work through the very cognitive content of the opposing pictures. Just as it is the thought of making love with other women that awakens Marcel's grief and love for Albertine, until that love, like a raging lion, takes over the heart with its own violent view of the world, so here it is the vision of undifferentiated flatness that summons the vision of the single point, which returns with triumphant force as, in pain, I embrace it.

Notice that we have here, subtly delineated, two conceptions of mourning: the mourning of time, which is compatible with the retention of recognition and acknowledgment, and the mourning of denial, which cuts short the natural process of grief's digestion by veering over to a different view of the world. If I mourn in the first way, the way most people mourn, I will find my grief diminishing gradually, as my judgment loses its 'freshness.' I will eventually stop grieving altogether, but I will continue to retain the very same judgment. I never tell myself that the person who died was not uniquely beloved. I never alter my fundamental commitment

to that love. I may in time find another love; but I will not for that reason give up my thought that the first person was unique and irreplaceable; I will not go over to Seneca's flattened view, and I will probably continue to find it a shocking view. This means that I will be likely to see my new love, too, as a unique and irreplaceable individual, qualitatively distinct from the other, and indeed from all other people in the universe. So I will still be loving in a way that leaves me vulnerable to loss in the future. Because I have not altered my judgments, I remain the sort of person for whom grief is possible and natural. If I mourn in the second way, the way described in my example, the extinction of grief is the result of a more fundamental restructuring of my cognitive commitments. The grief is extinguished by the refusal of the evaluative proposition and the acceptance of a contradictory proposition. By the time that grief is gone, I will have denied the value of something I once valued supremely; and my attitude to a new love can hardly fail to be different in consequence. (Proust, mourning in the second way, comes to understand that each beloved woman is simply an instantiation of the 'general form' of his needs and desires, and that love has, really, nothing to do with the individuating qualities of the loved ones) I will be removed in a global way, from the possibility of future grief. As Chrysippus would say (recommending second way), I will be that much closer to being really cured. We shall shortly see how he argues for the superior value of this second way.

IV

As we by now expect, the Stoic passions will be very close to one another, resting, as they all do, on some kind of high evaluation of externals. And they are classified accordingly in the formal definitional accounts that become canonical in the school, with reference to two distinctions: the distinction between good and bad, and the distinction between present and future, as these opposites figure in the propositions to whose content passion is a response. Thus, there are four basic emotions: (1) judgment that what is presently at hand is good: called delight (ἡδονή); (2) judgment that something still in the future is good or valuable: called longing or appetition (ἐπιθυμία); (3) judgment that what is presently at hand is bad: called distress (λύπη); and

(4) judgment that what is still in the future is bad: called fear (φόβος). (Note that to recognize that a possible or future item is good or valuable is ipso facto to reach out towards it; that's what it is really to have that recognition.) There are in each case numerous subspecies, depending upon the specific subject matter of the content of the proposition. Pity is distress at the undeserved sufferings of another; envy is distress at the good fortunes of another, viewed as a bad thing for me; mourning is defined as distress at the untimely death of a beloved person; and so forth.

In some cases as well, we find the definition mentioning the specific kinetic character of the recognition or judgment: depression (ἄχθος) is a distress 'that weighs us down'; exasperation (ἐνόχλησις) is 'a distress that coops us up and makes us feel that we haven't got enough room'; confusion or distraction (σύγχυσις) is 'an irrational distraction that scrapes away at us and prevents us from seeing what is at hand' (D.L5 VII.112 = SVF III.412; cf. Andronicus in SVF III.414). These wonderful phenomenological descriptions show us that the Stoics are not neglecting the way passions *feel*. What they insist is, that in each case, the thing that feels like this is an act of assent or acknowledgment. Some recognitions feel like embracing a nail; others like rubbing yourself across a rough, grating surface; other propositions 'cut' differently, so other acceptances have a different phenomenological content.

These emotions, we have said, are concrete episodes of passion, to be identified with highly specific evaluative beliefs about one's situation. But we have also said that the Stoics recognize the importance of more general beliefs in generating the passions: the entrenched beliefs about the value of certain sorts of externals that, internalized in a person's ongoing conception of value, are the stable bases for concrete outbursts of passion. This level of belief figures, as well, in their formal theory, which here relies explicitly on the medical analogy. The soul of an ordinary person, says Chrysippus, is like a body that is prone to various diseases, some large, some small, which may arise from chance causes (PHP V.23, 294D). These diseases are diseased conditions of belief. A νόσημα or chronic illness of the soul is a stable condition of the personality that consists in accepting a value-judgment that leaves its

holder susceptible to passions. It is defined as 'a belief in the desirability of something that gets strengthened into a disposition (ἕξις) and hardens, according to which they take things that are not choiceworthy to be strongly choiceworthy' (Stob Ecl II.93.1 = SVF III.421, cf. D.L. VII.122). The belief that money is extremely important, the belief that passionate love is extremely important, these would be νοσήματα.[1] So too, presumably, would be the more concrete belief that X is extremely important—an entrenched belief that could become the basis for a concrete episode of love, fear, or grief. Chrysippus added that when such an illness is deeply enough entrenched and generates psychological weakness, we should call the condition of νόσημα plus weakness an ἀρρώστημα, or infirmity.

What this schema implies, among other things, is that (if we confine ourselves to the big generic categories and some especially prominent subspecies) you cannot have one emotion without letting yourself in for many others: perhaps even, given the fullness of time, for all the others. Once you have hostages to fortune, the very course of life will bring you now to grief, now into fear, now into intense joy. 'Those same things in whose presence we experience distress are objects of fear when they are impending and approaching' (Cic TD III.14, cf. IV.8). 'If the wise man should be open to distress, he would also be open to anger . . . and also to pity and envy' (III.19-20). 'Where you take greatest joy you will also have the greatest fear.' Just as there is a unity among the virtues, all being forms of correct apprehension of the self-sufficient good, just so there is a unity to the passions—and also to their underlying dispositional states. But this means, too, that there is a unity to the cure of the passions. 'You will cease to fear, if you cease to hope . . . Both belong to a mind that is hanging in suspense, to a mind that is made anxious by concern with the future' (Sen Ep 5, 7-8). The world's vulnerable gifts, cherished, give rise to the passionate life; despised, to a life of calm. 'What fortune has not given, 'she cannot take away' (Sen Ep 59, 18).

---

1. Examples in Diogenes Laertius are love of fame and love of pleasure. Stobaeus adds love of women, love of wine, love of money—and also the hatreds corresponding to each of these.

V

The Stoics teach that the passions should be not moderated, but extirpated. Indeed, they view this as one of the greatest differences between their therapeutic teaching and that of their Aristotelian/Peripatetic rivals. 'It is often asked,' writes Seneca, 'whether is is better to have moderate passions or none. Our people drive out the passions altogether (*expellunt*); the Peripatetics moderate them' (*Ep* 116, 1 = *SVF* III.443). They must be pulled out root and branch (Lactantius, *SVF* III.444, 447). We must, that is, not only cut out the external manifestation but also tear out the roots of the passion that go deep into the soul (Cic *TD* III.13ff., cf. 61-3). Since they are beliefs, and not organic parts of our innate constitution, they *can* be so extirpated (III.31, etc.). Indeed, nature herself *demands* their removal, saying, 'What is all this? I brought you into the world without longing, without fear, without religious anxiety, without treachery and these other plagues; leave the you came in' (Sen *Ep* 22, 15).

So the Stoic does not hesitate to describe the wise man as totally free from passion (ἀπαθής cf. D.L. VII.117). Free, that is, from fear, distress, pity, hope, anger, jealousy, passionate love, intense joy, and all of the many relatives and subspecies of these. Free, as Seneca etymologizes, from all vulnerability and passivity towards the world (*Ep* 9.2-4). The wise man is totally self-sufficient. 'Distress never befalls him: his mind is serene, and nothing can happen that would cloud it' (Clement II.v.4, cf. D.L. VII.118, Cic *TD* III.10ff.)5 External happenings merely graze the surface of his mind (Sen *Ep* 72). Indeed, his spirit is 'like the country on the other side of the moon: it is always calm there' (*Ep* 59,16). Our task must now be to understand the reasons for this extreme view of the goal of therapy. What, then, could possibly justify this militant and obsessive opposition to the passions?

The first thing that we must record is that, in Stoic terms, the judgments with which the passions are identical are *false*. Externals do not have such great value; indeed, they have no intrinsic ethical value at all. If one had only true evaluative judgments, both general and particular, one would never have any of them. This is evident from the account we have given of the Stoic theory of value. But this, in a sense, does not take us very far. For the very judgments that are false according to the Stoic theory of value are true inside the Aristotelian theory, which appears to be closer to our intuitions. So far, then, we have no reason why someone not independently convinced of the truth of Stoic theory should wish to extirpate the passions. And it is also clear that, although the Stoics certainly do defend their account of value with arguments, including a complete view of the universe, that are in many ways independent of their analysis of passion, they view the account of passion as offering serious support to the theory of good. One of the major reasons repeatedly adduced in favor of going over from the Aristotelian to the Stoic theory is that it will free us from the domination of our passions. And Chrysippus explicitly maintains that Stoic arguments about the passions should prove convincing even to those who are not yet persuaded by, or even acquainted with, the Stoic theory of good. He tells us that Stoicism has arguments related to any major conception of the good that a pupil is likely to hold, so that even if the pupil is not ready to accept the Stoic conception he can be convinced in terms of his own conception that he has reasons to get rid of the passions (*SVF* 474 = Origen *contra Celsum* I.64, I, 117 Kü; VII.51, II, 266 Kü). Cicero's statements about therapy tell the same story. Epictetus goes even farther. For he says that if he discovered that the belief that the external is nothing to us was false, and the arguments that support it deceptions, he would still cling to those deceptions, since from them he is likely to live in a smooth and undisturbed way (*Disc* I.4.27). We need to find out, therefore, whether the Stoics really have what they claim they have: independent arguments for extirpation, arguments that would be powerful to the Aristotelian as well.

A second Stoic claim takes us a little further. This is that the passions are not as important as the Aristotelian thinks in motivating virtuous action. Insofar as anger is defended on the grounds that without it patriotic or other-defending action would be either non-existent or weak, the Stoics are able to answer that a healthy mind can be motivated to correct action by the thought of virtue and duty alone. Indeed, that these are far *more* secure and reliable than the motivations that come from passion. Aristotle describes the man without anger as a man who will allow himself to be trampled down in a slavish manner, who will not fight to defend his country or those he loves. Seneca's *On Anger* vividly rebuts this contention:

> What, you ask? Will the good man not be angry if he sees his father slaughtered and his mother raped? No, he will not be angry; but he will seek restitution, and he will protect them . . . The good man will perform his duties without upheaval, without fear. My father is being murdered; I shall defend him. He has been murdered; I shall pursue the offender—because it is right, not because I am in pain. (I.12.2)

The good man's actions, he later says, are like the operations of the law: secure, constant, reliable, passionless—and reliable *because* passionless, and therefore maximally capable of rational self-determination (I.16.6).

This argument has something to say to the Aristotelian insofar as he has built his case for the passions on their importance as forces motivating to correct action. But an Aristotelian is bound to feel at this point that the main point has been missed. He will, first of all, dispute the Stoic claim that emotional motives are unstable and unreliable, and he will be right to ask for more and better argument here. But, more important, he will insist that the moral value of an action depends in part *upon* its motives and upon the other reactive feelings accompanying it; and that motives of passion are in many cases more morally valuable than motives of duty, as revealing cares and commitments that are themselves ethically valuable, as showing a recognition of the proper and high importance of certain externals. He will insist that an action, in order to be really virtuous, must not only have the same content as the virtuous man's action; it must be done in the way that the person of practical wisdom would do it, with those very motives, those very reactive feelings. The man whom Seneca describes is not only less praiseworthy than a man who *is* moved to anger by the rape of a mother and the murder of a father; he is actually failing to perform a virtuous action. Anger is the *right* motive here; grief and pity will be the right accompanying reactions. Right, because these feelings are acknowledgments of the importance of family love in a correct view of the good human life. So it appears that this Stoic argument, like the first, rests, after all, on the prior acceptance

of a Stoic view of value, and can do little work independently of it.

A third argument is only partially circular. It concerns the intensely painful feeling of the experience of the passions. In making the case for seeing the passions as sick conditions of the personality, their underlying dispositional bases as forms of chronic illness, the Stoics like to point out that, after all, passions are *felt*, more often than not, as violent pains and upheavals of the organism; moreover, the person subject to them feels him or herself to be in a chronic condition of weakness and lassitude. Stoic writings continually put before us the discomforts of anxiety, the raging disorder of anger, the agony of fear, the torments of love. Treatises on particular passions characteristically begin with a description of the painful phenomenology of the passion in question, designed to convince even those who might think the passion an appropriate response that its cost in pain and upheaval is too great to bear. Consider, for example, this description of an angry man from the opening section of Seneca's *On Anger*:

> His eyes blaze and sparkle; his whole face is crimson with the blood that surges from the lowest depths of the heart; his lips quiver, his teeth are clenched, his hair bristles and stands on end, his breathing is forced and harsh, his joints crack from writhing; he groans and bellows, bursts into speech with scarcely audible words, strikes his hands together continually an stamps the ground with his feet; his whole body is excited and "performs great angry threats." It is an ugly and horrible picture of distorted and swollen frenzy. (I.1.3-5, trans. J. Basore)

Even the allegedly positive emotions, these writings stress, have a phenomenology of upheaval and disruption. Joy of the intense sort is experienced as a giddy inflation, a dangerous uplift that is never without the vertiginous sense that at any moment we may be dashed to the ground. It feels thin, ungrounded, terribly exposed and fragile. Love of the intensely passionate sort (as opposed to the calm affection that is aimed at friendship, which Stoics approve and foster) feels uncertain, scary, unpredictable. And Chrysippus perceptively insists that lovers demand this element of surprise and unpredictability, rejecting a more solid relation (*SVF* III.475 = *PHP* IV.6.29, 276D). But spontaneity brings with it the possibility of upset, and therefore a continued enervating anxiety. In general, the dispositional state of a person who is prone to strong passions is a state that feels infirm, debilitated, lacking in solidity (cf. § IV). It is the psychological analogue to the physical state of a person who is lacking in muscular tone, effete, neurasthenic. (And of course, given Stoic psychological theory, it is just such a physical state.) Epictetus tells us that this feeling of psychological weakness is felt as disease even by those who have not yet learned from philosophy that their beliefs about externals are false. They are led to seek out philosophy in the first place by 'an awareness of their own weakness and impotence' concerning the things that they consider most important (*Disc* II.11.1).

Here, I think, the Stoics begin to have a case against Aristotle. To some extent, the argument is, again, circular. For unless one is already convinced of the ethical value of freedom from disturbance and anxiety, one will be less than overwhelmed by the obvious fact that passions are disturbing. However, the Stoics' detailed and careful work on the phenomenology of particular strong passions does forcefully remind Aristotelians of the magnitude and the terror of these disturbances of the personality. It asks them whether having these forces around, with their ability to shatter reflection, to invade and shake up other areas of life, is not too great a price to pay for the ethical satisfactions they afford. The claim that uncontrolled externals have serious ethical value was defended by the Aristotelian not with any knock-down or even by any very detailed or systematic argument, but only by pointing directly to intuitions about value that most ordinary people seem to share. Those intuitions may begin to weaken if we confront the ordinary person vividly enough with the agony of passion and the disruption it leaves behind it. Especially in the case of anger—and especially when Stoic writers depict its baneful influence in the public sphere—the case for extirpation made through this line of argument begins to look pretty strong. Do we want Nero to feel 'appropriate' Aristotelian anger when we see truly how ghastly a disturbance of personality anger is? Do we want leaders and wise men whose souls are always being cut through by knives, even if we do have a view of the good that endorses this agony as a correct response?

The Stoics add to this argument two others that are even more impressive. The first, an argument from integrity, contains an element of circularity, but is still powerful internally against the Aristotelian position. The second, the argument from excess, seems free of even this limited circularity. The argument from integrity reminds the Aristotelian that he himself is committed to a good life that is, for each agent, 'one's own and hard to take away' (*EN* 1095b25-6). He defines his selfhood, his identity, in terms of the planning and ordering of such a life. Identified with several intrinsically good ways of acting and living, and with the practical reason that arranges for the orderly enactment of these, he views an impediment to these actions or to this reasoning as a diminution and even an invasion of his sphere of self-hood, of his person. The Aristotelian himself has, then, a deep abhorrence for the condition of slavery, a condition in which his own actions and relations are not under his own control, but are dictated by externals over which he has no control. It was on grounds such as these that Aristotle himself argued against ascribing supreme value to external items such as wealth or fame and in favor of ascribing such value to virtuous action. He too, then, wants to be 'at his own disposal, not someone else's' (Epictetus, *passim*). But then doesn't he have to grant that by opening himself up to external goods such as love and the other grounds of the passions, by valuing in such a way as to be living a passionate life, he opens his personality, the core of his self, to the possibility of invasion and control by the world—therefore to a possible loss of personal dignity and integrity? Distress, λύπη, Chrysippus etymologizes, gets its name from the verb λύω 'dissolve': it is a dissolution of the entire person (Cic *TD* III.61; cf. Plato *Crat* 419C). The self of the Aristotelian agent is extended out over parts of the world of change. Happenings in that world can then lacerate it, even rip it limb from limb. It can be enslaved, raped, even devoured by another. To cultivate such attachments, and the conception of the self that goes with them, is to go about inviting rape and enslavement, violations that abase and humiliate because they damage what is most intimately one's own. This spectacle of violation is just as repellant to the Aristotelian as it is to the Stoic; but he does not move to close off that possibility. The Stoic self, by contrast, feels external happenings as things that merely graze the surface of his skin (Sen *Ep* 72). They can never penetrate to the core. He and his good are safely at home together. As Seneca puts it, his good 'is cultivated at home, and is entirely self-sufficient; he begins to be the subject of fortune, the minute he looks for some part of himself outdoors' (*Ep* 9,15); again, 'all his good begins and ends inside him—and he can say, 'All my goods are with me' (9,18). Philosophy builds an impregnable wall around the self, fortifying it against all possible assaults of fortune (*Ep* 82,5).

To some extent, once more, this argument is circular. That is, unless one accords the enormous value the Stoics do to self-sufficiency and rational control, it will not seem to be a fatal objection to the passionate life that it opens us to violation by fortune. Again, unless one believes that virtue is the supreme good, one will not be disposed to grant that the Stoic *does* have all good things at home with him. But the argument has force against the Aristotelian nonetheless. For even if he does not ascribe supreme value to self-sufficiency and freedom from external control, he does ascribe considerable value to it—far more, it appears, than is compatible with his endorsement of the passionate life. He is charged with not having considered seriously enough the cost of his scheme of value in terms of his own conception of integrity. The suggestion is that once he considers this he will realize that the values he most seriously prizes can only be found within a Stoic life.

Finally, the Stoics charge the Aristotelian with naive optimism about the extent to which passion can be moderated and controlled. The Aristotelian seems to believe that a good upbringing and good habits can make love and anger into moderate, discerning, self-governing elements of good character, choosing just the occasion and degree of expression that reason also approves. The Stoics reply that if we really enter into the inner life of passion, we will understand that this is not the case. Passions have in their very nature a propensity to ungovernable excess. Chrysippus, in a long passage of *On Passions* quoted by Galen, invents a vivid metaphor. When a person is walking, the impulse of the limbs can be checked and changed as he wishes. But if he is running, it is no longer this way. The movement carries itself further, by its own impetus—so that even if he should wish to stop or change course, he will be unable to. The impulse of his motion will take him on ahead of the point at which he wished to stop. That

is the way passion is. The true judgments of Stoic reason, like walking, are governable by our will; anger, fear, and love, even when they can be stopped, cannot be reliably stopped at the place where virtue would want. They carry us further than our wish (*SVF* III.462 = *PHP* IV.213-19, 240-242D).

There are actually two subtly different points made by this set of arguments. One concerns the internal structure of each passion taken singly. Love leads on to excessive love, anger to excessive anger. You cannot say, 'I shall have anger in my life, but I shall educate myself so that anger will always manifest itself in the right way at the right time towards the right people in the right degree.' No, say the Stoics, that is not possible; for the passion is tumultuous and gets ahead of your plan. As Seneca vividly expresses this point:

> There are certain things which at the start are under our control, but later hurry us on further by their violence and leave us no retreat As a person who throws himself off a precipice has no control over himself and, once cast off, can neither stop nor stay but, speeding on irrevocably, is cut off from all reconsideration and repentance and cannot now avoid arriving at the goal toward which he might once have avoided starting, so with the mind—if it throws itself forward into anger, love, or the other passions, it has no power to check its own impetus; its very weight and the natural tendency of vice hurry it on and take it to the very bottom. (*Ir* 1.7.4, trans. J. Basore, with changes)

And Chrysippus has insisted that it is in the very nature of passion that those who are in it disdain planning and control. Absence of control is, indeed, a part of what people value in the experience of passion. We don't want lovers who obey a rational principle at all times. We like them to fling caution to the winds, to ignore sound advice, to follow their love in an 'uncalculated' spontaneous way—in short, to be carried away by love (*SVF* III.475 = *PHP* IV.6.29, 276D). They should have as their motto, he continues, the lines from Menander: 'I took my good sense and stuffed it into a jar.' For that is what it means to have those values and those beliefs about the good.

This rejection of limit and measure is most unfortunate in the case of anger: for the excesses of that passion are not just silly and wasteful, they are harmful, both to self and to others. In anger, Chrysippus observes:

We take such leave of ourselves and become so far outside of ourselves and are so completely blinded in our frustrations, that sometimes if we have a sponge or a piece of wool in our hands we lift it up and throw it, as if by doing this we could accomplish something. If we had happened to have a knife or some other object, we should have used it in the same way. (*PHP* IV.6.44-5 = *SVF* III.478, trans. De Lacy, with changes)

Seneca, too, insists that anger cannot reliably be stopped short of cruelty and murderousness (*Ir* II.5.3). The politics of his time lend support to these contentions. Nero's career is not a reassuring spectacle for even the most determined Aristotelian.

This argument is complicated and strengthened by the view we have already mentioned, concerning the close interrelationships among the passions. Suppose the Aristotelian tries to reply by conceding a part of the Stoic argument. All right, he says, I shall extirpate anger, and jealousy, and any other passions whose excessive form is likely to be especially brutal and dangerous. But surely I need not extinguish love, or pity—or perhaps even fear. For the first two may have no harmful excess; and the excess of the third is surely harmful to me alone. The Stoic now points out that this is neither plausible nor even consistent with the Aristotelian's own position. The very same evaluations that ground one group of passions ground—given a change of circumstances or a different temporal perspective—the others as well. You cannot love without being liable to hate and anger; unless you are extraordinarily lucky you cannot love without actual hate and anger. For your love may have an obstacle; another person may take from you the one you cherish; and then the love itself provides anger with most exquisite fuel. Nor can you be the sort of person who feels intense joy without being frequently immobilized and tormented by fear, without sometimes suffering all the agonies of grief. Seneca writes to Nero reproving the emotion of pity (*Clem* II.4.4, II.5.4, II.6.4; cf. D.L. VII.123). If the Aristotelian thinks this a moral and political error, he had better reflect further on the connections between that emotion and murderous rage. He will find them if he looks.

These seem to me to be the most powerful of the Stoic arguments against Aristotle. For they tell him that he cannot have forms of evaluation and action that he cherishes, without committing himself to what he himself abhors. If there is any argument that would persuade those among us who cherish our passions to rethink those commitments, it would, I believe, be the argument that it is only in the Stoic life of self-containment that we can have stable gentleness and beneficence, the avoidance of terrible acts. (—'Wise men are harmless: for they do no harm, either to others or to themselves' [D.L. VII.123].)

VI

What is the Stoic left with? As far as the passions themselves go, he has, as Zeno put it, the scars of his former condition, though the wound itself is closed. Seneca interprets this to mean that he will 'feel certain suggestions and shadows of the passions, but from the passions themselves he will be entirely free (*Ir* I.16). He will, on the other hand, be permitted to keep three so-called affective responses (cf. D.L. VII.115 = *SVF* III.431; Cic *TD* IV.12-14 = *SVF* III.438). These items, called εὐπάθειαι, are not passions and are not identified with any high evaluation of externals. But they are motivations that will help the wise man steer his way among things indifferent. There is no good affective form corresponding to distress: in other' words, no good way to register negatively the presence of a bad state of affairs. A response of prudent caution (εὐλάβεια) is, however, approved towards future negative possibilities. In other words, without ascribing to externals any intrinsic value at all, while keeping one's responses exactly in accordance with reason's judgment about their value, one can still appropriately be motivated to avoid death and other dispreferred indifferents. If they come, one will not mind; but one can sensibly avoid them. Towards their future opposites one can move under the guidance of rational wish βούλησις. And finally, if the good externals should arrive as one wishes, one is permitted to have a certain sort of joy (χαρά), namely the sort that is defined as 'rational uplift' (εὔλογος ἔπαρσις).

So it is a further point in the Stoic battle against Aristotelianism to insist that they have not done away with the thing that people value most in the emotional life. There is joy here; joy without enervating uncertainty, joy without fear and grief, a joy that really does move and lift up the heart. 'Do you think that I am now robbing you of many pleasures,' Seneca asks Lucilius, when I try to do away with the gifts of chance, when I counsel the avoidance of hope, the sweetest thing that gladdens our hearts? Quite the contrary: I do not wish you ever to be deprived of gladness. I would have it born in your own house; and it is born there, if only it be inside of you. Other objects of cheer do not fill a man's bosom; they merely smooth his brow and are inconstant—unless perhaps you believe that he who laughs has joy. The very soul must be happy and confident, lifted above every circumstance. (*Ep* 23,3, trans. R. Gummere)

Interpreters sometimes point to passages such as this in order to argue that Stoic extirpation is not the radical move against our emotional life that we might initially think. For though the tumult is undone, much happy affect still remains.

But I believe that we should not be lulled by this sort of Stoic rhetoric into thinking that extirpation will leave much of human happiness where we are accustomed to find it, while merely getting rid of many difficulties and tensions. The state that Seneca describes is indeed *called* joy. But consider how he describes it. It is like a child that is born inside of one and never leaves the womb to go out into the world. It has no commerce with laughter and elation. For wise men, we know, are severe, αὐστηροί, intolerant of idle pleasure in themselves and in others (D.L.VII.117); and it is difficult to laugh if one is never caught off guard. Indeed. the letter goes on,

Real joy believe me, is a stern matter. Can one, do you think, despise death with a carefree countenance, or with one that is full of mirth . . . Or can one thus open his door to poverty or hold the curb on his pleasures, or contemplate the endurance of pain? He who goes over these things with himself is indeed full of joy; but it is not a cheerful joy. It is just this joy, however, of which I would have you become the owner; for it will never fail you once you have found its source . . . The joy of which I speak . . . is something solid . . . Therefore I pray you, my dearest Lucilius, do the one thing that can render you really happy: cast aside, and trample under foot all those things that glitter outwardly and are held out to you by another or as obtainable from another; look toward the true good, and rejoice only in that which comes from what

is your own. And what do I mean by "from what is your own"? I mean from you yourself, and your own best part. (23,4-6, trans. R. Gummere, with changes)

The change to this joy from our own is vast. It is the change from suspense and elation to solid self-absorption; from surprise and spontaneity to measured watchfulness; from wonder at the separate and external to security in that which is oneself and one's own. To follow Seneca's sexual metaphors, it is the change from passionate intercourse, giving birth, and child-rearing to parthenogenetic conception, followed by the retention of the conceived child forever inside the womb. It is a change that leaves no part of life untouched. We are promised great good; perhaps more important, we are promised the avoidance of great evil; and for this good and this freedom from evil we are asked to give up what are now to us the most precious things, the very bases of our daily life. Epictetus imagines speaking to Medea, the unhappy heroine of Chrysippus' favorite tragedy. He gives her one simple formula for happiness: 'Stop wanting the man you love, and there is not one of the things you want that will fail to happen' (*Disc* II.17.22). I claim that this is not casual modification. Indeed, it is not modification at all. It is what the Stoics said it was. It is extirpation.

Department of Philosophy
Brown University
Providence, RI 02912
U.S.A.

Abbreviations

Cic *Fin* = Cicero, *de Finibus Bonorum et Malorum*
Cic *TD* = Cicero, *Tusculan Disputations*
Clem *Strom* = Clement, *Stromates*
D.L. = Diogenes Laertius, *Lives of the Philosophers*
Epict *Disc* = Epictetus, *Discourses*
Galen *PHP* = Galen, *de Placitis Hippocratis et Platonis*
Plut *St Repugn* = Plutarch, *de Stoicorum Repugnantus*
Plut *Virt Mor* = Plutarch, *de Virtute Morali*
Sen *Ir* = Seneca, *de Ira*
Sen *Tranq* = Seneca, *de Tranquillitate*
Sen *Ep* = Seneca, *Epistulae Morales*
Stob *Ecl* = Stobaeus, *Eclogae*

ANNETTE BAIER

Whom Can Women Trust?

Feminist ethical theory is a modern phenomenon. Feminist ethics is not a theory with historical roots; instead it has arisen out of the failure of traditional ethical theories to take seriously women's moral concerns. A feminist ethical theory is often identified as a morality of care and responsibility, distinguished from the morality of rights and duties familiar in traditional ethical theories. Growing awareness of the unique moral aspects of women's lives has resulted in the publication of numerous books and articles about women and morality, initiating the development of a feminist ethical theory.

In the following essay, Hume scholar Annette Baier combines a feminist perspective with Humean insights. The topic addresses the part that women play in perpetuating the inferior social status of women. Hume recognized that women may play a role in the male domination of women, and for that reason Baier turns to his writings for her starting point. Baier identifies a "confederacy of sexists," men and women who conspire, however unconsciously, to perpetuate the social institutions that restrict women. The conspiracy, she alleges, extends to the raising of sons and daughters who will, in their turn, contribute to the inequality between sexes. In light of this complicity in the tyranny of men over women, even by loving mothers who have been willing to be the primary caregiver to their children, Baier questions whether women can trust other women, even their own mothers.

For another work concerning issues of particular importance to feminist ethics, see Virginia Held, "Feminism and Moral Theory."

"But though the males, when united, have in all countries bodily force sufficient to maintain this severe tyranny, yet such are the insinuation, address and charms of their fair companions that women are commonly able to break the confederacy, and share with the other sex in all the rights and privileges of society. "[1] For years, decades even, I referred to this claim of Hume's as a claim about women's power to break male confederacies. It took a male reader of the passage, Chris Williams, to point out to me that Hume does not say that the confederacy to be broken is one of males only. Males are those accused of tyranny over women in many societies, but the confederacy that supports the tyranny that needs to be broken may not be an exclusively male one, indeed has not been an exclusively male one. Women must distrust not only the men who have the bodily force to maintain severe tyrannies but also the women whose insinuation, address, and charms are used to keep in favor with the tyrants, to help maintain rather than to break the confederacy that, in the extreme case, reduces women to slavery "incapable of all property, in opposition to their lordly masters."

Not only is this a pretty obvious truth once it is pointed out, but it is indeed one that Hume explicitly draws attention to in the essays that he addressed particularly to the women of his time and culture. In "Of Love and Marriage," for example, he gently chides them for taking satires on the institution of matrimony to be satires on themselves. "Do they mean that they are the parties principally concerned, and that if a backwardness to enter into that state should prevail in the world, they would be the greatest sufferers?"[2] Then there is his "pretty remarkable instance of a philosophic spirit," the young woman who, "observing the many unhappy marriages among her acquaintances, and hearing the complaints which her female friends made of the tyranny, inconstancy, jealousy, or indifference of their husbands, being a woman of strong spirit and an uncommon way of thinking," resolved to avoid matrimony without avoiding motherhood and resolutely did so.[3] "Our philosophical heroine" had to be fairly uncommon in her way of thinking, given the more usual female complicity in maintaining the institutions that perpetuated the inferior social position of women. The most thoroughgoing complicity consisted, and consists, not merely in vowing obedience but in bringing up daughters to do the same. But as Nancy Chodorow points out to us,[4] a woman's mere willingness to be the primary caregiver, however radically one might try to bring up daughters no differently than one brings up sons, may be enough to guarantee to one's daughters unequal ability to cope in "a man's world" and to one's sons unequal ability to cope in "a women's world." The confederacy of sexists is not easy to leave. In this chapter, I shall explore only some aspects of this confederacy. My title question, "Whom can women trust?" will be narrowed to "When can women trust women?" and that narrowed even further to trust between mothers and daughters.[5]

Should girls distrust their loving mothers simply because their love has been expressed in their loving care, their being willing to take the main responsibility for caring for them when they were infants and young children? Is the only trustworthy parent a co-parent who is very careful to keep the parental partnership, at least when it is a heterosexual one, from becoming unequal in time spent with the children? Maybe. But punctiliously coequal parents might still be abusive,[6] neglectful, unloving, bigoted, tyrannical, or themselves distrustful of their children, so that equal time with each parent is at best a necessary not a sufficient condition for the well-foundedness of children's trust in parents and of young daughters' trust in mothers.

Women, precisely because they have so often themselves been victims, should not be trusted too readily by other women or by men. The fact that they have been the victims of lies, exploitation, betrayal, cannot be expected to make them less ready

themselves to lie, cheat, and betray. Tit for tat is supposed to be a rational strategy. As Hume wrote, "Tyrants, we know, produce rebels; and all history informs us that rebels, when they prevail, are apt to become tyrants in their turn"[7] Women can scarcely be said to have "prevailed" in our culture, but there can be small rebel victories and so small temptations to tyranny, not just to engage in tit for tat against the earlier tyrants but to seize any opportunity for a bit of conspicuous exercise of power, to lord it over someone, male or female. This is the sorry lesson of history and of our known psychology. Toppling tyrants not enough to end tyranny-we have to have more than a mere rebellion, a mere switch of elites; we have to alter the structure of government, stage a revolution.

Have we done that? The governance that would need to be altered would be not merely that of parents over children but governance in all other places where the pernicious patriarchal model has affected structures of power. In this nation, we seem a very long way from having a woman president (and even if we did, if that were accompanied by no structural changes, it would not amount to much except a symbolic victory). Even the rebellion is badly incomplete as long as there is not equal representation of women at the top as well as in the lower levels of all power hierarchies, in universities, in the media, in the arts, in business, in banking, in the Senate and House, among the president's cabinet and advisers. But the rebellion, the replacement of at least half the powerful men by powerful women, is not likely to happen without some revolutionary structural changes of a sort that we have only begun to institute. Paid pregnancy leave for women, parental leave for both parents after the birth of their child, and proper allowance in promotion decisions for such parental time off are as necessary as equal educational opportunities, equitable divorce rights, settlements, and alimony. Equal pay for equal work is only the beginning—we need equal allowance and compensation for equal homemaking services, and we need to demand that the services in the home *be* equally shared.

As fathers take on more of their share of household drudgery, which women have always been expected to do even when they worked outside the home, and as both parents share the privilege of responsibility for child care, then of course the task and burden that used to be reserved for men—military service—must also be shared by women. This is only fair. However, it presents some problems. It might seem to be social suicide for a nation to put its pregnant young women and its nursing mothers into the front line along with the young fathers and fathers-to-be. Even Hitler realized that a nation needs its young women for more important tasks than killing and being killed. Decimating the ranks of young males need make no noticeable difference to the birth rate, but decimating the ranks of young females can decimate their collective offspring. As far as sheer biological reproduction is concerned, we do not need more than a few "studs."[8] This basic sociobiological fact will become relevant to decisions about conscription to military duty in war time, when it will be only sensible to find some alternative form of war work for pregnant women and breast-feeding mothers, perhaps also for any young women who prefer it to military service, just as any humane society will also provide such alternative service to any conscientious objectors to violent warfare. But that women must carry a fair share of the general burden of defense, and that military careers must be as open to women as to men, seems clear. If we want equality, we must refuse that historically fatal offer "Serve and obey us, and we will fight to defend you." We must defend ourselves or, at any rate, do our share of the collective defense.

If this still seems a crazy proposal, to allow the not-yet-pregnant young women to be conscripted and killed in wartime, just to satisfy the demands of equality, of equal burdens as well as equal rights, then we could well consider why in modern conditions of warfare it is still deemed socially desirable that the young, male or female, be the ones who run the greatest risk of death and injury. Is it really still the case, if it ever was, that it takes the hot blood of youth to do the sort of things that members of the military forces must do in war time? Why not conscript those between forty-five and fifty-five? Why not let the young live out their youth and let the older people, some of whom take the decisions to go to war, themselves face the greatest threats? Is is that we feel we need our "elder statesmen" more vitally than we need our young men? Once we have elder stateswomen, the whole rationale of sending the young to fight their elders' wars might well be radically rethought.

Whom, then, can women trust? If the ones most naturally expected to have their welfare at heart—

namely, their parents—are likely to be patriarchs and patriarchs' accomplices, then the outlook seems fairly bleak. Let me make it quite clear that when I say that daughters cannot necessarily trust either their fathers or their mothers, I am not necessarily imputing ill will to either. To trust is to take both the trusted's will and competence to be good enough for them to be relied upon to look after some aspect of one's well-being or something of importance to one that one entrusts to their care.[9] With the best will in the world, some parents may yet be untrustworthy because they lack some crucial *competence* that parents need. If to mold a child's aspirations and sense of herself and her future properly, it takes a mother who has herself an exemplary sense of her own worth and her own options, or indeed if Nancy Chodorow is right and it takes a mother who insists on *sharing* the child rearing, not claiming exclusive right to it, then many mothers will be incompetent, however great their goodwill and dedication to their children. "The reproduction of mothering is the reproduction of women's location and responsibilities in the domestic sphere. . .that women mother is a fundamental organizational feature of the sexual division of labor and generates a psychology and ideology of male dominance as well as an ideology about women's capacities and nature."[10]

Stereotypically maternal, attentive mothers and stereotypically paternal, distanced fathers reproduce their own psychology in their daughters and sons just as, according to folk wisdom on this matter, the victims of child abuse tend to become victimizers. Parenthood essentially is a matter of transmitting some of one's own traits, and of one's own inheritance of potentialities, to one's children. If it is true that the very fact that the mother has taken on the main responsibility of child care limits the daughter's ability to compete successfully for the opportunity to take on any responsibilities except those of child care, then this happens behaviorally as well as genetically and whether or not the parent intends it to happen. How is this self-replicating pattern of gender roles to be stopped from going on and on, generation after generation?

According to Nancy Chodorow's theory, we should expect that this will occur either through the against-the-grain efforts of some women to share their nurturing role equally with their children's fathers and to take on other roles outside the home or by the agency of the lucky few whose upbringing was fairly evenly shared by father and mother. "My expectation is that equal parenting would leave people of both genders with the positive capacities each has, but without the destructive extremes these currently tend towards."[11] These will be the points of leverage for change, particularly for change in the social structures that have reinforced the gender roles that perpetuate inequality.

I am no psychologist or psychotherapist, so I have no way, except casual observation, of knowing whether Nancy Chodorow's theses are empirically confirmed. I tread warily here, since even if by an large her theses are correct, it still seems evident that some daughters of mothers who took almost the full responsibility for their children' care do succeed in careers and are willing to share parental responsibility, to divide their time between career and home, expecting the father of their children to do the same. We all know of instances where the pattern has been broken—by good luck, by special help, or by special ambitions. My own mother, for example, was the very embodiment of the nurturing mother, devoting all her time and care to home and children, content to let my father take over child care only in the evenings and on weekends and then under fairly close supervision. But she imbued four daughters with career ambitions, and all four continued these careers after marriage, two of my sisters bringing up, with their husbands' help, five children each, the girls as career-bent as the boys. So my own observation closest to home does not make me gloomy about the prospects for women's equality and for men's chances to share the child-rearing. By Nancy Chodorow's theory, my own mother was *not* the sort who should have had ambitious daughters, but she did, and indeed it was to a large extent her sense of what she herself had not had—educational training for a career—that fired her with ambition for her daughters, that motivated the efforts she made to encourage our ambitions and to keep us at our schoolwork when other temptations beckoned. She was as trustworthy a mother as a daughter could have had, if will and competence to turn out ambitious daughters is the criterion of trustworthiness, and this despite the fact that she did not fit Nancy Chodorow's specifications.

The power of the negative should not be discounted. Women throughout history have occasionally broken the fetters that they inherited. Discontent is the first step. To communicate to one's daughters the discontent one feels with the way things were for oneself, and the hope one has of a different way for them, clearly can be enough to empower those daughters to take a different way from their mothers', and it can sometimes empower the discontented ones themselves to bring about change. The women activists whom we have to thank for women's suffrage and for other hard-won changes were not themselves the products of the better conditions they tried to bring into being and sustain. Servitude is not necessarily reproduced along with the reproduction of mothering. As Nancy Chodorow herself says, social advances "depend on the conscious organization and activity of all women and men who recognize that their interests lie in transforming the social organization of gender and eliminating sexual inequality."[12] Sometimes it is the daughters who recruit the mothers into the struggle rather than vice versa or, more generally, the younger women who spur the older women on to action.[13]

In Francine du Plessix Gray's "Reflections (Soviet Women),"[14] we get rather scary informal confirmation of some of Chodorow's general theses about the bad effect it has on girls to be brought up primarily by their mothers with little sharing of the responsibility by the fathers. Extensive interviews with contemporary Soviet women, most of them fairly successful career women and all of them women working outside as well as inside the home, revealed that their lives were spent in work outside the home (usually under men as top bosses), very time-consuming shopping for scarce food, and very hard work inside the home, where they live with their mothers and their children, occasionally with a temporary husband as a sort of tolerated guest in the matriarchal realm. Marriage is normal, but equally normal is its fairly fast dissolution. There is a Russian proverb, "Women can do everything; men can do the rest," and the women that Francine Gray spoke with were mostly scathing about men's contributions to their lives. A husband, one successful woman gynecologist said, is "how can I say . . . an elective obligation," and her felicitous wording was greeted with approving laughter from her women fellow-workers.[15] To tolerate a husband in the home is to "take on an extra child," so little contribution to home life is expected (or perhaps allowed) from a Soviet husband.

"Here's the way our order of priorities goes: first a career; second a child. As for a man, that's irrelevant. He can go his way as soon as the child is conceived," said one successful program editor of a television station, who lives with her mother and her twenty-year-old daughter.[16] Francine Gray, interviewing these superwomen who themselves speak of their own matriarchal ways as "chronic," finds the popular Russian gaily painted wooden *matryoshka* dolls-within-dolls a fitting symbol for Soviet women as she saw them. They were like these dolls with "generations of parthogenetic females fitting snugly into each other."

This matriarchal subsociety appears to be having a disheartening effect on the young sons of these superwomen, who perform less well than their sisters at school and seem passive and diffident in comparison with their more aggressive, more confident sisters. Their prospects do not include any permanent niche within the mutually supportive women's world; they are expected to become as burdensome to any women they will love when they are adult as their fathers proved to be to their mothers. Useless in the home, self-indulgent, exploitative, charmless, incapable of contributing anything important (except a child) to a woman's happiness, these miserable male creatures are nevertheless the ones to whom the running of the nation is relegated. A Leningrad woman, Olga Lipovskaya, who edits a feminist newsletter, told Francine Gray that "politics always struck me and my women friends as something deeply unethical, as dirty work."[17]

This division of function, where men do politics and, when they can, sponge off women and women look after each other and also look after those cowed, silent little boys, produces personality types that are neither those that Nancy Chodorow analyzed nor quite those that her theory would lead us to predict. The girls, reared mainly by strong women, become strong women—aggressive, competitive, and independent but not ambitious to enter the dirty male political arena. The boys, reared virtually without fathers, become like their absent fathers—boorish, domestically incompetent, sad, and drowning their sorrows in politics as well as vodka.

This is no improvement over having aggressive, ambitious boys and diffident, modest girls. The Soviet superwomen are not contented with their lot; neither are the men. Nor can there be much hope of

structural change if the strong women eschew politics and the politically strong men either avoid or are banished from the homes where their children are growing up. One Soviet woman suggested that "a good feminist movement would make our women more gentle,"[18] and one of the effects of *perestroika* was seen to have been to enable "our men to feel less superfluous" by encouraging some male individualism. Such sentiments may bring some changes, but whether they will be changes that break the cycle of the reproduction of matriarchs and rogue males is not at all clear. For the women's discontent is not really with the chronic matriarchy but with the overwork it brings. "Of course we are grossly overburdened. But we wouldn't give it up for the world. We take such pride in surviving it," said a Siberian woman factory worker to Francine Gray.[19] Such pride in being able to do without men is not the best basis for the sort of cooperation with them that on Nancy Chodorow's theory is an essential feature of competent parenting.[20] As long as the superwomen pride themselves on their own aggressive independence, or rather on the independence of the new family unit of grandmother, mother, and daughters, they are not likely to want to have the fathers of their children playing a more active parental role.

What of trust? Is there mutual trust among the superwomen? Between mothers and daughters, mutual trust seems the norm, but in a wider female circle the attitude seems more a mixture of mutual respect and mutual suspicion. Ironically enough, competition for the few relatively "bearable" (that is, civilized and house-trained) males contributes to the lack of general female solidarity. When one rare happily married woman whom Francine Gray interviewed explained how her older husband had helped make it possible for her to study and shared the cooking and diaper changing, her fellow students gasped with envy and incredulity.[21] Collective action by Soviet women on behalf of Soviet women and on behalf of their children, both male and female, was not seen by the women Gray interviewed as very likely.

The strong mother-daughter ties—what one woman termed "the normal and absolute return of love"[22]—contrasted with the weakness of other social ties. Should these daughters trust their mothers so absolutely? Should a Soviet daughter "give to my daughter what my mother gave to me"?[23] If what is given is this toughness, this very selective capacity for trust, gentleness, and sharing of responsibility, this self-verifying expectation that men, if allowed in their homes, will merely "look at television and occasionally remember to play with the children,"[24] does not seem an altogether benign inheritance to pass on, not such a great cause for filial gratitude. And certainly the sons seem to have very little reason to trust these mothers who make them feel so marginal and superfluous, fit only for dirty politics and for taking out the garbage. There may *be* mutual trust in the matriarchal Soviet family, but to an outside eye it appears to be misplaced trust.

It is instructive to consider the pathology of another society's gender relations, to compare it with our own pathological gender relations in the United States. For we, though surely different from these Soviet women, are certainly not superior. Our faults, especially those of white, middle-class women, may run more to contented dependency on men than to exclusionary independence of them, more to false buildup of male egos than to ruthless deflation of them. Many of us vacillate between making sisterhood powerful and turning on our sisters in displays of petty infighting, squabbles for ascendancy, and secret leagues with the supposed enemies. If the Soviet women look rather fearsome, we look just plain ridiculous. Most us have no good reason to trust ourselves to be trustworthy custodians of the welfare of women and children.

Are we at least *more* trustworthy custodians of our own and our children's welfare than those who traditionally put women and children first, at least in their protective activities? Even if we, or many of us, are part of any conspiracy to keep us from full equality, are we at least relatively innocuous members of that evil confederacy? Not if some of us voluntarily take on the role of spokeswoman for the paternalistic status quo, as some of us obviously do. Do we have more "excuse" for such action than do the men, who are the more obvious "confederates"?

If there were some advantage to men in keeping women down, commensurate with the disadvantage it entails for women, then we could treat women as an oppressed "class" whose interests are opposed to men as a "class" in the Marxist sense. It is difficult to see what clear overall advantage it did bring men to keep women uneducated or educated only in genteel womanly matters, to attempt to restrict woman's place to

the home, and then have to employ spies and jailers to try to enforce the restrictions. The only conceivable advantages it brought were monopoly of rule, monopoly of most of the interesting work, and what Grotius, Pufendorf, and others gave as the justification of that male monopoly within marriage—perceived assurance to men that their wives' children were really their own, "not spurious or suppositious."[25] Today, the last assurance is no longer one that men can reasonably expect to get by any coercive means, so it really falls out of account as a factor. A woman's assurance on this matter is not likely to be more trustworthy simply because she chooses the role of subservient wife rather than free woman. What of the monopoly of nondomestic work and of rule? Is the latter not always an advantage to the ruler? Is it not always a loss of advantage to compete with twice as many competitors for any job and to move from being ruler to becoming co-ruler?

As far as the last goes, it depends on the strength of one's hunger for power over others. Hume teases the women of his day with an over-valuing of the advantage of being boss. So restricted were his Scottish women contemporaries to a domestic realm in which to exercise any dominion that some of them were charged by Hume with the folly of taking "a fool for a mate, that she might govern with less control."[26] If the cost of being sole ruler is having fools as the ruled, the cost is too high. What is true for the women is as true for the men. If their monopoly of rule entailed their need to keep women as foolish as they could be—simpering sillies rather than full participants in "the feast of reason"—then the advantage was very dubious. As far as the monopoly of nondomestic work goes, males do lose some advantages once they compete with women. But to waste the reason and the passion of half the human population by narrowing their scope to domestic concerns is a pathological case of the division of labor. "By the conjunction of forces, our power is augmented: By the partition of employments, our ability increases: And by mutual succour we are less expos'd to fortune and accidents."[27] What abilities were increased by the partitioning of employment so that women got all and only the domestic work? Not child-rearing ability, if Nancy Chodorow is right. As for the ability to rule, that requires not just wisdom but power, and "by the conjunction of forces, our power is augmented."

Whom can women trust? Not ourselves, until we manage to get a partitioning of employments that really does increase the abilities that, on reflection, we really do want increased. We surely do want to increase our ability to raise free-spirited children, both boys and girls. To reflect properly on what abilities are worth increasing, we surely do need the power of conjoined forces, so we should be against *any* monopoly of rule, any sharp partition into ruler and ruled. The cooperative scheme, the conjunction of forces, cannot afford to exclude any, not even the old oppressors.[28] Soul-satisfying fantasies of reversing "the trade in women" so that those few desirable gentle men who like to cook[29] become a commodity that the women trade in while the rest are dumped as superfluous must, however reluctantly, be put aside if we really aim to give daughters good enough reason to want to pass on to their daughters what they got from their mothers.

Notes

I am grateful to Chris Williams for getting this essay started and Claudia Card for the correction of some of its errors.

1. This quotation and the next are from David Hume, *An Enquiry Concerning the Principles of Morals*, ed. L. A. Selby-Bigge and P. H. Nidditch (Oxford: Clarendon Press, 1975), 191.

2. David Hume, *Essays: Moral, Political, and Literary*, ed. Eugene Miller (Indianapolis: Liberty Classics, 1985), 557.

3. Ibid., 542.

4. Nancy Chodorow, *The Reproduction of Mothering* (Berkeley: University of California Press, 1978). Nancy Chodorow's study is of parenting by heterosexual couples.

5. Since I am appealing to Nancy Chodorow's findings and these are limited to parenting by heterosexual pairs of parents, my remarks will be yet further restricted to mothers and such daughters whose other provider of parental care is a father. I use "mother" and "father" and "parent" to include those who are not the child's biological parents. Since Nancy Chodorow's theory rests on acceptance of some Freudian views about the development of male and female self-identification, her findings cannot be generalized to cases where children are reared by homosexual parents.

6. For a sensational account of a trusting and trusted team of stepfather and mother in relation to a daughter, see Shelley Sessions and Peter Meyer, *Dark Obsession: A True Story of Incest and Justice* (New York: G. P. Putnam's Sons, 1990).

7. Hume, *Essays,* 560.

8. For a wonderfully informative account of "the mystery of males, why they're here and what they're for," see Fred Hapgood, *Why Males Exist* (New York: Morrow, 1979).

9. I develop this account of what trust is in "Trust and Antitrust," *Ethics* 96 (January 1986): 231-260.

10. Nancy Chodorow, *Reproduction of Mothering,* 208.

11. Ibid., 218. The heterosexual assumptions are very evident in this passage.

12. Ibid., 219.

13. My own consciousness of women's situation in this country is due largely to the influence of a succession of women students, among whom Carol Donovan, Lynne McFall, and Lynne Tirrell stand out as the ones who taught me most.

14. Francine du Plessix Gray, "Reflections (Soviet Women)," *New Yorker,* February 19, 1990, 48-81.

15. Ibid., 75.

16. Ibid., 74.

17. Ibid., 60.

18. Ibid., 74.

19. Ibid., 62.

20. If Nancy Chodorow is wrong in believing that the shared parenting must come from a male and a female parent, then of course such pride may not be so bad.

21. Francine Gray, "Reflections," 77.

22. Ibid., 81.

23. Ibid.

24. Ibid., 74.

25. Samuel Pufendorf, *The Duty of Man and Citizen*, tr. Frank Gardner Moore (Oxford: Oxford University Press, 1927), bk. 2, chap. 2. See also *The Law of Nature and Nations*, tr. C. H. Oldfather and W. A. Oldfather (Oxford: Oxford University Press, 1934), bk. 5, chap. 1.

26. Hume, *Essays*, 559.

27. David Hume, *A Treatise of Human Nature*, ed. L. A. Selby-Bigge (Oxford: Clarendon Press, 1975), 485.

28. Of course, if there is evidence that the old oppressors are still more prone to violence than their ex-victims, we will have to monitor the amount of parenting, of any sort, that they are permitted to do.

29. Hapgood, *Why Males Exist*, relates how the male eastern scorpion fly, *Bittacus apicalis*, must provide a "nuptial meal" before any self-respecting female will consent to mate with him and if the meal provided is inferior, she will still refuse.

CREDITS

Page 99, Aristotle, *Nichomachean Ethics,* Book I, II, III, VI, X, translated by W.D. Ross, 1925, Oxford University Press. Reprinted by permission of Oxford University Press. Page 144, Epicurus, "Letter to Menoeceus," "Principle Doctrines," from *Epicurus: The Extant Remains,* translated by Cyril Bailey, 1926, Oxford University Press. Reprinted by permission of Oxford University Press. Page 174, St. Thomas Aquinas, *Summa Theologica,* Second Part of the First Part, Q90~92, Q94~96, translated by Anton C. Pegis, NY: Random House, 1945, Vol. II. Reprinted by permission of the A.C. Pegis Estate. Page 345, Friedrich Nietzsche, from *Beyond Good and Evil,* Part Five, Sec. l86~203, Part Seven, Sec. 214~239, translated by Helen Zimmern; from *Genealogy of Morals,* First Essay, I-XVII, translated by Horace B. Samuel, HarperCollins Publishers. Page 386, G.E. Moore, *Principia Ethica,* Ch. 1-3, Cambridge University Press, 1903. Reprinted by permission of Cambridge University Press. Page 437, John Dewey, *The Quest for Certainty,* Ch. X, The Putnam Publishing Group, 1929. Copyright ©1929 by John Dewey; renewed ©1957 by Frederick A. Dewey. Reprinted by permission of The Putnam Publishing Group. Page 450, W.D. Ross, from *The Right and the Good,* Ch. 1-2, Oxford University Press, 1930. Reprinted by permission of Oxford University Press. Page 473, A. J. Ayer, from *Language, Truth and Logic,* Chs. 1, 6, Dover Publications, Inc. Reprinted with permission from Dover Publications, Inc. Page 490, Jean-Paul Sartre, from *Existentialism,* translated by Bernard Frechtman, NY: Philosophical Library, 1947, pp. 11-61. Reprinted with permission from Philosophical Library, New York. Page 503, R. M. Hare, from *Freedom and Reason,* Oxford University Press, 1963, Part II, Ch. 6. Reprinted with permission of Oxford University Press. Page 515, G. E. M. Anscombe, "Modern Moral Philosophy," *Philosophy, 33* (January 1958), pp. 1-19. Reprinted with permission of the publisher. Page 527, John Rawls, from *Theory of Justice,* Cambridge, MA: Harvard University Press, 1971. Copyright ©1971 by the President and Fellows of Harvard College. Reprinted by permission of the publisher. Page 544, Thomas E. Hill, Jr., "Servility and Self-Respect." Copyright ©1973 *The Monist,* La Salle, IL 61301. Reprinted by permission. Page 554, J. J. C. Smart and Bernard Williams, from *Utilitarianism: For and Against,* Cambridge University Press, 1973. Reprinted by permission of Cambridge University Press. Page 566, J. J. C. Smart and Bernard Williams, from *Utilitarianism: For and Against,* Cambridge University Press, 1973. Reprinted by permission of Cambridge University Press. Page 577, David Gauthier, "Morality and Advantage," *Philosophical Review,* 76, 1976, pp. 460~75. Copyright © 1976 Cornell University. Reprinted by permission of the publisher and the author. Page 585, Susan Wolf, "Moral Saints," *Journal of Philosophy,* 79:8 (1982), 419–39. Reprinted with permission of the publisher and the author. Page 597, Onora O'Neill, "Between Consenting Adults," *Philosophy and Public Affairs,* Vol. 14, Summer 1985, pp.252-277. Copyright ©1985 by Princeton University Press. Reprinted by permission of Princeton University Press. Page 612, Virginia Held, "Feminism and Moral Theory," from *Women and Moral Theory,* ed. Kittay, Rowman and Littlefield, 1987, pp. 111-128. Copyright ©1987 by Rowman and Littlefield Publishers. Used with permission of the publisher. Page 624, Martha Nussbaum, "The Stoics on the Extirpation of the Passions" from *Apeiron: A Journal for Ancient Philosophy and Science,* Vol.20, 1987, pp.129-175. Reprinted by permission of Academic Printing and Publishing. Page 643, Annette Baier, "Whom Can Women Trust?" from *Feminist Ethics,* Claudia Card, editor, University of Kansas Press, 1991, pp. 233-245. Reprinted with permission from the publisher.